core JAVA™ 2

Volume II – Advanced Features

Seventh Edition

CAY S. HORSTMANN • GARY CORNELL

Sun Microsystems Press
A Prentice Hall Title

Publisher: *John Wait*
Editor in Chief: *Don O'Hagan*
Acquisitions Editor: *Greg Doench*
Managing Editor: *John Fuller*
Manufacturing Buyer: *Carol Melville*

Project Editors: *Julie Nahil and Vanessa Moore*
Copyeditor: *Mary Lou Nohr*
Indexer: *Solveig Haugland*
Compositor: *Vanessa Moore*
Sun Microsystems Press Publisher: *Myrna Rivera*

The publisher offers excellent discounts on this book when ordered in quantity for bulk purchases or special sales, which may include electronic versions and/or custom covers and content particular to your business, training goals, marketing focus, and branding interests. For more information, please contact:

U. S. Corporate and Government Sales
(800) 382-3419
corpsales@pearsontechgroup.com

For sales outside the U. S., please contact:

International Sales
international@pearsoned.com

Visit us on the Web: www.phptr.com

Library of Congress Control Number: 2004109876

ISBN 0-13-111826-9

Text printed in the United States on recycled paper at Courier in Stoughton, Massachusetts.

First printing, November 2004

Sun Microsystems Press
A Prentice Hall Title

Contents

Chapter 1

Chapter 2

Contents

Chapter 8

Chapter 9

Chapter 12

Chapter 13

List of Code Examples

Preface

To the Reader

The book you have in your hands is the second volume of the seventh edition of *Core Java 2*. The first volume covers the essential features of the language; this volume covers the advanced topics that a programmer will need to know for professional software development. Thus, as with the first volume and the previous editions of this book, we still are targeting programmers who want to put Java technology to work on real projects.

Please note: If you are an experienced developer who is comfortable with advanced language features such as inner classes and generics, you need not have read the first volume in order to benefit from this volume. (While we do refer to sections of the previous volume when appropriate and, of course, hope you will buy or have bought Volume 1, you can find the needed background material in any comprehensive introductory book about the Java platform.)

Finally, when any book is being written, errors and inaccuracies are inevitable. We would very much like to hear about them. Of course, we would prefer to hear about them only once. For this reason, we have put up a web site at http://horstmann.com/corejava.html with an FAQ, bug fixes, and workarounds. Strategically placed at the end of the bug report web page (to encourage you to read the previous reports) is a form that you can use to report bugs or problems and to send suggestions for improvements to future editions.

About This Book

The chapters in this book are, for the most part, independent of each other. You should be able to delve into whatever topic interests you the most and read the chapters in any order.

Chapter 1 covers multithreading, which enables you to program tasks to be done in parallel. (A thread is a flow of control within a program.) We show you how to set up threads and how to deal with thread synchronization. Multithreading has changed a great deal in JDK 5.0, and we tell you all about the new mechanisms.

The topic of Chapter 2 is the collections framework of the Java 2 platform. Whenever you want to collect multiple objects and retrieve them later, you will want to use a collection that is best suited for your circumstances, instead of just tossing the elements into a Vector.

This chapter shows you how to take advantage of the standard collections that are prebuilt for your use. The chapter has been completely revised for the generic collections of JDK 5.0.

Chapter 3 covers the networking API. Java makes it phenomenally easy to do complex network programming. We show you how to make network connections to servers, how to implement your own servers, and how to make HTTP connections. We finish the chapter with advanced issues such as half-close and interruptible channels.

Chapter 4 covers database programming. The main focus is on JDBC, the Java database connectivity API that lets Java programs connect to relational databases. We show you how to write useful programs to handle realistic database chores, using a core subset of the JDBC API. (A complete treatment of the JDBC API would require a book almost as long as this one.) We finish the chapter with a brief introduction into hierarchical databases and discuss JNDI (the Java Naming and Directory Interface) and LDAP (the Lightweight Directory Access Protocol).

Chapter 5 covers distributed objects. We cover RMI (Remote Method Invocation) in detail. This API lets you work with Java objects that are distributed over multiple machines. We then briefly discuss CORBA (the Common Object Request Broker Architecture) and show you how objects written in C++ and Java can communicate. We finish the chapter with a discussion of SOAP (the Simple Object Access Protocol) and show you an example in which a Java program communicates with the Amazon Web Service.

Chapter 6 contains all the Swing material that didn't make it into Volume 1, especially the important but complex tree and table components. We show the basic uses of editor panes, the Java implementation of a "multiple document" interface, and the progress indicators that you use in multithreaded programs. Again, we focus on the most useful constructs that you are likely to encounter in practical programming, since an encyclopedic coverage of the entire Swing library would fill several volumes and would only be of interest to dedicated taxonomists.

Chapter 7 covers the Java 2D API that you can use to create realistic drawings. The chapter also covers some advanced features of the Abstract Windowing Toolkit (AWT) that seemed too specialized for coverage in Volume 1 but are, nonetheless, techniques that should be part of every programmer's toolkit. These features include printing and the APIs for cut-and-paste and drag-and-drop.

Chapter 8 shows you what you need to know about the component API for the Java platform—JavaBeans. You will see how to write your own beans that other programmers can manipulate in integrated builder environments. We conclude this chapter by showing you how you can use JavaBeans persistence to store your own data in a format that—unlike object serialization—is suitable for long-term storage.

Chapter 9 takes up the Java security model. The Java platform was designed from the ground up to be secure, and this chapter takes you under the hood to see how this design is implemented. We show you how to write your own class loaders and security managers for special-purpose applications. Then, we take up the security API that allows for such important features as message and code signing, authorization and authentication, and encryption. This chapter has been completely updated for JDK 5.0 to use the AES and RSA encryption algorithms.

Chapter 10 discusses a specialized feature that we believe can only grow in importance: internationalization. The Java programming language is one of the few languages designed from the start to handle Unicode, but the internationalization support in the Java platform goes much further. As a result, you can internationalize Java applications so that they not only cross platforms but cross country boundaries as well. For example, we show you how

to write a retirement calculator applet that uses either English, German, or Chinese—depending on the locale of the browser.

Chapter 11 takes up native methods, which let you call methods written for a specific machine such as the Microsoft Windows API. Obviously, this feature is controversial: Use native methods, and the cross-platform nature of the Java platform vanishes. Nonetheless, every serious programmer writing Java applications for specific platforms needs to know these techniques. There will be times when you need to turn to the operating system's API for your target platform when you are writing a serious application. We illustrate this by showing you how to access the registry API in Windows from a Java program.

Chapter 12 covers XML. We show you how to parse XML files, how to generate XML, and how to use XSL transformations. As a useful example, we show you how to specify the layout of a Swing form in XML. This chapter has been updated to include the XPath API that makes "finding needles in XML haystacks" much easier.

Chapter 13 is new to this edition. It discusses annotations and metadata, features that were added to JDK 5.0. Annotations allow you to add arbitrary information (the metadata) to a Java program. We show you how annotation processors can harvest these annotations at the source or class file level, and how annotations can be used to influence the behavior of classes at runtime. Annotations are only useful with tools, and we hope that our discussion will help you select useful annotation processing tools for your needs.

Conventions

As is common in many computer books, we use `monospace type` to represent computer code.

 NOTE: Notes are tagged with a "notepad" icon that looks like this.

 TIP: Helpful tips are tagged with this icon.

 CAUTION: Notes that warn of pitfalls or dangerous situations are tagged with a "caution" icon.

 C++ NOTE: There are a number of C++ notes that explain the difference between the Java programming language and C++. You can skip them if you aren't interested in C++.

 Application Programming Interface

The Java platform comes with a large programming library or Application Programming Interface (API). When using an API call for the first time, we add a short summary description, tagged with an API icon. These descriptions are a bit more informal but also a little more informative than those in the official on-line API documentation.

Programs whose source code is included in the companion code for this book are listed as examples; for instance,

Example 5–8: WarehouseServer.java

You can download the companion code from `http://www.phptr.com/corejava`.

Acknowledgments

Writing a book is always a monumental effort, and rewriting doesn't seem to be much easier, especially with such a rapid rate of change in Java technology. Making a book a reality takes many dedicated people, and it is my great pleasure to acknowledge the contributions of the entire Core Java team.

Our long-suffering editor Greg Doench of Prentice Hall PTR once again did a great job, coordinating all aspects of this complex project. Mary Lou Nohr copyedited the manuscript, with an excellent eye for consistency and always on the lookout for Teutonic constructions and violations of the Java trademark rules. Vanessa Moore once again did a wonderful job with the book production. A number of other individuals at Prentice Hall PTR and Sun Microsystems Press also provided valuable assistance, but they managed to stay behind the scenes. I'd like them all to know how much I appreciate their efforts. My thanks also go to my coauthor of earlier editions, Gary Cornell, who has since moved on to other ventures.

I am very grateful to the excellent reviewing team who found many embarrassing errors and made lots of thoughtful suggestions for improvement. This edition was reviewed by Chuck Allison (Contributing Editor, *C/C++ Users Journal*), Cliff Berg (iSavvix Corporation), Frank Cohen (PushToTest), Brian Goetz (Principal Consultant, Quiotix Corp.), Rob Gordon, John Gray (University of Hartford), Dan Harkey (San Jose State University), William Higgins (IBM), Angelika Langer, Mark Lawrence, Bob Lynch (Lynch Associates), Philip Milne (consultant), Hao Pham, Stephen Stelting (Sun Microsystems), Kim Topley (author of *Core JFC*), and Paul Tyma (consultant). Thank you very much for your generous help!

Reviewers of earlier editions are Alec Beaton (PointBase, Inc.), Joshua Bloch (Sun Microsystems), David Brown, Dr. Nicholas J. De Lillo (Manhattan College), Rakesh Dhoopar (Oracle), David Geary (Sabreware Inc.), Angela Gordon (Sun Microsystems), Dan Gordon (Sun Microsystems), Rob Gordon, Cameron Gregory (olabs.com), Marty Hall (The Johns Hopkins University Applied Physics Lab), Vincent Hardy (Sun Microsystems), Vladimir Ivanovic (PointBase, Inc.), Jerry Jackson (ChannelPoint Software), Tim Kimmet (Preview Systems), Chris Laffra, Charlie Lai (Sun Microsystems), Doug Langston, Doug Lea (SUNY Oswego), Gregory Longshore, Mark Morrissey (The Oregon Graduate Institute), Mahesh

Neelakanta (Florida Atlantic University), Paul Philion, Blake Ragsdell, Stuart Reges (University of Arizona), Peter Sanders (ESSI University, Nice, France), Devang Shah (Sun Microsystems), Christopher Taylor, Luke Taylor (Valtech), George Thiruvathukal, Janet Traub, Peter van der Linden (Sun Microsystems), and Burt Walsh.

Cay Horstmann
San Francisco, September 2004

Multithreading

You are probably familiar with *multitasking* in your operating system: the ability to have more than one program working at what seems like the same time. For example, you can print while editing or sending a fax. Of course, unless you have a multiple-processor machine, the operating system is really doling out CPU time to each program, giving the impression of parallel activity. This resource distribution is possible because although you may think you are keeping the computer busy by, for example, entering data, much of the CPU's time will be idle.

Multitasking can be done in two ways, depending on whether the operating system interrupts programs without consulting with them first or whether programs are only interrupted when they are willing to yield control. The former is called *preemptive multitasking*; the latter is called *cooperative* (or, simply, nonpreemptive) *multitasking*. Older operating systems such as Windows 3.x and Mac OS 9 are cooperative multitasking systems, as are the operating systems on simple devices such as cell phones. UNIX/Linux, Windows NT/XP (and Windows 9x for 32-bit programs), and OS X are preemptive. Although harder to implement, preemptive multitasking is much more effective. With cooperative multitasking, a badly behaved program can hog everything.

Multithreaded programs extend the idea of multitasking by taking it one level lower: individual programs will appear to do multiple tasks at the same time. Each task is usually called a *thread*—which is short for thread of control. Programs that can run more than one thread at once are said to be *multithreaded*.

So, what is the difference between multiple *processes* and multiple *threads*? The essential difference is that while each process has a complete set of its own variables, threads share the same data. This sounds somewhat risky, and indeed it can be, as you will see later in this chapter. However, shared variables make communication between threads more efficient and easier to program than interprocess communication. Moreover, on some operating systems, threads are more "lightweight" than processes—it takes less overhead to create and destroy individual threads than it does to launch new processes.

Multithreading is extremely useful in practice. For example, a browser should be able to simultaneously download multiple images. A web server needs to be able to serve concurrent requests. The Java programming language itself uses a thread to do garbage collection in the background—thus saving you the trouble of managing memory! Graphical user interface (GUI) programs have a separate thread for gathering user interface events from the host operating environment. This chapter shows you how to add multithreading capability to your Java applications.

Multithreading changed dramatically in JDK 5.0, with the addition of a large number of classes and interfaces that provide high-quality implementations of the mechanisms that most application programmers will need. In this chapter, we explain the new features of JDK 5.0 as well as the classic synchronization mechanisms, and help you choose between them.

Fair warning: multithreading can get very complex. In this chapter, we cover all the tools that an application programmer is likely to need. However, for more intricate system-level programming, we suggest that you turn to a more advanced reference, such as *Concurrent Programming in Java* by Doug Lea [Addison-Wesley 1999].

What Are Threads?

Let us start by looking at a program that does not use multiple threads and that, as a consequence, makes it difficult for the user to perform several tasks with that program. After we dissect it, we then show you how easy it is to have this program run separate threads. This program animates a bouncing ball by continually moving the ball, finding out if it bounces against a wall, and then redrawing it. (See Figure 1–1.)

As soon as you click the Start button, the program launches a ball from the upper-left corner of the screen and the ball begins bouncing. The handler of the Start button calls the addBall method. That method contains a loop running through 1,000 moves. Each call to move moves the ball by a small amount, adjusts the direction if it bounces against a wall, and then redraws the panel.

```
Ball ball = new Ball();
panel.add(ball);

for (int i = 1; i <= STEPS; i++)
{
   ball.move(panel.getBounds());
   panel.paint(panel.getGraphics());
   Thread.sleep(DELAY);
}
```

The static sleep method of the Thread class pauses for the given number of milliseconds.

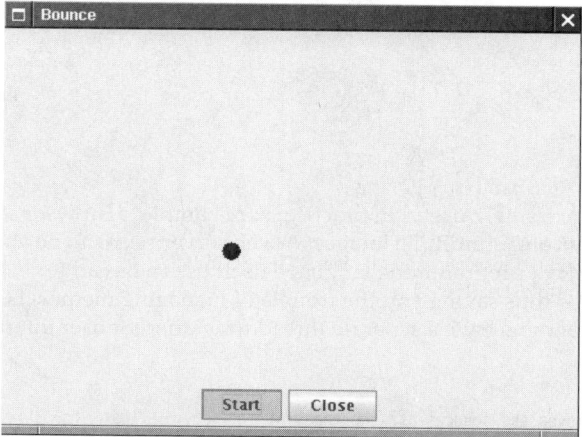

Figure 1–1: Using threads to animate bouncing balls

The call to Thread.sleep does not create a new thread—sleep is a static method of the Thread class that temporarily stops the activity of the current thread.

The sleep method can throw an InterruptedException. We discuss this exception and its proper handling later. For now, we simply terminate the bouncing if this exception occurs.

If you run the program, the ball bounces around nicely, but it completely takes over the application. If you become tired of the bouncing ball before it has finished its 1,000 moves and click the Close button, the ball continues bouncing anyway. You cannot interact with the program until the ball has finished bouncing.

 NOTE: If you carefully look over the code at the end of this section, you will notice the call

    panel.paint(panel.getGraphics())

inside the move method of the Ball class. That is pretty strange—normally, you'd call repaint and let the AWT worry about getting the graphics context and doing the painting. But if you try to call panel.repaint() in this program, you'll find that the panel is never repainted because the addBall method has completely taken over all processing. In the next program, in which we use a separate thread to compute the ball position, we'll again use the familiar repaint.

Obviously, the behavior of this program is rather poor. You would not want the programs that you use behaving in this way when you ask them to do a time-consuming job. After all, when you are reading data over a network connection, it is all too common to be stuck in a task that you would *really* like to interrupt. For example, suppose you download a large image and decide, after seeing a piece of it, that you do not need or want to see the rest; you certainly would like to be able to click a Stop or Back button to interrupt the loading process. In the next section, we show you how to keep the user in control by running crucial parts of the code in a separate *thread*.

Example 1–1 shows the code for the program.

Example 1–1: Bounce.java

```
1. import java.awt.*;
2. import java.awt.event.*;
3. import java.awt.geom.*;
4. import java.util.*;
```

```
 5. import javax.swing.*;
 6.
 7. /**
 8.    Shows an animated bouncing ball.
 9. */
10. public class Bounce
11. {
12.    public static void main(String[] args)
13.    {
14.       JFrame frame = new BounceFrame();
15.       frame.setDefaultCloseOperation(JFrame.EXIT_ON_CLOSE);
16.       frame.setVisible(true);
17.    }
18. }
19.
20. /**
21.    A ball that moves and bounces off the edges of a
22.    rectangle
23. */
24. class Ball
25. {
26.    /**
27.       Moves the ball to the next position, reversing direction
28.       if it hits one of the edges
29.    */
30.    public void move(Rectangle2D bounds)
31.    {
32.       x += dx;
33.       y += dy;
34.       if (x < bounds.getMinX())
35.       {
36.          x = bounds.getMinX();
37.          dx = -dx;
38.       }
39.       if (x + XSIZE >= bounds.getMaxX())
40.       {
41.          x = bounds.getMaxX() - XSIZE;
42.          dx = -dx;
43.       }
44.       if (y < bounds.getMinY())
45.       {
46.          y = bounds.getMinY();
47.          dy = -dy;
48.       }
49.       if (y + YSIZE >= bounds.getMaxY())
50.       {
51.          y = bounds.getMaxY() - YSIZE;
52.          dy = -dy;
53.       }
54.    }
55.
56.    /**
57.       Gets the shape of the ball at its current position.
58.    */
59.    public Ellipse2D getShape()
```

```
60.     {
61.         return new Ellipse2D.Double(x, y, XSIZE, YSIZE);
62.     }
63.
64.     private static final int XSIZE = 15;
65.     private static final int YSIZE = 15;
66.     private double x = 0;
67.     private double y = 0;
68.     private double dx = 1;
69.     private double dy = 1;
70. }
71.
72. /**
73.    The panel that draws the balls.
74. */
75. class BallPanel extends JPanel
76. {
77.    /**
78.       Add a ball to the panel.
79.       @param b the ball to add
80.    */
81.    public void add(Ball b)
82.    {
83.       balls.add(b);
84.    }
85.
86.    public void paintComponent(Graphics g)
87.    {
88.       super.paintComponent(g);
89.       Graphics2D g2 = (Graphics2D) g;
90.       for (Ball b : balls)
91.       {
92.          g2.fill(b.getShape());
93.       }
94.    }
95.
96.    private ArrayList<Ball> balls = new ArrayList<Ball>();
97. }
98.
99. /**
100.    The frame with panel and buttons.
101. */
102. class BounceFrame extends JFrame
103. {
104.    /**
105.       Constructs the frame with the panel for showing the
106.       bouncing ball and Start and Close buttons
107.    */
108.    public BounceFrame()
109.    {
110.       setSize(DEFAULT_WIDTH, DEFAULT_HEIGHT);
111.       setTitle("Bounce");
112.
113.       panel = new BallPanel();
114.       add(panel, BorderLayout.CENTER);
```

```
115.       JPanel buttonPanel = new JPanel();
116.       addButton(buttonPanel, "Start",
117.          new ActionListener()
118.          {
119.             public void actionPerformed(ActionEvent event)
120.             {
121.                addBall();
122.             }
123.          });
124.
125.       addButton(buttonPanel, "Close",
126.          new ActionListener()
127.          {
128.             public void actionPerformed(ActionEvent event)
129.             {
130.                System.exit(0);
131.             }
132.          });
133.       add(buttonPanel, BorderLayout.SOUTH);
134.    }
135.
136.    /**
137.       Adds a button to a container.
138.       @param c the container
139.       @param title the button title
140.       @param listener the action listener for the button
141.    */
142.    public void addButton(Container c, String title, ActionListener listener)
143.    {
144.       JButton button = new JButton(title);
145.       c.add(button);
146.       button.addActionListener(listener);
147.    }
148.
149.    /**
150.       Adds a bouncing ball to the panel and makes
151.       it bounce 1,000 times.
152.    */
153.    public void addBall()
154.    {
155.       try
156.       {
157.          Ball ball = new Ball();
158.          panel.add(ball);
159.
160.          for (int i = 1; i <= STEPS; i++)
161.          {
162.             ball.move(panel.getBounds());
163.             panel.paint(panel.getGraphics());
164.             Thread.sleep(DELAY);
165.          }
166.       }
167.       catch (InterruptedException e)
168.       {
169.       }
```

```
170.    }
171.
172.    private BallPanel panel;
173.    public static final int DEFAULT_WIDTH = 450;
174.    public static final int DEFAULT_HEIGHT = 350;
175.    public static final int STEPS = 1000;
176.    public static final int DELAY = 3;
177. }
```

API **java.lang.Thread 1.0**

- static void sleep(long millis)
  sleeps for the given number of milliseconds.

  Parameters: millis   The number of milliseconds to sleep

Using Threads to Give Other Tasks a Chance

We will make our bouncing-ball program more responsive by running the code that moves the ball in a separate thread. In fact, you will be able to launch multiple balls. Each of them is moved by its own thread. In addition, the AWT *event dispatch thread* continues running in parallel, taking care of user interface events. Because each thread gets a chance to run, the main thread has the opportunity to notice when a user clicks the Close button while the balls are bouncing. The thread can then process the "close" action.

Here is a simple procedure for running a task in a separate thread:

1. Place the code for the task into the run method of a class that implements the Runnable interface. That interface is very simple, with a single method:

    ```
    public interface Runnable
    {
       void run();
    }
    ```

    You simply implement a class, like this:

    ```
    class MyRunnable implements Runnable
    {
       public void run()
       {
          task code
       }
    }
    ```

2. Construct an object of your class:

    ```
    Runnable r = new MyRunnable();
    ```

3. Construct a Thread object from the Runnable:

    ```
    Thread t = new Thread(r);
    ```

4. Start the thread.

    ```
    t.start();
    ```

To make our bouncing-ball program into a separate thread, we need only implement a class BallRunnable and place the code for the animation inside the run method, as in the following code:

```
class BallRunnable implements Runnable
{
   . . .
```

```java
   public void run()
   {
      try
      {
         for (int i = 1; i <= STEPS; i++)
         {
            ball.move(component.getBounds());
            component.repaint();
            Thread.sleep(DELAY);
         }
      }
      catch (InterruptedException exception)
      {
      }
   }
   . . .
}
```

Again, we need to catch an InterruptedException that the sleep method threatens to throw. We discuss this exception in the next section. Typically, a thread is terminated by being interrupted. Accordingly, our run method exits when an InterruptedException occurs.

Whenever the Start button is clicked, the addBall method launches a new thread (see Figure 1–2):

```java
Ball b = new Ball();
panel.add(b);
Runnable r = new BallRunnable(b, panel);
Thread t = new Thread(r);
t.start();
```

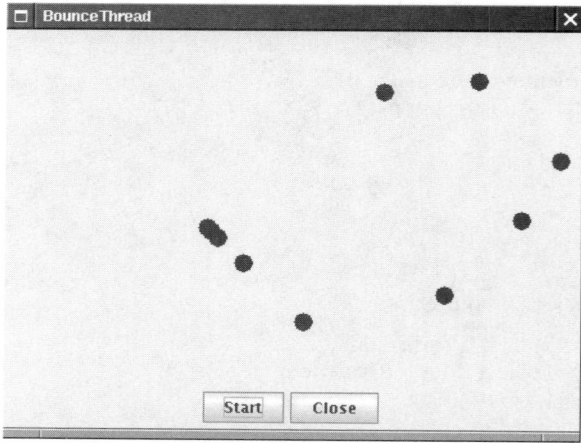

Figure 1–2: Running multiple threads

That's all there is to it! You now know how to run tasks in parallel. The remainder of this chapter tells you how to control the interaction between threads.

The complete code is shown in Example 1–2.

NOTE: You can also define a thread by forming a subclass of the Thread class, like this:

```
class MyThread extends Thread
{
    public void run()
    {
        task code
    }
}
```

Then you construct an object of the subclass and call its start method. However, this approach is no longer recommended. You should decouple the *task* that is to be run in parallel from the *mechanism* of running it. If you have many tasks, it is too expensive to create a separate thread for each one of them. Instead, you can use a thread pool—see page 59.

CAUTION: Do *not* call the run method of the Thread class or the Runnable object. Calling the run method directly merely executes the task in the *same* thread—no new thread is started. Instead, call the Thread.start method. It will create a new thread that executes the run method.

Example 1–2: BounceThread.java

```
1.  import java.awt.*;
2.  import java.awt.event.*;
3.  import java.awt.geom.*;
4.  import java.util.*;
5.  import javax.swing.*;
6.
7.  /**
8.     Shows an animated bouncing ball.
9.  */
10. public class BounceThread
11. {
12.    public static void main(String[] args)
13.    {
14.       JFrame frame = new BounceFrame();
15.       frame.setDefaultCloseOperation(JFrame.EXIT_ON_CLOSE);
16.       frame.setVisible(true);
17.    }
18. }
19.
20. /**
21.    A runnable that animates a bouncing ball.
22. */
23. class BallRunnable implements Runnable
24. {
25.    /**
26.       Constructs the runnable.
27.       @aBall the ball to bounce
28.       @aPanel the component in which the ball bounces
29.    */
30.    public BallRunnable(Ball aBall, Component aComponent)
31.    {
32.       ball = aBall;
33.       component = aComponent;
```

```
34.     }
35.
36.     public void run()
37.     {
38.        try
39.        {
40.           for (int i = 1; i <= STEPS; i++)
41.           {
42.              ball.move(component.getBounds());
43.              component.repaint();
44.              Thread.sleep(DELAY);
45.           }
46.        }
47.        catch (InterruptedException e)
48.        {
49.        }
50.     }
51.
52.     private Ball ball;
53.     private Component component;
54.     public static final int STEPS = 1000;
55.     public static final int DELAY = 5;
56. }
57.
58. /**
59.     A ball that moves and bounces off the edges of a
60.     rectangle
61. */
62. class Ball
63. {
64.     /**
65.        Moves the ball to the next position, reversing direction
66.        if it hits one of the edges
67.     */
68.     public void move(Rectangle2D bounds)
69.     {
70.        x += dx;
71.        y += dy;
72.        if (x < bounds.getMinX())
73.        {
74.           x = bounds.getMinX();
75.           dx = -dx;
76.        }
77.        if (x + XSIZE >= bounds.getMaxX())
78.        {
79.           x = bounds.getMaxX() - XSIZE;
80.           dx = -dx;
81.        }
82.        if (y < bounds.getMinY())
83.        {
84.           y = bounds.getMinY();
85.           dy = -dy;
86.        }
87.        if (y + YSIZE >= bounds.getMaxY())
88.        {
89.           y = bounds.getMaxY() - YSIZE;
```

```
90.            dy = -dy;
91.         }
92.      }
93.
94.      /**
95.         Gets the shape of the ball at its current position.
96.      */
97.      public Ellipse2D getShape()
98.      {
99.         return new Ellipse2D.Double(x, y, XSIZE, YSIZE);
100.     }
101.
102.     private static final int XSIZE = 15;
103.     private static final int YSIZE = 15;
104.     private double x = 0;
105.     private double y = 0;
106.     private double dx = 1;
107.     private double dy = 1;
108. }
109.
110. /**
111.    The panel that draws the balls.
112. */
113. class BallPanel extends JPanel
114. {
115.    /**
116.       Add a ball to the panel.
117.       @param b the ball to add
118.    */
119.    public void add(Ball b)
120.    {
121.       balls.add(b);
122.    }
123.
124.    public void paintComponent(Graphics g)
125.    {
126.       super.paintComponent(g);
127.       Graphics2D g2 = (Graphics2D) g;
128.       for (Ball b : balls)
129.       {
130.          g2.fill(b.getShape());
131.       }
132.    }
133.
134.    private ArrayList<Ball> balls = new ArrayList<Ball>();
135. }
136.
137. /**
138.    The frame with panel and buttons.
139. */
140. class BounceFrame extends JFrame
141. {
142.    /**
143.       Constructs the frame with the panel for showing the
144.       bouncing ball and Start and Close buttons
145.    */
```

```java
146.    public BounceFrame()
147.    {
148.       setSize(DEFAULT_WIDTH, DEFAULT_HEIGHT);
149.       setTitle("BounceThread");
150.
151.       panel = new BallPanel();
152.       add(panel, BorderLayout.CENTER);
153.       JPanel buttonPanel = new JPanel();
154.       addButton(buttonPanel, "Start",
155.          new ActionListener()
156.          {
157.             public void actionPerformed(ActionEvent event)
158.             {
159.                addBall();
160.             }
161.          });
162.
163.       addButton(buttonPanel, "Close",
164.          new ActionListener()
165.          {
166.             public void actionPerformed(ActionEvent event)
167.             {
168.                System.exit(0);
169.             }
170.          });
171.       add(buttonPanel, BorderLayout.SOUTH);
172.    }
173.
174.    /**
175.       Adds a button to a container.
176.       @param c the container
177.       @param title the button title
178.       @param listener the action listener for the button
179.    */
180.    public void addButton(Container c, String title, ActionListener listener)
181.    {
182.       JButton button = new JButton(title);
183.       c.add(button);
184.       button.addActionListener(listener);
185.    }
186.
187.    /**
188.       Adds a bouncing ball to the canvas and starts a thread
189.       to make it bounce
190.    */
191.    public void addBall()
192.    {
193.       Ball b = new Ball();
194.       panel.add(b);
195.       Runnable r = new BallRunnable(b, panel);
196.       Thread t = new Thread(r);
197.       t.start();
198.    }
199.
200.    private BallPanel panel;
201.    public static final int DEFAULT_WIDTH = 450;
```

```
202.   public static final int DEFAULT_HEIGHT = 350;
203.   public static final int STEPS = 1000;
204.   public static final int DELAY = 3;
205. }
```

 java.lang.Thread 1.0

- Thread(Runnable target)
  constructs a new thread that calls the run() method of the specified target.
- void start()
  starts this thread, causing the run() method to be called. This method will return immediately. The new thread runs concurrently.
- void run()
  calls the run method of the associated Runnable.

 java.lang.Runnable 1.0

- void run()
  You must override this method and supply the instructions for the task that you want to have executed.

Interrupting Threads

A thread terminates when its run method returns. In JDK 1.0, there also was a stop method that another thread could call to terminate a thread. However, that method is now deprecated. We discuss the reason on page 46.

There is no longer a way to *force* a thread to terminate. However, the interrupt method can be used to *request* termination of a thread.

When the interrupt method is called on a thread, the *interrupted status* of the thread is set. This is a Boolean flag that is present in every thread. Each thread should occasionally check whether it has been interrupted.

To find out whether the interrupted status was set, first call the static Thread.currentThread method to get the current thread and then call the isInterrupted method:

```
while (!Thread.currentThread().isInterrupted() && more work to do)
{
    do more work
}
```

However, if a thread is blocked, it cannot check the interrupted status. This is where the InterruptedException comes in. When the interrupt method is called on a blocked thread, the blocking call (such as sleep or wait) is terminated by an InterruptedException.

There is no language requirement that a thread that is interrupted should terminate. Interrupting a thread simply grabs its attention. The interrupted thread can decide how to react to the interruption. Some threads are so important that they should handle the exception and continue. But quite commonly, a thread will simply want to interpret an interruption as a request for termination. The run method of such a thread has the following form:

```
public void run()
{
    try
    {
        . . .
```

```
      while (!Thread.currentThread().isInterrupted() && more work to do)
      {
         do more work
      }
   }
   catch(InterruptedException e)
   {
      // thread was interrupted during sleep or wait
   }
   finally
   {
      cleanup, if required
   }
   // exiting the run method terminates the thread
}
```

The isInterrupted check is not necessary if you call the sleep method after every work iteration. The sleep method throws an InterruptedException if you call it when the interrupted status is set. Therefore, if your loop calls sleep, don't bother checking the interrupted status and simply catch the InterruptedException. Then your run method has the form

```
public void run()
{
   try
   {
      . . .
      while (more work to do)
      {
         do more work
         Thread.sleep(delay);
      }
   }
   catch(InterruptedException e)
   {
      // thread was interrupted during sleep or wait
   }
   finally
   {
      cleanup, if required
   }
   // exiting the run method terminates the thread
}
```

 CAUTION: When the sleep method throws an InterruptedException, it also *clears* the interrupted status.

 NOTE: There are two very similar methods, interrupted and isInterrupted. The interrupted method is a static method that checks whether the *current* thread has been interrupted. Furthermore, calling the interrupted method *clears* the interrupted status of the thread. On the other hand, the isInterrupted method is an instance method that you can use to check whether any thread has been interrupted. Calling it does not change the interrupted status.

You'll find lots of published code in which the InterruptedException is squelched at a low level, like this:

```
void mySubTask()
{
    . . .
    try { sleep(delay); }
    catch (InterruptedException e) {} // DON'T IGNORE!
    . . .
}
```

Don't do that! If you can't think of anything good to do in the catch clause, you still have two reasonable choices:

- In the catch clause, call Thread.currentThread().interrupt() to set the interrupted status. Then the caller can test it.

```
void mySubTask()
{
    . . .
    try { sleep(delay); }
    catch (InterruptedException e) { Thread().currentThread().interrupt(); }
    . . .
}
```

- Or, even better, tag your method with throws InterruptedException and drop the try block. Then the caller (or, ultimately, the run method) can catch it.

```
void mySubTask() throws InterruptedException
{
    . . .
    sleep(delay);
    . . .
}
```

 java.lang.Thread 1.0

- void interrupt()
  sends an interrupt request to a thread. The interrupted status of the thread is set to true. If the thread is currently blocked by a call to sleep, then an InterruptedException is thrown.

- static boolean interrupted()
  tests whether the *current* thread (that is, the thread that is executing this instruction) has been interrupted. Note that this is a static method. The call has a side effect—it resets the interrupted status of the current thread to false.

- boolean isInterrupted()
  tests whether a thread has been interrupted. Unlike the static interrupted method, this call does not change the interrupted status of the thread.

- static Thread currentThread()
  returns the Thread object representing the currently executing thread.

Thread States

Threads can be in one of four states:

- New
- Runnable

- Blocked
- Dead

Each of these states is explained in the sections that follow.

New Threads

When you create a thread with the new operator—for example, new Thread(r)—the thread is not yet running. This means that it is in the *new* state. When a thread is in the new state, the program has not started executing code inside of it. A certain amount of bookkeeping needs to be done before a thread can run.

Runnable Threads

Once you invoke the start method, the thread is *runnable*. A runnable thread may or may not actually be running. It is up to the operating system to give the thread time to run. (The Java specification does not call this a separate state, though. A running thread is still in the runnable state.)

 NOTE: The runnable state has nothing to do with the Runnable interface.

Once a thread is running, it doesn't necessarily keep running. In fact, it is desirable if running threads occasionally pause so that other threads have a chance to run. The details of thread scheduling depend on the services that the operating system provides. Preemptive scheduling systems give each runnable thread a slice of time to perform its task. When that slice of time is exhausted, the operating system *preempts* the thread and gives another thread an opportunity to work (see Figure 1–4 on page 27). When selecting the next thread, the operating system takes into account the thread *priorities*—see page 19 for more information on priorities.

All modern desktop and server operating systems use preemptive scheduling. However, small devices such as cell phones may use cooperative scheduling. In such a device, a thread loses control only when it calls a method such as sleep or yield.

On a machine with multiple processors, each processor can run a thread, and you can have multiple threads run in parallel. Of course, if there are more threads than processors, the scheduler still has to do time-slicing.

Always keep in mind that a runnable thread may or may not be running at any given time. (This is why the state is called "runnable" and not "running.")

Blocked Threads

A thread enters the *blocked* state when one of the following actions occurs:

- The thread goes to sleep by calling the sleep method.
- The thread calls an operation that is *blocking on input/output*, that is, an operation that will not return to its caller until input and output operations are complete.
- The thread tries to acquire a lock that is currently held by another thread. We discuss locks on page 27.
- The thread waits for a condition—see page 30.
- Someone calls the suspend method of the thread. However, this method is deprecated, and you should not call it in your code.

Figure 1–3 shows the states that a thread can have and the possible transitions from one state to another. When a thread is blocked (or, of course, when it dies), another thread can

be scheduled to run. When a blocked thread is reactivated (for example, because it has slept the required number of milliseconds or because the I/O it waited for is complete), the scheduler checks to see if it has a higher priority than the currently running thread. If so, it preempts the current thread and picks a new thread to run.

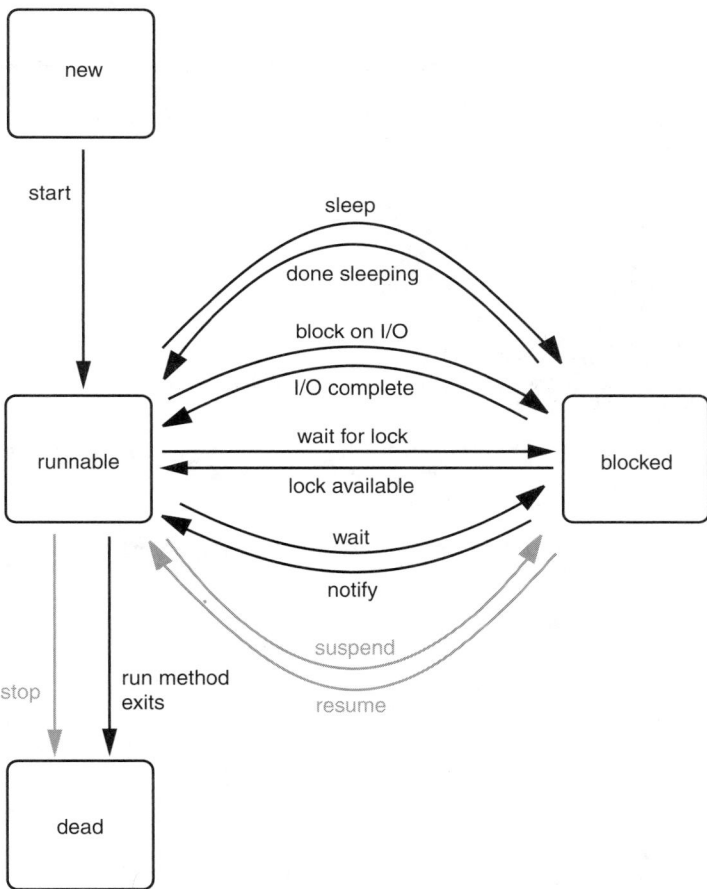

Figure 1–3: Thread states

A thread moves out of the blocked state and back into the runnable state by one of the following pathways.

1. If a thread has been put to sleep, the specified number of milliseconds must expire.

2. If a thread is waiting for the completion of an input or output operation, then the operation must have finished.

3. If a thread is waiting for a lock that was owned by another thread, then the other thread must relinquish ownership of the lock. (It is also possible to wait with a timeout. Then the thread unblocks when the timeout elapses.)

4. If a thread waits for a condition, then another thread must signal that the condition may have changed. (If the thread waits with a timeout, then the thread is unblocked when the timeout elapses.)

5. If a thread has been suspended, then someone must call its resume method. However, because the suspend method has been deprecated, the resume method has been deprecated as well, and you should not call it in your own code.

A blocked thread can only reenter the runnable state through the same route that blocked it in the first place. In particular, you cannot simply call the resume method to unblock a blocking thread.

 TIP: If you need to unblock an I/O operation, you should use the *channel* mechanism from the "new I/O" library. When another thread closes the channel, the blocked thread becomes runnable again, and the blocking operation throws a ClosedChannelException.

Dead Threads

A thread is dead for one of two reasons:

- It dies a natural death because the run method exits normally.
- It dies abruptly because an uncaught exception terminates the run method.

In particular, you can kill a thread by invoking its stop method. That method throws a ThreadDeath error object that kills the thread. However, the stop method is deprecated, and you should not call it in your own code.

To find out whether a thread is currently alive (that is, either runnable or blocked), use the isAlive method. This method returns true if the thread is runnable or blocked, false if the thread is still new and not yet runnable or if the thread is dead.

 NOTE: You cannot find out if an alive thread is runnable or blocked, or if a runnable thread is actually running. In addition, you cannot differentiate between a thread that has not yet become runnable and one that has already died.

 java.lang.Thread 1.0

- boolean isAlive()
  returns true if the thread has started and has not yet terminated.
- void stop()
  stops the thread. This method is deprecated.
- void suspend()
  suspends this thread's execution. This method is deprecated.
- void resume()
  resumes this thread. This method is only valid after suspend() has been invoked. This method is deprecated.
- void join()
  waits for the specified thread to die.
- void join(long millis)
  waits for the specified thread to die or for the specified number of milliseconds to pass.

Thread Properties

In the following sections, we discuss miscellaneous properties of threads: thread priorities, daemon threads, thread groups, and handlers for uncaught exceptions.

Thread Priorities

In the Java programming language, every thread has a *priority*. By default, a thread inherits the priority of its parent thread, that is, the thread that started it. You can increase or decrease the priority of any thread with the setPriority method. You can set the priority to any value between MIN_PRIORITY (defined as 1 in the Thread class) and MAX_PRIORITY (defined as 10). NORM_PRIORITY is defined as 5.

Whenever the thread-scheduler has a chance to pick a new thread, it prefers threads with higher priority. However, thread priorities are *highly system dependent*. When the virtual machine relies on the thread implementation of the host platform, the Java thread priorities are mapped to the priority levels of the host platform, which may have more or fewer thread priority levels.

For example, Windows NT/XP has seven priority levels. Some of the Java priorities will map to the same operating system level. In the Sun JVM for Linux, thread priorities are ignored altogether—all threads have the same priority.

Thus, it is best to treat thread priorities only as hints to the scheduler. You should never structure your programs so that their correct functioning depends on priority levels.

CAUTION: If you do use priorities, you should be aware of a common beginner's error. If you have several threads with a high priority that rarely block, the lower-priority threads may *never* execute. Whenever the scheduler decides to run a new thread, it will choose among the highest-priority threads first, even though that may starve the lower-priority threads completely.

---

 java.lang.Thread 1.0

- void setPriority(int newPriority)
  sets the priority of this thread. The priority must be between Thread.MIN_PRIORITY and Thread.MAX_PRIORITY. Use Thread.NORM_PRIORITY for normal priority.

- static int MIN_PRIORITY
  is the minimum priority that a Thread can have. The minimum priority value is 1.

- static int NORM_PRIORITY
  is the default priority of a Thread. The default priority is 5.

- static int MAX_PRIORITY
  is the maximum priority that a Thread can have. The maximum priority value is 10.

- static void yield()
  causes the currently executing thread to yield. If there are other runnable threads with a priority at least as high as the priority of this thread, they will be scheduled next. Note that this is a static method.

Daemon Threads

You can turn a thread into a *daemon thread* by calling

    t.setDaemon(true);

There is nothing demonic about such a thread. A daemon is simply a thread that has no other role in life than to serve others. Examples are timer threads that send regular "timer ticks" to other threads. When only daemon threads remain, the virtual machine exits. There is no point in keeping the program running if all remaining threads are daemons.

 java.lang.Thread 1.0

- `void setDaemon(boolean isDaemon)`
  marks this thread as a daemon thread or a user thread. This method must be called before the thread is started.

Thread Groups

Some programs contain quite a few threads. It then becomes useful to categorize them by functionality. For example, consider an Internet browser. If many threads are trying to acquire images from a server and the user clicks on a Stop button to interrupt the loading of the current page, then it is handy to have a way of interrupting all these threads simultaneously. The Java programming language lets you construct what it calls a *thread group* so that you can simultaneously work with a group of threads.

You construct a thread group with the constructor:

```
String groupName = . . .;
ThreadGroup g = new ThreadGroup(groupName)
```

The string argument of the `ThreadGroup` constructor identifies the group and must be unique. You then add threads to the thread group by specifying the thread group in the thread constructor.

```
Thread t = new Thread(g, threadName);
```

To find out whether any threads of a particular group are still runnable, use the `activeCount` method.

```
if (g.activeCount() == 0)
{
    // all threads in the group g have stopped
}
```

To interrupt all threads in a thread group, simply call `interrupt` on the group object.

```
g.interrupt(); // interrupt all threads in group g
```

However, executors let you achieve the same task without requiring the use of thread groups—see page 63.

Thread groups can have child subgroups. By default, a newly created thread group becomes a child of the current thread group. But you can also explicitly name the parent group in the constructor (see the API notes). Methods such as `activeCount` and `interrupt` refer to all threads in their group and all child groups.

 java.lang.Thread 1.0

- `Thread(ThreadGroup g, String name)`
  creates a new `Thread` that belongs to a given `ThreadGroup`.

Parameters:	g	The thread group to which the new thread belongs
	name	The name of the new thread

- `ThreadGroup getThreadGroup()`
  returns the thread group of this thread.

 java.lang.ThreadGroup 1.0

- `ThreadGroup(String name)`
  creates a new `ThreadGroup`. Its parent will be the thread group of the current thread.

Parameters:	name	The name of the new thread group

- `ThreadGroup(ThreadGroup parent, String name)`
  creates a new ThreadGroup.

  Parameters: parent   The parent thread group of the new thread group

  name   The name of the new thread group

- `int activeCount()`
  returns an upper bound for the number of active threads in the thread group.

- `int enumerate(Thread[] list)`
  gets references to every active thread in this thread group. You can use the `activeCount` method to get an upper bound for the array; this method returns the number of threads put into the array. If the array is too short (presumably because more threads were spawned after the call to `activeCount`), then as many threads as fit are inserted.

  Parameters: list   An array to be filled with the thread references

- `ThreadGroup getParent()`
  gets the parent of this thread group.

- `void interrupt()`
  interrupts all threads in this thread group and all of its child groups.

Handlers for Uncaught Exceptions

The `run` method of a thread cannot throw any checked exceptions, but it can be terminated by an unchecked exception. In that case, the thread dies.

However, there is no catch clause to which the exception can be propagated. Instead, just before the thread dies, the exception is passed to a handler for uncaught exceptions.

The handler must belong to a class that implements the `Thread.UncaughtExceptionHandler` interface. That interface has a single method,

```
void uncaughtException(Thread t, Throwable e)
```

As of JDK 5.0, you can install a handler into any thread with the `setUncaughtExceptionHandler` method. You can also install a default handler for all threads with the static method `setDefaultUncaughtExceptionHandler` of the `Thread` class. A replacement handler might use the logging API to send reports of uncaught exceptions into a log file.

If you don't install a default handler, the default handler is `null`. However, if you don't install a handler for an individual thread, the handler is the thread's `ThreadGroup` object.

The `ThreadGroup` class implements the `Thread.UncaughtExceptionHandler` interface. Its `uncaughtException` method takes the following action:

1. If the thread group has a parent, then the `uncaughtException` method of the parent group is called.
2. Otherwise, if the `Thread.getDefaultExceptionHandler` method returns a non-`null` handler, it is called.
3. Otherwise, if the `Throwable` is an instance of `ThreadDeath`, nothing happens.
4. Otherwise, the name of the thread and the stack trace of the `Throwable` are printed on `System.err`.

That is the stack trace that you have undoubtedly seen many times in your programs.

 NOTE: Prior to JDK 5.0, you could not install a handler for uncaught exceptions into each thread, nor could you specify a default handler. To install a handler, you needed to subclass the `ThreadGroup` class and override the `uncaughtException` method.

java.lang.Thread 1.0

- static void setDefaultUncaughtExceptionHandler(Thread.UncaughtExceptionHandler handler) 5.0
- static Thread.UncaughtExceptionHandler getDefaultUncaughtExceptionHandler() 5.0
  set or get the default handler for uncaught exceptions.

- void setUncaughtExceptionHandler(Thread.UncaughtExceptionHandler handler) 5.0
- Thread.UncaughtExceptionHandler getUncaughtExceptionHandler() 5.0
  set or get the handler for uncaught exceptions. If no handler is installed, the thread group object is the handler.

java.lang.Thread.UncaughtExceptionHandler 5.0

- void uncaughtException(Thread t, Throwable e)
  Define this method to log a custom report when a thread is terminated with an uncaught exception.

  Parameters: t   The thread that was terminated due to an uncaught exception

  e   The uncaught exception object

java.lang.ThreadGroup 1.0

- void uncaughtException(Thread t, Throwable e)
  calls this method of the parent thread group if there is a parent, or calls the default handler of the Thread class if there is a default handler, or otherwise prints a stack trace to the standard error stream. (However, if e is a ThreadDeath object, then the stack trace is suppressed. ThreadDeath objects are generated by the deprecated stop method.)

Synchronization

In most practical multithreaded applications, two or more threads need to share access to the same objects. What happens if two threads have access to the same object and each calls a method that modifies the state of the object? As you might imagine, the threads can step on each other's toes. Depending on the order in which the data were accessed, corrupted objects can result. Such a situation is often called a *race condition.*

An Example of a Race Condition

To avoid corruption of shared data by multiple threads, you must learn how to *synchronize the access*. In this section, you'll see what happens if you do not use synchronization. In the next section, you'll see how to synchronize data access.

In the next test program, we simulate a bank with a number of accounts. We randomly generate transactions that move money between these accounts. Each account has one thread. Each transaction moves a random amount of money from the account serviced by the thread to another random account.

The simulation code is straightforward. We have the class Bank with the method transfer. This method transfers some amount of money from one account to another. If the source account does not have enough money in it, then the call simply returns. Here is the code for the transfer method of the Bank class.

```
public void transfer(int from, int to, double amount)
   // CAUTION: unsafe when called from multiple threads
{
   System.out.print(Thread.currentThread());
   accounts[from] -= amount;
```

```
    System.out.printf(" %10.2f from %d to %d", amount, from, to);
    accounts[to] += amount;
    System.out.printf(" Total Balance: %10.2f%n", getTotalBalance());
}
```

Here is the code for the TransferRunnable class. Its run method keeps moving money out of a fixed bank account. In each iteration, the run method picks a random target account and a random amount, calls transfer on the bank object, and then sleeps.

```
class TransferRunnable implements Runnable
{
    . . .
    public void run()
    {
        try
        {
            int toAccount = (int) (bank.size() * Math.random());
            double amount = maxAmount * Math.random();
            bank.transfer(fromAccount, toAccount, amount);
            Thread.sleep((int) (DELAY * Math.random()));
        }
        catch(InterruptedException e) {}
    }
}
```

When this simulation runs, we do not know how much money is in any one bank account at any time. But we do know that the total amount of money in all the accounts should remain unchanged because all we do is move money from one account to another.

At the end of each transaction, the transfer method recomputes the total and prints it.

This program never finishes. Just press CTRL+C to kill the program.

Here is a typical printout:

```
. . .
Thread[Thread-11,5,main]      588.48 from 11 to 44 Total Balance:  100000.00
Thread[Thread-12,5,main]      976.11 from 12 to 22 Total Balance:  100000.00
Thread[Thread-14,5,main]      521.51 from 14 to 22 Total Balance:  100000.00
Thread[Thread-13,5,main]      359.89 from 13 to 81 Total Balance:  100000.00
. . .
Thread[Thread-36,5,main]      401.71 from 36 to 73 Total Balance:   99291.06
Thread[Thread-35,5,main]      691.46 from 35 to 77 Total Balance:   99291.06
Thread[Thread-37,5,main]       78.64 from 37 to 3 Total Balance:    99291.06
Thread[Thread-34,5,main]      197.11 from 34 to 69 Total Balance:   99291.06
Thread[Thread-36,5,main]       85.96 from 36 to 4 Total Balance:    99291.06
. . .
Thread[Thread-4,5,main]Thread[Thread-33,5,main]       7.31 from 31 to 32 Total Balance:   99979.24
        627.50 from 4 to 5 Total Balance:   99979.24
. . .
```

As you can see, something is very wrong. For a few transactions, the bank balance remains at $100,000, which is the correct total for 100 accounts of $1,000 each. But after some time, the balance changes slightly. When you run this program, you may find that errors happen quickly or it may take a very long time for the balance to become corrupted. This situation does not inspire confidence, and you would probably not want to deposit your hard-earned money in this bank.

Example 1–3 provides the complete source code. See if you can spot the problem with the code. We will unravel the mystery in the next section.

Example 1–3: UnsynchBankTest.java

```
1. /**
2.    This program shows data corruption when multiple threads access a data structure.
3. */
4. public class UnsynchBankTest
5. {
6.    public static void main(String[] args)
7.    {
8.       Bank b = new Bank(NACCOUNTS, INITIAL_BALANCE);
9.       int i;
10.      for (i = 0; i < NACCOUNTS; i++)
11.      {
12.         TransferRunnable r = new TransferRunnable(b, i, INITIAL_BALANCE);
13.         Thread t = new Thread(r);
14.         t.start();
15.      }
16.   }
17.
18.   public static final int NACCOUNTS = 100;
19.   public static final double INITIAL_BALANCE = 1000;
20. }
21.
22. /**
23.    A bank with a number of bank accounts.
24. */
25. class Bank
26. {
27.    /**
28.       Constructs the bank.
29.       @param n the number of accounts
30.       @param initialBalance the initial balance
31.       for each account
32.    */
33.    public Bank(int n, double initialBalance)
34.    {
35.       accounts = new double[n];
36.       for (int i = 0; i < accounts.length; i++)
37.          accounts[i] = initialBalance;
38.    }
39.
40.    /**
41.       Transfers money from one account to another.
42.       @param from the account to transfer from
43.       @param to the account to transfer to
44.       @param amount the amount to transfer
45.    */
46.    public void transfer(int from, int to, double amount)
47.    {
48.       if (accounts[from] < amount) return;
49.       System.out.print(Thread.currentThread());
50.       accounts[from] -= amount;
51.       System.out.printf(" %10.2f from %d to %d", amount, from, to);
52.       accounts[to] += amount;
53.       System.out.printf(" Total Balance: %10.2f%n", getTotalBalance());
54.    }
```

```
55.
56.    /**
57.       Gets the sum of all account balances.
58.       @return the total balance
59.    */
60.    public double getTotalBalance()
61.    {
62.       double sum = 0;
63.
64.       for (double a : accounts)
65.          sum += a;
66.
67.       return sum;
68.    }
69.
70.    /**
71.       Gets the number of accounts in the bank.
72.       @return the number of accounts
73.    */
74.    public int size()
75.    {
76.       return accounts.length;
77.    }
78.
79.    private final double[] accounts;
80. }
81.
82. /**
83.    A runnable that transfers money from an account to other
84.    accounts in a bank.
85. */
86. class TransferRunnable implements Runnable
87. {
88.    /**
89.       Constructs a transfer runnable.
90.       @param b the bank between whose account money is transferred
91.       @param from the account to transfer money from
92.       @param max the maximum amount of money in each transfer
93.    */
94.    public TransferRunnable(Bank b, int from, double max)
95.    {
96.       bank = b;
97.       fromAccount = from;
98.       maxAmount = max;
99.    }
100.
101.    public void run()
102.    {
103.       try
104.       {
105.          while (true)
106.          {
107.             int toAccount = (int) (bank.size() * Math.random());
108.             double amount = maxAmount * Math.random();
109.             bank.transfer(fromAccount, toAccount, amount);
110.             Thread.sleep((int) (DELAY * Math.random()));
```

```
111.          }
112.        }
113.        catch (InterruptedException e) {}
114.   }
115.
116.   private Bank bank;
117.   private int fromAccount;
118.   private double maxAmount;
119.   private int DELAY = 10;
120. }
```

The Race Condition Explained

In the previous section, we ran a program in which several threads updated bank account balances. After a while, errors crept in and some amount of money was either lost or spontaneously created. This problem occurs when two threads are simultaneously trying to update an account. Suppose two threads simultaneously carry out the instruction

```
accounts[to] += amount;
```

The problem is that these are not *atomic* operations. The instruction might be processed as follows:

1. Load accounts[to] into a register.
2. Add amount.
3. Move the result back to accounts[to].

Now, suppose the first thread executes Steps 1 and 2, and then it is interrupted. Suppose the second thread awakens and updates the same entry in the account array. Then, the first thread awakens and completes its Step 3.

That action wipes out the modification of the other thread. As a result, the total is no longer correct. (See Figure 1–4.)

Our test program detects this corruption. (Of course, there is a slight chance of false alarms if the thread is interrupted as it is performing the tests!)

 NOTE: You can actually peek at the virtual machine bytecodes that execute each statement in our class. Run the command

```
javap -c -v Bank
```

to decompile the Bank.class file. For example, the line

```
accounts[to] += amount;
```

is translated into the following bytecodes:

```
aload_0
getfield       #2; //Field accounts:[D
iload_2
dup2
daload
dload_3
dadd
dastore
```

What these codes mean does not matter. The point is that the increment command is made up of several instructions, and the thread executing them can be interrupted at the point of any instruction.

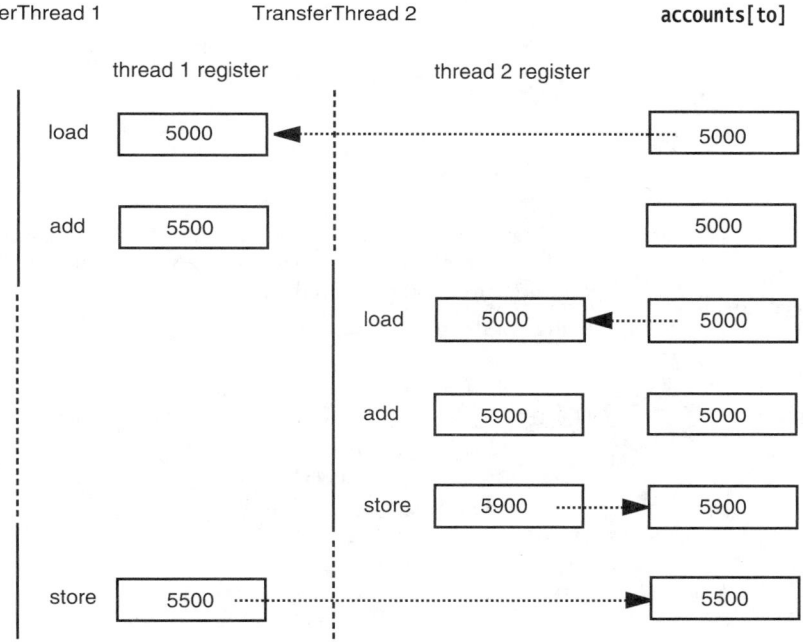

Figure 1–4: Simultaneous access by two threads

What is the chance of this corruption occurring? We boosted the chance of observing the problem by interleaving the print statements with the statements that update the balance.

If you omit the print statements, the risk of corruption is quite a bit lower because each thread does so little work before going to sleep again, and it is unlikely that the scheduler will preempt it in the middle of the computation. However, the risk of corruption does not completely go away. If you run lots of threads on a heavily loaded machine, then the program will still fail even after you have eliminated the print statements. The failure may take a few minutes or hours or days to occur. Frankly, there are few things worse in the life of a programmer than an error that only manifests itself once every few days.

The real problem is that the work of the transfer method can be interrupted in the middle. If we could ensure that the method runs to completion before the thread loses control, then the state of the bank account object would never be corrupted.

Lock Objects

Starting with JDK 5.0, there are two mechanisms for protecting a code block from concurrent access. Earlier versions of Java used the synchronized keyword for this purpose, and JDK 5.0 introduces the ReentrantLock class. The synchronized keyword automatically provides a lock as well as an associated "condition." We believe that it is easier to understand the synchronized keyword after you have seen locks and conditions in isolation. JDK 5.0 provides separate classes for these fundamental mechanisms, which we explain here and on page 30. We will discuss the synchronized keyword on page 35.

The basic outline for protecting a code block with a ReentrantLock is:

```
myLock.lock(); // a ReentrantLock object
try
{
    critical section
}
finally
{
    myLock.unlock(); // make sure the lock is unlocked even if an exception is thrown
}
```

This construct guarantees that only one thread at a time can enter the critical section. As soon as one thread locks the lock object, no other thread can get past the lock statement. When other threads call lock, they are blocked until the first thread unlocks the lock object.

Let us use a lock to protect the transfer method of the Bank class.

```
public class Bank
{
    public void transfer(int from, int to, int amount)
    {
        bankLock.lock();
        try
        {
            if (accounts[from] < amount) return;
            System.out.print(Thread.currentThread());
            accounts[from] -= amount;
            System.out.printf(" %10.2f from %d to %d", amount, from, to);
            accounts[to] += amount;
            System.out.printf(" Total Balance: %10.2f%n", getTotalBalance());
        }
        finally
        {
            bankLock.unlock();
        }
    }
    . . .
    private Lock bankLock = new ReentrantLock(); // ReentrantLock implements the Lock interface
}
```

Suppose one thread calls transfer and gets preempted before it is done. Suppose a second thread also calls transfer. The second thread cannot acquire the lock and is blocked in the call to the lock method. It is deactivated and must wait for the first thread to finish executing the transfer method. When the first thread unlocks the lock, then the second thread can proceed (see Figure 1–5).

Try it out. Add the locking code to the transfer method and run the program again. You can run it forever, and the bank balance will not become corrupted.

Note that each Bank object has its own ReentrantLock object. If two threads try to access the same Bank object, then the lock serves to serialize the access. However, if two threads access different Bank objects, then each thread acquires a different lock and neither thread is blocked. This is as it should be, because the threads cannot interfere with another when they manipulate different Bank instances.

The lock is called *reentrant* because a thread can repeatedly acquire a lock that it already owns. The lock keeps a *hold count* that keeps track of the nested calls to the lock method. The thread has to call unlock for every call to lock in order to relinquish the lock. Because of this feature, code that is protected by a lock can call another method that uses the same locks.

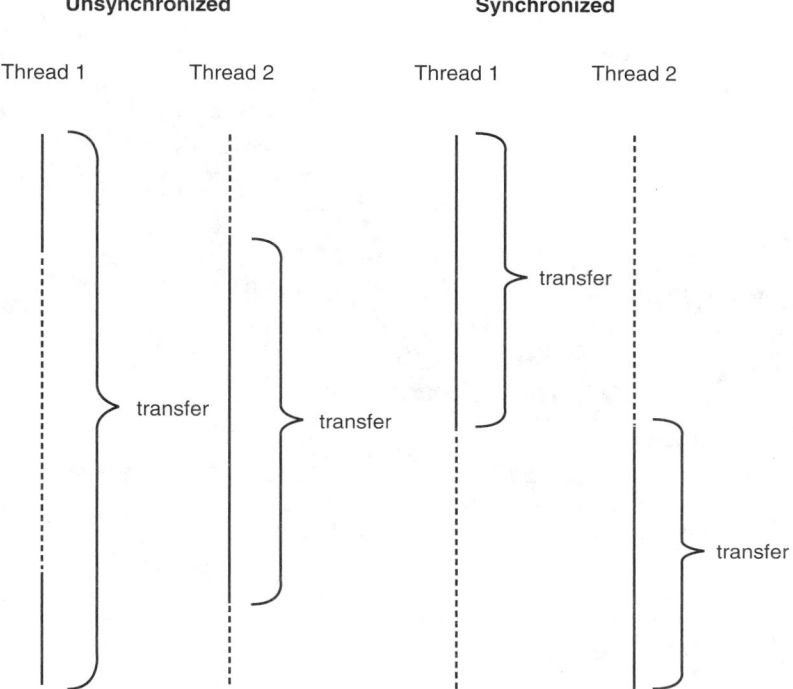

Unsynchronized   **Synchronized**

Thread 1   Thread 2   Thread 1   Thread 2

transfer

transfer   transfer

transfer

Figure 1–5: Comparison of unsynchronized and synchronized threads

For example, the transfer method calls the getTotalBalance method, which also locks the bankLock object, which now has a hold count of 2. When the getTotalBalance method exits, the hold count is back to 1. When the transfer method exits, the hold count is 0, and the thread relinquishes the lock.

In general, you will want to protect blocks of code that require multiple operations to update or inspect a data structure. You are then assured that these operations run to completion before another thread can use the same object.

CAUTION: You need to be careful that code in a critical section is not bypassed through the throwing of an exception. If an exception is thrown before the end of the section, then the finally clause will relinquish the lock but the object may be in a damaged state.

---

 java.util.concurrent.locks.Lock 5.0

- void lock()
  acquires this lock; blocks if the lock is currently owned by another thread.
- void unlock()
  releases this lock.

 java.util.concurrent.locks.ReentrantLock 5.0

- ReentrantLock()
  constructs a reentrant lock that can be used to protect a critical section.

Condition Objects

Often, a thread enters a critical section, only to discover that it can't proceed until a condition is fulfilled. You use a *condition object* to manage threads that have acquired a lock but cannot do useful work. In this section, we introduce the implementation of condition objects in the Java library. (For historical reasons, condition objects are often called *condition variables*.)

Let us refine our simulation of the bank. We do not want to transfer money out of an account that does not have the funds to cover the transfer. Note that we cannot use code like

```
if (bank.getBalance(from) >= amount)
    bank.transfer(from, to, amount);
```

It is entirely possible that the current thread will be deactivated between the successful outcome of the test and the call to transfer.

```
if (bank.getBalance(from) >= amount)
        // thread might be deactivated at this point
    bank.transfer(from, to, amount);
```

By the time the thread is running again, the account balance may have fallen below the withdrawal amount. You must make sure that the thread cannot be interrupted between the test and the insertion. You do so by protecting both the test and the transfer action with a lock:

```
public void transfer(int from, int to, int amount)
{
    bankLock.lock();
    try
    {
        while (accounts[from] < amount)
        {
            // wait
            . . .
        }
        // transfer funds
        . . .
    }
    finally
    {
        bankLock.unlock();
    }
}
```

Now, what do we do when there is not enough money in the account? We wait until some other thread has added funds. But this thread has just gained exclusive access to the bankLock, so no other thread has a chance to make a deposit. This is where condition objects come in.

A lock object can have one or more associated condition objects. You obtain a condition object with the newCondition method. It is customary to give each condition object a name that evokes the condition that it represents. For example, here we set up a condition object to represent the "sufficient funds" condition.

```
class Bank
{
    public Bank()
    {
```

```
        . . .
      sufficientFunds = bankLock.newCondition();
   }
      . . .
   private Condition sufficientFunds;
}
```

If the `transfer` method finds that sufficient funds are not available, it calls

```
sufficientFunds.await();
```

The current thread is now blocked and gives up the lock. This lets in another thread that can, we hope, increase the account balance.

There is an essential difference between a thread that is waiting to acquire a lock and a thread that has called `await`. Once a thread calls the `await` method, it enters a *wait set* for that condition. The thread is *not* unblocked when the lock is available. Instead, it stays blocked until another thread has called the `signalAll` method on the same condition.

When another thread transfers money, then it should call

```
sufficientFunds.signalAll();
```

This call unblocks all threads that are waiting for the condition. When the threads are removed from the wait set, they are again runnable and the scheduler will eventually activate them again. At that time, they will attempt to reenter the object. As soon as the lock is available, one of them will acquire the lock *and continue where it left off*, returning from the call to `await`.

At this time, the thread should test the condition again. There is no guarantee that the condition is now fulfilled—the `signalAll` method merely signals to the waiting threads that it *may be* fulfilled at this time and that it is worth checking for the condition again.

 NOTE: In general, a call to `await` should always be inside a loop of the form

```
while (!(ok to proceed))
    condition.await();
```

It is crucially important that *some* other thread calls the `signalAll` method eventually. When a thread calls `await`, it has no way of unblocking itself. It puts its faith in the other threads. If none of them bother to unblock the waiting thread, it will never run again. This can lead to unpleasant *deadlock* situations. If all other threads are blocked and the last active thread calls `await` without unblocking one of the others, then it also blocks. No thread is left to unblock the others, and the program hangs.

When should you call `signalAll`? The rule of thumb is to call `signalAll` whenever the state of an object changes in a way that might be advantageous to waiting threads. For example, whenever an account balance changes, the waiting threads should be given another chance to inspect the balance. In our example, we call `signalAll` when we have finished the funds transfer.

```
public void transfer(int from, int to, int amount)
{
   bankLock.lock();
   try
   {
      while (accounts[from] < amount)
         sufficientFunds.await();
      // transfer funds
      . . .
```

```
        sufficientFunds.signalAll();
      }
      finally
      {
        bankLock.unlock();
      }
    }
```

Note that the call to signalAll does not immediately activate a waiting thread. It only unblocks the waiting threads so that they can compete for entry into the object after the current thread has exited the synchronized method.

Another method, signal, unblocks only a single thread from the wait set, chosen at random. That is more efficient than unblocking all threads, but there is a danger. If the randomly chosen thread finds that it still cannot proceed, then it becomes blocked again. If no other thread calls signal again, then the system deadlocks.

 CAUTION: A thread can only call await, signalAll, or signal on a condition when it owns the lock of the condition.

If you run the sample program in Example 1–4, you will notice that nothing ever goes wrong. The total balance stays at $100,000 forever. No account ever has a negative balance. (Again, you need to press CTRL+C to terminate the program.) You may also notice that the program runs a bit slower—this is the price you pay for the added bookkeeping involved in the synchronization mechanism.

Example 1–4: SynchBankTest.java

```
1. import java.util.concurrent.locks.*;
2.
3. /**
4.    This program shows how multiple threads can safely access a data structure.
5. */
6. public class SynchBankTest
7. {
8.    public static void main(String[] args)
9.    {
10.       Bank b = new Bank(NACCOUNTS, INITIAL_BALANCE);
11.       int i;
12.       for (i = 0; i < NACCOUNTS; i++)
13.       {
14.          TransferRunnable r = new TransferRunnable(b, i, INITIAL_BALANCE);
15.          Thread t = new Thread(r);
16.          t.start();
17.       }
18.    }
19.
20.    public static final int NACCOUNTS = 100;
21.    public static final double INITIAL_BALANCE = 1000;
22. }
23.
24. /**
25.    A bank with a number of bank accounts.
26. */
27. class Bank
28. {
```

```
29.    /**
30.       Constructs the bank.
31.       @param n the number of accounts
32.       @param initialBalance the initial balance
33.       for each account
34.    */
35.    public Bank(int n, double initialBalance)
36.    {
37.       accounts = new double[n];
38.       for (int i = 0; i < accounts.length; i++)
39.          accounts[i] = initialBalance;
40.       bankLock = new ReentrantLock();
41.       sufficientFunds = bankLock.newCondition();
42.    }
43.
44.    /**
45.       Transfers money from one account to another.
46.       @param from the account to transfer from
47.       @param to the account to transfer to
48.       @param amount the amount to transfer
49.    */
50.    public void transfer(int from, int to, double amount)
51.       throws InterruptedException
52.    {
53.       bankLock.lock();
54.       try
55.       {
56.          while (accounts[from] < amount)
57.             sufficientFunds.await();
58.          System.out.print(Thread.currentThread());
59.          accounts[from] -= amount;
60.          System.out.printf(" %10.2f from %d to %d", amount, from, to);
61.          accounts[to] += amount;
62.          System.out.printf(" Total Balance: %10.2f%n", getTotalBalance());
63.          sufficientFunds.signalAll();
64.       }
65.       finally
66.       {
67.          bankLock.unlock();
68.       }
69.    }
70.
71.    /**
72.       Gets the sum of all account balances.
73.       @return the total balance
74.    */
75.    public double getTotalBalance()
76.    {
77.       bankLock.lock();
78.       try
79.       {
80.          double sum = 0;
81.
82.          for (double a : accounts)
83.             sum += a;
```

```
 84.
 85.        return sum;
 86.      }
 87.      finally
 88.      {
 89.        bankLock.unlock();
 90.      }
 91.   }
 92.
 93.   /**
 94.      Gets the number of accounts in the bank.
 95.      @return the number of accounts
 96.   */
 97.   public int size()
 98.   {
 99.      return accounts.length;
100.   }
101.
102.   private final double[] accounts;
103.   private Lock bankLock;
104.   private Condition sufficientFunds;
105. }
106.
107. /**
108.    A runnable that transfers money from an account to other
109.    accounts in a bank.
110. */
111. class TransferRunnable implements Runnable
112. {
113.   /**
114.      Constructs a transfer runnable.
115.      @param b the bank between whose account money is transferred
116.      @param from the account to transfer money from
117.      @param max the maximum amount of money in each transfer
118.   */
119.   public TransferRunnable(Bank b, int from, double max)
120.   {
121.      bank = b;
122.      fromAccount = from;
123.      maxAmount = max;
124.   }
125.
126.   public void run()
127.   {
128.      try
129.      {
130.         while (true)
131.         {
132.            int toAccount = (int) (bank.size() * Math.random());
133.            double amount = maxAmount * Math.random();
134.            bank.transfer(fromAccount, toAccount, amount);
135.            Thread.sleep((int) (DELAY * Math.random()));
136.         }
137.      }
138.      catch (InterruptedException e) {}
```

```
139.    }
140.
141.    private Bank bank;
142.    private int fromAccount;
143.    private double maxAmount;
144.    private int repetitions;
145.    private int DELAY = 10;
146. }
```

 java.util.concurrent.locks.Lock 5.0

- Condition newCondition()
  returns a condition object that is associated with this lock.

 java.util.concurrent.locks.Condition 5.0

- void await()
  puts this thread on the wait set for this condition.
- void signalAll()
  unblocks all threads in the wait set for this condition.
- void signal()
  unblocks one randomly selected thread in the wait set for this condition.

The *synchronized* Keyword

In the preceding sections, you saw how to use Lock and Condition objects. Before going any further, let us summarize the key points about locks and conditions:

- A lock protects sections of code, allowing only one thread to execute the code at a time.
- A lock manages threads that are trying to enter a protected code segment.
- A lock can have one or more associated condition objects.
- Each condition object manages threads that have entered a protected code section but that cannot proceed.

Before the Lock and Condition interfaces were added to JDK 5.0, the Java language used a different concurrency mechanism. Ever since version 1.0, *every object* in Java has an implicit lock. If a method is declared with the synchronized keyword, then the object's lock protects the entire method. That is, to call the method, a thread must acquire the object lock.

In other words,

```
public synchronized void method()
{
    method body
}
```

is the equivalent of

```
public void method()
{
    implicitLock.lock();
    try
    {
        method body
    }
    finally { implicitLock.unlock(); }
}
```

For example, instead of using an explicit lock, we can simply declare the transfer method of the Bank class as synchronized.

The implicit object lock has a single associated condition. The wait method adds a thread to the wait set, and the notifyAll/notify methods unblock waiting threads. In other words, calling wait or notifyAll is the equivalent of

```
implicitCondition.await();
implicitCondition.signalAll();
```

> **NOTE:** The wait and signal methods belong to the Object class. The Condition methods had to be named await and signalAll so that they don't conflict with the final methods wait and notify-All methods of the Object class.

For example, you can implement the Bank class in Java like this:

```
class Bank
{
    public synchronized void transfer(int from, int to, int amount) throws InterruptedException
    {
        while (accounts[from] < amount)
            wait(); // wait on object lock's single condition
        accounts[from] -= amount;
        accounts[to] += amount;
        notifyAll(); // notify all threads waiting on the condition
    }
    public synchronized double getTotalBalance() { . . . }
    private double accounts[];
}
```

As you can see, using the synchronized keyword yields code that is much more concise. Of course, to understand this code, you have to know that each object has an implicit lock, and that the lock has an implicit condition. The lock manages the threads that try to enter a synchronized method. The condition manages the threads that have called wait.

However, the implicit locks and conditions have some limitations. Among them are:

- You cannot interrupt a thread that is trying to acquire a lock.
- You cannot specify a timeout when trying to acquire a lock.
- Having a single condition per lock can be inefficient.
- The virtual machine locking primitives do not map well to the most efficient locking mechanisms available in hardware.

What should you use in your code—Lock and Condition objects or synchronized methods? Here is our recommendation:

1. It is best to use neither Lock/Condition nor the synchronized keyword. In many situations, you can use one of the mechanisms of the java.util.concurrent package that do all the locking for you. For example, on page 48, you will see how to use a blocking queue to synchronize threads that work on a common task.

2. If the synchronized keyword works for your situation, by all means, use it. You write less code and have less room for error. Example 1–5 shows the bank example, implemented with synchronized methods.

3. Use Lock/Condition if you specifically need the additional power that these constructs give you.

> **NOTE:** At least for now, using the `synchronized` keyword has an added benefit. Tools that monitor the virtual machine can report on the implicit locks and conditions, which is helpful for debugging deadlock problems. It will take some time for these tools to be extended to the `java.util.concurrent` mechanisms.

Example 1–5: SynchBankTest2.java

```
1.  /**
2.     This program shows how multiple threads can safely access a data structure, using
3.     synchronized methods.
4.  */
5.  public class SynchBankTest2
6.  {
7.     public static void main(String[] args)
8.     {
9.        Bank b = new Bank(NACCOUNTS, INITIAL_BALANCE);
10.       int i;
11.       for (i = 0; i < NACCOUNTS; i++)
12.       {
13.          TransferRunnable r = new TransferRunnable(b, i, INITIAL_BALANCE);
14.          Thread t = new Thread(r);
15.          t.start();
16.       }
17.    }
18.
19.    public static final int NACCOUNTS = 100;
20.    public static final double INITIAL_BALANCE = 1000;
21. }
22.
23. /**
24.    A bank with a number of bank accounts.
25. */
26. class Bank
27. {
28.    /**
29.       Constructs the bank.
30.       @param n the number of accounts
31.       @param initialBalance the initial balance
32.       for each account
33.    */
34.    public Bank(int n, double initialBalance)
35.    {
36.       accounts = new double[n];
37.       for (int i = 0; i < accounts.length; i++)
38.          accounts[i] = initialBalance;
39.    }
40.
41.    /**
42.       Transfers money from one account to another.
43.       @param from the account to transfer from
44.       @param to the account to transfer to
45.       @param amount the amount to transfer
46.    */
```

```java
47.    public synchronized void transfer(int from, int to, double amount)
48.        throws InterruptedException
49.    {
50.        while (accounts[from] < amount)
51.            wait();
52.        System.out.print(Thread.currentThread());
53.        accounts[from] -= amount;
54.        System.out.printf(" %10.2f from %d to %d", amount, from, to);
55.        accounts[to] += amount;
56.        System.out.printf(" Total Balance: %10.2f%n", getTotalBalance());
57.        notifyAll();
58.    }
59.
60.    /**
61.       Gets the sum of all account balances.
62.       @return the total balance
63.    */
64.    public synchronized double getTotalBalance()
65.    {
66.        double sum = 0;
67.
68.        for (double a : accounts)
69.            sum += a;
70.
71.        return sum;
72.    }
73.
74.    /**
75.       Gets the number of accounts in the bank.
76.       @return the number of accounts
77.    */
78.    public int size()
79.    {
80.        return accounts.length;
81.    }
82.
83.    private final double[] accounts;
84. }
85.
86. /**
87.    A runnable that transfers money from an account to other
88.    accounts in a bank.
89. */
90. class TransferRunnable implements Runnable
91. {
92.    /**
93.       Constructs a transfer runnable.
94.       @param b the bank between whose account money is transferred
95.       @param from the account to transfer money from
96.       @param max the maximum amount of money in each transfer
97.    */
98.    public TransferRunnable(Bank b, int from, double max)
99.    {
100.       bank = b;
```

```
101.      fromAccount = from;
102.      maxAmount = max;
103.   }
104.
105.   public void run()
106.   {
107.      try
108.      {
109.         while (true)
110.         {
111.            int toAccount = (int) (bank.size() * Math.random());
112.            double amount = maxAmount * Math.random();
113.            bank.transfer(fromAccount, toAccount, amount);
114.            Thread.sleep((int) (DELAY * Math.random()));
115.         }
116.      }
117.      catch (InterruptedException e) {}
118.   }
119.
120.   private Bank bank;
121.   private int fromAccount;
122.   private double maxAmount;
123.   private int repetitions;
124.   private int DELAY = 10;
125. }
```

java.lang.Object 1.0

- void notifyAll()

  unblocks the threads that called wait on this object. This method can only be called from within a synchronized method or block. The method throws an IllegalMonitorStateException if the current thread is not the owner of the object's lock.

- void notify()

  unblocks one randomly selected thread among the threads that called wait on this object. This method can only be called from within a synchronized method or block. The method throws an IllegalMonitorStateException if the current thread is not the owner of the object's lock.

- void wait()

  causes a thread to wait until it is notified. This method can only be called from within a synchronized method. It throws an IllegalMonitorStateException if the current thread is not the owner of the object's lock.

- void wait(long millis)
- void wait(long millis, int nanos)

  causes a thread to wait until it is notified or until the specified amount of time has passed. These methods can only be called from within a synchronized method. They throw an IllegalMonitorStateException if the current thread is not the owner of the object's lock.

Parameters:	millis	The number of milliseconds
	nanos	The number of nanoseconds, < 1,000,000

Monitors

The locks and conditions are powerful tools for thread synchronization, but they are not very object oriented. For many years, researchers have looked for ways to make multithreading safe without forcing programmers to think about explicit locks. One of the most successful solutions is the *monitor* concept that was pioneered by Per Brinch Hansen and Tony Hoare in the 1970s. In the terminology of Java, a monitor has these properties:

- A monitor is a class with only private fields.
- Each object of that class has an associated lock.
- All methods are locked by that lock. In other words, if a client calls `obj.method()`, then the lock for `obj` is automatically acquired at the beginning of the method call and relinquished when the method returns. Because all fields are private, this arrangement ensures that no thread can access the fields while another thread manipulates them.
- The lock can have any number of associated conditions.

Earlier versions of monitors had a single condition, with a rather elegant syntax. You can simply call `await accounts[from] >= balance` without using an explicit condition variable. However, research showed that indiscriminate retesting of conditions can be inefficient. This problem is solved with explicit condition variables, each managing a separate set of threads.

The Java designers loosely adapted the monitor concept. *Every object* in Java has an implicit lock and an implicit condition. If a method is declared with the `synchronized` keyword, then it acts like a monitor method. The condition variable is accessed by calling `wait/notify/notifyAll`.

However, a Java object differs from a monitor in two important ways, compromising its security:

- Fields are not required to be `private`.
- Methods are not required to be `synchronized`.

This disrespect for security enraged Per Brinch Hansen. In a scathing review of the multithreading primitives in Java, he wrote: "It is astounding to me that Java's insecure parallelism is taken seriously by the programming community, a quarter of a century after the invention of monitors and Concurrent Pascal. It has no merit." [Java's Insecure Parallelism, *ACM SIGPLAN Notices* 34:38–45, April 1999]

Synchronized Blocks

However, a Java object differs from a monitor in three ways:

- Fields are not required to be `private`.
- Methods are not required to be `synchronized`.
- The lock has only one condition.

If you deal with legacy code, you need to know something about the built-in synchronization primitives. Recall that each object has a lock. A thread can acquire the lock in one of two ways, by calling a synchronized method or by entering a *synchronized block*. If the thread calls `obj.method()`, it acquires the lock for `obj`. Similarly, if a thread enters a block of the form

```
synchronized (obj) // this is the syntax for a synchronized block
{
    critical section
}
```

then the thread acquires the lock for `obj`. The lock is reentrant. If a thread has acquired the lock, it can acquire it again, incrementing the hold count. In particular, a synchronized method can call other synchronized methods with the same implicit parameter without having to wait for the lock.

You will often find "ad hoc" locks in legacy code, such as

```
class Bank
{
   public void transfer(int from, int to, int amount)
   {
      synchronized (lock) // an ad-hoc lock
      {
         accounts[from] -= amount;
         accounts[to] += amount;
      }
      System.out.println(. . .);
   }
   . . .
   private double accounts[];
   private Object lock = new Object(); }
```

Here, the `lock` object is created only to use the lock that every Java object possesses.

It is legal to declare static methods as synchronized. If such a method is called, it acquires the lock of the associated class object. For example, if the `Bank` class has a static synchronized method, then the lock of the `Bank.class` object is locked when it is called.

Volatile Fields

Sometimes, it seems excessive to pay the cost of synchronization just to read or write an instance field or two. After all, what can go wrong? Unfortunately, with modern processors and compilers, there is plenty of room for error:

- Computers with multiple processors can temporarily hold memory values in registers or local memory caches. As a consequence, threads running in different processors may see different values for the same memory location!

- Compilers can reorder instructions for maximum throughput. Compilers won't choose an ordering that changes the meaning of the code, but they make the assumption that memory values are only changed when there are explicit instructions in the code. However, a memory value can be changed by another thread!

If you use locks to protect code that can be accessed by multiple threads, then you won't have these problems. Compilers are required to respect locks by flushing local caches as necessary and not inappropriately reordering instructions. The details are explained in the Java Memory Model and Thread Specification developed by JSR 133 (see http://www.jcp.org/en/jsr/detail?id=133). Much of the specification is highly complex and technical, but the document also contains a number of clearly explained examples. A more accessible overview article by Brian Goetz is available at http://www-106.ibm.com/developerworks/java/library/j-jtp02244.html.

 NOTE: Brian Goetz coined the following "synchronization motto": "If you write a variable which may next be read by another thread, or you read a variable which may have last been written by another thread, you must use synchronization."

The `volatile` keyword offers a lock-free mechanism for synchronizing access to an instance field. If you declare a field as `volatile`, then the compiler and the virtual machine take into account that the field may be concurrently updated by another thread.

For example, suppose an object has a `boolean` flag `done` that is set by one thread and queried by another thread. You have two choices:

1. Use a lock, for example:

   ```
   public synchronized boolean isDone() { return done; }
   private boolean done;
   ```

   (This approach has a potential drawback: the isDone method can block if another thread has locked the object.)

2. Declare the field as volatile:

   ```
   public boolean isDone() { return done; }
   private volatile boolean done;
   ```

Of course, accessing a volatile variable will be slower than accessing a regular variable—that is the price to pay for thread safety.

 NOTE: Prior to JDK 5.0, the semantics of volatile were rather permissive. The language designers attempted to give implementors leeway in optimizing the performance of code that uses volatile fields. However, the old specification was so complex that implementors didn't always follow it, and it allowed confusing and undesirable behavior, such as immutable objects that weren't truly immutable.

In summary, concurrent access to a field is safe in these three conditions:

- The field is volatile.
- The field is final, and it is accessed after the constructor has completed.
- The field access is protected by a lock.

Deadlocks

Locks and conditions cannot solve all problems that might arise in multithreading. Consider the following situation:

Account 1: $1,200

Account 2: $1,300

Thread 1: Transfer $300 from Account 1 to Account 2

Thread 2: Transfer $400 from Account 2 to Account 1

As Figure 1–6 indicates, Threads 1 and 2 are clearly blocked. Neither can proceed because the balances in Accounts 1 and 2 are insufficient.

Is it possible that all threads are blocked because each is waiting for more money? Such a situation is called a *deadlock*.

In our program, a deadlock cannot occur for a simple reason. Each transfer amount is for, at most, $1,000. Because there are 100 accounts and a total of $100,000 in them, at least one of the accounts must have more than $1,000 at any time. The thread moving money out of that account can therefore proceed.

But if you change the run method of the threads to remove the $1,000 transaction limit, deadlocks can occur quickly. Try it out. Set NACCOUNTS to 10. Construct each transfer thread with a maxAmount of 2000 and run the program. The program will run for a while and then hang.

 TIP: When the program hangs, type CTRL+\. You will get a thread dump that lists all threads. Each thread has a stack trace, telling you where it is currently blocked.

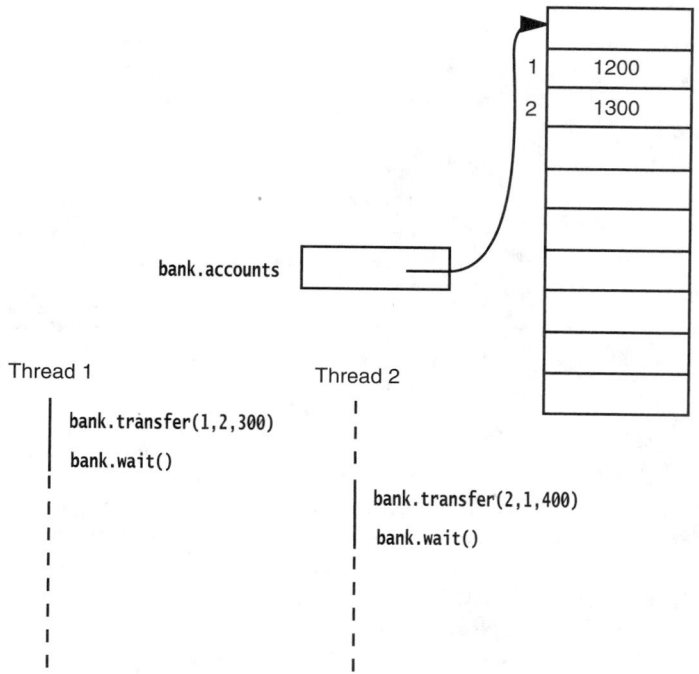

Figure 1–6: A deadlock situation

Another way to create a deadlock is to make the i'th thread responsible for putting money into the i'th account, rather than for taking it out of the i'th account. In this case, there is a chance that all threads will gang up on one account, each trying to remove more money from it than it contains. Try it out. In the SynchBankTest program, turn to the run method of the TransferRunnable class. In the call to transfer, flip fromAccount and toAccount. Run the program and see how it deadlocks almost immediately.

Here is another situation in which a deadlock can occur easily: Change the signalAll method to signal in the SynchBankTest program. You will find that the program hangs eventually. (Again, it is best to set NACCOUNTS to 10 to observe the effect more quickly.) Unlike signalAll, which notifies all threads that are waiting for added funds, the signal method unblocks only one thread. If that thread can't proceed, all threads can be blocked. Consider the following sample scenario of a developing deadlock.

    Account 1: $1,990

    All other accounts: $990 each

    Thread 1: Transfer $995 from Account 1 to Account 2

    All other threads: Transfer $995 from their account to another account

Clearly, all threads but Thread 1 are blocked, because there isn't enough money in their accounts.

Thread 1 proceeds. Afterward, we have the following situation:

    Account 1: $995

    Account 2: $1,985

All other accounts: $990 each

Then, Thread 1 calls signal. The signal method picks a thread at random to unblock. Suppose it picks Thread 3. That thread is awakened, finds that there isn't enough money in its account, and calls await again. But Thread 1 is still running. A new random transaction is generated, say,

Thread 1: Transfer $997 to from Account 1 to Account 2

Now, Thread 1 also calls await, and *all* threads are blocked. The system has deadlocked.

The culprit here is the call to signal. It only unblocks one thread, and it may not pick the thread that is essential to make progress. (In our scenario, Thread 2 must proceed to take money out of Account 2.)

Unfortunately, there is nothing in the Java programming language to avoid or break these deadlocks. You must design your program to ensure that a deadlock situation cannot occur.

Fairness

When you construct a ReentrantLock, you can specify that you want a *fair locking policy*:

```
Lock fairLock = new ReentrantLock(true);
```

A fair lock favors the thread that has been waiting for the longest time. However, this fairness guarantee can be a significant drag on performance. Therefore, by default, locks are not required to be fair.

Even if you use a fair lock, you have no guarantee that the thread scheduler is fair. If the thread scheduler chooses to neglect a thread that has been waiting a long time for the lock, then it doesn't get the chance to be treated fairly by the lock.

CAUTION: It sounds nicer to be fair, but fair locks are *a lot slower* than regular locks. You should only enable fair locking if you have a specific reason why fairness is essential for your problem. This is definitely an advanced technique.

---

 java.util.concurrent.locks.ReentrantLock 5.0

- ReentrantLock(boolean fair)
  constructs a lock with the given fairness policy.

Lock Testing and Timeouts

A thread blocks indefinitely when it calls the lock method to acquire a lock that is owned by another thread. You can be more cautious about acquiring a lock. The tryLock method tries to acquire a lock and returns true if it was successful. Otherwise, it immediately returns false, and the thread can go off and do something else.

```
if (myLock.tryLock())
    // now the thread owns the lock
    try { . . . }
    finally { myLock.unlock(); }
else
    // do something else
```

You can call tryLock with a timeout parameter, like this:

```
if (myLock.tryLock(100, TimeUnit.MILLISECONDS)) . . .
```

TimeUnit is an enumeration with values SECONDS, MILLISECONDS, MICROSECONDS, and NANOSECONDS.

These methods deal with fairness and thread interruption in subtly different ways.

The tryLock method with a timeout parameter respects fairness in the same way as the lock method. But the tryLock method without timeout can *barge in*—if the lock is available when the call is made, the current thread gets it, even if another thread has been waiting to lock it. If you don't want that behavior, you can always call

```
if (myLock.tryLock(0, TimeUnit.SECONDS)) . . .
```

The lock method cannot be interrupted. If a thread is interrupted while it is waiting to acquire a lock, the interrupted thread continues to be blocked until the lock is available. If a deadlock occurs, then the lock method can never terminate.

However, if you call tryLock with a timeout, then an InterruptedException is thrown if the thread is interrupted while it is waiting. This is clearly a useful feature because it allows a program to break up deadlocks.

You can also call the lockInterruptibly method. It has the same meaning as tryLock with an infinite timeout.

When you wait on a condition, you can also supply a timeout:

```
myCondition.await(100, TimeUnit.MILLISECONDS))
```

The await method returns if another thread has activated this thread by calling signalAll or signal, or if the timeout has elapsed, or if the thread was interrupted.

The await methods throw an InterruptedException if the waiting thread is interrupted. In the (perhaps unlikely) case that you'd rather continue waiting, use the awaitUninterruptibly method instead.

 ### java.util.concurrent.locks.Lock 5.0

- boolean tryLock()
  tries to acquire the lock without blocking; returns true if it was successful. This method grabs the lock if it is available even if it has a fair locking policy and other threads have been waiting.

- boolean tryLock(long time, TimeUnit unit)
  tries to acquire the lock, blocking no longer than the given time; returns true if it was successful.

- void lockInterruptibly()
  acquires the lock, blocking indefinitely. If the thread is interrupted, throws an InterruptedException.

 ### java.util.concurrent.locks.Condition 5.0

- boolean await(long time, TimeUnit unit)
  enters the wait set for this condition, blocking until the thread is removed from the wait set or the given time has elapsed. Returns false if the method returned because the time elapsed, true otherwise.

- void awaitUninterruptibly()
  enters the wait set for this condition, blocking until the thread is removed from the wait set. If the thread is interrupted, this method does not throw an InterruptedException.

Read/Write Locks

The java.util.concurrent.locks package defines two lock classes, the ReentrantLock that we already discussed and the ReentrantReadWriteLock class. The latter is useful when there are many threads that read from a data structure and fewer threads that modify it. In that

situation, it makes sense to allow shared access for the readers. Of course, a writer must still have exclusive access.

Here are the steps that are necessary to use read/write locks:

1. Construct a `ReentrantReadWriteLock` object:

   ```
   private ReentrantReadWriteLock rwl = new ReentrantReadWriteLock();
   ```

2. Extract read and write locks:

   ```
   private Lock readLock = rwl.readLock();
   private Lock writeLock = rwl.writeLock();
   ```

3. Use the read lock in all accessors:

   ```
   public double getTotalBalance()
   {
      readLock.lock();
      try { . . . }
      finally { readLock.unlock(); }
   }
   ```

4. Use the write lock in all mutators:

   ```
   public void transfer(. . .)
   {
      writeLock.lock();
      try { . . . }
      finally { writeLock.unlock(); }
   }
   ```

API   **java.util.concurrent.locks.ReentrantReadWriteLock 5.0**

- `Lock readLock()`
  gets a read lock that can be acquired by multiple readers, excluding all writers.
- `Lock writeLock()`
  gets a write lock that excludes all other readers and writers.

Why the *stop* and *suspend* Methods Are Deprecated

JDK 1.0 defined a stop method that simply terminates a thread, and a suspend method that blocks a thread until another thread calls resume. The stop and suspend methods have something in common: Both attempt to control the behavior of a given thread without the thread's cooperation.

Both of these methods have been deprecated since JDK 1.2. The stop method is inherently unsafe, and experience has shown that the suspend method frequently leads to deadlocks. In this section, you will see why these methods are problematic and what you can do to avoid problems.

Let us turn to the stop method first. This method terminates all pending methods, including the run method. When a thread is stopped, it immediately gives up the locks on all objects that it has locked. This can leave objects in an inconsistent state. For example, suppose a Transfer-Thread is stopped in the middle of moving money from one account to another, after the withdrawal and before the deposit. Now the bank object is *damaged*. Since the lock has been relinquished, the damage is observable from the other threads that have not been stopped.

When a thread wants to stop another thread, it has no way of knowing when the stop method is safe and when it leads to damaged objects. Therefore, the method has been deprecated. You should interrupt a thread when you want it to stop. The interrupted thread can then stop when it is safe to do so.

 NOTE: Some authors claim that the stop method has been deprecated because it can cause objects to be permanently locked by a stopped thread. However, that claim is not valid. A stopped thread exits all synchronized methods it has called—technically, by throwing a Thread-Death exception. As a consequence, the thread relinquishes the object locks that it holds.

Next, let us see what is wrong with the suspend method. Unlike stop, suspend won't damage objects. However, if you suspend a thread that owns a lock, then the lock is unavailable until the thread is resumed. If the thread that calls the suspend method tries to acquire the same lock, then the program deadlocks: The suspended thread waits to be resumed, and the suspending thread waits for the lock.

This situation occurs frequently in graphical user interfaces. Suppose we have a graphical simulation of our bank. A button labeled Pause suspends the transfer threads, and a button labeled Resume resumes them.

```
pauseButton.addActionListener(new
    ActionListener()
    {
        public void actionPerformed(ActionEvent event)
        {
            for (int i = 0; i < threads.length; i++)
                threads[i].suspend(); // Don't do this
        }
    });
resumeButton.addActionListener(. . .); // calls resume on all transfer threads
```

Suppose a paintComponent method paints a chart of each account, calling a getBalances method to get an array of balances.

As you will see on page 72, both the button actions and the repainting occur in the same thread, the *event dispatch thread.* Consider the following scenario:

1. One of the transfer threads acquires the lock of the bank object.
2. The user clicks the Pause button.
3. All transfer threads are suspended; one of them still holds the lock on the bank object.
4. For some reason, the account chart needs to be repainted.
5. The paintComponent method calls the getBalances method.
6. That method tries to acquire the lock of the bank object.

Now the program is frozen.

The event dispatch thread can't proceed because the lock is owned by one of the suspended threads. Thus, the user can't click the Resume button, and the threads won't ever resume.

If you want to safely suspend a thread, introduce a variable suspendRequested and test it in a safe place of your run method—somewhere your thread doesn't lock objects that other threads need. When your thread finds that the suspendRequested variable has been set, keep waiting until it becomes available again.

The following code framework implements that design:

```
public void run()
{
    while (. . .)
    {
```

```
      . . .
      if (suspendRequested)
      {
         suspendLock.lock();
         try { while (suspendRequested) suspendCondition.await(); }
         finally { suspendLock.unlock(); }
      }
   }
}
public void requestSuspend() { suspendRequested = true; }
public void requestResume()
{
   suspendRequested = false;
   suspendLock.lock();
   try { suspendCondition.signalAll(); }
   finally { suspendLock.unlock(); }
}
private volatile boolean suspendRequested = false;
private Lock suspendLock = new ReentrantLock();
private Condition suspendCondition = suspendLock.newCondition();
```

Blocking Queues

A *queue* is a data structure with two fundamental operations: to add an element to the *tail* of the queue and to remove an element from the *head*. That is, the queue manages the data in a first-in/first-out discipline. A *blocking queue* causes a thread to block when you try to add an element when the queue is currently full or to remove an element when the queue is empty. Blocking queues are a useful tool for coordinating the work of multiple threads. Worker threads can periodically deposit intermediate results in a blocking queue. Other worker threads remove the intermediate results and modify them further. The queue automatically balances the workload. If the first set of threads runs slower than the second, the second set blocks while waiting for the results. If the first set of threads runs faster, the queue fills up until the second set catches up. Table 1–1 shows the operations for blocking queues.

Table 1–1: Blocking Queue Operations

Method	Normal Action	Failure Action
add	Adds an element	Throws an IllegalStateException if the queue is full
remove	Removes and returns the head element	Throws a NoSuchElementException if the queue is empty
element	Returns the head element	Throws a NoSuchElementException if the queue is empty
offer	Adds an element and returns true	Returns false if the queue is full
poll	Removes and returns the head element	Returns null if the queue was empty
peek	Returns the head element	Returns null if the queue was empty
put	Adds an element	Blocks if the queue is full
take	Removes and returns the head element	Blocks if the queue is empty

The blocking queue operations fall into three categories, depending on their response. The add, remove, and element operations throw an exception when you try to add to a full queue or get the head of an empty queue. Of course, in a multithreaded program, the queue might become full or empty at any time, so you will instead want to use the offer, poll, and peek methods. These methods simply return with a failure indicator instead of throwing an exception if they cannot carry out their tasks.

NOTE: The poll and peek methods return null to indicate failure. Therefore, it is illegal to insert null values into these queues.

There are also variants of the offer and poll methods with a timeout. For example, the call

```
boolean success = q.offer(x, 100, TimeUnit.MILLISECONDS);
```

tries for 100 milliseconds to insert an element to the tail of the queue. If it succeeds, it immediately returns true; otherwise, it returns false when it times out. Similarly, the call

```
Object head = q.poll(100, TimeUnit.MILLISECONDS)
```

returns true for 100 milliseconds to remove the head of the queue. If it succeeds, it immediately returns the head; otherwise, it returns null when it times out.

Finally, we have blocking operations put and take. The put method blocks if the queue is full, and the take method blocks if the queue is empty. These are the equivalents of offer and poll with no timeout.

The java.util.concurrent package supplies four variations of blocking queues. By default, the LinkedBlockingQueue has no upper bound on its capacity, but a maximum capacity can be optionally specified. The ArrayBlockingQueue is constructed with a given capacity and an optional parameter to require fairness. If fairness is specified, then the longest-waiting threads are given preferential treatment. As always, fairness exacts a significant performance penalty, and you should only use it if your problem specifically requires it.

The PriorityBlockingQueue is a priority queue, not a first-in/first-out queue. Elements are removed in order of their priority. The queue has unbounded capacity, but retrieval will block if the queue is empty. (We discuss priority queues in greater detail in Chapter 2.)

Finally, a DelayQueue contains objects that implement the Delayed interface:

```
interface Delayed extends Comparable<Delayed>
{
    long getDelay(TimeUnit unit);
}
```

The getDelay method returns the remaining delay of the object. A negative value indicates that the delay has elapsed. Elements can only be removed from a DelayQueue if their delay has elapsed. You also need to implement the compareTo method. The DelayQueue uses that method to sort the entries.

The program in Example 1–6 shows how to use a blocking queue to control a set of threads. The program searches through all files in a directory and its subdirectories, printing lines that contain a given keyword.

A producer thread enumerates all files in all subdirectories and places them in a blocking queue. This operation is fast, and the queue would quickly fill up with all files in the file system if it was not bounded.

We also start a large number of search threads. Each search thread takes a file from the queue, opens it, prints all lines containing the keyword, and then takes the next file. We use a trick to terminate the application when no further work is required. In order to signal

completion, the enumeration thread places a dummy object into the queue. (This is similar to a dummy suitcase with a label "last bag" in a baggage claim belt.) When a search thread takes the dummy, it puts it back and terminates.

Note that no explicit thread synchronization is required. In this application, we use the queue data structure as a synchronization mechanism.

Example 1–6: BlockingQueueTest.java

```java
import java.io.*;
import java.util.*;
import java.util.concurrent.*;

public class BlockingQueueTest
{
   public static void main(String[] args)
   {
      Scanner in = new Scanner(System.in);
      System.out.print("Enter base directory (e.g. /usr/local/jdk5.0/src): ");
      String directory = in.nextLine();
      System.out.print("Enter keyword (e.g. volatile): ");
      String keyword = in.nextLine();

      final int FILE_QUEUE_SIZE = 10;
      final int SEARCH_THREADS = 100;

      BlockingQueue<File> queue = new ArrayBlockingQueue<File>(FILE_QUEUE_SIZE);

      FileEnumerationTask enumerator = new FileEnumerationTask(queue, new File(directory));
      new Thread(enumerator).start();
      for (int i = 1; i <= SEARCH_THREADS; i++)
         new Thread(new SearchTask(queue, keyword)).start();
   }
}

/**
   This task enumerates all files in a directory and its subdirectories.
*/
class FileEnumerationTask implements Runnable
{
   /**
      Constructs a FileEnumerationTask.
      @param queue the blocking queue to which the enumerated files are added
      @param startingDirectory the directory in which to start the enumeration
   */
   public FileEnumerationTask(BlockingQueue<File> queue, File startingDirectory)
   {
      this.queue = queue;
      this.startingDirectory = startingDirectory;
   }

   public void run()
   {
      try
      {
         enumerate(startingDirectory);
         queue.put(DUMMY);
```

```
 49.          }
 50.       catch (InterruptedException e) {}
 51.    }
 52.
 53.    /**
 54.       Recursively enumerates all files in a given directory and its subdirectories
 55.       @param directory the directory in which to start
 56.    */
 57.    public void enumerate(File directory) throws InterruptedException
 58.    {
 59.       File[] files = directory.listFiles();
 60.       for (File file : files)      {
 61.          if (file.isDirectory()) enumerate(file);
 62.          else queue.put(file);
 63.       }
 64.    }
 65.
 66.    public static File DUMMY = new File("");
 67.
 68.    private BlockingQueue<File> queue;
 69.    private File startingDirectory;
 70. }
 71.
 72. /**
 73.    This task searches files for a given keyword.
 74. */
 75. class SearchTask implements Runnable
 76. {
 77.    /**
 78.       Constructs a SearchTask.
 79.       @param queue the queue from which to take files
 80.       @param keyword the keyword to look for
 81.    */
 82.    public SearchTask(BlockingQueue<File> queue, String keyword)
 83.    {
 84.       this.queue = queue;
 85.       this.keyword = keyword;
 86.    }
 87.
 88.    public void run()
 89.    {
 90.       try
 91.       {
 92.          boolean done = false;
 93.          while (!done)
 94.          {
 95.             File file = queue.take();
 96.             if (file == FileEnumerationTask.DUMMY) { queue.put(file); done = true; }
 97.             else search(file);
 98.          }
 99.       }
100.       catch (IOException e) { e.printStackTrace(); }
101.       catch (InterruptedException e) {}
102.    }
103.
104.    /**
```

```
105.        Searches a file for a given keyword and prints all matching lines.
106.        @param file the file to search
107.    */
108.    public void search(File file) throws IOException
109.    {
110.        Scanner in = new Scanner(new FileInputStream(file));
111.        int lineNumber = 0;
112.        while (in.hasNextLine())
113.        {
114.            lineNumber++;
115.            String line = in.nextLine();
116.            if (line.contains(keyword))
117.                System.out.printf("%s:%d:%s%n", file.getPath(), lineNumber, line);
118.        }
119.        in.close();
120.    }
121.
122.    private BlockingQueue<File> queue;
123.    private String keyword;
124. }
```

java.util.concurrent.ArrayBlockingQueue<E> 5.0

- ArrayBlockingQueue(int capacity)
- ArrayBlockingQueue(int capacity, boolean fair)
  construct a blocking queue with the given capacity and fairness settings. The queue
  is implemented as a circular array.

java.util.concurrent.LinkedBlockingQueue<E> 5.0

- LinkedBlockingQueue()
  constructs an unbounded blocking queue, implemented as a linked list.
- LinkedBlockingQueue(int capacity)
  constructs a bounded blocking queue with the given capacity, implemented as a
  linked list.

java.util.concurrent.DelayQueue<E extends Delayed> 5.0

- DelayQueue()
  constructs an unbounded bounded blocking queue of Delayed elements. Only
  elements whose delay has expired can be removed from the queue.

java.util.concurrent.Delayed 5.0

- long getDelay(TimeUnit unit)
  gets the delay for this object, measured in the given time unit.

java.util.concurrent.PriorityBlockingQueue<E> 5.0

- PriorityBlockingQueue()
- PriorityBlockingQueue(int initialCapacity)
- PriorityBlockingQueue(int initialCapacity, Comparator<? super E> comparator)
  constructs an unbounded blocking priority queue implemented as a heap.

Parameters	initialCapacity	The initial capacity of the priority queue. Default is 11
	comparator	The comparator used to compare elements. If not specified, the elements must implement the Comparable interface

 java.util.concurrent.BlockingQueue<E> 5.0

- void put(E element)
  adds the element, blocking if necessary.

- boolean offer(E element)
- boolean offer(E element, long time, TimeUnit unit)
  adds the given element and returns true if successful, or returns without adding the element and returns false if the queue is full. The second method blocks if necessary, until the element has been added or the time has elapsed.

- E take()
  removes and returns the head element, blocking if necessary.

- E poll(long time, TimeUnit unit)
  removes and returns the head element, blocking if necessary until an element is available or the time has elapsed. Returns null upon failure.

 java.util.Queue<E> 5.0

- E poll()
  removes and returns the head element or null if the queue is empty.

- E peek()
  returns the head element or null if the queue is empty.

Thread-Safe Collections

If multiple threads concurrently modify a data structure such as a hash table, then it is easily possible to damage the data structure. (We discuss hash tables in greater detail in Chapter 2.) For example, one thread may begin to insert a new element. Suppose it is preempted while it is in the middle of rerouting the links between the hash table's buckets. If another thread starts traversing the same list, it may follow invalid links and create havoc, perhaps throwing exceptions or being trapped in an infinite loop.

You can protect a shared data structure by supplying a lock, but it is usually easier to choose a thread-safe implementation instead. The blocking queues that we discussed in the preceding section are, of course, thread-safe collections. In the following sections, we discuss the other thread-safe collections that the Java library provides.

Efficient Queues and Hash Tables

The java.util.concurrent package supplies efficient implementations for a queue and a hash table, ConcurrentLinkedQueue and ConcurrentHashMap. The concurrent hash map can efficiently support a large number of readers and a fixed number of writers. By default, it is assumed that there are up to 16 *simultaneous* writer threads. There can be many more writer threads, but if more than 16 write at the same time, the others are temporarily blocked. You can specify a higher number in the constructor, but it is unlikely that you will need to.

These collections use sophisticated algorithms that never lock the entire table and that minimize contention by allowing simultaneous access to different parts of the data structure.

The collections return *weakly consistent* iterators. That means that the iterators may or may not reflect all modifications that are made after they were constructed, but they will not return a value twice and they will not throw any exceptions.

 NOTE: In contrast, an iterator of a collection in the java.util package throws a ConcurrentModifi-cationException when the collection has been modified after construction of the iterator.

The ConcurrentHashMap has useful methods for atomic insertion and removal of associations. The putIfAbsent method adds a new association provided there wasn't one before. This is useful for a cache that is accessed by multiple threads, to ensure that only one thread adds an item into the cache:

```
cache.putIfAbsent(key, value);
```

The opposite operation is remove (which perhaps should have been called removeIfPresent). The call

```
cache.remove(key, value)
```

atomically removes the key and value if they are present in the map. Finally,

```
cache.replace(key, oldValue, newValue)
```

atomically replaces the old value with the new one, provided the old value was associated with the given key.

---

java.util.concurrent.ConcurrentLinkedQueue<E> 5.0

- ConcurrentLinkedQueue<E>()
  constructs an unbounded, nonblocking queue that can be safely accessed by multiple threads.

---

java.util.concurrent.ConcurrentHashMap<K, V> 5.0

- ConcurrentHashMap<K, V>()
- ConcurrentHashMap<K, V>(int initialCapacity)
- ConcurrentHashMap<K, V>(int initialCapacity, float loadFactor, int concurrencyLevel)
  construct a hash map that can be safely accessed by multiple threads.

Parameters	initialCapacity	The initial capacity for this collection. Default is 16
	loadFactor	Controls resizing: If the average load per bucket exceeds this factor, the table is resized. Default is 0.75
	concurrencyLevel	The estimated number of concurrent writer threads

- V putIfAbsent(K key, V value)
  if the key is not yet present in the map, associates the given value with the given key and returns null. Otherwise returns the existing value associated with the key.
- boolean remove(K key, V value)
  if the given key is currently associated with this value, removes the given key and value and returns true. Otherwise returns false.
- boolean replace(K key, V oldValue, V newValue)
  if the given key is currently associated with oldValue, associates it with newValue. Otherwise, returns false.

Copy on Write Arrays

The CopyOnWriteArrayList and CopyOnWriteArraySet are thread-safe collections in which all mutators make a copy of the underlying array. This arrangement is useful if the number of threads that iterate over the collection greatly outnumbers the threads that mutate it. When you construct an iterator, it contains a reference to the current array. If the array is later mutated, the iterator still has the old array, but the collection's array is replaced. As a consequence, the older iterator has a consistent (but potentially outdated) view that it can access without any synchronization expense.

Older Thread-Safe Collections

Ever since JDK 1.0, the Vector and Hashtable classes provided thread-safe implementations of a dynamic array and a hash table. In JDK 1.2, these classes were declared obsolete and replaced by the ArrayList and HashMap classes. Those classes are not thread-safe. Instead, a different mechanism is supplied in the collections library. Any collection class can be made thread-safe by means of a *synchronization wrapper*:

```
List synchArrayList = Collections.synchronizedList(new ArrayList());
Map synchHashMap = Collections.synchronizedMap(new HashMap());
```

The methods of the resulting collections are protected by a lock, providing thread-safe access. However, if you want to *iterate* over the collection, you need to use a synchronized block:

```
synchronized (synchHashMap)
{
    Iterator iter = synchHashMap.keySet().iterator();
    while (iter.hasNext()) . . .;
}
```

We discuss these wrappers in greater detail in Chapter 2.

Callables and Futures

A Runnable encapsulates a task that runs asynchronously; you can think of it as an asynchronous method with no parameters and no return value. A Callable is similar to a Runnable, but it returns a value. The Callable interface is a parameterized type, with a single method call.

```
public interface Callable<V>
{
    V call() throws Exception;
}
```

The type parameter is the type of the returned value. For example, a Callable<Integer> represents an asynchronous computation that eventually returns an Integer object.

A Future holds the *result* of an asynchronous computation. You use a Future object so that you can start a computation, give the result to someone, and forget about it. The owner of the Future object can obtain the result when it is ready.

The Future interface has the following methods:

```
public interface Future<V>
{
    V get() throws . . .;
    V get(long timeout, TimeUnit unit) throws . . .;
    void cancel(boolean mayInterrupt);
    boolean isCancelled();
    boolean isDone();
}
```

A call to the first get method blocks until the computation is finished. The second method throws a TimeoutException if the call timed out before the computation finished. If the thread running the computation is interrupted, both methods throw an InterruptedException. If the computation has already finished, then get returns immediately.

The isDone method returns false if the computation is still in progress, true if it is finished.

You can cancel the computation with the cancel method. If the computation has not yet started, it is canceled and will never start. If the computation is currently in progress, then it is interrupted if the mayInterrupt parameter is true.

The FutureTask wrapper is a convenient mechanism for turning a Callable into both a Future and a Runnable—it implements both interfaces. For example,

```
Callable<Integer> myComputation = . . .;
FutureTask<Integer> task = new FutureTask<Integer>(myComputation);
Thread t = new Thread(task); // it's a Runnable
t.start();
. . .
Integer result = task.get(); // it's a Future
```

The program in Example 1–7 puts these concepts to work. This program is similar to the preceding example that found files containing a given keyword. However, now we will merely count the number of matching files. Thus, we have a long-running task that yields an integer value—an example of a Callable<Integer>.

```
class MatchCounter implements Callable<Integer>
{
   public MatchCounter(File directory, String keyword) { . . . }
   public Integer call() { . . . } // returns the number of matching files
}
```

Then we construct a FutureTask object from the MatchCounter and use it to start a thread.

```
FutureTask<Integer> task = new FutureTask<Integer>(counter);
Thread t = new Thread(task);
t.start();
```

Finally, we print the result.

```
System.out.println(task.get() + " matching files.");
```

Of course, the call to get blocks until the result is actually available.

Inside the call method, we use the same mechanism recursively. For each subdirectory, we produce a new MatchCounter and launch a thread for it. We also stash the FutureTask objects away in an ArrayList<Future<Integer>>. At the end, we add up all results:

```
for (Future<Integer> result : results)
   count += result.get();
```

Each call to get blocks until the result is available. Of course, the threads run in parallel, so there is a good chance that the results will all be available at about the same time.

Example 1–7: FutureTest.java

```
1. import java.io.*;
2. import java.util.*;
3. import java.util.concurrent.*;
4.
5. public class FutureTest
6. {
7.    public static void main(String[] args)
8.    {
9.       Scanner in = new Scanner(System.in);
```

```
10.      System.out.print("Enter base directory (e.g. /usr/local/jdk5.0/src): ");
11.      String directory = in.nextLine();
12.      System.out.print("Enter keyword (e.g. volatile): ");
13.      String keyword = in.nextLine();
14.
15.      MatchCounter counter = new MatchCounter(new File(directory), keyword);
16.      FutureTask<Integer> task = new FutureTask<Integer>(counter);
17.      Thread t = new Thread(task);
18.      t.start();
19.      try
20.      {
21.         System.out.println(task.get() + " matching files.");
22.      }
23.      catch (ExecutionException e)
24.      {
25.         e.printStackTrace();
26.      }
27.      catch (InterruptedException e) {}
28.   }
29. }
30.
31. /**
32.    This task counts the files in a directory and its subdirectories that contain a given keyword.
33. */
34. class MatchCounter implements Callable<Integer>
35. {
36.    /**
37.       Constructs a MatchCounter.
38.       @param directory the directory in which to start the search
39.       @param keyword the keyword to look for
40.    */
41.    public MatchCounter(File directory, String keyword)
42.    {
43.       this.directory = directory;
44.       this.keyword = keyword;
45.    }
46.
47.    public Integer call()
48.    {
49.       count = 0;
50.       try
51.       {
52.          File[] files = directory.listFiles();
53.          ArrayList<Future<Integer>> results = new ArrayList<Future<Integer>>();
54.
55.          for (File file : files)
56.             if (file.isDirectory())
57.             {
58.                MatchCounter counter = new MatchCounter(file, keyword);
59.                FutureTask<Integer> task = new FutureTask<Integer>(counter);
60.                results.add(task);
61.                Thread t = new Thread(task);
62.                t.start();
63.             }
64.             else
65.             {
66.                if (search(file)) count++;
```

```
67.          }
68.
69.          for (Future<Integer> result : results)
70.             try
71.             {
72.                count += result.get();
73.             }
74.             catch (ExecutionException e)
75.             {
76.                e.printStackTrace();
77.             }
78.       }
79.       catch (InterruptedException e) {}
80.       return count;
81.    }
82.
83.    /**
84.       Searches a file for a given keyword.
85.       @param file the file to search
86.       @return true if the keyword is contained in the file
87.    */
88.    public boolean search(File file)
89.    {
90.       try
91.       {
92.          Scanner in = new Scanner(new FileInputStream(file));
93.          boolean found = false;
94.          while (!found && in.hasNextLine())
95.          {
96.             String line = in.nextLine();
97.             if (line.contains(keyword)) found = true;
98.          }
99.          in.close();
100.          return found;
101.       }
102.       catch (IOException e)
103.       {
104.          return false;
105.       }
106.    }
107.
108.    private File directory;
109.    private String keyword;
110.    private int count;
111. }
```

java.util.concurrent.Callable<V> 5.0

- V call()

  runs a task that yields a result.

java.util.concurrent.Future<V> 5.0

- V get()
- V get(long time, TimeUnit unit)

  gets the result, blocking until it is available or the given time has elapsed. The second method throws a TimeoutException if it was unsuccessful.

- boolean cancel(boolean mayInterrupt)
  attempts to cancel the execution of this task. If the task has already started and the mayInterrupt parameter is true, it is interrupted. Returns true if the cancellation was successful.
- boolean isCancelled()
  returns true if the task was canceled before it completed.
- boolean isDone()
  returns true if the task completed, through normal completion, cancellation, or an exception.

 java.util.concurrent.FutureTask<V> 5.0

- FutureTask(Callable<V> task)
- FutureTask(Runnable task, V result)
  constructs an object that is both a Future<V> and a Runnable.

Executors

Constructing a new thread is somewhat expensive because it involves interaction with the operating system. If your program creates a large number of short-lived threads, then it should instead use a *thread pool*. A thread pool contains a number of idle threads that are ready to run. You give a Runnable to the pool, and one of the threads calls the run method. When the run method exits, the thread doesn't die but stays around to serve the next request.

Another reason to use a thread pool is to throttle the number of concurrent threads. Creating a huge number of threads can greatly degrade performance and even crash the virtual machine. If you have an algorithm that creates lots of threads, then you should use a "fixed" thread pool that bounds the total number of concurrent threads.

The Executors class has a number of static factory methods for constructing thread pools; see Table 1–2 for a summary.

Table 1–2: Executors Factory Methods

Method	Description
newCachedThreadPool	New threads are created as needed; idle threads are kept for 60 seconds.
newFixedThreadPool	The pool contains a fixed set of threads; idle threads are kept indefinitely.
newSingleThreadExecutor	A "pool" with a single thread that executes the submitted tasks sequentially.
newScheduledThreadPool	A fixed-thread pool for scheduled execution.
newSingleThreadScheduledExecutor	A single-thread "pool" for scheduled execution.

Thread Pools

Let us look at the first three methods in Table 1–2. We discuss the remaining methods on page 63. The newCachedThreadPool method constructs a thread pool that executes each task immediately, using an existing idle thread when available and creating a new thread otherwise. The newFixedThreadPool method constructs a thread pool with a fixed size. If more tasks are submitted than there are idle threads, then the unserved tasks are placed on a queue. They are run when other tasks have completed. The newSingleThreadExecutor is a degenerate

pool of size 1: A single thread executes the submitted tasks, one after another. These three methods return an object of the ThreadPoolExecutor class that implements the ExecutorService interface.

You can submit a Runnable or Callable to an ExecutorService with one of the following methods:

```
Future<?> submit(Runnable task)
Future<T> submit(Runnable task, T result)
Future<T> submit(Callable<T> task)
```

The pool will run the submitted task at its earliest convenience. When you call submit, you get back a Future object that you can use to query the state of the task.

The first submit method returns an odd-looking Future<?>. You can use such an object to call isDone, cancel, or isCancelled. But the get method simply returns null upon completion.

The second version of submit also submits a Runnable, and the get method of the Future returns the given result object upon completion.

The third version submits a Callable, and the returned Future gets the result of the computation when it is ready.

When you are done with a connection pool, call shutdown. This method initiates the shutdown sequence for the pool. An executor that is shut down accepts no new tasks. When all tasks are finished, the threads in the pool die. Alternatively, you can call shutdownNow. The pool then cancels all tasks that have not yet begun and attempts to interrupt the running threads.

Here, in summary, is what you do to use a connection pool:

1. Call the static newCachedThreadPool or newFixedThreadPool method of the Executors class.
2. Call submit to submit Runnable or Callable objects.
3. If you want to be able to cancel a task or if you submit Callable objects, hang on to the returned Future objects.
4. Call shutdown when you no longer want to submit any tasks.

For example, the preceding example program produced a large number of short-lived threads, one per directory. The program in Example 1–8 uses a thread pool to launch the tasks instead.

For informational purposes, this program prints out the largest pool size during execution. This information is not available through the ExecutorService interface. For that reason, we had to cast the pool object to the ThreadPoolExecutor class.

Example 1–8: ThreadPoolTest.java

```
1.  import java.io.*;
2.  import java.util.*;
3.  import java.util.concurrent.*;
4.
5.  public class ThreadPoolTest
6.  {
7.     public static void main(String[] args) throws Exception
8.     {
9.        Scanner in = new Scanner(System.in);
10.       System.out.print("Enter base directory (e.g. /usr/local/jdk5.0/src): ");
11.       String directory = in.nextLine();
12.       System.out.print("Enter keyword (e.g. volatile): ");
13.       String keyword = in.nextLine();
14.
15.       ExecutorService pool = Executors.newCachedThreadPool();
```

```
16.
17.      MatchCounter counter = new MatchCounter(new File(directory), keyword, pool);
18.      Future<Integer> result = pool.submit(counter);
19.
20.      try
21.      {
22.         System.out.println(result.get() + " matching files.");
23.      }
24.      catch (ExecutionException e)
25.      {
26.         e.printStackTrace();
27.      }
28.      catch (InterruptedException e) {}
29.      pool.shutdown();
30.
31.      int largestPoolSize = ((ThreadPoolExecutor) pool).getLargestPoolSize();
32.      System.out.println("largest pool size=" + largestPoolSize);
33.   }
34. }
35.
36. /**
37.    This task counts the files in a directory and its subdirectories that contain a given keyword.
38. */
39. class MatchCounter implements Callable<Integer>
40. {
41.    /**
42.       Constructs a MatchCounter.
43.       @param directory the directory in which to start the search
44.       @param keyword the keyword to look for
45.       @param pool the thread pool for submitting subtasks
46.    */
47.    public MatchCounter(File directory, String keyword, ExecutorService pool)
48.    {
49.       this.directory = directory;
50.       this.keyword = keyword;
51.       this.pool = pool;
52.    }
53.
54.    public Integer call()
55.    {
56.       count = 0;
57.       try
58.       {
59.          File[] files = directory.listFiles();
60.          ArrayList<Future<Integer>> results = new ArrayList<Future<Integer>>();
61.
62.          for (File file : files)
63.             if (file.isDirectory())
64.             {
65.                MatchCounter counter = new MatchCounter(file, keyword, pool);
66.                Future<Integer> result = pool.submit(counter);
67.                results.add(result);
68.             }
69.             else
70.             {
71.                if (search(file)) count++;
```

```
72.              }
73.
74.          for (Future<Integer> result : results)
75.              try
76.              {
77.                  count += result.get();
78.              }
79.              catch (ExecutionException e)
80.              {
81.                  e.printStackTrace();
82.              }
83.      }
84.      catch (InterruptedException e) {}
85.      return count;
86.  }
87.
88.  /**
89.      Searches a file for a given keyword.
90.      @param file the file to search
91.      @return true if the keyword is contained in the file
92.  */
93.  public boolean search(File file)
94.  {
95.      try
96.      {
97.          Scanner in = new Scanner(new FileInputStream(file));
98.          boolean found = false;
99.          while (!found && in.hasNextLine())
100.         {
101.             String line = in.nextLine();
102.             if (line.contains(keyword)) found = true;
103.         }
104.         in.close();
105.         return found;
106.     }
107.     catch (IOException e)
108.     {
109.         return false;
110.     }
111. }
112.
113. private File directory;
114. private String keyword;
115. private ExecutorService pool;
116. private int count;
117. }
```

---

java.util.concurrent.Executors 5.0

- ExecutorService newCachedThreadPool()
  returns a cached thread pool that creates threads as needed and terminates threads that have been idle for 60 seconds.

- ExecutorService newFixedThreadPool(int threads)
  returns a thread pool that uses the given number of threads to execute tasks.

- ExecutorService newSingleThreadExecutor()
  returns an executor that executes tasks sequentially in a single thread.

java.util.concurrent.ExecutorService 5.0

- Future<T> submit(Callable<T> task)
- Future<T> submit(Runnable task, T result)
- Future<?> submit(Runnable task)
  submits the given task for execution.

- void shutdown()
  shuts down the service, completing the already submitted tasks but not accepting
  new submissions.

java.util.concurrent.ThreadPoolExecutor 5.0

- int getLargestPoolSize()
  returns the largest size of the thread pool during the life of this executor.

Scheduled Execution

The ScheduledExecutorService interface has methods for scheduled or repeated execution of
tasks. It is a generalization of java.util.Timer that allows for thread pooling. The newSched-
uledThreadPool and newSingleThreadScheduledExecutor methods of the Executors class return objects
that implement the ScheduledExecutorService interface.

You can schedule a Runnable or Callable to run once, after an initial delay. You can also schedule a Runnable to run periodically. See the API notes for details.

java.util.concurrent.Executors 5.0

- ScheduledExecutorService newScheduledThreadPool(int threads)
  returns a thread pool that uses the given number of threads to schedule tasks.
- ScheduledExecutorService newSingleThreadScheduledExecutor()
  returns an executor that schedules tasks in a single thread.

java.util.concurrent.ScheduledExecutorService 5.0

- ScheduledFuture<V> schedule(Callable<V> task, long time, TimeUnit unit)
- ScheduledFuture<?> schedule(Runnable task, long time, TimeUnit unit)
  schedules the given task after the given time has elapsed.

- ScheduledFuture<?> scheduleAtFixedRate(Runnable task, long initialDelay, long period, TimeUnit
  unit)
  schedules the given task to run periodically, every period units, after the initial delay
  has elapsed.

- ScheduledFuture<?> scheduleWithFixedDelay(Runnable task, long initialDelay, long delay, TimeUnit
  unit)
  schedules the given task to run periodically, with delay units between completion of
  one invocation and the start of the next, after the initial delay has elapsed.

Controlling Groups of Threads

You have seen how to use an executor service as a thread pool to increase the efficiency of
task execution. Sometimes, an executor is used for a more tactical reason, simply to control a group of related tasks. For example, you can cancel all tasks in an executor with the
shutdownNow method.

The invokeAny method submits all objects in a collection of Callable objects and returns the result of a completed task. You don't know which task that is—presumably, it was the one that finished most quickly. You would use this method for a search problem in which you are willing to accept any solution. For example, suppose that you need to factor a large integer—a computation that is required for breaking the RSA cipher. You could submit a number of tasks, each of which attempts a factorization by using numbers in a different range. As soon as one of these tasks has an answer, your computation can stop.

The invokeAll method submits all objects in a collection of Callable objects and returns a list of Future objects that represent the solutions to all tasks. You can combine the results of the computation when they are available, like this:

```
ArrayList<Callable<Integer>> tasks = . . .;
List<Future<Integer>> results = executor.invokeAll(tasks);
for (Future<Integer> result : results)
    count += result.get();
```

A disadvantage with this approach is that you may wait needlessly if the first task happens to take a long time. It would make more sense to obtain the results in the order in which they are available. This can be arranged with the ExecutorCompletionService.

Start with an executor, obtained in the usual way. Then construct an ExecutorCompletionService. Submit tasks to the completion service. The service manages a blocking queue of Future objects, containing the results of the submitted tasks as they become available. Thus, a more efficient organization for the preceding computation is the following:

```
ExecutorCompletionService service = new ExecutorCompletionService(executor);
for (Callable<Integer> task : tasks) service.submit(task);
for (int i = 0; i < taks.size(); i++)
    count += service.take().get();
```

 java.util.concurrent.ExecutorService 5.0

- T invokeAny(Collection<Callable<T>> tasks)
- T invokeAny(Collection<Callable<T>> tasks, long timeout, TimeUnit unit)
  executes the given tasks and returns the result of one of them. The second method throws a TimeoutException if a timeout occurs.
- List<Future<T>> invokeAll(Collection<Callable<T>> tasks)
- List<Future<T>> invokeAll(Collection<Callable<T>> tasks, long timeout, TimeUnit unit)
  executes the given tasks and returns the results of all of them. The second method throws a TimeoutException if a timeout occurs.

 java.util.concurrent.ExecutorCompletionService 5.0

- ExecutorCompletionService(Executor e)
  constructs an executor completion service that collects the results of the given executor.
- Future<T> submit(Callable<T> task)
- Future<T> submit(Runnable task, T result)
  submits a task to the underlying executor.
- Future<T> take()
  removes the next completed result, blocking if no completed results are available.
- Future<T> poll()
- Future<T> poll(long time, TimeUnit unit)
  removes the next completed result or null if no completed results are available. The second method waits for the given time.

Synchronizers

The java.util.concurrent package contains several classes that help manage a set of collaborating threads—see Table 1–3. These mechanisms have "canned functionality" for common rendezvous patterns between threads. If you have a set of collaborating threads that follows one of these behavior patterns, you should simply reuse the appropriate library class instead of trying to come up with a handcrafted collection of locks.

Table 1–3: Synchronizers

Class	What It Does	When To Use
CyclicBarrier	Allows a set of threads to wait until a predefined count of them has reached a common barrier, and then optionally executes a barrier action.	When a number of threads need to complete before their results can be used.
CountDownLatch	Allows a set of threads to wait until a count has been decremented to 0.	When one or more threads need to wait until a specified number of results are available.
Exchanger	Allows two threads to exchange objects when both are ready for the exchange.	When two threads work on two instances of the same data structure, one by filling an instance and the other by emptying the other.
SynchronousQueue	Allows a thread to hand off an object to another thread.	To send an object from one thread to another when both are ready, without explicit synchronization.
Semaphore	Allows a set of threads to wait until permits are available for proceeding.	To restrict the total number of threads that can access a resource. If permit count is one, use to block threads until another thread gives permission.

Barriers

The CyclicBarrier class implements a rendezvous called a *barrier*. Consider a number of threads that are working on parts of a computation. When all parts are ready, the results need to be combined. When a thread is done with its part, we let it run against the barrier. Once all threads have reached the barrier, the barrier gives way and the threads can proceed.

Here are the details. First, construct a barrier, giving the number of participating threads:

```
CyclicBarrier barrier = new CyclicBarrier(nthreads);
```

Each thread does some work and calls await on the barrier upon completion:

```
public void run()
{
   doWork();
   barrier.await();
   . . .
}
```

The await method takes an optional timeout parameter:

```
barrier.await(100, TimeUnit.MILLISECONDS);
```

If any of the threads waiting for the barrier leaves the barrier, then the barrier *breaks*. (A thread can leave because it called await with a timeout or because it was interrupted.) In that case, the await method for all other threads throws a BrokenBarrierException. Threads that are already waiting have their await call terminated immediately.

You can supply an optional *barrier action* that is executed when all threads have reached the barrier:

```
Runnable barrierAction = . . .;
CyclicBarrier barrier = new CyclicBarrier(nthreads, barrierAction);
```

The action can harvest the result of the individual threads.

The barrier is called *cyclic* because it can be reused after all waiting threads have been released.

Countdown Latches

A CountDownLatch lets a set of threads wait until a count has reached zero. It differs from a barrier in these respects:

- Not all threads need to wait for the latch until it can be opened.
- The latch can be counted down by external events.
- The countdown latch is one-time only. Once the count has reached 0, you cannot reuse it.

A useful special case is a latch with a count of 1. This implements a one-time *gate*. Threads are held at the gate until another thread sets the count to 0.

Imagine, for example, a set of threads that need some initial data to do their work. The worker threads are started and wait at the gate. Another thread prepares the data. When it is ready, it calls countDown, and all worker threads proceed.

Exchangers

An Exchanger is used when two threads are working on two instances of the same data buffer. Typically, one thread fills the buffer, and the other consumes its contents. When both are done, they exchange their buffers.

Synchronous Queues

A synchronous queue is a mechanism that pairs up producer and consumer threads. When a thread calls put on a SynchronousQueue, it blocks until another thread calls take, and vice versa. Unlike the case with an Exchanger, data are only transferred in one direction, from the producer to the consumer.

Even though the SynchronousQueue class implements the BlockingQueue interface, it is not conceptually a queue. It does not contain any elements—its size method always returns 0.

Semaphores

Conceptually, a semaphore manages a number of *permits*. To proceed past the semaphore, a thread requests a permit by calling acquire. Only a fixed number of permits are available, limiting the number of threads that are allowed to pass. Other threads may issue permits by calling release. There are no actual permit objects. The semaphore simply keeps a count. Moreover, a permit doesn't have to be released by the thread that acquires it. In fact, any thread can issue any number of permits. If it issues more than the maximum available, the semaphore is simply set to the maximum count. This generality makes semaphores both very flexible and potentially confusing.

Semaphores were invented by Edsger Dijkstra in 1968, for use as a *synchronization primitive*. Dijkstra showed that semaphores can be efficiently implemented and that they are powerful

enough to solve many common thread synchronization problems. In just about any operating systems textbook, you will find implementations of bounded queues using semaphores. Of course, application programmers shouldn't reinvent bounded queues. We suggest that you only use semaphores when their behavior maps well onto your synchronization problem, without your going through mental contortions.

For example, a semaphore with a permit count of 1 is useful as a gate that can be opened and closed by another thread. Imagine a program that does some work, then waits for a user to study the result and press a button to continue, then does the next unit of work. The worker thread calls `acquire` whenever it is ready to pause. The GUI thread calls `release` whenever the user clicks the Continue button.

What happens if the user clicks the button multiple times while the worker thread is ready? Because only one permit is available, the permit count stays at 1.

The program in Example 1–9 puts this idea to work. The program animates a sorting algorithm. A worker thread sorts an array, stopping periodically and waiting for the user to give permission to proceed. The user can admire a painting of the current state of the algorithm and press the Continue button to allow the worker thread to go to the next step.

We didn't want to bore you with the code for a sorting algorithm, so we simply call `Arrays.sort`. To pause the algorithm, we supply a `Comparator` object that waits for the semaphore. Thus, the animation is paused whenever the algorithm compares two elements. We paint the current values of the array and highlight the elements that are being compared (see Figure 1–7).

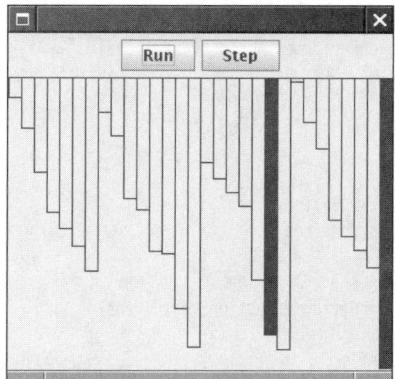

Figure 1–7: Animating a sort algorithm

Example 1–9: AlgorithmAnimation.java

```
1. import java.awt.*;
2. import java.awt.geom.*;
3. import java.awt.event.*;
4. import java.util.*;
5. import java.util.concurrent.*;
6. import javax.swing.*;
7.
8. /**
9.    This program animates a sort algorithm.
10. */
11. public class AlgorithmAnimation
```

```
12. {
13.    public static void main(String[] args)
14.    {
15.        JFrame frame = new AnimationFrame();
16.        frame.setDefaultCloseOperation(JFrame.EXIT_ON_CLOSE);
17.        frame.setVisible(true);
18.    }
19. }
20.
21. /**
22.    This frame shows the array as it is sorted, together with buttons to single-step the animation
23.    or to run it without interruption.
24. */
25. class AnimationFrame extends JFrame
26. {
27.    public AnimationFrame()
28.    {
29.        ArrayPanel panel = new ArrayPanel();
30.        add(panel, BorderLayout.CENTER);
31.
32.        Double[] values = new Double[VALUES_LENGTH];
33.        final Sorter sorter = new Sorter(values, panel);
34.
35.        JButton runButton = new JButton("Run");
36.        runButton.addActionListener(new
37.            ActionListener()
38.            {
39.                public void actionPerformed(ActionEvent event)
40.                {
41.                    sorter.setRun();
42.                }
43.            });
44.
45.        JButton stepButton = new JButton("Step");
46.        stepButton.addActionListener(new
47.            ActionListener()
48.            {
49.                public void actionPerformed(ActionEvent event)
50.                {
51.                    sorter.setStep();
52.                }
53.            });
54.
55.        JPanel buttons = new JPanel();
56.        buttons.add(runButton);
57.        buttons.add(stepButton);
58.        add(buttons, BorderLayout.NORTH);
59.        setSize(DEFAULT_WIDTH, DEFAULT_HEIGHT);
60.
61.        for (int i = 0; i < values.length; i++)
62.            values[i] = new Double(Math.random());
63.
64.        Thread t = new Thread(sorter);
65.        t.start();
66.    }
```

```
67.
68.    private static final int DEFAULT_WIDTH = 300;
69.    private static final int DEFAULT_HEIGHT = 300;
70.    private static final int VALUES_LENGTH = 30;
71. }
72.
73. /**
74.    This runnable executes a sort algorithm.
75.    When two elements are compared, the algorithm
76.    pauses and updates a panel.
77. */
78. class Sorter implements Runnable
79. {
80.    /**
81.       Constructs a Sorter.
82.       @param values the array to be sorted
83.       @param panel the panel on which to display the sorting progress
84.    */
85.    public Sorter(Double[] values, ArrayPanel panel)
86.    {
87.       this.values = values;
88.       this.panel = panel;
89.       this.gate = new Semaphore(1);
90.       this.run = false;
91.    }
92.
93.    /**
94.       Sets the sorter to "run" mode.
95.    */
96.    public void setRun()
97.    {
98.       run = true;
99.       gate.release();
100.   }
101.
102.   /**
103.      Sets the sorter to "step" mode.
104.   */
105.   public void setStep()
106.   {
107.      run = false;
108.      gate.release();
109.   }
110.
111.   public void run()
112.   {
113.      Comparator<Double> comp = new
114.         Comparator<Double>()
115.         {
116.            public int compare(Double i1, Double i2)
117.            {
118.               panel.setValues(values, i1, i2);
119.               try
120.               {
121.                  if (run)
```

```
122.                     Thread.sleep(DELAY);
123.                  else
124.                     gate.acquire();
125.               }
126.               catch (InterruptedException exception)
127.               {
128.                  Thread.currentThread().interrupt();
129.               }
130.               return i1.compareTo(i2);
131.            }
132.         };
133.      Arrays.sort(values, comp);
134.      panel.setValues(values, null, null);
135.   }
136.
137.   private Double[] values;
138.   private ArrayPanel panel;
139.   private Semaphore gate;
140.   private static final int DELAY = 100;
141.   private boolean run;
142. }
143.
144. /**
145.    This panel draws an array and marks two elements in the
146.    array.
147. */
148. class ArrayPanel extends JPanel
149. {
150.
151.   public void paintComponent(Graphics g)
152.   {
153.      if (values == null) return;
154.      super.paintComponent(g);
155.      Graphics2D g2 = (Graphics2D) g;
156.      int width = getWidth() / values.length;
157.      for (int i = 0; i < values.length; i++)
158.      {
159.         double height = values[i] * getHeight();
160.         Rectangle2D bar = new Rectangle2D.Double(width * i, 0, width, height);
161.         if (values[i] == marked1 || values[i] == marked2)
162.            g2.fill(bar);
163.         else
164.            g2.draw(bar);
165.      }
166.   }
167.
168.   /**
169.      Sets the values to be painted.
170.      @param values the array of values to display
171.      @param marked1 the first marked element
172.      @param marked2 the second marked element
173.   */
174.   public void setValues(Double[] values, Double marked1, Double marked2)
175.   {
176.      this.values = values;
177.      this.marked1 = marked1;
```

```
178.        this.marked2 = marked2;
179.        repaint();
180.    }
181.
182.    private Double marked1;
183.    private Double marked2;
184.    private Double[] values;
185. }
```

 java.util.concurrent.CyclicBarrier 5.0

- CyclicBarrier(int parties)
- CyclicBarrier(int parties, Runnable barrierAction)
  constructs a cyclic barrier for the given number of parties. The barrierAction is executed when all parties have called await on the barrier.
- int await()
- int await(long time, TimeUnit unit)
  waits until all parties have called await on the barrier or until the timeout has been reached, in which case a TimeoutException is thrown. Upon success, returns the arrival index of this party. The first party has index parties − 1, and the last party has index 0.

java.util.concurrent.CountDownLatch 5.0

- CountdownLatch(int count)
  constructs a countdown latch with the given count.
- void await()
  waits for this latch to count down to 0.
- boolean await(long time, TimeUnit unit)
  waits for this latch to count down to 0 or for the timeout to elapse. Returns true if the count is 0, false if the timeout elapsed.
- public void countDown()
  counts down the counter of this latch.

java.util.concurrent.Exchanger<V> 5.0

- V exchange(V item)
- V exchange(V item, long time, TimeUnit unit)
  blocks until another thread calls this method, and then exchanges the item with the other thread and returns the other thread's item. The second method throws a TimeoutException after the timeout has elapsed.

java.util.concurrent.SynchronousQueue<V> 5.0

- SynchronousQueue()
- SynchronousQueue(boolean fair)
  constructs a synchronous queue that allows threads to hand off items. If fair is true, the queue favors the longest-waiting threads.
- void put(V item)
  blocks until another thread calls take to take this item.
- V take()
  blocks until another thread calls put. Returns the item that the other thread provided.

java.util.concurrent.Semaphore 5.0

- `Semaphore(int permits)`
- `Semaphore(int permits, boolean fair)`
  construct a semaphore with the given maximum number of permits. If `fair` is `true`, the queue favors the longest-waiting threads.
- `void acquire()`
  waits to acquire a permit.
- `boolean tryAcquire()`
  tries to acquire a permit; returns `false` if none is available.
- `boolean tryAcquire(long time, TimeUnit unit)`
  tries to acquire a permit within the given time; returns `false` if none is available.
- `void release()`
  releases a permit.

Threads and Swing

As we mentioned in the introduction to this chapter, one of the reasons to use threads in your programs is to make your programs more responsive. When your program needs to do something time consuming, then you should fire up another worker thread instead of blocking the user interface.

However, you have to be careful what you do in a worker thread because, perhaps surprisingly, Swing is *not thread safe*. If you try to manipulate user interface elements from multiple threads, then your user interface can become corrupted.

To see the problem, run the test program in Example 1–10. When you click the Bad button, a new thread is started whose `run` method tortures a combo box, randomly adding and removing values.

```
public void run()
{
   try
   {
      while (true)
      {
         int i = Math.abs(generator.nextInt());
         if (i % 2 == 0)
            combo.insertItemAt(new Integer(i), 0);
         else if (combo.getItemCount() > 0)
            combo.removeItemAt(i % combo.getItemCount());
         sleep(1);
      }
      catch (InterruptedException e) {}
   }
}
```

Try it out. Click the Bad button. Click the combo box a few times. Move the scroll bar. Move the window. Click the Bad button again. Keep clicking the combo box. Eventually, you should see an exception report (see Figure 1–8).

What is going on? When an element is inserted into the combo box, the combo box fires an event to update the display. Then, the display code springs into action, reading the current size of the combo box and preparing to display the values. But the worker thread keeps going—occasionally resulting in a reduction of the count of the values in the combo box. The display code then thinks that there are more values in

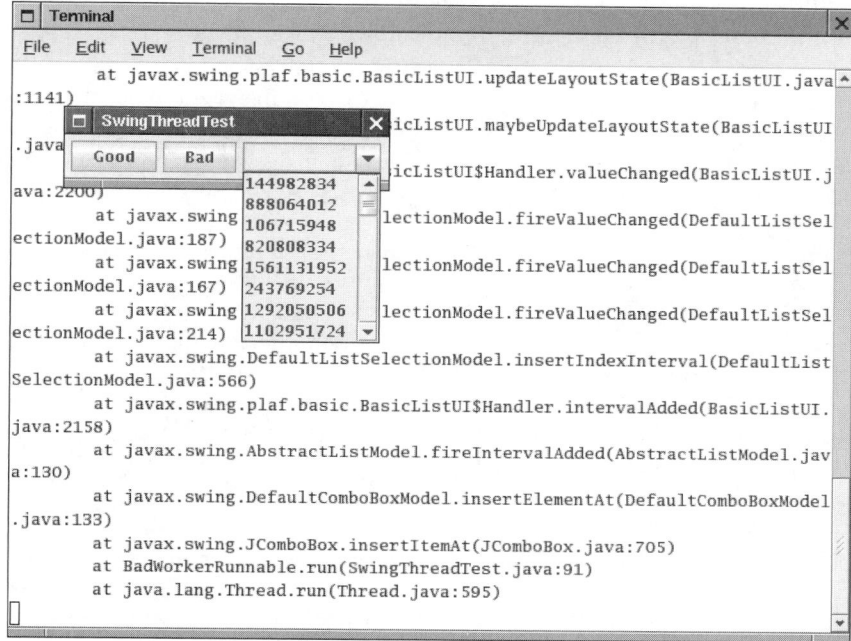

Figure 1–8: Exception reports in the console

the model than there actually are, asks for nonexistent values, and triggers an Array-IndexOutOfBounds exception.

This situation could have been avoided by enabling programmers to lock the combo box object while displaying it. However, the designers of Swing decided not to expend any effort to make Swing thread safe, for two reasons. First, synchronization takes time, and nobody wanted to slow down Swing any further. More important, the Swing team checked out the experience other teams had with thread-safe user interface toolkits. What they found was not encouraging. Builders of a user interface toolkit want it to be extensible so that other programmers can add their own user interface components. However, user interface programmers using thread-safe toolkits turned out to be confused by the demands for synchronization and tended to create components that were prone to deadlocks.

The "Single Thread" Rule

When you use threads together with Swing, you have to follow a few simple rules. First, however, let's see what threads are present in a Swing program.

Every Java application starts with a main method that runs in the *main thread*. In a Swing program, the main method typically does the following:

- First it calls a constructor that lays out components in a frame window;
- Then it invokes the setVisible method on the frame window.

When the first window is shown, a second thread is created, the *event dispatch thread*. All event notifications, such as calls to actionPerformed or paintComponent, run in the event dispatch thread. The main thread keeps running until the main method exits. Usually, of course, the main method exits immediately after displaying the frame window.

Other threads, such as the thread that posts events into the event queue, are running behind the scenes, but those threads are invisible to the application programmer.

In a Swing application, essentially all code is contained in event handlers to respond to user interface and repaint requests. All that code runs on the event dispatch thread. Here are the rules that you need to follow.

1. If an action takes a long time, fire up a new thread to do the work. If you take a long time in the event dispatch thread, the application seems "dead" because it cannot respond to any events.

2. If an action can block on input or output, fire up a new thread to do the work. You don't want to freeze the user interface for the potentially indefinite time that a network connection is unresponsive.

3. If you need to wait for a specific amount of time, don't sleep in the event dispatch thread. Instead, use timer events.

4. The work that you do in your threads cannot touch the user interface. Read any information from the UI before you launch your threads, launch them, and then update the user interface from the event dispatching thread once the threads have completed.

The last rule is often called the *single-thread rule* for Swing programming. There are a few exceptions to the single-thread rule.

1. A few Swing methods are thread safe. They are specially marked in the API documentation with the sentence *"This method is thread safe, although most Swing methods are not."* The most useful among these thread-safe methods are

   ```
   JTextComponent.setText
   JTextArea.insert
   JTextArea.append
   JTextArea.replaceRange
   ```

2. The following methods of the JComponent class can be called from any thread:

   ```
   repaint
   revalidate
   ```

   The repaint method schedules a repaint event. You use the revalidate method if the contents of a component have changed and the size and position of the component must be updated. The revalidate method marks the component's layout as invalid and schedules a layout event. (Just like paint events, layout events are *coalesced*. If multiple layout events are in the event queue, the layout is only recomputed once.)

 NOTE: We used the repaint method many times in Volume 1 of this book, but the revalidate method is less common. Its purpose is to force a layout of a component after the contents have changed. The traditional AWT has a validate method to force the layout of a component. For Swing components, you should simply call revalidate instead. (However, to force the layout of a JFrame, you still need to call validate—a JFrame is a Component but not a JComponent.)

---

3. You can safely add and remove event listeners in any thread. Of course, the listener methods will be invoked in the event dispatching thread.

4. You can construct components, set their properties, and add them into containers, as long as none of the components have been *realized*. A component has been realized if it can receive paint or validation events. This is the case as soon as the setVisible(true) or pack methods have been invoked on the component, or if the component has been added to a container that has been realized. Once a component has been realized, you can no longer manipulate it from another thread.

In particular, you can create the GUI of an application in the main method before calling setVisible(true), and you can create the GUI of an applet in the applet constructor or the init method.

Now suppose you fire up a separate thread to run a time-consuming task. You may want to update the user interface to indicate progress while your thread is working. When your task is finished, you want to update the GUI again. But you can't touch Swing components from your thread. For example, if you want to update a progress bar or a label text, then you can't simply set its value from your thread.

To solve this problem, you can use two convenient utility methods in any thread to add arbitrary actions to the event queue. For example, suppose you want to periodically update a label in a thread to indicate progress. You can't call label.setText from your thread. Instead, use the invokeLater and invokeAndWait methods of the EventQueue class to have that call executed in the event dispatching thread.

Here is what you do. You place the Swing code into the run method of a class that implements the Runnable interface. Then, you create an object of that class and pass it to the static invokeLater or invokeAndWait method. For example, here is how to update a label text.

```
EventQueue.invokeLater(new
    Runnable()
    {
        public void run()
        {
            label.setText(percentage + "% complete");
        }
    });
```

The invokeLater method returns immediately when the event is posted to the event queue. The run method is executed asynchronously. The invokeAndWait method waits until the run method has actually been executed.

In the situation of updating a progress label, the invokeLater method is more appropriate. Users would rather have the worker thread make more progress than have the most precise progress indicator.

Both methods execute the run method in the event dispatch thread. No new thread is created.

Example 1–10 demonstrates how to use the invokeLater method to safely modify the contents of a combo box. If you click on the Good button, a thread inserts and removes numbers. However, the actual modification takes place in the event dispatching thread.

Example 1–10: SwingThreadTest.java

```
1. import java.awt.*;
2. import java.awt.event.*;
3. import java.util.*;
4. import javax.swing.*;
5.
6. /**
7.    This program demonstrates that a thread that
8.    runs in parallel with the event dispatch thread
9.    can cause errors in Swing components.
10. */
11. public class SwingThreadTest
12. {
13.    public static void main(String[] args)
14.    {
15.       SwingThreadFrame frame = new SwingThreadFrame();
```

```
16.        frame.setDefaultCloseOperation(JFrame.EXIT_ON_CLOSE);
17.        frame.setVisible(true);
18.     }
19. }
20.
21. /**
22.    This frame has two buttons to fill a combo box from a
23.    separate thread. The "Good" button uses the event queue,
24.    the "Bad" button modifies the combo box directly.
25. */
26. class SwingThreadFrame extends JFrame
27. {
28.     public SwingThreadFrame()
29.     {
30.        setTitle("SwingThreadTest");
31.
32.        final JComboBox combo = new JComboBox();
33.        combo.insertItemAt(new Integer(Integer.MAX_VALUE), 0);
34.        combo.setPrototypeDisplayValue(combo.getItemAt(0));
35.        combo.setSelectedIndex(0);
36.
37.        JPanel panel = new JPanel();
38.
39.        JButton goodButton = new JButton("Good");
40.        goodButton.addActionListener(new ActionListener()
41.           {
42.              public void actionPerformed(ActionEvent event)
43.              {
44.                 new Thread(new GoodWorkerRunnable(combo)).start();
45.              }
46.           });
47.        panel.add(goodButton);
48.        JButton badButton = new JButton("Bad");
49.        badButton.addActionListener(new ActionListener()
50.           {
51.              public void actionPerformed(ActionEvent event)
52.              {
53.                 new Thread(new BadWorkerRunnable(combo)).start();
54.              }
55.           });
56.        panel.add(badButton);
57.        panel.add(combo);
58.        add(panel);
59.        pack();
60.     }
61. }
62.
63. /**
64.    This runnable modifies a combo box by randomly adding
65.    and removing numbers. This can result in errors because
66.    the combo box methods are not synchronized and both the worker
67.    thread and the event dispatch thread access the combo box.
68. */
69. class BadWorkerRunnable implements Runnable
70. {
```

```
71.   public BadWorkerRunnable(JComboBox aCombo)
72.   {
73.      combo = aCombo;
74.      generator = new Random();
75.   }
76.
77.   public void run()
78.   {
79.      try
80.      {
81.         while (true)
82.         {
83.            combo.showPopup();
84.            int i = Math.abs(generator.nextInt());
85.            if (i % 2 == 0)
86.               combo.insertItemAt(new Integer(i), 0);
87.            else if (combo.getItemCount() > 0)
88.               combo.removeItemAt(i % combo.getItemCount());
89.            Thread.sleep(1);
90.         }
91.      }
92.      catch (InterruptedException e) {}
93.   }
94.
95.   private JComboBox combo;
96.   private Random generator;
97. }
98.
99. /**
100.    This runnable modifies a combo box by randomly adding
101.    and removing numbers. In order to ensure that the
102.    combo box is not corrupted, the editing operations are
103.    forwarded to the event dispatch thread.
104. */
105. class GoodWorkerRunnable implements Runnable
106. {
107.    public GoodWorkerRunnable(JComboBox aCombo)
108.    {
109.       combo = aCombo;
110.       generator = new Random();
111.    }
112.
113.    public void run()
114.    {
115.       try
116.       {
117.          while (true)
118.          {
119.             EventQueue.invokeLater(new
120.                Runnable()
121.                {
122.                   public void run()
123.                   {
124.                      combo.showPopup();
125.                      int i = Math.abs(generator.nextInt());
```

```
126.                    if (i % 2 == 0)
127.                        combo.insertItemAt(new Integer(i), 0);
128.                    else if (combo.getItemCount() > 0)
129.                        combo.removeItemAt(i % combo.getItemCount());
130.                }
131.            });
132.            Thread.sleep(1);
133.        }
134.    }
135.    catch (InterruptedException e) {}
136. }
137.
138.    private JComboBox combo;
139.    private Random generator;
140. }
```

java.awt.EventQueue 1.0

- static void invokeLater(Runnable runnable) **1.2**
  causes the run method of the runnable object to be executed in the event dispatch thread after pending events have been processed.

- static void invokeAndWait(Runnable runnable) **1.2**
  causes the run method of the runnable object to be executed in the event dispatch thread after pending events have been processed. This call blocks until the run method has terminated.

A Swing Worker

When a user issues a command for which processing takes a long time, you will want to fire up a new thread to do the work. As you saw in the preceding section, that thread should use the EventQueue.invokeLater method to update the user interface.

Several authors have produced convenience classes to ease this task. A well-known example is Hans Muller's SwingWorker class, described in http://java.sun.com/docs/books/tutorial/uiswing/misc/threads.html. Here, we present a slightly different class that makes it easier for a thread to update the user interface after each unit of work.

The program in Example 1–11 has commands for loading a text file and for canceling the file loading process. You should try the program with a long file, such as the full text of *The Count of Monte Cristo*, supplied in the gutenberg directory of the book's companion code. The file is loaded in a separate thread. While the file is read, the Open menu item is disabled and the Cancel item is enabled (see Figure 1–9). After each line is read, a line counter in the status bar is updated. After the reading process is complete, the Open menu item is reenabled, the Cancel item is disabled, and the status line text is set to Done.

This example shows the typical UI activities of a worker thread:

- Make an initial update to the UI before starting the work.
- After each work unit, update the UI to show progress.
- After the work is finished, make a final change to the UI.

The SwingWorkerTask class in Example 1–11 makes it easy to implement such a task. You extend the class and override the init, update, and finish methods and implement the logic for the UI updates. The superclass contains convenience methods doInit, doUpdate, and doFinish that supply the unwieldy code for running these methods in the event dispatch thread. For example,

```
private void doInit()
{
   EventQueue.invokeLater(new
      Runnable()
      {
         public void run() { init(); }
      });
}
```

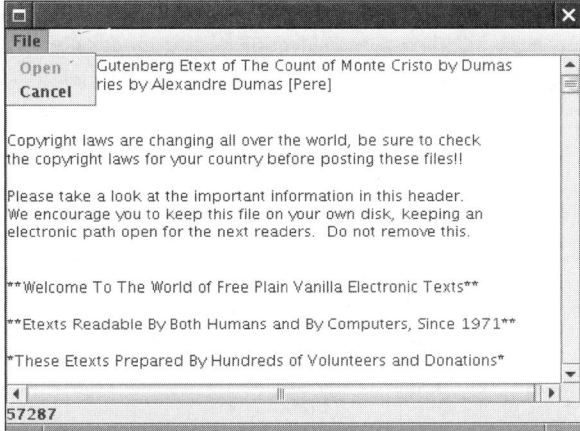

Figure 1–9: Loading a file in a separate thread

Then supply a work method that contains the work of the task. In the work method, you need to call doUpdate (not update) after every unit of work. For example, the file reading task has this work method:

```
public void work() // exception handling not shown
{
   Scanner in = new Scanner(new FileInputStream(file));
   textArea.setText("");
   while (!Thread.currentThread().isInterrupted() && in.hasNextLine())
   {
      lineNumber++;
      line = in.nextLine();
      textArea.append(line);
      textArea.append("\n");
      doUpdate();
   }
}
```

The SwingWorkerTask class implements the Runnable interface. The run method is straightforward:

```
public final void run()
{
   doInit();
   try
   {
      done = false;
      work();
   }
   catch (InterruptedException e)
```

```
        {
        }
        finally
        {
            done = true;
            doFinish();
        }
    }
}
```

You simply start a thread with an object of your SwingWorkerTask object or submit it to an Executor. The sample program does that in the handler for the Open menu item. The handler returns immediately, allowing the user to select other user interface elements.

This simple technique allows you to execute time-consuming tasks while keeping the user interface responsive.

Example 1–11: SwingWorkerTest.java

```
 1. import java.awt.*;
 2. import java.awt.event.*;
 3. import java.io.*;
 4. import java.util.*;
 5. import java.util.concurrent.*;
 6. import javax.swing.*;
 7.
 8. /**
 9.    This program demonstrates a worker thread that runs
10.    a potentially time-consuming task.
11. */
12. public class SwingWorkerTest
13. {
14.    public static void main(String[] args) throws Exception
15.    {
16.       JFrame frame = new SwingWorkerFrame();
17.       frame.setDefaultCloseOperation(JFrame.EXIT_ON_CLOSE);
18.       frame.setVisible(true);
19.    }
20. }
21.
22. /**
23.    This frame has a text area to show the contents of a text file,
24.    a menu to open a file and cancel the opening process, and
25.    a status line to show the file loading progress.
26. */
27. class SwingWorkerFrame extends JFrame
28. {
29.    public SwingWorkerFrame()
30.    {
31.       chooser = new JFileChooser();
32.       chooser.setCurrentDirectory(new File("."));
33.
34.       textArea = new JTextArea();
35.       add(new JScrollPane(textArea));
36.       setSize(DEFAULT_WIDTH, DEFAULT_HEIGHT);
37.
38.       statusLine = new JLabel();
39.       add(statusLine, BorderLayout.SOUTH);
40.
```

```
41.      JMenuBar menuBar = new JMenuBar();
42.      setJMenuBar(menuBar);
43.
44.      JMenu menu = new JMenu("File");
45.      menuBar.add(menu);
46.
47.      openItem = new JMenuItem("Open");
48.      menu.add(openItem);
49.      openItem.addActionListener(new
50.         ActionListener()
51.         {
52.            public void actionPerformed(ActionEvent event)
53.            {
54.               // show file chooser dialog
55.               int result = chooser.showOpenDialog(null);
56.
57.               // if file selected, set it as icon of the label
58.               if (result == JFileChooser.APPROVE_OPTION)
59.               {
60.                  readFile(chooser.getSelectedFile());
61.               }
62.            }
63.         });
64.
65.      cancelItem = new JMenuItem("Cancel");
66.      menu.add(cancelItem);
67.      cancelItem.setEnabled(false);
68.      cancelItem.addActionListener(new
69.         ActionListener()
70.         {
71.            public void actionPerformed(ActionEvent event)
72.            {
73.               if (workerThread != null) workerThread.interrupt();
74.            }
75.         });
76.   }
77.
78.   /**
79.      Reads a file asynchronously, updating the UI during the reading process.
80.      @param file the file to read
81.   */
82.   public void readFile(final File file)
83.   {
84.      Runnable task = new
85.         SwingWorkerTask()
86.         {
87.            public void init()
88.            {
89.               lineNumber = 0;
90.               openItem.setEnabled(false);
91.               cancelItem.setEnabled(true);
92.            }
93.
94.            public void update()
95.            {
96.               statusLine.setText("" + lineNumber);
```

```
97.            }
98.
99.         public void finish()
100.        {
101.            workerThread = null;
102.            openItem.setEnabled(true);
103.            cancelItem.setEnabled(false);
104.            statusLine.setText("Done");
105.        }
106.
107.        public void work()
108.        {
109.            try
110.            {
111.                Scanner in = new Scanner(new FileInputStream(file));
112.                textArea.setText("");
113.                while (!Thread.currentThread().isInterrupted() && in.hasNextLine())
114.                {
115.                    lineNumber++;
116.                    line = in.nextLine();
117.                    textArea.append(line);
118.                    textArea.append("\n");
119.                    doUpdate();
120.                }
121.            }
122.            catch (IOException e)
123.            {
124.                JOptionPane.showMessageDialog(null, "" + e);
125.            }
126.        }
127.
128.        private String line;
129.        private int lineNumber;
130.     };
131.
132.     workerThread = new Thread(task);
133.     workerThread.start();
134.  }
135.
136.  private JFileChooser chooser;
137.  private JTextArea textArea;
138.  private JLabel statusLine;
139.  private JMenuItem openItem;
140.  private JMenuItem cancelItem;
141.  private Thread workerThread;
142.
143.  public static final int DEFAULT_WIDTH = 450;
144.  public static final int DEFAULT_HEIGHT = 350;
145. }
146.
147. /**
148.    Extend this class to define an asynchronous task
149.    that updates a Swing UI.
150. */
151. abstract class SwingWorkerTask implements Runnable
152. {
```

```
153.    /**
154.       Place your task in this method. Be sure to call doUpdate(), not update(), to show the
155.       update after each unit of work.
156.    */
157.    public abstract void work() throws InterruptedException;
158.
159.    /**
160.       Override this method for UI operations before work commences.
161.    */
162.    public void init() {}
163.    /**
164.       Override this method for UI operations after each unit of work.
165.    */
166.    public void update() {}
167.    /**
168.       Override this method for UI operations after work is completed.
169.    */
170.    public void finish() {}
171.
172.    private void doInit()
173.    {
174.       EventQueue.invokeLater(new
175.          Runnable()
176.          {
177.             public void run() { init(); }
178.          });
179.    }
180.
181.    /**
182.       Call this method from work() to show the update after each unit of work.
183.    */
184.    protected final void doUpdate()
185.    {
186.       if (done) return;
187.       EventQueue.invokeLater(new
188.          Runnable()
189.          {
190.             public void run() { update(); }
191.          });
192.    }
193.
194.    private void doFinish()
195.    {
196.       EventQueue.invokeLater(new
197.          Runnable()
198.          {
199.             public void run() { finish(); }
200.          });
201.    }
202.
203.    public final void run()
204.    {
205.       doInit();
206.       try
207.       {
208.          done = false;
```

```
209.          work();
210.       }
211.    catch (InterruptedException ex)
212.    {
213.    }
214.    finally
215.    {
216.       done = true;
217.       doFinish();
218.    }
219. }
220.
221.    private boolean done;
222. }
```

Chapter 2

Collections

Object-oriented programming (OOP) encapsulates data inside classes, but this doesn't make the way in which you organize the data inside the classes any less important than in traditional programming languages. Of course, how you choose to structure the data depends on the problem you are trying to solve. Does your class need a way to easily search through thousands (or even millions) of items quickly? Does it need an ordered sequence of elements *and* the ability to rapidly insert and remove elements in the middle of the sequence? Does it need an array-like structure with random-access ability that can grow at run time? The way you structure your data inside your classes can make a big difference when it comes to implementing methods in a natural style, as well as for performance.

This chapter shows how Java technology can help you accomplish the traditional data structuring needed for serious programming. In college computer science programs, a course called *Data Structures* usually takes a semester to complete, so there are many, many books devoted to this important topic. Exhaustively covering all the data structures that may be useful is not our goal in this chapter; instead, we cover the fundamental ones that the standard Java library supplies. We hope that, after you finish this chapter, you will find it easy to translate any of your data structures to the Java programming language.

Collection Interfaces

Before the release of JDK 1.2, the standard library supplied only a small set of classes for the most useful data structures: Vector, Stack, Hashtable, BitSet, and the Enumeration interface that

provides an abstract mechanism for visiting elements in an arbitrary container. That was certainly a wise choice—it takes time and skill to come up with a comprehensive collection class library.

With the advent of JDK 1.2, the designers felt that the time had come to roll out a full-fledged set of data structures. They faced a number of conflicting design decisions. They wanted the library to be small and easy to learn. They did not want the complexity of the "Standard Template Library" (or STL) of C++, but they wanted the benefit of "generic algorithms" that STL pioneered. They wanted the legacy classes to fit into the new framework. As all designers of collection libraries do, they had to make some hard choices, and they came up with a number of idiosyncratic design decisions along the way. In this section, we will explore the basic design of the Java collections framework, show you how to put it to work, and explain the reasoning behind some of the more controversial features.

Separating Collection Interfaces and Implementation

As is common for modern data structure libraries, the Java collection library separates *interfaces* and *implementations*. Let us look at that separation with a familiar data structure, the *queue*.

A *queue interface* specifies that you can add elements at the tail end of the queue, remove them at the head, and find out how many elements are in the queue. You use a queue when you need to collect objects and retrieve them in a "first in, first out" fashion (see Figure 2–1).

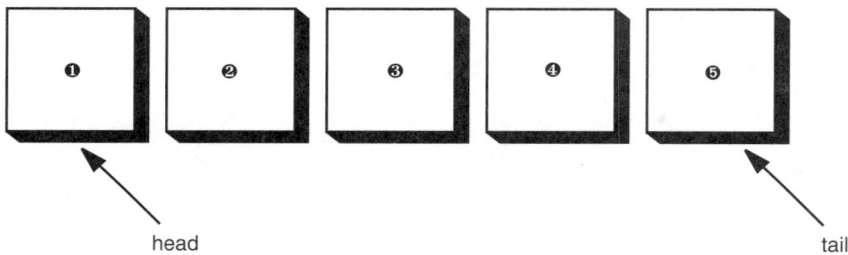

head   tail

Figure 2–1: A queue

A minimal form of a queue interface might look like this:

```
interface Queue<E> // a simplified form of the interface in the standard library
{
   void add(E element);
   E remove();
   int size();
}
```

The interface tells you nothing about how the queue is implemented. Of the two common implementations of a queue, one uses a "circular array" and one uses a linked list (see Figure 2–2).

 NOTE: As of JDK 5.0, the collection classes are generic classes with type parameters. If you use an older version of Java, you need to drop the type parameters and replace the generic types with the Object type. For more information on generic classes, please turn to Volume 1, Chapter 13.

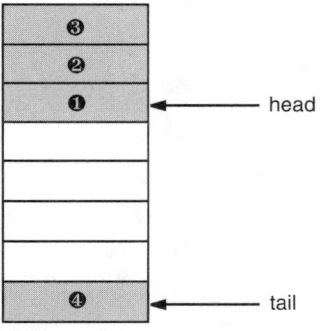

Circular Array

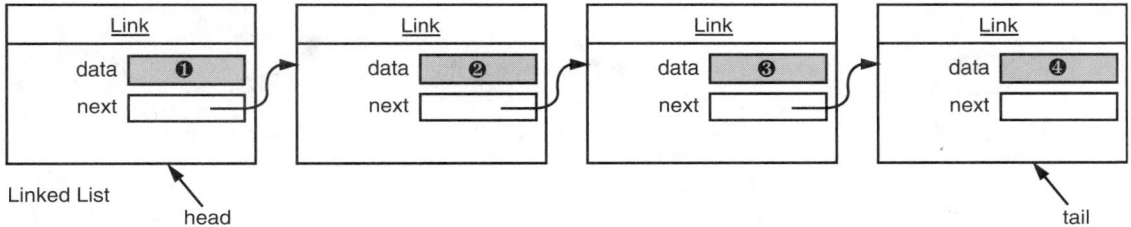

Linked List

Figure 2–2: Queue implementations

Each implementation can be expressed by a class that implements the Queue interface.

```
class CircularArrayQueue<E> implements Queue<E> // not an actual library class
{
   CircularArrayQueue(int capacity) { . . . }
   public void add(E element) { . . . }
   public E remove() { . . . }
   public int size() { . . . }

   private E[] elements;
   private int head;
   private int tail;
}

class LinkedListQueue<E> implements Queue<E>  // not an actual library class
{
   LinkedListQueue() { . . . }
   public void add(E element) { . . . }
   public E remove() { . . . }
   public int size() { . . . }

   private Link head;
   private Link tail;
}
```

 NOTE: The Java library doesn't actually have classes named `CircularArrayQueue` and `LinkedListQueue`. We use these classes as examples to explain the conceptual distinction between collection interfaces and implementations. If you need a circular array queue, you can use the `ArrayBlockingQueue` class described in Chapter 1 or the implementation described on page 128. For a linked list queue, simply use the `LinkedList` class—it implements the `Queue` interface.

When you use a queue in your program, you don't need to know which implementation is actually used once the collection has been constructed. Therefore, it makes sense to use the concrete class *only* when you construct the collection object. Use the *interface type* to hold the collection reference.

```
Queue<Customer> expressLane = new CircularArrayQueue<Customer>(100);
expressLane.add(new Customer("Harry"));
```

With this approach if you change your mind, you can easily use a different implementation. You only need to change your program in one place—the constructor. If you decide that a `LinkedListQueue` is a better choice after all, your code becomes

```
Queue<Customer> expressLane = new LinkedListQueue<Customer>();
expressLane.add(new Customer("Harry"));
```

Why would you choose one implementation over another? The interface says nothing about the efficiency of the implementation. A circular array is somewhat more efficient than a linked list, so it is generally preferable. However, as usual, there is a price to pay. The circular array is a *bounded* collection—it has a finite capacity. If you don't have an upper limit on the number of objects that your program will collect, you may be better off with a linked list implementation after all.

When you study the API documentation, you will find another set of classes whose name begins with `Abstract`, such as `AbstractQueue`. These classes are intended for library implementors. To implement your own queue class, you will find it easier to extend `AbstractQueue` than to implement all the methods of the `Queue` interface.

Collection and Iterator Interfaces in the Java Library

The fundamental interface for collection classes in the Java library is the `Collection` interface. The interface has two fundamental methods:

```
public interface Collection<E>
{
   boolean add(E element);
   Iterator<E> iterator();
   . . .
}
```

There are several methods in addition to these two; we discuss them later.

The `add` method adds an element to the collection. The `add` method returns `true` if adding the element actually changes the collection, and `false` if the collection is unchanged. For example, if you try to add an object to a set and the object is already present, then the `add` request has no effect because sets reject duplicates.

The `iterator` method returns an object that implements the `Iterator` interface. You can use the iterator object to visit the elements in the collection one by one.

Iterators

The `Iterator` interface has three methods:

```
public interface Iterator<E>
{
    E next();
    boolean hasNext();
    void remove();
}
```

By repeatedly calling the next method, you can visit the elements from the collection one by one. However, if you reach the end of the collection, the next method throws a NoSuchElement-Exception. Therefore, you need to call the hasNext method before calling next. That method returns true if the iterator object still has more elements to visit. If you want to inspect all elements in a collection, you request an iterator and then keep calling the next method while hasNext returns true. For example,

```
Collection<String> c = . . .;
Iterator<String> iter = c.iterator();
while (iter.hasNext())
{
    String element = iter.next();
    do something with element
}
```

As of JDK 5.0, there is an elegant shortcut for this loop. You write the same loop more concisely with the "for each" loop

```
for (String element : c)
{
    do something with element
}
```

The compiler simply translates the "for each" loop into a loop with an iterator.

The "for each" loop works with any object that implements the Iterable interface, an interface with a single method:

```
public interface Iterable<E>
{
    Iterator<E> iterator();
}
```

The Collection interface extends the Iterable interface. Therefore, you can use the "for each" loop with any collection in the standard library.

The order in which the elements are visited depends on the collection type. If you iterate over an ArrayList, the iterator starts at index 0 and increments the index in each step. However, if you visit the elements in a HashSet, you will encounter them in essentially random order. You can be assured that you will encounter all elements of the collection during the course of the iteration, but you cannot make any assumptions about their ordering. This is usually not a problem because the ordering does not matter for computations such as computing totals or counting matches.

NOTE: Old-timers will notice that the next and hasNext methods of the Iterator interface serve the same purpose as the nextElement and hasMoreElements methods of an Enumeration. The designers of the Java collection library could have chosen to make use of the Enumeration interface. But they disliked the cumbersome method names and instead introduced a new interface with shorter method names.

There is an important conceptual difference between iterators in the Java collection library and iterators in other libraries. In traditional collection libraries such as the Standard

Template Library of C++, iterators are modeled after array indexes. Given such an iterator, you can look up the element that is stored at that position, much like you can look up an array element a[i] if you have an array index i. Independently of the lookup, you can advance the iterator to the next position. This is the same operation as advancing an array index by calling i++, without performing a lookup. However, the Java iterators do not work like that. The lookup and position change are tightly coupled. The only way to look up an element is to call next, and that lookup advances the position.

Instead, you should think of Java iterators as being *between elements*. When you call next, the iterator *jumps over* the next element, and it returns a reference to the element that it just passed (see Figure 2–3).

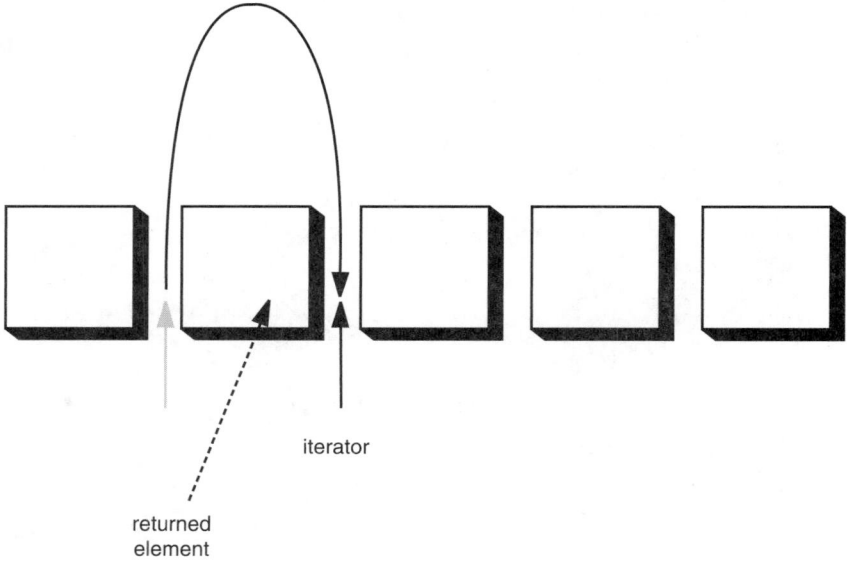

iterator

returned
element

Figure 2–3: Advancing an iterator

 NOTE: Here is another useful analogy. You can think of Iterator.next as the equivalent of InputStream.read. Reading a byte from a stream automatically "consumes" the byte. The next call to read consumes and returns the next byte from the input. Similarly, repeated calls to next let you read all elements in a collection.

Removing Elements

The remove method of the Iterator interface removes the element that was returned by the last call to next. In many situations, that makes sense—you need to see the element before you can decide that it is the one that should be removed. But if you want to remove an element in a particular position, you still need to skip past the element. For example, here is how you remove the first element in a collection of strings.

```
Iterator<String> it = c.iterator();
it.next(); // skip over the first element
it.remove(); // now remove it
```

More important, there is a dependency between calls to the next and remove methods. It is illegal to call remove if it wasn't preceded by a call to next. If you try, an IllegalStateException is thrown.

If you want to remove two adjacent elements, you cannot simply call

```
it.remove();
it.remove(); // Error!
```

Instead, you must first call next to jump over the element to be removed.

```
it.remove();
it.next();
it.remove(); // Ok
```

Generic Utility Methods

Because the Collection and Iterator interfaces are generic, you can write utility methods that operate on any kind of collection. For example, here is a generic method that tests whether an arbitrary collection contains a given element:

```
public static <E> boolean contains(Collection<E> c, Object obj)
{
   for (E element : c)
      if (element.equals(obj))
         return true;
   return false;
}
```

The designers of the Java library decided that some of these utility methods are so useful that the library should make them available. That way, library users don't have to keep reinventing the wheel. The contains method is one such method.

In fact, the Collection interface declares quite a few useful methods that all implementing classes must supply. Among them are:

```
int size()
boolean isEmpty()
boolean contains(Object obj)
boolean containsAll(Collection<?> c)
boolean equals(Object other)
boolean addAll(Collection<? extends E> from)
boolean remove(Object obj)
boolean removeAll(Collection<?> c)
void clear()
boolean retainAll(Collection<?> c)
Object[] toArray()
<T> T[] toArray(T[] arrayToFill)
```

Many of these methods are self-explanatory; you will find full documentation in the API notes at the end of this section.

Of course, it is a bother if every class that implements the Collection interface has to supply so many routine methods. To make life easier for implementors, the library supplies a class AbstractCollection that leaves the fundamental methods size and iterator abstract but implements the routine methods in terms of them. For example:

```
public abstract class AbstractCollection<E>
   implements Collection<E>
{
   . . .
   public abstract Iterator<E> iterator();

   public boolean contains(Object obj)
   {
      for (E element : c) // calls iterator()
         if (element.equals(obj))
```

```
                return = true;
        return false;
    }
    . . .
}
```

A concrete collection class can now extend the `AbstractCollection` class. It is now up to the concrete collection class to supply an `iterator` method, but the `contains` method has been taken care of by the `AbstractCollection` superclass. However, if the subclass has a more efficient way of implementing `contains`, it is free to do so.

This is a good design for a class framework. The users of the collection classes have a richer set of methods available in the generic interface, but the implementors of the actual data structures do not have the burden of implementing all the routine methods.

API **java.util.Collection<E>** 1.2

- `Iterator<E> iterator()`
  returns an iterator that can be used to visit the elements in the collection.
- `int size()`
  returns the number of elements currently stored in the collection.
- `boolean isEmpty()`
  returns true if this collection contains no elements.
- `boolean contains(Object obj)`
  returns true if this collection contains an object equal to `obj`.
- `boolean containsAll(Collection<?> other)`
  returns true if this collection contains all elements in the other collection.
- `boolean add(Object element)`
  adds an element to the collection. Returns true if the collection changed as a result of this call.
- `boolean addAll(Collection<? extends E> other)`
  adds all elements from the other collection to this collection. Returns true if the collection changed as a result of this call.
- `boolean remove(Object obj)`
  removes an object equal to `obj` from this collection. Returns true if a matching object was removed.
- `boolean removeAll(Collection<?> other)`
  removes from this collection all elements from the other collection. Returns true if the collection changed as a result of this call.
- `void clear()`
  removes all elements from this collection.
- `boolean retainAll(Collection<?> other)`
  removes all elements from this collection that do not equal one of the elements in the other collection. Returns true if the collection changed as a result of this call.
- `Object[] toArray()`
  returns an array of the objects in the collection.

API **java.util.Iterator<E>** 1.2

- `boolean hasNext()`
  returns true if there is another element to visit.

- `E next()`
  returns the next object to visit. Throws a `NoSuchElementException` if the end of the collection has been reached.
- `void remove()`
  removes the last visited object. This method must immediately follow an element visit. If the collection has been modified since the last element visit, then the method throws an `IllegalStateException`.

Concrete Collections

Rather than getting into more details about all the interfaces, we thought it would be helpful to first discuss the concrete data structures that the Java library supplies. Once we have thoroughly described the classes you might want to use, we will return to abstract considerations and see how the collections framework organizes these classes. Table 2–1 shows the collections in the Java library and briefly describes the purpose of each collection class. (For simplicity, we omit the thread-safe collections that were discussed in Chapter 1.) All classes in Table 2–1 implement the `Collection` interface, with the exception of the classes with names ending in `Map`. Those classes implement the `Map` interface instead. We will discuss the `Map` interface on page 110.

Table 2–1: Concrete Collections in the Java Library

Collection Type	Description	See Page
`ArrayList`	An indexed sequence that grows and shrinks dynamically	101
`LinkedList`	An ordered sequence that allows efficient insertions and removal at any location	93
`HashSet`	An unordered collection that rejects duplicates	101
`TreeSet`	A sorted set	104
`EnumSet`	A set of enumerated type values	116
`LinkedHashSet`	A set that remembers the order in which elements were inserted	115
`PriorityQueue`	A collection that allows efficient removal of the smallest element	109
`HashMap`	A data structure that stores key/value associations	110
`TreeMap`	A map in which the keys are sorted	110
`EnumMap`	A map in which the keys belong to an enumerated type	116
`LinkedHashMap`	A map that remembers the order in which entries were added	115
`WeakHashMap`	A map with values that can be reclaimed by the garbage collector if they are not used elsewhere	114
`IdentityHashMap`	A map with keys that are compared by ==, not equals	117

Linked Lists

We used arrays and their dynamic cousin, the `ArrayList` class, for many examples in Volume 1. However, arrays and array lists suffer from a major drawback. Removing an element from the middle of an array is expensive since all array elements beyond the removed one must be moved toward the beginning of the array (see Figure 2–4). The same is true for inserting elements in the middle.

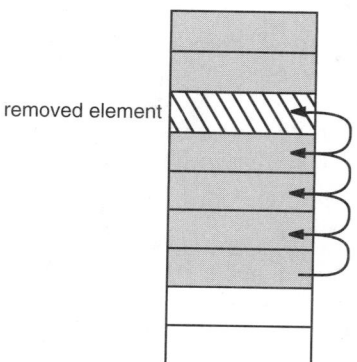

removed element

Figure 2–4: Removing an element from an array

Another well-known data structure, the *linked list,* solves this problem. Whereas an array stores object references in consecutive memory locations, a linked list stores each object in a separate *link*. Each link also stores a reference to the next link in the sequence. In the Java programming language, all linked lists are actually *doubly linked*; that is, each link also stores a reference to its predecessor (see Figure 2–5).

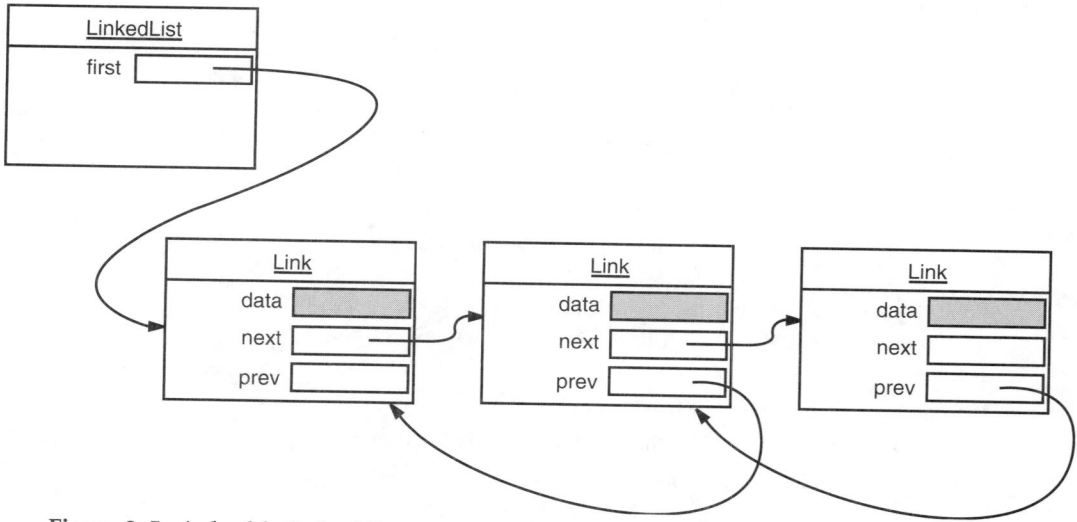

Figure 2–5: A doubly linked list

Removing an element from the middle of a linked list is an inexpensive operation—only the links around the element to be removed need to be updated (see Figure 2–6).

Perhaps you once took a data structures course in which you learned how to implement linked lists. You may have bad memories of tangling up the links when removing or adding elements in the linked list. If so, you will be pleased to learn that the Java collections library supplies a class LinkedList ready for you to use.

The following code example adds three elements and and then removes the second one.

```
List<String> staff = new LinkedList<String>(); // LinkedList implements List
staff.add("Amy");
staff.add("Bob");
staff.add("Carl");
Iterator iter = staff.iterator();
String first = iter.next(); // visit first element
String second = iter.next(); // visit second element
iter.remove(); // remove last visited element
```

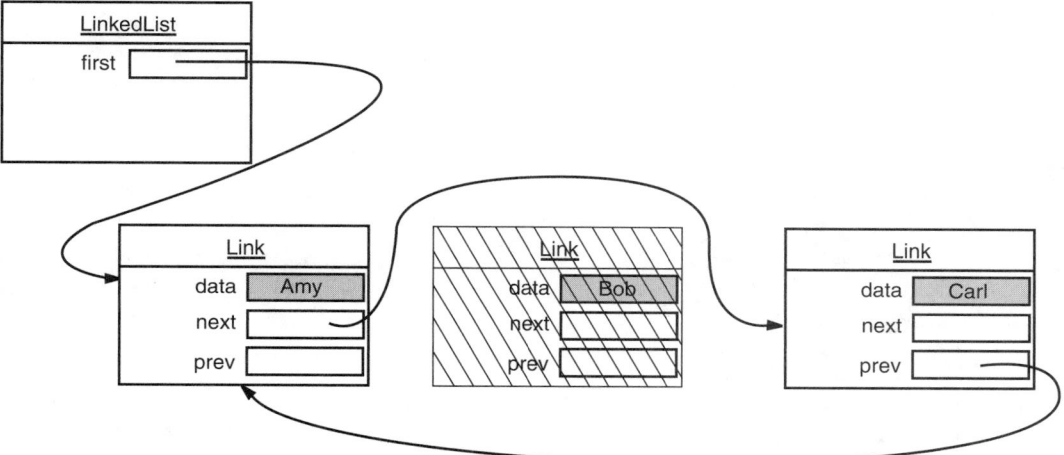

Figure 2–6: Removing an element from a linked list

There is, however, an important difference between linked lists and generic collections. A linked list is an *ordered collection* in which the position of the objects matters. The LinkedList.add method adds the object to the end of the list. But you often want to add objects somewhere in the middle of a list. This position-dependent add method is the responsibility of an iterator, since iterators describe positions in collections. Using iterators to add elements makes sense only for collections that have a natural ordering. For example, the *set* data type that we discuss in the next section does not impose any ordering on its elements. Therefore, there is no add method in the Iterator interface. Instead, the collections library supplies a subinterface ListIterator that contains an add method:

```
interface ListIterator<E> extends Iterator<E>
{
    void add(E element);
    . . .
}
```

Unlike Collection.add, this method does not return a boolean—it is assumed that the add operation always modifies the list.

In addition, the ListIterator interface has two methods that you can use for traversing a list backwards.

```
E previous()
boolean hasPrevious()
```

Like the next method, the previous method returns the object that it skipped over.

The listIterator method of the LinkedList class returns an iterator object that implements the ListIterator interface.

```
ListIterator<String> iter = staff.listIterator();
```

The add method adds the new element *before* the iterator position. For example, the following code skips past the first element in the linked list and adds "Juliet" before the second element (see Figure 2–7).

```
List<String> staff = new LinkedList<String>();
staff.add("Amy");
staff.add("Bob");
staff.add("Carl");
ListIterator<String> iter = staff.listIterator();
iter.next(); // skip past first element
iter.add("Juliet");
```

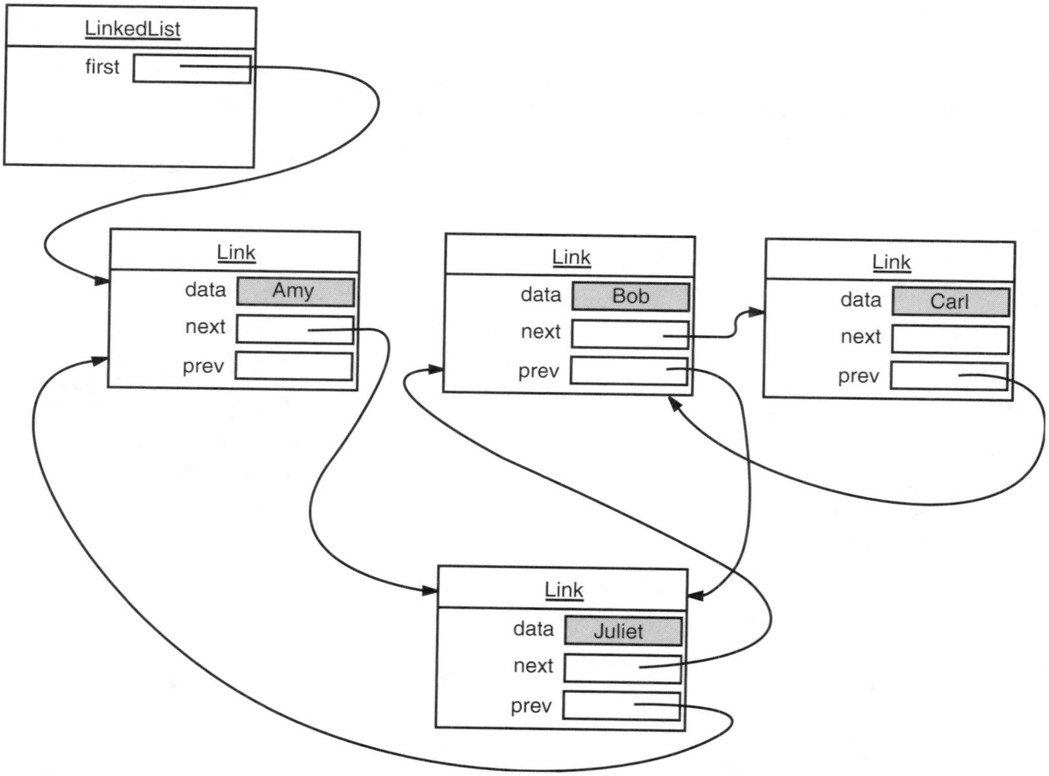

Figure 2–7: Adding an element to a linked list

If you call the add method multiple times, the elements are simply added in the order in which you supplied them. They are all added in turn before the current iterator position.

When you use the add operation with an iterator that was freshly returned from the list-Iterator method and that points to the beginning of the linked list, the newly added element becomes the new head of the list. When the iterator has passed the last element of the list (that is, when hasNext returns false), the added element becomes the new tail of the list. If the

linked list has *n* elements, there are *n*+1 spots for adding a new element. These spots correspond to the *n*+1 possible positions of the iterator. For example, if a linked list contains three elements, A, B, and C, then there are four possible positions (marked as |) for inserting a new element:

```
|ABC
A|BC
AB|C
ABC|
```

> **NOTE:** You have to be careful with the "cursor" analogy. The remove operation does not quite work like the BACKSPACE key. Immediately after a call to next, the remove method indeed removes the element to the left of the iterator, just like the BACKSPACE key would. However, if you just called previous, the element to the right is removed. And you can't call remove twice in a row.
>
> Unlike the add method, which depends only on the iterator position, the remove method depends on the iterator state.

Finally, a set method replaces the last element returned by a call to next or previous with a new element. For example, the following code replaces the first element of a list with a new value:

```
ListIterator<String> iter = list.listIterator();
String oldValue = iter.next(); // returns first element
iter.set(newValue); // sets first element to newValue
```

As you might imagine, if an iterator traverses a collection while another iterator is modifying it, confusing situations can occur. For example, suppose an iterator points before an element that another iterator has just removed. The iterator is now invalid and should no longer be used. The linked list iterators have been designed to detect such modifications. If an iterator finds that its collection has been modified by another iterator or by a method of the collection itself, then it throws a ConcurrentModificationException. For example, consider the following code:

```
List<String> list = . . .;
ListIterator<String> iter1 = list.listIterator();
ListIterator<String> iter2 = list.listIterator();
iter1.next();
iter1.remove();
iter2.next(); // throws ConcurrentModificationException
```

The call to iter2.next throws a ConcurrentModificationException since iter2 detects that the list was modified externally.

To avoid concurrent modification exceptions, follow this simple rule: You can attach as many iterators to a collection as you like, provided that all of them are only readers. Alternatively, you can attach a single iterator that can both read and write.

Concurrent modification detection is achieved in a simple way. The collection keeps track of the number of mutating operations (such as adding and removing elements). Each iterator keeps a separate count of the number of mutating operations that *it* was responsible for. At the beginning of each iterator method, the iterator simply checks whether its own mutation count equals that of the collection. If not, it throws a ConcurrentModificationException. This is an excellent check and a great improvement over the fundamentally unsafe iterators in the C++ STL framework.

NOTE: There is, however, a curious exception to the detection of concurrent modifications. The linked list only keeps track of *structural* modifications to the list, such as adding and removing links. The set method does *not* count as a structural modification. You can attach multiple iterators to a linked list, all of which call set to change the contents of existing links. This capability is required for a number of algorithms in the Collections class that we discuss later in this chapter.

Now you have seen the fundamental methods of the LinkedList class. You use a ListIterator to traverse the elements of the linked list in either direction and to add and remove elements.

As you saw in the preceding section, many other useful methods for operating on linked lists are declared in the Collection interface. These are, for the most part, implemented in the AbstractCollection superclass of the LinkedList class. For example, the toString method invokes toString on all elements and produces one long string of the format [A, B, C]. This is handy for debugging. Use the contains method to check whether an element is present in a linked list. For example, the call staff.contains("Harry") returns true if the linked list already contains a string that is equal to the string "Harry".

The library also supplies a number of methods that are, from a theoretical perspective, somewhat dubious. Linked lists do not support fast random access. If you want to see the *n*th element of a linked list, you have to start at the beginning and skip past the first $n - 1$ elements first. There is no shortcut. For that reason, programmers don't usually use linked lists in programming situations in which elements need to be accessed by an integer index.

Nevertheless, the LinkedList class supplies a get method that lets you access a particular element:

```
LinkedList<String> list = . . .;
String obj = list.get(n);
```

Of course, this method is not very efficient. If you find yourself using it, you are probably using the wrong data structure for your problem.

You should *never* use this illusory random access method to step through a linked list. The code

```
for (int i = 0; i < list.size(); i++)
   do something with list.get(i);
```

is staggeringly inefficient. Each time you look up another element, the search starts again from the beginning of the list. The LinkedList object makes no effort to cache the position information.

NOTE: The get method has one slight optimization: If the index is at least size() / 2, then the search for the element starts at the end of the list.

The list iterator interface also has a method to tell you the index of the current position. In fact, because Java iterators conceptually point between elements, it has two of them: The nextIndex method returns the integer index of the element that would be returned by the next call to next; the previousIndex method returns the index of the element that would be returned by the next call to previous. Of course, that is simply one less than nextIndex. These methods are efficient—the iterators keep a count of the current position. Finally, if you have an integer index n, then list.listIterator(n) returns an iterator that points just before the element with index n. That is, calling next yields the same element as list.get(n); obtaining that iterator is inefficient.

If you have a linked list with only a handful of elements, then you don't have to be overly paranoid about the cost of the get and set methods. But then why use a linked list in the first place? The only reason to use a linked list is to minimize the cost of insertion and removal in the middle of the list. If you have only a few elements, you can just use an ArrayList.

We recommend that you simply stay away from all methods that use an integer index to denote a position in a linked list. If you want random access into a collection, use an array or ArrayList, not a linked list.

The program in Example 2–1 puts linked lists to work. It simply creates two lists, merges them, then removes every second element from the second list, and finally tests the removeAll method. We recommend that you trace the program flow and pay special attention to the iterators. You may find it helpful to draw diagrams of the iterator positions, like this:

```
|ACE    |BDFG
A|CE    |BDFG
AB|CE   B|DFG
. . .
```

Note that the call

```
System.out.println(a);
```

prints all elements in the linked list a by invoking the toString method in AbstractCollection.

Example 2–1: LinkedListTest.java

```
1.  import java.util.*;
2.
3.  /**
4.     This program demonstrates operations on linked lists.
5.  */
6.  public class LinkedListTest
7.  {
8.     public static void main(String[] args)
9.     {
10.        List<String> a = new LinkedList<String>();
11.        a.add("Amy");
12.        a.add("Carl");
13.        a.add("Erica");
14.
15.        List<String> b = new LinkedList<String>();
16.        b.add("Bob");
17.        b.add("Doug");
18.        b.add("Frances");
19.        b.add("Gloria");
20.
21.        // merge the words from b into a
22.
23.        ListIterator<String> aIter = a.listIterator();
24.        Iterator<String> bIter = b.iterator();
25.
26.        while (bIter.hasNext())
27.        {
28.           if (aIter.hasNext()) aIter.next();
29.           aIter.add(bIter.next());
30.        }
31.
32.        System.out.println(a);
33.
```

```
34.        // remove every second word from b
35.
36.        bIter = b.iterator();
37.        while (bIter.hasNext())
38.        {
39.          bIter.next(); // skip one element
40.          if (bIter.hasNext())
41.          {
42.             bIter.next(); // skip next element
43.             bIter.remove(); // remove that element
44.          }
45.        }
46.
47.        System.out.println(b);
48.
49.        // bulk operation: remove all words in b from a
50.
51.        a.removeAll(b);
52.
53.        System.out.println(a);
54.     }
55. }
```

java.util.List<E> 1.2

- ListIterator<E> listIterator()
  returns a list iterator for visiting the elements of the list.
- ListIterator<E> listIterator(int index)
  returns a list iterator for visiting the elements of the list whose first call to next will return the element with the given index.
- void add(int i, E element)
  adds an element at the specified position.
- void addAll(int i, Collection<? extends E> elements)
  adds all elements from a collection to the specified position.
- E remove(int i)
  removes and returns an element at the specified position.
- E set(int i, E element)
  replaces the element at the specified position with a new element and returns the old element.
- int indexOf(Object element)
  returns the position of the first occurrence of an element equal to the specified element, or −1 if no matching element is found.
- int lastIndexOf(Object element)
  returns the position of the last occurrence of an element equal to the specified element, or −1 if no matching element is found.

java.util.ListIterator<E> 1.2

- void add(E newElement)
  adds an element before the current position.
- void set(E newElement)
  replaces the last element visited by next or previous with a new element. Throws an IllegalStateException if the list structure was modified since the last call to next or previous.

- `boolean hasPrevious()`
  returns true if there is another element to visit when iterating backwards through the list.
- `E previous()`
  returns the previous object. Throws a NoSuchElementException if the beginning of the list has been reached.
- `int nextIndex()`
  returns the index of the element that would be returned by the next call to next.
- `int previousIndex()`
  returns the index of the element that would be returned by the next call to previous.

API **java.util.LinkedList<E>** 1.2

- `LinkedList()`
  constructs an empty linked list.
- `LinkedList(Collection<? extends E> elements)`
  constructs a linked list and adds all elements from a collection.
- `void addFirst(E element)`
- `void addLast(E element)`
  add an element to the beginning or the end of the list.
- `E getFirst()`
- `E getLast()`
  return the element at the beginning or the end of the list.
- `E removeFirst()`
- `E removeLast()`
  remove and return the element at the beginning or the end of the list.

Array Lists

In the preceding section, you saw the List interface and the LinkedList class that implements it. The List interface describes an ordered collection in which the position of elements matters. There are two protocols for visiting the elements: through an iterator and by random access with methods get and set. The latter is not appropriate for linked lists, but of course get and set make a lot of sense for arrays. The collections library supplies the familiar ArrayList class that also implements the List interface. An ArrayList encapsulates a dynamically reallocated array of objects.

NOTE: If you are a veteran Java programmer, you may have used the Vector class whenever you needed a dynamic array. Why use an ArrayList instead of a Vector? For one simple reason: All methods of the Vector class are *synchronized*. It is safe to access a Vector object from two threads. But if you access a vector from only a single thread—by far the more common case—your code wastes quite a bit of time with synchronization. In contrast, the ArrayList methods are not synchronized. We recommend that you use an ArrayList instead of a Vector whenever you don't need synchronization.

Hash Sets

Linked lists and arrays let you specify the order in which you want to arrange the elements. However, if you are looking for a particular element and you don't remember its position, then you need to visit all elements until you find a match. That can be time consuming if the collection contains many elements. If you don't care about the ordering of the elements, then there are data structures that let you find elements much faster. The drawback is that those data structures give you no control over the order in which the elements

appear. The data structures organize the elements in an order that is convenient for their own purposes.

A well-known data structure for finding objects quickly is the *hash table*. A hash table computes an integer, called the *hash code*, for each object. A hash code is an integer that is somehow derived from the instance fields of an object, preferably such that objects with different data yield different codes. Table 2–2 lists a few examples of hash codes that result from the hashCode method of the String class.

Table 2–2: Hash Codes Resulting from the hashCode Function

String	Hash Code
"Lee"	76268
"lee"	107020
"eel"	100300

If you define your own classes, you are responsible for implementing your own hashCode method—see Volume 1, Chapter 5 for more information. Your implementation needs to be compatible with the equals method: If a.equals(b), then a and b must have the same hash code.

What's important for now is that hash codes can be computed quickly and that the computation depends only on the state of the object that needs to be hashed, and not on the other objects in the hash table.

A hash table is an array of linked lists. Each list is called a *bucket* (see Figure 2–8). To find the place of an object in the table, compute its hash code and reduce it modulo the total number of buckets. The resulting number is the index of the bucket that holds the element. For example, if an object has hash code 76268 and there are 128 buckets, then the object is placed in bucket 108 (because the remainder 76268 % 128 is 108). Perhaps you are lucky and there is no other element in that bucket. Then, you simply insert the element into that bucket. Of course, it is inevitable that you sometimes hit a bucket that is already filled. This is called a *hash collision*. Then, you compare the new object with all objects in that bucket to see if it is already present. Provided that the hash codes are reasonably randomly distributed and the number of buckets is large enough, only a few comparisons should be necessary.

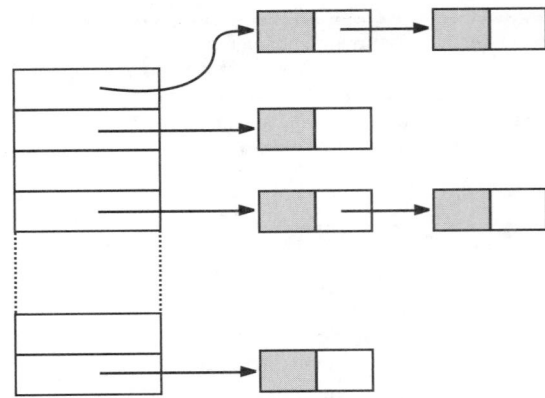

Figure 2–8: A hash table

If you want more control over the performance of the hash table, you can specify the initial bucket count. The bucket count gives the number of buckets that are used to collect objects with identical hash values. If too many elements are inserted into a hash table, the number of collisions increases and retrieval performance suffers.

If you know approximately how many elements will eventually be in the table, then you can set the bucket count. Typically, you set it to somewhere between 75% and 150% of the expected element count. Some researchers believe that it is a good idea to make the bucket count a prime number to prevent a clustering of keys. The evidence for this isn't conclusive, however. The standard library uses bucket counts that are a power of 2, with a default of 16. (Any value you supply for the table size is automatically rounded to the next power of 2.)

Of course, you do not always know how many elements you need to store, or your initial guess may be too low. If the hash table gets too full, it needs to be *rehashed*. To rehash the table, a table with more buckets is created, all elements are inserted into the new table, and the original table is discarded. The *load factor* determines when a hash table is rehashed. For example, if the load factor is 0.75 (which is the default) and the table is more than 75% full, then it is automatically rehashed, with twice as many buckets. For most applications, it is reasonable to leave the load factor at 0.75.

Hash tables can be used to implement several important data structures. The simplest among them is the *set* type. A set is a collection of elements without duplicates. The add method of a set first tries to find the object to be added, and adds it only if it is not yet present.

The Java collections library supplies a HashSet class that implements a set based on a hash table. You add elements with the add method. The contains method is redefined to make a fast lookup to find if an element is already present in the set. It checks only the elements in one bucket and not all elements in the collection.

The hash set iterator visits all buckets in turn. Because the hashing scatters the elements around in the table, they are visited in seemingly random order. You would only use a Hash-Set if you don't care about the ordering of the elements in the collection.

The sample program at the end of this section (Example 2–2) reads words from System.in, adds them to a set, and finally prints out all words in the set. For example, you can feed the program the text from *Alice in Wonderland* (which you can obtain from http://www.gutenberg.net) by launching it from a command shell as

```
java SetTest < alice30.txt
```

The program reads all words from the input and adds them to the hash set. It then iterates through the unique words in the set and finally prints out a count. (*Alice in Wonderland* has 5,909 unique words, including the copyright notice at the beginning.) The words appear in random order.

CAUTION: Be careful when you mutate set elements. If the hash code of an element were to change, then the element would no longer be in the correct position in the data structure.

Example 2–2: SetTest.java

```
1. import java.util.*;
2.
3. /**
4.    This program uses a set to print all unique words in
5.    System.in.
6. */
7. public class SetTest
```

```
 8. {
 9.    public static void main(String[] args)
10.    {
11.       Set<String> words = new HashSet<String>(); // HashSet implements Set
12.       long totalTime = 0;
13.
14.       Scanner in = new Scanner(System.in);
15.       while (in.hasNext())
16.       {
17.          String word = in.next();
18.          long callTime = System.currentTimeMillis();
19.          words.add(word);
20.          callTime = System.currentTimeMillis() - callTime;
21.          totalTime += callTime;
22.       }
23.
24.       Iterator<String> iter = words.iterator();
25.       for (int i = 1; i <= 20; i++)
26.          System.out.println(iter.next());
27.       System.out.println(". . .");
28.       System.out.println(words.size() + " distinct words. " + totalTime + " milliseconds.");
29.    }
30. }
```

 java.util.HashSet<E> 1.2

- HashSet()
  constructs an empty hash set.

- HashSet(Collection<? extends E> elements)
  constructs a hash set and adds all elements from a collection.

- HashSet(int initialCapacity)
  constructs an empty hash set with the specified capacity.

- HashSet(int initialCapacity, float loadFactor)
  constructs an empty hash set with the specified capacity and load factor (a number between 0.0 and 1.0 that determines at what percentage of fullness the hash table will be rehashed into a larger one).

java.lang.Object 1.0

- int hashCode()
  returns a hash code for this object. A hash code can be any integer, positive or negative. The definitions of equals and hashCode must be compatible: If x.equals(y) is true, then x.hashCode() must be the same value as y.hashCode().

Tree Sets

The TreeSet class is similar to the hash set, with one added improvement. A tree set is a *sorted collection*. You insert elements into the collection in any order. When you iterate through the collection, the values are automatically presented in sorted order. For example, suppose you insert three strings and then visit all elements that you added.

```
SortedSet<String> sorter = new TreeSet<String>(); // TreeSet implements SortedSet
sorter.add("Bob");
sorter.add("Amy");
sorter.add("Carl");
for (String s : sorter) System.out.println(s);
```

Then, the values are printed in sorted order: Amy Bob Carl. As the name of the class suggests, the sorting is accomplished by a tree data structure. (The current implementation uses a *red-black tree*. For a detailed description of red-black trees, see, for example, *Introduction to Algorithms* by Thomas Cormen, Charles Leiserson, Ronald Rivest, and Clifford Stein [The MIT Press 2001].) Every time an element is added to a tree, it is placed into its proper sorting position. Therefore, the iterator always visits the elements in sorted order.

Adding an element to a tree is slower than adding it to a hash table, but it is still much faster than adding it into the right place in an array or linked list. If the tree contains n elements, then an average of $\log_2 n$ comparisons are required to find the correct position for the new element. For example, if the tree already contains 1,000 elements, then adding a new element requires about 10 comparisons.

Thus, adding elements into a TreeSet is somewhat slower than adding into a HashSet—see Table 2–3 for a comparison—but the TreeSet automatically sorts the elements.

Table 2–3: Adding Elements into Hash and Tree Sets

Document	Total Number of Words	Number of Distinct Words	HashSet	TreeSet
Alice in Wonderland	28195	5909	5 sec	7 sec
The Count of Monte Cristo	466300	37545	75 sec	98 sec

java.util.TreeSet<E> 1.2

- TreeSet()
  constructs an empty tree set.
- TreeSet(Collection<? extends E> elements)
  constructs a tree set and adds all elements from a collection.

Object Comparison

How does the TreeSet know how you want the elements sorted? By default, the tree set assumes that you insert elements that implement the Comparable interface. That interface defines a single method:

```
public interface Comparable<T>
{
    int compareTo(T other);
}
```

The call a.compareTo(b) must return 0 if a and b are equal, a negative integer if a comes before b in the sort order, and a positive integer if a comes after b. The exact value does not matter; only its sign (>0, 0, or <0) matters. Several standard Java platform classes implement the Comparable interface. One example is the String class. Its compareTo method compares strings in dictionary order (sometimes called *lexicographic order*).

If you insert your own objects, you must define a sort order yourself by implementing the Comparable interface. There is no default implementation of compareTo in the Object class.

For example, here is how you can sort Item objects by part number.

```
class Item implements Comparable<Item>
{
    public int compareTo(Item other)
    {
        return partNumber - other.partNumber;
```

```
        }
          . . .
      }
```

If you compare two *positive* integers, such as part numbers in our example, then you can simply return their difference—it will be negative if the first item should come before the second item, zero if the part numbers are identical, and positive otherwise.

 CAUTION: This trick only works if the integers are from a small enough range. If x is a large positive integer and y is a large negative integer, then the difference x − y can overflow.

However, using the Comparable interface for defining the sort order has obvious limitations. A given class can implement the interface only once. But what can you do if you need to sort a bunch of items by part number in one collection and by description in another? Furthermore, what can you do if you need to sort objects of a class whose creator didn't bother to implement the Comparable interface?

In those situations, you tell the tree set to use a different comparison method, by passing a Comparator object into the TreeSet constructor. The Comparator interface declares a compare method with two explicit parameters:

```
public interface Comparator<T>
{
    int compare(T a, T b);
}
```

Just like the compareTo method, the compare method returns a negative integer if a comes before b, zero if they are identical, or a positive integer otherwise.

To sort items by their description, simply define a class that implements the Comparator interface:

```
class ItemComparator implements Comparator<Item>
{
    public int compare(Item a, Item b)
    {
        String descrA = a.getDescription();
        String descrB = b.getDescription();
        return descrA.compareTo(descrB);
    }
}
```

You then pass an object of this class to the tree set constructor:

```
ItemComparator comp = new ItemComparator();
SortedSet<Item> sortByDescription = new TreeSet<Item>(comp);
```

If you construct a tree with a comparator, it uses this object whenever it needs to compare two elements.

Note that this item comparator has no data. It is just a holder for the comparison method. Such an object is sometimes called a *function object*.

Function objects are commonly defined "on the fly," as instances of anonymous inner classes:

```
SortedSet<Item> sortByDescription = new TreeSet<Item>(new
    Comparator<Item>()
    {
        public int compare(Item a, Item b)
        {
```

```
        String descrA = a.getDescription();
        String descrB = b.getDescription();
        return descrA.compareTo(descrB);
    }
});
```

> NOTE: Actually, the Comparator<T> interface is declared to have two methods: compare and equals. Of course, *every* class has an equals method; thus, there seems little benefit in adding the method to the interface declaration. The API documentation explains that you need not override the equals method but that doing so may yield improved performance in some cases. For example, the addAll method of the TreeSet class can work more effectively if you add elements from another set that uses the same comparator.

If you look back at Table 2–3, you may well wonder if you should always use a tree set instead of a hash set. After all, adding elements does not seem to take much longer, and the elements are automatically sorted. The answer depends on the data that you are collecting. If you don't need the data sorted, there is no reason to pay for the sorting overhead. More important, with some data it is very difficult to come up with a sort order. Suppose you collect a bunch of rectangles. How do you sort them? By area? You can have two different rectangles with different positions but the same area. If you sort by area, the second one is not inserted into the set. The sort order for a tree must be a *total ordering* Any two elements must be comparable, and the comparison can only be zero if the elements are equal. There is such a sort order for rectangles (the lexicographic ordering on its coordinates), but it is unnatural and cumbersome to compute. In contrast, hash functions are usually easier to define. They only need to do a reasonably good job of scrambling the objects, whereas comparison functions must tell objects apart with complete precision.

The program in Example 2–3 builds two tree sets of Item objects. The first one is sorted by part number, the default sort order of Item objects. The second set is sorted by description, by means of a custom comparator.

Example 2–3: TreeSetTest.java

```
1. import java.util.*;
2.
3. /**
4.    This program sorts a set of items by comparing
5.    their descriptions.
6. */
7. public class TreeSetTest
8. {
9.    public static void main(String[] args)
10.   {
11.      SortedSet<Item> parts = new TreeSet<Item>();
12.      parts.add(new Item("Toaster", 1234));
13.      parts.add(new Item("Widget", 4562));
14.      parts.add(new Item("Modem", 9912));
15.      System.out.println(parts);
16.
17.      SortedSet<Item> sortByDescription = new TreeSet<Item>(new
18.         Comparator<Item>()
19.         {
20.            public int compare(Item a, Item b)
21.            {
22.               String descrA = a.getDescription();
```

```
23.              String descrB = b.getDescription();
24.              return descrA.compareTo(descrB);
25.          }
26.      });
27.
28.      sortByDescription.addAll(parts);
29.      System.out.println(sortByDescription);
30.   }
31. }
32.
33. /**
34.    An item with a description and a part number.
35. */
36. class Item implements Comparable<Item>
37. {
38.    /**
39.       Constructs an item.
40.       @param aDescription the item's description
41.       @param aPartNumber the item's part number
42.    */
43.    public Item(String aDescription, int aPartNumber)
44.    {
45.       description = aDescription;
46.       partNumber = aPartNumber;
47.    }
48.
49.    /**
50.       Gets the description of this item.
51.       @return the description
52.    */
53.    public String getDescription()
54.    {
55.       return description;
56.    }
57.
58.    public String toString()
59.    {
60.       return "[description=" + description
61.          + ", partNumber=" + partNumber + "]";
62.    }
63.
64.    public boolean equals(Object otherObject)
65.    {
66.       if (this == otherObject) return true;
67.       if (otherObject == null) return false;
68.       if (getClass() != otherObject.getClass()) return false;
69.       Item other = (Item) otherObject;
70.       return description.equals(other.description)
71.          && partNumber == other.partNumber;
72.    }
73.
74.    public int hashCode()
75.    {
76.       return 13 * description.hashCode() + 17 * partNumber;
77.    }
78.
```

```
79.   public int compareTo(Item other)
80.   {
81.      return partNumber - other.partNumber;
82.   }
83.
84.   private String description;
85.   private int partNumber;
86. }
```

 java.lang.Comparable<T> 1.2

- int compareTo(T other)

  compares this object with another object and returns a negative value if this comes before other, zero if they are considered identical in the sort order, and a positive value if this comes after other.

 java.util.Comparator<T> 1.2

- int compare(T a, T b)

  compares two objects and returns a negative value if a comes before b, zero if they are considered identical in the sort order, and a positive value if a comes after b.

 java.util.SortedSet<E> 1.2

- Comparator<? super E> comparator()

  returns the comparator used for sorting the elements, or null if the elements are compared with the compareTo method of the Comparable interface.

- E first()
- E last()

  return the smallest or largest element in the sorted set.

 java.util.TreeSet<E> 1.2

- TreeSet()

  constructs a tree set for storing Comparable objects.

- TreeSet(Comparator<? super E> c)

  constructs a tree set and uses the specified comparator for sorting its elements.

- TreeSet(SortedSet<? extends E> elements)

  constructs a tree set, adds all elements from a sorted set, and uses the same element comparator as the given sorted set.

Priority Queues

A priority queue retrieves elements in sorted order after they were inserted in arbitrary order. That is, whenever you call the remove method, you get the smallest element currently in the priority queue. However, the priority queue does not sort all its elements. If you iterate over the elements, they are not necessarily sorted. The priority queue makes use of an elegant and efficient data structure, called a *heap*. A heap is a self-organizing binary tree in which the add and remove operations cause the smallest element to gravitate to the root, without wasting time on sorting all elements.

Just like a TreeSet, a priority queue can either hold elements of a class that implements the Comparable interface or a Comparator object you supply in the constructor.

A typical use for a priority queue is job scheduling. Each job has a priority. Jobs are added in random order. Whenever a new job can be started, the highest-priority job is removed

from the queue. (Since it is traditional for priority 1 to be the "highest" priority, the remove operation yields the minimum element.)

Example 2–4 shows a priority queue in action. Unlike iteration in a TreeSet, the iteration here does not visit the elements in sorted order. However, removal always yields the smallest remaining element.

Example 2–4: PriorityQueueTest.java

```
1. import java.util.*;
2.
3. /**
4.    This program demonstrates the use of a priority queue.
5. */
6. public class PriorityQueueTest
7. {
8.    public static void main(String[] args)
9.    {
10.       PriorityQueue<GregorianCalendar> pq = new PriorityQueue<GregorianCalendar>();
11.       pq.add(new GregorianCalendar(1906, Calendar.DECEMBER, 9)); // G. Hopper
12.       pq.add(new GregorianCalendar(1815, Calendar.DECEMBER, 10)); // A. Lovelace
13.       pq.add(new GregorianCalendar(1903, Calendar.DECEMBER, 3)); // J. von Neumann
14.       pq.add(new GregorianCalendar(1910, Calendar.JUNE, 22)); // K. Zuse
15.
16.       System.out.println("Iterating over elements...");
17.       for (GregorianCalendar date : pq)
18.          System.out.println(date.get(Calendar.YEAR));
19.       System.out.println("Removing elements...");
20.       while (!pq.isEmpty())
21.          System.out.println(pq.remove().get(Calendar.YEAR));
22.    }
23. }
```

API   **java.util.PriorityQueue** 5.0

- PriorityQueue()
- PriorityQueue(int initialCapacity)
  construct a tree set for storing Comparable objects.

- PriorityQueue(int initialCapacity, Comparator<? super E> c)
  constructs a tree set and uses the specified comparator for sorting its elements.

Maps

A set is a collection that lets you quickly find an existing element. However, to look up an element, you need to have an exact copy of the element to find. That isn't a very common lookup—usually, you have some key information, and you want to look up the associated element. The *map* data structure serves that purpose. A map stores key/value pairs. You can find a value if you provide the key. For example, you may store a table of employee records, where the keys are the employee IDs and the values are Employee objects.

The Java library supplies two general-purpose implementations for maps: HashMap and TreeMap. Both classes implement the Map interface.

A hash map hashes the keys, and a tree map uses a total ordering on the keys to organize them in a search tree. The hash or comparison function is applied *only to the keys*. The values associated with the keys are not hashed or compared.

Should you choose a hash map or a tree map? As with sets, hashing is a bit faster, and it is the preferred choice if you don't need to visit the keys in sorted order.

Here is how you set up a hash map for storing employees.

```
Map<String, Employee> staff = new HashMap<String, Employee>(); // HashMap implements Map
Employee harry = new Employee("Harry Hacker");
staff.put("987-98-9996", harry);
    . . .
```

Whenever you add an object to a map, you must supply a key as well. In our case, the key is a string, and the corresponding value is an Employee object.

To retrieve an object, you must use (and, therefore, remember) the key.

```
String s = "987-98-9996";
e = staff.get(s); // gets harry
```

If no information is stored in the map with the particular key specified, then get returns null.

Keys must be unique. You cannot store two values with the same key. If you call the put method twice with the same key, then the second value replaces the first one. In fact, put returns the previous value stored with the key parameter.

The remove method removes an element with a given key from the map. The size method returns the number of entries in the map.

The collections framework does not consider a map itself as a collection. (Other frameworks for data structures consider a map as a collection of *pairs*, or as a collection of values that is indexed by the keys.) However, you can obtain *views* of the map, objects that implement the Collection interface, or one of its subinterfaces.

There are three views: the set of keys, the collection of values (which is not a set), and the set of key/value pairs. The keys and key/value pairs form a set because there can be only one copy of a key in a map. The methods

```
Set<K> keySet()
Collection<K> values()
Set<Map.Entry<K, V>> entrySet()
```

return these three views. (The elements of the entry set are objects of the static inner class Map.Entry.)

Note that the keySet is *not* a HashSet or TreeSet, but an object of some other class that implements the Set interface. The Set interface extends the Collection interface. Therefore, you can use a keySet as you would use any collection.

For example, you can enumerate all keys of a map:

```
Set<String> keys = map.keySet();
for (String key : keys)
{
    do something with key
}
```

TIP: If you want to look at both keys and values, then you can avoid value lookups by enumerating the *entries*. Use the following code skeleton:

```
for (Map.Entry<String, Employee> entry : staff.entrySet())
{
    String key = entry.getKey();
    Employee value = entry.getValue();
    do something with key, value
}
```

If you invoke the remove method of the iterator, you actually remove the key *and its associated value* from the map. However, you cannot *add* an element to the key set view. It makes no sense to add a key without also adding a value. If you try to invoke the add method, it throws an UnsupportedOperationException. The entry set view has the same restriction, even though it would make conceptual sense to add a new key/value pair.

Example 2–5 illustrates a map at work. We first add key/value pairs to a map. Then, we remove one key from the map, which removes its associated value as well. Next, we change the value that is associated with a key and call the get method to look up a value. Finally, we iterate through the entry set.

Example 2–5: MapTest.java

```
1. import java.util.*;
2.
3. /**
4.    This program demonstrates the use of a map with key type
5.    String and value type Employee.
6. */
7. public class MapTest
8. {
9.    public static void main(String[] args)
10.   {
11.      Map<String, Employee> staff = new HashMap<String, Employee>();
12.      staff.put("144-25-5464", new Employee("Amy Lee"));
13.      staff.put("567-24-2546", new Employee("Harry Hacker"));
14.      staff.put("157-62-7935", new Employee("Gary Cooper"));
15.      staff.put("456-62-5527", new Employee("Francesca Cruz"));
16.
17.      // print all entries
18.
19.      System.out.println(staff);
20.
21.      // remove an entry
22.
23.      staff.remove("567-24-2546");
24.
25.      // replace an entry
26.
27.      staff.put("456-62-5527", new Employee("Francesca Miller"));
28.
29.      // look up a value
30.
31.      System.out.println(staff.get("157-62-7935"));
32.
33.      // iterate through all entries
34.
35.      for (Map.Entry<String, Employee> entry : staff.entrySet())
36.      {
37.         String key = entry.getKey();
38.         Employee value = entry.getValue();
39.         System.out.println("key=" + key + ", value=" + value);
40.      }
41.   }
42. }
43.
```

```
44. /**
45.    A minimalist employee class for testing purposes.
46. */
47. class Employee
48. {
49.    /**
50.       Constructs an employee with $0 salary.
51.       @param n the employee name
52.    */
53.    public Employee(String n)
54.    {
55.       name = n;
56.       salary = 0;
57.    }
58.
59.    public String toString()
60.    {
61.       return "[name=" + name + ", salary=" + salary + "]";
62.    }
63.
64.    private String name;
65.    private double salary;
66. }
```

java.util.Map<K, V> 1.2

- V get(K key)

  gets the value associated with the key; returns the object associated with the key, or null if the key is not found in the map. The key may be null.

- V put(K key, V value)

  puts the association of a key and a value into the map. If the key is already present, the new object replaces the old one previously associated with the key. This method returns the old value of the key, or null if the key was not previously present. The key may be null, but the value must not be null.

- void putAll(Map<? extends K, ? extends V> entries)

  adds all entries from the specified map to this map.

- boolean containsKey(Object key)

  returns true if the key is present in the map.

- boolean containsValue(Object value)

  returns true if the value is present in the map.

- Set<Map.Entry<K, V>> entrySet()

  returns a set view of Map.Entry objects, the key/value pairs in the map. You can remove elements from this set and they are removed from the map, but you cannot add any elements.

- Set<K> keySet()

  returns a set view of all keys in the map. You can remove elements from this set and the keys and associated values are removed from the map, but you cannot add any elements.

- Collection<V> values()

  returns a collection view of all values in the map. You can remove elements from this set and the removed value and its key are removed from the map, but you cannot add any elements.

 java.util.Map.Entry<K, V> 1.2

- K getKey()
- V getValue()

  return the key or value of this entry.

- V setValue(V newValue)

  changes the value *in the associated map* to the new value and returns the old value.

 java.util.HashMap<K, V> 1.2

- HashMap()
- HashMap(int initialCapacity)
- HashMap(int initialCapacity, float loadFactor)

  construct an empty hash map with the specified capacity and load factor (a number between 0.0 and 1.0 that determines at what percentage of fullness the hash table will be rehashed into a larger one). The default load factor is 0.75.

java.util.TreeMap<K,V> 1.2

- TreeMap(Comparator<? super K> c)

  constructs a tree map and uses the specified comparator for sorting its keys.

- TreeMap(Map<? extends K, ? extends V> entries)

  constructs a tree map and adds all entries from a map.

- TreeMap(SortedMap<? extends K, ? extends V> entries)

  constructs a tree map, adds all entries from a sorted map, and uses the same element comparator as the given sorted map.

java.util.SortedMap<K, V> 1.2

- Comparator<? super K> comparator()

  returns the comparator used for sorting the keys, or null if the keys are compared with the compareTo method of the Comparable interface.

- K firstKey()
- K lastKey()

  return the smallest or largest key in the map.

Specialized Set and Map Classes

The collection class library has several map classes for specialized needs that we briefly discuss in this section.

Weak Hash Maps

The WeakHashMap class was designed to solve an interesting problem. What happens with a value whose key is no longer used anywhere in your program? Suppose the last reference to a key has gone away. Then, there is no longer any way to refer to the value object. But because no part of the program has the key any more, the key/value pair cannot be removed from the map. Why can't the garbage collector remove it? Isn't it the job of the garbage collector to remove unused objects?

Unfortunately, it isn't quite so simple. The garbage collector traces *live* objects. As long as the map object is live, then *all* buckets in it are live and they won't be reclaimed. Thus, your program should take care to remove unused values from long-lived maps. Or, you can use a WeakHashMap instead. This data structure cooperates with the garbage collector to remove key/value pairs when the only reference to the key is the one from the hash table entry.

Here are the inner workings of this mechanism. The WeakHashMap uses *weak references* to hold keys. A WeakReference object holds a reference to another object, in our case, a hash table key. Objects of this type are treated in a special way by the garbage collector. Normally, if the garbage collector finds that a particular object has no references to it, it simply reclaims the object. However, if the object is reachable *only* by a WeakReference, the garbage collector still reclaims the object, but it places the weak reference that led to it into a queue. The operations of the WeakHashMap periodically check that queue for newly arrived weak references. The arrival of a weak reference in the queue signifies that the key was no longer used by anyone and that it has been collected. The WeakHashMap then removes the associated entry.

Linked Hash Sets and Maps

JDK 1.4 adds classes LinkedHashSet and LinkedHashMap that remember in which order you inserted items. That way, you avoid the seemingly random order of items in a hash table. As entries are inserted into the table, they are joined in a doubly linked list (see Figure 2–9).

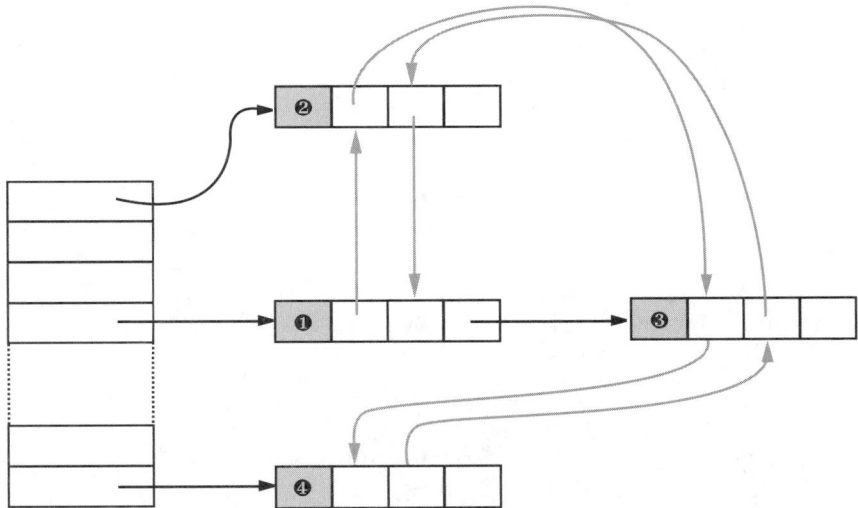

Figure 2–9: A linked hash table

For example, consider the following map insertions from Example 2–5:

```
Map staff = new LinkedHashMap();
staff.put("144-25-5464", new Employee("Amy Lee"));
staff.put("567-24-2546", new Employee("Harry Hacker"));
staff.put("157-62-7935", new Employee("Gary Cooper"));
staff.put("456-62-5527", new Employee("Francesca Cruz"));
```

Then staff.keySet().iterator() enumerates the keys in the order:

```
144-25-5464
567-24-2546
157-62-7935
456-62-5527
```

and staff.values().iterator() enumerates the values in the order:

```
Amy Lee
Harry Hacker
Gary Cooper
Francesca Cruz
```

A linked hash map can alternatively use *access order*, not insertion order, to iterate through the map entries. Every time you call get or put, the affected entry is removed from its current position and placed at the *end* of the linked list of entries. (Only the position in the linked list of entries is affected, not the hash table bucket. An entry always stays in the bucket that corresponds to the hash code of the key.) To construct such a hash map, call

```
LinkedHashMap<K, V>(initialCapacity, loadFactor, true)
```

Access order is useful for implementing a "least recently used" discipline for a cache. For example, you may want to keep frequently accessed entries in memory and read less frequently accessed objects from a database. When you don't find an entry in the table, and the table is already pretty full, then you can get an iterator into the table and remove the first few elements that it enumerates. Those entries were the least recently used ones.

You can even automate that process. Form a subclass of LinkedHashMap and override the method

```
protected boolean removeEldestEntry(Map.Entry<K, V> eldest)
```

Adding a new entry then causes the eldest entry to be removed whenever your method returns true. For example, the following cache is kept at a size of at most 100 elements:

```
Map<K, V> cache = new
   LinkedHashMap<K, V>(128, 0.75F, true)
   {
      protected boolean removeEldestEntry(Map.Entry<K, V> eldest)
      {
         return size() > 100;
      }
   };
```

Alternatively, you can consider the eldest entry to decide whether to remove it. For example, you may want to check a time stamp stored with the entry.

Enumeration Sets and Maps

The EnumSet is an efficient set implementation with elements that belong to an enumerated type. Because an enumerated type has a finite number of instances, the EnumSet is internally implemented simply as a sequence of bits. A bit is turned on if the corresponding value is present in the set.

The EnumSet class has no public constructors. You use a static factory method to construct the set:

```
enum Weekday { MONDAY, TUESDAY, WEDNESDAY, THURSDAY, FRIDAY, SATURDAY, SUNDAY };
EnumSet<Weekday> always = EnumSet.allOf(Weekday.class);
EnumSet<Weekday> never = EnumSet.noneOf(Weekday.class);
EnumSet<Weekday> workday = EnumSet.range(Weekday.MONDAY, Weekday.FRIDAY);
EnumSet<Weekday> mwf = EnumSet.of(Weekday.MONDAY, Weekday.WEDNESDAY, Weekday.FRIDAY);
```

You can use the usual methods of the Set interface to modify an EnumSet.

An EnumMap is a map with keys that belong to an enumerated type. It is simply and efficiently implemented as an array of values. You need to specify the key type in the constructor:

```
EnumMap<Weekday, Employee> personInCharge = new EnumMap<Weekday, Employee>(Weekday.class);
```

 NOTE: In the API documentation for EnumSet, you will see odd-looking type parameters of the form E extends Enum<E>. This simply means "E is an enumerated type." All enumerated types extend the generic Enum class. For example, Weekday extends Enum<Weekday>.

Identity Hash Maps

JDK 1.4 adds another class `IdentityHashMap` for another quite specialized purpose, where the hash values for the keys should not be computed by the `hashCode` method but by the `System.identityHashCode` method. That's the method that `Object.hashCode` uses to compute a hash code from the object's memory address. Also, for comparison of objects, the `IdentityHashMap` uses `==`, not `equals`.

In other words, different key objects are considered distinct even if they have equal contents. This class is useful for implementing object traversal algorithms (such as object serialization), in which you want to keep track of which objects have already been traversed.

 java.util.WeakHashMap<K, V> 1.2

- `WeakHashMap()`
- `WeakHashMap(int initialCapacity)`
- `WeakHashMap(int initialCapacity, float loadFactor)`
  construct an empty hash map with the specified capacity and load factor.

 java.util.LinkedHashSet<E> 1.4

- `LinkedHashSet()`
- `LinkedHashSet(int initialCapacity)`
- `LinkedHashSet(int initialCapacity, float loadFactor)`
  construct an empty linked hash set with the specified capacity and load factor.

 java.util.LinkedHashMap<K, V> 1.4

- `LinkedHashMap()`
- `LinkedHashMap(int initialCapacity)`
- `LinkedHashMap(int initialCapacity, float loadFactor)`
- `LinkedHashMap(int initialCapacity, float loadFactor, boolean accessOrder)`
  construct an empty linked hash map with the specified capacity, load factor, and ordering. The `accessOrder` parameter is `true` for access order, `false` for insertion order.

- `protected boolean removeEldestEntry(Map.Entry<K, V> eldest)`
  should be overridden to return `true` if you want the `eldest` entry to be removed. The `eldest` parameter is the entry whose removal is being contemplated. This method is called after an entry has been added to the map. The default implementation returns `false`—old elements are not removed by default. However, you can redefine this method to selectively return `true`; for example, if the eldest entry fits a certain condition or the map exceeds a certain size.

 java.util.EnumSet<E extends Enum<E>> 5.0

- `static <E extends Enum<E>> EnumSet<E> allOf(Class<E> enumType)`
  returns a set that contains all values of the given enumerated type.

- `static <E extends Enum<E>> EnumSet<E> noneOf(Class<E> enumType)`
  returns an empty set, capable of holding values of the given enumerated type.

- `static <E extends Enum<E>> EnumSet<E> range(E from, E to)`
  returns a set that contains all values between `from` and `to` (inclusive).

- `static <E extends Enum<E>> EnumSet<E> of(E value)`
- `static <E extends Enum<E>> EnumSet<E> of(E value, E... values)`
  return a set that contains the given values.

java.util.EnumMap<K extends Enum<K>, V> 5.0

- EnumMap(Class<K> keyType)
  constructs an empty map whose keys have the given type.

java.util.IdentityHashMap<K, V> 1.4

- IdentityHashMap()
- IdentityHashMap(int expectedMaxSize)
  construct an empty identity hash map whose capacity is the smallest power of 2 exceeding 1.5 * expectedMaxSize. (The default for expectedMaxSize is 21.)

java.lang.System 1.0

- static int identityHashCode(Object obj) 1.1
  returns the same hash code (derived from the object's memory address) that Object.hashCode computes, even if the class to which obj belongs has redefined the hashCode method.

The Collections Framework

A *framework* is a set of classes that form the basis for building advanced functionality. A framework contains superclasses with useful functionality, policies, and mechanisms. The user of a framework forms subclasses to extend the functionality without having to reinvent the basic mechanisms. For example, Swing is a framework for user interfaces.

The Java collections library forms a framework for collection classes. It defines a number of interfaces and abstract classes for implementors of collections (see Figure 2–10), and it prescribes certain mechanisms, such as the iteration protocol. You can use the collection classes without having to know much about the framework—we did just that in the preceding sections. However, if you want to implement generic algorithms that work for multiple collection types or if you want to add a new collection type, it is helpful to understand the framework.

There are two fundamental interfaces for collections: Collection and Map. You insert elements into a collection with a method:

    boolean add(E element)

However, maps hold key/value pairs, and you use the put method to insert them.

    V put(K key, V value)

To read elements from a collection, you visit them with an iterator. However, you can read values from a map with the get method:

    V get(K key)

A List is an *ordered collection*. Elements are added into a particular position in the container. An object can be placed into its position in two ways: by an integer index and by a list iterator. The List interface defines methods for random access:

    void add(int index, E element)
    E get(int index)
    void remove(int index)

As already discussed, the List interface provides these random access methods whether or not they are efficient for a particular implementation. To make it possible to avoid carrying out costly random access operations, JDK 1.4 introduces a tagging interface, RandomAccess. That interface has no methods, but you can use it to test whether a particular collection supports efficient random access:

```
if (c instanceof RandomAccess)
{
    use random access algorithm
}
else
{
    use sequential access algorithm
}
```

The ArrayList and Vector classes implement the RandomAccess interface.

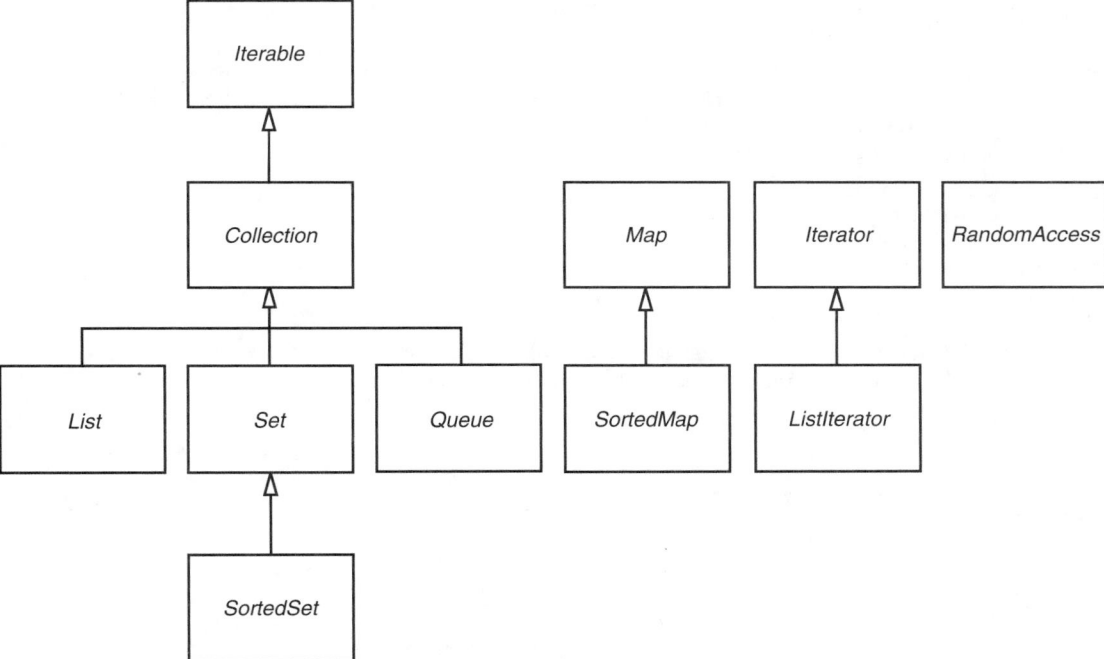

Figure 2–10: The interfaces of the collections framework

 NOTE: From a theoretical point of view, it would have made sense to have a separate Array interface that extends the List interface and declares the random access methods. If there were a separate Array interface, then those algorithms that require random access would use Array parameters and you could not accidentally apply them to collections with slow random access. However, the designers of the collections framework chose not to define a separate interface, because they wanted to keep the number of interfaces in the library small. Also, they did not want to take a paternalistic attitude toward programmers. You are free to pass a linked list to algorithms that use random access—you just need to be aware of the performance costs.

The ListIterator interface defines a method for adding an element before the iterator position:

```
void add(E element)
```

To get and remove elements at a particular position, you simply use the next and remove methods of the Iterator interface.

The Set interface is identical to the Collection interface, but the behavior of the methods is more tightly defined. The add method of a set should reject duplicates. The equals method of a set should be defined so that two sets are identical if they have the same elements, but not necessarily in the same order. The hashCode method should be defined such that two sets with the same elements yield the same hash code.

Why make a separate interface if the method signatures are the same? Conceptually, not all collections are sets. Making a Set interface enables programmers to write methods that accept only sets.

Finally, the SortedSet and SortedMap interfaces expose the comparison object used for sorting, and they define methods to obtain views of subsets of the collections. We discuss these views in the next section.

Now, let us turn from the interfaces to the classes that implement them. We already discussed that the collection interfaces have quite a few methods that can be trivially implemented from more fundamental methods. Abstract classes supply many of these routine implementations:

    AbstractCollection
    AbstractList
    AbstractSequentialList
    AbstractSet
    AbstractQueue
    AbstractMap

If you implement your own collection class, then you probably want to extend one of these classes so that you can pick up the implementations of the routine operations.

The Java library supplies concrete classes:

    LinkedList
    ArrayList
    HashSet
    TreeSet
    PriorityQueue
    HashMap
    TreeMap

Figure 2–11 shows the relationships between these classes.

Finally, a number of "legacy" container classes have been present since JDK 1.0, before there was a collections framework:

    Vector
    Stack
    Hashtable
    Properties

They have been integrated into the collections framework—see Figure 2–12. We discuss these classes later in this chapter.

Views and Wrappers

If you look at Figure 2–10 and Figure 2–11, you might think it is overkill to have lots of interfaces and abstract classes to implement a modest number of concrete collection classes. However, these figures don't tell the whole story. By using *views*, you can obtain other objects that implement the Collection or Map interfaces. You saw one example of this with the keySet method of the map classes. At first glance, it appears as if the method creates a new set, fills it with all keys of the map, and returns it. However, that is not the case. Instead, the keySet method returns an object of a class that implements the Set interface and whose methods manipulate the original map. Such a collection is called a *view*.

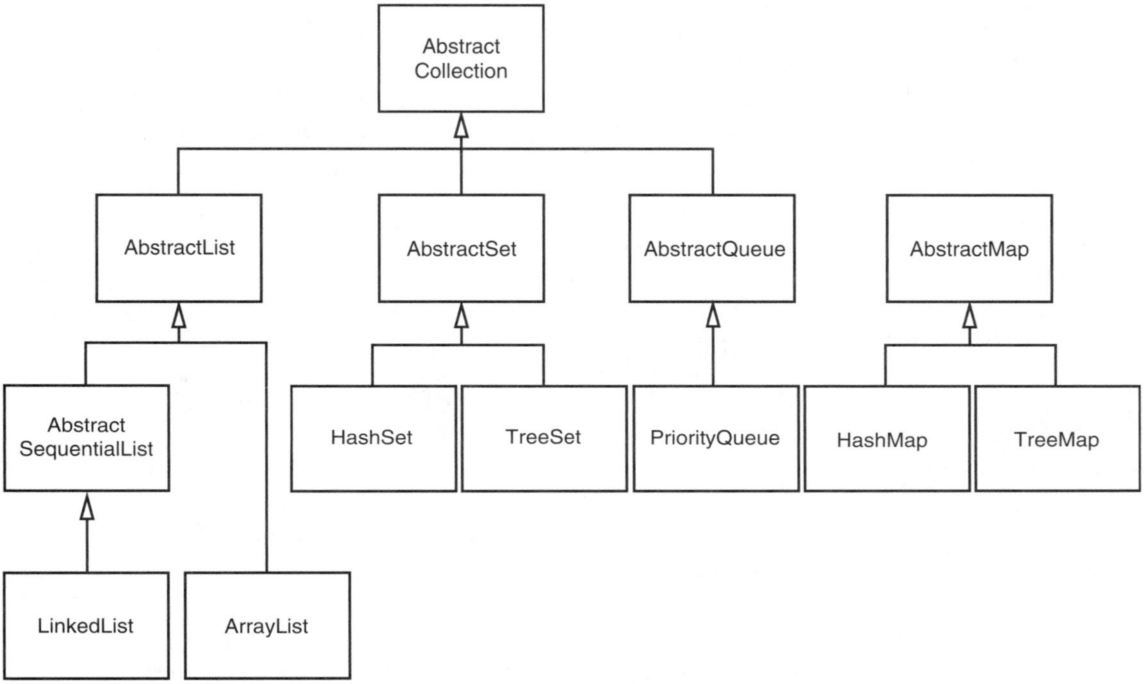

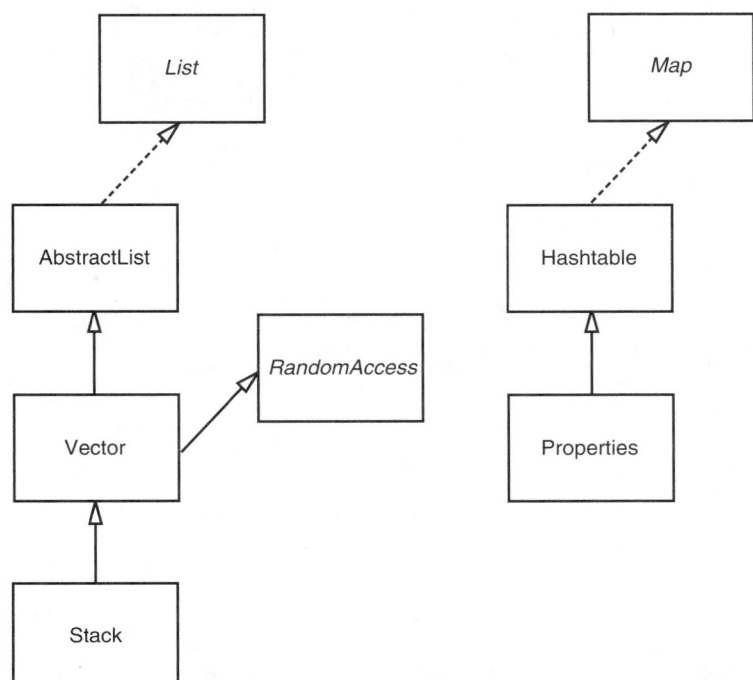

Figure 2–11: Classes in the collections framework

Figure 2–12: Legacy classes in the collections framework

The technique of views has a number of useful applications in the collections framework. We discuss these applications in the following sections.

Lightweight Collection Wrappers

The static asList method of the Arrays class returns a List wrapper around a plain Java array. This method lets you pass the array to a method that expects a list or collection argument. For example,

```
Card[] cardDeck = new Card[52];
. . .
List<Card> cardList = Arrays.asList(cardDeck);
```

The returned object is *not* an ArrayList. It is a view object with get and set methods that access the underlying array. All methods that would change the size of the array (such as add and the remove method of the associated iterator) throw an UnsupportedOperationException.

As of JDK 5.0, the asList method is declared to have a variable number of arguments. Instead of passing an array, you can also pass individual elements. For example,

```
List<String> names = Arrays.asList("Amy", "Bob", "Carl");
```

The method call

```
Collections.nCopies(n, anObject)
```

returns an immutable object that implements the List interface and gives the illusion of having n elements, each of which appears as anObject.

For example, the following call creates a List containing 100 strings, all set to "DEFAULT":

```
List<String> settings = Collections.nCopies(100, "DEFAULT");
```

There is very little storage cost—the object is stored only once. This is a cute application of the view technique.

 NOTE: The Collections class contains a number of utility methods with parameters or return values that are collections. Do not confuse it with the Collection interface.

The method call

```
Collections.singleton(anObject)
```

returns a view object that implements the Set interface (unlike ncopies, which produces a List). The returned object implements an immutable single-element set without the overhead of data structure. The methods singletonList and singletonMap behave similarly.

Subranges

You can form subrange views for a number of collections. For example, suppose you have a list staff and want to extract elements 10 to 19. You use the subList method to obtain a view into the subrange of the list.

```
List group2 = staff.subList(10, 20);
```

The first index is inclusive, the second exclusive—just like the parameters for the substring operation of the String class.

You can apply any operations to the subrange, and they automatically reflect the entire list. For example, you can erase the entire subrange:

```
group2.clear(); // staff reduction
```

The elements are now automatically cleared from the staff list, and group2 is empty.

For sorted sets and maps, you use the sort order, not the element position, to form subranges. The SortedSet interface declares three methods:

```
subSet(from, to)
headSet(to)
tailSet(from)
```

These return the subsets of all elements that are larger than or equal to from and strictly smaller than to. For sorted maps, the similar methods

```
subMap(from, to)
headMap(to)
tailMap(from)
```

return views into the maps consisting of all entries in which the *keys* fall into the specified ranges.

Unmodifiable Views

The Collections class has methods that produce *unmodifiable views* of collections. These views add a runtime check to an existing collection. If an attempt to modify the collection is detected, then an exception is thrown and the collection remains untouched.

You obtain unmodifiable views by six methods:

```
Collections.unmodifiableCollection
Collections.unmodifiableList
Collections.unmodifiableSet
Collections.unmodifiableSortedSet
Collections.unmodifiableMap
Collections.unmodifiableSortedMap
```

Each method is defined to work on an interface. For example, Collections.unmodifiableList works with an ArrayList, a LinkedList, or any other class that implements the List interface.

For example, suppose you want to let some part of your code look at, but not touch, the contents of a collection. Here is what you could do:

```
List<String> staff = new LinkedList<String>();
. . .
lookAt(new Collections.unmodifiableList(staff));
```

The Collections.unmodifiableList method returns an object of a class implementing the List interface. Its accessor methods retrieve values from the staff collection. Of course, the lookAt method can call all methods of the List interface, not just the accessors. But all mutator methods (such as add) have been redefined to throw an UnsupportedOperationException instead of forwarding the call to the underlying collection.

The unmodifiable view does not make the collection itself immutable. You can still modify the collection through its original reference (staff, in our case). And you can still call mutator methods on the elements of the collection.

Because the views wrap the *interface* and not the actual collection object, you only have access to those methods that are defined in the interface. For example, the LinkedList class has convenience methods, addFirst and addLast, that are not part of the List interface. These methods are not accessible through the unmodifiable view.

CAUTION: The unmodifiableCollection method (as well as the synchronizedCollection and checkedCollection methods discussed later in this section) returns a collection whose equals method does *not* invoke the equals method of the underlying collection. Instead, it inherits the equals method of the Object class, which just tests whether the objects are identical. If you turn a set or list into just a collection, you can no longer test for equal contents. The view acts in this way because equality testing is not well defined at this level of the hierarchy. The views treat the hashCode method in the same way.

However, the unmodifiableSet and unmodifiableList class do not hide the equals and hashCode methods of the underlying collections.

Synchronized Views

If you access a collection from multiple threads, you need to ensure that the collection is not accidentally damaged. For example, it would be disastrous if one thread tried to add to a hash table while another thread was rehashing the elements.

Instead of implementing thread-safe collection classes, the library designers used the view mechanism to make regular collections thread safe. For example, the static synchronizedMap method in the Collections class can turn any map into a Map with synchronized access methods:

```
HashMap<String, Employee> hashMap = new HashMap<String, Employee>();
Map<String, Employee> map = Collections.synchronizedMap(hashMap);
```

You can now access the map object from multiple threads. The methods such as get and put are serialized—each method call must be finished completely before another thread can call another method.

You should make sure that no thread accesses the data structure through the original unsynchronized methods. The easiest way to ensure this is not to save any reference to the original object:

```
map = Collections.synchronizedMap(new HashMap<String, Employee>());
```

Note that the views only serialize the methods of the *collection*. If you use an iterator, you need to manually acquire the lock on the collection object. For example,

```
synchronized (map)
{
    Iterator<String> iter = map.keySet().iterator();
    while (iter.hasNext()) . . .
}
```

You must use the same code if you use a "for each" loop since the loop uses an iterator. Note that the iterator will actually fail with a ConcurrentModificationException if another thread modifies the collection while the iteration is in progress. The synchronization is still required so that the concurrent modification can be reliably detected.

As a practical matter, the synchronization wrappers have limited utility. You are usually better off using the collections defined in the java.util.concurrent package—see Chapter 1 for more information. In particular, the ConcurrentHashMap map has been carefully implemented so that multiple threads can access it without blocking each other, provided they access different buckets.

Checked Views

JDK 5.0 adds a set of "checked" views that are intended as debugging support for a problem that can occur with generic types. As explained in Volume 1, Chapter 13, it is actually possible to smuggle elements of the wrong type into a generic collection. For example,

```
ArrayList<String> strings = new ArrayList<String>();
ArrayList rawList = strings; // get warning only, not an error, for compatibility with legacy code
rawList.add(new Date()); // now strings contains a Date object!
```

The erroneous add command is not detected at run time. Instead, a class cast exception will happen later when another part of the code calls get and casts the result to a String.

A checked view can detect this problem. Define

```
List<String> safeStrings = Collections.checkedList(strings, String.class);
```

The view's add method checks that the inserted object belongs to the given class and immediately throws a ClassCastException if it does not. The advantage is that the error is reported at the correct location:

```
ArrayList rawList = safeStrings;
rawList.add(new Date()); // Checked list throws a ClassCastException
```

> **CAUTION:** The checked views are limited by the runtime checks that the virtual machine can carry out. For example, if you have an ArrayList<Pair<String>>, you cannot protect it from inserting a Pair<Date> since the virtual machine has a single "raw" Pair class.

A Note on Optional Operations

A view usually has some restriction—it may be read-only, it may not be able to change the size, or it may support removal, but not insertion, as is the case for the key view of a map. A restricted view throws an UnsupportedOperationException if you attempt an inappropriate operation.

In the API documentation for the collection and iterator interfaces, many methods are described as "optional operations." This seems to be in conflict with the notion of an interface. After all, isn't the purpose of an interface to lay out the methods that a class *must* implement? Indeed, this arrangement is unsatisfactory from a theoretical perspective. A better solution might have been to design separate interfaces for read-only views and views that can't change the size of a collection. However, that would have tripled the number of interfaces, which the designers of the library found unacceptable.

Should you extend the technique of "optional" methods to your own designs? We think not. Even though collections are used frequently, the coding style for implementing them is not typical for other problem domains. The designers of a collection class library have to resolve a particularly brutal set of conflicting requirements. Users want the library to be easy to learn, convenient to use, completely generic, idiot proof, and at the same time as efficient as hand-coded algorithms. It is plainly impossible to achieve all these goals simultaneously, or even to come close. But in your own programming problems, you will rarely encounter such an extreme set of constraints. You should be able to find solutions that do not rely on the extreme measure of "optional" interface operations.

 java.util.Collections 1.2

- static <E> Collection unmodifiableCollection(Collection<E> c)
- static <E> List unmodifiableList(List<E> c)
- static <E> Set unmodifiableSet(Set<E> c)
- static <E> SortedSet unmodifiableSortedSet(SortedSet<E> c)
- static <K, V> Map unmodifiableMap(Map<K, V> c)
- static <K, V> SortedMap unmodifiableSortedMap(SortedMap<K, V> c)
  construct a view of the collection whose mutator methods throw an UnsupportedOperationException.

- static <E> Collection<E> synchronizedCollection(Collection<E> c)
- static <E> List synchronizedList(List<E> c)
- static <E> Set synchronizedSet(Set<E> c)
- static <E> SortedSet synchronizedSortedSet(SortedSet<E> c)
- static <K, V> Map<K, V> synchronizedMap(Map<K, V> c)
- static <K, V> SortedMap<K, V> synchronizedSortedMap(SortedMap<K, V> c)
  construct a view of the collection whose methods are synchronized.

- static <E> Collection checkedCollection(Collection<E> c, Class<E> elementType)
- static <E> List checkedList(List<E> c, Class<E> elementType)
- static <E> Set checkedSet(Set<E> c, Class<E> elementType)
- static <E> SortedSet checkedSortedSet(SortedSet<E> c, Class<E> elementType)
- static <K, V> Map checkedMap(Map<K, V> c, Class<K> keyType, Class<V> valueType)
- static <K, V> SortedMap checkedSortedMap(SortedMap<K, V> c, Class<K> keyType, Class<V> valueType)

  construct a view of the collection whose methods throw a ClassCastException if an element of the wrong type is inserted.

- static <E> List<E> nCopies(int n, E value)
- static <E> Set<E> singleton(E value)

  construct a view of the object as either an unmodifiable list with n identical elements, or a set with a single element.

 java.util.Arrays 1.2

- static <E> List<E> asList(E... array)

  returns a list view of the elements in an array that is modifiable but not resizable.

 java.util.List<E> 1.2

- List<E> subList(int firstIncluded, int firstExcluded)

  returns a list view of the elements within a range of positions.

 java.util.SortedSet<E> 1.2

- SortedSet<E> subSet(E firstIncluded, E firstExcluded)
- SortedSet<E> headSet(E firstExcluded)
- SortedSet<E> tailSet(E firstIncluded)

  return a view of the elements within a range.

java.util.SortedMap<K, V> 1.2

- SortedMap<K, V> subMap(K firstIncluded, K firstExcluded)
- SortedMap<K, V> headMap(K firstExcluded)
- SortedMap<K, V> tailMap(K firstIncluded)

  return a map view of the entries whose keys are within a range.

Bulk Operations

So far, most of our examples used an iterator to traverse a collection, one element at a time. However, you can often avoid iteration by using one of the *bulk operations* in the library.

Suppose you want to find the *intersection* of two sets, the elements that two sets have in common. First, make a new set to hold the result.

```
Set<String> result = new HashSet<String>(a);
```

Here, you use the fact that every collection has a constructor whose parameter is another collection that holds the initialization values.

Now, use the retainAll method:

```
result.retainAll(b);
```

It retains all elements that also happen to be in b. You have formed the intersection without programming a loop.

You can carry this idea further and apply a bulk operation to a *view*. For example, suppose you have a map that maps employee IDs to employee objects and you have a set of the IDs of all employees that are to be terminated.

```
Map<String, Employee> staffMap = . . .;
Set<String> terminatedIDs = . . .;
```

Simply form the key set and remove all IDs of terminated employees.

```
staffMap.keySet().removeAll(terminatedIDs);
```

Because the key set is a view into the map, the keys and associated employee names are automatically removed from the map.

By using a subrange view, you can restrict bulk operations to sublists and subsets. For example, suppose you want to add the first 10 elements of a list to another container. Form a sublist to pick out the first 10:

```
relocated.addAll(staff.subList(0, 10));
```

The subrange can also be a target of a mutating operation.

```
staff.subList(0, 10).clear();
```

Converting Between Collections and Arrays

Because large portions of the Java platform API were designed before the collections framework was created, you occasionally need to translate between traditional arrays and the more modern collections.

If you have an array, you need to turn it into a collection. The Arrays.asList wrapper serves this purpose. For example,

```
String[] values = . . .;
HashSet<String> staff = new HashSet<String>(Arrays.asList(values));
```

Obtaining an array from a collection is a bit trickier. Of course, you can use the toArray method:

```
Object[] values = staff.toArray();
```

But the result is an array of *objects*. Even if you know that your collection contained objects of a specific type, you cannot use a cast:

```
String[] values = (String[]) staff.toArray(); // Error!
```

The array returned by the toArray method was created as an Object[] array, and you cannot change its type. Instead, you use a variant of the toArray method. Give it an array of length 0 of the type that you'd like. The returned array is then created *as the same array type*:

```
String[] values = staff.toArray(new String[0]);
```

If you like, you can construct the array to have the correct size:

```
staff.toArray(new String[staff.size()]);
```

In this case, no new array is created.

 NOTE: You may wonder why you don't simply pass a Class object (such as String.class) to the toArray method. However, this method does "double duty," both to fill an existing array (provided it is long enough) and to create a new array.

---

 java.util.Collection<E> 1.2

* `<T> T[] toArray(T[] array)`
  checks whether the array parameter is larger than the size of the collection. If so, it adds all elements of the collection into the array, followed by a null terminator, and it returns the array. If the length of array equals the size of the collection, then the method adds all elements of the collection to the array but does not add a null

terminator. If there isn't enough room, then the method creates a new array, of the same type as array, and fills it with the elements of the collection.

Extending the Framework

The collections framework contains all data structures that most programmers will ever need. However, if you do need a specialized data structure, you can easily extend the framework. As an example, we implement a circular array queue—see Example 2–6.

The framework contains a class AbstractQueue that implements all methods of the Queue interface except for size, offer, poll, peek, and iterator. We make use of that class and only implement the missing methods. We then automatically inherit all the remaining methods from the AbstractQueue class.

Most of the methods are straightforward, with the exception of the iterator. We implement the queue iterator as an inner class. This enables the iterator methods to access the fields of the enclosing queue object, that is, the object that constructed the iterator. (As we discussed in Volume 1, Chapter 5, every object of a non-static inner class has a reference to the outer class object that created it.)

Also note the protection against concurrent modification. The queue keeps a count of all modifications. When the iterator is constructed, it makes a copy of that count. Whenever the iterator is used, it checks that the counts still match. If not, it throws a ConcurrentModification-Exception.

Example 2–6: CircularArrayQueueTest.java

```
1. import java.util.*;
2.
3. public class CircularArrayQueueTest
4. {
5.     public static void main(String[] args)
6.     {
7.         Queue<String> q = new CircularArrayQueue<String>(5);
8.         q.add("Amy");
9.         q.add("Bob");
10.        q.add("Carl");
11.        q.add("Deedee");
12.        q.add("Emile");
13.        q.remove();
14.        q.add("Fifi");
15.        q.remove();
16.        for (String s : q) System.out.println(s);
17.    }
18. }
19.
20. /**
21.    A first-in, first-out bounded collection.
22. */
23. class CircularArrayQueue<E> extends AbstractQueue<E>
24. {
25.    /**
26.       Constructs an empty queue.
27.       @param capacity the maximum capacity of the queue
28.    */
29.    public CircularArrayQueue(int capacity)
30.    {
31.        elements = (E[]) new Object[capacity];
```

```
32.        count = 0;
33.        head = 0;
34.        tail = 0;
35.     }
36.
37.     public boolean offer(E newElement)
38.     {
39.        assert newElement != null;
40.        if (count < elements.length)
41.        {
42.           elements[tail] = newElement;
43.           tail = (tail + 1) % elements.length;
44.           count++;
45.           modcount++;
46.           return true;
47.        }
48.        else
49.           return false;
50.     }
51.
52.     public E poll()
53.     {
54.        if (count == 0) return null;
55.        E r = elements[head];
56.        head = (head + 1) % elements.length;
57.        count--;
58.        modcount++;
59.        return r;
60.     }
61.
62.     public E peek()
63.     {
64.        if (count == 0) return null;
65.        return elements[head];
66.     }
67.
68.     public int size()
69.     {
70.        return count;
71.     }
72.
73.     public Iterator<E> iterator()
74.     {
75.        return new QueueIterator();
76.
77.     }
78.
79.     private class QueueIterator implements Iterator<E>
80.     {
81.        public QueueIterator()
82.        {
83.           modcountAtConstruction = modcount;
84.        }
85.
86.        public E next()
87.        {
```

```
88.          if (!hasNext()) throw new NoSuchElementException();
89.          E r = elements[(head + offset) % elements.length];
90.          offset++;
91.          return r;
92.       }
93.
94.       public boolean hasNext()
95.       {
96.          if (modcount != modcountAtConstruction)
97.             throw new ConcurrentModificationException();
98.          return offset < elements.length;
99.       }
100.
101.       public void remove()
102.       {
103.          throw new UnsupportedOperationException();
104.       }
105.
106.       private int offset;
107.       private int modcountAtConstruction;
108.    }
109.
110.    private E[] elements;
111.    private int head;
112.    private int tail;
113.    private int count;
114.    private int modcount;
115. }
```

Algorithms

Generic collection interfaces have a great advantage—you only need to implement your algorithms once. For example, consider a simple algorithm to compute the maximum element in a collection. Traditionally, programmers would implement such an algorithm as a loop. Here is how you find the largest element of an array.

```
if (a.length == 0) throw new NoSuchElementException();
T largest = a[0];
for (int i = 1; i < a.length; i++)
   if (largest.compareTo(a[i]) < 0)
      largest = a[i];
```

Of course, to find the maximum of an array list, you would write the code slightly differently.

```
if (v.size() == 0) throw new NoSuchElementException();
T largest = v.get(0);
for (int i = 1; i < v.size(); i++)
   if (largest.compareTo(v.get(i)) < 0)
      largest = v.get(i);
```

What about a linked list? You don't have efficient random access in a linked list, but you can use an iterator.

```
if (l.isEmpty()) throw new NoSuchElementException();
Iterator<T> iter = l.iterator();
T largest = iter.next();
while (iter.hasNext())
{
```

```
      T next = iter.next();
      if (largest.compareTo(next) < 0)
         largest = next;
   }
```

These loops are tedious to write, and they are just a bit error prone. Is there an off-by-one error? Do the loops work correctly for empty containers? For containers with only one element? You don't want to test and debug this code every time, but you also don't want to implement a whole slew of methods such as these:

```
static <T extends Comparable> T max(T[] a)
static <T extends Comparable> T max(ArrayList<T> v)
static <T extends Comparable> T max(LinkedList<T> l)
```

That's where the collection interfaces come in. Think of the *minimal* collection interface that you need to efficiently carry out the algorithm. Random access with get and set comes higher in the food chain than simple iteration. As you have seen in the computation of the maximum element in a linked list, random access is not required for this task. Computing the maximum can be done simply by iteration through the elements. Therefore, you can implement the max method to take *any* object that implements the Collection interface.

```
public static <T extends Comparable> T max(Collection<T> c)
{
   if (c.isEmpty()) throw new NoSuchElementException();
   Iterator<T> iter = c.iterator();
   T largest = iter.next();
   while (iter.hasNext())
   {
      T next = iter.next();
      if (largest.compareTo(next) < 0)
         largest = next;
   }
   return largest;
}
```

Now you can compute the maximum of a linked list, an array list, or an array, with a single method.

That's a powerful concept. In fact, the standard C++ library has dozens of useful algorithms, each of which operates on a generic collection. The Java library is not quite so rich, but it does contain the basics: sorting, binary search, and some utility algorithms.

Sorting and Shuffling

Computer old-timers will sometimes reminisce about how they had to use punched cards and how they actually had to program by hand algorithms for sorting. Nowadays, of course, sorting algorithms are part of the standard library for most programming languages, and the Java programming language is no exception.

The sort method in the Collections class sorts a collection that implements the List interface.

```
List<String> staff = new LinkedList<String>();
// fill collection . . .;
Collections.sort(staff);
```

This method assumes that the list elements implement the Comparable interface. If you want to sort the list in some other way, you can pass a Comparator object as a second parameter. (We discussed comparators on page 105.) Here is how you can sort a list of items.

```
Comparator<Item> itemComparator = new
   Comparator<Item>()
   {
      public int compare(Item a, Item b)
      {
         return a.partNumber - b.partNumber;
      }
   });
Collections.sort(items, itemComparator);
```

If you want to sort a list in *descending* order, then use the static convenience method Collections.reverseOrder(). It returns a comparator that returns b.compareTo(a). For example,

```
Collections.sort(staff, Collections.reverseOrder())
```

sorts the elements in the list staff in reverse order, according to the ordering given by the compareTo method of the element type. Similarly,

```
Collections.sort(items, Collections.reverseOrder(itemComparator))
```

reverses the ordering of the itemComparator.

You may wonder how the sort method sorts a list. Typically, when you look at a sorting algorithm in a book on algorithms, it is presented for arrays and uses random element access. However, random access in a list can be inefficient. You can actually sort lists efficiently by using a form of merge sort (see, for example, *Algorithms in C++* by Robert Sedgewick [Addison-Wesley 1998, pp. 366–369]). However, the implementation in the Java programming language does not do that. It simply dumps all elements into an array, sorts the array by using a different variant of merge sort, and then copies the sorted sequence back into the list.

The merge sort algorithm used in the collections library is a bit slower than *quick sort*, the traditional choice for a general-purpose sorting algorithm. However, it has one major advantage: It is *stable*, that is, it doesn't switch equal elements. Why do you care about the order of equal elements? Here is a common scenario. Suppose you have an employee list that you already sorted by name. Now you sort by salary. What happens to employees with equal salary? With a stable sort, the ordering by name is preserved. In other words, the outcome is a list that is sorted first by salary, then by name.

Because collections need not implement all of their "optional" methods, all methods that receive collection parameters must describe when it is safe to pass a collection to an algorithm. For example, you clearly cannot pass an unmodifiableList list to the sort algorithm. What kind of list *can* you pass? According to the documentation, the list must be modifiable but need not be resizable.

The terms are defined as follows:

- A list is *modifiable* if it supports the set method.
- A list is *resizable* if it supports the add and remove operations.

The Collections class has an algorithm shuffle that does the opposite of sorting—it randomly permutes the order of the elements in a list. You supply the list to be shuffled and a random number generator. For example,

```
ArrayList<Card> cards = . . .;
Collections.shuffle(cards);
```

If you supply a list that does not implement the RandomAccess interface, then the shuffle method copies the elements into an array, shuffles the array, and copies the shuffled elements back into the list.

The program in Example 2–7 fills an array list with 49 Integer objects containing the numbers 1 through 49. It then randomly shuffles the list and selects the first 6 values from the shuffled list. Finally, it sorts the selected values and prints them.

Example 2–7: ShuffleTest.java

```
1. import java.util.*;
2.
3. /**
4.    This program demonstrates the random shuffle and sort algorithms.
5. */
6. public class ShuffleTest
7. {
8.    public static void main(String[] args)
9.    {
10.       List<Integer> numbers = new ArrayList<Integer>();
11.       for (int i = 1; i <= 49; i++)
12.          numbers.add(i);
13.       Collections.shuffle(numbers);
14.       List<Integer> winningCombination = numbers.subList(0, 6);
15.       Collections.sort(winningCombination);
16.       System.out.println(winningCombination);
17.    }
18. }
```

API   **java.util.Collections** 1.2

- `static <T extends Comparable<? super T>> void sort(List<T> elements)`
- `static <T> void sort(List<T> elements, Comparator<? super T> c)`
  sort the elements in the list, using a stable sort algorithm. The algorithm is guaranteed to run in $O(n \log n)$ time, where n is the length of the list.

- `static void shuffle(List<?> elements)`
- `static void shuffle(List<?> elements, Random r)`
  randomly shuffle the elements in the list. This algorithm runs in $O(n \, a(n))$ time, where n is the length of the list and $a(n)$ is the average time to access an element.

- `static <T> Comparator<T> reverseOrder()`
  returns a comparator that sorts elements in the reverse order of the one given by the compareTo method of the Comparable interface.

- `static <T> Comparator<T> reverseOrder(Comparator<T> comp)`
  returns a comparator that sorts elements in the reverse order of the one given by comp.

Binary Search

To find an object in an array, you normally visit all elements until you find a match. However, if the array is sorted, then you can look at the middle element and check whether it is larger than the element that you are trying to find. If so, you keep looking in the first half of the array; otherwise, you look in the second half. That cuts the problem in half. You keep going in the same way. For example, if the array has 1024 elements, you will locate the match (or confirm that there is none) after 10 steps, whereas a linear search would have taken you an average of 512 steps if the element is present, and 1024 steps to confirm that it is not.

The binarySearch of the Collections class implements this algorithm. Note that the collection must already be sorted or the algorithm will return the wrong answer. To find an element, supply the collection (which must implement the List interface—more on that in the note

below) and the element to be located. If the collection is not sorted by the compareTo element of the Comparable interface, then you must supply a comparator object as well.

```
i = Collections.binarySearch(c, element);
i = Collections.binarySearch(c, element, comparator);
```

A return value of ≥ 0 from the binarySearch method denotes the index of the matching object. That is, c.get(i) is equal to element under the comparison order. If the value is negative, then there is no matching element. However, you can use the return value to compute the location where you *should* insert element into the collection to keep it sorted. The insertion location is

```
insertionPoint = -i - 1;
```

It isn't simply -i because then the value of 0 would be ambiguous. In other words, the operation

```
if (i < 0)
    c.add(-i - 1, element);
```

adds the element in the correct place.

To be worthwhile, binary search requires random access. If you have to iterate one by one through half of a linked list to find the middle element, you have lost all advantage of the binary search. Therefore, the binarySearch algorithm reverts to a linear search if you give it a linked list.

 NOTE: JDK 1.3 had no separate interface for an ordered collection with efficient random access, and the binarySearch method employed a very crude device, checking whether the list parameter extended the AbstractSequentialList class. This has been fixed in JDK 1.4. Now the binarySearch method checks whether the list parameter implements the RandomAccess interface. If it does, then the method carries out a binary search. Otherwise, it uses a linear search.

---

 java.util.Collections 1.2

- static <T extends Comparable<? super T>> int binarySearch(List<T> elements, T key)
- static <T> int binarySearch(List<T> elements, T key, Comparator<? super T> c)

  search for a key in a sorted list, using a linear search if elements extends the AbstractSequentialList class, and a binary search in all other cases. The methods are guaranteed to run in O($a(n)$ log n) time, where n is the length of the list and $a(n)$ is the average time to access an element. The methods return either the index of the key in the list, or a negative value i if the key is not present in the list. In that case, the key should be inserted at index -i - 1 for the list to stay sorted.

Simple Algorithms

The Collections class contains several simple but useful algorithms. Among them is the example from the beginning of this section, finding the maximum value of a collection. Others include copying elements from one list to another, filling a container with a constant value, and reversing a list. Why supply such simple algorithms in the standard library? Surely most programmers could easily implement them with simple loops. We like the algorithms because they make life easier for the programmer *reading* the code. When you read a loop that was implemented by someone else, you have to decipher the original programmer's intentions. When you see a call to a method such as Collections.max, you know right away what the code does.

The following API notes describe the simple algorithms in the Collections class.

- static <T extends Comparable<? super T>> T min(Collection<T> elements)
- static <T extends Comparable<? super T>> T max(Collection<T> elements)
- static <T> min(Collection<T> elements, Comparator<? super T> c)
- static <T> max(Collection<T> elements, Comparator<? super T> c)

  return the smallest or largest element in the collection. (The parameter bounds are simplified for clarity.)

- static <T> void copy(List<? super T> to, List<T> from)

  copies all elements from a source list to the same positions in the target list. The target list must be at least as long as the source list.

- static <T> void fill(List<? super T> l, T value)

  sets all positions of a list to the same value.

- static <T> boolean addAll(Collection<? super T> c, T... values) **5.0**

  adds all values to the given collection and returns true if the collection changed as a result.

- static <T> boolean replaceAll(List<T> l, T oldValue, T newValue) **1.4**

  replaces all elements equal to oldValue with newValue.

- static int indexOfSubList(List<?> l, List<?> s) **1.4**
- static int lastIndexOfSubList(List<?> l, List<?> s) **1.4**

  return the index of the first or last sublist of l equalling s, or −1 if no sublist of l equals s. For example, if l is [s, t, a, r] and s is [t, a, r], then both methods return the index 1.

- static void swap(List<?> l, int i, int j) **1.4**

  swaps the elements at the given offsets.

- static void reverse(List<?> l)

  reverses the order of the elements in a list. For example, reversing the list [t, a, r] yields the list [r, a, t]. This method runs in O(n) time, where n is the length of the list.

- static void rotate(List<?> l, int d) **1.4**

  rotates the elements in the list, moving the entry with index i to position (i + d) % l.size(). For example, rotating the list [t, a, r] by 2 yields the list [a, r, t]. This method runs in O(n) time, where n is the length of the list.

- static int frequency(Collection<?> c, Object o) **5.0**

  returns the count of elements in c that equal the object o.

- boolean disjoint(Collection<?> c1, Collection<?> c2) **5.0**

  returns true if the collections have no elements in common.

Writing Your Own Algorithms

If you write your own algorithm (or in fact, any method that has a collection as a parameter), you should work with *interfaces*, not concrete implementations, whenever possible. For example, suppose you want to fill a JMenu with a set of menu items. Traditionally, such a method might have been implemented like this:

```
void fillMenu(JMenu menu, ArrayList<JMenuItem> items)
{
   for (JMenuItem item : items)
      menu.addItem(item);
}
```

However, you now constrained the caller of your method—the caller must supply the choices in an ArrayList. If the choices happen to be in another container, they first need to be repackaged. It is much better to accept a more general collection.

You should ask yourself this: What is the most general collection interface that can do the job? In this case, you just need to visit all elements, a capability of the basic Collection interface. Here is how you can rewrite the fillMenu method to accept collections of any kind.

```
void fillMenu(JMenu menu, Collection<JMenuItem> items)
{
    for (JMenuItem item : items)
        menu.addItem(item);
}
```

Now, anyone can call this method, with an ArrayList or a LinkedList, or even with an array, wrapped with the Arrays.asList wrapper.

 NOTE: If it is such a good idea to use collection interfaces as method parameters, why doesn't the Java library follow this rule more often? For example, the JComboBox class has two constructors:

```
JComboBox(Object[] items)
JComboBox(Vector<?> items)
```

The reason is simply timing. The Swing library was created before the collections library.

If you write a method that *returns* a collection, you may also want to return an interface instead of a class because you can then change your mind and reimplement the method later with a different collection.

For example, let's write a method getAllItems that returns all items of a menu.

```
List<MenuItem> getAllItems(JMenu menu)
{
    ArrayList<MenuItem> items = new ArrayList<MenuItem>()
    for (int i = 0; i < menu.getItemCount(); i++)
        items.add(menu.getItem(i));
    return items;
}
```

Later, you can decide that you don't want to *copy* the items but simply provide a view into them. You achieve this by returning an anonymous subclass of AbstractList.

```
List<MenuItem> getAllItems(final JMenu menu)
{
    return new
        AbstractList<MenuItem>()
        {
            public MenuItem get(int i)
            {
                return item.getItem(i);
            }
            public int size()
            {
                return item.getItemCount();
            }
        };
}
```

Of course, this is an advanced technique. If you employ it, be careful to document exactly which "optional" operations are supported. In this case, you must advise the caller that the returned object is an unmodifiable list.

Legacy Collections

In this section, we discuss the collection classes that existed in the Java programming language since the beginning: the Hashtable class and its useful Properties subclass, the Stack subclass of Vector, and the BitSet class.

The *Hashtable* Class

The classic Hashtable class serves the same purpose as the HashMap and has essentially the same interface. Just like methods of the Vector class, the Hashtable methods are synchronized. If you do not require synchronization or compatibility with legacy code, you should use the HashMap instead.

> NOTE: The name of the class is Hashtable, with a lowercase t. Under Windows, you'll get strange error messages if you use HashTable, because the Windows file system is not case-sensitive but the Java compiler is.

Enumerations

The legacy collections use the Enumeration interface for traversing sequences of elements. The Enumeration interface has two methods, hasMoreElements and nextElement. These are entirely analogous to the hasNext and next methods of the Iterator interface.

For example, the elements method of the Hashtable class yields an object for enumerating the values in the table:

```
Enumeration<Employee> e = staff.elements();
while (e.hasMoreElements())
{
   Employee e = e.nextElement();
   . . .
}
```

You will occasionally encounter a legacy method that expects an enumeration parameter. The static method Collections.enumeration yields an enumeration object that enumerates the elements in the collection. For example,

```
ArrayList<InputStream> streams = . . .;
SequenceInputStream in = new SequenceInputStream(Collections.enumeration(streams));
   // the SequenceInputStream constructor expects an enumeration
```

> NOTE: In C++, it is quite common to use iterators as parameters. Fortunately, in programming for the Java platform, very few programmers use this idiom. It is much smarter to pass around the collection than to pass an iterator. The collection object is more useful. The recipients can always obtain the iterator from the collection when they need to do so, plus they have all the collection methods at their disposal. However, you will find enumerations in some legacy code because they were the only available mechanism for generic collections until the collections framework appeared in JDK 1.2.

 java.util.Enumeration<E> 1.0

- boolean hasMoreElements()

   returns true if there are more elements yet to be inspected.

- E nextElement()

   returns the next element to be inspected. Do not call this method if hasMoreElements() returned false.

 java.util.Hashtable<K, V> 1.0

- Enumeration<K> keys()
  returns an enumeration object that traverses the keys of the hash table.

- Enumeration<V> elements()
  returns an enumeration object that traverses the elements of the hash table.

 java.util.Vector<E> 1.0

- Enumeration<E> elements()
  returns an enumeration object that traverses the elements of the vector.

Property Sets

A *property set* is a map structure of a very special type. It has three particular characteristics.

- The keys and values are strings.
- The table can be saved to a file and loaded from a file.
- A secondary table for defaults is used.

The Java platform class that implements a property set is called Properties.

Property sets are commonly used in specifying configuration options for programs—see Volume 1, Chapter 10.

 java.util.Properties 1.0

- Properties()
  creates an empty property list.

- Properties(Properties defaults)
  creates an empty property list with a set of defaults.

- String getProperty(String key)
  gets a property association; returns the string associated with the key, or the string associated with the key in the default table if it wasn't present in the table.

- String getProperty(String key, String defaultValue)
  gets a property with a default value if the key is not found; returns the string associated with the key, or the default string if it wasn't present in the table.

- void load(InputStream in)
  loads a property set from an InputStream.

- void store(OutputStream out, String commentString)
  stores a property set to an OutputStream.

Stacks

Since version 1.0, the standard library had a Stack class with the familiar push and pop methods. However, the Stack class extends the Vector class, which is not satisfactory from a theoretical perspective—you can apply such un-stack-like operations as insert and remove to insert and remove values anywhere, not just at the top of the stack.

java.util.Stack<E> 1.0

- E push(E item)
  pushes item onto the stack and returns item.

- E pop()
  pops and returns the top item of the stack. Don't call this method if the stack is empty.

- E peek()
  returns the top of the stack without popping it. Don't call this method if the stack is empty.

Bit Sets

The Java platform BitSet class stores a sequence of bits. (It is not a *set* in the mathematical sense—bit *vector* or bit *array* would have been more appropriate terms.) Use a bit set if you need to store a sequence of bits (for example, flags) efficiently. Because a bit set packs the bits into bytes, it is far more efficient to use a bit set than to use an ArrayList of Boolean objects.

The BitSet class gives you a convenient interface for reading, setting, or resetting individual bits. Use of this interface avoids the masking and other bit-fiddling operations that would be necessary if you stored bits in int or long variables.

For example, for a BitSet named bucketOfBits,

    bucketOfBits.get(i)

returns true if the i'th bit is on, and false otherwise. Similarly,

    bucketOfBits.set(i)

turns the i'th bit on. Finally,

    bucketOfBits.clear(i)

turns the i'th bit off.

 C++ NOTE: The C++ bitset template has the same functionality as the Java platform BitSet.

API **java.util.BitSet** 1.0

- BitSet(int initialCapacity)
  constructs a bit set.

- int length()
  returns the "logical length" of the bit set: 1 plus the index of the highest set bit.

- boolean get(int bit)
  gets a bit.

- void set(int bit)
  sets a bit.

- void clear(int bit)
  clears a bit.

- void and(BitSet set)
  logically ANDs this bit set with another.

- void or(BitSet set)
  logically ORs this bit set with another.

- void xor(BitSet set)
  logically XORs this bit set with another.

- void andNot(BitSet set)
  clears all bits in this bit set that are set in the other bit set.

The "Sieve of Eratosthenes" Benchmark

As an example of using bit sets, we want to show you an implementation of the "sieve of Eratosthenes" algorithm for finding prime numbers. (A prime number is a number like 2,

3, or 5 that is divisible only by itself and 1, and the sieve of Eratosthenes was one of the first methods discovered to enumerate these fundamental building blocks.) This isn't a terribly good algorithm for finding the number of primes, but for some reason it has become a popular benchmark for compiler performance. (It isn't a good benchmark either, because it mainly tests bit operations.)

Oh well, we bow to tradition and include an implementation. This program counts all prime numbers between 2 and 2,000,000. (There are 148,933 primes, so you probably don't want to print them all out.)

Without going into too many details of this program, the key is to march through a bit set with 2 million bits. We first turn on all the bits. After that, we turn off the bits that are multiples of numbers known to be prime. The positions of the bits that remain after this process are themselves the prime numbers. Example 2–8 illustrates this program in the Java programming language, and Example 2–9 is the C++ code.

 NOTE: Even though the sieve isn't a good benchmark, we couldn't resist timing the two implementations of the algorithm. Here are the timing results on a 1.7-GHz IBM ThinkPad with 1 GB of RAM, running Red Hat Linux 9.

C++ (g++ 3.2.2): 330 milliseconds

Java (JDK 5.0): 105 milliseconds

We have run this test for six editions of *Core Java*, and in the last three editions Java easily beat C++. In previous editions, we pointed out, in all fairness, that the culprit for the bad C++ result is the lousy performance of the standard `bitset` template. When we reimplemented `bitset`, the time for C++ used to be faster than Java. Not anymore—with a handcrafted bitset, the C++ time was 140 milliseconds in our latest experiment.

Example 2–8: Sieve.java

```java
1. import java.util.*;
2.
3. /**
4.    This program runs the Sieve of Eratosthenes benchmark.
5.    It computes all primes up to 2,000,000.
6. */
7. public class Sieve
8. {
9.    public static void main(String[] s)
10.   {
11.      int n = 2000000;
12.      long start = System.currentTimeMillis();
13.      BitSet b = new BitSet(n + 1);
14.      int count = 0;
15.      int i;
16.      for (i = 2; i <= n; i++)
17.         b.set(i);
18.      i = 2;
19.      while (i * i <= n)
20.      {
21.         if (b.get(i))
22.         {
23.            count++;
24.            int k = 2 * i;
25.            while (k <= n)
```

```
26.           {
27.              b.clear(k);
28.              k += i;
29.           }
30.        }
31.        i++;
32.     }
33.     while (i <= n)
34.     {
35.        if (b.get(i))
36.           count++;
37.        i++;
38.     }
39.     long end = System.currentTimeMillis();
40.     System.out.println(count + " primes");
41.     System.out.println((end - start) + " milliseconds");
42.  }
43. }
```

Example 2–9: Sieve.cpp

```
1. #include <bitset>
2. #include <iostream>
3. #include <ctime>
4.
5. using namespace std;
6.
7. int main()
8. {
9.    const int N = 2000000;
10.   clock_t cstart = clock();
11.
12.   bitset<N + 1> b;
13.   int count = 0;
14.   int i;
15.   for (i = 2; i <= N; i++)
16.      b.set(i);
17.   i = 2;
18.   while (i * i <= N)
19.   {
20.      if (b.test(i))
21.      {
22.         count++;
23.         int k = 2 * i;
24.         while (k <= N)
25.         {
26.            b.reset(k);
27.            k += i;
28.         }
29.      }
30.      i++;
31.   }
32.   while (i <= N)
33.   {
34.      if (b.test(i))
35.         count++;
36.      i++;
```

```
37.    }
38.
39.    clock_t cend = clock();
40.    double millis = 1000.0
41.        * (cend - cstart) / CLOCKS_PER_SEC;
42.
43.    cout << count << " primes\n"
44.        << millis << " milliseconds\n";
45.
46.    return 0;
47. }
```

Chapter 3

Networking

- ▼ CONNECTING TO A SERVER
- ▼ IMPLEMENTING SERVERS
- ▼ SENDING E-MAIL
- ▼ MAKING URL CONNECTIONS
- ▼ ADVANCED SOCKET PROGRAMMING

We begin this chapter by reviewing basic networking concepts. We then move on to writing Java programs that connect to network services. We show you how to get information from a web server and how to send e-mail from a Java program. We conclude the chapter with a case study that combines an applet and a servlet to harvest information on the Internet.

In the first part of this chapter, we assume that you have no network programming experience. If you have written TCP/IP programs before and ports and sockets are no mystery to you, you should breeze through the sample code. Toward the end of this chapter, the code becomes complex and is geared more toward those with some experience in network programming.

Connecting to a Server

Before writing our first network program, let's learn about a great debugging tool for network programming that you already have, namely, telnet. Telnet is preinstalled on most systems (both UNIX and Windows). You should be able to launch it by typing telnet from a command shell.

You may have used telnet to connect to a remote computer, but you can use it to communicate with other services provided by Internet hosts as well. Here is an example of what you can do. Type

```
telnet time-A.timefreq.bldrdoc.gov 13
```

As Figure 3–1 shows, you should get back a line like this:

```
53221 04-08-04 02:19:40 50 0 0 513.0 UTC(NIST) *
```

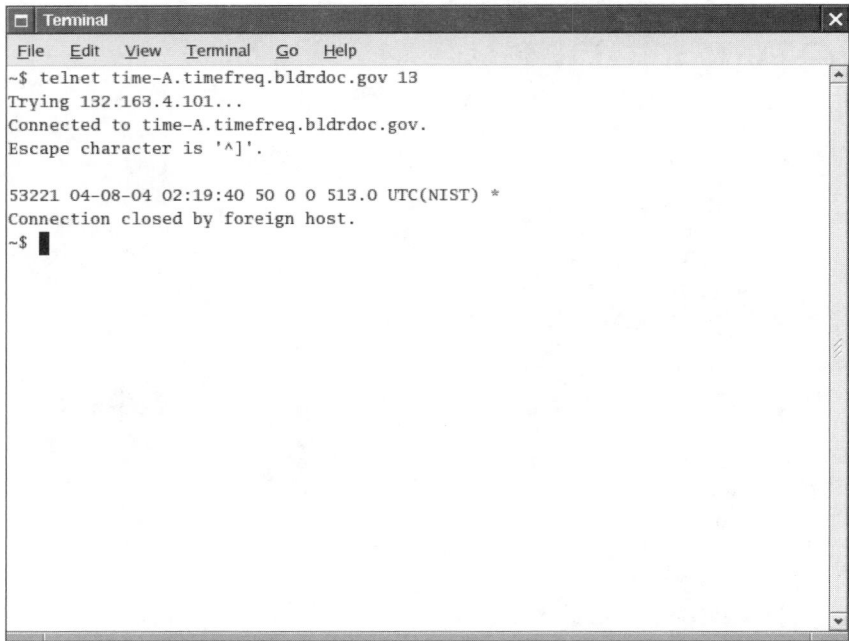

Figure 3–1: Output of the "time of day" service

What is going on? You have connected to the "time of day" service that most UNIX machines constantly run. The particular server that you connected to is operated by the National Institute of Standards and Technology in Boulder, Colorado, and gives the measurement of a Cesium atomic clock. (Of course, the reported time is not completely accurate due to network delays.)

By convention, the "time of day" service is always attached to "port" number 13.

 NOTE: In network parlance, a port is not a physical device, but an abstraction to facilitate communication between a server and a client (see Figure 3–2).

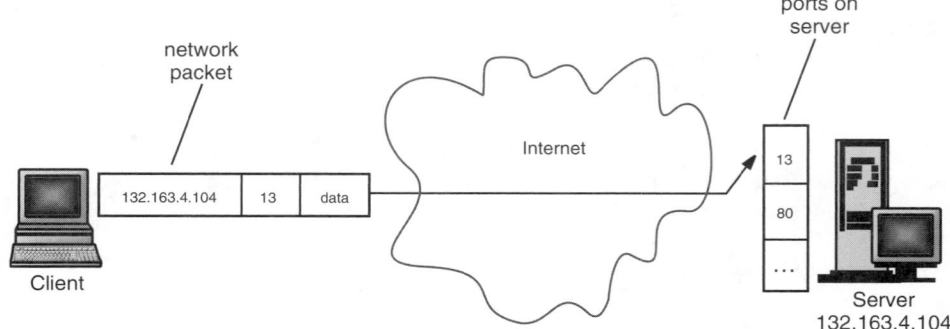

Figure 3–2: A client connecting to a server port

The server software is continuously running on the remote machine, waiting for any network traffic that wants to chat with port 13. When the operating system on the remote computer receives a network package that contains a request to connect to port number 13, it wakes up the listening server process and establishes the connection. The connection stays up until it is terminated by one of the parties.

When you began the telnet session with time-A.timefreq.bldrdoc.gov at port 13, an unrelated piece of network software knew enough to convert the string "time-A.timefreq.bldrdoc.gov" to its correct Internet Protocol address, 132.163.4.104. The software then sent a connection request to that computer, asking for a connection to port 13. Once the connection was established, the remote program sent back a line of data and then closed the connection. In general, of course, clients and servers engage in a more extensive dialog before one or the other closes the connection.

Here is another experiment, along the same lines, that is a bit more interesting. Do the following:

1. Use telnet to connect to java.sun.com on port 80.
2. Type the following, *exactly as it appears, without pressing backspace*. Note that there are spaces around the first slash but not the second.
3. `GET / HTTP/1.0`
4. Now, press the ENTER key *two times*.

Figure 3–3 shows the response. It should look eerily familiar—you got a page of HTML-formatted text, namely, the main web page for Java technology.

This is exactly the same process that your web browser goes through to get a web page. The only difference is that the browser displays the HTML code with nicer fonts.

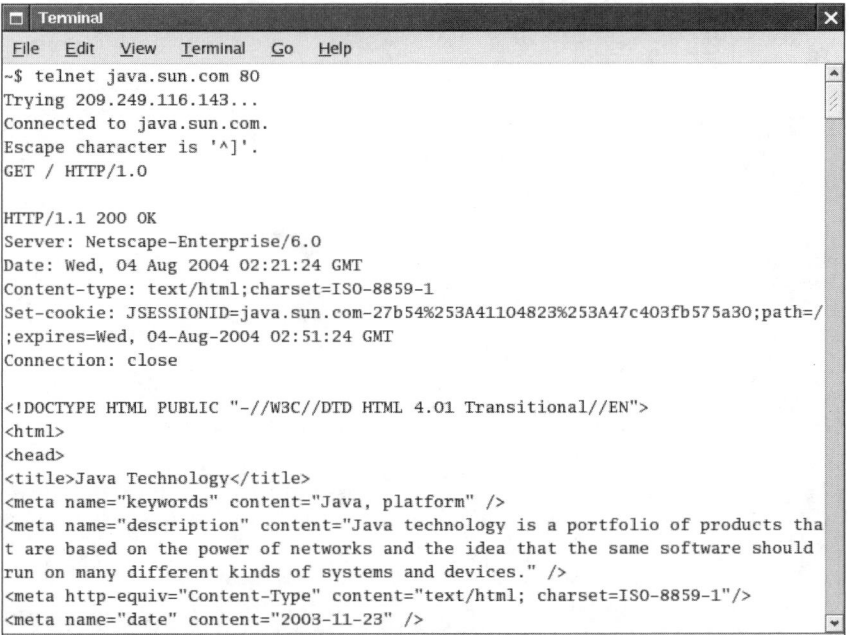

Figure 3–3: Using telnet to access an HTTP port

Our first network program in Example 3–1 will do the same thing we did using telnet—
connect to a port and print out what it finds.

Example 3–1: SocketTest.java

```java
1.  import java.io.*;
2.  import java.net.*;
3.  import java.util.*;
4.
5.  /**
6.     This program makes a socket connection to the atomic clock
7.     in Boulder, Colorado, and prints the time that the
8.     server sends.
9.  */
10. public class SocketTest
11. {
12.    public static void main(String[] args)
13.    {
14.       try
15.       {
16.          Socket s = new Socket("time-A.timefreq.bldrdoc.gov", 13);
17.          try
18.          {
19.             InputStream inStream = s.getInputStream();
20.             Scanner in = new Scanner(inStream);
21.
22.             while (in.hasNextLine())
23.             {
24.                String line = in.nextLine();
25.                System.out.println(line);
26.             }
27.          }
28.          finally
29.          {
30.             s.close();
31.          }
32.       }
33.       catch (IOException e)
34.       {
35.          e.printStackTrace();
36.       }
37.    }
38. }
```

The key statements of this simple program are as follows:

```java
Socket s = new Socket("time-A.timefreq.bldrdoc.gov", 13);
InputStream inStream = s.getInputStream();
```

The first line opens a *socket*, which is an abstraction for the network software that enables
communication out of and into this program. We pass the remote address and the port
number to the socket constructor. If the connection fails, then an UnknownHostException is
thrown. If there is another problem, then an IOException occurs. Because UnknownHostException is
a subclass of IOException and this is a sample program, we just catch the superclass.

Once the socket is open, the getInputStream method in java.net.Socket returns an InputStream
object that you can use just like any other stream. (See Volume 1, Chapter 12 for information about streams.) Once you have grabbed the stream, this program simply:

1. Uses a Scanner to read a line of characters sent by the server; and

2. Prints each line out to standard output.

This process continues until the stream is finished and the server disconnects.

 NOTE: This program works only with very simple servers, such as a "time of day" service. In more complex networking programs, the client sends request data to the server, and the server may not immediately disconnect at the end of a response. You will see how to implement that behavior in several examples throughout this chapter.

The Socket class is pleasant and easy to use because Java technology hides the complexities of establishing a networking connection and sending data across it. The java.net package essentially gives you the same programming interface you would use to work with a file.

 java.net.Socket 1.0

- Socket(String host, int port)
  constructs a socket to connect to the given host and port.

- InputStream getInputStream()
- OutputStream getOutputStream()
  get streams to read data from the socket and write data to the socket.

Implementing Servers

Now that we have implemented a basic network client that receives data from the Internet, let's implement a simple server that can send information to clients. Once you start the server program, it waits for some client to attach to its port. We chose port number 8189, which is not used by any of the standard services. The ServerSocket class establishes a socket. In our case, the command

```
ServerSocket s = new ServerSocket(8189);
```

establishes a server that monitors port 8189. The command

```
Socket incoming = s.accept();
```

tells the program to wait indefinitely until a client connects to that port. Once someone connects to this port by sending the correct request over the network, this method returns a Socket object that represents the connection that was made. You can use this object to get input and output streams, as is shown in the following code:

```
InputStream inStream = incoming.getInputStream();
OutputStream outStream = incoming.getOutputStream();
```

Everything that the server sends to the server output stream becomes the input of the client program, and all the output from the client program ends up in the server input stream.

In all the examples in this chapter, we will transmit text through sockets. We therefore turn the streams into scanners and writers.

```
Scanner in = new Scanner(inStream);
PrintWriter out = new PrintWriter(outStream, true /* autoFlush */);
```

Let's send the client a greeting:

```
out.println("Hello! Enter BYE to exit.");
```

When you use telnet to connect to this server program at port 8189, you will see the preceding greeting on the terminal screen.

In this simple server, we just read the client input, a line at a time, and echo it. This demonstrates that the program receives the client's input. An actual server would obviously compute and return an answer that depended on the input.

```
String line = in.nextLine();
out.println("Echo: " + line);
if (line.trim().equals("BYE")) done = true;
```

In the end, we close the incoming socket.

```
incoming.close();
```

That is all there is to it. Every server program, such as an HTTP web server, continues performing this loop:

1. It receives a command from the client ("get me this information") through an incoming data stream.
2. It somehow fetches the information.
3. It sends the information to the client through the outgoing data stream.

Example 3–2 is the complete program.

Example 3–2: EchoServer.java

```
1. import java.io.*;
2. import java.net.*;
3. import java.util.*;
4.
5. /**
6.    This program implements a simple server that listens to port 8189 and echoes back all
7.    client input.
8. */
9. public class EchoServer
10. {
11.    public static void main(String[] args )
12.    {
13.       try
14.       {
15.          // establish server socket
16.          ServerSocket s = new ServerSocket(8189);
17.
18.          // wait for client connection
19.          Socket incoming = s.accept( );
20.          try
21.          {
22.             InputStream inStream = incoming.getInputStream();
23.             OutputStream outStream = incoming.getOutputStream();
24.
25.             Scanner in = new Scanner(inStream);
26.             PrintWriter out = new PrintWriter(outStream, true /* autoFlush */);
27.
28.             out.println( "Hello! Enter BYE to exit." );
29.
30.             // echo client input
31.             boolean done = false;
32.             while (!done && in.hasNextLine())
33.             {
34.                String line = in.nextLine();
35.                out.println("Echo: " + line);
36.                if (line.trim().equals("BYE"))
```

```
37.                 done = true;
38.             }
39.         }
40.         finally
41.         {
42.             incoming.close();
43.         }
44.     }
45.     catch (IOException e)
46.     {
47.         e.printStackTrace();
48.     }
49.   }
50. }
```

To try it out, compile and run the program. Then, use telnet to connect to the following server and port:

> Server: 127.0.0.1

> Port: 8189

The IP address 127.0.0.1 is a special address, the *local loopback address*, that denotes the local machine. Because you are running the echo server locally, that is where you want to connect.

If you are connected directly to the Internet, then anyone in the world can access your echo server, provided they know your IP address and the magic port number.

When you connect to the port, you will see the message shown in Figure 3–4:

```
Hello! Enter BYE to exit.
```

Type anything and watch the input echo on your screen. Type BYE (all uppercase letters) to disconnect. The server program will terminate as well.

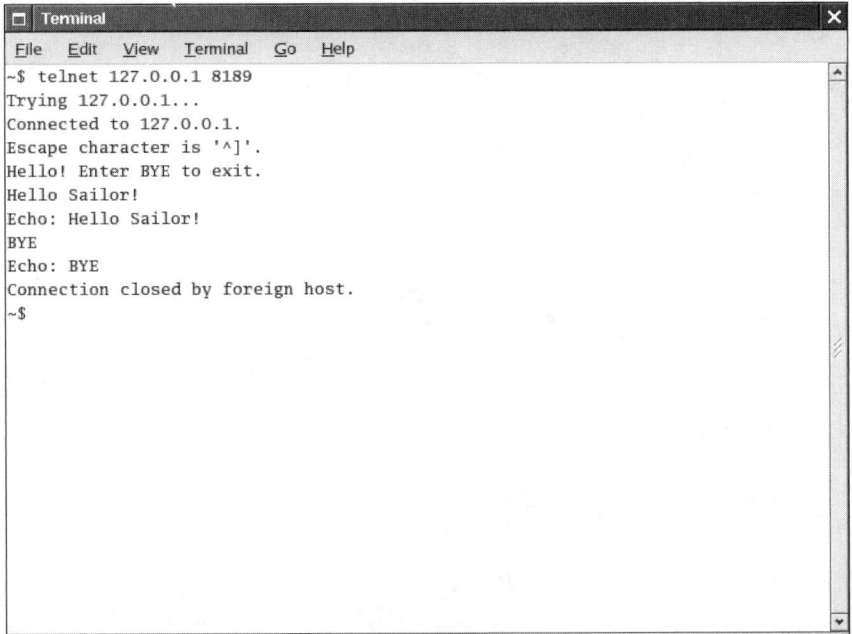

Figure 3–4: Accessing an echo server

API **java.net.ServerSocket** 1.0

- ServerSocket(int port)
  creates a server socket that monitors a port.

- Socket accept()
  waits for a connection. This method blocks (that is, idles) the current thread until the connection is made. The method returns a Socket object through which the program can communicate with the connecting client.

- void close()
  closes the server socket.

Serving Multiple Clients

There is one problem with the simple server in the preceding example. Suppose we want to allow multiple clients to connect to our server at the same time. Typically, a server runs constantly on a server computer, and clients from all over the Internet may want to use the server at the same time. Rejecting multiple connections allows any one client to monopolize the service by connecting to it for a long time. We can do much better through the magic of threads.

Every time we know the program has established a new socket connection, that is, when the call to accept was successful, we will launch a new thread to take care of the connection between the server and *that* client. The main program will just go back and wait for the next connection. For this to happen, the main loop of the server should look like this:

```
while (true)
{
   Socket incoming = s.accept();
   Runnable r = new ThreadedEchoHandler(incoming);

   Thread t = new Thread(r);
   t.start();
}
```

The ThreadedEchoHandler class implements Runnable and contains the communication loop with the client in its run method.

```
class ThreadedEchoHandler implements Runnable
{  . . .
   public void run()
   {
      try
      {
         InputStream inStream = incoming.getInputStream();
         OutputStream outStream = incoming.getOutputStream();
         process input and send response
         incoming.close();
      }
      catch(IOException e)
      {
         handle exception
      }
   }
}
```

Because each connection starts a new thread, multiple clients can connect to the server at the same time. You can easily check this out. Compile and run the server program

(Example 3–3). Open several telnet windows as we have in Figure 3–5. You can communicate through all of them simultaneously. The server program never dies. Use CTRL+C to kill it.

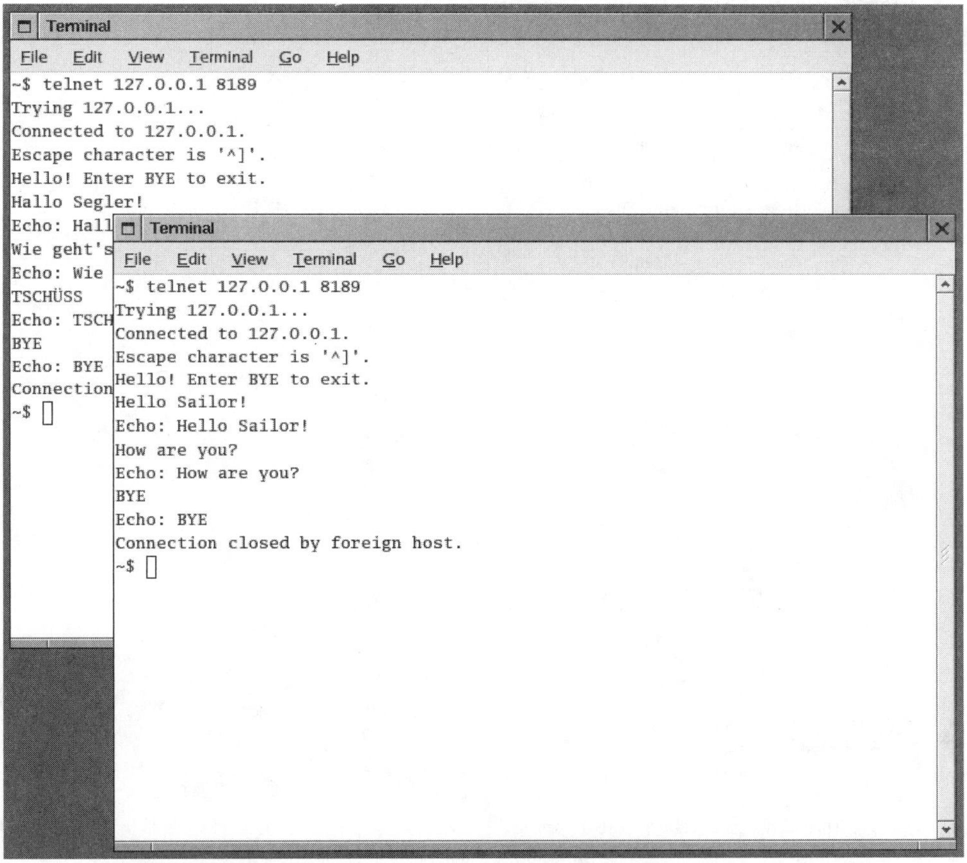

Figure 3–5: **Several telnet windows communicating simultaneously**

> NOTE: In this program, we spawn a separate thread for each connection. This approach is not satisfactory for high-performance servers. You can achieve greater server throughput by using features of the java.nio package. See http://www-106.ibm.com/developerworks/java/library/j-javaio for more information.

Example 3–3: ThreadedEchoServer.java

```
1. import java.io.*;
2. import java.net.*;
3. import java.util.*;
4.
5. /**
6.    This program implements a multithreaded server that listens to port 8189 and echoes back
7.    all client input.
8. */
9. public class ThreadedEchoServer
```

```
10. {
11.    public static void main(String[] args )
12.    {
13.       try
14.       {
15.          int i = 1;
16.          ServerSocket s = new ServerSocket(8189);
17.
18.          while (true)
19.          {
20.             Socket incoming = s.accept();
21.             System.out.println("Spawning " + i);
22.             Runnable r = new ThreadedEchoHandler(incoming, i);
23.             Thread t = new Thread(r);
24.             t.start();
25.             i++;
26.          }
27.       }
28.       catch (IOException e)
29.       {
30.          e.printStackTrace();
31.       }
32.    }
33. }
34.
35. /**
36.    This class handles the client input for one server socket connection.
37. */
38. class ThreadedEchoHandler implements Runnable
39. {
40.    /**
41.       Constructs a handler.
42.       @param i the incoming socket
43.       @param c the counter for the handlers (used in prompts)
44.    */
45.    public ThreadedEchoHandler(Socket i, int c)
46.    {
47.       incoming = i; counter = c;
48.    }
49.
50.    public void run()
51.    {
52.       try
53.       {
54.          try
55.          {
56.             InputStream inStream = incoming.getInputStream();
57.             OutputStream outStream = incoming.getOutputStream();
58.
59.             Scanner in = new Scanner(inStream);
60.             PrintWriter out = new PrintWriter(outStream, true /* autoFlush */);
61.
62.             out.println( "Hello! Enter BYE to exit." );
63.
64.             // echo client input
65.             boolean done = false;
```

```
66.        while (!done && in.hasNextLine())
67.        {
68.           String line = in.nextLine();
69.           out.println("Echo: " + line);
70.           if (line.trim().equals("BYE"))
71.              done = true;
72.        }
73.     }
74.     finally
75.     {
76.        incoming.close();
77.     }
78.  }
79.  catch (IOException e)
80.  {
81.     e.printStackTrace();
82.  }
83.  }
84.
85.  private Socket incoming;
86.  private int counter;
87. }
```

Sending E-Mail

In this section, we show you a practical example of socket programming: a program that sends e-mail to a remote site.

To send e-mail, you make a socket connection to port 25, the SMTP port. SMTP is the Simple Mail Transport Protocol that describes the format for e-mail messages. You can connect to any server that runs an SMTP service. On UNIX machines, that service is typically implemented by the sendmail daemon. However, the server must be willing to accept your request. It used to be that sendmail servers were routinely willing to route e-mail from anyone, but in these days of spam floods, most servers now have built-in checks and accept requests only from users, domains, or IP address ranges that they trust.

Once you are connected to the server, send a mail header (in the SMTP format, which is easy to generate), followed by the mail message.

Here are the details:

1. Open a socket to your host.
    ```
    Socket s = new Socket("mail.yourserver.com", 25); // 25 is SMTP
    PrintWriter out = new PrintWriter(s.getOutputStream());
    ```

2. Send the following information to the print stream:
    ```
    HELO sending host
    MAIL FROM: <sender e-mail address>
    RCPT TO: <>recipient e-mail address>
    DATA
    mail message
    (any number of lines)

    .
    QUIT
    ```

The SMTP specification (RFC 821) states that lines must be terminated with \r followed by \n.

Most SMTP servers do not check the veracity of the information—you may be able to supply any sender you like. (Keep this in mind the next time you get an e-mail message from president@whitehouse.gov inviting you to a black-tie affair on the front lawn. Anyone could have connected to an SMTP server and created a fake message.)

The program in Example 3–4 is a simple e-mail program. As you can see in Figure 3–6, you type in the sender, recipient, mail message, and SMTP server. Then, click the Send button, and your message is sent.

The program simply sends the sequence of commands that we just discussed. It displays the commands that it sends to the SMTP server and the responses that it receives. Note that the communication with the mail server occurs in a separate thread so that the user interface thread is not blocked when the program tries to connect to the mail server. (See Chapter 1 for more details on threads in Swing applications.)

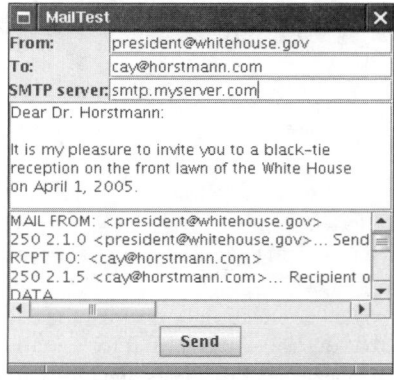

Figure 3–6: The MailTest program

Example 3–4: MailTest.java

```
1.  import java.awt.*;
2.  import java.awt.event.*;
3.  import java.util.*;
4.  import java.net.*;
5.  import java.io.*;
6.  import javax.swing.*;
7.
8.  /**
9.     This program shows how to use sockets to send plain text
10.    mail messages.
11. */
12. public class MailTest
13. {
14.    public static void main(String[] args)
15.    {
16.       JFrame frame = new MailTestFrame();
17.       frame.setDefaultCloseOperation(JFrame.EXIT_ON_CLOSE);
18.       frame.setVisible(true);
19.    }
20. }
21.
22. /**
```

```
23.     The frame for the mail GUI.
24. */
25. class MailTestFrame extends JFrame
26. {
27.     public MailTestFrame()
28.     {
29.         setSize(DEFAULT_WIDTH, DEFAULT_HEIGHT);
30.         setTitle("MailTest");
31.
32.         setLayout(new GridBagLayout());
33.
34.         // we use the GBC convenience class of Core Java Volume 1 Chapter 9
35.         add(new JLabel("From:"), new GBC(0, 0).setFill(GBC.HORIZONTAL));
36.
37.         from = new JTextField(20);
38.         add(from, new GBC(1, 0).setFill(GBC.HORIZONTAL).setWeight(100, 0));
39.
40.         add(new JLabel("To:"), new GBC(0, 1).setFill(GBC.HORIZONTAL));
41.
42.         to = new JTextField(20);
43.         add(to, new GBC(1, 1).setFill(GBC.HORIZONTAL).setWeight(100, 0));
44.
45.         add(new JLabel("SMTP server:"), new GBC(0, 2).setFill(GBC.HORIZONTAL));
46.
47.         smtpServer = new JTextField(20);
48.         add(smtpServer, new GBC(1, 2).setFill(GBC.HORIZONTAL).setWeight(100, 0));
49.
50.         message = new JTextArea();
51.         add(new JScrollPane(message), new GBC(0, 3, 2, 1).setFill(GBC.BOTH).setWeight(100, 100));
52.
53.         comm = new JTextArea();
54.         add(new JScrollPane(comm), new GBC(0, 4, 2, 1).setFill(GBC.BOTH).setWeight(100, 100));
55.
56.         JPanel buttonPanel = new JPanel();
57.         add(buttonPanel, new GBC(0, 5, 2, 1));
58.
59.         JButton sendButton = new JButton("Send");
60.         buttonPanel.add(sendButton);
61.         sendButton.addActionListener(new
62.             ActionListener()
63.             {
64.                 public void actionPerformed(ActionEvent event)
65.                 {
66.                     new Thread(new
67.                         Runnable()
68.                         {
69.                             public void run()
70.                             {
71.                                 comm.setText("");
72.                                 sendMail();
73.                             }
74.                         }).start();
75.                 }
76.             });
77.     }
78.
```

```
79.    /**
80.        Sends the mail message that has been authored in the GUI.
81.    */
82.    public void sendMail()
83.    {
84.       try
85.       {
86.          Socket s = new Socket(smtpServer.getText(), 25);
87.
88.          InputStream inStream = s.getInputStream();
89.          OutputStream outStream = s.getOutputStream();
90.
91.          in = new Scanner(inStream);
92.          out = new PrintWriter(outStream, true /* autoFlush */);
93.
94.          String hostName = InetAddress.getLocalHost().getHostName();
95.
96.          receive();
97.          send("HELO " + hostName);
98.          receive();
99.          send("MAIL FROM: <" + from.getText() + ">");
100.         receive();
101.         send("RCPT TO: <" + to.getText() + ">");
102.         receive();
103.         send("DATA");
104.         receive();
105.         send(message.getText());
106.         send(".");
107.         receive();
108.         s.close();
109.      }
110.      catch (IOException e)
111.      {
112.         comm.append("Error: " + e);
113.      }
114.   }
115.
116.   /**
117.       Sends a string to the socket and echoes it in the
118.       comm text area.
119.       @param s the string to send.
120.   */
121.   public void send(String s) throws IOException
122.   {
123.      comm.append(s);
124.      comm.append("\n");
125.      out.print(s.replaceAll("\n", "\r\n"));
126.      out.print("\r\n");
127.      out.flush();
128.   }
129.
130.   /**
131.       Receives a string from the socket and displays it
132.       in the comm text area.
133.   */
134.   public void receive() throws IOException
```

```
135.    {
136.        if (in.hasNextLine());
137.        {
138.            String line = in.nextLine();
139.            comm.append(line);
140.            comm.append("\n");
141.        }
142.    }
143.
144.    private Scanner in;
145.    private PrintWriter out;
146.    private JTextField from;
147.    private JTextField to;
148.    private JTextField smtpServer;
149.    private JTextArea message;
150.    private JTextArea comm;
151.
152.    public static final int DEFAULT_WIDTH = 300;
153.    public static final int DEFAULT_HEIGHT = 300;
154. }
```

Making URL Connections

In the last section, you saw how to use socket-level programming to connect to an SMTP server and send an e-mail message. It is nice to know that this can be done and to get a glimpse of what goes on "under the hood" of an Internet service such as e-mail. However, if you are planning an application that incorporates e-mail, you will probably want to work at a higher level and use a library that encapsulates the protocol details. For example, Sun Microsystems has developed the JavaMail API as a standard extension of the Java platform. In the JavaMail API, you simply issue a call such as

```
Transport.send(message);
```

to send a message. The library takes care of message protocols, multiple recipients, handling attachments, and so on.

For the remainder of this chapter, we concentrate on higher-level services that the standard edition of the Java platform provides. Of course, the runtime library uses sockets to implement these services, but you don't have to worry about the protocol details when you use the higher-level services.

URLs and URIs

The URL and URLConnection classes encapsulate much of the complexity of retrieving information from a remote site. You can construct a URL object from a string:

```
URL url = new URL(urlString);
```

If you simply want to fetch the contents of the resource, then you can use the openStream method of the URL class. This method yields an InputStream object. Use it in the usual way, for example, to construct a Scanner:

```
InputStream inStream = url.openStream();
Scanner in = new Scanner(inStream);
```

As of JDK 1.4, the java.net package makes a useful distinction between URLs (uniform resource *locators*) and URIs (uniform resource *identifiers*).

A URI is a purely syntactical construct that specifies the various parts of the string specifying a web resource. A URL is a special kind of URI, namely, one with sufficient information to *locate* a resource. Other URIs, such as

```
mailto:cay@horstmann.com
```

are not locators—there is no data to locate from this identifier. Such a URI is called a URN (uniform resource *name*).

In the Java library, the URI class has no methods for accessing the resource that the identifier specifies—its sole purpose is parsing. In contrast, the URL class can open a stream to the resource. For that reason, the URL class only works with schemes that the Java library knows how to handle, such as http:, https:, ftp: the local file system (file:), and JAR files (jar:).

To see why parsing is not trivial, consider how complex URIs can be. For example,

```
http://maps.yahoo.com/py/maps.py?csz=Cupertino+CA
ftp://username:password@ftp.yourserver.com/pub/file.txt
```

The URI specification gives rules for the makeup of these identifiers. A URI has the syntax

[*scheme:*]*schemeSpecificPart*[*#fragment*]

Here, the [. . .] denotes an optional part, and the : and # are included literally in the identifier.

If the *scheme:* part is present, the URI is called *absolute*. Otherwise, it is called *relative*.

An absolute URI is *opaque* if the schemeSpecificPart does not begin with a / such as

```
mailto:cay@horstmann.com
```

All absolute nonopaque URIs and all relative URIs are *hierarchical*. Examples are

```
http://java.sun.com/index.html
../../java/net/Socket.html#Socket()
```

The schemeSpecificPart of a hierarchical URI has the structure

[*//authority*][*path*][*?query*]

where again [. . .] denotes optional parts.

For server-based URIs, the authority part has the form

[*user-info@*]*host*[*:port*]

The *port* must be an integer.

RFC 2396, which standardizes URIs, also supports a registry-based mechanism by which the authority has a different format, but they are not in common use.

One of the purposes of the URI class is to parse an identifier and break it up into its various components. You can retrieve them with the methods

```
getScheme
getSchemeSpecificPart
getAuthority
getUserInfo
getHost
getPort
getPath
getQuery
getFragment
```

The other purpose of the URI class is the handling of absolute and relative identifiers. If you have an absolute URI such as

```
http://docs.mycompany.com/api/java/net/ServerSocket.html
```

and a relative URI such as

```
../../java/net/Socket.html#Socket()
```

then you can combine the two into an absolute URI.

```
http://docs.mycompany.com/api/java/net/Socket.html#Socket()
```

This process is called *resolving* a relative URL.

The opposite process is called *relativization*. For example, suppose you have a *base* URI

```
http://docs.mycompany.com/api
```

and a URI

```
http://docs.mycompany.com/api/java/lang/String.html
```

Then the relativized URI is

```
java/lang/String.html
```

The URI class supports both of these operations:

```
relative = base.relativize(combined);
combined = base.resolve(relative);
```

Using a URLConnection to Retrieve Information

If you want additional information about a web resource, then you should use the URLConnection class, which gives you much more control than the basic URL class.

When working with a URLConnection object, you must carefully schedule your steps, as follows:

1. Call the openConnection method of the URL class to obtain the URLConnection object:

    ```
    URLConnection connection = url.openConnection();
    ```

2. Set any request properties, using the methods

    ```
    setDoInput
    setDoOutput
    setIfModifiedSince
    setUseCaches
    setAllowUserInteraction
    setRequestProperty
    setConnectTimeout
    setReadTimeout
    ```

    We discuss these methods later in this section and in the API notes.

3. Connect to the remote resource by calling the connect method.

    ```
    connection.connect();
    ```

    Besides making a socket connection to the server, this method also queries the server for *header information*.

4. After connecting to the server, you can query the header information. Two methods, getHeaderFieldKey and getHeaderField, enumerate all fields of the header. As of JDK 1.4, the method getHeaderFields gets a standard Map object containing the header fields. For your convenience, the following methods query standard fields.

    ```
    getContentType
    getContentLength
    getContentEncoding
    getDate
    getExpiration
    getLastModified
    ```

5. Finally, you can access the resource data. Use the getInputStream method to obtain an input stream for reading the information. (This is the same input stream that the openStream method of the URL class returns.) The other method, getContent, isn't very useful in practice. The objects that are returned by standard content types such as text/plain and image/gif require classes in the com.sun hierarchy for processing. You could register your own content handlers, but we do not discuss that technique in this book.

> **CAUTION:** Some programmers form the wrong mental image when using the URLConnection
> class, thinking that the getInputStream and getOutputStream methods are similar to those of the
> Socket class. But that isn't quite true. The URLConnection class does quite a bit of magic behind
> the scenes, in particular the handling of request and response headers. For that reason, it is
> important that you follow the setup steps for the connection.

Let us now look at some of the URLConnection methods in detail. Several methods set properties of the connection before connecting to the server. The most important ones are setDoInput and setDoOutput. By default, the connection yields an input stream for reading from the server but no output stream for writing. If you want an output stream (for example, for posting data to a web server), then you need to call

```
connection.setDoOutput(true);
```

Next, you may want to set some of the request headers. The request headers are sent together with the request command to the server. Here is an example:

```
GET www.server.com/index.html HTTP/1.0
Referer: http://www.somewhere.com/links.html
Proxy-Connection: Keep-Alive
User-Agent: Mozilla/4.76 (Windows ME; U) [en]
Host: www.server.com
Accept: text/html, image/gif, image/jpeg, image/png, */*
Accept-Language: en
Accept-Charset: iso-8859-1,*,utf-8
Cookie: orangemilano=192218887821987
```

The setIfModifiedSince method tells the connection that you are only interested in data that have been modified since a certain date. The setUseCaches and setAllowUserInteraction are only used inside applets. The setUseCaches method directs the browser to first check the browser cache. The setAllowUserInteraction method allows an applet to pop up a dialog box for querying the user name and password for password-protected resources (see Figure 3–7). These settings have no effect outside of applets.

Figure 3–7: A network password dialog box

Finally, you can use the catch-all setRequestProperty method to set any name/value pair that is meaningful for the particular protocol. For the format of the HTTP request headers, see RFC 2616. Some of these parameters are not well documented and are passed around by word of mouth from one programmer to the next. For example, if you want to access a password-protected web page, you must do the following:

1. Concatenate the user name, a colon, and the password.

   ```
   String input = username + ":" + password;
   ```

2. Compute the base64 encoding of the resulting string. (The base64 encoding encodes a sequence of bytes into a sequence of printable ASCII characters.)

   ```
   String encoding = base64Encode(input);
   ```

3. Call the setRequestProperty method with a name of "Authorization" and value "Basic " + encoding:

   ```
   connection.setRequestProperty("Authorization", "Basic " + encoding);
   ```

 TIP: You just saw how to access a password-protected web page. To access a password-protected file by FTP, you use an entirely different method. You simply construct a URL of the form

```
ftp://username:password@ftp.yourserver.com/pub/file.txt
```

Once you call the connect method, you can query the response header information. First, let us see how to enumerate all response header fields. The implementors of this class felt a need to express their individuality by introducing yet another iteration protocol. The call

```
String key = connection.getHeaderFieldKey(n);
```

gets the nth key from the response header, where n starts from 1! It returns null if n is zero or larger than the total number of header fields. There is no method to return the number of fields; you simply keep calling getHeaderFieldKey until you get null. Similarly, the call

```
String value = connection.getHeaderField(n);
```

returns the nth value.

Mercifully, as of JDK 1.4, the method getHeaderFields returns a Map of response header fields that you can access as explained in Chapter 2.

```
Map<String,List<String>> headerFields = connection.getHeaderFields();
```

Here is a set of response header fields from a typical HTTP request.

```
Date: Wed, 29 Aug 2004 00:15:48 GMT
Server: Apache/1.3.31 (Unix)
Last-Modified: Sun, 24 Jun 2004 20:53:38 GMT
Accept-Ranges: bytes
Content-Length: 4813
Connection: close
Content-Type: text/html
```

As a convenience, six methods query the values of the most common header types and convert them to numeric types when appropriate. Table 3–1 shows these convenience methods. The methods with return type long return the number of seconds since January 1, 1970 GMT.

The program in Example 3–5 lets you experiment with URL connections. Supply a URL and an optional user name and password on the command line when running the program, for example:

```
java URLConnectionTest http://www.yourserver.com user password
```

Table 3–1: Convenience Methods for Response Header Values

Key Name	Method Name	Return Type
Date	getDate	long
Expires	getExpiration	long
Last-Modified	getLastModified	long
Content-Length	getContentLength	int
Content-Type	getContentType	String
Content-Encoding	getContentEncoding	String

The program prints

- All keys and values of the header;
- The return values of the six convenience methods in Table 3–1;
- The first 10 lines of the requested resource.

The program is straightforward, except for the computation of the base64 encoding. There is an undocumented class, sun.misc.Base64Encoder, that you can use instead of the one that we provide in the example program. Simply replace the call to base64Encode with

```
String encoding = new sun.misc.BASE64Encoder().encode(input.getBytes());
```

However, we supplied our own class because we do not like to rely on the classes in the sun or com.sun packages.

 NOTE: The javax.mail.internet.MimeUtility class in the JavaMail standard extension package also has a method for Base64 encoding. JDK 1.4 has a class java.util.prefs.Base64 for the same purpose, but it is not public, so you cannot use it in your code.

Example 3–5: URLConnectionTest.java

```
1. import java.io.*;
2. import java.net.*;
3. import java.util.*;
4.
5. /**
6.    This program connects to a URL and displays the
7.    response header data and the first 10 lines of the
8.    requested data.
9.
10.   Supply the URL and an optional username and password (for
11.   HTTP basic authentication) on the command line.
12. */
13. public class URLConnectionTest
14. {
15.    public static void main(String[] args)
16.    {
17.       try
18.       {
19.          String urlName;
20.          if (args.length > 0)
21.             urlName = args[0];
22.          else
23.             urlName = "http://java.sun.com";
24.
```

```
25.      URL url = new URL(urlName);
26.      URLConnection connection = url.openConnection();
27.
28.      // set username, password if specified on command line
29.
30.      if (args.length > 2)
31.      {
32.         String username = args[1];
33.         String password = args[2];
34.         String input = username + ":" + password;
35.         String encoding = base64Encode(input);
36.         connection.setRequestProperty("Authorization", "Basic " + encoding);
37.      }
38.
39.      connection.connect();
40.
41.      // print header fields
42.
43.      Map<String, List<String>> headers = connection.getHeaderFields();
44.      for (Map.Entry<String, List<String>> entry : headers.entrySet())
45.      {
46.         String key = entry.getKey();
47.         for (String value : entry.getValue())
48.            System.out.println(key + ": " + value);
49.      }
50.
51.      // print convenience functions
52.
53.      System.out.println("----------");
54.      System.out.println("getContentType: " + connection.getContentType());
55.      System.out.println("getContentLength: " + connection.getContentLength());
56.      System.out.println("getContentEncoding: " + connection.getContentEncoding());
57.      System.out.println("getDate: " + connection.getDate());
58.      System.out.println("getExpiration: " + connection.getExpiration());
59.      System.out.println("getLastModifed: " + connection.getLastModified());
60.      System.out.println("----------");
61.
62.      Scanner in = new Scanner(connection.getInputStream());
63.
64.      // print first ten lines of contents
65.
66.      for (int n = 1; in.hasNextLine() && n <= 10; n++)
67.         System.out.println(in.nextLine());
68.      if (in.hasNextLine()) System.out.println(". . .");
69.      }
70.   catch (IOException e)
71.      {
72.         e.printStackTrace();
73.      }
74.   }
75.
76.   /**
77.      Computes the Base64 encoding of a string
78.      @param s a string
79.      @return the Base 64 encoding of s
80.   */
81.   public static String base64Encode(String s)
```

```
82.     {
83.         ByteArrayOutputStream bOut = new ByteArrayOutputStream();
84.         Base64OutputStream out = new Base64OutputStream(bOut);
85.         try
86.         {
87.             out.write(s.getBytes());
88.             out.flush();
89.         }
90.         catch (IOException e)
91.         {
92.         }
93.         return bOut.toString();
94.     }
95. }
96.
97. /**
98.     This stream filter converts a stream of bytes to their
99.     Base64 encoding.
100.
101.    Base64 encoding encodes 3 bytes into 4 characters.
102.    |11111122|22223333|33444444|
103.    Each set of 6 bits is encoded according to the
104.    toBase64 map. If the number of input bytes is not
105.    a multiple of 3, then the last group of 4 characters
106.    is padded with one or two = signs. Each output line
107.    is at most 76 characters.
108. */
109. class Base64OutputStream extends FilterOutputStream
110. {
111.    /**
112.        Constructs the stream filter
113.        @param out the stream to filter
114.    */
115.    public Base64OutputStream(OutputStream out)
116.    {
117.        super(out);
118.    }
119.
120.    public void write(int c) throws IOException
121.    {
122.        inbuf[i] = c;
123.        i++;
124.        if (i == 3)
125.        {
126.            super.write(toBase64[(inbuf[0] & 0xFC) >> 2]);
127.            super.write(toBase64[((inbuf[0] & 0x03) << 4) | ((inbuf[1] & 0xF0) >> 4)]);
128.            super.write(toBase64[((inbuf[1] & 0x0F) << 2) | ((inbuf[2] & 0xC0) >> 6)]);
129.            super.write(toBase64[inbuf[2] & 0x3F]);
130.            col += 4;
131.            i = 0;
132.            if (col >= 76)
133.            {
134.                super.write('\n');
135.                col = 0;
136.            }
137.        }
138.    }
```

```
139.
140.    public void flush() throws IOException
141.    {
142.       if (i == 1)
143.       {
144.          super.write(toBase64[(inbuf[0] & 0xFC) >> 2]);
145.          super.write(toBase64[(inbuf[0] & 0x03) << 4]);
146.          super.write('=');
147.          super.write('=');
148.       }
149.       else if (i == 2)
150.       {
151.          super.write(toBase64[(inbuf[0] & 0xFC) >> 2]);
152.          super.write(toBase64[((inbuf[0] & 0x03) << 4) | ((inbuf[1] & 0xF0) >> 4)]);
153.          super.write(toBase64[(inbuf[1] & 0x0F) << 2]);
154.          super.write('=');
155.       }
156.    }
157.
158.    private static char[] toBase64 =
159.    {
160.       'A', 'B', 'C', 'D', 'E', 'F', 'G', 'H', 'I', 'J', 'K', 'L', 'M', 'N', 'O', 'P',
161.       'Q', 'R', 'S', 'T', 'U', 'V', 'W', 'X', 'Y', 'Z', 'a', 'b', 'c', 'd', 'e', 'f',
162.       'g', 'h', 'i', 'j', 'k', 'l', 'm', 'n', 'o', 'p', 'q', 'r', 's', 't', 'u', 'v',
163.       'w', 'x', 'y', 'z', '0', '1', '2', '3', '4', '5', '6', '7', '8', '9', '+', '/'
164.    };
165.
166.    private int col = 0;
167.    private int i = 0;
168.    private int[] inbuf = new int[3];
169. }
```

> **NOTE:** A commonly asked question is whether the Java platform supports access of secure web pages (https: URLs). As of JDK 1.4, SSL support is a part of the standard library. Before JDK 1.4, you were only able to make SSL connections from applets by taking advantage of the SSL implementation of the browser.

 java.net.URL 1.0

- InputStream openStream()
  opens an input stream for reading the resource data.
- URLConnection openConnection();
  returns a URLConnection object that manages the connection to the resource.

 java.net.URLConnection 1.0

- void setDoInput(boolean doInput)
- boolean getDoInput()
  If doInput is true, then the user can receive input from this URLConnection.
- void setDoOutput(boolean doOutput)
- boolean getDoOutput()
  If doOutput is true, then the user can send output to this URLConnection.

- void setIfModifiedSince(long time)
- long getIfModifiedSince()
  The ifModifiedSince property configures this URLConnection to fetch only data that have been modified since a given time. The time is given in seconds from midnight, GMT, January 1, 1970.
- void setUseCaches(boolean useCaches)
- boolean getUseCaches()
  If useCaches is true, then data can be retrieved from a local cache. Note that the URLConnection itself does not maintain such a cache. The cache must be supplied by an external program such as a browser.
- void setAllowUserInteraction(boolean allowUserInteraction)
- boolean getAllowsUserInteraction()
  If allowUserInteraction is true, then the user can be queried for passwords. Note that the URLConnection itself has no facilities for executing such a query. The query must be carried out by an external program such as a browser or browser plug-in.
- void setConnectTimeout(int timeout) **5.0**
- int getConnectTimeout() **5.0**
  set or get the timeout for the connection (in milliseconds). If the timeout has elapsed before a connection was established, the read method of the associated input stream throws a SocketTimeoutException.
- void setReadTimeout(int timeout) **5.0**
- int getReadTimeout() **5.0**
  set the timeout for reading data (in milliseconds). If the timeout has elapsed before a read operation was successful, the connect method throws a SocketTimeoutException.
- void setRequestProperty(String key, String value)
  sets a request header field.
- Map<String,List<String>> getRequestProperties() **1.4**
  returns a map of request properties. All values for the same key are placed in a list.
- void connect()
  connects to the remote resource and retrieves response header information.
- Map<String,List<String>> Map getHeaderFields() **1.4**
  returns a map of response headers. All values for the same key are placed in a map.
- String getHeaderFieldKey(int n)
  gets the key for the nth response header field, or null if n is ≤ 0 or larger than the number of response header fields.
- String getHeaderField(int n)
  gets value of the nth response header field, or null if n is ≤ 0 or larger than the number of response header fields.
- int getContentLength()
  gets the content length if available, or –1 if unknown.
- String getContentType
  gets the content type, such as text/plain or image/gif.
- String getContentEncoding()
  gets the content encoding, such as gzip. This value is not commonly used, because the default identity encoding is not supposed to be specified with a Content-Encoding header.
- long getDate()
- long getExpiration()
- long getLastModifed()
  get the date of creation, expiration, and last modification of the resource. The dates are specified as seconds from midnight, GMT, January 1, 1970.

- `InputStream getInputStream()`
- `OutputStream getOutputStream()`

  return a stream for reading from the resource or writing to the resource.

- `Object getContent()`

  selects the appropriate content handler to read the resource data and convert it into an object. This method is not useful for reading standard types such as text/plain or image/gif unless you install your own content handler.

Posting Form Data

In the preceding section, you saw how to read data from a web server. Now we will show you how your programs can send data back to a web server and to programs that the web server invokes.

To send information from a web browser to the web server, a user fills out a *form*, like the one in Figure 3–8.

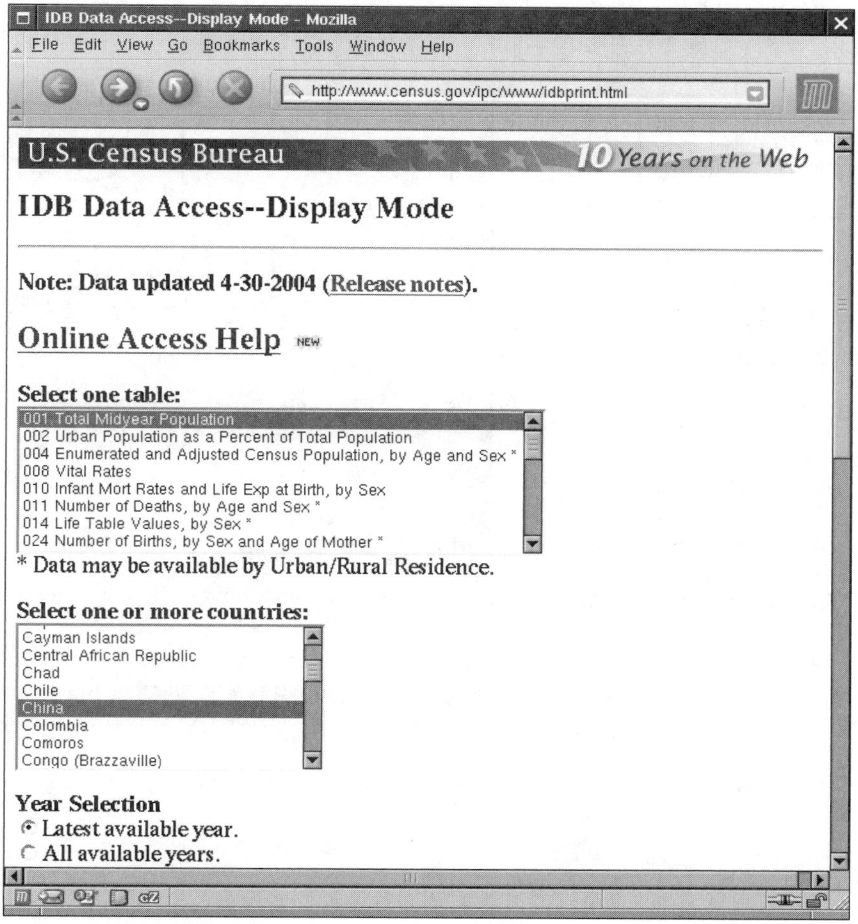

Figure 3–8: An HTML form

When the user clicks the Submit button, the text in the text fields and the settings of the checkboxes and radio buttons are sent back to the web server. The web server invokes a program that processes the user input.

Many technologies enable web servers to invoke programs. Among the best known ones are Java servlets, JavaServer Faces, Microsoft ASP (Active Server Pages), and CGI (Common Gateway Interface) scripts. For simplicity, we use the generic term *script* for a server-side program, no matter what technology is used.

The server-side script processes the form data and produces another HTML page that the web server sends back to the browser. This sequence is illustrated in Figure 3–9. The response page can contain new information (for example, in an information-search program) or just an acknowledgment. The web browser then displays the response page.

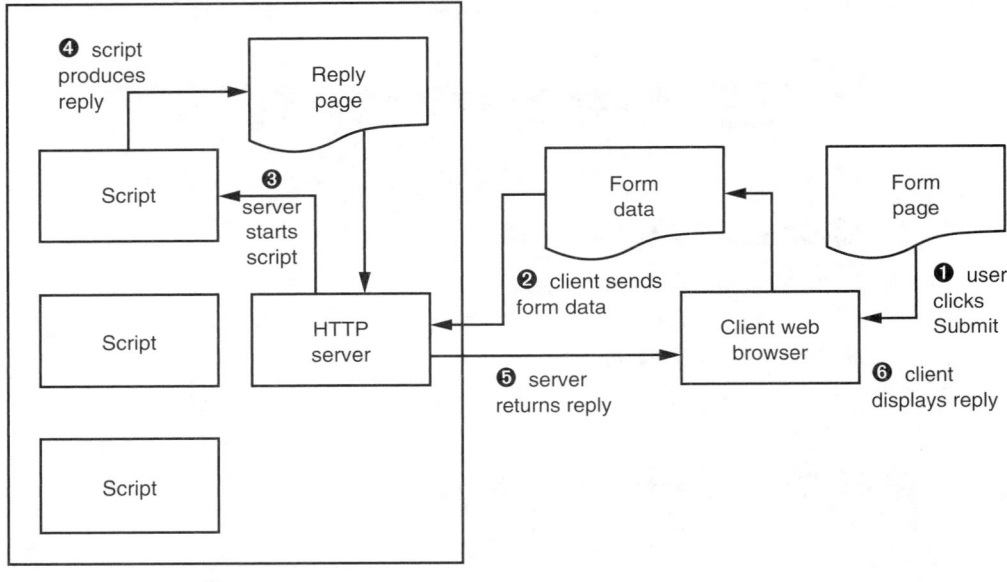

Figure 3–9: Data flow during execution of a server-side script

We do not discuss the implementation of server-side scripts in this book. Our interest is merely in writing client programs that interact with existing server-side scripts.

When form data is sent to a web server, it does not matter whether the data are interpreted by a servlet, a CGI script, or some other server-side technology. The client sends the data to the web server in a standard format, and the web server takes care of passing it on to the program that generates the response.

Two commands, called GET and POST, are commonly used to send information to a web server.

In the GET command, you simply attach parameters to the end of the URL. The URL has the form

> http://*host*/*script*?*parameters*

For example, at the time of this writing, the Yahoo! web site has a script, py/maps.py, at the host maps.yahoo.com. The script requires two parameters, addr and csz. You separate the parameters by an & and encode the parameters, using the following scheme.

Replace all spaces with a +. Replace all nonalphanumeric characters by a %, followed by a two-digit hexadecimal number. For example, to transmit the street name *S. Main,* you use S%2e+Main, since the hexadecimal number 2e (or decimal 46) is the ASCII code of the "." character. This encoding keeps any intermediate programs from messing with spaces and interpreting other special characters. This encoding scheme is called *URL encoding.*

For example, to get a map of 1 Infinite Loop, Cupertino, CA, simply request the following URL:

```
http://maps.yahoo.com/py/maps.py?addr=1+Infinite+Loop&csz=Cupertino+CA
```

The GET command is simple, but it has a major limitation that makes it relatively unpopular: Most browsers have a limit on the number of characters that you can include in a GET request.

In the POST command, you do not attach parameters to a URL. Instead, you get an output stream from the URLConnection and write name/value pairs to the output stream. You still have to URL-encode the values and separate them with & characters.

Let us look at this process in more detail. To post data to a script, you first establish a URL-Connection.

```
URL url = new URL("http://host/script");
URLConnection connection = url.openConnection();
```

Then, you call the setDoOutput method to set up the connection for output.

```
connection.setDoOutput(true);
```

Next, you call getOutputStream to get a stream through which you can send data to the server. If you are sending text to the server, it is convenient to wrap that stream into a PrintWriter.

```
PrintWriter out = new PrintWriter(connection.getOutputStream());
```

Now you are ready to send data to the server:

```
out.print(name1 + "=" + URLEncoder.encode(value1, "UTF-8") + "&");
out.print(name2 + "=" + URLEncoder.encode(value2, "UTF-8"));
```

Close the output stream.

```
out.close();
```

Finally, call getInputStream and read the server response.

Let us run through a practical example. The web site at http://www.census.gov/ipc/www/idb-print.html contains a form to request population data (see Figure 3–8 on page 167). If you look at the HTML source, you will see the following HTML tag:

```
<form method=post action="/cgi-bin/ipc/idbsprd">
```

This tag means that the name of the script executed when the user clicks the Submit button is /cgi-bin/ipc/idbsprd and that you need to use the POST command to send data to the script.

Next, you need to find out the field names that the script expects. Look at the user interface components. Each of them has a name attribute, for example,

```
<select name="tbl" size=8>
<option value="001">001 Total Midyear Population</option>
more options . . .
</select>
```

This tells you that the name of the field is tbl. This field specifies the population table type. If you specify the table type 001, you will get a table of the total midyear population. If you look further, you will also find a country field name cty with values such as US for the United States and CH (!) for China. (Sadly, the Census Bureau seems to be unaware of the ISO-3166 standard for country codes.)

Finally, a field named `optyr` allows selection of the year range. For this example, we will just set it to `latest checked`. For example, to get the latest data for the total midyear population of China, you construct this string:

```
tbl=1&cty=CH&optyr=latest+checked
```

Send the string to the URL

```
http://www.census.gov/cgi-bin/ipc/idbsprd:
```

The script sends back the following reply:

```
<PRE>
U.S. Bureau of the Census, International Data Base


Table 001. Total Midyear Population
---------------- --------------------

Country or area/
Year                    Population
---------------- --------------------

China


2004                    1,298,847,624
---------------- --------------------

Source: U.S. Bureau of the Census, International
        Data Base.

</PRE>
```

As you can see, this particular script doesn't bother with constructing a pretty table. That is the reason we picked it as an example—it is easy to see what happens with this script, whereas it can be confusing to decipher a complex set of HTML tags that other scripts produce.

The program in Example 3–6 sends POST data to the census bureau. We provide a simple GUI to pick a country and view the report (see Figure 3–10).

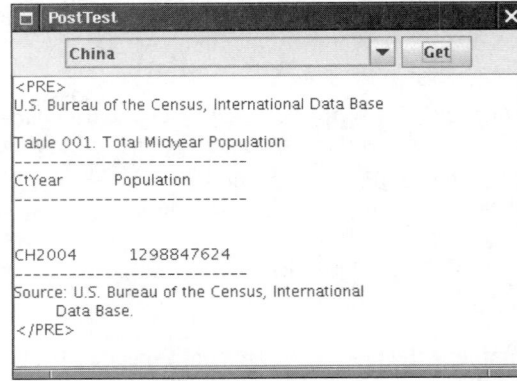

Figure 3–10: Harvesting information from a server

In the doPost method, we first open the connection, call setDoOutput(true), and open the output stream. We then enumerate the names and values in a Map object. For each of them, we send the name, = character, value, and & separator character:

```
out.print(name);
out.print('=');
out.print(URLEncoder.encode(value, "UTF-8"));
if (more pairs) out.print('&');
```

Finally, we read the response from the server.

There is one twist with reading the response. If a script error occurs, then the call to connection.getInputStream() throws a FileNotFoundException. However, the server still sends an error page back to the browser (such as the ubiquitous "Error 404 -page not found"). To capture this error page, you cast the URLConnection object to the HttpURLConnection class and call its getErrorStream method:

```
InputStream err = ((HttpURLConnection) connection).getErrorStream();
```

The technique that this program displays is useful whenever you need to query information from an existing web site. Simply find out the parameters that you need to send (usually by inspecting the HTML source of a web page that carries out the same query), and then strip out the HTML tags and other unnecessary information from the reply.

Example 3–6: PostTest.java

```
 1. import java.io.*;
 2. import java.net.*;
 3. import java.util.*;
 4. import java.awt.*;
 5. import java.awt.event.*;
 6. import javax.swing.*;
 7.
 8. /**
 9.    This program demonstrates how to use the URLConnection class for a POST request.
10. */
11. public class PostTest
12. {
13.    public static void main(String[] args)
14.    {
15.       JFrame frame = new PostTestFrame();
16.       frame.setDefaultCloseOperation(JFrame.EXIT_ON_CLOSE);
17.       frame.setVisible(true);
18.    }
19. }
20.
21. class PostTestFrame extends JFrame
22. {
23.    /**
24.       Makes a POST request and returns the server response.
25.       @param urlString the URL to post to
26.       @param nameValuePairs a map of name/value pairs to supply in the request.
27.       @return the server reply (either from the input stream or the error stream)
28.    */
29.    public static String doPost(String urlString, Map<String, String> nameValuePairs)
30.       throws IOException
31.    {
32.       URL url = new URL(urlString);
33.       URLConnection connection = url.openConnection();
```

```
34.      connection.setDoOutput(true);
35.
36.      PrintWriter out = new PrintWriter(connection.getOutputStream());
37.
38.      boolean first = true;
39.      for (Map.Entry<String, String> pair : nameValuePairs.entrySet())
40.      {
41.         if (first) first = false;
42.         else out.print('&');
43.         String name = pair.getKey();
44.         String value = pair.getValue();
45.         out.print(name);
46.         out.print('=');
47.         out.print(URLEncoder.encode(value, "UTF-8"));
48.      }
49.
50.      out.close();
51.
52.      Scanner in;
53.      StringBuilder response = new StringBuilder();
54.      try
55.      {
56.         in = new Scanner(connection.getInputStream());
57.      }
58.      catch (IOException e)
59.      {
60.         if (!(connection instanceof HttpURLConnection)) throw e;
61.         InputStream err
62.            = ((HttpURLConnection)connection).getErrorStream();
63.         if (err == null) throw e;
64.         in = new Scanner(err);
65.      }
66.      while (in.hasNextLine())
67.      {
68.         response.append(in.nextLine());
69.         response.append("\n");
70.      }
71.
72.      in.close();
73.      return response.toString();
74.   }
75.
76.   public PostTestFrame()
77.   {
78.      setSize(DEFAULT_WIDTH, DEFAULT_HEIGHT);
79.      setTitle("PostTest");
80.
81.      JPanel northPanel = new JPanel();
82.      add(northPanel, BorderLayout.NORTH);
83.
84.      final JComboBox combo = new JComboBox();
85.      for (int i = 0; i < countries.length; i += 2)
86.      combo.addItem(countries[i]);
87.      northPanel.add(combo);
88.
89.      final JTextArea result = new JTextArea();
```

```
90.      add(new JScrollPane(result));
91.
92.      JButton getButton = new JButton("Get");
93.      northPanel.add(getButton);
94.      getButton.addActionListener(new
95.         ActionListener()
96.         {
97.            public void actionPerformed(ActionEvent event)
98.            {
99.               new Thread(new
100.                  Runnable()
101.                  {
102.                     public void run()
103.                     {
104.                        final String SERVER_URL = "http://www.census.gov/cgi-bin/ipc/idbsprd";
105.                        result.setText("");
106.                        Map<String, String> post = new HashMap<String, String>();
107.                        post.put("tbl", "001");
108.                        post.put("cty", countries[2 * combo.getSelectedIndex() + 1]);
109.                        post.put("optyr", "latest checked");
110.                        try
111.                        {
112.                           result.setText(doPost(SERVER_URL, post));
113.                        }
114.                        catch (IOException e)
115.                        {
116.                           result.setText("" + e);
117.                        }
118.                     }
119.                  }).start();
120.            }
121.         });
122.   }
123.
124.   private static String[] countries = {
125.      "Afghanistan", "AF", "Albania", "AL", "Algeria", "AG", "American Samoa", "AQ",
126.      "Andorra", "AN", "Angola", "AO", "Anguilla", "AV", "Antigua and Barbuda", "AC",
127.      "Argentina", "AR", "Armenia", "AM", "Aruba", "AA", "Australia", "AS", "Austria", "AU",
128.      "Azerbaijan", "AJ", "Bahamas, The", "BF", "Bahrain", "BA", "Bangladesh", "BG",
129.      "Barbados", "BB", "Belarus", "BO", "Belgium", "BE", "Belize", "BH", "Benin", "BN",
130.      "Bermuda", "BD", "Bhutan", "BT", "Bolivia", "BL", "Bosnia and Herzegovina", "BK",
131.      "Botswana", "BC", "Brazil", "BR", "Brunei", "BX", "Bulgaria", "BU", "Burkina Faso", "UV",
132.      "Burma", "BM", "Burundi", "BY", "Cambodia", "CB", "Cameroon", "CM", "Canada", "CA",
133.      "Cape Verde", "CV", "Cayman Islands", "CJ", "Central African Republic", "CT", "Chad", "CD",
134.      "Chile", "CI", "China", "CH", "Colombia", "CO", "Comoros", "CN", "Congo (Brazzaville)", "CF",
135.      "Congo (Kinshasa)", "CG", "Cook Islands", "CW", "Costa Rica", "CS", "Cote d'Ivoire", "IV",
136.      "Croatia", "HR", "Cuba", "CU", "Cyprus", "CY", "Czech Republic", "EZ", "Denmark", "DA",
137.      "Djibouti", "DJ", "Dominica", "DO", "Dominican Republic", "DR", "East Timor", "TT",
138.      "Ecuador", "EC", "Egypt", "EG", "El Salvador", "ES", "Equatorial Guinea", "EK",
139.      "Eritrea", "ER", "Estonia", "EN", "Ethiopia", "ET", "Faroe Islands", "FO", "Fiji", "FJ",
140.      "Finland", "FI", "France", "FR", "French Guiana", "FG", "French Polynesia", "FP",
141.      "Gabon", "GB", "Gambia, The", "GA", "Gaza Strip", "GZ", "Georgia", "GG", "Germany", "GM",
142.      "Ghana", "GH", "Gibraltar", "GI", "Greece", "GR", "Greenland", "GL", "Grenada", "GJ",
143.      "Guadeloupe", "GP", "Guam", "GQ", "Guatemala", "GT", "Guernsey", "GK", "Guinea", "GV",
144.      "Guinea-Bissau", "PU", "Guyana", "GY", "Haiti", "HA", "Honduras", "HO",
145.      "Hong Kong S.A.R", "HK", "Hungary", "HU", "Iceland", "IC", "India", "IN", "Indonesia", "ID",
```

```
146.    "Iran", "IR", "Iraq", "IZ", "Ireland", "EI", "Israel", "IS", "Italy", "IT", "Jamaica", "JM",
147.    "Japan", "JA", "Jersey", "JE", "Jordan", "JO", "Kazakhstan", "KZ", "Kenya", "KE",
148.    "Kiribati", "KR", "Korea, North", "KN", "Korea, South", "KS", "Kuwait", "KU",
149.    "Kyrgyzstan", "KG", "Laos", "LA", "Latvia", "LG", "Lebanon", "LE", "Lesotho", "LT",
150.    "Liberia", "LI", "Libya", "LY", "Liechtenstein", "LS", "Lithuania", "LH", "Luxembourg", "LU",
151.    "Macau S.A.R", "MC", "Macedonia, The Former Yugo. Rep. of", "MK", "Madagascar", "MA",
152.    "Malawi", "MI", "Malaysia", "MY", "Maldives", "MV", "Mali", "ML", "Malta", "MT",
153.    "Man, Isle of", "IM", "Marshall Islands", "RM", "Martinique", "MB", "Mauritania", "MR",
154.    "Mauritius", "MP", "Mayotte", "MF", "Mexico", "MX", "Micronesia, Federated States of", "FM",
155.    "Moldova", "MD", "Monaco", "MN", "Mongolia", "MG", "Montserrat", "MH", "Morocco", "MO",
156.    "Mozambique", "MZ", "Namibia", "WA", "Nauru", "NR", "Nepal", "NP", "Netherlands", "NL",
157.    "Netherlands Antilles", "NT", "New Caledonia", "NC", "New Zealand", "NZ", "Nicaragua", "NU",
158.    "Niger", "NG", "Nigeria", "NI", "Northern Mariana Islands", "CQ", "Norway", "NO",
159.    "Oman", "MU", "Pakistan", "PK", "Palau", "PS", "Panama", "PM", "Papua New Guinea", "PP",
160.    "Paraguay", "PA", "Peru", "PE", "Philippines", "RP", "Poland", "PL", "Portugal", "PO",
161.    "Puerto Rico", "RQ", "Qatar", "QA", "Reunion", "RE", "Romania", "RO", "Russia", "RS",
162.    "Rwanda", "RW", "Saint Helena", "SH", "Saint Kitts and Nevis", "SC", "Saint Lucia", "ST",
163.    "Saint Pierre and Miquelon", "SB", "Saint Vincent and the Grenadines", "VC", "Samoa", "WS",
164.    "San Marino", "SM", "Sao Tome and Principe", "TP", "Saudi Arabia", "SA", "Senegal", "SG",
165.    "Serbia and Montenegro", "YI", "Seychelles", "SE", "Sierra Leone", "SL", "Singapore", "SN",
166.    "Slovakia", "LO", "Slovenia", "SI", "Solomon Islands", "BP", "Somalia", "SO",
167.    "South Africa", "SF", "Spain", "SP", "Sri Lanka", "CE", "Sudan", "SU", "Suriname", "NS",
168.    "Swaziland", "WZ", "Sweden", "SW", "Switzerland", "SZ", "Syria", "SY", "Taiwan", "TW",
169.    "Tajikistan", "TI", "Tanzania", "TZ", "Thailand", "TH", "Togo", "TO", "Tonga", "TN",
170.    "Trinidad and Tobago", "TD", "Tunisia", "TS", "Turkey", "TU", "Turkmenistan", "TX",
171.    "Turks and Caicos Islands", "TK", "Tuvalu", "TV", "Uganda", "UG", "Ukraine", "UP",
172.    "United Arab Emirates", "TC", "United Kingdom", "UK", "United States", "US", "Uruguay", "UY",
173.    "Uzbekistan", "UZ", "Vanuatu", "NH", "Venezuela", "VE", "Vietnam", "VM",
174.    "Virgin Islands", "VQ", "Virgin Islands, British", "VI", "Wallis and Futuna", "WF",
175.    "West Bank", "WE", "Western Sahara", "WI", "Yemen", "YM", "Zambia", "ZA", "Zimbabwe", "ZI"
176.    };
177.
178.    public static final int DEFAULT_WIDTH = 400;
179.    public static final int DEFAULT_HEIGHT = 300;
180. }
```

Our example program uses the URLConnection class to post data to a web site. More for curiosity's sake than for practical use, you may like to know exactly what information the URLConnection sends to the server in addition to the data that you supply.

The URLConnection object first sends a request header to the server. When you post form data, the header must include

```
Content-Type: application/x-www-form-urlencoded
```

You must also specify the content length, for example,

```
Content-Length: 124
```

The end of the header is indicated by a blank line. Then, the data portion follows. The web server strips off the header and routes the data portion to the server-side script.

Note that the URLConnection object buffers all data that you send to the output stream since it must first determine the total content length.

 java.net.HttpURLConnection 1.0

- InputStream getErrorStream()
  returns a stream from which you can read web server error messages.

 java.net.URLEncoder 1.0

- static String encode(String s, String encoding) **1.4**
  returns the URL-encoded form of the string s, using the given character encoding scheme. (The recommended scheme is "UTF-8".) In URL encoding, the characters 'A' - 'Z', 'a'- 'z', '0'- '9', '-', '_', '.' and '*' are left unchanged. Space is encoded into '+', and all other characters are encoded into sequences of encoded bytes of the form "%XY", where 0xXY is the hexadecimal value of the byte.

 java.net.URLDecoder 1.2

- static string decode(String s, String encoding) **1.4**
  returns the decoding of the URL encoded string s under the given character encoding scheme.

Advanced Socket Programming

In the following sections, we cover advanced issues that arise in real-world programs. We first show you how to use timeouts and interrupts to deal with connection errors. We show how the "half-close" mechanism can simplify request protocol, and we finish with a section on Internet addresses.

Socket Timeouts

In real-life programs, you don't just want to read from a socket, because the read methods will block until data are available. If the host is unreachable, then your application waits for a long time and you are at the mercy of the underlying operating system to time out eventually.

Instead, you should decide what timeout value is reasonable for your particular application. Then, call the setSoTimeout method to set a timeout value (in milliseconds).

```
Socket s = new Socket(. . .);
s.setSoTimeout(10000); // time out after 10 seconds
```

If the timeout value has been set for a socket, then all subsequent read and write operations throw a SocketTimeoutException when the timeout has been reached before the operation has completed its work. You can catch that exception and react to the timeout.

```
try
{
   Scanner in = new Scanner(s.getInputStream());
   String line = in.nextLine();
   . . .
}
catch (InterruptedIOException exception)
{
   react to timeout
}
```

There is one additional timeout issue that you need to address: The constructor

```
Socket(String host, int port)
```

can block indefinitely until an initial connection to the host is established.

As of JDK 1.4, you can overcome this problem by first constructing an unconnected socket and then connecting it with a timeout:

```
Socket s = new Socket();
s.connect(new InetSocketAddress(host, port), timeout);
```

Interruptible Sockets

When you connect to a socket, the current thread blocks until the connection has been established or a timeout has elapsed. Similarly, when you read or write data through a socket, the current thread blocks until the operation is successful or has timed out.

In interactive applications, you would like to give users an option to simply cancel a socket connection that does not appear to produce results. However, if a thread blocks on an unresponsive socket, you cannot unblock it by calling `interrupt`.

To interrupt a socket operation, you use a `SocketChannel`, a feature of the `java.nio` package. Open the `SocketChannel` like this:

```
SocketChannel channel = SocketChannel.open(new InetSocketAddress(host, port));
```

A channel does not have associated streams. Instead, it has read and `write` methods that make use of `Buffer` objects. (See Volume 1, Chapter 12 for more information about NIO buffers.) These methods are declared in interfaces `ReadableByteChannel` and `WritableByteChannel`.

If you don't want to deal with buffers, you can use the `Scanner` class to read from a `SocketChannel` because `Scanner` has a constructor with a `ReadableByteChannel` parameter:

```
Scanner in = new Scanner(channel);
```

To turn a channel into an output stream, use the static `Channels.newOutputStream` method.

```
OutputStream outStream = Channels.newOutputStream(channel);
```

That's all you need to do. Whenever a thread is interrupted during an open, read, or write operation, the operation does not block but is terminated with an exception.

The program in Example 3–7 shows how a thread that reads from a server can be interrupted. The server sends a stream of random numbers to the client. However, if the Busy checkbox is checked, then the server pretends to be busy and doesn't send anything. In either case, you can click the Cancel button, and the connection is terminated (see Figure 3–11).

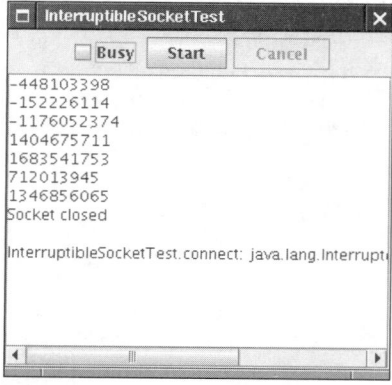

Figure 3–11: Interrupting a socket

Example 3–7: InterruptibleSocketTest.java

```java
1. import java.awt.*;
2. import java.awt.event.*;
3. import java.util.*;
4. import java.net.*;
5. import java.io.*;
6. import java.nio.channels.*;
7. import javax.swing.*;
```

```
8.
9.  /**
10.    This program shows how to interrupt a socket channel.
11.  */
12.  public class InterruptibleSocketTest
13.  {
14.     public static void main(String[] args)
15.     {
16.        JFrame frame = new InterruptibleSocketFrame();
17.        frame.setDefaultCloseOperation(JFrame.EXIT_ON_CLOSE);
18.        frame.setVisible(true);
19.     }
20.  }
21.
22.  class InterruptibleSocketFrame extends JFrame
23.  {
24.     public InterruptibleSocketFrame()
25.     {
26.        setSize(WIDTH, HEIGHT);
27.        setTitle("InterruptibleSocketTest");
28.
29.        JPanel northPanel = new JPanel();
30.        add(northPanel, BorderLayout.NORTH);
31.
32.        messages = new JTextArea();
33.        add(new JScrollPane(messages));
34.
35.        busyBox = new JCheckBox("Busy");
36.        northPanel.add(busyBox);
37.
38.        startButton = new JButton("Start");
39.        northPanel.add(startButton);
40.        startButton.addActionListener(new
41.           ActionListener()
42.           {
43.              public void actionPerformed(ActionEvent event)
44.              {
45.                 startButton.setEnabled(false);
46.                 cancelButton.setEnabled(true);
47.                 connectThread = new Thread(new
48.                    Runnable()
49.                    {
50.                       public void run()
51.                       {
52.                          connect();
53.                       }
54.                    });
55.                 connectThread.start();
56.              }
57.           });
58.
59.        cancelButton = new JButton("Cancel");
60.        cancelButton.setEnabled(false);
61.        northPanel.add(cancelButton);
62.        cancelButton.addActionListener(new
63.           ActionListener()
64.           {
```

```
65.        public void actionPerformed(ActionEvent event)
66.        {
67.           connectThread.interrupt();
68.           startButton.setEnabled(true);
69.           cancelButton.setEnabled(false);
70.        }
71.     });
72.     server = new TestServer();
73.     new Thread(server).start();
74.  }
75.
76.  /**
77.     Connects to the test server.
78.  */
79.  public void connect()
80.  {
81.     try
82.     {
83.        SocketChannel channel = SocketChannel.open(new InetSocketAddress("localhost", 8189));
84.        try
85.        {
86.           in = new Scanner(channel);
87.           while (true)
88.           {
89.              if (in.hasNextLine())
90.              {
91.                 String line = in.nextLine();
92.                 messages.append(line);
93.                 messages.append("\n");
94.              }
95.              else Thread.sleep(100);
96.           }
97.        }
98.        finally
99.        {
100.          channel.close();
101.          messages.append("Socket closed\n");
102.       }
103.    }
104.    catch (IOException e)
105.    {
106.       messages.append("\nInterruptibleSocketTest.connect: " + e);
107.    }
108.    catch (InterruptedException e)
109.    {
110.       messages.append("\nInterruptibleSocketTest.connect: " + e);
111.    }
112. }
113.
114. /**
115.    A multithreaded server that listens to port 8189 and sends random numbers to the client.
116. */
117. class TestServer implements Runnable
118. {
119.    public void run()
120.    {
121.       try
```

```
122.          {
123.              int i = 1;
124.              ServerSocket s = new ServerSocket(8189);
125.
126.              while (true)
127.              {
128.                  Socket incoming = s.accept();
129.                  Runnable r = new RandomNumberHandler(incoming);
130.                  Thread t = new Thread(r);
131.                  t.start();
132.              }
133.          }
134.          catch (IOException e)
135.          {
136.              messages.append("\nTestServer.run: " + e);
137.          }
138.      }
139.  }
140.
141.  /**
142.     This class handles the client input for one server socket connection.
143.  */
144.  class RandomNumberHandler implements Runnable
145.  {
146.     /**
147.        Constructs a handler.
148.        @param i the incoming socket
149.     */
150.     public RandomNumberHandler(Socket i)
151.     {
152.        incoming = i;
153.     }
154.
155.     public void run()
156.     {
157.        try
158.        {
159.           OutputStream outStream = incoming.getOutputStream();
160.           PrintWriter out = new PrintWriter(outStream, true /* autoFlush */);
161.           Random generator = new Random();
162.           while (true)
163.           {
164.              if (!busyBox.isSelected()) out.println(generator.nextInt());
165.              Thread.sleep(100);
166.           }
167.        }
168.        catch (IOException e)
169.        {
170.           messages.append("\nRandomNumberHandler.run: " + e);
171.        }
172.        catch (InterruptedException e)
173.        {
174.           messages.append("\nRandomNumberHandler.run: " + e);
175.        }
176.     }
177.
178.     private Socket incoming;
```

```
179.     }
180.
181.     private Scanner in;
182.     private PrintWriter out;
183.     private JButton startButton;
184.     private JButton cancelButton;
185.     private JCheckBox busyBox;
186.     private JTextArea messages;
187.     private TestServer server;
188.     private Thread connectThread;
189.
190.     public static final int WIDTH = 300;
191.     public static final int HEIGHT = 300;
192. }
```

Half-Close

When a client program sends a request to the server, the server needs to be able to determine when the end of the request occurs. For that reason, many Internet protocols (such as SMTP) are line oriented. Other protocols contain a header that specifies the size of the request data. Otherwise, indicating the end of the request data is harder than writing data to a file. With a file, you'd just close the file at the end of the data. However, if you close a socket, then you immediately disconnect from the server.

The *half-close* overcomes this problem. You can close the output stream of a socket, thereby indicating to the server the end of the request data, but keep the input stream open so that you can read the response.

The client side looks like this:

```
Socket socket = new Socket(host, port);
Scanner in = new Scanner(socket.getInputStream());
PrintWriter writer = new PrintWriter(socket.getOutputStream());
// send request data
writer.print(. . .);
writer.flush();
socket.shutdownOutput();
// now socket is half closed
// read response data
while (in.hasNextLine()) != null) { String line = in.nextLine(); . . . }
socket.close();
```

The server side simply reads input until the end of the input stream is reached.

Of course, this protocol is only useful for one-shot services such as HTTP where the client connects, issues a request, catches the response, and then disconnects.

Internet Addresses

Usually, you don't have to worry too much about Internet addresses—the numerical host addresses that consist of four bytes (or, with IPv6, 16 bytes) such as 132.163.4.102. However, you can use the InetAddress class if you need to convert between host names and Internet addresses.

As of JDK 1.4, the java.net package supports IPv6 Internet addresses, provided the host operating system does.

The static getByName method returns an InetAddress object of a host. For example,

```
InetAddress address = InetAddress.getByName("time-A.timefreq.bldrdoc.gov");
```

returns an InetAddress object that encapsulates the sequence of four bytes 132.163.4.104. You can access the bytes with the getAddress method.

```
byte[] addressBytes = address.getAddress();
```

Some host names with a lot of traffic correspond to multiple Internet addresses, to facilitate load balancing. For example, at the time of this writing, the host name java.sun.com corresponds to three different Internet addresses. One of them is picked at random when the host is accessed. You can get all hosts with the getAllByName method.

```
InetAddress[] addresses = InetAddress.getAllByName(host);
```

Finally, you sometimes need the address of the local host. If you simply ask for the address of localhost, you always get the address 127.0.0.1, which isn't very useful. Instead, use the static getLocalHost method to get the address of your local host.

```
InetAddress address = InetAddress.getLocalHost();
```

Example 3–8 is a simple program that prints the Internet address of your local host if you do not specify any command-line parameters, or all Internet addresses of another host if you specify the host name on the command line, such as

```
java InetAddressTest java.sun.com
```

Example 3–8: InetAddressTest.java

```
 1. import java.net.*;
 2.
 3. /**
 4.    This program demonstrates the InetAddress class.
 5.    Supply a host name as command-line argument, or run
 6.    without command-line arguments to see the address of the
 7.    local host.
 8. */
 9. public class InetAddressTest
10. {
11.    public static void main(String[] args)
12.    {
13.       try
14.       {
15.          if (args.length > 0)
16.          {
17.             String host = args[0];
18.             InetAddress[] addresses = InetAddress.getAllByName(host);
19.             for (InetAddress a : addresses)
20.                System.out.println(a);
21.          }
22.          else
23.          {
24.             InetAddress localHostAddress = InetAddress.getLocalHost();
25.             System.out.println(localHostAddress);
26.          }
27.       }
28.       catch (Exception e)
29.       {
30.          e.printStackTrace();
31.       }
32.    }
33. }
```

> **NOTE:** In this book, we cover only the TCP (Transmission Control Protocol) networking protocol. TCP establishes a reliable connection between two computers. The Java platform also supports the so-called UDP (User Datagram Protocol) protocol, which can be used to send packets (also called *datagrams*) with much less overhead than that for TCP. The drawback is that the packets can be delivered in random order or even dropped altogether. It is up to the recipient to put the packets in order and to request retransmission of missing packets. UDP is most suited for applications in which missing packets can be tolerated, for example, in audio or video streams, or for continuous measurements.

 java.net.Socket 1.0

- `Socket()`
  creates a socket that has not yet been connected.
- `void connect(SocketAddress address)` 1.4
  connects this socket to the given address.
- `void connect(SocketAddress address, int timeoutInMilliseconds)` 1.4
  connects this socket to the given address or returns if the time interval expired.
- `boolean isConnected()` 1.4
  returns true if the socket is connected.
- `boolean isClosed()` 1.4
  returns true if the socket is closed.
- `void setSoTimeout(int timeoutInMilliseconds)` 1.1
  sets the blocking time for read requests on this socket. If the timeout is reached, then an `InterruptedIOException` is raised.
- `void shutdownOutput()` 1.3
  sets the output stream to "end of stream."
- `void shutdownInput()` 1.3
  sets the input stream to "end of stream."
- `boolean isOutputShutdown()` 1.4
  returns true if output has been shut down.
- `boolean isInputShutdown()` 1.4
  returns true if input has been shut down.

java.net.InetAddress 1.0

- `static InetAddress getByName(String host)`
- `static InetAddress[] getAllByName(String host)`
  construct an `InetAddress`, or an array of all Internet addresses, for the given host name.
- `static InetAddress getLocalHost()`
  constructs an `InetAddress` for the local host.
- `byte[] getAddress()`
  returns an array of bytes that contains the numerical address.
- `String getHostAddress()`
  returns a string with decimal numbers, separated by periods, for example, `"132.163.4.102"`.
- `String getHostName()`
  returns the host name.

 java.net.InetSocketAddress 1.4

- InetSocketAddress(String hostname, int port)
  constructs an address object with the given host and port, resolving the host name during construction. If the host name cannot be resolved, then the address object's unresolved property is set to true.
- boolean isUnresolved()
  returns true if this address object could not be resolved.

java.nio.channels.SocketChannel 1.4

- static SocketChannel open(SocketAddress address)
  opens a socket channel and connects it to a remote address.

java.nio.channels.Channels 1.4

- static InputStream newInputStream(ReadableByteChannel channel)
  constructs an input stream that reads from the given channel.
- static OutputStream newOutputStream(WritableByteChannel channel)
  constructs an output stream that writes to the given channel.

Chapter 4

Database Programming

▼ The Design of JDBC
▼ The Structured Query Language
▼ JDBC Installation
▼ Basic JDBC Programming Concepts
▼ Query Execution
▼ Scrollable and Updatable Result Sets
▼ Metadata
▼ Row Sets
▼ Transactions
▼ Advanced Connection Management
▼ Introduction to LDAP

In the summer of 1996, Sun released the first version of the Java Database Connectivity (JDBC) API. This API lets programmers connect to a database and then query or update it, using the Structured Query Language or SQL. (SQL, usually pronounced like "sequel," is an industry standard for relational database access.)

Java and JDBC have an essential advantage over other database programming environments: Programs developed with Java and JDBC are platform independent and vendor independent.

The same database program written in Java can run on an NT box, a Solaris server, or a database appliance powered by the Java platform. You can move your data from one database to another, for example, from Microsoft SQL Server to Oracle, or even to a tiny database embedded in a device, and the same program can still read your data. This capability is in sharp contrast to traditional database programming. Too often, developers write database applications in a proprietary database language, using a database management system that is available only from a single vendor.

JDBC has been updated several times. As part of the release of JDK 1.2 in 1998, a second version of JDBC was issued. As this book is published, JDBC 3 is the most current version, with JDBC 4 under development. JDBC 3 is included with JDK 1.4 and 5.0.

We must caution you that the JDK offers no tools for "visual" database program development. For form designers, query builders, and report generators, you need to turn to third-party tools.

In this chapter:

- We explain some of the ideas behind JDBC—the Java Database Connectivity API.
- We introduce you to (or refresh your memory of) SQL, the industry-standard Structured Query Language for relational databases.
- We provide enough details and examples to let you start using JDBC for common programming situations.
- We finish with a brief introduction to hierarchical databases, the LDAP protocol, and JNDI (the Java Naming and Directory Interface).

 NOTE: Over the years, many technologies were invented to make database access more efficient and fail-safe. Standard relational databases support indexes, triggers, stored procedures, and transaction management. JDBC supports all these features, but we do not discuss them in detail in this chapter. One can fill an entire book with a discussion of advanced database programming for the Java platform, and many such books have been written. For further study, we recommend *JDBC API Tutorial and Reference* by Maydene Fisher, Jon Ellis, and Jonathan Bruce [Addison-Wesley 2003].

The Design of JDBC

From the start, the developers of the Java technology at Sun were aware of the potential that Java showed for working with databases. Starting in 1995, they began working on extending the standard Java library to deal with SQL access to databases. What they first hoped to do was to extend Java so that it could talk to any random database, using only "pure" Java. It didn't take them long to realize that this is an impossible task: There are simply too many databases out there, using too many protocols. Moreover, while database vendors were all in favor of Sun providing a standard network protocol for database access, they were only in favor of it if Sun decided to use *their* network protocol.

What all the database vendors and tool vendors *did* agree on was that it would be useful if Sun provided a pure Java API for SQL access along with a driver manager to allow third-party drivers to connect to specific databases. Database vendors could provide their own drivers to plug in to the driver manager. There would then be a simple mechanism for registering third-party drivers with the driver manager—the point being that all the drivers needed to do was follow the requirements laid out in the driver manager API.

As a result, two interfaces were created. Application programmers use the JDBC API, and database vendors and tool providers use the JDBC Driver API.

This organization follows the very successful model of Microsoft's ODBC, which provided a C programming language interface for database access. Both JDBC and ODBC are based on the same idea: Programs written according to the API talk to the driver manager, which, in turn, uses the drivers that are plugged in to it to talk to the actual database.

All this means the JDBC API is all that most programmers will ever have to deal with—see Figure 4–1.

 NOTE: A list of currently available JDBC drivers can be found at the web site
http://industry.java.sun.com/products/jdbc/drivers.

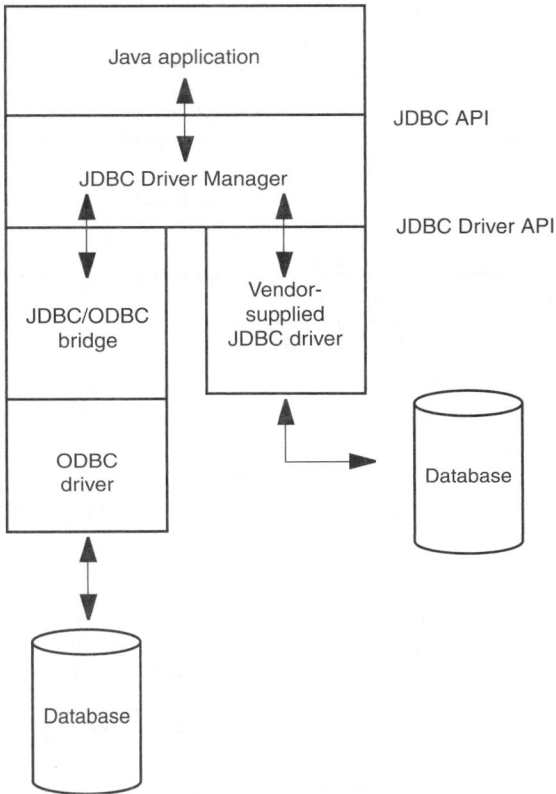

Figure 4–1: JDBC-to-database communication path

JDBC Driver Types

JDBC drivers are classified into the following *types*:

- A *type 1 driver* translates JDBC to ODBC and relies on an ODBC driver to communicate with the database. Sun includes one such driver, the *JDBC/ODBC bridge,* with the JDK. However, the bridge requires deployment and proper configuration of an ODBC driver. When JDBC was first released, the bridge was handy for testing, but it was never intended for production use. At this point, plenty of better drivers are available, and we advise against using the JDBC/ODBC bridge.

- A *type 2 driver* is written partly in Java and partly in native code; it communicates with the client API of a database. When you use such a driver, you must install some platform-specific code in addition to a Java library.

- A *type 3 driver* is a pure Java client library that uses a database-independent protocol to communicate database requests to a server component, which then translates the requests into a database-specific protocol. This can simplify deployment since the database-dependent code is located only on the server.

- A *type 4 driver* is a pure Java library that translates JDBC requests directly to a database-specific protocol.

Most database vendors supply either a type 3 or type 4 driver with their database. Furthermore, a number of third-party companies specialize in producing drivers with better

standards conformance, support for more platforms, better performance, or, in some cases, simply better reliability than the drivers that are provided by the database vendors.

In summary, the ultimate goal of JDBC is to make possible the following:

- Programmers can write applications in the Java programming language to access any database, using standard SQL statements—or even specialized extensions of SQL— while still following Java language conventions.

- Database vendors and database tool vendors can supply the low-level drivers. Thus, they can optimize their drivers for their specific products.

 NOTE: If you are curious as to why Sun just didn't adopt the ODBC model, their response, as given at the JavaOne conference in May 1996, was this:

- ODBC is hard to learn.

- ODBC has a few commands with lots of complex options. The preferred style in the Java programming language is to have simple and intuitive methods, but to have lots of them.

- ODBC relies on the use of void* pointers and other C features that are not natural in the Java programming language.

- An ODBC-based solution is inherently less safe and harder to deploy than a pure Java solution.

Typical Uses of JDBC

The traditional client/server model has a rich GUI on the client and a database on the server (see Figure 4–2). In this model, a JDBC driver is deployed on the client.

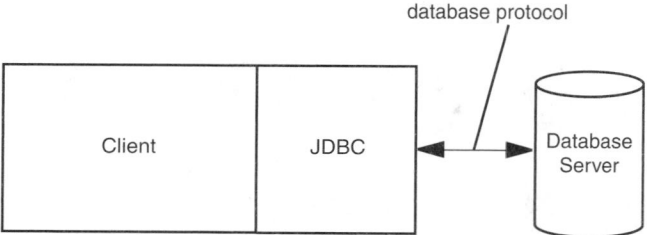

Figure 4–2: A traditional client/server application

However, the world is moving away from client/server and toward a "three-tier model" or even more advanced "*n*-tier models." In the three-tier model, the client does not make database calls. Instead, it calls on a middleware layer on the server that in turn makes the database queries. The three-tier model has a couple of advantages. It separates *visual presentation* (on the client) from the *business logic* (in the middle tier) and the raw data (in the database). Therefore, it becomes possible to access the same data and the same business rules from multiple clients, such as a Java application or applet or a web form.

Communication between the client and middle tier can occur through HTTP (when you use a web browser as the client), RMI (when you use an application or applet— see Chapter 5), or another mechanism. JDBC manages the communication between the middle tier and the back-end database. Figure 4–3 shows the basic architecture. There are, of course, many variations of this model. In particular, the Java 2 Enterprise Edition defines a structure for *application servers* that manage code modules called *Enterprise JavaBeans*, and provides valuable services such as load balancing, request

caching, security, and simple database access. In that architecture, JDBC still plays an important role for issuing complex database queries. (For more information on the Enterprise Edition, see http://java.sun.com/j2ee.)

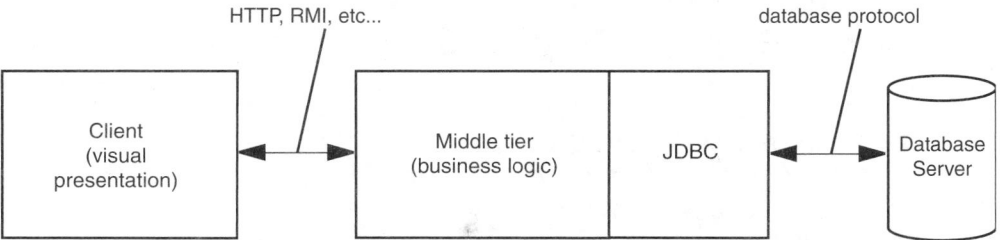

Figure 4–3: A three-tier application

 NOTE: You can use JDBC in applets, but you probably don't want to. By default, the security manager permits a database connection only to the server from which the applet is downloaded. That means the web server and the database server must be the same machine, which is not a typical setup. You would need to sign the applet to overcome this problem. Moreover, the applet would need to include the JDBC driver.

The Structured Query Language

JDBC lets you communicate with databases using SQL, which is the command language for essentially all modern relational databases. Desktop databases usually have a graphical user interface that lets users manipulate the data directly, but server-based databases are accessed purely through SQL. Most desktop databases have a SQL interface as well, but it often does not support the full SQL standard.

The JDBC package can be thought of as nothing more than an application programming interface (API) for communicating SQL statements to databases. We briefly introduce SQL in this section. If you have never seen SQL before, you may not find this material sufficient. If so, you should turn to one of the many books on the topic. We recommend *Client/Server Databases* by James Martin and Joe Leben [Prentice-Hall 1998] or the opinionated classic, *A Guide to the SQL Standard* by C. J. Date and Hugh Darwen [Addison-Wesley 1997].

You can think of a database as a bunch of named tables with rows and columns. Each column has a *column name*. The rows contain the actual data. These are sometimes called *records*.

As the example database for this book, we use a set of tables that describe a collection of classic computer science books.

Table 4–1: The **Authors** Table

Author_ID	Name	Fname
ALEX	Alexander	Christopher
BROO	Brooks	Frederick P.
...	...	...

Table 4–2: The Books Table

Title	ISBN	Publisher_ID	Price
A Guide to the SQL Standard	0-201-96426-0	0201	47.95
A Pattern Language: Towns, Buildings, Construction	0-19-501919-9	019	65.00
…	…	…	…

Table 4–3: The BooksAuthors Table

ISBN	Author_ID	Seq_No
0-201-96426-0	DATE	1
0-201-96426-0	DARW	2
0-19-501919-9	ALEX	1
…	…	…

Table 4–4: The Publishers Table

Publisher_ID	Name	URL
0201	Addison-Wesley	www.aw-bc.com
0407	John Wiley & Sons	www.wiley.com
…	…	…

Figure 4–4 shows a view of the Books table. Figure 4–5 shows the result of *joining* this table with the Publishers table. Both the Books and the Publishers table contain an identifier for the publisher. When we join both tables on the publisher code, we obtain a *query result* made up of values from the joined tables. Each row in the result contains the information about a book, together with the publisher name and web page URL. Note that the publisher names and URLs are duplicated across several rows because we have several rows with the same publisher.

The benefit of joining tables is to avoid unnecessary duplication of data in the database tables. For example, a naive database design might have had columns for the publisher name and URL right in the Books table. But then the database itself, and not just the query result, would have many duplicates of these entries. If a publisher's web address changed, *all* entries would need to be updated. Clearly, this is somewhat error prone. In the relational model, we distribute data into multiple tables such that no information is ever unnecessarily duplicated. For example, each publisher URL is contained only once in the publisher table. If the information needs to be combined, then the tables are joined.

In the figures, you can see a graphical tool to inspect and link the tables. Many vendors have tools to express queries in a simple form by connecting column names and filling information into forms. Such tools are often called *query by example* (QBE) tools. In contrast, a query that uses SQL is written out in text, with SQL syntax. For example,

```
SELECT Books.Title, Books.Publisher_Id, Books.Price, Publishers.Name, Publishers.URL
FROM Books, Publishers
WHERE Books.Publisher_Id = Publishers.Publisher_Id
```

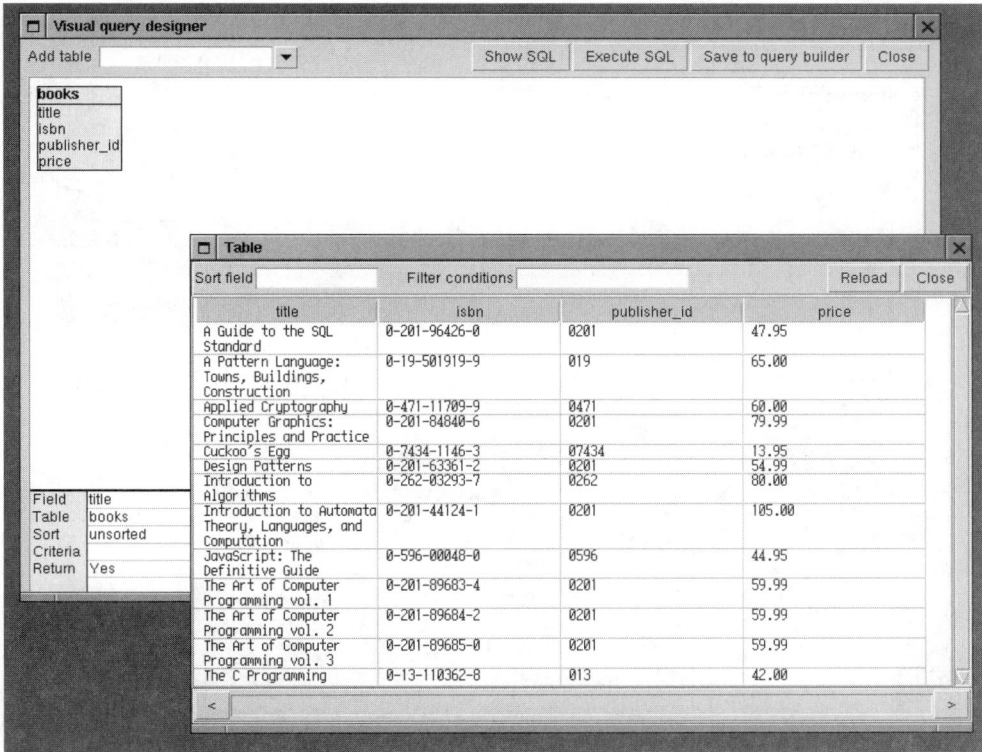

Figure 4–4: Sample table containing books

In the remainder of this section, you will learn how to write such queries. If you are already familiar with SQL, just skip this section.

By convention, SQL keywords are written in capital letters, although this is not necessary.

The SELECT statement is quite flexible. You can simply select all rows in the Books table with the following query:

```
SELECT * FROM Books
```

The FROM clause is required in every SQL SELECT statement. The FROM clause tells the database which tables to examine to find the data.

You can choose the columns that you want.

```
SELECT ISBN, Price, Title
FROM Books
```

You can restrict the rows in the answer with the WHERE clause.

```
SELECT ISBN, Price, Title
FROM Books
WHERE Price <= 29.95
```

Be careful with the "equals" comparison. SQL uses = and <> rather than == or != as in the Java programming language, for equality testing.

Figure 4–5: Two tables joined together

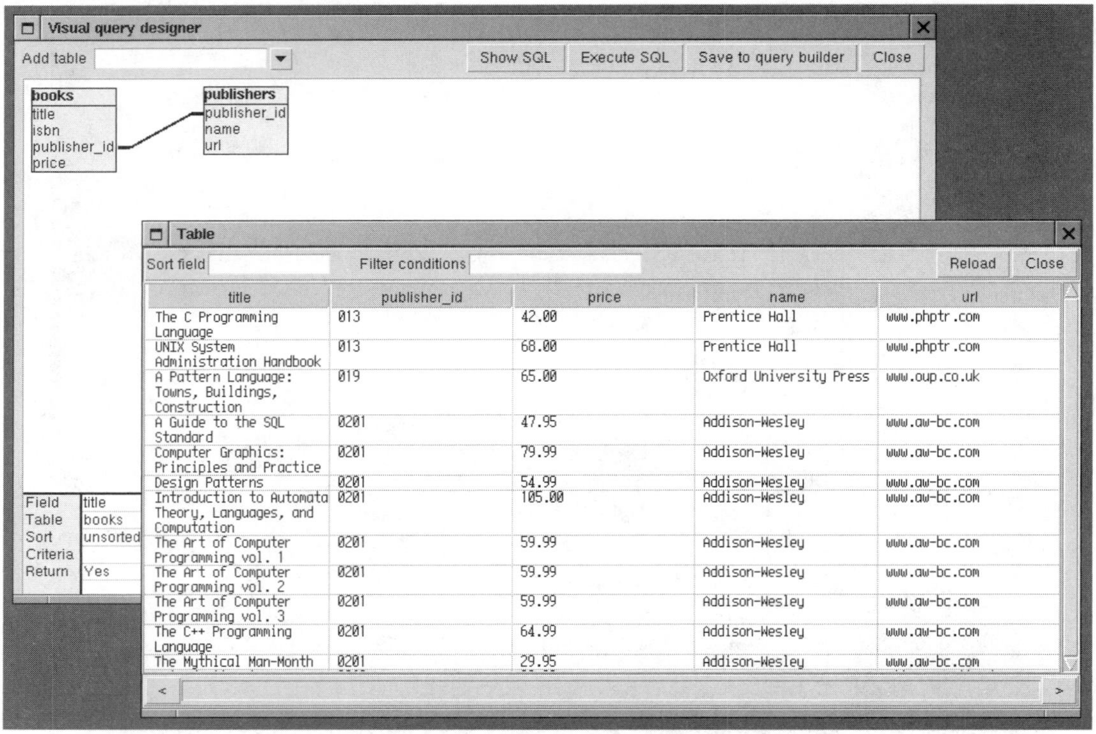

NOTE: Some database vendors support the use of != for inequality testing. This is not standard SQL, so we recommend against such use.

The WHERE clause can also use pattern matching by means of the LIKE operator. The wildcard characters are not the usual * and ?, however. Use a % for zero or more characters and an underscore for a single character. For example,

```
SELECT ISBN, Price, Title
FROM Books
WHERE Title NOT LIKE '%n_x%'
```

excludes books with titles that contain words such as UNIX or Linux.

Note that strings are enclosed in single quotes, not double quotes. A single quote inside a string is denoted as a pair of single quotes. For example,

```
SELECT Title
FROM Books
WHERE Title LIKE '%''%'
```

reports all titles that contain a single quote.

You can select data from multiple tables.

```
SELECT * FROM Books, Publishers
```

Without a WHERE clause, this query is not very interesting. It lists *all combinations* of rows from both tables. In our case, where Books has 20 rows and Publishers has 8 rows, the result is a set of rows with 20 × 8 entries and lots of duplications. We really want to constrain the query to say that we are only interested in *matching* books with their publishers.

```
SELECT * FROM Books, Publishers
WHERE Books.Publisher_Id = Publishers.Publisher_Id
```

This query result has 20 rows, one for each book, because each book has one publisher in the Publisher table.

Whenever you have multiple tables in a query, the same column name can occur in two different places. That happened in our example. There is a column called Publisher_Id in both the Books and the Publishers table. When an ambiguity would otherwise result, you must prefix each column name with the name of the table to which it belongs, such as Books.Publisher_Id.

You can use SQL to change the data inside a database as well by using so-called *action queries* (i.e., queries that move or change data). For example, suppose you want to reduce by $5.00 the current price of all books that have "C++" in their title.

```
UPDATE Books
SET Price = Price - 5.00
WHERE Title LIKE '%C++%'
```

Probably the most important action besides UPDATE is DELETE, which allows the query to delete those records that satisfy the criteria of the WHERE clause.

Moreover, SQL comes with built-in functions for taking averages, finding maximums and minimums in a column, and a lot more. A good source for this information is http://sqlzoo.net. (That site also contains a nifty interactive SQL tutorial.)

Typically, to insert values into a table, you use the INSERT statement:

```
INSERT INTO Books
VALUES ('A Guide to the SQL Standard', '0-201-96426-0', '0201', 47.95)
```

You need a separate INSERT statement for every row being inserted in the table.

Of course, before you can query, modify, and insert data, you must have a place to store data. Use the CREATE TABLE statement to make a new table. You specify the name and data type for each column. For example,

```
CREATE TABLE Books
(
   Title CHAR(60),
   ISBN CHAR(13),
   Publisher_Id CHAR(6),
   Price DECIMAL(10,2)
)
```

Table 4–5 shows the most common SQL data types.

Table 4–5: SQL Data Types

Data Types	Description
INTEGER or INT	Typically, a 32-bit integer
SMALLINT	Typically, a 16-bit integer
NUMERIC(m,n), DECIMAL(m,n) or DEC(m,n)	Fixed-point decimal number with m total digits and n digits after the decimal point

Table 4–5: SQL Data Types (continued)

Data Types	Description
FLOAT(n)	A floating-point number with n binary digits of precision
REAL	Typically, a 32-bit floating-point number
DOUBLE	Typically, a 64-bit floating-point number
CHARACTER(n) or CHAR(n)	Fixed-length string of length n
VARCHAR(n)	Variable-length strings of maximum length n
BOOLEAN	A boolean value
DATE	Calendar date, implementation dependent
TIME	Time of day, implementation dependent
TIMESTAMP	Date and time of day, implementation dependent
BLOB	A binary large object
CLOB	A character large object

In this book, we do not discuss the additional clauses, such as keys and constraints, that you can use with the CREATE TABLE command.

JDBC Installation

First, you need a database program that is compatible with JDBC. There are many excellent choices, such as IBM DB2, Microsoft SQL Server, MySQL, Oracle, and PostgreSQL.

You must also create a database for your experimental use. We assume you name it COREJAVA. Create a new database, or have your database administrator create one with the appropriate permissions. You need to be able to create, update, and drop tables in the database.

If you have never installed a client/server database before, you may find that setting up the database is somewhat complex and that diagnosing the cause for failure can be difficult. It may be best to seek expert help if your setup is not working correctly.

If this is your first experience with databases, we recommend that you install a pure Java database such as McKoi (http://mckoi.com/database), HSQLDB (http://hsqldb.sourceforge.net), or Derby (http://incubator.apache.org/derby). These databases are less powerful but are simple to set up.

Essentially all database vendors already have JDBC drivers. You need to locate the vendor's instructions to load the driver into your program and to connect to the database. In the next section, we explain the setups for two typical databases that are available on a variety of platforms:

- McKoi
- PostgreSQL

Instructions for other databases are similar, although, of course, the details will vary.

We recommend against using the JDBC/ODBC bridge driver that comes with the Java 2 SDK. We recommend even more strongly against using that driver with a desktop database such as Microsoft Access. Not only are the installation and configuration somewhat cumbersome, but both the bridge driver and desktop databases have restrictions that can easily lead to confusion. Ultimately, one learns very little about real databases from this setup.

Basic JDBC Programming Concepts

Programming with the JDBC classes is, by design, not very different from programming with the usual Java platform classes: You build objects from the JDBC core classes, extending them by inheritance if need be. This section takes you through the details.

 NOTE: The classes that you use for JDBC programming are contained in the `java.sql` and `javax.sql` packages.

Database URLs

When connecting to a database, you must specify the data source and you may need to specify additional parameters. For example, network protocol drivers may need a port, and ODBC drivers may need various attributes.

As you might expect, JDBC uses a syntax similar to that of ordinary URLs to describe data sources. Here are examples of the syntax:

```
jdbc:mckoi://localhost/
jdbc:postgresql:COREJAVA
```

These JDBC URLs specify a local McKoi database and a PostgreSQL database named COREJAVA. The general syntax is

```
jdbc:subprotocol:other stuff
```

where a subprotocol selects the specific driver for connecting to the database.

The format for the *other stuff* parameter depends on the subprotocol used. Look up your vendor's documentation for the specific format.

Making the Connection

Find out the names of the JDBC driver classes used by your vendor. Typical driver names are

```
org.postgresql.Driver
com.mckoi.JDBCDriver
```

Next, find the library in which the driver is located, such as `pg74jdbc3.jar` or `mkjdbc.jar`. Use one of the following three mechanisms:

- Launch your database programs with the -classpath command-line argument.
- Modify the CLASSPATH environment variable.
- Copy the database library into the *jre*/lib/ext directory.

The DriverManager class selects database drivers and creates a new database connection. However, before the driver manager can activate a driver, the driver must be registered.

The jdbc.drivers property contains a list of class names for the drivers that the driver manager will register at startup. Two methods can set that property.

You can specify the property with a command-line argument, such as

```
java -Djdbc.drivers=org.postgresql.Driver MyProg
```

Or your application can set the system property with a call such as

```
System.setProperty("jdbc.drivers", "org.postgresql.Driver");
```

You can also supply multiple drivers; separate them with colons, such as

```
org.postgresql.Driver:com.mckoi.JDBCDriver
```

 NOTE: Alternatively, you can manually register a driver by loading its class. For example,

```
Class.forName("org.postgresql.Driver"); // force registration of driver
```

You may need to use this approach if the driver manager cannot load the driver. This can happen because of limitations in a particular driver or because your program executes inside a container such as a servlet engine.

After registering drivers, you open a database connection with code that is similar to the following example:

```
String url = "jdbc:postgresql:COREJAVA";
String username = "dbuser";
String password = "secret";
Connection conn = DriverManager.getConnection(url, username, password);
```

The driver manager iterates through the available drivers currently registered with it to find a driver that can use the subprotocol specified in the database URL.

For our example programs, we find it convenient to use a properties file to specify the URL, user name, and password in addition to the database driver. A typical properties file has the following contents:

```
jdbc.drivers=org.postgresql.Driver
jdbc.url=jdbc:postgresql:COREJAVA
jdbc.username=dbuser
jdbc.password=secret
```

Here is the code for reading a properties file and opening the database connection.

```
Properties props = new Properties();
FileInputStream in = new FileInputStream("database.properties");
props.load(in);
in.close();
String drivers = props.getProperty("jdbc.drivers");
if (drivers != null) System.setProperty("jdbc.drivers", drivers);
String url = props.getProperty("jdbc.url");
String username = props.getProperty("jdbc.username");
String password = props.getProperty("jdbc.password");
return DriverManager.getConnection(url, username, password);
```

The getConnection method returns a Connection object. In the following sections, you will see how to use the Connection object to execute SQL statements.

 TIP: A good way to debug JDBC-related problems is to enable JDBC tracing. Call the Driver-Manager.setLogWriter method to send trace messages to a PrintWriter. The trace output contains a detailed listing of the JDBC activity.

Testing Your Database Installation

Setting up JDBC for the first time can be a bit tricky. You need several pieces of vendor-specific information, and the slightest configuration error can lead to very bewildering error messages. You should first test your database setup without JDBC. Follow these instructions.

Step 1. Start the database. With McKoi, run

```
java -jar mckoidb.jar
```

from the installation directory. With PostgreSQL, run

```
postmaster -i -D /usr/share/pgsql/data
```

Testing Your Database Installation (continued)

Step 2. Set up a user and a database. With McKoi, call

```
java -jar mckoidb.jar -create dbuser secret
```

For PostgreSQL, issue the commands

```
createuser -d -U dbuser
createdb -U dbuser COREJAVA
```

Step 3. Start the SQL interpreter for your database. With McKoi, call

```
java -classpath mckoidb.jar com.mckoi.tools.JDBCQueryTool
```

With PostgreSQL, call

```
psql COREJAVA
```

Step 4. Enter the following SQL commands:

```
CREATE TABLE Greetings (Message CHAR(20))
INSERT INTO Greetings VALUES ('Hello, World!')
SELECT * FROM Greetings
```

At this point, you should see a display of the "Hello, World!" entry.

Step 5. Clean up:

```
DROP TABLE Greetings
```

Once you know that your database installation is working and that you can log on to the database, you need to gather five pieces of information:

- The database user name and password
- The name of the database to use (such as COREJAVA)
- The JDBC URL format
- The JDBC driver name
- The location of the library files with the driver code

The first two depend on your database setup. The other three are supplied in the JDBC-specific documentation from your database vendor.

For McKoi, typical values are

- Database user name = dbuser, password = secret
- Database name = (none)
- JDBC URL format = jdbc:mckoi://localhost/
- JDBC driver = com.mckoi.JDBCDriver
- Library file = mkjdbc.jar

For PostgreSQL, you may have

- Database user name = dbuser, password = (none)
- Database name = COREJAVA
- JDBC URL format = jdbc:postgresql:COREJAVA
- JDBC driver = org.postgresql.Driver
- Library file = pg74jdbc3.jar

Example 4–1 is a small test program that you can use to test your JDBC setup. Prepare the database.properties file with the information that you collected. Then start the test program with the driver library on the class path, such as

```
java -classpath .:driverPath TestDB
```

(Remember to use a semicolon instead of a colon as the path separator on Windows.)

This program executes the same SQL instructions as the manual test. If you get an SQL error message, you need to keep working on your setup. It is extremely common to make one or more small errors with capitalization, path names, the JDBC URL format, or the database configuration. Once the test program displays "Hello, World!", everything is fine and you can move on to the next section.

Example 4–1: TestDB.java

```
1.  import java.sql.*;
2.  import java.io.*;
3.  import java.util.*;
4.
5.  /**
6.     This program tests that the database and the JDBC
7.     driver are correctly configured.
8.  */
9.  class TestDB
10. {
11.    public static void main (String args[])
12.    {
13.       try
14.       {
15.          runTest();
16.       }
17.       catch (SQLException ex)
18.       {
19.          while (ex != null)
20.          {
21.             ex.printStackTrace();
22.             ex = ex.getNextException();
23.          }
24.       }
25.       catch (IOException ex)
26.       {
27.          ex.printStackTrace();
28.       }
29.    }
30.
31.    /**
32.       Runs a test by creating a table, adding a value, showing the table contents, and
33.       removing the table.
34.    */
35.    public static void runTest()
36.       throws SQLException, IOException
37.    {
38.       Connection conn = getConnection();
39.       try
40.       {
41.          Statement stat = conn.createStatement();
42.
43.          stat.execute("CREATE TABLE Greetings (Message CHAR(20))");
44.          stat.execute("INSERT INTO Greetings VALUES ('Hello, World!')");
45.
46.          ResultSet result = stat.executeQuery("SELECT * FROM Greetings");
47.          result.next();
48.          System.out.println(result.getString(1));
49.          stat.execute("DROP TABLE Greetings");
50.       }
51.       finally
52.       {
53.          conn.close();
54.       }
55.    }
```

```
56.
57.    /**
58.       Gets a connection from the properties specified
59.       in the file database.properties
60.       @return the database connection
61.    */
62.    public static Connection getConnection()
63.       throws SQLException, IOException
64.    {
65.       Properties props = new Properties();
66.       FileInputStream in = new FileInputStream("database.properties");
67.       props.load(in);
68.       in.close();
69.
70.       String drivers = props.getProperty("jdbc.drivers");
71.       if (drivers != null)
72.          System.setProperty("jdbc.drivers", drivers);
73.       String url = props.getProperty("jdbc.url");
74.       String username = props.getProperty("jdbc.username");
75.       String password = props.getProperty("jdbc.password");
76.
77.       return DriverManager.getConnection(url, username, password);
78.    }
79. }
```

Executing SQL Commands

To execute a SQL command, you first create a Statement object. To create statement objects, use the Connection object that you obtained from the call to DriverManager.getConnection.

```
Statement stat = conn.createStatement();
```

Next, place the statement that you want to execute into a string, for example,

```
String command = "UPDATE Books"
   + " SET Price = Price - 5.00"
   + " WHERE Title NOT LIKE '%Introduction%'";
```

Then call the executeUpdate method of the Statement class:

```
stat.executeUpdate(command);
```

The executeUpdate method returns a count of the rows that were affected by the SQL command. For example, the call to executeUpdate in the preceding example returns the number of book records whose price was lowered by $5.00.

The executeUpdate method can execute actions such as INSERT, UPDATE, and DELETE as well as data definition commands such as CREATE TABLE and DROP TABLE. However, you need to use the executeQuery method to execute SELECT queries. There is also a catch-all execute statement to execute arbitrary SQL statements. It's commonly used only for queries that a user supplies interactively.

When you execute a query, you are interested in the result. The executeQuery object returns an object of type ResultSet that you use to walk through the result one row at a time.

```
ResultSet rs = stat.executeQuery("SELECT * FROM Books")
```

The basic loop for analyzing a result set looks like this:

```
while (rs.next())
{
   look at a row of the result set
}
```

 CAUTION: The iteration protocol of the ResultSet class is subtly different from the protocol of the Iterator interface that we discussed in Chapter 2. Here, the iterator is initialized to a position *before* the first row. You must call the next method once to move the iterator to the first row.

 NOTE: The order of the rows in a result set is completely arbitrary. Unless you specifically ordered the result with an ORDER BY clause, you should not attach any significance to the row order.

When inspecting an individual row, you will want to know the contents of the fields. A large number of accessor methods give you this information.

```
String isbn = rs.getString(1);
double price = rs.getDouble("Price");
```

There are accessors for various *types*, such as getString and getDouble. Each accessor has two forms, one that takes a numeric argument and one that takes a string argument. When you supply a numeric argument, you refer to the column with that number. For example, rs.get-String(1) returns the value of the first column in the current row.

 CAUTION: Unlike array indexes, database column numbers start at 1.

When you supply a string argument, you refer to the column in the result set with that name. For example, rs.getDouble("Price") returns the value of the column with name Price. Using the numeric argument is a bit more efficient, but the string arguments make the code easier to read and maintain.

Each get method makes reasonable type conversions when the type of the method doesn't match the type of the column. For example, the call rs.getString("Price") converts the floating-point value of the Price column to a string.

 NOTE: SQL data types and Java data types are not exactly the same. See Table 4–6 for a listing of the basic SQL data types and their equivalents in the Java programming language.

Table 4–6: SQL Data Types and Their Corresponding Java Types

SQL Data Type	Java Data Type
INTEGER or INT	int
SMALLINT	short
NUMERIC(m,n), DECIMAL(m,n) or DEC(m,n)	java.math.BigDecimal
FLOAT(n)	double
REAL	float
DOUBLE	double
CHARACTER(n) or CHAR(n)	String
VARCHAR(n)	String
BOOLEAN	boolean
DATE	java.sql.Date

Table 4–6: SQL Data Types and Their Corresponding Java Types (continued)

SQL Data Type	Java Data Type
TIME	java.sql.Time
TIMESTAMP	java.sql.Timestamp
BLOB	java.sql.Blob
CLOB	java.sql.Clob
ARRAY	java.sql.Array

Advanced SQL Types

In addition to numbers, strings, and dates, many databases can store *large objects* such as images or other data. In SQL, binary large objects are called BLOBs, and character large objects are called CLOBs. The getBlob and getClob methods return objects of type java.sql.Blob and java.sql.Clob. These classes have methods to fetch the bytes or characters in the large objects.

A SQL ARRAY is a sequence of values. For example, in a Student table, you can have a Scores column that is an ARRAY OF INTEGER. The getArray method returns an object of type java.sql.Array (which is different from the java.lang.reflect.Array class that we discussed in Volume 1). The java.sql.Array interface has methods to fetch the array values.

When you get a BLOB or an array from a database, the actual contents are fetched from the database only when you request individual values. This is a useful performance enhancement, since the data can be quite voluminous.

Some databases can store user-defined structured types. JDBC supports a mechanism for automatically mapping structured SQL types to Java objects. We do not discuss BLOBs, arrays, and user-defined types any further. You can find more information on these topics in the book *JDBC(TM) API Tutorial and Reference: Universal Data Access for the Java 2 Platform* (2nd Edition) by Seth White, Maydene Fisher, Rick Cattell, Graham Hamilton, and Mark Hapner [Addison-Wesley 1999].

 java.sql.DriverManager 1.1

- static Connection getConnection(String url, String user, String password)
  establishes a connection to the given database and returns a Connection object.

 java.sql.Connection 1.1

- Statement createStatement()
  creates a Statement object that can be used to execute SQL queries and updates without parameters.

- void close()
  immediately closes the current connection and the JDBC resources that it created.

 java.sql.Statement 1.1

- ResultSet executeQuery(String sqlQuery)
  executes the SQL statement given in the string and returns a ResultSet object to view the query result.

- int executeUpdate(String sqlStatement)
  executes the SQL INSERT, UPDATE, or DELETE statement specified by the string. Also executes Data Definition Language (DDL) statements such as CREATE TABLE. Returns the number of records affected, or −1 for a statement without an update count.

- boolean execute(String sqlStatement)
  executes the SQL statement specified by the string. Returns true if the statement returns a result set, false otherwise. Use the getResultSet or getUpdateCount method to obtain the statement outcome.

- int getUpdateCount()
  returns the number of records affected by the preceding update statement, or −1 if the preceding statement was a statement without an update count. Call this method only once per executed statement.

- ResultSet getResultSet()
  returns the result set of the preceding query statement, or null if the preceding statement did not have a result set. Call this method only once per executed statement.

- void close()
  closes this statement object and its associated result set.

java.sql.ResultSet 1.1

- boolean next()
  makes the current row in the result set move forward by one. Returns false after the last row. Note that you must call this method to advance to the first row.

- *Xxx* get*Xxx*(int columnNumber)
- *Xxx* get*Xxx*(String columnName)
  (*Xxx* is a type such as int, double, String, Date, etc.)
  return the value of the column with the given column number or name, converted to the specified type. Not all type conversions are legal. See documentation for details.

- int findColumn(String columnName)
  gives the column index associated with a column name.

- void close()
  immediately closes the current result set.

java.sql.SQLException 1.1

- String getSQLState()
  gets the "SQL state," a five-digit error code associated with the error.

- int getErrorCode()
  gets the vendor-specific exception code.

- SQLException getNextException()
  gets the exception chained to this one. It may contain more information about the error.

Managing Connections, Statements, and Result Sets

Every Connection object can create one or more Statement objects. You can use the same Statement object for multiple, unrelated commands and queries. However, a statement has *at most one* open result set. If you issue multiple queries whose results you analyze concurrently, then you need multiple Statement objects.

Be forewarned, though, that at least one commonly used database (Microsoft SQL Server) has a JDBC driver that allows only one active statement at a time. Use the getMaxStatements method of the DatabaseMetaData class to find out the number of concurrently open statements that your JDBC driver supports.

This sounds restrictive, but in practice, you should probably not fuss with multiple concurrent result sets. If the result sets are related, then you should be able to issue a combined query and analyze a single result. It is much more efficient to let the database combine queries than it is for a Java program to iterate through multiple result sets.

When you are done using a ResultSet, Statement, or Connection, you should call the close method immediately. These objects use large data structures, and you don't want to wait for the garbage collector to deal with them.

The close method of a Statement object automatically closes the associated result set if the statement has an open result set. Similarly, the close method of the Connection class closes all statements of the connection.

If your connections are short-lived, you don't have to worry about closing statements and result sets. Just make absolutely sure that a connection object cannot possibly remain open, by placing the close statement in a finally block:

```
Connection conn = . . .;
try
{
    Statement stat = conn.createStatement();
    ResultSet result = stat.executeQuery(queryString);
    process query result
}
finally
{
    conn.close();
}
```

 TIP: Use the try/finally block just to close the connection, and use a separate try/catch block to deal with exceptions. Separating the try blocks makes your code easier to read.

Populating a Database

We now want to write our first, real, JDBC program. Of course, it would be nice if we could execute some of the fancy queries that we discussed earlier. Unfortunately, we have a problem: Right now, there are no data in the database. And you won't find a database file on the CD-ROM that you can simply copy onto your hard disk for the database program to read, because no database file format lets you interchange SQL relational databases from one vendor to another. SQL does not have anything to do with files. It is a language to issue queries and updates to a database. How the database executes these statements most efficiently and what file formats it uses toward that goal are entirely up to the *implementation* of the database. Database vendors try hard to come up with clever strategies for query optimization and data storage, and different vendors arrive at different mechanisms. Thus, although SQL statements are portable, the underlying data representation is not.

To get around our problem, we provide a small set of data in a series of text files that contain the raw SQL instructions to create the tables and insert the values. We also give you a program that reads a file with SQL instructions, one instruction per line, and executes them.

. Specifically, the program reads data from a text file in a format such as

```
CREATE TABLE Publisher (Publisher_Id CHAR(6), Name CHAR(30), URL CHAR(80))
INSERT INTO Publishers VALUES ('0201', 'Addison-Wesley', 'www.aw-bc.com')
INSERT INTO Publishers VALUES ('0471', 'John Wiley & Sons', 'www.wiley.com')
. . .
```

At the end of this section, you can see the code for the program that reads the SQL statement file and executes the statements. Even if you are not interested in looking at the implementation, you must run this program if you want to execute the more interesting examples in the remainder of this chapter. Run the program as follows:

```
java -classpath .:driverPath ExecSQL Books.sql
java -classpath .:driverPath ExecSQL Authors.sql
java -classpath .:driverPath ExecSQL Publishers.sql
java -classpath .:driverPath ExecSQL BooksAuthors.sql
```

Before running the program, check that the file database.properties is set up properly for your environment—see page 195.

The following steps briefly describe the ExecSQL program:

1. Connect to the database. The getConnection method reads the properties in the file database.properties and adds the jdbc.drivers property to the system properties. The driver manager uses the jdbc.drivers property to load the appropriate database driver. The getConnection method uses the jdbc.url, jdbc.username, and jdbc.password properties to open the database connection.

2. Open the file with the SQL commands. If no file name was supplied, then prompt the user to enter the commands on the console.

3. Execute each command with the generic execute method. If it returns true, the command had a result set. The four SQL files that we provide for the book database all end in a SELECT * statement so that you can see that the data were successfully inserted.

4. If there was a result set, print out the result. Because this is a generic result set, we need to use metadata to find out how many columns the result has. You will learn more about metadata on page 221.

5. If there is any SQL exception, print the exception and any chained exceptions that may be contained in it.

6. Close the connection to the database.

Example 4–2 lists the code for the program.

Example 4–2: ExecSQL.java

```
 1. import java.io.*;
 2. import java.util.*;
 3. import java.sql.*;
 4.
 5. /**
 6.    Executes all SQL statements in a file.
 7.    Call this program as
 8.       java -classpath driverPath:. ExecSQL commandFile
 9. */
10. class ExecSQL
11. {
12.    public static void main (String args[])
13.    {
14.       try
15.       {
```

```
16.        Scanner in;
17.        if (args.length == 0)
18.           in = new Scanner(System.in);
19.        else
20.           in = new Scanner(new File(args[0]));
21.
22.        Connection conn = getConnection();
23.        try
24.        {
25.           Statement stat = conn.createStatement();
26.
27.           while (true)
28.           {
29.              if (args.length == 0) System.out.println("Enter command or EXIT to exit:");
30.
31.              if (!in.hasNextLine()) return;
32.
33.              String line = in.nextLine();
34.              if (line.equalsIgnoreCase("EXIT")) return;
35.              try
36.              {
37.                 boolean hasResultSet = stat.execute(line);
38.                 if (hasResultSet)
39.                    showResultSet(stat);
40.              }
41.              catch (SQLException e)
42.              {
43.                 while (e != null)
44.                 {
45.                    e.printStackTrace();
46.                    e = e.getNextException();
47.                 }
48.              }
49.           }
50.        }
51.        finally
52.        {
53.           conn.close();
54.        }
55.     }
56.     catch (SQLException e)
57.     {
58.        while (e != null)
59.        {
60.           e.printStackTrace();
61.           e = e.getNextException();
62.        }
63.     }
64.     catch (IOException e)
65.     {
66.        e.printStackTrace();
67.     }
68.  }
69.
70.  /**
```

```
71.      Gets a connection from the properties specified
72.      in the file database.properties
73.      @return the database connection
74.   */
75.   public static Connection getConnection()
76.       throws SQLException, IOException
77.   {
78.      Properties props = new Properties();
79.      FileInputStream in = new FileInputStream("database.properties");
80.      props.load(in);
81.      in.close();
82.
83.      String drivers = props.getProperty("jdbc.drivers");
84.      if (drivers != null) System.setProperty("jdbc.drivers", drivers);
85.
86.      String url = props.getProperty("jdbc.url");
87.      String username = props.getProperty("jdbc.username");
88.      String password = props.getProperty("jdbc.password");
89.
90.      return DriverManager.getConnection(url, username, password);
91.   }
92.
93.   /**
94.      Prints a result set.
95.      @param stat the statement whose result set should be
96.      printed
97.   */
98.   public static void showResultSet(Statement stat)
99.       throws SQLException
100.   {
101.      ResultSet result = stat.getResultSet();
102.      ResultSetMetaData metaData = result.getMetaData();
103.      int columnCount = metaData.getColumnCount();
104.
105.      for (int i = 1; i <= columnCount; i++)
106.      {
107.         if (i > 1) System.out.print(", ");
108.         System.out.print(metaData.getColumnLabel(i));
109.      }
110.      System.out.println();
111.
112.      while (result.next())
113.      {
114.         for (int i = 1; i <= columnCount; i++)
115.         {
116.            if (i > 1) System.out.print(", ");
117.            System.out.print(result.getString(i));
118.         }
119.         System.out.println();
120.      }
121.      result.close();
122.   }
123. }
```

Query Execution

In this section, we write a program that executes queries against the COREJAVA database. For this program to work, you must have populated the COREJAVA database with tables, as described in the preceding section. Figure 4–6 shows the QueryDB application in action.

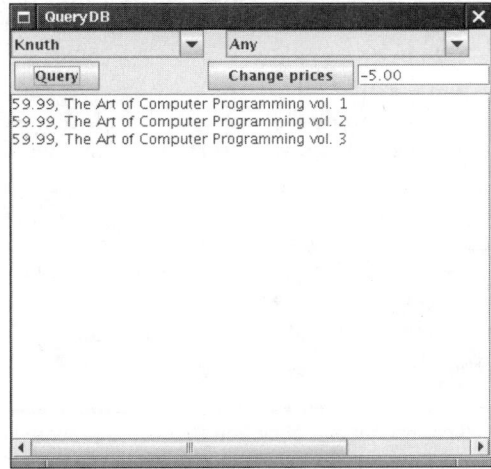

Figure 4–6: The QueryDB application

You can select the author and the publisher or leave either of them as "Any." Click the Query button; all books matching your selection will be displayed in the text area.

You can also change the data in the database. Select a publisher and type an amount into the text box next to the Change prices button. When you click the button, all prices of that publisher are adjusted by the amount you entered, and the text area contains a message indicating how many records were changed. However, to minimize unintended changes to the database, you can't change all prices at once. The author field is ignored when you change prices. After a price change, you may want to run a query to verify the new prices.

Prepared Statements

In this program, we use one new feature, *prepared statements*. Consider the query for all books by a particular publisher, independent of the author. The SQL query is

```
SELECT Books.Price, Books.Title
FROM Books, Publishers
WHERE Books.Publisher_Id = Publishers.Publisher_Id
AND Publishers.Name = the name from the list box
```

Rather than build a separate query statement every time the user launches such a query, we can *prepare* a query with a host variable and use it many times, each time filling in a different string for the variable. That technique benefits performance. Whenever the database executes a query, it first computes a strategy of how to efficiently execute the query. By preparing the query and reusing it, you ensure that the planning step is done only once.

Each host variable in a prepared query is indicated with a ?. If there is more than one variable, then you must keep track of the positions of the ? when setting the values. For example, our prepared query becomes

```
String publisherQuery =
   "SELECT Books.Price, Books.Title" +
   " FROM Books, Publishers" +
   " WHERE Books.Publisher_Id = Publishers.Publisher_Id AND Publishers.Name = ?";
PreparedStatement publisherQueryStat = conn.prepareStatement(publisherQuery);
```

Before executing the prepared statement, you must bind the host variables to actual values with a set method. As with the ResultSet get methods, there are different set methods for the various types. Here, we want to set a string to a publisher name.

```
publisherQueryStat.setString(1, publisher);
```

The first argument is the position number of the host variable that we want to set. The position 1 denotes the first ?. The second argument is the value that we want to assign to the host variable.

If you reuse a prepared query that you have already executed and the query has more than one host variable, all host variables stay bound as you set them unless you change them with a set method. That means you only need to call a set*Xxx* method on those host variables that change from one query to the next.

Once all variables have been bound to values, you can execute the query

```
ResultSet rs = publisherQueryStat.executeQuery();
```

 TIP: Even if you don't care about efficiency, you should use prepared statements whenever your query involves variables. If you build a query by hand, you have to worry about special characters (such as quotes). That is more trouble than using a prepared statement.

The price update feature is implemented as an UPDATE statement. Note that we call executeUpdate, not executeQuery, because the UPDATE statement does not return a result set. The return value of executeUpdate is the count of changed rows. We display the count in the text area.

```
int r = priceUpdateStmt.executeUpdate();
result.setText(r + " records updated");
```

 NOTE: A PreparedStatement object becomes invalid after the associated Connection object is closed. However, many database drivers automatically *cache* prepared statements. If the same query is prepared twice, the database simply reuses the query strategy. Therefore, don't worry about the overhead of calling prepareStatement.

The following steps briefly describe the example program.

1. Arrange the components in the frame, using a grid bag layout (see Volume 1, Chapter 9).
2. Populate the author and publisher text boxes by running two queries that return all author and publisher names in the database.
3. When the user clicks the Query button, find which of the four query types needs to be executed. If this is the first time this query type is executed, then the prepared statement variable is null, and the prepared statement is constructed. Then, the values are bound to the query and the query is executed.

   The queries involving authors are more complex. Because a book can have multiple authors, the BooksAuthors table gives the correspondence between authors and books. For example, the book with ISBN number 0-201-96426-0 has two authors with codes DATE and DARW. The BooksAuthors table has the rows

```
0-201-96426-0, DATE, 1
0-201-96426-0, DARW, 2
```

to indicate this fact. The third column lists the order of the authors. (We can't just use the position of the records in the table. There is no fixed row ordering in a relational table.) Thus, the query has to join the Books, BooksAuthors, and Authors tables to compare the author name with the one selected by the user.

```
SELECT Books.Price, Books.Title FROM Books, BooksAuthors, Authors, Publishers
WHERE Authors.Author_Id = BooksAuthors.Author_Id AND BooksAuthors.ISBN = Books.ISBN
AND Books.Publisher_Id = Publishers.Publisher_Id AND Authors.Name = ? AND Publishers.Name = ?
```

 TIP: Some Java programmers avoid complex SQL statements such as this one. A surprisingly common, but very inefficient, workaround is to write lots of Java code that iterates through multiple result sets. But the database is *a lot* better at executing query code than a Java program can be—that's the core competency of a database. A rule of thumb: If you can do it in SQL, don't do it in Java.

4. The results of the query are displayed in the results text box.

5. When the user clicks the Change prices button, then the update command is constructed and executed. The command is quite complex because the WHERE clause of the UPDATE statement needs the publisher *code* and we know only the publisher *name*. This problem is solved with a nested subquery.

```
UPDATE Books
SET Price = Price + ?
WHERE Books.Publisher_Id = (SELECT Publisher_Id FROM Publishers WHERE Name = ?)
```

6. We initialize the connection and statement objects in the constructor. We hang on to them for the life of the program. Just before the program exits, we trap the "window closing" event, and these objects are closed.

```java
class QueryDBFrame extends JFrame
{
   public QueryDBFrame()
   {
      conn = getConnection();
      stat = conn.createStatement();
      . . .
      add(new
         WindowAdapter()
         {
            public void windowClosing(WindowEvent event)
            {
               try
               {
                  stat.close();
                  conn.close();
               }
               catch (SQLException e)
               {
                  while (e != null)
                  {
                     e.printStackTrace();
                     e = e.getNextException();
                  }
               }
            }
         }
```

```
            });
        }
        . . .
        private Connection conn;
        private Statement stat;
    }
```

Example 4–3 is the complete program code.

Example 4–3: QueryDB.java

```
 1. import java.net.*;
 2. import java.sql.*;
 3. import java.awt.*;
 4. import java.awt.event.*;
 5. import java.io.*;
 6. import java.util.*;
 7. import javax.swing.*;
 8.
 9. /**
10.    This program demonstrates several complex database queries.
11. */
12. public class QueryDB
13. {
14.    public static void main(String[] args)
15.    {
16.       JFrame frame = new QueryDBFrame();
17.       frame.setDefaultCloseOperation(JFrame.EXIT_ON_CLOSE);
18.       frame.setVisible(true);
19.    }
20. }
21.
22. /**
23.    This frame displays combo boxes for query parameters, a text area for command results,
24.    and buttons to launch a query and an update.
25. */
26. class QueryDBFrame extends JFrame
27. {
28.    public QueryDBFrame()
29.    {
30.       setTitle("QueryDB");
31.       setSize(DEFAULT_WIDTH, DEFAULT_HEIGHT);
32.       setLayout(new GridBagLayout());
33.
34.       authors = new JComboBox();
35.       authors.setEditable(false);
36.       authors.addItem("Any");
37.
38.       publishers = new JComboBox();
39.       publishers.setEditable(false);
40.       publishers.addItem("Any");
41.
42.       result = new JTextArea(4, 50);
43.       result.setEditable(false);
44.
45.       priceChange = new JTextField(8);
46.       priceChange.setText("-5.00");
```

```
47.
48.      try
49.      {
50.         conn = getConnection();
51.         Statement stat = conn.createStatement();
52.
53.         String query = "SELECT Name FROM Authors";
54.         ResultSet rs = stat.executeQuery(query);
55.         while (rs.next())
56.            authors.addItem(rs.getString(1));
57.         rs.close();
58.
59.         query = "SELECT Name FROM Publishers";
60.         rs = stat.executeQuery(query);
61.         while (rs.next())
62.            publishers.addItem(rs.getString(1));
63.         rs.close();
64.         stat.close();
65.      }
66.      catch (SQLException e)
67.      {
68.         result.setText("");
69.         while (e != null)
70.         {
71.            result.append("" + e);
72.            e = e.getNextException();
73.         }
74.      }
75.      catch (IOException e)
76.      {
77.         result.setText("" + e);
78.      }
79.
80.      // we use the GBC convenience class of Core Java Volume 1, Chapter 9
81.      add(authors, new GBC(0, 0, 2, 1));
82.
83.      add(publishers, new GBC(2, 0, 2, 1));
84.
85.      JButton queryButton = new JButton("Query");
86.      queryButton.addActionListener(new
87.         ActionListener()
88.         {
89.            public void actionPerformed(ActionEvent event)
90.            {
91.               executeQuery();
92.            }
93.         });
94.      add(queryButton, new GBC(0, 1, 1, 1).setInsets(3));
95.
96.      JButton changeButton = new JButton("Change prices");
97.      changeButton.addActionListener(new
98.         ActionListener()
99.         {
100.           public void actionPerformed(ActionEvent event)
101.           {
102.              changePrices();
```

```
103.            }
104.        });
105.     add(changeButton, new GBC(2, 1, 1, 1).setInsets(3));
106.
107.     add(priceChange, new GBC(3, 1, 1, 1).setFill(GBC.HORIZONTAL));
108.
109.     add(new JScrollPane(result), new GBC(0, 2, 4, 1).setFill(GBC.BOTH).setWeight(100, 100));
110.
111.     addWindowListener(new
112.        WindowAdapter()
113.        {
114.           public void windowClosing(WindowEvent event)
115.           {
116.              try
117.              {
118.                 if (conn != null) conn.close();
119.              }
120.              catch (SQLException e)
121.              {
122.                 while (e != null)
123.                 {
124.                    e.printStackTrace();
125.                    e = e.getNextException();
126.                 }
127.              }
128.           }
129.        });
130.  }
131.
132.  /**
133.     Executes the selected query.
134.  */
135.  private void executeQuery()
136.  {
137.     ResultSet rs = null;
138.     try
139.     {
140.        String author = (String) authors.getSelectedItem();
141.        String publisher = (String) publishers.getSelectedItem();
142.        if (!author.equals("Any") && !publisher.equals("Any"))
143.        {
144.           if (authorPublisherQueryStmt == null)
145.              authorPublisherQueryStmt = conn.prepareStatement(authorPublisherQuery);
146.           authorPublisherQueryStmt.setString(1, author);
147.           authorPublisherQueryStmt.setString(2, publisher);
148.           rs = authorPublisherQueryStmt.executeQuery();
149.        }
150.        else if (!author.equals("Any") && publisher.equals("Any"))
151.        {
152.           if (authorQueryStmt == null)
153.              authorQueryStmt = conn.prepareStatement(authorQuery);
154.           authorQueryStmt.setString(1, author);
155.           rs = authorQueryStmt.executeQuery();
156.        }
157.        else if (author.equals("Any") && !publisher.equals("Any"))
158.        {
```

```
159.        if (publisherQueryStmt == null)
160.           publisherQueryStmt = conn.prepareStatement(publisherQuery);
161.        publisherQueryStmt.setString(1, publisher);
162.        rs = publisherQueryStmt.executeQuery();
163.     }
164.     else
165.     {
166.        if (allQueryStmt == null)
167.           allQueryStmt = conn.prepareStatement(allQuery);
168.        rs = allQueryStmt.executeQuery();
169.     }
170.
171.     result.setText("");
172.     while (rs.next())
173.     {
174.        result.append(rs.getString(1));
175.        result.append(", ");
176.        result.append(rs.getString(2));
177.        result.append("\n");
178.     }
179.     rs.close();
180.  }
181.  catch (SQLException e)
182.  {
183.     result.setText("");
184.     while (e != null)
185.     {
186.        result.append("" + e);
187.        e = e.getNextException();
188.     }
189.  }
190. }
191.
192. /**
193.    Executes an update statement to change prices.
194. */
195. public void changePrices()
196. {
197.    String publisher = (String) publishers.getSelectedItem();
198.    if (publisher.equals("Any"))
199.    {
200.       result.setText("I am sorry, but I cannot do that.");
201.       return;
202.    }
203.    try
204.    {
205.       if (priceUpdateStmt == null)
206.          priceUpdateStmt = conn.prepareStatement(priceUpdate);
207.       priceUpdateStmt.setString(1, priceChange.getText());
208.       priceUpdateStmt.setString(2, publisher);
209.       int r = priceUpdateStmt.executeUpdate();
210.       result.setText(r + " records updated.");
211.    }
212.    catch (SQLException e)
213.    {
214.       result.setText("");
```

```
215.        while (e != null)
216.        {
217.           result.append("" + e);
218.           e = e.getNextException();
219.        }
220.     }
221.  }
222.
223.  /**
224.     Gets a connection from the properties specified
225.     in the file database.properties
226.     @return the database connection
227.  */
228.  public static Connection getConnection()
229.     throws SQLException, IOException
230.  {
231.     Properties props = new Properties();
232.     FileInputStream in = new FileInputStream("database.properties");
233.     props.load(in);
234.     in.close();
235.
236.     String drivers = props.getProperty("jdbc.drivers");
237.     if (drivers != null) System.setProperty("jdbc.drivers", drivers);
238.     String url = props.getProperty("jdbc.url");
239.     String username = props.getProperty("jdbc.username");
240.     String password = props.getProperty("jdbc.password");
241.
242.     return DriverManager.getConnection(url, username, password);
243.  }
244.
245.  public static final int DEFAULT_WIDTH = 400;
246.  public static final int DEFAULT_HEIGHT = 400;
247.
248.  private JComboBox authors;
249.  private JComboBox publishers;
250.  private JTextField priceChange;
251.  private JTextArea result;
252.  private Connection conn;
253.  private PreparedStatement authorQueryStmt;
254.  private PreparedStatement authorPublisherQueryStmt;
255.  private PreparedStatement publisherQueryStmt;
256.  private PreparedStatement allQueryStmt;
257.  private PreparedStatement priceUpdateStmt;
258.
259.  private static final String authorPublisherQuery =
260.     "SELECT Books.Price, Books.Title FROM Books, BooksAuthors, Authors, Publishers" +
261.     " WHERE Authors.Author_Id = BooksAuthors.Author_Id AND BooksAuthors.ISBN = Books.ISBN" +
262.     " AND Books.Publisher_Id = Publishers.Publisher_Id AND Authors.Name = ?" +
263.     " AND Publishers.Name = ?";
264.
265.  private static final String authorQuery =
266.     "SELECT Books.Price, Books.Title FROM Books, BooksAuthors, Authors" +
267.     " WHERE Authors.Author_Id = BooksAuthors.Author_Id AND BooksAuthors.ISBN = Books.ISBN" +
268.     " AND Authors.Name = ?";
269.
270.  private static final String publisherQuery =
```

```
271.        "SELECT Books.Price, Books.Title FROM Books, Publishers" +
272.        " WHERE Books.Publisher_Id = Publishers.Publisher_Id AND Publishers.Name = ?";
273.
274.    private static final String allQuery = "SELECT Books.Price, Books.Title FROM Books";
275.
276.    private static final String priceUpdate =
277.        "UPDATE Books " + "SET Price = Price + ? " +
278.        " WHERE Books.Publisher_Id = (SELECT Publisher_Id FROM Publishers WHERE Name = ?)";
279. }
```

API `java.sql.Connection` 1.1

- `PreparedStatement prepareStatement(String sql)`
  returns a `PreparedStatement` object containing the precompiled statement. The string `sql` contains a SQL statement that can contain one or more parameter placeholders denoted by `?` characters.

API `java.sql.PreparedStatement` 1.1

- `void setXxx(int n, Xxx x)`
  (*Xxx* is a type such as `int`, `double`, `String`, `Date`, etc.)
  sets the value of the nth parameter to x.
- `void clearParameters()`
  clears all current parameters in the prepared statement.
- `ResultSet executeQuery()`
  executes a prepared SQL query and returns a `ResultSet` object.
- `int executeUpdate()`
  executes the prepared SQL `INSERT`, `UPDATE`, or `DELETE` statement represented by the `PreparedStatement` object. Returns the number of rows affected, or 0 for Data Definition Language (DDL) statements such as `CREATE TABLE`.

Scrollable and Updatable Result Sets

As you have seen, the `next` method of the `ResultSet` class iterates over the rows in a result set. That is certainly adequate for a program that needs to analyze the data. However, consider a visual data display that shows a table or query result (see Figure 4–7). You usually want the user to be able to move both forward and backward in the result set. But JDBC 1 had no `previous` method. Programmers who wanted to implement backward iteration had to manually cache the result set data. The *scrollable* result set in JDBC 2 lets you move forward and backward through a result set and jump to any position in the result set.

Furthermore, once users see the contents of a result set displayed, they may be tempted to edit it. If you supply an editable view to your users, you must ensure that the user edits are posted back to the database. In JDBC 1, you had to program `UPDATE` statements. In JDBC 2, you can simply update the result set entries, and the database is automatically updated.

JDBC 2 delivers further enhancements to result sets, such as the capability of updating a result set with the most recent data if the data have been modified by another concurrent database connection. JDBC 3 adds yet another refinement, specifying the behavior of result sets when a transaction is committed. However, these advanced features are outside the scope of this introductory chapter. We refer you to the *JDBC API Tutorial and Reference* and the JDBC specification documents at `http://java.sun.com/products/jdbc` for more information.

title	isbn	name	price
Design Patterns	0-201-63361-2	Addison-Wesley	54.99
Introduction to Automata Theory, Languages, and Computation	0-201-44124-1	Addison-Wesley	105.00
The Art of Computer Programming vol. 1	0-201-89683-4	Addison-Wesley	59.99
The Art of Computer Programming vol. 2	0-201-89684-2	Addison-Wesley	59.99
The Art of Computer Programming vol. 3	0-201-89685-0	Addison-Wesley	59.99
The C++ Programming Language	0-201-70073-5	Addison-Wesley	64.99
The Mythical Man-Month	0-201-83595-9	Addison-Wesley	29.95
Introduction to Algorithms	0-262-03293-7	MIT Press	80.00
Applied Cryptography	0-471-11709-9	John Wiley & Sons	60.00
JavaScript: The Definitive Guide	0-596-00048-0	O'Reilly	44.95
The Cathedral and the Bazaar	0-596-00108-8	O'Reilly	16.95
The Soul of a New Machine	0-679-60261-5	Random House	18.95
Cuckoo's Egg	0-7434-1146-3	Simon & Schuster	13.95
The Codebreakers	0-684-83130-9	Simon & Schuster	70.00

Sort field | Filter conditions | Reload | Close

Figure 4–7: A GUI view of a query result

Scrollable Result Sets

To obtain scrollable result sets from your queries, you must obtain a different Statement object with the method

```
Statement stat = conn.createStatement(type, concurrency);
```

For a prepared statement, use the call

```
PreparedStatement stat = conn.prepareStatement(command, type, concurrency);
```

The possible values of type and concurrency are listed in Table 4–7 and Table 4–8. You have the following choices:

- Do you want the result set to be scrollable or not? If not, use ResultSet.TYPE_FORWARD_ONLY.
- If the result set is scrollable, do you want it to be able to reflect changes in the database that occurred after the query that yielded it? (In our discussion, we assume the ResultSet.TYPE_SCROLL_INSENSITIVE setting for scrollable result sets. This assumes that the result set does not "sense" database changes that occurred after execution of the query.)
- Do you want to be able to update the database by editing the result set? (See the next section for details.)

For example, if you simply want to be able to scroll through a result set but you don't want to edit its data, you use:

```
Statement stat = conn.createStatement(
    ResultSet.TYPE_SCROLL_INSENSITIVE, ResultSet.CONCUR_READ_ONLY);
```

Table 4–7: ResultSet Type Values

TYPE_FORWARD_ONLY	The result set is not scrollable.
TYPE_SCROLL_INSENSITIVE	The result set is scrollable but not sensitive to database changes.
TYPE_SCROLL_SENSITIVE	The result set is scrollable and sensitive to database changes.

Table 4–8: ResultSet Concurrency Values

CONCUR_READ_ONLY	The result set cannot be used to update the database.
CONCUR_UPDATABLE	The result set can be used to update the database.

All result sets that are returned by method calls

```
ResultSet rs = stat.executeQuery(query)
```

are now scrollable. A scrollable result set has a *cursor* that indicates the current position.

NOTE: Actually, a database driver might not be able to honor your request for a scrollable or updatable cursor. (The supportsResultSetType and supportsResultSetConcurrency methods of the DatabaseMetaData class tell you which types and concurrency modes are supported by a particular database.) Even if a database supports all result set modes, a particular query might not be able to yield a result set with all the properties that you requested. (For example, the result set of a complex query may not be updatable.) In that case, the executeQuery method returns a ResultSet of lesser capabilities and adds an SQLWarning to the connection object. You can retrieve warnings with the getWarnings method of the Connection class. Alternatively, you can use the getType and getConcurrency methods of the ResultSet class to find out what mode a result set actually has. If you do not check the result set capabilities and issue an unsupported operation, such as previous on a result set that is not scrollable, then the operation throws a SQLException.

CAUTION: In JDBC 1 drivers, the Connection class does not have a method

```
Statement createStatement(int type, int concurrency);
```

If a program that you compiled for JDBC 2 inadvertently loads a JDBC 1 driver and then calls this nonexistent method, the program will crash. Unfortunately, there is no JDBC 2 mechanism for querying a driver as to whether it is JDBC 2 compliant. In JDBC 3, you can use the getJDBCMajorVersion and getJDBCMinorVersion methods of the DatabaseMetaData class to find the JDBC version number of the driver.

Scrolling is very simple. You use

```
if (rs.previous()) . . .
```

to scroll backward. The method returns true if the cursor is positioned on an actual row; false if it now is positioned before the first row.

You can move the cursor backward or forward by a number of rows with the command

```
rs.relative(n);
```

If n is positive, the cursor moves forward. If n is negative, it moves backward. If n is zero, the call has no effect. If you attempt to move the cursor outside the current set of rows, it is set to point either after the last row or before the first row, depending on the sign of n. Then, the method returns false and the cursor does not move. The method returns true if the cursor is positioned on an actual row.

Alternatively, you can set the cursor to a particular row number:

```
rs.absolute(n);
```

You get the current row number with the call

```
int currentRow = rs.getRow();
```

The first row in the result set has number 1. If the return value is 0, the cursor is not currently on a row—it is either before the first row or after the last row.

The convenience methods

```
first
last
beforeFirst
afterLast
```

move the cursor to the first, to the last, before the first, or after the last position.

Finally, the methods

```
isFirst
isLast
isBeforeFirst
isAfterLast
```

test whether the cursor is at one of these special positions.

Using a scrollable result set is very simple. The hard work of caching the query data is carried out behind the scenes by the database driver.

Updatable Result Sets

If you want to be able to edit result set data and have the changes automatically reflected in the database, you create an updatable result set. Updatable result sets don't have to be scrollable, but if you present data to a user for editing, you usually want to allow scrolling as well.

To obtain updatable result sets, you create a statement as follows.

```
Statement stat = conn.createStatement(
    ResultSet.TYPE_SCROLL_INSENSITIVE, ResultSet.CONCUR_UPDATABLE);
```

The result sets returned by a call to executeQuery are then updatable.

 NOTE: Not all queries return updatable result sets. If your query is a join that involves multiple tables, the result may not be updatable. If your query involves only a single table or if it joins multiple tables by their primary keys, you should expect the result set to be updatable. Call the getConcurrency method of the ResultSet class to find out for sure.

For example, suppose you want to raise the prices of some books, but you don't have a simple criterion for issuing an UPDATE command. Then, you can iterate through all books and update prices, based on arbitrary conditions.

```
String query = "SELECT * FROM Books";
ResultSet rs = stat.executeQuery(query);
while (rs.next())
{
    if (. . .)
    {
        double increase = . . .
        double price = rs.getDouble("Price");
        rs.updateDouble("Price", price + increase);
        rs.updateRow();
    }
}
```

There are updateXxx methods for all data types that correspond to SQL types, such as update-Double, updateString, and so on. As with the getXxx methods, you specify the name or the number of the column. You then specify the new value for the field.

 NOTE: If you use the update*Xxx* method whose first parameter is the column number, be aware that this is the column number in the *result set*. It may well be different from the column number in the database.

The update*Xxx* method changes only the row values, not the database. When you are done with the field updates in a row, you must call the updateRow method. That method sends all updates in the current row to the database. If you move the cursor to another row without calling updateRow, all updates are discarded from the row set and they are never communicated to the database. You can also call the cancelRowUpdates method to cancel the updates to the current row.

The preceding example shows how you modify an existing row. If you want to add a new row to the database, you first use the moveToInsertRow method to move the cursor to a special position, called the *insert row*. You build up a new row in the insert row position by issuing update*Xxx* instructions. Finally, when you are done, call the insertRow method to deliver the new row to the database. When you are done inserting, call moveToCurrentRow to move the cursor back to the position before the call to moveToInsertRow. Here is an example:

```
rs.moveToInsertRow();
rs.updateString("Title", title);
rs.updateString("ISBN", isbn);
rs.updateString("Publisher_Id", pubid);
rs.updateDouble("Price", price);
rs.insertRow();
rs.moveToCurrentRow();
```

Note that you cannot influence *where* the new data is added in the result set or the database.

Finally, you can delete the row under the cursor.

```
rs.deleteRow();
```

The deleteRow method immediately removes the row from both the result set and the database.

The updateRow, insertRow, and deleteRow methods of the ResultSet class give you the same power as executing UPDATE, INSERT, and DELETE SQL commands. However, programmers who are accustomed to the Java programming language may find it more natural to manipulate the database contents through result sets than by constructing SQL statements.

CAUTION: If you are not careful, you can write staggeringly inefficient code with updatable result sets. It is *much* more efficient to execute an UPDATE statement than it is to make a query and iterate through the result, changing data along the way. Updatable result sets make sense for interactive programs in which a user can make arbitrary changes, but for most programmatic changes, a SQL UPDATE is more appropriate.

 java.sql.Connection 1.1

- Statement createStatement(int type, int concurrency) **1.2**
- PreparedStatement prepareStatement(String command, int type, int concurrency) **1.2**
  create a statement or prepared statement that yields result sets with the given type and concurrency.

  Parameters: command   The command to prepare

type	One of the constants TYPE_FORWARD_ONLY, TYPE_SCROLL_INSENSITIVE, or TYPE_SCROLL_SENSITIVE of the ResultSet interface
concurrency	One of the constants CONCUR_READ_ONLY or CONCUR_UPDATABLE of the ResultSet interface

- SQLWarning getWarnings()
  returns the first of the pending warnings on this connection, or null if no warnings are pending. The warnings are chained together—keep calling getNextWarning on the returned SQLWarning object until that method returns null. This call does not consume the warnings. The SQLWarning class extends SQLException. Use the inherited getErrorCode and getSQLState to analyze the warnings.

- void clearWarnings()
  clears all warnings that have been reported on this connection.

 java.sql.ResultSet 1.1

- int getType() **1.2**
  returns the type of this result set, one of TYPE_FORWARD_ONLY, TYPE_SCROLL_INSENSITIVE, or TYPE_SCROLL_SENSITIVE.

- int getConcurrency() **1.2**
  returns the concurrency setting of this result set, one of CONCUR_READ_ONLY or CONCUR_UPDATABLE.

- boolean previous() **1.2**
  moves the cursor to the preceding row. Returns true if the cursor is positioned on a row or false if the cursor is positioned before the first row.

- int getRow() **1.2**
  gets the number of the current row. Rows are numbered starting with 1.

- boolean absolute(int r) **1.2**
  moves the cursor to row r. Returns true if the cursor is positioned on a row.

- boolean relative(int d) **1.2**
  moves the cursor by d rows. If d is negative, the cursor is moved backward. Returns true if the cursor is positioned on a row.

- boolean first() **1.2**
- boolean last() **1.2**
  move the cursor to the first or last row. Return true if the cursor is positioned on a row.

- void beforeFirst() **1.2**
- void afterLast() **1.2**
  move the cursor before the first or after the last row.

- boolean isFirst() **1.2**
- boolean isLast() **1.2**
  test whether the cursor is at the first or last row.

- boolean isBeforeFirst() **1.2**
- boolean isAfterLast() **1.2**
  test whether the cursor is before the first or after the last row.

- void moveToInsertRow() **1.2**
  moves the cursor to the insert row. The insert row is a special row for inserting new data with the update*Xxx* and insertRow methods.

- void moveToCurrentRow() **1.2**
  moves the cursor back from the insert row to the row that it occupied when the moveToInsertRow method was called.
- void insertRow() **1.2**
  inserts the contents of the insert row into the database and the result set.
- void deleteRow() **1.2**
  deletes the current row from the database and the result set.
- void update*Xxx*(int column, *Xxx* data) **1.2**
- void update*Xxx*(String columnName, *Xxx* data) **1.2**
  (*Xxx* is a type such as int, double, String, Date, etc.)
  update a field in the current row of the result set.
- void updateRow() **1.2**
  sends the current row updates to the database.
- void cancelRowUpdates() **1.2**
  cancels the current row updates.

 java.sql.DatabaseMetaData 1.1

- boolean supportsResultSetType(int type) **1.2**
  returns true if the database can support result sets of the given type.

Parameters:	type	One of the constants TYPE_FORWARD_ONLY, TYPE_SCROLL_INSENSITIVE, or TYPE_SCROLL_SENSITIVE of the ResultSet interface

- boolean supportsResultSetConcurrency(int type, int concurrency) **1.2**
  returns true if the database can support result sets of the given combination of type and concurrency.

Parameters:	type	One of the constants TYPE_FORWARD_ONLY, TYPE_SCROLL_INSENSITIVE, or TYPE_SCROLL_SENSITIVE of the ResultSet interface
	concurrency	One of the constants CONCUR_READ_ONLY or CONCUR_UPDATABLE of the ResultSet interface

Metadata

In the preceding sections, you saw how to populate, query, and update database tables. However, JDBC can give you additional information about the *structure* of a database and its tables. For example, you can get a list of the tables in a particular database or the column names and types of a table. This information is not useful when you are implementing a business application with a predefined database. After all, if you design the tables, you know their structure. Structural information is, however, extremely useful for programmers who write tools that work with any database.

In this section, we show you how to write such a simple tool. This tool lets you browse all tables in a database.

The combo box on top displays all tables in the database. Select one of them, and the center of the frame is filled with the field names of that table and the values of the first record, as shown in Figure 4–8. Click Next to scroll through the records in the table.

Figure 4–8: The ViewDB application

Many databases come with much more sophisticated tools for viewing and editing tables. If your database doesn't, check out iSQL-Viewer (http://isql.sourceforge.net) or SQuirreL (http://squirrel-sql.sourceforge.net). These programs can view the tables in any JDBC database. Our example program is not intended as a replacement for these tools, but it shows you how to implement a tool for working with arbitrary tables.

In SQL, data that describe the database or one of its parts are called *metadata* (to distinguish them from the actual data stored in the database). You can get three kinds of metadata: about a database, about a result set, and about parameters of prepared statements.

To find out more about the database, you request an object of type DatabaseMetaData from the database connection.

```
DatabaseMetaData meta = conn.getMetaData();
```

Now you are ready to get some metadata. For example, the call

```
ResultSet mrs = meta.getTables(null, null, null, new String[] { "TABLE" });
```

returns a result set that contains information about all tables in the database. (See the API note for other parameters to this method.)

Each row in the result set contains information about a table in the database. We only care about the third column, the name of the table. (Again, see the API note for the other columns.) Thus, rs.getString(3) is the table name. Here is the code that populates the combo box.

```
while (mrs.next())
    tableNames.addItem(mrs.getString(3));
rs.close();
```

The DatabaseMetaData class gives data about the database. A second metadata class, ResultSetMetaData, reports information about a result set. Whenever you have a result set from a query, you can inquire about the number of columns and each column's name, type, and field width.

We use this information to make a label for each column name and a text field of sufficient size for each value.

```
ResultSet mrs = stat.executeQuery("SELECT * FROM " + tableName);
ResultSetMetaData meta = mrs.getMetaData();
for (int i = 1; i <= meta.getColumnCount(); i++)
{
    String columnName = meta.getColumnLabel(i);
    int columnWidth = meta.getColumnDisplaySize(i);
    JLabel l = new Label (columnName);
    JTextField tf = new TextField (columnWidth);
    . . .
}
```

There is a second important use for database metadata. Databases are complex, and the SQL standard leaves plenty of room for variability. Well over a hundred methods in the DatabaseMetaData class can inquire about the database, including calls with exotic names such as

```
meta.supportsCatalogsInPrivilegeDefinitions()
```

and

```
meta.nullPlusNonNullIsNull()
```

Clearly, these are geared toward advanced users with special needs, in particular, those who need to write highly portable code that works with multiple databases. In our sample program, we give only one example of this technique. We ask the database metadata whether the JDBC driver supports scrollable result sets. If so, we open a scrollable result set and add a Previous button for scrolling backward.

```
if (meta.supportsResultSetType(ResultSet.TYPE_SCROLL_INSENSITIVE)) . . .
```

The following steps briefly describe the sample program.

1. Add the table name combo box, the panel that displays the table values, and the button panel.

2. Connect to the database. Find out if it supports scrollable result sets. If so, create the Statement object to yield scrollable result sets. Otherwise, just create a default Statement.

3. Get the table names and fill them into the choice component.

4. If scrolling is supported, add the Previous button. Always add the Next button.

5. When the user selects a table, make a query to see all its values. Get the result set metadata. Throw out the old scroll pane from the center panel. Create a panel containing a grid bag layout of labels and text fields. Add it to the frame and call the validate method to recompute the frame layout. Then, call showNextRow to show the first row.

6. Call the showNextRow method to show the first record and also whenever the user clicks the Next button. The showNextRow method gets the next row from the table and fills the column values into the text boxes.

7. There is a slight subtlety in detecting the end of the result set. When the result set is scrollable, we can simply use the isLast method. But when it isn't scrollable, that method call will cause an exception (or even a JVM error if the driver is a JDBC 1 driver). Therefore, we use a different strategy for non-scrollable result sets. When rs.next() returns false, we close the result set and set rs to null.

8. The Previous button calls showPreviousRow, which moves the result set backwards. Because this button is only installed when the result set is scrollable, we know that the previous and isFirst method are supported.

9. The showRow method simply fills in all the result set fields into the text fields of the data panel.

Example 4–4 is the program.

Example 4–4: ViewDB.java

```
1. import java.net.*;
2. import java.sql.*;
3. import java.awt.*;
4. import java.awt.event.*;
5. import java.io.*;
6. import java.util.*;
```

```
 7. import javax.swing.*;
 8.
 9. /**
10.    This program uses metadata to display arbitrary tables
11.    in a database.
12. */
13. public class ViewDB
14. {
15.    public static void main(String[] args)
16.    {
17.       JFrame frame = new ViewDBFrame();
18.       frame.setDefaultCloseOperation(JFrame.EXIT_ON_CLOSE);
19.       frame.setVisible(true);
20.    }
21. }
22.
23. /**
24.    The frame that holds the data panel and the navigation
25.    buttons.
26. */
27. class ViewDBFrame extends JFrame
28. {
29.    public ViewDBFrame()
30.    {
31.       setTitle("ViewDB");
32.       setSize(DEFAULT_WIDTH, DEFAULT_HEIGHT);
33.
34.       tableNames = new JComboBox();
35.       tableNames.addActionListener(new
36.          ActionListener()
37.          {
38.             public void actionPerformed(ActionEvent event)
39.             {
40.                showTable((String) tableNames.getSelectedItem());
41.             }
42.          });
43.       add(tableNames, BorderLayout.NORTH);
44.
45.       try
46.       {
47.          conn = getConnection();
48.          meta = conn.getMetaData();
49.          createStatement();
50.          getTableNames();
51.       }
52.       catch (SQLException e)
53.       {
54.          JOptionPane.showMessageDialog(this, e);
55.       }
56.       catch (IOException e)
57.       {
58.          JOptionPane.showMessageDialog(this, e);
59.       }
60.
61.       JPanel buttonPanel = new JPanel();
62.       add(buttonPanel, BorderLayout.SOUTH);
```

```
63.
64.        if (scrolling)
65.        {
66.           previousButton = new JButton("Previous");
67.           previousButton.addActionListener(new
68.              ActionListener()
69.              {
70.                 public void actionPerformed(ActionEvent event)
71.                 {
72.                    showPreviousRow();
73.                 }
74.              });
75.           buttonPanel.add(previousButton);
76.        }
77.
78.        nextButton = new JButton("Next");
79.        nextButton.addActionListener(new
80.           ActionListener()
81.           {
82.              public void actionPerformed(ActionEvent event)
83.              {
84.                 showNextRow();
85.              }
86.           });
87.        buttonPanel.add(nextButton);
88.
89.        addWindowListener(new
90.           WindowAdapter()
91.           {
92.              public void windowClosing(WindowEvent event)
93.              {
94.                 try
95.                 {
96.                    if (conn != null) conn.close();
97.                 }
98.                 catch (SQLException e)
99.                 {
100.                    while (e != null)
101.                    {
102.                       e.printStackTrace();
103.                       e = e.getNextException();
104.                    }
105.                 }
106.              }
107.           });
108.     }
109.
110.     /**
111.        Creates the statement object used for executing queries.
112.        If the database supports scrolling cursors, the statement
113.        is created to yield them.
114.     */
115.     public void createStatement() throws SQLException
116.     {
117.        if (meta.supportsResultSetType(
118.           ResultSet.TYPE_SCROLL_INSENSITIVE))
```

```
119.      {
120.          stat = conn.createStatement(
121.              ResultSet.TYPE_SCROLL_INSENSITIVE,
122.              ResultSet.CONCUR_READ_ONLY);
123.          scrolling = true;
124.      }
125.      else
126.      {
127.          stat = conn.createStatement();
128.          scrolling = false;
129.      }
130.  }
131.
132.  /**
133.     Gets all table names of this database and adds them
134.     to the combo box.
135.  */
136.  public void getTableNames() throws SQLException
137.  {
138.      ResultSet mrs = meta.getTables(null, null, null, new String[] { "TABLE" });
139.      while (mrs.next())
140.          tableNames.addItem(mrs.getString(3));
141.      mrs.close();
142.  }
143.
144.  /**
145.     Prepares the text fields for showing a new table, and
146.     shows the first row.
147.     @param tableName the name of the table to display
148.  */
149.  public void showTable(String tableName)
150.  {
151.      try
152.      {
153.          if (rs != null) rs.close();
154.          rs = stat.executeQuery("SELECT * FROM " + tableName);
155.          if (scrollPane != null)
156.              remove(scrollPane);
157.          dataPanel = new DataPanel(rs);
158.          scrollPane = new JScrollPane(dataPanel);
159.          add(scrollPane, BorderLayout.CENTER);
160.          validate();
161.          showNextRow();
162.      }
163.      catch (SQLException e)
164.      {
165.          JOptionPane.showMessageDialog(this, e);
166.      }
167.  }
168.
169.  /**
170.     Moves to the previous table row.
171.  */
172.  public void showPreviousRow()
173.  {
174.      try
```

```
175.        {
176.           if (rs == null || rs.isFirst()) return;
177.           rs.previous();
178.           dataPanel.showRow(rs);
179.        }
180.        catch (SQLException e)
181.        {
182.           JOptionPane.showMessageDialog(this, e);
183.        }
184.     }
185.
186.     /**
187.        Moves to the next table row.
188.     */
189.     public void showNextRow()
190.     {
191.        try
192.        {
193.           if (rs == null || scrolling && rs.isLast()) return;
194.
195.           if (!rs.next() && !scrolling)
196.           {
197.              rs.close();
198.              rs = null;
199.              return;
200.           }
201.
202.           dataPanel.showRow(rs);
203.        }
204.        catch (SQLException e)
205.        {
206.           JOptionPane.showMessageDialog(this, e);
207.        }
208.     }
209.
210.     /**
211.        Gets a connection from the properties specified
212.        in the file database.properties
213.        @return the database connection
214.     */
215.     public static Connection getConnection()
216.        throws SQLException, IOException
217.     {
218.        Properties props = new Properties();
219.        FileInputStream in
220.           = new FileInputStream("database.properties");
221.        props.load(in);
222.        in.close();
223.
224.        String drivers = props.getProperty("jdbc.drivers");
225.        if (drivers != null) System.setProperty("jdbc.drivers", drivers);
226.        String url = props.getProperty("jdbc.url");
227.        String username = props.getProperty("jdbc.username");
228.        String password = props.getProperty("jdbc.password");
229.
230.        return DriverManager.getConnection(url, username, password);
```

```
231.    }
232.
233.    public static final int DEFAULT_WIDTH = 300;
234.    public static final int DEFAULT_HEIGHT = 200;
235.
236.    private JButton previousButton;
237.    private JButton nextButton;
238.    private DataPanel dataPanel;
239.    private Component scrollPane;
240.    private JComboBox tableNames;
241.
242.    private Connection conn;
243.    private Statement stat;
244.    private DatabaseMetaData meta;
245.    private ResultSet rs;
246.    private boolean scrolling;
247. }
248.
249. /**
250.    This panel displays the contents of a result set.
251. */
252. class DataPanel extends JPanel
253. {
254.    /**
255.       Constructs the data panel.
256.       @param rs the result set whose contents this panel displays
257.    */
258.    public DataPanel(ResultSet rs) throws SQLException
259.    {
260.       fields = new ArrayList<JTextField>();
261.       setLayout(new GridBagLayout());
262.       GridBagConstraints gbc = new GridBagConstraints();
263.       gbc.gridwidth = 1;
264.       gbc.gridheight = 1;
265.
266.       ResultSetMetaData rsmd = rs.getMetaData();
267.       for (int i = 1; i <= rsmd.getColumnCount(); i++)
268.       {
269.          gbc.gridy = i - 1;
270.
271.          String columnName = rsmd.getColumnLabel(i);
272.          gbc.gridx = 0;
273.          gbc.anchor = GridBagConstraints.EAST;
274.          add(new JLabel(columnName), gbc);
275.
276.          int columnWidth = rsmd.getColumnDisplaySize(i);
277.          JTextField tb = new JTextField(columnWidth);
278.          fields.add(tb);
279.
280.          gbc.gridx = 1;
281.          gbc.anchor = GridBagConstraints.WEST;
282.          add(tb, gbc);
283.       }
284.    }
285.
286.    /**
```

```
287.        Shows a database row by populating all text fields
288.        with the column values.
289.    */
290.    public void showRow(ResultSet rs) throws SQLException
291.    {
292.        for (int i = 1; i <= fields.size(); i++)
293.        {
294.            String field = rs.getString(i);
295.            JTextField tb = (JTextField) fields.get(i - 1);
296.            tb.setText(field);
297.        }
298.    }
299.
300.    private ArrayList<JTextField> fields;
301. }
```

 java.sql.Connection 1.1

- DatabaseMetaData getMetaData()
  returns the metadata for the connection as a DatabaseMetaData object.

 java.sql.DatabaseMetaData 1.1

- ResultSet getTables(String catalog, String schemaPattern, String tableNamePattern, String types[])

  gets a description of all tables in a catalog that match the schema and table name patterns and the type criteria. (A *schema* describes a group of related tables and access permissions. A *catalog* describes a related group of schemas. These concepts are important for structuring large databases.)

  The catalog and schema parameters can be "" to retrieve those tables without a catalog or schema, or null to return tables regardless of catalog or schema.

  The types array contains the names of the table types to include. Typical types are TABLE, VIEW, SYSTEM TABLE, GLOBAL TEMPORARY, LOCAL TEMPORARY, ALIAS, and SYNONYM. If types is null, then tables of all types are returned.

  The result set has five columns, all of which are of type String, as shown in Table 4–9.

Table 4–9: Five Columns of the getTables Method

1	TABLE_CAT	Table catalog (may be null)
2	TABLE_SCHEM	Table schema (may be null)
3	TABLE_NAME	Table name
4	TABLE_TYPE	Table type
5	REMARKS	Comment on the table

- int getJDBCMajorVersion()
- int getJDBCMinorVersion()
  (JDBC 3) return the major and minor JDBC version numbers of the driver that established the database connection. For example, a JDBC 3.0 driver has major version number 3 and minor version number 0.
- int getMaxConnections()
  returns the maximum number of concurrent connections to this database.

- `int getMaxStatements()`
  returns the maximum number of concurrently open statements per database connection, or 0 if the number is unlimited or unknown.

 java.sql.ResultSet 1.1

- `ResultSetMetaData getMetaData()`
  gives you the metadata associated with the current ResultSet columns.

 java.sql.ResultSetMetaData 1.1

- `int getColumnCount()`
  returns the number of columns in the current ResultSet object.
- `int getColumnDisplaySize(int column)`
  tells you the maximum width of the column specified by the index parameter.

  Parameters:　　　column　　　　The column number

- `String getColumnLabel(int column)`
  gives you the suggested title for the column.

  Parameters:　　　column　　　　The column number

- `String getColumnName(int column)`
  gives the column name associated with the column index specified.

  Parameters:　　　column　　　　The column number

Row Sets

Scrollable result sets are powerful, but they have a major drawback. You need to keep the database connection open during the entire user interaction. However, users can walk away from their computer for a long time, leaving the connection occupied. That is not good—database connections are scarce resources. In such a situation, use a *row set*. The RowSet interface extends the ResultSet interface, but row sets don't have to be tied to a database connection.

Row sets are also suitable if you need to move a query result to a different tier of a complex application, or to another device such as a cell phone. You would never want to move a result set—its data structures can be huge, and it is tethered to the database connection.

The javax.sql.rowset package provides the following interfaces that extend the RowSet interface:

- A CachedRowSet allows disconnected operation. We discuss cached row sets in the following section.
- A WebRowSet is a cached row set that can be saved to an XML file. The XML file can be moved to another tier of a web application, where it is opened by another WebRowSet object.
- The FilteredRowSet and JoinRowSet interfaces support lightweight operations on row sets that are equivalent to SQL SELECT and JOIN operations. These operations are carried out on the data stored in row sets, without having to make a database connection.
- A JdbcRowSet is a thin wrapper around a ResultSet. It adds useful getters and setters from the RowSet interface, turning a result set into a "bean." (See Chapter 8 for more information on beans.)

Sun Microsystems expects database vendors to produce efficient implementations of these interfaces. Fortunately, they also supply reference implementations so that you can use row

sets even if your database vendor doesn't support them. The reference implementations are part of JDK 5.0. You can also download them from http://java.sun.com/jdbc. The reference implementations are in the package com.sun.rowset. The class names end in Impl, for example, CachedRowSetImpl.

Cached Row Sets

A cached row set contains all data from a result set. Because CachedRowSet extends the Result-Set interface, you can use a cached row set exactly as you would use a result set. Cached row sets confer an important benefit: You can close the connection and still use the row set. As you will see in our sample program, this greatly simplifies the implementation of inter-active applications. Each user command simply opens the database connection, issues a query, puts the result in a row set, and then closes the database connection.

It is even possible to modify the data in a cached row set. Of course, the modifications are not immediately reflected in the database. Instead, you need to make an explicit request to accept the accumulated changes. The CachedRowSet then reconnects to the database and issues SQL commands to write the accumulated changes.

Of course, cached row sets are not appropriate for large query results. It would be very inefficient to move large numbers of records from the database into memory, particularly if users only look at a few of them.

You can populate a CachedRowSet from a result set:

```
ResultSet result = stat.executeQuery(queryString);
CachedRowSet rowset = new com.sun.rowset.CachedRowSetImpl();
    // or use an implementation from your database vendor
rowset.populate(result);
conn.close(); // now ok to close the database connection
```

Alternatively, you can let the CachedRowSet object establish a connection automatically. Set up the database parameters:

```
rowset.setURL("jdbc:mckoi://localhost/");
rowset.setUsername("dbuser");
rowset.setPassword("secret");
```

Then set the query command.

```
rowset.setCommand("SELECT * FROM Books");
```

Finally, populate the row set with the query result:

```
rowset.execute();
```

This call establishes a database connection, issues the query, populates the row set, and disconnects.

You can inspect and modify the row set with the same commands you use for result sets. If you modified the row set contents, you must write it back to the database by calling

```
rowset.acceptChanges(conn);
```

or

```
rowset.acceptChanges();
```

The second call works only if you configured the row set with the information (such as URL, user name, and password) that is required to connect to a database.

On page 218, you saw that not all result sets are updatable. Similarly, a row set that contains the result of a complex query will not be able to write back changes to the database. You should be safe if your row set contains data from a single table.

> CAUTION: If you populated the row set from a result set, the row set does not know the name of the table to update. You need to call setTable to set the table name.

Another complexity arises if data in the database have changed after you populated the row set. This is clearly a sign of trouble that could lead to inconsistent data. The reference implementation checks whether the original row set values (that is, the values before editing) are identical to the current values in the database. If so, they are replaced with the edited values. Otherwise, a SyncProviderException is thrown, and none of the changes are written. Other implementations may use other strategies for synchronization.

The program in Example 4–5 is identical to the database viewer in Example 4–4. However, we now use a cached row set. The program logic is now greatly simplified.

- We simply open and close the connection in every action listener.
- We no longer need to trap the "window closing" event to close the connection.
- We no longer worry whether the result set is scrollable. Row sets are always scrollable.

Example 4–5: RowSetTest.java

```
1. import com.sun.rowset.*;
2. import java.net.*;
3. import java.sql.*;
4. import java.awt.*;
5. import java.awt.event.*;
6. import java.io.*;
7. import java.util.*;
8. import javax.swing.*;
9. import javax.sql.*;
10. import javax.sql.rowset.*;
11.
12. /**
13.    This program uses metadata to display arbitrary tables
14.    in a database.
15. */
16. public class RowSetTest
17. {
18.    public static void main(String[] args)
19.    {
20.       JFrame frame = new RowSetFrame();
21.       frame.setDefaultCloseOperation(JFrame.EXIT_ON_CLOSE);
22.       frame.setVisible(true);
23.    }
24. }
25.
26. /**
27.    The frame that holds the data panel and the navigation
28.    buttons.
29. */
30. class RowSetFrame extends JFrame
31. {
32.    public RowSetFrame()
33.    {
34.       setTitle("RowSetTest");
35.       setSize(DEFAULT_WIDTH, DEFAULT_HEIGHT);
36.
```

```
37.     tableNames = new JComboBox();
38.     tableNames.addActionListener(new
39.        ActionListener()
40.        {
41.           public void actionPerformed(ActionEvent event)
42.           {
43.              showTable((String) tableNames.getSelectedItem());
44.           }
45.        });
46.     add(tableNames, BorderLayout.NORTH);
47.
48.     try
49.     {
50.        Connection conn = getConnection();
51.        try
52.        {
53.           DatabaseMetaData meta = conn.getMetaData();
54.           ResultSet mrs = meta.getTables(null, null, null, new String[] { "TABLE" });
55.           while (mrs.next())
56.              tableNames.addItem(mrs.getString(3));
57.        }
58.        finally
59.        {
60.           conn.close();
61.        }
62.     }
63.     catch (SQLException e)
64.     {
65.        JOptionPane.showMessageDialog(this, e);
66.     }
67.     catch (IOException e)
68.     {
69.        JOptionPane.showMessageDialog(this, e);
70.     }
71.
72.     JPanel buttonPanel = new JPanel();
73.     add(buttonPanel, BorderLayout.SOUTH);
74.
75.     previousButton = new JButton("Previous");
76.     previousButton.addActionListener(new
77.        ActionListener()
78.        {
79.           public void actionPerformed(ActionEvent event)
80.           {
81.              showPreviousRow();
82.           }
83.        });
84.     buttonPanel.add(previousButton);
85.
86.     nextButton = new JButton("Next");
87.     nextButton.addActionListener(new
88.        ActionListener()
89.        {
90.           public void actionPerformed(ActionEvent event)
91.           {
92.              showNextRow();
```

```
93.           }
94.        });
95.     buttonPanel.add(nextButton);
96.
97.     deleteButton = new JButton("Delete");
98.     deleteButton.addActionListener(new
99.        ActionListener()
100.       {
101.          public void actionPerformed(ActionEvent event)
102.          {
103.             deleteRow();
104.          }
105.       });
106.    buttonPanel.add(deleteButton);
107.
108.    saveButton = new JButton("Save");
109.    saveButton.addActionListener(new
110.       ActionListener()
111.       {
112.          public void actionPerformed(ActionEvent event)
113.          {
114.             saveChanges();
115.          }
116.       });
117.    buttonPanel.add(saveButton);
118. }
119.
120. /**
121.    Prepares the text fields for showing a new table, and
122.    shows the first row.
123.    @param tableName the name of the table to display
124. */
125. public void showTable(String tableName)
126. {
127.    try
128.    {
129.       // open connection
130.       Connection conn = getConnection();
131.       try
132.       {
133.          // get result set
134.          Statement stat = conn.createStatement();
135.          ResultSet result = stat.executeQuery("SELECT * FROM " + tableName);
136.          // copy into row set
137.          rs = new CachedRowSetImpl();
138.          rs.setTableName(tableName);
139.          rs.populate(result);
140.       }
141.       finally
142.       {
143.          conn.close();
144.       }
145.
146.       if (scrollPane != null)
147.          remove(scrollPane);
148.       dataPanel = new DataPanel(rs);
```

```
149.        scrollPane = new JScrollPane(dataPanel);
150.        add(scrollPane, BorderLayout.CENTER);
151.        validate();
152.        showNextRow();
153.     }
154.     catch (SQLException e)
155.     {
156.        JOptionPane.showMessageDialog(this, e);
157.     }
158.     catch (IOException e)
159.     {
160.        JOptionPane.showMessageDialog(this, e);
161.     }
162.  }
163.
164.  /**
165.     Moves to the previous table row.
166.  */
167.  public void showPreviousRow()
168.  {
169.     try
170.     {
171.        if (rs == null || rs.isFirst()) return;
172.        rs.previous();
173.        dataPanel.showRow(rs);
174.     }
175.     catch (SQLException e)
176.     {
177.        System.out.println("Error " + e);
178.     }
179.  }
180.
181.  /**
182.     Moves to the next table row.
183.  */
184.  public void showNextRow()
185.  {
186.     try
187.     {
188.        if (rs == null || rs.isLast()) return;
189.        rs.next();
190.        dataPanel.showRow(rs);
191.     }
192.     catch (SQLException e)
193.     {
194.        JOptionPane.showMessageDialog(this, e);
195.     }
196.  }
197.
198.  /**
199.     Deletes current table row.
200.  */
201.  public void deleteRow()
202.  {
203.     try
204.     {
```

```
205.        rs.deleteRow();
206.        if (!rs.isLast()) rs.next();
207.        else if (!rs.isFirst()) rs.previous();
208.        else rs = null;
209.        dataPanel.showRow(rs);
210.     }
211.     catch (SQLException e)
212.     {
213.        JOptionPane.showMessageDialog(this, e);
214.     }
215.  }
216.
217.  /**
218.     Saves all changes.
219.  */
220.  public void saveChanges()
221.  {
222.     try
223.     {
224.        Connection conn = getConnection();
225.        try
226.        {
227.           rs.acceptChanges(conn);
228.        }
229.        finally
230.        {
231.           conn.close();
232.        }
233.     }
234.     catch (SQLException e)
235.     {
236.        JOptionPane.showMessageDialog(this, e);
237.     }
238.     catch (IOException e)
239.     {
240.        JOptionPane.showMessageDialog(this, e);
241.     }
242.  }
243.
244.  /**
245.     Gets a connection from the properties specified
246.     in the file database.properties
247.     @return the database connection
248.  */
249.  public static Connection getConnection()
250.     throws SQLException, IOException
251.  {
252.     Properties props = new Properties();
253.     FileInputStream in
254.        = new FileInputStream("database.properties");
255.     props.load(in);
256.     in.close();
257.
258.     String drivers = props.getProperty("jdbc.drivers");
259.     if (drivers != null) System.setProperty("jdbc.drivers", drivers);
260.     String url = props.getProperty("jdbc.url");
```

```
261.      String username = props.getProperty("jdbc.username");
262.      String password = props.getProperty("jdbc.password");
263.
264.      return DriverManager.getConnection(url, username, password);
265.   }
266.
267.   public static final int DEFAULT_WIDTH = 400;
268.   public static final int DEFAULT_HEIGHT = 200;
269.
270.   private JButton previousButton;
271.   private JButton nextButton;
272.   private JButton deleteButton;
273.   private JButton saveButton;
274.   private DataPanel dataPanel;
275.   private Component scrollPane;
276.   private JComboBox tableNames;
277.
278.   private CachedRowSet rs;
279. }
280.
281. /**
282.    This panel displays the contents of a result set.
283. */
284. class DataPanel extends JPanel
285. {
286.    /**
287.       Constructs the data panel.
288.       @param rs the result set whose contents this panel displays
289.    */
290.    public DataPanel(RowSet rs) throws SQLException
291.    {
292.       fields = new ArrayList<JTextField>();
293.       setLayout(new GridBagLayout());
294.       GridBagConstraints gbc = new GridBagConstraints();
295.       gbc.gridwidth = 1;
296.       gbc.gridheight = 1;
297.
298.       ResultSetMetaData rsmd = rs.getMetaData();
299.       for (int i = 1; i <= rsmd.getColumnCount(); i++)
300.       {
301.          gbc.gridy = i - 1;
302.
303.          String columnName = rsmd.getColumnLabel(i);
304.          gbc.gridx = 0;
305.          gbc.anchor = GridBagConstraints.EAST;
306.          add(new JLabel(columnName), gbc);
307.
308.          int columnWidth = rsmd.getColumnDisplaySize(i);
309.          JTextField tb = new JTextField(columnWidth);
310.          fields.add(tb);
311.
312.          gbc.gridx = 1;
313.          gbc.anchor = GridBagConstraints.WEST;
314.          add(tb, gbc);
315.       }
316.    }
```

```
317.
318.    /**
319.       Shows a database row by populating all text fields
320.       with the column values.
321.    */
322.    public void showRow(ResultSet rs) throws SQLException
323.    {
324.       for (int i = 1; i <= fields.size(); i++)
325.       {
326.          String field = rs.getString(i);
327.          JTextField tb = (JTextField) fields.get(i - 1);
328.          tb.setText(field);
329.       }
330.    }
331.
332.    private ArrayList<JTextField> fields;
333. }
```

 javax.sql.RowSet 1.4

- • String getURL()
- • void setURL(String url)
  get or set the database URL.
- • String getUsername()
- • void setUsername(String username)
  get or set the user name for connecting to the database.
- • String getPassword()
- • void setPassword(String password)
  get or set the password for connecting to the database.
- • String getCommand()
- • void setCommand(String command)
  get or set the command that is executed to populate this row set.
- • void execute()
  populates this row set by issuing the command set with setCommand. For the driver
  manager to obtain a connection, the URL, user name, and password must be set.

 javax.sql.rowset.CachedRowSet 5.0

- • void execute(Connection conn)
  populates this row set by issuing the command set with setCommand. This method uses
  the given connection *and closes it.*
- • void populate(ResultSet result)
  populates this cached row set with the data from the given result set.
- • String getTableName()
- • void setTableName(String tableName)
  get or set the name of the table from which this cached row set was populated.
- • void acceptChanges()
- • void acceptChanges(Connection conn)
  reconnect to the database and write the changes that are the result of editing the row
  set. May throw a SyncProviderException if the data cannot be written back because the
  database data have changed.

Transactions

You can group a set of statements to form a *transaction*. The transaction can be *committed* when all has gone well. Or, if an error has occurred in one of them, it can be *rolled back* as if none of the commands had been issued.

The major reason for grouping commands into transactions is *database integrity*. For example, suppose we want to transfer money from one bank account to another. Then, it is important that we simultaneously debit one account and credit another. If the system fails before crediting the other account, the debit needs to be undone.

If you group update statements to a transaction, then the transaction either succeeds in its entirety and it can be *committed*, or it fails somewhere in the middle. In that case, you can carry out a *rollback* and the database automatically undoes the effect of all updates that occurred since the last committed transaction.

By default, a database connection is in *autocommit mode,* and each SQL command is committed to the database as soon as it is executed. Once a command is committed, you cannot roll it back.

To check the current autocommit mode setting, call the getAutoCommit method of the Connection class.

You turn off autocommit mode with the command

```
conn.setAutoCommit(false);
```

Now you create a statement object in the normal way:

```
Statement stat = conn.createStatement();
```

Call executeUpdate any number of times:

```
stat.executeUpdate(command1);
stat.executeUpdate(command2);
stat.executeUpdate(command3);
. . .
```

When all commands have been executed, call the commit method:

```
conn.commit();
```

However, if an error occurred, call

```
conn.rollback();
```

Then, all commands until the last commit are automatically reversed. You typically issue a rollback when your transaction was interrupted by a SQLException.

Save Points

You can gain finer-grained control over the rollback process by using *save points*. Creating a save point marks a point to which you can later return without having to return to the start of the transaction. For example,

```
Statement stat = conn.createStatement(); // start transaction; rollback() goes here
stat.executeUpdate(command1);
Savepoint svpt = conn.setSavepoint(); // set savepoint; rollback(svpt) goes here
stat.executeUpdate(command2);
if (. . .) conn.rollback(svpt); // undo effect of command2
. . .
conn.commit();
```

Here, we used an anonymous save point. You can also give the save point a name, such as

```
Savepoint svpt = conn.setSavepoint("stage1");
```

When you are done with a save point, you should release it:

```
stat.releaseSavepoint(svpt);
```

Batch Updates

Suppose a program needs to execute many INSERT statements to populate a database table. In JDBC 2, you can improve the performance of the program by using a *batch update*. In a batch update, a sequence of commands is collected and submitted as a batch.

> NOTE: Use the supportsBatchUpdates method of the DatabaseMetaData class to find out if your database supports this feature.

The commands in a batch can be actions such as INSERT, UPDATE, and DELETE as well as data definition commands such as CREATE TABLE and DROP TABLE. However, you cannot add SELECT commands to a batch since executing a SELECT statement returns a result set.

To execute a batch, you first create a Statement object in the usual way:

```
Statement stat = conn.createStatement();
```

Now, instead of calling executeUpdate, you call the addBatch method:

```
String command = "CREATE TABLE . . ."
stat.addBatch(command);

while (. . .)
{
   command = "INSERT INTO . . . VALUES (" + . . . + ")";
   stat.addBatch(command);
}
```

Finally, you submit the entire batch:

```
int[] counts = stat.executeBatch();
```

The call to executeBatch returns an array of the row counts for all submitted commands. (Recall that an individual call to executeUpdate returns an integer, namely, the count of the rows that are affected by the command.) In our example, the executeBatch method returns an array with first element equal to 0 (because the CREATE TABLE command yields a row count of 0) and all other elements equal to 1 (because each INSERT command affects one row).

For proper error handling in batch mode, you want to treat the batch execution as a single transaction. If a batch fails in the middle, you want to roll back to the state before the beginning of the batch.

First, turn autocommit mode off, then collect the batch, execute it, commit it, and finally restore the original autocommit mode:

```
boolean autoCommit = conn.getAutoCommit();
conn.setAutoCommit(false);
Statement stat = conn.getStatement();
. . .
// keep calling stat.addBatch(. . .);
. . .
stat.executeBatch();
conn.commit();
conn.setAutoCommit(autoCommit);
```

> NOTE: You can only issue update statements in a batch. If you issue a SELECT query, an exception is thrown.

 java.sql.Connection 1.1

- void setAutoCommit(boolean b)
  sets the autocommit mode of this connection to b. If autocommit is true, all statements are committed as soon as their execution is completed.
- boolean getAutoCommit()
  gets the autocommit mode of this connection.
- void commit()
  commits all statements that were issued since the last commit.
- void rollback()
  undoes the effect of all statements that were issued since the last commit.
- Savepoint setSavepoint() 1.4
  sets an unnamed save point.
- Savepoint setSavepoint(String name) 1.4
  sets a named save point.
- void rollback(Savepoint svpt) 1.4
  rolls back until the given save point.
- void releaseSavepoint(Savepoint svpt) 1.4
  releases the given save point.

 java.sql.Savepoint 1.4

- int getSavepointId()
  gets the ID of this unnamed save point, or throws a SQLException if this is a named save point.
- String getSavepointName()
  gets the name of this save point, or throws a SQLException if this is an unnamed save point.

 java.sql.Statement 1.1

- void addBatch(String command) 1.2
  adds the command to the current batch of commands for this statement.
- int[] executeBatch() 1.2
  executes all commands in the current batch. Returns an array of row counts, containing an element for each command in the batch that denotes the number of rows affected by that command.

 java.sql.DatabaseMetaData 1.1

- boolean supportsBatchUpdates() 1.2
  returns true if the driver supports batch updates.

Advanced Connection Management

The simplistic database connection setup with a database.properties file, as described in the preceding sections, is suitable for small test programs, but it won't scale for larger applications.

When a JDBC application is deployed in an enterprise environment, the management of database connections is integrated with the Java Naming and Directory Interface (JNDI). The properties of data sources across the enterprise can be stored in a directory. Using a directory allows for centralized management of user names, passwords, database names, and JDBC URLs.

In such an environment, you use the following code to establish a database connection:

```
Context jndiContext = new InitialContext();
DataSource source = (DataSource) jndiContext.lookup("java:comp/env/jdbc/corejava");
Connection conn = source.getConnection();
```

Note that the `DriverManager` is no longer involved. Instead, the JNDI service locates a *data source*. A data source is an interface that allows for simple JDBC connections as well as more advanced services, such as executing distributed transactions that involve multiple databases. The `DataSource` interface is defined in the `javax.sql` standard extension package.

Of course, the data source needs to be configured somewhere. If you write database programs that execute in a servlet container such as Apache Tomcat or in an application server such as BEA WebLogic, then you place the database configuration (including the JDBC URL, user name, and password) in a configuration file.

Management of user names and logins is just one of the issues that require special attention. A second issue involves the cost of establishing database connections.

Our simple database programs established a single database connection at the start of the program and closed it at the end of the program. However, in many programming situations, this approach won't work. Consider a typical web application. Such an application serves multiple page requests in parallel. Multiple requests may need simultaneous access the database. With many databases, a connection is not intended to be shared by multiple threads. Thus, each request needs its own connection. A simplistic approach would be to establish a connection for each page request and close it afterward, but that would be very costly. Establishing a database connection can be quite time consuming. Connections are intended to be used for multiple queries, not to be closed after one or two queries.

The solution is to *pool* the connections. This means that database connections are not physically closed but are kept in a queue and reused. Connection pooling is an important service, and the JDBC specification provides hooks for implementors to supply it. However, the Java SDK itself does not provide any implementation, and database vendors don't usually include one with their JDBC driver either. Instead, vendors of application servers such as BEA WebLogic or IBM WebSphere supply connection pool implementations as part of the application server package.

Using a connection pool is completely transparent to the programmer. You acquire a connection from a source of pooled connections by obtaining a data source and calling `getConnection`. When you are done using the connection, call `close`. That doesn't close the physical connection but tells the pool that you are done using it.

You have now learned about the JDBC fundamentals and know enough to implement simple database applications. However, as we mentioned at the beginning of this chapter, databases are complex and quite a few of its advanced topics are beyond the scope of an introductory chapter. For an overview of advanced JDBC capabilities, check out the *JDBC API Tutorial and Reference* or the JDBC specifications at http://java.sun.com/products/jdbc.

Introduction to LDAP

In the preceding sections, you have seen how to interact with a *relational* database. In this section, we briefly look at *hierarchical* databases that use LDAP, the Lightweight Directory Access Protocol. This section is adapted from *Core JavaServer Faces* by Geary and Horstmann [Sun Microsystems Press 2004].

LDAP is preferred over relational databases when the application data naturally follows a tree structure and when read operations greatly outnumber write operations. LDAP is most commonly used for the storage of directories that contain data such as user names, passwords, and permissions.

NOTE: For an in-depth discussion of LDAP, we recommend the "LDAP bible": *Understanding and Deploying LDAP Directory Services*, 2nd ed., by Timothy Howes et al. [Macmillan 2003].

An LDAP database keeps all data in a tree structure, not in a set of tables as a relational database would. Each entry in the tree has the following:

- Zero or more *attributes*. An attribute has an ID and a value. An example attribute is cn=John Q. Public. (The ID cn stores the "common name." See Table 4–10 for the meaning of commonly used LDAP attributes.)
- One or more *object classes*. An object class defines the set of required and optional attributes for this element. For example, the object class person defines a required attribute cn and an optional attribute telephoneNumber. Of course, the object classes are different from Java classes, but they also support a notion of inheritance. For example, organizationalPerson is a subclass of person with additional attributes.
- A *distinguished name* (for example, uid=jqpublic,ou=people,dc=mycompany,dc=com). The distinguished name is a sequence of attributes that trace a path joining the entry with the root of the tree. There may be alternate paths, but one of them must be specified as distinguished.

Table 4–10: Commonly Used LDAP Attributes

Attribute ID	Meaning
dc	Domain component
cn	Common name
sn	Surname
dn	Distinguished name
o	Organization
ou	Organizational unit
uid	Unique identifier

Figure 4–9 shows an example of a directory tree.

How to organize a directory tree, and what information to put in it, can be a matter of intense debate. We do not discuss the issues here. Instead, we simply assume that an organizational scheme has been established and that the directory has been populated with the relevant user data.

Configuring an LDAP Server

You have several options for running an LDAP server to try out the programs in this section. Here are the most common choices:

- IBM Tivoli Directory Server
- Microsoft Active Directory
- Novell eDirectory
- OpenLDAP (http://openldap.org), a free server available for Linux and Windows and built into Mac OS X
- Sun Java System Directory Server

We give you brief instructions for configuring OpenLDAP. If you use another directory server, the basic steps are similar.

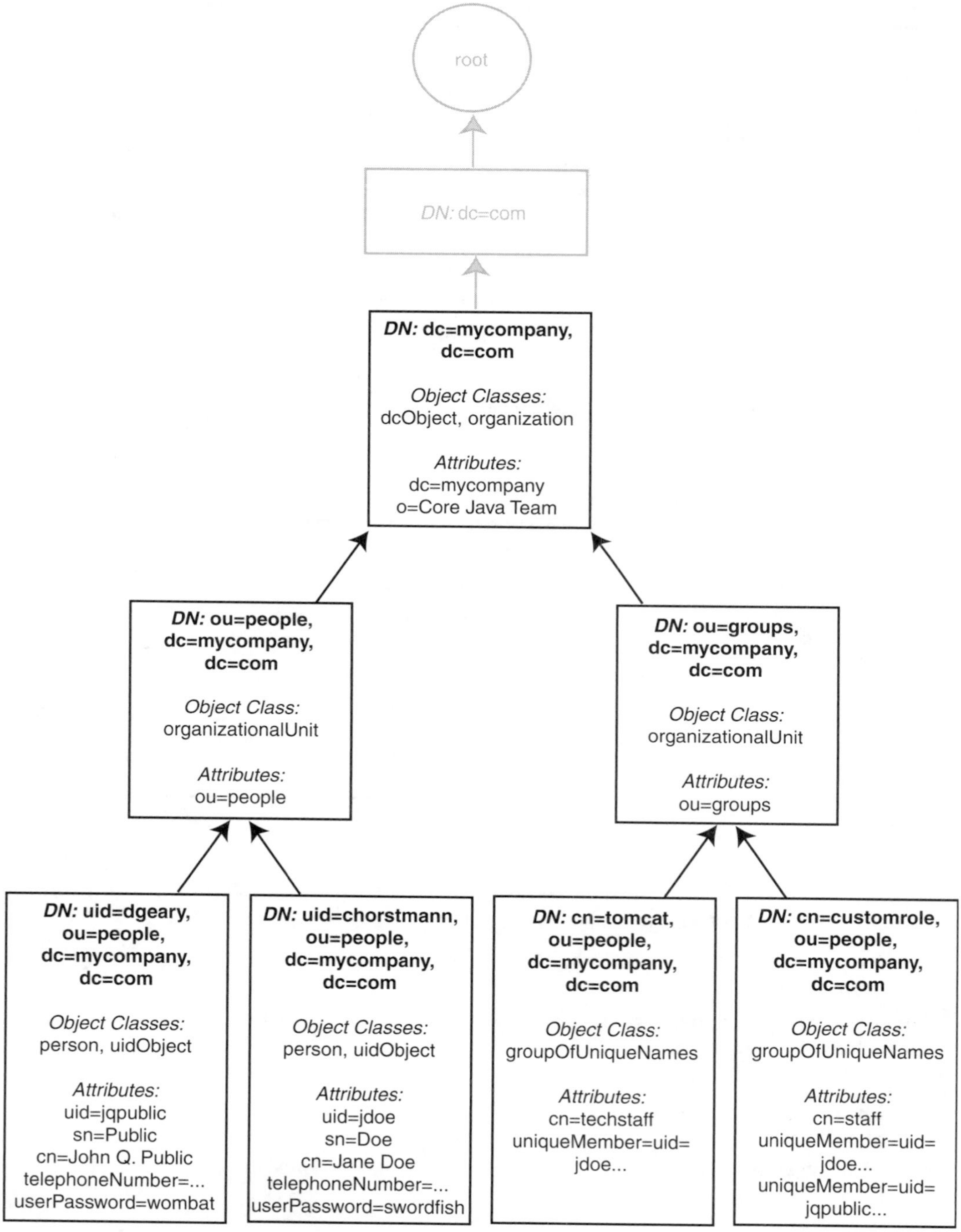

Figure 4–9: A directory tree

If you use OpenLDAP, you need to edit the `slapd.conf` file before starting the LDAP server. (On Linux, the default location for the `slapd.conf` file is `/usr/local/etc/openldap`.) Edit the `suffix` entry in `slapd.conf` to match the sample data set. This entry specifies the distinguished name suffix for this server. It should read

```
suffix  "dc=mycompany,dc=com"
```

You also need to configure an LDAP user with administrative rights to edit the directory data. In OpenLDAP, add these lines to `slapd.conf`:

```
rootdn  "cn=Manager,dc=mycompany,dc=com"
rootpw  secret
```

You can now start the LDAP server. On Linux, run `/usr/local/libexec/slapd`.

Next, populate the server with the sample data. Most LDAP servers allow the import of LDIF (Lightweight Directory Interchange Format) data. LDIF is a human-readable format that simply lists all directory entries, including their distinguished names, object classes, and attributes. Example 4–6 shows an LDIF file that describes our sample data.

Example 4–6: sample.ldif

```
 1. # Define top-level entry
 2. dn: dc=mycompany,dc=com
 3. objectClass: dcObject
 4. objectClass: organization
 5. dc: mycompany
 6. o: Core Java Team
 7.
 8. # Define an entry to contain people
 9. # searches for users are based on this entry
10. dn: ou=people,dc=mycompany,dc=com
11. objectClass: organizationalUnit
12. ou: people
13.
14. # Define a user entry for John Q. Public
15. dn: uid=jqpublic,ou=people,dc=mycompany,dc=com
16. objectClass: person
17. objectClass: uidObject
18. uid: jqpublic
19. sn: Public
20. cn: John Q. Public
21. telephoneNumber: +1 408 555 0017
22. userPassword: wombat
23.
24. # Define a user entry for Jane Doe
25. dn: uid=jdoe,ou=people,dc=mycompany,dc=com
26. objectClass: person
27. objectClass: uidObject
28. uid: jdoe
29. sn: Doe
30. cn: Jane Doe
31. telephoneNumber: +1 408 555 0029
32. userPassword: heffalump
33.
34. # Define an entry to contain LDAP groups
35. # searches for roles are based on this entry
36. dn: ou=groups,dc=mycompany,dc=com
37. objectClass: organizationalUnit
```

```
38. ou: groups
39.
40. # Define an entry for the "techstaff" group
41. dn: cn=techstaff,ou=groups,dc=mycompany,dc=com
42. objectClass: groupOfUniqueNames
43. cn: techstaff
44. uniqueMember: uid=jdoe,ou=people,dc=mycompany,dc=com
45.
46. # Define an entry for the "staff" group
47. dn: cn=staff,ou=groups,dc=mycompany,dc=com
48. objectClass: groupOfUniqueNames
49. cn: staff
50. uniqueMember: uid=jqpublic,ou=people,dc=mycompany,dc=com
51. uniqueMember: uid=jdoe,ou=people,dc=mycompany,dc=com
```

For example, with OpenLDAP, you use the ldapadd tool to add the data to the directory:

```
ldapadd -f sample.ldif -x -D "cn=Manager,dc=mycompany,dc=com" -w secret
```

Before proceeding, it is a good idea to double-check that the directory contains the data that you need. We suggest that you download Jarek Gawor's LDAP Browser\Editor from http://www-unix.mcs.anl.gov/~gawor/ldap/. This convenient Java program lets you browse the contents of any LDAP server. Launch the program and configure it with the following options:

- Host: localhost
- Base DN: dc=mycompany,dc=com
- Anonymous bind: unchecked
- User DN: cn=Manager
- Append base DN: checked
- Password: secret

Make sure the LDAP server has started, then connect. If everything is in order, you should see a directory tree similar to that shown in Figure 4–10.

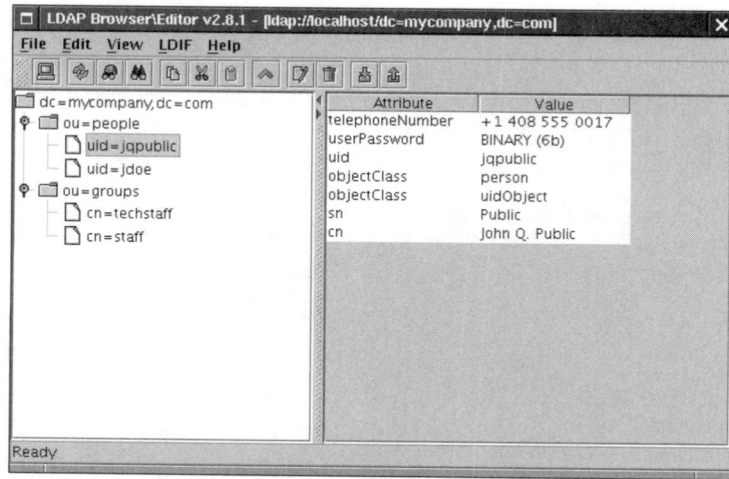

Figure 4–10: Inspecting an LDAP directory tree

Accessing LDAP Directory Information

Once your LDAP database is populated, connect to it with a Java program. You use the Java Naming and Directory Interface (JNDI), an interface that unifies various directory protocols.

Start by getting a *directory context* to the LDAP directory, with the following incantation:

```
Hashtable env = new Hashtable();
env.put(Context.SECURITY_PRINCIPAL, username);
env.put(Context.SECURITY_CREDENTIALS, password);
DirContext initial = new InitialDirContext(env);
DirContext context = (DirContext) initial.lookup("ldap://localhost:389");
```

Here, we connect to the LDAP server at the local host. The port number 389 is the default LDAP port.

If you connect to the LDAP database with an invalid user/password combination, an AuthenticationException is thrown.

NOTE: Sun's JNDI tutorial suggests an alternative way to connect to the server:

```
Hashtable env = new Hashtable();
env.put(Context.INITIAL_CONTEXT_FACTORY, "com.sun.jndi.ldap.LdapCtxFactory");
env.put(Context.PROVIDER_URL, "ldap://localhost:389");
env.put(Context.SECURITY_PRINCIPAL, userDN);
env.put(Context.SECURITY_CREDENTIALS, password);
DirContext context = new InitialDirContext(env);
```

However, it seems undesirable to hardwire the Sun LDAP provider into your code. JNDI has an elaborate mechanism for configuring providers, and you should not lightly bypass it.

To list the attributes of a given entry, specify its distinguished name and then use the get-Attributes method:

```
Attributes attrs = context.getAttributes("uid=jqpublic,ou=people,dc=mycompany,dc=com");
```

You can get a specific attribute with the get method, for example,

```
Attribute commonNameAttribute = attrs.get("cn");
```

To enumerate all attributes, you use the NamingEnumeration class. The designers of this class felt that they too could improve on the standard Java iteration protocol, and they gave us this usage pattern:

```
NamingEnumeration<? extends Attribute> attrEnum = attrs.getAll();
while (attrEnum.hasMore())
{
    Attribute attr = attrEnum.next();
    String id = attr.getID();
    . . .
}
```

Note the use of hasMore instead of hasNext.

If you know that an attribute has a single value, you can call the get method to retrieve it:

```
String commonName = (String) commonNameAttribute.get();
```

If an attribute can have multiple values, you need to use another NamingEnumeration to list them all:

```
NamingEnumeration<?> valueEnum = attr.getAll();
while (valueEnum.hasMore())
{
    Object value = valueEnum.next();
    . . .
}
```

 NOTE: As of JDK 5.0, `NamingEnumeration` is a generic type. The type bound `<? extends Attribute>` means that the enumeration yields objects of some unknown type that is a subtype of `Attribute`. Therefore, you don't need to cast the value that `next` returns—it has type `Attribute`. Without generics, you would write

```
NamingEnumeration attrEnum = attrs.getAll();
Attribute attr = (Attribute) attrEnum.next();
```

However, a `NamingEnumeration<?>` has no idea what it enumerates. Its `next` method returns an `Object`.

You now know how to query the directory for user data. Next, let us take up operations for modifying the directory contents.

To add a new entry, gather the set of attributes in a `BasicAttributes` object. (The `BasicAttributes` class implements the `Attributes` interface.)

```
Attributes attrs = new BasicAttributes();
attrs.put("uid", "alee");
attrs.put("sn", "Lee");
attrs.put("cn", "Amy Lee");
attrs.put("telephoneNumber", "+1 408 555 0033");
String password = "redqueen";
attrs.put("userPassword", password.getBytes());
// the following attribute has two values
Attribute objclass = new BasicAttribute("objectClass");
objclass.add("uidObject");
objclass.add("person");
attrs.put(objclass);
```

Then call the `createSubcontext` method. Provide the distinguished name of the new entry and the attribute set.

```
context.createSubcontext("uid=alee,ou=people,dc=mycompany,dc=com", attrs);
```

 CAUTION: When assembling the attributes, remember that the attributes are checked against the schema. Don't supply unknown attributes, and be sure to supply all attributes that are required by the object class. For example, if you omit the `sn` of `person`, the `createSubcontext` method will fail.

To remove an entry, call `destroySubcontext`:

```
context.destroySubcontext("uid=jdoe,ou=people,dc=mycompany,dc=com");
```

Finally, you may want to edit the attributes of an existing entry. You call the method

```
context.modifyAttributes(distinguishedName, flag, attrs);
```

Here, `flag` is one of

```
DirContext.ADD_ATTRIBUTE
DirContext.REMOVE_ATTRIBUTE
DirContext.REPLACE_ATTRIBUTE
```

The attrs parameter contains a set of the attributes to be added, removed, or replaced.

Conveniently, the BasicAttributes(String, Object) constructor constructs an attribute set with a single attribute. For example,

```
context.modifyAttributes("uid=alee,ou=people,dc=mycompany,dc=com",
   DirContext.ADD_ATTRIBUTE,
   new BasicAttributes("title", "CTO"));

context.modifyAttributes("uid=alee,ou=people,dc=mycompany,dc=com",
   DirContext.REMOVE_ATTRIBUTE,
   new BasicAttributes("telephoneNumber", "+1 408 555 0033"));

context.modifyAttributes("uid=alee,ou=people,dc=mycompany,dc=com",
   DirContext.REPLACE_ATTRIBUTE,
   new BasicAttributes("userPassword", password.getBytes()));
```

Finally, when you are done with a context, you should close it:

```
context.close();
```

The program in Example 4–7 demonstrates how to access a hierarchical database through LDAP. The program lets you view, modify, and delete information in a database with the sample data in Example 4–6.

Enter a uid into the text field and click the Find button to find an entry. If you edit the entry and click Save, your changes are saved. If you edited the uid field, a new entry is created. Otherwise, the existing entry is updated. You can also delete the entry by clicking the Delete button (see Figure 4–11).

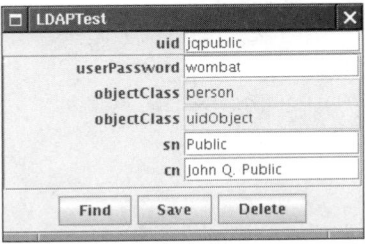

Figure 4–11: Accessing a hierarchical database

The following steps briefly describe the program.

1. The configuration for the LDAP server is contained in the file ldapserver.properties. The file defines the URL, user name, and password of the server, like this:

   ```
   ldap.username=cn=Manager,dc=mycompany,dc=com
   ldap.password=secret
   ldap.url=ldap://localhost:389
   ```

   The getContext method reads the file and obtains the directory context.

2. When the user clicks the Find button, the findEntry method fetches the attribute set for the entry with the given uid. The attribute set is used to construct a new DataPanel.

3. The DataPanel constructor iterates over the attribute set and adds a label and text field for each ID/value pair.

4. When the user clicks the Delete button, the deleteEntry method deletes the entry with the given uid and discards the data panel.

5. When the user clicks the Save button, the DataPanel constructs a BasicAttributes object with the current contents of the text fields. The saveEntry method checks whether the uid has changed. If the user edited the uid, a new entry is created. Otherwise, the modified attributes are updated. The modification code is simple because we have only one attribute with multiple values, namely, objectClass. In general, you would need to work harder to handle multiple values for each attribute.

6. Similar to the program in Example 4–4, we close the directory context when the frame window is closing.

You now know enough about directory operations to carry out the tasks that you will commonly need when working with LDAP directories. A good source for more advanced information is the JNDI tutorial at http://java.sun.com/products/jndi/tutorial.

Example 4–7: LDAPTest.java

```java
1. import java.net.*;
2. import java.awt.*;
3. import java.awt.event.*;
4. import java.io.*;
5. import java.util.*;
6. import javax.naming.*;
7. import javax.naming.directory.*;
8. import javax.swing.*;
9.
10. /**
11.    This program demonstrates access to a hierarchical database through LDAP
12. */
13. public class LDAPTest
14. {
15.    public static void main(String[] args)
16.    {
17.       JFrame frame = new LDAPFrame();
18.       frame.setDefaultCloseOperation(JFrame.EXIT_ON_CLOSE);
19.       frame.setVisible(true);
20.    }
21. }
22.
23. /**
24.    The frame that holds the data panel and the navigation buttons.
25. */
26. class LDAPFrame extends JFrame
27. {
28.    public LDAPFrame()
29.    {
30.       setTitle("LDAPTest");
31.       setSize(DEFAULT_WIDTH, DEFAULT_HEIGHT);
32.
33.       JPanel northPanel = new JPanel();
34.       northPanel.setLayout(new java.awt.GridLayout(1, 2, 3, 1));
35.       northPanel.add(new JLabel("uid", SwingConstants.RIGHT));
36.       uidField = new JTextField();
37.       northPanel.add(uidField);
38.       add(northPanel, BorderLayout.NORTH);
39.
40.       JPanel buttonPanel = new JPanel();
41.       add(buttonPanel, BorderLayout.SOUTH);
42.
```

```
43.     findButton = new JButton("Find");
44.     findButton.addActionListener(new
45.        ActionListener()
46.        {
47.           public void actionPerformed(ActionEvent event)
48.           {
49.              findEntry();
50.           }
51.        });
52.     buttonPanel.add(findButton);
53.
54.     saveButton = new JButton("Save");
55.     saveButton.addActionListener(new
56.        ActionListener()
57.        {
58.           public void actionPerformed(ActionEvent event)
59.           {
60.              saveEntry();
61.           }
62.        });
63.     buttonPanel.add(saveButton);
64.
65.     deleteButton = new JButton("Delete");
66.     deleteButton.addActionListener(new
67.        ActionListener()
68.        {
69.           public void actionPerformed(ActionEvent event)
70.           {
71.              deleteEntry();
72.           }
73.        });
74.     buttonPanel.add(deleteButton);
75.
76.     addWindowListener(new
77.        WindowAdapter()
78.        {
79.           public void windowClosing(WindowEvent event)
80.           {
81.              try
82.              {
83.                 if (context != null) context.close();
84.              }
85.              catch (NamingException e)
86.              {
87.                 e.printStackTrace();
88.              }
89.           }
90.        });
91.  }
92.
93.  /**
94.     Finds the entry for the uid in the text field.
95.  */
96.  public void findEntry()
97.  {
98.     try
```

```
 99.     {
100.         if (scrollPane != null) remove(scrollPane);
101.         String dn = "uid=" + uidField.getText() + ",ou=people,dc=mycompany,dc=com";
102.         if (context == null) context = getContext();
103.         attrs = context.getAttributes(dn);
104.         dataPanel = new DataPanel(attrs);
105.         scrollPane = new JScrollPane(dataPanel);
106.         add(scrollPane, BorderLayout.CENTER);
107.         validate();
108.         uid = uidField.getText();
109.     }
110.     catch (NamingException e)
111.     {
112.         JOptionPane.showMessageDialog(this, e);
113.     }
114.     catch (IOException e)
115.     {
116.         JOptionPane.showMessageDialog(this, e);
117.     }
118. }
119.
120. /**
121.     Saves the changes that the user made.
122. */
123. public void saveEntry()
124. {
125.     try
126.     {
127.         if (dataPanel == null) return;
128.         if (context == null) context = getContext();
129.         if (uidField.getText().equals(uid)) // update existing entry
130.         {
131.             String dn = "uid=" + uidField.getText() + ",ou=people,dc=mycompany,dc=com";
132.             Attributes editedAttrs = dataPanel.getEditedAttributes();
133.             NamingEnumeration<? extends Attribute> attrEnum = attrs.getAll();
134.             while (attrEnum.hasMore())
135.             {
136.                 Attribute attr = attrEnum.next();
137.                 String id = attr.getID();
138.                 Object value = attr.get();
139.                 Attribute editedAttr = editedAttrs.get(id);
140.                 if (editedAttr != null && !attr.get().equals(editedAttr.get()))
141.                     context.modifyAttributes(dn, DirContext.REPLACE_ATTRIBUTE,
142.                         new BasicAttributes(id, editedAttr.get()));
143.             }
144.         }
145.         else // create new entry
146.         {
147.             String dn = "uid=" + uidField.getText() + ",ou=people,dc=mycompany,dc=com";
148.             attrs = dataPanel.getEditedAttributes();
149.             Attribute objclass = new BasicAttribute("objectClass");
150.             objclass.add("uidObject");
151.             objclass.add("person");
152.             attrs.put(objclass);
153.             attrs.put("uid", uidField.getText());
154.             context.createSubcontext(dn, attrs);
```

```
155.        }
156.
157.        findEntry();
158.      }
159.    catch (NamingException e)
160.    {
161.       JOptionPane.showMessageDialog(LDAPFrame.this, e);
162.       e.printStackTrace();
163.    }
164.    catch (IOException e)
165.    {
166.       JOptionPane.showMessageDialog(LDAPFrame.this, e);
167.       e.printStackTrace();
168.    }
169.  }
170.
171.  /**
172.     Deletes the entry for the uid in the text field.
173.  */
174.  public void deleteEntry()
175.  {
176.     try
177.     {
178.        String dn = "uid=" + uidField.getText() + ",ou=people,dc=mycompany,dc=com";
179.        if (context == null) context = getContext();
180.        context.destroySubcontext(dn);
181.        uidField.setText("");
182.        remove(scrollPane);
183.        scrollPane = null;
184.        repaint();
185.     }
186.    catch (NamingException e)
187.    {
188.       JOptionPane.showMessageDialog(LDAPFrame.this, e);
189.       e.printStackTrace();
190.    }
191.    catch (IOException e)
192.    {
193.       JOptionPane.showMessageDialog(LDAPFrame.this, e);
194.       e.printStackTrace();
195.    }
196.  }
197.
198.  /**
199.     Gets a context from the properties specified in the file ldapserver.properties
200.     @return the directory context
201.  */
202.  public static DirContext getContext()
203.     throws NamingException, IOException
204.  {
205.     Properties props = new Properties();
206.     FileInputStream in = new FileInputStream("ldapserver.properties");
207.     props.load(in);
208.     in.close();
209.
210.     String url = props.getProperty("ldap.url");
```

```
211.      String username = props.getProperty("ldap.username");
212.      String password = props.getProperty("ldap.password");
213.
214.      Hashtable<String, String> env = new Hashtable<String, String>();
215.      env.put(Context.SECURITY_PRINCIPAL, username);
216.      env.put(Context.SECURITY_CREDENTIALS, password);
217.      DirContext initial = new InitialDirContext(env);
218.      DirContext context = (DirContext) initial.lookup(url);
219.
220.      return context;
221.   }
222.
223.   public static final int DEFAULT_WIDTH = 300;
224.   public static final int DEFAULT_HEIGHT = 200;
225.
226.   private JButton findButton;
227.   private JButton saveButton;
228.   private JButton deleteButton;
229.
230.   private JTextField uidField;
231.   private DataPanel dataPanel;
232.   private Component scrollPane;
233.
234.   private DirContext context;
235.   private String uid;
236.   private Attributes attrs;
237. }
238.
239. /**
240.    This panel displays the contents of a result set.
241. */
242. class DataPanel extends JPanel
243. {
244.    /**
245.       Constructs the data panel.
246.       @param attributes the attributes of the given entry
247.    */
248.    public DataPanel(Attributes attrs) throws NamingException
249.    {
250.       setLayout(new java.awt.GridLayout(0, 2, 3, 1));
251.
252.       NamingEnumeration<? extends Attribute> attrEnum = attrs.getAll();
253.       while (attrEnum.hasMore())
254.       {
255.          Attribute attr = attrEnum.next();
256.          String id = attr.getID();
257.
258.          NamingEnumeration<?> valueEnum = attr.getAll();
259.          while (valueEnum.hasMore())
260.          {
261.             Object value = valueEnum.next();
262.             if (id.equals("userPassword"))
263.                value = new String((byte[]) value);
264.
265.             JLabel idLabel = new JLabel(id, SwingConstants.RIGHT);
266.             JTextField valueField = new JTextField("" + value);
```

```
267.          if (id.equals("objectClass"))
268.             valueField.setEditable(false);
269.          if (!id.equals("uid"))
270.          {
271.             add(idLabel);
272.             add(valueField);
273.          }
274.       }
275.    }
276. }
277.
278. public Attributes getEditedAttributes()
279. {
280.    Attributes attrs = new BasicAttributes();
281.    for (int i = 0; i < getComponentCount(); i += 2)
282.    {
283.       JLabel idLabel = (JLabel) getComponent(i);
284.       JTextField valueField = (JTextField) getComponent(i + 1);
285.       String id = idLabel.getText();
286.       String value = valueField.getText();
287.       if (id.equals("userPassword"))
288.          attrs.put("userPassword", value.getBytes());
289.       else if (!id.equals("") && !id.equals("objectClass"))
290.          attrs.put(id, value);
291.    }
292.    return attrs;
293. }
294. }
```

 javax.naming.directory.InitialDirContext 1.3

- InitialDirContext(Hashtable env)
  constructs a directory context, using the given environment settings. The hash table
  can contain bindings for Context.SECURITY_PRINCIPAL, Context.SECURITY_CREDENTIALS, and other
  keys—see the API documentation for the javax.naming.Context interface for details.

 javax.naming.Context 1.3

- Object lookup(String name)
  looks up the object with the given name. The return value depends on the nature of
  this context. It commonly is a subtree context or a leaf object.

- Context createSubcontext(String name)
  creates a subcontext with the given name. The subcontext becomes a child of this
  context. All path components of the name, except for the last one, must exist.

- void destroySubcontext(String name)
  destroys the subcontext with the given name. All path components of the name,
  except for the last one, must exist.

- void close()
  closes this context.

 javax.naming.directory.DirContext 1.3

- Attributes getAttributes(String name)
  gets the attributes of the entry with the given name.

- void modifyAttributes(String name, int flag, Attributes modes)
  modifies the attributes of the entry with the given name. The value flag is one of DirContext.ADD_ATTRIBUTE, DirContext.REMOVE_ATTRIBUTE, or DirContext.REPLACE_ATTRIBUTE.

 javax.naming.directory.Attributes 1.3

- Attribute get(String id)
  gets the attribute with the given ID.
- NamingEnumeration<? extends Attribute> getAll()
  yields an enumeration that iterates through all attributes in this attribute set.
- Attribute put(Attribute attr)
- Attribute put(String id, Object value)
  add an attribute to this attribute set.

javax.naming.directory.BasicAttributes 1.3

- BasicAttributes(String id, Object value)
  constructs an attribute set that contains a single attribute with the given ID and value.

javax.naming.directory.Attribute 1.3

- String getID()
  gets the ID of this attribute.
- Object get()
  gets the first attribute value of this attribute if the values are ordered or an arbitrary value if they are unordered.
- NamingEnumeration<?> getAll()
  yields an enumeration that iterates through all values of this attribute.

javax.naming.NamingEnumeration<T> 1.3

- boolean hasMore()
  returns true if this enumeration object has more elements.
- T next()
  returns the next element of this enumeration.

Chapter **5**

Distributed Objects

Periodically, the programming community starts thinking of "objects everywhere" as the solution to all its problems. The idea is to have a happy family of collaborating objects that can be located anywhere. These objects are, of course, supposed to communicate through standard protocols across a network. For example, you'll have an object on the client where the user can fill in a request for data. The client object sends a message to an object on the server that contains the details of the request. The server object gathers the requested information, perhaps by accessing a database or by communicating with additional objects. Once the server object has the answer to the client request, it sends the answer back to the client. Like most bandwagons in programming, this plan contains a fair amount of hype that can obscure the utility of the concept. This chapter

- Explains the models that make interobject communication possible;
- Explains situations in which distributed objects can be useful;
- Shows you how to use remote objects and the associated *remote method invocation* (RMI) for communicating between two Java virtual machines (which may run on different computers); and
- Introduces you to CORBA and SOAP, technologies that allow communication between objects that are written in different programming languages.

The Roles of Client and Server

Let's go back to that idea of locally collecting information on a client computer and sending the information across a network to a server. We are supposing that a user on a local

machine will fill out an information request form. The data is sent to the vendor's server. The server processes the request and will, in turn, want to send back product information the client can view, as shown in Figure 5–1.

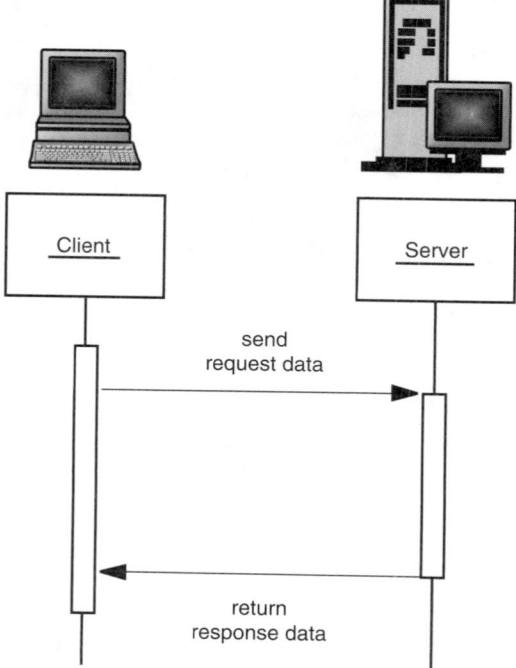

Figure 5–1: Transmitting objects between client and server

In the traditional client/server model, the client translates the request to an intermediary transmission format and sends the request data to the server. The server parses the request format, computes the response, and formats the response for transmission to the client. The client then parses the response and displays it to the user.

If you implement this approach by hand, there is a significant coding hassle: You have to design a transmission format, and you have to write code for conversion between your data and the transmission format.

 NOTE: In this particular example, we assume that the client is a computer that interacts with a human user. However, the client could equally be a computer that runs a web application and that requires a service from a program that runs on another computer. You again have two communicating objects, the client object in the web application and the server object that implements the service. This is a very common model in practice. In the examples of this chapter, we stick to a more traditional client/server example because it makes the roles of the client and server more intuitive.

What we want is a mechanism by which the client programmer makes a regular method call, without worrying about sending data across the network or parsing the response. The problem is, of course, that the object that carries out the work is *not* located in the same virtual machine. It might not even be implemented in the Java programming language.

The solution is to install a *proxy* for the server object on the client. The client calls the proxy, making a regular method call. The client proxy contacts the server.

Similarly, the programmer of the server object doesn't want to fuss with client communication. The solution is to install a second proxy object on the server. The server proxy communicates with the client proxy, and it makes regular method calls to the server object (see Figure 5–2).

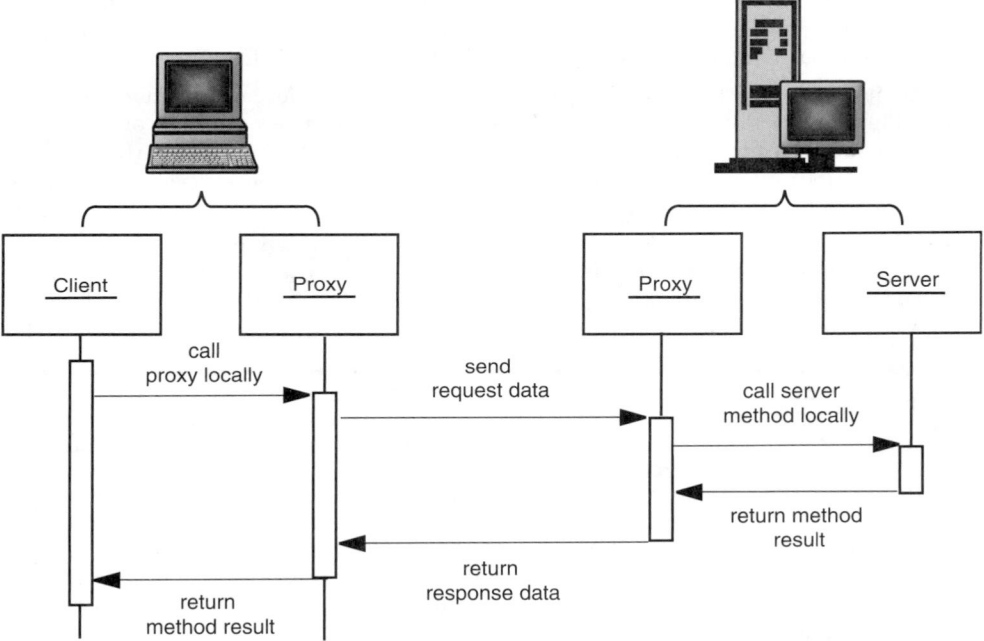

Figure 5–2: Remote method call with proxies

How do the proxies communicate with each other? That depends on the implementation technology. There are three common choices:

- RMI, the Java Remote Method Invocation technology, supports method calls between distributed Java objects.
- CORBA, the Common Object Request Broker Architecture, supports method calls between objects of any programming language. CORBA uses the Internet Inter-ORB Protocol, or IIOP, to communicate between objects.
- SOAP, the Simple Object Access Protocol, is also programming-language neutral. However, SOAP uses an XML-based transmission format.

 NOTE: Microsoft uses COM, a different, lower-level protocol for interobject communication. ORB-like services are bundled into the Windows operating system. In the past, Microsoft positioned COM as a competitor to CORBA. However, at the time of this writing, Microsoft is deemphasizing COM and focusing on SOAP.

CORBA and SOAP are completely language neutral. Client and server programs can be written in C, C++, Java, or any other language. You supply an *interface description* to specify the signatures of the methods and the types of the data your objects can handle. These descriptions are formatted in a special language, called Interface Definition Language (IDL) for CORBA and Web Services Description Language (WSDL) for SOAP.

Quite a few people believe that CORBA is the object model of the future. Frankly, though, CORBA has had a reputation—sometimes deserved—for complex implementations and interoperability problems. After running into quite a few CORBA problems while writing this chapter, our sentiments about CORBA are similar to those expressed by French president Charles De Gaulle about Brazil: It has a great future . . . and always will.

SOAP may have once been simple, but it too has become complex, as it acquires more of the features that CORBA had all along. The XML protocol has the advantage of being (barely) human-readable, which helps with debugging. On the other hand, XML processing is a significant performance bottleneck. Overall, CORBA is more efficient, although SOAP is a better fit for a web architecture.

If both communicating objects are implemented in Java code, then the full generality and complexity of CORBA and SOAP is not required. Sun developed a simpler mechanism, called Remote Method Invocation (RMI), specifically for communication between Java applications.

 NOTE: CORBA supporters initially did not like RMI because it completely ignored the CORBA standard. However, starting with JDK 1.3, CORBA and RMI have become more interoperable. In particular, you can use RMI with the IIOP protocol instead of the proprietary Java Remote Method Protocol. For more information on RMI over IIOP, see the introductory article at http://www.javaworld.com/javaworld/jw-12-1999/jw-12-iiop.html and the tutorial at http://java.sun.com/j2se/1.4/docs/guide/rmi-iiop/rmiiiopexample.html. A very thorough example is at http://www.ociweb.com/jnb/jnbApr2004.html.

Because RMI is easier to understand than CORBA or SOAP, we start this chapter with a thorough discussion of RMI. In the last sections of this chapter, we briefly introduce CORBA and SOAP. We show you how to use CORBA for communicating between Java and C++ programs and how to access a web service with SOAP.

Remote Method Invocations

The Remote Method Invocation mechanism lets you do something that sounds simple. If you have access to an object on a different machine, you can call methods of the remote object. Of course, the method parameters must somehow be shipped to the other machine, the server must be informed to execute the method, and the return value must be shipped back. RMI handles these details.

For example, the client seeking product information can query a Warehouse object on the server. It calls a remote method, find, which has one parameter: a Customer object. The find method returns an object to the client: the Product object (see Figure 5–3).

In RMI terminology, the object whose method makes the remote call is called the *client object*. The remote object is called the *server object*. It is important to remember that the client/server terminology applies only to a single method call. The computer running the Java code that calls the remote method is the client for *that* call, and the computer hosting the object that processes the call is the server for *that* call. It is entirely possible that the roles are reversed somewhere down the road. The server of a previous call can itself become the client when it invokes a remote method on an object residing on another computer.

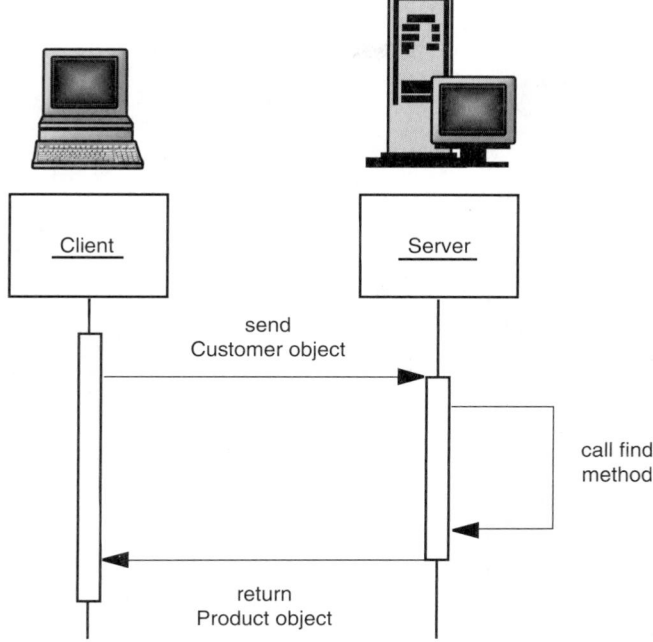

Figure 5–3: Invoking a remote method on a server object

Stubs and Parameter Marshalling

When client code wants to invoke a remote method on a remote object, it actually calls an ordinary method on a proxy object called a *stub*. The stub resides on the client machine, not on the server. The stub packages the parameters used in the remote method into a block of bytes. This packaging uses a device-independent encoding for each parameter. For example, in the RMI protocol, numbers are always sent in big-endian byte ordering, and objects are encoded with the serialization mechanism that is described in Volume 1, Chapter 12. The process of encoding the parameters is called *parameter marshalling*. The purpose of parameter marshalling is to convert the parameters into a format suitable for transport from one virtual machine to another.

To sum up, the stub method on the client builds an information block that consists of

- An identifier of the remote object to be used;
- A description of the method to be called; and
- The marshalled parameters.

The stub then sends this information to the server. On the server side, a receiver object performs the following actions for every remote method call:

- It unmarshals the parameters.
- It locates the object to be called.
- It calls the desired method.
- It captures and marshals the return value or exception of the call.
- It sends a package consisting of the marshalled return data back to the stub on the client.

The client stub unmarshals the return value or exception from the server. This value becomes the return value of the stub call. Or, if the remote method threw an exception, the stub rethrows it in the process space of the caller. Figure 5–4 shows the information flow of a remote method invocation.

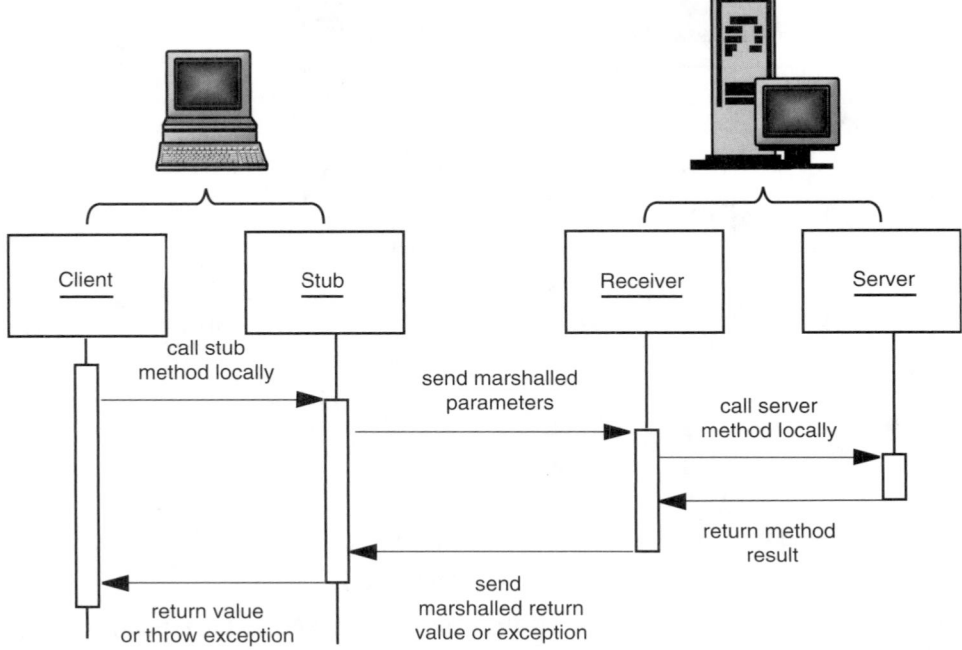

Figure 5–4: Parameter marshalling

This process is obviously complex, but the good news is that it is completely automatic and, to a large extent, transparent for the programmer. Moreover, the designers of the remote Java object tried hard to give remote objects the same "look and feel" as local objects.

The syntax for a remote method call is the same as for a local call. If centralWarehouse references a stub object for a central warehouse object on a remote machine and getQuantity is the method you want to invoke on it, then a typical call looks like this:

```
int q = centralWarehouse.getQuantity("SuperSucker 100 Vacuum Cleaner");
```

The client code always uses object variables whose type is an interface to access remote objects. For example, associated to this call would be an interface:

```
interface Warehouse
{
   int getQuantity(String description)
      throws RemoteException;
   Product getProduct(Customer cust)
      throws RemoteException;
   . . .
}
```

An object declaration for a variable that will implement the interface is

```
Warehouse centralWarehouse = . . .;
```

Of course, interfaces are abstract entities that only spell out what methods can be called along with their signatures. Variables whose type is an interface must always be bound to an actual object of some type. When remote methods are called, the object variable refers to a *stub object*. The client program does not actually know the type of those objects. The stub classes and the associated objects are created automatically.

Although the designers did a good job of hiding many details of remote method invocation from the programmer, a number of techniques and caveats still must be mastered.

 NOTE: Remote objects are garbage-collected automatically, just as local objects are. However, the current distributed collector uses reference counting and cannot detect cycles of objects that refer to each other but have no external reference into the cycle. Cycles must be explicitly broken by the programmer before the remote objects can be reclaimed.

Dynamic Class Loading

When you pass a remote object to another program, either as a parameter or return value of a remote method, then that program must have the class file for that object. For example, consider a method with return type Product. Of course, the client program needs the class file Product.class to compile. But now suppose the server constructs and returns a Book object, and Book is a subtype of Product. The client may have never seen the Book class, and it may have no idea where to find the class file Book.class. Therefore, a class loader that will load required classes from the server is required. The process is similar to the class loading process of applets that run in a browser.

Whenever a program loads new code from another network location, there is a security issue. For that reason, you need to use a *security manager* in RMI client applications. This is a safety mechanism that protects the program from viruses in stub code. For specialized applications, programmers can substitute their own class loaders and security managers, but those provided by the RMI system suffice for normal usage. (See Chapter 9 for more information on class loaders and security managers.)

Setup for Remote Method Invocation

Running even the simplest remote object example requires quite a bit more setup than does running a standalone program or applet. You must run programs on both the server and client computers. The necessary object information must be separated into client-side interfaces and server-side implementations. Also, a special lookup mechanism allows the client to locate objects on the server.

To get started with the actual coding, we walk through each of these requirements, using a simple example. In our first example, we generate a couple of objects of a type Product on the server computer. We then run a program on a client computer that locates and queries these objects.

Interfaces and Implementations

Your client program needs to manipulate server objects, but it doesn't actually have copies of them. The objects themselves reside on the server. The client code must still know what it can do with those objects. Their capabilities are expressed in an interface that is shared between the client and server and so resides simultaneously on both machines.

```
interface Product // shared by client and server
   extends Remote
{
   String getDescription() throws RemoteException;
}
```

Just as in this example, *all* interfaces for remote objects must extend the Remote interface defined in the java.rmi package. All the methods in those interfaces must also declare that they will throw a RemoteException. The reason for the declaration is that remote method calls are inherently less reliable than local calls—it is always possible that a remote call will fail. For example, the server or the network connection may be temporarily unavailable, or there may be a network problem. Your client code must be prepared to deal with these possibilities. For these reasons, the Java programming language forces you to catch the RemoteException with *every* remote method call and to specify the appropriate action to take when the call does not succeed.

The client accesses the server object through a stub that implements this interface.

```
Product p = . . .; // see below how the client gets a stub reference
String d = p.getDescription();
System.out.println(d);
```

In the next section, you will see how the client can obtain a reference to this kind of remote object.

Next, on the server side, you must implement the class that actually carries out the methods advertised in the remote interface.

```
public class ProductImpl // server
    extends UnicastRemoteObject
    implements Product
{
    public ProductImpl(String d)
        throws RemoteException
    {
        descr = d;
    }

    public String getDescription()
        throws RemoteException
    {
        return "I am a " + descr + ". Buy me!";
    }

    private String descr;
}
```

 NOTE: The ProductImpl constructor is declared to throw a RemoteException because the UnicastRemoteObject might throw that exception if it can't connect to the network service that keeps track of server objects.

This class has a single method, getDescription, that can be called from the remote client.

You can tell that the class is a server for remote methods because it extends UnicastRemoteObject, which is a concrete Java platform class that makes objects remotely accessible.

 NOTE: The ProductImpl class is *not* a typical server class because it does so little work. Normally, you only want to have server classes that do some heavy-duty work that a client could not carry out locally. We just use the Product example to walk you through the mechanics of calling remote methods.

Server classes generally extend the class RemoteServer from the java.rmi.server package, but RemoteServer is an abstract class that defines only the basic mechanisms for the communication between server objects and their remote stubs. The UnicastRemoteObject class that comes with RMI extends the RemoteServer abstract class and is concrete—so you can use it without writing any code. The "path of least resistance" for a server class is to derive from Unicast-RemoteObject, and all server classes in this chapter do so. Figure 5–5 shows the inheritance relationship between these classes.

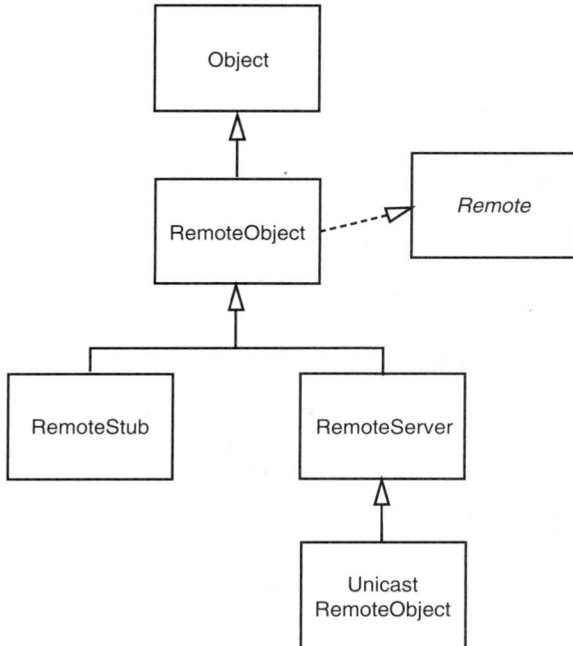

Figure 5–5: Fundamental RMI classes

A UnicastRemoteObject object resides on a server. It must be alive when a service is requested and must be reachable through the TCP/IP protocol. This is the class that we extend for all the server classes in this book and is the only server class available in the current version of the RMI package. Sun or third-party vendors may, in the future, design other classes for use by servers for RMI.

 NOTE: Occasionally, you may not want a server class that extends the UnicastRemoteObject class, perhaps because it already extends another class. In that situation, you need to manually instantiate the server objects and pass them to the static exportObject method. Instead of extending UnicastRemoteObject, call

```
UnicastRemoteObject.exportObject(this, 0);
```

in the constructor of the server object. The second parameter is 0 to indicate that any suitable port can be used to listen to client connections.

When you use RMI (or any distributed object mechanism, for that matter), you will have to master a somewhat bewildering set of classes. In this chapter, we use a uniform naming

convention for all of our examples that we hope makes it easier to recognize the purpose of each class (see Table 5–1).

Table 5–1: Naming Conventions for RMI Classes

No suffix (e.g., Product)	A remote interface
Impl suffix (e.g., ProductImpl)	A server class implementing that interface
Server suffix (e.g., ProductServer)	A server program that creates server objects
Client suffix (e.g., ProductClient)	A client program that calls remote methods
_Stub suffix (e.g., ProductImpl_Stub)	A stub class that is located on the client (needed prior to JDK 5.0)
_Skel suffix (e.g., ProductImpl_Skel)	A skeleton class that is located on the server (needed prior to JDK 1.2)

Stub Class Generation

As of JDK 5.0, all stub classes are generated automatically, using the proxy mechanism discussed in Volume 1, Chapter 6. However, before JDK 5.0, you had to manually generate stubs with the rmic tool, as in the following example.

```
rmic -v1.2 ProductImpl
```

This call to the rmic tool generates a class file ProductImpl_Stub.class.

If you still use JDK 1.1, call

```
rmic -v1.1 ProductImpl
```

Two files are generated: the stub file and a second class file named ProductImpl_Skel.class.

 NOTE: Remember to first compile the source file with javac before running rmic. If you are generating stubs for a class in a package, you must give rmic the full package name.

Locating Server Objects

To access a remote object that exists on the server, the client needs a local stub object. How can the client request such a stub? The most common method is to call a remote method of another server object and get a stub object as a return value. There is, however, a chicken-and-egg problem here. The *first* server object has to be located some other way. The Sun RMI library provides a *bootstrap registry service* to locate the first server object.

A server program registers objects with the bootstrap registry service, and the client retrieves stubs to those objects. You register a server object by giving the bootstrap registry service a reference to the object and a *name*. The name is a string that is (hopefully) unique.

```
// server
ProductImpl p1 = new ProductImpl("Blackwell Toaster");
Context namingContext = new InitialContext();
namingContext.bind("rmi:toaster", p1);
```

The client code gets a stub to access that server object by specifying the server name and the object name in the following way:

```
// client
Product p = (Product) namingContext.lookup("rmi://yourserver.com/toaster");
```

RMI URLs start with rmi:// and are followed by a server, an optional port number, another slash, and the name of the remote object. Another example is:

```
rmi://localhost:99/central_warehouse
```

By default, the server is localhost and the port number is 1099.

> **NOTE:** Because it is notoriously difficult to keep names unique in a global registry, you should not use this technique as the general method for locating objects on the server. Instead, there should be relatively few named server objects registered with the bootstrap service. These should be objects that can locate other objects for you. In our example, we temporarily violate this rule and register relatively trivial objects to show you the mechanics for registering and locating objects.

For security reasons, an application can bind, unbind, or rebind registry object references only if it runs on the same host as the registry. This prevents hostile clients from changing the registry information. However, any client can look up objects.

The RMI naming service is integrated into the Java Naming and Directory Information (JNDI) service. In JDK 1.3 and below, you use a standalone RMI naming service, like this:

```
Naming.bind("toaster", p1); // on the server
Product p = (Product) Naming.lookup("rmi://yourserver.com/toaster");
```

The code in Example 5–1 through Example 5–3 shows a complete server program that registers two Product objects under the names toaster and microwave.

> **TIP:** If you compare our server with the server examples in the Sun tutorial documentation, you will note that we do not install a security manager in the server. Contrary to the statements in the tutorial, a security manager is not necessary for RMI servers. You do need a security manager if the client sends to the server objects that belong to classes that the server doesn't know. However, in our service, the client only sends String parameters. In general, it seems wise to limit dynamic class loading on servers.

Example 5–1: ProductServer.java

```java
1.  import java.rmi.*;
2.  import java.rmi.server.*;
3.  import javax.naming.*;
4.
5.  /**
6.     This server program instantiates two remote objects,
7.     registers them with the naming service, and waits for
8.     clients to invoke methods on the remote objects.
9.  */
10. public class ProductServer
11. {
12.    public static void main(String args[])
13.    {
14.       try
15.       {
16.          System.out.println("Constructing server implementations...");
17.
18.          ProductImpl p1 = new ProductImpl("Blackwell Toaster");
19.          ProductImpl p2 = new ProductImpl("ZapXpress Microwave Oven");
20.
21.          System.out.println("Binding server implementations to registry...");
22.          Context namingContext = new InitialContext();
```

```
23.        namingContext.bind("rmi:toaster", p1);
24.        namingContext.bind("rmi:microwave", p2);
25.        System.out.println("Waiting for invocations from clients...");
26.     }
27.     catch (Exception e)
28.     {
29.        e.printStackTrace();
30.     }
31.   }
32. }
```

Example 5–2: ProductImpl.java

```
1. import java.rmi.*;
2. import java.rmi.server.*;
3.
4. /**
5.    This is the implementation class for the remote product
6.    objects.
7. */
8. public class ProductImpl
9.    extends UnicastRemoteObject
10.   implements Product
11. {
12.   /**
13.      Constructs a product implementation
14.      @param n the product name
15.   */
16.   public ProductImpl(String n) throws RemoteException
17.   {
18.      name = n;
19.   }
20.
21.   public String getDescription() throws RemoteException
22.   {
23.      return "I am a " + name + ". Buy me!";
24.   }
25.
26.   private String name;
27. }
```

Example 5–3: Product.java

```
1. import java.rmi.*;
2.
3. /**
4.    The interface for remote product objects.
5. */
6. public interface Product extends Remote
7. {
8.    /**
9.       Gets the description of this product.
10.      @return the product description
11.   */
12.   String getDescription() throws RemoteException;
13. }
```

Starting the Server

Our server program isn't quite ready to run yet. Because it uses the bootstrap RMI registry, that service must be available. To start the RMI registry under UNIX, execute the
statement

```
rmiregistry &
```

Under Windows, call

```
start rmiregistry
```

at a DOS prompt or from the Run dialog box. (The start command is a Windows command
that starts a program in a new window.)

Now you are ready to start the server. Under UNIX, use the command:

```
java ProductServer &
```

Under Windows, use the command:

```
start java ProductServer
```

If you run the server program as

```
java ProductServer
```

then the program will never exit normally. This seems strange—after all, the program just
creates two objects and registers them. Actually, the main function does exit immediately
after registration, as you would expect. However, when you create an object of a class that
extends UnicastRemoteObject, a separate thread that keeps the program alive indefinitely is
started. Thus, the program stays around to allow clients to connect to it.

> TIP: The Windows version of the JDK contains a command, javaw, that starts the bytecode
> interpreter as a separate Windows process and keeps it running. Some sources recommend
> that you use javaw, not start java, to run a Java session in the background in Windows for
> RMI. Doing so is not a good idea, for two reasons. Windows has no tool to kill a javaw back-
> ground process—it does not show up in the task list. It turns out that you need to kill and
> restart the bootstrap registry service when you change the stub of a registered class. To kill a
> process that you started with the start command, all you have to do is click on the window
> and press CTRL+C.
>
> There is another important reason to use the start command. When you run a server process
> by using javaw, messages sent to the output or error streams are discarded. In particular, they
> *are not* displayed *anywhere*. If you want to see output or error messages, use start instead.
> Then, error messages at least show up on the console. And trust us, you will want to see these
> messages. Lots of things can go wrong when you experiment with RMI. The most common
> error probably is that you forget to run rmic. Then, the server complains about missing stubs. If
> you use javaw, you won't see that error message, and you'll scratch your head wondering why
> the client can't find the server objects.

Listing Remote Objects

Before writing the client program, let's verify that we have succeeded in registering the
remote objects. Call

```
NamingEnumeration<NameClassPair> e = namingContext.list("rmi:");
```

to get an enumeration of all server objects with an rmi: URL. The enumeration yields objects
of type NameClassPair, a helper class that contains both the name of the bound object and the
name of its class. We only care about the names:

```
while (e.hasMore()) System.out.println(e.next().getName());
```

Example 5–4 contains the complete program. The output should be

```
toaster
microwave
```

Example 5–4: ShowBindings.java

```java
1. import java.rmi.*;
2. import java.rmi.server.*;
3. import javax.naming.*;
4.
5. /**
6.    This programs shows all RMI bindings.
7. */
8. public class ShowBindings
9. {
10.    public static void main(String[] args)
11.    {
12.       try
13.       {
14.          Context namingContext = new InitialContext();
15.          NamingEnumeration<NameClassPair> e = namingContext.list("rmi:");
16.          while (e.hasMore())
17.             System.out.println(e.next().getName());
18.       }
19.       catch (Exception e)
20.       {
21.          e.printStackTrace();
22.       }
23.    }
24. }
```

The Client Side

Now, we can write the client program that asks each newly registered product object to print its description.

Client programs that use RMI should install a security manager to control the activities of the dynamically loaded stubs. The RMISecurityManager is such a security manager. You install it with the instruction

```java
System.setSecurityManager(new RMISecurityManager());
```

 NOTE: If all classes (including stubs) are available locally, then you do not actually need a security manager. If you know all class files of your program at deployment time, you can deploy them all locally. However, it often happens that the server program evolves and new classes are added over time. Then you benefit from dynamic class loading. Any time you load code from another source, you need a security manager.

 NOTE: Applets already have a security manager that can control the loading of the stub classes. When using RMI from an applet, you do not install another security manager.

Example 5–5 shows the complete client program. The client simply obtains references to two Product objects in the RMI registry and invokes the getDescription method on both objects.

Example 5–5: ProductClient.java

```
1. import java.rmi.*;
2. import java.rmi.server.*;
3. import javax.naming.*;
4.
5. /**
6.    This program demonstrates how to call a remote method
7.    on two objects that are located through the naming service.
8. */
9. public class ProductClient
10. {
11.    public static void main(String[] args)
12.    {
13.       System.setProperty("java.security.policy", "client.policy");
14.       System.setSecurityManager(new RMISecurityManager());
15.       String url = "rmi://localhost/";
16.          // change to "rmi://yourserver.com/" when server runs on remote machine yourserver.com
17.       try
18.       {
19.          Context namingContext = new InitialContext();
20.          Product c1 = (Product) namingContext.lookup(url + "toaster");
21.          Product c2 = (Product) namingContext.lookup(url + "microwave");
22.
23.          System.out.println(c1.getDescription());
24.          System.out.println(c2.getDescription());
25.       }
26.       catch (Exception e)
27.       {
28.          e.printStackTrace();
29.       }
30.    }
31. }
```

Running the Client

By default, the RMISecurityManager restricts all code in the program from establishing network connections. However, the program needs to make network connections

- To reach the RMI registry; and
- To contact the server objects.

 NOTE: Once the client program is deployed, it also needs permission to load its stub classes. We address this issue later when we discuss deployment.

To allow the client to connect to the RMI registry and the server object, you supply a *policy file*. We discuss policy files in greater detail in Chapter 9. For now, just use and modify the samples that we supply. Here is a policy file that allows an application to make any network connection to a port with port number of at least 1024. (The RMI port is 1099 by default, and the server objects also use ports ≥ 1024.)

```
grant
{
   permission java.net.SocketPermission
      "*:1024-65535", "connect";
};
```

 NOTE: Multiple server objects on the same server can share a port. However, if a remote call is made and the port is busy, another port is opened automatically. Thus, you should expect some-what fewer ports to be used than there are remote objects on the server.

In the client program, we instruct the security manager to read the policy file by setting the java.security.policy property to the file name. (We use the file client.policy in our example programs.)

```
System.setProperty("java.security.policy", "client.policy");
```

Alternatively, you can specify the system property setting on the command line:

```
java -Djava.security.policy=client.policy ProductClient
```

 NOTE: In JDK 1.1, a policy file was not required for RMI clients. You don't need a policy file for applets either, provided the RMI server and the RMI registry are both located on the host that serves the applet code.

If the RMI registry and server are still running, you can proceed to run the client. Or, if you want to start from scratch, kill the RMI registry and the server. Then follow these steps:

1. Compile the source files for the interface, implementation, client, and server classes.
    ```
    javac Product*.java
    ```
2. If you use JDK 1.4 or below, run rmic on the implementation class.
    ```
    rmic -v1.2 ProductImpl
    ```
3. Start the RMI registry.
    ```
    rmiregistry &
    ```
    or
    ```
    start rmiregistry
    ```
4. Start the server.
    ```
    java ProductServer &
    ```
    or
    ```
    start java ProductServer
    ```
5. Run the client.
    ```
    java ProductClient
    ```
    (Make sure the client.policy file is in the current directory.)

The program simply prints

```
I am a Blackwell Toaster. Buy me!
I am a ZapXpress Microwave Oven. Buy me!
```

This output doesn't seem all that impressive, but consider what goes on behind the scenes when the client program executes the call to the getDescription method. The client program has a reference to a stub object that it obtained from the lookup method. It calls the getDescription method, which sends a network message to a receiver object on the server side. The receiver object invokes the getDescription method on the ProductImpl object located on the server. That method computes a string. The receiver sends that string across the network. The stub receives it and returns it as the result (see Figure 5–6).

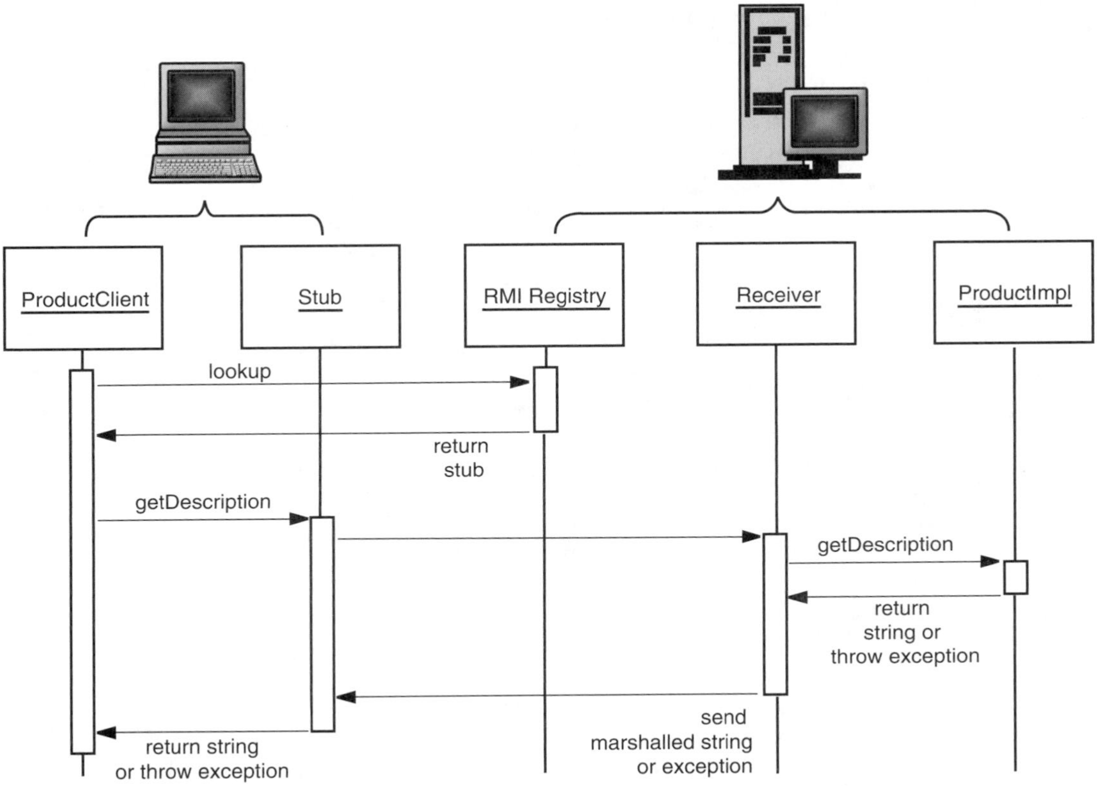

Figure 5–6: Calling the remote `getDescription` **method**

---

 javax.naming.InitialContext 1.3

- `InitialContext()`
  constructs a naming context that can be used for accessing the RMI registry.

 javax.naming.Context 1.3

- `static Object lookup(String name)`
  returns the object for the given name. Throws a `NamingException` if the name is not currently bound.
- `static void bind(String name, Object obj)`
  binds `name` to the object `obj`. Throws a `NameAlreadyBoundException` if the object is already bound.
- `static void unbind(String name)`
  unbinds the name. It is legal to unbind a name that doesn't exist.
- `static void rebind(String name, Object obj)`
  binds `name` to the object `obj`. Replaces any existing binding.
- `NamingEnumeration<NameClassPair> list(String name)`
  returns an enumeration listing all matching bound objects. To list all RMI objects, call with `"rmi:"`.

 javax.naming.NamingEnumeration<T> 1.3

- boolean hasMore()
  returns true if this enumeration has more elements.
- T next()
  returns the next element of this enumeration.

 javax.naming.NameClassPair 1.3

- String getName()
  gets the name of the named object.
- String getClassName()
  gets the name of the class to which the named object belongs.

 java.rmi.Naming 1.1

- static Remote lookup(String url)
  returns the remote object for the URL. Throws a NotBoundException if the name is not currently bound.
- static void bind(String name, Remote obj)
  binds name to the remote object obj. Throws an AlreadyBoundException if the object is already bound.
- static void unbind(String name)
  unbinds the name. Throws the NotBound exception if the name is not currently bound.
- static void rebind(String name, Remote obj)
  binds name to the remote object obj. Replaces any existing binding.
- static String[] list(String url)
  returns an array of strings of the URLs in the registry located at the given URL. The array contains a snapshot of the names present in the registry.

Preparing for Deployment

Deploying an application that uses RMI can be tricky because so many things can go wrong and the error messages that you get when something does go wrong are so poor. We have found that it really pays off to stage the deployment locally. In this preparatory step, separate the class files into three subdirectories:

```
server
download
client
```

The server directory contains all files that are needed to *run the server*. You will later move these files to the machine running the server process. In our example, the server directory contains the following files:

```
server/
    ProductServer.class
    ProductImpl.class
    Product.class
```

 CAUTION: If you use JDK 1.4 or below, add the stub classes (such as ProductImpl_Stub.class) to the server directory. They are needed when the server registers the implementation object. Contrary to popular belief, the server will not locate them in the download directory, even if you set the codebase.

The client directory contains the files that are needed to *start the client*. These are

```
client/
    ProductClient.class
    Product.class
    client.policy
```

You will deploy these files on the client computer.

Finally, the download directory contains those class files needed by the RMI registry, the client, and the server, *as well as the classes they depend on*. In our example, the download directory looks like this:

```
download/
    Product.class
```

If your clients run JDK 1.4 or lower, also supply the stub classes (such as ProductImpl_Stub.class). If the server runs JDK 1.1, then you need to supply the skeleton classes (such as ProductImpl_Skel.class). You will later place these files on a web server.

 CAUTION: Keep in mind that *three* virtual machines use the download directory: the client, the server, and the RMI registry. The RMI registry needs the class files for the remote interfaces of the objects that it binds. The client and server need the class files for parameters and return values.

Now you have all class files partitioned correctly, and you can test that they can all be loaded.

You need to run a web server to serve the class files on your computer. If you don't have a web server installed, download Tomcat from http://jakarta.apache.org/tomcat and install it. Make a directory *tomcat*/webapps/download, where *tomcat* is the base directory of your Tomcat installation. Make a subdirectory *tomcat*/webapps/download/WEB-INF, and place the following minimal web.xml file inside the WEB-INF subdirectory:

```
<?xml version="1.0" encoding="utf-8"?>
<!DOCTYPE web-app PUBLIC "-//Sun Microsystems, Inc.//DTD Web Application 2.3//EN"
    "http://java.sun.com/dtd/web-app_2_3.dtd">
<web-app>
</web-app>
```

Then copy the class files from the download staging directory into the directory *tomcat*/webapps/ download.

Next, edit the client.policy file. It must give the client these permissions:

- To connect to ports 1024 and above to reach the RMI registry and the server implementations;
- To connect to port 80 (the standard HTTP port) to load the stub class files. You can omit this permission if you use Tomcat as a web server—it uses port 8080 by default.

Change the file to look like this:

```
grant
{
    permission java.net.SocketPermission
        "*:1024-65535", "connect";
    permission java.net.SocketPermission
        "*:80", "connect";
};
```

Finally, you are ready to test your setup.

1. Start the web server.

2. Point a web browser to the download URL (`http://localhost:8080/download/Product.class` for Tomcat) to verify that the web server is running.

3. Start a new shell. Make sure that the *class path is not set* to anything. Change to a directory that contains *no class files*. Then start the RMI registry.

 CAUTION: If you just want to test out your program and have client, server, and stub class files in a single directory, then you can start the RMI registry in that directory. However, for deployment, make sure to start the registry in a shell with *no class path* and in a directory with *no class files*. Otherwise, the RMI registry may find spurious class files that will confuse it when it should download additional classes from a different source. There is a reason for this behavior; see `http://java.sun.com/j2se/5.0/docs/guide/rmi/codebase.html`.

RMI registry confusion is a major source of grief for RMI deployment. The easiest way of protecting yourself is to make sure that the RMI registry cannot find any classes.

---

4. Start a new shell. Change to the `server` directory. Start the server, giving a URL to the download directory as the value of the `java.rmi.server.codebase` property:

   ```
   java -Djava.rmi.server.codebase=http://localhost:8080/download/ ProductServer &
   ```

 CAUTION: It is very important that you make sure that *the URL ends with a slash* (/).

---

5. Change to the `client` directory. Make sure the `client.policy` file is in that directory. Start the client.

   ```
   java -Djava.security.policy=client.policy ProductClient
   ```

If both the server and the client started up without a hitch, then you are ready to go to the next step and deploy the classes on a separate client and server. If not, you need to do some more tweaking.

 TIP: If you do not want to install a web server locally, you can use a file URL to test class loading. However, the setup is a bit trickier. Add the line

```
permission java.io.FilePermission
   "downloadDirectory", "read";
```

to your client policy file. Here, the download directory is the full path name to the download directory, enclosed in quotes, and ending in a minus sign (to denote all files in that directory and its subdirectories). For example,

```
permission java.io.FilePermission "/home/test/download/-", "read";
```

In Windows file names, you have to double each backslash. For example,

```
permission java.io. FilePermission "c:\\home\\test\\download\\-", "read";
```

Start the RMI registry, then the server with

```
java -Djava.rmi.server.codebase=file://home/test/download/ ProductServer &
```

or

```
start java -Djava.rmi.server.codebase=file:/c:\home\test\download/ ProductServer
```

(Remember to add a slash at the end of the URL.) Then start the client.

Deploying the Program

Now that you have tested the deployment of your program, you are ready to distribute it onto the actual clients and servers.

Move the classes in the download directory to the web server. Make sure to use that URL when starting the server. Move the classes in the server directory onto your server and start the RMI registry and the server.

Your server setup is now finalized, but you need to make two changes in the client. First, edit the policy file and replace * with your server name:

```
grant
{
   permission java.net.SocketPermission
      "yourserver.com:1024-65535", "connect";
   permission java.net.SocketPermission
      "yourserver.com:80", "connect";
};
```

Finally, replace localhost in the RMI URL of the client program with the actual server.

```
String url = "rmi://yourserver.com/";
Product c1 = (Product) namingContext.lookup(url + "toaster");
. . .
```

Then, recompile the client and try it. If everything works, then congratulations are in order. If not, you may find the sidebar checklist helpful. It lists a number of problems that can commonly arise when you are trying to get RMI to work.

TIP: In practice, you would not want to hardcode the RMI URLs into your program. Instead, you can store them in a property file. We use that technique in Example 5–13.

RMI Deployment Checklist

Deploying RMI is tough because it either works or it fails with a cryptic error message. Judging from the traffic on the RMI discussion list at http://archives.java.sun.com/archives/rmi-users.html, many programmers initially run into grief. If you do too, you may find it helpful to check out the following issues. We managed to get every one of them wrong at least once during testing.

- Did you put the interface class files into the download and client directory?
- Did you put the stub class files into the server directory (for JDK 1.4 or below)?
- Did you include the dependent classes for each class? For example, in the next section, you will see an interface Warehouse that has a method with a parameter of type Customer. Be sure to include Customer.class whenever you deploy Warehouse.class.
- When you started rmiregistry, was the CLASSPATH unset? Was the current directory free from class files?
- Did you use a policy file when starting the client? Does the policy file contain the correct server names (or * to connect to any host)?
- If you used a file: URL for testing, did you specify the correct file name in the policy file? Does it end in a /- or \\- ? Did you remember to use \\ for Windows file names?
- Does your codebase URL end in a slash?

Finally, note that the RMI registry remembers the class files that it found as well as those that it failed to find. If you keep adding or removing various class files to test which files are really necessary, make sure to restart rmiregistry each time.

Logging RMI Activity

The Sun RMI implementation is instrumented to produce logging messages, using the standard Java logging API. (See Volume 1, Chapter 11 for more information on logging.)

To see the logging in action, make a file `logging.properties` with the following content:

```
handlers=java.util.logging.ConsoleHandler
.level=FINEST
java.util.logging.ConsoleHandler.level=FINEST
java.util.logging.ConsoleHandler.formatter=java.util.logging.SimpleFormatter
```

You can fine-tune the settings by setting individual levels for each logger rather than setting the global level to FINEST. Table 5–2 lists the RMI loggers.

Table 5–2: RMI Loggers

Logger Name	Logged Activity
sun.rmi.server.call	Server-side remote calls
sun.rmi.server.ref	Server-side remote references
sun.rmi.client.call	Client-side remote calls
sun.rmi.client.ref	Client-side remote references
sun.rmi.dgc	Distributed garbage collection
sun.rmi.loader	RMIClassLoader
sun.rmi.transport.misc	Transport layer
sun.rmi.transport.tcp	TCP binding and connection
sun.rmi.transport.proxy	HTTP tunneling

Start the RMI registry with the option

```
-J-Djava.util.logging.config.file=directory/logging.properties
```

Start the client and server with

```
-Djava.util.logging.config.file=directory/logging.properties
```

It is best to start the RMI registry, client, and server in different windows. Alternatively, you can log the messages to a file—see Volume 1, Chapter 11 for instructions.

Here is an example of a logging message that shows a class loading problem: The RMI registry cannot find the Product class. It needs it to build a dynamic proxy.

```
Aug 15, 2004 10:44:07 AM sun.rmi.server.LoaderHandler loadProxyClass
FINE: RMI TCP Connection(1)-127.0.0.1: interfaces = [java.rmi.Remote, Product],
codebase = "http://localhost:8080/download/"
Aug 15, 2004 10:44:07 AM sun.rmi.server.LoaderHandler loadProxyClass
FINER: RMI TCP Connection(1)-127.0.0.1: (thread context class loader: java.net.URLClassLoader@6ca1c)
Aug 15, 2004 10:44:07 AM sun.rmi.server.LoaderHandler loadProxyClass
FINE: RMI TCP Connection(1)-127.0.0.1: proxy class resolution failed
java.lang.ClassNotFoundException: Product
```

Parameter Passing in Remote Methods

You often want to pass parameters to remote objects. This section explains some of the techniques for doing so—along with some of the pitfalls.

Passing Nonremote Objects

When a remote object is passed from the server to the client, the client receives a stub. Using the stub, it can manipulate the server object by invoking remote methods. The object,

however, stays on the server. It is also possible to pass and return *any* objects with a remote method call, not just those that implement the Remote interface. For example, the getDescription method of the preceding section returned a String object. That string was created on the server and had to be transported to the client. Because String does not implement the Remote interface, the server cannot return a string stub object. Instead, the client gets a *copy* of the string. Then, after the call, the client has its own String object to work with. This means that there is no need for any further connection to any object on the server to deal with that string.

Whenever an object that is not a remote object needs to be transported from one Java virtual machine to another, the Java virtual machine makes a copy and sends that copy across the network connection. This technique is very different from parameter passing in a local method. When you pass objects into a local method or return them as method results, only object *references* are passed. However, object references are memory addresses of objects in the local Java virtual machine. This information is meaningless to a different Java virtual machine.

It is not difficult to imagine how a copy of a string can be transported across a network. The RMI mechanism can also make copies of more complex objects, provided they are *serializable*. RMI uses the serialization mechanism described in Volume 1, Chapter 12 to send objects across a network connection. This means that only the information in any classes that implement the Serializable interface can be copied.

The following program shows the copying of parameters and return values in action. This program is a simple application that lets a user shop for a gift. On the client, the user runs a program that gathers information about the gift recipient, in this case, age, sex, and hobbies (see Figure 5–7).

 NOTE: Figure 5–7 has a curious banner "Java Applet Window". This is a consequence of running the program with a security manager. This warning banner is provided to defend against "phishing" applets. A hostile applet might pop up a window, prompt for a password or credit card number, and then send the information back to its host. To turn off the warning, add the following lines to the client.policy file:

```
permission java.awt.AWTPermission
    "showWindowWithoutWarningBanner";
```

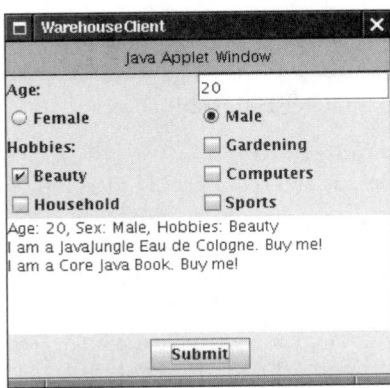

Figure 5–7: Obtaining product suggestions from the server

An object of type Customer is then sent to the server. Because Customer is not a remote object, a copy of the object is made on the server. The server program sends back an array list of products. The array list contains those products that match the customer profile, and it always contains that one item that will delight anyone, namely, a copy of the book *Core Java*. Again, ArrayList is not a remote class, so the array list is copied from the server back to its client. As described in Volume 1, Chapter 12, the serialization mechanism makes copies of all objects that are referenced inside a copied object. In our case, it makes a copy of all array list entries as well. We added an extra complexity: The entries are actually remote Product objects. Thus, the recipient gets a copy of the array list, filled with stub objects to the products on the server (see Figure 5–8).

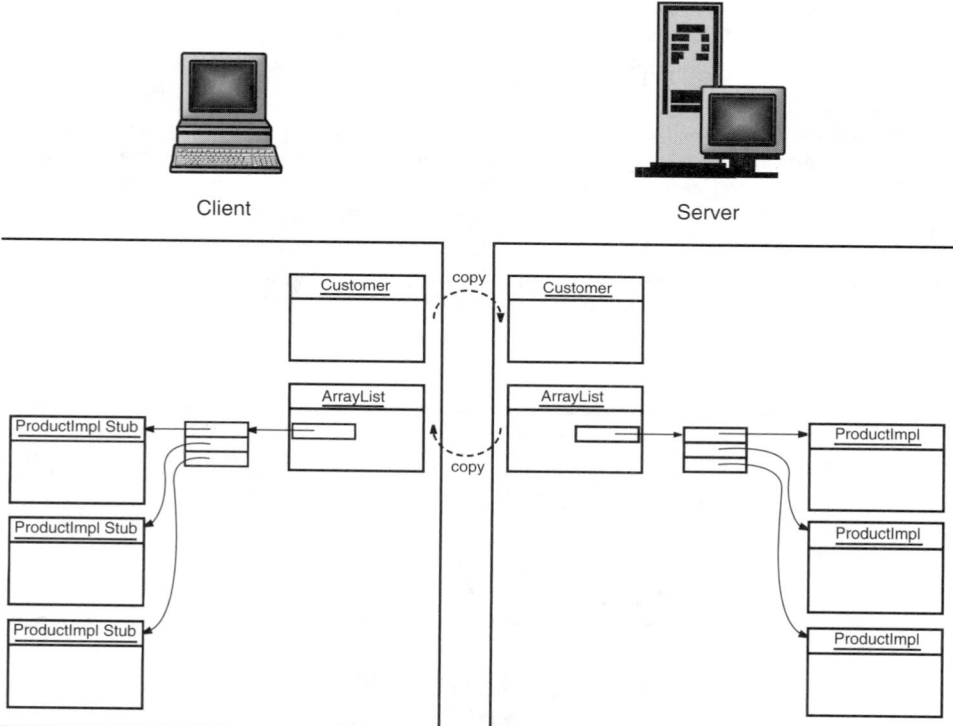

Figure 5–8: Copying local parameter and result objects

To summarize, remote objects are passed across the network as stubs. Nonremote objects are copied. All of this is automatic and requires no programmer intervention.

Whenever code calls a remote method, the stub makes a package that contains copies of all parameter values and sends it to the server, using the object serialization mechanism to marshal the parameters. The server unmarshals them. Naturally, the process can be quite slow—especially when the parameter objects are large.

Let's look at the complete program. First, we have the interfaces for the product and ware-house services, as shown in Example 5–6 and Example 5–7.

Example 5–6: Product.java

```
1. import java.rmi.*;
2.
3. /**
4.    The interface for remote product objects.
5. */
6. public interface Product extends Remote
7. {
8.    /**
9.       Gets the description of this product.
10.      @return the product description
11.   */
12.   String getDescription() throws RemoteException;
13. }
```

Example 5–7: Warehouse.java

```
1. import java.rmi.*;
2. import java.util.*;
3.
4. /**
5.    The remote interface for a warehouse with products.
6. */
7. public interface Warehouse extends Remote
8. {
9.    /**
10.      Gets products that are good matches for a customer.
11.      @param c the customer to match
12.      @return an array list of matching products
13.   */
14.   ArrayList<Product> find(Customer c) throws RemoteException;
15. }
```

Example 5–8 shows the implementation for the product service. Products store a description, an age range, the gender targeted (male, female, or both), and the matching hobby. Note that this class implements the getDescription method advertised in the Product interface, and it also implements another method, match, which is not a part of that interface. The match method is an example of a *local method*, a method that can be called only from the local program, not remotely. Because the match method is local, it need not be prepared to throw a RemoteException.

Example 5–9 contains the code for the Customer class. Note once again that Customer is not a remote class—none of its methods can be executed remotely. However, the class is serializable. Therefore, objects of this class can be transported from one virtual machine to another.

Examples 5–10 and 5–11 show the interface and implementation for the warehouse service. Like the ProductImpl class, the WarehouseImpl class has local and remote methods. The add method is local; it is used by the server to add products to the warehouse. The find method is remote; it is used by the client to find items in the warehouse.

To illustrate that the Customer object is actually copied, the find method of the WarehouseImpl class clears the customer object it receives. When the remote method returns, the Warehouse-Client displays the customer object that it sent to the server. As you will see, that object has not changed. The server cleared only *its copy*. In this case, the reset operation serves no useful purpose except to demonstrate that local objects are copied when they are passed as parameters.

It is possible for multiple client stubs to make simultaneous calls to a server object, even if some of the methods change the state of the server. In Example 5–11, we use a ReadWrite-

Lock in the `WarehouseImpl` class because it is conceivable that the local `add` and the remote `find` methods are called simultaneously. Example 5–12 shows the server program that creates a warehouse object and registers it with the bootstrap registry service.

 NOTE: Remember that you must start the registry and the server program and keep both running before you start the client.

Example 5–13 shows the code for the client. When the user clicks the Submit button, a new customer object is generated and passed to the remote `find` method. The customer record is then displayed in the text area (to prove that the `reset` call in the server did not affect it). Finally, the product descriptions of the returned products in the array list are added to the text area. Note that each `getDescription` call is again a remote method invocation. That would not be a good design in practice—you would normally pass small objects such as product descriptions by value. However, we want to demonstrate that a remote object is automatically replaced by a stub during marshalling.

 TIP: If you start the server with

    `java -Djava.rmi.server.logCalls=true WarehouseServer &`

then the server logs all remote method calls on its console. Try it—you'll get a good impression of the RMI traffic.

Example 5–8: ProductImpl.java

```
1. import java.rmi.*;
2. import java.rmi.server.*;
3.
4. /**
5.    This is the implementation class for the remote product
6.    objects.
7. */
8. public class ProductImpl
9.    extends UnicastRemoteObject
10.    implements Product
11. {
12.    /**
13.       Constructs a product implementation
14.       @param n the product name
15.    */
16.    public ProductImpl(String n) throws RemoteException
17.    {
18.       name = n;
19.    }
20.
21.    public String getDescription() throws RemoteException
22.    {
23.       return "I am a " + name + ". Buy me!";
24.    }
25.
26.    private String name;
27. }
```

Example 5–9: Customer.java

```
1. import java.io.*;
2.
3. /**
4.    Description of a customer. Note that customer objects are not
5.    remote--the class does not implement a remote interface.
6. */
7. public class Customer implements Serializable
8. {
9.    /**
10.      Constructs a customer.
11.      @param theAge the customer's age
12.      @param theSex the customer's sex (MALE or FEMALE)
13.      @param theHobbies the customer's hobbies
14.   */
15.   public Customer(int theAge, int theSex, String[] theHobbies)
16.   {
17.      age = theAge;
18.      sex = theSex;
19.      hobbies = theHobbies;
20.   }
21.
22.   /**
23.      Gets the customer's age.
24.      @return the age
25.   */
26.   public int getAge() { return age; }
27.
28.   /**
29.      Gets the customer's sex
30.      @return MALE or FEMALE
31.   */
32.   public int getSex() { return sex; }
33.
34.   /**
35.      Tests whether this customer has a particular hobby.
36.      @param aHobby the hobby to test
37.      @return true if this customer has the hobby
38.   */
39.   public boolean hasHobby(String aHobby)
40.   {
41.      if (aHobby == "") return true;
42.      for (int i = 0; i < hobbies.length; i++)
43.         if (hobbies[i].equals(aHobby)) return true;
44.
45.      return false;
46.   }
47.
48.   /**
49.      Resets this customer record to default values.
50.   */
51.   public void reset()
52.   {
53.      age = 0;
54.      sex = 0;
```

```
55.       hobbies = null;
56.    }
57.
58.    public String toString()
59.    {
60.       String result = "Age: " + age + ", Sex: ";
61.       if (sex == Product.MALE) result += "Male";
62.       else if (sex == Product.FEMALE) result += "Female";
63.       else result += "Male or Female";
64.       result += ", Hobbies:";
65.       for (int i = 0; i < hobbies.length; i++)
66.          result += " " + hobbies[i];
67.       return result;
68.    }
69.
70.    private int age;
71.    private int sex;
72.    private String[] hobbies;
73. }
```

Example 5–10: Warehouse.java

```
1. import java.rmi.*;
2. import java.util.*;
3.
4. /**
5.    The remote interface for a warehouse with products.
6. */
7. public interface Warehouse extends Remote
8. {
9.    /**
10.      Gets products that are good matches for a customer.
11.      @param c the customer to match
12.      @return an array list of matching products
13.   */
14.   ArrayList<Product> find(Customer c) throws RemoteException;
15. }
```

Example 5–11: WarehouseImpl.java

```
1. import java.io.*;
2. import java.rmi.*;
3. import java.util.*;
4. import java.rmi.server.*;
5. import java.util.*;
6. import java.util.concurrent.locks.*;
7.
8. /**
9.    This class is the implementation for the remote
10.   Warehouse interface.
11. */
12. public class WarehouseImpl
13.    extends UnicastRemoteObject
14.    implements Warehouse
15. {
16.    /**
17.      Constructs a warehouse implementation.
18.   */
```

```
19.    public WarehouseImpl()
20.       throws RemoteException
21.    {
22.       products = new ArrayList<ProductImpl>();
23.       add(new ProductImpl("Core Java Book", 0, 200, Product.BOTH, "Computers"));
24.    }
25.
26.    /**
27.       Add a product to the warehouse. Note that this is a local method.
28.       @param p the product to add
29.    */
30.    public void add(ProductImpl p)
31.    {
32.       Lock wlock = rwlock.writeLock();
33.       wlock.lock();
34.       try
35.       {
36.          products.add(p);
37.       }
38.       finally
39.       {
40.          wlock.unlock();
41.       }
42.    }
43.
44.    public ArrayList<Product> find(Customer c)
45.       throws RemoteException
46.    {
47.       Lock rlock = rwlock.readLock();
48.       rlock.lock();
49.       try
50.       {
51.          ArrayList<Product> result = new ArrayList<Product>();
52.          // add all matching products
53.          for (ProductImpl p : products)
54.          {
55.             if (p.match(c)) result.add(p);
56.          }
57.          // add the product that is a good match for everyone, a copy of Core Java
58.          if (!result.contains(products.get(0)))
59.             result.add(products.get(0));
60.
61.          // we reset c just to show that c is a copy of the client object
62.          c.reset();
63.          return result;
64.       }
65.       finally
66.       {
67.          rlock.unlock();
68.       }
69.    }
70.
71.    private ArrayList<ProductImpl> products;
72.    private ReadWriteLock rwlock = new ReentrantReadWriteLock();
73. }
```

Example 5–12: WarehouseServer.java

```
1.  import java.rmi.*;
2.  import java.rmi.server.*;
3.  import javax.naming.*;
4.
5.  /**
6.     This server program instantiates a remote warehouse
7.     object, registers it with the naming service, and waits
8.     for clients to invoke methods.
9.  */
10. public class WarehouseServer
11. {
12.    public static void main(String[] args)
13.    {
14.       try
15.       {
16.          System.out.println("Constructing server implementations...");
17.          WarehouseImpl w = new WarehouseImpl();
18.          w.add(new ProductImpl("Blackwell Toaster", Product.BOTH, 18, 200, "Household"));
19.          w.add(new ProductImpl("ZapXpress Microwave Oven", Product.BOTH, 18, 200, "Household"));
20.          w.add(new ProductImpl("DirtDigger Steam Shovel", Product.MALE, 20, 60, "Gardening"));
21.          w.add(new ProductImpl("U238 Weed Killer", Product.BOTH, 20, 200, "Gardening"));
22.          w.add(new ProductImpl("Persistent Java Fragrance", Product.FEMALE, 15, 45, "Beauty"));
23.          w.add(new ProductImpl("Rabid Rodent Computer Mouse", Product.BOTH, 6, 40, "Computers"));
24.          w.add(new ProductImpl("My first Espresso Maker", Product.FEMALE, 6, 10, "Household"));
25.          w.add(new ProductImpl("JavaJungle Eau de Cologne", Product.MALE, 15, 45, "Beauty"));
26.          w.add(new ProductImpl("FireWire Espresso Maker", Product.BOTH, 20, 50, "Computers"));
27.          w.add(new ProductImpl("Learn Bad Java Habits in 21 Days Book", Product.BOTH, 20, 200,
28.             "Computers"));
29.
30.          System.out.println("Binding server implementations to registry...");
31.          Context namingContext = new InitialContext();
32.          namingContext.bind("rmi:central_warehouse", w);
33.
34.          System.out.println("Waiting for invocations from clients...");
35.       }
36.       catch (Exception e)
37.       {
38.          e.printStackTrace();
39.       }
40.    }
41. }
```

Example 5–13: WarehouseClient.java

```
1.  import java.awt.*;
2.  import java.awt.event.*;
3.  import java.io.*;
4.  import java.rmi.*;
5.  import java.rmi.server.*;
6.  import java.util.*;
7.  import javax.naming.*;
8.  import javax.swing.*;
9.
10. /**
```

```
11.    The client for the warehouse program.
12. */
13. public class WarehouseClient
14. {
15.    public static void main(String[] args)
16.    {
17.       try
18.       {
19.          System.setProperty("java.security.policy", "client.policy");
20.          System.setSecurityManager(new RMISecurityManager());
21.
22.          Properties props = new Properties();
23.          String fileName = "WarehouseClient.properties";
24.          FileInputStream in = new FileInputStream(fileName);
25.          props.load(in);
26.          String url = props.getProperty("warehouse.url");
27.          if (url == null)
28.             url = "rmi://localhost/central_warehouse";
29.
30.          Context namingContext = new InitialContext();
31.          Warehouse centralWarehouse = (Warehouse) namingContext.lookup(url);
32.          JFrame frame = new WarehouseClientFrame(centralWarehouse);
33.          frame.setDefaultCloseOperation(JFrame.EXIT_ON_CLOSE);
34.          frame.setVisible(true);
35.       }
36.       catch (Exception e)
37.       {
38.          e.printStackTrace();
39.       }
40.    }
41. }
42.
43. /**
44.    A frame to select the customer's age, sex, and hobbies, and to
45.    show the matching products resulting from a remote call to the
46.    warehouse.
47. */
48. class WarehouseClientFrame extends JFrame
49. {
50.    public WarehouseClientFrame(Warehouse warehouse)
51.    {
52.       this.warehouse = warehouse;
53.       setTitle("WarehouseClient");
54.       setSize(DEFAULT_WIDTH, DEFAULT_HEIGHT);
55.
56.       JPanel panel = new JPanel();
57.       panel.setLayout(new GridLayout(0, 2));
58.
59.       panel.add(new JLabel("Age:"));
60.       age = new JTextField(4);
61.       age.setText("20");
62.       panel.add(age);
63.
64.       female = new JRadioButton("Female", true);
```

```
65.    male = new JRadioButton("Male", true);
66.    ButtonGroup group = new ButtonGroup();
67.    panel.add(female); group.add(female);
68.    panel.add(male); group.add(male);
69.
70.    panel.add(new JLabel("Hobbies: "));
71.    hobbies = new ArrayList<JCheckBox>();
72.    for (String h : new String[] { "Gardening", "Beauty", "Computers", "Household", "Sports" })
73.    {
74.       JCheckBox checkBox = new JCheckBox(h);
75.       hobbies.add(checkBox);
76.       panel.add(checkBox);
77.    }
78.
79.    result = new JTextArea(4, 40);
80.    result.setEditable(false);
81.
82.    JPanel buttonPanel = new JPanel();
83.    JButton submitButton = new JButton("Submit");
84.    buttonPanel.add(submitButton);
85.    submitButton.addActionListener(new
86.       ActionListener()
87.       {
88.          public void actionPerformed(ActionEvent event)
89.          {
90.             callWarehouse();
91.          }
92.       });
93.
94.    add(panel, BorderLayout.NORTH);
95.    add(result, BorderLayout.CENTER);
96.    add(buttonPanel, BorderLayout.SOUTH);
97. }
98.
99. /**
100.    Call the remote warehouse to find matching products.
101. */
102. private void callWarehouse()
103. {
104.    try
105.    {
106.       ArrayList<String> selected = new ArrayList<String>();
107.       for (JCheckBox checkBox : hobbies)
108.          if (checkBox.isSelected()) selected.add(checkBox.getText());
109.       Customer c = new Customer(Integer.parseInt(age.getText()),
110.          (male.isSelected() ? Product.MALE : 0)
111.          + (female.isSelected() ? Product.FEMALE : 0),
112.          selected.toArray(new String[selected.size()]));
113.       ArrayList<Product> recommendations = warehouse.find(c);
114.       result.setText(c + "\n");
115.       for (Product p : recommendations)
116.       {
117.          String t = p.getDescription() + "\n";
118.          result.append(t);
```

```
119.            }
120.        }
121.        catch (Exception e)
122.        {
123.            e.printStackTrace();
124.            result.setText("Exception: " + e);
125.        }
126.    }
127.
128.    private static final int DEFAULT_WIDTH = 300;
129.    private static final int DEFAULT_HEIGHT = 300;
130.
131.    private Warehouse warehouse;
132.    private JTextField age;
133.    private JRadioButton male;
134.    private JRadioButton female;
135.    private ArrayList<JCheckBox> hobbies;
136.    private JTextArea result;
137. }
```

Passing Remote Objects

Passing remote objects from the server to the client is simple. The client receives a stub object, then saves it in an object variable with the same type as the remote interface. The client can now access the actual object on the server through the variable. The client can copy this variable in its own local machine—all those copies are simply references to the same stub. It is important to note that only the *remote interfaces* can be accessed through the stub. A remote interface is any interface extending Remote. All local methods are inaccessible through the stub. (A local method is any method that is not defined in a remote interface.) Local methods can run only on the virtual machine containing the actual object.

Next, stubs are generated only from classes that implement a remote interface, and only the methods specified in the interfaces are provided in the stub classes. If a subclass doesn't implement a remote interface but a superclass does, and an object of the subclass is passed to a remote method, only the superclass methods are accessible. To understand this better, consider the following example. We derive a class BookImpl from ProductImpl.

```
class BookImpl extends ProductImpl
{
    public BookImpl(String title, String theISBN, int sex, int age1, int age2, String hobby)
    {
        super(title + " Book", sex, age1, age2, hobby);
        ISBN = theISBN;
    }
    public String getStockCode() { return ISBN; }
    private String ISBN;
}
```

Now, suppose we pass a book object to a remote method, either as a parameter or as a return value. The recipient obtains a stub object, but that stub is not a book stub. Instead, it is a stub to the superclass ProductImpl because only that class implements a remote interface (see Figure 5–9). Thus, in this case, the getStockCode method isn't available remotely.

A remote class can implement multiple interfaces. For example, the BookImpl class can implement a second interface in addition to Product. Here, we define a remote interface StockUnit and have the BookImpl class implement it.

```
interface StockUnit extends Remote
{
    public String getStockCode() throws RemoteException;
}

class BookImpl extends ProductImpl implements StockUnit
{
    public BookImpl(String title, String theISBN, int sex, int age1, int age2, String hobby)
        throws RemoteException
    {
        super(title + " Book", sex, age1, age2, hobby);
        ISBN = theISBN;
    }

    public String getStockCode() throws RemoteException
    {
        return ISBN;
    }

    private String ISBN;
}
```

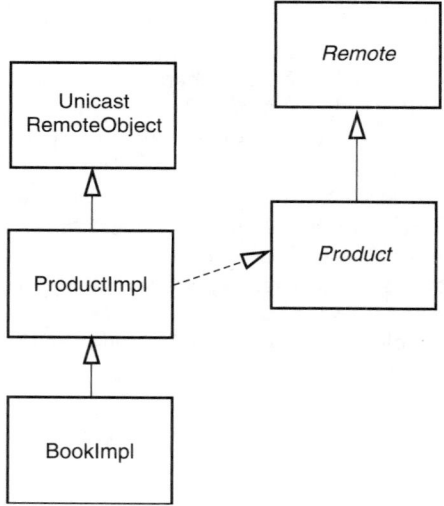

Figure 5–9: Only the ProductImpl methods are remote

Figure 5–10 shows the inheritance diagram.

Now, when a book object is passed to a remote method, the recipient obtains a stub that has access to the remote methods in both the Product and the StockUnit class. In fact, you can use the instanceof operator to find out whether a particular remote object implements an interface. Here is a typical situation in which you will use this feature. Suppose you receive a remote object through a variable of type Product.

```
ArrayList<Product> result = centralWarehouse.find(c);
for (Product p : result)
{
    . . .
}
```

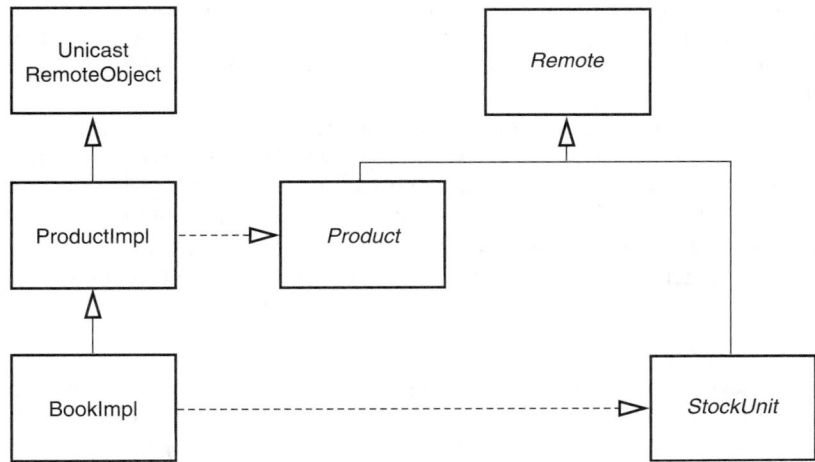

Figure 5–10: `BookImpl` has additional remote methods

The remote object may or may not be a book. We'd like to use `instanceof` to find out whether it is or not, but we can't test

```
if (p instanceof BookImpl) // wrong
{
   BookImpl b = (BookImpl) p;
   . . .
}
```

The object `p` refers to a stub object, and `BookImpl` is the class of the server object. Instead, cast to the second interface:

```
if (p instanceof StockUnit)
{
   StockUnit s = (StockUnit) p;
   String c = s.getStockCode();
   . . .
}
```

This code tests whether the stub object to which `p` refers implements the `StockUnit` interface. If so, it calls the `getStockCode` remote method of that interface.

To summarize:

- If an object belonging to a class that implements a remote interface is passed to a remote method, the remote method receives a stub object.
- You can cast that stub object to any of the remote interfaces that the implementation class implements.
- You can call all remote methods defined in those interfaces, but you cannot call any local methods through the stub.

Remote Objects and the `equals` and `hashCode` *Methods*

As you saw in Chapter 2, objects inserted in sets must override the `equals` method. In the case of a hash set or hash map, the `hashCode` method must be defined as well. However, there is a problem when trying to compare remote objects. To find out if two remote objects have the same contents, the call to `equals` would need to contact the servers containing the objects and compare their contents. And that call could fail. But the `equals` method in the class `Object`

is not declared to throw a RemoteException, whereas all methods in a remote interface must throw that exception. Because a subclass method cannot throw more exceptions than the superclass method it replaces, you cannot define an equals method in a remote interface. The same holds for hashCode.

Instead, the equals and hashCode methods on stub objects simply look at the location of the server objects. The equals method deems two stubs equal if they refer to the same server object. Two stubs that refer to different server objects are never equal, even if those objects have identical contents. Similarly, the hash code is computed only from the object identifier.

To summarize, you can use stub objects in sets and hash tables, but you must remember that equality testing and hashing do not take into account the contents of the remote objects.

Cloning Remote Objects

Stubs do not have a clone method, so you cannot clone a remote object by invoking clone on the stub. The reason is again somewhat technical. If clone were to make a remote call to tell the server to clone the implementation object, then the clone method would need to throw a RemoteException. However, the clone method in the Object superclass promised never to throw any exception other than CloneNotSupportedException. That is the same limitation that you encountered in the previous section: equals and hashCode don't look up the remote object value at all but just compare stub references. However, it makes no sense for clone to make another clone of a stub—if you wanted to have another reference to the remote object, you could just copy the stub variable. Therefore, clone is simply not defined for stubs.

Server Object Activation

In the preceding sample programs, we used a server program to instantiate and register objects so that clients could make remote calls on them. However, in some cases, it may be wasteful to instantiate lots of server objects and have them wait for connections, whether or not client objects use them. The *activation* mechanism lets you delay the object construction so that a server object is only constructed when at least one client invokes a remote method on it.

To take advantage of activation, the client code is completely unchanged. The client simply requests a remote reference and makes calls through it.

However, the server program is replaced by an activation program that constructs *activation descriptors* of the objects that are to be constructed at a later time, and binds receivers for remote method calls with the naming service. When a call is made for the first time, the information in the activation descriptor is used to construct the object.

A server object that is used in this way should extend the Activatable class and, of course, implement one or more remote interfaces. For example,

```
class ProductImpl
    extends Activatable
    implements Product
{
    . . .
}
```

Because the object construction is delayed until a later time, it must happen in a standardized form. Therefore, you must provide a constructor that takes two parameters:

- An activation ID (which you simply pass to the superclass constructor)
- A single object containing all construction information, wrapped in a MarshalledObject

If you need multiple construction parameters, you must package them in a single object. You can always use an Object[] array or an ArrayList. As you will soon see, you place a serialized (or marshalled) copy of the construction information inside the activation descriptor. Your server object constructor should use the get method of the MarshalledObject class to deserialize the construction information.

In the case of the ProductImpl class, this procedure is quite simple—only one piece of information is necessary for construction, namely, the product name. That information can be wrapped into a MarshalledObject and unwrapped in the constructor:

```
public ProductImpl(ActivationID id, MarshalledObject data)
{
   super(id, 0);
   name = (String) data.get();;
   System.out.println("Constructed " + name);
}
```

By passing 0 as the second parameter of the superclass constructor, we indicate that the RMI library should assign a suitable port number to the listener port.

This constructor prints a message so that you can see that the product objects are activated on demand.

 NOTE: Your server objects don't actually have to extend the Activatable class. If they don't, then place the static method call

```
Activatable.exportObject(this, id, 0)
```

in the constructor of the server class.

Now let us turn to the activation program. First, you need to define an activation group. An activation group describes common parameters for launching the virtual machine that contains the server objects. The most important parameter is the security policy.

As with our other server objects, we do not check for security. (Presumably, the objects come from a trusted source.) However, the virtual machine in which the activated objects run has a security manager installed. To enable all permissions, supply a file server.policy with the following contents:

```
grant
{
   permission java.security.AllPermission;
};
```

Construct an activation group descriptor as follows:

```
Properties props = new Properties();
props.put("java.security.policy", "/server/server.policy");
ActivationGroupDesc group = new ActivationGroupDesc(props, null);
```

The second parameter describes special command options; we don't need any for this example, so we pass a null reference.

Next, create a group ID with the call

```
ActivationGroupID id = ActivationGroup.getSystem().registerGroup(group);
```

Now you are ready to construct the activation descriptors. For each object that should be constructed on demand, you need the following:

- The activation group ID for the virtual machine in which the object should be constructed;
- The name of the class (such as "ProductImpl" or "com.mycompany.MyClassImpl");
- The URL string from which to load the class files. This should be the base URL, not including package paths;
- The marshalled construction information.

For example,

```
MarshalledObject param = new MarshalledObject("Blackwell Toaster");
ActivationDesc desc = new ActivationDesc(id, "ProductImpl", "http://myserver.com/download/", param);
```

Pass the descriptor to the static `Activatable.register` method. It returns an object of some class that implements the remote interfaces of the implementation class. You can bind that object with the naming service:

```
Product p = (Product) Activatable.register(desc);
namingContext.bind("toaster", p);
```

Unlike the server programs of the preceding examples, the activation program exits after registering and binding the activation receivers. The server objects are constructed only when the first remote method call occurs.

Examples 5–14 and 5–15 show the code for the activatable product implementation and the activation program. The product interface and the client program are unchanged.

To launch this program, follow these steps:

1. Compile all source files.
2. If you use JDK 1.4 or below, run `rmic` to generate a stub for the `ProductImpl` class:
   ```
   rmic -v1.2 ProductImpl
   ```
3. Start the RMI registry.
4. Start the RMI activation daemon.
   ```
   rmid -J-Djava.security.policy=rmid.policy &
   ```
   or
   ```
   start rmid -J-Djava.security.policy=rmid.policy
   ```
   The `rmid` program listens to activation requests and activates objects in a separate virtual machine. To launch a virtual machine, the `rmid` program needs certain permissions. These are specified in a policy file (see Example 5–16). Use the -J option to pass an option to the virtual machine running the activation daemon.
5. Run the activation program. In this setup, we assume that you start the program in the directory that contains the class files and the server policy file.
   ```
   java ProductActivator
   ```
   The program exits after the activation receivers have been registered with the naming service.
6. Run the client program
   ```
   java -Djava.security.policy=client.policy ProductClient
   ```
   The client will print the familiar product descriptions. When you run the client for the first time, you will also see the constructor messages in the server shell window.

Example 5–14: ProductImpl.java

```
1. import java.rmi.*;
2. import java.rmi.server.*;
3.
4. /**
```

```
5.    This is the implementation class for the remote product
6.    objects.
7.  */
8.  public class ProductImpl
9.     extends UnicastRemoteObject
10.    implements Product
11. {
12.    /**
13.       Constructs a product implementation
14.       @param n the product name
15.    */
16.    public ProductImpl(String n) throws RemoteException
17.    {
18.       name = n;
19.    }
20.
21.    public String getDescription() throws RemoteException
22.    {
23.       return "I am a " + name + ". Buy me!";
24.    }
25.
26.    private String name;
27. }
```

Example 5–15: ProductActivator.java

```
1.  import java.io.*;
2.  import java.net.*;
3.  import java.rmi.*;
4.  import java.rmi.activation.*;
5.  import java.util.*;
6.  import javax.naming.*;
7.
8.  /**
9.     This server program activates two remote objects and
10.    registers them with the naming service.
11. */
12. public class ProductActivator
13. {
14.    public static void main(String args[])
15.    {
16.       try
17.       {
18.          System.out.println("Constructing activation descriptors...");
19.
20.          Properties props = new Properties();
21.          // use the server.policy file in the current directory
22.          props.put("java.security.policy", new File("server.policy").getCanonicalPath());
23.          ActivationGroupDesc group = new ActivationGroupDesc(props, null);
24.          ActivationGroupID id = ActivationGroup.getSystem().registerGroup(group);
25.          MarshalledObject p1param = new MarshalledObject("Blackwell Toaster");
26.          MarshalledObject p2param = new MarshalledObject("ZapXpress Microwave Oven");
27.
28.          String classDir = ".";
29.          // turn the class directory into a file URL
30.          // for this demo we assume that the classes are in the current dir
31.          // we use toURI so that spaces and other special characters in file names are escaped
```

```
32.        String classURL = new File(classDir).getCanonicalFile().toURI().toString();
33.
34.        ActivationDesc desc1 = new ActivationDesc(id, "ProductImpl", classURL, p1param);
35.        ActivationDesc desc2 = new ActivationDesc(id, "ProductImpl", classURL, p2param);
36.
37.        Product p1 = (Product) Activatable.register(desc1);
38.        Product p2 = (Product) Activatable.register(desc2);
39.
40.        System.out.println("Binding activable implementations to registry...");
41.        Context namingContext = new InitialContext();
42.        namingContext.bind("rmi:toaster", p1);
43.        namingContext.bind("rmi:microwave", p2);
44.        System.out.println("Exiting...");
45.     }
46.     catch (Exception e)
47.     {
48.        e.printStackTrace();
49.     }
50.   }
51. }
```

Example 5–16: rmid.policy

```
1. grant
2. {
3.    permission com.sun.rmi.rmid.ExecPermission
4.       "${java.home}${/}bin${/}java";
5.    permission com.sun.rmi.rmid.ExecOptionPermission
6.       "-Djava.security.policy=*";
7. };
```

Example 5–17: server.policy

```
1. grant
2. {
3.    permission java.security.AllPermission;
4. };
```

 java.rmi.activation.Activatable 1.2

- protected Activatable(ActivationID id, int port)
  constructs the activatable object and establishes a listener on the given port. Use 0 for the port to have a port assigned automatically.

- static Remote exportObject(Remote obj, ActivationID id, int port)
  makes a remote object activatable. Returns the activation receiver that should be made available to remote callers. Use 0 for the port to have a port assigned automatically.

- static Remote register(ActivationDescriptor desc)
  registers the descriptor for an activatable object and prepares it for receiving remote calls. Returns the activation receiver that should be made available to remote callers.

java.rmi.MarshalledObject 1.2

- MarshalledObject(Object obj)
  constructs an object containing the serialized data of a given object.

- Object get()
  deserializes the stored object data and returns the object.

 java.rmi.activation.ActivationGroupDesc 1.2

- ActivationGroupDesc(Properties props, ActivationGroupDesc.CommandEnvironment env)
  constructs an activation group descriptor that specifies virtual machine properties
  for a virtual machine that hosts activated objects. The env parameter contains the path
  to the virtual machine executable and command-line options, or it is null if no special
  settings are required.

 java.rmi.activation.ActivationGroup 1.2

- static ActivationSystem getSystem()
  returns a reference to the activation system.

 java.rmi.activation.ActivationSystem 1.2

- ActivationGroupID registerGroup(ActivationGroupDesc group)
  registers an activation group and returns the group ID.

 java.rmi.activation.ActivationDesc 1.2

- ActivationDesc(ActivationGroupID id, String className, String classFileURL,
  MarshalledObject data)
  constructs an activation descriptor.

Java IDL and CORBA

Unlike RMI, CORBA lets you make calls between Java objects and objects written in other
languages. CORBA depends on having an Object Request Broker (ORB) available on both
client and server. You can think of an ORB as a kind of universal translator for interobject
CORBA communication. The CORBA 2 specification defines more than a dozen "services"
that the ORB can use for various kinds of housekeeping tasks. These range from a "startup
service" to get the process going, to a "life cycle service" that you use to create, copy, move,
or destroy objects, to a "naming service" that allows you to search for objects if you know
their name.

JDK 1.2 introduced an implementation of a CORBA 2-compliant ORB, giving Java applications and applets the ability to connect to remote CORBA objects.

> NOTE: Sun refers to the CORBA support as "Java IDL." That term is really a misnomer. IDL refers
> to the interface definition language, a language for describing class interfaces. The important
> aspect of the technology is connectivity with CORBA, not just support for IDL.

Here are the steps for implementing CORBA objects:

1. Write the interface that specifies how the object works, using IDL, the *interface definition
   language* for defining CORBA interfaces. IDL is a special language to specify interfaces in
   a language-neutral form.
2. Using the IDL compiler(s) for the target language(s), generate the needed stub and
   helper classes.
3. Add the implementation code for the server objects, using the language of your choice.
   (The skeleton created by the IDL compiler is only glue code. You still need to provide
   the actual implementation code for the server methods.) Compile the implementation
   code.

4. Write a server program that creates and registers the server objects. The most convenient method for registration is to use the CORBA *naming service*, a service that is similar to the rmiregistry.

5. Write a client program that locates the server objects and invokes services on them.

6. Start the naming service and the server program on the server, and start the client program on the client.

These steps are quite similar to the steps that you use to build distributed applications with RMI, but with two important differences:

- You can use any language with a CORBA binding to implement clients and servers.
- You use IDL to specify interfaces.

In the following sections, you will see how to use IDL to define CORBA interfaces, and how to connect clients implemented in Java with C++ servers and C++ clients with servers implemented in Java.

However, CORBA is a complex subject, and we give you only a couple of basic examples to show you how to get started. For more information, we recommend *Client/Server Programming with Java and CORBA* by Robert Orfali and Dan Harkey [John Wiley & Sons 1998]. More advanced, and definitely not for the faint of heart, is *Advanced CORBA Programming with C++* by Michi Henning and Steve Vinoski [Addison-Wesley 1999].

The Interface Definition Language

To introduce the IDL syntax, we quickly run through the same example that we used for RMI. In RMI, you started out with an interface in the Java programming language. With CORBA, the starting point is an interface in IDL syntax:

```
interface Product
{
    string getDescription();
};
```

There are a few subtle differences between IDL and Java. In IDL, the interface definition ends with a semicolon. Note that string is written in lower case. In fact, the string class refers to the CORBA notion of a string, which is different from a Java string. In the Java programming language, strings contain 16-bit Unicode characters. In CORBA, strings contain only 8-bit characters. If you send the 16-bit string through the ORB and the string has characters with nonzero high byte, an exception is thrown. This kind of type mismatch problem is the price you pay for interoperability between programming languages.

 NOTE: CORBA also has wchar and wstring types for "wide" characters. However, there is no guarantee that wide character strings use the Unicode encoding.

The "IDL to Java" compiler (Java IDL compiler) translates IDL definitions to definitions for Java interfaces. For example, suppose you place the IDL Product definition into a file Product.idl and run

```
idlj Product.idl
```

The result is a file ProductOperations.java with the following contents—

```
interface ProductOperations
{
    String getDescription();
}
```

—and a file Product.java that defines an interface

```
public interface Product extends
    ProductOperations,
    org.omg.CORBA.Object,
    org.omg.CORBA.portable.IDLEntity
{
}
```

 NOTE: In JDK1.2, the idltojava program is used to translate IDL files.

The IDL compiler also generates a number of other source files—the stub class for communicating with the ORB and three helper classes that you will encounter later in this section and the next.

 NOTE: You cannot do any programming in IDL. IDL can only express interfaces. The CORBA objects that IDL describes must still be implemented, for example, in C++ or Java.

The rules that govern the translation from IDL to the Java programming language are collectively called the *Java programming language binding*. Language bindings are standardized by the OMG; all CORBA vendors are required to use the same rules for mapping IDL constructs to a particular programming language.

We do not discuss all aspects of IDL or the Java programming language binding—see the CORBA documentation at the web site of the Object Management Group (http://www.omg.org) for a full description. However, there are a number of important concepts that every IDL user needs to know.

When defining a method, you have more choices for parameter passing than the Java programming language offers. Every parameter can be declared as in, out, or inout. An in parameter is simply passed to the method—this is the same parameter-passing mechanism as in Java. However, Java has no analog to an out parameter. A method stores a value in each out parameter before it returns. The caller can retrieve the values stored in out parameters.

For example, a find method might store the product object that it has found:

```
interface Warehouse
{
    boolean locate(in String descr, out Product p);
    . . .
};
```

If the parameter is declared as out only, then the method should not expect the parameter to be initialized. However, if it is declared as inout, then the caller needs to supply a value for the method, and the method can change that value so that the caller can retrieve the changed value. In Java, these parameters are simulated with special *holder classes* that are generated by the Java IDL compiler.

The IDL compiler generates a class with suffix Holder for every interface. For example, when the Product interface is compiled, it automatically generates a ProductHolder class. Every holder class has a public instance variable called value.

When a method has an out parameter, the IDL compiler changes the method signature to use a holder, for example,

```
interface Warehouse
{
    boolean locate(String descr, ProductHolder p);
    . . .
};
```

When calling the method, you must pass in a holder object. After the method returns, you retrieve the value of the out parameter from the holder object. Here is how you call the locate method.

```
Warehouse w = . . .;
String descr = . . .;
Product p;
ProductHolder pHolder = new ProductHolder();
if (w.locate(descr, pHolder))
    p = pHolder.value;
```

Holder classes are predefined for fundamental types (such as IntHolder, DoubleHolder, and so on).

 NOTE: IDL does not support overloaded methods, so you must come up with a different name for each method.

In IDL, you use the sequence construct to define arrays of variable size. You must first define a type before you can declare sequence parameters or return values. For example, here is the definition of a "sequence of products" type.

```
typedef sequence<Product> ProductSeq;
```

You then use that type in method declarations:

```
interface Warehouse
{
    ProductSeq find(in Customer c);
    . . .
};
```

In the Java programming language, sequences correspond to arrays. For example, the find method is mapped to

```
Product[] find(Customer c)
```

If a method can throw an exception, you first define the exception type and then use a raises declaration. In the following example, the find method can raise a BadCustomer exception.

```
interface Warehouse
{
    exception BadCustomer { string reason; };
    ProductSeq find(in Customer c) raises BadCustomer;
    . . .
};
```

The IDL compiler translates the exception type into a class.

```
final public class BadCustomer
    extends org.omg.CORBA.UserException
{
    public BadCustomer() {}
    public BadCustomer(String __reason) { reason = __reason; }
    public String reason;
}
```

If you catch such an exception, you can look into its public instance variables.

The raises specifier becomes a throws specifier of the Java method

```
ProductSeq find(Customer c) throws BadCustomer
```

Interfaces can contain constants, for example,

```
interface Warehouse
{
   const int SOLD_OUT = 404;
   . . .
};
```

Interfaces can also contain attributes. Attributes look like instance variables, but they are actually shorthand for a pair of accessor and mutator methods. For example, here is a Book interface with an isbn attribute:

```
interface Book
{
   attribute string isbn;
   . . .
};
```

The Java equivalent is a pair of methods, both with the name isbn:

```
String isbn() // accessor
void isbn(String __isbn) // mutator
```

If the attribute is declared as readonly, then no mutator method is generated.

You cannot specify variables in CORBA interfaces—the data representation for objects is part of the implementation strategy, and IDL does not address implementation at all.

CORBA supports interface inheritance, for example,

```
interface Book : Product { /* . . . */ };
```

You use the colon (:) to denote inheritance. An interface can inherit multiple interfaces.

In IDL, you can group definitions of interfaces, types, constants, and exceptions into *modules*.

```
module corejava
{
   interface Product
   {
      . . .
   };

   interface Warehouse
   {
      . . .
   };
};
```

In Java, modules are translated to packages.

Once you have the IDL file, you run the IDL compiler that your ORB vendor supplies to get stubs and helper classes for your target programming language (such as Java or C++).

For example, to convert IDL files to Java, you run the idlj program. Supply the name of the IDL file on the command line:

```
idlj Product.idl
```

The program creates five source files:

- `Product.java`, the interface definition;
- `ProductOperations.java`, the interface that contains the actual operations (`Product` extends `ProductOperations` as well as a couple of CORBA-specific interfaces);
- `ProductHolder.java`, the holder class for out parameters;
- `ProductHelper.java`, a helper class, which we use in the next section;
- `_ProductStub.java`, the stub class for communicating with the ORB.

The same IDL file can be compiled to C++. We use a freely available ORB called omniORB for our examples. The omniORB package contains an IDL-to-C++ compiler called `omniidl`. To generate C++ stubs, invoke it as

```
omniidl -bcxx Product.idl
```

You get two C++ files:

- `Product.hh`, a header file that defines classes `Product`, `Product_Helper`, and `POA_Product` (the superclass for the server implementation class);
- `ProductSK.cc`, a C++ file that contains the source code for these classes.

 NOTE: Although the language binding is standardized, it is up to each vendor to decide how to generate and package the code that realizes the binding. IDL-to-C++ compilers of other vendors will generate a different set of files.

A CORBA Example

In our first example, we show you how to call a C++ server object from a Java client, using the CORBA support that is built into the JDK. On the server side, we use omniORB, an open-source ORB that is available from `http://omniorb.sourceforge.net`.

 NOTE: You can use any CORBA 2-compliant ORB on the server. However, you need to make changes to the C++ code if you use a different ORB.

Our example C++ server object simply reports the value of an environment variable on the server. The interface is

```
interface Env
{
    string getenv(in string name);
};
```

For example, the following Java program fragment obtains the value of the `PATH` environment variable of the process in which the server object runs.

```
Env env = . . .;
String value = env.getenv("PATH")
```

The C++ implementation code for this interface is straightforward. We simply call the `getenv` method in the standard C library.

```cpp
class EnvImpl
  : public POA_Env, public PortableServer::RefCountServantBase
{
public:
    virtual char* getenv(const char *name)
    {
        char* value = std::getenv(name);
        return CORBA::string_dup(value);
```

```
    }
};
```

You don't need to understand the C++ code to follow this section—just treat it as a bit of legacy code that you want to encapsulate in a CORBA object so that you can call it from Java programs.

On the server side, you write a C++ program that does the following:

1. Starts the ORB;
2. Creates an object of the `EnvImpl` class and registers it with the ORB;
3. Uses the name server to bind the object to a name;
4. Waits for invocations from a client.

You can find that program in Example 5–19 at the end of this section. We do not discuss the C++ code in detail. If you are interested, consult the omniORB documentation for more information. The documentation contains a good tutorial that explains each step in detail.

Let us now turn to the client code. You already saw how to invoke a method on the server object once you have a reference to the remote object. However, to get to that reference, you have to go through a different set of mumbo-jumbo than in RMI.

First, you initialize the ORB. The ORB is simply a code library that knows how to talk to other ORBs and how to marshal and unmarshal parameters.

```
ORB orb = ORB.init(args, null);
```

Next, you locate the naming service that helps you locate other objects. However, in CORBA, the naming service is just another CORBA object. To call the naming service, you first need to locate it. In the days of CORBA 1, this was a major problem because there was no standard way of getting a reference to it. However, a CORBA 2 ORB lets you locate certain standard services by name. The call

```
String[] services = orb.list_initial_services();
```

lists the names of the standard services to which the ORB can connect. The naming service has the standard name `NameService`. Most ORBs have additional initial services, such as the `RootPOA` service that accesses the root Portable Object Adaptor.

To obtain an object reference to the service, you use the `resolve_initial_references` method. It returns a generic CORBA object, an instance of the class `org.omg.corba.Object`. Use the full package prefix; if you just use `Object`, then the compiler assumes that you mean `java.lang.Object`.

```
org.omg.CORBA.Object object = orb.resolve_initial_references("NameService");
```

Next, convert this reference to a `NamingContext` reference so that you can invoke the methods of the `NamingContext` interface. In RMI, you would simply cast the reference to a different type. However, in CORBA, you cannot simply cast references.

```
NamingContext namingContext = (NamingContext) object; // ERROR
```

Instead, you have to use the `narrow` method of the helper class of the target interface.

```
NamingContext namingContext = NamingContextHelper.narrow(object);
```

CAUTION: Casting a CORBA object reference to a subtype will *sometimes* succeed. Many `org.omg.CORBA.Object` references already point to objects that implement the appropriate interface. However, an object reference can also hold a delegate to another object that actually implements the interface. Because you don't have any way of knowing how the stub objects were generated, you should always use the `narrow` method to convert a CORBA object reference to a subtype.

Now that you have the naming context, you can use it to locate the object that the server placed into it. The naming context associates names with server objects. Names are nested sequences of *name components*. You can use the nesting levels to organize hierarchies of names, much like you use directories in a file system.

A name component consists of an *ID* and a *kind*. The ID is a name for the component that is unique among all names with the same parent component. The kind is some indication of the type of the component. These kinds are not standardized; we use "Context" for name components that have nested names, and "Object" for object names.

In our example, the server program has placed the `EnvImpl` object into the name expressed by the sequence

```
(id="corejava", kind="Context"), (id="Env", kind="Object")
```

We retrieve a remote reference to it by building an array of name components and passing it to the `resolve` method of the `NamingContext` interface.

```
NameComponent[] path =
    {
        new NameComponent("corejava", "Context"),
        new NameComponent("Env", "Object")
    };
org.omg.CORBA.Object envObj = namingContext.resolve(path);
```

Once again, we must narrow the resulting object reference:

```
Env env = EnvHelper.narrow(envObj);
```

Now we are ready to call the remote method:

```
String value = env.getenv("PATH");
```

You will find the complete code in Example 5–18.

This example shows the steps to follow in a typical client program:

1. Start the ORB.
2. Locate the naming service by retrieving an initial reference to "NameService" and narrowing it to a `NamingContext` reference.
3. Locate the object whose methods you want to call by assembling its name and calling the `resolve` method of the `NamingContext`.
4. Narrow the returned object to the correct type and invoke your methods.

To actually test this program, do the following. The C++ instructions depend on the ORB. We give instructions for omniORB; modify them if you use another ORB.

1. Compile the IDL file, using both the C++ and Java IDL compilers:

```
omniidl -bcxx Env.idl
idlj Env.idl
```

2. Compile the C++ server program. The compilation instructions depend on the ORB. For example, with OmniORB on Linux, you use

```
g++
    -o EnvServer
    -D__x86__ -D__linux__ -D__OSVERSION__=2
    -I/usr/local/include/omniORB4
    EnvServer.cpp EnvSK.cc
    -lomniORB4 -lomnithread -lpthread
```

To find out what you need with your particular ORB, compile one of the example programs that are supplied with your installation and make the appropriate modifications to compile your own programs.

3. Compile the Java client program.

4. Start the naming service on the server. You can either use the `orbd` program that comes with the JDK, or the naming service of your ORB (for example, `omniNames` if you use omniORB). The naming service runs until you kill it.

   To start `orbd`, run

   ```
   orbd -ORBInitialPort 2809 &
   ```

   Alternatively, to start `omniNames`, run

   ```
   omniNames -ORBsupportBootstrapAgent 1 &
   ```

5. Start the server:

   ```
   ./EnvServer -ORBInitRef NameService=corbaname::localhost:2809 &
   ```

   The server also runs until you kill it.

6. Run the client:

   ```
   java EnvClient -ORBInitialPort 2809
   ```

   The client program should report the `PATH` of the server process.

If the server is on a remote machine or if the initial port of the server ORB is not the same as the Java IDL default of 900, then set the `ORBInitialHost` and `ORBInitialPort` properties. For example, OmniORB uses port 2809. When using `orbd`, we also used port 2809 because we need to have root privileges to start a service on a port below 1024 on UNIX/Linux.

There are two methods for setting these properties. You can set the system properties

```
org.omg.CORBA.ORBInitialHost
org.omg.CORBA.ORBInitialPort
```

for example, by starting the `java` interpreter with the `-D` option. Or, you can specify the values on the command line:

```
java EnvClient -ORBInitialHost warthog -ORBInitialPort 2809
```

The command-line parameters are passed to the ORB by the call

```
ORB orb = ORB.init(args, null);
```

In principle, your ORB vendor should tell you with great clarity how its bootstrap process works. In practice, we have found that vendors blithely assume that you would never dream of mixing their precious ORB with another, and they tend to be less than forthcoming with this information. If your client won't find the naming service, try forcing the initial ports for both the server and the client to the same value.

 TIP: If you have trouble connecting to the naming service, print a list of initial services that your ORB can locate.

```
public class ListServices
{
   public static void main(String args[]) throws Exception
   {
      ORB orb = ORB.init(args, null);
      String[] services = orb.list_initial_services();
      for (int i = 0; i < services.length; i++)
         System.out.println(services[i]);
   }
}
```

With some ORBs, `NameService` isn't among the listed services, no matter how much you tweak the configuration. In that case, switch to Plan B and locate the server object by its Interoperable Object Reference, or IOR. See the sidebar for more information.

In this section, you saw how to connect to a server that was implemented in C++. We believe that is a particularly useful scenario. You can wrap legacy services into CORBA objects and access them from your Java programs, without having to deploy additional system software on the client. In the next section, you will see the opposite scenario, where the server is implemented in Java and the client in C++.

Example 5–18: EnvClient.java

```
1.  import org.omg.CosNaming.*;
2.  import org.omg.CORBA.*;
3.
4.  public class EnvClient
5.  {
6.     public static void main(String args[])
7.     {
8.        try
9.        {
10.          ORB orb = ORB.init(args, null);
11.          org.omg.CORBA.Object namingContextObj = orb.resolve_initial_references("NameService");
12.          NamingContext namingContext = NamingContextHelper.narrow(namingContextObj);
13.
14.          NameComponent[] path =
15.             {
16.                new NameComponent("corejava", "Context"),
17.                new NameComponent("Env", "Object")
18.             };
19.          org.omg.CORBA.Object envObj = namingContext.resolve(path);
20.          Env env = EnvHelper.narrow(envObj);
21.          System.out.println(env.getenv("PATH"));
22.       }
23.       catch (Exception e)
24.       {
25.          e.printStackTrace();
26.       }
27.    }
28. }
```

Example 5–19: EnvServer.cpp

```
1.  #include <iostream>
2.  #include <cstdlib>
3.
4.  #include "Env.hh"
5.
6.  using namespace std;
7.
8.  class EnvImpl :
9.     public POA_Env,
10.    public PortableServer::RefCountServantBase
11. {
12. public:
13.    virtual char* getenv(const char *name);
14. };
15.
16. char* EnvImpl::getenv(const char *name)
17. {
18.    char* value = std::getenv(name);
```

```
19.    return CORBA::string_dup(value);
20. }
21.
22. static void bindObjectToName(CORBA::ORB_ptr orb, const char name[], CORBA::Object_ptr objref)
23. {
24.    CosNaming::NamingContext_var rootContext;
25.
26.    try
27.    {
28.       // Obtain a reference to the root context of the name service:
29.       CORBA::Object_var obj;
30.       obj = orb->resolve_initial_references("NameService");
31.
32.       // Narrow the reference returned.
33.       rootContext = CosNaming::NamingContext::_narrow(obj);
34.       if(CORBA::is_nil(rootContext))
35.       {
36.          cerr << "Failed to narrow the root naming context." << endl;
37.          return;
38.       }
39.    }
40.    catch (CORBA::ORB::InvalidName& ex)
41.    {
42.       // This should not happen!
43.       cerr << "Service required is invalid [does not exist]." << endl;
44.       return;
45.    }
46.
47.    try
48.    {
49.       CosNaming::Name contextName;
50.       contextName.length(1);
51.       contextName[0].id   = (const char*) "corejava";
52.       contextName[0].kind = (const char*) "Context";
53.
54.       CosNaming::NamingContext_var corejavaContext;
55.       try
56.       {
57.          // Bind the context to root.
58.          corejavaContext = rootContext->bind_new_context(contextName);
59.       }
60.       catch (CosNaming::NamingContext::AlreadyBound& ex)
61.       {
62.          // If the context already exists, this exception will be raised. In this case, just
63.          // resolve the name and assign the context to the object returned:
64.          CORBA::Object_var obj;
65.          obj = rootContext->resolve(contextName);
66.          corejavaContext = CosNaming::NamingContext::_narrow(obj);
67.          if( CORBA::is_nil(corejavaContext) )
68.          {
69.             cerr << "Failed to narrow naming context." << endl;
70.             return;
71.          }
72.       }
```

```
73.
74.        // Bind objref with given name to the context:
75.        CosNaming::Name objectName;
76.        objectName.length(1);
77.        objectName[0].id = name;
78.        objectName[0].kind = (const char*) "Object";
79.
80.        try
81.        {
82.            corejavaContext->bind(objectName, objref);
83.        }
84.        catch (CosNaming::NamingContext::AlreadyBound& ex)
85.        {
86.            corejavaContext->rebind(objectName, objref);
87.        }
88.    }
89.    catch (CORBA::COMM_FAILURE& ex)
90.    {
91.        cerr << "Caught system exception COMM_FAILURE--unable to contact the naming service."
92.            << endl;
93.    }
94.    catch (CORBA::SystemException&)
95.    {
96.        cerr << "Caught a CORBA::SystemException while using the naming service." << endl;
97.    }
98. }
99.
100. int main(int argc, char *argv[])
101. {
102.    cout << "Creating and initializing the ORB..." << endl;
103.
104.    CORBA::ORB_var orb = CORBA::ORB_init(argc, argv, "omniORB4");
105.
106.    CORBA::Object_var obj = orb->resolve_initial_references("RootPOA");
107.    PortableServer::POA_var poa = PortableServer::POA::_narrow(obj);
108.    poa->the_POAManager()->activate();
109.
110.    EnvImpl* envImpl = new EnvImpl();
111.    poa->activate_object(envImpl);
112.
113.    // Obtain a reference to the object, and register it in the naming service.
114.    obj = envImpl->_this();
115.
116.    cout << orb->object_to_string(obj) << endl;
117.    cout << "Binding server implementations to registry..." << endl;
118.    bindObjectToName(orb, "Env", obj);
119.    envImpl->_remove_ref();
120.
121.    cout << "Waiting for invocations from clients..." << endl;
122.    orb->run();
123.
124.    return 0;
125. }
```

Locating Objects Through IORs

If you can't configure your server ORB and name service so that your client can invoke it, you can still locate CORBA objects by using an *Interoperable Object Reference,* or IOR. An IOR is a long string starting with IOR: and followed by many hexadecimal digits, for example:

```
IOR:012020201000000049444c3a4163636f756e743a312e30000100000000000004e000000010100200f0000003
231362e31352e3131322e3137390020350420202e00000001504d43000000001000000049444c3a4163636f756e74
3a312e30000e0000004a61636b6b20422e20517569636b6b00
```

An IOR describes an object uniquely. By convention, many server classes print out the IORs of all objects they register, to enable clients to locate them. You can then paste the server IOR into the client program. Specifically, use the following code:

```
String ref = "IOR:012020201000000049444c3a4163636f...";
   // paste IOR from server
org.omg.CORBA.Object object = orb.string_to_object(ref);
```

Then, narrow the returned object to the appropriate type, for example:

```
Env env = EnvHelper.narrow(object);
```

or

```
NamingContext context = NamingContextHelper.narrow(object);
```

When testing the code for this book, we successfully used this method to connect clients with Visibroker and OmniORB.

org.omg.CORBA.ORB 1.2

- `static ORB init(String[] commandLineArgs, Properties orbConfigurationprops)`
  creates a new ORB and initializes it.
- `String[] list_initial_services()`
  returns a list of the initially available services such as "NameService".
- `org.omg.CORBA.Object resolve_initial_references(String initialServiceName)`
  returns an object that carries out one of the initial services.
- `org.omg.CORBA.Object string_to_object(String ior)`
  locates the object with a given IOR.

org.omg.CosNaming.NamingContext 1.2

- `org.omg.CORBA.Object resolve(NameComponent[] name)`
  returns the object that is bound to the given name.

org.omg.CosNaming.NameComponent 1.2

- `NameComponent(String componentId, String componentType)`
  constructs a new name component.

Implementing CORBA Servers

If you are deploying a CORBA infrastructure, you will find that Java is a good implementation language for CORBA server objects. The language binding is natural, and robust server software is more easily built with Java than with C++. This section describes how to implement a CORBA server in the Java programming language.

The example program in this section is similar to that of the preceding section. We supply a service to look up a system property of a Java virtual machine. Here is the IDL description:

```
interface SysProp
{
    string getProperty(in string name);
};
```

For example, our client test program calls the server as follows:

```
CORBA::String_var key = "java.vendor";
CORBA::String_var value = sysProp->getProperty(key);
```

The result is a string describing the vendor of the Java virtual machine that is executing the server program. We don't look into the details of the C++ client program. Example 5–21 lists the code.

To implement the server, you run the idlj compiler with the -fall option. (By default, idlj only creates client-side stubs.)

```
idlj -fall SysProp.idl
```

Then you extend the SysPropPOA class that the idlj compiler generated from the IDL file. Here is the implementation:

```
class SysPropImpl extends SysPropPOA
{
    public String getProperty(String key)
    {
        return System.getProperty(key);
    }
}
```

 NOTE: You can choose any name you like for the implementation class. In this book, we follow the RMI convention and use the suffix Impl for the implementation class name. Other programmers use a suffix Servant or _i.

 NOTE: If your implementation class already extends another class, you cannot simultaneously extend the implementation base class. In that case, you can instruct the idlj compiler to create a *tie* class. Your server class then implements the operations interface instead of extending the implementation base class. However, any server objects must be created by means of the tie class. For details, check out the idlj documentation at http://java.sun.com/j2se/5.0/docs/guide/rmi-iiop/toJavaPortableUG.html.

Next, write a server program that carries out the following tasks:

1. Start the ORB.
2. Locate and activate the root Portable Object Adaptor (POA).
3. Create the server implementation.
4. Use the POA to convert the servant reference to a CORBA object reference. (The server implementation class extends SysPropPOA, which itself extends org.omg.PortableServer.Servant.)
5. Print its IOR (for name-service-challenged clients—see the sidebar on page 309).
6. Bind the server implementation to the naming service.
7. Wait for invocations from clients.

You will find the complete code in Example 5–20. Here are the highlights.

Start the ORB as you would for a client program:

```
ORB orb = ORB.init(args, null);
```

Next, activate the root POA:

```
POA rootpoa = (POA) orb.resolve_initial_references("RootPOA");
rootpoa.the_POAManager().activate();
```

Construct the server object and convert it to a CORBA object:

```
SysPropImpl impl = new SysPropImpl();
org.omg.CORBA.Object ref = rootpoa.servant_to_reference(impl);
```

Next, obtain the IOR with the `object_to_string` method and print it:

```
System.out.println(orb.object_to_string(impl));
```

You obtain a reference to the naming service in exactly the same way as with a client program:

```
org.omg.CORBA.Object namingContextObj = orb.resolve_initial_references("NameService");
NamingContext namingContext = NamingContextHelper.narrow(namingContextObj);
```

You then build the desired name for the object. Here, we call the object `SysProp`:

```
NameComponent[] path =
    {
        new NameComponent("SysProp", "Object")
    };
```

You use the `rebind` method to bind the object to the name:

```
namingContext.rebind(path, impl);
```

Finally, you wait for client invocations:

```
orb.run();
```

To test this program, do the following.

1. Compile the IDL file, using both the C++ and Java IDL compilers.
   ```
   omniidl -bcxx SysProp.idl
   idlj -fall SysProp.idl
   ```

2. Compile the server program.
   ```
   javac SysPropServer.java
   ```

3. Compile the C++ client program. On Linux, use the command
   ```
   g++ -o SysPropClient -D__x86__ -D__linux__ -D__OSVERSION__=2 -I /usr/local/include/omniORB4/
       SysPropClient.cpp SysPropSK.cc -lomniORB4 -lomnithread -lpthread
   ```

4. Start the orbd naming service on the server. This program is a part of the JDK.
   ```
   orbd -ORBInitialPort 2809 &
   ```

5. Start the server.
   ```
   java SysPropServer -ORBInitialPort 2809 &
   ```
   The server also runs until you kill it.

6. Run the client.
   ```
   ./SysPropClient -ORBInitRef NameService=corbaname::localhost
   ```
   It should print the JVM vendor of the server.

You have now seen how to use CORBA to connect clients and servers that were written in different programming languages.

This concludes our discussion of CORBA. CORBA has other interesting features, such as dynamic method invocation and a number of standard services such as transaction handling and persistence. We refer you to *Client/Server Programming with Java and CORBA* by Robert Orfali and Dan Harkey [John Wiley & Sons 1998] for an in-depth discussion of advanced CORBA issues.

Example 5–20: SysPropServer.java

```java
1.  import org.omg.CosNaming.*;
2.  import org.omg.CORBA.*;
3.  import org.omg.PortableServer.*;
4.
5.  class SysPropImpl extends SysPropPOA
6.  {
7.     public String getProperty(String key)
8.     {
9.        return System.getProperty(key);
10.    }
11. }
12.
13. public class SysPropServer
14. {
15.    public static void main(String args[])
16.    {
17.       try
18.       {
19.          System.out.println("Creating and initializing the ORB...");
20.
21.          ORB orb = ORB.init(args, null);
22.
23.          System.out.println("Registering server implementation with the ORB...");
24.
25.          POA rootpoa = (POA) orb.resolve_initial_references("RootPOA");
26.          rootpoa.the_POAManager().activate();
27.
28.          SysPropImpl impl = new SysPropImpl();
29.          org.omg.CORBA.Object ref = rootpoa.servant_to_reference(impl);
30.
31.          System.out.println(orb.object_to_string(ref));
32.
33.          org.omg.CORBA.Object namingContextObj = orb.resolve_initial_references("NameService");
34.          NamingContext namingContext = NamingContextHelper.narrow(namingContextObj);
35.          NameComponent[] path =
36.             {
37.                new NameComponent("SysProp", "Object")
38.             };
39.
40.          System.out.println("Binding server implemenation to name service...");
41.          namingContext.rebind(path, ref);
42.
43.          System.out.println("Waiting for invocations from clients...");
44.          orb.run();
45.       }
46.       catch (Exception e)
47.       {
48.          e.printStackTrace(System.out);
49.       }
50.    }
51. }
```

Example 5–21: SysPropClient.cpp

```cpp
1. #include <iostream>
2.
3. #include "SysProp.hh"
4.
5. using namespace std;
6.
7. CORBA::Object_ptr getObjectReference(CORBA::ORB_ptr orb, const char serviceName[])
8. {
9.     CosNaming::NamingContext_var rootContext;
10.
11.     try
12.     {
13.         // Obtain a reference to the root context of the name service:
14.         CORBA::Object_var initServ;
15.         initServ = orb->resolve_initial_references("NameService");
16.
17.         // Narrow the object returned by resolve_initial_references() to a CosNaming::NamingContext
18.         // object
19.         rootContext = CosNaming::NamingContext::_narrow(initServ);
20.         if (CORBA::is_nil(rootContext))
21.         {
22.             cerr << "Failed to narrow naming context." << endl;
23.             return CORBA::Object::_nil();
24.         }
25.     }
26.     catch (CORBA::ORB::InvalidName&)
27.     {
28.         cerr << "Name service does not exist." << endl;
29.         return CORBA::Object::_nil();
30.     }
31.
32.     // Create a name object, containing the name corejava/SysProp:
33.     CosNaming::Name name;
34.     name.length(1);
35.
36.     name[0].id   = serviceName;
37.     name[0].kind = "Object";
38.
39.     CORBA::Object_ptr obj;
40.     try
41.     {
42.         // Resolve the name to an object reference, and assign the returned reference to a
43.         // CORBA::Object:
44.         obj = rootContext->resolve(name);
45.     }
46.     catch (CosNaming::NamingContext::NotFound&)
47.     {
48.         // This exception is thrown if any of the components of the path [contexts or the object]
49.         // aren't found:
50.         cerr << "Context not found." << endl;
51.         return CORBA::Object::_nil();
52.     }
53.     return obj;
54. }
```

```
55.
56.  int main (int argc, char *argv[])
57.  {
58.      CORBA::ORB_ptr orb = CORBA::ORB_init(argc, argv, "omniORB4");
59.
60.      CORBA::Object_var obj = getObjectReference(orb, "SysProp");
61.      SysProp_var sysProp = SysProp::_narrow(obj);
62.
63.      if (CORBA::is_nil(sysProp))
64.      {
65.          cerr << "Cannot invoke on a nil object reference." << endl;
66.          return 1;
67.      }
68.
69.      CORBA::String_var key = "java.vendor";
70.      CORBA::String_var value = sysProp->getProperty(key);
71.
72.      cerr << key << "=" << value << endl;
73.
74.      return 0;
75.  }
```

org.omg.CORBA.ORB 1.2

- void connect(org.omg.CORBA.Object obj)
  connects the given implementation object to this ORB, enabling the ORB to forward calls to the object's methods.
- String object_to_string(org.omg.CORBA.Object obj)
  returns the IOR string of the given object.

org.omg.CosNaming.NamingContext 1.2

- void bind(NameComponent[] name, org.omg.CORBA.Object obj)
- void rebind(NameComponent[] name, org.omg.CORBA.Object obj)
  bind an object to a name. The bind method throws an AlreadyBound exception if the object has previously been bound. The rebind method replaces any previously bound objects.

Remote Method Calls with SOAP

This section is adapted from Geary and Horstmann, *Core JavaServer Faces* [Sun Microsystems Press 2004].

In recent years, *web services* have emerged as a popular technology for remote method calls. Technically, a web service has two components:

- A server that can be accessed with the Simple Object Access Protocol (SOAP) transport protocol
- A description of the service in the Web Service Description Language (WSDL) format

SOAP is an XML protocol that, like CORBA's IIOP, provides a protocol for invoking remote methods. Just as you can program CORBA clients and servers without knowing anything about IIOP, you don't really need to know any details about SOAP to call a web service.

WSDL is analogous to IDL. It describes the interface of the web service: the methods that can be called, and their parameter and return types. In this section, we discuss only the implementation of a client that connects to an existing web service. Someone else has already prepared the WSDL file in this situation.

Implementing a web service is beyond the scope of this book. For more information on this topic, see Chapter 8 of the J2EE tutorial at `http://java.sun.com/j2ee/1.4/docs/tutorial/doc/index.html`.

To make web services easy to understand, we look at a concrete example: the Amazon web service, described at `http://www.amazon.com/gp/aws/landing.html`. The Amazon web service allows a programmer to interact with the Amazon system for a wide variety of purposes. For example, you can get listings of all books with a given author or title, or you can fill shopping carts and place orders. Amazon makes this service available for use by companies that want to sell items to their customers, using the Amazon system as a fulfillment backend. To run our example program, you will need to sign up with Amazon and get a free developer token that lets you connect to the service.

Alternatively, you can adapt the technique described in this section to any other web service. The site `http://www.xmethods.com` lists many freely available web services that you can try.

A primary attraction of web services is that they are language-neutral. We access the Amazon Web Services by using Java programs, but other developers can equally well use C++ or Visual Basic. The WSDL descriptor describes the services in a language-independent manner. For example, the WSDL for the Amazon Web Services (located at `http://soap.amazon.com/schemas3/AmazonWebServices.wsdl`) describes an `AuthorSearchRequest` operation as follows:

```
<operation name="AuthorSearchRequest">
   <input message="typens:AuthorSearchRequest"/>
   <output message="typens:AuthorSearchResponse"/>
</operation>
   . . .
<message name="AuthorSearchRequest">
   <part name="AuthorSearchRequest" type="typens:AuthorRequest"/>
</message>
<message name="AuthorSearchResponse">
   <part name="return" type="typens:ProductInfo"/>
</message>
```

Elsewhere, it defines the data types. Here is the definition of `AuthorRequest`:

```
<xsd:complexType name="AuthorRequest">
   <xsd:all>
      <xsd:element name="author" type="xsd:string"/>
      <xsd:element name="page" type="xsd:string"/>
      <xsd:element name="mode" type="xsd:string"/>
      <xsd:element name="tag" type="xsd:string"/>
      <xsd:element name="type" type="xsd:string"/>
      <xsd:element name="devtag" type="xsd:string"/>
      <xsd:element name="sort" type="xsd:string" minOccurs="0"/>
      <xsd:element name="locale" type="xsd:string" minOccurs="0"/>
      <xsd:element name="keywords" type="xsd:string" minOccurs="0"/>
      <xsd:element name="price" type="xsd:string" minOccurs="0"/>
   </xsd:all>
</xsd:complexType>
```

When this description is translated into Java, the `AuthorRequest` type becomes a class.

```
public class AuthorRequest
{
   public AuthorRequest(String author, String page, String mode, String tag, String type,
      String devtag, String sort, String locale, String keyword, String price) { . . . }
   public String getAuthor() { . . . }
   public void setAuthor(String newValue) { . . . }
```

```
public String getPage() { . . . }
public void setPage(String) { . . . }
    . . .
}
```

To call the search service, construct an `AuthorRequest` object and call the `authorSearchRequest` of a "port" object.

```
AmazonSearchPort port = (AmazonSearchPort) (new AmazonSearchService_Impl().getAmazonSearchPort());
AuthorRequest request = new AuthorRequest(name, "1", "books", "", "lite", "", token, "", "", "");
ProductInfo response = port.authorSearchRequest(request);
```

The port object translates the Java object into a SOAP message, passes it to the Amazon server, and translates the returned message into a `ProductInfo` object. The port classes are automatically generated.

 NOTE: The WSDL file does not specify *what* the service does. It only specifies the parameter and return types.

Download the Java Web Services Developer Pack (JWSDP) from http://java.sun.com/webservices/webservicespack.html and install it.

To generate the required Java classes, place a `config.xml` file with the following contents into the directory of the client program:

```
<?xml version="1.0" encoding="UTF-8"?>
<configuration
    xmlns="http://java.sun.com/xml/ns/jax-rpc/ri/config">
        <wsdl
            location="http://soap.amazon.com/schemas3/AmazonWebServices.wsdl"
            packageName="com.amazon" />
</configuration>
```

Then run these commands:

```
jwsdp/jaxrpc/bin/wscompile.sh -import config.xml
jwsdp/jaxrpc/bin/wscompile.sh -gen -keep config.xml
```

Here, *jwsdp* is the directory into which you installed the JWSDP, such as /usr/local/jwsdp-1.4 or c:\jwsdp-1.4. (As usual, Windows users need to use \ instead of / and .bat instead of .sh.)

The first command imports the WSDL file from the given location. The second command generates the classes that the client needs. The -keep option keeps the source files. This is not strictly necessary, but you may find it interesting to look at some of them. As a result of these commands, a large number of classes are created in the specified package directory (here, com/amazon). Have a look at some of them, in particular com/amazon/AuthorRequest.java and com/amazon/Details.java. We use these classes in the sample application.

Our sample application (in Example 5–22) is straightforward. The user specifies an author name and clicks the Search button. We simply show the first page of the response (see Figure 5–11). This shows that the web service is successful. We leave it as the proverbial exercise for the reader to extend the functionality of the application.

To compile this application, add the library file *jwsdp*/jaxrpc/lib/jaxrpc-impl.jar to your class path.

To run this application, your class file must contain the following:

```
. (the current directory)
jwsdp/jaxrpc/lib/jaxrpc-api.jar
jwsdp/jaxrpc/lib/jaxrpc-impl.jar
```

jwsdp/jaxrpc/lib/jaxrpc-spi.jar
jwsdp/jwsdp-shared/lib/activation.jar
jwsdp/jwsdp-shared/lib/mail.jar
jwsdp/saaj/lib/saaj-api.jar
jwsdp/saaj/lib/saaj-impl.jar

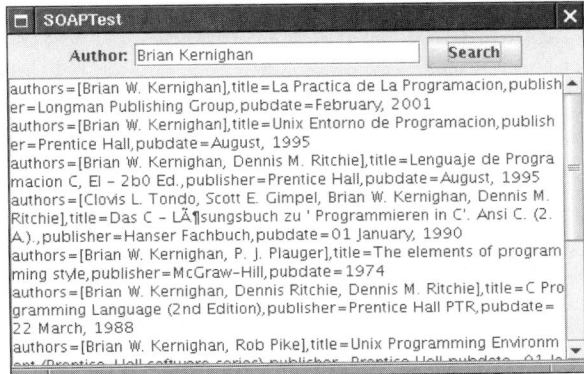

Figure 5–11: Connecting to a web service

If you compile and run from the command line, you may want to use a shell script to automate this task.

This example shows that calling a web service is fundamentally the same as making any other remote method call. The programmer calls a local method on a proxy object, and the proxy connects to a server. Since web services are springing up everywhere, this is clearly an interesting technology for application programmers. Web services will become even easier to use when the tools and libraries are bundled into a future version of the JDK.

Example 5–22: SOAPTest.java

```
 1. import com.amazon.*;
 2. import java.awt.*;
 3. import java.awt.event.*;
 4. import java.rmi.*;
 5. import java.util.*;
 6. import javax.swing.*;
 7.
 8. /**
 9.    The client for the warehouse program.
10. */
11. public class SOAPTest
12. {
13.    public static void main(String[] args)
14.    {
15.       JFrame frame = new SOAPTestFrame();
16.       frame.setDefaultCloseOperation(JFrame.EXIT_ON_CLOSE);
17.       frame.setVisible(true);
18.    }
19. }
20.
21. /**
22.    A frame to select the book author and to display the server response.
23. */
```

```
24. class SOAPTestFrame extends JFrame
25. {
26.    public SOAPTestFrame()
27.    {
28.       setTitle("SOAPTest");
29.       setSize(DEFAULT_WIDTH, DEFAULT_HEIGHT);
30.
31.       JPanel panel = new JPanel();
32.
33.       panel.add(new JLabel("Author:"));
34.       author = new JTextField(20);
35.       panel.add(author);
36.
37.       JButton searchButton = new JButton("Search");
38.       panel.add(searchButton);
39.       searchButton.addActionListener(new
40.          ActionListener()
41.          {
42.             public void actionPerformed(ActionEvent event)
43.             {
44.                result.setText("Please wait...");
45.                new Thread(new
46.                   Runnable()
47.                   {
48.                      public void run()
49.                      {
50.                         String name = author.getText();
51.                         String books = searchByAuthor(name);
52.                         result.setText(books);
53.                      }
54.                   }).start();
55.             }
56.          });
57.
58.       result = new JTextArea();
59.       result.setLineWrap(true);
60.       result.setEditable(false);
61.
62.       add(panel, BorderLayout.NORTH);
63.       add(new JScrollPane(result), BorderLayout.CENTER);
64.    }
65.
66.    /**
67.       Calls the Amazon web service to find titles that match the author.
68.       @param name the author name
69.       @return a description of the matching titles
70.    */
71.    private String searchByAuthor(String name)
72.    {
73.       try
74.       {
75.          AmazonSearchPort port = (AmazonSearchPort)
76.             (new AmazonSearchService_Impl().getAmazonSearchPort());
77.
78.          AuthorRequest request
79.             = new AuthorRequest(name, "1", "books", "", "lite", "", token, "", "", "");
```

```
80.        ProductInfo response = port.authorSearchRequest(request);
81.
82.        Details[] details = response.getDetails();
83.        StringBuilder r = new StringBuilder();
84.        for (Details d : details)
85.        {
86.           r.append("authors=");
87.           String[] authors = d.getAuthors();
88.           if (authors == null) r.append("[]");
89.           else r.append(Arrays.asList(d.getAuthors()));
90.           r.append(",title=");
91.           r.append(d.getProductName());
92.           r.append(",publisher=");
93.           r.append(d.getManufacturer());
94.           r.append(",pubdate=");
95.           r.append(d.getReleaseDate());
96.           r.append("\n");
97.        }
98.        return r.toString();
99.     }
100.    catch (RemoteException e)
101.    {
102.        return "Exception: " + e;
103.    }
104. }
105.
106. private static final int DEFAULT_WIDTH = 450;
107. private static final int DEFAULT_HEIGHT = 300;
108.
109. private static final String token = "your token goes here";
110.
111. private JTextField author;
112. private JTextArea result;
113. }
```

Chapter **6**

Advanced Swing

In this chapter, we continue our discussion of the Swing user interface toolkit from Volume 1. Swing is a rich toolkit, and Volume 1 covered only basic and commonly used components. That leaves us with three significantly more complex components for lists, trees, and tables, the exploration of which occupies the bulk of this chapter. Components for styled text, in particular HTML, are internally even more complex, and we show you how to put them to practical use. We then discuss how to display progress of a slow activity that runs in a separate thread. We finish the chapter by covering component organizers such as tabbed panes and desktop panes with internal frames.

Lists

If you want to present a set of choices to a user, and a radio button or checkbox set consumes too much space, you can use a combo box or a list. Combo boxes were covered in Volume 1 because they are relatively simple. The JList component has many more features, and its design is similar to that of the tree and table components. For that reason, it is our starting point for the discussion of complex Swing components.

Of course, you can have lists of strings, but you can also have lists of arbitrary objects, with full control of how they appear. The internal architecture of the list component that makes this generality possible is rather elegant. Unfortunately, the designers at Sun felt that they needed to show off that elegance, rather than hiding it from the programmer who just wants to use the component. You will find that the list control is somewhat awkward to use for common cases because you need to manipulate some of the machinery that makes the

general cases possible. We walk you through the simple and most common case, a list box of strings, and then give a more complex example that shows off the flexibility of the list component.

The JList Component

The JList component is similar to a set of checkboxes or radio buttons, except that the items are placed inside a single box and are selected by clicking on the items themselves, not on buttons. If you permit multiple selection for a list box, the user can select any combination of the items in the box.

Figure 6–1 shows an admittedly silly example. The user can select the attributes for the fox, such as "quick," "brown," "hungry," "wild," and, because we ran out of attributes, "static," "private," and "final." You can thus have the *static final* fox jump over the lazy dog.

To construct this list component, you first start out with an array of strings, then pass the array to the JList constructor:

```
String[] words= { "quick", "brown", "hungry", "wild", ... };
JList wordList = new JList(words);
```

Alternatively, you can use an anonymous array:

```
JList wordList = new JList(new String[] {"quick", "brown", "hungry", "wild", ... });
```

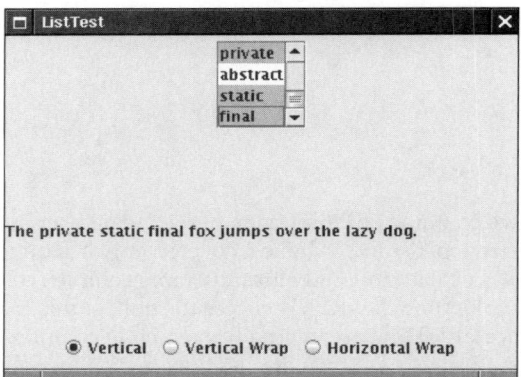

Figure 6–1: A list box

List boxes do not scroll automatically. To make a list box scroll, you must insert it into a scroll pane:

```
JScrollPane scrollPane = new JScrollPane(wordList);
```

You then add the scroll pane, not the list, into the surrounding panel.

We must admit that the separation of the list display and the scrolling mechanism is elegant in theory, but it is a pain in practice. Essentially all lists that we ever encountered needed scrolling. It seems cruel to force programmers to go through hoops in the default case just so they can appreciate that elegance.

By default, the list component displays eight items; use the setVisibleRowCount method to change that value:

```
wordList.setVisibleRowCount(4); // display 4 items
```

You can set the *layout orientation* to one of three values:

- JList.VERTICAL (the default): arrange all items vertically

- `JList.VERTICAL_WRAP`: start new columns if there are more items than the visible row count (see Figure 6–2)
- `JList.HORIZONTAL_WRAP`: start new columns if there are more items than the visible row count, but fill them horizontally. Look at the placement of the words "quick," "brown," and "hungry" in Figure 6–2 to see the difference between vertical and horizontal wrap.

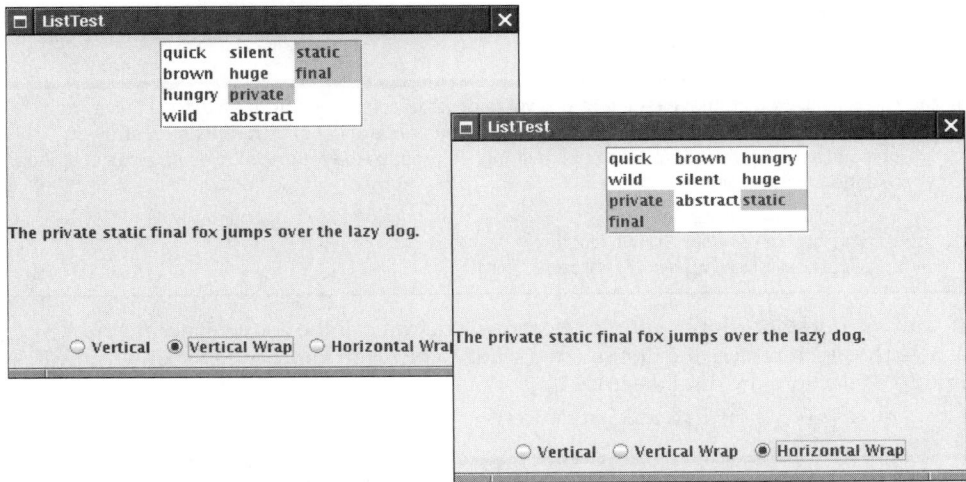

Figure 6–2: Lists with vertical and horizontal wrap

By default, a user can select multiple items. This requires some knowledge of mouse technique: To add more items to a selection, press the CTRL key while clicking on each item. To select a contiguous range of items, click on the first one, then hold down the SHIFT key and click on the last one.

You can also restrict the user to a more limited selection mode with the `setSelectionMode` method:

```
wordList.setSelectionMode(ListSelectionModel.SINGLE_SELECTION);
    // select one item at a time
wordList.setSelectionMode(ListSelectionModel.SINGLE_INTERVAL_SELECTION);
    // select one item or one range of items
```

You may recall from Volume 1 that the basic user interface components send out action events when the user activates them. List boxes use a different notification mechanism. Rather than listening to action events, you need to listen to list selection events. Add a list selection listener to the list component, and implement the method

```
public void valueChanged(ListSelectionEvent evt)
```

in the listener.

When the user selects items, a flurry of list selection events is generated. For example, suppose the user clicks on a new item. When the mouse button goes down, an event reports a change in selection. This is a transitional event—the call

```
event.isAdjusting()
```

returns `true` if the selection is not yet final. Then, when the mouse button goes up, there is another event, this time with `isAdjusting` returning `false`. If you are not interested in the transitional events, then you can wait for the event for which `isAdjusting` is `false`. However, if you

want to give the user instant feedback as soon as the mouse button is clicked, then you need to process all events.

Once you are notified that an event has happened, you will want to find out what items are currently selected. The getSelectedValues method returns an *array of objects* containing all selected items. Cast *each* array element to a string.

```
Object[] values = list.getSelectedValues();
for (Object value : values)
    do something with (String) value;
```

CAUTION: You cannot cast the return value of getSelectedValues from an Object[] array to a String[] array. The return value was not created as an array of strings, but as an array of objects, each of which happens to be a string. To process the return value as an array of strings, use the following code:

```
int length = values.length;
String[] words = new String[length];
System.arrayCopy(values, 0, words, 0, length);
```

If your list does not allow multiple selections, you can call the convenience method getSelectedValue. It returns the first selected value (which you know to be the only value if multiple selections are disallowed).

```
String value = (String) list.getSelectedValue();
```

NOTE: List components do not react to double clicks from a mouse. As envisioned by the designers of Swing, you use a list to select an item, and then you click a button to make something happen. However, some user interfaces allow a user to double-click on a list item as a shortcut for item selection and acceptance of a default action. If you want to implement this behavior, you have to add a mouse listener to the list box, then trap the mouse event as follows:

```
public void mouseClicked(MouseEvent evt)
{
    if (evt.getClickCount() == 2)
    {
        JList source = (JList) evt.getSource();
        Object[] selection = source.getSelectedValues();
        doAction(selection);
    }
}
```

Example 6–1 is the listing of the program that demonstrates a list box filled with strings. Notice how the valueChanged method builds up the message string from the selected items.

Example 6–1: ListTest.java

```
1. import java.awt.*;
2. import java.awt.event.*;
3. import javax.swing.*;
4. import javax.swing.event.*;
5.
6. /**
7.    This program demonstrates a simple fixed list of strings.
8. */
9. public class ListTest
10. {
```

```
11.    public static void main(String[] args)
12.    {
13.       JFrame frame = new ListFrame();
14.       frame.setDefaultCloseOperation(JFrame.EXIT_ON_CLOSE);
15.       frame.setVisible(true);
16.    }
17. }
18.
19. /**
20.    This frame contains a word list and a label that shows a
21.    sentence made up from the chosen words. Note that you can
22.    select multiple words with Ctrl+click and Shift+click.
23. */
24. class ListFrame extends JFrame
25. {
26.    public ListFrame()
27.    {
28.       setTitle("ListTest");
29.       setSize(DEFAULT_WIDTH, DEFAULT_HEIGHT);
30.
31.       String[] words =
32.       {
33.          "quick","brown","hungry","wild","silent",
34.          "huge","private","abstract","static","final"
35.       };
36.
37.       wordList = new JList(words);
38.       wordList.setVisibleRowCount(4);
39.       JScrollPane scrollPane = new JScrollPane(wordList);
40.
41.       listPanel = new JPanel();
42.       listPanel.add(scrollPane);
43.       wordList.addListSelectionListener(new
44.          ListSelectionListener()
45.          {
46.             public void valueChanged(ListSelectionEvent event)
47.             {
48.                Object[] values = wordList.getSelectedValues();
49.
50.                StringBuilder text = new StringBuilder(prefix);
51.                for (int i = 0; i < values.length; i++)
52.                {
53.                   String word = (String) values[i];
54.                   text.append(word);
55.                   text.append(" ");
56.                }
57.                text.append(suffix);
58.
59.                label.setText(text.toString());
60.             }
61.          });
62.
63.       buttonPanel = new JPanel();
64.       group = new ButtonGroup();
65.       makeButton("Vertical", JList.VERTICAL);
66.       makeButton("Vertical Wrap", JList.VERTICAL_WRAP);
```

```
67.      makeButton("Horizontal Wrap", JList.HORIZONTAL_WRAP);
68.
69.      add(listPanel, BorderLayout.NORTH);
70.      label = new JLabel(prefix + suffix);
71.      add(label, BorderLayout.CENTER);
72.      add(buttonPanel, BorderLayout.SOUTH);
73.   }
74.
75.   /**
76.      Makes a radio button to set the layout orientation.
77.      @param label the button label
78.      @param orientation the orientation for the list
79.   */
80.   private void makeButton(String label, final int orientation)
81.   {
82.      JRadioButton button = new JRadioButton(label);
83.      buttonPanel.add(button);
84.      if (group.getButtonCount() == 0) button.setSelected(true);
85.      group.add(button);
86.      button.addActionListener(new
87.         ActionListener()
88.         {
89.            public void actionPerformed(ActionEvent event)
90.            {
91.               wordList.setLayoutOrientation(orientation);
92.               listPanel.revalidate();
93.            }
94.         });
95.   }
96.
97.   private static final int DEFAULT_WIDTH = 400;
98.   private static final int DEFAULT_HEIGHT = 300;
99.   private JPanel listPanel;
100.  private JList wordList;
101.  private JLabel label;
102.  private JPanel buttonPanel;
103.  private ButtonGroup group;
104.  private String prefix = "The ";
105.  private String suffix = "fox jumps over the lazy dog.";
106. }
```

javax.swing.JList 1.2

- JList(Object[] items)
  constructs a list that displays these items.

- int getVisibleRowCount()
- void setVisibleRowCount(int c)
  get or set the preferred number of rows in the list that can be displayed without a scroll bar.

- int getLayoutOrientation() **1.4**
- void setLayoutOrientation(int orientation) **1.4**
  get or set the layout orientation

  Parameters: orientation   One of VERTICAL, VERTICAL_WRAP, HORIZONTAL_WRAP

- int getSelectionMode()
- void setSelectionMode(int mode)
  get or set the mode that determines whether single-item or multiple-item selections are allowed.

  Parameters: mode   One of SINGLE_SELECTION, SINGLE_INTERVAL_SELECTION, MULTIPLE_INTERVAL_SELECTION

- void addListSelectionListener(ListSelectionListener listener)
  adds to the list a listener that's notified each time a change to the selection occurs.
- Object[] getSelectedValues()
  returns the selected values or an empty array if the selection is empty.
- Object getSelectedValue()
  returns the first selected value or null if the selection is empty.

 javax.swing.event.ListSelectionListener 1.2

- void valueChanged(ListSelectionEvent e)
  is called whenever the list selection changes.

List Models

In the preceding section, you saw the most common method for using a list component:

- Specify a fixed set of strings for display in the list,
- Place the list inside a scroll pane, and
- Trap the list selection events.

In the remainder of the section on lists, we cover more complex situations that require a bit more finesse:

- Very long lists
- Lists with changing contents
- Lists that don't contain strings

In the first example, we constructed a JList component that held a fixed collection of strings. However, the collection of choices in a list box is not always fixed. How do we add or remove items in the list box? Somewhat surprisingly, there are no methods in the JList class to achieve this. Instead, you have to understand a little more about the internal design of the list component. As with text components, the list component uses the model-view-controller design pattern to separate the visual appearance (a column of items that are rendered in some way) from the underlying data (a collection of objects).

The JList class is responsible for the visual appearance of the data. It actually knows very little about how the data are stored—all it knows is that it can retrieve the data through some object that implements the ListModel interface:

```
public interface ListModel
{
    int getSize();
    Object getElementAt(int i);
    void addListDataListener(ListDataListener l);
    void removeListDataListener(ListDataListener l);
}
```

Through this interface, the JList can get a count of elements and retrieve each one of the elements. Also, the JList object can add itself as a *list data listener*. That way, if the collection of elements changes, JList gets notified so that it can repaint the list.

Why is this generality useful? Why doesn't the JList object simply store a vector of objects?

Note that the interface doesn't specify how the objects are stored. In particular, it doesn't force them to be stored at all! The getElementAt method is free to recompute each value whenever it is called. This is potentially useful if you want to show a very large collection without having to store the values.

Here is a somewhat silly example: We let the user choose among *all three-letter words* in a list box (see Figure 6–3).

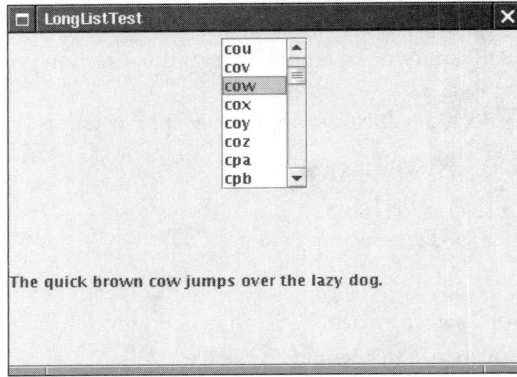

Figure 6–3: Choosing from a very long list of selections

There are $26 \times 26 \times 26 = 17{,}576$ three-letter combinations. Rather than storing all these combinations, we recompute them as requested when the user scrolls through them.

This turns out to be easy to implement. The tedious part, adding and removing listeners, has been done for us in the AbstractListModel class, which we extend. We only need to supply the getSize and getElementAt methods:

```
class WordListModel extends AbstractListModel
{
    public WordListModel(int n) { length = n; }
    public int getSize() { return (int) Math.pow(26, length); }
    public Object getElementAt(int n)
    {
        // compute nth string
        . . .
    }
    . . .
}
```

The computation of the *n*th string is a bit technical—you'll find the details in the code listing in Example 6–2.

Now that we have supplied a model, we can simply build a list that lets the user scroll through the elements supplied by the model:

```
JList wordList = new JList(new WordListModel(3));
wordList.setSelectionMode(ListSelectionModel.SINGLE_SELECTION);
JScrollPane scrollPane = new JScrollPane(wordList);
```

The point is that the strings are never *stored*. Only those strings that the user actually requests to see are generated.

We must make one other setting. We must tell the list component that all items have a fixed width and height. The easiest way to set the cell dimensions is to specify a *prototype cell value*:

```
wordList.setPrototypeCellValue("www");
```

The prototype cell value is used to determine the size for all cells. Alternatively, you can set a fixed cell size:

```
wordList.setFixedCellWidth(50);
wordList.setFixedCellHeight(15);
```

If you don't set a prototype value or a fixed cell size, the list component computes the width and height of each item. That would take a long time.

As a practical matter, very long lists are rarely useful. It is extremely cumbersome for a user to scroll through a huge selection. For that reason, we believe that the list control has been completely overengineered. A selection that a user can comfortably manage on the screen is certainly small enough to be stored directly in the list component. That arrangement would have saved programmers from the pain of having to deal with the list model as a separate entity. On the other hand, the JList class is consistent with the JTree and JTable class where this generality is useful.

Example 6–2: LongListTest.java

```
 1. import java.awt.*;
 2. import java.awt.event.*;
 3. import javax.swing.*;
 4. import javax.swing.event.*;
 5.
 6. /**
 7.    This program demonstrates a list that dynamically computes
 8.    list entries.
 9. */
10. public class LongListTest
11. {
12.    public static void main(String[] args)
13.    {
14.       JFrame frame = new LongListFrame();
15.       frame.setDefaultCloseOperation(JFrame.EXIT_ON_CLOSE);
16.       frame.setVisible(true);
17.    }
18. }
19.
20. /**
21.    This frame contains a long word list and a label that shows a
22.    sentence made up from the chosen word.
23. */
24. class LongListFrame extends JFrame
25. {
26.    public LongListFrame()
27.    {
28.       setTitle("LongListTest");
29.       setSize(DEFAULT_WIDTH, DEFAULT_HEIGHT);
30.
31.       wordList = new JList(new WordListModel(3));
32.       wordList.setSelectionMode(ListSelectionModel.SINGLE_SELECTION);
33.       wordList.setPrototypeCellValue("www");
34.       JScrollPane scrollPane = new JScrollPane(wordList);
35.
36.       JPanel p = new JPanel();
37.       p.add(scrollPane);
38.       wordList.addListSelectionListener(new
39.          ListSelectionListener()
```

```
40.        {
41.            public void valueChanged(ListSelectionEvent evt)
42.            {
43.                StringBuilder word = (StringBuilder) wordList.getSelectedValue();
44.                setSubject(word.toString());
45.            }
46.
47.        });
48.
49.        Container contentPane = getContentPane();
50.        contentPane.add(p, BorderLayout.NORTH);
51.        label = new JLabel(prefix + suffix);
52.        contentPane.add(label, BorderLayout.CENTER);
53.        setSubject("fox");
54.    }
55.
56.    /**
57.        Sets the subject in the label.
58.        @param word the new subject that jumps over the lazy dog
59.    */
60.    public void setSubject(String word)
61.    {
62.        StringBuilder text = new StringBuilder(prefix);
63.        text.append(word);
64.        text.append(suffix);
65.        label.setText(text.toString());
66.    }
67.
68.    private static final int DEFAULT_WIDTH = 400;
69.    private static final int DEFAULT_HEIGHT = 300;
70.    private JList wordList;
71.    private JLabel label;
72.    private String prefix = "The quick brown ";
73.    private String suffix = " jumps over the lazy dog.";
74. }
75.
76. /**
77.    A model that dynamically generates n-letter words.
78. */
79. class WordListModel extends AbstractListModel
80. {
81.    /**
82.        Constructs the model.
83.        @param n the word length
84.    */
85.    public WordListModel(int n) { length = n; }
86.
87.    public int getSize()
88.    {
89.        return (int) Math.pow(LAST - FIRST + 1, length);
90.    }
91.
92.    public Object getElementAt(int n)
93.    {
94.        StringBuilder r = new StringBuilder();;
95.        for (int i = 0; i < length; i++)
96.        {
```

```
97.          char c = (char)(FIRST + n % (LAST - FIRST + 1));
98.          r.insert(0, c);
99.          n = n / (LAST - FIRST + 1);
100.       }
101.       return r;
102.    }
103.
104.    private int length;
105.    public static final char FIRST = 'a';
106.    public static final char LAST = 'z';
107. }
```

API **`javax.swing.JList`** 1.2

- JList(ListModel dataModel)
  constructs a list that displays the elements in the specified model.

- void setPrototypeCellValue(Object newValue)
- Object getPrototypeCellValue()
  set or get the prototype cell value that is used to determine the width and height of each cell in the list. The default is null, which forces the size of each cell to be measured.

- void setFixedCellWidth(int width)
  if the width is greater than zero, specifies the width of every cell in the list. The default value is –1, which forces the size of each cell to be measured.

- void setFixedCellHeight(int height)
  if the height is greater than zero, specifies the height of every cell in the list. The default value is –1, which forces the size of each cell to be measured.

API *`javax.swing.ListModel`* 1.2

- int getSize()
  returns the number of elements of the model.

- Object getElementAt(int position)
  returns an element of the model at the given position.

Inserting and Removing Values

You cannot directly edit the collection of list values. Instead, you must access the *model* and then add or remove elements. That, too, is easier said than done. Suppose you want to add more values to a list. You can obtain a reference to the model:

```
ListModel model = list.getModel();
```

But that does you no good—as you saw in the preceding section, the ListModel interface has no methods to insert or remove elements because, after all, the whole point of having a list model is that it need not *store* the elements.

Let's try it the other way around. One of the constructors of JList takes a vector of objects:

```
Vector<String> values = new Vector<String>();
values.addElement("quick");
values.addElement("brown");
. . .
JList list = new JList(values);
```

You can now edit the vector and add or remove elements, but the list does not know that this is happening, so it cannot react to the changes. In particular, the list cannot update its view when you add the values. Therefore, this constructor is not very useful.

Instead, you should construct a DefaultListModel object, fill it with the initial values, and associate it with the list.

```
DefaultListModel model = new DefaultListModel();
model.addElement("quick");
model.addElement("brown");
    . . .
JList list = new JList(model);
```

Now you can add or remove values from the model object. The model object then notifies the list of the changes, and the list repaints itself.

```
model.removeElement("quick");
model.addElement("slow");
```

For historical reasons, the DefaultListModel class doesn't use the same method names as the collection classes.

The default list model uses a vector internally to store the values.

 CAUTION: There are JList constructors that construct a list from an array or vector of objects or strings. You might think that these constructors use a DefaultListModel to store these values. That is not the case—the constructors build a trivial model that can access the values without any provisions for notification if the content changes. For example, here is the code for the constructor that constructs a JList from a Vector:

```
public JList(final Vector<?> listData)
{
    this (new AbstractListModel()
    {
        public int getSize() { return listData.size(); }
        public Object getElementAt(int i) { return listData.elementAt(i); }
    });
}
```

That means, if you change the contents of the vector after the list is constructed, then the list may show a confusing mix of old and new values until it is completely repainted. (The keyword final in the constructor above does not prevent you from changing the vector elsewhere—it only means that the constructor itself won't modify the value of the listData reference; the keyword is required because the listData object is used in the inner class.)

---

 javax.swing.JList 1.2

- ListModel getModel()
  gets the model of this list.

 javax.swing.DefaultListModel 1.2

- void addElement(Object obj)
  adds the object to the end of the model.
- boolean removeElement(Object obj)
  removes the first occurrence of the object from the model. Returns true if the object was contained in the model, false otherwise.

Rendering Values

So far, all lists that you saw in this chapter contained only strings. It is actually just as easy to show a list of icons—simply pass an array or vector filled with Icon objects. More interestingly, you can easily represent your list values with any drawing whatsoever.

Although the JList class can display strings and icons automatically, you need to install a
list cell renderer into the JList object for all custom drawing. A list cell renderer is any class
that implements the following interface:

```
interface ListCellRenderer
{
    Component getListCellRendererComponent(JList list, Object value, int index,
        boolean isSelected, boolean cellHasFocus);
}
```

This method is called for each cell. It returns a component that paints the cell contents. The
component is placed at the appropriate location whenever a cell needs to be rendered.

One way to implement a cell renderer is to create a class that extends JPanel, like this:

```
class MyCellRenderer extends JPanel implements ListCellRenderer
{
    public Component getListCellRendererComponent(JList list, Object value, int index,
        boolean isSelected, boolean cellHasFocus)
    {
        // stash away information that is needed for painting and size measurement
        return this;
    }
    public void paintComponent(Graphics g)
    {
        // paint code goes here
    }
    public Dimension getPreferredSize()
    {
        // size measurement code goes here
    }
    // instance fields
}
```

In Example 6–3, we display the font choices graphically by showing the actual appearance of
each font (see Figure 6–4). In the paintComponent method, we display each name in its own font.
We also need to make sure to match the usual colors of the look and feel of the JList class. We
obtain these colors by calling the getForeground/getBackground and getSelectionForeground/getSelec-
tionBackground methods of the JList class. In the getPreferredSize method, we need to measure the
size of the string, using the techniques that you saw in Volume 1, Chapter 7.

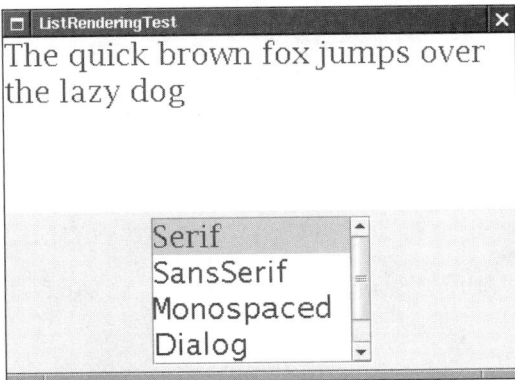

Figure 6–4: A list box with rendered cells

To install the cell renderer, simply call the setCellRenderer method:

```
fontList.setCellRenderer(new FontCellRenderer());
```

Now all list cells are drawn with the custom renderer.

Actually, a simpler method for writing custom renderers works in many cases. If the rendered image just contains text, an icon, and possibly a change of color, then you can get by with configuring a JLabel. For example, to show the font name in its own font, we can use the following renderer:

```
class FontCellRenderer extends JLabel implements ListCellRenderer
{
    public Component getListCellRendererComponent(JList list, Object value, int index,
        boolean isSelected, boolean cellHasFocus)
    {
        JLabel label = new JLabel();
        Font font = (Font) value;
        setText(font.getFamily());
        setFont(font);
        setOpaque(true);
        setBackground(isSelected ? list.getSelectionBackground() : list.getBackground());
        setForeground(isSelected ? list.getSelectionForeground() : list.getForeground());
        return this;
    }
}
```

Note that here we don't write any paintComponent or getPreferredSize methods; the JLabel class already implements these methods to our satisfaction. All we do is configure the label appropriately by setting its text, font, and color.

This code is a convenient shortcut for those cases in which an existing component—in this case, JLabel—already provides all functionality needed to render a cell value.

 CAUTION: It is not a good idea to construct a new component in each call to getListCellRendererComponent. If the user scrolls through many list entries, a new component would be constructed every time. Reconfiguring an existing component is safe and much more efficient.

Example 6–3: ListRenderingTest.java

```
1. import java.util.*;
2. import java.awt.*;
3. import java.awt.event.*;
4. import javax.swing.*;
5. import javax.swing.event.*;
6.
7. /**
8.    This program demonstrates the use of cell renderers in
9.    a list box.
10. */
11. public class ListRenderingTest
12. {
13.    public static void main(String[] args)
14.    {
15.       JFrame frame = new ListRenderingFrame();
16.       frame.setDefaultCloseOperation(JFrame.EXIT_ON_CLOSE);
17.       frame.setVisible(true);
18.    }
19. }
```

```
20.
21.  /**
22.     This frame contains a list with a set of fonts and a text
23.     area that is set to the selected font.
24.  */
25.  class ListRenderingFrame extends JFrame
26.  {
27.     public ListRenderingFrame()
28.     {
29.        setTitle("ListRenderingTest");
30.        setSize(DEFAULT_WIDTH, DEFAULT_HEIGHT);
31.
32.        ArrayList<Font> fonts = new ArrayList<Font>();
33.        final int SIZE = 24;
34.        fonts.add(new Font("Serif", Font.PLAIN, SIZE));
35.        fonts.add(new Font("SansSerif", Font.PLAIN, SIZE));
36.        fonts.add(new Font("Monospaced", Font.PLAIN, SIZE));
37.        fonts.add(new Font("Dialog", Font.PLAIN, SIZE));
38.        fonts.add(new Font("DialogInput", Font.PLAIN, SIZE));
39.        fontList = new JList(fonts.toArray());
40.        fontList.setVisibleRowCount(4);
41.        fontList.setSelectionMode(ListSelectionModel.SINGLE_SELECTION);
42.        fontList.setCellRenderer(new FontCellRenderer());
43.        JScrollPane scrollPane = new JScrollPane(fontList);
44.
45.        JPanel p = new JPanel();
46.        p.add(scrollPane);
47.        fontList.addListSelectionListener(new
48.           ListSelectionListener()
49.           {
50.              public void valueChanged(ListSelectionEvent evt)
51.              {
52.                 Font font = (Font) fontList.getSelectedValue();
53.                 text.setFont(font);
54.              }
55.
56.           });
57.
58.        Container contentPane = getContentPane();
59.        contentPane.add(p, BorderLayout.SOUTH);
60.        text = new JTextArea("The quick brown fox jumps over the lazy dog");
61.        text.setFont((Font) fonts.get(0));
62.        text.setLineWrap(true);
63.        text.setWrapStyleWord(true);
64.        contentPane.add(text, BorderLayout.CENTER);
65.     }
66.
67.     private JTextArea text;
68.     private JList fontList;
69.     private static final int DEFAULT_WIDTH = 400;
70.     private static final int DEFAULT_HEIGHT = 300;
71.  }
72.
73.  /**
74.     A cell renderer for Font objects that renders the font name in its own font.
75.  */
```

```
76. class FontCellRenderer extends JPanel implements ListCellRenderer
77. {
78.    public Component getListCellRendererComponent(JList list, Object value, int index,
79.       boolean isSelected, boolean cellHasFocus)
80.    {
81.       font = (Font) value;
82.       background = isSelected ? list.getSelectionBackground() : list.getBackground();
83.       foreground = isSelected ? list.getSelectionForeground() : list.getForeground();
84.       return this;
85.    }
86.
87.    public void paintComponent(Graphics g)
88.    {
89.       String text = font.getFamily();
90.       FontMetrics fm = g.getFontMetrics(font);
91.       g.setColor(background);
92.       g.fillRect(0, 0, getWidth(), getHeight());
93.       g.setColor(foreground);
94.       g.setFont(font);
95.       g.drawString(text, 0, fm.getAscent());
96.    }
97.
98.    public Dimension getPreferredSize()
99.    {
100.      String text = font.getFamily();
101.      Graphics g = getGraphics();
102.      FontMetrics fm = g.getFontMetrics(font);
103.      return new Dimension(fm.stringWidth(text), fm.getHeight());
104.   }
105.
106.   private Font font;
107.   private Color background;
108.   private Color foreground;
109. }
```

 javax.swing.JList 1.2

- `Color getBackground()`
  returns the background color for unselected cells.

- `Color getSelectionBackground()`
  returns the background color for selected cells.

- `Color getForeground()`
  returns the foreground color for unselected cells.

- `Color getSelectionForeground()`
  returns the foreground color for selected cells.

- `void setCellRenderer(ListCellRenderer cellRenderer)`
  sets the renderer that paints the cells in the list.

javax.swing.ListCellRenderer 1.2

- `Component getListCellRendererComponent(JList list, Object item, int index, boolean isSelected, boolean hasFocus)`
  returns a component whose paint method draws the cell contents. If the list cells do not have fixed size, that component must also implement getPreferredSize.

Parameters:	list	The list whose cell is being drawn
	item	The item to be drawn
	index	The index where the item is stored in the model
	isSelected	true if the specified cell was selected
	hasFocus	true if the specified cell has the focus

Trees

Every computer user who uses a hierarchical file system has encountered *tree* displays such as the one in Figure 6–5. Of course, directories and files form only one of the many examples of treelike organizations. Programmers are familiar with inheritance trees for classes. Many tree structures arise in everyday life, such as the hierarchy of countries, states, and cities shown in Figure 6–6.

▾ 📁 /	20 files	Aug 14 17:35
▷ 📁 bin	92 files	Apr 10 04:52
▷ 📁 boot	16 files	Apr 10 04:33
▷ 📁 dev	7524 files	Aug 19 14:08
▷ 📁 etc	205 files	Aug 19 14:08
▷ 📁 home	7 files	May 28 17:54
▷ 📁 initrd	0 files	Jan 24 2003
▷ 📁 lib	94 files	Apr 10 04:58
▷ ⊘ lost+found		Apr 10 00:24
▷ 📁 misc	0 files	Jan 27 2003
▷ 📁 mnt	4 files	Aug 8 19:25
▷ 📁 opt	0 files	Jan 24 2003
▷ 📁 proc	246 files	Aug 14 10:34
▷ ⊘ root		Aug 16 07:38
▷ 📁 sbin	263 files	Apr 10 04:36
▷ 📁 tftpboot	1 file	Apr 10 04:58
▷ 📁 tmp	52 files	Aug 21 04:03
▾ 📁 usr	14 files	Apr 10 04:31
▷ 📁 X11R6	6 files	Apr 10 04:54
▷ 📁 bin	1688 files	Aug 10 16:58
▷ 📁 dict	0 files	Jan 24 2003
▷ 📁 etc	0 files	Jan 24 2003
▷ 📁 games	0 files	Jan 24 2003
▷ 📁 include	372 files	Apr 10 04:59
▷ 📁 kerberos	6 files	Apr 10 04:52
▷ 📁 lib	1263 files	Aug 10 16:58
▷ 📁 libexec	43 files	Apr 10 04:59
▾ 📁 local	18 files	Aug 10 16:56
▷ 📁 BerkeleyDB.4.2	4 files	Apr 20 09:36
▷ 📁 GNUstep	1 file	Apr 11 15:36
▷ 📁 bin	121 files	Aug 15 21:14
▷ 📁 etc	8 files	May 11 10:42
▷ 📁 games	0 files	Jan 24 2003

Figure 6–5: A directory tree

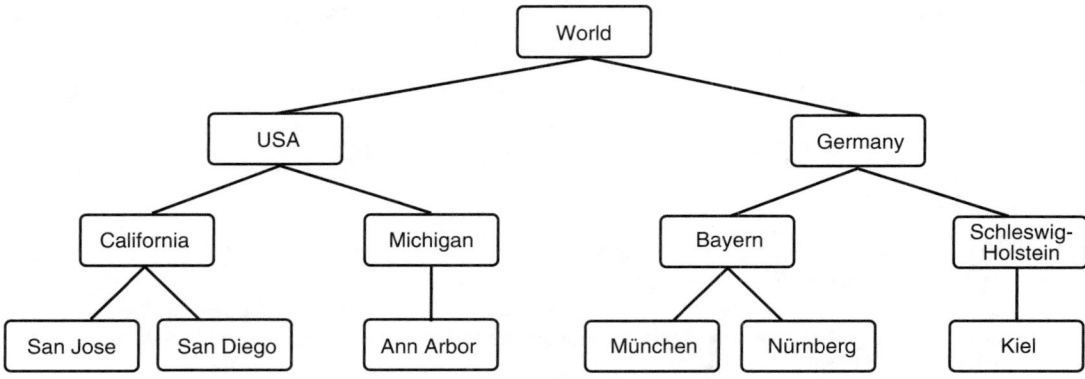

Figure 6–6: A hierarchy of countries, states, and cities

As programmers, we often have to display these tree structures. Fortunately, the Swing library has a JTree class for this purpose. The JTree class (together with its helper classes) takes care of laying out the tree and processing user requests for expanding and collapsing nodes. In this section, you will learn how to put the JTree class to use.

As with the other complex Swing components, we must focus on the common and useful cases and cannot cover every nuance. If you want to achieve an unusual effect, we recommend that you consult *Graphic Java 2* by David M. Geary [Prentice-Hall 1999], *Core Java Foundation Classes* by Kim Topley [Prentice-Hall 1998], or *Core Swing: Advanced Programming* by Kim Topley [Prentice-Hall 1999].

Before going any further, let's settle on some terminology (see Figure 6–7). A *tree* is composed of *nodes*. Every node is either a *leaf* or it has *child nodes*. Every node, with the exception of the root node, has exactly one *parent*. A tree has exactly one root node. Sometimes you have a collection of trees, each of which has its own root node. Such a collection is called a *forest*.

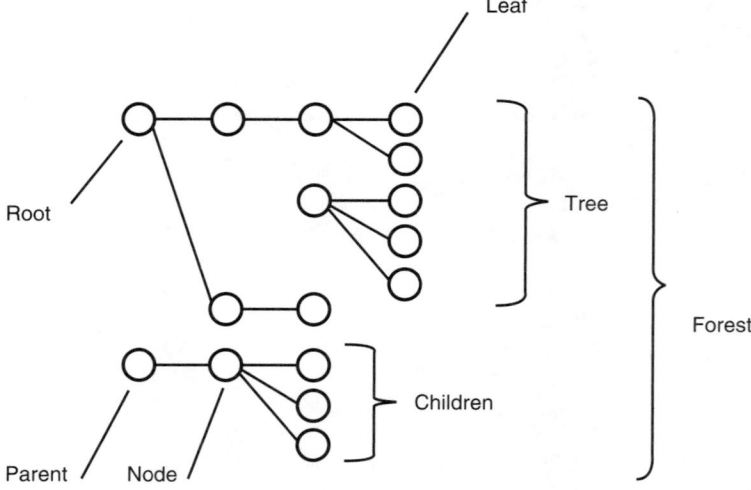

Figure 6–7: Tree terminology

Simple Trees

In our first example program, we simply display a tree with a few nodes (see Figure 6–9 on page 340). As with most other Swing components, the JTree component follows the model-view-controller pattern. You provide a model of the hierarchical data, and the component displays it for you. To construct a JTree, you supply the tree model in the constructor:

```
TreeModel model = . . .;
JTree tree = new JTree(model);
```

NOTE: There are also constructors that construct trees out of a collection of elements:

```
JTree(Object[] nodes)
JTree(Vector<?> nodes)
JTree(Hashtable<?, ?> nodes) // the values become the nodes
```

These constructors are not very useful. They merely build a forest of trees, each with a single node. The third constructor seems particularly useless since the nodes appear in the essentially random order given by the hash codes of the keys.

How do you obtain a tree model? You can construct your own model by creating a class that implements the TreeModel interface. You see later in this chapter how to do that. For now, we stick with the DefaultTreeModel that the Swing library supplies.

To construct a default tree model, you must supply a root node.

```
TreeNode root = . . .;
DefaultTreeModel model = new DefaultTreeModel(root);
```

TreeNode is another interface. You populate the default tree model with objects of any class that implements the interface. For now, we use the concrete node class that Swing supplies, namely, DefaultMutableTreeNode. This class implements the MutableTreeNode interface, a subinterface of TreeNode (see Figure 6–8).

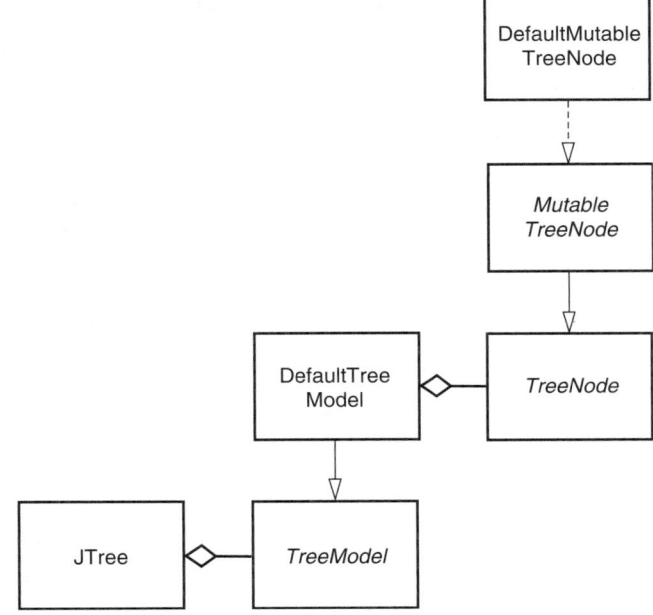

Figure 6–8: Tree classes

A default mutable tree node holds an object, the *user object*. The tree renders the user objects for all nodes. Unless you specify a renderer, the tree simply displays the string that is the result of the toString method.

In our first example, we use strings as user objects. In practice, you would usually populate a tree with more expressive user objects. For example, when displaying a directory tree, it makes sense to use File objects for the nodes.

You can specify the user object in the constructor, or you can set it later with the setUserObject method.

```
DefaultMutableTreeNode node = new DefaultMutableTreeNode("Texas");
node.setUserObject("California");
```

Next, you establish the parent/child relationships between the nodes. Start with the root node, and use the add method to add the children:

```
DefaultMutableTreeNode root = new DefaultMutableTreeNode("World");
DefaultMutableTreeNode country = new DefaultMutableTreeNode("USA");
root.add(country);
DefaultMutableTreeNode state = new DefaultMutableTreeNode("California");
country.add(state);
```

Figure 6–9 illustrates how the tree will look.

Link up all nodes in this fashion. Then, construct a DefaultTreeModel with the root node. Finally, construct a JTree with the tree model.

```
DefaultTreeModel treeModel = new DefaultTreeModel(root);
JTree tree = new JTree(treeModel);
```

Or, as a shortcut, you can simply pass the root node to the JTree constructor. Then the tree automatically constructs a default tree model:

```
JTree tree = new JTree(root);
```

Figure 6–9: A simple tree

Example 6–4 contains the complete code.

Example 6–4: SimpleTree.java

```
1. import java.awt.*;
2. import java.awt.event.*;
3. import javax.swing.*;
4. import javax.swing.tree.*;
5.
6. /**
7.    This program shows a simple tree.
8. */
9. public class SimpleTree
10. {
```

```
11.    public static void main(String[] args)
12.    {
13.       JFrame frame = new SimpleTreeFrame();
14.       frame.setDefaultCloseOperation(JFrame.EXIT_ON_CLOSE);
15.       frame.setVisible(true);
16.    }
17. }
18.
19. /**
20.    This frame contains a simple tree that displays a
21.    manually constructed tree model.
22. */
23. class SimpleTreeFrame extends JFrame
24. {
25.    public SimpleTreeFrame()
26.    {
27.       setTitle("SimpleTree");
28.       setSize(DEFAULT_WIDTH, DEFAULT_HEIGHT);
29.
30.       // set up tree model data
31.
32.       DefaultMutableTreeNode root
33.          = new DefaultMutableTreeNode("World");
34.       DefaultMutableTreeNode country
35.          = new DefaultMutableTreeNode("USA");
36.       root.add(country);
37.       DefaultMutableTreeNode state
38.          = new DefaultMutableTreeNode("California");
39.       country.add(state);
40.       DefaultMutableTreeNode city
41.          = new DefaultMutableTreeNode("San Jose");
42.       state.add(city);
43.       city = new DefaultMutableTreeNode("Cupertino");
44.       state.add(city);
45.       state = new DefaultMutableTreeNode("Michigan");
46.       country.add(state);
47.       city = new DefaultMutableTreeNode("Ann Arbor");
48.       state.add(city);
49.       country = new DefaultMutableTreeNode("Germany");
50.       root.add(country);
51.       state = new DefaultMutableTreeNode("Schleswig-Holstein");
52.       country.add(state);
53.       city = new DefaultMutableTreeNode("Kiel");
54.       state.add(city);
55.
56.       // construct tree and put it in a scroll pane
57.
58.       JTree tree = new JTree(root);
59.       Container contentPane = getContentPane();
60.       contentPane.add(new JScrollPane(tree));
61.    }
62.
63.    private static final int DEFAULT_WIDTH = 300;
64.    private static final int DEFAULT_HEIGHT = 200;
65. }
```

When you run the program, the tree first looks as in Figure 6–10. Only the root node and its children are visible. Click on the circle icons (the *handles*) to open up the subtrees. The line sticking out from the handle icon points to the right when the subtree is collapsed, and it points down when the subtree is expanded (see Figure 6–11). We don't know what the designers of the Metal look and feel had in mind, but we think of the icon as a door handle. You push down on the handle to open the subtree.

 NOTE: Of course, the display of the tree depends on the selected look and feel. We just described the Metal look and feel. In the Windows and Motif look and feel, the handles have the more familiar look—a "-" or "+" in a box (see Figure 6–12).

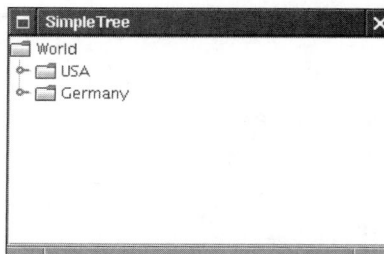

Figure 6–10: The initial tree display

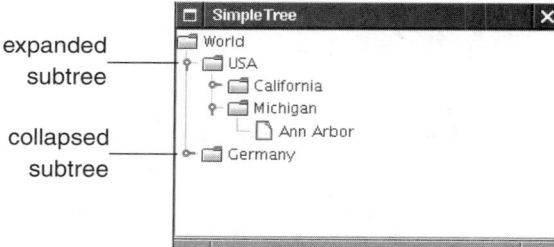

Figure 6–11: Collapsed and expanded subtrees

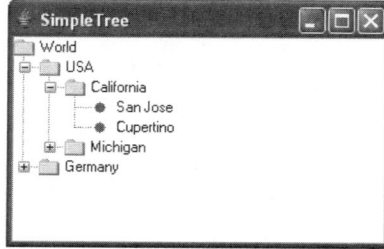

Figure 6–12: A tree with the Windows look and feel

Up to JDK 1.3, the Metal look and feel does not display the tree outline by default (see Figure 6–13). As of JDK 1.4, the default line style is "angled."

In JDK 1.4, use the following magic incantation to turn off the lines joining parents and children:

```
tree.putClientProperty("JTree.lineStyle", "None");
```

Conversely, to make sure that the lines are shown, use

```
tree.putClientProperty("JTree.lineStyle", "Angled");
```

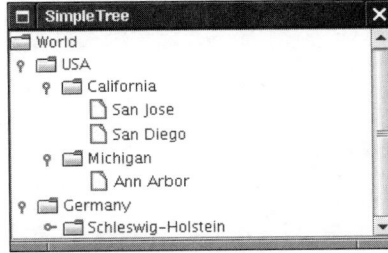

Figure 6–13: A tree with no connecting lines

Another line style, "Horizontal", is shown in Figure 6–14. The tree is displayed with horizontal lines separating only the children of the root. We aren't quite sure what it is good for.

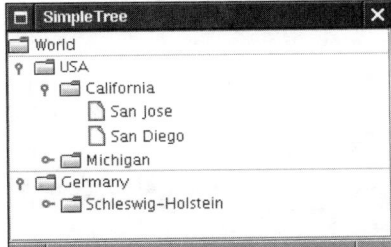

Figure 6–14: A tree with the horizontal line style

By default, there is no handle for collapsing the root of the tree. If you like, you can add one with the call

```
tree.setShowsRootHandles(true);
```

Figure 6–15 shows the result. Now you can collapse the entire tree into the root node.

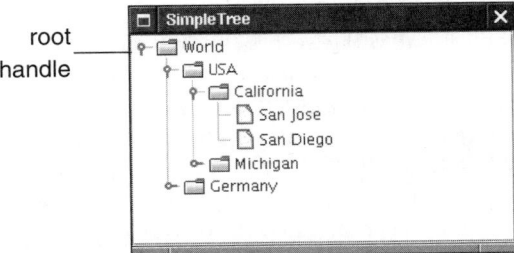

Figure 6–15: A tree with a root handle

Conversely, you can hide the root altogether. You do that to display a *forest*, a set of trees, each of which has its own root. You still must join all trees in the forest to a common root. Then, you hide the root with the instruction

```
tree.setRootVisible(false);
```

Look at Figure 6–16. There appear to be two roots, labeled "USA" and "Germany." The actual root that joins the two is made invisible.

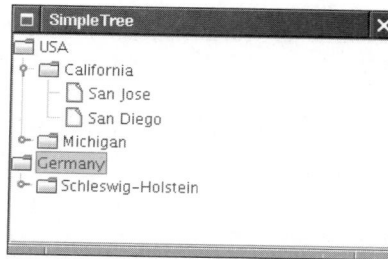

Figure 6–16: A forest

Let's turn from the root to the leaves of the tree. Note that the leaves have a different icon from the other nodes (see Figure 6–17).

When the tree is displayed, each node is drawn with an icon. There are actually three kinds of icons: a leaf icon, an opened non-leaf icon, and a closed non-leaf icon. For simplicity, we refer to the last two as folder icons.

The node renderer needs to know which icon to use for each node. By default, the decision process works like this: If the isLeaf method of a node returns true, then the leaf icon is used. Otherwise, a folder icon is used.

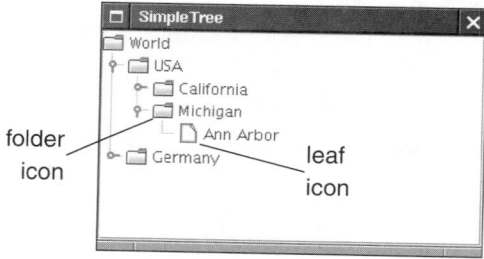

Figure 6–17: Leaf and folder icons

The isLeaf method of the DefaultMutableTreeNode class returns true if the node has no children. Thus, nodes with children get folder icons, and nodes without children get leaf icons.

Sometimes, that behavior is not appropriate. Suppose we added a node "Montana" to our sample tree, but we're at a loss as to what cities to add. We would not want the state node to get a leaf icon because conceptually only the cities are leaves.

The JTree class has no idea which nodes should be leaves. It asks the tree model. If a childless node isn't automatically a conceptual leaf, you can ask the tree model to use a different criterion for leafiness, namely, to query the "allows children" node property.

For those nodes that should not have children, call

```
node.setAllowsChildren(false);
```

Then, tell the tree model to ask the value of the "allows children" property to determine whether a node should be displayed with a leaf icon. You use the setAsksAllowsChildren method of the DefaultTreeModel class to set this behavior:

```
model.setAsksAllowsChildren(true);
```

With this decision criterion, nodes that allow children get folder icons, and nodes that don't allow children get leaf icons.

Alternatively, if you construct the tree by supplying the root node, supply the setting for the "asks allows children" property in the constructor.

```
JTree tree = new JTree(root, true); // nodes that don't allow children get leaf icons
```

javax.swing.JTree 1.2

- JTree(TreeModel model)
  constructs a tree from a tree model.

- JTree(TreeNode root)
- JTree(TreeNode root, boolean asksAllowChildren)
  construct a tree with a default tree model that displays the root and its children.

Parameters:	root	The root node
	asksAllowsChildren	true to use the "allows children" node property for determining whether a node is a leaf

- void setShowsRootHandles(boolean b)
  If b is true, then the root node has a handle for collapsing or expanding its children.

- void setRootVisible(boolean b)
  If b is true, then the root node is displayed. Otherwise, it is hidden.

javax.swing.tree.TreeNode 1.2

- boolean isLeaf()
  returns true if this node is conceptually a leaf.

- boolean getAllowsChildren()
  returns true if this node can have child nodes.

javax.swing.tree.MutableTreeNode 1.2

- void setUserObject(Object userObject)
  sets the "user object" that the tree node uses for rendering.

javax.swing.tree.TreeModel 1.2

- boolean isLeaf(Object node)
  returns true if node should be displayed as a leaf node.

javax.swing.tree.DefaultTreeModel 1.2

- void setAsksAllowsChildren(boolean b)
  If b is true, then nodes are displayed as leaves when their getAllowsChildren method returns false. Otherwise, they are displayed as leaves when their isLeaf method returns true.

javax.swing.tree.DefaultMutableTreeNode 1.2

- DefaultMutableTreeNode(Object userObject)
  constructs a mutable tree node with the given user object.

- void add(MutableTreeNode child)
  adds a node as the last child of this node.

- void setAllowsChildren(boolean b)
  If b is true, then children can be added to this node.

 javax.swing.JComponent 1.2

- void putClientProperty(Object key, Object value)
  adds a key/value pair to a small table that each component manages. This is an "escape hatch" mechanism that some Swing components use for storing look-and-feel–specific properties.

Editing Trees and Tree Paths

In the next example program, you see how to edit a tree. Figure 6–18 shows the user interface. If you click the Add Sibling or Add Child button, the program adds a new node (with title New) to the tree. If you click the Delete button, the program deletes the currently selected node.

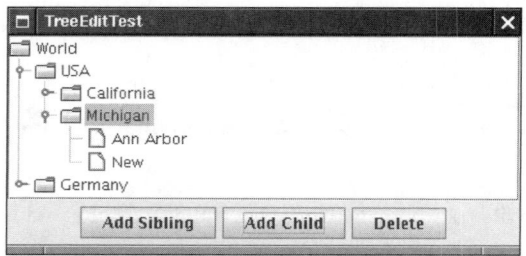

Figure 6–18: Editing a tree

To implement this behavior, you need to find out which tree node is currently selected. The JTree class has a surprising way of identifying nodes in a tree. It does not deal with tree nodes, but with *paths of objects*, called *tree paths*. A tree path starts at the root and consists of a sequence of child nodes—see Figure 6–19.

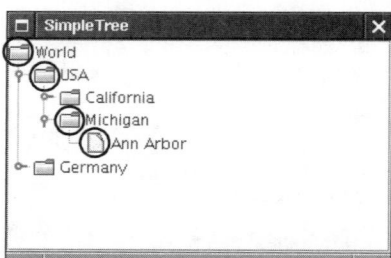

Figure 6–19: A tree path

You may wonder why the JTree class needs the whole path. Couldn't it just get a TreeNode and keep calling the getParent method? In fact, the JTree class knows nothing about the Tree-Node interface. That interface is never used by the TreeModel interface; it is only used by the DefaultTreeModel implementation. You can have other tree models in which the nodes do not implement the TreeNode interface at all. If you use a tree model that manages other types of objects, then those objects may not have getParent and getChild methods. They would of course need to have some other connection to each other. It is the job of the tree model to link nodes together. The JTree class itself has no clue about the nature of their linkage. For that reason, the JTree class always needs to work with complete paths.

The `TreePath` class manages a sequence of `Object` (not `TreeNode`!) references. A number of `JTree` methods return `TreePath` objects. When you have a tree path, you usually just need to know the terminal node, which you get with the `getLastPathComponent` method. For example, to find out the currently selected node in a tree, you use the `getSelectionPath` method of the `JTree` class. You get a `TreePath` object back, from which you can retrieve the actual node.

```
TreePath selectionPath = tree.getSelectionPath();
DefaultMutableTreeNode selectedNode
    = (DefaultMutableTreeNode) selectionPath.getLastPathComponent();
```

Actually, because this particular query is so common, there is a convenience method that gives the selected node immediately.

```
DefaultMutableTreeNode selectedNode
    = (DefaultMutableTreeNode) tree.getLastSelectedPathComponent();
```

This method is not called `getSelectedNode` because the tree does not know that it contains nodes—its tree model deals only with paths of objects.

 NOTE: Tree paths are one of two ways in which the `JTree` class describes nodes. Quite a few `JTree` methods take or return an integer index, the *row position*. A row position is simply the row number (starting with 0) of the node in the tree display. Only visible nodes have row numbers, and the row number of a node changes if other nodes before it are expanded, collapsed, or modified. For that reason, you should avoid row positions. All `JTree` methods that use rows have equivalents that use tree paths instead.

Once you have the selected node, you can edit it. However, do not simply add children to a tree node:

```
selectedNode.add(newNode); // NO!
```

If you change the structure of the nodes, you change the model but the associated view is not notified. You could send out a notification yourself, but if you use the `insertNodeInto` method of the `DefaultTreeModel` class, the model class takes care of that. For example, the following call appends a new node as the last child of the selected node and notifies the tree view.

```
model.insertNodeInto(newNode, selectedNode, selectedNode.getChildCount());
```

The analogous call `removeNodeFromParent` removes a node and notifies the view:

```
model.removeNodeFromParent(selectedNode);
```

If you keep the node structure in place but you changed the user object, you should call the following method:

```
model.nodeChanged(changedNode);
```

The automatic notification is a major advantage of using the `DefaultTreeModel`. If you supply your own tree model, you have to implement automatic notification by hand. (See *Core Java Foundation Classes* by Kim Topley for details.)

 CAUTION: The `DefaultTreeModel` class has a `reload` method that reloads the entire model. However, don't call `reload` simply to update the tree after making a few changes. When the tree is regenerated, all nodes beyond the root's children are collapsed again. It is quite disconcerting to your users if they have to keep expanding the tree after every change.

When the view is notified of a change in the node structure, it updates the display but it does not automatically expand a node to show newly added children. In particular, if a user in our sample program adds a new child node to a node whose children are currently

collapsed, then the new node is silently added to the collapsed subtree. This gives the user no feedback that the command was actually carried out. In such a case, you should make a special effort to expand all parent nodes so that the newly added node becomes visible. You use the `makeVisible` method of the `JTree` class for this purpose. The `makeVisible` method expects a tree path leading to the node that should become visible.

Thus, you need to construct a tree path from the root to the newly inserted node. To get a tree path, you first call the `getPathToRoot` method of the `DefaultTreeModel` class. It returns a `TreeNode[]` array of all nodes from a node to the root node. You pass that array to a `TreePath` constructor.

For example, here is how you make the new node visible:

```
TreeNode[] nodes = model.getPathToRoot(newNode);
TreePath path = new TreePath(nodes);
tree.makeVisible(path);
```

 NOTE: It is curious that the `DefaultTreeModel` class feigns almost complete ignorance about the `TreePath` class, even though its job is to communicate with a `JTree`. The `JTree` class uses tree paths a lot, and it never uses arrays of node objects.

But now suppose your tree is contained inside a scroll pane. After the tree node expansion, the new node may still not be visible because it falls outside the viewport. To overcome that problem, call

```
tree.scrollPathToVisible(path);
```

instead of calling `makeVisible`. This call expands all nodes along the path, and it tells the ambient scroll pane to scroll the node at the end of the path into view (see Figure 6–20).

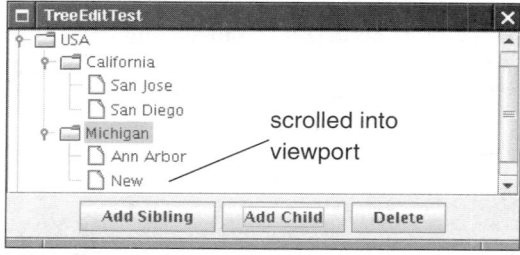

Figure 6–20: The scroll pane scrolls to display a new node

By default, tree nodes cannot be edited. However, if you call

```
tree.setEditable(true);
```

then the user can edit a node simply by double-clicking, editing the string, and pressing the ENTER key. Double-clicking invokes the *default cell editor*, which is implemented by the `DefaultCellEditor` class (see Figure 6–21). It is possible to install other cell editors, but we defer our discussion of cell editors until the section on tables, where cell editors are more commonly used.

Example 6–5 shows the complete source code of the tree editing program. Run the program, add a few nodes, and edit them by double-clicking them. Observe how collapsed nodes expand to show added children and how the scroll pane keeps added nodes in the viewport.

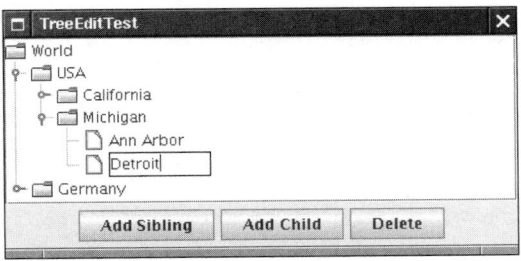

Figure 6–21: The default cell editor

Example 6–5: TreeEditTest.java

```
1. import java.awt.*;
2. import java.awt.event.*;
3. import javax.swing.*;
4. import javax.swing.tree.*;
5.
6. /**
7.    This program demonstrates tree editing.
8. */
9. public class TreeEditTest
10. {
11.    public static void main(String[] args)
12.    {
13.       JFrame frame = new TreeEditFrame();
14.       frame.setDefaultCloseOperation(JFrame.EXIT_ON_CLOSE);
15.       frame.setVisible(true);
16.    }
17. }
18.
19. /**
20.    A frame with a tree and buttons to edit the tree.
21. */
22. class TreeEditFrame extends JFrame
23. {
24.    public TreeEditFrame()
25.    {
26.       setTitle("TreeEditTest");
27.       setSize(DEFAULT_WIDTH, DEFAULT_HEIGHT);
28.
29.       // construct tree
30.
31.       TreeNode root = makeSampleTree();
32.       model = new DefaultTreeModel(root);
33.       tree = new JTree(model);
34.       tree.setEditable(true);
35.
36.       // add scroll pane with tree
37.
38.       JScrollPane scrollPane = new JScrollPane(tree);
39.       add(scrollPane, BorderLayout.CENTER);
40.
41.       makeButtons();
42.    }
```

```
43.
44.    public TreeNode makeSampleTree()
45.    {
46.        DefaultMutableTreeNode root = new DefaultMutableTreeNode("World");
47.        DefaultMutableTreeNode country = new DefaultMutableTreeNode("USA");
48.        root.add(country);
49.        DefaultMutableTreeNode state = new DefaultMutableTreeNode("California");
50.        country.add(state);
51.        DefaultMutableTreeNode city = new DefaultMutableTreeNode("San Jose");
52.        state.add(city);
53.        city = new DefaultMutableTreeNode("San Diego");
54.        state.add(city);
55.        state = new DefaultMutableTreeNode("Michigan");
56.        country.add(state);
57.        city = new DefaultMutableTreeNode("Ann Arbor");
58.        state.add(city);
59.        country = new DefaultMutableTreeNode("Germany");
60.        root.add(country);
61.        state = new DefaultMutableTreeNode("Schleswig-Holstein");
62.        country.add(state);
63.        city = new DefaultMutableTreeNode("Kiel");
64.        state.add(city);
65.        return root;
66.    }
67.
68.    /**
69.        Makes the buttons to add a sibling, add a child, and
70.        delete a node.
71.    */
72.    public void makeButtons()
73.    {
74.        JPanel panel = new JPanel();
75.        JButton addSiblingButton = new JButton("Add Sibling");
76.        addSiblingButton.addActionListener(new
77.            ActionListener()
78.            {
79.                public void actionPerformed(ActionEvent event)
80.                {
81.                    DefaultMutableTreeNode selectedNode
82.                        = (DefaultMutableTreeNode) tree.getLastSelectedPathComponent();
83.
84.                    if (selectedNode == null) return;
85.
86.                    DefaultMutableTreeNode parent
87.                        = (DefaultMutableTreeNode) selectedNode.getParent();
88.
89.                    if (parent == null) return;
90.
91.                    DefaultMutableTreeNode newNode = new DefaultMutableTreeNode("New");
92.
93.                    int selectedIndex = parent.getIndex(selectedNode);
94.                    model.insertNodeInto(newNode, parent, selectedIndex + 1);
95.
96.                    // now display new node
97.
98.                    TreeNode[] nodes = model.getPathToRoot(newNode);
```

```
99.          TreePath path = new TreePath(nodes);
100.         tree.scrollPathToVisible(path);
101.       }
102.    });
103.    panel.add(addSiblingButton);
104.
105.    JButton addChildButton = new JButton("Add Child");
106.    addChildButton.addActionListener(new
107.       ActionListener()
108.       {
109.          public void actionPerformed(ActionEvent event)
110.          {
111.             DefaultMutableTreeNode selectedNode = (DefaultMutableTreeNode)
112.                tree.getLastSelectedPathComponent();
113.
114.             if (selectedNode == null) return;
115.
116.             DefaultMutableTreeNode newNode = new DefaultMutableTreeNode("New");
117.             model.insertNodeInto(newNode, selectedNode, selectedNode.getChildCount());
118.
119.             // now display new node
120.
121.             TreeNode[] nodes = model.getPathToRoot(newNode);
122.             TreePath path = new TreePath(nodes);
123.             tree.scrollPathToVisible(path);
124.          }
125.       });
126.    panel.add(addChildButton);
127.
128.    JButton deleteButton = new JButton("Delete");
129.    deleteButton.addActionListener(new
130.       ActionListener()
131.       {
132.          public void actionPerformed(ActionEvent event)
133.          {
134.             DefaultMutableTreeNode selectedNode
135.                = (DefaultMutableTreeNode) tree.getLastSelectedPathComponent();
136.
137.             if (selectedNode != null && selectedNode.getParent() != null)
138.                model.removeNodeFromParent(selectedNode);
139.          }
140.       });
141.    panel.add(deleteButton);
142.    add(panel, BorderLayout.SOUTH);
143. }
144.
145. private DefaultTreeModel model;
146. private JTree tree;
147. private static final int DEFAULT_WIDTH = 400;
148. private static final int DEFAULT_HEIGHT = 200;
149. }
```

`javax.swing.JTree` `1.2`

- TreePath getSelectionPath()

  gets the path to the currently selected node, or the path to the first selected node if multiple nodes are selected. Returns `null` if no node is selected.

- Object getLastSelectedPathComponent()
  gets the node object that represents the currently selected node, or the first node if multiple nodes are selected. Returns null if no node is selected.
- void makeVisible(TreePath path)
  expands all nodes along the path.
- void scrollPathToVisible(TreePath path)
  expands all nodes along the path and, if the tree is contained in a scroll pane, scrolls to ensure that the last node on the path is visible.

 javax.swing.tree.TreePath 1.2

- Object getLastPathComponent()
  gets the last object on this path, that is, the node object that the path represents.

 javax.swing.tree.TreeNode 1.2

- TreeNode getParent()
  returns the parent node of this node.
- TreeNode getChildAt(int index)
  looks up the child node at the given index. The index must be between 0 and getChildCount() − 1.
- int getChildCount()
  returns the number of children of this node.
- Enumeration children()
  returns an enumeration object that iterates through all children of this node.

 javax.swing.tree.DefaultTreeModel 1.2

- void insertNodeInto(MutableTreeNode newChild, MutableTreeNode parent, int index)
  inserts newChild as a new child node of parent at the given index and notifies the tree model listeners.
- void removeNodeFromParent(MutableTreeNode node)
  removes node from this model and notifies the tree model listeners.
- void nodeChanged(TreeNode node)
  notifies the tree model listeners that node has changed.
- void nodesChanged(TreeNode parent, int[] changedChildIndexes)
  notifies the tree model listeners that all child nodes of parent with the given indexes have changed.
- void reload()
  reloads all nodes into the model. This is a drastic operation that you should use only if the nodes have changed completely because of some outside influence.

Node Enumeration

Sometimes you need to find a node in a tree by starting at the root and visiting all children until you have found a match. The DefaultMutableTreeNode class has several convenience methods for iterating through nodes.

The breadthFirstEnumeration and depthFirstEnumeration methods return enumeration objects whose nextElement method visits all children of the current node, using either a breadth-first or depth-first traversal. Figure 6–22 shows the traversals for a sample tree—the node labels indicate the order in which the nodes are traversed.

Breadth-first enumeration is the easiest to visualize. The tree is traversed in layers. The root is visited first, followed by all of its children, then followed by the grandchildren, and so on.

To visualize depth-first enumeration, imagine a rat trapped in a tree-shaped maze. It rushes along the first path until it comes to a leaf. Then, it backtracks and turns around to the next path, and so on.

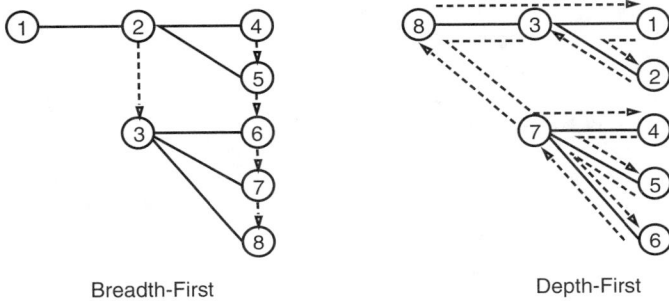

Breadth-First   Depth-First

Figure 6–22: Tree traversal orders

Computer scientists also call this *postorder traversal* because the search process visits the children before visiting the parents. The postOrderTraversal method is a synonym for depthFirstTraversal. For completeness, there is also a preOrderTraversal, a depth-first search that enumerates parents before the children.

Here is the typical usage pattern:

```
Enumeration breadthFirst = node.breadthFirstEnumeration();
while (breadthFirst.hasMoreElements())
    do something with breadthFirst.nextElement();
```

Finally, a related method, pathFromAncestorEnumeration, finds a path from an ancestor to a given node and then enumerates the nodes along that path. That's no big deal—it just keeps calling getParent until the ancestor is found and then presents the path in reverse order.

In our next example program, we put node enumeration to work. The program displays inheritance trees of classes. Type the name of a class into the text field on the bottom of the frame. The class and all of its superclasses are added to the tree (see Figure 6–23).

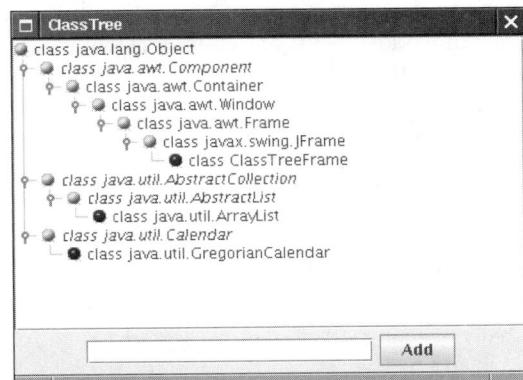

Figure 6–23: An inheritance tree

In this example, we take advantage of the fact that the user objects of the tree nodes can be objects of any type. Because our nodes describe classes, we store Class objects in the nodes.

Of course, we don't want to add the same class object twice, so we need to check whether a class already exists in the tree. The following method finds the node with a given user object if it exists in the tree.

```java
public DefaultMutableTreeNode findUserObject(Object obj)
{
   Enumeration e = root.breadthFirstEnumeration();
   while (e.hasMoreElements())
   {
      DefaultMutableTreeNode node = (DefaultMutableTreeNode) e.nextElement();
      if (node.getUserObject().equals(obj))
         return node;
   }
   return null;
}
```

Rendering Nodes

In your applications, you will often need to change the way in which a tree component draws the nodes. The most common change is, of course, to choose different icons for nodes and leaves. Other changes might involve changing the font of the node labels or drawing images at the nodes. All these changes are made possible by installing a new *tree cell renderer* into the tree. By default, the JTree class uses DefaultTreeCellRenderer objects to draw each node. The DefaultTreeCellRenderer class extends the JLabel class. The label contains the node icon and the node label.

 NOTE: The cell renderer does not draw the "handles" for expanding and collapsing subtrees. The handles are part of the look and feel, and it is recommended that you not change them.

You can customize the display in three ways.

1. You can change the icons, font, and background color used by a DefaultTreeCellRenderer. These settings are used for all nodes in the tree.
2. You can install a renderer that extends the DefaultTreeCellRenderer class and vary the icons, fonts, and background color for each node.
3. You can install a renderer that implements the TreeCellRenderer interface, to draw a custom image for each node.

Let us look at these possibilities one by one. The easiest customization is to construct a DefaultTreeCellRenderer object, change the icons, and install it into the tree:

```java
DefaultTreeCellRenderer renderer = new DefaultTreeCellRenderer();
renderer.setLeafIcon(new ImageIcon("blue-ball.gif")); // used for leaf nodes
renderer.setClosedIcon(new ImageIcon("red-ball.gif")); // used for collapsed nodes
renderer.setOpenIcon(new ImageIcon("yellow-ball.gif")); // used for expanded nodes
tree.setCellRenderer(renderer);
```

You can see the effect in Figure 6–23. We just use the "ball" icons as placeholders—presumably your user interface designer would supply you with appropriate icons to use for your applications.

We don't recommend that you change the font or background color for an entire tree—that is really the job of the look and feel.

However, it can be useful to change the font for individual nodes in a tree to highlight some of them. If you look carefully at Figure 6–23, you will notice that the *abstract* classes are set in italics.

To change the appearance of individual nodes, you install a tree cell renderer. Tree cell renderers are very similar to the list cell renderers we discussed earlier in this chapter. The TreeCellRenderer interface has a single method

```
Component getTreeCellRendererComponent(JTree tree, Object value, boolean selected,
    boolean expanded, boolean leaf, int row, boolean hasFocus)
```

The getTreeCellRendererComponent method of the DefaultTreeCellRenderer class returns this—in other words, a label. (The DefaultTreeCellRenderer class extends the JLabel class.) To customize the component, extend the DefaultTreeCellRenderer class. Override the getTreeCellRendererComponent method as follows: Call the superclass method, so that it can prepare the label data. Customize the label properties, and finally return this.

```
class MyTreeCellRenderer extends DefaultTreeCellRenderer
{
    public Component getTreeCellRendererComponent(JTree tree, Object value, boolean selected,
        boolean expanded, boolean leaf, int row, boolean hasFocus)
    {
        super.getTreeCellRendererComponent(tree, value, selected, expanded, leaf, row, hasFocus);
        DefaultMutableTreeNode node = (DefaultMutableTreeNode) value;
        look at node.getUserObject();
        Font font = appropriate font;
        setFont(font);
        return this;
    }
};
```

CAUTION: The value parameter of the getTreeCellRendererComponent method is the *node* object, *not* the user object! Recall that the user object is a feature of the DefaultMutableTreeNode, and that a JTree can contain nodes of an arbitrary type. If your tree uses DefaultMutableTreeNode nodes, then you must retrieve the user object in a second step, as we did in the preceding code sample.

CAUTION: The DefaultTreeCellRenderer uses the *same* label object for all nodes, only changing the label text for each node. If you change the font for a particular node, you must set it back to its default value when the method is called again. Otherwise, all subsequent nodes will be drawn in the changed font! Look at the code in Example 6–6 to see how to restore the font to the default.

We do not show an example for a tree cell renderer that draws arbitrary graphics. If you need this capability, you can adapt the list cell renderer in Example 6–3; the technique is entirely analogous.

Let's put tree cell renderers to work. Example 6–6 shows the complete source code for the class tree program. The program displays inheritance hierarchies, and it customizes the display to show abstract classes in italics. You can type the name of any class into the text field at the bottom of the frame. Press the ENTER key or click the Add button to add the class and its superclasses to the tree. You must enter the full package name, such as java.util.ArrayList.

This program is a bit tricky because it uses reflection to construct the class tree. This work is contained inside the addClass method. (The details are not that important. We use the class tree in this example because inheritance trees yield a nice supply of trees without laborious coding. If you display trees in your own applications, you will have your own source of hierarchical data.) The method uses the breadth-first search algorithm to find whether the current class is already in the tree by calling the findUserObject method that we implemented in the preceding section. If the class is not already in the tree, we add the superclasses to the tree, then make the new class node a child and make that node visible.

The ClassNameTreeCellRenderer sets the class name in either the normal or italic font, depending on the ABSTRACT modifier of the Class object. We don't want to set a particular font because we don't want to change whatever font the look and feel normally uses for labels. For that reason, we use the font from the label and *derive* an italic font from it. Recall that only a single shared JLabel object is returned by all calls. We need to hang on to the original font and restore it in the next call to the getTreeCellRendererComponent method.

Finally, note how we change the node icons in the ClassTreeFrame constructor.

Example 6–6: ClassTree.java

```
1. import java.awt.*;
2. import java.awt.event.*;
3. import java.lang.reflect.*;
4. import java.util.*;
5. import javax.swing.*;
6. import javax.swing.event.*;
7. import javax.swing.tree.*;
8.
9. /**
10.    This program demonstrates cell rendering by showing
11.    a tree of classes and their superclasses.
12. */
13. public class ClassTree
14. {
15.    public static void main(String[] args)
16.    {
17.       JFrame frame = new ClassTreeFrame();
18.       frame.setDefaultCloseOperation(JFrame.EXIT_ON_CLOSE);
19.       frame.setVisible(true);
20.    }
21. }
22.
23. /**
24.    This frame displays the class tree, a text field and
25.    add button to add more classes into the tree.
26. */
27. class ClassTreeFrame extends JFrame
28. {
29.    public ClassTreeFrame()
30.    {
31.       setTitle("ClassTree");
32.       setSize(DEFAULT_WIDTH, DEFAULT_HEIGHT);
33.
34.       // the root of the class tree is Object
35.       root = new DefaultMutableTreeNode(java.lang.Object.class);
36.       model = new DefaultTreeModel(root);
37.       tree = new JTree(model);
```

```
38.
39.       // add this class to populate the tree with some data
40.       addClass(getClass());
41.
42.       // set up node icons
43.       ClassNameTreeCellRenderer renderer = new ClassNameTreeCellRenderer();
44.       renderer.setClosedIcon(new ImageIcon("red-ball.gif"));
45.       renderer.setOpenIcon(new ImageIcon("yellow-ball.gif"));
46.       renderer.setLeafIcon(new ImageIcon("blue-ball.gif"));
47.       tree.setCellRenderer(renderer);
48.
49.       add(new JScrollPane(tree), BorderLayout.CENTER);
50.
51.       addTextField();
52.    }
53.
54.    /**
55.       Add the text field and "Add" button to add a new class.
56.    */
57.    public void addTextField()
58.    {
59.       JPanel panel = new JPanel();
60.
61.       ActionListener addListener = new
62.          ActionListener()
63.          {
64.             public void actionPerformed(ActionEvent event)
65.             {
66.                // add the class whose name is in the text field
67.                try
68.                {
69.                   String text = textField.getText();
70.                   addClass(Class.forName(text)); // clear text field to indicate success
71.                   textField.setText("");
72.                }
73.                catch (ClassNotFoundException e)
74.                {
75.                   JOptionPane.showMessageDialog(null, "Class not found");
76.                }
77.             }
78.          };
79.
80.       // new class names are typed into this text field
81.       textField = new JTextField(20);
82.       textField.addActionListener(addListener);
83.       panel.add(textField);
84.
85.       JButton addButton = new JButton("Add");
86.       addButton.addActionListener(addListener);
87.       panel.add(addButton);
88.
89.       add(panel, BorderLayout.SOUTH);
90.    }
91.
92.    /**
93.       Finds an object in the tree.
```

```
94.        @param obj the object to find
95.        @return the node containing the object or null
96.        if the object is not present in the tree
97.     */
98.     public DefaultMutableTreeNode findUserObject(Object obj)
99.     {
100.       // find the node containing a user object
101.       Enumeration e = root.breadthFirstEnumeration();
102.       while (e.hasMoreElements())
103.       {
104.          DefaultMutableTreeNode node = (DefaultMutableTreeNode) e.nextElement();
105.          if (node.getUserObject().equals(obj))
106.             return node;
107.       }
108.       return null;
109.     }
110.
111.     /**
112.        Adds a new class and any parent classes that aren't
113.        yet part of the tree
114.        @param c the class to add
115.        @return the newly added node.
116.     */
117.     public DefaultMutableTreeNode addClass(Class c)
118.     {
119.       // add a new class to the tree
120.
121.       // skip non-class types
122.       if (c.isInterface() || c.isPrimitive()) return null;
123.
124.       // if the class is already in the tree, return its node
125.       DefaultMutableTreeNode node = findUserObject(c);
126.       if (node != null) return node;
127.
128.       // class isn't present--first add class parent recursively
129.
130.       Class s = c.getSuperclass();
131.
132.       DefaultMutableTreeNode parent;
133.       if (s == null)
134.          parent = root;
135.       else
136.          parent = addClass(s);
137.
138.       // add the class as a child to the parent
139.       DefaultMutableTreeNode newNode = new DefaultMutableTreeNode(c);
140.       model.insertNodeInto(newNode, parent, parent.getChildCount());
141.
142.       // make node visible
143.       TreePath path = new TreePath(model.getPathToRoot(newNode));
144.       tree.makeVisible(path);
145.
146.       return newNode;
147.     }
148.
149.     private DefaultMutableTreeNode root;
```

```
150.    private DefaultTreeModel model;
151.    private JTree tree;
152.    private JTextField textField;
153.    private static final int DEFAULT_WIDTH = 400;
154.    private static final int DEFAULT_HEIGHT = 300;
155. }
156.
157. /**
158.    This class renders a class name either in plain or italic.
159.    Abstract classes are italic.
160. */
161. class ClassNameTreeCellRenderer extends DefaultTreeCellRenderer
162. {
163.    public Component getTreeCellRendererComponent(JTree tree, Object value, boolean selected,
164.       boolean expanded, boolean leaf, int row, boolean hasFocus)
165.    {
166.       super.getTreeCellRendererComponent(tree, value, selected, expanded, leaf, row, hasFocus);
167.       // get the user object
168.       DefaultMutableTreeNode node = (DefaultMutableTreeNode) value;
169.       Class c = (Class) node.getUserObject();
170.
171.       // the first time, derive italic font from plain font
172.       if (plainFont == null)
173.       {
174.          plainFont = getFont();
175.          // the tree cell renderer is sometimes called with a label that has a null font
176.          if (plainFont != null) italicFont = plainFont.deriveFont(Font.ITALIC);
177.       }
178.
179.       // set font to italic if the class is abstract, plain otherwise
180.       if ((c.getModifiers() & Modifier.ABSTRACT) == 0)
181.          setFont(plainFont);
182.       else
183.          setFont(italicFont);
184.       return this;
185.    }
186.
187.    private Font plainFont = null;
188.    private Font italicFont = null;
189. }
```

API   **javax.swing.tree.DefaultMutableTreeNode 1.2**

- Enumeration breadthFirstEnumeration()
- Enumeration depthFirstEnumeration()
- Enumeration preOrderEnumeration()
- Enumeration postOrderEnumeration()

return enumeration objects for visiting all nodes of the tree model in a particular order. In breadth-first traversal, children that are closer to the root are visited before those that are farther away. In depth-first traversal, all children of a node are completely enumerated before its siblings are visited. The postOrderEnumeration method is a synonym for depthFirstEnumeration. The preorder traversal is identical to the postorder traversal except that parents are enumerated before their children.

 javax.swing.tree.TreeCellRenderer 1.2

- Component getTreeCellRendererComponent(JTree tree, Object value, boolean selected, boolean expanded, boolean leaf, int row, boolean hasFocus)
  returns a component whose paint method is invoked to render a tree cell.

Parameters:	tree	The tree containing the node to be rendered
	value	The node to be rendered
	selected	true if the node is currently selected
	expanded	true if the children of the node are visible
	leaf	true if the node needs to be displayed as a leaf
	row	The display row containing the node
	hasFocus	true if the node currently has input focus

 javax.swing.tree.DefaultTreeCellRenderer 1.2

- void setLeafIcon(Icon icon)
- void setOpenIcon(Icon icon)
- void setClosedIcon(Icon icon)
  set the icon to show for a leaf node, an expanded node, and a collapsed node.

Listening to Tree Events

Most commonly, a tree component is paired with some other component. When the user selects tree nodes, some information shows up in another window. See Figure 6–24 for an example. When the user selects a class, the instance and static variables of that class are displayed in the text area to the right.

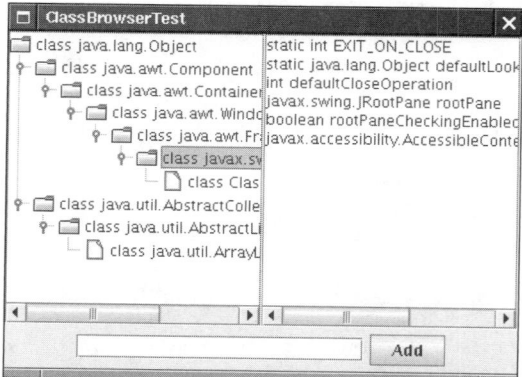

Figure 6–24: A class browser

To obtain this behavior, you install a *tree selection listener*. The listener must implement the TreeSelectionListener interface, an interface with a single method

```
void valueChanged(TreeSelectionEvent event)
```

That method is called whenever the user selects or deselects tree nodes.

You add the listener to the tree in the normal way:

```
tree.addTreeSelectionListener(listener);
```

You can specify whether the user is allowed to select a single node, a contiguous range of nodes, or an arbitrary, potentially discontiguous, set of nodes. The JTree class uses a Tree-SelectionModel to manage node selection. You need to retrieve the model to set the selection state to one of SINGLE_TREE_SELECTION, CONTIGUOUS_TREE_SELECTION, or DISCONTIGUOUS_TREE_SELECTION. (Discontiguous selection mode is the default.) For example, in our class browser, we want to allow selection of only a single class:

```
int mode = TreeSelectionModel.SINGLE_TREE_SELECTION;
tree.getSelectionModel().setSelectionMode(mode);
```

Apart from setting the selection mode, you need not worry about the tree selection model.

 NOTE: How the user selects multiple items depends on the look and feel. In the Metal look and feel, hold down the CTRL key while clicking on an item to add the item to the selection, or to remove it if it was currently selected. Hold down the SHIFT key while clicking on an item to select a *range* of items, extending from the previously selected item to the new item.

To find out the current selection, you query the tree with the getSelectionPaths method:

```
TreePath[] selectedPaths = tree.getSelectionPaths();
```

If you restricted the user to a single selection, you can use the convenience method getSelectionPath, which returns the first selected path, or null if no path was selected.

 CAUTION: The TreeSelectionEvent class has a getPaths method that returns an array of TreePath objects, but that array describes *selection changes*, not the current selection.

Example 6–7 puts tree selection to work. This program builds on Example 6–6; however, to keep the program short, we did not use a custom tree cell renderer. In the frame constructor, we restrict the user to single item selection and add a tree selection listener. When the valueChanged method is called, we ignore its event parameter and simply ask the tree for the current selection path. As always, we need to get the last node of the path and look up its user object. We then call the getFieldDescription method, which uses reflection to assemble a string with all fields of the selected class. Finally, that string is displayed in the text area.

Example 6–7: ClassBrowserTest.java

```
1. import java.awt.*;
2. import java.awt.event.*;
3. import java.lang.reflect.*;
4. import java.util.*;
5. import javax.swing.*;
6. import javax.swing.event.*;
7. import javax.swing.tree.*;
8.
9. /**
10.    This program demonstrates tree selection events.
11. */
12. public class ClassBrowserTest
13. {
14.    public static void main(String[] args)
15.    {
16.       JFrame frame = new ClassBrowserTestFrame();
17.       frame.setDefaultCloseOperation(JFrame.EXIT_ON_CLOSE);
18.       frame.setVisible(true);
19.    }
```

```
20.  }
21.
22.  /**
23.     A frame with a class tree, a text area to show the properties
24.     of the selected class, and a text field to add new classes.
25.  */
26.  class ClassBrowserTestFrame extends JFrame
27.  {
28.     public ClassBrowserTestFrame()
29.     {
30.        setTitle("ClassBrowserTest");
31.        setSize(DEFAULT_WIDTH, DEFAULT_HEIGHT);
32.
33.        // the root of the class tree is Object
34.        root = new DefaultMutableTreeNode(java.lang.Object.class);
35.        model = new DefaultTreeModel(root);
36.        tree = new JTree(model);
37.
38.        // add this class to populate the tree with some data
39.        addClass(getClass());
40.
41.        // set up selection mode
42.        tree.addTreeSelectionListener(new
43.           TreeSelectionListener()
44.           {
45.              public void valueChanged(TreeSelectionEvent event)
46.              {
47.                 // the user selected a different node--update description
48.                 TreePath path = tree.getSelectionPath();
49.                 if (path == null) return;
50.                 DefaultMutableTreeNode selectedNode
51.                    = (DefaultMutableTreeNode) path.getLastPathComponent();
52.                 Class c = (Class) selectedNode.getUserObject();
53.                 String description = getFieldDescription(c);
54.                 textArea.setText(description);
55.              }
56.           });
57.        int mode = TreeSelectionModel.SINGLE_TREE_SELECTION;
58.        tree.getSelectionModel().setSelectionMode(mode);
59.
60.        // this text area holds the class description
61.        textArea = new JTextArea();
62.
63.        // add tree and text area
64.        JPanel panel = new JPanel();
65.        panel.setLayout(new GridLayout(1, 2));
66.        panel.add(new JScrollPane(tree));
67.        panel.add(new JScrollPane(textArea));
68.
69.        add(panel, BorderLayout.CENTER);
70.
71.        addTextField();
72.     }
73.
74.     /**
75.        Add the text field and "Add" button to add a new class.
```

```
76.    */
77.    public void addTextField()
78.    {
79.       JPanel panel = new JPanel();
80.
81.       ActionListener addListener = new
82.          ActionListener()
83.          {
84.             public void actionPerformed(ActionEvent event)
85.             {
86.                // add the class whose name is in the text field
87.                try
88.                {
89.                   String text = textField.getText();
90.                   addClass(Class.forName(text));
91.                   // clear text field to indicate success
92.                   textField.setText("");
93.                }
94.                catch (ClassNotFoundException e)
95.                {
96.                   JOptionPane.showMessageDialog(null, "Class not found");
97.                }
98.             }
99.          };
100.
101.      // new class names are typed into this text field
102.      textField = new JTextField(20);
103.      textField.addActionListener(addListener);
104.      panel.add(textField);
105.
106.      JButton addButton = new JButton("Add");
107.      addButton.addActionListener(addListener);
108.      panel.add(addButton);
109.
110.      add(panel, BorderLayout.SOUTH);
111.   }
112.
113.   /**
114.      Finds an object in the tree.
115.      @param obj the object to find
116.      @return the node containing the object or null
117.      if the object is not present in the tree
118.   */
119.   public DefaultMutableTreeNode findUserObject(Object obj)
120.   {
121.      // find the node containing a user object
122.      Enumeration e = root.breadthFirstEnumeration();
123.      while (e.hasMoreElements())
124.      {
125.         DefaultMutableTreeNode node = (DefaultMutableTreeNode) e.nextElement();
126.         if (node.getUserObject().equals(obj))
127.            return node;
128.      }
129.      return null;
130.   }
131.
```

```
132.    /**
133.       Adds a new class and any parent classes that aren't
134.       yet part of the tree
135.       @param c the class to add
136.       @return the newly added node.
137.    */
138.    public DefaultMutableTreeNode addClass(Class c)
139.    {
140.       // add a new class to the tree
141.
142.       // skip non-class types
143.       if (c.isInterface() || c.isPrimitive()) return null;
144.
145.       // if the class is already in the tree, return its node
146.       DefaultMutableTreeNode node = findUserObject(c);
147.       if (node != null) return node;
148.
149.       // class isn't present--first add class parent recursively
150.
151.       Class s = c.getSuperclass();
152.
153.       DefaultMutableTreeNode parent;
154.       if (s == null)
155.          parent = root;
156.       else
157.          parent = addClass(s);
158.
159.       // add the class as a child to the parent
160.       DefaultMutableTreeNode newNode = new DefaultMutableTreeNode(c);
161.       model.insertNodeInto(newNode, parent, parent.getChildCount());
162.
163.       // make node visible
164.       TreePath path = new TreePath(model.getPathToRoot(newNode));
165.       tree.makeVisible(path);
166.
167.       return newNode;
168.    }
169.
170.    /**
171.       Returns a description of the fields of a class.
172.       @param the class to be described
173.       @return a string containing all field types and names
174.    */
175.    public static String getFieldDescription(Class c)
176.    {
177.       // use reflection to find types and names of fields
178.       StringBuilder r = new StringBuilder();
179.       Field[] fields = c.getDeclaredFields();
180.       for (int i = 0; i < fields.length; i++)
181.       {
182.          Field f = fields[i];
183.          if ((f.getModifiers() & Modifier.STATIC) != 0) r.append("static ");
184.          r.append(f.getType().getName());
185.          r.append(" ");
186.          r.append(f.getName());
187.          r.append("\n");
```

```
188.        }
189.      return r.toString();
190.    }
191.
192.    private DefaultMutableTreeNode root;
193.    private DefaultTreeModel model;
194.    private JTree tree;
195.    private JTextField textField;
196.    private JTextArea textArea;
197.    private static final int DEFAULT_WIDTH = 400;
198.    private static final int DEFAULT_HEIGHT = 300;
199. }
```

 javax.swing.JTree 1.2

- TreePath getSelectionPath()
- TreePath[] getSelectionPaths()

  return the first selected path, or an array of paths to all selected nodes. If no paths are selected, both methods return null.

 javax.swing.event.TreeSelectionListener 1.2

- void valueChanged(TreeSelectionEvent event)

  is called whenever nodes are selected or deselected.

 javax.swing.event.TreeSelectionEvent 1.2

- TreePath getPath()
- TreePath[] getPaths()

  get the first path or all paths that have *changed* in this selection event. If you want to know the current selection, not the selection change, you should call JTree.getSelectionPaths instead.

Custom Tree Models

In the final example, we implement a program that inspects the contents of a variable, just like a debugger does (see Figure 6–25).

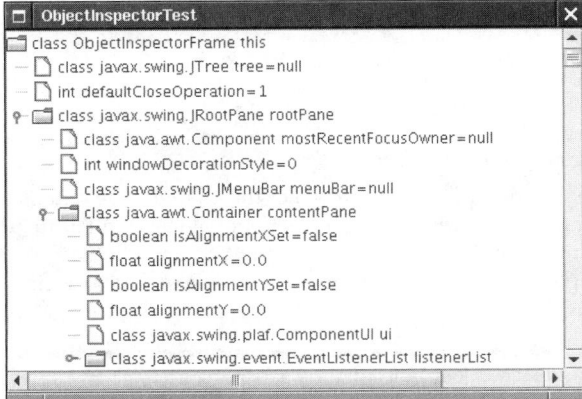

Figure 6–25: An object inspection tree

Before going further, compile and run the example program. Each node corresponds to an instance variable. If the variable is an object, expand it to see *its* instance variables. The program inspects the contents of the frame window. If you poke around a few of the instance variables, you should be able to find some familiar classes. You'll also gain some respect for how complex the Swing user interface components are under the hood.

What's remarkable about the program is that the tree does not use the `DefaultTreeModel`. If you already have data that is hierarchically organized, you may not want to build a duplicate tree and worry about keeping both trees synchronized. That is the situation in our case—the inspected objects are already linked to each other through the object references, so there is no need to replicate the linking structure.

The `TreeModel` interface has only a handful of methods. The first group of methods enables the `JTree` to find the tree nodes by first getting the root, then the children. The `JTree` class calls these methods only when the user actually expands a node.

```
Object getRoot()
int getChildCount(Object parent)
Object getChild(Object parent, int index)
```

This example shows why the `TreeModel` interface, like the `JTree` class itself, does not need an explicit notion of nodes. The root and its children can be any objects. The `TreeModel` is responsible for telling the `JTree` how they are connected.

The next method of the `TreeModel` interface is the reverse of `getChild`:

```
int getIndexOfChild(Object parent, Object child)
```

Actually, this method can be implemented in terms of the first three—see the code in Example 6–8.

The tree model tells the `JTree` which nodes should be displayed as leaves:

```
boolean isLeaf(Object node)
```

If your code changes the tree model, then the tree needs to be notified so that it can redraw itself. The tree adds itself as a `TreeModelListener` to the model. Thus, the model must support the usual listener management methods:

```
void addTreeModelListener(TreeModelListener l)
void removeTreeModelListener(TreeModelListener l)
```

You can see implementations for these methods in Example 6–8.

When the model modifies the tree contents, it calls one of the four methods of the `TreeModelListener` interface:

```
void treeNodesChanged(TreeModelEvent e)
void treeNodesInserted(TreeModelEvent e)
void treeNodesRemoved(TreeModelEvent e)
void treeStructureChanged(TreeModelEvent e)
```

The `TreeModelEvent` object describes the location of the change. The details of assembling a tree model event that describes an insertion or removal event are quite technical. You only need to worry about firing these events if your tree can actually have nodes added and removed. In Example 6–8, we show you how to fire one event: replacing the root with a new object.

 TIP: To simplify the code for event firing, we use the `javax.swing.EventListenerList` convenience class that collects listeners. See Volume 1, Chapter 8 for more information on this class.

Finally, if the user edits a tree node, your model is called with the change:

```
void valueForPathChanged(TreePath path, Object newValue)
```

If you don't allow editing, this method is never called.

If you don't need to support editing, then constructing a tree model is easily done. Implement the three methods

```
Object getRoot()
int getChildCount(Object parent)
Object getChild(Object parent, int index)
```

These methods describe the structure of the tree. Supply routine implementations of the other five methods, as in Example 6–8. You are then ready to display your tree.

Now let's turn to the implementation of the example program. Our tree will contain objects of type `Variable`.

 NOTE: Had we used the `DefaultTreeModel`, our nodes would have been objects of type `Default-MutableTreeNode` with *user objects* of type `Variable`.

For example, suppose you inspect the variable

```
Employee joe;
```

That variable has a *type* `Employee.class`, a *name* `"joe"`, and a *value*, the value of the object reference joe. We define a class `Variable` that describes a variable in a program:

```
Variable v = new Variable(Employee.class, "joe", joe);
```

If the type of the variable is a primitive type, you must use an object wrapper for the value.

```
new Variable(double.class, "salary", new Double(salary));
```

If the type of the variable is a class, then the variable has *fields*. Using reflection, we enumerate all fields and collect them in an `ArrayList`. Since the `getFields` method of the `Class` class does not return fields of the superclass, we need to call `getFields` on all superclasses as well. You can find the code in the `Variable` constructor. The `getFields` method of our `Variable` class returns the array of fields. Finally, the `toString` method of the `Variable` class formats the node label. The label always contains the variable type and name. If the variable is not a class, the label also contains the value.

 NOTE: If the type is an array, then we do not display the elements of the array. This would not be difficult to do; we leave it as the proverbial "exercise for the reader."

Let's move on to the tree model. The first two methods are simple.

```
public Object getRoot()
{
    return root;
}

public int getChildCount(Object parent)
{
    return ((Variable) parent).getFields().size();
}
```

The getChild method returns a new `Variable` object that describes the field with the given index. The getType and getName method of the `Field` class yield the field type and name. By using reflection, you can read the field value as f.get(parentValue). That method can throw an

IllegalAccessException. However, we made all fields accessible in the Variable constructor, so this won't happen in practice.

Here is the complete code of the getChild method.

```
public Object getChild(Object parent, int index)
{
   ArrayList fields = ((Variable) parent).getFields();
   Field f = (Field) fields.get(index);
   Object parentValue = ((Variable) parent).getValue();
   try
   {
      return new Variable(f.getType(), f.getName(), f.get(parentValue));
   }
   catch (IllegalAccessException e)
   {
      return null;
   }
}
```

These three methods reveal the structure of the object tree to the JTree component. The remaining methods are routine—see the source code in Example 6–8.

There is one remarkable fact about this tree model: It actually describes an *infinite* tree. You can verify this by following one of the WeakReference objects. Click on the variable named referent. It leads you right back to the original object. You get an identical subtree, and you can open its WeakReference object again, ad infinitum. Of course, you cannot *store* an infinite set of nodes. The tree model simply generates the nodes on demand as the user expands the parents.

This example concludes our discussion on trees. We move on to the table component, another complex Swing component. Superficially, trees and tables don't seem to have much in common, but you will find that they both use the same concepts for data models and cell rendering.

Example 6–8: ObjectInspectorTest.java

```
1. import java.awt.*;
2. import java.awt.event.*;
3. import java.lang.reflect.*;
4. import java.util.*;
5. import javax.swing.*;
6. import javax.swing.event.*;
7. import javax.swing.tree.*;
8.
9. /**
10.    This program demonstrates how to use a custom tree
11.    model. It displays the fields of an object.
12. */
13. public class ObjectInspectorTest
14. {
15.    public static void main(String[] args)
16.    {
17.       JFrame frame = new ObjectInspectorFrame();
18.       frame.setDefaultCloseOperation(JFrame.EXIT_ON_CLOSE);
19.       frame.setVisible(true);
20.    }
21. }
22.
```

```
23. /**
24.    This frame holds the object tree.
25. */
26. class ObjectInspectorFrame extends JFrame
27. {
28.    public ObjectInspectorFrame()
29.    {
30.       setTitle("ObjectInspectorTest");
31.       setSize(DEFAULT_WIDTH, DEFAULT_HEIGHT);
32.
33.       // we inspect this frame object
34.
35.       Variable v = new Variable(getClass(), "this", this);
36.       ObjectTreeModel model = new ObjectTreeModel();
37.       model.setRoot(v);
38.
39.       // construct and show tree
40.
41.       tree = new JTree(model);
42.       add(new JScrollPane(tree), BorderLayout.CENTER);
43.    }
44.
45.    private JTree tree;
46.    private static final int DEFAULT_WIDTH = 400;
47.    private static final int DEFAULT_HEIGHT = 300;
48. }
49.
50. /**
51.    This tree model describes the tree structure of a Java
52.    object. Children are the objects that are stored in instance
53.    variables.
54. */
55. class ObjectTreeModel implements TreeModel
56. {
57.    /**
58.       Constructs an empty tree.
59.    */
60.    public ObjectTreeModel()
61.    {
62.       root = null;
63.    }
64.
65.    /**
66.       Sets the root to a given variable.
67.       @param v the variable that is being described by this tree
68.    */
69.    public void setRoot(Variable v)
70.    {
71.       Variable oldRoot = v;
72.       root = v;
73.       fireTreeStructureChanged(oldRoot);
74.    }
75.
76.    public Object getRoot()
77.    {
78.       return root;
```

```
79.      }
80.
81.     public int getChildCount(Object parent)
82.     {
83.        return ((Variable) parent).getFields().size();
84.     }
85.
86.     public Object getChild(Object parent, int index)
87.     {
88.        ArrayList<Field> fields = ((Variable) parent).getFields();
89.        Field f = (Field) fields.get(index);
90.        Object parentValue = ((Variable) parent).getValue();
91.        try
92.        {
93.           return new Variable(f.getType(), f.getName(), f.get(parentValue));
94.        }
95.        catch (IllegalAccessException e)
96.        {
97.           return null;
98.        }
99.     }
100.
101.    public int getIndexOfChild(Object parent, Object child)
102.    {
103.       int n = getChildCount(parent);
104.       for (int i = 0; i < n; i++)
105.          if (getChild(parent, i).equals(child))
106.             return i;
107.       return -1;
108.    }
109.
110.    public boolean isLeaf(Object node)
111.    {
112.       return getChildCount(node) == 0;
113.    }
114.
115.    public void valueForPathChanged(TreePath path,
116.       Object newValue)
117.    {}
118.
119.    public void addTreeModelListener(TreeModelListener l)
120.    {
121.       listenerList.add(TreeModelListener.class, l);
122.    }
123.
124.    public void removeTreeModelListener(TreeModelListener l)
125.    {
126.       listenerList.remove(TreeModelListener.class, l);
127.    }
128.
129.    protected void fireTreeStructureChanged(Object oldRoot)
130.    {
131.       TreeModelEvent event = new TreeModelEvent(this, new Object[] {oldRoot});
132.       EventListener[] listeners = listenerList.getListeners(TreeModelListener.class);
133.       for (int i = 0; i < listeners.length; i++)
134.          ((TreeModelListener) listeners[i]).treeStructureChanged(event);
```

```
135.     }
136.
137.     private Variable root;
138.     private EventListenerList listenerList = new EventListenerList();
139. }
140.
141. /**
142.    A variable with a type, name, and value.
143. */
144. class Variable
145. {
146.    /**
147.       Construct a variable
148.       @param aType the type
149.       @param aName the name
150.       @param aValue the value
151.    */
152.    public Variable(Class aType, String aName, Object aValue)
153.    {
154.       type = aType;
155.       name = aName;
156.       value = aValue;
157.       fields = new ArrayList<Field>();
158.
159.       // find all fields if we have a class type except we don't expand strings and null values
160.
161.       if (!type.isPrimitive() && !type.isArray() && !type.equals(String.class) && value != null)
162.       {
163.          // get fields from the class and all superclasses
164.          for (Class c = value.getClass(); c != null; c = c.getSuperclass())
165.          {
166.             Field[] fs = c.getDeclaredFields();
167.             AccessibleObject.setAccessible(fs, true);
168.
169.             // get all nonstatic fields
170.             for (Field f : fs)
171.                if ((f.getModifiers() & Modifier.STATIC) == 0)
172.                   fields.add(f);
173.          }
174.       }
175.    }
176.
177.    /**
178.       Gets the value of this variable.
179.       @return the value
180.    */
181.    public Object getValue() { return value; }
182.
183.    /**
184.       Gets all nonstatic fields of this variable.
185.       @return an array list of variables describing the fields
186.    */
187.    public ArrayList<Field> getFields() { return fields; }
188.
189.    public String toString()
```

```
190.    {
191.        String r = type + " " + name;
192.        if (type.isPrimitive()) r += "=" + value;
193.        else if (type.equals(String.class)) r += "=" + value;
194.        else if (value == null) r += "=null";
195.        return r;
196.    }
197.
198.    private Class type;
199.    private String name;
200.    private Object value;
201.    private ArrayList<Field> fields;
202. }
```

API **javax.swing.tree.TreeModel** 1.2

- Object getRoot()
  returns the root node.
- int getChildCount(Object parent)
  gets the number of children of the parent node.
- Object getChild(Object parent, int index)
  gets the child node of the parent node at the given index.
- int getIndexOfChild(Object parent, Object child)
  gets the index of the child node in the parent node, or −1 if child is not a child of parent in this tree model.
- boolean isLeaf(Object node)
  returns true if node is conceptually a leaf of the tree.
- void addTreeModelListener(TreeModelListener l)
- void removeTreeModelListener(TreeModelListener l)
  add and remove listeners that are notified when the information in the tree model changes.
- void valueForPathChanged(TreePath path, Object newValue)
  is called when a cell editor has modified the value of a node.

Parameters:	path	The path to the node that has been edited
	newValue	The replacement value returned by the editor

API **javax.swing.event.TreeModelListener** 1.2

- void treeNodesChanged(TreeModelEvent e)
- void treeNodesInserted(TreeModelEvent e)
- void treeNodesRemoved(TreeModelEvent e)
- void treeStructureChanged(TreeModelEvent e)
  are called by the tree model when the tree has been modified.

API **javax.swing.event.TreeModelEvent** 1.2

- TreeModelEvent(Object eventSource, TreePath node)
  constructs a tree model event.

Parameters:	eventSource	The tree model generating this event
	node	The path to the node that is being changed

Tables

The JTable component displays a two-dimensional grid of objects. Of course, tables are common in user interfaces. The Swing team has put a lot of effort into the table control. Tables are inherently complex, but—perhaps more successfully than with other Swing classes—the JTable component hides much of that complexity. You can produce fully functional tables with rich behavior by writing a few lines of code. Of course, you can write more code and customize the display and behavior for your specific applications.

In this section, we explain how to make simple tables, how the user interacts with them, and how to make some of the most common adjustments. As with the other complex Swing controls, it is impossible to cover all aspects in complete detail. For more information, look in *Graphic Java 2* by David Geary or *Core Java Foundation Classes* by Kim Topley.

A Simple Table

As with the tree control, a JTable does not store its own data but obtains its data from a *table model*. The JTable class has a constructor that wraps a two-dimensional array of objects into a default model. That is the strategy that we use in our first example. Later in this chapter, we turn to table models.

Figure 6–26 shows a typical table, describing properties of the planets of the solar system. (A planet is *gaseous* if it consists mostly of hydrogen and helium. You should take the "Color" entries with a grain of salt—that column was added because it will be useful in a later code example.)

Planet	Radius	Moons	Gaseous	Color
Mercury	2440.0	0	false	java.awt.C...
Venus	6052.0	0	false	java.awt.C...
Earth	6378.0	1	false	java.awt.C...
Mars	3397.0	2	false	java.awt.C...
Jupiter	71492.0	16	true	java.awt.C...
Saturn	60268.0	18	true	java.awt.C...
Uranus	25559.0	17	true	java.awt.C...

Print

Figure 6–26: A simple table

As you can see from the code in Example 6–9, the data of the table is stored as a two-dimensional array of Object values:

```
Object[][] cells =
{
    { "Mercury", 2440.0, 0, false, Color.yellow },
    { "Venus", 6052.0, 0, false, Color.yellow },
    . . .
}
```

 NOTE: Here, we take advantage of autoboxing. The entries in the second, third, and fourth column are automatically converted into objects of type Double, Integer, and Boolean.

The table simply invokes the toString method on each object to display it. That's why the colors show up as java.awt.Color[r=...,g=...,b=...].

You supply the column names in a separate array of strings:

```
String[] columnNames = {  "Planet", "Radius", "Moons", "Gaseous", "Color" };
```

Then, you construct a table from the cell and column name arrays. Finally, add scroll bars in the usual way, by wrapping the table in a JScrollPane.

```
JTable table = new JTable(cells, columnNames);
JScrollPane pane = new JScrollPane(table);
```

The resulting table already has surprisingly rich behavior. Resize the table vertically until the scroll bar shows up. Then, scroll the table. Note that the column headers don't scroll out of view!

Next, click on one of the column headers and drag it to the left or right. See how the entire column becomes detached (see Figure 6–27). You can drop it to a different location. This rearranges the columns *in the view only*. The data model is not affected.

Planet	Radius	oons	Gaseous	Color
Mercury	2440.0		false	java.awt.C...
Venus	6052.0		false	java.awt.C...
Earth	6378.0		false	java.awt.C...
Mars	3397.0		false	java.awt.C...
Jupiter	71492.0		true	java.awt.C...
Saturn	60268.0		true	java.awt.C...
Uranus	25559.0		true	java.awt.C...

Print

Figure 6–27: Moving a column

To *resize* columns, simply place the cursor between two columns until the cursor shape changes to an arrow. Then, drag the column boundary to the desired place (see Figure 6–28).

Planet	Radius	Moons	Gas	Color
Mercury	2440.0	0	false	java.awt.Color[r=...
Venus	6052.0	0	false	java.awt.Color[r=...
Earth	6378.0	1	false	java.awt.Color[r=...
Mars	3397.0	2	false	java.awt.Color[r=...
Jupiter	71492.0	16	true	java.awt.Color[r=...
Saturn	60268.0	18	true	java.awt.Color[r=...
Uranus	25559.0	17	true	java.awt.Color[r=...

Print

Figure 6–28: Resizing columns

Users can select rows by clicking anywhere in a row. The selected rows are highlighted; you will see later how to get selection events. Users can also edit the table entries by clicking on a cell and typing into it. However, in this code example, the edits do not change the underlying data. In your programs, you should either make cells uneditable or handle cell editing events and update your model. We discuss those topics later in this section.

As of JDK 5.0, you can print a table with the print method:

```
table.print();
```

A print dialog box appears, and the table is sent to the printer. We discuss custom printing options in Chapter 7.

Example 6–9: PlanetTable.java

```
1. import java.awt.*;
2. import java.awt.event.*;
3. import javax.swing.*;
```

```
4.  import javax.swing.table.*;
5.
6.  /**
7.     This program demonstrates how to show a simple table
8.  */
9.  public class PlanetTable
10. {
11.    public static void main(String[] args)
12.    {
13.       JFrame frame = new PlanetTableFrame();
14.       frame.setDefaultCloseOperation(JFrame.EXIT_ON_CLOSE);
15.       frame.setVisible(true);
16.    }
17. }
18.
19. /**
20.    This frame contains a table of planet data.
21. */
22. class PlanetTableFrame extends JFrame
23. {
24.    public PlanetTableFrame()
25.    {
26.       setTitle("PlanetTable");
27.       setSize(DEFAULT_WIDTH, DEFAULT_HEIGHT);
28.       final JTable table = new JTable(cells, columnNames);
29.       add(new JScrollPane(table), BorderLayout.CENTER);
30.       JButton printButton = new JButton("Print");
31.       printButton.addActionListener(new
32.          ActionListener()
33.          {
34.             public void actionPerformed(ActionEvent event)
35.             {
36.                try
37.                {
38.                   table.print();
39.                }
40.                catch (java.awt.print.PrinterException e)
41.                {
42.                   e.printStackTrace();
43.                }
44.             }
45.          });
46.       JPanel buttonPanel = new JPanel();
47.       buttonPanel.add(printButton);
48.       add(buttonPanel, BorderLayout.SOUTH);
49.    }
50.
51.    private Object[][] cells =
52.    {
53.       { "Mercury", 2440.0,  0, false, Color.yellow },
54.       { "Venus", 6052.0, 0, false, Color.yellow },
55.       { "Earth", 6378.0, 1, false, Color.blue },
56.       { "Mars", 3397.0, 2, false, Color.red },
57.       { "Jupiter", 71492.0, 16, true, Color.orange },
```

```
58.        { "Saturn", 60268.0, 18, true, Color.orange },
59.        { "Uranus", 25559.0, 17, true, Color.blue },
60.        { "Neptune", 24766.0, 8, true, Color.blue },
61.        { "Pluto", 1137.0, 1, false, Color.black }
62.     };
63.
64.     private String[] columnNames = { "Planet", "Radius", "Moons", "Gaseous", "Color" };
65.
66.     private static final int DEFAULT_WIDTH = 400;
67.     private static final int DEFAULT_HEIGHT = 200;
68.  }
```

javax.swing.JTable 1.2

- JTable(Object[][] entries, Object[] columnNames)
  constructs a table with a default table model.

- void print() **5.0**
  displays a print dialog box and prints the table.

Table Models

In the preceding example, the table-rendered objects were stored in a two-dimensional array. However, you should generally not use that strategy in your own code. If you find yourself dumping data into an array to display it as a table, you should instead think about implementing your own table model.

Table models are particularly simple to implement because you can take advantage of the AbstractTableModel class that implements most of the required methods. You only need to supply three methods:

```
public int getRowCount();
public int getColumnCount();
public Object getValueAt(int row, int column);
```

There are many ways for implementing the getValueAt method. You can simply compute the answer. Or you can look up the value from a database or some other repository. Let us look at a couple of examples.

In the first example, we construct a table that simply shows some computed values, namely, the growth of an investment under different interest rate scenarios (see Figure 6–29).

5%	6%	7%	8%	9%	10%
100000.00	100000.00	100000.00	100000.00	100000.00	100000.00
105000.00	106000.00	107000.00	108000.00	109000.00	110000.00
110250.00	112360.00	114490.00	116640.00	118810.00	121000.00
115762.50	119101.60	122504.30	125971.20	129502.90	133100.00
121550.63	126247.70	131079.60	136048.90	141158.16	146410.00
127628.16	133822.56	140255.17	146932.81	153862.40	161051.00
134009.56	141851.91	150073.04	158687.43	167710.01	177156.10
140710.04	150363.03	160578.15	171382.43	182803.91	194871.71
147745.54	159384.81	171818.62	185093.02	199256.26	214358.88
155132.82	168947.90	183845.92	199900.46	217189.33	235794.77
162889.46	179084.77	196715.14	215892.50	236736.37	259374.25
171033.94	189829.86	210485.20	233163.90	258042.64	285311.67
179585.63	201219.65	225219.16	251817.01	281266.48	313842.84
188564.91	213292.83	240984.50	271962.37	306580.46	345227.12
197993.16	226090.40	257853.42	293719.36	334172.70	379749.83
207892.82	239655.82	275903.15	317216.91	364248.25	417724.82

Figure 6–29: Growth of an investment

The getValueAt method computes the appropriate value and formats it:

```
public Object getValueAt(int r, int c)
{
    double rate = (c + minRate) / 100.0;
    int nperiods = r;
    double futureBalance = INITIAL_BALANCE * Math.pow(1 + rate, nperiods);
    return String.format("%.2f", futureBalance);
}
```

The getRowCount and getColumnCount methods simply return the number of rows and columns.

```
public int getRowCount() { return years; }
public int getColumnCount() { return maxRate - minRate + 1; }
```

If you don't supply column names, the getColumnName method of the AbstractTableModel names the columns A, B, C, and so on. To change column names, override the getColumnName method. You will usually want to override that default behavior. In this example, we simply label each column with the interest rate.

```
public String getColumnName(int c) { return (c + minRate) + "%"; }
```

You can find the complete source code in Example 6–10.

Example 6–10: InvestmentTable.java

```
1.  import java.awt.*;
2.  import java.awt.event.*;
3.  import java.text.*;
4.  import javax.swing.*;
5.  import javax.swing.table.*;
6.
7.  /**
8.     This program shows how to build a table from a table model.
9.  */
10. public class InvestmentTable
11. {
12.    public static void main(String[] args)
13.    {
14.       JFrame frame = new InvestmentTableFrame();
15.       frame.setDefaultCloseOperation(JFrame.EXIT_ON_CLOSE);
16.       frame.setVisible(true);
17.    }
18. }
19.
20. /**
21.    This frame contains the investment table.
22. */
23. class InvestmentTableFrame extends JFrame
24. {
25.    public InvestmentTableFrame()
26.    {
27.       setTitle("InvestmentTable");
28.       setSize(DEFAULT_WIDTH, DEFAULT_HEIGHT);
29.
30.       TableModel model = new InvestmentTableModel(30, 5, 10);
31.       JTable table = new JTable(model);
32.       add(new JScrollPane(table));
33.    }
```

```
34.
35.    private static final int DEFAULT_WIDTH = 600;
36.    private static final int DEFAULT_HEIGHT = 300;
37. }
38.
39. /**
40.    This table model computes the cell entries each time they
41.    are requested. The table contents shows the growth of
42.    an investment for a number of years under different interest
43.    rates.
44. */
45. class InvestmentTableModel extends AbstractTableModel
46. {
47.    /**
48.       Constructs an investment table model.
49.       @param y the number of years
50.       @param r1 the lowest interest rate to tabulate
51.       @param r2 the highest interest rate to tabulate
52.    */
53.    public InvestmentTableModel(int y, int r1, int r2)
54.    {
55.       years = y;
56.       minRate = r1;
57.       maxRate = r2;
58.    }
59.
60.    public int getRowCount() { return years; }
61.
62.    public int getColumnCount() { return maxRate - minRate + 1; }
63.
64.    public Object getValueAt(int r, int c)
65.    {
66.       double rate = (c + minRate) / 100.0;
67.       int nperiods = r;
68.       double futureBalance = INITIAL_BALANCE * Math.pow(1 + rate, nperiods);
69.       return String.format("%.2f", futureBalance);
70.    }
71.
72.    public String getColumnName(int c) { return (c + minRate) + "%"; }
73.
74.    private int years;
75.    private int minRate;
76.    private int maxRate;
77.
78.    private static double INITIAL_BALANCE = 100000.0;
79. }
```

Displaying Database Records

Probably the most common information to be displayed in a table is a set of records from a database. If you use a professional development environment, it almost certainly includes convenient JavaBeans components (beans) for accessing database information. However, if you don't have database beans or if you are simply curious about what goes on under the hood, you will find the next example interesting. Figure 6–30 shows the output—the result of a query for all rows in a database table.

Title	ISBN	Publisher_Id	Price
A Guide to th...	0-201-9642...	0201	47.95
A Pattern Lan...	0-19-50191...	019	65.00
Applied Crypt...	0-471-1170...	0471	60.00
Computer Gr...	0-201-8484...	0201	79.99
Cuckoo's Egg ...	0-7434-114...	07434	13.95
Design Patter...	0-201-6336...	0201	54.99
Introduction t...	0-262-0329...	0262	80.00
Introduction t...	0-201-4412...	0201	105.00
JavaScript: Th...	0-596-0004...	0596	44.95
The Art of Co...	0-201-8968...	0201	59.99
The Art of Co...	0-201-8968...	0201	59.99
The Art of Co...	0-201-8968...	0201	59.99
The C Progra...	0-13-11036...	013	42.00
The C++ Pro	0-201-7007	0201	64.99

Figure 6–30: Displaying a query result in a table

In the example program, we define a ResultSetTableModel that fetches data from the result set of a database query. (See Chapter 4 for more information on Java database access and result sets.)

You can obtain the column count and the column names from the ResultSetMetaData object:

```
public String getColumnName(int c)
{
   try
   {
      return rsmd.getColumnName(c + 1);
   }
   catch (SQLException e)
   {
      . . .
   }
}

public int getColumnCount()
{
   try
   {
      return rsmd.getColumnCount();
   }
   catch (SQLException e)
   {
      . . .
   }
}
```

If the database supports scrolling cursors, then it is particularly easy to get a cell value: Just move the cursor to the requested row and fetch the column value.

```
public Object getValueAt(int r, int c)
{
   try
   {
      ResultSet rs = getResultSet();
      rs.absolute(r + 1);
      return rs.getObject(c + 1);
```

```
        }
        catch (SQLException e)
        {
            e.printStackTrace();
            return null;
        }
    }
```

It makes a lot of sense to use this data model instead of the DefaultTableModel. If you created an array of values, then you would duplicate the cache that the database driver is already managing.

If the database does not support scrolling cursors, our example program puts the data in a row set instead.

Example 6–11: ResultSetTable.java

```
 1. import com.sun.rowset.*;
 2. import java.awt.*;
 3. import java.awt.event.*;
 4. import java.io.*;
 5. import java.sql.*;
 6. import java.util.*;
 7. import javax.swing.*;
 8. import javax.swing.table.*;
 9. import javax.sql.rowset.*;
10.
11. /**
12.    This program shows how to display the result of a
13.    database query in a table.
14. */
15. public class ResultSetTable
16. {
17.    public static void main(String[] args)
18.    {
19.        JFrame frame = new ResultSetFrame();
20.        frame.setDefaultCloseOperation(JFrame.EXIT_ON_CLOSE);
21.        frame.setVisible(true);
22.    }
23. }
24.
25. /**
26.    This frame contains a combo box to select a database table
27.    and a table to show the data stored in the table
28. */
29. class ResultSetFrame extends JFrame
30. {
31.    public ResultSetFrame()
32.    {
33.        setTitle("ResultSet");
34.        setSize(DEFAULT_WIDTH, DEFAULT_HEIGHT);
35.
36.        /* find all tables in the database and add them to
37.           a combo box
38.        */
39.
40.        tableNames = new JComboBox();
41.        tableNames.addActionListener(new
```

```
42.        ActionListener()
43.        {
44.           public void actionPerformed(ActionEvent event)
45.           {
46.              try
47.              {
48.                 if (scrollPane != null) remove(scrollPane);
49.                 String tableName = (String) tableNames.getSelectedItem();
50.                 if (rs != null) rs.close();
51.                 String query = "SELECT * FROM " + tableName;
52.                 rs = stat.executeQuery(query);
53.                 if (scrolling)
54.                    model = new ResultSetTableModel(rs);
55.                 else
56.                 {
57.                    CachedRowSet crs = new CachedRowSetImpl();
58.                    crs.populate(rs);
59.                    model = new ResultSetTableModel(crs);
60.                 }

62.                 JTable table = new JTable(model);
63.                 scrollPane = new JScrollPane(table);
64.                 add(scrollPane, BorderLayout.CENTER);
65.                 validate();
66.              }
67.              catch (SQLException e)
68.              {
69.                 e.printStackTrace();
70.              }
71.           }
72.        });
73.        JPanel p = new JPanel();
74.        p.add(tableNames);
75.        add(p, BorderLayout.NORTH);

77.        try
78.        {
79.           conn = getConnection();
80.           DatabaseMetaData meta = conn.getMetaData();
81.           if (meta.supportsResultSetType(ResultSet.TYPE_SCROLL_INSENSITIVE))
82.           {
83.              scrolling = true;
84.              stat = conn.createStatement(ResultSet.TYPE_SCROLL_INSENSITIVE,
85.                 ResultSet.CONCUR_READ_ONLY);
86.           }
87.           else
88.           {
89.              stat = conn.createStatement();
90.              scrolling = false;
91.           }
92.           ResultSet tables = meta.getTables(null, null, null, new String[] { "TABLE" });
93.           while (tables.next())
94.              tableNames.addItem(tables.getString(3));
95.           tables.close();
96.        }
97.        catch (IOException e)
```

```
 98.         {
 99.             e.printStackTrace();
100.         }
101.         catch (SQLException e)
102.         {
103.             e.printStackTrace();
104.         }
105.
106.         addWindowListener(new
107.             WindowAdapter()
108.             {
109.                 public void windowClosing(WindowEvent event)
110.                 {
111.                     try
112.                     {
113.                         if (conn != null) conn.close();
114.                     }
115.                     catch (SQLException e)
116.                     {
117.                         e.printStackTrace();
118.                     }
119.                 }
120.             });
121.     }
122.
123.     /**
124.         Gets a connection from the properties specified in
125.         the file database.properties.
126.         @return the database connection
127.     */
128.     public static Connection getConnection()
129.         throws SQLException, IOException
130.     {
131.         Properties props = new Properties();
132.         FileInputStream in = new FileInputStream("database.properties");
133.         props.load(in);
134.         in.close();
135.
136.         String drivers = props.getProperty("jdbc.drivers");
137.         if (drivers != null) System.setProperty("jdbc.drivers", drivers);
138.         String url = props.getProperty("jdbc.url");
139.         String username = props.getProperty("jdbc.username");
140.         String password = props.getProperty("jdbc.password");
141.
142.         return DriverManager.getConnection(url, username, password);
143.     }
144.
145.     private JScrollPane scrollPane;
146.     private ResultSetTableModel model;
147.     private JComboBox tableNames;
148.     private ResultSet rs;
149.     private Connection conn;
150.     private Statement stat;
151.     private boolean scrolling;
152.
```

```
153.    private static final int DEFAULT_WIDTH = 400;
154.    private static final int DEFAULT_HEIGHT = 300;
155. }
156.
157. /**
158.    This class is the superclass for the scrolling and the
159.    caching result set table model. It stores the result set
160.    and its metadata.
161. */
162. class ResultSetTableModel extends AbstractTableModel
163. {
164.    /**
165.       Constructs the table model.
166.       @param aResultSet the result set to display.
167.    */
168.    public ResultSetTableModel(ResultSet aResultSet)
169.    {
170.       rs = aResultSet;
171.       try
172.       {
173.          rsmd = rs.getMetaData();
174.       }
175.       catch (SQLException e)
176.       {
177.          e.printStackTrace();
178.       }
179.    }
180.
181.    public String getColumnName(int c)
182.    {
183.       try
184.       {
185.          return rsmd.getColumnName(c + 1);
186.       }
187.       catch (SQLException e)
188.       {
189.          e.printStackTrace();
190.          return "";
191.       }
192.    }
193.
194.    public int getColumnCount()
195.    {
196.       try
197.       {
198.          return rsmd.getColumnCount();
199.       }
200.       catch (SQLException e)
201.       {
202.          e.printStackTrace();
203.          return 0;
204.       }
205.    }
206.
207.    public Object getValueAt(int r, int c)
```

```
208.    {
209.        try
210.        {
211.            rs.absolute(r + 1);
212.            return rs.getObject(c + 1);
213.        }
214.        catch(SQLException e)
215.        {
216.            e.printStackTrace();
217.            return null;
218.        }
219.    }
220.
221.    public int getRowCount()
222.    {
223.        try
224.        {
225.            rs.last();
226.            return rs.getRow();
227.        }
228.        catch(SQLException e)
229.        {
230.            e.printStackTrace();
231.            return 0;
232.        }
233.    }
234.
235.    private ResultSet rs;
236.    private ResultSetMetaData rsmd;
237. }
```

A Sort Filter

The last two examples drove home the point that tables don't store the cell data; they get them from a model. The model need not store the data either. It can compute the cell values or fetch them from somewhere else.

In this section, we introduce another useful technique, a *filter model* that presents information from another table in a different form. In our example, we *sort* the rows in a table. Run the program in Example 6–12 and *double-click* on one of the column headers. You will see how the rows are rearranged so that the column entries are sorted (see Figure 6–31).

Planet	Radius	Moons	Gaseous	Color
Mercury	2440.0	0	false	java.awt.C...
Venus	6052.0	0	false	java.awt.C...
Earth	6378.0	1	false	java.awt.C...
Pluto	1137.0	1	false	java.awt.C...
Mars	3397.0	2	false	java.awt.C...
Neptune	24766.0	8	true	java.awt.C...
Jupiter	71492.0	16	true	java.awt.C...
Uranus	25559.0	17	true	java.awt.C...
Saturn	60268.0	18	true	java.awt.C...

TableSortTest

Figure 6–31: Sorting the rows of a table

However, we don't physically rearrange the rows in the data model. Instead, we use a *filter model* that keeps an array with the permuted row indexes.

The filter model stores a reference to the actual table model. When the `JTable` needs to look up a value, the filter model computes the actual row index and gets the value from the model. For example,

```
public Object getValueAt(int r, int c) {  return model.getValueAt(actual row index, c); }
```

All other methods are simply passed on to the original model.

```
public String getColumnName(int c) {  return model.getColumnName(c); }
```

Figure 6–32 shows how the filter sits between the `JTable` object and the actual table model.

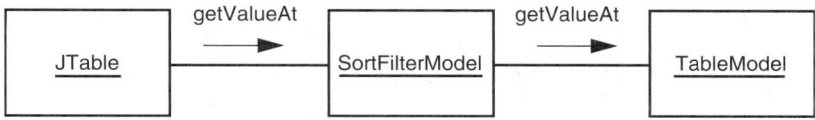

Figure 6–32: A table model filter

There are two complexities when you implement such a sort filter. First, you need to be notified when the user double-clicks on one of the column headers. We don't want to go into too much detail on this technical point. You can find the code in the `addMouseListener` method of the `SortFilterModel` in Example 6–12. Here is the idea behind the code. First, get the table header component and attach a mouse listener. When a double click is detected, you need to find out in which table column the mouse click fell. Then, you need to translate the table column to the model column—they can be different if the user moved the table columns around. Once you know the model column, you can start sorting the table rows.

The second complexity lies in sorting the table rows. We don't want to physically rearrange the rows. What we want is a sequence of row indexes that tells us how we would rearrange them if they were being sorted. However, the sort algorithms in the `Arrays` and `Collections` classes don't tell us how they rearrange the elements. Of course, you could reimplement a sorting algorithm and keep track of the object rearrangements, but there is a much smarter way. The trick is to come up with custom objects and a custom comparison method so that the library sorting algorithm can be pressed into service.

We will sort objects of type `Row`. A `Row` object contains the index r of a row in the model. Compare two such objects as follows: Find the elements in the model and compare them. In other words, the `compareTo` method for `Row` objects computes

```
model.getValueAt(r1, c).compareTo(model.getValueAt(r2, c))
```

Here r_1 and r_2 are the row indexes of the `Row` objects, and c is the column whose elements should be sorted.

If the entries of a particular column aren't comparable, we simply compare their string representations. That way, the column with `Color` values can still be sorted. (The `Color` class does not implement the `Comparable` interface.)

We make the `Row` class into an inner class of the `SortFilterModel` because the `compareTo` method needs to access the current model and column. Here is the code:

```
class SortFilterModel extends AbstractTableModel
{
    . . .
    private class Row implements Comparable<Row>
    {
        public int index;
        public int compareTo(Row other)
        {
            Object a = model.getValueAt(index, sortColumn);
```

```
          Object b = model.getValueAt(other.index, sortColumn);
          if (a instanceof Comparable)
             return ((Comparable) a).compareTo(b);
          else
             return a.toString().compareTo(b.toString());
       }
    }

    private TableModel model;
    private int sortColumn;
    private Row[] rows;
 }
```

In the constructor, we build an array rows, initialized such that rows[i].index is set to i:

```
public SortFilterModel(TableModel m)
{
   model = m;
   rows = new Row[model.getRowCount()];
   for (int i = 0; i < rows.length; i++)
   {
      rows[i] = new Row();
      rows[i].index = i;
   }
}
```

In the sort method, we invoke the Arrays.sort algorithm. It sorts the Row objects. Because the comparison criterion looks at the model elements in the appropriate column, the elements are arranged so that afterward row[0] contains the index of the smallest element in the column, row[1] contains the index of the next-smallest element, and so on.

When the array is sorted, we notify all table model listeners (in particular, the JTable) that the table contents have changed and must be redrawn.

```
public void sort(int c)
{
   sortColumn = c;
   Arrays.sort(rows);
   fireTableDataChanged();
}
```

Finally, we can show you the exact computation of the getValueAt method of the filter class. It simply translates a row index r to the model row index rows[r].index:

```
public Object getValueAt(int r, int c) { return model.getValueAt(rows[r].index, c); }
```

The sort model filter shows again the power of the model-view-controller pattern. Because the data and the display are separated, we are able to change the mapping between the two.

 TIP: You can find a more elaborate version of a table sorter at http://java.sun.com/docs/books/ tutorial/uiswing/components/table.html#sorting. That implementation listens to the table model and updates the sorted view when the table model changes.

Example 6–12: TableSortTest.java

```
1.  import java.awt.*;
2.  import java.awt.event.*;
3.  import java.util.*;
4.  import javax.swing.*;
5.  import javax.swing.event.*;
```

```
6.  import javax.swing.table.*;
7.
8.  /**
9.     This program demonstrates how to sort a table column.
10.    Double-click on a table column's header to sort it.
11. */
12. public class TableSortTest
13. {
14.    public static void main(String[] args)
15.    {
16.       JFrame frame = new TableSortFrame();
17.       frame.setDefaultCloseOperation(JFrame.EXIT_ON_CLOSE);
18.       frame.setVisible(true);
19.    }
20. }
21.
22. /**
23.    This frame contains a table of planet data.
24. */
25. class TableSortFrame extends JFrame
26. {
27.    public TableSortFrame()
28.    {
29.       setTitle("TableSortTest");
30.       setSize(DEFAULT_WIDTH, DEFAULT_HEIGHT);
31.
32.       // set up table model and interpose sorter
33.
34.       DefaultTableModel model = new DefaultTableModel(cells, columnNames);
35.       final SortFilterModel sorter = new SortFilterModel(model);
36.
37.       // show table
38.
39.       final JTable table = new JTable(sorter);
40.       add(new JScrollPane(table), BorderLayout.CENTER);
41.
42.       // set up double-click handler for column headers
43.
44.       table.getTableHeader().addMouseListener(new
45.          MouseAdapter()
46.          {
47.             public void mouseClicked(MouseEvent event)
48.             {
49.                // check for double click
50.                if (event.getClickCount() < 2) return;
51.
52.                // find column of click and
53.                int tableColumn = table.columnAtPoint(event.getPoint());
54.
55.                // translate to table model index and sort
56.                int modelColumn = table.convertColumnIndexToModel(tableColumn);
57.                sorter.sort(modelColumn);
58.             }
59.          });
60.    }
61.
```

```
62.    private Object[][] cells =
63.    {
64.       { "Mercury", 2440.0,  0, false, Color.yellow },
65.       { "Venus", 6052.0, 0, false, Color.yellow },
66.       { "Earth", 6378.0, 1, false, Color.blue },
67.       { "Mars", 3397.0, 2, false, Color.red },
68.       { "Jupiter", 71492.0, 16, true, Color.orange },
69.       { "Saturn", 60268.0, 18, true, Color.orange },
70.       { "Uranus", 25559.0, 17, true, Color.blue },
71.       { "Neptune", 24766.0, 8, true, Color.blue },
72.       { "Pluto", 1137.0, 1, false, Color.black }
73.    };
74.
75.    private String[] columnNames = { "Planet", "Radius", "Moons", "Gaseous", "Color" };
76.
77.    private static final int DEFAULT_WIDTH = 400;
78.    private static final int DEFAULT_HEIGHT = 200;
79. }
80.
81. /**
82.    This table model takes an existing table model and produces a new model that sorts the rows
83.    so that the entries in a given column are sorted.
84. */
85. class SortFilterModel extends AbstractTableModel
86. {
87.    /**
88.       Constructs a sort filter model.
89.       @param m the table model whose rows should be sorted
90.    */
91.    public SortFilterModel(TableModel m)
92.    {
93.       model = m;
94.       rows = new Row[model.getRowCount()];
95.       for (int i = 0; i < rows.length; i++)
96.       {
97.          rows[i] = new Row();
98.          rows[i].index = i;
99.       }
100.   }
101.
102.   /**
103.      Sorts the rows.
104.      @param c the column that should become sorted
105.   */
106.   public void sort(int c)
107.   {
108.      sortColumn = c;
109.      Arrays.sort(rows);
110.      fireTableDataChanged();
111.   }
112.
113.   // Compute the moved row for the three methods that access model elements
114.
115.   public Object getValueAt(int r, int c) { return model.getValueAt(rows[r].index, c); }
116.
117.   public boolean isCellEditable(int r, int c) { return model.isCellEditable(rows[r].index, c); }
```

```
118.
119.    public void setValueAt(Object aValue, int r, int c)
120.    {
121.        model.setValueAt(aValue, rows[r].index, c);
122.    }
123.
124.    // delegate all remaining methods to the model
125.
126.    public int getRowCount() { return model.getRowCount(); }
127.    public int getColumnCount() { return model.getColumnCount(); }
128.    public String getColumnName(int c) { return model.getColumnName(c); }
129.    public Class getColumnClass(int c) { return model.getColumnClass(c); }
130.
131.    /**
132.        This inner class holds the index of the model row
133.        Rows are compared by looking at the model row entries
134.        in the sort column.
135.    */
136.    private class Row implements Comparable<Row>
137.    {
138.        public int index;
139.        public int compareTo(Row other)
140.        {
141.            Object a = model.getValueAt(index, sortColumn);
142.            Object b = model.getValueAt(other.index, sortColumn);
143.            if (a instanceof Comparable)
144.                return ((Comparable) a).compareTo(b);
145.            else
146.                return a.toString().compareTo(b.toString());
147.        }
148.    }
149.
150.    private TableModel model;
151.    private int sortColumn;
152.    private Row[] rows;
153. }
```

 javax.swing.table.TableModel 1.2

- int getRowCount()
- int getColumnCount()
  get the number of rows and columns in the table model.

- Object getValueAt(int row, int column)
  gets the value at the given row and column.

- void setValueAt(Object newValue, int row, int column)
  sets a new value at the given row and column.

- boolean isCellEditable(int row, int column)
  returns true if the cell at the given row and column is editable.

- String getColumnName(int column)
  gets the column title.

javax.swing.table.AbstractTableModel 1.2

- void fireTableDataChanged()
  notifies all table model listeners that the table data has changed.

 javax.swing.JTable 1.2

- JTableHeader getTableHeader()
  returns the table header component of this table.

- int columnAtPoint(Point p)
  returns the number of the table column that falls under the pixel position p.

- int convertColumnIndexToModel(int tableColumn)
  returns the model index of the column with the given index. This value is different from tableColumn if some of the table columns are moved or hidden.

Cell Rendering and Editing

In the next example, we again display our planet data, but this time, we want to give the table more information about the *column types*. If you define the method

```
Class getColumnClass(int columnIndex)
```

of your table model to return the class that describes the column type, then the JTable class picks an appropriate *renderer* for the class. Table 6–1 shows how the JTable class renders types by default.

Table 6–1: Default Rendering Actions

Type	Rendered As
Icon	Image
Boolean	Checkbox
Object	String

You can see the checkboxes and images in Figure 6–33. (Thanks to Jim Evins, http://www.snaught.com/JimsCoolIcons/Planets, for providing the planet images!)

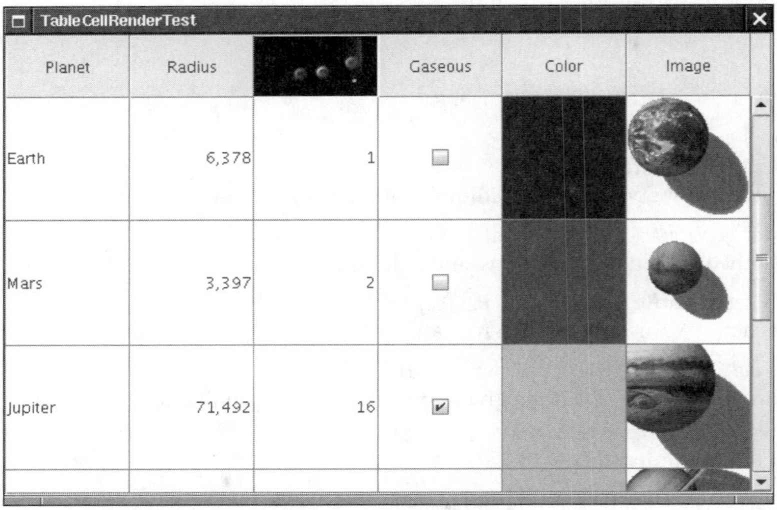

Figure 6–33: A table with cell renderers

For other types, you can supply your own cell renderers. Table cell renderers are similar to the tree cell renderers that you saw earlier. They implement the `TableCellRenderer` interface, which has a single method

```
Component getTableCellRendererComponent(JTable table, Object value, boolean isSelected,
    boolean hasFocus, int row, int column)
```

That method is called when the table needs to draw a cell. You return a component whose paint method is then invoked to fill the cell area.

To display a cell of type `Color`, you can simply return a panel with a background color you set to the color object stored in the cell. The color is passed as the value parameter.

```
class ColorTableCellRenderer extends JPanel implements TableCellRenderer
{
    public Component getTableCellRendererComponent(JTable table, Object value, boolean isSelected,
        boolean hasFocus, int row, int column)
    {
        setBackground((Color) value);
        if (hasFocus)
            setBorder(UIManager.getBorder("Table.focusCellHighlightBorder"));
        else
            setBorder(null);
    }
}
```

As you can see, the renderer installs a border when the cell has focus. (We ask the `UIManager` for the correct border. To find the lookup key, we peeked into the source code of the `Default-TableCellRenderer` class.)

Generally, you will also want to set the background color of the cell to indicate whether it is currently selected. We skip this step because it would interfere with the displayed color. The `ListRenderingTest` example on page 334 shows how to indicate the selection status in a renderer.

 TIP: If your renderer simply draws a text string or an icon, you can extend the `DefaultTableCell-Renderer` class. It takes care of rendering the focus and selection status for you.

You need to tell the table to use this renderer with all objects of type `Color`. The `setDefaultRen-derer` method of the `JTable` class lets you establish this association. You supply a `Class` object and the renderer:

```
table.setDefaultRenderer(Color.class, new ColorTableCellRenderer());
```

That renderer is now used for all objects of the given type.

Cell Editing

To enable cell editing, the table model must indicate which cells are editable by defining the `isCellEditable` method. Most commonly, you will want to make certain columns editable. In the example program, we allow editing in four columns.

```
public boolean isCellEditable(int r, int c)
{
    return c == PLANET_COLUMN || c == MOONS_COLUMN || c == GASEOUS_COLUMN || c == COLOR_COLUMN;
}

private static final int PLANET_COLUMN = 0;
private static final int MOONS_COLUMN = 2;
private static final int GASEOUS_COLUMN = 3;
private static final int COLOR_COLUMN = 4;
```

> **NOTE:** The AbstractTableModel defines the isCellEditable method to always return false. The DefaultTableModel overrides the method to always return true.

If you run the program in Example 6–13, note that you can click on the checkboxes in the Gaseous column and turn the check marks on and off. If you click on a cell in the Moons column, a combo box appears (see Figure 6–34). You will shortly see how to install such a combo box as a cell editor.

Finally, click on a cell in the first column. The cell gains focus. You can start typing and the cell contents change.

Planet	Radius		Gaseous	Color	Image
Mercury	2,440	0 ▼	☐		
Venus	6,052	0 1 2 3 4 5 6 7	☐		
Earth	6,378	1	☐		

Figure 6–34: A cell editor

What you just saw in action are the three variations of the DefaultCellEditor class. A DefaultCellEditor can be constructed with a JTextField, a JCheckBox, or a JComboBox. The JTable class automatically installs a checkbox editor for Boolean cells and a text field editor for all editable cells that don't supply their own renderer. The text fields let the user edit the strings that result from applying toString to the return value of the getValueAt method of the table model.

When the edit is complete, the edited value is retrieved by calling the getCellEditorValue method of your editor. That method should return a value of the correct type (that is, the type returned by the getColumnType method of the model).

To get a combo box editor, you set a cell editor manually—the JTable component has no idea what values might be appropriate for a particular type. For the Moons column, we wanted to enable the user to pick any value between 0 and 20. Here is the code for initializing the combo box.

```
JComboBox moonCombo = new JComboBox();
for (int i = 0; i <= 20; i++)
    moonCombo.addItem(i);
```

To construct a DefaultCellEditor, supply the combo box in the constructor:

```
TableCellEditor moonEditor = new DefaultCellEditor(moonCombo);
```

Next, we need to install the editor. Unlike the color cell renderer, this editor does not depend on the object *type*—we don't necessarily want to use it for all objects of type Integer. Instead, we need to install it into a particular column.

The JTable class stores information about table columns in objects of type TableColumn. A Table-ColumnModel object manages the columns. (Figure 6–35 shows the relationships among the most important table classes.) If you don't want to insert or remove columns dynamically, you won't use the table column model much. However, to get a particular TableColumn object, you need to get the column model to ask it for the column object:

```
TableColumnModel columnModel = table.getColumnModel()
TableColumn moonColumn = columnModel.getColumn(PlanetTableModel.MOONS_COLUMN);
```

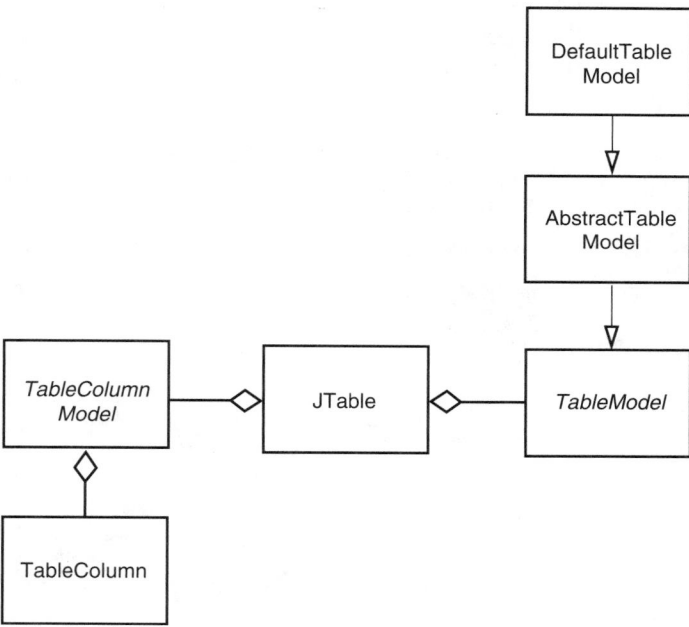

Figure 6–35: Relationship between Table classes

Finally, you can install the cell editor:

```
moonColumn.setCellEditor(moonEditor);
```

If your cells are taller than the default, you also want to set the row height:

```
table.setRowHeight(height);
```

By default, all rows of the table have the same height. You can set the heights of individual rows with the call

```
table.setRowHeight(row, height);
```

The actual row height equals the row height that has been set with these methods, reduced by the row margin. The default row margin is 1, but you can change it with the call

```
table.setRowMargin(margin);
```

To display an icon in the header, set the header value:

```
moonColumn.setHeaderValue(new ImageIcon("Moons.gif"));
```

However, the table header isn't smart enough to choose an appropriate renderer for the header value. You have to install the renderer manually. For example, to show an image icon in a column header, call

```
moonColumn.setHeaderRenderer(table.getDefaultRenderer(ImageIcon.class));
```

Custom Editors

Run the example program again and click on a color. A *color chooser* pops up to let you pick a new color for the planet. Select a color and click OK. The cell color is updated (see Figure 6–36).

The color cell editor is not a standard table cell editor but a custom implementation. To create a custom cell editor, you implement the `TableCellEditor` interface. That interface is a bit tedious, and as of JDK 1.3, an `AbstractCellEditor` class is provided to take care of the event handling details.

The `getTableCellEditorComponent` method of the `TableCellEditor` interface requests a component to render the cell. It is exactly the same as the `getTableCellRendererComponent` method of the `TableCellRenderer` interface, except that there is no focus parameter. Because the cell is being edited, it is presumed to have focus. The editor component temporarily *replaces* the renderer when the editing is in progress. In our example, we return a blank panel that is not colored. This is an indication to the user that the cell is currently being edited.

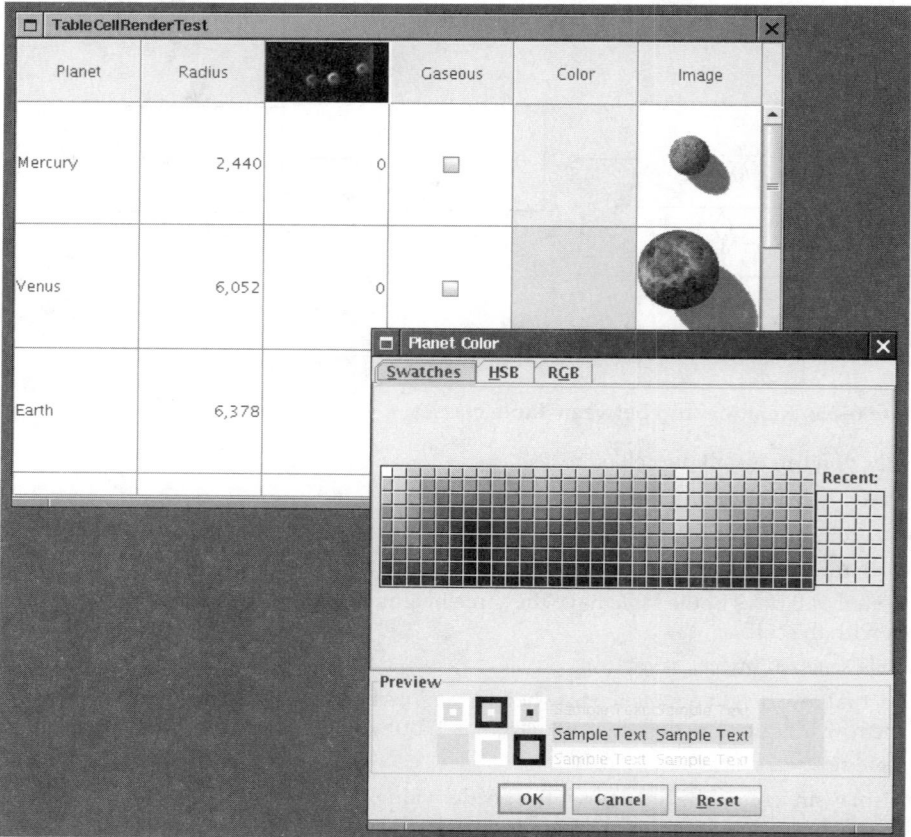

Figure 6–36: Editing the cell color with a color chooser

Next, you want to have your editor pop up when the user clicks on the cell.

The JTable class calls your editor with an event (such as a mouse click) to find out if that event is acceptable to initiate the editing process. The AbstractCellEditor class defines the method to accept all events.

```
public boolean isCellEditable(EventObject anEvent)
{
    return true;
}
```

However, if you override this method to false, then the table would not go through the trouble of inserting the editor component.

Once the editor component is installed, the shouldSelectCell method is called, presumably with the same event. You should initiate editing in this method, for example, by popping up an external edit dialog box.

```
public boolean shouldSelectCell(EventObject anEvent)
{
    colorDialog.setVisible(true);
    return true;
}
```

If the user cancels the edit, the table calls the cancelCellEditing method. If the user has clicked on another table cell, the table calls the stopCellEditing method. In both cases, you should hide the dialog box. When your stopCellEditing method is called, the table would like to use the partially edited value. You should return true if the current value is valid. In the color chooser, any value is valid. But if you edit other data, you can ensure that only valid data is retrieved from the editor.

Also, you should call the superclass methods that take care of event firing—otherwise, the editing won't be properly canceled.

```
public void cancelCellEditing()
{
    colorDialog.setVisible(false);
    super.cancelCellEditing();
}
```

Finally, you need to supply a method that yields the value that the user supplied in the editing process:

```
public Object getCellEditorValue()
{
    return colorChooser.getColor();
}
```

To summarize, your custom editor should do the following:

1. Extend the AbstractCellEditor class and implement the TableCellEditor interface.
2. Define the getTableCellEditorComponent method to supply a component. This can either be a dummy component (if you pop up a dialog box) or a component for in-place editing such as a combo box or text field.
3. Define the shouldSelectCell, stopCellEditing, and cancelCellEditing methods to handle the start, completion, and cancellation of the editing process. The stopCellEditing and cancel-CellEditing should call the superclass methods to ensure that listeners are notified.
4. Define the getCellEditorValue method to return the value that is the result of the editing process.

Finally, you indicate when the user is finished editing by calling the stopCellEditing and cancelCellEditing methods. When constructing the color dialog box, we install accept and cancel callbacks that fire these events.

```
colorDialog = JColorChooser.createDialog(null, "Planet Color", false, colorChooser,
   new
      ActionListener() // OK button listener
      {
         public void actionPerformed(ActionEvent event)
         {
            stopCellEditing();
         }
      },
   new
      ActionListener() // Cancel button listener
      {
         public void actionPerformed(ActionEvent event)
         {
            cancelCellEditing();
         }
      });
```

Also, when the user closes the dialog box, editing should be canceled. This is achieved by installation of a window listener:

```
colorDialog.addWindowListener(new
   WindowAdapter()
   {
      public void windowClosing(WindowEvent event)
      {
         cancelCellEditing();
      }
   });
```

This completes the implementation of the custom editor.

You now know how to make a cell editable and how to install an editor. There is one remaining issue—how to update the model with the value that the user edited. When editing is complete, the JTable class calls the following method of the table model:

```
void setValueAt(Object value, int r, int c)
```

You need to override the method to store the new value. The value parameter is the object that was returned by the cell editor. If you implemented the cell editor, then you know the type of the object that you return from the getCellEditorValue method. In the case of the DefaultCellEditor, there are three possibilities for that value. It is a Boolean if the cell editor is a checkbox, a string if it is a text field. If the value comes from a combo box, then it is the object that the user selected.

If the value object does not have the appropriate type, you need to convert it. That happens most commonly when a number is edited in a text field. In our example, we populated the combo box with Integer objects so that no conversion is necessary.

Example 6–13: TableCellRenderTest.java

```
1. import java.awt.*;
2. import java.awt.event.*;
3. import java.util.*;
4. import javax.swing.*;
5. import javax.swing.border.*;
6. import javax.swing.event.*;
```

```
 7. import javax.swing.table.*;
 8.
 9. /**
10.    This program demonstrates cell rendering and editing
11.    in a table.
12. */
13. public class TableCellRenderTest
14. {
15.    public static void main(String[] args)
16.    {
17.       JFrame frame = new TableCellRenderFrame();
18.       frame.setDefaultCloseOperation(JFrame.EXIT_ON_CLOSE);
19.       frame.setVisible(true);
20.    }
21. }
22.
23. /**
24.    This frame contains a table of planet data.
25. */
26. class TableCellRenderFrame extends JFrame
27. {
28.    public TableCellRenderFrame()
29.    {
30.       setTitle("TableCellRenderTest");
31.       setSize(DEFAULT_WIDTH, DEFAULT_HEIGHT);
32.
33.       TableModel model = new PlanetTableModel();
34.       JTable table = new JTable(model);
35.       table.setRowSelectionAllowed(false);
36.
37.       // set up renderers and editors
38.
39.       table.setDefaultRenderer(Color.class, new ColorTableCellRenderer());
40.       table.setDefaultEditor(Color.class, new ColorTableCellEditor());
41.
42.       JComboBox moonCombo = new JComboBox();
43.       for (int i = 0; i <= 20; i++)
44.          moonCombo.addItem(i);
45.
46.       TableColumnModel columnModel = table.getColumnModel();
47.       TableColumn moonColumn = columnModel.getColumn(PlanetTableModel.MOONS_COLUMN);
48.       moonColumn.setCellEditor(new DefaultCellEditor(moonCombo));
49.       moonColumn.setHeaderRenderer(table.getDefaultRenderer(ImageIcon.class));
50.       moonColumn.setHeaderValue(new ImageIcon("Moons.gif"));
51.
52.       // show table
53.
54.       table.setRowHeight(100);
55.       add(new JScrollPane(table), BorderLayout.CENTER);
56.    }
57.
58.    private static final int DEFAULT_WIDTH = 600;
59.    private static final int DEFAULT_HEIGHT = 400;
60. }
61.
62. /**
```

```
63.    The planet table model specifies the values, rendering
64.    and editing properties for the planet data.
65. */
66. class PlanetTableModel extends AbstractTableModel
67. {
68.    public String getColumnName(int c) { return columnNames[c]; }
69.    public Class getColumnClass(int c) { return cells[0][c].getClass(); }
70.    public int getColumnCount() { return cells[0].length; }
71.    public int getRowCount() { return cells.length; }
72.    public Object getValueAt(int r, int c) { return cells[r][c]; }
73.    public void setValueAt(Object obj, int r, int c) { cells[r][c] = obj; }
74.    public boolean isCellEditable(int r, int c)
75.    {
76.       return c == PLANET_COLUMN || c == MOONS_COLUMN || c == GASEOUS_COLUMN || c == COLOR_COLUMN;
77.    }
78.
79.    public static final int PLANET_COLUMN = 0;
80.    public static final int MOONS_COLUMN = 2;
81.    public static final int GASEOUS_COLUMN = 3;
82.    public static final int COLOR_COLUMN = 4;
83.
84.    private Object[][] cells =
85.    {
86.       { "Mercury", 2440.0,  0, false, Color.yellow, new ImageIcon("Mercury.gif") },
87.       { "Venus", 6052.0, 0, false, Color.yellow, new ImageIcon("Venus.gif") },
88.       { "Earth", 6378.0, 1, false, Color.blue, new ImageIcon("Earth.gif") },
89.       { "Mars", 3397.0, 2, false, Color.red, new ImageIcon("Mars.gif") },
90.       { "Jupiter", 71492.0, 16, true, Color.orange, new ImageIcon("Jupiter.gif") },
91.       { "Saturn", 60268.0, 18, true, Color.orange, new ImageIcon("Saturn.gif") },
92.       { "Uranus", 25559.0, 17, true, Color.blue, new ImageIcon("Uranus.gif") },
93.       { "Neptune", 24766.0, 8, true, Color.blue, new ImageIcon("Neptune.gif") },
94.       { "Pluto", 1137.0, 1, false, Color.black, new ImageIcon("Pluto.gif") }
95.    };
96.
97.    private String[] columnNames = { "Planet", "Radius", "Moons", "Gaseous", "Color", "Image" };
98. }
99.
100. /**
101.    This renderer renders a color value as a panel with the
102.    given color.
103. */
104. class ColorTableCellRenderer extends JPanel implements TableCellRenderer
105. {
106.    public Component getTableCellRendererComponent(JTable table, Object value, boolean isSelected,
107.       boolean hasFocus, int row, int column)
108.    {
109.       setBackground((Color) value);
110.       if (hasFocus)
111.          setBorder(UIManager.getBorder("Table.focusCellHighlightBorder"));
112.       else
113.          setBorder(null);
114.       return this;
115.    }
116. }
117.
118. /**
```

```
119.   This editor pops up a color dialog to edit a cell value
120. */
121. class ColorTableCellEditor extends AbstractCellEditor implements TableCellEditor
122. {
123.    public ColorTableCellEditor()
124.    {
125.       panel = new JPanel();
126.       // prepare color dialog
127.
128.       colorChooser = new JColorChooser();
129.       colorDialog = JColorChooser.createDialog(null, "Planet Color", false, colorChooser,
130.          new
131.             ActionListener() // OK button listener
132.             {
133.                public void actionPerformed(ActionEvent event) { stopCellEditing(); }
134.             },
135.          new
136.             ActionListener() // Cancel button listener
137.             {
138.                public void actionPerformed(ActionEvent event) { cancelCellEditing(); }
139.             });
140.       colorDialog.addWindowListener(new
141.          WindowAdapter()
142.          {
143.             public void windowClosing(WindowEvent event) { cancelCellEditing(); }
144.          });
145.    }
146.
147.    public Component getTableCellEditorComponent(JTable table,
148.       Object value, boolean isSelected, int row, int column)
149.    {
150.       // this is where we get the current Color value. We store it in the dialog in case the user
151.       // starts editing
152.       colorChooser.setColor((Color) value);
153.       return panel;
154.    }
155.
156.    public boolean shouldSelectCell(EventObject anEvent)
157.    {
158.       // start editing
159.       colorDialog.setVisible(true);
160.
161.       // tell caller it is ok to select this cell
162.       return true;
163.    }
164.
165.    public void cancelCellEditing()
166.    {
167.       // editing is canceled--hide dialog
168.       colorDialog.setVisible(false);
169.       super.cancelCellEditing();
170.    }
171.
172.    public boolean stopCellEditing()
173.    {
174.       // editing is complete--hide dialog
```

```
175.        colorDialog.setVisible(false);
176.        super.stopCellEditing();
177.
178.        // tell caller is is ok to use color value
179.        return true;
180.    }
181.
182.    public Object getCellEditorValue()
183.    {
184.        return colorChooser.getColor();
185.    }
186.
187.    private Color color;
188.    private JColorChooser colorChooser;
189.    private JDialog colorDialog;
190.    private JPanel panel;
191. }
```

 javax.swing.JTable 1.2

- void setRowHeight(int height)
  sets the height of all rows of the table to height pixels.
- void setRowHeight(int row, int height)
  sets the height of the given row of the table to height pixels.
- void setRowMargin(int margin)
  sets the amount of empty space between cells in adjacent rows.
- int getRowHeight()
  gets the default height of all rows of the table.
- int getRowHeight(int row)
  gets the height of the given row of the table.
- int getRowMargin()
  gets the amount of empty space between cells in adjacent rows.
- Rectangle getCellRect(int row, int column, boolean includeSpacing)
  returns the bounding rectangle of a table cell.

  | *Parameters:* | row, column | The row and column of the cell |
  | | includeSpacing | true if the space around the cell should be included |

- Color getSelectionBackground()
- Color getSelectionForeground()
  return the background and foreground colors to use for selected cells.
- TableCellRenderer getDefaultRenderer(Class<?> type)
  gets the default renderer for the given type.
- TableCellEditor getDefaultEditor(Class<?> type)
  gets the default editor for the given type.

javax.swing.table.TableModel 1.2

- Class getColumnClass(int columnIndex)
  gets the class for the values in this column. This information is used by the cell renderer and editor.

javax.swing.table.TableCellRenderer 1.2

- Component getTableCellRendererComponent(JTable table, Object value, boolean selected, boolean hasFocus, int row, int column)
  returns a component whose paint method is invoked to render a table cell.

Parameters:	table	The table containing the cell to be rendered
	value	The cell to be rendered
	selected	true if the cell is currently selected
	hasFocus	true if the cell currently has focus
	row, column	The row and column of the cell

javax.swing.table.TableColumnModel 1.2

- TableColumn getColumn(int index)
  gets the table column object that describes the column with the given index.

javax.swing.table.TableColumn 1.2

- void setCellEditor(TableCellEditor editor)
- void setCellRenderer(TableCellRenderer renderer)
  set the cell editor or renderer for all cells in this column.

- void setHeaderRenderer(TableCellRenderer renderer)
  sets the cell renderer for the header cell in this column.

- void setHeaderValue(Object value)
  sets the value to be displayed for the header in this column.

javax.swing.DefaultCellEditor 1.2

- DefaultCellEditor(JComboBox comboBox)
  constructs a cell editor that presents the combo box for selecting cell values.

javax.swing.CellEditor 1.2

- boolean isCellEditable(EventObject event)
  returns true if the event is suitable for initiating the editing process for this cell.

- boolean shouldSelectCell(EventObject anEvent)
  starts the editing process. Returns true if the edited cell should be *selected*. Normally, you want to return true, but you can return false if you don't want the editing process to change the cell selection.

- void cancelCellEditing()
  cancels the editing process. You can abandon partial edits.

- boolean stopCellEditing()
  stops the editing process, with the intent of using the result. Returns true if the edited value is in a proper state for retrieval.

- Object getCellEditorValue()
  returns the edited result.

- void addCellEditorListener(CellEditorListener l)
- void removeCellEditorListener(CellEditorListener l)
  add and remove the obligatory cell editor listener.

javax.swing.table.TableCellEditor 1.2

- Component getTableCellEditorComponent(JTable table, Object value, boolean selected, int row, int column)

  returns a component whose paint method renders a table cell.

Parameters:	table	The table containing the cell to be rendered
	value	The cell to be rendered
	selected	true if the cell is currently selected
	row, column	The row and column of the cell

Working with Rows and Columns

In this subsection, you will see how to manipulate the rows and columns in a table. As you read through this material, keep in mind that a Swing table is quite asymmetric—there are different operations that you can carry out on rows and columns. The table component was optimized to display rows of information with the same structure, such as the result of a database query, not an arbitrary two-dimensional grid of objects. You will see this asymmetry throughout this subsection.

Resizing Columns

The TableColumn class gives you control over the resizing behavior of columns. You can set the preferred, minimum, and maximum width with the methods

```
void setPreferredWidth(int width)
void setMinWidth(int width)
void setMaxWidth(int width)
```

This information is used by the table component to lay out the columns.

Use the method

```
void setResizable(boolean resizable)
```

to control whether the user is allowed to resize the column.

You can programmatically resize a column with the method

```
void setWidth(int width)
```

When a column is resized, the default is to leave the total size of the table unchanged. Of course, the width increase or decrease of the resized column must then be distributed over other columns. The default behavior is to change the size of all columns to the right of the resized column. That's a good default because it allows a user to adjust all columns to a desired width, moving from left to right.

You can set another behavior from Table 6–2 by using the method

```
void setAutoResizeMode(int mode)
```

of the JTable class.

Table 6–2: Resize Modes

Mode	Behavior
AUTO_RESIZE_OFF	Don't resize other columns; change the table size
AUTO_RESIZE_NEXT_COLUMN	Resize the next column only
AUTO_RESIZE_SUBSEQUENT_COLUMNS	Resize all subsequent columns equally; this is the default behavior

Table 6–2: Resize Modes (continued)

AUTO_RESIZE_LAST_COLUMN	Resize the last column only
AUTO_RESIZE_ALL_COLUMNS	Resize all columns in the table; this is not a good choice because it poses challenges to the user to adjust multiple columns to a desired size

Selecting Rows, Columns, and Cells

Depending on the selection mode, the user can select rows, columns, or individual cells in the table. By default, row selection is enabled. Clicking inside a cell selects the entire row (see Figure 6–37). Call

```
table.setRowSelectionAllowed(false)
```

to disable row selection.

When row selection is enabled, you can control whether the user is allowed to select a single row, a contiguous set of rows, or any set of rows. You need to retrieve the *selection model* and use its setSelectionMode method:

```
table.getSelectionModel().setSelectionMode(mode);
```

Figure 6–37: Selecting a row

Here, mode is one of the three values:

```
ListSelectionModel.SINGLE_SELECTION
ListSelectionModel.SINGLE_INTERVAL_SELECTION
ListSelectionModel.MULTIPLE_INTERVAL_SELECTION
```

Column selection is disabled by default. You turn it on with the call

```
table.setColumnSelectionAllowed(true)
```

Enabling both row and column selection is equivalent to enabling cell selection. The user then selects ranges of cells (see Figure 6–38). You can also enable that setting with the call

```
table.setCellSelectionEnabled(true)
```

NOTE: In early versions of the Swing toolkit, when you set both row and column selections, every mouse click selected a "+" shaped area consisting of both the row and the column containing the cursor.

Figure 6–38: Selecting a range of cells

You can find out which rows and columns are selected by calling the getSelectedRows and get-SelectedColumns methods. Both return an int[] array of the indexes of the selected items.

You can run the program in Example 6–14 to watch cell selection in action. Enable row, column, or cell selection in the Selection menu and watch how the selection behavior changes.

Hiding and Displaying Columns

The removeColumn method of the JTable class removes a column from the table view. The column data is not actually removed from the model—it is just hidden from view. The remove-Column method takes a TableColumn argument. If you have the column number (for example, from a call to getSelectedColumns), you need to ask the table model for the actual table column object:

```
TableColumnModel columnModel = table.getColumnModel();
TableColumn column = columnModel.getColumn(i);
table.removeColumn(column);
```

If you remember the column, you can later add it back in:

```
table.addColumn(column);
```

This method adds the column to the end. If you want it to appear elsewhere, you call the moveColumn method.

You can also add a new column that corresponds to a column index in the table model, by adding a new TableColumn object:

```
table.addColumn(new TableColumn(modelColumnIndex));
```

You can have multiple table columns that view the same column of the model.

There are no JTable methods for hiding or showing rows. If you want to hide rows, you can create a filter model similar to the sort filter that you saw earlier.

Adding and Removing Rows in the Default Table Model

The DefaultTableModel class is a concrete class that implements the TableModel interface. It stores a two-dimensional grid of objects. If your data are already in a tabular arrangement, then there is no point in copying all the data into a DefaultTableModel, but the class is handy if you quickly need to make a table from a small data set. The DefaultTableModel class has methods for adding rows and columns, and for removing rows.

The addRow and addColumn methods add a row or column of new data. You supply an Object[] array or a vector that holds the new data. With the addColumn method, you also supply a name for the new column. These methods add the new data to the end of the grid. To insert

a row in the middle, use the insertRow method. There is no method for inserting a column in the middle of the grid.

Conversely, the removeRow method removes a row from the model. There is no method for removing a column.

Because the JTable object registers itself as a table model listener, the model notifies the table when data are inserted or removed. At that time, the table refreshes the display.

The program in Example 6–14 shows both selection and editing at work. A default table model contains a simple data set (a multiplication table). The Edit menu contains these commands:

- Hide all selected columns.
- Show all columns that you've ever hidden.
- Remove selected rows from the model.
- Add a row of data to the end of the model.

This example concludes the discussion of Swing tables. Tables are conceptually a bit easier to grasp than trees because the underlying data model—a grid of objects—is easy to visualize. However, under the hood, the table component is actually quite a bit more complex than the tree component. Column headers, resizable columns, and column-specific renderers and editors all add to the complexity. In this section, we focused on those topics that you are most likely to encounter in practice: displaying database information, sorting, and custom cell rendering and editing. If you have special advanced needs, we once again refer you to *Core Java Foundation Classes* by Kim Topley and *Graphic Java 2* by David Geary.

Example 6–14: TableSelectionTest.java

```
1. import java.awt.*;
2. import java.awt.event.*;
3. import java.util.*;
4. import java.text.*;
5. import javax.swing.*;
6. import javax.swing.table.*;
7.
8. /**
9.    This program demonstrates selection, addition, and removal of rows and columns.
10. */
11. public class TableSelectionTest
12. {
13.    public static void main(String[] args)
14.    {
15.       JFrame frame = new TableSelectionFrame();
16.       frame.setDefaultCloseOperation(JFrame.EXIT_ON_CLOSE);
17.       frame.setVisible(true);
18.    }
19. }
20.
21. /**
22.    This frame shows a multiplication table and has menus for setting the row/column/cell selection
23.    modes, and for adding and removing rows and columns.
24. */
25. class TableSelectionFrame extends JFrame
26. {
27.    public TableSelectionFrame()
28.    {
29.       setTitle("TableSelectionTest");
```

```
30.     setSize(DEFAULT_WIDTH, DEFAULT_HEIGHT);
31.
32.     // set up multiplication table
33.
34.     model = new DefaultTableModel(10, 10);
35.
36.     for (int i = 0; i < model.getRowCount(); i++)
37.        for (int j = 0; j < model.getColumnCount(); j++)
38.           model.setValueAt((i + 1) * (j + 1), i, j);
39.
40.     table = new JTable(model);
41.
42.     add(new JScrollPane(table), "Center");
43.
44.     removedColumns = new ArrayList<TableColumn>();
45.
46.     // create menu
47.
48.     JMenuBar menuBar = new JMenuBar();
49.     setJMenuBar(menuBar);
50.
51.     JMenu selectionMenu = new JMenu("Selection");
52.     menuBar.add(selectionMenu);
53.
54.     final JCheckBoxMenuItem rowsItem = new JCheckBoxMenuItem("Rows");
55.     final JCheckBoxMenuItem columnsItem = new JCheckBoxMenuItem("Columns");
56.     final JCheckBoxMenuItem cellsItem = new JCheckBoxMenuItem("Cells");
57.
58.     rowsItem.setSelected(table.getRowSelectionAllowed());
59.     columnsItem.setSelected(table.getColumnSelectionAllowed());
60.     cellsItem.setSelected(table.getCellSelectionEnabled());
61.
62.     rowsItem.addActionListener(new
63.        ActionListener()
64.        {
65.           public void actionPerformed(ActionEvent event)
66.           {
67.              table.clearSelection();
68.              table.setRowSelectionAllowed(rowsItem.isSelected());
69.              cellsItem.setSelected(table.getCellSelectionEnabled());
70.           }
71.        });
72.     selectionMenu.add(rowsItem);
73.
74.     columnsItem.addActionListener(new
75.        ActionListener()
76.        {
77.           public void actionPerformed(ActionEvent event)
78.           {
79.              table.clearSelection();
80.              table.setColumnSelectionAllowed(columnsItem.isSelected());
81.              cellsItem.setSelected(table.getCellSelectionEnabled());
82.           }
83.        });
84.     selectionMenu.add(columnsItem);
```

```
85.
86.    cellsItem.addActionListener(new
87.       ActionListener()
88.       {
89.          public void actionPerformed(ActionEvent event)
90.          {
91.             table.clearSelection();
92.             table.setCellSelectionEnabled(cellsItem.isSelected());
93.             rowsItem.setSelected(table.getRowSelectionAllowed());
94.             columnsItem.setSelected(table.getColumnSelectionAllowed());
95.          }
96.       });
97.    selectionMenu.add(cellsItem);
98.
99.    JMenu tableMenu = new JMenu("Edit");
100.   menuBar.add(tableMenu);
101.
102.   JMenuItem hideColumnsItem = new JMenuItem("Hide Columns");
103.   hideColumnsItem.addActionListener(new
104.      ActionListener()
105.      {
106.         public void actionPerformed(ActionEvent event)
107.         {
108.            int[] selected = table.getSelectedColumns();
109.            TableColumnModel columnModel = table.getColumnModel();
110.
111.            // remove columns from view, starting at the last
112.            // index so that column numbers aren't affected
113.
114.
115.            for (int i = selected.length - 1; i >= 0; i--)
116.            {
117.               TableColumn column = columnModel.getColumn(selected[i]);
118.               table.removeColumn(column);
119.
120.               // store removed columns for "show columns" command
121.
122.               removedColumns.add(column);
123.            }
124.         }
125.      });
126.   tableMenu.add(hideColumnsItem);
127.
128.   JMenuItem showColumnsItem = new JMenuItem("Show Columns");
129.   showColumnsItem.addActionListener(new
130.      ActionListener()
131.      {
132.         public void actionPerformed(ActionEvent event)
133.         {
134.            // restore all removed columns
135.            for (TableColumn tc : removedColumns)
136.               table.addColumn(tc);
137.            removedColumns.clear();
138.         }
139.      });
```

```
140.        tableMenu.add(showColumnsItem);
141.
142.        JMenuItem addRowItem = new JMenuItem("Add Row");
143.        addRowItem.addActionListener(new
144.           ActionListener()
145.           {
146.              public void actionPerformed(ActionEvent event)
147.              {
148.                 // add a new row to the multiplication table in
149.                 // the model
150.
151.                 Integer[] newCells = new Integer[model.getColumnCount()];
152.                 for (int i = 0; i < newCells.length; i++)
153.                    newCells[i] = (i + 1) * (model.getRowCount() + 1);
154.                 model.addRow(newCells);
155.              }
156.           });
157.        tableMenu.add(addRowItem);
158.
159.        JMenuItem removeRowsItem = new  JMenuItem("Remove Rows");
160.        removeRowsItem.addActionListener(new
161.           ActionListener()
162.           {
163.              public void actionPerformed(ActionEvent event)
164.              {
165.                 int[] selected = table.getSelectedRows();
166.
167.                 for (int i = selected.length - 1; i >= 0; i--)
168.                    model.removeRow(selected[i]);
169.              }
170.           });
171.        tableMenu.add(removeRowsItem);
172.
173.        JMenuItem clearCellsItem = new  JMenuItem("Clear Cells");
174.        clearCellsItem.addActionListener(new
175.           ActionListener()
176.           {
177.              public void actionPerformed(ActionEvent event)
178.              {
179.                 for (int i = 0; i < table.getRowCount(); i++)
180.                    for (int j = 0; j < table.getColumnCount(); j++)
181.                       if (table.isCellSelected(i, j))
182.                          table.setValueAt(0, i, j);
183.              }
184.           });
185.        tableMenu.add(clearCellsItem);
186.     }
187.
188.     private DefaultTableModel model;
189.     private JTable table;
190.     private ArrayList<TableColumn> removedColumns;
191.
192.     private static final int DEFAULT_WIDTH = 400;
193.     private static final int DEFAULT_HEIGHT = 300;
194. }
```

API **javax.swing.JTable** 1.2

- void setAutoResizeMode(int mode)
  sets the mode for automatic resizing of table columns.

  Parameters: mode   One of AUTO_RESIZE_OFF, AUTO_RESIZE_NEXT_COLUMN,
                                    AUTO_RESIZE_SUBSEQUENT_COLUMNS, AUTO_RESIZE_LAST_COLUMN,
                                    AUTO_RESIZE_ALL_COLUMNS

- ListSelectionModel getSelectionModel()
  returns the list selection model. You need that model to choose between row, column, and cell selection.

- void setRowSelectionAllowed(boolean b)
  If b is true, then rows can be selected when the user clicks on cells.

- void setColumnSelectionAllowed(boolean b)
  If b is true, then columns can be selected when the user clicks on cells.

- void setCellSelectionEnabled(boolean b)
  If b is true, then individual cells are selected. This is equivalent to calling both setRowSelectionAllowed(b) and setColumnSelectionAllowed(b).

- boolean getRowSelectionAllowed()
  returns true if row selection is allowed.

- boolean getColumnSelectionAllowed()
  returns true if column selection is allowed.

- boolean getCellSelectionEnabled()
  returns true if both row and column selection are allowed.

- void clearSelection()
  unselects all selected rows and columns.

- void addColumn(TableColumn column)
  adds a column to the table view.

- void moveColumn(int from, int to)
  moves the column at table index from so that its index becomes to. Only the view is affected.

- void removeColumn(TableColumn column)
  removes the given column from the view.

API **javax.swing.table.TableColumn** 1.2

- TableColumn(int modelColumnIndex)
  constructs a table column for viewing the model column with the given index.

- void setPreferredWidth(int width)
- void setMinWidth(int width)
- void setMaxWidth(int width)
  set the preferred, minimum, and maximum width of this table column to width.

- void setWidth(int width)
  sets the actual width of this column to width.

- void setResizable(boolean b)
  If b is true, this column is resizable.

 javax.swing.ListSelectionModel 1.2

- void setSelectionMode(int mode)

  Parameters: mode   One of SINGLE_SELECTION, SINGLE_INTERVAL_SELECTION, and MULTIPLE_INTERVAL_SELECTION

 javax.swing.table.DefaultTableModel 1.2

- void addRow(Object[] rowData)
- void addColumn(Object columnName, Object[] columnData)

  add a row or column of data to the end of the table model.

- void insertRow(int row, Object[] rowData)

  adds a row of data at index row.

- void removeRow(int row)

  removes the given row from the model.

- void moveRow(int start, int end, int to)

  moves all rows with indexes between start and end to a new location starting at to.

Styled Text Components

In Volume 1, we discussed the basic text component classes JTextField and JTextArea. Of course, these classes are very useful for obtaining text input from the user. Another useful class, JEditorPane, displays and edits text in HTML and RTF format. (RTF is the "rich text format" that is used by a number of Microsoft applications for document interchange. It is a poorly documented format that doesn't work well even between Microsoft's own applications. We do not cover the RTF capabilities in this book.)

Frankly, at this point, the JEditorPane is limited. The HTML renderer can display simple files, but it chokes at many complex pages that you typically find on the Web. The HTML editor is limited and unstable.

We think that the perfect application for the JEditorPane is to display program help in HTML format. Because you have control over the help files that you provide, you can stay away from features that the JEditorPane does not display well.

 NOTE: For more information on an industrial-strength help system, check out JavaHelp at http://java.sun.com/products/javahelp/index.html.

 NOTE: The subclass JTextPane of JEditorPane can hold styled text with special fonts and text formats, as well as embedded components. We do not cover that component in this book. If you need to implement a component that allows users of your program to enter styled text, look at the implementation of the StylePad demo that is included in the JDK.

The program in Example 6–15 contains an editor pane that shows the contents of an HTML page. Type a URL into the text field. The URL must start with http: or file:. Then, click the Load button. The selected HTML page is displayed in the editor pane (see Figure 6–39).

The hyperlinks are active: If you click on a link, the application loads it. The Back button returns to the previous page.

This program is in fact a very simple browser. Of course, it does not have any of the comfort features, such as page caching or bookmark lists, that you expect from a commercial browser. The editor pane does not even display applets!

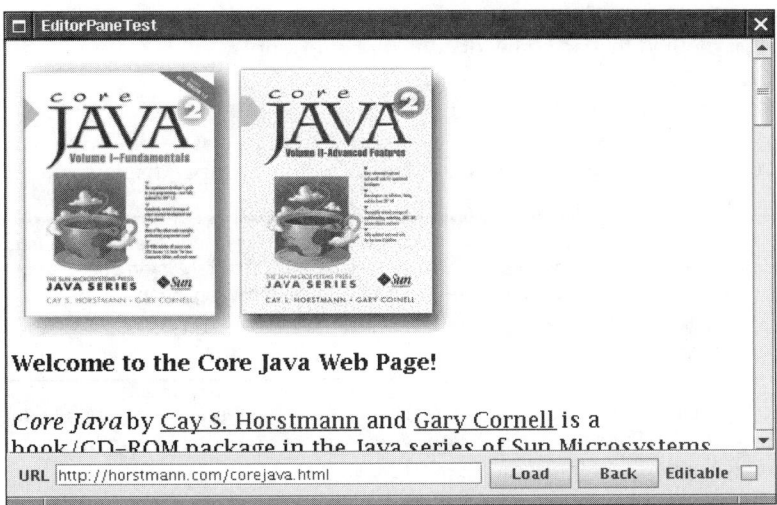

Figure 6–39: The editor pane displaying an HTML page

If you click on the Editable checkbox, then the editor pane becomes editable. You can type in text and use the BACKSPACE key to delete text. The component also understands the CTRL+X, CTRL+C, and CTRL+V shortcuts for cut, copy, and paste. However, you would have to do quite a bit of programming to add support for fonts and formatting.

When the component is editable, then hyperlinks are not active. Also, with some web pages you can see JavaScript commands, comments, and other tags when edit mode is turned on (see Figure 6–40). The example program lets you investigate the editing feature, but we recommend that you omit that feature in your programs.

 TIP: By default, the JEditorPane is in edit mode. You should call editorPane.setEditable(false) to turn it off.

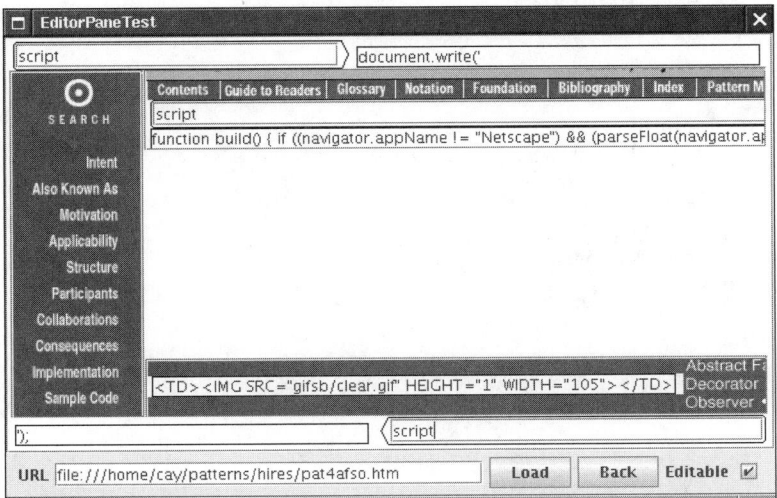

Figure 6–40: The editor pane in edit mode

The features of the editor pane that you saw in the example program are easy to use. You use the setPage method to load a new document. For example,

```
JEditorPane editorPane = new JEditorPane();
editorPane.setPage(url);
```

The parameter is either a string or a URL object. The JEditorPane class extends the JTextComponent class. Therefore, you can call the setText method as well—it simply displays plain text.

 TIP: The API documentation is unclear about whether setPage loads the new document in a separate thread (which is generally what you want—the JEditorPane is no speed demon). However, you can force loading in a separate thread with the following incantation:

```
AbstractDocument doc = (AbstractDocument) editorPane.getDocument();
doc.setAsynchronousLoadPriority(0);
```

To listen to hyperlink clicks, you add a HyperlinkListener. The HyperlinkListener interface has a single method, hyperlinkUpdate, that is called when the user moves over or clicks on a link. The method has a parameter of type HyperlinkEvent.

You need to call the getEventType method to find out what kind of event occurred. There are three possible return values:

```
HyperlinkEvent.EventType.ACTIVATED
HyperlinkEvent.EventType.ENTERED
HyperlinkEvent.EventType.EXITED
```

The first value indicates that the user clicked on the hyperlink. In that case, you typically want to open the new link. You can use the second and third values to give some visual feedback, such as a tooltip, when the mouse hovers over the link.

 NOTE: It is a complete mystery why there aren't three separate methods to handle activation, entry, and exit in the HyperlinkListener interface.

The getURL method of the HyperlinkEvent class returns the URL of the hyperlink. For example, here is how you can install a hyperlink listener that follows the links that a user activates:

```
editorPane.addHyperlinkListener(new
   HyperlinkListener()
   {
      public void hyperlinkUpdate(HyperlinkEvent event)
      {
         if (event.getEventType()
            == HyperlinkEvent.EventType.ACTIVATED)
         {
            try
            {
               editorPane.setPage(event.getURL());
            }
            catch (IOException e)
            {
               editorPane.setText("Exception: " + e);
            }
         }
      }
   });
```

The event handler simply gets the URL and updates the editor pane. The setPage method can throw an IOException. In that case, we display an error message as plain text.

The program in Example 6–15 shows all the features that you need to put together an HTML help system. Under the hood, the JEditorPane is even more complex than the tree and table components. However, if you don't need to write a text editor or a renderer of a custom text format, that complexity is hidden from you.

Example 6–15: EditorPaneTest.java

```
1.  import java.awt.*;
2.  import java.awt.event.*;
3.  import java.io.*;
4.  import java.net.*;
5.  import java.util.*;
6.  import javax.swing.*;
7.  import javax.swing.event.*;
8.
9.  /**
10.    This program demonstrates how to display HTML documents
11.    in an editor pane.
12.  */
13.  public class EditorPaneTest
14.  {
15.     public static void main(String[] args)
16.     {
17.        JFrame frame = new EditorPaneFrame();
18.        frame.setDefaultCloseOperation(JFrame.EXIT_ON_CLOSE);
19.        frame.setVisible(true);
20.     }
21.  }
22.
23.  /**
24.    This frame contains an editor pane, a text field and button
25.    to enter a URL and load a document, and a Back button to
26.    return to a previously loaded document.
27.  */
28.  class EditorPaneFrame extends JFrame
29.  {
30.     public EditorPaneFrame()
31.     {
32.        setTitle("EditorPaneTest");
33.        setSize(DEFAULT_WIDTH, DEFAULT_HEIGHT);
34.
35.        final Stack<String> urlStack = new Stack<String>();
36.        final JEditorPane editorPane = new JEditorPane();
37.        final JTextField url = new JTextField(30);
38.
39.        // set up hyperlink listener
40.
41.        editorPane.setEditable(false);
42.        editorPane.addHyperlinkListener(new
43.           HyperlinkListener()
44.           {
45.              public void hyperlinkUpdate(HyperlinkEvent event)
46.              {
47.                 if (event.getEventType() == HyperlinkEvent.EventType.ACTIVATED)
```

```
48.               {
49.                   try
50.                   {
51.                       // remember URL for back button
52.                       urlStack.push(event.getURL().toString());
53.                       // show URL in text field
54.                       url.setText(event.getURL().toString());
55.                       editorPane.setPage(event.getURL());
56.                   }
57.                   catch (IOException e)
58.                   {
59.                       editorPane.setText("Exception: " + e);
60.                   }
61.               }
62.           }
63.       });
64.
65.       // set up checkbox for toggling edit mode
66.
67.       final JCheckBox editable = new JCheckBox();
68.       editable.addActionListener(new
69.           ActionListener()
70.           {
71.               public void actionPerformed(ActionEvent event)
72.               {
73.                   editorPane.setEditable(editable.isSelected());
74.               }
75.           });
76.
77.       // set up load button for loading URL
78.
79.       ActionListener listener = new
80.           ActionListener()
81.           {
82.               public void actionPerformed(ActionEvent event)
83.               {
84.                   try
85.                   {
86.                       // remember URL for back button
87.                       urlStack.push(url.getText());
88.                       editorPane.setPage(url.getText());
89.                   }
90.                   catch (IOException e)
91.                   {
92.                       editorPane.setText("Exception: " + e);
93.                   }
94.               }
95.           };
96.
97.       JButton loadButton = new JButton("Load");
98.       loadButton.addActionListener(listener);
99.       url.addActionListener(listener);
100.
101.      // set up back button and button action
102.
103.      JButton backButton = new JButton("Back");
```

```
104.    backButton.addActionListener(new
105.        ActionListener()
106.        {
107.           public void actionPerformed(ActionEvent event)
108.           {
109.              if (urlStack.size() <= 1) return;
110.              try
111.              {
112.                 // get URL from back button
113.                 urlStack.pop();
114.                 // show URL in text field
115.                 String urlString = urlStack.peek();
116.                 url.setText(urlString);
117.                 editorPane.setPage(urlString);
118.              }
119.              catch (IOException e)
120.              {
121.                 editorPane.setText("Exception: " + e);
122.              }
123.           }
124.        });
125.
126.    add(new JScrollPane(editorPane), BorderLayout.CENTER);
127.
128.    // put all control components in a panel
129.
130.    JPanel panel = new JPanel();
131.    panel.add(new JLabel("URL"));
132.    panel.add(url);
133.    panel.add(loadButton);
134.    panel.add(backButton);
135.    panel.add(new JLabel("Editable"));
136.    panel.add(editable);
137.
138.    add(panel, BorderLayout.SOUTH);
139.    }
140.
141.    private static final int DEFAULT_WIDTH = 600;
142.    private static final int DEFAULT_HEIGHT = 400;
143. }
```

---

javax.swing.JEditorPane 1.2

- void setPage(URL url)

  loads the page from url into the editor pane.

- void addHyperlinkListener(HyperLinkListener listener)

  adds a hyperlink listener to this editor pane.

javax.swing.event.HyperlinkListener 1.2

- void hyperlinkUpdate(HyperlinkEvent event)

  is called whenever a hyperlink was selected.

javax.swing.HyperlinkEvent 1.2

- URL getURL()

  returns the URL of the selected hyperlink.

Progress Indicators

In the following sections, we discuss three classes for indicating the progress of a slow activity. A JProgressBar is a Swing component that indicates progress. A ProgressMonitor is a dialog box that contains a progress bar. A ProgressMonitorInputStream displays a progress monitor dialog box while the stream is read.

Progress Bars

A *progress bar* is a simple component—just a rectangle that is partially filled with color to indicate the progress of an operation. By default, progress is indicated by a string *"n%"*. You can see a progress bar in the bottom right of Figure 6–41.

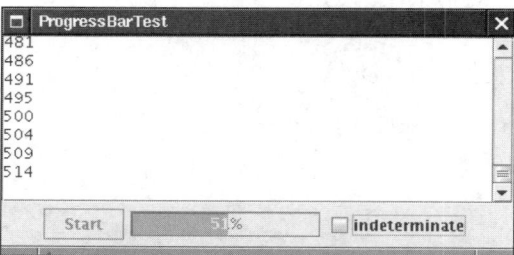

Figure 6–41: A progress bar

You construct a progress bar much as you construct a slider, by supplying the minimum and maximum value and an optional orientation:

```
progressBar = new JProgressBar(0, 1000);
progressBar = new JProgressBar(SwingConstants.VERTICAL, 0, 1000);
```

You can also set the minimum and maximum with the setMinimum and setMaximum methods.

Unlike a slider, the progress bar cannot be adjusted by the user. Your program needs to call setValue to update it.

If you call

```
progressBar.setStringPainted(true);
```

the progress bar computes the completion percentage and displays a string *"n%"*. If you want to show a different string, you can supply it with the setString method:

```
if (progressBar.getValue() > 900)
   progressBar.setString("Almost Done");
```

The program in Example 6–16 shows a progress bar that monitors a simulated time-consuming activity.

The SimulatedActivity class implements a thread that increments a value current 10 times per second. When it reaches a target value, the thread finishes. To terminate the thread before it has reached its target, you interrupt it.

```
class SimulatedActivity implements Runnable
{
   . . .
   public void run()
   {
      try
      {
         while (current < target && !interrupted())
```

```
        {
            Thread.sleep(100);
            current++;
        }
    }
    catch (InterruptedException e)
    {
    }
}

int current;
int target;
}
```

When you click the Start button, a new SimulatedActivity thread is started. Updating the progress bar would appear to be an easy matter—the simulated activity thread calls the setValue method. But that is not thread safe: Recall that you should call Swing methods only from the event dispatch thread. In practice, the apparent approach is also unrealistic: In general, a worker thread is not aware of the existence of the progress bar. Instead, the example program shows how to launch a timer that periodically polls the thread for a progress status and updates the progress bar.

 CAUTION: Remember that a worker thread cannot set the progress bar value directly. A worker thread must use the SwingUtilities.invokeLater method to set the progress bar value in the event dispatch thread.

Recall that a Swing timer calls the actionPerformed method of its listeners and that these calls occur in the event dispatch thread. That means it is safe to update Swing components in the timer callback. Here is the timer callback from the example program. The current value of the simulated activity is displayed both in the text area and the progress bar. If the end of the simulation has been reached, the timer is stopped and the Start button is reenabled.

```
public void actionPerformed(ActionEvent event)
{
    int current = activity.getCurrent();
    // show progress

    textArea.append(current + "\n");
    progressBar.setValue(current);

    // check if task is completed
    if (current == activity.getTarget())
    {
        activityMonitor.stop();
        startButton.setEnabled(true);
    }
}
```

JDK 1.4 adds support for an *indeterminate* progress bar that shows an animation indicating some kind of progress, without giving an indication of the percentage of completion. That is the kind of progress bar that you see in your browser—it indicates that the browser is waiting for the server and has no idea how long the wait may be. To display the "indeterminate wait" animation, call the setIndeterminate method.

Example 6–16 shows the full program code.

Example 6–16: ProgressBarTest.java

```java
1.  import java.awt.*;
2.  import java.awt.event.*;
3.  import java.util.*;
4.  import javax.swing.*;
5.  import javax.swing.event.*;
6.  import javax.swing.Timer;
7.
8.  /**
9.     This program demonstrates the use of a progress bar
10.    to monitor the progress of a thread.
11. */
12. public class ProgressBarTest
13. {
14.    public static void main(String[] args)
15.    {
16.       JFrame frame = new ProgressBarFrame();
17.       frame.setDefaultCloseOperation(JFrame.EXIT_ON_CLOSE);
18.       frame.setVisible(true);
19.    }
20. }
21.
22. /**
23.    A frame that contains a button to launch a simulated activity,
24.    a progress bar, and a text area for the activity output.
25. */
26. class ProgressBarFrame extends JFrame
27. {
28.    public ProgressBarFrame()
29.    {
30.       setTitle("ProgressBarTest");
31.       setSize(DEFAULT_WIDTH, DEFAULT_HEIGHT);
32.
33.       // this text area holds the activity output
34.       textArea = new JTextArea();
35.
36.       // set up panel with button and progress bar
37.
38.       JPanel panel = new JPanel();
39.       startButton = new JButton("Start");
40.       progressBar = new JProgressBar();
41.       progressBar.setStringPainted(true);
42.       panel.add(startButton);
43.       panel.add(progressBar);
44.
45.       checkBox = new JCheckBox("indeterminate");
46.       checkBox.addActionListener(new
47.          ActionListener()
48.          {
49.             public void actionPerformed(ActionEvent event)
50.             {
51.                progressBar.setIndeterminate(checkBox.isSelected());
52.             }
53.          });
54.       panel.add(checkBox);
```

```
55.         add(new JScrollPane(textArea), BorderLayout.CENTER);
56.         add(panel, BorderLayout.SOUTH);
57.
58.         // set up the button action
59.
60.         startButton.addActionListener(new
61.            ActionListener()
62.            {
63.               public void actionPerformed(ActionEvent event)
64.               {
65.                  progressBar.setMaximum(1000);
66.                  activity = new SimulatedActivity(1000);
67.                  new Thread(activity).start();
68.                  activityMonitor.start();
69.                  startButton.setEnabled(false);
70.               }
71.            });
72.
73.
74.         // set up the timer action
75.
76.         activityMonitor = new Timer(500, new
77.            ActionListener()
78.            {
79.               public void actionPerformed(ActionEvent event)
80.               {
81.                  int current = activity.getCurrent();
82.
83.                  // show progress
84.                  textArea.append(current + "\n");
85.                  progressBar.setStringPainted(!progressBar.isIndeterminate());
86.                  progressBar.setValue(current);
87.
88.                  // check if task is completed
89.                  if (current == activity.getTarget())
90.                  {
91.                     activityMonitor.stop();
92.                     startButton.setEnabled(true);
93.                  }
94.               }
95.            });
96.      }
97.
98.      private Timer activityMonitor;
99.      private JButton startButton;
100.     private JProgressBar progressBar;
101.     private JCheckBox checkBox;
102.     private JTextArea textArea;
103.     private SimulatedActivity activity;
104.
105.     public static final int DEFAULT_WIDTH = 400;
106.     public static final int DEFAULT_HEIGHT = 200;
107. }
108.
109. /**
110.     A simulated activity runnable.
```

```
111. */
112. class SimulatedActivity implements Runnable
113. {
114.    /**
115.       Constructs the simulated activity thread object. The
116.       thread increments a counter from 0 to a given target.
117.       @param t the target value of the counter.
118.    */
119.    public SimulatedActivity(int t)
120.    {
121.       current = 0;
122.       target = t;
123.    }
124.
125.    public int getTarget()
126.    {
127.       return target;
128.    }
129.
130.    public int getCurrent()
131.    {
132.       return current;
133.    }
134.
135.    public void run()
136.    {
137.       try
138.       {
139.          while (current < target)
140.          {
141.             Thread.sleep(100);
142.             current++;
143.          }
144.       }
145.       catch(InterruptedException e)
146.       {
147.       }
148.    }
149.
150.    private volatile int current;
151.    private int target;
152. }
```

Progress Monitors

A progress bar is a simple component that can be placed inside a window. In contrast, a ProgressMonitor is a complete dialog box that contains a progress bar (see Figure 6–42). The dialog box contains a Cancel button. If you click it, the monitor dialog box is closed. In addition, your program can query whether the user has canceled the dialog box and terminate the monitored action. (Note that the class name does not start with a "J".)

You construct a progress monitor by supplying the following:

- The parent component over which the dialog box should pop up;
- An object (which should be a string, icon, or component) that is displayed on the dialog box;

- An optional note to display below the object;
- The minimum and maximum values.

However, the progress monitor cannot measure progress or cancel an activity by itself. You still need to periodically set the progress value by calling the setProgress method. (This is the equivalent of the setValue method of the JProgressBar class.) As you update the progress value, you should also call the isCanceled method to see if the program user has clicked the Cancel button.

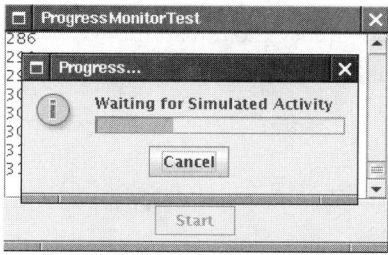

Figure 6–42: A progress monitor dialog box

When the monitored activity has concluded, call the close method to dismiss the dialog box. You can reuse the same dialog box by calling start again.

The example program looks very similar to that of the preceding section. We still need to launch a timer to watch over the progress of the simulated activity and update the progress monitor. Here is the timer callback.

```
public void actionPerformed(ActionEvent event)
{
    int current = activity.getCurrent();

    // show progress
    textArea.append(current + "\n");
    progressDialog.setProgress(current);

    // check if task is completed or canceled
    if (current == activity.getTarget() || progressDialog.isCanceled())
    {
        activityMonitor.stop();
        progressDialog.close();
        activity.interrupt();
        startButton.setEnabled(true);
    }
}
```

Note that there are two conditions for termination. The activity might have completed, or the user might have canceled it. In each of these cases, we close down

- the timer that monitored the activity;
- the progress dialog box;
- the activity itself (by interrupting the thread).

If you run the program in Example 6–17, you can observe an interesting feature of the progress monitor dialog box. The dialog box doesn't come up immediately. Instead, it waits for a short interval to see if the activity has already been completed or is likely to complete in less time than it would take for the dialog box to appear.

You control the timing as follows. Use the setMillisToDecideToPopup method to set the number of milliseconds to wait between the construction of the dialog object and the decision whether to show the pop-up at all. The default value is 500 milliseconds. The setMillisTo-Popup is your estimation of the time the dialog box needs to pop up. The Swing designers set this value to a default of 2 seconds. Clearly they were mindful of the fact that Swing dialogs don't always come up as snappily as we all would like. You should probably not touch this value.

Example 6–17 shows the progress monitor in action, again measuring the progress of a simulated activity. As you can see, the progress monitor is convenient to use and only requires that you periodically query the thread that you want to monitor.

Example 6–17: ProgressMonitorTest.java

```
 1. import java.awt.*;
 2. import java.awt.event.*;
 3. import java.util.*;
 4. import javax.swing.*;
 5. import javax.swing.event.*;
 6. import javax.swing.Timer;
 7.
 8. /**
 9.    A program to test a progress monitor dialog.
10. */
11. public class ProgressMonitorTest
12. {
13.    public static void main(String[] args)
14.    {
15.       JFrame frame = new ProgressMonitorFrame();
16.       frame.setDefaultCloseOperation(JFrame.EXIT_ON_CLOSE);
17.       frame.setVisible(true);
18.    }
19. }
20.
21. /**
22.    A frame that contains a button to launch a simulated activity
23.    and a text area for the activity output.
24. */
25. class ProgressMonitorFrame extends JFrame
26. {
27.    public ProgressMonitorFrame()
28.    {
29.       setTitle("ProgressMonitorTest");
30.       setSize(DEFAULT_WIDTH, DEFAULT_HEIGHT);
31.
32.       // this text area holds the activity output
33.       textArea = new JTextArea();
34.
35.       // set up a button panel
36.       JPanel panel = new JPanel();
37.       startButton = new JButton("Start");
38.       panel.add(startButton);
39.
40.       add(new JScrollPane(textArea), BorderLayout.CENTER);
41.       add(panel, BorderLayout.SOUTH);
42.
```

```
43.      // set up the button action
44.
45.      startButton.addActionListener(new
46.         ActionListener()
47.         {
48.            public void actionPerformed(ActionEvent event)
49.            {
50.               // start activity
51.               activity = new SimulatedActivity(1000);
52.               activityThread = new Thread(activity);
53.               activityThread.start();
54.
55.               // launch progress dialog
56.               progressDialog = new ProgressMonitor(ProgressMonitorFrame.this,
57.                  "Waiting for Simulated Activity", null, 0, activity.getTarget());
58.
59.               // start timer
60.               activityMonitor.start();
61.
62.               startButton.setEnabled(false);
63.            }
64.         });
65.
66.      // set up the timer action
67.
68.      activityMonitor = new Timer(500, new
69.         ActionListener()
70.         {
71.            public void actionPerformed(ActionEvent event)
72.            {
73.               int current = activity.getCurrent();
74.
75.               // show progress
76.               textArea.append(current + "\n");
77.               progressDialog.setProgress(current);
78.
79.               // check if task is completed or canceled
80.               if (current == activity.getTarget() || progressDialog.isCanceled())
81.               {
82.                  activityMonitor.stop();
83.                  progressDialog.close();
84.                  activityThread.interrupt();
85.                  startButton.setEnabled(true);
86.               }
87.            }
88.         });
89.   }
90.
91.   private Timer activityMonitor;
92.   private JButton startButton;
93.   private ProgressMonitor progressDialog;
94.   private JTextArea textArea;
95.   private Thread activityThread;
96.   private SimulatedActivity activity;
97.
98.   public static final int DEFAULT_WIDTH = 300;
```

```
 99.    public static final int DEFAULT_HEIGHT = 200;
100. }
101.
102. /**
103.    A simulated activity runnable.
104. */
105. class SimulatedActivity implements Runnable
106. {
107.    /**
108.       Constructs the simulated activity thread object. The
109.       thread increments a counter from 0 to a given target.
110.       @param t the target value of the counter.
111.    */
112.    public SimulatedActivity(int t)
113.    {
114.       current = 0;
115.       target = t;
116.    }
117.
118.    public int getTarget()
119.    {
120.       return target;
121.    }
122.
123.    public int getCurrent()
124.    {
125.       return current;
126.    }
127.
128.    public void run()
129.    {
130.       try
131.       {
132.          while (current < target)
133.          {
134.             Thread.sleep(100);
135.             current++;
136.          }
137.       }
138.       catch(InterruptedException e)
139.       {
140.       }
141.    }
142.
143.    private volatile int current;
144.    private int target;
145. }
```

Monitoring the Progress of Input Streams

The Swing package contains a useful stream filter, ProgressMonitorInputStream, that automatically pops up a dialog box that monitors how much of the stream has been read.

This filter is extremely easy to use. You sandwich in a ProgressMonitorInputStream between your usual sequence of filtered streams. (See Volume 1, Chapter 12 for more information on streams.)

For example, suppose you read text from a file. You start out with a FileInputStream:

```
FileInputStream in = new FileInputStream(f);
```

Normally, you would convert in to an InputStreamReader:

```
InputStreamReader reader = new InputStreamReader(in);
```

However, to monitor the stream, first turn the file input stream into a stream with a progress monitor:

```
ProgressMonitorInputStream progressIn = new ProgressMonitorInputStream(parent, caption, in);
```

You supply the parent component, a caption, and, of course, the stream to monitor. The read method of the progress monitor stream simply passes along the bytes and updates the progress dialog box.

You now go on building your filter sequence:

```
InputStreamReader reader = new InputStreamReader(progressIn);
```

That's all there is to it. When the file is read, the progress monitor automatically pops up (see Figure 6–43). This is a very nice application of stream filtering.

 CAUTION: The progress monitor stream uses the available method of the InputStream class to determine the total number of bytes in the stream. However, the available method only reports the number of bytes in the stream that are available *without blocking.* Progress monitors work well for files and HTTP URLs because their length is known in advance, but they don't work with all streams.

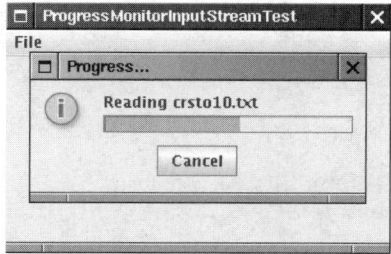

Figure 6–43: A progress monitor for an input stream

The program in Example 6–18 counts the lines in a file. If you read in a large file (such as "The Count of Monte Cristo" on the CD), then the progress dialog box pops up.

Note that the program doesn't use a very efficient way of filling up the text area. It would be faster to first read the file into a StringBuffer and then set the text of the text area to the string buffer contents. However, in this example program, we actually like this slow approach—it gives you more time to admire the progress dialog box.

To avoid flicker, we do not display the text area while it is filling up.

Example 6–18: ProgressMonitorInputStreamTest.java

```
1. import java.awt.*;
2. import java.awt.event.*;
3. import java.io.*;
4. import java.util.*;
5. import javax.swing.*;
6. import javax.swing.event.*;
7.
```

```
8.  /**
9.     A program to test a progress monitor input stream.
10. */
11. public class ProgressMonitorInputStreamTest
12. {
13.    public static void main(String[] args)
14.    {
15.       JFrame frame = new TextFrame();
16.       frame.setDefaultCloseOperation(JFrame.EXIT_ON_CLOSE);
17.       frame.setVisible(true);
18.    }
19. }
20.
21. /**
22.    A frame with a menu to load a text file and a text area
23.    to display its contents. The text area is constructed
24.    when the file is loaded and set as the content pane of
25.    the frame when the loading is complete. That avoids flicker
26.    during loading.
27. */
28. class TextFrame extends JFrame
29. {
30.    public TextFrame()
31.    {
32.       setTitle("ProgressMonitorInputStreamTest");
33.       setSize(DEFAULT_WIDTH, DEFAULT_HEIGHT);
34.
35.       // set up menu
36.
37.       JMenuBar menuBar = new JMenuBar();
38.       setJMenuBar(menuBar);
39.       JMenu fileMenu = new JMenu("File");
40.       menuBar.add(fileMenu);
41.       openItem = new JMenuItem("Open");
42.       openItem.addActionListener(new
43.          ActionListener()
44.          {
45.             public void actionPerformed(ActionEvent event)
46.             {
47.                try
48.                {
49.                   openFile();
50.                }
51.                catch(IOException exception)
52.                {
53.                   exception.printStackTrace();
54.                }
55.             }
56.          });
57.
58.       fileMenu.add(openItem);
59.       exitItem = new JMenuItem("Exit");
60.       exitItem.addActionListener(new
61.          ActionListener()
62.          {
63.             public void actionPerformed(ActionEvent event)
```

```
64.            {
65.                System.exit(0);
66.            }
67.        });
68.        fileMenu.add(exitItem);
69.    }
70.
71.    /**
72.       Prompts the user to select a file, loads the file into
73.       a text area, and sets it as the content pane of the frame.
74.    */
75.    public void openFile() throws IOException
76.    {
77.        JFileChooser chooser = new JFileChooser();
78.        chooser.setCurrentDirectory(new File("."));
79.        chooser.setFileFilter(
80.            new javax.swing.filechooser.FileFilter()
81.                {
82.                    public boolean accept(File f)
83.                    {
84.                        String fname = f.getName().toLowerCase();
85.                        return fname.endsWith(".txt") || f.isDirectory();
86.                    }
87.                    public String getDescription()
88.                    {
89.                        return "Text Files";
90.                    }
91.                });
92.
93.        int r = chooser.showOpenDialog(this);
94.        if (r != JFileChooser.APPROVE_OPTION) return;
95.        final File f = chooser.getSelectedFile();
96.
97.        // set up stream and reader filter sequence
98.
99.        FileInputStream fileIn = new FileInputStream(f);
100.       ProgressMonitorInputStream progressIn
101.           = new ProgressMonitorInputStream(this, "Reading " + f.getName(), fileIn);
102.       final Scanner in = new Scanner(progressIn);
103.
104.       // the monitored activity must be in a new thread.
105.
106.       Runnable readRunnable = new
107.           Runnable()
108.           {
109.               public void run()
110.               {
111.                   final JTextArea textArea = new JTextArea();
112.
113.                   while (in.hasNextLine())
114.                   {
115.                       String line = in.nextLine();
116.                       textArea.append(line);
117.                       textArea.append("\n");
118.                   }
119.                   in.close();
```

```
120.
121.                    // set content pane in the event dispatch thread
122.                    EventQueue.invokeLater(new
123.                       Runnable()
124.                       {
125.                          public void run()
126.                          {
127.                             setContentPane(new JScrollPane(textArea));
128.                             validate();
129.                          }
130.                       });
131.
132.               }
133.            };
134.
135.        Thread readThread = new Thread(readRunnable);
136.        readThread.start();
137.     }
138.
139.     private JMenuItem openItem;
140.     private JMenuItem exitItem;
141.
142.     public static final int DEFAULT_WIDTH = 300;
143.     public static final int DEFAULT_HEIGHT = 200;
144. }
```

API javax.swing.JProgressBar 1.2

- JProgressBar()
- JProgressBar(int direction)
- JProgressBar(int min, int max)
- JProgressBar(int direction, int min, int max)

  construct a slider with the given direction, minimum, and maximum.

Parameters:	direction	One of SwingConstants.HORIZONTAL or SwingConstants.VERTICAL. The default is horizontal
	min, max	The minimum and maximum for the progress bar values. Defaults are 0 and 100

- int getMinimum()
- int getMaximum()
- void setMinimum(int value)
- void setMaximum(int value)

  get and set the minimum and maximum values.

- int getValue()
- void setValue(int value)

  get and set the current value.

- String getString()
- void setString(String s)

  get and set the string to be displayed in the progress bar. If the string is null, then a default string "*n*%" is displayed.

- boolean isStringPainted()
- void setStringPainted(boolean b)

  get and set the "string painted" property. If this property is true, then a string is painted on top of the progress bar. The default is false; no string is painted.

- boolean isIndeterminate() **1.4**
- void setIndeterminate(boolean b) **1.4**
  get and set the "indeterminate" property. If this property is true, then the progress bar becomes a block that moves backward and forward, indicating a wait of unknown duration. The default is false.

 javax.swing.ProgressMonitor 1.2

- ProgressMonitor(Component parent, Object message, String note, int min, int max)
  constructs a progress monitor dialog box.

Parameters:	parent	The parent component over which this dialog box pops up
	message	The message object to display in the dialog box
	note	The optional string to display under the message. If this value is null, then no space is set aside for the note, and a later call to setNote has no effect
	min, max	The minimum and maximum values of the progress bar

- void setNote(String note)
  changes the note text.
- void setProgress(int value)
  sets the progress bar value to the given value.
- void close()
  closes this dialog box.
- boolean isCanceled()
  returns true if the user canceled this dialog box.

 javax.swing.ProgressMonitorInputStream 1.2

- ProgressMonitorInputStream(Component parent, Object message, InputStream in)
  constructs an input stream filter with an associated progress monitor dialog box.

Parameters:	parent	The parent component over which this dialog box pops up
	message	The message object to display in the dialog box
	in	The input stream that is being monitored

Component Organizers

We conclude the discussion of advanced Swing features with a presentation of components that help organize other components. These include the *split pane*, a mechanism for splitting an area into multiple parts whose boundaries can be adjusted, the *tabbed pane*, which uses tab dividers to allow a user to flip through multiple panels, and the *desktop pane*, which can be used to implement applications that display multiple *internal frames*.

Split Panes

Split panes split a component into two parts, with an adjustable boundary in between. Figure 6–44 shows a frame with two split panes. The outer pane is split vertically, with a text area on the bottom and another split pane on the top. That pane is split horizontally, with a list on the left and a label containing an image on the right.

You construct a split pane by specifying the orientation, one of JSplitPane.HORIZONTAL_SPLIT or JSplitPane.VERTICAL_SPLIT, followed by the two components. For example,

```
JSplitPane innerPane = new JSplitPane(JSplitPane.HORIZONTAL_SPLIT, planetList, planetImage);
```

That's all you have to do. If you like, you can add "one-touch expand" icons to the splitter bar. You see those icons in the top pane in Figure 6–44. In the Metal look and feel, they are small triangles. If you click one of them, the splitter moves all the way in the direction to which the triangle is pointing, expanding one of the panes completely.

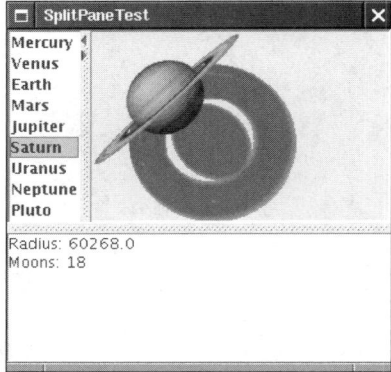

Figure 6–44: A frame with two nested split panes

To add this capability, call

```
innerPane.setOneTouchExpandable(true);
```

The "continuous layout" feature continuously repaints the contents of both components as the user adjusts the splitter. That looks classier, but it can be slow. You turn on that feature with the call

```
innerPane.setContinuousLayout(true);
```

In the example program, we left the bottom splitter at the default (no continuous layout). When you drag it, you only move a black outline. When you release the mouse, the components are repainted.

The straightforward program in Example 6–19 populates a list box with planets. When the user makes a selection, the planet image is displayed to the right and a description is placed in the text area on the bottom. When you run the program, adjust the splitters and try out the one-touch expansion and continuous layout features.

Example 6–19: SplitPaneTest.java

```
1. import java.awt.*;
2. import java.awt.event.*;
3. import java.util.*;
4. import javax.swing.*;
5. import javax.swing.event.*;
6.
7. /**
8.    This program demonstrates the split pane component
9.    organizer.
10. */
11. public class SplitPaneTest
12. {
```

```
13.   public static void main(String[] args)
14.   {
15.      JFrame frame = new SplitPaneFrame();
16.      frame.setDefaultCloseOperation(JFrame.EXIT_ON_CLOSE);
17.      frame.setVisible(true);
18.   }
19. }
20.
21. /**
22.    This frame consists of two nested split panes to demonstrate
23.    planet images and data.
24. */
25. class SplitPaneFrame extends JFrame
26. {
27.    public SplitPaneFrame()
28.    {
29.       setTitle("SplitPaneTest");
30.       setSize(DEFAULT_WIDTH, DEFAULT_HEIGHT);
31.
32.       // set up components for planet names, images, descriptions
33.
34.       final JList planetList = new JList(planets);
35.       final JLabel planetImage = new JLabel();
36.       final JTextArea planetDescription = new JTextArea();
37.
38.       planetList.addListSelectionListener(new
39.          ListSelectionListener()
40.          {
41.             public void valueChanged(ListSelectionEvent event)
42.             {
43.                Planet value = (Planet) planetList.getSelectedValue();
44.
45.                // update image and description
46.
47.                planetImage.setIcon(value.getImage());
48.                planetDescription.setText(value.getDescription());
49.             }
50.          });
51.
52.       // set up split panes
53.
54.       JSplitPane innerPane
55.          = new JSplitPane(JSplitPane.HORIZONTAL_SPLIT, planetList, planetImage);
56.
57.       innerPane.setContinuousLayout(true);
58.       innerPane.setOneTouchExpandable(true);
59.
60.       JSplitPane outerPane
61.          = new JSplitPane(JSplitPane.VERTICAL_SPLIT, innerPane, planetDescription);
62.
63.       add(outerPane, BorderLayout.CENTER);
64.    }
65.
66.    private Planet[] planets =
67.       {
68.          new Planet("Mercury", 2440, 0),
```

```
 69.            new Planet("Venus", 6052, 0),
 70.            new Planet("Earth", 6378, 1),
 71.            new Planet("Mars", 3397, 2),
 72.            new Planet("Jupiter", 71492, 16),
 73.            new Planet("Saturn", 60268, 18),
 74.            new Planet("Uranus", 25559, 17),
 75.            new Planet("Neptune", 24766, 8),
 76.            new Planet("Pluto", 1137, 1),
 77.         };
 78.      private static final int DEFAULT_WIDTH = 300;
 79.      private static final int DEFAULT_HEIGHT = 300;
 80. }
 81.
 82. /**
 83.    Describes a planet.
 84. */
 85. class Planet
 86. {
 87.      /**
 88.         Constructs a planet.
 89.         @param n the planet name
 90.         @param r the planet radius
 91.         @param m the number of moons
 92.      */
 93.      public Planet(String n, double r, int m)
 94.      {
 95.         name = n;
 96.         radius = r;
 97.         moons = m;
 98.         image = new ImageIcon(name + ".gif");
 99.      }
100.
101.      public String toString()
102.      {
103.         return name;
104.      }
105.
106.      /**
107.         Gets a description of the planet.
108.         @return the description
109.      */
110.      public String getDescription()
111.      {
112.         return "Radius: " + radius + "\nMoons: " + moons + "\n";
113.      }
114.
115.      /**
116.         Gets an image of the planet.
117.         @return the image
118.      */
119.      public ImageIcon getImage()
120.      {
121.         return image;
122.      }
123.
124.      private String name;
```

```
125.    private double radius;
126.    private int moons;
127.    private ImageIcon image;
128. }
```

API **javax.swing.JSplitPane** 1.2

- JSplitPane()
- JSplitPane(int direction)
- JSplitPane(int direction, boolean continuousLayout)
- JSplitPane(int direction, Component first, Component second)
- JSplitPane(int direction, boolean continuousLayout, Component first, Component second)
  construct a new split pane.

Parameters:	direction	One of HORIZONTAL_SPLIT or VERTICAL_SPLIT
	continuousLayout	true if the components are continuously updated when the splitter is moved
	first, second	The components to add

- boolean isOneTouchExpandable()
- void setOneTouchExpandable(boolean b)
  get and set the "one-touch expandable" property. When this property is set, the splitter has two icons to completely expand one or the other component.
- boolean isContinuousLayout()
- void setContinuousLayout(boolean b)
  get and set the "continuous layout" property. When this property is set, then the components are continuously updated when the splitter is moved.
- void setLeftComponent(Component c)
- void setTopComponent(Component c)
  These operations have the same effect, to set c as the first component in the split pane.
- void setRightComponent(Component c)
- void setBottomComponent(Component c)
  These operations have the same effect, to set c as the second component in the split pane.

Tabbed Panes

Tabbed panes are a familiar user interface device to break up a complex dialog box into subsets of related options. You can also use tabs to let a user flip through a set of documents or images (see Figure 6–45). That is what we do in our sample program.

To create a tabbed pane, you first construct a JTabbedPane object, then you add tabs to it.

```
JTabbedPane tabbedPane = new JTabbedPane();
tabbedPane.addTab(title, icon, component);
```

The last parameter of the addTab method has type Component. To add multiple components into the same tab, you first pack them up in a container, such as a JPanel.

The icon is optional; for example, the addTab method does not require an icon:

```
tabbedPane.addTab(title, component);
```

You can also add a tab in the middle of the tab collection with the insertTab method:

```
tabbedPane.insertTab(title, icon, component, tooltip, index);
```

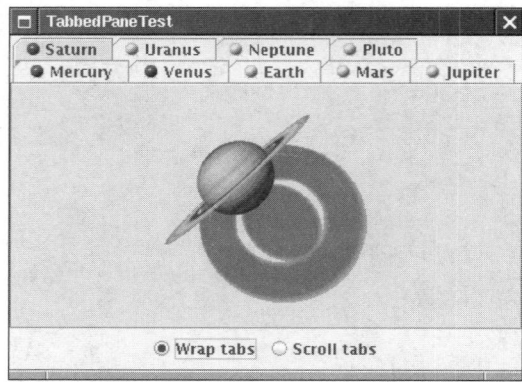

Figure 6–45: A tabbed pane

To remove a tab from the tab collection, use

```
tabPane.removeTabAt(index);
```

When you add a new tab to the tab collection, it is not automatically displayed. You must select it with the setSelectedIndex method. For example, here is how you show a tab that you just added to the end:

```
tabbedPane.setSelectedIndex(tabbedPane.getTabCount() - 1);
```

If you have a lot of tabs, then they can take up quite a bit of space. Starting with JDK 1.4, you can display the tabs in scrolling mode, in which only one row of tabs is displayed, together with a set of arrow buttons that allow the user to scroll through the tab set (see Figure 6–46).

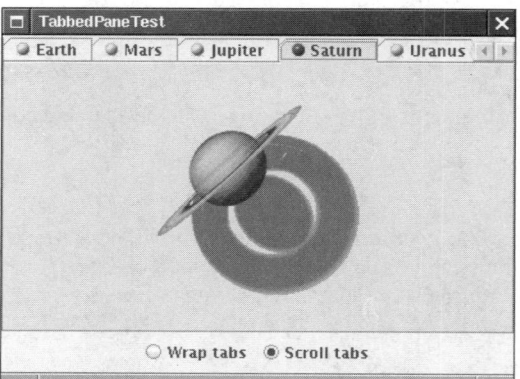

Figure 6–46: A tabbed pane with scrolling tabs

You set the tab layout to wrapped or scrolling mode by calling

```
tabbedPane.setTabLayoutPolicy(JTabbedPane.WRAP_TAB_LAYOUT);
```

or

```
tabbedPane.setTabLayoutPolicy(JTabbedPane.SCROLL_TAB_LAYOUT);
```

The example program shows a useful technique with tabbed panes. Sometimes, you want to update a component just before it is displayed. In our example program, we load the planet image only when the user actually clicks on a tab.

To be notified whenever the user clicks on a new tab, you install a ChangeListener with the tabbed pane. Note that you must install the listener with the tabbed pane itself, not with any of the components.

```
tabbedPane.addChangeListener(listener);
```

When the user selects a tab, the stateChanged method of the change listener is called. You retrieve the tabbed pane as the source of the event. Call the getSelectedIndex method to find out which pane is about to be displayed.

```
public void stateChanged(ChangeEvent event)
{
    int n = tabbedPane.getSelectedIndex();
    loadTab(n);
}
```

In Example 6–20, we first set all tab components to null. When a new tab is selected, we test whether its component is still null. If so, we replace it with the image. (This happens instantaneously when you click on the tab. You will not see an empty pane.) Just for fun, we also change the icon from a yellow ball to a red ball to indicate which panes have been visited.

Example 6–20: TabbedPaneTest.java

```
1. import java.awt.*;
2. import java.awt.event.*;
3. import java.util.*;
4. import javax.swing.*;
5. import javax.swing.event.*;
6.
7. /**
8.    This program demonstrates the tabbed pane component organizer.
9. */
10. public class TabbedPaneTest
11. {
12.    public static void main(String[] args)
13.    {
14.       JFrame frame = new TabbedPaneFrame();
15.       frame.setDefaultCloseOperation(JFrame.EXIT_ON_CLOSE);
16.       frame.setVisible(true);
17.    }
18. }
19.
20. /**
21.    This frame shows a tabbed pane and radio buttons to
22.    switch between wrapped and scrolling tab layout.
23. */
24. class TabbedPaneFrame extends JFrame
25. {
26.    public TabbedPaneFrame()
27.    {
28.       setTitle("TabbedPaneTest");
29.       setSize(DEFAULT_WIDTH, DEFAULT_HEIGHT);
30.
31.       tabbedPane = new JTabbedPane();
32.       // we set the components to null and delay their loading until the tab is shown
33.       // for the first time
34.
35.       ImageIcon icon = new ImageIcon("yellow-ball.gif");
36.
```

```
37.        tabbedPane.addTab("Mercury", icon, null);
38.        tabbedPane.addTab("Venus", icon, null);
39.        tabbedPane.addTab("Earth", icon, null);
40.        tabbedPane.addTab("Mars", icon, null);
41.        tabbedPane.addTab("Jupiter", icon, null);
42.        tabbedPane.addTab("Saturn", icon, null);
43.        tabbedPane.addTab("Uranus", icon, null);
44.        tabbedPane.addTab("Neptune", icon, null);
45.        tabbedPane.addTab("Pluto", icon, null);
46.
47.        add(tabbedPane, "Center");
48.
49.        tabbedPane.addChangeListener(new
50.           ChangeListener()
51.           {
52.              public void stateChanged(ChangeEvent event)
53.              {
54.
55.                 // check if this tab still has a null component
56.
57.                 if (tabbedPane.getSelectedComponent() == null)
58.                 {
59.                    // set the component to the image icon
60.
61.                    int n = tabbedPane.getSelectedIndex();
62.                    loadTab(n);
63.                 }
64.              }
65.           });
66.
67.        loadTab(0);
68.
69.        JPanel buttonPanel = new JPanel();
70.        ButtonGroup buttonGroup = new ButtonGroup();
71.        JRadioButton wrapButton = new JRadioButton("Wrap tabs");
72.        wrapButton.addActionListener(new
73.           ActionListener()
74.           {
75.              public void actionPerformed(ActionEvent event)
76.              {
77.                 tabbedPane.setTabLayoutPolicy(JTabbedPane.WRAP_TAB_LAYOUT);
78.              }
79.           });
80.        buttonPanel.add(wrapButton);
81.        buttonGroup.add(wrapButton);
82.        wrapButton.setSelected(true);
83.        JRadioButton scrollButton = new JRadioButton("Scroll tabs");
84.        scrollButton.addActionListener(new
85.           ActionListener()
86.           {
87.              public void actionPerformed(ActionEvent event)
88.              {
89.                 tabbedPane.setTabLayoutPolicy(JTabbedPane.SCROLL_TAB_LAYOUT);
90.              }
91.           });
92.        buttonPanel.add(scrollButton);
93.        buttonGroup.add(scrollButton);
```

```
94.       add(buttonPanel, BorderLayout.SOUTH);
95.    }
96.
97.    /**
98.       Loads the tab with the given index.
99.       @param n the index of the tab to load
100.   */
101.   private void loadTab(int n)
102.   {
103.      String title = tabbedPane.getTitleAt(n);
104.      ImageIcon planetIcon = new ImageIcon(title + ".gif");
105.      tabbedPane.setComponentAt(n, new JLabel(planetIcon));
106.
107.      // indicate that this tab has been visited--just for fun
108.
109.      tabbedPane.setIconAt(n, new ImageIcon("red-ball.gif"));
110.   }
111.
112.   private JTabbedPane tabbedPane;
113.
114.   private static final int DEFAULT_WIDTH = 400;
115.   private static final int DEFAULT_HEIGHT = 300;
116. }
```

API `javax.swing.JTabbedPane` 1.2

- `JTabbedPane()`
- `JTabbedPane(int placement)`
  construct a tabbed pane.

  Parameters: placement   One of SwingConstants.TOP, SwingConstants.LEFT,
                               SwingConstants.RIGHT, or SwingConstants.BOTTOM

- `void addTab(String title, Component c)`
- `void addTab(String title, Icon icon, Component c)`
- `void addTab(String title, Icon icon, Component c, String tooltip)`
  add a tab to the end of the tabbed pane.

- `void insertTab(String title, Icon icon, Component c, String tooltip, int index)`
  inserts a tab to the tabbed pane at the given index.

- `void removeTabAt(int index)`
  removes the tab at the given index.

- `void setSelectedIndex(int index)`
  selects the tab at the given index.

- `int getSelectedIndex()`
  returns the index of the selected tab.

- `Component getSelectedComponent()`
  returns the component of the selected tab.

- `String getTitleAt(int index)`
- `void setTitleAt(int index, String title)`
- `Icon getIconAt(int index)`
- `void setIconAt(int index, Icon icon)`
- `Component getComponentAt(int index)`
- `void setComponentAt(int index, Component c)`
  get or set the title, icon, or component at the given index.

- `int indexOfTab(String title)`
- `int indexOfTab(Icon icon)`
- `int indexOfComponent(Component c)`
  return the index of the tab with the given title, icon, or component.

- `int getTabCount()`
  returns the total number of tabs in this tabbed pane.

- `int getTabLayoutPolicy()`
- `void setTabLayoutPolicy(int policy)` **1.4**
  get or set the tab layout policy. Tabs can be wrapped or scrolling.

  Parameters: policy   One of `JTabbedPane.WRAP_TAB_LAYOUT` or
                                      `JTabbedPane.SCROLL_TAB_LAYOUT`

- `void addChangeListener(ChangeListener listener)`
  adds a change listener that is notified when the user selects a different tab.

Desktop Panes and Internal Frames

Many applications present information in multiple windows that are all contained inside a large frame. If you minimize the application frame, then all of its windows are hidden at the same time. In the Windows environment, this user interface is sometimes called the *multiple document interface* or MDI. Figure 6–47 shows a typical application that uses this interface.

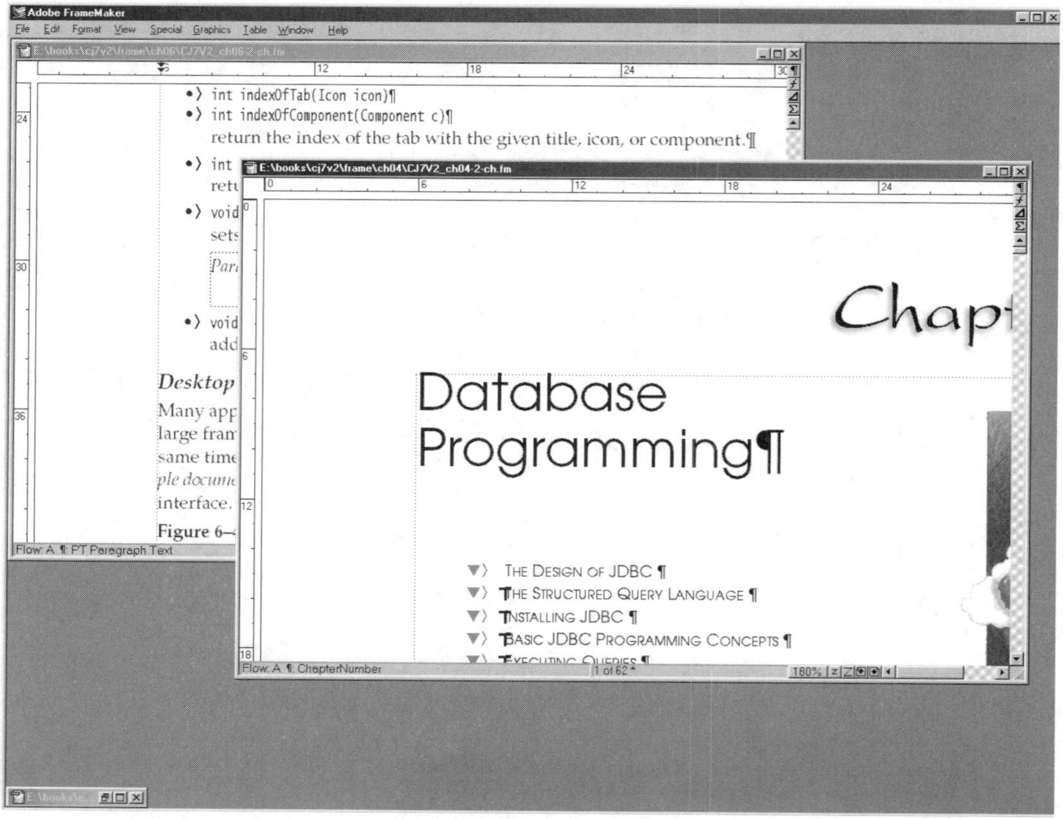

Figure 6–47: A multiple document interface application

For some time, this user interface style was popular, but it has become less prevalent in recent years. Nowadays, many applications simply display a separate top-level frame for each document. Which is better? MDI reduces window clutter, but having separate top-level windows means that you can use the buttons and hotkeys of the host windowing system to flip through your windows.

In the world of Java, where you can't rely on a rich host windowing system, it makes a lot of sense to have your application manage its frames.

Figure 6–48 shows a Java application with three internal frames. Two of them have decorations on the border to maximize and iconify them. The third is in its iconified state.

In the Metal look and feel, the internal frames have distinctive "grabber" areas that you use to move the frames around. You can resize the windows by dragging the resize corners.

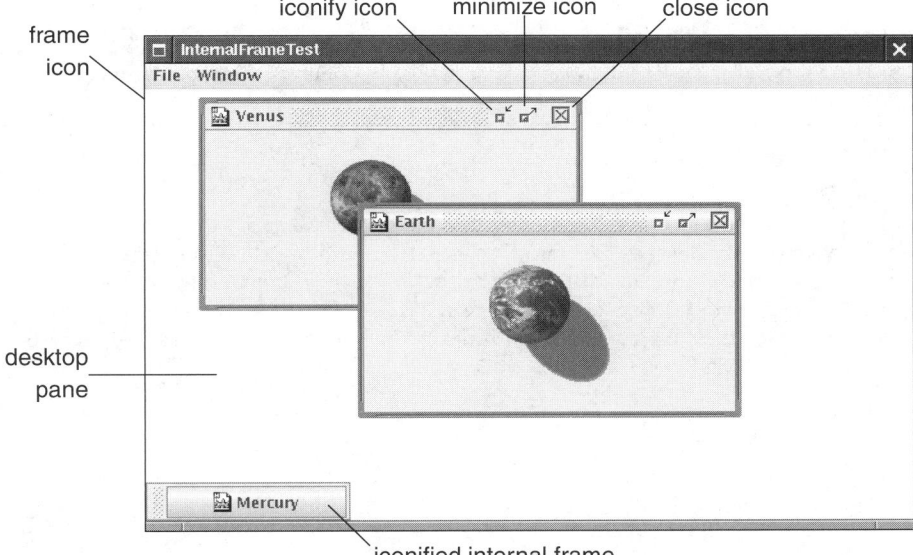

Figure 6–48: A Java application with three internal frames

To achieve this capability, follow these steps:

1. Use a regular JFrame window for the application.
2. Add the JDesktopPane to the JFrame.

    ```
    desktop = new JDesktopPane();
    add(desktop, BorderLayout.CENTER);
    ```

3. Construct JInternalFrame windows. You can specify whether you want the icons for resizing or closing the frame. Normally, you want all icons.

    ```
    JInternalFrame iframe = new JInternalFrame(title,
        true, // resizable
        true, // closable
        true, // maximizable
        true); // iconifiable
    ```

4. Add components to the frame.

    ```
    iframe.add(c, BorderLayout.CENTER);
    ```

5. Set a frame icon. The icon is shown in the top-left corner of the frame.

```
iframe.setFrameIcon(icon);
```

> **NOTE:** In the current version of the Metal look and feel, the frame icon is not displayed in iconized frames.

6. Set the size of the internal frame. As with regular frames, internal frames initially have a size of 0 by 0 pixels. Because you don't want internal frames to be displayed on top of each other, use a variable position for the next frame. Use the reshape method to set both the position and size of the frame:

```
iframe.reshape(nextFrameX, nextFrameY, width, height);
```

7. As with JFrames, you need to make the frame visible.

```
iframe.setVisible(true);
```

> **NOTE:** In earlier versions of Swing, internal frames were automatically visible and this call was not necessary.

8. Add the frame to the JDesktopPane:

```
desktop.add(iframe);
```

9. You probably want to make the new frame the *selected frame*. Of the internal frames on the desktop, only the selected frame receives keyboard focus. In the Metal look and feel, the selected frame has a blue title bar, whereas the other frames have a gray title bar. You use the setSelected method to select a frame. However, the "selected" property can be *vetoed*—the currently selected frame can refuse to give up focus. In that case, the setSelected method throws a PropertyVetoException that you need to handle.

```
try
{
   iframe.setSelected(true);
}
catch (PropertyVetoException e)
{
   // attempt was vetoed
}
```

10. You probably want to move the position for the next internal frame down so that it won't overlay the existing frame. A good distance between frames is the height of the title bar, which you can obtain as

```
int frameDistance = iframe.getHeight() - iframe.getContentPane().getHeight()
```

11. Use that distance to determine the next internal frame position.

```
nextFrameX += frameDistance;
nextFrameY += frameDistance;
if (nextFrameX + width > desktop.getWidth())
   nextFrameX = 0;
if (nextFrameY + height > desktop.getHeight())
   nextFrameY = 0;
```

Cascading and Tiling

In Windows, there are standard commands for *cascading* and *tiling* windows (see Figures 6–49 and 6–50). The Java JDesktopPane and JInternalFrame classes have no built-in support for these operations. In Example 6–21, we show you how to implement these operations yourself.

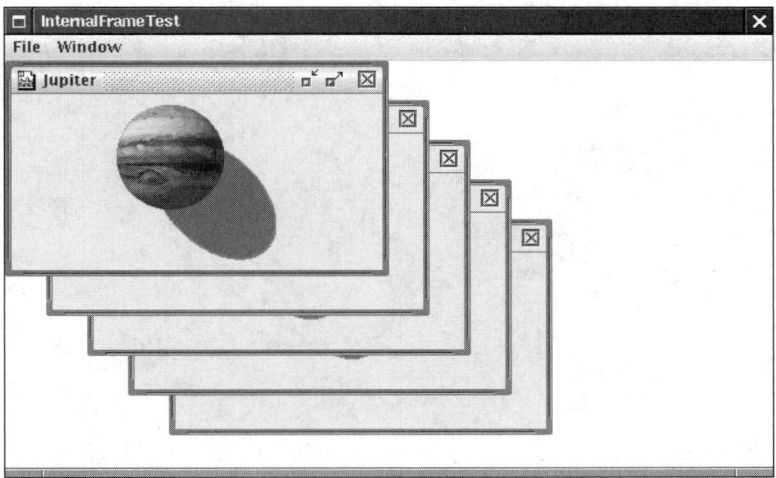

Figure 6–49: Cascaded internal frames

To cascade all windows, you reshape windows to the same size and stagger their positions. The getAllFrames method of the JDesktopPane class returns an array of all internal frames.

```
JInternalFrame[] frames = desktop.getAllFrames();
```

However, you need to pay attention to the frame state. An internal frame can be in one of three states:

- Icon
- Resizable
- Maximum

You use the isIcon method to find out which internal frames are currently icons and should be skipped. However, if a frame is in the maximum state, you first set it to be resizable by calling setMaximum(false). This is another property that can be vetoed, so you must catch the PropertyVetoException.

The following loop cascades all internal frames on the desktop:

```
for (JInternalFrame frame : desktop.getAllFrames())
{
   if (!frame.isIcon())
   {
      try
      {
         // try to make maximized frames resizable; this might be vetoed
         frame.setMaximum(false);
         frame.reshape(x, y, width, height);
         x += frameDistance;
         y += frameDistance;
         // wrap around at the desktop edge
         if (x + width > desktop.getWidth()) x = 0;
         if (y + height > desktop.getHeight()) y = 0;
      }
      catch (PropertyVetoException e)
      {}
   }
}
```

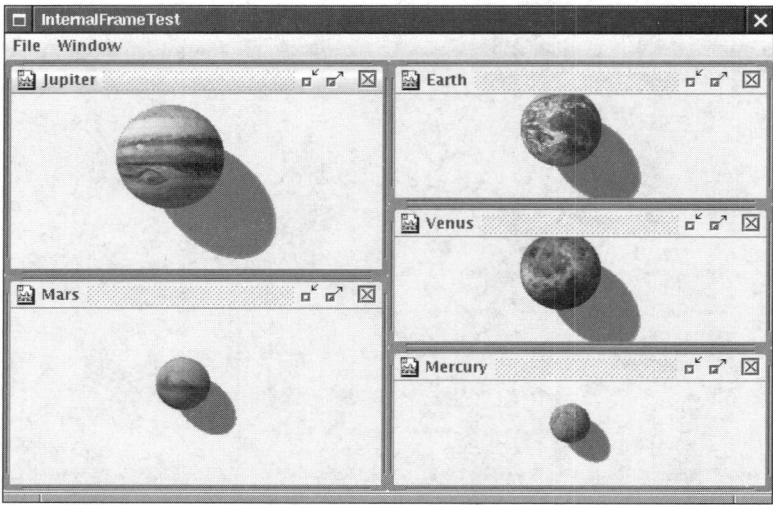

Figure 6–50: Tiled internal frames

Tiling frames is trickier, particularly if the number of frames is not a perfect square. First, count the number of frames that are not icons. Then, compute the number of rows as

```
int rows = (int) Math.sqrt(frameCount);
```

Then the number of columns is

```
int cols = frameCount / rows;
```

except that the last

```
int extra = frameCount % rows;
```

columns have rows + 1 rows.

Here is the loop for tiling all frames on the desktop.

```
int width = desktop.getWidth() / cols;
int height = desktop.getHeight() / rows;
int r = 0;
int c = 0;
for (JInternalFrame frame : desktop.getAllFrames())
{
   if (!frame.isIcon())
   {
      try
      {
         frame.setMaximum(false);
         frame.reshape(c * width, r * height, width, height);
         r++;
         if (r == rows)
         {
            r = 0;
            c++;
            if (c == cols - extra)
            {
               // start adding an extra row
               rows++;
```

```
            height = desktop.getHeight() / rows;
         }
      }
   }
   catch (PropertyVetoException e)
   {}
  }
}
```

The example program shows another common frame operation: moving the selection from the current frame to the next frame that isn't an icon. The JDesktopPane class has no method to return the selected frame. Instead, you must traverse all frames and call isSelected until you find the currently selected frame. Then, look for the next frame in the sequence that isn't an icon, and try to select it by calling

```
frames[next].setSelected(true);
```

As before, that method can throw a PropertyVetoException, in which case you keep looking. If you come back to the original frame, then no other frame was selectable, and you give up. Here is the complete loop:

```
JInternalFrame[] frames = desktop.getAllFrames();
for (int i = 0; i < frames.length; i++)
{
   if (frames[i].isSelected())
   {
      // find next frame that isn't an icon and can be selected
      int next = (i + 1) % frames.length;
      while (next != i)
      {
         if (!frames[next].isIcon())
         {
            try
            {
               // all other frames are icons or veto selection
               frames[next].setSelected(true);
               frames[next].toFront();
               frames[i].toBack();
               return;
            }
            catch (PropertyVetoException e)
            {}
         }
         next = (next + 1) % frames.length;
      }
   }
}
```

Vetoing Property Settings

Now that you have seen all these veto exceptions, you may wonder how your frames can issue a veto. The JInternalFrame class uses a general *JavaBeans* mechanism for monitoring the setting of properties. We discuss this mechanism in full detail in Chapter 8. For now, we just want to show you how your frames can veto requests for property changes.

Frames don't usually want to use a veto to protest iconization or loss of focus, but it is very common for frames to check whether it is okay to *close* them. You close a frame with the set-Closed method of the JInternalFrame class. Because the method is vetoable, it calls all registered *vetoable change listeners* before proceeding to make the change. That gives each of the

listeners the opportunity to throw a PropertyVetoException and thereby terminate the call to setClosed before it changed any settings.

In our example program, we put up a dialog box to ask the user whether it is okay to close the window (see Figure 6–51). If the user doesn't agree, the window stays open.

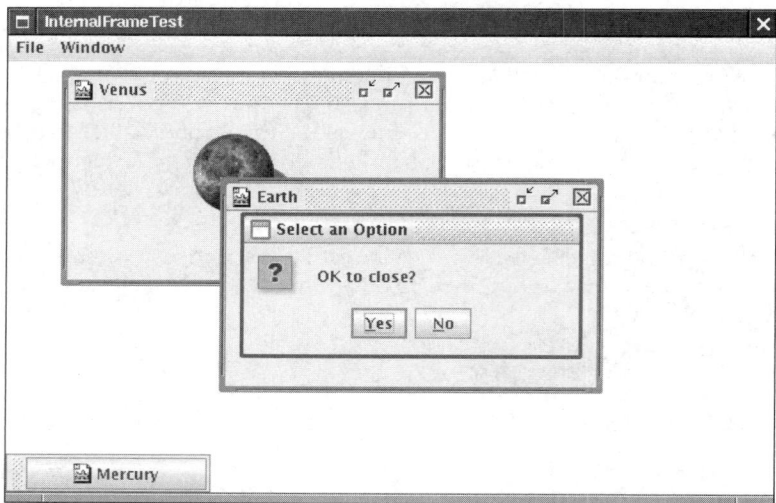

Figure 6–51: The user can veto the close property

Here is how you achieve such a notification.

1. Add a listener object to each frame. The object must belong to some class that implements the VetoableChangeListener interface. It is best to add the listener right after constructing the frame. In our example, we use the frame class that constructs the internal frames. Another option would be to use an anonymous inner class.

    ```
    iframe.addVetoableChangeListener(listener);
    ```

2. Implement the vetoableChange method, the only method required by the VetoableChangeListener interface. The method receives a PropertyChangeEvent object. Use the getName method to find the name of the property that is about to be changed (such as "closed" if the method call to veto is setClosed(true)). As you see in Chapter 8, you obtain the property name by removing the "set" prefix from the method name and changing the next letter to lowercase.

    Use the getNewValue method to get the proposed new value.

    ```
    String name = event.getPropertyName();
    Object value = event.getNewValue();
    if (name.equals("closed") && value.equals(true))
    {
       ask user for confirmation
    }
    ```

3. Simply throw a PropertyVetoException to block the property change. Return normally if you don't want to veto the change.

    ```
    class DesktopFrame extends JFrame
       implements VetoableChangeListener
    {
       . . .
    ```

```
    public void vetoableChange(PropertyChangeEvent event)
       throws PropertyVetoException
    {
       . . .
       if (not ok)
          throw new PropertyVetoException(reason, event);
       // return normally if ok
    }
 }
```

Dialogs in Internal Frames

If you use internal frames, you should not use the JDialog class for dialog boxes. Those dialog boxes have two disadvantages:

- They are heavyweight because they create a new frame in the windowing system.
- The windowing system does not know how to position them relative to the internal frame that spawned them.

Instead, for simple dialog boxes, use the showInternal*Xxx*Dialog methods of the JOptionPane class. They work exactly like the show*Xxx*Dialog methods, except they position a lightweight window over an internal frame.

As for more complex dialog boxes, construct them with a JInternalFrame. Unfortunately, you then have no built-in support for modal dialog boxes.

In our sample program, we use an internal dialog box to ask the user whether it is okay to close a frame.

```
int result = JOptionPane.showInternalConfirmDialog(
   iframe, "OK to close?", "Select an Option", JOptionPane.YES_NO_OPTION);;
```

 NOTE: If you simply want to be *notified* when a frame is closed, then you should not use the veto mechanism. Instead, install an InternalFrameListener. An internal frame listener works just like a WindowListener. When the internal frame is closing, the internalFrameClosing method is called instead of the familiar windowClosing method. The other six internal frame notifications (opened/closed, iconified/deiconified, activated/deactivated) also correspond to the window listener methods.

Outline Dragging

One criticism that developers have leveled against internal frames is that performance has not been great. By far the slowest operation is to drag a frame with complex content across the desktop. The desktop manager keeps asking the frame to repaint itself as it is being dragged, which is quite slow.

Actually, if you use Windows or X Windows with a poorly written video driver, you'll experience the same problem. Window dragging appears to be fast on most systems because the video hardware supports the dragging operation by mapping the image inside the frame to a different screen location during the dragging process.

To improve performance without greatly degrading the user experience, you can set "outline dragging" on. When the user drags the frame, only the outline of the frame is continuously updated. The inside is repainted only when the user drops the frame to its final resting place.

To turn on outline dragging, call

```
desktop.setDragMode(JDesktopPane.OUTLINE_DRAG_MODE);
```

This setting is the equivalent of "continuous layout" in the JSplitPane class.

 NOTE: In early versions of Swing, you had to use the magic incantation

```
desktop.putClientProperty("JDesktopPane.dragMode", "outline");
```

to turn on outline dragging.

In the sample program, you can use the Window -> Drag Outline checkbox menu selection to toggle outline dragging on or off.

 NOTE: The internal frames on the desktop are managed by a DesktopManager class. You don't need to know about this class for normal programming. It is possible to implement different desktop behavior by installing a new desktop manager, but we don't cover that.

Example 6–21 populates a desktop with internal frames that show HTML pages. The File -> Open menu option pops up a file dialog box for reading a local HTML file into a new internal frame. If you click on any link, the linked document is displayed in another internal frame. Try out the Window -> Cascade and Window -> Tile commands. This example concludes our discussion of advanced Swing features.

Example 6–21: InternalFrameTest.java

```
 1. import java.awt.*;
 2. import java.awt.event.*;
 3. import java.beans.*;
 4. import java.io.*;
 5. import java.net.*;
 6. import java.util.*;
 7. import javax.swing.*;
 8. import javax.swing.event.*;
 9.
10. /**
11.    This program demonstrates the use of internal frames.
12. */
13. public class InternalFrameTest
14. {
15.    public static void main(String[] args)
16.    {
17.       JFrame frame = new DesktopFrame();
18.       frame.setDefaultCloseOperation(JFrame.EXIT_ON_CLOSE);
19.       frame.setVisible(true);
20.    }
21. }
22.
23. /**
24.    This desktop frame contains editor panes that show HTML
25.    documents.
26. */
27. class DesktopFrame extends JFrame
28. {
29.    public DesktopFrame()
30.    {
31.       setTitle("InternalFrameTest");
32.       setSize(DEFAULT_WIDTH, DEFAULT_HEIGHT);
33.
34.       desktop = new JDesktopPane();
```

```
35.     add(desktop, BorderLayout.CENTER);
36.
37.     // set up menus
38.
39.     JMenuBar menuBar = new JMenuBar();
40.     setJMenuBar(menuBar);
41.     JMenu fileMenu = new JMenu("File");
42.     menuBar.add(fileMenu);
43.     JMenuItem openItem = new JMenuItem("New");
44.     openItem.addActionListener(new
45.        ActionListener()
46.        {
47.           public void actionPerformed(ActionEvent event)
48.           {
49.              createInternalFrame(
50.                 new JLabel(new ImageIcon(planets[counter] + ".gif")),
51.                 planets[counter]);
52.              counter = (counter + 1) % planets.length;
53.           }
54.        });
55.     fileMenu.add(openItem);
56.     JMenuItem exitItem = new JMenuItem("Exit");
57.     exitItem.addActionListener(new
58.        ActionListener()
59.        {
60.           public void actionPerformed(ActionEvent event)
61.           {
62.              System.exit(0);
63.           }
64.        });
65.     fileMenu.add(exitItem);
66.     JMenu windowMenu = new JMenu("Window");
67.     menuBar.add(windowMenu);
68.     JMenuItem nextItem = new JMenuItem("Next");
69.     nextItem.addActionListener(new
70.        ActionListener()
71.        {
72.           public void actionPerformed(ActionEvent event)
73.           {
74.              selectNextWindow();
75.           }
76.        });
77.     windowMenu.add(nextItem);
78.     JMenuItem cascadeItem = new JMenuItem("Cascade");
79.     cascadeItem.addActionListener(new
80.        ActionListener()
81.        {
82.           public void actionPerformed(ActionEvent event)
83.           {
84.              cascadeWindows();
85.           }
86.        });
87.     windowMenu.add(cascadeItem);
88.     JMenuItem tileItem = new JMenuItem("Tile");
89.     tileItem.addActionListener(new
90.        ActionListener()
```

```
91.          {
92.             public void actionPerformed(ActionEvent event)
93.             {
94.                tileWindows();
95.             }
96.          });
97.       windowMenu.add(tileItem);
98.       final JCheckBoxMenuItem dragOutlineItem = new JCheckBoxMenuItem("Drag Outline");
99.       dragOutlineItem.addActionListener(new
100.         ActionListener()
101.         {
102.            public void actionPerformed(ActionEvent event)
103.            {
104.               desktop.setDragMode(dragOutlineItem.isSelected()
105.                  ? JDesktopPane.OUTLINE_DRAG_MODE
106.                  : JDesktopPane.LIVE_DRAG_MODE);
107.            }
108.         });
109.      windowMenu.add(dragOutlineItem);
110.   }
111.
112.   /**
113.      Creates an internal frame on the desktop.
114.      @param c the component to display in the internal frame
115.      @param t the title of the internal frame.
116.   */
117.   public void createInternalFrame(Component c, String t)
118.   {
119.      final JInternalFrame iframe = new JInternalFrame(t,
120.         true, // resizable
121.         true, // closable
122.         true, // maximizable
123.         true); // iconifiable
124.
125.      iframe.add(c, BorderLayout.CENTER);
126.      desktop.add(iframe);
127.
128.      iframe.setFrameIcon(new ImageIcon("document.gif"));
129.
130.      // add listener to confirm frame closing
131.      iframe.addVetoableChangeListener(new
132.         VetoableChangeListener()
133.         {
134.            public void vetoableChange(PropertyChangeEvent event)
135.               throws PropertyVetoException
136.            {
137.               String name = event.getPropertyName();
138.               Object value = event.getNewValue();
139.
140.               // we only want to check attempts to close a frame
141.               if (name.equals("closed") && value.equals(true))
142.               {
143.                  // ask user if it is ok to close
144.                  int result = JOptionPane.showInternalConfirmDialog(
145.                     iframe, "OK to close?", "Select an Option", JOptionPane.YES_NO_OPTION);
146.
```

```
147.                        // if the user doesn't agree, veto the close
148.                        if (result != JOptionPane.YES_OPTION)
149.                            throw new PropertyVetoException("User canceled close", event);
150.                    }
151.                }
152.            });
153.
154.        // position frame
155.        int width = desktop.getWidth() / 2;
156.        int height = desktop.getHeight() / 2;
157.        iframe.reshape(nextFrameX, nextFrameY, width, height);
158.
159.        iframe.show();
160.
161.        // select the frame--might be vetoed
162.        try
163.        {
164.            iframe.setSelected(true);
165.        }
166.        catch (PropertyVetoException e)
167.        {}
168.
169.        frameDistance = iframe.getHeight() - iframe.getContentPane().getHeight();
170.
171.        // compute placement for next frame
172.
173.        nextFrameX += frameDistance;
174.        nextFrameY += frameDistance;
175.        if (nextFrameX + width > desktop.getWidth()) nextFrameX = 0;
176.        if (nextFrameY + height > desktop.getHeight()) nextFrameY = 0;
177.    }
178.
179.    /**
180.        Cascades the non-iconified internal frames of the desktop.
181.    */
182.    public void cascadeWindows()
183.    {
184.        int x = 0;
185.        int y = 0;
186.        int width = desktop.getWidth() / 2;
187.        int height = desktop.getHeight() / 2;
188.
189.        for (JInternalFrame frame : desktop.getAllFrames())
190.        {
191.            if (!frame.isIcon())
192.            {
193.                try
194.                {
195.                    // try to make maximized frames resizable; this might be vetoed
196.                    frame.setMaximum(false);
197.                    frame.reshape(x, y, width, height);
198.
199.                    x += frameDistance;
200.                    y += frameDistance;
201.                    // wrap around at the desktop edge
202.                    if (x + width > desktop.getWidth()) x = 0;
```

```
203.              if (y + height > desktop.getHeight()) y = 0;
204.           }
205.           catch (PropertyVetoException e)
206.           {}
207.       }
208.    }
209. }
210.
211. /**
212.    Tiles the non-iconified internal frames of the desktop.
213. */
214. public void tileWindows()
215. {
216.    // count frames that aren't iconized
217.    int frameCount = 0;
218.    for (JInternalFrame frame : desktop.getAllFrames())
219.       if (!frame.isIcon()) frameCount++;
220.    if (frameCount == 0) return;
221.
222.    int rows = (int) Math.sqrt(frameCount);
223.    int cols = frameCount / rows;
224.    int extra = frameCount % rows;
225.       // number of columns with an extra row
226.
227.    int width = desktop.getWidth() / cols;
228.    int height = desktop.getHeight() / rows;
229.    int r = 0;
230.    int c = 0;
231.    for (JInternalFrame frame : desktop.getAllFrames())
232.    {
233.       if (!frame.isIcon())
234.       {
235.          try
236.          {
237.             frame.setMaximum(false);
238.             frame.reshape(c * width, r * height, width, height);
239.             r++;
240.             if (r == rows)
241.             {
242.                r = 0;
243.                c++;
244.                if (c == cols - extra)
245.                {
246.                   // start adding an extra row
247.                   rows++;
248.                   height = desktop.getHeight() / rows;
249.                }
250.             }
251.          }
252.          catch (PropertyVetoException e)
253.          {}
254.       }
255.    }
256. }
257.
258. /**
```

```
259.      Brings the next non-iconified internal frame to the front.
260.   */
261.   public void selectNextWindow()
262.   {
263.      JInternalFrame[] frames = desktop.getAllFrames();
264.      for (int i = 0; i < frames.length; i++)
265.      {
266.         if (frames[i].isSelected())
267.         {
268.            // find next frame that isn't an icon and can be selected
269.            int next = (i + 1) % frames.length;
270.            while (next != i)
271.            {
272.               if (!frames[next].isIcon())
273.               {
274.                  try
275.                  {
276.                     // all other frames are icons or veto selection
277.                     frames[next].setSelected(true);
278.                     frames[next].toFront();
279.                     frames[i].toBack();
280.                     return;
281.                  }
282.                  catch (PropertyVetoException e)
283.                  {}
284.               }
285.               next = (next + 1) % frames.length;
286.            }
287.         }
288.      }
289.   }
290.
291.   private JDesktopPane desktop;
292.   private int nextFrameX;
293.   private int nextFrameY;
294.   private int frameDistance;
295.   private int counter;
296.   private static final String[] planets =
297.   {
298.      "Mercury",
299.      "Venus",
300.      "Earth",
301.      "Mars",
302.      "Jupiter",
303.      "Saturn",
304.      "Uranus",
305.      "Neptune",
306.      "Pluto",
307.   };
308.
309.   private static final int DEFAULT_WIDTH = 600;
310.   private static final int DEFAULT_HEIGHT = 400;
311. }
```

 javax.swing.JDesktopPane 1.2

- JInternalFrame[] getAllFrames()
  gets all internal frames in this desktop pane.
- void setDragMode(int mode)
  sets the drag mode to live or outline drag mode.

Parameters:	mode	One of JDesktopPane.LIVE_DRAG_MODE or
		JDesktopPane.OUTLINE_DRAG_MODE

 javax.swing.JInternalFrame 1.2

- JInternalFrame()
- JInternalFrame(String title)
- JInternalFrame(String title, boolean resizable)
- JInternalFrame(String title, boolean resizable, boolean closable)
- JInternalFrame(String title, boolean resizable, boolean closable, boolean maximizable)
- JInternalFrame(String title, boolean resizable, boolean closable, boolean maximizable, boolean iconifiable)
  construct a new internal frame.

Parameters:	title	The string to display in the title bar
	resizable	true if the frame can be resized
	closable	true if the frame can be closed
	maximizable	true if the frame can be maximized
	iconifiable	true if the frame can be iconified

- boolean isResizable()
- void setResizable(boolean b)
- boolean isClosable()
- void setClosable(boolean b)
- boolean isMaximizable()
- void setMaximizable(boolean b)
- boolean isIconifiable()
- void setIconifiable(boolean b)
  get and set the resizable, closable, maximizable, and iconifiable properties. When the property is true, an icon appears in the frame title to resize, close, maximize, or iconify the internal frame.
- boolean isIcon()
- void setIcon(boolean b)
- boolean isMaximum()
- void setMaximum(boolean b)
- boolean isClosed()
- void setClosed(boolean b)
  get or set the icon, maximum, or closed property. When this property is true, the internal frame is iconified, maximized, or closed.
- boolean isSelected()
- void setSelected(boolean b)
  get or set the selected property. When this property is true, the current internal frame becomes the selected frame on the desktop.
- void moveToFront()
- void moveToBack()
  move this internal frame to the front or the back of the desktop.

- void reshape(int x, int y, int width, int height)
  moves and resizes this internal frame.

  Parameters: x, y   The top-left corner of the frame

                    width, height   The width and height of the frame

- Container getContentPane()
- void setContentPane(Container c)
  get and set the content pane of this internal frame.
- JDesktopPane getDesktopPane()
  gets the desktop pane of this internal frame.
- Icon getFrameIcon()
- void setFrameIcon(Icon anIcon)
  get and set the frame icon that is displayed in the title bar.
- boolean isVisible()
- void setVisible(boolean b)
  get and set the "visible" property.
- void show()
  makes this internal frame visible and brings it to the front.

 javax.swing.JComponent 1.2

- void addVetoableChangeListener(VetoableChangeListener listener)
  adds a vetoable change listener that is notified when an attempt is made to change a constrained property.

 java.beans.VetoableChangeListener 1.1

- void vetoableChange(PropertyChangeEvent event)
  is called when the set method of a constrained property notifies the vetoable change listeners.

 java.beans.PropertyChangeEvent 1.1

- String getPropertyName()
  returns the name of the property that is about to be changed.
- Object getNewValue()
  returns the proposed new value for the property.

 java.beans.PropertyVetoException 1.1

- PropertyVetoException(String reason, PropertyChangeEvent event)
  constructs a property veto exception.

  Parameters: reason   The reason for the veto

                    event   The vetoed event

Advanced AWT

You can use the methods of the Graphics class to create simple drawings. Those methods are sufficient for simple applets and applications, but they fall short when you create complex shapes or when you require complete control over the appearance of the graphics. The Java 2D API is a more sophisticated class library that you can use to produce high-quality drawings. In this chapter, we give you an overview of that API.

We then turn to the topic of printing and show how you can implement printing capabilities into your programs.

Finally, we cover two techniques for transferring data between programs: the system clipboard and the drag-and-drop mechanism. You can use these techniques to transfer data between two Java applications or between a Java application and a native program.

The Rendering Pipeline

The original JDK 1.0 had a very simple mechanism for drawing shapes. You select color and paint mode, and call methods of the Graphics class such as drawRect or fillOval. The Java 2D API supports many more options.

- You can easily produce a wide variety of *shapes*.
- You have control over the *stroke*, the pen that traces shape boundaries.
- You can *fill* shapes with solid colors, varying hues, and repeating patterns.
- You can use *transformations* to move, scale, rotate, or stretch shapes.

- You can *clip* shapes to restrict them to arbitrary areas.
- You can select *composition rules* to describe how to combine the pixels of a new shape with existing pixels.
- You can give *rendering hints* to make trade-offs between speed and drawing quality.

To draw a shape, you go through the following steps:

1. Obtain an object of the Graphics2D class. This class is a subclass of the Graphics class. If you use a version of the JDK that is enabled for Java 2D technology, methods such as paint and paintComponent automatically receive an object of the Graphics2D class. Simply use a cast, as follows:

```
public void paintComponent(Graphics g)
{
    Graphics2D g2 = (Graphics2D) g;
    . . .
}
```

2. Use the setRenderingHints method to set *rendering hints*: trade-offs between speed and drawing quality.

```
RenderingHints hints = . . .;
g2.setRenderingHints(hints);
```

3. Use the setStroke method to set the *stroke*. The stroke draws the outline of the shape. You can select the thickness and choose among solid and dotted lines.

```
Stroke stroke = . . .;
g2.setStroke(stroke);
```

4. Use the setPaint method to set the *paint*. The paint fills areas such as the stroke path or the interior of a shape. You can create solid color paint, paint with changing hues, or tiled fill patterns.

```
Paint paint = . . .;
g2.setPaint(paint);
```

5. Use the clip method to set the *clipping region*.

```
Shape clip = . . .;
g2.clip(clip);
```

6. Use the transform method to set a *transformation* from user space to device space. You use transformations if it is easier for you to define your shapes in a custom coordinate system than by using pixel coordinates.

```
AffineTransform transform = . . .;
g2.transform(transform);
```

7. Use the setComposite method to set a *composition rule* that describes how to combine the new pixels with the existing pixels.

```
Composite composite = . . .;
g2.setComposite(composite);
```

8. Create a shape. The Java 2D API supplies many shape objects and methods to combine shapes.

```
Shape shape = . . .;
```

9. Draw or fill the shape. If you draw the shape, its outline is stroked. If you fill the shape, the interior is painted.

```
g2.draw(shape);
g2.fill(shape);
```

Of course, in many practical circumstances, you don't need all these steps. There are reasonable defaults for the settings of the 2D graphics context. You would change the settings only if you want to change the defaults.

In the following sections, you will see how to describe shapes, strokes, paints, transformations, and composition rules.

The various set methods simply set the state of the 2D graphics context. They don't cause any drawing. Similarly, when you construct Shape objects, no drawing takes place. A shape is only rendered when you call draw or fill. At that time, the new shape is computed in a *rendering pipeline* (see Figure 7–1).

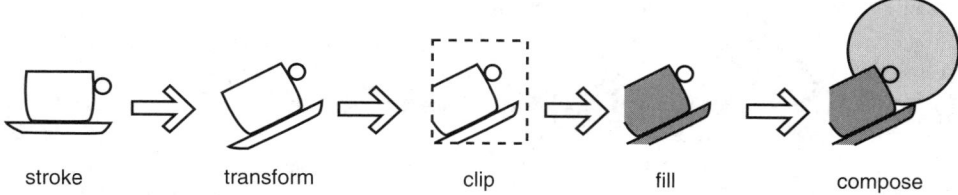

stroke   transform   clip   fill   compose

Figure 7–1: The rendering pipeline

In the rendering pipeline, the following steps take place to render a shape:

1. The path of the shape is stroked.
2. The shape is transformed.
3. The shape is clipped. If there is no intersection between the shape and the clipping area, then the process stops.
4. The remainder of the shape after clipping is filled.
5. The pixels of the filled shape are composed with the existing pixels. (In Figure 7–1, the circle is part of the existing pixels, and the cup shape is superimposed over it.)

In the next section, you will see how to define shapes. Then, we turn to the 2D graphics context settings.

 java.awt.Graphics2D 1.2

- void draw(Shape s)
  draws the outline of the given shape with the current stroke.
- void fill(Shape s)
  fills the interior of the given shape with the current paint.

Shapes

Here are some of the methods in the Graphics class to draw shapes:

```
drawLine
drawRectangle
drawRoundRect
draw3DRect
drawPolygon
drawPolyline
drawOval
drawArc
```

There are also corresponding `fill` methods. These methods have been in the `Graphics` class ever since JDK 1.0. The Java 2D API uses a completely different, object-oriented approach. Instead of methods, there are classes:

```
Line2D
Rectangle2D
RoundRectangle2D
Ellipse2D
Arc2D
QuadCurve2D
CubicCurve2D
GeneralPath
```

These classes all implement the `Shape` interface.

Finally, the `Point2D` class describes a point with an *x*- and a *y*-coordinate. Points are useful to define shapes, but they aren't themselves shapes.

To draw a shape, you first create an object of a class that implements the `Shape` interface and then call the `draw` method of the `Graphics2D` class.

The `Line2D`, `Rectangle2D`, `RoundRectangle2D`, `Ellipse2D`, and `Arc2D` classes correspond to the `draw-Line`, `drawRectangle`, `drawRoundRect`, `drawOval`, and `drawArc` methods. (The concept of a "3D rectangle" has died the death that it so richly deserved—there is no analog to the `draw3DRect` method.) The Java 2D API supplies two additional classes: quadratic and cubic curves. We discuss these shapes later in this section. There is no `Polygon2D` class. Instead, the `GeneralPath` class describes paths that are made up from lines, quadratic and cubic curves. You can use a `GeneralPath` to describe a polygon; we show you how later in this section.

The classes

```
Rectangle2D
RoundRectangle2D
Ellipse2D
Arc2D
```

all inherit from a common superclass `RectangularShape`. Admittedly, ellipses and arcs are not rectangular, but they have a *bounding rectangle* (see Figure 7–2).

Figure 7–2: The bounding rectangle of an ellipse and an arc

Each of the classes with a name ending in "2D" has two subclasses for specifying coordinates as `float` or `double` quantities. In Volume 1, you already encountered `Rectangle2D.Float` and `Rectangle2D.Double`.

The same scheme is used for the other classes, such as `Arc2D.Float` and `Arc2D.Double`.

Internally, all graphics classes use `float` coordinates because `float` numbers use less storage space and they have sufficient precision for geometric computations. However, the Java programming language makes it a bit more tedious to manipulate `float` numbers. For that reason, most methods of the graphics classes use `double` parameters and return values. Only when constructing a 2D object must you choose between a constructor with `float` or `double` coordinates. For example,

```
Rectangle2D floatRect = new Rectangle2D.Float(5F, 10F, 7.5F, 15F);
Rectangle2D doubleRect = new Rectangle2D.Double(5, 10, 7.5, 15);
```

The *Xxx*2D.Float and *Xxx*2D.Double classes are subclasses of the *Xxx*2D classes. After object construction, essentially no benefit accrues from remembering the subclass, and you can just store the constructed object in a superclass variable, just as in the code example.

As you can see from the curious names, the *Xxx*2D.Float and *Xxx*2D.Double classes are also inner classes of the *Xxx*2D classes. That is just a minor syntactical convenience, to avoid an inflation of outer class names.

Figure 7–3 shows the relationships between the shape classes. However, the Double and Float subclasses are omitted. Legacy classes from the pre-2D library are marked with a gray fill.

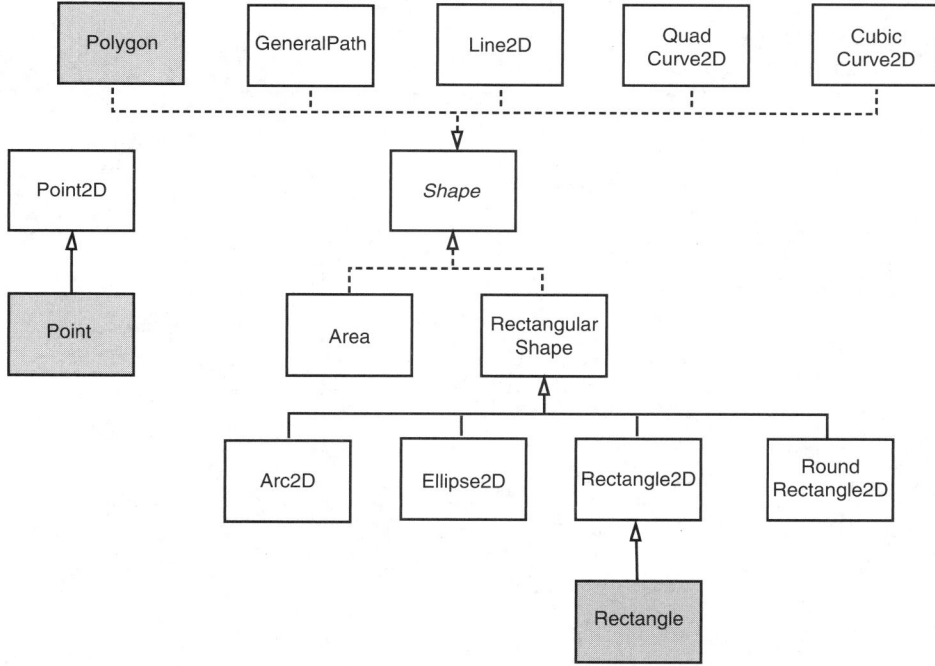

Figure 7–3: Relationships between the shape classes

Using the Shape Classes

You already saw how to use the Rectangle2D, Ellipse2D, and Line2D classes in Volume 1, Chapter 7. In this section, you will learn how to work with the remaining 2D shapes.

For the RoundRectangle2D shape, you specify the top-left corner, width and height, and the x- and y-dimension of the corner area that should be rounded (see Figure 7–4). For example, the call

```
RoundRectangle2D r = new RoundRectangle2D.Double(150, 200, 100, 50, 20, 20);
```

produces a rounded rectangle with circles of radius 20 at each of the corners.

To construct an arc, you specify the bounding box, the start angle, the angle swept out by the arc (see Figure 7–5), and the closure type, one of Arc2D.OPEN, Arc2D.PIE, or Arc2D.CHORD.

```
Arc2D a = new Arc2D(x, y, width, height, startAngle, arcAngle, closureType);
```

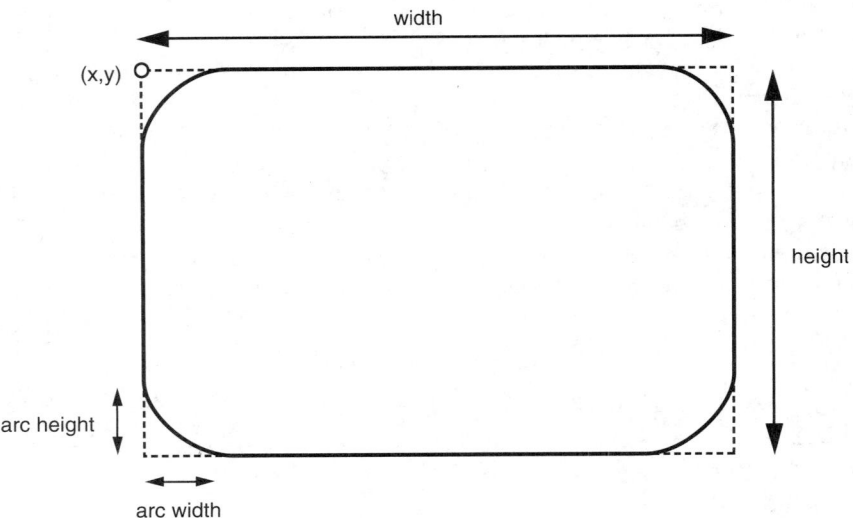

Figure 7–4: Constructing a `RoundRectangle2D`

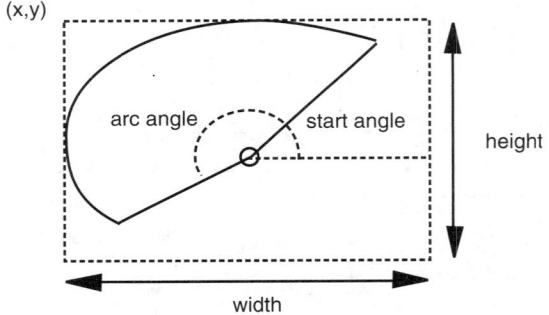

Figure 7–5: Constructing an elliptical arc

Figure 7–6 illustrates the arc types.

However, the angles are not simply given in degrees, but they are distorted such that a 45-degree angle denotes the diagonal position, *even if width and height are not the same.* If you draw circular arcs (for example, in a pie chart), then you don't need to worry about this. However, for elliptical arcs, be prepared for an adventure in trigonometry—see the sidebar for details.

The Java 2D API supports *quadratic* and *cubic* curves. In this chapter, we do not get into the mathematics of these curves. We suggest you get a feel for how the curves look by running the program in Example 7–1. As you can see in Figures 7–7 and 7–8, quadratic and cubic curves are specified by two *end points* and one or two *control points.* Moving the control points changes the shape of the curves.

To construct quadratic and cubic curves, you give the coordinates of the end points and the control points. For example,

```
QuadCurve2D q = new QuadCurve2D.Double(startX, startY, controlX, controlY, endX, endY);
CubicCurve2D c = new CubicCurve2D.Double(startX, startY, control1X, control1Y,
    control2X, control2Y, endX, endY);
```

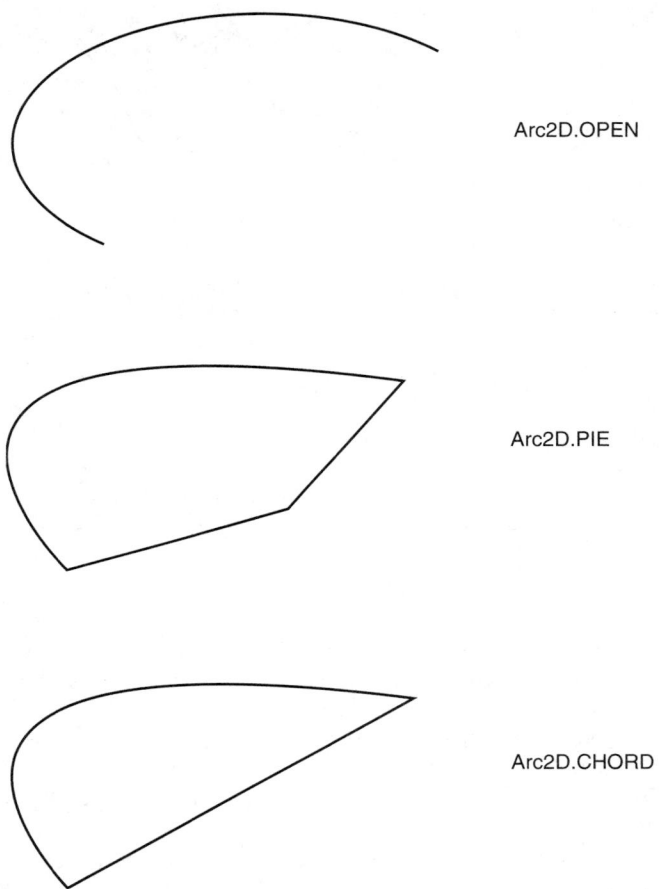

Arc2D.OPEN

Arc2D.PIE

Arc2D.CHORD

Figure 7–6: Arc types

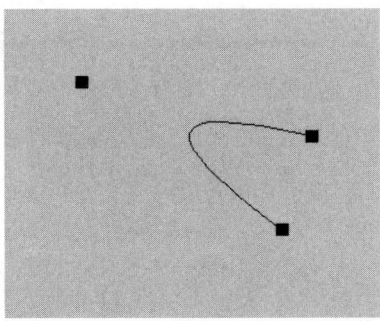

Figure 7–7: A quadratic curve

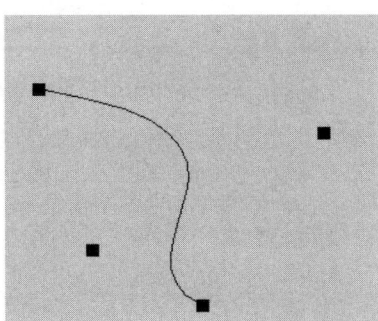

Figure 7–8: A cubic curve

Specifying Angles for Elliptical Arcs

The algorithm for drawing elliptical arcs uses distorted angles, which the caller must precompute. This sidebar tells you how. If you belong to the large majority of programmers who never draw elliptical arcs, just skip the sidebar. However, because the official documentation completely glosses over this topic, we thought it worth recording, to save those who need this information from a few hours of trigonometric agony.

You convert actual angles to distorted angles with the following formula:

```
distortedAngle = Math.atan2(Math.sin(angle) * width, Math.cos(angle) * height);
```

Sometimes (such as in the example program at the end of this section), you know an end point of the arc, or another point on the line joining the center of the ellipse and that end point. In that case, first compute

```
dx = p.getX() - center.getX();
dy = p.getY() - center.getY();
```

Then, the distorted angle is

```
distortedAngle = Math.atan2(-dy * width, dx * height);
```

(The minus sign in front of dy is necessary because in the pixel coordinate system, the y-axis points downward, which leads to angle measurements that are clockwise, but you need to supply an angle that is measured counterclockwise.)

Convert the result from radians to degrees:

```
distortedAngle = Math.toDegrees(distortedAngle);
```

The result is a value between 2180 and 180.

Compute both the distorted start and end angles in this way. Then, compute the difference between the two distorted angles.

If either the start angle or the difference is negative, add 360. Then, supply the start angle and the angle difference to the arc constructor.

```
Arc2D a = new Arc2D(x, y, width, height, distortedStartAngle, distortedAngleDifference,
    closureType);
```

Not only is the documentation vague on the exact nature of the distortion, it is also quite misleading in calling the distorted angle difference value the "arc angle." Except for the case of a circular arc, that value is neither the actual arc angle nor its distortion.

If you run the example program at the end of this section, then you can visually check that this calculation yields the correct values for the arc constructor (see Figure 7–9 on page 464).

Quadratic curves are not very flexible, and they are not commonly used in practice. Cubic curves (such as the Bezier curves drawn by the CubicCurve3D class) are, however, very common. By combining many cubic curves so that the slopes at the connection points match, you can create complex, smooth-looking curved shapes. For more information, we refer you to *Computer Graphics: Principles and Practice, Second Edition in C* by James D. Foley, Andries van Dam, Steven K. Feiner, et al. [Addison Wesley 1995].

You can build arbitrary sequences of line segments, quadratic curves, and cubic curves, and store them in a GeneralPath object. You specify the first coordinate of the path with the moveTo method. For example,

```
GeneralPath path = new GeneralPath();
path.moveTo(10, 20);
```

You then extend the path by calling one of the methods lineTo, quadTo, or curveTo. These methods extend the path by a line, a quadratic curve, or a cubic curve. To call lineTo, supply

the end point. For the two curve methods, supply the control points, then the end point. For example,

```
path.lineTo(20, 30);
path.curveTo(control1X, control1Y, control2X, control2Y, endX, endY);
```

You close the path by calling the `closePath` method. It draws a line back to the last `moveTo`.

To make a polygon, simply call `moveTo` to go to the first corner point, followed by repeated calls to `lineTo` to visit the other corner points. Finally, call `closePath` to close the polygon. The program in Example 7–1 shows this in more detail.

A general path does not have to be connected. You can call `moveTo` at any time to start a new path segment.

Finally, you can use the `append` method to add arbitrary `Shape` objects to a general path. The outline of the shape is added to the end to the path. The second parameter of the `append` method is `true` if the new shape should be connected to the last point on the path, `false` if it should not be connected. For example, the call

```
Rectangle2D r = . . .;
path.append(r, false);
```

appends the outline of a rectangle to the path without connecting it to the existing path. But

```
path.append(r, true);
```

adds a straight line from the end point of the path to the starting point of the rectangle, and then adds the rectangle outline to the path.

The program in Example 7–1 lets you create sample paths. Figures 7–7 and 7–8 show sample runs of the program. You pick a shape maker from the combo box. The program contains shape makers for

- Straight lines;
- Rectangles, round rectangles, and ellipses;
- Arcs (showing lines for the bounding rectangle and the start and end angles, in addition to the arc itself);
- Polygons (using a `GeneralPath`); and
- Quadratic and cubic curves.

Use the mouse to adjust the control points. As you move them, the shape continuously repaints itself.

The program is a bit complex because it handles a multiplicity of shapes and supports dragging of the control points.

An abstract superclass `ShapeMaker` encapsulates the commonality of the shape maker classes. Each shape has a fixed number of control points that the user can move around. The `get-PointCount` method returns that value. The abstract method

```
Shape makeShape(Point2D[] points)
```

computes the actual shape, given the current positions of the control points. The `toString` method returns the class name so that the `ShapeMaker` objects can simply be dumped into a `JComboBox`.

To enable dragging of the control points, the `ShapePanel` class handles both mouse and mouse motion events. If the mouse is pressed on top of a rectangle, subsequent mouse drags move the rectangle.

The majority of the shape maker classes are simple—their makeShape methods just construct and return the requested shape. However, the ArcMaker class needs to compute the distorted start and end angles. Furthermore, to demonstrate that the computation is indeed correct, the returned shape is a GeneralPath containing the arc itself, the bounding rectangle, and the lines from the center of the arc to the angle control points (see Figure 7–9).

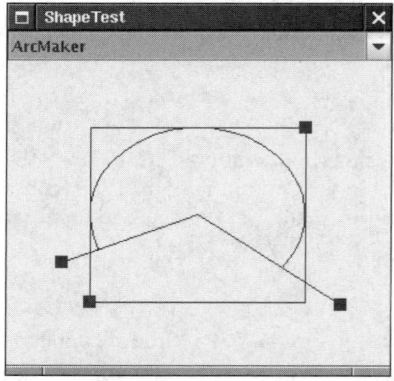

Figure 7–9: The ShapeTest program

Example 7–1: ShapeTest.java

```
1. import java.awt.*;
2. import java.awt.event.*;
3. import java.awt.geom.*;
4. import java.util.*;
5. import javax.swing.*;
6.
7. /**
8.    This program demonstrates the various 2D shapes.
9. */
10. public class ShapeTest
11. {
12.    public static void main(String[] args)
13.    {
14.       JFrame frame = new ShapeTestFrame();
15.       frame.setDefaultCloseOperation(JFrame.EXIT_ON_CLOSE);
16.       frame.setVisible(true);
17.    }
18. }
19.
20. /**
21.    This frame contains a combo box to select a shape
22.    and a panel to draw it.
23. */
24. class ShapeTestFrame extends JFrame
25. {
26.    public ShapeTestFrame()
27.    {
28.       setTitle("ShapeTest");
29.       setSize(DEFAULT_WIDTH, DEFAULT_HEIGHT);
30.
```

```
31.      final ShapePanel panel = new ShapePanel();
32.      add(panel, BorderLayout.CENTER);
33.      final JComboBox comboBox = new JComboBox();
34.      comboBox.addItem(new LineMaker());
35.      comboBox.addItem(new RectangleMaker());
36.      comboBox.addItem(new RoundRectangleMaker());
37.      comboBox.addItem(new EllipseMaker());
38.      comboBox.addItem(new ArcMaker());
39.      comboBox.addItem(new PolygonMaker());
40.      comboBox.addItem(new QuadCurveMaker());
41.      comboBox.addItem(new CubicCurveMaker());
42.      comboBox.addActionListener(new
43.         ActionListener()
44.         {
45.            public void actionPerformed(ActionEvent event)
46.            {
47.               ShapeMaker shapeMaker = (ShapeMaker) comboBox.getSelectedItem();
48.               panel.setShapeMaker(shapeMaker);
49.            }
50.         });
51.      add(comboBox, BorderLayout.NORTH);
52.      panel.setShapeMaker((ShapeMaker) comboBox.getItemAt(0));
53.   }
54.
55.   private static final int DEFAULT_WIDTH = 300;
56.   private static final int DEFAULT_HEIGHT = 300;
57. }
58.
59. /**
60.    This panel draws a shape and allows the user to
61.    move the points that define it.
62. */
63. class ShapePanel extends JPanel
64. {
65.    public ShapePanel()
66.    {
67.       addMouseListener(new
68.          MouseAdapter()
69.          {
70.             public void mousePressed(MouseEvent event)
71.             {
72.                Point p = event.getPoint();
73.                for (int i = 0; i < points.length; i++)
74.                {
75.                   double x = points[i].getX() - SIZE / 2;
76.                   double y = points[i].getY() - SIZE / 2;
77.                   Rectangle2D r = new Rectangle2D.Double(x, y, SIZE, SIZE);
78.                   if (r.contains(p))
79.                   {
80.                      current = i;
81.                      return;
82.                   }
83.                }
84.             }
85.
86.             public void mouseReleased(MouseEvent event)
```

```
87.            {
88.                current = -1;
89.            }
90.         });
91.      addMouseMotionListener(new
92.         MouseMotionAdapter()
93.         {
94.            public void mouseDragged(MouseEvent event)
95.            {
96.               if (current == -1) return;
97.               points[current] = event.getPoint();
98.               repaint();
99.            }
100.        });
101.     current = -1;
102.   }
103.
104.   /**
105.      Set a shape maker and initialize it with a random
106.      point set.
107.      @param aShapeMaker a shape maker that defines a shape
108.      from a point set
109.   */
110.   public void setShapeMaker(ShapeMaker aShapeMaker)
111.   {
112.      shapeMaker = aShapeMaker;
113.      int n = shapeMaker.getPointCount();
114.      points = new Point2D[n];
115.      for (int i = 0; i < n; i++)
116.      {
117.         double x = generator.nextDouble() * getWidth();
118.         double y = generator.nextDouble() * getHeight();
119.         points[i] = new Point2D.Double(x, y);
120.      }
121.      repaint();
122.   }
123.
124.   public void paintComponent(Graphics g)
125.   {
126.      super.paintComponent(g);
127.      if (points == null) return;
128.      Graphics2D g2 = (Graphics2D) g;
129.      for (int i = 0; i < points.length; i++)
130.      {  double x = points[i].getX() - SIZE / 2;
131.         double y = points[i].getY() - SIZE / 2;
132.         g2.fill(new Rectangle2D.Double(x, y, SIZE, SIZE));
133.      }
134.
135.      g2.draw(shapeMaker.makeShape(points));
136.   }
137.
138.   private Point2D[] points;
139.   private static Random generator = new Random();
140.   private static int SIZE = 10;
141.   private int current;
142.   private ShapeMaker shapeMaker;
```

```
143.  }
144.
145.  /**
146.     A shape maker can make a shape from a point set.
147.     Concrete subclasses must return a shape in the makeShape
148.     method.
149.  */
150.  abstract class ShapeMaker
151.  {
152.     /**
153.        Constructs a shape maker.
154.        @param aPointCount the number of points needed to define
155.        this shape.
156.     */
157.     public ShapeMaker(int aPointCount)
158.     {
159.        pointCount = aPointCount;
160.     }
161.
162.     /**
163.        Gets the number of points needed to define this shape.
164.        @return the point count
165.     */
166.     public int getPointCount()
167.     {
168.        return pointCount;
169.     }
170.
171.     /**
172.        Makes a shape out of the given point set.
173.        @param p the points that define the shape
174.        @return the shape defined by the points
175.     */
176.     public abstract Shape makeShape(Point2D[] p);
177.
178.     public String toString()
179.     {
180.        return getClass().getName();
181.     }
182.
183.     private int pointCount;
184.  }
185.
186.  /**
187.     Makes a line that joins two given points.
188.  */
189.  class LineMaker extends ShapeMaker
190.  {
191.     public LineMaker() { super(2); }
192.
193.     public Shape makeShape(Point2D[] p)
194.     {
195.        return new Line2D.Double(p[0], p[1]);
196.     }
197.  }
198.
```

```
199. /**
200.    Makes a rectangle that joins two given corner points.
201. */
202. class RectangleMaker extends ShapeMaker
203. {
204.    public RectangleMaker() { super(2); }
205.
206.    public Shape makeShape(Point2D[] p)
207.    {
208.       Rectangle2D s = new Rectangle2D.Double();
209.       s.setFrameFromDiagonal(p[0], p[1]);
210.       return s;
211.    }
212. }
213.
214. /**
215.    Makes a round rectangle that joins two given corner points.
216. */
217. class RoundRectangleMaker extends ShapeMaker
218. {
219.    public RoundRectangleMaker() { super(2); }
220.
221.    public Shape makeShape(Point2D[] p)
222.    {
223.       RoundRectangle2D s = new RoundRectangle2D.Double(0, 0, 0, 0, 20, 20);
224.       s.setFrameFromDiagonal(p[0], p[1]);
225.       return s;
226.    }
227. }
228.
229. /**
230.    Makes an ellipse contained in a bounding box with two given
231.    corner points.
232. */
233. class EllipseMaker extends ShapeMaker
234. {
235.    public EllipseMaker() { super(2); }
236.
237.    public Shape makeShape(Point2D[] p)
238.    {
239.       Ellipse2D s = new Ellipse2D.Double();
240.       s.setFrameFromDiagonal(p[0], p[1]);
241.       return s;
242.    }
243. }
244.
245. /**
246.    Makes an arc contained in a bounding box with two given
247.    corner points, and with starting and ending angles given
248.    by lines emanating from the center of the bounding box and
249.    ending in two given points. To show the correctness of
250.    the angle computation, the returned shape contains the arc,
251.    the bounding box, and the lines.
252. */
253. class ArcMaker extends ShapeMaker
254. {
```

```
255.    public ArcMaker() { super(4); }
256.
257.    public Shape makeShape(Point2D[] p)
258.    {
259.       double centerX = (p[0].getX() + p[1].getX()) / 2;
260.       double centerY = (p[0].getY() + p[1].getY()) / 2;
261.       double width = Math.abs(p[1].getX() - p[0].getX());
262.       double height = Math.abs(p[1].getY() - p[0].getY());
263.
264.       double distortedStartAngle = Math.toDegrees(Math.atan2(-(p[2].getY() - centerY)
265.             * width, (p[2].getX() - centerX) * height));
266.       double distortedEndAngle = Math.toDegrees(Math.atan2(-(p[3].getY() - centerY)
267.             * width, (p[3].getX() - centerX) * height));
268.       double distortedAngleDifference = distortedEndAngle - distortedStartAngle;
269.       if (distortedStartAngle < 0) distortedStartAngle += 360;
270.       if (distortedAngleDifference < 0) distortedAngleDifference += 360;
271.
272.       Arc2D s = new Arc2D.Double(0, 0, 0, 0,
273.          distortedStartAngle, distortedAngleDifference, Arc2D.OPEN);
274.       s.setFrameFromDiagonal(p[0], p[1]);
275.
276.       GeneralPath g = new GeneralPath();
277.       g.append(s, false);
278.       Rectangle2D r = new Rectangle2D.Double();
279.       r.setFrameFromDiagonal(p[0], p[1]);
280.       g.append(r, false);
281.       Point2D center = new Point2D.Double(centerX, centerY);
282.       g.append(new Line2D.Double(center, p[2]), false);
283.       g.append(new Line2D.Double(center, p[3]), false);
284.       return g;
285.    }
286. }
287.
288. /**
289.    Makes a polygon defined by six corner points.
290. */
291. class PolygonMaker extends ShapeMaker
292. {
293.    public PolygonMaker() { super(6); }
294.
295.    public Shape makeShape(Point2D[] p)
296.    {
297.       GeneralPath s = new GeneralPath();
298.       s.moveTo((float) p[0].getX(), (float) p[0].getY());
299.       for (int i = 1; i < p.length; i++)
300.          s.lineTo((float) p[i].getX(), (float) p[i].getY());
301.       s.closePath();
302.       return s;
303.    }
304. }
305.
306. /**
307.    Makes a quad curve defined by two end points and a control
308.    point.
309. */
310. class QuadCurveMaker extends ShapeMaker
```

```
311.  {
312.      public QuadCurveMaker() { super(3); }
313.
314.      public Shape makeShape(Point2D[] p)
315.      {
316.          return new QuadCurve2D.Double(p[0].getX(), p[0].getY(), p[1].getX(), p[1].getY(),
317.              p[2].getX(), p[2].getY());
318.      }
319.  }
320.
321.  /**
322.     Makes a cubic curve defined by two end points and two control
323.     points.
324.  */
325.  class CubicCurveMaker extends ShapeMaker
326.  {
327.      public CubicCurveMaker() { super(4); }
328.
329.      public Shape makeShape(Point2D[] p)
330.      {
331.          return new CubicCurve2D.Double(p[0].getX(), p[0].getY(), p[1].getX(), p[1].getY(),
332.              p[2].getX(), p[2].getY(), p[3].getX(), p[3].getY());
333.      }
334.  }
```

 java.awt.geom.RoundRectangle2D.Double 1.2

- RoundRectangle2D.Double(double x, double y, double w, double h, double arcWidth, double arcHeight)

  constructs a round rectangle with the given bounding rectangle and arc dimensions.

Parameters:		
	x, y	Top-left corner of bounding rectangle
	w, h	Width and height of bounding rectangle
	arcWidth	The horizontal distance from the center to the end of the elliptical boundary arc
	arcHeight	The vertical distance from the center to the end of the elliptical boundary arc

 java.awt.geom.Arc2D.Double 1.2

- Arc2D.Double(double x, double y, double w, double h, double startAngle, double arcAngle, int type)

  constructs an arc with the given bounding rectangle, start, and arc angle and arc type.

Parameters:		
	x, y	Top-left corner of bounding rectangle.
	w, h	Width and height of bounding rectangle.
	startAngle	The angular measurement between the x-axis and the line joining the center of the bounding rectangle with the starting point of the arc, in degrees. The angle is distorted so that an "angle" of 45° corresponds to the angle between the x-axis and the line joining the center and top-right corner of the bounding rectangle.

arcAngle	The difference between the distorted end and start angles—see the sidebar on page 462. For a circular arc, this value equals the angle swept out by the arc.
type	One of Arc2D.OPEN, Arc2D.PIE, and Arc2D.CHORD

 java.awt.geom.QuadCurve2D.Double 1.2

- QuadCurve2D.Double(double x1, double y1, double ctrlx, double ctrly, double x2, double y2)
  constructs a quadratic curve from a start point, a control point, and an end point.

  Parameters:

x1, y1	The start point
ctrlx, ctrly	The control point
x2, y2	The end points

 java.awt.geom.CubicCurve2D.Double 1.2

- CubicCurve2D.Double(double x1, double y1, double ctrlx1, double ctrly1, double ctrlx2, double ctrly2, double x2, double y2)
  constructs a cubic curve from a start point, two control points, and an end point.

  Parameters:

x1, y1	The start point
ctrlx1, ctrly1	The first control point
ctrlx2, ctrly2	The second control point
x2, y2	The end points

 java.awt.geom.GeneralPath 1.2

- GeneralPath()
  constructs an empty general path.
- void moveTo(float x, float y)
  makes (x, y) the *current point*, that is, the starting point of the next segment.
- void lineTo(float x, float y)
- void quadTo(float ctrlx, float ctrly, float x, float y)
- void curveTo(float ctrl1x, float ctrl1y, float ctrl2x, float ctrl2y, float x, float y)
  draw a line, quadratic curve, or cubic curve from the current point to the end point (x, y), and make that end point the current point.
- void append(Shape s, boolean connect)
  adds the outline of the given shape to the general path. If connect is true, the current point of the general path is connected to the starting point of the added shape by a straight line.
- void closePath()
  closes the path by drawing a straight line from the current point to the first point in the path.

Areas

In the preceding section, you saw how you can specify complex shapes by constructing general paths that are composed of lines and curves. By using a sufficient number of lines and curves, you can draw essentially any shape. For example, the shapes of characters in the fonts that you see on the screen and on your printouts are all made up of lines and cubic curves.

Occasionally, it is easier to describe a shape by composing it from *areas,* such as rectangles, polygons, or ellipses. The Java 2D API supports four *constructive area geometry* operations that combine two areas to a new area:

- add—The combined area contains all points that are in the first or the second area.
- subtract—The combined area contains all points that are in the first but not the second area.
- intersect—The combined area contains all points that are in the first and the second area.
- exclusiveOr—The combined area contains all points that are in either the first or the second area, but not in both.

Figure 7–10 shows these operations.

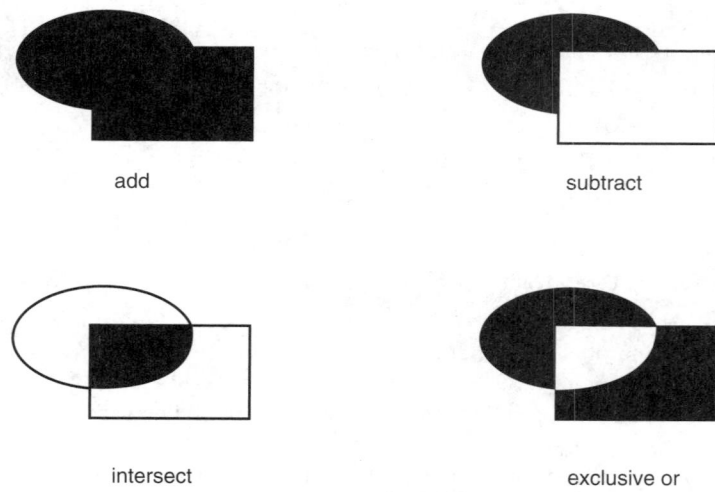

add

subtract

intersect

exclusive or

Figure 7–10: Constructive area geometry operations

To construct a complex area, you start out with a default area object.

```
Area a = new Area();
```

Then, you combine the area with any shape:

```
a.add(new Rectangle2D.Double(. . .));
a.subtract(path);
. . .
```

The Area class implements the Shape interface. You can stroke the boundary of the area with the draw method or paint the interior with the fill method of the Graphics2D class.

The program in Example 7–2 shows the constructive area geometry operations. Select one of the four operations, and see the result of combining an ellipse and a rectangle with the operation that you selected (see Figure 7–11).

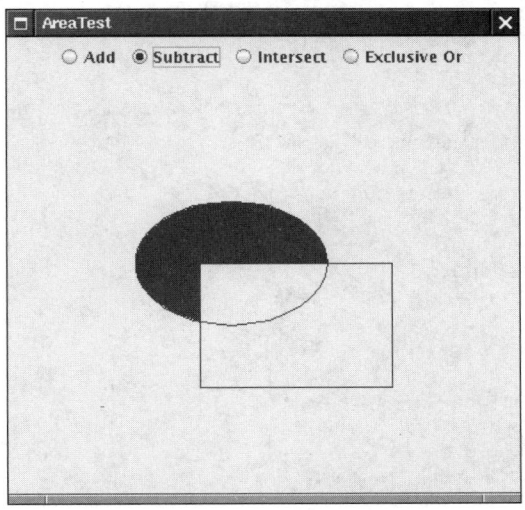

Figure 7–11: The AreaTest program

Example 7–2: AreaTest.java

```
1. import java.awt.*;
2. import java.awt.event.*;
3. import java.awt.geom.*;
4. import java.util.*;
5. import javax.swing.*;
6.
7. /**
8.    This program demonstrates constructive area geometry
9.    operations.
10. */
11. public class AreaTest
12. {
13.    public static void main(String[] args)
14.    {
15.       JFrame frame = new AreaTestFrame();
16.       frame.setDefaultCloseOperation(JFrame.EXIT_ON_CLOSE);
17.       frame.setVisible(true);
18.    }
19. }
20.
21. /**
22.    This frame contains a set of radio buttons to define
23.    area operations and a panel to show their result.
24. */
25. class AreaTestFrame extends JFrame
26. {
27.    public AreaTestFrame()
28.    {
29.       setTitle("AreaTest");
30.       setSize(DEFAULT_WIDTH, DEFAULT_HEIGHT);
31.
32.       area1 = new Area(new Ellipse2D.Double(100, 100, 150, 100));
```

```
33.         area2 = new Area(new Rectangle2D.Double(150, 150, 150, 100));
34.
35.         panel = new
36.            JPanel()
37.            {
38.               public void paintComponent(Graphics g)
39.               {
40.                  super.paintComponent(g);
41.                  Graphics2D g2 = (Graphics2D)g;
42.                  g2.draw(area1);
43.                  g2.draw(area2);
44.                  if (area != null) g2.fill(area);
45.               }
46.            };
47.
48.         add(panel, BorderLayout.CENTER);
49.
50.         JPanel buttonPanel = new JPanel();
51.         ButtonGroup group = new ButtonGroup();
52.
53.         JRadioButton addButton = new JRadioButton("Add", false);
54.         buttonPanel.add(addButton);
55.         group.add(addButton);
56.         addButton.addActionListener(new
57.            ActionListener()
58.            {
59.               public void actionPerformed(ActionEvent event)
60.               {
61.                  area = new Area();
62.                  area.add(area1);
63.                  area.add(area2);
64.                  panel.repaint();
65.               }
66.            });
67.
68.         JRadioButton subtractButton = new JRadioButton("Subtract", false);
69.         buttonPanel.add(subtractButton);
70.         group.add(subtractButton);
71.         subtractButton.addActionListener(new
72.            ActionListener()
73.            {
74.               public void actionPerformed(ActionEvent event)
75.               {
76.                  area = new Area();
77.                  area.add(area1);
78.                  area.subtract(area2);
79.                  panel.repaint();
80.               }
81.            });
82.
83.         JRadioButton intersectButton = new JRadioButton("Intersect", false);
84.         buttonPanel.add(intersectButton);
85.         group.add(intersectButton);
86.         intersectButton.addActionListener(new
87.            ActionListener()
88.            {
```

```
89.      public void actionPerformed(ActionEvent event)
90.      {
91.         area = new Area();
92.         area.add(area1);
93.         area.intersect(area2);
94.         panel.repaint();
95.      }
96.   });
97.
98.   JRadioButton exclusiveOrButton = new JRadioButton("Exclusive Or", false);
99.   buttonPanel.add(exclusiveOrButton);
100.  group.add(exclusiveOrButton);
101.  exclusiveOrButton.addActionListener(new
102.     ActionListener()
103.     {
104.        public void actionPerformed(ActionEvent event)
105.        {
106.           area = new Area();
107.           area.add(area1);
108.           area.exclusiveOr(area2);
109.           panel.repaint();
110.        }
111.     });
112.
113.  add(buttonPanel, BorderLayout.NORTH);
114. }
115.
116. private JPanel panel;
117. private Area area;
118. private Area area1;
119. private Area area2;
120.
121. private static final int DEFAULT_WIDTH = 400;
122. private static final int DEFAULT_HEIGHT = 400;
123. }
```

java.awt.geom.Area

- void add(Area other)
- void subtract(Area other)
- void intersect(Area other)
- void exclusiveOr(Area other)

  carry out the constructive area geometry operation with this area and the other area and set this area to the result.

Strokes

The draw operation of the Graphics2D class draws the boundary of a shape by using the currently selected *stroke*. By default, the stroke is a solid line that is one pixel wide. You can select a different stroke by calling the setStroke method. You supply an object of a class that implements the Stroke interface. The Java 2D API defines only one such class, called BasicStroke. In this section, we look at the capabilities of the BasicStroke class.

You can construct strokes of arbitrary thickness. For example, here is how you draw lines that are 10 pixels wide.

```
g2.setStroke(new BasicStroke(10.0F));
g2.draw(new Line2D.Double(. . .));
```

When a stroke is more than a pixel thick, then the *end* of the stroke can have different styles. Figure 7–12 shows these so-called *end cap styles*. You have three choices:

- A *butt cap* simply ends the stroke at its end point.
- A *round cap* adds a half-circle to the end of the stroke.
- A *square cap* adds a half-square to the end of the stroke.

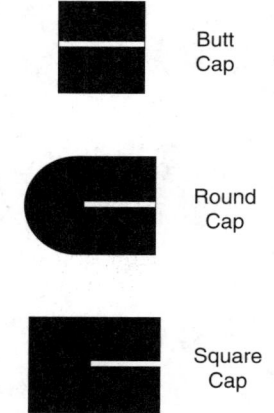

Butt Cap

Round Cap

Square Cap

Figure 7–12: End cap styles

When two thick strokes meet, there are three choices for the *join style* (see Figure 7–13).

- A *bevel join* joins the strokes with a straight line that is perpendicular to the bisector of the angle between the two strokes.
- A *round join* extends each stroke to have a round cap.
- A *miter join* extends both strokes by adding a "spike."

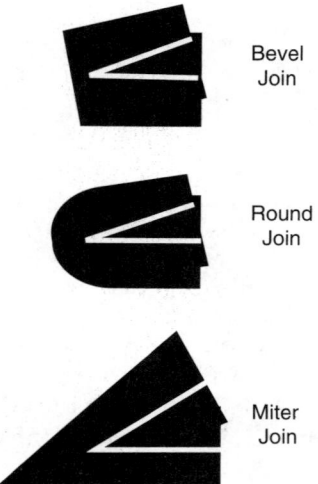

Bevel Join

Round Join

Miter Join

Figure 7–13: Join styles

The miter join is not suitable for lines that meet at small angles. If two lines join with an angle that is less than the *miter limit,* then a bevel join is used instead. That usage prevents extremely long spikes. By default, the miter limit is 10 degrees.

You specify these choices in the `BasicStroke` constructor, for example:

```
g2.setStroke(new BasicStroke(10.0F, BasicStroke.CAP_ROUND, BasicStroke.JOIN_ROUND));
g2.setStroke(new BasicStroke(10.0F, BasicStroke.CAP_BUTT, BasicStroke.JOIN_MITER,
    15.0F /* miter limit */));
```

Finally, you can specify dashed lines by setting a *dash pattern.* In the program in Example 7–3, you can select a dash pattern that spells out SOS in Morse code. The dash pattern is a `float[]` array of numbers that contains the lengths of the "on" and "off" strokes (see Figure 7–14).

Figure 7–14: A dash pattern

You specify the dash pattern and a *dash phase* when constructing the `BasicStroke`. The dash phase indicates where in the dash pattern each line should start. Normally, you set this value to 0.

```
float[] dashPattern = { 10, 10, 10, 10, 10, 10, 30, 10, 30, ... };
g2.setStroke(new BasicStroke(10.0F, BasicStroke.CAP_BUTT, BasicStroke.JOIN_MITER,
    10.0F /* miter limit */, dashPattern, 0 /* dash phase */));
```

 NOTE: End cap styles are applied to the ends of *each dash* in a dash pattern.

The program in Example 7–3 lets you specify end cap styles, join styles, and dashed lines (see Figure 7–15). You can move the ends of the line segments to test the miter limit: Select the miter join, then move the line segment to form a very acute angle. You will see the miter join turn into a bevel join.

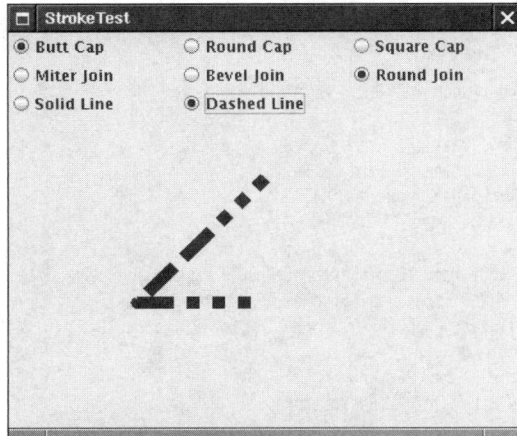

Figure 7–15: The StrokeTest program

The program is similar to the program in Example 7–1. The mouse listener remembers if you click on the end point of a line segment, and the mouse motion listener monitors the dragging of the end point. A set of radio buttons signal the user choices for the end cap style, join style, and solid or dashed line. The `paintComponent` method of the `StrokePanel` class constructs a `GeneralPath` consisting of the two line segments that join the three points that the user can move with the mouse. It then constructs a `BasicStroke`, according to the selections that the user made, and finally draws the path.

Example 7–3: StrokeTest.java

```java
1. import java.awt.*;
2. import java.awt.event.*;
3. import java.awt.geom.*;
4. import java.util.*;
5. import javax.swing.*;
6.
7. /**
8.    This program demonstrates different stroke types.
9. */
10. public class StrokeTest
11. {
12.    public static void main(String[] args)
13.    {
14.       JFrame frame = new StrokeTestFrame();
15.       frame.setDefaultCloseOperation(JFrame.EXIT_ON_CLOSE);
16.       frame.setVisible(true);
17.    }
18. }
19.
20. /**
21.    This frame lets the user choose the cap, join, and
22.    line style, and shows the resulting stroke.
23. */
24. class StrokeTestFrame extends JFrame
25. {
26.    public StrokeTestFrame()
27.    {
28.       setTitle("StrokeTest");
29.       setSize(DEFAULT_WIDTH, DEFAULT_HEIGHT);
30.
31.       canvas = new StrokePanel();
32.       add(canvas, BorderLayout.CENTER);
33.
34.       buttonPanel = new JPanel();
35.       buttonPanel.setLayout(new GridLayout(3, 3));
36.       add(buttonPanel, BorderLayout.NORTH);
37.
38.       ButtonGroup group1 = new ButtonGroup();
39.       makeCapButton("Butt Cap", BasicStroke.CAP_BUTT, group1);
40.       makeCapButton("Round Cap", BasicStroke.CAP_ROUND, group1);
41.       makeCapButton("Square Cap", BasicStroke.CAP_SQUARE, group1);
42.
43.       ButtonGroup group2 = new ButtonGroup();
44.       makeJoinButton("Miter Join", BasicStroke.JOIN_MITER, group2);
45.       makeJoinButton("Bevel Join", BasicStroke.JOIN_BEVEL, group2);
46.       makeJoinButton("Round Join", BasicStroke.JOIN_ROUND, group2);
```

```
47.
48.        ButtonGroup group3 = new ButtonGroup();
49.        makeDashButton("Solid Line", false, group3);
50.        makeDashButton("Dashed Line", true, group3);
51.     }
52.
53.     /**
54.        Makes a radio button to change the cap style.
55.        @param label the button label
56.        @param style the cap style
57.        @param group the radio button group
58.     */
59.     private void makeCapButton(String label, final int style, ButtonGroup group)
60.     {
61.        // select first button in group
62.        boolean selected = group.getButtonCount() == 0;
63.        JRadioButton button = new JRadioButton(label, selected);
64.        buttonPanel.add(button);
65.        group.add(button);
66.        button.addActionListener(new
67.           ActionListener()
68.           {
69.              public void actionPerformed(ActionEvent event)
70.              {
71.                 canvas.setCap(style);
72.              }
73.           });
74.     }
75.
76.     /**
77.        Makes a radio button to change the join style.
78.        @param label the button label
79.        @param style the join style
80.        @param group the radio button group
81.     */
82.     private void makeJoinButton(String label, final int style,
83.        ButtonGroup group)
84.     {
85.        // select first button in group
86.        boolean selected = group.getButtonCount() == 0;
87.        JRadioButton button = new JRadioButton(label, selected);
88.        buttonPanel.add(button);
89.        group.add(button);
90.        button.addActionListener(new
91.           ActionListener()
92.           {
93.              public void actionPerformed(ActionEvent event)
94.              {
95.                 canvas.setJoin(style);
96.              }
97.           });
98.     }
99.
100.    /**
101.       Makes a radio button to set solid or dashed lines
102.       @param label the button label
```

```
103.      @param style false for solid, true for dashed lines
104.      @param group the radio button group
105.    */
106.    private void makeDashButton(String label, final boolean style,
107.       ButtonGroup group)
108.    {
109.       // select first button in group
110.       boolean selected = group.getButtonCount() == 0;
111.       JRadioButton button = new JRadioButton(label, selected);
112.       buttonPanel.add(button);
113.       group.add(button);
114.       button.addActionListener(new
115.          ActionListener()
116.          {
117.             public void actionPerformed(ActionEvent event)
118.             {
119.                canvas.setDash(style);
120.             }
121.          });
122.    }
123.
124.    private StrokePanel canvas;
125.    private JPanel buttonPanel;
126.
127.    private static final int DEFAULT_WIDTH = 400;
128.    private static final int DEFAULT_HEIGHT = 400;
129. }
130.
131. /**
132.    This panel draws two joined lines, using different
133.    stroke objects, and allows the user to drag the three
134.    points defining the lines.
135. */
136. class StrokePanel extends JPanel
137. {
138.    public StrokePanel()
139.    {
140.       addMouseListener(new
141.          MouseAdapter()
142.          {
143.             public void mousePressed(MouseEvent event)
144.             {
145.                Point p = event.getPoint();
146.                for (int i = 0; i < points.length; i++)
147.                {
148.                   double x = points[i].getX() - SIZE / 2;
149.                   double y = points[i].getY() - SIZE / 2;
150.                   Rectangle2D r = new Rectangle2D.Double(x, y, SIZE, SIZE);
151.                   if (r.contains(p))
152.                   {
153.                      current = i;
154.                      return;
155.                   }
156.                }
157.             }
158.
```

```
159.        public void mouseReleased(MouseEvent event)
160.        {
161.           current = -1;
162.        }
163.     });
164.
165.    addMouseMotionListener(new
166.       MouseMotionAdapter()
167.       {
168.          public void mouseDragged(MouseEvent event)
169.          {
170.             if (current == -1) return;
171.             points[current] = event.getPoint();
172.             repaint();
173.          }
174.       });
175.
176.    points = new Point2D[3];
177.    points[0] = new Point2D.Double(200, 100);
178.    points[1] = new Point2D.Double(100, 200);
179.    points[2] = new Point2D.Double(200, 200);
180.    current = -1;
181.    width = 8.0F;
182. }
183.
184. public void paintComponent(Graphics g)
185. {
186.    super.paintComponent(g);
187.    Graphics2D g2 = (Graphics2D) g;
188.    GeneralPath path = new GeneralPath();
189.    path.moveTo((float) points[0].getX(), (float) points[0].getY());
190.    for (int i = 1; i < points.length; i++)
191.       path.lineTo((float) points[i].getX(), (float) points[i].getY());
192.    BasicStroke stroke;
193.    if (dash)
194.    {
195.       float miterLimit = 10.0F;
196.       float[] dashPattern = { 10F, 10F, 10F, 10F, 10F, 10F,
197.          30F, 10F, 30F, 10F, 30F, 10F, 10F, 10F, 10F, 10F, 10F, 30F };
198.       float dashPhase = 0;
199.       stroke = new BasicStroke(width, cap, join, miterLimit, dashPattern, dashPhase);
200.    }
201.    else
202.       stroke = new BasicStroke(width, cap, join);
203.    g2.setStroke(stroke);
204.    g2.draw(path);
205. }
206.
207. /**
208.    Sets the join style.
209.    @param j the join style
210. */
211. public void setJoin(int j)
212. {
213.    join = j;
214.    repaint();
```

```
215.   }
216.
217.   /**
218.      Sets the cap style.
219.      @param c the cap style
220.   */
221.   public void setCap(int c)
222.   {
223.      cap = c;
224.      repaint();
225.   }
226.
227.   /**
228.      Sets solid or dashed lines
229.      @param d false for solid, true for dashed lines
230.   */
231.   public void setDash(boolean d)
232.   {
233.      dash = d;
234.      repaint();
235.   }
236.
237.   private Point2D[] points;
238.   private static int SIZE = 10;
239.   private int current;
240.   private float width;
241.   private int cap;
242.   private int join;
243.   private boolean dash;
244. }
```

 java.awt.Graphics2D 1.2

- void setStroke(Stroke s)
  sets the stroke of this graphics context to the given object that implements the Stroke interface.

java.awt.BasicStroke 1.2

- BasicStroke(float width)
- BasicStroke(float width, int cap, int join)
- BasicStroke(float width, int cap, int join, float miterlimit)
- BasicStroke(float width, int cap, int join, float miterlimit, float[] dash, float dashPhase)
  construct a stroke object with the given attributes.

Parameters:	width	The width of the pen
	cap	The end cap style, one of CAP_BUTT, CAP_ROUND, and CAP_SQUARE
	join	The join style, one of JOIN_BEVEL, JOIN_MITER, and JOIN_ROUND
	miterlimit	The angle, in degrees, below which a miter join is rendered as a bevel join
	dash	An array of the lengths of the alternating filled and blank portions of a dashed stroke

dashPhase	The "phase" of the dash pattern; a segment of this length, preceding the starting point of the stroke, is assumed to have the dash pattern already applied

Paint

When you fill a shape, its inside is covered with *paint*. You use the setPaint method to set the paint style to an object with a class that implements the Paint interface. The Java 2D API provides three such classes:

- The Color class implements the Paint interface. To fill shapes with a solid color, simply call setPaint with a Color object, such as

  g2.setPaint(Color.red);

- The GradientPaint class varies colors by interpolating between two given color values (see Figure 7–16).

- The TexturePaint class fills an area with repetitions of an image (see Figure 7–17).

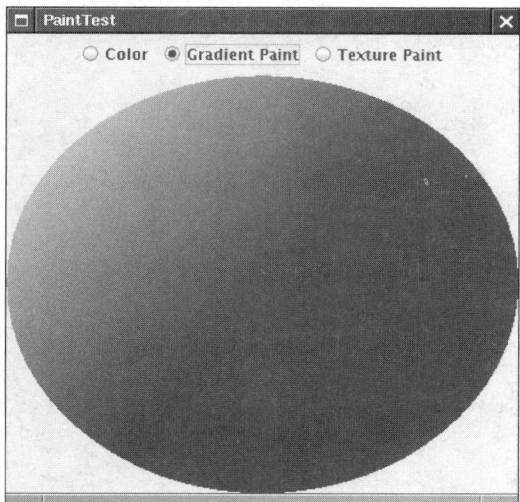

Figure 7–16: Gradient paint

You construct a GradientPaint object by specifying two points and the colors that you want at these two points.

    g2.setPaint(new GradientPaint(p1, Color.red, p2, Color.blue));

Colors are interpolated along the line joining the two points. Colors are constant along lines that are perpendicular to that joining line. Points beyond an end point of the line are given the color at the end point.

Alternatively, if you call the GradientPaint constructor with true for the cyclic parameter,

    g2.setPaint(new GradientPaint(p1, Color.red, p2, Color.blue, true));

then the color variation *cycles* and keeps varying beyond the end points.

To construct a TexturePaint object, you specify a BufferedImage and an *anchor* rectangle. The anchor rectangle is extended indefinitely in x- and y-directions to tile the entire coordinate plane. The image is scaled to fit into the anchor and then replicated into each tile.

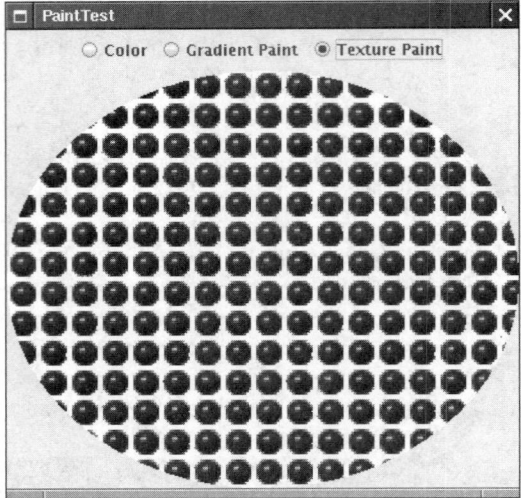

Figure 7–17: Texture paint

We introduce the BufferedImage class later in this chapter when we discuss images in detail. You create a BufferedImage object by giving the image size and the *image type*. The most common image type is TYPE_INT_ARGB, in which each pixel is specified by an integer that describes the *alpha*, or transparency, red, green, and blue values. For example,

```
BufferedImage bufferedImage = new BufferedImage(width,height, BufferedImage.TYPE_INT_ARGB);
```

You then obtain a graphics context to draw into the buffered image.

```
Graphics2D g2 = bufferedImage.createGraphics();
```

Any drawing operations on g2 now fill the buffered image with pixels. When you are done, you can create your TexturePaint object:

```
g2.setPaint(new TexturePaint(bufferedImage, anchorRectangle));
```

The program in Example 7–4 lets the user choose between a solid color paint, a gradient paint, and a texture paint. Then, an ellipse is filled with the specified paint.

The texture paint uses an image that is read from a GIF file. As you will see later in this chapter, the ImageIO class makes it simple to read a graphics file into a buffered image by calling

```
bufferedImage = ImageIO.read(new File("blue-ball.gif"));
```

 NOTE: The ImageIO class was added in JDK version 1.4. If you have an older version of the JDK, use the following code instead:

```
Image image = Toolkit.getDefaultToolkit().getImage("blue-ball.gif");
MediaTracker tracker = new MediaTracker(this);
tracker.addImage(image, 0);
try { tracker.waitForID(0); }
catch (InterruptedException e) {}
bufferedImage = new BufferedImage(image.getWidth(null), image.getHeight(null),
    BufferedImage.TYPE_INT_ARGB);
Graphics2D g2 = bufferedImage.createGraphics();
g2.drawImage(image, 0, 0, null);
```

To show the significance of the anchor rectangle, we specify the anchor to have twice the size of the image:

```
Rectangle2D anchor = new Rectangle2D.Double(0, 0,
   2 * bufferedImage.getWidth(),
   2 * bufferedImage.getHeight());
paint = new TexturePaint(bufferedImage, anchor);
```

As you can see when you select Texture Paint, the image is scaled to fit the anchor, and it is then replicated to fill the shape. Tiles that meet the boundary of the shape are clipped.

Example 7–4: PaintTest.java

```
 1. import java.awt.*;
 2. import java.awt.event.*;
 3. import java.awt.geom.*;
 4. import java.awt.image.*;
 5. import java.io.*;
 6. import java.util.*;
 7. import javax.imageio.*;
 8. import javax.swing.*;
 9.
10. /**
11.    This program demonstrates the various paint modes.
12. */
13. public class PaintTest
14. {
15.    public static void main(String[] args)
16.    {
17.       JFrame frame = new PaintTestFrame();
18.       frame.setDefaultCloseOperation(JFrame.EXIT_ON_CLOSE);
19.       frame.setVisible(true);
20.    }
21. }
22.
23. /**
24.    This frame contains radio buttons to choose the paint mode
25.    and a panel that draws a circle in the selected paint mode.
26. */
27. class PaintTestFrame extends JFrame
28. {
29.    public PaintTestFrame()
30.    {
31.       setTitle("PaintTest");
32.       setSize(DEFAULT_WIDTH, DEFAULT_HEIGHT);
33.
34.       canvas = new PaintPanel();
35.       add(canvas, BorderLayout.CENTER);
36.
37.       JPanel buttonPanel = new JPanel();
38.       ButtonGroup group = new ButtonGroup();
39.
40.       JRadioButton colorButton = new JRadioButton("Color", true);
41.       buttonPanel.add(colorButton);
42.       group.add(colorButton);
43.       colorButton.addActionListener(new
44.          ActionListener()
45.          {
46.             public void actionPerformed(ActionEvent event)
```

```
47.          {
48.              canvas.setColor();
49.          }
50.      });
51.
52.      JRadioButton gradientPaintButton = new JRadioButton("Gradient Paint", false);
53.      buttonPanel.add(gradientPaintButton);
54.      group.add(gradientPaintButton);
55.      gradientPaintButton.addActionListener(new
56.          ActionListener()
57.          {
58.              public void actionPerformed(ActionEvent event)
59.              {
60.                  canvas.setGradientPaint();
61.              }
62.          });
63.
64.      JRadioButton texturePaintButton = new JRadioButton("Texture Paint", false);
65.      buttonPanel.add(texturePaintButton);
66.      group.add(texturePaintButton);
67.      texturePaintButton.addActionListener(new
68.          ActionListener()
69.          {
70.              public void actionPerformed(ActionEvent event)
71.              {
72.                  canvas.setTexturePaint();
73.              }
74.          });
75.
76.      add(buttonPanel, BorderLayout.NORTH);
77.  }
78.
79.  private PaintPanel canvas;
80.  private static final int DEFAULT_WIDTH = 400;
81.  private static final int DEFAULT_HEIGHT = 400;
82. }
83.
84. /**
85.    This panel paints a circle in various paint modes.
86. */
87. class PaintPanel extends JPanel
88. {
89.    public PaintPanel()
90.    {
91.       try
92.       {
93.          bufferedImage = ImageIO.read(new File("blue-ball.gif"));
94.       }
95.       catch (IOException e)
96.       {
97.          e.printStackTrace();
98.       }
99.       setColor();
100.   }
101.
102.   public void paintComponent(Graphics g)
103.   {
104.      super.paintComponent(g);
```

```
105.       Graphics2D g2 = (Graphics2D) g;
106.       g2.setPaint(paint);
107.       Ellipse2D circle = new Ellipse2D.Double(0, 0, getWidth(), getHeight());
108.       g2.fill(circle);
109.    }
110.
111.    /**
112.       Paints in a plain color.
113.    */
114.    public void setColor()
115.    {
116.       paint = Color.red; // Color implements Paint
117.       repaint();
118.    }
119.
120.    /**
121.       Sets the paint mode to gradient paint.
122.    */
123.    public void setGradientPaint()
124.    {
125.       paint = new GradientPaint(0, 0, Color.red,
126.          (float) getWidth(), (float) getHeight(), Color.blue);
127.       repaint();
128.    }
129.
130.    /**
131.       Sets the paint mode to texture paint.
132.    */
133.    public void setTexturePaint()
134.    {
135.       Rectangle2D anchor = new Rectangle2D.Double(0, 0,
136.          2 * bufferedImage.getWidth(),
137.          2 * bufferedImage.getHeight());
138.       paint = new TexturePaint(bufferedImage, anchor);
139.       repaint();
140.    }
141.
142.    private Paint paint;
143.    private BufferedImage bufferedImage;
144. }
```

java.awt.Graphics2D 1.2

- void setPaint(Paint s)
  sets the paint of this graphics context to the given object that implements the Paint interface.

java.awt.GradientPaint 1.2

- GradientPaint(float x1, float y1, Color color1, float x2, float y2, Color color2)
- GradientPaint(float x1, float y1, Color color1, float x2, float y2, Color color2, boolean cyclic)
- GradientPaint(Point2D p1, Color color1, Point2D p2, Color color2)
- GradientPaint(Point2D p1, Color color1, Point2D p2, Color color2, boolean cyclic)
  construct a gradient paint object that fills shapes with color such that the start point is colored with color1, the end point is colored with color2, and the colors in between are linearly interpolated. Colors are constant along lines that are perpendicular to the line joining the start and the end point. By default, the gradient paint is not cyclic;

that is, points beyond the start and end points are colored with the same color as the start and end point. If the gradient paint is *cyclic,* then colors continue to be interpolated, first returning to the starting point color and then repeating indefinitely in both directions.

Parameters:	x1, y1, or p1	The start point
	color1	The color to use for the start point
	x2, y2, or p2	The end point
	color2	The color to use for the end point
	cyclic	true if the color change pattern repeats, false if the colors beyond the start and end point are constant

 java.awt.TexturePaint 1.2

- TexturePaint(BufferedImage texture, Rectangle2D anchor)
  creates a texture paint object.

| *Parameters:* | texture | The texture to use for filling shapes |
| | anchor | The anchor rectangle that defines the tiling of the space to be painted; it is repeated indefinitely in x- and y-directions, and the texture image is scaled to fill each tile |

Coordinate Transformations

Suppose you need to draw an object such as an automobile. You know, from the manufacturer's specifications, the height, wheelbase, and total length. You could, of course, figure out all pixel positions, assuming some number of pixels per meter. However, there is an easier way: You can ask the graphics context to carry out the conversion for you.

```
g2.scale(pixelsPerMeter, pixelsPerMeter);
g2.draw(new Line2D.Double(coordinates in meters)); // converts to pixels and draws scaled line
```

The scale method of the Graphics2D class sets the *coordinate transformation* of the graphics context to a scaling transformation. That transformation changes *user coordinates* (user-specified units) to *device coordinates* (pixels). Figure 7–18 shows how the transformation works.

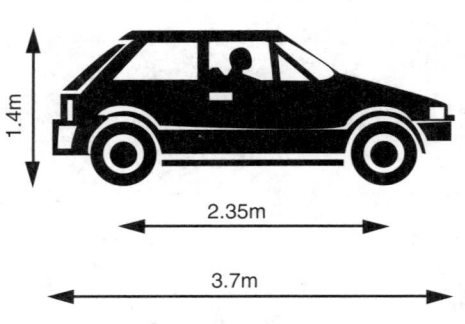 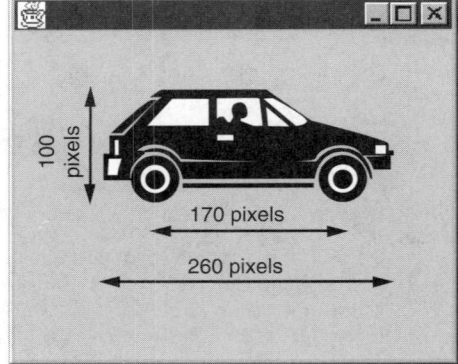

User coordinates   Device coordinates

Figure 7–18: User and device coordinates

Coordinate transformations are very useful in practice. They allow you to work with convenient coordinate values. The graphics context takes care of the dirty work of transforming them to pixels.

There are four fundamental transformations.

- Scaling: blowing up, or shrinking, all distances from a fixed point
- Rotation: rotating all points around a fixed center
- Translation: moving all points by a fixed amount
- Shear: leaving one line fixed and "sliding" the lines parallel to it by an amount that is proportional to the distance from the fixed line

Figure 7–19 shows how these four fundamental transformations act on a unit square.

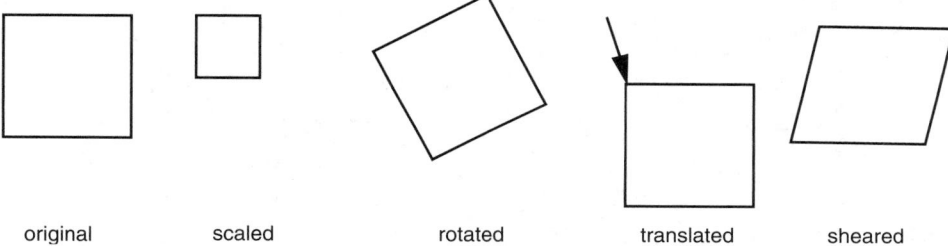

original   scaled   rotated   translated   sheared

Figure 7–19: The fundamental transformations

The scale, rotate, translate, and shear methods of the Graphics2D class set the coordinate transformation of the graphics context to one of these fundamental transformations.

You can *compose* the transformations. For example, you may want to rotate shapes *and* double their size. Then, you supply both a rotation and a scaling transformation.

```
g2.rotate(angle);
g2.scale(2, 2);
g2.draw(. . .);
```

In this case, it does not matter in which order you supply the transformations. However, with most transformations, order does matter. For example, if you want to rotate and shear, then it makes a difference which of the transformations you supply first. You need to figure out what your intention is. The graphics context will apply the transformations in the opposite order in which you supplied them. That is, the last transformation that you supply is applied first.

You can supply as many transformations as you like. For example, consider the following sequence of transformations:

```
g2.translate(x, y);
g2.rotate(a);
g2.translate(-x, -y);
```

The last transformation (which is applied first) moves the point (x, y) to the origin. The second transformation rotates with an angle a around the origin. The final transformation moves the origin back to (x, y). The overall effect is a rotation with center point (x, y)—see Figure 7–20. Because rotating about a point other than the origin is such a common operation, there is a shortcut:

```
g2.rotate(a, x, y);
```

If you know some matrix theory, you are probably aware that all rotations, translations, scalings, shears, and their compositions can be expressed by matrix transformations of the form:

$$
\begin{bmatrix} x_{\text{new}} \\ y_{\text{new}} \\ 1 \end{bmatrix} = \begin{bmatrix} a & c & e \\ b & d & f \\ 0 & 0 & 1 \end{bmatrix} \cdot \begin{bmatrix} x \\ y \\ 1 \end{bmatrix}
$$

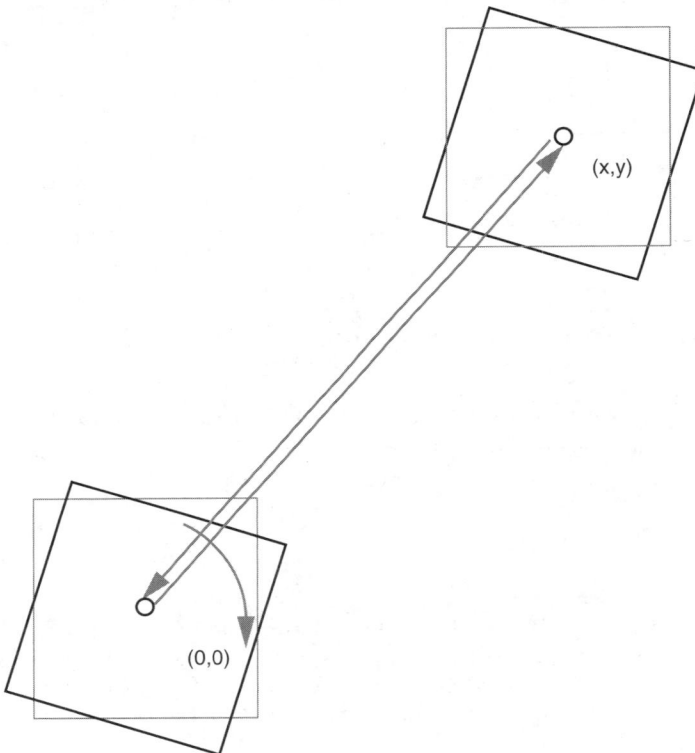

Figure 7–20: Composing transformations

Such a transformation is called an *affine transformation*. In the Java 2D API, the AffineTransform class describes such a transformation. If you know the components of a particular transformation matrix, you can construct it directly as

```
AffineTransform t = new AffineTransform(a, b, c, d, e, f);
```

Additionally, the factory methods getRotateInstance, getScaleInstance, getTranslateInstance, and getShearInstance construct the matrices that represent these transformation types. For example, the call

```
t = AffineTransform.getScaleInstance(2.0F, 0.5F);
```

returns a transformation that corresponds to the matrix

$$\begin{bmatrix} 2 & 0 & 0 \\ 0 & 0.5 & 0 \\ 0 & 0 & 1 \end{bmatrix}$$

Finally, the instance methods setToRotation, setToScale, setToTranslation, and setToShear set a transformation object to a new type. Here is an example.

```
t.setToRotation(angle); // sets t to a rotation
```

You can set the coordinate transformation of the graphics context to an AffineTransform object.

```
g2.setTransform(t); // replaces current transformation
```

However, in practice, you shouldn't call the setTransform operation, since it replaces any existing transformation that the graphics context may have. For example, a graphics context for printing in landscape mode already contains a 90-degree rotation transformation. If you call setTransform, you obliterate that rotation. Instead, call the transform method.

```
g2.transform(t); // composes current transformation with t
```

It composes the existing transformation with the new AffineTransform object.

If you just want to apply a transformation temporarily, then you first get the old transformation, compose with your new transformation, and finally restore the old transformation when you are done.

```
AffineTransform oldTransform = g2.getTransform(); // save old transform
g2.transform(t); // apply temporary transform // now draw on g2
g2.setTransform(oldTransform); // restore old transform
```

The program in Example 7–5 lets the user choose among the four fundamental transformations. The paintComponent method draws a square, then applies the selected transformation and redraws the square. However, for a good visual appearance, we want to have the square and its transform appear on the *center* of the display panel. For that reason, the paintComponent method first sets the coordinate transformation to a translation.

```
g2.translate(getWidth() / 2, getHeight() / 2);
```

This translation moves the origin to the center of the component.

Then, the paintComponent method draws a square that is centered around the origin.

```
square = new Rectangle2D.Double(-50, -50, 100, 100);
. . .
g2.setPaint(Color.gray);
g2.draw(square);
```

However, because the graphics context applies the translation to the shape, the square is actually drawn with its center lying at the center of the component.

Next, the transformation that the user selected is composed with the current transformation, and the square is drawn once again.

```
g2.transform(t);
g2.setPaint(Color.black);
g2.draw(square);
```

The original square is drawn in gray, and the transformed one in black (see Figure 7–21).

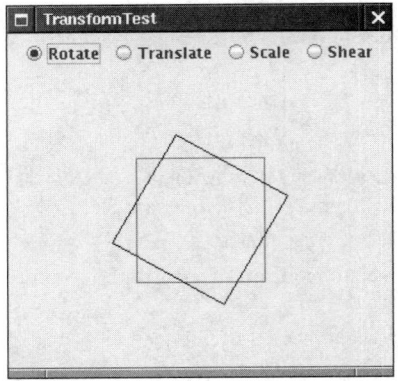

Figure 7–21: The TransformTest program

Example 7–5: TransformTest.java

```java
1.  import java.awt.*;
2.  import java.awt.event.*;
3.  import java.awt.geom.*;
4.  import java.util.*;
5.  import javax.swing.*;
6.
7.  /**
8.     This program displays the effects of various transformations.
9.  */
10. public class TransformTest
11. {
12.    public static void main(String[] args)
13.    {
14.       JFrame frame = new TransformTestFrame();
15.       frame.setDefaultCloseOperation(JFrame.EXIT_ON_CLOSE);
16.       frame.setVisible(true);
17.    }
18. }
19.
20. /**
21.    This frame contains radio buttons to choose a transformation
22.    and a panel to display the effect of the chosen
23.    transformation.
24. */
25. class TransformTestFrame extends JFrame
26. {
27.    public TransformTestFrame()
28.    {
29.       setTitle("TransformTest");
30.       setSize(DEFAULT_WIDTH, DEFAULT_HEIGHT);
31.
32.       canvas = new TransformPanel();
33.       add(canvas, BorderLayout.CENTER);
34.
35.       JPanel buttonPanel = new JPanel();
36.       ButtonGroup group = new ButtonGroup();
37.
```

```
38.        JRadioButton rotateButton = new JRadioButton("Rotate", true);
39.        buttonPanel.add(rotateButton);
40.        group.add(rotateButton);
41.        rotateButton.addActionListener(new
42.           ActionListener()
43.           {
44.              public void actionPerformed(ActionEvent event)
45.              {
46.                 canvas.setRotate();
47.              }
48.           });
49.
50.        JRadioButton translateButton = new JRadioButton("Translate", false);
51.        buttonPanel.add(translateButton);
52.        group.add(translateButton);
53.        translateButton.addActionListener(new
54.           ActionListener()
55.           {
56.              public void actionPerformed(ActionEvent event)
57.              {
58.                 canvas.setTranslate();
59.              }
60.           });
61.
62.        JRadioButton scaleButton = new JRadioButton("Scale", false);
63.        buttonPanel.add(scaleButton);
64.        group.add(scaleButton);
65.        scaleButton.addActionListener(new
66.           ActionListener()
67.           {
68.              public void actionPerformed(ActionEvent event)
69.              {
70.                 canvas.setScale();
71.              }
72.           });
73.
74.        JRadioButton shearButton = new JRadioButton("Shear", false);
75.        buttonPanel.add(shearButton);
76.        group.add(shearButton);
77.        shearButton.addActionListener(new
78.           ActionListener()
79.           {
80.              public void actionPerformed(ActionEvent event)
81.              {
82.                 canvas.setShear();
83.              }
84.           });
85.
86.        add(buttonPanel, BorderLayout.NORTH);
87.     }
88.
89.     private TransformPanel canvas;
90.     private static final int DEFAULT_WIDTH = 300;
91.     private static final int DEFAULT_HEIGHT = 300;
92.  }
```

```
93.
94.  /**
95.     This panel displays a square and its transformed image
96.     under a transformation.
97.  */
98.  class TransformPanel extends JPanel
99.  {
100.    public TransformPanel()
101.    {
102.       square = new Rectangle2D.Double(-50, -50, 100, 100);
103.       t = new AffineTransform();
104.       setRotate();
105.    }
106.
107.    public void paintComponent(Graphics g)
108.    {
109.       super.paintComponent(g);
110.       Graphics2D g2 = (Graphics2D) g;
111.       g2.translate(getWidth() / 2, getHeight() / 2);
112.       g2.setPaint(Color.gray);
113.       g2.draw(square);
114.       g2.transform(t);
115.       // we don't use setTransform because we want to compose with the current translation
116.       g2.setPaint(Color.black);
117.       g2.draw(square);
118.    }
119.
120.    /**
121.       Set the transformation to a rotation.
122.    */
123.    public void setRotate()
124.    {
125.       t.setToRotation(Math.toRadians(30));
126.       repaint();
127.    }
128.
129.    /**
130.       Set the transformation to a translation.
131.    */
132.    public void setTranslate()
133.    {
134.       t.setToTranslation(20, 15);
135.       repaint();
136.    }
137.
138.    /**
139.       Set the transformation to a scale transformation.
140.    */
141.    public void setScale()
142.    {
143.       t.setToScale(2.0, 1.5);
144.       repaint();
145.    }
146.
147.    /**
```

```
148.      Set the transformation to a shear transformation.
149.   */
150.   public void setShear()
151.   {
152.      t.setToShear(-0.2, 0);
153.      repaint();
154.   }
155.
156.   private Rectangle2D square;
157.   private AffineTransform t;
158. }
```

java.awt.geom.AffineTransform 1.2

- AffineTransform(double a, double b, double c, double d, double e, double f)
- AffineTransform(float a, float b, float c, float d, float e, float f)
  construct the affine transform with matrix

$$\begin{bmatrix} a & c & e \\ b & d & f \\ 0 & 0 & 1 \end{bmatrix}$$

- AffineTransform(double[] m)
- AffineTransform(float[] m)
  construct the affine transform with matrix

$$\begin{bmatrix} m[0] & m[2] & m[4] \\ m[1] & m[3] & m[5] \\ 0 & 0 & 1 \end{bmatrix}$$

- static AffineTransform getRotateInstance(double a)
  creates a rotation around the origin by the angle a (in radians). The transformation matrix is

$$\begin{bmatrix} \cos(a) & -\sin(a) & 0 \\ \sin(a) & \cos(a) & 0 \\ 0 & 0 & 1 \end{bmatrix}$$

  If a is between 0 and $\pi / 2$, the rotation moves the positive x-axis toward the positive y-axis.
- static AffineTransform getRotateInstance(double a, double x, double y)
  creates a rotation around the point (x,y) by the angle a (in radians).
- static AffineTransform getScaleInstance(double sx, double sy)
  creates a scaling transformation that scales the x-axis by sx and the y-axis by sy. The transformation matrix is

$$\begin{bmatrix} sx & 0 & 0 \\ 0 & sy & 0 \\ 0 & 0 & 1 \end{bmatrix}$$

- static AffineTransform getShearInstance(double shx, double shy)
  creates a shear transformation that shears the x-axis by shx and the y-axis by shy. The transformation matrix is

$$\begin{bmatrix} 1 & shx & 0 \\ shy & 1 & 0 \\ 0 & 0 & 1 \end{bmatrix}$$

- static AffineTransform getTranslateInstance(double tx, double ty)
  creates a translation that moves the x-axis by tx and the y-axis by ty. The transformation matrix is

$$\begin{bmatrix} 1 & 0 & tx \\ 0 & 1 & ty \\ 0 & 0 & 1 \end{bmatrix}$$

- void setToRotation(double a)
- void setToRotation(double a, double x, double y)
- void setToScale(double sx, double sy)
- void setToShear(double sx, double sy)
- void setToTranslation(double tx, double ty)
  set this affine transformation to a basic transformation with the given parameters. See the get*Xxx*Instance method for an explanation of the basic transformations and their parameters.

 java.awt.Graphics2D 1.2

- void setTransform(AffineTransform t)
  replaces the existing coordinate transformation of this graphics context with t.
- void transform(AffineTransform t)
  composes the existing coordinate transformation of this graphics context with t.
- void rotate(double a)
- void rotate(double a, double x, double y)
- void scale(double sx, double sy)
- void shear(double sx, double sy)
- void translate(double tx, double ty)
  compose the existing coordinate transformation of this graphics context with a basic transformation with the given parameters. See the AffineTransform.get*Xxx*Instance method for an explanation of the basic transformations and their parameters.

Clipping

By setting a *clipping shape* in the graphics context, you constrain all drawing operations to the interior of that clipping shape.

```
g2.setClip(clipShape); // but see below
g2.draw(shape); // draws only the part that falls inside the clipping shape
```

However, in practice, you don't want to call the setClip operation, since it replaces any existing clipping shape that the graphics context may have. For example, as you will see later in this chapter, a graphics context for printing comes with a clip rectangle that ensures that you don't draw on the margins. Instead, call the clip method.

```
g2.clip(clipShape); // better
```

The clip method intersects the existing clipping shape with the new one that you supply.

If you just want to apply a clipping area temporarily, then you should first get the old clip, then add your new clip, and finally restore the old clip when you are done:

```
Shape oldClip = g2.getClip(); // save old clip
g2.clip(clipShape); // apply temporary clip
draw on g2
g2.setClip(oldClip); // restore old clip
```

In Example 7–6, we show off the clipping capability with a rather dramatic drawing of a line pattern that is clipped by a complex shape, namely, the outline of a set of characters (see Figure 7–22).

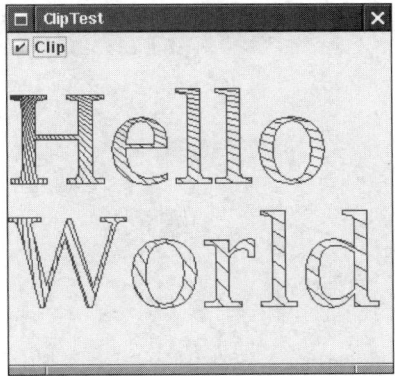

Figure 7–22: The ClipTest program

To obtain character outlines, you need a *font render context.* Use the getFontRenderContext method of the Graphics2D class.

```
FontRenderContext context = g2.getFontRenderContext();
```

Next, using a string, a font, and the font render context, create a TextLayout object:

```
TextLayout layout = new TextLayout("Hello", font, context);
```

This text layout object describes the layout of a sequence of characters, as rendered by a particular font render context. The layout depends on the font render context—the same characters will look different on a screen or a printer.

More important for our current application, the getOutline method returns a Shape object that describes the shape of the outline of the characters in the text layout. The outline shape starts at the origin (0, 0), which is not suitable for most drawing operations. Therefore, you need to supply an affine transform to the getOutline operation that specifies where you would like the outline to appear. We simply supply a translation that moves the base point to the point (0, 100).

```
AffineTransform transform = AffineTransform.getTranslateInstance(0, 100);
Shape outline = layout.getOutline(transform);
```

Then, we append the outline to the clipping shape.

```
GeneralPath clipShape = new GeneralPath();
clipShape.append(outline, false);
```

Finally, we set the clipping shape and draw a set of lines. The lines appear only inside the character boundaries.

```
g2.setClip(clipShape);
Point2D p = new Point2D.Double(0, 0);
for (int i = 0; i < NLINES; i++)
{
    double x = . . .;
    double y = . . .;
    Point2D q = new Point2D.Double(x, y);
    g2.draw(new Line2D.Double(p, q)); // lines are clipped
}
```

Here is the complete program.

Example 7–6: ClipTest.java

```
1. import java.awt.*;
2. import java.awt.event.*;
3. import java.awt.font.*;
4. import java.awt.geom.*;
5. import java.util.*;
6. import javax.swing.*;
7.
8. /**
9.    This program demonstrates the use of a clip shape.
10. */
11. public class ClipTest
12. {
13.    public static void main(String[] args)
14.    {
15.       JFrame frame = new ClipTestFrame();
16.       frame.setDefaultCloseOperation(JFrame.EXIT_ON_CLOSE);
17.       frame.setVisible(true);
18.    }
19. }
20.
21. /**
22.    This frame contains a checkbox to turn a clip off
23.    and on, and a panel to draw a set of lines with or without
24.    clipping.
25. */
26. class ClipTestFrame extends JFrame
27. {
28.    public ClipTestFrame()
29.    {
30.       setTitle("ClipTest");
31.       setSize(DEFAULT_WIDTH, DEFAULT_HEIGHT);
32.
33.       final JCheckBox checkBox = new JCheckBox("Clip");
34.       checkBox.addActionListener(new
35.          ActionListener()
36.          {
37.             public void actionPerformed(ActionEvent event)
38.             {
39.                panel.repaint();
40.             }
41.          });
42.       add(checkBox, BorderLayout.NORTH);
43.
44.       panel = new
```

```
45.        JPanel()
46.        {
47.           public void paintComponent(Graphics g)
48.           {
49.              super.paintComponent(g);
50.              Graphics2D g2 = (Graphics2D)g;
51.
52.              if (clipShape == null) clipShape = makeClipShape(g2);
53.
54.              g2.draw(clipShape);
55.
56.              if (checkBox.isSelected()) g2.clip(clipShape);
57.
58.              // draw line pattern
59.              final int NLINES = 50;
60.              Point2D p = new Point2D.Double(0, 0);
61.              for (int i = 0; i < NLINES; i++)
62.              {
63.                 double x = (2 * getWidth() * i) / NLINES;
64.                 double y = (2 * getHeight() * (NLINES - 1 - i)) / NLINES;
65.                 Point2D q = new Point2D.Double(x, y);
66.                 g2.draw(new Line2D.Double(p, q));
67.              }
68.           }
69.        };
70.        add(panel, BorderLayout.CENTER);
71.     }
72.
73.     /**
74.        Makes the clip shape.
75.        @param g2 the graphics context
76.        @return the clip shape
77.     */
78.     Shape makeClipShape(Graphics2D g2)
79.     {
80.        FontRenderContext context = g2.getFontRenderContext();
81.        Font f = new Font("Serif", Font.PLAIN, 100);
82.        GeneralPath clipShape = new GeneralPath();
83.
84.        TextLayout layout = new TextLayout("Hello", f, context);
85.        AffineTransform transform = AffineTransform.getTranslateInstance(0, 100);
86.        Shape outline = layout.getOutline(transform);
87.        clipShape.append(outline, false);
88.
89.        layout = new TextLayout("World", f, context);
90.        transform = AffineTransform.getTranslateInstance(0, 200);
91.        outline = layout.getOutline(transform);
92.        clipShape.append(outline, false);
93.        return clipShape;
94.     }
95.
96.     private JPanel panel;
97.     private Shape clipShape;
98.     private static final int DEFAULT_WIDTH = 300;
99.     private static final int DEFAULT_HEIGHT = 300;
100. }
```

API **java.awt.Graphics** 1.0

- `void setClip(Shape s)` **1.2**
  sets the current clipping shape to the shape s.
- `Shape getClip()` **1.2**
  returns the current clipping shape.

API **java.awt.Graphics2D** 1.2

- `void clip(Shape s)`
  intersects the current clipping shape with the shape s.
- `FontRenderContext getFontRenderContext()`
  returns a font render context that is necessary for constructing TextLayout objects.

API **java.awt.font.TextLayout** 1.2

- `TextLayout(String s, Font f, FontRenderContext context)`
  constructs a text layout object from a given string and font, using the font render context to obtain font properties for a particular device.
- `float getAdvance()`
  returns the width of this text layout.
- `float getAscent()`
- `float getDescent()`
  return the height of this text layout above and below the baseline.
- `float getLeading()`
  returns the distance between successive lines in the font used by this text layout.

Transparency and Composition

In the standard RGB color model, every color is described by its red, green, and blue components. However, it is also convenient to be able to describe areas of an image that are *transparent* or partially transparent. When you superimpose an image onto an existing drawing, the transparent pixels do not obscure the pixels under them at all, whereas partially transparent pixels are mixed with the pixels under them. Figure 7–23 shows the effect of overlaying a partially transparent rectangle on an image. You can still see the details of the image shine through from under the rectangle.

In the Java 2D API, transparency is described by an *alpha channel*. Each pixel has, in addition to its red, green, and blue color components, an alpha value between 0 (fully transparent) and 1 (fully opaque). For example, the rectangle in Figure 7–23 was filled with a pale yellow color with 50% transparency:

```
new Color(0.7F, 0.7F, 0.0F, 0.5F);
```

Figure 7–23: Overlaying a partially transparent rectangle on an image

Now let us look at what happens if you superimpose two shapes. You need to blend or *compose* the colors and alpha values of the source and destination pixels. Porter and Duff,

two researchers in the field of computer graphics, have formulated 12 possible *composition rules* for this blending process. The Java 2D API implements all of these rules. Before we go any further, we want to point out that only two of these rules have practical significance. If you find the rules arcane or confusing, just use the SRC_OVER rule. It is the default rule for a Graphics2D object, and it gives the most intuitive results.

Here is the theory behind the rules. Suppose you have a *source pixel* with alpha value a_S. In the image, there is already a *destination pixel* with alpha value a_D. You want to compose the two. The diagram in Figure 7–24 shows how to design a composition rule.

Porter and Duff consider the alpha value as the probability that the pixel color should be used. From the perspective of the source, there is a probability a_S that it wants to use the source color and a probability of $1 - a_S$ that it doesn't care. The same holds for the destination. When composing the colors, let us assume that the probabilities are independent. Then there are four cases, as shown in Figure 7–24. If the source wants to use the source color and the destination doesn't care, then it seems reasonable to let the source have its way. That's why the upper-right corner of the diagram is labeled "S." The probability for that event is $a_S \cdot (1 - a_D)$. Similarly, the lower-left corner is labeled "D." What should one do if both destination and source would like to select their color? That's where the Porter-Duff rules come in. If we decide that the source is more important, then we label the lower-right corner with an "S" as well. That rule is called SRC_OVER. In that rule, you combine the source colors with a weight of a_S and the destination colors with a weight of $(1 - a_S) \cdot a_D$.

The visual effect is a blending of the source and destination, with preference given to the source. In particular, if a_S is 1, then the destination color is not taken into account at all. If a_S is 0, then the source pixel is completely transparent and the destination color is unchanged.

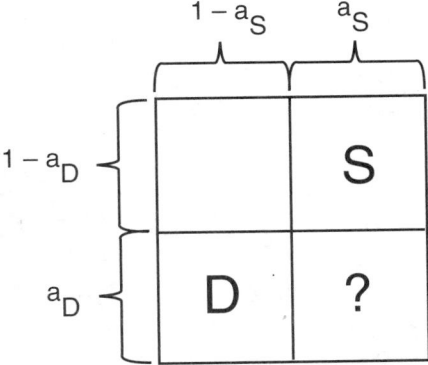

Figure 7–24: Designing a composition rule

The other rules depend on what letters you put in the boxes of the probability diagram. Table 7–1 and Figure 7–25 show all rules that are supported by the Java 2D API. The images in the figure show the results of the rules when a rectangular source region with an alpha of 0.75 is combined with an elliptical destination region with an alpha of 1.0.

As you can see, most of the rules aren't very useful. Consider, as an extreme case, the DST_IN rule. It doesn't take the source color into account at all, but it uses the alpha of the source to affect the destination. The SRC rule is potentially useful—it forces the source color to be used, turning off blending with the destination.

The DST, SRC_ATOP, DST_ATOP, and XOR rules have been added in JDK 1.4.

For more information on the Porter-Duff rules, see, for example, Foley, van Dam, Feiner, et al., Section 17.6.1.

Table 7–1: The Porter-Duff Composition Rules

CLEAR	Source clears destination.
SRC	Source overwrites destination and empty pixels.
DST	Source does not affect destination.
SRC_OVER	Source blends with destination and overwrites empty pixels.
DST_OVER	Source does not affect destination and overwrites empty pixels.
SRC_IN	Source overwrites destination.
SRC_OUT	Source clears destination and overwrites empty pixels.
DST_IN	Source alpha modifies destination.
DST_OUT	Source alpha complement modifies destination.
SRC_ATOP	Source blends with destination.
DST_ATOP	Source alpha modifies destination. Source overwrites empty pixels.
XOR	Source alpha complement modifies destination. Source overwrites empty pixels.

You use the setComposite method of the Graphics2D class to install an object of a class that implements the Composite interface. The Java 2D API supplies one such class, AlphaComposite, that implements all the Porter-Duff rules in Figure 7–25.

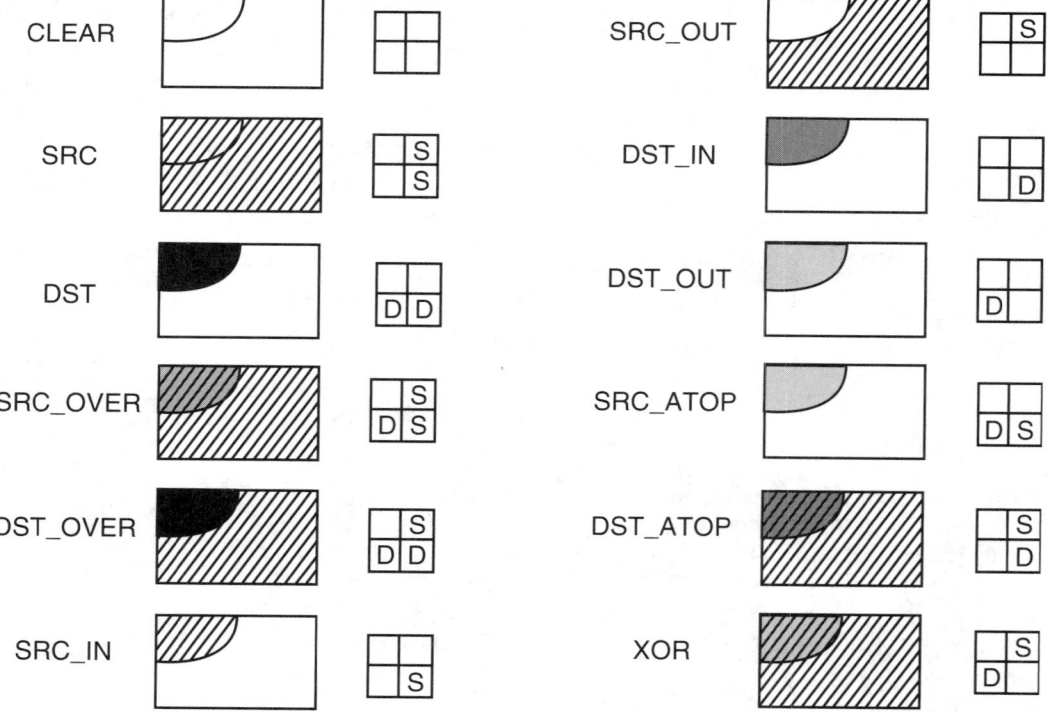

Figure 7–25: Porter-Duff composition rules

The factory method getInstance of the AlphaComposite class yields an AlphaComposite object. You supply the rule and the alpha value to be used for source pixels. For example, consider the following code:

```
int rule = AlphaComposite.SRC_OVER;
float alpha = 0.5f;
g2.setComposite(AlphaComposite.getInstance(rule, alpha));
g2.setPaint(Color.blue);
g2.fill(rectangle);
```

The rectangle is then painted with blue color and an alpha value of 0.5. Because the composition rule is SRC_OVER, it is transparently overlaid on the existing image.

The program in Example 7–7 lets you explore these composition rules. Pick a rule from the combo box and use the slider to set the alpha value of the AlphaComposite object.

Furthermore, the program displays a verbal description of each rule. Note that the descriptions are computed from the composition rule diagrams. For example, a "DS" in the second row stands for "blends with destination."

The program has one important twist. There is no guarantee that the graphics context that corresponds to the screen has an alpha channel. (In fact, it generally does not.) When pixels are deposited to a destination without an alpha channel, then the pixel colors are multiplied with the alpha value and the alpha value is discarded. Because several of the Porter-Duff rules use the alpha values of the destination, a destination alpha channel is important. For that reason, we use a buffered image with the ARGB color model to compose the shapes. After the images have been composed, we draw the resulting image to the screen.

```
BufferedImage image = new BufferedImage(getWidth(), getHeight(), BufferedImage.TYPE_INT_ARGB);
Graphics2D gImage = image.createGraphics();
// now draw to gImage
g2.drawImage(image, null, 0, 0);
```

Here is the complete code for the program. Figure 7–26 shows the screen display. As you run the program, move the alpha slider from left to right to see the effect on the composed shapes. In particular, note that the only difference between the DST_IN and DST_OUT rules is how the destination (!) color changes when you change the source alpha.

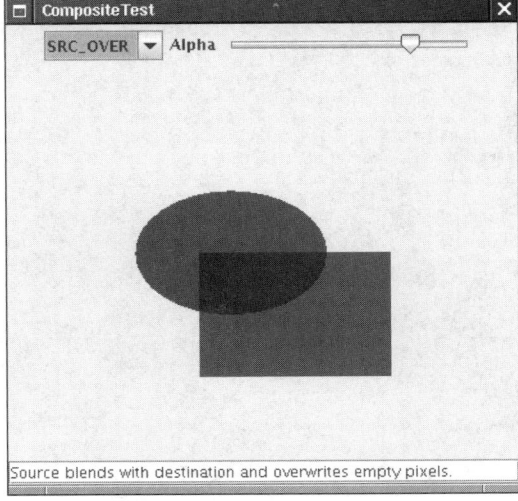

Figure 7–26: The CompositeTest program

Example 7–7: CompositeTest.java

```java
1.  import java.awt.*;
2.  import java.awt.event.*;
3.  import java.awt.image.*;
4.  import java.awt.geom.*;
5.  import java.util.*;
6.  import javax.swing.*;
7.  import javax.swing.event.*;
8.
9.  /**
10.    This program demonstrates the Porter-Duff composition rules.
11. */
12. public class CompositeTest
13. {
14.    public static void main(String[] args)
15.    {
16.       JFrame frame = new CompositeTestFrame();
17.       frame.setDefaultCloseOperation(JFrame.EXIT_ON_CLOSE);
18.       frame.setVisible(true);
19.    }
20. }
21.
22. /**
23.    This frame contains a combo box to choose a composition
24.    rule, a slider to change the source alpha channel,
25.    and a panel that shows the composition.
26. */
27. class CompositeTestFrame extends JFrame
28. {
29.    public CompositeTestFrame()
30.    {
31.       setTitle("CompositeTest");
32.       setSize(DEFAULT_WIDTH, DEFAULT_HEIGHT);
33.
34.       canvas = new CompositePanel();
35.       add(canvas, BorderLayout.CENTER);
36.
37.       ruleCombo = new JComboBox(new
38.          Object[]
39.          {
40.             new Rule("CLEAR",    "  ", "  "),
41.             new Rule("SRC",      " S", " S"),
42.             new Rule("DST",      "  ", "DD"),
43.             new Rule("SRC_OVER", " S", "DS"),
44.             new Rule("DST_OVER", " S", "DD"),
45.             new Rule("SRC_IN",   "  ", " S"),
46.             new Rule("SRC_OUT",  " S", "  "),
47.             new Rule("DST_IN",   "  ", " D"),
48.             new Rule("DST_OUT",  "  ", "D "),
49.             new Rule("SRC_ATOP", "  ", "DS"),
50.             new Rule("DST_ATOP", " S", " D"),
51.             new Rule("XOR",      " S", "D "),
52.          });
53.       ruleCombo.addActionListener(new
54.          ActionListener()
```

```
55.            {
56.                public void actionPerformed(ActionEvent event)
57.                {
58.                    Rule r = (Rule)ruleCombo.getSelectedItem();
59.                    canvas.setRule(r.getValue());
60.                    explanation.setText(r.getExplanation());
61.                }
62.            });
63.
64.        alphaSlider = new JSlider(0, 100, 75);
65.        alphaSlider.addChangeListener(new
66.            ChangeListener()
67.            {
68.                public void stateChanged(ChangeEvent event)
69.                {
70.                    canvas.setAlpha(alphaSlider.getValue());
71.                }
72.            });
73.        JPanel panel = new JPanel();
74.        panel.add(ruleCombo);
75.        panel.add(new JLabel("Alpha"));
76.        panel.add(alphaSlider);
77.        add(panel, BorderLayout.NORTH);
78.
79.        explanation = new JTextField();
80.        add(explanation, BorderLayout.SOUTH);
81.
82.        canvas.setAlpha(alphaSlider.getValue());
83.        Rule r = (Rule) ruleCombo.getSelectedItem();
84.        canvas.setRule(r.getValue());
85.        explanation.setText(r.getExplanation());
86.    }
87.
88.    private CompositePanel canvas;
89.    private JComboBox ruleCombo;
90.    private JSlider alphaSlider;
91.    private JTextField explanation;
92.    private static final int DEFAULT_WIDTH = 400;
93.    private static final int DEFAULT_HEIGHT = 400;
94. }
95.
96. /**
97.    This class describes a Porter-Duff rule.
98. */
99. class Rule
100. {
101.    /**
102.       Constructs a Porter-Duff rule
103.       @param n the rule name
104.       @param pd1 the first row of the Porter-Duff square
105.       @param pd2 the second row of the Porter-Duff square
106.    */
107.    public Rule(String n, String pd1, String pd2)
108.    {
109.        name = n;
110.        porterDuff1 = pd1;
```

```
111.        porterDuff2 = pd2;
112.    }
113.
114.    /**
115.       Gets an explanation of the behavior of this rule.
116.       @return the explanation
117.    */
118.    public String getExplanation()
119.    {
120.        StringBuilder r = new StringBuilder("Source ");
121.        if (porterDuff2.equals("  ")) r.append("clears");
122.        if (porterDuff2.equals(" S")) r.append("overwrites");
123.        if (porterDuff2.equals("DS")) r.append("blends with");
124.        if (porterDuff2.equals(" D")) r.append("alpha modifies");
125.        if (porterDuff2.equals("D ")) r.append("alpha complement modifies");
126.        if (porterDuff2.equals("DD")) r.append("does not affect");
127.        r.append(" destination");
128.        if (porterDuff1.equals(" S")) r.append(" and overwrites empty pixels");
129.        r.append(".");
130.        return r.toString();
131.    }
132.
133.    public String toString() { return name; }
134.
135.    /**
136.       Gets the value of this rule in the AlphaComposite class
137.       @return the AlphaComposite constant value, or -1 if
138.       there is no matching constant.
139.    */
140.    public int getValue()
141.    {
142.        try
143.        {
144.            return (Integer) AlphaComposite.class.getField(name).get(null);
145.        }
146.        catch (Exception e)
147.        {
148.            return -1;
149.        }
150.    }
151.
152.    private String name;
153.    private String porterDuff1;
154.    private String porterDuff2;
155. }
156.
157. /**
158.    This panel draws two shapes, composed with a
159.    composition rule.
160. */
161. class CompositePanel extends JPanel
162. {
163.    public CompositePanel()
164.    {
165.        shape1 = new Ellipse2D.Double(100, 100, 150, 100);
166.        shape2 = new Rectangle2D.Double(150, 150, 150, 100);
```

```
167.      }
168.
169.      public void paintComponent(Graphics g)
170.      {
171.         super.paintComponent(g);
172.         Graphics2D g2 = (Graphics2D)g;
173.
174.         BufferedImage image = new BufferedImage(getWidth(), getHeight(),
175.            BufferedImage.TYPE_INT_ARGB);
176.         Graphics2D gImage = image.createGraphics();
177.         gImage.setPaint(Color.red);
178.         gImage.fill(shape1);
179.         AlphaComposite composite = AlphaComposite.getInstance(rule, alpha);
180.         gImage.setComposite(composite);
181.         gImage.setPaint(Color.blue);
182.         gImage.fill(shape2);
183.         g2.drawImage(image, null, 0, 0);
184.      }
185.
186.      /**
187.         Sets the composition rule.
188.         @param r the rule (as an AlphaComposite constant)
189.      */
190.      public void setRule(int r)
191.      {
192.         rule = r;
193.         repaint();
194.      }
195.
196.      /**
197.         Sets the alpha of the source
198.         @param a the alpha value between 0 and 100
199.      */
200.      public void setAlpha(int a)
201.      {
202.         alpha = (float) a / 100.0F;
203.         repaint();
204.      }
205.
206.      private int rule;
207.      private Shape shape1;
208.      private Shape shape2;
209.      private float alpha;
210.   }
```

📖 **java.awt.Graphics2D** 1.2

- void setComposite(Composite s)
  sets the composite of this graphics context to the given object that implements the Composite interface.

📖 **java.awt.AlphaComposite** 1.2

- static AlphaComposite getInstance(int rule)
- static AlphaComposite getInstance(int rule, float alpha)
  construct an alpha composite object.

Parameters:	rule	One of CLEAR, SRC, SRC_OVER, DST_OVER, SRC_IN, SRC_OUT, DST_IN, DST_OUT, DST, DST_ATOP, SRC_ATOP, XOR
	alpha	The alpha value for the source pixels

Rendering Hints

In the preceding sections you have seen that the rendering process is quite complex. Though the Java 2D API is surprisingly fast in most cases, there are cases when you would like to have control over trade-offs between speed and quality. You achieve this by setting *rendering hints*. The setRenderingHint method of the Graphics2D class lets you set a single hint. The hint keys and values are declared in the RenderingHints class. Table 7–2 summarizes the choices.

The most useful of these settings involves *antialiasing*. This technique removes the "jaggies" from slanted lines and curves. As you can see in Figure 7–27, a slanted line must be drawn as a "staircase" of pixels. Especially on low-resolution screens, this line can look ugly. But if, rather than drawing each pixel completely on or off, you color in the pixels that are partially covered, with the color value proportional to the area of the pixel that the line covers, then the result looks much smoother. This technique is called antialiasing. Of course, antialiasing takes a bit longer because it takes time to compute all those color values.

Table 7–2: Rendering Hints

Key	Values	Explanation
KEY_ANTIALIASING	VALUE_ANTIALIAS_ON VALUE_ANTIALIAS_OFF VALUE_ANTIALIAS_DEFAULT	Turn antialiasing for shapes on or off.
KEY_RENDERING	VALUE_RENDER_QUALITY VALUE_RENDER_SPEED VALUE_RENDER_DEFAULT	When available, select rendering algorithms for greater quality or speed.
KEY_DITHERING	VALUE_DITHER_ENABLE VALUE_DITHER_DISABLE VALUE_DITHER_DEFAULT	Turn dithering for colors on or off. Dithering approximates color values by drawing groups of pixels of similar colors.
KEY_TEXT_ANTIALIASING	VALUE_TEXT_ANTIALIAS_ON VALUE_TEXT_ANTIALIAS_OFF VALUE_TEXT_ANTIALIAS_DEFAULT	Turn antialiasing for fonts on or off.
KEY_FRACTIONALMETRICS	VALUE_FRACTIONALMETRICS_ON VALUE_FRACTIONALMETRICS_OFF VALUE_FRACTIONALMETRICS_DEFAULT	Turn the computation of fractional character dimensions on or off. Fractional character dimensions lead to better placement of characters.
KEY_ALPHA_INTERPOLATION	VALUE_ALPHA_INTERPOLATION_QUALITY VALUE_ALPHA_INTERPOLATION_SPEED VALUE_ALPHA_INTERPOLATION_DEFAULT	Turn precise computation of alpha composites on or off.
KEY_COLOR_RENDERING	VALUE_COLOR_RENDER_QUALITY VALUE_COLOR_RENDER_SPEED VALUE_COLOR_RENDER_DEFAULT	Select quality or speed for color rendering.

Table 7–2: Rendering Hints (continued)

Key	Values	Explanation
KEY_INTERPOLATION	VALUE_INTERPOLATION_NEAREST_NEIGHBOR VALUE_INTERPOLATION_BILINEAR VALUE_INTERPOLATION_BICUBIC	Select a rule for interpolating pixels when scaling or rotating images.
KEY_STROKE_CONTROL	VALUE_STROKE_NORMALIZE VALUE_STROKE_PURE VALUE_STROKE_DEFAULT	Select a rule for combining strokes.

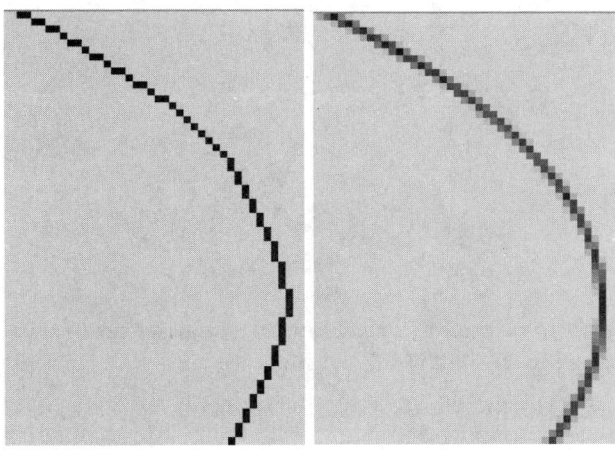

Figure 7–27: Antialiasing

For example, here is how you can request the use of antialiasing.

```
g2.setRenderingHint(RenderingHints.KEY_ANTIALIASING, RenderingHints.VALUE_ANTIALIAS_ON);
```

It also makes sense to use antialiasing for fonts.

```
g2.setRenderingHint(RenderingHints.KEY_TEXT_ANTIALIASING, RenderingHints.VALUE_TEXT_ANTIALIAS_ON);
```

The other rendering hints are not as commonly used.

You can also put a bunch of key/value hint pairs into a map and set them all at once by calling the setRenderingHints method. Any collection class implementing the map interface will do, but you may as well use the RenderingHints class itself. It implements the Map interface and supplies a default map implementation if you pass null to the constructor. For example,

```
RenderingHints hints = new RenderingHints(null);
hints.put(RenderingHints.KEY_ANTIALIASING, RenderingHints.VALUE_ANTIALIAS_ON);
hints.put(RenderingHints.KEY_TEXT_ANTIALIASING, RenderingHints.VALUE_TEXT_ANTIALIAS_ON);
g2.setRenderingHints(hints);
```

That is the technique we use in Example 7–8. The program draws an image that we thought might benefit from some of the hints. You can turn various rendering hints on or off. Not all platforms support all the hints, so you should not expect every one of the settings to have an effect. On Windows and Linux, antialiasing smooths out the ellipse, and text antialiasing improves the look of the italic font. The other hints seemed to have no effect, but they might with other platforms or with more complex images.

Figure 7–28 shows a screen capture of the program.

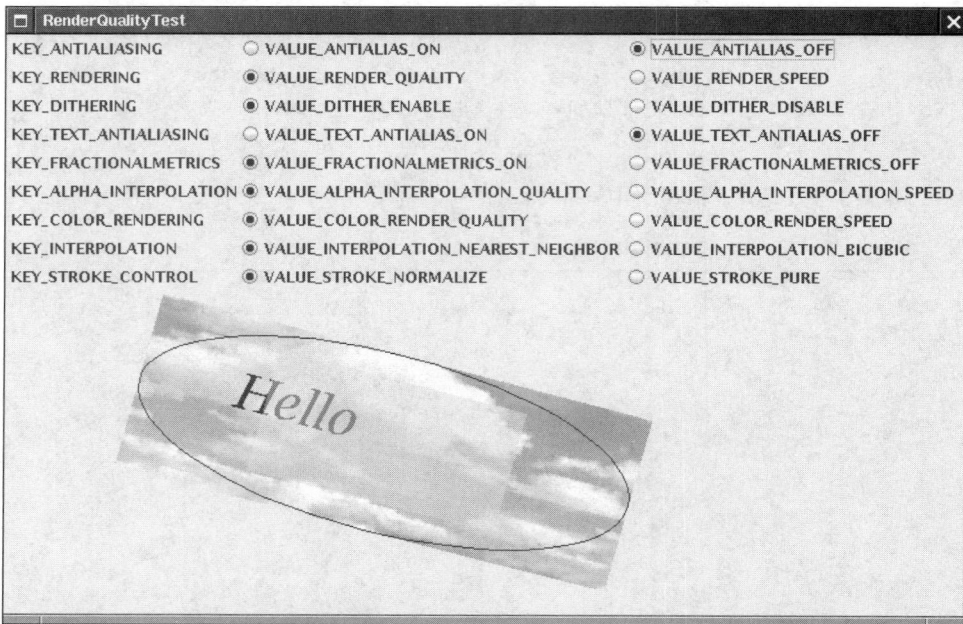

Figure 7–28: Testing the effect of rendering hints

Example 7–8: RenderQualityTest.java

```java
1. import java.awt.*;
2. import java.awt.event.*;
3. import java.awt.geom.*;
4. import java.io.*;
5. import java.util.*;
6. import javax.imageio.*;
7. import javax.swing.*;
8.
9. /**
10.    This program demonstrates the effect of the various
11.    rendering hints.
12. */
13. public class RenderQualityTest
14. {
15.    public static void main(String[] args)
16.    {
17.       JFrame frame = new RenderQualityTestFrame();
18.       frame.setDefaultCloseOperation(JFrame.EXIT_ON_CLOSE);
19.       frame.setVisible(true);
20.    }
21. }
22.
23. /**
24.    This frame contains buttons to set rendering hints
25.    and an image that is drawn with the selected hints.
26. */
27. class RenderQualityTestFrame extends JFrame
```

```
28. {
29.    public RenderQualityTestFrame()
30.    {
31.       setTitle("RenderQualityTest");
32.       setSize(DEFAULT_WIDTH, DEFAULT_HEIGHT);
33.
34.       buttonBox = new JPanel();
35.       buttonBox.setLayout(new GridBagLayout());
36.       hints = new RenderingHints(null);
37.
38.       makeButtons("KEY_ANTIALIASING", "VALUE_ANTIALIAS_ON", "VALUE_ANTIALIAS_OFF");
39.       makeButtons("KEY_RENDERING", "VALUE_RENDER_QUALITY", "VALUE_RENDER_SPEED");
40.       makeButtons("KEY_DITHERING", "VALUE_DITHER_ENABLE", "VALUE_DITHER_DISABLE");
41.       makeButtons("KEY_TEXT_ANTIALIASING", "VALUE_TEXT_ANTIALIAS_ON", "VALUE_TEXT_ANTIALIAS_OFF");
42.       makeButtons("KEY_FRACTIONALMETRICS",
43.          "VALUE_FRACTIONALMETRICS_ON", "VALUE_FRACTIONALMETRICS_OFF");
44.       makeButtons("KEY_ALPHA_INTERPOLATION",
45.          "VALUE_ALPHA_INTERPOLATION_QUALITY", "VALUE_ALPHA_INTERPOLATION_SPEED");
46.      makeButtons("KEY_COLOR_RENDERING", "VALUE_COLOR_RENDER_QUALITY", "VALUE_COLOR_RENDER_SPEED");
47.       makeButtons("KEY_INTERPOLATION",
48.          "VALUE_INTERPOLATION_NEAREST_NEIGHBOR", "VALUE_INTERPOLATION_BICUBIC");
49.       makeButtons("KEY_STROKE_CONTROL", "VALUE_STROKE_NORMALIZE", "VALUE_STROKE_PURE");
50.       canvas = new RenderQualityPanel();
51.       canvas.setRenderingHints(hints);
52.
53.       add(canvas, BorderLayout.CENTER);
54.       add(buttonBox, BorderLayout.NORTH);
55.    }
56.
57.    /**
58.       Makes a set of buttons for a rendering hint key and values
59.       @param key the key name
60.       @param value1 the name of the first value for the key
61.       @param value2 the name of the second value for the key
62.    */
63.    void makeButtons(String key, String value1, String value2)
64.    {
65.       try
66.       {
67.          final RenderingHints.Key k
68.             = (RenderingHints.Key) RenderingHints.class.getField(key).get(null);
69.          final Object v1 = RenderingHints.class.getField(value1).get(null);
70.          final Object v2 = RenderingHints.class.getField(value2).get(null);
71.          JLabel label = new JLabel(key);
72.
73.          buttonBox.add(label, new GBC(0, r).setAnchor(GBC.WEST));
74.          ButtonGroup group = new ButtonGroup();
75.          JRadioButton b1 = new JRadioButton(value1, true);
76.
77.          buttonBox.add(b1, new GBC(1, r).setAnchor(GBC.WEST));
78.          group.add(b1);
79.          b1.addActionListener(new
80.             ActionListener()
81.             {
82.                public void actionPerformed(ActionEvent event)
83.                {
```

```
84.              hints.put(k, v1);
85.              canvas.setRenderingHints(hints);
86.           }
87.        });
88.        JRadioButton b2 = new JRadioButton(value2, false);
89.
90.        buttonBox.add(b2, new GBC(2, r).setAnchor(GBC.WEST));
91.        group.add(b2);
92.        b2.addActionListener(new
93.           ActionListener()
94.           {
95.              public void actionPerformed(ActionEvent event)
96.              {
97.                 hints.put(k, v2);
98.                 canvas.setRenderingHints(hints);
99.              }
100.        });
101.        hints.put(k, v1);
102.        r++;
103.     }
104.     catch (Exception e)
105.     {
106.        e.printStackTrace();
107.     }
108.   }
109.
110.   private RenderQualityPanel canvas;
111.   private JPanel buttonBox;
112.   private RenderingHints hints;
113.   private int r;
114.   private static final int DEFAULT_WIDTH = 750;
115.   private static final int DEFAULT_HEIGHT = 500;
116. }
117.
118. /**
119.    This panel produces a drawing that hopefully shows some
120.    of the difference caused by rendering hints.
121. */
122. class RenderQualityPanel extends JPanel
123. {
124.   public RenderQualityPanel()
125.   {
126.     try
127.     {
128.        image = ImageIO.read(new File("clouds.jpg"));
129.     }
130.     catch (IOException e)
131.     {
132.        e.printStackTrace();
133.     }
134.   }
135.
136.   public void paintComponent(Graphics g)
137.   {
138.     super.paintComponent(g);
139.     Graphics2D g2 = (Graphics2D) g;
```

```
140.      g2.setRenderingHints(hints);
141.
142.      g2.scale(1.05, 1.05);
143.      g2.rotate(Math.PI / 12);
144.      g2.translate(120, -30);
145.      g2.drawImage(image, 0, 0, null);
146.
147.      g2.draw(new Ellipse2D.Double(0, 0, image.getWidth(null), image.getHeight(null)));
148.      g2.setFont(new Font("Serif", Font.ITALIC, 40));
149.      g2.drawString("Hello", 75, 75);
150.      g2.setPaint(Color.YELLOW);
151.      g2.translate(0,-80);
152.      g2.setComposite(AlphaComposite.getInstance(AlphaComposite.SRC_OVER, 0.5f));
153.      g2.fill(new Rectangle2D.Double(100, 100, 200, 100));
154.   }
155.
156.   /**
157.      Sets the hints and repaints.
158.      @param h the rendering hints
159.   */
160.   public void setRenderingHints(RenderingHints h)
161.   {
162.      hints = h;
163.      repaint();
164.   }
165.
166.   private RenderingHints hints = new RenderingHints(null);
167.   private Image image;
168. }
```

 java.awt.Graphics2D 1.2

- void setRenderingHint(RenderingHints.Key key, Object value)
  sets a rendering hint for this graphics context.
- void setRenderingHints(Map m)
  sets all rendering hints whose key/value pairs are stored in the map.

 java.awt.RenderingHints 1.2

- RenderingHints(Map<RenderingHints.Key, ?> m)
  constructs a rendering hints map for storing rendering hints. If m is null, then a
  default map implementation is provided.

Readers and Writers for Images

Prior to version 1.4, the JDK had very limited capabilities for reading and writing image files. It was possible to read GIF and JPEG images, but there was no official support for writing images at all.

This situation is now much improved. JDK 1.4 introduces the javax.imageio package that contains "out of the box" support for reading and writing several common file formats, as well as a framework that enables third parties to add readers and writers for other formats. Specifically, the JDK contains readers for the GIF, JPEG, and PNG formats and writers for JPEG and PNG. (We suspect that writing GIF files is not supported because of patent issues.)

 NOTE: You can find a GIF encoder at http://www.acme.com/java.

The basics of the library are extremely straightforward. To load an image, use the static read method of the ImageIO class:

```
File f = . . .;
BufferedImage image = ImageIO.read(f);
```

The ImageIO class picks an appropriate reader, based on the file type. It may consult the file extension and the "magic number" at the beginning of the file for that purpose. If no suitable reader can be found or the reader can't decode the file contents, then the read method returns null.

Writing an image to a file is just as simple:

```
File f = . . .;
String format = . . .;
ImageIO.write(image, format, f);
```

Here the format string is a string identifying the image format, such as "JPEG" or "PNG". The ImageIO class picks an appropriate writer and saves the file.

Obtaining Readers and Writers for Image File Types

For more advanced image reading and writing operations that go beyond the static read and write methods of the ImageIO class, you first need to get the appropriate ImageReader and ImageWriter objects. The ImageIO class enumerates readers and writers that match one of the following:

- An image format (such as "JPEG")
- A file suffix (such as "jpg")
- A MIME type (such as "image/jpeg")

 NOTE: MIME is the Multipurpose Internet Mail Extensions standard. The MIME standard defines common data formats such as "image/jpeg" and "application/pdf". For an HTML version of the RFC (Request for Comments) that defines the MIME format, see http://www.oac.uci.edu/indiv/ehood/MIME.

For example, you can obtain a reader that reads JPEG files as follows:

```
ImageReader reader = null;
Iterator<ImageReader> iter = ImageIO.getImageReadersByFormatName("JPEG");
if (iter.hasNext()) reader = iter.next();
```

The getImageReadersBySuffix and getImageReadersByMIMEType method enumerate readers that match a file extension or MIME type.

It is possible that the ImageIO class can locate multiple readers that can all read a particular image type. In that case, you have to pick one of them, but it isn't clear how you can decide which one is the best. To find out more information about a reader, obtain its *service provider interface*:

```
ImageReaderSpi spi = reader.getOriginatingProvider();
```

Then you can get the vendor name and version number:

```
String vendor = spi.getVendor();
String version = spi.getVersion();
```

Perhaps that information can help you decide among the choices, or you may just present a list of readers to your program users and let them choose. However, for now, we assume that the first enumerated reader is at least adequate.

In the sample program at the end of this section, we have a couple of problems that the API doesn't address well. First, we want to find all file suffixes of all available readers so that we can use them in a file filter. The `IOImage` class is willing to tell us the names of all reader formats and the names of all supported MIME types. But we can't enumerate all supported file suffixes, nor can we get all readers. So, we first enumerate all format names, then we get all readers for a given format name. An `ImageReader` won't reveal the supported file suffixes, but the associated service provider interface object does. With a couple of nested loops and the handy `addAll` method of the `Set` interface, we manage to collect all file suffixes. You can find the full code in the `getReaderSuffixes` method in Example 7–9.

For saving files, we have a similar problem. We'd like to present the user with a menu of all supported image types. Unfortunately, the `getWriterFormatNames` of the `IOImage` class returns a rather curious list with redundant names, such as

```
JPG
jpeg
jpg
PNG
JPEG
png
```

That's not something one would want to present in a menu. It would be nice if there were some notion of a "preferred" format name. To pare down the list, we pick the first format name and look up the first writer associated with it. Then we ask it what its format names are, in the hope that it will list the most popular one first. Indeed, for the JPEG writer, this works fine: It lists `"JPEG"` before the other options. The PNG writer, on the other hand, lists `"png"` in lower case before `"PNG"`. We hope this behavior will be addressed at some time in the future. (We don't want to force the format name into upper case—that wouldn't work for a format such as "PostScript".)

Once we pick a writer, we add the first format name to the format name set and remove all its format names from the original set. We keep going until all format names are handled. The details are in the `getWriterFormats` method of Example 7–9. Note that this method would break down should someone provide a single writer that can write multiple image formats.

As a practical matter, most programmers won't be bothered by these issues. If you have a fixed number of file formats that your application supports, then you can simply find the appropriate readers, writers, and file suffixes for them.

Reading and Writing Files with Multiple Images

Some files, in particular, animated GIF files, contain multiple images. The `read` method of the `ImageIO` class reads a single image. To read multiple images, turn the input source (for example, an input stream or file) into an `ImageInputStream`.

```
InputStream in = . . .;
ImageInputStream imageIn = ImageIO.createImageInputStream(in);
```

Then attach the image input stream to the reader:

```
reader.setInput(imageIn, true);
```

The second parameter indicates that the input is in "seek forward only" mode. Otherwise, random access is used, either by buffering stream input as it is read or by using random file access. Random access is required for certain operations. For example, to find out the

number of images in a GIF file, you need to read the entire file. If you then want to fetch an image, the input must be read again.

This consideration is only important if you read from a stream, if the input contains multiple images, and if the image format doesn't have the information that you request (such as the image count) in the header. If you read from a file, simply use

```
File f = . . .;
ImageInputStream imageIn = ImageIO.createImageInputStream(f);
reader.setInput(imageIn);
```

Once you have a reader, you can read the images in the input by calling

```
BufferedImage image = reader.read(index);
```

where index is the image index, starting with 0.

If the input is in "seek forward only" mode, you keep reading images until the read method throws an IndexOutOfBoundsException. Otherwise, you can call the getNumImages method:

```
int n = reader.getNumImages(true);
```

Here, the parameter indicates that you allow a search of the input to determine the number of images. That method throws an IllegalStateException if the input is in "seek forward only" mode. Alternatively, you can set the "allow search" parameter to false. Then the getNumImages method returns –1 if it can't determine the number of images without a search. In that case, you'll have to switch to Plan B and keep reading images until you get an IndexOutOfBounds-Exception.

Some files contain thumbnails, smaller versions of an image for preview purposes. You can get the number of thumbnails of an image with the call

```
int count = reader.getNumThumbnails(index);
```

Then you get a particular index as

```
BufferedImage thumbnail = reader.getThumbnail(index, thumbnailIndex);
```

Another consideration is that you sometimes want to get the image size before actually getting the image, in particular, if the image comes from a slow network connection. Use the calls

```
int width = reader.getWidth(index);
int height = reader.getHeight(index);
```

to get the dimensions of an image with a given index. The image dimensions should be available before the actual image data. If there is no image with the given index, the methods throw an IndexOutOfBoundsException.

To write a file with multiple images, you first need an ImageWriter. The ImageIO class can enumerate the writers that are capable of writing a particular image format:

```
String format = . . .;
ImageWriter writer = null;
Iterator<ImageWriter> iter =  ImageIO.getImageWritersByFormatName( format );
if (iter.hasNext()) writer = iter.next();
```

Next, turn an output stream or file into an ImageOutputStream and attach it to the writer. For example,

```
File f = . . .;
ImageOutputStream imageOut = ImageIO.createImageOutputStream(f);
writer.setOutput(imageOut);
```

You must wrap each image into an IIOImage object. You can optionally supply a list of thumbnails and image metadata (such as compression algorithms and color information).

In this example, we just use null for both; see the JDK documentation for additional information.

```
IIOImage iioImage = new IIOImage(images[i], null, null);
```

Write out the *first* image, using the write method:

```
writer.write(new IIOImage(images[0], null, null));
```

For subsequent images, use

```
if (writer.canInsertImage(i))
    writer.writeInsert(i, iioImage, null);
```

The third parameter can contain an ImageWriteParam object to set image writing details such as tiling and compression; use null for default values.

Not all file formats can handle multiple images. In that case, the canInsertImage method returns false for i > 0, and only a single image is saved.

The program in Example 7–9 lets you load and save files in the formats for which the JDK supplies readers and writers. The program displays multiple images (see Figure 7–29), but not thumbnails.

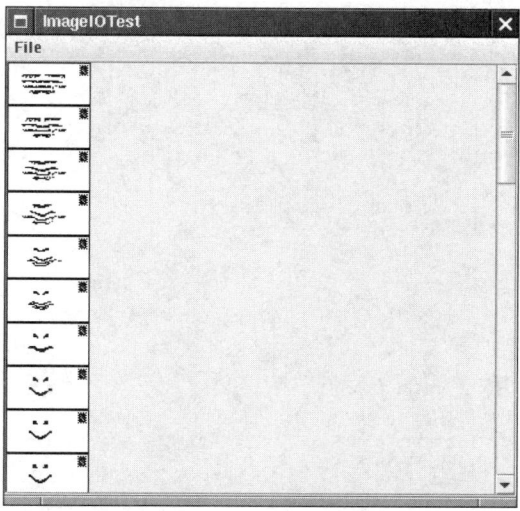

Figure 7–29: An animated GIF image

Example 7–9: ImageIOTest.java

```
1.  import java.awt.*;
2.  import java.awt.event.*;
3.  import java.awt.image.*;
4.  import java.io.*;
5.  import java.util.*;
6.  import java.util.List;
7.  import javax.imageio.*;
8.  import javax.imageio.stream.*;
9.  import javax.swing.*;
10.
11. /**
12.    This program lets you read and write image files in the
13.    formats that the JDK supports. Multifile images are
14.    supported.
```

```
15. */
16. public class ImageIOTest
17. {
18.    public static void main(String[] args)
19.    {
20.       JFrame frame = new ImageIOFrame();
21.       frame.setDefaultCloseOperation(JFrame.EXIT_ON_CLOSE);
22.       frame.setVisible(true);
23.    }
24. }
25.
26. /**
27.    This frame displays the loaded images. The menu has items
28.    for loading and saving files.
29. */
30. class ImageIOFrame extends JFrame
31. {
32.    public ImageIOFrame()
33.    {
34.       setTitle("ImageIOTest");
35.       setSize(DEFAULT_WIDTH, DEFAULT_HEIGHT);
36.
37.       JMenu fileMenu = new JMenu("File");
38.       JMenuItem openItem = new JMenuItem("Open");
39.       openItem.addActionListener(new
40.          ActionListener()
41.          {
42.             public void actionPerformed(ActionEvent event)
43.             {
44.                openFile();
45.             }
46.          });
47.       fileMenu.add(openItem);
48.
49.       JMenu saveMenu = new JMenu("Save");
50.       fileMenu.add(saveMenu);
51.       Iterator<String> iter = writerFormats.iterator();
52.       while (iter.hasNext())
53.       {
54.          final String formatName = iter.next();
55.          JMenuItem formatItem = new JMenuItem(formatName);
56.          saveMenu.add(formatItem);
57.          formatItem.addActionListener(new
58.             ActionListener()
59.             {
60.                public void actionPerformed(ActionEvent event)
61.                {
62.                   saveFile(formatName);
63.                }
64.             });
65.       }
66.
67.       JMenuItem exitItem = new JMenuItem("Exit");
68.       exitItem.addActionListener(new
69.          ActionListener()
70.          {
```

```
71.      public void actionPerformed(ActionEvent event)
72.      {
73.         System.exit(0);
74.      }
75.   });
76.   fileMenu.add(exitItem);
77.
78.
79.   JMenuBar menuBar = new JMenuBar();
80.   menuBar.add(fileMenu);
81.   setJMenuBar(menuBar);
82. }
83.
84. /**
85.    Open a file and load the images.
86. */
87. public void openFile()
88. {
89.   JFileChooser chooser = new JFileChooser();
90.   chooser.setCurrentDirectory(new File("."));
91.
92.   chooser.setFileFilter(new
93.      javax.swing.filechooser.FileFilter()
94.      {
95.         public boolean accept(File f)
96.         {
97.            if (f.isDirectory()) return true;
98.            String name = f.getName();
99.            int p = name.lastIndexOf('.');
100.           if (p == -1) return false;
101.           String suffix = name.substring(p + 1).toLowerCase();
102.           return readerSuffixes.contains(suffix);
103.        }
104.        public String getDescription()
105.        {
106.           return "Image files";
107.        }
108.     });
109.   int r = chooser.showOpenDialog(this);
110.   if (r != JFileChooser.APPROVE_OPTION) return;
111.   File f = chooser.getSelectedFile();
112.   Box box = Box.createVerticalBox();
113.   try
114.   {
115.      String name = f.getName();
116.      String suffix = name.substring(name.lastIndexOf('.') + 1);
117.      Iterator<ImageReader> iter = ImageIO.getImageReadersBySuffix(suffix);
118.      ImageReader reader = iter.next();
119.      ImageInputStream imageIn = ImageIO.createImageInputStream(f);
120.      reader.setInput(imageIn);
121.      int count = reader.getNumImages(true);
122.      images = new BufferedImage[count];
123.      for (int i = 0; i < count; i++)
124.      {
125.         images[i] = reader.read(i);
126.         box.add(new JLabel(new ImageIcon(images[i])));
```

```
127.            }
128.          }
129.          catch (IOException e)
130.          {
131.             JOptionPane.showMessageDialog(this, e);
132.          }
133.          setContentPane(new JScrollPane(box));
134.          validate();
135.       }
136.
137.       /**
138.          Save the current image in a file
139.          @param formatName the file format
140.       */
141.       public void saveFile(final String formatName)
142.       {
143.          if (images == null) return;
144.          Iterator<ImageWriter> iter = ImageIO.getImageWritersByFormatName(formatName);
145.          ImageWriter writer = iter.next();
146.          final List<String> writerSuffixes
147.             = Arrays.asList(writer.getOriginatingProvider().getFileSuffixes());
148.          JFileChooser chooser = new JFileChooser();
149.          chooser.setCurrentDirectory(new File("."));
150.
151.          chooser.setFileFilter(new
152.             javax.swing.filechooser.FileFilter()
153.             {
154.                public boolean accept(File f)
155.                {
156.                   if (f.isDirectory()) return true;
157.                   String name = f.getName();
158.                   int p = name.lastIndexOf('.');
159.                   if (p == -1) return false;
160.                   String suffix = name.substring(p + 1).toLowerCase();
161.                   return writerSuffixes.contains(suffix);
162.                }
163.                public String getDescription()
164.                {
165.                   return formatName + " files";
166.                }
167.             });
168.
169.          int r = chooser.showSaveDialog(this);
170.          if (r != JFileChooser.APPROVE_OPTION) return;
171.          File f = chooser.getSelectedFile();
172.          try
173.          {
174.             ImageOutputStream imageOut = ImageIO.createImageOutputStream(f);
175.             writer.setOutput(imageOut);
176.
177.             writer.write(new IIOImage(images[0], null, null));
178.             for (int i = 1; i < images.length; i++)
179.             {
180.                IIOImage iioImage = new IIOImage(images[i], null, null);
181.                if (writer.canInsertImage(i))
182.                   writer.writeInsert(i, iioImage, null);
```

```
183.           }
184.       }
185.       catch (IOException e)
186.       {
187.           JOptionPane.showMessageDialog(this, e);
188.       }
189.    }
190.
191.    /**
192.       Gets a set of all file suffixes that are recognized by image readers.
193.       @return the file suffix set
194.    */
195.    public static Set<String> getReaderSuffixes()
196.    {
197.       TreeSet<String> readerSuffixes = new TreeSet<String>();
198.       for (String name : ImageIO.getReaderFormatNames())
199.       {
200.          Iterator<ImageReader> iter = ImageIO.getImageReadersByFormatName(name);
201.          while (iter.hasNext())
202.          {
203.             ImageReader reader = iter.next();
204.             String[] s = reader.getOriginatingProvider().getFileSuffixes();
205.             readerSuffixes.addAll(Arrays.asList(s));
206.          }
207.       }
208.       return readerSuffixes;
209.    }
210.
211.    /**
212.       Gets a set of "preferred" format names of all image writers. The preferred format name is
213.       the first format name that a writer specifies.
214.       @return the format name set
215.    */
216.    public static Set<String> getWriterFormats()
217.    {
218.       TreeSet<String> writerFormats = new TreeSet<String>();
219.       TreeSet<String> formatNames
220.          = new TreeSet<String>(Arrays.asList(ImageIO.getWriterFormatNames()));
221.       while (formatNames.size() > 0)
222.       {
223.          String name = formatNames.iterator().next();
224.          Iterator<ImageWriter> iter = ImageIO.getImageWritersByFormatName(name);
225.          ImageWriter writer = iter.next();
226.          String[] names = writer.getOriginatingProvider().getFormatNames();
227.          writerFormats.add(names[0]);
228.          formatNames.removeAll(Arrays.asList(names));
229.       }
230.       return writerFormats;
231.    }
232.
233.    private BufferedImage[] images;
234.    private static Set<String> readerSuffixes = getReaderSuffixes();
235.    private static Set<String> writerFormats = getWriterFormats();
236.    private static final int DEFAULT_WIDTH = 400;
237.    private static final int DEFAULT_HEIGHT = 400;
238. }
```

 javax.imageio.ImageIO 1.4

- static BufferedImage read(File input)
- static BufferedImage read(InputStream input)
- static BufferedImage read(URL input)
  read an image from input.

- static boolean write(RenderedImage image, String formatName, File output)
- static boolean write(RenderedImage image, String formatName, OutputStream output)
  write an image in the given format to output. Return false if no appropriate writer was found.

- static Iterator<ImageReader> getImageReadersByFormatName(String formatName)
- static Iterator<ImageReader> getImageReadersBySuffix(String fileSuffix)
- static Iterator<ImageReader> getImageReadersByMIMEType(String mimeType)
- static Iterator<ImageWriter> getImageWritersByFormatName(String formatName)
- static Iterator<ImageWriter> getImageWritersBySuffix(String fileSuffix)
- static Iterator<ImageWriter> getImageWritersByMIMEType(String mimeType)
  get all readers and writers that are able to handle the given format (e.g., "JPEG"), file suffix (e.g., "jpg"), or MIME type (e.g., "image/jpeg").

- static String[] getReaderFormatNames()
- static String[] getReaderMIMETypes()
- static String[] getWriterFormatNames()
- static String[] getWriterMIMETypes()
  get all format names and MIME type names supported by readers and writers.

- ImageInputStream createImageInputStream(Object input)
- ImageOutputStream createImageOutputStream(Object output)
  create an image input or image output stream from the given object. The object can be a file, a stream, a RandomAccessFile, or another object for which a service provider exists. Return null if no registered service provider can handle the object.

 javax.imageio.ImageReader 1.4

- void setInput(Object input)
- void setInput(Object input, boolean seekForwardOnly)
  set the input source of the reader.

Parameters:	input	An ImageInputStream object or another object that this reader can accept.
	seekForwardOnly	true if the reader should read forward only. By default, the reader uses random access and, if necessary, buffers image data.

- BufferedImage read(int index)
  reads the image with the given image index (starting at 0). Throws an IndexOutOfBoundsException if no such image is available.

- int getNumImages(boolean allowSearch)
  gets the number of images in this reader. If allowSearch is false and the number of images cannot be determined without reading forward, then –1 is returned. If allowSearch is true and the reader is in "seek forward only" mode, then an IllegalStateException is thrown.

- int getNumThumbnails(int index)
  gets the number of thumbnails of the image with the given index.

- BufferedImage readThumbnail(int index, int thumbnailIndex)
  gets the thumbnail with index thumbnailIndex of the image with the given index.
- int getWidth(int index)
- int getHeight(int index)
  get the image width and height. Throw an IndexOutOfBoundsException if no such image is available.
- ImageReaderSpi getOriginatingProvider()
  gets the service provider that constructed this reader.

javax.imageio.spi.IIOServiceProvider 1.4

- String getVendorName()
- String getVersion()
  get the vendor name and version of this service provider.

javax.imageio.spi.ImageReaderWriterSpi 1.4

- String[] getFormatNames()
- String[] getFileSuffixes()
- String[] getMIMETypes()
  get the format names, file suffixes, and MIME types supported by the readers or writers that this service provider creates.

javax.imageio.ImageWriter 1.4

- void setOutput(Object output)
  sets the output target of this writer.

  | *Parameters:* | output | An ImageOutputStream object or another object that this writer can accept |

- void write(IIOImage image)
- void write(RenderedImage image)
  write a single image to the output.
- void writeInsert(int index, IIOImage image, ImageWriteParam param)
  write an image into a multi-image file.

Parameters:	index	The image index
	image	The image to write
	param	The write parameters, or null

- boolean canInsertImage(int index)
  returns true if it is possible to insert an image at the given index.
- ImageWriterSpi getOriginatingProvider()
  gets the service provider that constructed this writer.

javax.imageio.IIOImage 1.4

- IIOImage(RenderedImage image, List thumbnails, IIOMetadata metadata)
  constructs an IIOImage from an image, optional thumbnails, and optional metadata.

Parameters:	image	An image
	thumbnails	A list of BufferedImage objects, or null
	metadata	Metadata, or null

Image Manipulation

Suppose you have an image and you would like to improve its appearance. You then need to access the individual pixels of the image and replace them with other pixels. Or perhaps you want to compute the pixels of an image from scratch, for example, to show the result of physical measurements or a mathematical computation. The BufferedImage class gives you control over the pixels in an image, and classes that implement the BufferedImageOp interface let you transform images.

This is a major change from the image support in JDK 1.0. At that time, the image classes were optimized to support *incremental rendering*. The original purpose of the classes was to render GIF and JPEG images that are downloaded from the Web, a scan line at a time, as soon as partial image data is available. In fact, scan lines can be *interlaced,* with all even scan lines coming first, followed by the odd scan lines. That mechanism lets a browser quickly display an approximation of the image while fetching the remainder of the image data. The ImageProducer, ImageFilter, and ImageConsumer interfaces in JDK 1.0 expose all the complexities of incremental rendering. Writing an image manipulation that fit well into that framework was quite complex.

Fortunately, the need for using these classes has completely gone away. JDK 1.2 replaced the "push model" of JDK 1.0 with a "direct" model that lets you access pixels directly and conveniently. We cover only the direct model in this chapter. The only disadvantage of the direct model is that it requires all image pixels to be in memory. (In practice, the "push model" had the same restriction. It would have required fiendish cunning to write image manipulation algorithms that processed pixels as they became available. Most users of the old model simply buffered the entire image before processing it.) Future versions of the Java platform may support a "pull" model with which a processing pipeline can reduce memory consumption and increase speed by fetching and processing pixels only when they are actually needed.

Accessing Image Data

Most of the images that you manipulate are simply read in from an image file—they were either produced by a device such as a digital camera or scanner, or constructed by a drawing program. In this section, we show you a different technique for constructing an image, namely, to build up an image a pixel at a time.

To create an image, construct a BufferedImage object in the usual way.

```
image = new BufferedImage(width, height, BufferedImage.TYPE_INT_ARGB);
```

Now, call the getRaster method to obtain an object of type WritableRaster. You use this object to access and modify the pixels of the image.

```
WritableRaster raster = image.getRaster();
```

The setPixel method lets you set an individual pixel. The complexity here is that you can't simply set the pixel to a Color value. You must know how the buffered image specifies color values. That depends on the *type* of the image. If your image has a type of TYPE_INT_ARGB, then each pixel is described by four values, for red, green, blue, and alpha, each of which is between 0 and 255. You supply them in an array of four integers.

```
int[] black = { 0, 0, 0, 255 };
raster.setPixel(i, j, black);
```

In the lingo of the Java 2D API, these values are called the *sample values* of the pixel.

CAUTION: There are also setPixel methods that take array parameters of types float[] and double[]. However, the values that you need to place into these arrays are *not* normalized color values between 0.0 and 1.0.

```
float[] red = { 1.0F, 0.0F, 0.0F, 1.0F };
raster.setPixel(i, j, red); // ERROR
```

You need to supply values between 0 and 255, no matter what the type of the array is.

You can supply batches of pixels with the setPixels method. Specify the starting pixel position and the width and height of the rectangle that you want to set. Then, supply an array that contains the sample values for all pixels. For example, if your buffered image has a type of TYPE_INT_ARGB, then you supply the red, green, blue, and alpha value of the first pixel, then the red, green, blue, and alpha value for the second pixel, and so on.

```
int[] pixels = new int[4 * width * height];
pixels[0] = . . . // red value for first pixel
pixels[1] = . . . // green value for first pixel
pixels[2] = . . . // blue value for first pixel
pixels[3] = . . . // alpha value for first pixel
. . .
raster.setPixels(x, y, width, height, pixels);
```

Conversely, to read a pixel, you use the getPixel method. Supply an array of four integers to hold the sample values.

```
int[] sample = new int[4];
raster.getPixel(x, y, sample);
Color c = new Color(sample[0], sample[1], sample[2], sample[3]);
```

You can read multiple pixels with the getPixels method.

```
raster.getPixels(x, y, width, height, samples);
```

If you use an image type other than TYPE_INT_ARGB and you know how that type represents pixel values, then you can still use the getPixel/setPixel methods. However, you have to know the encoding of the sample values in the particular image type.

If you need to manipulate an image with an arbitrary, unknown image type, then you have to work a bit harder. Every image type has a *color model* that can translate between sample value arrays and the standard RGB color model.

NOTE: The RGB color model isn't as standard as you might think. The exact look of a color value depends on the characteristics of the imaging device. Digital cameras, scanners, monitors, and LCD displays all have their own idiosyncrasies. As a result, the same RGB value can look quite different on different devices. The International Color Consortium (http://www.color.org) recommends that all color data be accompanied by an *ICC profile* that specifies how the colors map to a standard form such as the 1931 CIE XYZ color specification. That specification was designed by the Commission Internationale de l'Eclairage or CIE (http://www.cie.co.at/cie), the international organization in charge of providing technical guidance in all matters of illumination and color. The specification is a standard method for representing all colors that the human eye can perceive as a triple of coordinates called X, Y, Z. (See, for example, Foley, van Dam, Feiner, et al., Chapter 13, for more information on the 1931 CIE XYZ specification.)

ICC profiles are complex, however. A simpler proposed standard, called sRGB (http://www.w3.org/Graphics/Color/sRGB.html), specifies an exact mapping between RGB values and the 1931 CIE XYZ values that was designed to work well with typical color monitors. The Java 2D API uses that mapping when converting between RGB and other color spaces.

The getColorModel method returns the color model:

```
ColorModel model = image.getColorModel();
```

To find the color value of a pixel, you call the getDataElements method of the Raster class. That call returns an Object that contains a color-model-specific description of the color value.

```
Object data = raster.getDataElements(x, y, null);
```

 NOTE: The object that is returned by the getDataElements method is actually an array of sample values. You don't need to know this to process the object, but it explains why the method is called getDataElements.

The color model can translate the object to standard ARGB values. The getRGB method returns an int value that has the alpha, red, green, and blue values packed in four blocks of 8 bits each. You can construct a Color value out of that integer with the Color(int argb, boolean hasAlpha) constructor.

```
int argb = model.getRGB(data);
Color color = new Color(argb, true);
```

To set a pixel to a particular color, you reverse these steps. The getRGB method of the Color class yields an int value with the alpha, red, green, and blue values. Supply that value to the getDataElements method of the ColorModel class. The return value is an Object that contains the color-model-specific description of the color value. Pass the object to the setDataElements method of the WritableRaster class.

```
int argb = color.getRGB();
Object data = model.getDataElements(argb, null);
raster.setDataElements(x, y, data);
```

To illustrate how to use these methods to build an image from individual pixels, we bow to tradition and draw a Mandelbrot set, as shown in Figure 7–30.

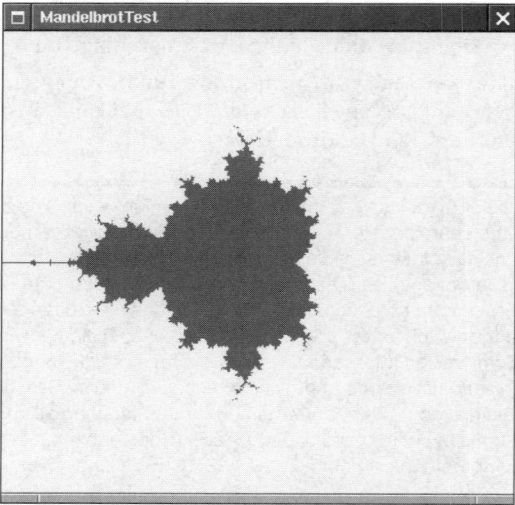

Figure 7–30: A Mandelbrot set

The idea of the Mandelbrot set is that you associate with each point in the plane a sequence of numbers. If that sequence stays bounded, you color the point. If it "escapes to infinity,"

you leave it transparent. The formulas for the number sequences come ultimately from the mathematics of complex numbers. We just take them for granted. For more on the mathematics of fractals, choose from the hundreds of books out there; one that is quite thick and comprehensive is *Chaos and Fractals: New Frontiers of Science* by Heinz-Otto Peitgen, Dietmar Saupe, and Hartmut Jürgens [Springer Verlag 1992].

Here is how you can construct the simplest Mandelbrot set. For each point (a, b), you look at sequences that start with $(x, y) = (0, 0)$ and iterate:

$$x_{new} = x^2 - y^2 + a$$
$$y_{new} = 2 \cdot x \cdot y + b$$

Check whether the sequence stays bounded or "escapes to infinity," that is, whether x and y keep getting larger. It turns out that if x or y ever gets larger than 2, then the sequence escapes to infinity. Only the pixels that correspond to points (a, b) leading to a bounded sequence are colored.

Example 7–10 shows the code. In this program, we demonstrate how to use the `ColorModel` class for translating `Color` values into pixel data. That process is independent of the image type. Just for fun, change the color type of the buffered image to `TYPE_BYTE_GRAY`. You don't need to change any other code—the color model of the image automatically takes care of the conversion from colors to sample values.

Example 7–10: MandelbrotTest.java

```
 1. import java.awt.*;
 2. import java.awt.event.*;
 3. import java.awt.image.*;
 4. import javax.swing.*;
 5.
 6. /**
 7.    This program demonstrates how to build up an image from individual pixels.
 8. */
 9. public class MandelbrotTest
10. {
11.    public static void main(String[] args)
12.    {
13.       JFrame frame = new MandelbrotFrame();
14.       frame.setDefaultCloseOperation(JFrame.EXIT_ON_CLOSE);
15.       frame.setVisible(true);
16.    }
17. }
18.
19. /**
20.    This frame shows an image with a Mandelbrot set.
21. */
22. class MandelbrotFrame extends JFrame
23. {
24.    public MandelbrotFrame()
25.    {
26.       setTitle("MandelbrotTest");
27.       setSize(DEFAULT_WIDTH, DEFAULT_HEIGHT);
28.       BufferedImage image = makeMandelbrot(DEFAULT_WIDTH, DEFAULT_HEIGHT);
29.       add(new JLabel(new ImageIcon(image)), BorderLayout.CENTER);
30.    }
```

```
31.
32.    /**
33.       Makes the Mandelbrot image.
34.       @param width the width
35.       @parah height the height
36.       @return the image
37.    */
38.    public BufferedImage makeMandelbrot(int width, int height)
39.    {
40.       BufferedImage image = new BufferedImage(width, height, BufferedImage.TYPE_INT_ARGB);
41.       WritableRaster raster = image.getRaster();
42.       ColorModel model = image.getColorModel();
43.
44.       Color fractalColor = Color.red;
45.       int argb = fractalColor.getRGB();
46.       Object colorData = model.getDataElements(argb, null);
47.
48.       for (int i = 0; i < width; i++)
49.          for (int j = 0; j < height; j++)
50.          {
51.             double a = XMIN + i * (XMAX - XMIN) / width;
52.             double b = YMIN + j * (YMAX - YMIN) / height;
53.             if (!escapesToInfinity(a, b))
54.                raster.setDataElements(i, j, colorData);
55.          }
56.       return image;
57.    }
58.
59.    private boolean escapesToInfinity(double a, double b)
60.    {
61.       double x = 0.0;
62.       double y = 0.0;
63.       int iterations = 0;
64.       do
65.       {
66.          double xnew = x * x - y * y + a;
67.          double ynew = 2 * x * y + b;
68.          x = xnew;
69.          y = ynew;
70.          iterations++;
71.          if (iterations == MAX_ITERATIONS) return false;
72.       }
73.       while (x <= 2 && y <= 2);
74.       return true;
75.    }
76.
77.    private static final double XMIN = -2;
78.    private static final double XMAX = 2;
79.    private static final double YMIN = -2;
80.    private static final double YMAX = 2;
81.    private static final int MAX_ITERATIONS = 16;
82.    private static final int DEFAULT_WIDTH = 400;
83.    private static final int DEFAULT_HEIGHT = 400;
84. }
```

---

java.awt.image.BufferedImage 1.2

- BufferedImage(int width, int height, int imageType)
  constructs a buffered image object.

Parameters:	width, height	The image dimensions
	imageType	A type such as TYPE_INT_RGB, TYPE_INT_ARGB, TYPE_BYTE_GRAY, TYPE_BYTE_INDEXED, TYPE_USHORT_555_RGB, and so on

- ColorModel getColorModel()
  returns the color model of this buffered image.

- WritableRaster getRaster()
  gets the raster for accessing and modifying pixels of this buffered image.

java.awt.image.Raster 1.2

- Object getDataElements(int x, int y, Object data)
  returns the sample data for a raster point, in an array whose element type and length depend on the color model. If data is not null, it is assumed to be an array that is appropriate for holding sample data and it is filled. If data is null, a new array is allocated.

Parameters:	x, y	The pixel location.
	data	null or an array that is suitable for being filled with the sample data for a pixel. Its element type and length depend on the color model.

- int[] getPixel(int x, int y, int[] sampleValues)
- float[] getPixel(int x, int y, float[] sampleValues)
- double[] getPixel(int x, int y, double[] sampleValues)
- int[] getPixels(int x, int y, int w, int h, int[] sampleValues)
- float[] getPixels(int x, int y, int w, int h, float[] sampleValues)
- double[] getPixels(int x, int y, int w, int h, double[] sampleValues)
  return the sample values for a raster point, or a rectangle of raster points, in an array whose length depends on the color model. If sampleValues is not null, it is assumed to be sufficiently long for holding the sample values and it is filled. If sampleValues is null, a new array is allocated. These methods are only useful if you know the meaning of the sample values for a color model.

Parameters:	x, y	The raster point location, or the top-left corner of the rectangle
	w, h	The width and height of the rectangle of raster points
	sampleValues	null or an array that is sufficiently long to be filled with the sample values

 java.awt.image.WritableRaster 1.2

- void setDataElements(int x, int y, Object data)
  sets the sample data for a raster point.

Parameters:	x, y	The pixel location.

data	An array filled with the sample data for a pixel. Its element type and length depend on the color model.

- void setPixel(int x, int y, int[] sampleValues)
- void setPixel(int x, int y, float[] sampleValues)
- void setPixel(int x, int y, double[] sampleValues)
- void setPixels(int x, int y, int w, int h, int[] sampleValues)
- void setPixels(int x, int y, int w, int h, float[] sampleValues)
- void setPixels(int x, int y, int w, int h, double[] sampleValues)

set the sample values for a raster point or a rectangle of raster points. These methods are only useful if you know the encoding of the sample values for a color model.

Parameters:	x, y	The raster point location, or the top-left corner of the rectangle.
	w, h	The width and height of the rectangle of raster points.
	sampleValues	An array filled with the sample data. Its element type and length depend on the color model.

 java.awt.image.ColorModel 1.2

- int getRGB(Object data)
  returns the ARGB value that corresponds to the sample data passed in data.

Parameters:	data	An array filled with the sample data for a pixel. Its element type and length depend on the color model.

- Object getDataElements(int argb, Object data);
  returns the sample data for a color value. If data is not null, it is assumed to be an array that is appropriate for holding sample data and it is filled. If data is null, a new array is allocated.

Parameters:	argb	The color value.
	data	null or an array that is suitable for being filled with the sample data for a color value. Its element type and length depend on the color model.

 java.awt.Color 1.0

- Color(int argb, boolean hasAlpha) **1.2**
  creates a color with the specified combined ARGB value if hasAlpha is true, or the specified RGB value if hasAlpha is false.
- int getRGB()
  returns the ARGB color value corresponding to this color.

Filtering Images

In the preceding section, you saw how to build up an image from scratch. However, often you want to access image data for a different reason: You already have an image and you want to improve it in some way.

Of course, you can use the getPixel/getDataElements methods that you saw in the preceding section to read the image data, manipulate them, and then write them back. But fortunately, the Java 2D API already supplies a number of *filters* that carry out common image processing operations for you.

The image manipulations all implement the BufferedImageOp interface. After you construct the operation, you simply call the filter method to transform an image into another.

```
BufferedImageOp op = . . .;
BufferedImage filteredImage
    = new BufferedImage(image.getWidth(), image.getHeight(), image.getType());
op.filter(image, filteredImage);
```

Some operations can transform an image in place (op.filter(image, image)), but most can't.

Five classes implement the BufferedImageOp interface:

```
AffineTransformOp
RescaleOp
LookupOp
ColorConvertOp
ConvolveOp
```

The AffineTransformOp carries out an affine transformation on the pixels. For example, here is how you can rotate an image about its center.

```
AffineTransform transform = AffineTransform.getRotateInstance(Math.toRadians(angle),
    image.getWidth() / 2, image.getHeight() / 2);
AffineTransformOp op = new AffineTransformOp(transform, interpolation);
op.filter(image, filteredImage);
```

The AffineTransformOp constructor requires an affine transform and an *interpolation* strategy. Interpolation is necessary to determine pixels in the target image if the source pixels are transformed somewhere between target pixels. For example, if you rotate source pixels, then they will generally not fall exactly onto target pixels. There are two interpolation strategies: AffineTransformOp.TYPE_BILINEAR and AffineTransformOp.TYPE_NEAREST_NEIGHBOR. Bilinear interpolation takes a bit longer but looks better.

The program in Example 7–11 lets you rotate an image by 5 degrees (see Figure 7–31).

Figure 7–31: A rotated image

The RescaleOp carries out a rescaling operation

$$x_{new} = a \cdot x + b$$

for all sample values x in the image. Sample values that are too large or small after the rescaling are set to the largest or smallest legal value. If the image is in ARGB format, the scaling is carried out separately for the red, green, and blue values, but not for the alpha values. The effect of rescaling with $a > 1$ is to brighten the image. You construct the RescaleOp by specifying the scaling parameters and optional rendering hints. In Example 7–11, we use:

```
float a = 1.5f;
float b = -20.0f;
RescaleOp op = new RescaleOp(a, b, null);
```

The LookupOp operation lets you specify an arbitrary mapping of sample values. You supply a table that specifies how each value should be mapped. In the example program, we compute the *negative* of all colors, changing the color c to $255 - c$.

The LookupOp constructor requires an object of type LookupTable and a map of optional hints. The LookupTable class is abstract, with two concrete subclasses: ByteLookupTable and ShortLookupTable. Because RGB color values are bytes, we use the ByteLookupTable. You construct such a table from an array of bytes and an integer offset into that array. Here is how we construct the LookupOp for the example program:

```
byte negative[] = new byte[256];
for (int i = 0; i < 256; i++) negative[i] = (byte) (255 - i);
ByteLookupTable table = new ByteLookupTable(0, negative);
LookupOp op = new LookupOp(table, null);
```

The lookup is applied to each color value separately, but not to the alpha value.

 NOTE: You cannot apply a LookupOp to an image with an indexed color model. (In those images, each sample value is an offset into a color palette.)

The ColorConvertOp is useful for color space conversions. We do not discuss it here.

The most powerful of the transformations is the ConvolveOp, which carries out a mathematical *convolution*. We do not want to get too deeply into the mathematical details of convolution, but the basic idea is simple. Consider, for example, the *blur filter* (see Figure 7–32).

Figure 7–32: Blurring an image

The blurring is achieved by replacement of each pixel with the *average* value from the pixel and its eight neighbors. Intuitively, it makes sense why this operation would blur out the picture. Mathematically, the averaging can be expressed as a convolution operation with the following *kernel:*

$$\begin{bmatrix} \frac{1}{9} & \frac{1}{9} & \frac{1}{9} \\ \frac{1}{9} & \frac{1}{9} & \frac{1}{9} \\ \frac{1}{9} & \frac{1}{9} & \frac{1}{9} \end{bmatrix}$$

The kernel of a convolution is a matrix that tells what weights should be applied to the neighboring values. The kernel above leads to a blurred image. A different kernel carries out *edge detection,* locating areas of color changes:

$$\begin{bmatrix} 0 & -1 & 0 \\ -1 & 4 & -1 \\ 0 & -1 & 0 \end{bmatrix}$$

Edge detection is an important technique for analyzing photographic images (see Figure 7–33).

Figure 7–33: Edge detection

To construct a convolution operation, you first set up an array of the values for the kernel and construct a `Kernel` object. Then, construct a `ConvolveOp` object from the kernel and use it for filtering.

```
float[] elements =
    {
        0.0f, -1.0f, 0.0f,
        -1.0f,  4.f, -1.0f,
        0.0f, -1.0f, 0.0f
    };
Kernel kernel = new Kernel(3, 3, elements);
ConvolveOp op = new ConvolveOp(kernel);
op.filter(image, filteredImage);
```

The program in Example 7–11 allows a user to load in a GIF or JPEG image and carry out the image manipulations that we discussed. Thanks to the power of the image operations that the Java 2D API provides, the program is very simple.

Example 7–11: ImageProcessingTest.java

```
1.  import java.awt.*;
2.  import java.awt.event.*;
3.  import java.awt.geom.*;
4.  import java.awt.image.*;
5.  import java.io.*;
6.  import javax.imageio.*;
7.  import javax.swing.*;
8.
9.  /**
10.    This program demonstrates various image processing operations.
11. */
12. public class ImageProcessingTest
13. {
14.    public static void main(String[] args)
15.    {
16.       JFrame frame = new ImageProcessingFrame();
17.       frame.setDefaultCloseOperation(JFrame.EXIT_ON_CLOSE);
```

```
18.        frame.setVisible(true);
19.     }
20. }
21.
22. /**
23.    This frame has a menu to load an image and to specify
24.    various transformations, and a panel to show the resulting
25.    image.
26. */
27. class ImageProcessingFrame extends JFrame
28. {
29.    public ImageProcessingFrame()
30.    {
31.       setTitle("ImageProcessingTest");
32.       setSize(DEFAULT_WIDTH, DEFAULT_HEIGHT);
33.
34.       JPanel panel = new
35.          JPanel()
36.          {
37.             public void paintComponent(Graphics g)
38.             {
39.                super.paintComponent(g);
40.                if (image != null) g.drawImage(image, 0, 0, null);
41.             }
42.          };
43.
44.       add(panel, BorderLayout.CENTER);
45.
46.       JMenu fileMenu = new JMenu("File");
47.       JMenuItem openItem = new JMenuItem("Open");
48.       openItem.addActionListener(new
49.          ActionListener()
50.          {
51.             public void actionPerformed(ActionEvent event)
52.             {
53.                openFile();
54.             }
55.          });
56.       fileMenu.add(openItem);
57.
58.       JMenuItem exitItem = new JMenuItem("Exit");
59.       exitItem.addActionListener(new
60.          ActionListener()
61.          {
62.             public void actionPerformed(ActionEvent event)
63.             {
64.                System.exit(0);
65.             }
66.          });
67.       fileMenu.add(exitItem);
68.
69.       JMenu editMenu = new JMenu("Edit");
70.       JMenuItem blurItem = new JMenuItem("Blur");
71.       blurItem.addActionListener(new
72.          ActionListener()
73.          {
```

```
74.    public void actionPerformed(ActionEvent event)
75.    {
76.       float weight = 1.0f / 9.0f;
77.       float[] elements = new float[9];
78.       for (int i = 0; i < 9; i++) elements[i] = weight;
79.       convolve(elements);
80.    }
81. });
82. editMenu.add(blurItem);
83.
84. JMenuItem sharpenItem = new JMenuItem("Sharpen");
85. sharpenItem.addActionListener(new
86.    ActionListener()
87.    {
88.       public void actionPerformed(ActionEvent event)
89.       {
90.          float[] elements =
91.          {
92.             0.0f, -1.0f, 0.0f,
93.             -1.0f,  5.f, -1.0f,
94.             0.0f, -1.0f, 0.0f
95.          };
96.          convolve(elements);
97.       }
98.    });
99. editMenu.add(sharpenItem);
100.
101. JMenuItem brightenItem = new JMenuItem("Brighten");
102. brightenItem.addActionListener(new
103.    ActionListener()
104.    {
105.       public void actionPerformed(ActionEvent event)
106.       {
107.          float a = 1.1f;
108.          float b = -20.0f;
109.          RescaleOp op = new RescaleOp(a, b, null);
110.          filter(op);
111.       }
112.    });
113. editMenu.add(brightenItem);
114.
115. JMenuItem edgeDetectItem = new JMenuItem("Edge detect");
116. edgeDetectItem.addActionListener(new
117.    ActionListener()
118.    {
119.       public void actionPerformed(ActionEvent event)
120.       {
121.          float[] elements =
122.          {
123.             0.0f, -1.0f, 0.0f,
124.             -1.0f,  4.f, -1.0f,
125.             0.0f, -1.0f, 0.0f
126.          };
127.          convolve(elements);
128.       }
129.    });
```

```
130.    editMenu.add(edgeDetectItem);
131.
132.    JMenuItem negativeItem = new JMenuItem("Negative");
133.    negativeItem.addActionListener(new
134.        ActionListener()
135.        {
136.            public void actionPerformed(ActionEvent event)
137.            {
138.                byte negative[] = new byte[256];
139.                for (int i = 0; i < 256; i++) negative[i] = (byte) (255 - i);
140.                ByteLookupTable table  = new ByteLookupTable(0, negative);
141.                LookupOp op = new LookupOp(table, null);
142.                filter(op);
143.            }
144.        });
145.    editMenu.add(negativeItem);
146.
147.    JMenuItem rotateItem = new JMenuItem("Rotate");
148.    rotateItem.addActionListener(new
149.        ActionListener()
150.        {
151.            public void actionPerformed(ActionEvent event)
152.            {
153.                if (image == null) return;
154.                AffineTransform transform = AffineTransform.getRotateInstance(
155.                    Math.toRadians(5), image.getWidth() / 2,  image.getHeight() / 2);
156.                AffineTransformOp op  = new AffineTransformOp(transform,
157.                    AffineTransformOp.TYPE_BILINEAR);
158.                filter(op);
159.            }
160.        });
161.    editMenu.add(rotateItem);
162.
163.    JMenuBar menuBar = new JMenuBar();
164.    menuBar.add(fileMenu);
165.    menuBar.add(editMenu);
166.    setJMenuBar(menuBar);
167.    }
168.
169.    /**
170.       Open a file and load the image.
171.    */
172.    public void openFile()
173.    {
174.        JFileChooser chooser = new JFileChooser();
175.        chooser.setCurrentDirectory(new File("."));
176.
177.        chooser.setFileFilter(new
178.            javax.swing.filechooser.FileFilter()
179.            {
180.                public boolean accept(File f)
181.                {
182.                    String name = f.getName().toLowerCase();
183.                    return name.endsWith(".gif") || name.endsWith(".jpg") || name.endsWith(".jpeg")
184.                        || f.isDirectory();
185.                }
```

```
186.          public String getDescription() {  return "Image files"; }
187.       });
188.
189.       int r = chooser.showOpenDialog(this);
190.       if(r != JFileChooser.APPROVE_OPTION) return;
191.
192.       try
193.       {
194.          image = ImageIO.read(chooser.getSelectedFile());
195.       }
196.       catch (IOException e)
197.       {
198.          JOptionPane.showMessageDialog(this, e);
199.       }
200.       repaint();
201.    }
202.
203.    /**
204.       Apply a filter and repaint.
205.       @param op the image operation to apply
206.    */
207.    private void filter(BufferedImageOp op)
208.    {
209.       if (image == null) return;
210.       BufferedImage filteredImage
211.          = new BufferedImage(image.getWidth(), image.getHeight(), image.getType());
212.       op.filter(image, filteredImage);
213.       image = filteredImage;
214.       repaint();
215.    }
216.
217.    /**
218.       Apply a convolution and repaint.
219.       @param elements the convolution kernel (an array of
220.       9 matrix elements)
221.    */
222.    private void convolve(float[] elements)
223.    {
224.       Kernel kernel = new Kernel(3, 3, elements);
225.       ConvolveOp op = new ConvolveOp(kernel);
226.       filter(op);
227.    }
228.
229.    private BufferedImage image;
230.    private static final int DEFAULT_WIDTH = 400;
231.    private static final int DEFAULT_HEIGHT = 400;
232. }
```

API	**java.awt.image.BufferedImageOp** 1.2

* BufferedImage filter(BufferedImage source, BufferedImage dest)
  applies the image operation to the source image and stores the result in the
  destination image. If dest is null, a new destination image is created. The destination
  image is returned.

 java.awt.image.AffineTransformOp 1.2

- AffineTransformOp(AffineTransform t, int interpolationType)
constructs an affine transform operator.

| *Parameters:* | t | An affine transform |
| | interpolationType | One of TYPE_BILINEAR or TYPE_NEAREST_NEIGHBOR |

 java.awt.image.RescaleOp 1.2

- RescaleOp(float a, float b, RenderingHints hints)
constructs a rescale operator.

| *Parameters:* | a, b | Coefficients of the transformation $x_{new} = a \cdot x + b$ that is applied to the sample values |
| | hints | Rendering hints for color matching; can be null |

 java.awt.image.LookupOp 1.2

- LookupOp(LookupTable table, RenderingHints hints)
constructs a lookup operator.

| *Parameters:* | table | The table for mapping the sample values |
| | hints | Rendering hints for color matching; can be null |

 java.awt.image.ByteLookupTable 1.2

- ByteLookupTable(int offset, byte[] data)
constructs a byte lookup table.

| *Parameters:* | offset | Position of first data value to be used |
| | data | The table data |

 java.awt.image.ConvolveOp 1.2

- ConvolveOp(Kernel kernel)
- ConvolveOp(Kernel kernel, int edgeCondition, RenderingHints hints)
construct a convolution operator.

Parameters:	kernel	The kernel matrix for the convolution.
	edgeCondition	Specifies how edge values should be treated: one of EDGE_NO_OP and EDGE_ZERO_FILL. Edge values need to be treated specially because they don't have sufficient neighboring values to compute the convolution. The default is EDGE_ZERO_FILL.
	hints	Rendering hints for color matching; can be null.

`java.awt.image.Kernel` 1.2

- `Kernel(int width, int height, float[] data)`
  constructs a kernel.

Parameters:	`width, height`	Dimensions of the kernel matrix
	`data`	Entries of the kernel matrix

Printing

The original Java Development Kit had no support for printing at all. It was not possible to print from applets, and you had to get a third-party library if you wanted to print in an application. JDK 1.1 introduced very lightweight printing support, just enough to produce simple printouts, as long as you were not too particular about the print quality. The 1.1 printing model was designed to allow browser vendors to print the surface of an applet as it appears on a web page (which, however, the browser vendors have not embraced).

JDK 1.2 introduced the beginnings of a robust printing model that is fully integrated with 2D graphics, and JDK 1.3 provided minor improvements. JDK 1.4 adds important enhancements, such as discovery of printer features and streaming print jobs for server-side print management.

In this section, we show you how you can easily print a drawing on a single sheet of paper, how you can manage a multipage printout, and how you can benefit from the elegance of the Java 2D imaging model and easily generate a print preview dialog box.

NOTE: The Java platform also supports the printing of user interface components. We do not cover this topic because it is mostly of interest to implementors of browsers, screen grabbers, and so on. For more information on printing components, see `http://java.sun.com/developer/onlineTraining/Programming/JDCBook/render.html`.

Graphics Printing

In this section, we tackle what is probably the most common printing situation: to print a 2D graphic. Of course, the graphic can contain text in various fonts or even consist entirely of text.

To generate a printout, you take care of these two tasks:

- Supply an object that implements the `Printable` interface.
- Start a print job.

The `Printable` interface has a single method:

```
int print(Graphics g, PageFormat format, int page)
```

That method is called whenever the print engine needs to have a page formatted for printing. Your code draws the text and image that are to be printed onto the graphics context. The page format tells you the paper size and the print margins. The page number tells you which page to render.

To start a print job, you use the `PrinterJob` class. First, you call the static `getPrinterJob` method to get a print job object. Then set the `Printable` object that you want to print.

```
Printable canvas = . . . .;
PrinterJob job = PrinterJob.getPrinterJob();
job.setPrintable(canvas);
```

> CAUTION: The class `PrintJob` handles JDK 1.1-style printing. That class is now obsolete. Do not confuse it with the `PrinterJob` class.

Before starting the print job, you should call the `printDialog` method to display a print dialog box (see Figure 7–34). That dialog box gives the user a chance to select the printer to be used (in case multiple printers are available), the page range that should be printed, and various printer settings.

You collect printer settings in an object of a class that implements the `PrintRequestAttribute-Set` interface to the `printDialog` method. The JDK provides a `HashPrintRequestAttributeSet` class for that purpose.

```
HashPrintRequestAttributeSet attributes = new HashPrintRequestAttributeSet();
```

Add attribute settings and pass the `attributes` object to the `printDialog` method.

The `printDialog` method returns `true` if the user clicked OK and `false` if the user canceled the dialog box. If the user accepted, call the `print` method of the `PrinterJob` class to start the printing process. The `print` method may throw a `PrinterException`. Here is the outline of the printing code:

```
if (job.printDialog(attributes))
{
   try
   {
      job.print(attributes);
   }
   catch (PrinterException exception)
   {
      . . .
   }
}
```

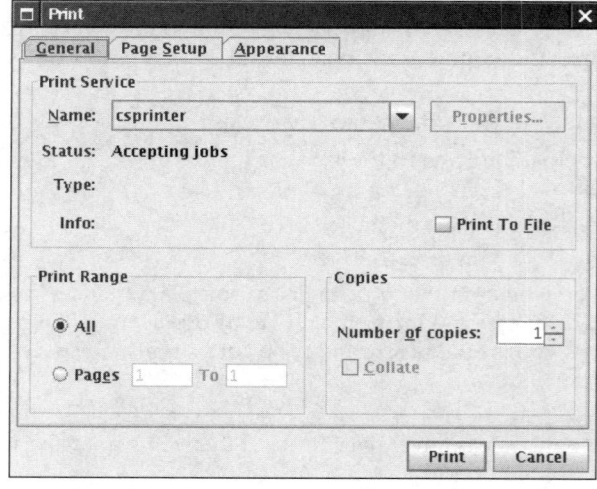

Figure 7–34: A cross-platform print dialog box

 NOTE: If you must support JDK 1.2 or 1.3, modify your program to display the native print dialog box instead of the cross-platform dialog box that was added in JDK 1.4. See the sidebar at the end of this section for details.

During printing, the `print` method of the `PrinterJob` class makes repeated calls to the `print` method of the `Printable` object associated with the job.

Because the job does not know how many pages you want to print, it simply keeps calling the `print` method. As long as the `print` method returns the value `Printable.PAGE_EXISTS`, the print job keeps producing pages. When the `print` method returns `Printable.NO_SUCH_PAGE`, the print job stops.

 CAUTION: The page numbers that the print job passes to the `print` method start with page 0.

Therefore, the print job doesn't have an accurate page count until after the printout is complete. For that reason, the print dialog box can't display the correct page range and instead displays a page range of "Pages 1 to 1." You will see in the next section how to avoid this blemish by supplying a `Book` object to the print job.

During the printing process, the print job repeatedly calls the `print` method of the `Printable` object. The print job is allowed to make multiple calls *for the same page*. You should therefore not count pages inside the `print` method but always rely on the page number parameter. There is a good reason why the print job may call the `print` method repeatedly for the same page. Some printers, in particular dot-matrix and inkjet printers, use *banding*. They print one band at a time, advance the paper, and then print the next band. The print job may use banding even for laser printers that print a full page at a time—it gives the print job a way of managing the size of the spool file.

If the print job needs the `Printable` object to print a band, then it sets the clip area of the graphics context to the requested band and calls the `print` method. Its drawing operations are clipped against the band rectangle, and only those drawing elements that show up in the band are rendered. Your `print` method need not be aware of that process, with one caveat: It should *not* interfere with the clip area.

 CAUTION: The `Graphics` object that your `print` method gets is also clipped against the page margins. If you replace the clip area, you can draw outside the margins. Especially in a printer graphics context, the clipping area must be respected. Call `clip`, not `setClip`, to further restrict the clipping area. If you must remove a clip area, then make sure to call `getClip` at the beginning of your `print` method and restore that clip area.

The `PageFormat` parameter of the `print` method contains information about the printed page. The methods `getWidth` and `getHeight` return the paper size, measured in *points*. One point is 1/72 of an inch. (An inch equals 25.4 millimeters.) For example, A4 paper is approximately 595 by 842 points, and U.S. letter-size paper is 612 by 792 points.

Points are a common measurement in the printing trade in the United States. Much to the chagrin of the rest of the world, the printing package uses point units for two purposes. Paper sizes and paper margins are measured in points. And the default unit for all print graphics contexts is one point. You can verify that in the example program at the end of

this section. The program prints two lines of text that are 72 units apart. Run the example program and measure the distance between the baselines. They are exactly 1 inch or 25.4 millimeters apart.

The getWidth and getHeight methods of the PageFormat class give you the complete paper size. Not all of the paper area is printable. Users typically select margins, and even if they don't, printers need to somehow grip the sheets of paper on which they print and therefore have a small unprintable area around the edges.

The methods getImageableWidth and getImageableHeight tell you the dimensions of the area that you can actually fill. However, the margins need not be symmetrical, so you must also know the top-left corner of the imageable area (see Figure 7–35), which you obtain by the methods getImageableX and getImageableY.

 TIP: The graphics context that you receive in the print method is clipped to exclude the margins, but the origin of the coordinate system is nevertheless the top-left corner of the paper. It makes sense to translate the coordinate system to start at the top-left corner of the imageable area. Simply start your print method with

```
g.translate(pageFormat.getImageableX(), pageFormat.getImageableY());
```

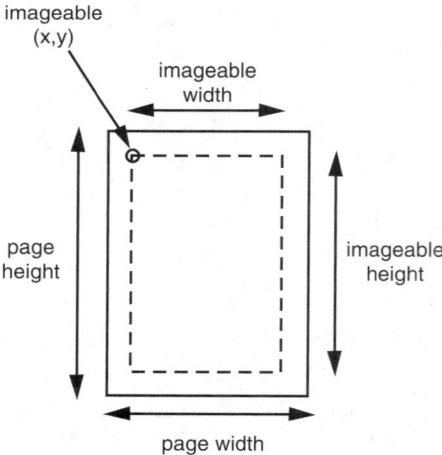

Figure 7–35: Page format measurements

If you want your users to choose the settings for the page margins or to switch between portrait and landscape orientation without setting other printing attributes, then you can call the pageDialog method of the PrinterJob class:

```
PageFormat format = job.pageDialog(attributes);
```

 NOTE: One of the tabs of the print dialog box contains the page setup dialog box (see Figure 7–36). You may still want to give users an option to set the page format before printing, especially if your program presents a "what you see is what you get" display of the pages to be printed. The pageDialog method returns a PageFormat object with the user settings.

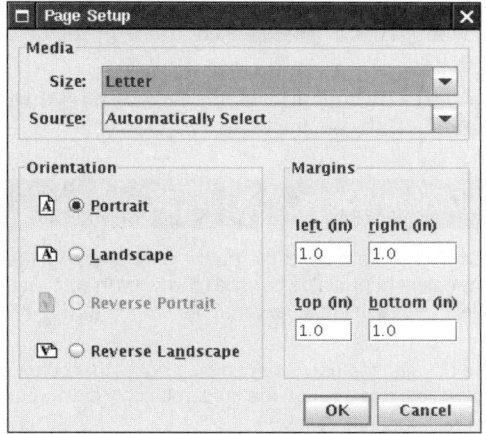

Figure 7–36: A cross-platform page setup dialog box

Example 7–12 shows how to render the same set of shapes on the screen and on the printed page. A subclass of JPanel implements the Printable interface. Both the paintComponent and the print methods call the same method to carry out the actual drawing.

```java
class PrintPanel extends JPanel implements Printable
{
   public void paintComponent(Graphics g)
   {
      super.paintComponent(g);
      Graphics2D g2 = (Graphics2D) g;
      drawPage(g2);
   }

   public int print(Graphics g, PageFormat pf, int page)
      throws PrinterException
   {
      if (page >= 1) return Printable.NO_SUCH_PAGE;
      Graphics2D g2 = (Graphics2D) g;
      g2.translate(pf.getImageableX(), pf.getImageableY());
      drawPage(g2);
      return Printable.PAGE_EXISTS;
   }

   public void drawPage(Graphics2D g2)
   {
      // shared drawing code goes here
      . . .
   }
   . . .
}
```

 CAUTION: JDK 1.2 does not set the paint to black when setting up a printer graphics context. If your pages come out all white, add a line g2.setPaint(Color.black) at the top of the print method. This problem has been fixed in JDK 1.3.

This example displays and prints the same image as Example 7–6 on page 498, namely, the outline of the message "Hello, World" that is used as a clipping area for a pattern of lines (see Figure 7–22 on page 497).

Click the Print button to start printing, or click the Page setup button to open the page setup dialog box. Example 7–12 shows the code. .

Using Native Print Dialog Boxes

Prior to JDK 1.4, the printing system used the native print and page setup dialog boxes of the host platform. To show a native print dialog box, call the `printDialog` method with no parameters. (There is no way to collect user settings in an attribute set.) Figure 7–37 shows a Windows print dialog box.

One potential advantage of using the native print dialog box is that some printer drivers have special features that are not accessible through the cross-platform dialog box. At any rate, to support JDK 1.2 and 1.3, show the native dialog boxes.

To show a native page setup dialog box, you pass a default `PageFormat` object to the `pageDialog` method. The method clones that object, modifies it according to the user selections in the dialog bpx, and returns the cloned object.

```
PageFormat defaultFormat = printJob.defaultPage();
PageFormat selectedFormat = printJob.pageDialog(defaultFormat);
```

Figure 7–38 shows a page setup dialog box for the Windows operating system.

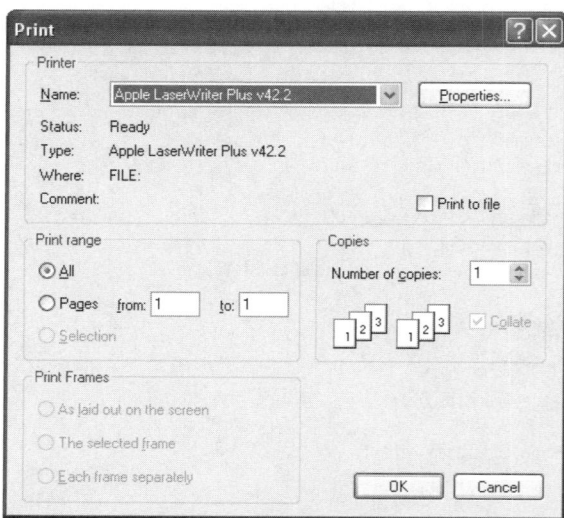

Figure 7–37: A Windows print dialog box

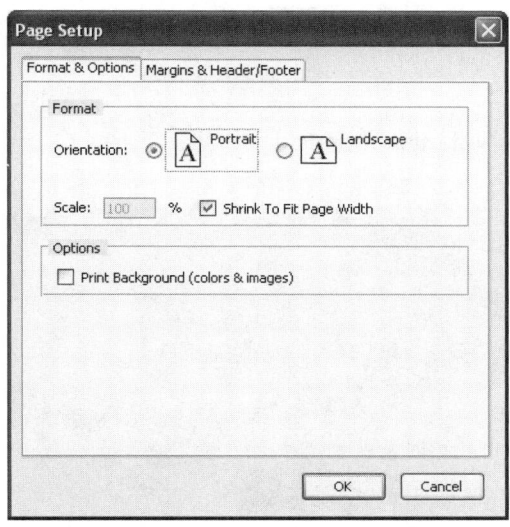

Figure 7–38: A Windows page setup dialog box

Example 7–12: PrintTest.java

```java
1.  import java.awt.*;
2.  import java.awt.event.*;
3.  import java.awt.font.*;
4.  import java.awt.geom.*;
5.  import java.awt.print.*;
6.  import java.util.*;
7.  import javax.print.*;
8.  import javax.print.attribute.*;
9.  import javax.swing.*;
10.
11. /**
12.    This program demonstrates how to print 2D graphics
13. */
14. public class PrintTest
15. {
16.    public static void main(String[] args)
17.    {
18.       JFrame frame = new PrintTestFrame();
19.       frame.setDefaultCloseOperation(JFrame.EXIT_ON_CLOSE);
20.       frame.setVisible(true);
21.    }
22. }
23.
24. /**
25.    This frame shows a panel with 2D graphics and buttons
26.    to print the graphics and to set up the page format.
27. */
28. class PrintTestFrame extends JFrame
29. {
30.    public PrintTestFrame()
31.    {
32.       setTitle("PrintTest");
```

```
33.     setSize(DEFAULT_WIDTH, DEFAULT_HEIGHT);
34.
35.     canvas = new PrintPanel();
36.     add(canvas, BorderLayout.CENTER);
37.
38.     attributes = new HashPrintRequestAttributeSet();
39.
40.     JPanel buttonPanel = new JPanel();
41.     JButton printButton = new JButton("Print");
42.     buttonPanel.add(printButton);
43.     printButton.addActionListener(new
44.        ActionListener()
45.        {
46.           public void actionPerformed(ActionEvent event)
47.           {
48.              try
49.              {
50.                 PrinterJob job = PrinterJob.getPrinterJob();
51.                 job.setPrintable(canvas);
52.                 if (job.printDialog(attributes))
53.                    job.print(attributes);
54.              }
55.              catch (PrinterException e)
56.              {
57.                 JOptionPane.showMessageDialog(PrintTestFrame.this, e);
58.              }
59.           }
60.        });
61.
62.     JButton pageSetupButton = new JButton("Page setup");
63.     buttonPanel.add(pageSetupButton);
64.     pageSetupButton.addActionListener(new
65.        ActionListener()
66.        {
67.           public void actionPerformed(ActionEvent event)
68.           {
69.              PrinterJob job = PrinterJob.getPrinterJob();
70.              job.pageDialog(attributes);
71.           }
72.        });
73.
74.     add(buttonPanel, BorderLayout.NORTH);
75.   }
76.
77.   private PrintPanel canvas;
78.   private PrintRequestAttributeSet attributes;
79.
80.   private static final int DEFAULT_WIDTH = 300;
81.   private static final int DEFAULT_HEIGHT = 300;
82. }
83.
84. /**
85.    This panel generates a 2D graphics image for screen display
86.    and printing.
87. */
88. class PrintPanel extends JPanel implements Printable
```

```
89.  {
90.     public void paintComponent(Graphics g)
91.     {
92.        super.paintComponent(g);
93.        Graphics2D g2 = (Graphics2D) g;
94.        drawPage(g2);
95.     }
96.
97.     public int print(Graphics g, PageFormat pf, int page)
98.        throws PrinterException
99.     {
100.       if (page >= 1) return Printable.NO_SUCH_PAGE;
101.       Graphics2D g2 = (Graphics2D) g;
102.       g2.translate(pf.getImageableX(), pf.getImageableY());
103.       g2.draw(new Rectangle2D.Double(0, 0, pf.getImageableWidth(), pf.getImageableHeight()));
104.
105.       drawPage(g2);
106.       return Printable.PAGE_EXISTS;
107.    }
108.
109.    /**
110.       This method draws the page both on the screen and the
111.       printer graphics context.
112.       @param g2 the graphics context
113.    */
114.    public void drawPage(Graphics2D g2)
115.    {
116.       FontRenderContext context = g2.getFontRenderContext();
117.       Font f = new Font("Serif", Font.PLAIN, 72);
118.       GeneralPath clipShape = new GeneralPath();
119.
120.       TextLayout layout = new TextLayout("Hello", f, context);
121.       AffineTransform transform = AffineTransform.getTranslateInstance(0, 72);
122.       Shape outline = layout.getOutline(transform);
123.       clipShape.append(outline, false);
124.
125.       layout = new TextLayout("World", f, context);
126.       transform  = AffineTransform.getTranslateInstance(0, 144);
127.       outline = layout.getOutline(transform);
128.       clipShape.append(outline, false);
129.
130.       g2.draw(clipShape);
131.       g2.clip(clipShape);
132.
133.       final int NLINES =50;
134.       Point2D p = new Point2D.Double(0, 0);
135.       for (int i = 0; i < NLINES; i++)
136.       {
137.          double x = (2 * getWidth() * i) / NLINES;
138.          double y = (2 * getHeight() * (NLINES - 1 - i))
139.             / NLINES;
140.          Point2D q = new Point2D.Double(x, y);
141.          g2.draw(new Line2D.Double(p, q));
142.       }
143.    }
144. }
```

 java.awt.print.Printable 1.2

- int print(Graphics g, PageFormat format, int pageNumber)
  renders a page and returns PAGE_EXISTS, or returns NO_SUCH_PAGE.

  Parameters: g   The graphics context onto which the page is
  rendered

                       format   The format of the page to draw on

                       pageNumber   The number of the requested page

java.awt.print.PrinterJob 1.2

- static PrinterJob getPrinterJob()
  returns a printer job object.

- PageFormat defaultPage()
  returns the default page format for this printer.

- boolean printDialog(PrintRequestAttributeSet attributes)
- boolean printDialog()
  open print dialog boxes to allow a user to select the pages to be printed and to
  change print settings. The first method displays a cross-platform dialog box, the
  second a native dialog box. The first method modifies the attributes object to reflect
  the user settings. Both methods return true if the user accepts the dialog box.

- PageFormat pageDialog(PrintRequestAttributeSet attributes)
- PageFormat pageDialog(PageFormat defaults)
  display page setup dialog boxes. The first method displays a cross-platform dialog box,
  the second a native dialog box. Both methods return a PageFormat object with the format
  that the user requested in the dialog. The first method modifies the attributes object to
  reflect the user settings. The second method does not modify the defaults object.

- void setPrintable(Printable p)
- void setPrintable(Printable p, PageFormat format)
  set the Printable of this print job and an optional page format.

- void print()
- void print(PrintRequestAttributeSet attributes)
  prints the current Printable by repeatedly calling its print method and sending the
  rendered pages to the printer, until no more pages are available.

 java.awt.print.PageFormat 1.2

- double getWidth()
- double getHeight()
  return the width and height of the page.

- double getImageableWidth()
- double getImageableHeight()
  return the width and height of the imageable area of the page.

- double getImageableX()
- double getImageableY()
  return the position of the top-left corner of the imageable area.

- int getOrientation()
  returns one of PORTRAIT, LANDSCAPE, REVERSE_LANDSCAPE. Page orientation is transparent to
  programmers since the page format and graphics context settings automatically
  reflect the page orientation.

Multiple-Page Printing

In practice, you usually shouldn't pass a raw Printable object to a print job. Instead, you should obtain an object of a class that implements the Pageable interface. The Java platform supplies one such class, called Book. A book is made up of sections, each of which is a Printable object. You make a book by adding Printable objects and their page counts.

```
Book book = new Book();
Printable coverPage = . . .;
Printable bodyPages = . . .;
book.append(coverPage, pageFormat); // append 1 page
book.append(bodyPages, pageFormat, pageCount);
```

Then, you use the setPageable method to pass the Book object to the print job.

```
printJob.setPageable(book);
```

Now the print job knows exactly how many pages to print. Then, the print dialog box displays an accurate page range, and the user can select the entire range or subranges.

 CAUTION: When the print job calls the print methods of the Printable sections, it passes the current page number of the *book*, and not of each *section*, as the current page number. That is a huge pain—each section must know the page counts of the preceding sections to make sense of the page number parameter.

From your perspective as a programmer, the biggest challenge about using the Book class is that you must know how many pages each section will have when you print it. Your Printable class needs a *layout algorithm* that computes the layout of the material on the printed pages. Before printing starts, invoke that algorithm to compute the page breaks and the page count. You can retain the layout information so you have it handy during the printing process.

You must guard against the possibility that the user has changed the page format. If that happens, you must recompute the layout, even if the information that you want to print has not changed.

Example 7–13 shows how to produce a multipage printout. This program prints a message in very large characters on a number of pages (see Figure 7–39). You can then trim the margins and tape the pages together to form a banner.

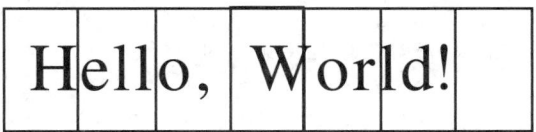

Figure 7–39: A banner

The layoutPages method of the Banner class computes the layout. We first lay out the message string in a 72-point font. We then compute the height of the resulting string and compare it with the imageable height of the page. We derive a scale factor from these two measurements. When printing the string, we magnify it by that scale factor.

 CAUTION: To lay out your information precisely, you usually need access to the printer graphics context. Unfortunately, there is no way to obtain that graphics context until printing actually starts. In our example program, we make do with the screen graphics context and hope that the font metrics of the screen and printer match.

The getPageCount method of the Banner class first calls the layout method. Then it scales up the width of the string and divides it by the imageable width of each page. The quotient, rounded up to the next integer, is the page count.

It sounds like it might be difficult to print the banner since characters can be broken across multiple pages. However, thanks to the power of the Java 2D API, this turns out not to be a problem at all. When a particular page is requested, we simply use the translate method of the Graphics2D class to shift the top-left corner of the string to the left. Then, we set a clip rectangle that equals the current page (see Figure 7–40). Finally, we scale the graphics context with the scale factor that the layout method computed.

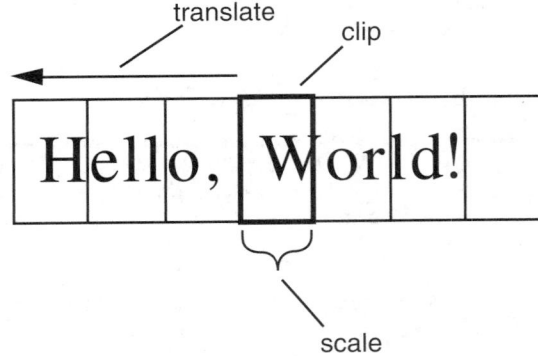

Figure 7–40: Printing a page of a banner

This example shows the power of transformations. The drawing code is kept simple, and the transformation does all the work of placing the drawing at the appropriate place. Finally, the clip cuts away the part of the image that falls outside the page. In the next section, you will see another compelling use of transformations, to display a print preview.

Print Preview

Most professional programs have a print preview mechanism that lets you look at your pages on the screen so that you won't waste paper on a printout that you don't like. The printing classes of the Java platform do not supply a standard "print preview" dialog box, but it is easy to design your own (see Figure 7–41). In this section, we show you how. The PrintPreviewDialog class in Example 7–13 is completely generic—you can reuse it to preview any kind of printout.

To construct a PrintPreviewDialog, you supply either a Printable or a Book, together with a Page-Format object. The surface of the dialog box contains a PrintPreviewCanvas. As you use the Next and Previous buttons to flip through the pages, the paintComponent method calls the print method of the Printable object for the requested page.

Normally, the print method draws the page context on a printer graphics context. However, we supply the screen graphics context, suitably scaled so that the entire printed page fits inside a small screen rectangle.

```
float xoff = . . .; // left of page
float yoff = . . .; // top of page
float scale = . . .; // to fit printed page onto screen
g2.translate(xoff, yoff);
g2.scale(scale, scale);
```

```
Printable printable = book.getPrintable(currentPage);
printable.print(g2, pageFormat, currentPage);
```

The print method never knows that it doesn't actually produce printed pages. It simply draws onto the graphics context, thereby producing a microscopic print preview on the screen. This is a compelling demonstration of the power of the Java 2D imaging model.

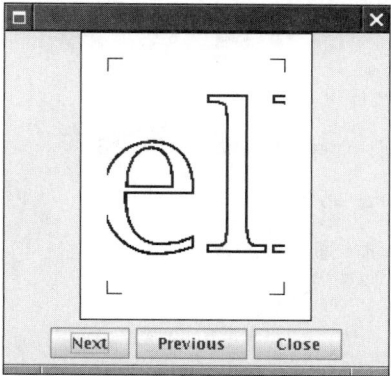

Figure 7–41: A print preview dialog box

Example 7–13 contains the code for the banner printing program and the print preview dialog box. Type "Hello, World!" into the text field and look at the print preview, then print the banner.

Example 7–13: BookTest.java

```
 1. import java.awt.*;
 2. import java.awt.event.*;
 3. import java.awt.font.*;
 4. import java.awt.geom.*;
 5. import java.awt.print.*;
 6. import java.util.*;
 7. import javax.print.*;
 8. import javax.print.attribute.*;
 9. import javax.swing.*;
10.
11. /**
12.    This program demonstrates the printing of a multipage
13.    book. It prints a "banner," by blowing up a text string
14.    to fill the entire page vertically. The program also
15.    contains a generic print preview dialog box.
16. */
17. public class BookTest
18. {
19.    public static void main(String[] args)
20.    {
21.       JFrame frame = new BookTestFrame();
22.       frame.setDefaultCloseOperation(JFrame.EXIT_ON_CLOSE);
23.       frame.setVisible(true);
24.    }
25. }
26.
27. /**
```

```
28.    This frame has a text field for the banner text and
29.    buttons for printing, page setup, and print preview.
30. */
31. class BookTestFrame extends JFrame
32. {
33.    public BookTestFrame()
34.    {
35.       setTitle("BookTest");
36.
37.       text = new JTextField();
38.       add(text, BorderLayout.NORTH);
39.
40.       attributes = new HashPrintRequestAttributeSet();
41.
42.       JPanel buttonPanel = new JPanel();
43.
44.       JButton printButton = new JButton("Print");
45.       buttonPanel.add(printButton);
46.       printButton.addActionListener(new
47.          ActionListener()
48.          {
49.             public void actionPerformed(ActionEvent event)
50.             {
51.                try
52.                {
53.                   PrinterJob job = PrinterJob.getPrinterJob();
54.                   job.setPageable(makeBook());
55.                   if (job.printDialog(attributes))
56.                   {
57.                      job.print(attributes);
58.                   }
59.                }
60.                catch (PrinterException e)
61.                {
62.                   JOptionPane.showMessageDialog(
63.                      BookTestFrame.this, e);
64.                }
65.             }
66.          });
67.
68.       JButton pageSetupButton = new JButton("Page setup");
69.       buttonPanel.add(pageSetupButton);
70.       pageSetupButton.addActionListener(new
71.          ActionListener()
72.          {
73.             public void actionPerformed(ActionEvent event)
74.             {
75.                PrinterJob job = PrinterJob.getPrinterJob();
76.                pageFormat = job.pageDialog(attributes);
77.             }
78.          });
79.
80.       JButton printPreviewButton = new JButton("Print preview");
81.       buttonPanel.add(printPreviewButton);
82.       printPreviewButton.addActionListener(new
```

```
83.        ActionListener()
84.        {
85.           public void actionPerformed(ActionEvent event)
86.           {
87.              PrintPreviewDialog dialog = new PrintPreviewDialog(makeBook());
88.              dialog.setVisible(true);
89.           }
90.        });
91.
92.     add(buttonPanel, BorderLayout.SOUTH);
93.     pack();
94.  }
95.
96.  /**
97.     Makes a book that contains a cover page and the
98.     pages for the banner.
99.  */
100. public Book makeBook()
101. {
102.    if (pageFormat == null)
103.    {
104.       PrinterJob job = PrinterJob.getPrinterJob();
105.       pageFormat = job.defaultPage();
106.    }
107.    Book book = new Book();
108.    String message = text.getText();
109.    Banner banner = new Banner(message);
110.    int pageCount = banner.getPageCount((Graphics2D)getGraphics(), pageFormat);
111.    book.append(new CoverPage(message + " (" + pageCount + " pages)"), pageFormat);
112.    book.append(banner, pageFormat, pageCount);
113.    return book;
114. }
115.
116. private JTextField text;
117. private PageFormat pageFormat;
118. private PrintRequestAttributeSet attributes;
119. }
120.
121. /**
122.    A banner that prints a text string on multiple pages.
123. */
124. class Banner implements Printable
125. {
126.    /**
127.       Constructs a banner
128.       @param m the message string
129.    */
130.    public Banner(String m)
131.    {
132.       message = m;
133.    }
134.
135.    /**
136.       Gets the page count of this section.
137.       @param g2 the graphics context
```

```
138.        @param pf the page format
139.        @return the number of pages needed
140.     */
141.     public int getPageCount(Graphics2D g2, PageFormat pf)
142.     {
143.        if (message.equals("")) return 0;
144.        FontRenderContext context = g2.getFontRenderContext();
145.        Font f = new Font("Serif", Font.PLAIN, 72);
146.        Rectangle2D bounds = f.getStringBounds(message, context);
147.        scale = pf.getImageableHeight() / bounds.getHeight();
148.        double width = scale * bounds.getWidth();
149.        int pages = (int)Math.ceil(width / pf.getImageableWidth());
150.        return pages;
151.     }
152.
153.     public int print(Graphics g, PageFormat pf, int page)
154.        throws PrinterException
155.     {
156.        Graphics2D g2 = (Graphics2D)g;
157.        if (page > getPageCount(g2, pf))
158.           return Printable.NO_SUCH_PAGE;
159.        g2.translate(pf.getImageableX(), pf.getImageableY());
160.
161.        drawPage(g2, pf, page);
162.        return Printable.PAGE_EXISTS;
163.     }
164.
165.     public void drawPage(Graphics2D g2, PageFormat pf, int page)
166.     {
167.        if (message.equals("")) return;
168.        page--; // account for cover page
169.
170.        drawCropMarks(g2, pf);
171.        g2.clip(new Rectangle2D.Double(0, 0, pf.getImageableWidth(), pf.getImageableHeight()));
172.        g2.translate(-page * pf.getImageableWidth(), 0);
173.        g2.scale(scale, scale);
174.        FontRenderContext context = g2.getFontRenderContext();
175.        Font f = new Font("Serif", Font.PLAIN, 72);
176.        TextLayout layout = new TextLayout(message, f, context);
177.        AffineTransform transform = AffineTransform.getTranslateInstance(0, layout.getAscent());
178.        Shape outline = layout.getOutline(transform);
179.        g2.draw(outline);
180.     }
181.
182.     /**
183.        Draws 1/2" crop marks in the corners of the page.
184.        @param g2 the graphics context
185.        @param pf the page format
186.     */
187.     public void drawCropMarks(Graphics2D g2, PageFormat pf)
188.     {
189.        final double C = 36; // crop mark length = 1/2 inch
190.        double w = pf.getImageableWidth();
191.        double h = pf.getImageableHeight();
192.        g2.draw(new Line2D.Double(0, 0, 0, C));
```

```
193.        g2.draw(new Line2D.Double(0, 0, C, 0));
194.        g2.draw(new Line2D.Double(w, 0, w, C));
195.        g2.draw(new Line2D.Double(w, 0, w - C, 0));
196.        g2.draw(new Line2D.Double(0, h, 0, h - C));
197.        g2.draw(new Line2D.Double(0, h, C, h));
198.        g2.draw(new Line2D.Double(w, h, w, h - C));
199.        g2.draw(new Line2D.Double(w, h, w - C, h));
200.    }
201.
202.    private String message;
203.    private double scale;
204. }
205.
206. /**
207.    This class prints a cover page with a title.
208. */
209. class CoverPage implements Printable
210. {
211.    /**
212.       Constructs a cover page.
213.       @param t the title
214.    */
215.    public CoverPage(String t)
216.    {
217.       title = t;
218.    }
219.
220.    public int print(Graphics g, PageFormat pf, int page)
221.       throws PrinterException
222.    {
223.       if (page >= 1) return Printable.NO_SUCH_PAGE;
224.       Graphics2D g2 = (Graphics2D)g;
225.       g2.setPaint(Color.black);
226.       g2.translate(pf.getImageableX(), pf.getImageableY());
227.       FontRenderContext context = g2.getFontRenderContext();
228.       Font f = g2.getFont();
229.       TextLayout layout = new TextLayout(title, f, context);
230.       float ascent = layout.getAscent();
231.       g2.drawString(title, 0, ascent);
232.       return Printable.PAGE_EXISTS;
233.    }
234.
235.    private String title;
236. }
237.
238. /**
239.    This class implements a generic print preview dialog.
240. */
241. class PrintPreviewDialog extends JDialog
242. {
243.    /**
244.       Constructs a print preview dialog.
245.       @param p a Printable
246.       @param pf the page format
247.       @param pages the number of pages in p
```

```
248.   */
249.   public PrintPreviewDialog(Printable p, PageFormat pf, int pages)
250.   {
251.      Book book = new Book();
252.      book.append(p, pf, pages);
253.      layoutUI(book);
254.   }
255.
256.   /**
257.      Constructs a print preview dialog.
258.      @param b a Book
259.   */
260.   public PrintPreviewDialog(Book b)
261.   {
262.      layoutUI(b);
263.   }
264.
265.   /**
266.      Lays out the UI of the dialog.
267.      @param book the book to be previewed
268.   */
269.   public void layoutUI(Book book)
270.   {
271.      setSize(DEFAULT_WIDTH, DEFAULT_HEIGHT);
272.
273.      canvas = new PrintPreviewCanvas(book);
274.      add(canvas, BorderLayout.CENTER);
275.
276.      JPanel buttonPanel = new JPanel();
277.
278.      JButton nextButton = new JButton("Next");
279.      buttonPanel.add(nextButton);
280.      nextButton.addActionListener(new
281.         ActionListener()
282.         {
283.            public void actionPerformed(ActionEvent event)
284.            {
285.               canvas.flipPage(1);
286.            }
287.         });
288.
289.      JButton previousButton = new JButton("Previous");
290.      buttonPanel.add(previousButton);
291.      previousButton.addActionListener(new
292.         ActionListener()
293.         {
294.            public void actionPerformed(ActionEvent event)
295.            {
296.               canvas.flipPage(-1);
297.            }
298.         });
299.
300.      JButton closeButton = new JButton("Close");
301.      buttonPanel.add(closeButton);
302.      closeButton.addActionListener(new
```

```
303.        ActionListener()
304.        {
305.           public void actionPerformed(ActionEvent event)
306.           {
307.              setVisible(false);
308.           }
309.        });
310.
311.     add(buttonPanel, BorderLayout.SOUTH);
312.   }
313.
314.   private PrintPreviewCanvas canvas;
315.
316.   private static final int DEFAULT_WIDTH = 300;
317.   private static final int DEFAULT_HEIGHT = 300;
318. }
319.
320. /**
321.    The canvas for displaying the print preview.
322. */
323. class PrintPreviewCanvas extends JPanel
324. {
325.    /**
326.       Constructs a print preview canvas.
327.       @param b the book to be previewed
328.    */
329.    public PrintPreviewCanvas(Book b)
330.    {
331.       book = b;
332.       currentPage = 0;
333.    }
334.
335.    public void paintComponent(Graphics g)
336.    {
337.       super.paintComponent(g);
338.       Graphics2D g2 = (Graphics2D)g;
339.       PageFormat pageFormat = book.getPageFormat(currentPage);
340.
341.       double xoff; // x offset of page start in window
342.       double yoff; // y offset of page start in window
343.       double scale; // scale factor to fit page in window
344.       double px = pageFormat.getWidth();
345.       double py = pageFormat.getHeight();
346.       double sx = getWidth() - 1;
347.       double sy = getHeight() - 1;
348.       if (px / py < sx / sy) // center horizontally
349.       {
350.          scale = sy / py;
351.          xoff = 0.5 * (sx - scale * px);
352.          yoff = 0;
353.       }
354.       else // center vertically
355.       {
356.          scale = sx / px;
357.          xoff = 0;
```

```
358.          yoff = 0.5 * (sy - scale * py);
359.       }
360.       g2.translate((float)xoff, (float)yoff);
361.       g2.scale((float)scale, (float)scale);
362.
363.       // draw page outline (ignoring margins)
364.       Rectangle2D page = new Rectangle2D.Double(0, 0, px, py);
365.       g2.setPaint(Color.white);
366.       g2.fill(page);
367.       g2.setPaint(Color.black);
368.       g2.draw(page);
369.
370.       Printable printable = book.getPrintable(currentPage);
371.       try
372.       {
373.          printable.print(g2, pageFormat, currentPage);
374.       }
375.       catch (PrinterException e)
376.       {
377.          g2.draw(new Line2D.Double(0, 0, px, py));
378.          g2.draw(new Line2D.Double(px, 0, 0, py));
379.       }
380.    }
381.
382.    /**
383.       Flip the book by the given number of pages.
384.       @param by the number of pages to flip by. Negative
385.       values flip backwards.
386.    */
387.    public void flipPage(int by)
388.    {
389.       int newPage = currentPage + by;
390.       if (0 <= newPage && newPage < book.getNumberOfPages())
391.       {
392.          currentPage = newPage;
393.          repaint();
394.       }
395.    }
396.
397.    private Book book;
398.    private int currentPage;
399. }
```

API   **java.awt.print.PrinterJob 1.2**

- void setPageable(Pageable p)
  sets a Pageable (such as a Book) to be printed.

API   **java.awt.print.Book 1.2**

- void append(Printable p, PageFormat format)
- void append(Printable p, PageFormat format, int pageCount)
  append a section to this book. If the page count is not specified, the first page is added.

- Printable getPrintable(int page)
  gets the printable for the specified page.

Print Services

So far, you have seen how to print 2D graphics. However, the printing API introduced in JDK 1.4 affords far greater flexibility. The API defines a number of data types and lets you find print services that are able to print them. Among the data types:

- Images in GIF, JPEG, or PNG format
- Documents in text, HTML, PostScript, or PDF format
- Raw printer code data
- Objects of a class that implements `Printable`, `Pageable`, or `RenderableImage`

The data themselves can be stored in a source of bytes or characters such as an input stream, a URL, or an array. A *document flavor* describes the combination of a data source and a data type. The `DocFlavor` class defines a number of inner classes for the various data sources. Each of the inner classes defines constants to specify the flavors. For example, the constant

```
DocFlavor.INPUT_STREAM.GIF
```

describes a GIF image that is read from an input stream. Table 7–3 lists the combinations.

Suppose you want to print a GIF image that is located in a file. First find out whether there is a *print service* that is capable of handling the task. The static `lookupPrintServices` method of the `PrintServiceLookup` class returns an array of `PrintService` objects that can handle the given document flavor.

```
DocFlavor flavor = DocFlavor.INPUT_STREAM.GIF;
PrintService[] services
    = PrintServiceLookup.lookupPrintServices(flavor, null);
```

The second parameter of the `lookupPrintServices` method is `null` to indicate that we don't want to constrain the search by specifying printer attributes. We cover attributes in the next section.

 NOTE: JDK 1.4 supplies print services for basic document flavors such as images and 2D graphics, but if you try to print text or HTML documents, the lookup will return an empty array.

If the lookup yields an array with more than one element, you select from the listed print services. You can call the `getName` method of the `PrintService` class to get the printer names, and then let the user choose.

Next, get a document print job from the service:

```
DocPrintJob job = services[i].createPrintJob();
```

Table 7–3: Document Flavors for Print Services

Data Source	Data Type	MIME Type
INPUT_STREAM	GIF	image/gif
URL	JPEG	image/jpeg
BYTE_ARRAY	PNG	image/png
	POSTSCRIPT	application/postscript
	PDF	application/pdf
	TEXT_HTML_HOST	text/html (using host encoding)
	TEXT_HTML_US_ASCII	text/html; charset=us-ascii

Table 7–3: Document Flavors for Print Services (continued)

Data Source	Data Type	MIME Type
	TEXT_HTML_UTF_8	text/html; charset=utf-8
	TEXT_HTML_UTF_16	text/html; charset=utf-16
	TEXT_HTML_UTF_16LE	text/html; charset=utf-16le (little-endian)
	TEXT_HTML_UTF_16BE	text/html; charset=utf-16be (big-endian)
	TEXT_PLAIN_HOST	text/plain (using host encoding)
	TEXT_PLAIN_US_ASCII	text/plain; charset=us-ascii
	TEXT_PLAIN_UTF_8	text/plain; charset=utf-8
	TEXT_PLAIN_UTF_16	text/plain; charset=utf-16
	TEXT_PLAIN_UTF_16LE	text/plain; charset=utf-16le (little-endian)
	TEXT_PLAIN_UTF_16BE	text/plain; charset=utf-16be (big-endian)
	PCL	application/vnd.hp-PCL (Hewlett Packard Printer Control Language)
	AUTOSENSE	application/octet-stream (raw printer data)
READER	TEXT_HTML	text/html; charset=utf-16
STRING	TEXT_PLAIN	text/plain; charset=utf-16
CHAR_ARRAY		
SERVICE_FORMATTED	PRINTABLE	N/A
	PAGEABLE	N/A
	RENDERABLE_IMAGE	N/A

For printing, you need an object that implements the `Doc` interface. The JDK supplies a class `SimpleDoc` for that purpose. The `SimpleDoc` constructor requires the data source object, the document flavor, and an optional attribute set. For example,

```
InputStream in = new FileInputStream(fileName);
Doc doc = new SimpleDoc(in, flavor, null);
```

Finally, you are ready to print:

```
job.print(doc, null);
```

As before, the `null` parameter can be replaced by an attribute set.

Note that this printing process is quite different from that of the preceding section. There is no user interaction through print dialog boxes. For example, you can implement a server-side printing mechanism in which users submit print jobs through a web form.

The program in Example 7–14 demonstrates how to use a print service to print an image file.

Example 7–14: PrintServiceTest.java

```
1. import java.awt.*;
2. import java.awt.event.*;
3. import java.awt.image.*;
4. import java.io.*;
5. import java.util.*;
6. import javax.print.*;
7. import javax.swing.*;
```

```
8.
9.  /**
10.     This program demonstrates the use of print services. The program lets you print a GIF image
11.     to any of the print services that support the GIF document flavor.
12.  */
13.  public class PrintServiceTest
14.  {
15.     public static void main(String[] args)
16.     {
17.        JFrame frame = new PrintServiceFrame();
18.        frame.setDefaultCloseOperation(JFrame.EXIT_ON_CLOSE);
19.        frame.setVisible(true);
20.     }
21.  }
22.
23.  /**
24.     This frame displays the image to be printed. It contains
25.     menus for opening an image file, printing, and selecting
26.     a print service.
27.  */
28.  class PrintServiceFrame extends JFrame
29.  {
30.     public PrintServiceFrame()
31.     {
32.        setTitle("PrintServiceTest");
33.        setSize(DEFAULT_WIDTH, DEFAULT_HEIGHT);
34.
35.        // set up menu bar
36.        JMenuBar menuBar = new JMenuBar();
37.        setJMenuBar(menuBar);
38.
39.        JMenu menu = new JMenu("File");
40.        menuBar.add(menu);
41.
42.        JMenuItem openItem = new JMenuItem("Open");
43.        menu.add(openItem);
44.        openItem.addActionListener(new
45.           ActionListener()
46.           {
47.              public void actionPerformed(ActionEvent event)
48.              {
49.                 openFile();
50.              }
51.           });
52.
53.        JMenuItem printItem = new JMenuItem("Print");
54.        menu.add(printItem);
55.        printItem.addActionListener(new
56.           ActionListener()
57.           {
58.              public void actionPerformed(ActionEvent event)
59.              {
60.                 printFile();
61.              }
62.           });
63.
64.        JMenuItem exitItem = new JMenuItem("Exit");
```

```
65.        menu.add(exitItem);
66.        exitItem.addActionListener(new
67.          ActionListener()
68.          {
69.             public void actionPerformed(ActionEvent event)
70.             {
71.                System.exit(0);
72.             }
73.          });
74.
75.        menu = new JMenu("Printer");
76.        menuBar.add(menu);
77.        DocFlavor flavor = DocFlavor.INPUT_STREAM.GIF;
78.        addPrintServices(menu, flavor);
79.
80.        // use a label to display the images
81.        label = new JLabel();
82.        add(label);
83.     }
84.
85.     /**
86.        Adds print services to a menu
87.        @param menu the menu to which to add the services
88.        @param flavor the flavor that the services need to support
89.     */
90.     public void addPrintServices(JMenu menu, DocFlavor flavor)
91.     {
92.        PrintService[] services = PrintServiceLookup.lookupPrintServices(flavor, null);
93.        ButtonGroup group = new ButtonGroup();
94.        for (int i = 0; i < services.length; i++)
95.        {
96.           final PrintService service = services[i];
97.           JRadioButtonMenuItem item = new JRadioButtonMenuItem(service.getName());
98.           menu.add(item);
99.           if (i == 0)
100.          {
101.             item.setSelected(true);
102.             currentService = service;
103.          }
104.          group.add(item);
105.          item.addActionListener(new
106.            ActionListener()
107.            {
108.               public void actionPerformed(ActionEvent event)
109.               {
110.                  currentService = service;
111.               }
112.            });
113.        }
114.     }
115.
116.    /**
117.       Open a GIF file and display the image.
118.    */
119.    public void openFile()
120.    {
121.       // set up file chooser
```

```
122.    JFileChooser chooser = new JFileChooser();
123.    chooser.setCurrentDirectory(new File("."));
124.
125.    // accept all files ending with .gif
126.    chooser.setFileFilter(new
127.       javax.swing.filechooser.FileFilter()
128.       {
129.          public boolean accept(File f)
130.          {
131.             return f.getName().toLowerCase().endsWith(".gif") || f.isDirectory();
132.          }
133.
134.          public String getDescription() { return "GIF Images"; }
135.       });
136.
137.    // show file chooser dialog
138.    int r = chooser.showOpenDialog(PrintServiceFrame.this);
139.
140.    // if image file accepted, set it as icon of the label
141.    if(r == JFileChooser.APPROVE_OPTION)
142.    {
143.       fileName = chooser.getSelectedFile().getPath();
144.       label.setIcon(new ImageIcon(fileName));
145.    }
146. }
147.
148. /**
149.    Print the current file using the current print service.
150. */
151. public void printFile()
152. {
153.    try
154.    {
155.       if (fileName == null) return;
156.       if (currentService == null) return;
157.       FileInputStream in = new FileInputStream(fileName);
158.       DocFlavor flavor = DocFlavor.INPUT_STREAM.GIF;
159.       Doc doc = new SimpleDoc(in, flavor, null);
160.       DocPrintJob job = currentService.createPrintJob();
161.       job.print(doc, null);
162.    }
163.    catch (FileNotFoundException e)
164.    {
165.       JOptionPane.showMessageDialog(this, e);
166.    }
167.    catch (PrintException e)
168.    {
169.       JOptionPane.showMessageDialog(this, e);
170.    }
171. }
172.
173. private JLabel label;
174. private String fileName;
175. private PrintService currentService;
176. private static final int DEFAULT_WIDTH = 300;
177. private static final int DEFAULT_HEIGHT = 400;
178. }
```

 javax.print.PrintServiceLookup 1.4

- PrintService[] lookupPrintServices(DocFlavor flavor, AttributeSet attributes)
  looks up the print services that can handle the given document flavor and attributes.

  Parameters: flavor   The document flavor

                    attributes   The required printing attributes, or null if attributes
  should not be considered

 javax.print.PrintService 1.4

- DocPrintJob createPrintJob()
  creates a print job for printing an object of a class that implements the Doc interface,
  such as a SimpleDoc.

 javax.print.DocPrintJob 1.4

- void print(Doc doc, PrintRequestAttributeSet attributes)
  prints the given document with the given attributes.

  Parameters: doc   The Doc to be printed

                    attributes   The required printing attributes, or null if no printing
  attributes are required

 javax.print.SimpleDoc 1.4

- SimpleDoc(Object data, DocFlavor flavor, DocAttributeSet attributes)
  constructs a SimpleDoc object that can be printed with a DocPrintJob.

  Parameters: data   The object with the print data, such as an input stream
  or a Printable

                    flavor   The document flavor of the print data

                    attributes   Document attributes, or null if attributes are not
  required

Stream Print Services

A print service sends print data to a printer. A stream print service generates the same print
data but instead sends them to a stream, perhaps for delayed printing or because the print
data format can be interpreted by other programs. In particular, if the print data format is
PostScript, then it is useful to save the print data to a file because many programs can process PostScript files.

JDK 1.4 includes a stream print service that can produce PostScript output from images
and 2D graphics. You can use that service on all systems, even if there are no local printers.

Enumerating stream print services is a bit more tedious than locating regular print services.
You need both the DocFlavor of the object to be printed and the MIME type of the stream output. You then get a StreamPrintServiceFactory array of factories.

```
DocFlavor flavor = DocFlavor.SERVICE_FORMATTED.PRINTABLE;
String mimeType = "application/postscript";
StreamPrintServiceFactory[] factories
   = StreamPrintServiceFactory.lookupStreamPrintServiceFactories(flavor, mimeType);
```

The StreamPrintServiceFactory class has no methods that would help us distinguish any one factory from another, so we just take factories[0]. We call the getPrintService method with an output stream parameter to get a StreamPrintService object.

```
OutputStream out = new FileOutputStream(fileName);
StreamPrintService service = factories[0].getPrintService(out);
```

The StreamPrintService class is a subclass of PrintService. To produce a printout, simply follow the steps of the preceding section.

Example 7–15 prints the "Hello, World" graphic from the preceding examples to a PostScript file (see Figure 7–42).

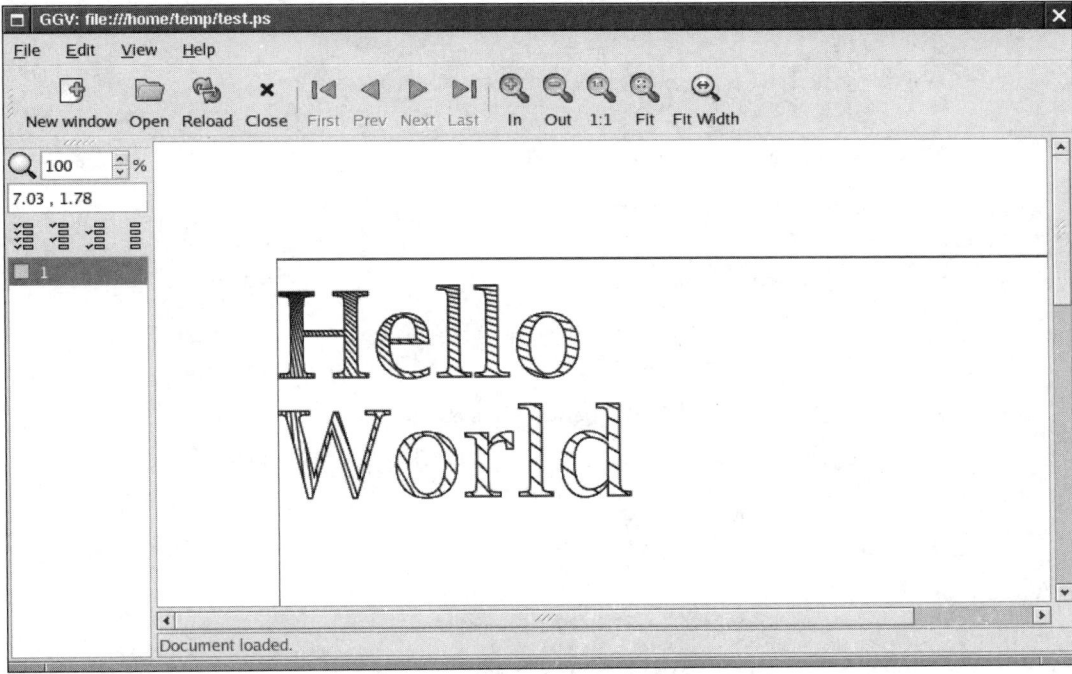

Figure 7–42: Viewing a PostScript file

Example 7–15: StreamPrintServiceTest.java

```
 1. import java.awt.*;
 2. import java.awt.event.*;
 3. import java.awt.font.*;
 4. import java.awt.geom.*;
 5. import java.awt.print.*;
 6. import java.io.*;
 7. import java.util.*;
 8. import javax.print.*;
 9. import javax.print.attribute.*;
10. import javax.swing.*;
11.
12.
13. /**
```

```
14.    This program demonstrates the use of a stream print service.
15.    It prints a 2D graphic to a PostScript file.
16. */
17. public class StreamPrintServiceTest
18. {
19.    public static void main(String[] args)
20.    {
21.       JFrame frame = new StreamPrintServiceFrame();
22.       frame.setDefaultCloseOperation(JFrame.EXIT_ON_CLOSE);
23.       frame.setVisible(true);
24.    }
25. }
26.
27. /**
28.    This frame shows a panel with 2D graphics and buttons
29.    to print the graphics to a PostScript file and to set up
30.    the page format.
31. */
32. class StreamPrintServiceFrame extends JFrame
33. {
34.    public StreamPrintServiceFrame()
35.    {
36.       setTitle("StreamPrintServiceTest");
37.       setSize(DEFAULT_WIDTH, DEFAULT_HEIGHT);
38.
39.       canvas = new PrintPanel();
40.       add(canvas, BorderLayout.CENTER);
41.
42.       attributes = new HashPrintRequestAttributeSet();
43.
44.       JPanel buttonPanel = new JPanel();
45.       JButton printButton = new JButton("Print");
46.       buttonPanel.add(printButton);
47.       printButton.addActionListener(new
48.          ActionListener()
49.          {
50.             public void actionPerformed(ActionEvent event)
51.             {
52.                String fileName = getFile();
53.                if (fileName != null)
54.                   printPostScript(fileName);
55.             }
56.          });
57.
58.       JButton pageSetupButton = new JButton("Page setup");
59.       buttonPanel.add(pageSetupButton);
60.       pageSetupButton.addActionListener(new
61.          ActionListener()
62.          {
63.             public void actionPerformed(ActionEvent event)
64.             {
65.                PrinterJob job = PrinterJob.getPrinterJob();
66.                job.pageDialog(attributes);
67.             }
68.          });
69.
```

```
70.         add(buttonPanel, BorderLayout.NORTH);
71.      }
72.
73.      /**
74.         Allows the user to select a PostScript file.
75.         @return the file name, or null if the user didn't
76.         select a file.
77.      */
78.      public String getFile()
79.      {
80.         // set up file chooser
81.         JFileChooser chooser = new JFileChooser();
82.         chooser.setCurrentDirectory(new File("."));
83.
84.         // accept all files ending with .ps
85.         chooser.setFileFilter(new
86.            javax.swing.filechooser.FileFilter()
87.            {
88.               public boolean accept(File f)
89.               {
90.                  return f.getName().toLowerCase().endsWith(".ps") || f.isDirectory();
91.               }
92.
93.               public String getDescription() { return "PostScript Files"; }
94.            });
95.
96.         // show file chooser dialog
97.         int r = chooser.showSaveDialog(this);
98.
99.         // if file accepted, return path
100.        if(r == JFileChooser.APPROVE_OPTION)
101.           return chooser.getSelectedFile().getPath();
102.        else
103.           return null;
104.     }
105.
106.     /**
107.        Prints the 2D graphic to a PostScript file.
108.        @param fileName the name of the PostScript file
109.     */
110.     public void printPostScript(String fileName)
111.     {
112.        try
113.        {
114.           DocFlavor flavor = DocFlavor.SERVICE_FORMATTED.PRINTABLE;
115.           String mimeType = "application/postscript";
116.           StreamPrintServiceFactory[] factories =
117.              StreamPrintServiceFactory.lookupStreamPrintServiceFactories(flavor, mimeType);
118.
119.           FileOutputStream out = new FileOutputStream(fileName);
120.           if (factories.length == 0) return;
121.           StreamPrintService service = factories[0].getPrintService(out);
122.
123.           Doc doc = new SimpleDoc(canvas, flavor, null);
124.           DocPrintJob job = service.createPrintJob();
125.           job.print(doc, attributes);
```

```
126.        }
127.        catch (FileNotFoundException e)
128.        {
129.           JOptionPane.showMessageDialog(this, e);
130.        }
131.        catch (PrintException e)
132.        {
133.           JOptionPane.showMessageDialog(this, e);
134.        }
135.
136.     }
137.
138.     private PrintPanel canvas;
139.     private PrintRequestAttributeSet attributes;
140.
141.     private static final int DEFAULT_WIDTH = 300;
142.     private static final int DEFAULT_HEIGHT = 300;
143. }
144.
145. /**
146.     This panel generates a 2D graphics image for screen display
147.     and printing.
148. */
149. class PrintPanel extends JPanel implements Printable
150. {
151.     public void paintComponent(Graphics g)
152.     {
153.        super.paintComponent(g);
154.        Graphics2D g2 = (Graphics2D) g;
155.        drawPage(g2);
156.     }
157.
158.     public int print(Graphics g, PageFormat pf, int page)
159.        throws PrinterException
160.     {
161.        if (page >= 1) return Printable.NO_SUCH_PAGE;
162.        Graphics2D g2 = (Graphics2D) g;
163.        g2.translate(pf.getImageableX(), pf.getImageableY());
164.        g2.draw(new Rectangle2D.Double(0, 0, pf.getImageableWidth(), pf.getImageableHeight()));
165.
166.        drawPage(g2);
167.        return Printable.PAGE_EXISTS;
168.     }
169.
170.     /**
171.        This method draws the page both on the screen and the
172.        printer graphics context.
173.        @param g2 the graphics context
174.     */
175.     public void drawPage(Graphics2D g2)
176.     {
177.        FontRenderContext context = g2.getFontRenderContext();
178.        Font f = new Font("Serif", Font.PLAIN, 72);
179.        GeneralPath clipShape = new GeneralPath();
180.
181.        TextLayout layout = new TextLayout("Hello", f, context);
```

```
182.        AffineTransform transform = AffineTransform.getTranslateInstance(0, 72);
183.        Shape outline = layout.getOutline(transform);
184.        clipShape.append(outline, false);
185.
186.        layout = new TextLayout("World", f, context);
187.        transform = AffineTransform.getTranslateInstance(0, 144);
188.        outline = layout.getOutline(transform);
189.        clipShape.append(outline, false);
190.
191.        g2.draw(clipShape);
192.        g2.clip(clipShape);
193.
194.        final int NLINES =50;
195.        Point2D p = new Point2D.Double(0, 0);
196.        for (int i = 0; i < NLINES; i++)
197.        {
198.           double x = (2 * getWidth() * i) / NLINES;
199.           double y = (2 * getHeight() * (NLINES - 1 - i))
200.              / NLINES;
201.           Point2D q = new Point2D.Double(x, y);
202.           g2.draw(new Line2D.Double(p, q));
203.        }
204.     }
205. }
```

javax.print.StreamPrintServiceFactory 1.4

- `StreamPrintServiceFactory[] lookupStreamPrintServiceFactories(DocFlavor flavor, String mimeType)`
  looks up the stream print service factories that can print the given document flavor and produce an output stream of the given MIME type.
- `StreamPrintService getPrintService(OutputStream out)`
  gets a print service that sends the printing output to the given output stream.

Printing Attributes

The print service API contains a complex set of interfaces and classes to specify various kinds of attributes. There are four important groups of attributes. The first two specify requests to the printer.

- *Print request attributes* request particular features for all doc objects in a print job, such as two-sided printing or the paper size.
- *Doc attributes* are request attributes that apply only to a single doc object.

The other two attributes contain information about the printer and job status.

- *Print service attributes* give information about the print service, such as the printer make and model or whether the printer is currently accepting jobs.
- *Print job attributes* give information about the status of a particular print job, such as whether the job is already completed.

To describe the various attributes there is an interface Attribute with subinterfaces:

```
PrintRequestAttribute
DocAttribute
PrintServiceAttribute
PrintJobAttribute
SupportedValuesAttribute
```

Individual attribute classes implement one or more of these interfaces. For example, objects of the Copies class describe the number of copies of a printout. That class implements both the PrintRequestAttribute and the PrintJobAttribute interfaces. Clearly, a print request may contain a request for multiple copies. Conversely, an attribute of the print job may be how many of these copies were actually printed. That number might be lower, perhaps because of printer limitations or because the printer ran out of paper.

The SupportedValuesAttribute interface indicates that an attribute value does not reflect actual request or status data but rather the capability of a service. For example, the CopiesSupported class implements the SupportedValuesAttribute interface. An object of that class might describe that a printer supports 1 through 99 copies of a printout.

Figure 7–43 shows a class diagram of the attribute hierarchy.

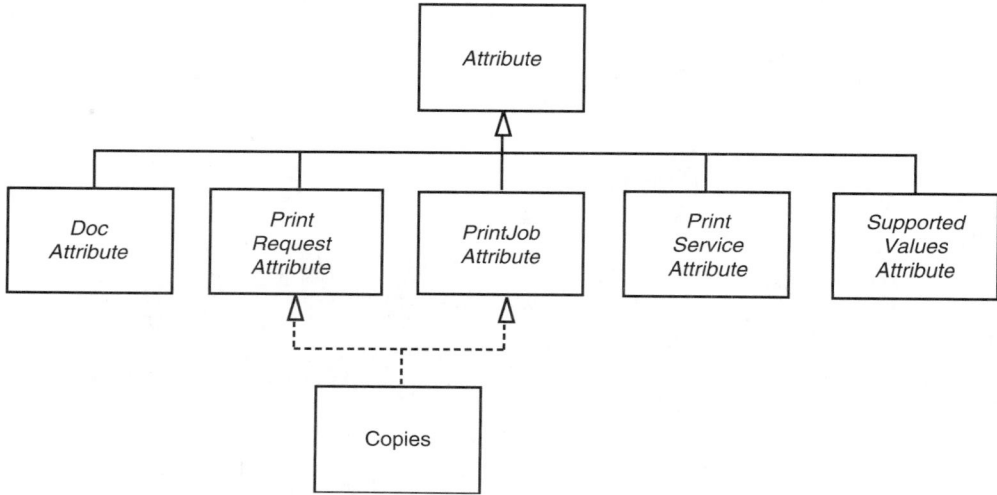

Figure 7–43: The attribute hierarchy

In addition to the interfaces and classes for individual attributes, the print service API defines interfaces and classes for attribute sets. A superinterface, AttributeSet, has four sub-interfaces:

```
PrintRequestAttributeSet
DocAttributeSet
PrintServiceAttributeSet
PrintJobAttributeSet
```

Each of these interfaces has an implementing class, yielding the five classes:

```
HashAttributeSet
HashPrintRequestAttributeSet
HashDocAttributeSet
HashPrintServiceAttributeSet
HashPrintJobAttributeSet
```

Figure 7–44 shows a class diagram of the attribute set hierarchy.

For example, you construct a print request attribute set like this:

```
PrintRequestAttributeSet attributes = new HashPrintRequestAttributeSet();
```

After constructing the set, you are freed from worry about the Hash prefix.

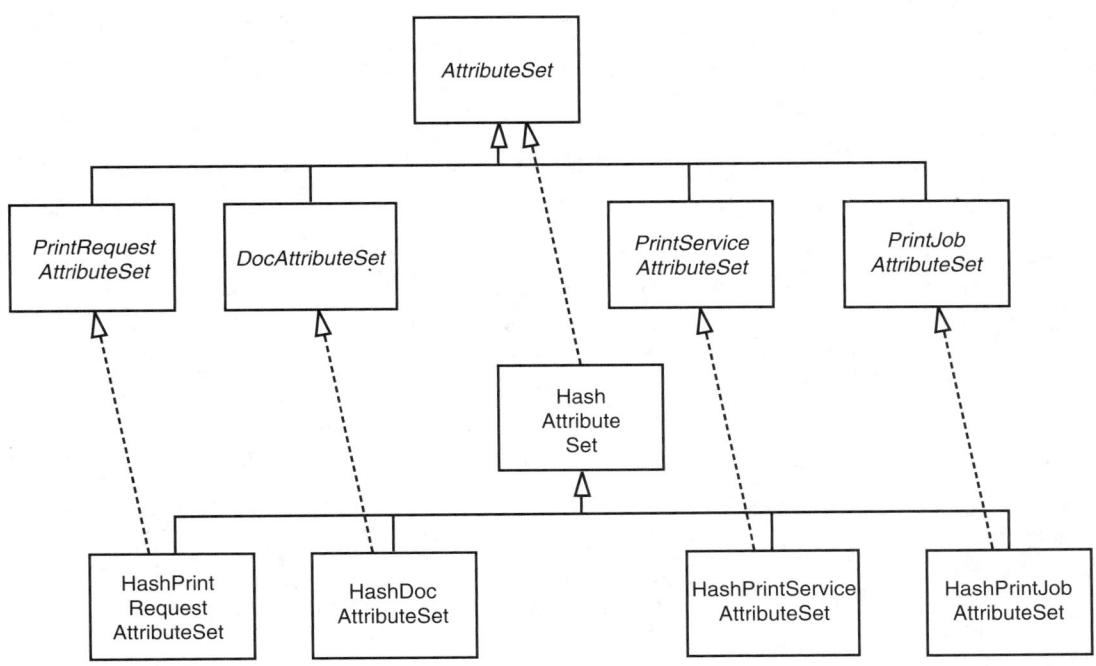

Figure 7–44: The attribute set hierarchy

Why have all these interfaces? They make it possible to check for correct attribute usage. For example, a DocAttributeSet accepts only objects that implement the DocAttribute interface. Any attempt to add another attribute results in a runtime error.

An attribute set is a specialized kind of map, where the keys are of type Class and the values belong to a class that implements the Attribute interface. For example, if you insert an object

```
new Copies(10)
```

into an attribute set, then its key is the Class object Copies.class. That key is called the *category* of the attribute. The Attribute interface declares a method

```
Class getCategory()
```

that returns the category of an attribute. The Copies class defines the method to return the object Copies.class, but it isn't a requirement that the category be the same as the class of the attribute.

When an attribute is added to an attribute set, the category is extracted automatically. You just add the attribute value:

```
attributes.add(new Copies(10));
```

If you subsequently add another attribute with the same category, it overwrites the first one.

To retrieve an attribute, you need to use the category as the key, for example,

```
AttributeSet attributes = job.getAttributes();
Copies copies = (Copies) attribute.get(Copies.class);
```

Finally, attributes are organized by the values they can have. The `Copies` attribute can have any integer value. The `Copies` class extends the `IntegerSyntax` class that takes care of all integer-valued attributes. The `getValue` method returns the integer value of the attribute, for example,

```
int n = copies.getValue();
```

The classes

- `TextSyntax`
  `DateTimeSyntax`
  `URISyntax`

encapsulate a string, date and time, or URI (Uniform Resource Identifier).

Finally, many attributes can take a finite number of values. For example, the `PrintQuality` attribute has three settings: draft, normal, and high. They are represented by three constants:

```
PrintQuality.DRAFT
PrintQuality.NORMAL
PrintQuality.HIGH
```

Attribute classes with a finite number of values extend the `EnumSyntax` class, which provides a number of convenience methods to set up these enumerations in a typesafe manner. You need not worry about the mechanism when using such an attribute. Simply add the named values to attribute sets:

```
attributes.add(PrintQuality.HIGH);
```

Here is how you check the value of an attribute:

```
if (attributes.get(PrintQuality.class) == PrintQuality.HIGH)
    . . .
```

Table 7–4 lists the printing attributes. The second column lists the superclass of the attribute class (for example, `IntegerSyntax` for the `Copies` attribute) or the set of enumeration values for the attributes with a finite set of values. The last four columns indicate whether the attribute class implements the `DocAttribute` (DA), `PrintJobAttribute` (PJA), `PrintRequest-Attribute` (PRA), and `PrintServiceAttribute` (PSA) interfaces.

 NOTE: As you can see, there are lots of attributes, many of which are quite specialized. The source for most of the attributes is the Internet Printing Protocol 1.1 (RFC 2911).

 NOTE: JDK 1.3 introduced the `JobAttributes` and `PageAttributes` classes, whose purpose is similar to the printing attributes covered in this section. Unless you need to specifically support JDK 1.3, you should instead use the more robust JDK 1.4 print service mechanism.

Table 7–4: Printing Attributes

Attribute	Superclass or Enumeration Constants	DA	PJA	PRA	PSA
Chromaticity	MONOCHROME, COLOR	✔	✔	✔	
ColorSupported	SUPPORTED, NOT_SUPPORTED				✔
Compression	COMPRESS, DEFLATE, GZIP, NONE	✔			
Copies	IntegerSyntax		✔	✔	
DateTimeAtCompleted	DateTimeSyntax		✔		

Table 7–4: Printing Attributes (continued)

Attribute	Superclass or Enumeration Constants	DA	PJA	PRA	PSA
DateTimeAtCreation	DateTimeSyntax		✔		
DateTimeAtProcessing	DateTimeSyntax		✔		
Destination	URISyntax		✔	✔	
DocumentName	TextSyntax	✔			
Fidelity	FIDELITY_TRUE, FIDELITY_FALSE		✔	✔	
Finishings	NONE, STAPLE, EDGE_STITCH, BIND, SADDLE_STITCH, COVER, . . .	✔	✔	✔	
JobHoldUntil	DateTimeSyntax		✔	✔	
JobImpressions	IntegerSyntax		✔	✔	
JobImpressionsCompleted	IntegerSyntax		✔		
JobKOctets	IntegerSyntax		✔	✔	
JobKOctetsProcessed	IntegerSyntax		✔		
JobMediaSheets	IntegerSyntax		✔	✔	
JobMediaSheetsCompleted	IntegerSyntax		✔		
JobMessageFromOperator	TextSyntax		✔		
JobName	TextSyntax		✔	✔	
JobOriginatingUserName	TextSyntax		✔		
JobPriority	IntegerSyntax		✔	✔	
JobSheets	STANDARD, NONE		✔	✔	
JobState	ABORTED, CANCELED, COMPLETED, PENDING, PENDING_HELD, PROCESSING, PROCESSING_STOPPED		✔		
JobStateReason	ABORTED_BY_SYSTEM, DOCUMENT_FORMAT_ERROR, many others				
JobStateReasons	HashSet		✔		
MediaName	ISO_A4_WHITE, ISO_A4_TRANSPARENT, NA_LETTER_WHITE, NA_LETTER_TRANSPARENT	✔	✔	✔	
MediaSize	ISO.A0 - ISO.A10, ISO.B0 - ISO.B10, ISO.C0 - ISO.C10, NA.LETTER, NA.LEGAL, various other paper and envelope sizes				
MediaSizeName	ISO_A0 - ISO_A10, ISO_B0 - ISO_B10, ISO_C0 - ISO_C10, NA_LETTER, NA_LEGAL, various other paper and envelope size names	✔	✔	✔	

Table 7–4: Printing Attributes (continued)

Attribute	Superclass or Enumeration Constants	DA	PJA	PRA	PSA
MediaTray	TOP, MIDDLE, BOTTOM, SIDE, ENVELOPE, LARGE_CAPACITY, MAIN, MANUAL,	✔	✔	✔	
MultipleDocumentHandling	SINGLE_DOCUMENT, SINGLE_DOCUMENT_NEW_SHEET, SEPARATE_DOCUMENTS_COLLATED_ COPIES, SEPARATE_DOCUMENTS_UNCOLLATED_ COPIES		✔	✔	
NumberOfDocuments	IntegerSyntax		✔		
NumberOfInterveningJobs	IntegerSyntax		✔		
NumberUp	IntegerSyntax	✔	✔	✔	
OrientationRequested	PORTRAIT, LANDSCAPE, REVERSE_PORTRAIT, REVERSE_LANDSCAPE	✔	✔	✔	
OutputDeviceAssigned	TextSyntax		✔		
PageRanges	SetOfInteger	✔	✔	✔	
PagesPerMinute	IntegerSyntax				✔
PagesPerMinuteColor	IntegerSyntax				✔
PDLOverrideSupported	ATTEMPTED, NOT_ATTEMPTED				✔
PresentationDirection	TORIGHT_TOBOTTOM, TORIGHT_TOTOP, TOBOTTOM_TORIGHT, TOBOTTOM_TOLEFT, TOLEFT_TOBOTTOM, TOLEFT_TOTOP, TOTOP_TORIGHT, TOTOP_TOLEFT		✔	✔	
PrinterInfo	TextSyntax				✔
PrinterIsAcceptingJobs	ACCEPTING_JOBS, NOT_ACCEPTING_JOBS				✔
PrinterLocation	TextSyntax				✔
PrinterMakeAndModel	TextSyntax				✔
PrinterMessageFromOperator	TextSyntax				✔
PrinterMoreInfo	URISyntax				✔
PrinterMoreInfoManufacturer	URISyntax				✔
PrinterName	TextSyntax				✔
PrinterResolution	ResolutionSyntax	✔	✔	✔	
PrinterState	PROCESSING, IDLE, STOPPED, UNKNOWN				✔
PrinterStateReason	COVER_OPEN, FUSER_OVER_TEMP, MEDIA_JAM, and many others				
PrinterStateReasons	HashMap				
PrinterURI	URISyntax				✔

Table 7–4: Printing Attributes (continued)

Attribute	Superclass or Enumeration Constants	DA	PJA	PRA	PSA
PrintQuality	DRAFT, NORMAL, HIGH	✔	✔	✔	
QueuedJobCount	IntegerSyntax				✔
ReferenceUriSchemes-Supported	FILE, FTP, GOPHER, HTTP, HTTPS, NEWS, NNTP, WAIS				
RequestingUserName	TextSyntax			✔	
Severity	ERROR, REPORT, WARNING				
SheetCollate	COLLATED, UNCOLLATED	✔	✔	✔	
Sides	ONE_SIDED, DUPLEX (=TWO_SIDED_LONG_EDGE), TUMBLE (=TWO_SIDED_SHORT_EDGE)	✔	✔	✔	

 javax.print.attribute.Attribute 1.4

- `Class getCategory()`
  gets the category of this attribute.
- `String getName()`
  gets the name of this attribute.

 javax.print.attribute.AttributeSet 1.4

- `boolean add(Attribute attr)`
  adds an attribute to this set. If the set has another attribute with the same category, that attribute is replaced by the given attribute. Returns `true` if the set changed as a result of this operation.
- `Attribute get(Class category)`
  retrieves the attribute with the given category key, or `null` if no such attribute exists.
- `boolean remove(Attribute attr)`
- `boolean remove(Class category)`
  remove the given attribute, or the attribute with the given category, from the set. Return `true` if the set changed as a result of this operation.
- `Attribute[] toArray()`
  returns an array with all attributes in this set.

 javax.print.PrintService 1.4

- `PrintServiceAttributeSet getAttributes()`
  gets the attributes of this print service.

 javax.print.DocPrintJob 1.4

- `PrintJobAttributeSet getAttributes()`
  gets the attributes of this print job.

This concludes our discussion on printing. You now know how to print 2D graphics and other document types, how to enumerate printers and stream print services, and how to set and retrieve attributes. Next, we turn to two important user interface issues, the clipboard and support for the drag-and-drop mechanism.

The Clipboard

One of the most useful and convenient user interface mechanisms of graphical user interface environments (such as Windows and the X Window System) *is cut and paste.* You select some data in one program and cut or copy them to the clipboard. Then, you select another program and paste the clipboard contents into that application. Using the clipboard, you can transfer text, images, or other data from one document to another, or, of course, from one place in a document to another place in the same document. Cut and paste is so natural that most computer users never think about it.

However, JDK 1.0 did not support cut and paste. JDK 1.1 implemented a rudimentary clipboard mechanism. That mechanism has been gradually improved and is now quite usable on a number of platforms.

Even though the clipboard is conceptually simple, implementing clipboard services is actually harder than you might think. Suppose you copy text from a word processor to the clipboard. If you paste that text into another word processor, then you expect that the fonts and formatting will stay intact. That is, the text in the clipboard needs to retain the formatting information. But if you paste the text into a plain text field, then you expect that just the characters are pasted in, without additional formatting codes. To support this flexibility, the data provider can offer the clipboard data in multiple formats, and the data consumer can pick one of them.

The system clipboard implementations of Microsoft Windows and the Macintosh are similar, but, of course, there are slight differences. However, the X Window System clipboard mechanism is much more limited—cutting and pasting of anything but plain text is only sporadically supported. You should consider these limitations when trying out the programs in this section.

 NOTE: Check out the file *jre*/lib/flavormap.properties on your platform to get an idea about what kinds of objects can be transferred between Java programs and the system clipboard.

Often, programs need to support cut and paste of data types that the system clipboard cannot handle. The data transfer API supports the transfer of arbitrary local object references in the same virtual machine. Between different virtual machines, you can transfer serialized objects and references to remote objects.

Table 7–5 summarizes the data transfer capabilities of the clipboard mechanism.

Table 7–5: Capabilities of the Java Data Transfer Mechanism

Transfer	Format
Between a Java program and a native program	Text, images, file lists, . . . (depending on the host platform)
Between two cooperating Java programs	Serialized and remote objects
Within one Java program	Any object

Classes and Interfaces for Data Transfer

Data transfer in the Java technology is implemented in a package called java.awt.datatrans-fer. Here is an overview of the most important classes and interfaces of that package.

- Objects that can be transferred via a clipboard must implement the Transferable interface.
- The Clipboard class describes a clipboard. Transferable objects are the only items that can be put on or taken off a clipboard. The system clipboard is a concrete example of a Clipboard.
- The DataFlavor class describes data flavors that can be placed on the clipboard.
- The StringSelection class is a concrete class that implements the Transferable interface. It transfers text strings.
- A class must implement the ClipboardOwner interface if it wants to be notified when the clipboard contents have been overwritten by someone else. Clipboard ownership enables "delayed formatting" of complex data. If a program transfers simple data (such as a string), then it simply sets the clipboard contents and moves on to do the next thing. However, if a program will place complex data that can be formatted in multiple flavors onto the clipboard, then it may not actually want to prepare all the flavors, since there is a good chance that most of them are never needed. However, then it needs to hang on to the clipboard data so that it can create the flavors later when they are requested. The clipboard owner is notified (by a call to its lostOwnership method) when the contents of the clipboard change. That tells it that the information is no longer needed. In our sample programs, we don't worry about clipboard ownership.

Transferring Text

The best way to get comfortable with the data transfer classes is to start with the simplest situation: transferring text to and from the system clipboard. The idea of the following program is simple. First, get a reference to the system clipboard.

```
Clipboard clipboard = Toolkit.getDefaultToolkit().getSystemClipboard();
```

For strings to be transferred to the clipboard, they must be wrapped into StringSelection objects. The constructor takes the text you want to transfer.

```
String text = . . .
StringSelection selection = new StringSelection(text);
```

The actual transfer is done by a call to setContents, which takes a StringSelection object and a ClipBoardOwner as parameters. If you are not interested in designating a clipboard owner, set the second parameter to null.

```
clipboard.setContents(selection, null);
```

Starting with JDK 5.0, you can bypass the Transferable and query the clipboard directly.

Let us look at the reverse operation, reading a string from the clipboard. Starting with JDK 5.0, this is quite simple:

```
DataFlavor flavor = DataFlavor.stringFlavor;
if (clipboard.isDataFlavorAvailable(flavor)
   String text = (String) clipboard.getData(flavor);
```

Before JDK 5.0, you had to retrieve the Transferable and query it for the available flavors:

```
Transferable contents = clipBoard.getContents(null);
if (contents != null && contents.isDataFlavorSupported(flavor))
   String text = (String) contents.getTransferData(flavor);
```

According to the API documentation, the parameter of the getContents call is an Object reference of the requesting object. It is not clear why the clipboard collects this information.

The return value of getContents may be null. That indicates that the clipboard is either empty or that it has no data that the Java platform knows how to retrieve.

Example 7–16 is a program that demonstrates cutting and pasting between a Java application and the system clipboard. Figure 7–45 shows a screen shot. If you select an area of text in the text area and click Copy, then the selected text is copied to the system clipboard. As Figure 7–46 shows, the copied text is indeed stored on the system clipboard. (Run the program c:\windows\system32\clipbrd to display the clipboard viewer in Windows.) When you subsequently click the Paste button, the contents of the clipboard (which may come from a native program) are pasted at the cursor position.

Figure 7–45: The TextTransferTest program

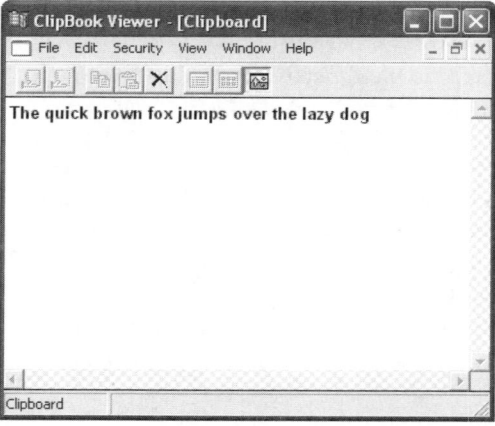

Figure 7–46: The Windows clipboard viewer after a copy

Example 7–16: TextTransferTest.java

```
1. import java.awt.*;
2. import java.awt.datatransfer.*;
3. import java.awt.event.*;
4. import java.io.*;
5. import javax.swing.*;
6.
7. /**
```

```
 8.     This program demonstrates the transfer of text
 9.     between a Java application and the system clipboard.
10. */
11. public class TextTransferTest
12. {
13.    public static void main(String[] args)
14.    {
15.       JFrame frame = new TextTransferFrame();
16.       frame.setDefaultCloseOperation(JFrame.EXIT_ON_CLOSE);
17.       frame.setVisible(true);
18.    }
19. }
20.
21. /**
22.    This frame has a text area and buttons for copying and
23.    pasting text.
24. */
25. class TextTransferFrame extends JFrame
26. {
27.    public TextTransferFrame()
28.    {
29.       setTitle("TextTransferTest");
30.       setSize(DEFAULT_WIDTH, DEFAULT_HEIGHT);
31.
32.       textArea = new JTextArea();
33.       add(new JScrollPane(textArea), BorderLayout.CENTER);
34.       JPanel panel = new JPanel();
35.
36.       JButton copyButton = new JButton("Copy");
37.       panel.add(copyButton);
38.       copyButton.addActionListener(new
39.          ActionListener()
40.          {
41.             public void actionPerformed(ActionEvent event)
42.             {
43.                copy();
44.             }
45.          });
46.
47.       JButton pasteButton = new JButton("Paste");
48.       panel.add(pasteButton);
49.       pasteButton.addActionListener(new
50.          ActionListener()
51.          {
52.             public void actionPerformed(ActionEvent event)
53.             {
54.                paste();
55.             }
56.          });
57.
58.       add(panel, BorderLayout.SOUTH);
59.    }
60.
61.    /**
62.       Copies the selected text to the system clipboard.
63.    */
```

```
64.    private void copy()
65.    {
66.       Clipboard clipboard = Toolkit.getDefaultToolkit().getSystemClipboard();
67.       String text = textArea.getSelectedText();
68.       if (text == null) text = textArea.getText();
69.       StringSelection selection = new StringSelection(text);
70.       clipboard.setContents(selection, null);
71.    }
72.
73.    /**
74.       Pastes the text from the system clipboard into the
75.       text area.
76.    */
77.    private void paste()
78.    {
79.       Clipboard clipboard = Toolkit.getDefaultToolkit().getSystemClipboard();
80.       DataFlavor flavor = DataFlavor.stringFlavor;
81.       if (clipboard.isDataFlavorAvailable(flavor))
82.       {
83.          try
84.          {
85.             String text = (String) clipboard.getData(flavor);
86.             textArea.replaceSelection(text);
87.          }
88.          catch (UnsupportedFlavorException e)
89.          {
90.             JOptionPane.showMessageDialog(this, e);
91.          }
92.          catch (IOException e)
93.          {
94.             JOptionPane.showMessageDialog(this, e);
95.          }
96.       }
97.    }
98.
99.    private JTextArea textArea;
100.
101.   private static final int DEFAULT_WIDTH = 300;
102.   private static final int DEFAULT_HEIGHT = 300;
103. }
```

---

java.awt.Toolkit 1.0

- Clipboard getSystemClipboard() **1.1**
  gets the system clipboard.

java.awt.datatransfer.Clipboard 1.1

- Transferable getContents(Object requester)
  gets the clipboard contents.

  Parameters: requester   The object requesting the clipboard contents; this value is not actually used

- void setContents(Transferable contents, ClipboardOwner owner)
  puts contents on the clipboard.

Parameters: contents   The Transferable encapsulating the contents

owner   The object to be notified (via its lostOwnership method) when new information is placed on the clipboard, or null if no notification is desired

- boolean isDataFlavorAvailable(DataFlavor flavor) **5.0**
  returns true if the clipboard has data in the given flavor.
- Object getData(DataFlavor flavor) **5.0**
  gets the data in the given flavor, or throws an UnsupportedFlavorException if no data are available in the given flavor.

 java.awt.datatransfer.ClipboardOwner 1.1

- void lostOwnership(Clipboard clipboard, Transferable contents)
  notifies this object that it is no longer the owner of the contents of the clipboard.

  Parameters: clipboard   The clipboard onto which the contents were placed

  contents   The item that this owner had placed onto the clipboard

 java.awt.datatransfer.Transferable 1.1

- boolean isDataFlavorSupported(DataFlavor flavor)
  returns true if the specified flavor is one of the supported data flavors; false otherwise.
- Object getTransferData(DataFlavor flavor)
  returns the data, formatted in the requested flavor. Throws an UnsupportedFlavorException if the flavor requested is not supported.

The Transferable Interface and Data Flavors

As of JDK 5.0, you can ask the clipboard to list all available flavors:

```
DataFlavor[] flavors = clipboard.getAvailableDataFlavors()
```

In older versions of the JDK, you first got the clipboard contents—an object that implements the Transferable interface—and queried it for the available flavors:

```
Transferable contents = clipBoard.getContents(null);
if (contents != null)
    flavors = transferable.getTransferDataFlavors();
```

You can also install a FlavorListener onto the clipboard. The listener is notified when the collection of data flavors on the clipboard changes. See the API notes for details.

A DataFlavor is defined by two characteristics:

- A MIME type name (such as "image/gif")
- A representation class for accessing the data (such as java.awt.Image)

In addition, every data flavor has a human-readable name (such as "GIF Image").

The representation class can be specified with a class parameter in the MIME type, for example,

```
image/gif;class=java.awt.Image
```

 NOTE: This is just an example to show the syntax. There is no standard data flavor for transferring GIF image data.

If no class parameter is given, then the representation class is InputStream.

For transferring local, serialized, and remote Java objects, Sun Microsystems defines three MIME types:

```
application/x-java-jvm-local-objectref
application/x-java-serialized-object
application/x-java-remote-object
```

> NOTE: The x- prefix indicates that this is an experimental name, not one that is sanctioned by IANA, the organization that assigns standard MIME type names.

For example, the standard stringFlavor data flavor is described by the MIME type

```
application/x-java-serialized-object;class=java.lang.String
```

 java.awt.datatransfer.DataFlavor 1.1

- DataFlavor(String mimeType, String humanPresentableName)
  creates a data flavor that describes stream data in a format described by a MIME type.

Parameters:	mimeType	A MIME type string
	humanPresentableName	A more readable version of the name

- DataFlavor(Class class, String humanPresentableName)
  creates a data flavor that describes a Java platform class. Its MIME type is application/x-java-serialized-object;class=className.

Parameters:	class	The class that is retrieved from the Transferable
	humanPresentableName	A readable version of the name

- String getMimeType()
  returns the MIME type string for this data flavor.
- boolean isMimeTypeEqual(String mimeType)
  tests whether this data flavor has the given MIME type.
- String getHumanPresentableName()
  returns the human-presentable name for the data format of this data flavor.
- Class getRepresentationClass()
  returns a Class object that represents the class of the object that a Transferable object will return when called with this data flavor. This is either the class parameter of the MIME type or InputStream.

 java.awt.datatransfer.Clipboard 1.1

- DataFlavor[] getAvailableDataFlavors() 5.0
  returns an array of the available flavors.
- void addFlavorListener(FlavorListener listener) 5.0
  adds a listener that is notified when the set of available flavors changes.

 java.awt.datatransfer.Transferable 1.1

- DataFlavor[] getTransferDataFlavors()
  returns an array of the supported flavors.

 java.awt.datatransfer.FlavorListener 5.0

- void flavorsChanged(FlavorEvent event)
  is called when a clipboard's set of available flavors changes.

Building an Image Transferable

Objects that you want to transfer via the clipboard must implement the Transferable interface. The StringSelection class is currently the only public class in the Java standard library that implements the Transferable interface. In this section, you will see how to transfer images into the clipboard. Because the JDK does not supply a class for image transfer, you must implement it yourself.

The class is completely trivial. It simply reports that the only available data format is DataFlavor.imageFlavor, and it holds an image object.

```java
class ImageSelection implements Transferable
{
    public ImageSelection(Image image)
    {
        theImage = image;
    }

    public DataFlavor[] getTransferDataFlavors()
    {
        return new DataFlavor[] { DataFlavor.imageFlavor };
    }

    public boolean isDataFlavorSupported(DataFlavor flavor)
    {
        return flavor.equals(DataFlavor.imageFlavor);
    }

    public Object getTransferData(DataFlavor flavor)
        throws UnsupportedFlavorException
    {
        if(flavor.equals(DataFlavor.imageFlavor))
        {
            return theImage;
        }
        else
        {
            throw new UnsupportedFlavorException(flavor);
        }
    }

    private Image theImage;
}
```

 NOTE: The JDK supplies the DataFlavor.imageFlavor constant and does all the heavy lifting to convert between Java images and native clipboard images. But, curiously, it does not supply the wrapper class that is necessary to place images onto the clipboard.

The program of Example 7–17 demonstrates the transfer of images between a Java application and the system clipboard. When the program starts, it generates a Mandelbrot image. Click the Copy button to copy the image to the clipboard and then paste it into another application. (See Figure 7–47.) From another application, copy an image into the system clipboard. Then click the Paste button and see the image being pasted into the example program. (See Figure 7–48.)

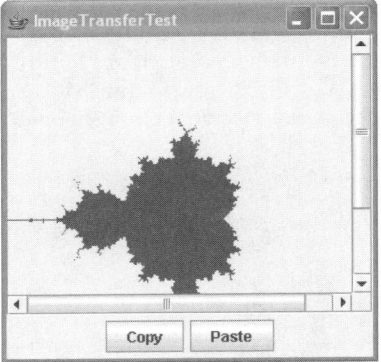

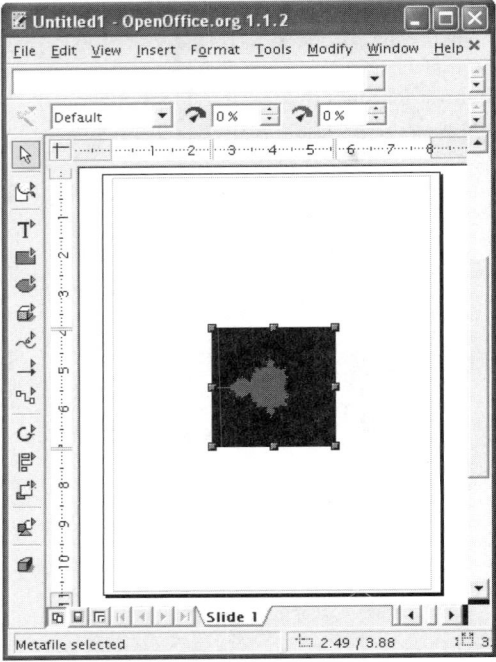

Figure 7–47: Copying from a Java program to a native program

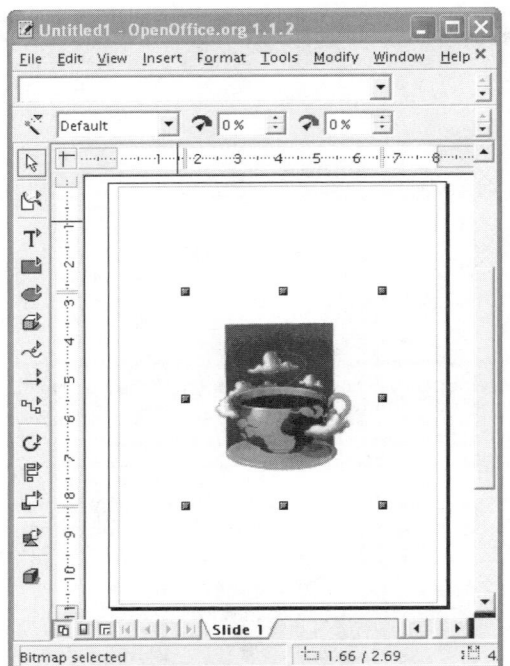

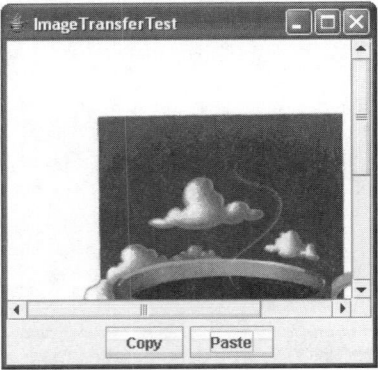

Figure 7–48: Copying from a native program to a Java program

The program is a straightforward modification of the text transfer program. The data flavor is now DataFlavor.imageFlavor, and we use the ImageSelection class to transfer an image to the system clipboard.

Example 7–17: ImageTransferTest.java

```
1. import java.io.*;
2. import java.awt.*;
3. import java.awt.datatransfer.*;
4. import java.awt.event.*;
5. import java.awt.image.*;
6. import javax.swing.*;
7.
8. /**
9.    This program demonstrates the transfer of images between a Java application
10.    and the system clipboard.
11. */
12. public class ImageTransferTest
13. {
14.    public static void main(String[] args)
15.    {
16.       JFrame frame = new ImageTransferFrame();
17.       frame.setDefaultCloseOperation(JFrame.EXIT_ON_CLOSE);
18.       frame.setVisible(true);
19.    }
20. }
21.
22. /**
23.    This frame has an image label and buttons for copying and pasting an image.
24. */
25. class ImageTransferFrame extends JFrame
26. {
27.    public ImageTransferFrame()
28.    {
29.       setTitle("ImageTransferTest");
30.       setSize(DEFAULT_WIDTH, DEFAULT_HEIGHT);
31.
32.       label = new JLabel();
33.       image = makeMandelbrot(DEFAULT_WIDTH, DEFAULT_HEIGHT);
34.       label.setIcon(new ImageIcon(image));
35.       add(new JScrollPane(label), BorderLayout.CENTER);
36.       JPanel panel = new JPanel();
37.
38.       JButton copyButton = new JButton("Copy");
39.       panel.add(copyButton);
40.       copyButton.addActionListener(new
41.          ActionListener()
42.          {
43.             public void actionPerformed(ActionEvent event) { copy(); }
44.          });
45.
46.       JButton pasteButton = new JButton("Paste");
47.       panel.add(pasteButton);
48.       pasteButton.addActionListener(new
49.          ActionListener()
50.          {
51.             public void actionPerformed(ActionEvent event) { paste(); }
```

```
52.          });
53.
54.      add(panel, BorderLayout.SOUTH);
55.   }
56.
57.   /**
58.      Copies the current image to the system clipboard.
59.   */
60.   private void copy()
61.   {
62.      Clipboard clipboard = Toolkit.getDefaultToolkit().getSystemClipboard();
63.      ImageSelection selection = new ImageSelection(image);
64.      clipboard.setContents(selection, null);
65.   }
66.
67.   /**
68.      Pastes the image from the system clipboard into the
69.      image label.
70.   */
71.   private void paste()
72.   {
73.      Clipboard clipboard = Toolkit.getDefaultToolkit().getSystemClipboard();
74.      DataFlavor flavor = DataFlavor.imageFlavor;
75.      if (clipboard.isDataFlavorAvailable(flavor))
76.      {
77.         try
78.         {
79.            image = (Image) clipboard.getData(flavor);
80.            label.setIcon(new ImageIcon(image));
81.         }
82.         catch (UnsupportedFlavorException exception)
83.         {
84.            JOptionPane.showMessageDialog(this, exception);
85.         }
86.         catch (IOException exception)
87.         {
88.            JOptionPane.showMessageDialog(this, exception);
89.         }
90.      }
91.   }
92.
93.   /**
94.      Makes the Mandelbrot image.
95.      @param width the width
96.      @parah height the height
97.      @return the image
98.   */
99.   public BufferedImage makeMandelbrot(int width, int height)
100.  {
101.     BufferedImage image = new BufferedImage(width, height, BufferedImage.TYPE_INT_ARGB);
102.     WritableRaster raster = image.getRaster();
103.     ColorModel model = image.getColorModel();
104.
105.     Color fractalColor = Color.red;
106.     int argb = fractalColor.getRGB();
107.     Object colorData = model.getDataElements(argb, null);
```

```
108.
109.      for (int i = 0; i < width; i++)
110.        for (int j = 0; j < height; j++)
111.        {
112.            double a = XMIN + i * (XMAX - XMIN) / width;
113.            double b = YMIN + j * (YMAX - YMIN) / height;
114.            if (!escapesToInfinity(a, b))
115.                raster.setDataElements(i, j, colorData);
116.        }
117.      return image;
118.    }
119.
120.    private boolean escapesToInfinity(double a, double b)
121.    {
122.      double x = 0.0;
123.      double y = 0.0;
124.      int iterations = 0;
125.      do
126.      {
127.        double xnew = x * x - y * y + a;
128.        double ynew = 2 * x * y + b;
129.        x = xnew;
130.        y = ynew;
131.        iterations++;
132.        if (iterations == MAX_ITERATIONS) return false;
133.      }
134.      while (x <= 2 && y <= 2);
135.      return true;
136.    }
137.
138.    private JLabel label;
139.    private Image image;
140.
141.    private static final double XMIN = -2;
142.    private static final double XMAX = 2;
143.    private static final double YMIN = -2;
144.    private static final double YMAX = 2;
145.    private static final int MAX_ITERATIONS = 16;
146.
147.    private static final int DEFAULT_WIDTH = 300;
148.    private static final int DEFAULT_HEIGHT = 300;
149. }
150.
151. /**
152.    This class is a wrapper for the data transfer of image
153.    objects.
154. */
155. class ImageSelection implements Transferable
156. {
157.    /**
158.       Constructs the selection.
159.       @param image an image
160.    */
161.    public ImageSelection(Image image)
162.    {
163.       theImage = image;
```

```
164.    }
165.
166.    public DataFlavor[] getTransferDataFlavors()
167.    {
168.       return new DataFlavor[] { DataFlavor.imageFlavor };
169.    }
170.
171.    public boolean isDataFlavorSupported(DataFlavor flavor)
172.    {
173.       return flavor.equals(DataFlavor.imageFlavor);
174.    }
175.
176.    public Object getTransferData(DataFlavor flavor)
177.       throws UnsupportedFlavorException
178.    {
179.       if(flavor.equals(DataFlavor.imageFlavor))
180.       {
181.          return theImage;
182.       }
183.       else
184.       {
185.          throw new UnsupportedFlavorException(flavor);
186.       }
187.    }
188.
189.    private Image theImage;
190. }
```

Using a Local Clipboard to Transfer Object References

Suppose you want to copy and paste a data type that isn't one of the data types supported by the system clipboard. For example, in a drawing program, you may want to allow your users to copy and paste arbitrary shapes.

The program in Example 7–18 demonstrates this capability. As you can see in Figure 7–49, the program displays two panels. By moving the rectangle "grabbers" in the left panel, you can change the shape of a cubic curve. The panel on the right side can display an arbitrary shape.

When you click the Copy button, the current cubic curve shape is copied. Click Paste, and the Shape object on the clipboard is displayed in the panel on the right-hand side. You can see that the shape is held on a clipboard by the actions of copying a curve and then modifying the curve before pasting. The copied shape, and not the current shape of the curve, is pasted into the right-side panel.

To transfer an arbitrary Java object reference within the same JVM, you use the MIME type

```
application/x-java-jvm-local-objectref;class=className
```

However, the JDK doesn't include a Transferable wrapper for this type. You can find the code for the wrapper in the example program. It is entirely analogous to the ImageSelection wrapper of the preceding section.

An object reference is only meaningful within a single virtual machine. For that reason, you cannot copy the shape object to the system clipboard. Instead, this program uses a local clipboard:

```
Clipboard clipboard = new Clipboard("local");
```

The construction parameter is the clipboard name.

However, using a local clipboard has one major disadvantage. You need to synchronize the local and the system clipboard, so that users don't confuse the two. Currently, the Java platform doesn't do that synchronization for you.

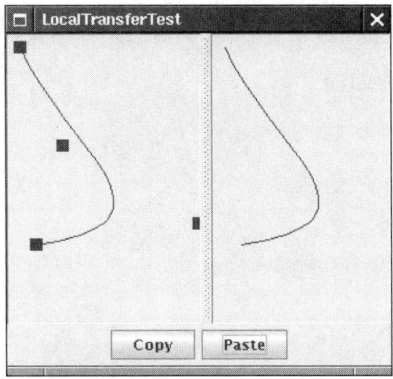

Figure 7–49: Transferring local objects

Example 7–18: LocalTransferTest.java

```
1.  import java.awt.*;
2.  import java.awt.datatransfer.*;
3.  import java.awt.event.*;
4.  import java.awt.geom.*;
5.  import java.io.*;
6.  import java.util.*;
7.  import javax.swing.*;
8.
9.  /**
10.    This program demonstrates the transfer of object references within the same virtual machine.
11. */
12. public class LocalTransferTest
13. {
14.    public static void main(String[] args)
15.    {
16.       JFrame frame = new LocalTransferFrame();
17.       frame.setDefaultCloseOperation(JFrame.EXIT_ON_CLOSE);
18.       frame.setVisible(true);
19.    }
20. }
21.
22. /**
23.    This frame contains a panel to edit a cubic curve, a
24.    panel that can display an arbitrary shape, and copy and
25.    paste buttons.
26. */
27. class LocalTransferFrame extends JFrame
28. {
29.    public LocalTransferFrame()
30.    {
31.       setTitle("LocalTransferTest");
32.       setSize(DEFAULT_WIDTH, DEFAULT_HEIGHT);
```

```
33.
34.       curvePanel = new CubicCurvePanel();
35.       curvePanel.setPreferredSize(new Dimension(DEFAULT_WIDTH / 2, DEFAULT_HEIGHT));
36.       shapePanel = new ShapePanel();
37.
38.       add(new JSplitPane(JSplitPane.HORIZONTAL_SPLIT, curvePanel, shapePanel),
39.          BorderLayout.CENTER);
40.       JPanel panel = new JPanel();
41.
42.       JButton copyButton = new JButton("Copy");
43.       panel.add(copyButton);
44.       copyButton.addActionListener(new
45.          ActionListener()
46.          {
47.             public void actionPerformed(ActionEvent event)
48.             {
49.                copy();
50.             }
51.          });
52.
53.       JButton pasteButton = new JButton("Paste");
54.       panel.add(pasteButton);
55.       pasteButton.addActionListener(new
56.          ActionListener()
57.          {
58.             public void actionPerformed(ActionEvent event)
59.             {
60.                paste();
61.             }
62.          });
63.
64.       add(panel, BorderLayout.SOUTH);
65.    }
66.
67.    /**
68.       Copies the current cubic curve to the local clipboard.
69.    */
70.    private void copy()
71.    {
72.       LocalSelection selection = new LocalSelection(curvePanel.getShape());
73.       clipboard.setContents(selection, null);
74.    }
75.
76.    /**
77.       Pastes the shape from the local clipboard into the
78.       shape panel.
79.    */
80.    private void paste()
81.    {
82.       try
83.       {
84.          DataFlavor flavor
85.             = new DataFlavor("application/x-java-jvm-local-objectref;class=java.awt.Shape");
86.          if (clipboard.isDataFlavorAvailable(flavor))
87.             shapePanel.setShape((Shape) clipboard.getData(flavor));
```

```
88.         }
89.         catch (ClassNotFoundException e)
90.         {
91.            JOptionPane.showMessageDialog(this, e);
92.         }
93.         catch (UnsupportedFlavorException e)
94.         {
95.            JOptionPane.showMessageDialog(this, e);
96.         }
97.         catch (IOException e)
98.         {
99.            JOptionPane.showMessageDialog(this, e);
100.        }
101.     }
102.
103.     private CubicCurvePanel curvePanel;
104.     private ShapePanel shapePanel;
105.     private Clipboard clipboard = new Clipboard("local");
106.
107.     private static final int DEFAULT_WIDTH = 300;
108.     private static final int DEFAULT_HEIGHT = 300;
109. }
110.
111.
112. /**
113.    This panel draws a shape and allows the user to
114.    move the points that define it.
115. */
116. class CubicCurvePanel extends JPanel
117. {
118.     public CubicCurvePanel()
119.     {
120.        addMouseListener(new
121.           MouseAdapter()
122.           {
123.              public void mousePressed(MouseEvent event)
124.              {
125.                 for (int i = 0; i < p.length; i++)
126.                 {
127.                    double x = p[i].getX() - SIZE / 2;
128.                    double y = p[i].getY() - SIZE / 2;
129.                    Rectangle2D r = new Rectangle2D.Double(x, y, SIZE, SIZE);
130.                    if (r.contains(event.getPoint()))
131.                    {
132.                       current = i;
133.                       return;
134.                    }
135.                 }
136.              }
137.
138.              public void mouseReleased(MouseEvent event)
139.              {
140.                 current = -1;
141.              }
142.           });
```

```
143.
144.    addMouseMotionListener(new
145.       MouseMotionAdapter()
146.       {
147.          public void mouseDragged(MouseEvent event)
148.          {
149.             if (current == -1) return;
150.             p[current] = event.getPoint();
151.             repaint();
152.          }
153.       });
154.
155.    current = -1;
156. }
157.
158. public void paintComponent(Graphics g)
159. {
160.    super.paintComponent(g);
161.    Graphics2D g2 = (Graphics2D)g;
162.    for (int i = 0; i < p.length; i++)
163.    {
164.       double x = p[i].getX() - SIZE / 2;
165.       double y = p[i].getY() - SIZE / 2;
166.       g2.fill(new Rectangle2D.Double(x, y, SIZE, SIZE));
167.    }
168.
169.    g2.draw(getShape());
170. }
171.
172. /**
173.    Gets the current cubic curve.
174.    @return the curve shape
175. */
176. public Shape getShape()
177. {
178.    return new CubicCurve2D.Double(p[0].getX(), p[0].getY(), p[1].getX(), p[1].getY(),
179.       p[2].getX(), p[2].getY(), p[3].getX(), p[3].getY());
180. }
181.
182. private Point2D[] p =
183. {
184.    new Point2D.Double(10, 10),
185.    new Point2D.Double(10, 100),
186.    new Point2D.Double(100, 10),
187.    new Point2D.Double(100, 200)
188. };
189. private static int SIZE = 10;
190. private int current;
191. }
192.
193. /**
194.    This panel displays an arbitrary shape.
195. */
196. class ShapePanel extends JPanel
197. {
```

```
198.   /**
199.      Set the shape to be displayed in this panel.
200.      @param aShape any shape
201.   */
202.   public void setShape(Shape aShape)
203.   {
204.      shape = aShape;
205.      repaint();
206.   }
207.
208.   public void paintComponent(Graphics g)
209.   {
210.      super.paintComponent(g);
211.      Graphics2D g2 = (Graphics2D) g;
212.      if (shape != null) g2.draw(shape);
213.   }
214.
215.   private Shape shape;
216. }
217.
218. /**
219.    This class is a wrapper for the data transfer of
220.    object references that are transferred within the same
221.    virtual machine.
222. */
223. class LocalSelection implements Transferable
224. {
225.    /**
226.       Constructs the selection.
227.       @param o any object
228.    */
229.    LocalSelection(Object o)
230.    {
231.       obj = o;
232.    }
233.
234.    public DataFlavor[] getTransferDataFlavors()
235.    {
236.       DataFlavor[] flavors = new DataFlavor[1];
237.       Class type = obj.getClass();
238.       String mimeType = "application/x-java-jvm-local-objectref;class=" + type.getName();
239.       try
240.       {
241.          flavors[0] = new DataFlavor(mimeType);
242.          return flavors;
243.       }
244.       catch (ClassNotFoundException e)
245.       {
246.          return new DataFlavor[0];
247.       }
248.    }
249.
250.    public boolean isDataFlavorSupported(DataFlavor flavor)
251.    {
252.       return "application".equals(flavor.getPrimaryType())
```

```
253.          && "x-java-jvm-local-objectref".equals(flavor.getSubType())
254.          && flavor.getRepresentationClass().isAssignableFrom(obj.getClass());
255.    }
256.
257.    public Object getTransferData(DataFlavor flavor)
258.       throws UnsupportedFlavorException
259.    {
260.       if (! isDataFlavorSupported(flavor))
261.          throw new UnsupportedFlavorException(flavor);
262.
263.       return obj;
264.    }
265.
266.    private Object obj;
267. }
```

 java.awt.datatransfer.Clipboard 1.1

- Clipboard(String name)

  constructs a local clipboard with the given name.

Transferring Java Objects via the System Clipboard

Suppose you want to copy and paste objects from one Java application to another. In that case, you cannot use local clipboards. Fortunately, you can place serialized Java objects onto the system clipboard.

The program in Example 7–19 demonstrates this capability. The program shows a color chooser. The Copy button copies the current color to the system clipboard as a serialized Color object. The Paste button checks whether the system clipboard contains a serialized Color object. If so, it fetches the color and sets it as the current choice of the color chooser.

You can transfer the serialized object between two Java applications (see Figure 7–50). Run two copies of the SerialTransferTest program. Click Copy in the first program, then click Paste in the second program. The Color object is transferred from one virtual machine to the other.

To enable the data transfer, the Java platform places binary data on the system clipboard that contains the serialized object. Another Java program—not necessarily of the same type as the one that generated the clipboard data—can retrieve the clipboard data and deserialize the object.

Of course, a non-Java application will not know what to do with the clipboard data. For that reason, the example program offers the clipboard data in a second flavor, as text. The text is simply the result of the toString method, applied to the transferred object. To see the second flavor, run the program, click on a color, and then select the Paste command in your text editor. A string such as

```
java.awt.Color[r=255,g=51,b=51]
```

will be inserted into your document.

Essentially no additional programming is required to transfer a serializable object. You use the MIME type

```
application/x-java-serialized-object;class=className
```

As before, you have to build your own transfer wrapper—see the example code for details.

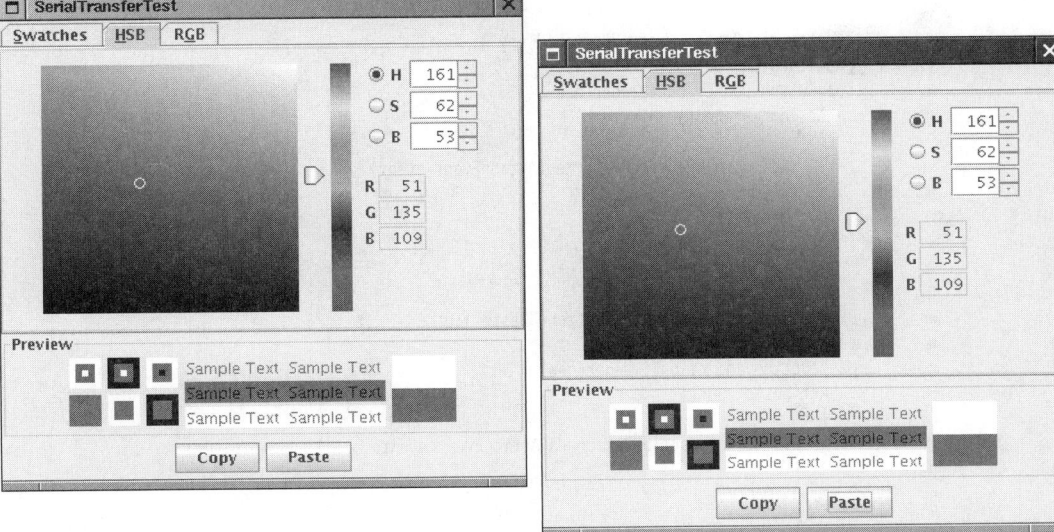

Figure 7–50: Data are copied between two instances of a Java application

Example 7–19: SerialTransferTest.java

```
1.  import java.io.*;
2.  import java.awt.*;
3.  import java.awt.datatransfer.*;
4.  import java.awt.event.*;
5.  import java.awt.image.*;
6.  import javax.swing.*;
7.
8.  /**
9.     This program demonstrates the transfer of serialized objects between virtual machines.
10. */
11. public class SerialTransferTest
12. {
13.    public static void main(String[] args)
14.    {
15.       JFrame frame = new SerialTransferFrame();
16.       frame.setDefaultCloseOperation(JFrame.EXIT_ON_CLOSE);
17.       frame.setVisible(true);
18.    }
19. }
20.
21. /**
22.    This frame contains a color chooser, and copy and paste buttons.
23. */
24. class SerialTransferFrame extends JFrame
25. {
26.    public SerialTransferFrame()
27.    {
28.       setTitle("SerialTransferTest");
29.
30.       chooser = new JColorChooser();
31.       add(chooser, BorderLayout.CENTER);
```

```
32.     JPanel panel = new JPanel();
33.
34.     JButton copyButton = new JButton("Copy");
35.     panel.add(copyButton);
36.     copyButton.addActionListener(new
37.        ActionListener()
38.        {
39.           public void actionPerformed(ActionEvent event)
40.           {
41.              copy();
42.           }
43.        });
44.
45.     JButton pasteButton = new JButton("Paste");
46.     panel.add(pasteButton);
47.     pasteButton.addActionListener(new
48.        ActionListener()
49.        {
50.           public void actionPerformed(ActionEvent event)
51.           {
52.              paste();
53.           }
54.        });
55.
56.     add(panel, BorderLayout.SOUTH);
57.     pack();
58.  }
59.
60.  /**
61.     Copies the chooser's color into the system clipboard.
62.  */
63.  private void copy()
64.  {
65.     Clipboard clipboard = Toolkit.getDefaultToolkit().getSystemClipboard();
66.     Color color = chooser.getColor();
67.     SerialSelection selection = new SerialSelection(color);
68.     clipboard.setContents(selection, null);
69.  }
70.
71.  /**
72.     Pastes the color from the system clipboard into the chooser.
73.  */
74.  private void paste()
75.  {
76.     Clipboard clipboard = Toolkit.getDefaultToolkit().getSystemClipboard();
77.     try
78.     {
79.        DataFlavor flavor
80.           = new DataFlavor("application/x-java-serialized-object;class=java.awt.Color");
81.        if (clipboard.isDataFlavorAvailable(flavor))
82.        {
83.           Color color = (Color) clipboard.getData(flavor);
84.           chooser.setColor(color);
85.        }
86.     }
87.     catch (ClassNotFoundException e)
88.     {
```

```
89.          JOptionPane.showMessageDialog(this, e);
90.       }
91.       catch (UnsupportedFlavorException e)
92.       {
93.          JOptionPane.showMessageDialog(this, e);
94.       }
95.       catch (IOException e)
96.       {
97.          JOptionPane.showMessageDialog(this, e);
98.       }
99.    }
100.
101.    private JColorChooser chooser;
102. }
103.
104. /**
105.    This class is a wrapper for the data transfer of serialized objects.
106. */
107. class SerialSelection implements Transferable
108. {
109.    /**
110.       Constructs the selection.
111.       @param o any serializable object
112.    */
113.    SerialSelection(Serializable o)
114.    {
115.       obj = o;
116.    }
117.
118.    public DataFlavor[] getTransferDataFlavors()
119.    {
120.       DataFlavor[] flavors = new DataFlavor[2];
121.       Class type = obj.getClass();
122.       String mimeType = "application/x-java-serialized-object;class=" + type.getName();
123.       try
124.       {
125.          flavors[0] = new DataFlavor(mimeType);
126.          flavors[1] = DataFlavor.stringFlavor;
127.          return flavors;
128.       }
129.       catch (ClassNotFoundException e)
130.       {
131.          return new DataFlavor[0];
132.       }
133.    }
134.
135.    public boolean isDataFlavorSupported(DataFlavor flavor)
136.    {
137.       return
138.          DataFlavor.stringFlavor.equals(flavor)
139.          || "application".equals(flavor.getPrimaryType())
140.          && "x-java-serialized-object".equals(flavor.getSubType())
141.          && flavor.getRepresentationClass().isAssignableFrom(obj.getClass());
142.    }
143.
144.    public Object getTransferData(DataFlavor flavor)
145.       throws UnsupportedFlavorException
```

```
146.    {
147.       if (!isDataFlavorSupported(flavor))
148.          throw new UnsupportedFlavorException(flavor);
149.
150.       if (DataFlavor.stringFlavor.equals(flavor))
151.          return obj.toString();
152.
153.       return obj;
154.    }
155.
156.    private Serializable obj;
157. }
```

Drag and Drop

When you use cut and paste to transmit information between two programs, the clipboard acts as an intermediary. The *drag and drop* metaphor cuts out the middleman and lets two programs communicate directly. The Java platform offers basic support for drag and drop. You can carry out drag and drop operations between Java applications and native applications. This section shows you how to write a Java application that is a drop target, and an application that is a drag source.

Before going deeper into the Java platform support for drag and drop, let us quickly look at the drag and drop user interface. We use the Windows Explorer and WordPad programs as examples—on another platform, you can experiment with locally available programs with drag and drop capabilities.

You initiate a *drag operation* with a *gesture* inside a *drag source*—usually, by first selecting one or more elements and then dragging the selection away from its initial location (see Figure 7–51).

Name ▲	Size	Type	Date Modified
ProcessBuilder.java	18 KB	JAVA File	8/26/2004 7:41 AM
ProcessEnvironment.java	10 KB	JAVA File	8/26/2004 7:41 AM
ProcessImpl.java	4 KB	JAVA File	8/26/2004 7:41 AM
Readable.java	2 KB	JAVA File	8/26/2004 7:41 AM
Runnable.java	2 KB	JAVA File	8/26/2004 7:42 AM
Runtime.java	37 KB	JAVA File	8/26/2004 7:42 AM
RuntimeException.java	3 KB	JAVA File	8/26/2004 7:42 AM
RuntimePermission.java	13 KB	JAVA File	8/26/2004 7:42 AM
SecurityException.java	2 KB	JAVA File	8/26/2004 7:42 AM
SecurityManager.java	69 KB	JAVA File	8/26/2004 7:42 AM
Short.java	16 KB	JAVA File	8/26/2004 7:42 AM
Shutdown.java	7 KB	JAVA File	8/26/2004 7:42 AM
StackOverflowError.java	1 KB	JAVA File	8/26/2004 7:42 AM
StackTraceElement.java	9 KB	JAVA File	8/26/2004 7:42 AM
StrictMath.java	44 KB	JAVA File	8/26/2004 7:42 AM
String.java	107 KB	JAVA File	8/26/2004 7:42 AM
StringBuffer.java	18 KB	JAVA File	8/26/2004 7:42 AM
StringBuilder.java	13 KB	JAVA File	8/26/2004 7:42 AM
StringCoding.java	11 KB	JAVA File	8/26/2004 7:42 AM
StringIndexOutOfBoundsExce...	2 KB	JAVA File	8/26/2004 7:42 AM
SuppressWarnings.java	2 KB	JAVA File	8/26/2004 7:42 AM
System.java	45 KB	JAVA File	8/26/2004 7:42 AM
Terminator.java	2 KB	JAVA File	8/26/2004 7:42 AM
Thread.java	68 KB	JAVA File	8/26/2004 7:42 AM
ThreadDeath.java	2 KB	JAVA File	8/26/2004 7:42 AM
ThreadGroup.java	35 KB	JAVA File	8/26/2004 7:42 AM
ThreadLocal.java	25 KB	JAVA File	8/26/2004 7:42 AM

Figure 7–51: Initiating a drag operation

When you release the mouse button over a drop target that accepts the drop operation, the drop target queries the drag source for information about the dropped elements and initiates some operation. For example, if you drop a file icon from Windows Explorer to WordPad, then WordPad opens the file. However, if you drag a file icon on top of a directory icon in Windows Explorer, then Explorer moves the file into that directory.

If you hold down the SHIFT or CTRL key while dragging, then the type of the drop action changes from a *move action* to a *copy action,* and a copy of the file is placed into the directory. If you hold down *both* SHIFT and CTRL keys, then a *link* to the file is placed into the directory. (Other platforms may use other keyboard combinations for these operations.)

Thus, there are three types of drop actions with different gestures:

- Move
- Copy
- Link

The intention of the link action is to establish a reference to the dropped element. Such links typically require support from the host operating system (such as symbolic links for files, or object linking for document components) and don't usually make a lot of sense in cross-platform programs. In this section, we focus on using drag and drop for copying and moving.

There is usually some visual feedback for the drag operation. Minimally, the cursor shape changes. As the cursor moves over possible *drop targets,* the cursor shape indicates whether the drop is possible or not. If a drop is possible, the cursor shape also indicates the type of the drop action. Figure 7–52 shows several cursor shapes over drop targets.

Figure 7–52: **Cursor shapes over drop targets**

You can also drag other elements besides file icons. For example, you can select text in WordPad and drag it. Try dropping text fragments into willing drop targets and see how they react.

 NOTE: This experiment shows a disadvantage of drag and drop as a user interface mechanism. It can be difficult for users to anticipate what they can drag, where they can drop it, and what happens when they do. Because the default "move" action can remove the original, many users are understandably cautious about experimenting with drag and drop.

Drop Targets

In this section, we construct a simple Java application that is a drop target. The example program does nothing useful; it simply demonstrates how you can detect that a user would like to initiate a drop, how to accept the drop, and how to analyze the data that are being dropped.

You can designate any AWT component to be a drop target. To do so, you construct a DropTarget object and pass the component and a drop target listener to the constructor. The constructor registers the object with the drag and drop system.

```
DropTarget target = new DropTarget(component, listener);
```

You can activate or deactivate the target with the setActive method. By default, the target is active.

```
target.setActive(b);
```

You can call the setDefaultActions method to set the following drop operations that you want to accept by default:

```
DndConstants.ACTION_COPY
DndConstants.ACTION_MOVE
DndConstants.ACTION_COPY_OR_MOVE
DndConstants.ACTION_LINK
```

By default, all operations are allowed.

Now you need to implement a drop target listener. The DropTargetListener interface has five methods:

```
void dragEnter(DropTargetDragEvent event)
void dragExit(DropTargetEvent event)
void dragOver(DropTargetDragEvent event)
void dropActionChanged(DropTargetDragEvent event)
void drop(DropTargetDropEvent event)
```

The dragEnter and dragExit methods are called when the cursor enters or exits the drop target component. In the dragEnter method, you can set the cursor shape to indicate whether the drop target is willing to accept the drop.

You don't usually worry about the dragExit method. However, if you built up some elaborate mechanism for visual feedback, then you can dispose of it in this method.

The dragOver method is called continuously as the user moves the mouse over the drop target component. You can use it to give detailed visual feedback about the effect of a drop. For example, if the drop target is a tree component, you can highlight the node under the cursor or even open up a subtree if the cursor hovers over a node.

The dropActionChanged method is called if the user changes the action gesture. For example, if the user presses or lifts the SHIFT or CTRL keys while moving the mouse over the drop target component, then this method is called. That gives you a chance to modify the visual feedback and match it to the changed action.

The most important method is the drop method. It is called when the user has committed to a drop by finishing the drop gesture, usually by releasing the mouse button. Note that this method is called whether or not you previously indicated that you would accept the drop.

Look carefully at the parameters of the DropTargetListener methods. Three of them are a DropTargetDragEvent. However, the drop method receives a DropTargetDropEvent, and the dragExit method receives a DropTargetEvent. The DropTargetEvent class is the superclass of the other two event classes. It has only one method, getDropTargetContext, which returns a class with no interesting public methods. Since the purpose of a dragExit method is to clean up, you probably won't even look at the parameter.

The DropTargetDragEvent and DropTargetDropEvent classes each have the following methods:

```
int getDropAction()
Point getLocation()
DataFlavor[] getCurrentDataFlavors()
boolean isDataFlavorSupported(DataFlavor flavor)
```

You need these methods to test whether to encourage a drag or allow a drop, and to specify how to give visual feedback.

Unfortunately, because the methods are not available in the common superclass, you'll have to implement the test logic twice, once for the drag and then again for the drop.

If you don't want to encourage a drag, you call the rejectDrag method of the DropTargetDragEvent class in the dragEnter or dropActionChanged method. As a result, the cursor changes to a warning icon. If the user drops an item despite the warning, then you call the rejectDrop method of the DropTargetDropEvent class.

The getDropAction method returns the drop action that the user intends to carry out. In many drag and drop operations, you don't want the action taken literally. For example, if you move a file icon into WordPad, then you don't want the drag source to delete the file. But you also don't want the drop target to insist that the user hold down a key when dragging. In this situation, the drop target should accept either copy or move actions. In the drop method, call the acceptDrop method of the DropTargetDropEvent with the *actual* action. If you call

```
event.acceptDrop(DnDConstants.ACTION_MOVE); // drag source deletes dragged items!
```

then the drag source will *delete* the dragged items.

TIP: Are you certain that your users understand the distinction between move and copy operations and the role of the SHIFT and CTRL modifiers? Do they realize that the default drag gesture (without a modifier) deletes the dragged items from the source? If not, you should accept a drop as

```
event.acceptDrop(DnDConstants.ACTION_COPY);
```

On the other hand, if you really want to make a distinction between move and copy, simply call

```
event.acceptDrop(event.getDropAction()).
```

Here is an overview of a typical drop target listener:

```
class ADropTargetListener implements DropTargetListener
{
   // convenience methods
   public boolean isDragAcceptable(DropTargetDragEvent event)
   {
      look at drop action and available data flavors
   }

   public boolean isDropAcceptable(DropTargetDropEvent event)
   {
      carry out the same test as in isDragAcceptable
   }

   // listener methods
   public void dragEnter(DropTargetDragEvent event)
   {
      if (!isDragAcceptable(event))
      {
         event.rejectDrag();
         return;
      }
   }

   public void dragExit(DropTargetEvent event)
   {
   }

   public void dragOver(DropTargetDragEvent event)
```

```
   {
      // you can provide visual feedback here
   }

   public void dropActionChanged(DropTargetDragEvent event)
   {
      if (!isDragAcceptable(event))
      {
         event.rejectDrag();
         return;
      }
   }

   public void drop(DropTargetDropEvent event)
   {
      if (!isDropAcceptable(event))
      {
         event.rejectDrop();
         return;
      }
      event.acceptDrop(actual action);
      process data from drag source
      event.dropComplete(true);
   }
   . . .
}
```

Once you accept a drop, you need to analyze the data from the drag source. The getTransferable method of the DropTargetDropEvent class returns a reference to a Transferable object. This is the same interface that is used for copy and paste.

One data type that is more commonly used for drag and drop than for copy and paste is the DataFlavor.javaFileListFlavor. A file list describes a set of file icons that was dropped onto the target. The Transferable object yields an object of type java.util.List whose items are File objects. Here is the code for retrieving the files:

```
DataFlavor[] flavors = transferable.getTransferDataFlavors();
DataFlavor flavor = flavors[i];
if (flavor.equals(DataFlavor.javaFileListFlavor))
{
   java.util.List<File> fileList = (java.util.List<File>) transferable.getTransferData(flavor);
   Iterator iterator = fileList.iterator();
   for (File f : fileList)
   {
      do something with f;
   }
}
```

Another flavor that can be dropped is text. You can retrieve the text in various flavors. The most convenient is DataFlavor.stringFlavor. The other flavors have a MIME type of text/plain and a variety of representation classes, including InputStream and [B (byte array).

 CAUTION: Earlier versions of the Java platform did not go through the effort of converting dragged text to Unicode and giving you a stringFlavor. Instead, you had to retrieve the text through an InputStream. The text/plain MIME type contains a charset parameter that indicates the character encoding. To compound the inconvenience, those Java platform versions also

used character encoding names that were different from the names that the InputStreamReader constructor expects. In particular, you had to convert ascii to ISO-8859-1 and unicode to Unicode.

Under Windows, you ran into additional problems. The end of input was indicated by a null character, and you should not read past it. The Unicode data didn't start with a Unicode byte order marker that the InputStreamReader expects, resulting in a sun.io.MalformedInputException. Thus, programmers had to bypass the InputStreamReader and construct the Unicode characters from pairs of bytes.

Fortunately, these growing pains have been overcome in JDK 1.4.

Depending on the drag source, you might also find data in other formats such as

```
text/html
text/rtf
```

To read the data in that format, pick a convenient flavor, for example, an input stream, and obtain the data like this:

```
if (flavor.isMimeTypeEqual("text/html") && flavor.getRepresentationClass() == InputStream.class)
{
    String charset = flavor.getParameter("charset");
    InputStreamReader in = new InputStreamReader(transferable.getTransferData(flavor), charset);
    read data from in
}
```

Our sample program does not attempt to do anything useful. It simply lets you drop items onto a text area. When you start dragging over the text area, the drop action is displayed. Once you initiate a drop, the dropped data are displayed. If the data are in text format, the program reads both ascii and unicode encodings.

In our sample program, we do not give any visual feedback of the dragging process beyond the change to a warning cursor that automatically happens when the rejectDrag method is called.

This program simply gives you a drop target for experimentation. Try dropping a selection of file names from Windows Explorer or a text fragment from WordPad (see Figure 7–53). Also see how a link attempt is rejected. If you press both the SHIFT and CTRL keys, then a warning icon appears when you drag an item over the text area.

Example 7–20 shows the complete program.

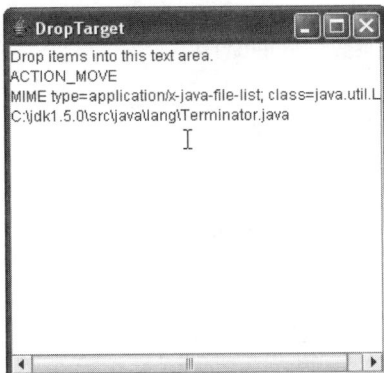

Figure 7–53: The DropTargetTest program

Example 7–20: DropTargetTest.java

```java
1.  import java.awt.*;
2.  import java.awt.datatransfer.*;
3.  import java.awt.event.*;
4.  import java.awt.dnd.*;
5.  import java.io.*;
6.  import java.util.*;
7.  import javax.swing.*;
8.
9.  /**
10.    This is a test class to test drag and drop behavior. Drop items into the text area to see the
11.    MIME types of the drop target.
12.  */
13.  public class DropTargetTest
14.  {
15.     public static void main(String[] args)
16.     {
17.        JFrame frame = new DropTargetFrame();
18.        frame.setDefaultCloseOperation(JFrame.EXIT_ON_CLOSE);
19.        frame.setVisible(true);
20.     }
21.  }
22.
23.  /**
24.    This frame contains a text area that is a simple drop target.
25.  */
26.  class DropTargetFrame extends JFrame
27.  {
28.     public DropTargetFrame()
29.     {
30.        setTitle("DropTarget");
31.        setSize(DEFAULT_WIDTH, DEFAULT_HEIGHT);
32.
33.        JTextArea textArea = new JTextArea("Drop items into this text area.\n");
34.
35.        new DropTarget(textArea, new TextDropTargetListener(textArea));
36.        add(new JScrollPane(textArea), "Center");
37.     }
38.
39.     private static final int DEFAULT_WIDTH = 300;
40.     private static final int DEFAULT_HEIGHT = 300;
41.  }
42.
43.  /**
44.    This listener displays the properties of a dropped object.
45.  */
46.  class TextDropTargetListener implements DropTargetListener
47.  {
48.     /**
49.        Constructs a listener.
50.        @param aTextArea the text area in which to display the
51.        properties of the dropped object.
52.     */
53.     public TextDropTargetListener(JTextArea aTextArea)
54.     {
```

```
55.     textArea = aTextArea;
56.   }
57.
58.   public void dragEnter(DropTargetDragEvent event)
59.   {
60.      int a = event.getDropAction();
61.      if ((a & DnDConstants.ACTION_COPY) != 0)
62.         textArea.append("ACTION_COPY\n");
63.      if ((a & DnDConstants.ACTION_MOVE) != 0)
64.         textArea.append("ACTION_MOVE\n");
65.      if ((a & DnDConstants.ACTION_LINK) != 0)
66.         textArea.append("ACTION_LINK\n");
67.
68.      if (!isDragAcceptable(event))
69.      {
70.         event.rejectDrag();
71.         return;
72.      }
73.   }
74.
75.   public void dragExit(DropTargetEvent event)
76.   {
77.   }
78.
79.   public void dragOver(DropTargetDragEvent event)
80.   {
81.      // you can provide visual feedback here
82.   }
83.
84.   public void dropActionChanged(DropTargetDragEvent event)
85.   {
86.      if (!isDragAcceptable(event))
87.      {
88.         event.rejectDrag();
89.         return;
90.      }
91.   }
92.
93.   public void drop(DropTargetDropEvent event)
94.   {
95.      if (!isDropAcceptable(event))
96.      {
97.         event.rejectDrop();
98.         return;
99.      }
100.
101.     event.acceptDrop(DnDConstants.ACTION_COPY);
102.
103.     Transferable transferable = event.getTransferable();
104.
105.     DataFlavor[] flavors = transferable.getTransferDataFlavors();
106.     for (int i = 0; i < flavors.length; i++)
107.     {
108.        DataFlavor d = flavors[i];
109.        textArea.append("MIME type=" + d.getMimeType() + "\n");
110.
```

```
111.         try
112.         {
113.            if (d.equals(DataFlavor.javaFileListFlavor))
114.            {
115.               java.util.List<File> fileList
116.                  = (java.util.List<File>) transferable.getTransferData(d);
117.               for (File f : fileList)
118.               {
119.                  textArea.append(f + "\n");
120.               }
121.            }
122.            else if (d.equals(DataFlavor.stringFlavor))
123.            {
124.               String s = (String) transferable.getTransferData(d);
125.               textArea.append(s + "\n");
126.            }
127.         }
128.         catch (Exception e)
129.         {
130.            textArea.append(e + "\n");
131.         }
132.      }
133.      textArea.append("\n");
134.      event.dropComplete(true);
135.   }
136.
137.   public boolean isDragAcceptable(DropTargetDragEvent event)
138.   {
139.      // usually, you check the available data flavors here
140.      // in this program, we accept all flavors
141.      return (event.getDropAction() & DnDConstants.ACTION_COPY_OR_MOVE) != 0;
142.   }
143.
144.   public boolean isDropAcceptable(DropTargetDropEvent event)
145.   {
146.      // usually, you check the available data flavors here
147.      // in this program, we accept all flavors
148.      return (event.getDropAction() & DnDConstants.ACTION_COPY_OR_MOVE) != 0;
149.   }
150.
151.   private JTextArea textArea;
152. }
```

---

java.awt.dnd.DropTarget 1.2

- DropTarget(Component c, DropTargetListener listener)
  constructs a drop target that coordinates the drag and drop action onto
  a component.

  Parameters: c   The drop target

                  listener   The listener to be notified in the drop process

- void setActive(boolean b)
  activates or deactivates this drop target.

- void setDefaultActions(int actions)

  sets the actions that are permissible by default for this drop target. actions is a bit mask composed of constants defined in the DnDConstants class such as ACTION_COPY, ACTION_MOVE, ACTION_COPY_OR_MOVE, or ACTION_LINK.

java.awt.dnd.DropTargetListener 1.2

- void dragEnter(DropTargetDragEvent event)

  is called when the cursor enters the drop target.

- void dragExit(DropTargetEvent event)

  is called when the cursor exits the drop target.

- void dragOver(DropTargetDragEvent event)

  is called when the cursor moves over the drop target.

- void dropActionChanged(DropTargetDragEvent event)

  is called when the user changes the drop action while the cursor is over the drop target.

- void drop(DropTargetDropEvent event)

  is called when the user drops items into the drop target.

java.awt.dnd.DropTargetDragEvent 1.2

- int getDropAction()

  gets the currently selected drop action. Possible values are defined in the DnDConstants class.

- void acceptDrag(int action)

  should be called if the drop target wants to accept a drop action that is different from the currently selected action.

- void rejectDrag()

  notifies the drag and drop mechanism that this component rejects the current drop attempt.

- Point getLocation()

  returns the current location of the mouse over the drop target.

- DataFlavor[] getCurrentDataFlavors()

  returns the data flavors that the drag source can deliver.

- boolean isDataFlavorSupported(DataFlavor flavor)

  tests whether drag source supports the given flavor.

- Transferable getTransferable() 5.0

  gets the Transferable object that represents the dragged value.

java.awt.dnd.DropTargetDropEvent 1.2

- int getDropAction()

  gets the currently selected drop action. Possible values are defined in the DnDConstants class.

- void acceptDrop(int action)

  should be called if the drop target has carried out a drop action that is different from the currently selected action.

- void rejectDrop()

  notifies the drag and drop mechanism that this component rejects the drop.

- void dropComplete(boolean success)

  notifies the drag source that the drop is complete and that it was or was not successful.

- `Point getLocation()`
  returns the current location of the mouse over the drop target.
- `DataFlavor[] getCurrentDataFlavors()`
  returns the data flavors that the drag source can deliver.
- `boolean isDataFlavorSupported(DataFlavor flavor)`
  tests whether the drag source supports the given flavor.

Drag Sources

Now that you saw how to implement a program that contains a drop target, we show you how to implement a drag source.

The program in Example 7–21 fills a `JList` with all files in the current directory (see Figure 7–54). The list component is a drag source. You can drag file items from the list component to any drop target that is willing to accept a list of files.

To turn a component into a drag source, obtain a `DragSource` object—you can simply call the static `DragSource.getDefaultDragSource` method. Then, call the `createDefaultDragGestureRecognizer` method and supply it with

- The component that you want to turn into a drag source;
- The drop actions that you want to allow; and
- An object that implements the `DragGestureListener` interface.

For example,

```
DragSource dragSource = DragSource.getDefaultDragSource();
dragSource.createDefaultDragGestureRecognizer(component,
    DnDConstants.ACTION_COPY_OR_MOVE, dragGestureListener);
```

The `DragGestureListener` interface has a single method, `dragGestureRecognized`. The gesture recognizer calls that method as soon as it has noticed that the user wants to initiate a drag operation. In that method, you build the `Transferable` object that the drop target will ultimately read in its `drop` method. Once you have assembled the `Transferable` object, you call the `startDrag` method of the `DragGestureEvent` class. You supply an optional cursor, or `null` if you want to use the default drag cursor, followed by the `Transferable` object and an object that implements the `DragSourceListener` interface. For example,

```
event.startDrag(null, transferable, dragSourceListener);
```

You then do the usual busywork of defining a `Transferable` wrapper—see the code in the example program for details.

The drag source listener is notified repeatedly as the drag operation progresses. The interface has five methods:

```
void dragEnter(DragSourceDragEvent event)
void dragOver(DragSourceDragEvent event)
void dragExit(DragSourceEvent event)
void dropActionChanged(DragSourceDragEvent event)
void dragDropEnd(DragSourceDropEvent event)
```

You can use the first four methods to give the user visual feedback of the drag operation. However, generally, such feedback should be the role of the drop target. Only the last method, `dragDropEnd`, is important. This method is called when the `drop` method has finished. For a move operation, you check whether the drop has succeeded. In that case, you update the drag source. (For a copy operation, you probably don't have to do anything.)

 NOTE: JDK 1.4 introduces a `DragSourceAdapter` helper class that implements all methods of the `DragSourceListener` interface as do-nothing methods.

Here is the dragDropEnd method for our example program. When a move has succeeded, we remove the moved items from the list model.

```
public void dragDropEnd(DragSourceDropEvent event)
{
    if (event.getDropSuccess())
    {
        int action = event.getDropAction();
        if (action == DnDConstants.ACTION_MOVE)
        {
            for (Object v : draggedValues)
                model.removeElement(v);
        }
    }
}
```

In this method, we rely on the drop method to tell us what drop was actually carried out. Recall that the drop method can change a move action to a copy action if the source allowed both actions. The event.getDropAction of the DragSourceDropEvent class returns the action that the drop target reported when calling the acceptDrop method of the DropTargetDropEvent.

Try out the program in Example 7–21 and drag file items to various drop targets, such as the program in Example 7–20 or a native program such as Windows Explorer or WordPad.

 NOTE: When you try the dragging, be careful that the drag gesture doesn't interfere with the normal mouse effects of the list control. Select one or more items. Press the mouse button on a selected item and move the mouse *sideways*, until it leaves the list component. Now the drag gesture is recognized. *After* the mouse has left the list component, press the SHIFT or CTRL key to modify the drop action.

 CAUTION: The default drop action is a *move*. If you drag a file item from the list component and drop it into Windows Explorer, then Explorer moves the file into the target folder.

As you have seen, support for the system clipboard and the drag and drop mechanism are still very much a work in progress. The basics work on all platforms, but future versions of the Java platform will, we hope, offer more robust and comprehensive support.

In this section, we have covered the basic mechanics of the drag and drop mechanism. For more information, particularly about programming visual feedback, we recommend *Core Swing: Advanced Programming* by Kim Topley [Prentice Hall 1999].

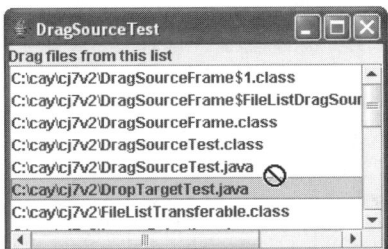

Figure 7–54: The DragSourceTest program

Example 7–21: DragSourceTest.java

```java
1. import java.awt.*;
2. import java.awt.datatransfer.*;
3. import java.awt.dnd.*;
4. import java.awt.event.*;
5. import java.io.*;
6. import java.util.*;
7. import java.util.List;
8. import javax.swing.*;
9.
10.
11. /**
12.    This is a sample drag source for testing purposes. It consists of a list of files
13.    in the current directory.
14. */
15. public class DragSourceTest
16. {
17.    public static void main(String[] args)
18.    {
19.       JFrame frame = new DragSourceFrame();
20.       frame.setDefaultCloseOperation(JFrame.EXIT_ON_CLOSE);
21.       frame.setVisible(true);
22.    }
23. }
24.
25. /**
26.    This frame contains a list of files in the current
27.    directory with support for dragging files to a drop target.
28.    Moved files are removed from the list.
29. */
30. class DragSourceFrame extends JFrame
31. {
32.    public DragSourceFrame()
33.    {
34.       setTitle("DragSourceTest");
35.       setSize(DEFAULT_WIDTH, DEFAULT_HEIGHT);
36.
37.       File f = new File(".").getAbsoluteFile();
38.       File[] files = f.listFiles();
39.       model = new DefaultListModel();
40.       for (File file : files)
41.          try
42.          {
43.             model.addElement(file.getCanonicalFile());
44.          }
45.          catch (IOException e)
46.          {
47.             JOptionPane.showMessageDialog(this, e);
48.          }
49.       fileList = new JList(model);
50.       add(new JScrollPane(fileList), BorderLayout.CENTER);
51.       add(new JLabel("Drag files from this list"), BorderLayout.NORTH);
52.
53.       DragSource dragSource = DragSource.getDefaultDragSource();
54.       dragSource.createDefaultDragGestureRecognizer(fileList,
```

```
55.          DnDConstants.ACTION_COPY_OR_MOVE, new
56.             DragGestureListener()
57.             {
58.                public void dragGestureRecognized(DragGestureEvent event)
59.                {
60.                   draggedValues = fileList.getSelectedValues();
61.                   Transferable transferable = new FileListTransferable(draggedValues);
62.                   event.startDrag(null, transferable, new FileListDragSourceListener());
63.                }
64.          });
65.    }
66.
67.    /**
68.       A drag source listener that removes moved files from the file list.
69.    */
70.    private class FileListDragSourceListener
71.       extends DragSourceAdapter
72.    {
73.       public void dragDropEnd(DragSourceDropEvent event)
74.       {
75.          if (event.getDropSuccess())
76.          {
77.             int action = event.getDropAction();
78.             if (action == DnDConstants.ACTION_MOVE)
79.             {
80.                for (Object v : draggedValues)
81.                   model.removeElement(v);
82.             }
83.          }
84.       }
85.    }
86.
87.    private JList fileList;
88.    private DefaultListModel model;
89.    private Object[] draggedValues;
90.    private static final int DEFAULT_WIDTH = 300;
91.    private static final int DEFAULT_HEIGHT = 200;
92. }
93.
94. class FileListTransferable implements Transferable
95. {
96.    public FileListTransferable(Object[] files)
97.    {
98.       fileList = new ArrayList<Object>(Arrays.asList(files));
99.    }
100.
101.   public DataFlavor[] getTransferDataFlavors()
102.   {
103.      return flavors;
104.   }
105.
106.   public boolean isDataFlavorSupported(DataFlavor flavor)
107.   {
108.      return Arrays.asList(flavors).contains(flavor);
109.   }
110.
```

```
111.   public Object getTransferData(DataFlavor flavor)
112.      throws UnsupportedFlavorException
113.   {
114.      if(flavor.equals(DataFlavor.javaFileListFlavor))
115.         return fileList;
116.      else if(flavor.equals(DataFlavor.stringFlavor))
117.         return fileList.toString();
118.      else
119.         throw new UnsupportedFlavorException(flavor);
120.   }
121.
122.   private static DataFlavor[] flavors =
123.   {
124.      DataFlavor.javaFileListFlavor,
125.      DataFlavor.stringFlavor
126.   };
127.
128.   private java.util.List<Object> fileList;
129. }
```

 java.awt.dnd.DragSource 1.2

- static DragSource getDefaultDragSource()
  gets a DragSource object to coordinate drag actions on components.

- DragGestureRecognizer createDefaultDragGestureRecognizer(Component component, int actions,
  DragGestureListener listener)
  creates a drag gesture recognizer.

Parameters:	component	The drag source
	actions	The permissible drop actions
	listener	The listener to be notified when a drag gesture has been recognized

 java.awt.dnd.DragGestureListener 1.2

- void dragGestureRecognized(DragGestureEvent event)
  is called when the drag gesture recognizer has recognized a gesture.

java.awt.dnd.DragGestureEvent 1.2

- void startDrag(Cursor dragCursor, Transferable transferable, DragSourceListener listener)
  starts the drag action.

Parameters:	dragCursor	An optional cursor to use for the drag; may be null, in which case a default cursor is used
	transferable	The data to be transferred to the drop target
	listener	The listener to be notified of the drag process

 java.awt.dnd.DragSourceListener 1.2

- void dragEnter(DragSourceDragEvent event)
  is called when the drag cursor enters the drag source.

- void dragExit(DragSourceEvent event)
  is called when the drag cursor exits the drag source.

- void dragOver(DragSourceDragEvent event)
  is called when the drag cursor moves over the drag source.
- void dropActionChanged(DragSourceDragEvent event)
  is called when the user changes the drop action.
- void dragDropEnd(DragSourceDropEvent event)
  is called after the drag and drop operation is completed or canceled.

 java.awt.dnd.DragSourceDropEvent 1.2

- boolean getDropSuccess()
  returns true if the drop target reported a successful drop.
- int getDropAction()
  returns the action that the drop target actually carried out.

Data Transfer Support in Swing

Starting with JDK 1.4, Swing components have built-in support for data transfer. That frees programmers from much of the burden of implementing copy and paste or drag and drop.

For example, start the TableSelectionTest program from Chapter 6 and highlight a range of cells. Then press CTRL+C and paste the clipboard contents into a text editor. The result is HTML-formatted text like this:

```
<html>
<table>
<tr>
  <th id=2>C
  <th id=3>D
  <th id=4>E
  <th id=5>F
<tr id=3>
  <td>12
  <td>16
  <td>20
  <td>24
. . .
</table>
</html>
```

If you add the line

```
table.setDragEnabled(true);
```

after the table constructor and recompile the program, then you can drag the selection area to drop targets. The drop target receives the table selection as HTML-formatted data.

Table 7–6 summarizes the Swing components that are sources and targets for data transfer. The standard Cut, Copy, and Paste keyboard shortcuts are enabled for all components except the JColorChooser. Dragging is not enabled by default. You must call the setDragEnabled method to activate it.

Table 7–6: Data Transfer Support in Swing Components

Component	Transfer Source	Transfer Target
JFileChooser	Exports file list	N/A
JColorChooser	Exports local reference to color object	Accepts any color object

Table 7–6: Data Transfer Support in Swing Components (continued)

Component	Transfer Source	Transfer Target
JTextField JFormattedTextField	Exports selected text	Accepts text
JPasswordField	N/A (for security)	Accepts text
JTextArea JTextPane JEditorPane	Exports selected text	Accepts text and file lists. Text is inserted. Files are opened.
JList JTable JTree	Exports HTML description of selection	N/A

The Swing package provides a potentially useful mechanism to quickly turn a component into a drop target. If the component has a method

```
void setName(Type t)
```

then you turn it into a drop target for data flavors with representation class Type simply by calling

```
component.setTransferHandler(new TransferHandler("name"));
```

When a drop occurs, then the transfer handler checks whether one of the data flavors has representation class *Type*. If so, it invokes the set*Name* method.

 NOTE: In JavaBeans terminology, the transfer handler sets the value of the *name* property. JavaBeans component properties are covered in Chapter 8.

For example, suppose you want to use drag and drop to change the background color of a text field. You need a transfer handler that invokes the method

```
void setBackground(Color c)
```

when a Color object is dragged onto the text field. Simply call

```
textField.setTransferHandler(new TransferHandler("background"));
```

Example 7–22 demonstrates this behavior. As you can see in Figure 7–55, the top of the frame contains a color chooser, and the bottom, a text field with the text "Drag color here." You drag the color from the inside of the Preview panel, not from one of the color swatches. When you drag it onto the text field, its background color changes.

 CAUTION: By installing this transfer handler into the text field, you disable the standard transfer handler. You can no longer cut, copy, paste, drag, or drop text in the text field. A Swing component can have only one transfer handler.

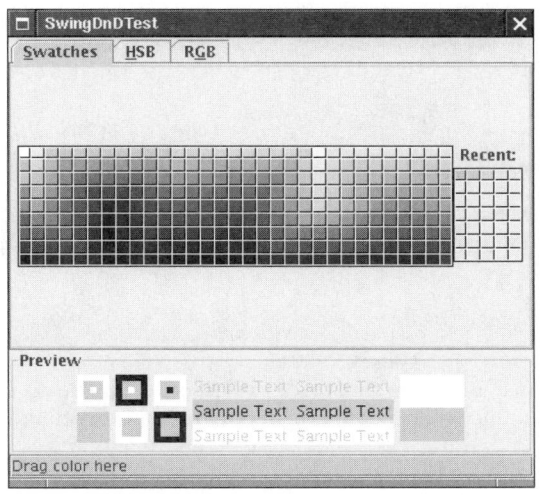

Figure 7–55: The Swing drag and drop test program

Example 7–22: SwingDnDTest.java

```
 1. import java.awt.*;
 2. import javax.swing.*;
 3.
 4. /**
 5.    This program demonstrates how to easily add data transfer
 6.    capabilities to Swing components. Drag a color from the
 7.    "Preview" panel of the color chooser into the text field.
 8. */
 9. public class SwingDnDTest
10. {
11.    public static void main(String[] args)
12.    {
13.       JFrame frame = new SwingDnDFrame();
14.       frame.setDefaultCloseOperation(JFrame.EXIT_ON_CLOSE);
15.       frame.setVisible(true);
16.    }
17. }
18.
19. /**
20.    This frame contains a color chooser and a text field. Dragging
21.    a color into the text field changes its background color.
22. */
23. class SwingDnDFrame extends JFrame
24. {
25.    public SwingDnDFrame()
26.    {
27.       setTitle("SwingDnDTest");
28.
29.       JColorChooser chooser = new JColorChooser();
30.       chooser.setDragEnabled(true);
31.       add(chooser, BorderLayout.CENTER);
32.       JTextField textField = new JTextField("Drag color here");
33.       textField.setDragEnabled(true);
```

```
34.    textField.setTransferHandler(new TransferHandler("background"));
35.    add(textField, BorderLayout.SOUTH);
36.    pack();
37.    }
38. }
```

 javax.swing.JComponent 1.2

- void setTransferHandler(TransferHandler handler) **1.4**
  sets a transfer handler to handle data transfer operations (cut, copy, paste, drag, drop).

 javax.swing.TransferHandler 1.4

- TransferHandler(String propertyName)
  constructs a transfer handler that reads or writes the JavaBeans component property with the given name when a data transfer operation is executed.

 javx.swing.JFileChooser 1.2

 javax.swing.JColorChooser 1.2

 javax.swing.JTextComponent 1.2

 javax.swing.JList 1.2

 javax.swing.JTable 1.2

 javax.swing.JTree 1.2

- void setDragEnabled(boolean b) **1.4**
  enables or disables dragging of data out of this component.

Chapter **8**

JavaBeans Components

- ▼ WHY BEANS?
- ▼ THE BEAN-WRITING PROCESS
- ▼ USING BEANS TO BUILD AN APPLICATION
- ▼ NAMING PATTERNS FOR BEAN PROPERTIES AND EVENTS
- ▼ BEAN PROPERTY TYPES
- ▼ BEANINFO CLASSES
- ▼ PROPERTY EDITORS
- ▼ CUSTOMIZERS
- ▼ JAVABEANS PERSISTENCE

The official definition of a bean, as given in the JavaBeans specification, is: "A bean is a reusable software component based on Sun's JavaBeans specification that can be manipulated visually in a builder tool."

Once you implement a bean, others can use it in a builder environment such as NetBeans or JBuilder to produce GUI applications more efficiently.

We do not tell you in detail how to use those environments—you should refer to the documentation that the vendors provide. This chapter explains what you need to know about beans in order to *implement* them so that other programmers can use your beans easily.

 NOTE: We'd like to address a common confusion before going any further: The JavaBeans that we discuss in this chapter have little in common with "Enterprise JavaBeans" or EJB. Enterprise JavaBeans are server-side components with support for transactions, persistence, replication, and security. At a very basic level, they too are components that can be manipulated in builder tools. However, the Enterprise JavaBeans technology is quite a bit more complex than the "Standard Edition" JavaBeans technology.

That does not mean that standard JavaBeans components are limited to client-side programming. Web technologies such as JavaServer Faces (JSF) and JavaServer Pages (JSP) rely heavily on the JavaBeans component model.

Why Beans?

Programmers coming from a Windows background (specifically, Visual Basic or C#) will immediately know why beans are so important. Programmers coming from an environment in which the tradition is to "roll your own" for everything may not understand at once. In

617

our experience, programmers who do not come from a Visual Basic background often find it hard to believe that Visual Basic is one of the most successful examples of reusable object technology. One reason for the popularity of Visual Basic becomes clear if you consider how you build a Visual Basic application. For those who have never worked with Visual Basic, here, in a nutshell, is how you do it:

1. You build the interface by dropping components (called *controls* in Visual Basic) onto a form window.

2. Through *property sheets,* you set properties of the components such as height, color, or other behavior.

3. The property sheets also list the events to which components can react. For some of those events, you write short snippets of event handling code.

For example, in Volume 1, Chapter 2, we wrote a program that displays an image in a frame. It took over a page of code. Here's what you would do in Visual Basic to create a program with pretty much the same functionality:

1. Add two controls to a window: an *Image* control for displaying graphics and a *Common Dialog* control for selecting a file.

2. Set the *Filter* properties of the CommonDialog control so that only files that the Image control can handle will show up. This is done in what Visual Basic calls the Properties window, as shown in Figure 8–1.

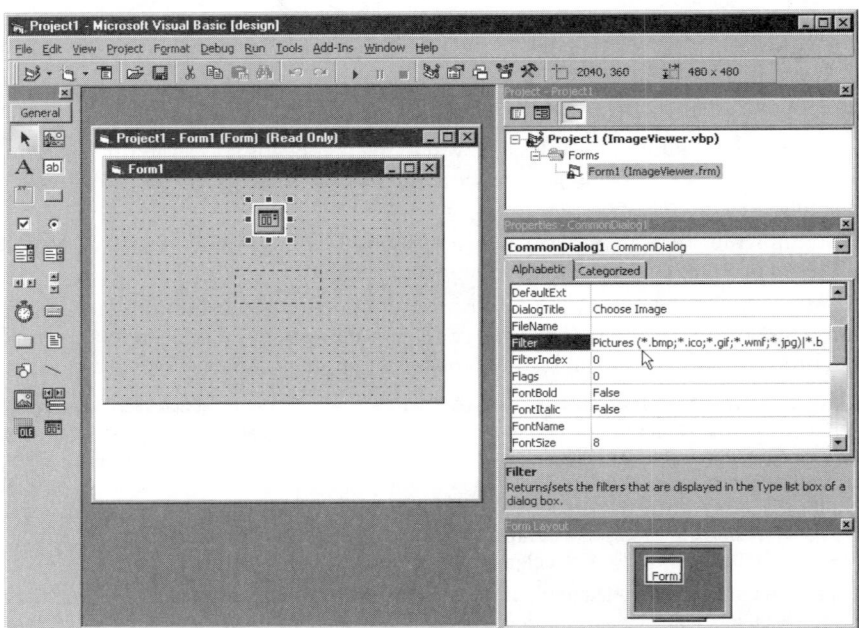

Figure 8–1: The Properties window in Visual Basic for an image application

Now, we need to write the four lines of Visual Basic code that will be activated when the project first starts running. The following code pops up the file dialog box—but only files with the right extension are shown because of how we set the filter property. After the user selects an image file, the code then tells the Image control to display it. All the code you need for this sequence looks like this:

```
Private Sub Form_Load()
  CommonDialog1.ShowOpen
  Image1.Picture = LoadPicture(CommonDialog1.FileName)
End Sub
```

That's it. The layout activity, combined with these statements, gives essentially the same functionality as a page of Java code. Clearly, it is a lot easier to learn how to drop down components and set properties than it is to write a page of code.

We do not want to imply that Visual Basic is a good solution for every problem. It is clearly optimized for a particular kind of problem—UI-intensive Windows programs. The Java-Beans technology was invented to make Java technology competitive in this arena. It enables vendors to create Visual Basic-style environments for developing Java user interfaces with a minimum of programming.

The Bean-Writing Process

Most of the rest of this chapter shows you the techniques that you use to write beans. Before we go into details, we give an overview of the process. First, we want to stress that writing a bean is not technically difficult—there are only a few new classes and interfaces for you to master.

In particular, the simplest kind of bean is really nothing more than a Java class that follows some fairly strict naming conventions for its methods.

 NOTE: Some authors claim that a bean must have a default constructor. The JavaBeans specification is actually silent on this issue. However, most builder tools require a default constructor for each bean, so that they can instantiate beans without construction parameters.

Example 8–1 at the end of this section shows the code for an ImageViewer bean that could give a Java builder environment the same functionality as the Visual Basic image control we mentioned in the previous section. When you look at this code, notice that the ImageViewerBean class really doesn't look any different from any other class. For example, all accessor methods begin with get, and all mutator methods begin with set. As you will soon see, builder tools use this standard naming convention to discover *properties*. For example, file-Name is a property of this bean because it has get and set methods.

Note that a property is not the same as an instance field. In this particular example, the fileName property is computed from the file instance field. Properties are conceptually at a higher level than instance fields—they are features of the interface, whereas instance fields belong to the implementation of the class.

One point that you need to keep in mind when you read through the examples in this chapter is that real-world beans are much more elaborate and tedious to code than our brief examples, for two reasons.

1. Beans must be usable by less-than-expert programmers. You need to expose *lots of properties* so that your users can access most of the functionality of your bean with a visual design tool and without programming.

2. The same bean must be usable in a wide *variety of contexts*. Both the behavior and the appearance of your bean must be customizable. Again, this means exposing lots of properties.

A good example of a bean with rich behavior is CalendarBean by Kai Tödter (see Figure 8–2). The bean and its source code are freely available from http://www.toedter.com/en/jcalendar. This bean gives users a convenient way of entering dates, simply by locating them in a calendar

display. This is obviously pretty complex and not something one would want to program from scratch. By using a bean such as this one, you can take advantage of the work of others, simply by dropping the bean into a builder tool.

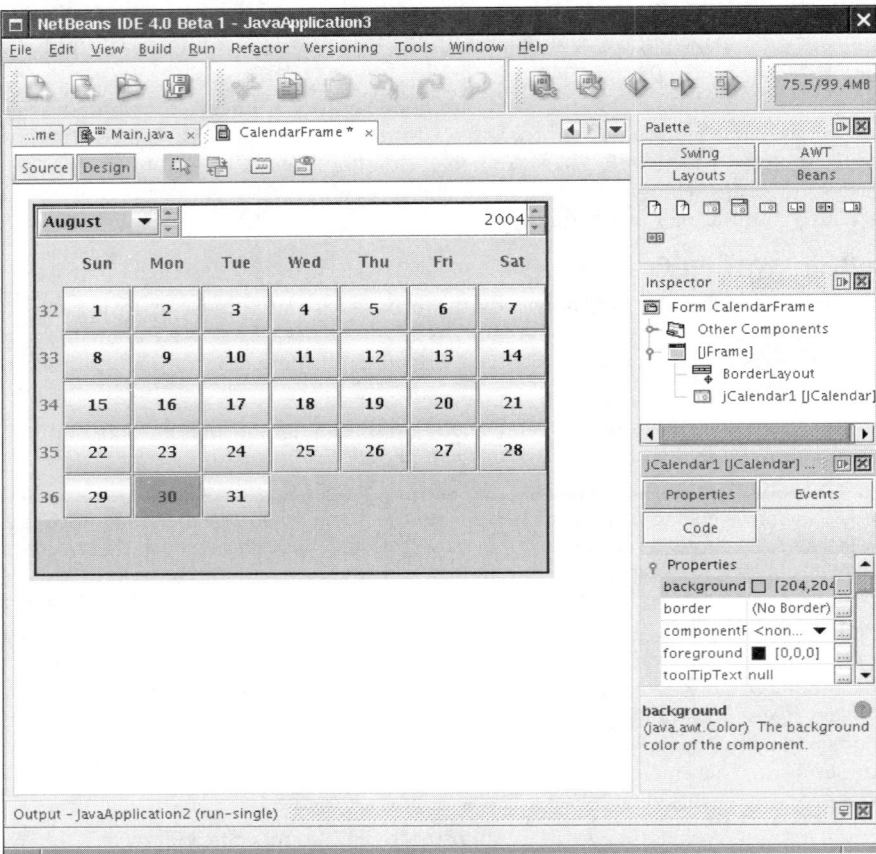

Figure 8–2: A calendar bean

Fortunately, you need to master only a small number of concepts to write beans with a rich set of behaviors. The example beans in this chapter, although not trivial, are kept simple enough to illustrate the necessary concepts.

Example 8–1: ImageViewerBean.java

```
 1. package com.horstmann.corejava;
 2.
 3. import java.awt.*;
 4. import java.io.*;
 5. import javax.imageio.*;
 6. import javax.swing.*;
 7.
 8. /**
 9.    A bean for viewing an image.
10. */
11. public class ImageViewerBean extends JLabel
```

```
12. {
13.
14.    public ImageViewerBean()
15.    {
16.       setBorder(BorderFactory.createEtchedBorder());
17.    }
18.
19.    /**
20.       Sets the fileName property.
21.       @param fileName the image file name
22.    */
23.    public void setFileName(String fileName)
24.    {
25.       try
26.       {
27.          file = new File(fileName);
28.          setIcon(new ImageIcon(ImageIO.read(file)));
29.       }
30.       catch (IOException e)
31.       {
32.          file = null;
33.          setIcon(null);
34.       }
35.    }
36.
37.    /**
38.       Gets the fileName property.
39.       @return the image file name
40.    */
41.    public String getFileName()
42.    {
43.       if (file == null) return null;
44.       else return file.getPath();
45.    }
46.
47.    public Dimension getPreferredSize()
48.    {
49.       return new Dimension(XPREFSIZE, YPREFSIZE);
50.    }
51.
52.    private File file = null;
53.    private static final int XPREFSIZE = 200;
54.    private static final int YPREFSIZE = 200;
55. }
```

Using Beans to Build an Application

Before we get into the mechanics of writing beans, we want you to see how you might use or test them. ImageViewerBean is a perfectly usable bean, but outside a builder environment it can't show off its special features. In particular, the only way to use it in an ordinary program in the Java programming language would be to write code that constructs an object of the bean class, places the object into a container, and calls the setFileName method. That's not rocket science, but it is more code than an overworked programmer may want to write. Builder environments aim to reduce the amount of drudgery that is involved in wiring together components into an application.

Each builder environment uses its own set of strategies to ease the programmer's life. We cover one environment, the NetBeans integrated development environment, available from

http://netbeans.org. We don't want to claim that NetBeans is better than other products—in fact, as you will see, it has its share of idiosyncrasies. We simply use NetBeans because it is a fairly typical programming environment and because it is freely available.

If you prefer another builder environment, you can still follow the steps of the next sections. The basic principles are the same for most environments. Of course, the details differ.

In this example, we use two beans, ImageViewerBean and FileNameBean. You have already seen the code for ImageViewerBean. The code for FileNameBean is a bit more sophisticated. We analyze it in depth later in this chapter. For now, all you have to know is that clicking the button with the "..." label opens a standard File Open dialog box where you can select a file.

Before we can go any further with showing you how to use these beans, we need to explain how to package the bean for import into a builder tool.

Packaging Beans in JAR Files

To make any bean usable in a builder tool, package into a JAR file all class files that are used by the bean code. Unlike the JAR files for an applet that you saw previously, a JAR file for a bean needs a manifest file that specifies which class files in the archive are beans and should be included in the Toolbox. For example, here is the manifest file ImageViewerBean.mf for ImageViewerBean.

```
Manifest-Version: 1.0

Name: com/horstmann/corejava/ImageViewerBean.class
Java-Bean: True
```

Note the blank line between the manifest version and bean name.

 NOTE: We place our example beans into the package com.horstmann.corejava because some builder environments have problems loading beans from the default package.

If your bean contains multiple class files, you just mention in the manifest those class files that are beans and that you want to have displayed in the Toolbox. For example, you could place ImageViewerBean and FileNameBean into the same JAR file and use the manifest

```
Manifest-Version: 1.0

Name: com/horstmann/corejava/ImageViewerBean.class
Java-Bean: True

Name: com/horstmann/corejava/FileNameBean.class
Java-Bean: True
```

 CAUTION: Some builder tools are extremely fussy about manifests. Make sure that there are no spaces after the ends of each line, that there are blank lines after the version and between bean entries, and that the last line ends in a newline.

To make the JAR file, follow these steps:

1. Edit the manifest file.
2. Gather all needed class files in a directory.
3. Run the jar tool as follows:
   ```
   jar cvfm JarFile ManifestFile ClassFiles
   ```
   For example,
   ```
   jar cvfm ImageViewerBean.jar ImageViewerBean.mf com/horstmann/corejava/*.class
   ```

You can also add other items, such as GIF files for icons, to the JAR file. We discuss bean icons later in this chapter.

 CAUTION: Make sure to include all files that your bean needs in the JAR file. In particular, pay attention to inner class files such as `FileNameBean$1.class`.

Builder environments have a mechanism for adding new beans, typically by loading JAR files. Here is what you do to import beans into NetBeans.

Compile the `ImageViewerBean` and `FileNameBean` classes and package them into JAR files. Then start NetBeans and follow these steps.

1. Select Tools -> Palette Manager from the menu.
2. Click the Add from JAR button.
3. In the file dialog box, move to the `ImageViewerBean` directory and select `ImageViewerBean.jar`.
4. Now a dialog box pops up that lists all the beans that were found in the JAR file. Select `ImageViewerBean`.
5. Finally, you are asked into which palette you want to place the beans. Select Beans. (There are other palettes for Swing components, AWT components, and so on.)
6. Have a look at the Beans palette. It now contains an icon representing the new bean However, the icon is just a default icon—you will see later how to add icons to a bean.

Repeat these steps with `FileNameBean`. Now you are ready to compose these beans into an application.

Composing Beans in a Builder Environment

In NetBeans, select File -> New Project from the menu. A dialog box pops up. Select Standard, then Java Application (see Figure 8–3).

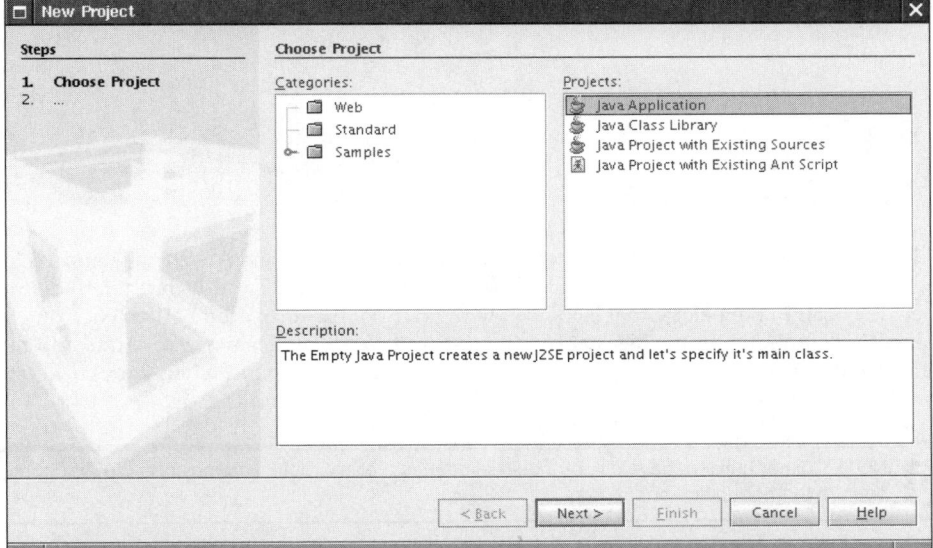

Figure 8–3: Creating a new project

Click the Next button. In the following screen, set a name for your application (such as ImageViewer), and click the Finish button. Now you see a project viewer on the left and the source code editor in the middle.

Right-click on the project name in the project viewer and select New -> JFrame Form from the menu (see Figure 8–4).

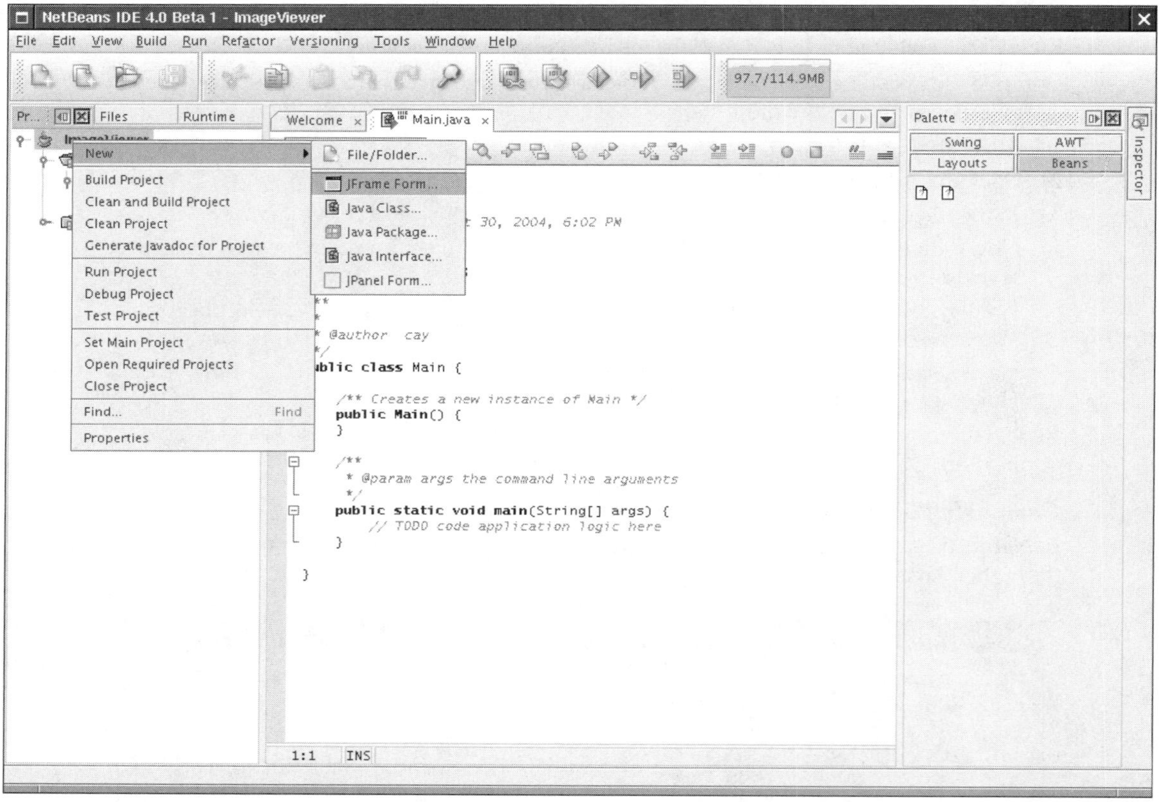

Figure 8–4: Creating a form view

A dialog box pops up. Enter a name for the frame class (such as ImageViewerFrame), and click the Finish button. You now get a form editor with a blank frame. To add a bean to the form, select the bean in the palette that is located to the right of the form editor. Then click on the frame. By default, the frame has a border layout, and NetBeans is smart enough to add the component to the center, north, south, east, or west position, depending on your click location. You can always change the layout position in the property editor.

> NOTE: Other builders have different user interfaces. For example, you may need to drag the bean to the right place on the form.

Figure 8–5 shows the result of adding an ImageViewerBean at the center position of the frame.

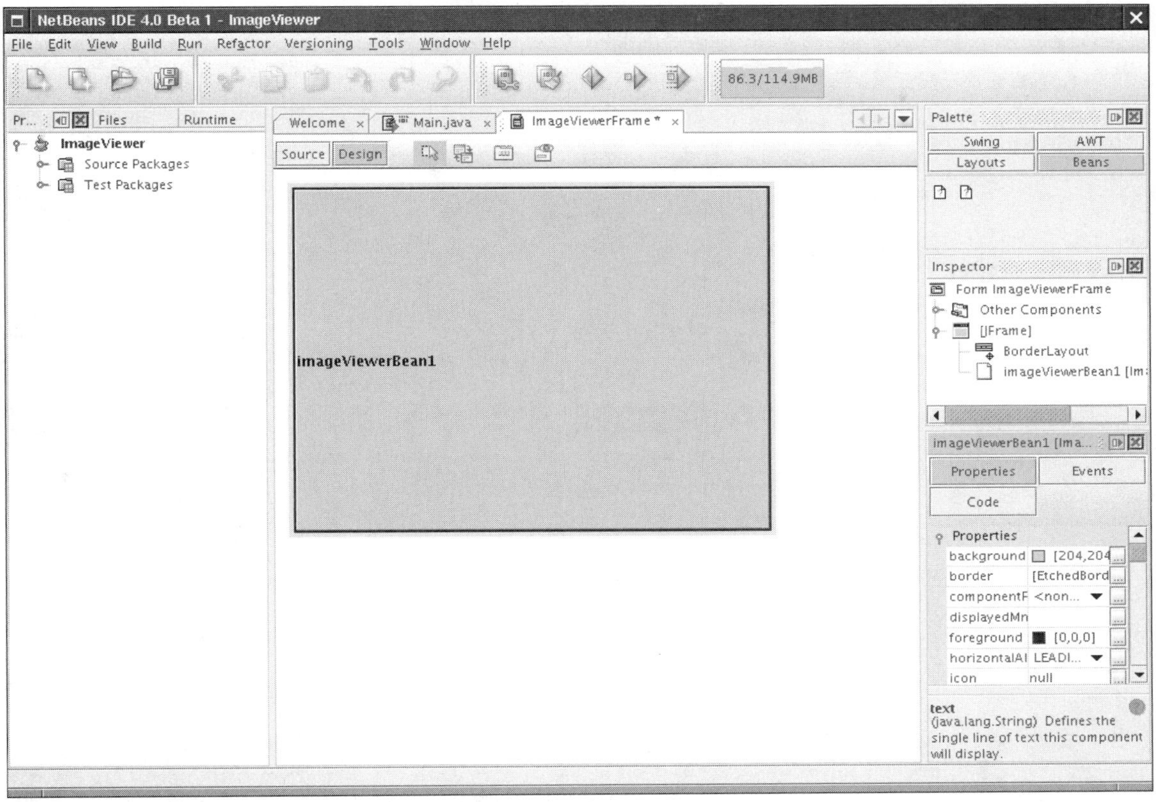

Figure 8–5: Adding a bean

If you look into the code editor window, you will find that the source code now contains the Java instructions to add the bean objects to the frame (see Figure 8–6). The source code is bracketed by dire warnings that you should not edit it. Any edits would be lost when the builder environment updates the code as you modify the form.

> NOTE: A builder environment is not required to update source code as you build an application. A builder environment may generate source code when you are done editing, serialize the beans you customized, or perhaps produce an entirely different description of your building activity.
>
> For example, the experimental Bean Builder at `http://bean-builder.dev.java.net` lets you design GUI applications without writing any source code at all.
>
> The JavaBeans mechanism doesn't attempt to force an implementation strategy on a builder tool. Instead, it aims to supply information about beans to builder tools that can choose to take advantage of the information in one way or another. In the following sections we show you how to program beans so that tools accurately discover that information.

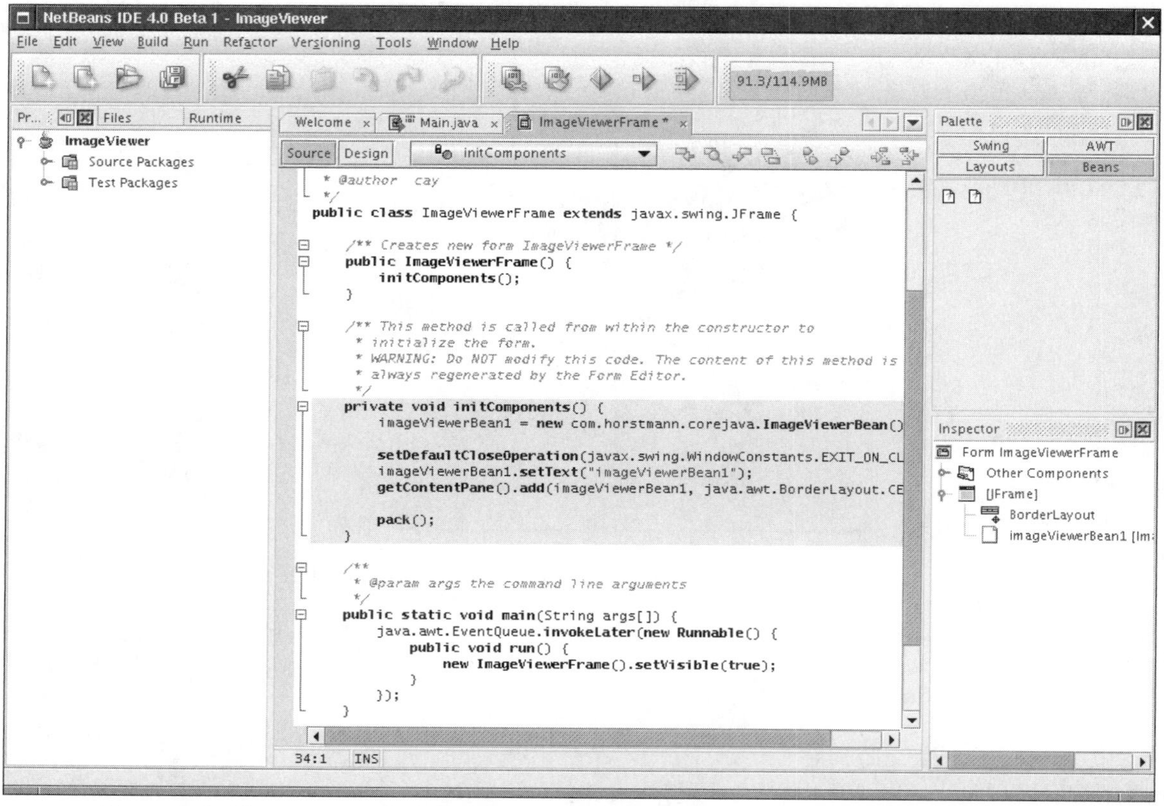

```
  NetBeans IDE 4.0 Beta 1 - ImageViewer                                                    X
File  Edit  View  Build  Run  Refactor  Versioning  Tools  Window  Help

                                                              91.3/114.9MB

Pr... 40 X  Files      Runtime     Welcome  x   Main.java  x   ImageViewerFrame *  x        Palette          D X
○   ImageViewer                  Source  Design      initComponents                          Swing      AWT
 ○   Source Packages                                                                        Layouts    Beans
 ○   Test Packages              * @author  cay
                               */
                             public class ImageViewerFrame extends javax.swing.JFrame {

                               /** Creates new form ImageViewerFrame */
                               public ImageViewerFrame() {
                                   initComponents();
                               }

                               /** This method is called from within the constructor to
                                * initialize the form.
                                * WARNING: Do NOT modify this code. The content of this method is
                                * always regenerated by the Form Editor.
                                */                                                          Inspector         D X
                               private void initComponents() {                              Form ImageViewerFrame
                                   imageViewerBean1 = new com.horstmann.corejava.ImageViewerBean() ○  Other Components
                                                                                           ○  [JFrame]
                                   setDefaultCloseOperation(javax.swing.WindowConstants.EXIT_ON_CL    BorderLayout
                                   imageViewerBean1.setText("imageViewerBean1");                  imageViewerBean1 [Im
                                   getContentPane().add(imageViewerBean1, java.awt.BorderLayout.CE

                                   pack();
                               }

                               /**
                                * @param args the command line arguments
                                */
                               public static void main(String args[]) {
                                   java.awt.EventQueue.invokeLater(new Runnable() {
                                       public void run() {
                                           new ImageViewerFrame().setVisible(true);
                                       }
                                   });
                               }
34:1    INS
```

Figure 8–6: The source code for adding the bean

Now go back to the form view and click ImageViewerBean in the form. On the right-hand side is a property inspector that lists the bean property names and their current values (see Figure 8–7). This is a vital part of component-based development tools since setting properties at design time is how you set the initial state of a component.

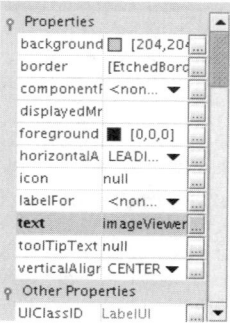

Figure 8–7: A property inspector

For example, you can modify the text property of the label used for the image bean by simply typing a new name into the property inspector. Changing the text property is simple—you just edit a string in a text field. Try it out—set the label text to "Hello". The form is immediately updated to reflect your change.

NOTE: When you change the setting of a property, the NetBeans environment updates the source code to reflect your action. For example, if you set the text field to Hello, the instruction

```
imageViewerBean.setText("Hello");
```

is added to the initComponents method. As already mentioned, other builder tools may have different strategies for recording property settings.

Properties don't have to be strings; they can be values of any Java type. To make it possible for users to set values for properties of any type, builder tools use specialized *property editors*. (Property editors either come with the builder or are supplied by the bean developer. You see how to write your own property editors later in this chapter.)

To see a simple property editor at work, look at the foreground property. The property type is Color. You can see the color editor, with a text field containing a string [0,0,0] and a button labeled ". . ." that brings up a color chooser. Go ahead and change the foreground color. Notice that you'll immediately see the change to the property value—the label text changes color.

More interestingly, choose a file name for an image file in the property inspector. Once you do so, ImageViewerBean automatically displays the image (see Figure 8–8).

NOTE: If you look at the property inspector in Figure 8–8, you will find a large number of mysterious properties such as focusCycleRoot and iconTextGap. These are inherited from the JLabel superclass. You will see later in this chapter how you can suppress them from the property inspector.

To complete our application, place a FileNameBean object at the south end of the frame. Now we want the image to be loaded when the fileName property of FileNameBean is changed. This happens through a PropertyChange event; we discuss these kinds of events later in this chapter.

To react to the event, select FileNameBean and select the Events tab from its property inspector (see Figure 8–9). Then click the "..." button next to the propertyChange entry. A dialog box appears that shows that no handlers are currently associated with this event. Click the Add button of the dialog box. You are prompted for a method name. Type loadImage.

Now look at the code editor. Event handling code has been added, and there is a new method:

```
private void loadImage(java.beans.PropertyChange evt)
{
    // TODO add your handling code here
}
```

Add the following line of code to that method:

```
imageViewerBean1.setFileName(fileNameBean1.getFileName());
```

Then compile and execute the frame class. You now have a complete image viewer application. Click the button with the ". . ." label and select an image file. The image is displayed in the image viewer.

This process demonstrates that you can create a Java application from beans by setting properties and providing a small amount of code for event handlers.

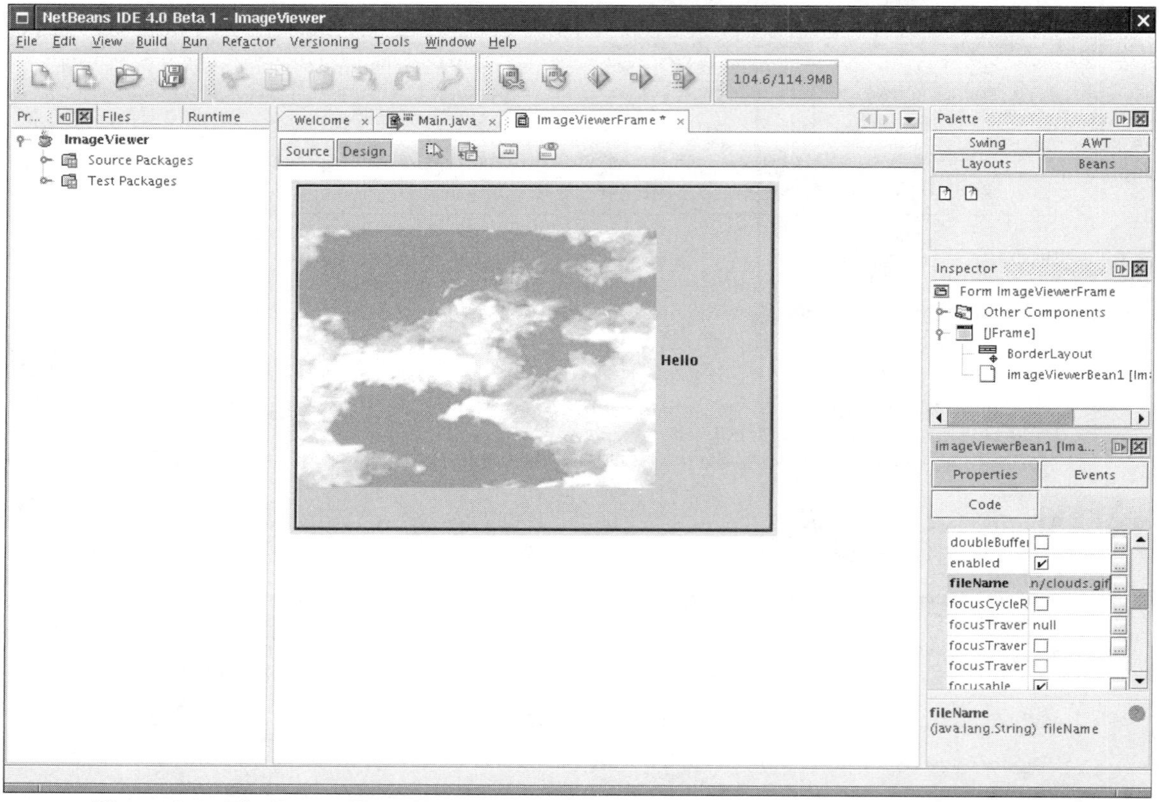

Figure 8–8: The ImageViewerBean at work

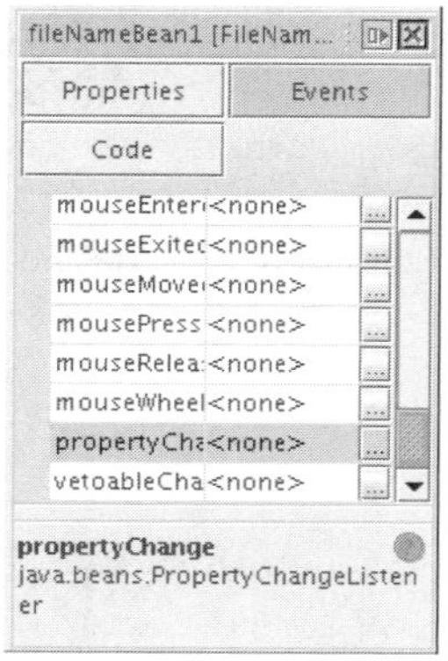

Figure 8–9: The events tab of the property inspector

Naming Patterns for Bean Properties and Events

In this section, we cover the basic rules for designing your own beans. First, we want to stress there is *no* cosmic beans class that you extend to build your beans. Visual beans directly or indirectly extend the Component class, but nonvisual beans don't have to extend any particular superclass. Remember, a bean is simply *any* class that can be manipulated in a builder tool. The builder tool does not look at the superclass to determine the bean nature of a class, but it analyzes the names of its methods. To enable this analysis, the method names for beans must follow certain patterns.

> NOTE: There is a java.beans.Beans class, but all methods in it are static. Extending it would, therefore, be rather pointless, even though you will see it done occasionally, supposedly for greater "clarity." Clearly, because a bean can't extend both Beans and Component, this approach can't work for visual beans. In fact, the Beans class contains methods that are designed to be called by builder tools, for example, to check whether the tool is operating at design time or run time.

Other languages for visual design environments, such as Visual Basic and C#, have special keywords such as "Property" and "Event" to express these concepts directly. The designers of the Java specification decided not to add keywords to the language to support visual programming. Therefore, they needed an alternative so that a builder tool could analyze a bean to learn its properties or events. Actually, there are two alternative mechanisms. If the bean writer uses standard naming patterns for properties and events, then the builder tool can use the reflection mechanism to understand what properties and events the bean is supposed to expose. Alternatively, the bean writer can supply a *bean information* class that tells the builder tool about the properties and events of the bean. We start out using the naming patterns because they are easy to use. You'll see later in this chapter how to supply a bean information class.

> NOTE: Although the documentation calls these standard naming patterns "design patterns," these are really only naming conventions and have nothing to do with the design patterns that are used in object-oriented programming.

The naming pattern for properties is simple: Any pair of methods

```
public Type getPropertyName()
public void setPropertyName(Type newValue)
```

corresponds to a read/write property.

For example, in our ImageViewerBean, there is only one read/write property (for the file name to be viewed), with the following methods:

```
public String getFileName()
public void setFileName(String newValue)
```

If you have a get method but not an associated set method, you define a read-only property. Conversely, a set method without an associated get method defines a write-only property.

> NOTE: The get and set methods you create can do more than simply get and set a private data field. Like any Java method, they can carry out arbitrary actions. For example, the setFileName method of the ImageViewerBean class not only sets the value of the fileName data field, but also opens the file and loads the image.

 NOTE: In Visual Basic and C#, properties also come from get and set methods. However, in both these languages, you explicitly define properties rather than having builder tools second-guess the programmer's intentions by analyzing method names. In those languages, properties have another advantage: Using a property name on the left side of an assignment automatically calls the set method. Using a property name in an expression automatically calls the get method. For example, in Visual Basic you can write

```
imageBean.fileName = "corejava.gif"
```

instead of

```
imageBean.setFileName("corejava.gif");
```

This syntax was considered for Java, but the language designers felt that it was a poor idea to hide a method call behind syntax that looks like field access.

There is one exception to the get/set naming pattern. Properties that have Boolean values should use an is/set naming pattern, as in the following examples:

```
public boolean isPropertyName()
public void setPropertyName(boolean b)
```

For example, an animation might have a property running, with two methods

```
public boolean isRunning()
public void setRunning(boolean b)
```

The setRunning method would start and stop the animation. The isRunning method would report its current status.

 NOTE: It is legal to use a get prefix for a Boolean property accessor (such as getRunning), but the is prefix is preferred.

Be careful with the capitalization pattern you use for your method names. The designers of the JavaBeans specification decided that the name of the property in our example would be fileName, with a lowercase f, even though the get and set methods contain an uppercase F (getFileName, setFileName). The bean analyzer performs a process called *decapitalization* to derive the property name. (That is, the first character after get or set is converted to lower case.) The rationale is that this process results in method and property names that are more natural to programmers.

However, if the first *two* letters are uppercase (such as in getURL), then the first letter of the property is not changed to lower case. After all, a property name of uRL would look ridiculous.

 NOTE: What do you do if your class has a pair of get and set methods that doesn't correspond to a property that you want users to manipulate in a property inspector? In your own classes, you can of course avoid that situation by renaming your methods. However, if you extend another class, then you inherit the method names from the superclass. This happens, for example, when your bean extends JPanel or JLabel—a large number of uninteresting properties show up in the property inspector. You will see later in this chapter how you can override the automatic property discovery process by supplying *bean information*. In the bean information, you can specify exactly which properties your bean should expose.

For events, the naming patterns are equally simple. A bean builder environment will infer that your bean generates events when you supply methods to add and remove event listeners. All event class names must end in Event, and the classes must extend the EventObject class.

Suppose your bean generates events of type *EventName*Event. The listener interface must be called *EventName*Listener, and the methods to add and remove a listener must be called

```
public void addEventNameListener(EventNameListener e)
public void removeEventNameListener(EventNameListener e)
```

If you look at the code for ImageViewerBean, you'll see that it has no events to expose. However, many Swing components generate events, and they follow this pattern. For example, the AbstractButton class generates ActionEvent objects, and it has the following methods to manage ActionListener objects:

```
public void addActionListener(ActionListener e)
public void removeActionListener(ActionListener e)
```

CAUTION: If your event class doesn't extend EventObject, chances are that your code will compile just fine because none of the methods of the EventObject class are actually needed. However, your bean will mysteriously fail—the introspection mechanism will not recognize the events.

Bean Property Types

A sophisticated bean will have lots of different kinds of properties that it should expose in a builder tool for a user to set at design time or get at run time. It can also trigger both standard and custom events. Properties can be as simple as the fileName property that you saw in ImageViewerBean and FileNameBean or as sophisticated as a color value or even an array of data points—we encounter both of these cases later in this chapter. Furthermore, properties can fire events, as you will see in this section.

Getting the properties of your beans right is probably the most complex part of building a bean because the model is quite rich. The JavaBeans specification allows four types of properties, which we illustrate by various examples.

Simple Properties

A simple property is one that takes a single value such as a string or a number. The fileName property of the ImageViewer is an example of a simple property. Simple properties are easy to program: Just use the set/get naming convention we indicated earlier. For example, if you look at the code in Example 8–1, you can see that all it took to implement a simple string property is the following:

```
public void setFileName(String f)
{
    fileName = f;
    image = . . .
    repaint();
}

public String getFileName()
{
    if (file == null) return null;
    else return file.getPath();
}
```

Notice that, as far as the JavaBeans specification is concerned, we also have a read-only property of this bean because we have a method with this signature inside the class

```
public Dimension getPreferredSize()
```

without a corresponding setPreferredSize method. You would not normally be able to see read-only properties at design time in a property inspector.

Indexed Properties

An indexed property is one that gets or sets an array. A chart bean (see below) would use an indexed property for the data points. With an indexed property, you supply two pairs of get and set methods: one for the array and one for individual entries. They must follow this pattern:

```
Type[] getPropertyName()
void setPropertyName(Type[] x)
Type getPropertyName(int i)
void setPropertyName(int i, Type x)
```

Here's an example of the indexed property we use in the chart bean that you will see later in this chapter.

```
public double[] getValues() { return values; }
public void setValues(double[] v) { values = v; }
public double getValues(int i)
{
   if (0 <= i && i < values.length) return values[i];
   return 0;
}
public void setValues(int i, double value)
{
   if (0 <= i && i < values.length) values[i] = value;
}
. . .
private double[] values;
```

The

```
setPropertyName(int i, Type x)
```

method cannot be used to *grow* the array. To grow the array, you must manually build a new array and then pass it to this method:

```
setPropertyName(Type[] x)
```

NOTE: As we write this, NetBeans does not support indexed properties in the property inspector. You see later in this chapter how to overcome this limitation by supplying a custom property editor for arrays.

Bound Properties

Bound properties tell interested listeners that their value has changed. For example, the fileName property in FileNameBean is a bound property. When the file name changes, then ImageViewerBean is automatically notified and it loads the new file.

To implement a bound property, you must implement two mechanisms.

1. Whenever the value of the property changes, the bean must send a PropertyChange event to all registered listeners. This change can occur when the set method is called or when the program user carries out an action, such as editing text or selecting a file.

2. To enable interested listeners to register themselves, the bean has to implement the following two methods:

```
void addPropertyChangeListener(PropertyChangeListener listener)
void removePropertyChangeListener(PropertyChangeListener listener)
```

The java.beans package has a convenience class, called PropertyChangeSupport, that manages the listeners for you. To use this convenience class, your bean must have a data field of this class that looks like this:

```
private PropertyChangeSupport changeSupport = new PropertyChangeSupport(this);
```
You delegate the task of adding and removing property change listeners to that object.
```
public void addPropertyChangeListener(PropertyChangeListener listener)
{
    changeSupport.addPropertyChangeListener(listener);
}

public void removePropertyChangeListener(PropertyChangeListener listener)
{
    changeSupport.removePropertyChangeListener(listener);
}
```
Whenever the value of the property changes, use the firePropertyChange method of the PropertyChangeSupport object to deliver an event to all the registered listeners. That method has three parameters: the name of the property, the old value, and the new value. For example,
```
changeSupport.firePropertyChange("fileName", oldValue, newValue);
```
The values must be objects. If the property type is not an object, then you must use an object wrapper. For example,
```
changeSupport.firePropertyChange("running", false, true);
```

 TIP: If your bean extends any Swing class that ultimately extends the JComponent class, then you do *not* need to implement the addPropertyChangeListener and removePropertyChangeListener methods. These methods are already implemented in the JComponent superclass.

To notify the listeners of a property change, simply call the firePropertyChange method of the JComponent superclass:
```
firePropertyChange("propertyName", oldValue, newValue);
```
For your convenience, that method is overloaded for the types boolean, byte, char, double, float, int, long, and short. If oldValue and newValue belong to these types, you do not need to use object wrappers.

Other beans that want to be notified when the property value changes must implement the PropertyChangeListener interface. That interface contains only one method:
```
void propertyChange(PropertyChangeEvent event)
```
The code in the propertyChange method is triggered whenever the property value changes, provided, of course, that you have added the recipient to the property change listeners of the bean that generates the event. The PropertyChangeEvent object encapsulates the old and new value of the property, obtainable with
```
Object oldValue = event.getOldValue();
Object newValue = event.getNewValue();
```
If the property type is not a class type, then the returned objects are the usual wrapper types. For example, if a boolean property is changed, then a Boolean is returned and you need to retrieve the Boolean value with the booleanValue method.

Thus, a listening object must follow this model:
```
class Listener
{
    public Listener()
    {
        bean.addPropertyChangeListener(new
            PropertyChangeListener()
```

```
        {
            void propertyChange(PropertyChangeEvent event)
            {
                Object newValue = event.getNewValue();
                . . .
            }
        });
    }
    . . .
}
```

Constrained Properties

A *constrained property* is constrained by the fact that *any* listener can "veto" proposed changes, forcing it to revert to the old setting. The Java library contains only a few examples of constrained properties. One of them is the closed property of the JInternalFrame class. If someone tries to call setClosed(true) on an internal frame, then all of its VetoableChangeListeners are notified. If any of them throws a PropertyVetoException, then the closed property is *not* changed, and the setClosed method throws the same exception. For example, a VetoableChangeListener may veto closing the frame if its contents have not been saved.

To build a constrained property, your bean must have the following two methods to manage VetoableChangeListener objects:

```
public void addVetoableChangeListener(VetoableChangeListener listener);
public void removeVetoableChangeListener(VetoableChangeListener listener);
```

Just as there is a convenience class to manage property change listeners, there is a convenience class, called VetoableChangeSupport, that manages vetoable change listeners. Your bean should contain an object of this class.

```
private VetoableChangeSupport vetoSupport = new VetoableChangeSupport(this);
```

Adding and removing listeners should be delegated to this object. For example:

```
public void addVetoableChangeListener(VetoableChangeListener listener)
{
    vetoSupport.addVetoableChangeListener(listener);
}
public void removeVetoableChangeListener(VetoableChangeListener listener)
{
    vetoSupport.removeVetoableChangeListener(listener);
}
```

 TIP: The JComponent class has some support for constrained properties, but it is not as extensive as that for bound properties. The JComponent class keeps a single listener list for vetoable change listeners, not a separate list for each property. And the fireVetoableChange method is not overloaded for basic types. If your bean extends JComponent and has a single constrained property, then the listener support of the JComponent superclass is entirely adequate, and you do not need a separate VetoableChangeSupport object.

To update a constrained property value, a bean uses the following three-phase approach:

1. Notify all vetoable change listeners of the *intent* to change the property value. (Use the fireVetoableChange method of the VetoableChangeSupport class.)

2. If none of the vetoable change listeners has thrown a PropertyVetoException, then update the value of the property.

3. Notify all property change listeners to *confirm* that a change has occurred.

For example,

```
public void setValue(Type newValue) throws PropertyVetoException
{
    Type oldValue = getValue();
    vetoSupport.fireVetoableChange("value", oldValue, newValue);
    // survived, therefore no veto
    value = newValue;
    changeSupport.firePropertyChange("value", oldValue, newValue);
}
```

It is important that you don't change the property value until all the registered vetoable change listeners have agreed to the proposed change. Conversely, a vetoable change listener should never assume that a change that it agrees to is actually happening. The only reliable way to get notified when a change is actually happening is through a property change listener.

We end our discussion of JavaBeans properties by showing the full code for FileNameBean (see Example 8–2). The FileNameBean has a constrained filename property. Because FileNameBean extends the JPanel class, we did not have to explicitly use a PropertyChangeSupport object. Instead, we rely on the ability of the JPanel class to manage property change listeners.

Example 8–2: FileNameBean.java

```
1. package com.horstmann.corejava;
2.
3. import java.awt.*;
4. import java.awt.event.*;
5. import java.beans.*;
6. import java.io.*;
7. import javax.swing.*;
8.
9. /**
10.    A bean for specifying file names.
11. */
12. public class FileNameBean extends JPanel
13. {
14.    public FileNameBean()
15.    {
16.       dialogButton = new JButton("...");
17.       nameField = new JTextField(30);
18.
19.       chooser = new JFileChooser();
20.
21.       chooser.setFileFilter(new
22.          javax.swing.filechooser.FileFilter()
23.          {
24.             public boolean accept(File f)
25.             {
26.                String name = f.getName().toLowerCase();
27.                return name.endsWith("." + defaultExtension) || f.isDirectory();
28.             }
29.             public String getDescription()
30.             {
31.                return defaultExtension + " files";
32.             }
33.          });
```

```
34.
35.        setLayout(new GridBagLayout());
36.        GridBagConstraints gbc = new GridBagConstraints();
37.        gbc.weightx = 100;
38.        gbc.weighty = 100;
39.        gbc.anchor = GridBagConstraints.WEST;
40.        gbc.fill = GridBagConstraints.BOTH;
41.        gbc.gridwidth = 1;
42.        gbc.gridheight = 1;
43.        add(nameField, gbc);
44.
45.        dialogButton.addActionListener(
46.           new ActionListener()
47.              {
48.                 public void actionPerformed(ActionEvent event)
49.                 {
50.                    int r = chooser.showOpenDialog(null);
51.                    if(r == JFileChooser.APPROVE_OPTION)
52.                    {
53.                       File f = chooser.getSelectedFile();
54.                       try
55.                       {
56.                          String name = f.getCanonicalPath();
57.                          setFileName(name);
58.                       }
59.                       catch (IOException e)
60.                       {
61.                       }
62.                    }
63.                 }
64.              });
65.        nameField.setEditable(false);
66.
67.        gbc.weightx = 0;
68.        gbc.anchor = GridBagConstraints.EAST;
69.        gbc.fill = GridBagConstraints.NONE;
70.        gbc.gridx = 1;
71.        add(dialogButton, gbc);
72.     }
73.
74.     /**
75.        Sets the fileName property.
76.        @param newValue the new file name
77.     */
78.     public void setFileName(String newValue)
79.     {
80.        String oldValue = nameField.getText();
81.        nameField.setText(newValue);
82.        firePropertyChange("fileName", oldValue, newValue);
83.     }
84.
85.     /**
86.        Gets the fileName property.
87.        @return the name of the selected file
88.     */
```

```
 89.   public String getFileName()
 90.   {
 91.      return nameField.getText();
 92.   }
 93.
 94.   /**
 95.      Sets the defaultExtension property.
 96.      @param s the new default extension
 97.   */
 98.   public void setDefaultExtension(String s)
 99.   {
100.      defaultExtension = s;
101.   }
102.
103.   /**
104.      Gets the defaultExtension property.
105.      @return the default extension in the file chooser
106.   */
107.   public String getDefaultExtension()
108.   {
109.      return defaultExtension;
110.   }
111.
112.   public Dimension getPreferredSize()
113.   {
114.      return new Dimension(XPREFSIZE, YPREFSIZE);
115.   }
116.
117.   private static final int XPREFSIZE = 200;
118.   private static final int YPREFSIZE = 20;
119.   private JButton dialogButton;
120.   private JTextField nameField;
121.   private JFileChooser chooser;
122.   private String defaultExtension = "gif";
123. }
```

API   **java.beans.PropertyChangeListener 1.1**

- void propertyChange(PropertyChangeEvent event)
  is called when a property change event is fired.

  Parameters: event   The property change event

API   **java.beans.PropertyChangeSupport 1.1**

- PropertyChangeSupport(Object sourceBean)
  constructs a PropertyChangeSupport object that manages listeners for bound property changes of the given bean.
- void addPropertyChangeListener(PropertyChangeListener listener)
- void addPropertyChangeListener(String propertyName, PropertyChangeListener listener) **1.2**
  register an interested listener for changes in all bound properties, or only the named bound property.
- void removePropertyChangeListener(PropertyChangeListener listener)
- void removePropertyChangeListener(String propertyName, PropertyChangeListener listener) **1.2**
  remove a previously registered property change listener.

- void firePropertyChange(String propertyName, Object oldValue, Object newValue)
- void firePropertyChange(String propertyName, int oldValue, int newValue) **1.2**
- void firePropertyChange(String propertyName, boolean oldValue, boolean newValue) **1.2**

  send a PropertyChangeEvent to registered listeners.

- void fireIndexedPropertyChange(String propertyName, int index, Object oldValue, Object newValue) **5.0**
- void fireIndexedPropertyChange(String propertyName, int index, int oldValue, int newValue) **5.0**
- void fireIndexedPropertyChange(String propertyName, int index, boolean oldValue, boolean newValue) **5.0**

  send an IndexedPropertyChangeEvent to registered listeners.

- PropertyChangeListener[] getPropertyChangeListeners() **1.4**
- PropertyChangeListener[] getPropertyChangeListeners(String propertyName) **1.4**

  get the listeners for changes in all bound properties, or only the named bound property.

 java.beans.PropertyChangeEvent 1.1

- PropertyChangeEvent(Object sourceBean, String propertyName, Object oldValue, Object newValue)

  constructs a new PropertyChangeEvent object, describing that the given property has changed from oldValue to newValue.

- Object getNewValue()

  returns the new value of the property.

- Object getOldValue();

  returns the previous value of the property.

- String getPropertyName()

  returns the name of the property.

 java.beans.IndexedPropertyChangeEvent 5.0

- IndexedPropertyChangeEvent(Object sourceBean, String propertyName, int index, Object oldValue, Object newValue)

  constructs a new IndexedPropertyChangeEvent object, describing that the given property has changed from oldValue to newValue at the given index.

- int getIndex()

  returns the index at which the change occurred.

 java.beans.VetoableChangeListener **1.1**

- void vetoableChange(PropertyChangeEvent event)

  is called when a property is about to be changed. It should throw a PropertyVetoException if the change is not acceptable.

  Parameters: event   The event object describing the property change

 java.beans.VetoableChangeSupport 1.1

- VetoableChangeSupport(Object sourceBean)

  constructs a PropertyChangeSupport object that manages listeners for constrained property changes of the given bean.

- void addVetoableChangeListener(VetoableChangeListener listener)
- void addVetoableChangeListener(String propertyName, VetoableChangeListener listener) **1.2**

  register an interested listener for changes in all constrained properties, or only the named constrained property.

- void removeVetoableChangeListener(VetoableChangeListener listener)
- void removeVetoableChangeListener(String propertyName, VetoableChangeListener listener) **1.2**
  remove a previously registered vetoable change listener.

- void fireVetoableChange(String propertyName, Object oldValue, Object newValue)
- void fireVetoableChange(String propertyName, int oldValue, int newValue) **1.2**
- void fireVetoableChange(String propertyName, boolean oldValue, boolean newValue) **1.2**
  send a VetoableChangeEvent to registered listeners.

- VetoableChangeListener[] getVetoableChangeListeners() **1.4**
- VetoableChangeListener[] getVetoableChangeListeners(String propertyName) **1.4**
  get the listeners for changes in all constrained properties, or only the named bound property.

 javax.swing.JComponent 1.2

- void addPropertyChangeListener(PropertyChangeListener listener)
- void addPropertyChangeListener(String propertyName, PropertyChangeListener listener)
  register an interested listener for changes in all bound properties, or only the named bound property.

- void removePropertyChangeListener(PropertyChangeListener listener)
- void removePropertyChangeListener(String propertyName, PropertyChangeListener listener) **1.2**
  remove a previously registered property change listener.

- void firePropertyChange(String propertyName, Object oldValue, Object newValue)
  sends a PropertyChangeEvent to registered listeners.

- void addVetoableChangeListener(VetoableChangeListener listener)
  registers an interested listener for changes in all constrained properties, or only the named constrained property.

- void removeVetoableChangeListener(VetoableChangeListener listener)
  removes a previously registered vetoable change listener.

- void fireVetoableChange(String propertyName, Object oldValue, Object newValue)
  sends a VetoableChangeEvent to registered listeners.

 java.beans.PropertyVetoException 1.1

- PropertyVetoException(String reason, PropertyChangeEvent event)
  creates a new PropertyVetoException.

Parameters:	reason	A string that describes the reason for the veto
	event	The PropertyChangeEvent for the constrained property you want to veto

- PropertyChangeEvent getPropertyChangeEvent()
  returns the PropertyChangeEvent used to construct the exception.

BeanInfo Classes

You have already seen that if you use the standard naming patterns for the methods of your bean class, then a builder tool can use reflection to determine features such as properties and events. This process makes it simple to get started with bean programming, but naming patterns are rather limiting in the end. As your beans become complex, there may be features of your bean that naming patterns will not reveal. Moreover, as we already mentioned, many beans have get/set method pairs that should *not* correspond to bean properties.

Luckily, the JavaBeans specification allows a far more flexible and powerful mechanism for storing information about your bean for use by a builder. You can define an object that implements the BeànInfo interface to describe your bean. When you implement this interface, a builder tool will look to the methods from the BeanInfo interface to tell it about the features that your bean supports.

Even though you can use a BeanInfo class to avoid naming patterns, you need to follow a naming pattern to associate a BeanInfo object to the bean: The name of the bean info class must be formed by adding BeanInfo to the name of the bean. For example, the bean info class associated to the class ImageViewerBean *must* be named ImageViewerBeanBeanInfo. The bean info class must be part of the same package as the bean itself.

You won't normally write a class that implements all methods of the BeanInfo interface. Instead, you should extend the SimpleBeanInfo convenience class that has default implementations for all the methods in the BeanInfo interface.

The most common reason for supplying a BeanInfo class is to gain control of the bean properties. You construct a PropertyDescriptor for each property by supplying the name of the property and the class of the bean that contains it.

```
PropertyDescriptor descriptor = new PropertyDescriptor("fileName", ImageViewerBean.class);
```

Then implement the getPropertyDescriptors method of your BeanInfo class to return an array of all property descriptors.

For example, suppose ImageViewerBean wants to hide all properties that it inherits from the JLabel superclass and expose only the fileName property. The following BeanInfo class does just that:

```
// bean info class for ImageViewerBean
class ImageViewerBeanBeanInfo extends SimpleBeanInfo
{
   public PropertyDescriptor[] getPropertyDescriptors()
   {
      return new PropertyDescriptor[]
      {
         new PropertyDescriptor("fileName", ImageViewerBean.class);
      };
   }
}
```

Other methods also return EventSetDescriptor and MethodDescriptor arrays, but they are less commonly used. If one of these methods returns null (as is the case for the SimpleBeanInfo methods), then the standard naming patterns apply. However, if you override a method to return a non-null array, then you must include *all* properties, events, or methods in your array.

 NOTE: Sometimes, you may want to write generic code that discovers properties or events of an arbitrary bean. Call the static getBeanInfo method of the Introspector class. The Introspector constructs a BeanInfo class that completely describes the bean, taking into account the information in BeanInfo companion classes.

Another useful method in the BeanInfo interface is the getIcon method that lets you give your bean a custom icon. Builder tools will display the icon in a palette. Actually, you can specify four separate icon bitmaps. The BeanInfo interface has four constants that cover the standard sizes:

```
ICON_COLOR_16x16
ICON_COLOR_32x32
```

```
ICON_MONO_16x16
ICON_MONO_32x32
```

Here is an example of how you might use the loadImage convenience method in the Simple-BeanInfo class to add an icon to a class:

```
public Image getIcon(int iconType)
{
    String name = "";
    if (iconType == BeanInfo.ICON_COLOR_16x16) name = "COLOR_16x16";
    else if (iconType == BeanInfo.ICON_COLOR_32x32) name = "COLOR_32x32";
    else if (iconType == BeanInfo.ICON_MONO_16x16) name = "MONO_16x16";
    else if (iconType == BeanInfo.ICON_MONO_32x32) name = "MONO_32x32";
    else return null;
    return loadImage("ImageViewerBean_" + name + ".gif");
}
```

This works, provided you cleverly name the image files to be

```
ImageViewerBean_COLOR_16x16.gif
ImageViewerBean_COLOR_32x32.gif
```

and so on.

 java.beans.Introspector 1.1

- static BeanInfo getBeanInfo(Class<?> beanClass)
  gets the bean information of the given class.

 java.beans.BeanInfo 1.1

- EventSetDescriptor[] getEventSetDescriptors()
- MethodDescriptor[] getMethodDescriptors()
- PropertyDescriptor[] getPropertyDescriptors()
  return an array of the specified descriptor objects. A return of null signals the builder to use the naming conventions and reflection to find the member. The getPropertyDescriptors method returns a mixture of plain and indexed property descriptors. Use instanceof to check whether a specific PropertyDescriptor is an IndexedPropertyDescriptor.

- Image getIcon(int iconType)
  returns an image object that can represent the bean in toolboxes, tool bars, and the like. There are four constants, as described earlier, for the standard types of icons.

- int getDefaultEventIndex()
- int getDefaultPropertyIndex()
  A bean can have a default event or property. Both of these methods return the array index that specifies which element of the descriptor array to use as that default member, or –1 if no default exists. A bean builder environment can visually enhance the default feature, for example, by placing it first in a list of features or by displaying its name in boldface.

- BeanInfo[] getAdditionalBeanInfo()
  returns an array of BeanInfo objects or null. Use this method when you want some information about your bean to come from BeanInfo classes for other beans. For example, you might use this method if your bean aggregated lots of other beans. The current BeanInfo class rules in case of conflict.

 java.beans.SimpleBeanInfo 1.1

- Image loadImage(String resourceName)
returns an image object file associated to the resource. Currently only GIFs are supported.

  Parameters: resourceName   A path name (taken relative to the directory containing the current class)

 java.beans.FeatureDescriptor 1.1

- String getName()
- void setName(String name)
get or set the programmatic name for the feature.

- String getDisplayName()
- void setDisplayName(String displayName)
get or set a display name for the feature. The default value is the value returned by getName. However, currently there is no explicit support for supplying feature names in multiple locales.

- String getShortDescription()
- void setShortDescription(String text)
get or set a string that a builder tool can use to provide a short description for this feature. The default value is the return value of getDisplayName.

- Object getValue(String attributeName)
- void setValue(String attributeName, Object value)
get or set a named value that is associated with this feature.

- Enumeration attributeNames()
returns an enumeration object that contains names of any attributes registered with setValue.

- boolean isExpert()
- void setExpert(boolean b)
get or set an expert flag that a builder can use to determine whether to hide the feature from a naive user. (Not every builder is likely to support this feature.)

- boolean isHidden()
- void setHidden(boolean b)
get or set a flag that a builder tool should hide this feature.

 java.beans.PropertyDescriptor 1.1

- PropertyDescriptor(String propertyName, Class<?> beanClass)
- PropertyDescriptor(String propertyName, Class<?> beanClass, String getMethod, String setMethod)
construct a PropertyDescriptor object. The methods throw an IntrospectionException if an error occurred during introspection. The first constructor assumes that you follow the standard convention for the names of the get and set methods.

- Class<?> getPropertyType()
returns a Class object for the property type.

- Method getReadMethod()
returns the get method.

- Method getWriteMethod()
returns the set method.

- `boolean isBound()`
- `void setBound(boolean b)`
  get or set a flag that determines whether this property is a bound property.
- `boolean isConstrained()`
- `void setConstrained(boolean b)`
  get or set a flag that determines whether this property is a constrained property.

 java.beans.IndexedPropertyDescriptor 1.1

- `IndexedPropertyDescriptor(String propertyName, Class<?> beanClass)`
- `IndexedPropertyDescriptor(String propertyName, Class<?> beanClass, String getMethod, String setMethod, String indexedGetMethod, String indexedSetMethod)`
  construct an `IndexedPropertyDescriptor` for the index property. The methods throw an `IntrospectionException` if an error occurred during introspection. The first constructor assumes that you follow the standard convention for the names of the get and set methods.
- `Class<?> getIndexedPropertyType()`
  returns the class that describes the type of the indexed values of the property, that is, the return type of the indexed get method.
- `Method getIndexedReadMethod()`
  returns the indexed get method.
- `Method getIndexedWriteMethod()`
  returns the indexed set method.

java.beans.EventSetDescriptor 1.1

- `EventSetDescriptor(Class<?> sourceClass, String eventSetName, Class<?> listener, String listenerMethod)`
  constructs an `EventSetDescriptor`. This constructor assumes that you follow the standard pattern for the names of the event class and the names of the methods to add and remove event listeners. Throws an `IntrospectionException` if an error occurred during introspection.
- `EventSetDescriptor(Class<?> sourceClass, String eventSetName, Class<?> listener, String[] listenerMethods, String addListenerMethod, String removeListenerMethod)`
  constructs an `EventSetDescriptor` with multiple listener methods and custom methods for adding and removing listeners. Throws an `IntrospectionException` if an error occurred during introspection.
- `Method getAddListenerMethod()`
  returns the method used to register the listener.
- `Method getRemoveListenerMethod()`
  returns the method used to remove a registered listener for the event.
- `Method[] getListenerMethods()`
- `MethodDescriptor[] getListenerMethodDescriptors()`
  return an array of `Method` or `MethodDescriptor` objects for the methods triggered in the listener interface.
- `Class<?> getListenerType()`
  returns the type of the listener interface associated with the event.
- `boolean isUnicast()`
- `void setUnicast(boolean b)`
  get or set a flag that is true if this event can be propagated to only one listener.

Property Editors

If you add an integer or string property to a bean, then that property is automatically displayed in the bean's property inspector. But what happens if you add a property whose values cannot easily be edited in a text field, for example, a date or a Color? Then, you need to provide a separate component by which the user can specify the property value. Such components are called *property editors*. For example, a property editor for a date object might be a calendar that lets the user scroll through the months and pick a date. A property editor for a Color object would let the user select the red, green, and blue components of the color.

Actually, NetBeans already has a property editor for colors. Also, of course, there are property editors for basic types such as String (a text field) and boolean (a checkbox). These property editors are registered with the *property editor manager*.

The process for supplying a new property editor is slightly involved. First, you create a bean info class to accompany your bean. Override the getPropertyDescriptors method. That method returns an array of PropertyDescriptor objects. You create one object for each property that should be displayed on a property editor, *even those for which you just want the default editor*.

You construct a PropertyDescriptor by supplying the name of the property and the class of the bean that contains it.

```
PropertyDescriptor descriptor = new PropertyDescriptor("titlePosition", ChartBean.class);
```

Then you call the setPropertyEditorClass method of the PropertyDescriptor class.

```
descriptor.setPropertyEditorClass(TitlePositionEditor.class);
```

Next, you build an array of descriptors for properties of your bean. For example, the chart bean that we discuss in this section has five properties:

- A Color property, graphColor
- A String property, title
- An int property, titlePosition
- A double[] property, values
- A boolean property, inverse

The code in Example 8–3 shows the ChartBeanBeanInfo class that specifies the property editors for these properties. It achieves the following:

1. The getPropertyDescriptors method returns a descriptor for each property. The title and graphColor properties are used with the default editors, that is, the string and color editors that come with the builder tool.

2. The titlePosition, values, and inverse properties use special editors of type TitlePositionEditor, DoubleArrayEditor, and InverseEditor, respectively.

Figure 8–10 shows the chart bean. You can see the title on the top. Its position can be set to left, center, or right. The values property specifies the graph values. If the inverse property is true, then the background is colored and the bars of the chart are white. Example 8–4 lists the code for the chart bean; the bean is simply a modification of the chart applet in Volume 1, Chapter 10.

The static registerEditor method of the PropertyEditorManager class sets a property editor for all properties of a given type. Here is an example:

```
PropertyEditorManager.registerEditor(Date.class, CalendarSelector.class);
```

 NOTE: You should not call the registerEditor method in your beans—the default editor for a type is a global setting that is properly the responsibility of the builder environment.

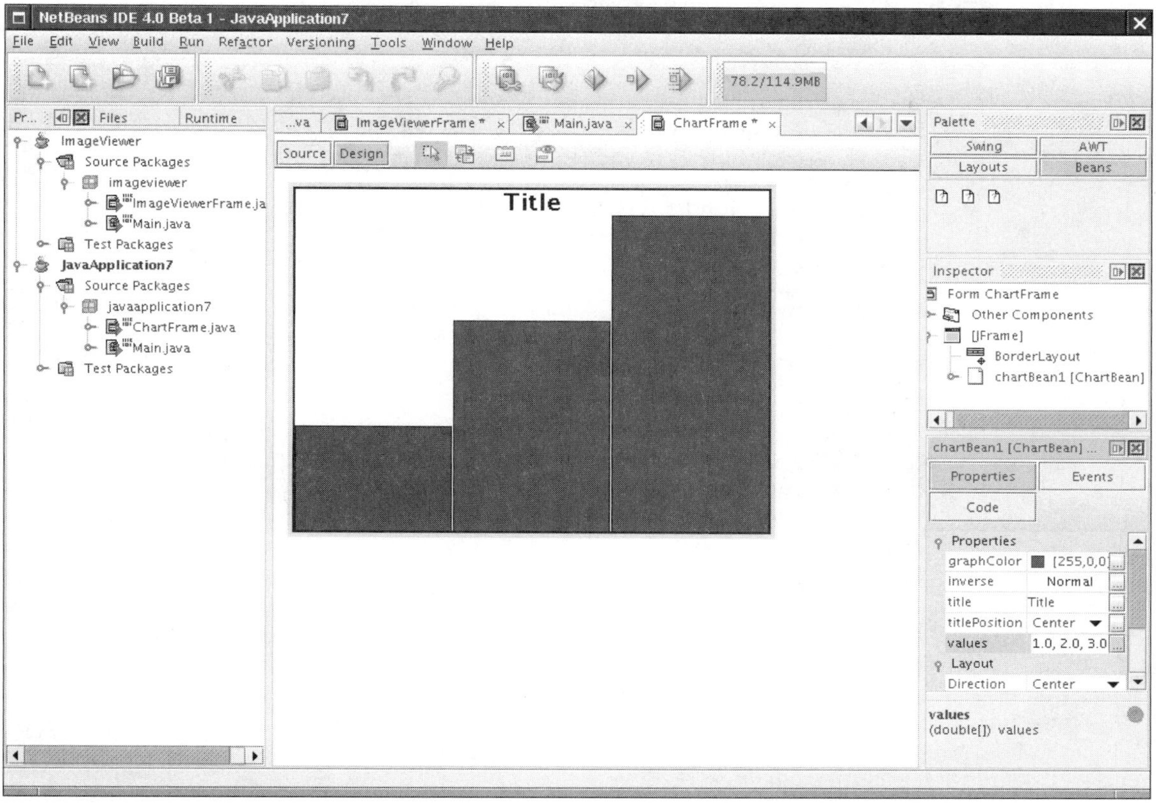

Figure 8–10: The chart bean

You use the findEditor method in the PropertyEditorManager class to check whether a property editor exists for a given type in your builder tool. That method does the following:

1. It looks first to see which property editors are already registered with it. (These are the editors supplied by the builder tool and by calls to the registerEditor method.)

2. Then, it looks for a class with a name that consists of the name of the type plus the word Editor.

3. If neither lookup succeeds, then findEditor returns null.

For example, if a CalendarSelector class is registered for java.util.Date objects, then it would be used to edit a Date property. Otherwise, a java.util.DateEditor would be searched.

Example 8–3: ChartBeanBeanInfo.java

```
 1. package com.horstmann.corejava;
 2.
 3. import java.beans.*;
 4.
 5. /**
 6.    The bean info for the chart bean, specifying the property editors.
 7. */
 8. public class ChartBeanBeanInfo extends SimpleBeanInfo
 9. {
```

```
10.    public PropertyDescriptor[] getPropertyDescriptors()
11.    {
12.       try
13.       {
14.          PropertyDescriptor titlePositionDescriptor
15.             = new PropertyDescriptor("titlePosition", ChartBean.class);
16.          titlePositionDescriptor.setPropertyEditorClass(TitlePositionEditor.class);
17.          PropertyDescriptor inverseDescriptor
18.             = new PropertyDescriptor("inverse", ChartBean.class);
19.          inverseDescriptor.setPropertyEditorClass(InverseEditor.class);
20.          PropertyDescriptor valuesDescriptor
21.             = new PropertyDescriptor("values", ChartBean.class);
22.          valuesDescriptor.setPropertyEditorClass(DoubleArrayEditor.class);
23.
24.          return new PropertyDescriptor[]
25.          {
26.             new PropertyDescriptor("title", ChartBean.class),
27.             titlePositionDescriptor,
28.             valuesDescriptor,
29.             new PropertyDescriptor("graphColor", ChartBean.class),
30.             inverseDescriptor
31.          };
32.       }
33.       catch (IntrospectionException e)
34.       {
35.          e.printStackTrace();
36.          return null;
37.       }
38.    }
39. }
```

Example 8–4: ChartBean.java

```
1. package com.horstmann.corejava;
2.
3. import java.awt.*;
4. import java.awt.font.*;
5. import java.awt.geom.*;
6. import java.util.*;
7. import java.beans.*;
8. import java.io.*;
9. import javax.swing.*;
10.
11. /**
12.    A bean to draw a bar chart.
13. */
14. public class ChartBean extends JPanel
15. {
16.    public void paint(Graphics g)
17.    {
18.       Graphics2D g2 = (Graphics2D) g;
19.
20.       if (values == null || values.length == 0) return;
21.       double minValue = 0;
22.       double maxValue = 0;
23.       for (int i = 0; i < values.length; i++)
24.       {
```

```
25.        if (minValue > getValues(i)) minValue = getValues(i);
26.        if (maxValue < getValues(i)) maxValue = getValues(i);
27.     }
28.     if (maxValue == minValue) return;
29.
30.     Dimension d = getSize();
31.     Rectangle2D bounds = getBounds();
32.     double clientWidth = bounds.getWidth();
33.     double clientHeight = bounds.getHeight();
34.     double barWidth = clientWidth / values.length;
35.
36.     g2.setPaint(inverse ? color : Color.white);
37.     g2.fill(bounds);
38.     g2.setPaint(Color.black);
39.
40.     Font titleFont = new Font("SansSerif", Font.BOLD, 20);
41.     FontRenderContext context = g2.getFontRenderContext();
42.     Rectangle2D titleBounds = titleFont.getStringBounds(title, context);
43.
44.     double titleWidth = titleBounds.getWidth();
45.     double y = -titleBounds.getY();
46.     double x;
47.     if (titlePosition == LEFT) x = 0;
48.     else if (titlePosition == CENTER) x = (clientWidth - titleWidth) / 2;
49.     else x = clientWidth - titleWidth;
50.
51.     g2.setFont(titleFont);
52.     g2.drawString(title, (float) x, (float) y);
53.
54.     double top = titleBounds.getHeight();
55.     double scale = (clientHeight - top) / (maxValue - minValue);
56.     y = clientHeight;
57.
58.     for (int i = 0; i < values.length; i++)
59.     {
60.        double x1 = i * barWidth + 1;
61.        double y1 = top;
62.        double value = getValues(i);
63.        double height =  value * scale;
64.        if (value >= 0)
65.           y1 += (maxValue - value) * scale;
66.        else
67.        {
68.           y1 += (int)(maxValue * scale);
69.           height = -height;
70.        }
71.
72.        g2.setPaint(inverse ? Color.white : color);
73.        Rectangle2D bar = new Rectangle2D.Double(x1, y1, barWidth - 2, height);
74.        g2.fill(bar);
75.        g2.setPaint(Color.black);
76.        g2.draw(bar);
77.     }
78.  }
79.
80.  /**
```

```
81.        Sets the title property.
82.        @param t the new chart title.
83.     */
84.     public void setTitle(String t) { title = t; }
85.
86.     /**
87.        Gets the title property.
88.        @return the chart title.
89.     */
90.     public String getTitle() { return title; }
91.
92.     /**
93.        Sets the indexed values property.
94.        @param v the values to display in the chart.
95.     */
96.     public void setValues(double[] v) { values = v; }
97.
98.     /**
99.        Gets the indexed values property.
100.        @return the values to display in the chart.
101.     */
102.     public double[] getValues() { return values; }
103.
104.     /**
105.        Sets the indexed values property.
106.        @param i the index of the value to set
107.        @param value the new value for that index
108.     */
109.     public void setValues(int i, double value)
110.     {
111.        if (0 <= i && i < values.length) values[i] = value;
112.     }
113.
114.     /**
115.        Gets the indexed values property.
116.        @param i the index of the value to get
117.        @return the value for that index
118.     */
119.     public double getValues(int i)
120.     {
121.        if (0 <= i && i < values.length) return values[i];
122.        return 0;
123.     }
124.
125.     /**
126.        Sets the inverse property.
127.        @param b true if the display is inverted (white bars
128.        on colored background)
129.     */
130.     public void setInverse(boolean b) { inverse = b; }
131.
132.     /**
133.        Gets the inverse property.
134.        @return true if the display is inverted
135.     */
136.     public boolean isInverse() { return inverse; }
```

```
137.
138.    /**
139.       Sets the titlePosition property.
140.       @param p LEFT, CENTER, or RIGHT
141.    */
142.    public void setTitlePosition(int p) { titlePosition = p; }
143.
144.    /**
145.       Gets the titlePosition property.
146.       @return LEFT, CENTER, or RIGHT
147.    */
148.    public int getTitlePosition() { return titlePosition; }
149.
150.    /**
151.       Sets the graphColor property.
152.       @param c the color to use for the graph
153.    */
154.    public void setGraphColor(Color c) { color = c; }
155.
156.    /**
157.       Gets the graphColor property.
158.       @param c the color to use for the graph
159.    */
160.    public Color getGraphColor() { return color; }
161.
162.    public Dimension getPreferredSize()
163.    {
164.       return new Dimension(XPREFSIZE, YPREFSIZE);
165.    }
166.
167.    private static final int LEFT = 0;
168.    private static final int CENTER = 1;
169.    private static final int RIGHT = 2;
170.
171.    private static final int XPREFSIZE = 300;
172.    private static final int YPREFSIZE = 300;
173.    private double[] values = { 1, 2, 3 };
174.    private String title = "Title";
175.    private int titlePosition = CENTER;
176.    private boolean inverse;
177.    private Color color = Color.red;
178. }
```

API java.beans.PropertyEditorManager 1.1

- static PropertyEditor findEditor(Class targetType)
  returns a property editor for the given type, or null if none is registered.

  Parameters: targetType   The Class object for the type to be edited, such as
                                       Color.class

- static void registerEditor(Class targetType, Class editorClass)
  registers an editor class to edit values of the given type.

  Parameters: targetType   The Class object for the type to be edited

                   editorClass   The Class object for the editor class (null unregis-
                                       ters the current editor)

java.beans.PropertyDescriptor 1.1

- PropertyDescriptor(String name, Class beanClass)
  constructs a PropertyDescriptor object.

Parameters:	name	The name of the property
	beanClass	The class of the bean to which the property belongs

- void setPropertyEditorClass(Class editorClass)
  sets the class of the property editor to be used with this property.

java.beans.BeanInfo 1.1

- PropertyDescriptor[] getPropertyDescriptors()
  returns a descriptor for each property that should be displayed in the property inspector for the bean.

Writing a Property Editor

Before we begin showing you how to write a property editor, we want to point out that although each property editor works with a value of one specific type, it can nonetheless be quite elaborate. For example, a font property editor (which edits an object of type Font) could show font samples to allow the user to pick a font in a more congenial way.

Next, any property editor you write must implement the PropertyEditor interface, an interface with 12 methods. As with the BeanInfo interface, you will not want to do this directly. Instead, it is far more convenient to extend the convenience PropertyEditorSupport class that is supplied with the standard library. This support class comes with methods to add and remove property change listeners, and with default versions of all other methods of the PropertyEditor interface. For example, our editor for editing the title position of a chart in our chart bean starts out like this:

```
// property editor class for title position
class TitlePositionEditor extends PropertyEditorSupport
{
    . . .
}
```

Note that if a property editor class has a constructor, it must also supply a default constructor, that is, one without arguments.

Finally, before we get into the mechanics of actually writing a property editor, we should point out that the editor is under the control of the builder, not the bean. The builder adheres to the following procedure to display the current value of the property:

1. It instantiates property editors for each property of the bean.
2. It asks the *bean* to tell it the current value of the property.
3. It then asks the *property editor* to display the value.

The property editor can use either text-based or graphics-based methods to actually display the value. We discuss these methods next.

Simple Property Editors

Simple property editors work with text strings. You override the setAsText and getAsText methods. For example, our chart bean has a property that lets you set where the title should be displayed: Left, Center, or Right. These choices are implemented as integer constants.

```
private static final int LEFT = 0;
private static final int CENTER = 1;
private static final int RIGHT = 2;
```

But of course, we don't want them to appear as numbers 0, 1, 2 in the text field—unless we are trying to enter the User Interface Hall of Horrors. Instead, we define a property editor whose getAsText method returns the value as a string. The method calls the getValue method of the PropertyEditor to find the value of the property. Because this is a generic method, the value is returned as an Object. If the property type is a basic type, we need to return a wrapper object. In our case, the property type is int, and the call to getValue returns an Integer.

```
class TitlePositionEditor extends PropertyEditorSupport
{
   public String getAsText()
   {
      int value = (Integer) getValue();
      return options[value];
   }
   . . .
   private String[] options = { "Left", "Center", "Right" };
}
```

Now, the text field displays one of these fields. When the user edits the text field, this triggers a call to the setAsText method to update the property value by invoking the setValue method. It, too, is a generic method whose parameter is of type Object. To set the value of a numeric type, we need to pass a wrapper object.

```
public void setAsText(String s)
{
   for (int i = 0; i < options.length; i++)
   {
      if (options[i].equals(s))
      {
         setValue(i);
         return;
      }
   }
}
```

Actually, this property editor is not a good choice for the titlePosition property, unless, of course, we are also competing for entry into the User Interface Hall of Shame. The user may not know what the legal choices are. It would be better to display all valid settings (see Figure 8–11). The PropertyEditorSupport class gives a simple method to display the selections in a property editor. We simply write a getTags method that returns an array of strings.

```
public String[] getTags() { return options; }
```

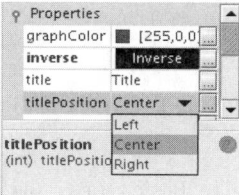

Figure 8–11: Custom property editors at work

The default getTags method returns null. By returning a non-null value, we indicate a choice field instead of a text field.

We still need to supply the getAsText and setAsText methods. The getTags method simply specifies the values to be displayed in a combo box. The getAsText/setAsText methods translate between the strings and the data type of the property (which may be a string, an integer, or a completely different type).

Example 8–5 lists the complete code for this property editor.

Example 8–5: TitlePositionEditor.java

```
1.  package com.horstmann.corejava;
2.
3.  import java.beans.*;
4.
5.  /**
6.     A custom editor for the titlePosition property of the
7.     ChartBean. The editor lets the user choose between
8.     Left, Center, and Right
9.  */
10. public class TitlePositionEditor
11.    extends PropertyEditorSupport
12. {
13.    public String[] getTags() { return options; }
14.    private String[] options = { "Left", "Center", "Right" };
15.    public String getJavaInitializationString() { return "" + getValue(); }
16.
17.    public String getAsText()
18.    {
19.       int value = (Integer) getValue();
20.       return options[value];
21.    }
22.
23.    public void setAsText(String s)
24.    {
25.       for (int i = 0; i < options.length; i++)
26.       {
27.          if (options[i].equals(s))
28.          {
29.             setValue(i);
30.             return;
31.          }
32.       }
33.    }
34. }
```

---

java.beans.PropertyEditorSupport 1.1

- Object getValue()
  returns the current value of the property. Basic types are wrapped into object wrappers.

- void setValue(Object newValue)
  sets the property to a new value. Basic types must be wrapped into object wrappers.

  Parameters: newValue   The new value of the object; should be a newly created object that the property can own

- `String getAsText()`
  Override this method to return a string representation of the current value of the property. The default returns `null` to indicate that the property cannot be represented as a string.

- `void setAsText(String text)`
  Override this method to set the property to a new value that is obtained by parsing the text. May throw an `IllegalArgumentException` if the text does not represent a legal value or if this property cannot be represented as a string.

- `String[] getTags()`
  Override this method to return an array of all possible string representations of the property values so they can be displayed in a Choice box. The default returns `null` to indicate that there is not a finite set of string values.

GUI-Based Property Editors

More sophisticated property types can't be edited as text. Instead, they are represented in two ways. The property inspector contains a small area (which otherwise would hold a text box or combo box) onto which the property editor will draw a graphical representation of the current value. When the user clicks on that area, a custom editor dialog box pops up (see Figure 8–12). The dialog box contains a component to edit the property values, supplied by the property editor, and various buttons, supplied by the builder environment.

To build a GUI-based property editor:

1. Tell the builder tool that you will paint the value and not use a string.
2. "Paint" the value the user enters onto the GUI.
3. Tell the builder tool that you will be using a GUI-based property editor.
4. Build the GUI.
5. Write the code to validate what the user tries to enter as the value.

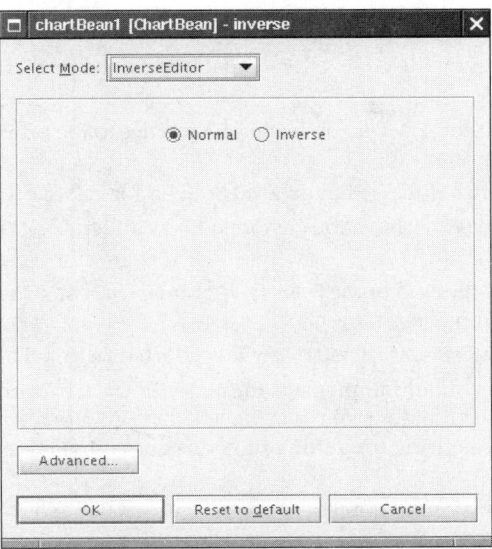

Figure 8–12: A custom editor dialog box

For the first step, you override the getAsText method in the PropertyEditor interface to return null and the isPaintable method to return true.

```
public String getAsText() { return null; }
public boolean isPaintable() { return true; }
```

Then, you implement the paintValue method. It receives a Graphics context and the coordinates of the rectangle inside which you can paint. Note that this rectangle is typically small, so you can't have a very elaborate representation. To graphically represent the inverse property, we draw the string "Inverse" in white letters with a black background, or the string "Normal" in black letters with a white background (see Figure 8–11).

```
public void paintValue(Graphics g, Rectangle box)
{
    Graphics2D g2 = (Graphics2D) g;
    boolean isInverse = (Boolean) getValue();
    String s = isInverse ? "Inverse" : "Normal";
    g2.setColor(isInverse ? Color.black : Color.white);
    g2.fill(box);
    g2.setColor(isInverse ? Color.white : Color.black);
    // compute string position to center string
    . . .
    g2.drawString(s, (float) x, (float) y);
}
```

Of course, this graphical representation is not editable. The user must click on it to pop up a custom editor.

You indicate that you will have a custom editor by overriding the supportsCustomEditor in the PropertyEditor interface to return true.

```
public boolean supportsCustomEditor() { return true; }
```

Now, you write the code that builds up the component that will hold the custom editor. You must build a separate custom editor class for every property. For example, associated to our InverseEditor class is an InverseEditorPanel class (see Example 8–7) that describes a GUI with two radio buttons to toggle between normal and inverse mode. That code is straightforward. However, the GUI actions must update the property values. We did this as follows:

1. Have the custom editor constructor receive a reference to the property editor object and store it in a variable editor.
2. To read the property value, we have the custom editor call editor.getValue().
3. To set the object value, we have the custom editor call editor.setValue(newValue) followed by editor.firePropertyChange().

Next, the getCustomEditor method of the PropertyEditor interface constructs and returns an object of the custom editor class.

```
public Component getCustomEditor() { return new InverseEditorPanel(this); }
```

Finally, property editors should implement the getJavaInitializationString method. With this method, you can give the builder tool the Java code that sets a property to its current value. The builder tool uses this string for automatic code generation. For example, here is the method for the InverseEditor:

```
public String getJavaInitializationString() { return "" + getValue(); }
```

This method returns the string "false" or "true". Try it out in NetBeans: If you edit the inverse property, NetBeans inserts code such as

```
chartBean1.setInverse(true);
```

 NOTE: If a property has a custom editor that does not implement the `getJavaInitialization-String` method, NetBeans does not know how to generate code and produces a setter with parameter ???.

Example 8–6 shows the complete code for the `InverseEditor` that displays the current setting in the property inspector. Example 8–7 lists the code implementing the pop-up editor panel.

The code for the property editor class (shown in Example 8–8) is almost identical to that of the `InverseEditor`, except that we simply paint a string consisting of the first few array values, followed by . . . in the `paintValue` method. And, of course, we return a different custom editor in the `getCustomEditor` method.

The other custom editor that we built for the chart bean class lets you edit a `double[]` array. NetBeans cannot edit array properties. We developed this custom editor to fill this obvious gap. Figure 8–13 shows the custom editor in action. All array values are shown in the list box, prefixed by their array index. Clicking on an array value places it into the text field above it, and you can edit it. You can also resize the array. The code for the `DoubleArrayPanel` class that implements the GUI is listed in Example 8–9.

These examples complete the code for the chart bean.

 NOTE: Unfortunately, we have to *paint* the array values. It would be more convenient to return a string with the `getAsText` method. However, some builder environments (including NetBeans) get confused when both `getAsText` and `getCustomEditor` return non-`null` values.

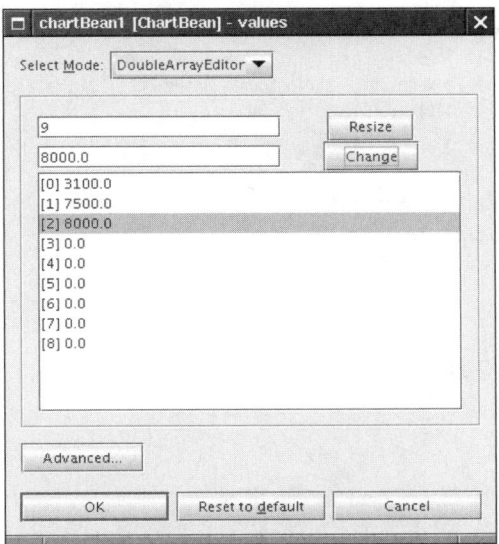

Figure 8–13: The custom editor dialog box for editing an array

Example 8–6: InverseEditor.java

```
1. package com.horstmann.corejava;
2.
3. import java.awt.*;
```

```
 4. import java.awt.font.*;
 5. import java.awt.geom.*;
 6. import java.beans.*;
 7.
 8. /**
 9.    The property editor for the inverse property of the ChartBean.
10.    The inverse property toggles between colored graph bars
11.    and colored background.
12. */
13. public class InverseEditor extends PropertyEditorSupport
14. {
15.    public Component getCustomEditor() { return new InverseEditorPanel(this); }
16.    public boolean supportsCustomEditor() { return true; }
17.    public boolean isPaintable() { return true; }
18.    public String getAsText() { return null; }
19.    public String getJavaInitializationString() { return "" + getValue(); }
20.
21.    public void paintValue(Graphics g, Rectangle box)
22.    {
23.       Graphics2D g2 = (Graphics2D) g;
24.       boolean isInverse = (Boolean) getValue();
25.       String s = isInverse ? "Inverse" : "Normal";
26.       g2.setPaint(isInverse ? Color.black : Color.white);
27.       g2.fill(box);
28.       g2.setPaint(isInverse ? Color.white : Color.black);
29.       FontRenderContext context = g2.getFontRenderContext();
30.       Rectangle2D stringBounds = g2.getFont().getStringBounds(s, context);
31.       double w = stringBounds.getWidth();
32.       double x = box.x;
33.       if (w < box.width) x += (box.width - w) / 2;
34.       double ascent = -stringBounds.getY();
35.       double y = box.y + (box.height - stringBounds.getHeight()) / 2 + ascent;
36.       g2.drawString(s, (float) x, (float) y);
37.    }
38. }
```

Example 8–7: InverseEditorPanel.java

```
 1. package com.horstmann.corejava;
 2.
 3. import java.awt.*;
 4. import java.awt.event.*;
 5. import java.text.*;
 6. import java.lang.reflect.*;
 7. import java.beans.*;
 8. import javax.swing.*;
 9.
10. /**
11.    The panel for setting the inverse property. It contains
12.    radio buttons to toggle between normal and inverse coloring.
13. */
14. public class InverseEditorPanel extends JPanel
15. {
16.    public InverseEditorPanel(PropertyEditorSupport ed)
17.    {
18.       editor = ed;
19.       ButtonGroup g = new ButtonGroup();
```

```
20.     boolean isInverse = (Boolean) editor.getValue();
21.     normal = new JRadioButton("Normal", !isInverse);
22.     inverse = new JRadioButton("Inverse", isInverse);
23.
24.     g.add(normal);
25.     g.add(inverse);
26.     add(normal);
27.     add(inverse);
28.
29.     ActionListener buttonListener =
30.        new ActionListener()
31.        {
32.           public void actionPerformed(ActionEvent event)
33.           {
34.              editor.setValue(
35.                 new Boolean(inverse.isSelected()));
36.              editor.firePropertyChange();
37.           }
38.        };
39.
40.     normal.addActionListener(buttonListener);
41.     inverse.addActionListener(buttonListener);
42.  }
43.
44.  private JRadioButton normal;
45.  private JRadioButton inverse;
46.  private PropertyEditorSupport editor;
47. }
```

Example 8–8: DoubleArrayEditor.java

```
1. package com.horstmann.corejava;
2.
3. import java.awt.*;
4. import java.awt.font.*;
5. import java.awt.geom.*;
6. import java.beans.*;
7.
8. /**
9.    A custom editor for an array of floating point numbers.
10. */
11. public class DoubleArrayEditor extends PropertyEditorSupport
12. {
13.    public Component getCustomEditor() { return new DoubleArrayEditorPanel(this); }
14.    public boolean supportsCustomEditor() { return true; }
15.    public boolean isPaintable() { return true; }
16.    public String getAsText() { return null; }
17.
18.    public void paintValue(Graphics g, Rectangle box)
19.    {
20.       Graphics2D g2 = (Graphics2D) g;
21.       double[] values = (double[]) getValue();
22.       StringBuilder s = new StringBuilder();
23.       for (int i = 0; i < 3; i++)
24.       {
25.          if (values.length > i) s.append(values[i]);
26.          if (values.length > i + 1) s.append(", ");
```

```
27.        }
28.        if (values.length > 3) s.append("...");
29.
30.        g2.setPaint(Color.white);
31.        g2.fill(box);
32.        g2.setPaint(Color.black);
33.        FontRenderContext context = g2.getFontRenderContext();
34.        Rectangle2D stringBounds = g2.getFont().getStringBounds(s.toString(), context);
35.        double w = stringBounds.getWidth();
36.        double x = box.x;
37.        if (w < box.width) x += (box.width - w) / 2;
38.        double ascent = -stringBounds.getY();
39.        double y = box.y + (box.height - stringBounds.getHeight()) / 2 + ascent;
40.        g2.drawString(s.toString(), (float) x, (float) y);
41.     }
42.
43.     public String getJavaInitializationString()
44.     {
45.        double[] values = (double[]) getValue();
46.        StringBuilder s = new StringBuilder();
47.        s.append("new double[] {");
48.        for (int i = 0; i < values.length; i++)
49.        {
50.           if (i > 0) s.append(", ");
51.           s.append(values[i]);
52.        }
53.        s.append("}");
54.        return s.toString();
55.     }
56. }
```

Example 8–9: DoubleArrayEditorPanel.java

```
1. package com.horstmann.corejava;
2.
3. import java.awt.*;
4. import java.awt.event.*;
5. import java.text.*;
6. import java.lang.reflect.*;
7. import java.beans.*;
8. import javax.swing.*;
9. import javax.swing.event.*;
10.
11. /**
12.    The panel inside the DoubleArrayEditor. It contains
13.    a list of the array values, together with buttons to
14.    resize the array and change the currently selected list value.
15. */
16. public class DoubleArrayEditorPanel extends JPanel
17. {
18.    public DoubleArrayEditorPanel(PropertyEditorSupport ed)
19.    {
20.       editor = ed;
21.       setArray((double[])ed.getValue());
22.
23.       setLayout(new GridBagLayout());
24.
```

```
25.     add(sizeField, new GBC(0, 0, 1, 1).setWeight(100, 0).setFill(GBC.HORIZONTAL));
26.     add(valueField, new GBC(0, 1, 1, 1).setWeight(100, 0).setFill(GBC.HORIZONTAL));
27.     add(sizeButton, new GBC(1, 0, 1, 1).setWeight(100, 0));
28.     add(valueButton, new GBC(1, 1, 1, 1).setWeight(100, 0));
29.     add(new JScrollPane(elementList), new GBC(0, 2, 2, 1).setWeight(100, 100).setFill(GBC.BOTH));
30.
31.     sizeButton.addActionListener(new
32.        ActionListener()
33.        {
34.           public void actionPerformed(ActionEvent event) { changeSize(); }
35.        });
36.
37.     valueButton.addActionListener(new
38.        ActionListener()
39.        {
40.           public void actionPerformed(ActionEvent event) { changeValue(); }
41.        });
42.
43.
44.     elementList.setSelectionMode(
45.        ListSelectionModel.SINGLE_SELECTION);
46.
47.     elementList.addListSelectionListener(new
48.        ListSelectionListener()
49.        {
50.           public void valueChanged(ListSelectionEvent event)
51.           {
52.              int i = elementList.getSelectedIndex();
53.              if (i < 0) return;
54.              valueField.setText("" + array[i]);
55.           }
56.        });
57.
58.     elementList.setModel(model);
59.     elementList.setSelectedIndex(0);
60.  }
61.
62.  /**
63.     This method is called when the user wants to change
64.     the size of the array.
65.  */
66.  public void changeSize()
67.  {
68.     fmt.setParseIntegerOnly(true);
69.     int s = 0;
70.     try
71.     {
72.        s = fmt.parse(sizeField.getText()).intValue();
73.        if (s < 0) throw new ParseException("Out of bounds", 0);
74.     }
75.     catch (ParseException e)
76.     {
77.        JOptionPane.showMessageDialog(this, "" + e, "Input Error", JOptionPane.WARNING_MESSAGE);
78.        sizeField.requestFocus();
79.        return;
80.     }
```

```
81.        if (s == array.length) return;
82.        setArray((double[])arrayGrow(array, s));
83.        editor.setValue(array);
84.        editor.firePropertyChange();
85.     }
86.
87.     /**
88.        This method is called when the user wants to change
89.        the currently selected array value.
90.     */
91.     public void changeValue()
92.     {
93.        double v = 0;
94.        fmt.setParseIntegerOnly(false);
95.        try
96.        {
97.           v = fmt.parse(valueField.getText()).doubleValue();
98.        }
99.        catch (ParseException e)
100.       {
101.          JOptionPane.showMessageDialog(this, "" + e, "Input Error", JOptionPane.WARNING_MESSAGE);
102.          valueField.requestFocus();
103.          return;
104.       }
105.       int currentIndex = elementList.getSelectedIndex();
106.       setArray(currentIndex, v);
107.       editor.firePropertyChange();
108.    }
109.
110.    /**
111.       Sets the indexed array property.
112.       @param v the array to edit
113.    */
114.    public void setArray(double[] v)
115.    {
116.       if (v == null) array = new double[0];
117.       else array = v;
118.       model.setArray(array);
119.       sizeField.setText("" + array.length);
120.       if (array.length > 0)
121.       {
122.          valueField.setText("" + array[0]);
123.          elementList.setSelectedIndex(0);
124.       }
125.       else
126.          valueField.setText("");
127.    }
128.
129.    /**
130.       Gets the indexed array property.
131.       @return the array being edited
132.    */
133.    public double[] getArray()
134.    {
135.       return (double[]) array.clone();
136.    }
```

```
137.
138.    /**
139.       Sets the indexed array property.
140.       @param i the index whose value to set
141.       @param value the new value for the given index
142.    */
143.    public void setArray(int i, double value)
144.    {
145.       if (0 <= i && i < array.length)
146.       {
147.          model.setValue(i, value);
148.          elementList.setSelectedIndex(i);
149.          valueField.setText("" + value);
150.       }
151.    }
152.
153.    /**
154.       Gets the indexed array property.
155.       @param i the index whose value to get
156.       @return the value at the given index
157.    */
158.    public double getArray(int i)
159.    {
160.       if (0 <= i && i < array.length) return array[i];
161.       return 0;
162.    }
163.
164.    /**
165.       Resizes an array
166.       @param a the array to grow
167.       @param newLength the new length
168.       @return an array with the given length and the same
169.       elements as a in the common positions
170.    */
171.    private static Object arrayGrow(Object a, int newLength)
172.    {
173.       Class cl = a.getClass();
174.       if (!cl.isArray()) return null;
175.       Class componentType = a.getClass().getComponentType();
176.       int length = Array.getLength(a);
177.
178.       Object newArray = Array.newInstance(componentType, newLength);
179.       System.arraycopy(a, 0, newArray, 0, Math.min(length, newLength));
180.       return newArray;
181.    }
182.
183.    private PropertyEditorSupport editor;
184.    private double[] array;
185.    private NumberFormat fmt = NumberFormat.getNumberInstance();
186.    private JTextField sizeField = new JTextField(4);
187.    private JTextField valueField = new JTextField(12);
188.    private JButton sizeButton = new JButton("Resize");
189.    private JButton valueButton = new JButton("Change");
190.    private JList elementList = new JList();
191.    private DoubleArrayListModel model = new DoubleArrayListModel();
192. }
```

```
193.
194. /**
195.    The list model for the element list in the editor.
196. */
197. class DoubleArrayListModel extends AbstractListModel
198. {
199.    public int getSize() { return array.length; }
200.    public Object getElementAt(int i) { return "[" + i + "] " + array[i]; }
201.
202.    /**
203.       Sets a new array to be displayed in the list.
204.       @param a the new array
205.    */
206.    public void setArray(double[] a)
207.    {
208.       int oldLength = array == null ? 0 : array.length;
209.       array = a;
210.       int newLength = array == null ? 0 : array.length;
211.       if (oldLength > 0) fireIntervalRemoved(this, 0, oldLength);
212.       if (newLength > 0) fireIntervalAdded(this, 0, newLength);
213.    }
214.
215.    /**
216.       Changes a value in the array to be displayed in the list.
217.       @param i the index whose value to change
218.       @param value the new value for the given index
219.    */
220.    public void setValue(int i, double value)
221.    {
222.       array[i] = value;
223.       fireContentsChanged(this, i, i);
224.    }
225.
226.    private double[] array;
227. }
```

Summing Up

For every property editor you write, you have to choose one of three ways to display and edit the property value:

- As a text string (define getAsText and setAsText)
- As a choice field (define getAsText, setAsText, and getTags)
- Graphically, by painting it (define isPaintable, paintValue, supportsCustomEditor, and getCustomEditor)

You saw examples of all three cases in the chart bean.

 java.beans.PropertyEditorSupport 1.1

- boolean isPaintable()
  should be overridden to return true if the class uses the paintValue method to display the property.

- void paintValue(Graphics g, Rectangle box)
  should be overridden to represent the value by drawing into a graphics context in the specified place on the component used for the property inspector.

Parameters: g   The graphics object to draw onto

           box   A rectangle object that represents where on the property inspector component to draw the value

- `boolean supportsCustomEditor()`
  should be overridden to return `true` if the property editor has a custom editor.
- `Component getCustomEditor()`
  should be overridden to return the component that contains a customized GUI for editing the property value.
- `String getJavaInitializationString()`
  should be overridden to return a Java code string that can be used to generate code that initializes the property value. Examples are "`0`", "`new Color(64, 64, 64)`".

Customizers

A property editor, no matter how sophisticated, is responsible for allowing the user to set one property at a time. Especially if certain properties of a bean relate to each other, it may be more user friendly to give users a way to edit multiple properties at the same time. To enable this feature, you supply a *customizer* instead of (or in addition to) multiple property editors.

In the example program for this section, we develop a customizer for the chart bean. The customizer lets you set several properties of the chart bean at once, and it lets you specify a file from which to read the data points for the chart. Figure 8–14 shows you one pane of the customizer for the chart bean.

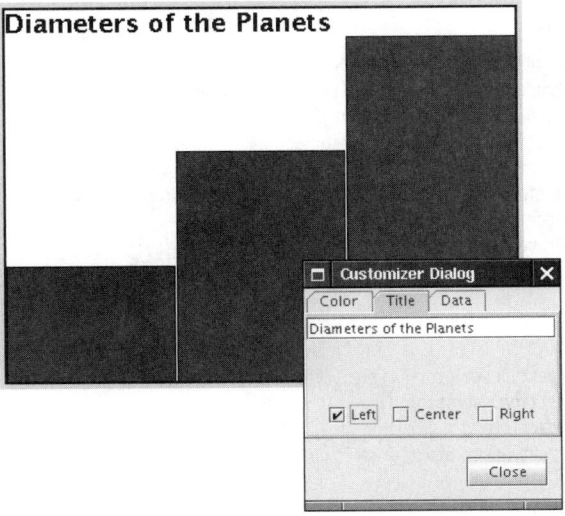

Figure 8–14: The customizer for the ChartBean

To add a customizer to your bean, you *must* supply a `BeanInfo` class and override the `getBean-Descriptor` method, as shown in the following example.

```
public ChartBean2BeanInfo extends SimpleBeanInfo
{
   public BeanDescriptor getBeanDescriptor()
   {
```

```
        return new BeanDescriptor(ChartBean2.class, ChartBean2Customizer.class);
      }
      . . .
    }
```

Note that you need not follow any naming pattern for the customizer class. The builder can locate it by

1. Finding the associated BeanInfo class;
2. Invoking its getBeanDescriptor method; and
3. Calling the getCustomizerClass method.

(Nevertheless, it is customary to name the customizer as *BeanName*Customizer.)

Example 8–10 has the code for the ChartBean2BeanInfo class that references the ChartBean2-Customizer. You see in the next section how that customizer is implemented.

Example 8–10: ChartBean2BeanInfo.java

```
1.  package com.horstmann.corejava;
2.
3.  import java.beans.*;
4.
5.  /**
6.     The bean info for the chart bean, specifying the property editors.
7.  */
8.  public class ChartBeanBeanInfo extends SimpleBeanInfo
9.  {
10.     public PropertyDescriptor[] getPropertyDescriptors()
11.     {
12.        try
13.        {
14.           PropertyDescriptor titlePositionDescriptor
15.              = new PropertyDescriptor("titlePosition", ChartBean.class);
16.           titlePositionDescriptor.setPropertyEditorClass(TitlePositionEditor.class);
17.           PropertyDescriptor inverseDescriptor
18.              = new PropertyDescriptor("inverse", ChartBean.class);
19.           inverseDescriptor.setPropertyEditorClass(InverseEditor.class);
20.           PropertyDescriptor valuesDescriptor
21.              = new PropertyDescriptor("values", ChartBean.class);
22.           valuesDescriptor.setPropertyEditorClass(DoubleArrayEditor.class);
23.
24.           return new PropertyDescriptor[]
25.           {
26.              new PropertyDescriptor("title", ChartBean.class),
27.              titlePositionDescriptor,
28.              valuesDescriptor,
29.              new PropertyDescriptor("graphColor", ChartBean.class),
30.              inverseDescriptor
31.           };
32.        }
33.        catch (IntrospectionException e)
34.        {
35.           e.printStackTrace();
36.           return null;
37.        }
38.     }
39. }
```

 java.beans.BeanInfo 1.1

- BeanDescriptor getBeanDescriptor()
  returns a BeanDescriptor object that describes features of the bean.

 java.beans.BeanDescriptor 1.1

- BeanDescriptor(Class beanClass, Class customizerClass)
  constructs a BeanDescriptor object for a bean that has a customizer.

Parameters:	beanClass	The Class object for the bean
	customizerClass	The Class object for the bean's customizer

- Class getBeanClass()
  returns the Class object that defines the bean.
- Class getCustomizerClass()
  returns the Class object that defines the bean's customizer.

Writing a Customizer Class

Any customizer class you write must implement the Customizer interface. The interface has only three methods:

- The setObject method, which takes a parameter that specifies the bean being customized
- The addPropertyChangeListener and removePropertyChangeListener methods, which manage the collection of listeners that are notified when a property is changed in the customizer

It is a good idea to update the visual appearance of the target bean by broadcasting a PropertyChangeEvent whenever the user changes any of the property values, not just when the user is at the end of the customization process.

Unlike property editors, customizers are not automatically displayed. In NetBeans, you must right-click on the bean and select the Customize menu option to pop up the customizer. At that point, the builder calls the setObject method of the customizer that takes the bean being customized as a parameter. Notice that your customizer is thus created before it is actually linked to an instance of your bean. Therefore, you cannot assume any information about the state of a bean in the customizer, and you must provide a default constructor, that is, one without arguments.

Writing a customizer class is done in three parts:

1. Building the visual interface
2. Initializing the customizer in the setObject method
3. Updating the bean by firing property change events when the user changes properties in the interface

By definition, a customizer class is visual. It must, therefore, extend Component or a subclass of Component, such as JPanel. Because customizers typically present the user with many options, it is often handy to use the tabbed pane user interface. We use this approach and have the customizer extend the JTabbedPane class.

The customizer gathers the following information in three panes:

- Graph color and inverse mode
- Title and title position
- Data points

Of course, developing this kind of user interface can be tedious to code—our example devotes over 100 lines just to set it up in the constructor. However, this task requires only the usual Swing programming skills, and we don't dwell on the details here.

One trick is worth keeping in mind. You often need to edit property values in a customizer. Rather than implementing a new interface for setting the property value of a particular class, you can simply locate an existing property editor and add it to your user interface! For example, in our ChartBean2 customizer, we need to set the graph color. Since we know that the BeanBox has a perfectly good property editor for colors, we locate it as follows:

```
PropertyEditor colorEditor = PropertyEditorManager.findEditor(Color.Class);
```

We then call getCustomEditor to get the component that contains the user interface for setting the colors.

```
Component colorEditorComponent = colorEditor.getCustomEditor();
// now add this component to the UI
```

Once we have all components laid out, we initialize their values in the setObject method. The setObject method is called when the customizer is displayed. Its parameter is the bean that is being customized. To proceed, we store that bean reference—we'll need it later to notify the bean of property changes. Then, we initialize each user interface component. Here is a part of the setObject method of the chart bean customizer that does this initialization.

```
public void setObject(Object obj)
{
   bean = (ChartBean2) obj;
   titleField.setText(bean.getTitle());
   colorEditor.setValue(bean.getGraphColor());
   . . .
}
```

Finally, we hook up event handlers to track the user's activities. Whenever the user changes the value of a component, the component fires an event that our customizer must handle. The event handler must update the value of the property in the bean and must also fire a PropertyChangeEvent so that other listeners (such as the property inspector) can be updated. Let us follow that process with a couple of user interface elements in the chart bean customizer.

When the user types a new title, we want to update the title property. We attach a DocumentListener to the text field into which the user types the title.

```
titleField.getDocument().addDocumentListener(new
   DocumentListener()
   {
      public void changedUpdate(DocumentEvent event)
      {
         setTitle(titleField.getText());
      }
      public void insertUpdate(DocumentEvent event)
      {
         setTitle(titleField.getText());
      }
      public void removeUpdate(DocumentEvent event)
      {
         setTitle(titleField.getText());
      }
   });
```

The three listener methods call the setTitle method of the customizer. That method calls the bean to update the property value and then fires a property change event. (This update is necessary only for properties that are not bound.) Here is the code for the setTitle method.

```
public void setTitle(String newValue)
{
   if (bean == null) return;
   String oldValue = bean.getTitle();
   bean.setTitle(newValue);
   firePropertyChange("title", oldValue, newValue);
}
```

When the color value changes in the color property editor, we want to update the graph color of the bean. We track the color changes by attaching a listener to the property editor. Perhaps confusingly, that editor also sends out property change events.

```
colorEditor.addPropertyChangeListener(new
   PropertyChangeListener()
   {
      public void propertyChange(PropertyChangeEvent event)
      {
         setGraphColor((Color) colorEditor.getValue());
      }
   });
```

Whenever the color value of the color property editor changes, we call the setGraphColor method of the customizer. That method updates the graphColor property of the bean and fires a different property change event that is associated with the graphColor property.

```
public void setGraphColor(Color newValue)
{
   if (bean == null) return;
   Color oldValue = bean.getGraphColor();
   bean.setGraphColor(newValue);
   firePropertyChange("graphColor", oldValue, newValue);
}
```

Example 8–11 provides the full code of the chart bean customizer.

This particular customizer just sets properties of the bean. In general, customizers can call any methods of the bean, whether or not they are property setters. That is, customizers are more general than property editors. (Some beans may have features that are not exposed as properties and that can be edited only through the customizer.)

Example 8–11: ChartBean2Customizer.java

```
 1. package com.horstmann.corejava;
 2.
 3. import java.awt.*;
 4. import java.awt.event.*;
 5. import java.beans.*;
 6. import java.io.*;
 7. import java.text.*;
 8. import java.util.*;
 9. import javax.swing.*;
10. import javax.swing.event.*;
11.
12. /**
13.    A customizer for the chart bean that allows the user to
14.    edit all chart properties in a single tabbed dialog.
15. */
16. public class ChartBean2Customizer extends JTabbedPane
17.    implements Customizer
18. {
```

```
19.    public ChartBean2Customizer()
20.    {
21.       data = new JTextArea();
22.       JPanel dataPane = new JPanel();
23.       dataPane.setLayout(new BorderLayout());
24.       dataPane.add(new JScrollPane(data), BorderLayout.CENTER);
25.       JButton dataButton = new JButton("Set data");
26.       dataButton.addActionListener(new
27.          ActionListener()
28.          {
29.             public void actionPerformed(ActionEvent event) { setData(data.getText()); }
30.          });
31.       JPanel p = new JPanel();
32.       p.add(dataButton);
33.       dataPane.add(p, BorderLayout.SOUTH);
34.
35.       JPanel colorPane = new JPanel();
36.       colorPane.setLayout(new BorderLayout());
37.
38.       normal = new JCheckBox("Normal", true);
39.       inverse = new JCheckBox("Inverse", false);
40.       p = new JPanel();
41.       p.add(normal);
42.       p.add(inverse);
43.       ButtonGroup g = new ButtonGroup();
44.       g.add(normal);
45.       g.add(inverse);
46.       normal.addActionListener(new
47.          ActionListener()
48.          {
49.             public void actionPerformed(ActionEvent event) { setInverse(false); }
50.          });
51.
52.       inverse.addActionListener(
53.          new ActionListener()
54.          {
55.             public void actionPerformed(ActionEvent event) { setInverse(true); }
56.          });
57.
58.       colorEditor = PropertyEditorManager.findEditor(Color.class);
59.       colorEditor.addPropertyChangeListener(
60.          new PropertyChangeListener()
61.          {
62.             public void propertyChange(PropertyChangeEvent event)
63.             {
64.                setGraphColor((Color) colorEditor.getValue());
65.             }
66.          });
67.
68.       colorPane.add(p, BorderLayout.NORTH);
69.       colorPane.add(colorEditor.getCustomEditor(), BorderLayout.CENTER);
70.
71.       JPanel titlePane = new JPanel();
72.       titlePane.setLayout(new BorderLayout());
73.
74.       g = new ButtonGroup();
```

```
75.      position = new JCheckBox[3];
76.      position[0] = new JCheckBox("Left", false);
77.      position[1] = new JCheckBox("Center", true);
78.      position[2] = new JCheckBox("Right", false);
79.
80.      p = new JPanel();
81.      for (int i = 0; i < position.length; i++)
82.      {
83.         final int value = i;
84.         p.add(position[i]);
85.         g.add(position[i]);
86.         position[i].addActionListener(new
87.            ActionListener()
88.            {
89.               public void actionPerformed(ActionEvent event) { setTitlePosition(value); }
90.            });
91.      }
92.
93.      titleField = new JTextField();
94.      titleField.getDocument().addDocumentListener(
95.         new DocumentListener()
96.         {
97.            public void changedUpdate(DocumentEvent evt) {  setTitle(titleField.getText()); }
98.            public void insertUpdate(DocumentEvent evt) { setTitle(titleField.getText()); }
99.            public void removeUpdate(DocumentEvent evt) { setTitle(titleField.getText()); }
100.        });
101.
102.     titlePane.add(titleField, BorderLayout.NORTH);
103.     titlePane.add(p, BorderLayout.SOUTH);
104.     addTab("Color", colorPane);
105.     addTab("Title", titlePane);
106.     addTab("Data", dataPane);
107.  }
108.
109.  /**
110.     Sets the data to be shown in the chart.
111.     @param s a string containing the numbers to be displayed,
112.     separated by white space
113.  */
114.  public void setData(String s)
115.  {
116.     StringTokenizer tokenizer = new StringTokenizer(s);
117.
118.     int i = 0;
119.     double[] values = new double[tokenizer.countTokens()];
120.     while (tokenizer.hasMoreTokens())
121.     {
122.        String token = tokenizer.nextToken();
123.        try
124.        {
125.           values[i] = Double.parseDouble(token);
126.           i++;
127.        }
128.        catch (NumberFormatException e)
129.        {
130.        }
```

```
131.        }
132.        setValues(values);
133.    }
134.
135.    /**
136.        Sets the title of the chart.
137.        @param newValue the new title
138.    */
139.    public void setTitle(String newValue)
140.    {
141.        if (bean == null) return;
142.        String oldValue = bean.getTitle();
143.        bean.setTitle(newValue);
144.        firePropertyChange("title", oldValue, newValue);
145.    }
146.
147.    /**
148.        Sets the title position of the chart.
149.        @param i the new title position (ChartBean2.LEFT,
150.        ChartBean2.CENTER, or ChartBean2.RIGHT)
151.    */
152.    public void setTitlePosition(int i)
153.    {
154.        if (bean == null) return;
155.        Integer oldValue = new Integer(bean.getTitlePosition());
156.        Integer newValue = new Integer(i);
157.        bean.setTitlePosition(i);
158.        firePropertyChange("titlePosition", oldValue, newValue);
159.    }
160.
161.    /**
162.        Sets the inverse setting of the chart.
163.        @param b true if graph and background color are inverted
164.    */
165.    public void setInverse(boolean b)
166.    {
167.        if (bean == null) return;
168.        Boolean oldValue = new Boolean(bean.isInverse());
169.        Boolean newValue = new Boolean(b);
170.        bean.setInverse(b);
171.        firePropertyChange("inverse", oldValue, newValue);
172.    }
173.
174.    /**
175.        Sets the values to be shown in the chart.
176.        @param newValue the new value array
177.    */
178.    public void setValues(double[] newValue)
179.    {
180.        if (bean == null) return;
181.        double[] oldValue = bean.getValues();
182.        bean.setValues(newValue);
183.        firePropertyChange("values", oldValue, newValue);
184.    }
185.
186.    /**
```

```
187.        Sets the color of the chart
188.        @param newValue the new color
189.     */
190.     public void setGraphColor(Color newValue)
191.     {
192.        if (bean == null) return;
193.        Color oldValue = bean.getGraphColor();
194.        bean.setGraphColor(newValue);
195.        firePropertyChange("graphColor", oldValue, newValue);
196.     }
197.
198.     public void setObject(Object obj)
199.     {
200.        bean = (ChartBean2) obj;
201.
202.        data.setText("");
203.        for (double value : bean.getValues())
204.           data.append(value + "\n");
205.
206.        normal.setSelected(!bean.isInverse());
207.        inverse.setSelected(bean.isInverse());
208.
209.        titleField.setText(bean.getTitle());
210.
211.        for (int i = 0; i < position.length; i++)
212.           position[i].setSelected(i == bean.getTitlePosition());
213.
214.        colorEditor.setValue(bean.getGraphColor());
215.     }
216.
217.     public Dimension getPreferredSize() { return new Dimension(XPREFSIZE, YPREFSIZE); }
218.
219.     private static final int XPREFSIZE = 200;
220.     private static final int YPREFSIZE = 120;
221.     private ChartBean2 bean;
222.     private PropertyEditor colorEditor;
223.
224.     private JTextArea data;
225.     private JCheckBox normal;
226.     private JCheckBox inverse;
227.     private JCheckBox[] position;
228.     private JTextField titleField;
229. }
```

java.beans.Customizer 1.1

- void setObject(Object bean)
  specifies the bean to customize.

JavaBeans Persistence

JavaBeans persistence uses JavaBeans properties to save beans to a stream and to read them back at a later time or in a different virtual machine. In this regard, JavaBeans persistence is similar to object serialization. (See Volume 1, Chapter 12 for more information on serialization.) However, there is an important difference: JavaBeans persistence is *suitable for long-term storage.*

When an object is serialized, its instance fields are written to a stream. If the implementation of a class changes, then its instance fields may change. You cannot simply read files that contain serialized objects of older versions. It is possible to detect version differences and translate between old and new data representations. However, the process is extremely tedious and should only be applied in desperate situations. Plainly, serialization is unsuitable for long-term storage. For that reason, all Swing components have the following message in their documentation: "Warning: Serialized objects of this class will not be compatible with future Swing releases. The current serialization support is appropriate for short term storage or RMI between applications."

The long-term persistence mechanism was invented as a solution for this problem. It was originally intended for drag-and-drop GUI design tools. The design tool saves the result of mouse clicks—a collection of frames, panels, buttons, and other Swing components—in a file, using the long-term persistence format. The running program simply opens that file. This approach cuts out the tedious source code for laying out and wiring up Swing components. Sadly, it has not been widely implemented.

 NOTE: The Bean Builder at `http://bean-builder.dev.java.net` is an experimental GUI builder with support for long-term persistence.

The basic idea behind JavaBeans persistence is simple. Suppose you want to save a `JFrame` object to a file so that you can retrieve it later. If you look into the source code of the `JFrame` class and its superclasses, then you see dozens of instance fields. If the frame were to be serialized, all of the field values would need to be written. But think about how a frame is constructed:

```
JFrame frame = new JFrame();
frame.setTitle("My Application");
frame.setVisible(true);
```

The default constructor initializes all instance fields, and a couple of properties are set. If you archive the `frame` object, the JavaBeans persistence mechanism saves exactly these statements in XML format:

```
<object class="javax.swing.JFrame">
  <void property="title">
    <string>My Application</string>
  </void>
  <void property="visible">
    <boolean>true</boolean>
  </void>
</object>
```

When the object is read back, the statements are *executed*: A `JFrame` object is constructed, and its `title` and `visible` properties are set to the given values. It does not matter if the internal representation of the `JFrame` has changed in the meantime. All that matters is that you can restore the object by setting properties.

Note that only those properties that are different from the default are archived. The `XMLEncoder` makes a default `JFrame` and compares its property with the frame that is being archived. Property setter statements are generated only for properties that are different from the default. This process is called *redundancy elimination*. As a result, the archives are generally smaller than the result of serialization. (When serializing Swing components, the difference is particularly dramatic since Swing objects have a lot of state, most of which is never changed from the default.)

Of course, there are minor technical hurdles with this approach. For example, the call

```
frame.setSize(600, 400);
```

is not a property setter. However, the XMLEncoder can cope with this: It writes the statement

```
<void property="bounds">
   <object class="java.awt.Rectangle">
       <int>0</int>
       <int>0</int>
       <int>600</int>
       <int>400</int>
   </object>
</void>
```

To save an object to a stream, use an XMLEncoder:

```
XMLEncoder out = new XMLEncoder(new FileOutputStream(. . .));
out.writeObject(frame);
out.close();
```

To read it back, use an XMLDecoder:

```
XMLDecoder in = new XMLDecoder(new FileInputStream(. . .));
JFrame newFrame = (JFrame) in.readObject();
in.close();
```

The program in Example 8–12 shows how a frame can load and save *itself* (see Figure 8–15). When you run the program, first click the Save button and save the frame to a file. Then move the original frame to a different position and click Load to see another frame pop up at the original location. Have a look inside the XML file that the program produces.

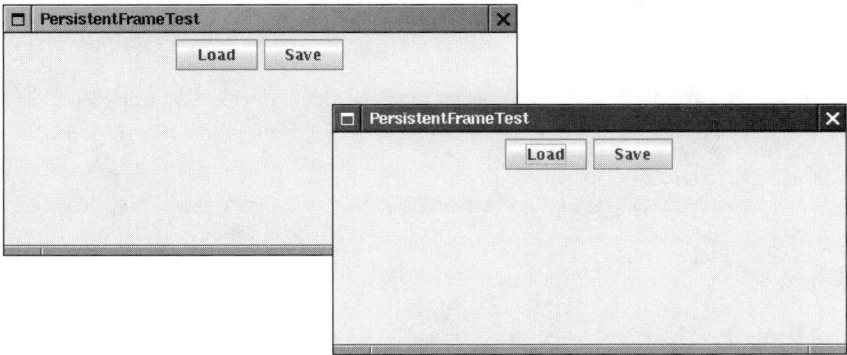

Figure 8–15: The PersistentFrameTest program

If you look closely at the XML output, you will find that the XMLEncoder carries out an amazing amount of work when it saves the frame. The XMLEncoder produces statements that carry out the following actions:

- Set various frame properties: size, layout, defaultCloseOperation, title, and so on.
- Add buttons to the frame.
- Add action listeners to the buttons.

Here, we had to construct the action listers with the EventHandler class. The XMLEncoder cannot archive arbitrary inner classes, but it knows how to handle EventHandler objects.

Example 8–12: PersistentFrameTest.java

```java
1.  import java.awt.*;
2.  import java.awt.event.*;
3.  import java.beans.*;
4.  import java.io.*;
5.  import javax.swing.*;
6.
7.  /**
8.     This program demonstrates the use of an XML encoder and decoder to save and restore a frame.
9.  */
10. public class PersistentFrameTest
11. {
12.    public static void main(String[] args)
13.    {
14.       chooser = new JFileChooser();
15.       chooser.setCurrentDirectory(new File("."));
16.       PersistentFrameTest test = new PersistentFrameTest();
17.       test.init();
18.    }
19.
20.    public void init()
21.    {
22.       frame = new JFrame();
23.       frame.setLayout(new FlowLayout());
24.       frame.setDefaultCloseOperation(JFrame.EXIT_ON_CLOSE);
25.       frame.setTitle("PersistentFrameTest");
26.       frame.setSize(400, 200);
27.
28.       JButton loadButton = new JButton("Load");
29.       frame.add(loadButton);
30.       loadButton.addActionListener(EventHandler.create(ActionListener.class, this, "load"));
31.
32.       JButton saveButton = new JButton("Save");
33.       frame.add(saveButton);
34.       saveButton.addActionListener(EventHandler.create(ActionListener.class, this, "save"));
35.
36.       frame.setVisible(true);
37.    }
38.
39.    public void load()
40.    {
41.       // show file chooser dialog
42.       int r = chooser.showOpenDialog(null);
43.
44.       // if file selected, open
45.       if(r == JFileChooser.APPROVE_OPTION)
46.       {
47.          try
48.          {
49.             File file = chooser.getSelectedFile();
50.             XMLDecoder decoder = new XMLDecoder(new FileInputStream(file));
51.             JFrame newFrame = (JFrame) decoder.readObject();
52.             decoder.close();
53.          }
```

```
54.        catch (IOException e)
55.        {
56.            JOptionPane.showMessageDialog(null, e);
57.        }
58.     }
59.  }
60.
61.  public void save()
62.  {
63.     // show file chooser dialog
64.     int r = chooser.showSaveDialog(null);
65.
66.     // if file selected, save
67.     if(r == JFileChooser.APPROVE_OPTION)
68.     {
69.        try
70.        {
71.           File file = chooser.getSelectedFile();
72.           XMLEncoder encoder = new XMLEncoder(new FileOutputStream(file));
73.           encoder.writeObject(frame);
74.           encoder.close();
75.        }
76.        catch (IOException e)
77.        {
78.           JOptionPane.showMessageDialog(null, e);
79.        }
80.     }
81.  }
82.
83.  private static JFileChooser chooser;
84.  private JFrame frame;
85. }
```

Using JavaBeans Persistence for Arbitrary Data

JavaBeans persistence is not limited to the storage of Swing components. You can use the mechanism to store *any* collection of objects, provided you follow a few simple rules. In the following sections, you learn how you can use JavaBeans persistence as a long-term storage format for your own data.

Writing a Persistence Delegate to Construct an Object

Using JavaBeans persistence is trivial if one can obtain the state of every object by setting properties. But in real programs, there are always classes that don't work that way. Consider, for example, the Employee class of Volume 1, Chapter 4. Employee isn't a well-behaved bean. It doesn't have a default constructor, and it doesn't have methods setName, setSalary, setHireDay. To overcome this problem, you install a *persistence delegate* into the XMLWriter that knows how to write Employee objects:

```
out.setPersistenceDelegate(Employee.class, delegate);
```

The persistence delegate for the Employee class overrides the instantiate method to produce an *expression* that constructs an object.

```
PersistenceDelegate delegate = new
    DefaultPersistenceDelegate()
    {
        protected Expression instantiate(Object oldInstance, Encoder out)
```

```
    {
        Employee e = (Employee) oldInstance;
        GregorianCalendar c = new GregorianCalendar();
        c.setTime(e.getHireDay());
        return new Expression(oldInstance, Employee.class, "new",
            new Object[]
            {
                e.getName(),
                e.getSalary(),
                c.get(Calendar.YEAR),
                c.get(Calendar.MONTH),
                c.get(Calendar.DATE)
            });
    }
};
```

This means: "To re-create oldInstance, call the new method (i.e., the constructor) on the Employee.class object, and supply the given parameters." The parameter name oldInstance is a bit misleading—this is simply the instance that is being saved.

Once the delegate is installed, you can save Employee objects. For example, the statements

```
Object myData = new Employee("Harry Hacker", 50000, 1989, 10, 1);
out.writeObject(myData);
```

generate the following output:

```
<object class="Employee">
    <string>Harry Hacker</string>
    <double>50000.0</double>
    <int>1989</int>
    <int>9</int>
    <int>1</int>
</object>
```

 NOTE: You only need to tweak the *encoding* process. There are no special decoding methods. The decoder simply executes the statements and expressions that it finds in its XML input.

Constructing an Object from Properties

Often, you can use this shortcut: If all constructor parameters can be obtained by accessing properties of oldInstance, then you need not write the instantiate method yourself. Instead, simply construct a DefaultPersistenceDelegate and supply the property names.

For example, the following statement sets the persistence delegate for the Rectangle2D.Double class:

```
out.setPersistenceDelegate(Rectangle2D.Double.class,
    new DefaultPersistenceDelegate(new String[] { "x", "y", "width", "height" }));
```

This tells the encoder: "To encode a Rectangle2D.Double object, get its x, y, width, and height properties and call the constructor with those four values." As a result, the output contains an element such as the following:

```
<object class="java.awt.geom.Rectangle2D$Double">
    <double>5.0</double>
    <double>10.0</double>
    <double>20.0</double>
    <double>30.0</double>
</object>
```

Constructing an Object with a Factory Method

Sometimes, you need to save objects that are obtained from factory methods, not constructors. Consider, for example, how you get an `InetAddress` object:

```
byte[] bytes = new byte[] { 127, 0, 0, 1};
InetAddress address = InetAddress.getByAddress(bytes);
```

The `instantiate` method of the `PersistenceDelegate` produces a call to the factory method.

```
protected Expression instantiate(Object oldInstance, Encoder out)
{
   return new Expression(oldInstance, InetAddress.class, "getByAddress",
      new Object[] { ((InetAddress) oldInstance).getAddress() });
}
```

A sample output is

```
<object class="java.net.Inet4Address" method="getByAddress">
   <array class="byte" length="4">
      <void index="0">
         <byte>127</byte>
      </void>
      <void index="3">
         <byte>1</byte>
      </void>
   </array>
</object>
```

 CAUTION: You must install this delegate with the concrete subclass, such as `Inet4Address`, not with the abstract `InetAddress` class!

Enumerations

To save an `enum` value, you supply a very simple delegate:

```
enum Mood { SAD, HAPPY };
. . .
out.setPersistenceDelegate(Mood.class, new EnumDelegate());
```

You find the `EnumDelegate` class in Example 8–14 on page 680. For example, if you save `Mood.SAD`, the delegate writes an expression that is equivalent to `Enum.valueOf(Mood.class, "SAD")`:

```
<object class="java.lang.Enum" method="valueOf">
   <class>Mood</class>
   <string>SAD</string>
</object>
```

Post-Construction Work

The state of some classes is built up by calls to methods that are not property setters. You can cope with that situation by overriding the `initialize` method of the `DefaultPersistenceDelegate`. The `initialize` method is called after the `instantiate` method. You can generate a sequence of *statements* that are recorded in the archive.

For example, consider the `BitSet` class. To re-create a `BitSet` object, you set all the bits that were present in the original. The following `initialize` method generates the necessary statements:

```
protected void initialize(Class type, Object oldInstance, Object newInstance, Encoder out)
{
   super.initialize(type, oldInstance, newInstance, out);
   BitSet bs = (BitSet) oldInstance;
```

```
    for (int i = bs.nextSetBit(0); i >= 0; i = bs.nextSetBit(i + 1))
        out.writeStatement(new Statement(bs, "set", new Object[] { i, i + 1, true } ));
}
```

A sample output is

```
<object class="java.util.BitSet">
    <void method="set">
        <int>1</int>
        <int>2</int>
        <boolean>true</boolean>
    </void>
    <void method="set">
        <int>4</int>
        <int>5</int>
        <boolean>true</boolean>
    </void>
</object>
```

 NOTE: It would make more sense to write new Statement(bs, "set", new Object[] { i }), but then the XMLWriter produces an unsightly statement that sets a property with an empty name.

Predefined Delegates

You do not have to provide your own delegates for every class. The XMLEncoder has built-in delegates for the following types:

- null
- All primitive types and their wrappers
- String
- Arrays
- Collections and maps
- The reflection types Class, Field, Method, and Proxy
- The AWT types Color, Cursor, Dimension, Font, Insets, Point, Rectangle , and ImageIcon
- AWT and Swing components, borders, layout managers, and models
- Event handlers

Transient Properties

Occasionally, a class has a property with a getter and setter that the XMLDecoder discovers, but you don't want to include the property value in the archive. To suppress archiving of a property, mark it as *transient* in the property descriptor. For example, the following statement tells the GregorianCalendar class not to archive the gregorianChange property:

```
BeanInfo info = Introspector.getBeanInfo(GregorianCalendar.class);
for (PropertyDescriptor desc : info.getPropertyDescriptors())
    if (desc.getName().equals("gregorianChange"))
        desc.setValue("transient", Boolean.TRUE);
```

The setValue method can store arbitrary information with a property descriptor. The XML-Encoder queries the transient attribute before generating a property setter statement.

The program in Example 8–13 shows the various persistence delegates at work. Keep in mind that this program shows a worst-case scenario—in actual applications, many classes can be archived without the use of delegates.

Example 8–13: PersistenceDelegateTest.java

```
 1. import java.awt.*;
 2. import java.awt.geom.*;
 3. import java.beans.*;
 4. import java.io.*;
 5. import java.net.*;
 6. import java.util.*;
 7.
 8. /**
 9.    This program demonstrates various persistence delegates.
10. */
11. public class PersistenceDelegateTest
12. {
13.    public enum Mood { SAD, HAPPY };
14.
15.    public static void main(String[] args) throws Exception
16.    {
17.       XMLEncoder out = new XMLEncoder(System.out);
18.       out.setExceptionListener(new
19.          ExceptionListener()
20.          {
21.             public void exceptionThrown(Exception e)
22.             {
23.                e.printStackTrace();
24.             }
25.          });
26.
27.       PersistenceDelegate delegate = new
28.          DefaultPersistenceDelegate()
29.          {
30.             protected Expression instantiate(Object oldInstance, Encoder out)
31.             {
32.                Employee e = (Employee) oldInstance;
33.                GregorianCalendar c = new GregorianCalendar();
34.                c.setTime(e.getHireDay());
35.                return new Expression(oldInstance, Employee.class, "new",
36.                   new Object[]
37.                   {
38.                      e.getName(),
39.                      e.getSalary(),
40.                      c.get(Calendar.YEAR),
41.                      c.get(Calendar.MONTH),
42.                      c.get(Calendar.DATE)
43.                   });
44.             }
45.          };
46.
47.       out.setPersistenceDelegate(Employee.class, delegate);
48.
49.       out.setPersistenceDelegate(Rectangle2D.Double.class,
50.          new DefaultPersistenceDelegate(new String[] { "x", "y", "width", "height" }));
51.
52.       out.setPersistenceDelegate(Inet4Address.class, new
53.          DefaultPersistenceDelegate()
54.          {
```

```
55.         protected Expression instantiate(Object oldInstance, Encoder out)
56.         {
57.            return new Expression(oldInstance, InetAddress.class, "getByAddress",
58.               new Object[] { ((InetAddress) oldInstance).getAddress() });
59.         }
60.      });
61.
62.      out.setPersistenceDelegate(BitSet.class, new
63.         DefaultPersistenceDelegate()
64.         {
65.            protected void initialize(Class type, Object oldInstance, Object newInstance,
66.               Encoder out)
67.            {
68.               super.initialize(type, oldInstance, newInstance, out);
69.               BitSet bs = (BitSet) oldInstance;
70.               for(int i = bs.nextSetBit(0); i >= 0; i = bs.nextSetBit(i + 1))
71.                  out.writeStatement(new Statement(bs, "set", new Object[]{ i, i + 1, true }));
72.            }
73.         });
74.
75.      out.setPersistenceDelegate(Mood.class, new EnumDelegate());
76.
77.      out.writeObject(new Employee("Harry Hacker", 50000, 1989, 10, 1));
78.      out.writeObject(new java.awt.geom.Rectangle2D.Double(5, 10, 20, 30));
79.      out.writeObject(InetAddress.getLocalHost());
80.      out.writeObject(Mood.SAD);
81.      BitSet bs = new BitSet(); bs.set(1, 4); bs.clear(2, 3);
82.      out.writeObject(bs);
83.      out.writeObject(Color.PINK);
84.      out.writeObject(new GregorianCalendar());
85.      out.close();
86.   }
87.
88.   static
89.   {
90.      try
91.      {
92.         BeanInfo info = Introspector.getBeanInfo(GregorianCalendar.class);
93.         for (PropertyDescriptor desc : info.getPropertyDescriptors())
94.            if (desc.getName().equals("gregorianChange"))
95.               desc.setValue("transient", Boolean.TRUE);
96.      }
97.      catch (IntrospectionException e)
98.      {
99.         e.printStackTrace();
100.      }
101.   }
102. }
```

Example 8–14: EnumDelegate.java

```
1. import java.beans.*;
2.
3. /**
4.    This class can be used to save any enum type in a JavaBeans archive.
5. */
6. public class EnumDelegate extends DefaultPersistenceDelegate
```

```
7.  {
8.      protected Expression instantiate(Object oldInstance, Encoder out)
9.      {
10.         return new Expression(Enum.class,
11.             "valueOf",
12.             new Object[] { oldInstance.getClass(), ((Enum) oldInstance).name() });
13.     }
14. }
```

A Complete Example for JavaBeans Persistence

We end the description of JavaBeans persistence with a complete example (see Figure 8–16). This application writes a damage report for a rental car. The rental car agent enters the rental record, selects the car type, uses the mouse to click on damaged areas on the car, and saves the report. The application can also load existing damage reports. Example 8–15 contains the code for the program.

The application uses JavaBeans persistence to save and load DamageReport objects (see Example 8–16). It illustrates the following aspects of the persistence technology:

• Properties are automatically saved and restored. Nothing needs to be done for the rentalRecord and carType properties.

• Post-construction work is required to restore the damage locations. The persistence delegate generates statements that call the click method.

• The Point2D.Double class needs a DefaultPersistenceDelegate that constructs a point from its x and y properties.

• An EnumDelegate is required to handle the enumerated type CarType.

• The removeMode property (which specifies whether mouse clicks add or remove damage marks) is transient since it should not be saved in damage reports.

Here is a sample damage report:

```
<?xml version="1.0" encoding="UTF-8"?>
<java version="1.5.0" class="java.beans.XMLDecoder">
    <object class="DamageReport">
        <object class="java.lang.Enum" method="valueOf">
            <class>DamageReport$CarType</class>
            <string>SEDAN</string>
        </object>
        <void property="rentalRecord">
            <string>12443-19</string>
        </void>
        <void method="click">
            <object class="java.awt.geom.Point2D$Double">
                <double>181.0</double>
                <double>84.0</double>
            </object>
        </void>
        <void method="click">
            <object class="java.awt.geom.Point2D$Double">
                <double>162.0</double>
                <double>66.0</double>
            </object>
        </void>
    </object>
</java>
```

 NOTE: The sample application does *not* use JavaBeans persistence to save the GUI of the application. That may be of interest to creators of development tools, but here we are focusing on how to use the persistence mechanism to store *application data*.

 CAUTION: At the time of this writing, JavaBeans persistence is not compatible with Java Web Start—see bug 4741757 in the "bug parade" at http://bugs.sun.com.

This example ends our discussion of JavaBeans persistence. In summary, JavaBeans persistence archives are

- Suitable for long-term storage;
- Small and fast;
- Easy to create;
- Human editable; and
- A part of standard Java.

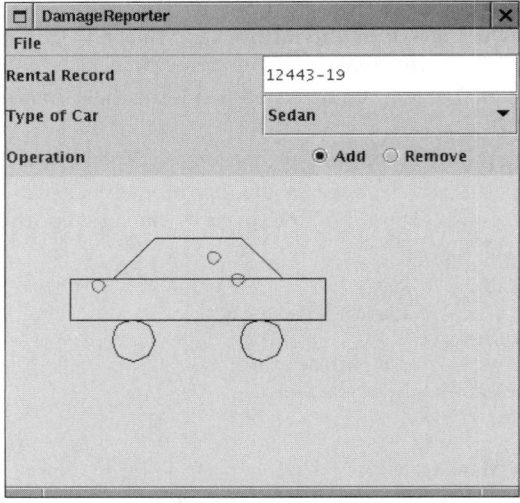

Figure 8–16: The DamageReporter application

Example 8–15: DamageReporter.java

```
1. import java.awt.*;
2. import java.awt.event.*;
3. import java.awt.geom.*;
4. import java.beans.*;
5. import java.io.*;
6. import java.util.*;
7. import javax.swing.*;
8.
9. /**
10.    This program demonstrates the use of an XML encoder and decoder.
11.    All GUI and drawing code is collected in this class. The only
12.    interesting pieces are the action listeners for openItem and
13.    saveItem. Look inside the DamageReport class for encoder customizations.
```

```
14.  */
15.  public class DamageReporter extends JFrame
16.  {
17.     public static void main(String[] args)
18.     {
19.        JFrame frame = new DamageReporter();
20.        frame.setDefaultCloseOperation(JFrame.EXIT_ON_CLOSE);
21.        frame.setVisible(true);
22.     }
23.
24.     public DamageReporter()
25.     {
26.        setTitle("DamageReporter");
27.        setSize(DEFAULT_WIDTH, DEFAULT_HEIGHT);
28.
29.        chooser = new JFileChooser();
30.        chooser.setCurrentDirectory(new File("."));
31.
32.        report = new DamageReport();
33.        report.setCarType(DamageReport.CarType.SEDAN);
34.
35.        // set up the menu bar
36.        JMenuBar menuBar = new JMenuBar();
37.        setJMenuBar(menuBar);
38.
39.        JMenu menu = new JMenu("File");
40.        menuBar.add(menu);
41.
42.        JMenuItem openItem = new JMenuItem("Open");
43.        menu.add(openItem);
44.        openItem.addActionListener(new
45.           ActionListener()
46.           {
47.              public void actionPerformed(ActionEvent evt)
48.              {
49.                 // show file chooser dialog
50.                 int r = chooser.showOpenDialog(null);
51.
52.                 // if file selected, open
53.                 if(r == JFileChooser.APPROVE_OPTION)
54.                 {
55.                    try
56.                    {
57.                       File file = chooser.getSelectedFile();
58.                       XMLDecoder decoder = new XMLDecoder(new FileInputStream(file));
59.                       report = (DamageReport) decoder.readObject();
60.                       decoder.close();
61.                       repaint();
62.                    }
63.                    catch (IOException e)
64.                    {
65.                       JOptionPane.showMessageDialog(null, e);
66.                    }
67.                 }
68.              }
69.           });
70.
```

```
71.    JMenuItem saveItem = new JMenuItem("Save");
72.    menu.add(saveItem);
73.    saveItem.addActionListener(new
74.       ActionListener()
75.       {
76.          public void actionPerformed(ActionEvent evt)
77.          {
78.             report.setRentalRecord(rentalRecord.getText());
79.             chooser.setSelectedFile(new File(rentalRecord.getText() + ".xml"));
80.
81.             // show file chooser dialog
82.             int r = chooser.showSaveDialog(null);
83.
84.             // if file selected, save
85.             if(r == JFileChooser.APPROVE_OPTION)
86.             {
87.                try
88.                {
89.                   File file = chooser.getSelectedFile();
90.                   XMLEncoder encoder = new XMLEncoder(new FileOutputStream(file));
91.                   report.configureEncoder(encoder);
92.                   encoder.writeObject(report);
93.                   encoder.close();
94.                }
95.                catch (IOException e)
96.                {
97.                   JOptionPane.showMessageDialog(null, e);
98.                }
99.             }
100.         }
101.      });
102.
103.   JMenuItem exitItem = new JMenuItem("Exit");
104.   menu.add(exitItem);
105.   exitItem.addActionListener(new
106.      ActionListener()
107.      {
108.         public void actionPerformed(ActionEvent event)
109.         {
110.            System.exit(0);
111.         }
112.      });
113.
114.   // combo box for car type
115.   rentalRecord = new JTextField();
116.   carType = new JComboBox();
117.   carType.addItem(DamageReport.CarType.SEDAN);
118.   carType.addItem(DamageReport.CarType.WAGON);
119.   carType.addItem(DamageReport.CarType.SUV);
120.
121.   carType.addActionListener(new
122.      ActionListener()
123.      {
124.         public void actionPerformed(ActionEvent event)
125.         {
126.            DamageReport.CarType item = (DamageReport.CarType) carType.getSelectedItem();
```

```
127.              report.setCarType(item);
128.              repaint();
129.           }
130.        });
131.
132.        // panel for showing car
133.        carPanel = new
134.           JPanel()
135.           {
136.              public void paintComponent(Graphics g)
137.              {
138.                 super.paintComponent(g);
139.                 Graphics2D g2 = (Graphics2D) g;
140.                 g2.draw((Shape) shapes.get(report.getCarType()));
141.                 report.drawDamage(g2);
142.              }
143.           };
144.        carPanel.addMouseListener(new
145.           MouseAdapter()
146.           {
147.              public void mousePressed(MouseEvent event)
148.              {
149.                 report.click(new Point2D.Double(event.getX(), event.getY()));
150.                 repaint();
151.              }
152.           });
153.        carPanel.setBackground(new Color(0.9f, 0.9f, 0.45f));
154.
155.        // radio buttons for click action
156.        addButton = new JRadioButton("Add");
157.        removeButton = new JRadioButton("Remove");
158.        ButtonGroup group = new ButtonGroup();
159.        JPanel buttonPanel = new JPanel();
160.        group.add(addButton);
161.        buttonPanel.add(addButton);
162.        group.add(removeButton);
163.        buttonPanel.add(removeButton);
164.        addButton.setSelected(!report.getRemoveMode());
165.        removeButton.setSelected(report.getRemoveMode());
166.        addButton.addActionListener(new
167.           ActionListener()
168.           {
169.              public void actionPerformed(ActionEvent event)
170.              {
171.                 report.setRemoveMode(false);
172.              }
173.           });
174.        removeButton.addActionListener(new
175.           ActionListener()
176.           {
177.              public void actionPerformed(ActionEvent event)
178.              {
179.                 report.setRemoveMode(true);
180.              }
181.           });
182.
```

```
183.    // layout components
184.    JPanel gridPanel = new JPanel();
185.    gridPanel.setLayout(new GridLayout(0, 2));
186.    gridPanel.add(new JLabel("Rental Record"));
187.    gridPanel.add(rentalRecord);
188.    gridPanel.add(new JLabel("Type of Car"));
189.    gridPanel.add(carType);
190.    gridPanel.add(new JLabel("Operation"));
191.    gridPanel.add(buttonPanel);
192.
193.    add(gridPanel, BorderLayout.NORTH);
194.    add(carPanel, BorderLayout.CENTER);
195.  }
196.
197.  private JTextField rentalRecord;
198.  private JComboBox carType;
199.  private JPanel carPanel;
200.  private JRadioButton addButton;
201.  private JRadioButton removeButton;
202.  private DamageReport report;
203.  private JFileChooser chooser;
204.
205.  private static final int DEFAULT_WIDTH = 400;
206.  private static final int DEFAULT_HEIGHT = 400;
207.
208.  private static Map<DamageReport.CarType, Shape> shapes
209.     = new EnumMap<DamageReport.CarType, Shape>(DamageReport.CarType.class);
210.
211.  static
212.  {
213.     int width = 200;
214.     int height = 100;
215.     int x = 50;
216.     int y = 50;
217.     Rectangle2D.Double body = new Rectangle2D.Double(x, y + width / 6, width - 1, width / 6);
218.     Ellipse2D.Double frontTire = new Ellipse2D.Double(x + width / 6, y + width / 3,
219.         width / 6, width / 6);
220.     Ellipse2D.Double rearTire = new Ellipse2D.Double(x + width * 2 / 3, y + width / 3,
221.         width / 6, width / 6);
222.
223.     Point2D.Double p1 = new Point2D.Double(x + width / 6, y + width / 6);
224.     Point2D.Double p2 = new Point2D.Double(x + width / 3, y);
225.     Point2D.Double p3 = new Point2D.Double(x + width * 2 / 3, y);
226.     Point2D.Double p4 = new Point2D.Double(x + width * 5 / 6, y + width / 6);
227.
228.     Line2D.Double frontWindshield = new Line2D.Double(p1, p2);
229.     Line2D.Double roofTop = new Line2D.Double(p2, p3);
230.     Line2D.Double rearWindshield = new Line2D.Double(p3, p4);
231.
232.     GeneralPath sedanPath = new GeneralPath();
233.     sedanPath.append(frontTire, false);
234.     sedanPath.append(rearTire, false);
235.     sedanPath.append(body, false);
236.     sedanPath.append(frontWindshield, false);
237.     sedanPath.append(roofTop, false);
238.     sedanPath.append(rearWindshield, false);
```

```
239.    shapes.put(DamageReport.CarType.SEDAN, sedanPath);
240.
241.    Point2D.Double p5 = new Point2D.Double(x + width * 11 / 12, y);
242.    Point2D.Double p6 = new Point2D.Double(x + width, y + width / 6);
243.    roofTop = new Line2D.Double(p2, p5);
244.    rearWindshield = new Line2D.Double(p5, p6);
245.
246.    GeneralPath wagonPath = new GeneralPath();
247.    wagonPath.append(frontTire, false);
248.    wagonPath.append(rearTire, false);
249.    wagonPath.append(body, false);
250.    wagonPath.append(frontWindshield, false);
251.    wagonPath.append(roofTop, false);
252.    wagonPath.append(rearWindshield, false);
253.    shapes.put(DamageReport.CarType.WAGON, wagonPath);
254.
255.    Point2D.Double p7 = new Point2D.Double(x + width / 3, y - width / 6);
256.    Point2D.Double p8 = new Point2D.Double(x + width * 11 / 12, y - width / 6);
257.    frontWindshield = new Line2D.Double(p1, p7);
258.    roofTop = new Line2D.Double(p7, p8);
259.    rearWindshield = new Line2D.Double(p8, p6);
260.
261.    GeneralPath suvPath = new GeneralPath();
262.    suvPath.append(frontTire, false);
263.    suvPath.append(rearTire, false);
264.    suvPath.append(body, false);
265.    suvPath.append(frontWindshield, false);
266.    suvPath.append(roofTop, false);
267.    suvPath.append(rearWindshield, false);
268.    shapes.put(DamageReport.CarType.SUV, suvPath);
269.    }
270. }
```

Example 8–16: DamageReport.java

```
1. import java.awt.*;
2. import java.awt.geom.*;
3. import java.beans.*;
4. import java.util.*;
5.
6. /**
7.    This class describes a vehicle damage report that will be
8.    saved and loaded with the long-term persistence mechanism.
9. */
10. public class DamageReport
11. {
12.    public enum CarType { SEDAN, WAGON, SUV }
13.
14.    // this property is saved automatically
15.    public void setRentalRecord(String newValue)
16.    {
17.       rentalRecord = newValue;
18.    }
19.
20.    public String getRentalRecord()
21.    {
22.       return rentalRecord;
23.    }
```

```
24.
25.    // this property is saved automatically
26.    public void setCarType(CarType newValue)
27.    {
28.       carType = newValue;
29.    }
30.
31.    public CarType getCarType()
32.    {
33.       return carType;
34.    }
35.
36.    // this property is set to be transient
37.    public void setRemoveMode(boolean newValue)
38.    {
39.       removeMode = newValue;
40.    }
41.
42.    public boolean getRemoveMode()
43.    {
44.       return removeMode;
45.    }
46.
47.    public void click(Point2D p)
48.    {
49.       if (removeMode)
50.       {
51.          for (Point2D center : points)
52.          {
53.             Ellipse2D circle = new Ellipse2D.Double(
54.                center.getX() - MARK_SIZE, center.getY() - MARK_SIZE,
55.                2 * MARK_SIZE, 2 * MARK_SIZE);
56.             if (circle.contains(p))
57.             {
58.                points.remove(center);
59.                return;
60.             }
61.          }
62.       }
63.       else points.add(p);
64.    }
65.
66.    public void drawDamage(Graphics2D g2)
67.    {
68.       g2.setPaint(Color.RED);
69.       for (Point2D center : points)
70.       {
71.          Ellipse2D circle = new Ellipse2D.Double(
72.             center.getX() - MARK_SIZE, center.getY() - MARK_SIZE,
73.             2 * MARK_SIZE, 2 * MARK_SIZE);
74.          g2.draw(circle);
75.       }
76.    }
77.
78.    public void configureEncoder(XMLEncoder encoder)
79.    {
```

```
80.      // this step is necessary to save Point2D.Double objects
81.      encoder.setPersistenceDelegate(
82.         Point2D.Double.class,
83.         new DefaultPersistenceDelegate(new String[]{ "x", "y" }) );
84.
85.      // this step is necessary to save the enumerated Type CarType
86.      encoder.setPersistenceDelegate(CarType.class, new EnumDelegate());
87.
88.      // this step is necessary because the array list of points is not
89.      // (and should not be) exposed as a property
90.      encoder.setPersistenceDelegate(
91.         DamageReport.class, new
92.            DefaultPersistenceDelegate()
93.            {
94.               protected void initialize(Class type, Object oldInstance, Object newInstance,
95.                  Encoder out)
96.               {
97.                  super.initialize(type, oldInstance, newInstance, out);
98.                  DamageReport r = (DamageReport) oldInstance;
99.
100.                 for (Point2D p : r. points)
101.                    out.writeStatement(new Statement(oldInstance,"click", new Object[]{ p }) );
102.               }
103.           });
104.
105.   }
106.
107.   // this step is necessary to make the removeMode property transient
108.   static
109.   {
110.      try
111.      {
112.         BeanInfo info = Introspector.getBeanInfo(DamageReport.class);
113.         for (PropertyDescriptor desc : info.getPropertyDescriptors())
114.            if (desc.getName().equals("removeMode"))
115.               desc.setValue("transient", Boolean.TRUE);
116.      }
117.      catch (IntrospectionException e)
118.      {
119.         e.printStackTrace();
120.      }
121.   }
122.
123.   private String rentalRecord;
124.   private CarType carType;
125.   private boolean removeMode;
126.   private ArrayList<Point2D> points = new ArrayList<Point2D>();
127.
128.   private static final int MARK_SIZE = 5;
129. }
```

API   **java.beans.XMLEncoder 1.4**

- XMLEncoder(OutputStream out)

  constructs an XMLEncoder that sends its output to the given stream.

- void writeObject(Object obj)
  archives the given object.

- void writeStatement(Statement stat)
  writes the given statement to the archive. This method should only be called from a persistence delegate.

 java.beans.Encoder 1.4

- void setPersistenceDelegate(Class<?> type, PersistenceDelegate delegate)
- PersistenceDelegate getPersistenceDelegate(Class<?> type)
  set or get the delegate for archiving objects of the given type.

- void setExceptionListener(ExceptionListener listener)
- ExceptionListener getExceptionListener()
  set or get the exception listener that is notified if an exception occurs during the encoding process.

 java.beans.ExceptionListener 1.4

- void exceptionThrown(Exception e)
  is called when an exception was thrown during the encoding or decoding process.

 java.beans.XMLDecoder 1.4

- XMLDecoder(InputStream in)
  constructs an XMLDecoder that reads an archive from the given input stream.

- Object readObject()
  reads the next object from the archive.

- void setExceptionListener(ExceptionListener listener)
- ExceptionListener getExceptionListener()
  set or get the exception listener that is notified if an exception occurs during the encoding process.

 java.beans.PersistenceDelegate 1.4

- protected abstract Expression instantiate(Object oldInstance, Encoder out)
  returns an expression for instantiating an object that is equivalent to oldInstance.

- protected void initialize(Class<?> type, Object oldInstance, Object newInstance, Encoder out)
  writes statements to out that turn newInstance into an object that is equivalent to oldInstance.

 java.beans.DefaultPersistenceDelegate 1.4

- DefaultPersistenceDelegate()
  constructs a persistence delegate for a class with a zero-parameter constructor.

- DefaultPersistenceDelegate(String[] propertyNames)
  constructs a persistence delegate for a class whose construction parameters are the values of the given properties.

- protected Expression instantiate(Object oldInstance, Encoder out)
  returns an expression for invoking the constructor with either no parameters or the values of the properties specified in the constructor.

- `protected void initialize(Class<?> type, Object oldInstance, Object newInstance, Encoder out)`
  writes statements to out that apply property setters to newInstance, attempting to turn it into an object that is equivalent to oldInstance.

 java.beans.Expression 1.4

- `Expression(Object value, Object target, String methodName, Object[] parameters)`
  constructs an expression that calls the given method on target, with the given parameters. The result of the expression is assumed to be value. To call a constructor, target should be a Class object and methodName should be "new".

java.beans.Statement 1.4

- `Statement(Object target, String methodName, Object[] parameters)`
  constructs a statement that calls the given method on target, with the given parameters.

Chapter 9

Security

- ▼ CLASS LOADERS
- ▼ BYTECODE VERIFICATION
- ▼ SECURITY MANAGERS AND PERMISSIONS
- ▼ DIGITAL SIGNATURES
- ▼ CODE SIGNING
- ▼ ENCRYPTION

When Java technology first appeared on the scene, the excitement was not about a well-crafted programming language but about the possibility of safely executing applets that are delivered over the Internet (see Volume 1, Chapter 10 for more information about applets). Obviously, delivering executable applets is practical only when the recipients are sure that the code can't wreak havoc on their machines. For this reason, security was and is a major concern of both the designers and the users of Java technology. This means that unlike the case with other languages and systems where security was implemented as an afterthought or a reaction to break-ins, security mechanisms are an integral part of Java technology.

Three mechanisms help ensure safety:

- Language design features (bounds checking on arrays, legal type conversions only, no pointer arithmetic, and so on);
- An access control mechanism that controls what the code can do (such as file access, network access, and so on);
- Code signing, whereby code authors can use standard cryptographic algorithms to authenticate Java code. Then, the users of the code can determine exactly who created the code and whether the code has been altered after it was signed.

The Java virtual machine checks for bad pointers, invalid array offsets, and so on. The other steps require controlling what goes to the Java virtual machine.

When class files are loaded into the virtual machine, they are checked for integrity. We show you in detail how that process works, and we show you how to implement your own *class loader*.

For maximum security, both the default mechanism for loading a class and a custom class loader need to work with a *security manager* class that controls what actions code can perform. You'll see how to write your own security manager class.

Finally, you'll see the cryptographic algorithms supplied in the java.security package, which allow for code signing and user authentication.

As always, we focus on those topics that are of greatest interest to application programmers. For an in-depth view, we recommend the book *Inside Java 2 Platform Security* by Li Gong [Addison-Wesley 1999].

Class Loaders

A Java compiler converts source into the machine language of a hypothetical machine, called the *virtual machine*. The virtual machine code is stored in a class file with a .class extension. Each class file contains the definition and implementation code for one class or interface. These class files must be interpreted by a program that can translate the instruction set of the virtual machine into the machine language of the target machine.

Note that the virtual machine loads only those class files that are needed for the execution of a program. For example, suppose program execution starts with MyProgram.class. Here are the steps that the virtual machine carries out.

1. The virtual machine has a mechanism for loading class files, for example, by reading the files from disk or by requesting them from the Web; it uses this mechanism to load the contents of the MyProgram class file.

2. If the MyProgram class has instance variables or superclasses of another class type, these class files are loaded as well. (The process of loading all the classes that a given class depends on is called *resolving* the class.)

3. The virtual machine then executes the main method in MyProgram (which is static, so no instance of a class needs to be created).

4. If the main method or a method that main calls requires additional classes, these are loaded next.

The class loading mechanism doesn't just use a single class loader, however. Every Java program has at least three class loaders:

• The bootstrap class loader
• The extension class loader
• The system class loader (also sometimes called the application class loader)

The bootstrap class loader loads the system classes (typically, from the JAR file rt.jar). It is an integral part of the virtual machine and is usually implemented in C. There is no Class-Loader object corresponding to the bootstrap class loader. For example,

```
String.class.getClassLoader()
```

returns null.

The extension class loader loads "standard extensions" from the *jre*/lib/ext directory. You can drop JAR files into that directory, and the extension class loader will find the classes in them, even without any class path. (Some people recommend this mechanism to avoid the "class path from hell," but see the cautionary notes below.)

The system class loader loads the application classes. It locates classes in the directories and JAR/ZIP files on the class path, as set by the CLASSPATH environment variable or the -classpath command-line option.

In Sun's Java implementation, the extension and system class loaders are implemented in Java. Both are instances of the URLClassLoader class.

 CAUTION: You can run into grief if you drop a JAR file into the *jre*/lib/ext directory and one of its classes needs to load a class that is not a system or extension class. The extension class loader *does not use the class path*. Keep that in mind before you use the extension directory as a way to manage your class file hassles.

 CAUTION: There is a second pitfall with dropping JAR files into the *jre*/lib/ext directory. Sometimes, programmers forget about the files they placed there months ago. Then they scratch their heads when the class loader seems to ignore the class path, when it is actually loading long-forgotten classes from the extension directory.

Class loaders have a *parent/child* relationship. Every class loader except for the bootstrap class loader has a parent class loader. A class loader is supposed to give its parent a chance to load any given class and only load it if the parent has failed. For example, when the system class loader is asked to load a system class (say, java.util.ArrayList), then it first asks the extension class loader. That class loader first asks the bootstrap class loader. The bootstrap class loader finds and loads the class in rt.jar, and neither of the other class loaders searches any further.

 NOTE: When implementing a class loader, you should always delegate class loading to the parent first. Otherwise, there is a potential security risk: The custom class loader can accidentally load a version of a system class that bypasses important security checks.

Applets, servlets, and RMI stubs are loaded with custom class loaders. You can even write your own class loader for specialized purposes. That lets you carry out specialized security checks before you pass the bytecodes to the virtual machine. For example, you can write a class loader that can refuse to load a class that has not been marked as "paid for." The next section shows you how.

Most of the time, you don't have to worry about class loaders. Most classes are loaded because they are required by other classes, and that process is transparent to you.

If you load a class programmatically, by calling Class.forName, then the new class is loaded with the same class loader that loaded the code that calls Class.forName. Generally, this is the right behavior. However, it fails in the following circumstances:

1. You implement a library class with a method that calls Class.forName.
2. Your method is called from an application class that was loaded with a different class loader than the library class.
3. The loaded class is not visible from the class loader that loaded the library class.

In that case, the library class needs to work harder and retrieve the application's class loader:

```
Thread t = Thread.currentThread();
ClassLoader loader = t.getContextClassLoader();
Class cl = loader.loadClass(className);
```

Using Class Loaders as Namespaces

Every Java programmer knows that package names are used to eliminate name conflicts. There are two classes called Date in the standard library, but of course their real names are java.util.Date and java.sql.Date. The simple name is only a programmer convenience and requires the inclusion of appropriate import statements. In a running program, all class names contain their package name.

It may surprise you, however, that you can have two classes in the same virtual machine that have the same class *and package* name. A class is determined by its full name *and* the class loader. This technique is useful for loading code from multiple sources. For example, a browser uses separate instances of the applet class loader class for each web page. This allows the virtual machine to separate classes from different web pages, no matter what they are named.

 NOTE: This technique has other uses as well, such as "hot deployment" of servlets and Enterprise JavaBeans. See http://java.sun.com/developer/TechTips/2000/tt1027.html for more information.

Writing Your Own Class Loader

To write your own class loader, you simply extend the ClassLoader class and override the method.

```
findClass(String className)
```

The loadClass method of the ClassLoader superclass takes care of the delegation to the parent and calls findClass only if the class hasn't already been loaded and if the parent class loader was unable to load the class.

 NOTE: In earlier versions of the JDK, programmers had to override the loadClass method. That practice is no longer recommended.

Your implementation of this method must do the following:

1. Load the bytecodes for the class from the local file system or from some other source.
2. Call the defineClass method of the ClassLoader superclass to present the bytecodes to the virtual machine.

In the program of Example 9–1, we implement a class loader that loads encrypted class files. The program asks the user for the name of the first class to load (that is, the class containing main) and the decryption key. It then uses a special class loader to load the specified class and calls the main method. The class loader decrypts the specified class and all nonsystem classes that are referenced by it. Finally, the program calls the main method of the loaded class (see Figure 9–1).

For simplicity, we ignore 2,000 years of progress in the field of cryptography and use the venerable Caesar cipher for encrypting the class files.

 NOTE: David Kahn's wonderful book *The Codebreakers* [Macmillan, NY, 1967, p. 84] refers to Suetonius as a historical source for the Caesar cipher. Caesar shifted the 24 letters of the Roman alphabet by 3 letters. When this chapter was first written, the U.S. government restricted the export of strong encryption methods. Therefore, we used Caesar's method for our example since it was clearly legal for export.

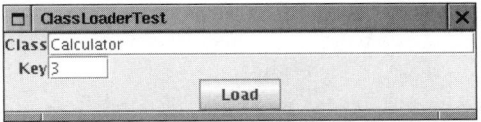

Figure 9–1: The ClassLoaderTest program

Our version of the Caesar cipher has as a key a number between 1 and 255. To decrypt, simply add that key to every byte and reduce modulo 256. The Caesar.java program of Example 9–2 carries out the encryption.

So that we do not confuse the regular class loader, we use a different extension, .caesar, for the encrypted class files.

To decrypt, the class loader simply subtracts the key from every byte. In the companion code for this book, you will find four class files, encrypted with a key value of 3—the traditional choice. To run the encrypted program, you need the custom class loader defined in our ClassLoaderTest program.

Encrypting class files has a number of practical uses (provided, of course, that you use a cipher stronger than the Caesar cipher). Without the decryption key, the class files are useless. They can neither be executed by a standard virtual machine nor readily disassembled.

This means that you can use a custom class loader to authenticate the user of the class or to ensure that a program has been paid for before it will be allowed to run. Of course, encryption is only one application of a custom class loader. You can use other types of class loaders to solve other problems, for example, storing class files in a database.

Example 9–1: ClassLoaderTest.java

```
1. import java.util.*;
2. import java.io.*;
3. import java.lang.reflect.*;
4. import java.awt.*;
5. import java.awt.event.*;
6. import javax.swing.*;
7.
8. /**
9.    This program demonstrates a custom class loader that decrypts
10.   class files.
11. */
12. public class ClassLoaderTest
13. {
14.    public static void main(String[] args)
15.    {
16.       JFrame frame = new ClassLoaderFrame();
17.       frame.setDefaultCloseOperation(JFrame.EXIT_ON_CLOSE);
18.       frame.setVisible(true);
```

```
19.          }
20.    }
21.
22.    /**
23.       This frame contains two text fields for the name of the class
24.       to load and the decryption key.
25.    */
26.    class ClassLoaderFrame extends JFrame
27.    {
28.       public ClassLoaderFrame()
29.       {
30.          setTitle("ClassLoaderTest");
31.          setSize(DEFAULT_WIDTH, DEFAULT_HEIGHT);
32.          setLayout(new GridBagLayout());
33.          add(new JLabel("Class"), new GBC(0, 0).setAnchor(GBC.EAST));
34.          add(nameField, new GBC(1, 0).setWeight(100, 0).setAnchor(GBC.WEST));
35.          add(new JLabel("Key"), new GBC(0, 1).setAnchor(GBC.EAST));
36.          add(keyField, new GBC(1, 1).setWeight(100, 0).setAnchor(GBC.WEST));
37.          JButton loadButton = new JButton("Load");
38.          add(loadButton, new GBC(0, 2, 2, 1));
39.          loadButton.addActionListener(new
40.             ActionListener()
41.             {
42.                public void actionPerformed(ActionEvent event)
43.                {
44.                   runClass(nameField.getText(), keyField.getText());
45.                }
46.             });
47.          pack();
48.       }
49.
50.       /**
51.          Runs the main method of a given class.
52.          @param name the class name
53.          @param key the decryption key for the class files
54.       */
55.       public void runClass(String name, String key)
56.       {
57.          try
58.          {
59.             ClassLoader loader = new CryptoClassLoader(Integer.parseInt(key));
60.             Class c = loader.loadClass(name);
61.             String[] args = new String[] {};
62.
63.             Method m = c.getMethod("main", args.getClass());
64.             m.invoke(null, (Object) args);
65.          }
66.          catch (Throwable e)
67.          {
68.             JOptionPane.showMessageDialog(this, e);
69.          }
70.       }
71.
72.       private JTextField keyField = new JTextField("3", 4);
73.       private JTextField nameField = new JTextField(30);
74.       private static final int DEFAULT_WIDTH = 300;
75.       private static final int DEFAULT_HEIGHT = 200;
```

```
 76.   }
 77.
 78.   /**
 79.      This class loader loads encrypted class files.
 80.   */
 81.   class CryptoClassLoader extends ClassLoader
 82.   {
 83.      /**
 84.         Constructs a crypto class loader.
 85.         @param k the decryption key
 86.      */
 87.      public CryptoClassLoader(int k)
 88.      {
 89.         key = k;
 90.      }
 91.
 92.      protected Class findClass(String name)
 93.         throws ClassNotFoundException
 94.      {
 95.         byte[] classBytes = null;
 96.         try
 97.         {
 98.            classBytes = loadClassBytes(name);
 99.         }
100.         catch (IOException e)
101.         {
102.            throw new ClassNotFoundException(name);
103.         }
104.
105.         Class cl = defineClass(name, classBytes, 0, classBytes.length);
106.         if (cl == null)
107.            throw new ClassNotFoundException(name);
108.         return cl;
109.      }
110.
111.      /**
112.         Loads and decrypt the class file bytes.
113.         @param name the class name
114.         @return an array with the class file bytes
115.      */
116.      private byte[] loadClassBytes(String name)
117.         throws IOException
118.      {
119.         String cname = name.replace('.', '/') + ".caesar";
120.         FileInputStream in = null;
121.         in = new FileInputStream(cname);
122.         try
123.         {
124.            ByteArrayOutputStream buffer = new ByteArrayOutputStream();
125.            int ch;
126.            while ((ch = in.read()) != -1)
127.            {
128.               byte b = (byte) (ch - key);
129.               buffer.write(b);
130.            }
131.            in.close();
132.            return buffer.toByteArray();
```

```
133.         }
134.      finally
135.      {
136.         in.close();
137.      }
138.    }
139.
140.    private int key;
141. }
```

Example 9–2: Caesar.java

```
1. import java.io.*;
2.
3. /**
4.    Encrypts a file using the Caesar cipher.
5. */
6. public class Caesar
7. {
8.    public static void main(String[] args)
9.    {
10.      if (args.length != 3)
11.      {
12.         System.out.println("USAGE: java Caesar in out key");
13.         return;
14.      }
15.
16.      try
17.      {
18.         FileInputStream in = new FileInputStream(args[0]);
19.         FileOutputStream out = new FileOutputStream(args[1]);
20.         int key = Integer.parseInt(args[2]);
21.         int ch;
22.         while ((ch = in.read()) != -1)
23.         {
24.            byte c = (byte)(ch + key);
25.            out.write(c);
26.         }
27.         in.close();
28.         out.close();
29.      }
30.      catch (IOException exception)
31.      {
32.         exception.printStackTrace();
33.      }
34.    }
35. }
```

API   **java.lang.Class 1.0**

- ClassLoader getClassLoader()
  gets the class loader that loaded this class.

API   **java.lang.ClassLoader 1.0**

- ClassLoader getParent() **1.2**
  returns the parent class loader, or null if the parent class loader is the bootstrap class loader.

- `static ClassLoader getSystemClassLoader()` **1.2**
  gets the system class loader, that is, the class loader that was used to load the first application class.
- `protected Class findClass(String name)` **1.2**
  should be overridden by a class loader to find the bytecodes for a class and present them to the virtual machine by calling the `defineClass` method.

Parameters:	name	The name of the class; use . as package name separator, and don't use a .class suffix

- `Class defineClass(String name, byte[] data, int offset, int length)`
  adds a new class to the virtual machine.

Parameters:	name	The name of the class; use . as package name separator, and don't use a .class suffix
	data	An array holding the bytecodes of the class
	offset	The start of the bytecodes in the array
	length	The length of the bytecodes in the array

 java.lang.Thread 1.0

- `ClassLoader getContextClassLoader()` **1.2**
  gets the class loader that the creator of this thread has designated as the most reasonable class loader to use when executing this thread.
- `void setContextClassLoader(ClassLoader loader)` **1.2**
  sets a class loader for code in this thread to retrieve for loading classes. If no context class loader is set explicitly when a thread is started, the parent's context class loader is used.

Bytecode Verification

When a class loader presents the bytecodes of a newly loaded Java platform class to the virtual machine, these bytecodes are first inspected by a *verifier.* The verifier checks that the instructions cannot perform actions that are obviously damaging. All classes except for system classes are verified. You can, however, deactivate verification with the undocumented `-noverify` option.

For example,

```
java -noverify Hello
```

Here are some of the checks that the verifier carries out:

- That variables are initialized before they are used
- That method calls match the types of object references
- That rules for accessing private data and methods are not violated
- That local variable accesses fall within the runtime stack
- That the runtime stack does not overflow

If any of these checks fails, then the class is considered corrupted and will not be loaded.

 NOTE: If you are familiar with Gödel's theorem, you may wonder how the verifier can prove that a class file is free from type mismatches, uninitialized variables, and stack overflows. Gödel's theorem states that it is impossible to design algorithms whose inputs are program files and whose output is a Boolean value that states whether the input program has a particular property

(such as being free from stack overflows). Is this a conflict between the public relations department at Sun Microsystems and the laws of logic? No—in fact, the verifier is *not* a decision algorithm in the sense of Gödel. If the verifier accepts a program, it is indeed safe. However, the verifier may reject many programs even though they would actually be safe.

This strict verification is an important security consideration. Accidental errors, such as uninitialized variables, can easily wreak havoc if they are not caught. More important, in the wide open world of the Internet, you must be protected against malicious programmers who create evil effects on purpose. For example, by modifying values on the runtime stack or by writing to the private data fields of system objects, a program can break through the security system of a browser.

You may wonder, however, why a special verifier checks all these features. After all, the compiler would never allow you to generate a class file in which an uninitialized variable is used or in which a private data field is accessed from another class. Indeed, a class file generated by a compiler for the Java programming language always passes verification. However, the bytecode format used in the class files is well documented, and it is an easy matter for someone with some experience in assembly programming and a hex editor to manually produce a class file that contains valid but unsafe instructions for the Java virtual machine. Once again, keep in mind that the verifier is always guarding against maliciously altered class files, not just checking the class files produced by a compiler.

Here's an example of how to construct such an altered class file. We start with the program VerifierTest.java of Example 9–3. This is a simple program that calls a method and displays the method result. The program can be run both as a console program and as an applet. The fun method itself just computes 1 + 2.

```
static int fun()
{
   int m;
   int n;
   m = 1;
   n = 2;
   int r = m + n;
   return r;
}
```

As an experiment, try to compile the following modification of this program:

```
static int fun()
{
   int m = 1;
   int n;
   m = 1;
   m = 2;
   int r = m + n;
   return r;
}
```

In this case, n is not initialized, and it could have any random value. Of course, the compiler detects that problem and refuses to compile the program. To create a bad class file, we have to work a little harder. First, run the javap program to find out how the compiler translates the fun method. The command

```
javap -c VerifierTest
```

shows the bytecodes in the class file in mnemonic form.

```
Method int fun()
   0 iconst_1
   1 istore_0
   2 iconst_2
   3 istore_1
   4 iload_0
   5 iload_1
   6 iadd
   7 istore_2
   8 iload_2
   9 ireturn
```

We use a hex editor to change instruction 3 from istore_1 to istore_0. That is, local variable 0 (which is m) is initialized twice, and local variable 1 (which is n) is not initialized at all. We need to know the hexadecimal values for these instructions. These values are readily available from *The Java Virtual Machine Specification* by Tim Lindholm and Frank Yellin [Addison-Wesley 1999].

```
   0 iconst_1 04
   1 istore_0 3B
   2 iconst_2 05
   3 istore_1 3C
   4 iload_0  1A
   5 iload_1  1B
   6 iadd     60
   7 istore_2 3D
   8 iload_2  1C
   9 ireturn  AC
```

You can use a hex editor (such as DataWorkshop, which you can download from http://www.dataworkshop.de) to carry out the modification. Or, of course, you can use emacs in hexl-mode. In Figure 9–2, you see the class file VerifierTest.class loaded into DataWorkshop, with the bytecodes of the fun method highlighted.

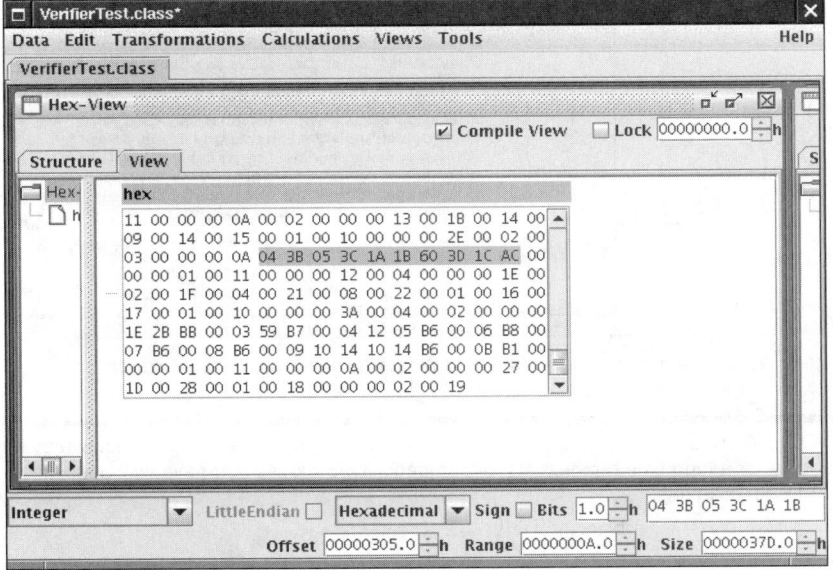

Figure 9–2: Modifying bytecodes with a hex editor

Change 3C to 3B and save the class file. Then try running the VerifierTest program. You get an error message:

```
Exception in thread "main" java.lang.VerifyError: (class: VerifierTest, method:fun signature: ()I)
Accessing value from uninitialized register 1
```

That is good—the virtual machine detected our modification.

Now run the program with the -noverify (or -Xverify:none) option.

```
java -noverify VerifierTest
```

The fun method returns a seemingly random value. This is actually 2 plus the value that happened to be stored in the variable n, which never was initialized. Here is a typical printout:

```
1 + 2 = 15102330
```

To see how browsers handle verification, we wrote this program to run either as an application or an applet. Load the applet into a browser, using a file URL such as

```
file:///C:/CoreJavaBook/v2ch9/VerifierTest/VerifierTest.html
```

You then see an error message displayed indicating that verification has failed (see Figure 9–3).

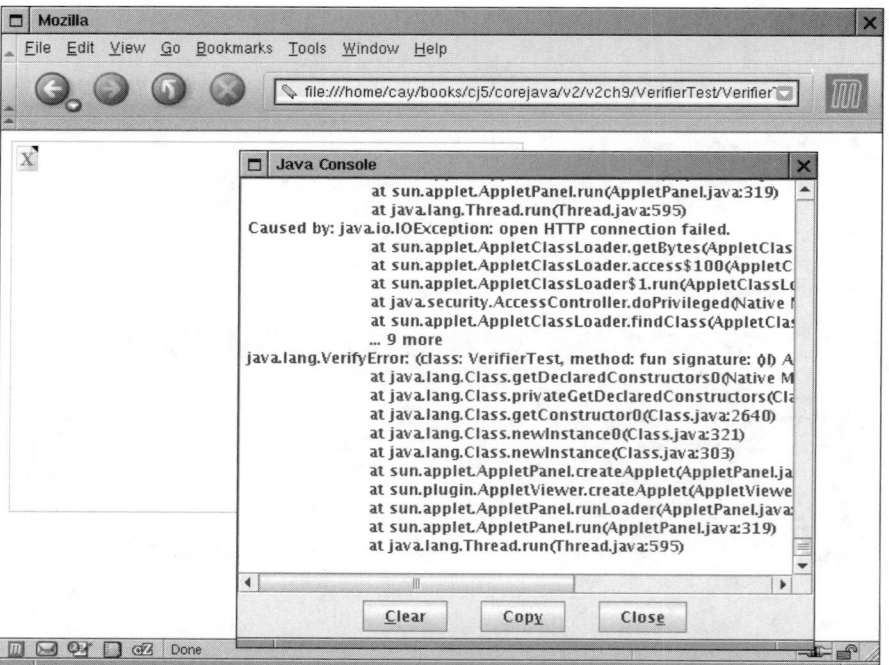

Figure 9–3: Loading a corrupted class file raises a method verification error

 NOTE: A curious hole in the verifier in the Java virtual machine has been known by many people for a long time but persists for compatibility. Suppose you have two class files A.java and B.java like this:

```
public class A { public int field; }

public class B
```

```
    {
       public static void main(String[] args)
       {
          System.out.println(new A().field);
       }
    }
```

This program compiles and runs, of course. Now edit *only* the file A.java to make field private. Recompile only that file. The resulting program should fail verification since B now attempts to access a private field of A. However, up to JDK 5.0, the program will run and merrily access the private field. Only if you run the Java virtual machine with the -verify option will the error be caught.

The reason is backward compatibility with an obscure and ill-considered optimization in JDK 1.0—see http://bugs.sun.com/developer/bugParade/bugs/4030988.html. This flaw is not considered a security risk because only classes loaded from the local file system are exempt from verification.

Example 9–3: VerifierTest.java

```java
1.  import java.awt.*;
2.  import java.applet.*;
3.
4.  /**
5.     This application demonstrates the bytecode verifier of
6.     the virtual machine. If you use a hex editor to modify the
7.     class file, then the virtual machine should detect the
8.     tampering.
9.  */
10. public class VerifierTest extends Applet
11. {
12.    public static void main(String[] args)
13.    {
14.       System.out.println("1 + 2 == " + fun());
15.    }
16.
17.    /**
18.       A function that computes 1 + 2
19.       @return 3, if the code has not been corrupted
20.    */
21.    public static int fun()
22.    {
23.       int m;
24.       int n;
25.       m = 1;
26.       n = 2;
27.       // use hex editor to change to "m = 2" in class file
28.       int r = m + n;
29.       return r;
30.    }
31.
32.    public void paint(Graphics g)
33.    {
34.       g.drawString("1 + 2 == " + fun(), 20, 20);
35.    }
36. }
```

Security Managers and Permissions

Once a class has been loaded into the virtual machine by a class loader or by the default class loading mechanism and checked by the verifier, the third security mechanism of the Java platform springs into action: the *security manager.* A security manager is a class that controls whether a specific operation is permitted. Operations checked by a security manager include the following:

- Whether the current thread can create a new class loader
- Whether the current thread can halt the virtual machine
- Whether a class can access a member of another class
- Whether the current thread can access a local file
- Whether the current thread can open a socket connection to an external host
- Whether a class can start a print job
- Whether a class can access the system clipboard
- Whether a class can access the AWT event queue
- Whether the current thread is trusted to bring up a top-level window

There are many other checks such as these throughout the Java library.

The default behavior when running Java applications is that *no* security manager is installed, so all these operations are permitted. The applet viewer, on the other hand, immediately installs a security manager that is quite restrictive.

For example, applets are not allowed to exit the virtual machine. If they try calling the exit method, then a security exception is thrown. Here is what happens in detail. The exit method of the Runtime class calls the checkExit method of the security manager. Here is the entire code of the exit method:

```
public void exit(int status)
{
   SecurityManager security = System.getSecurityManager();
   if (security != null)
       security.checkExit(status);
   exitInternal(status);
}
```

The security manager now checks if the exit request came from the browser or an individual applet. If the security manager agrees with the exit request, then the checkExit method simply returns and normal processing continues. However, if the security manager doesn't want to grant the request, the checkExit method throws a SecurityException.

The exit method continues only if no exception occurred. It then calls the *private native* exitInternal method that actually terminates the virtual machine. There is no other way of terminating the virtual machine, and because the exitInternal method is private, it cannot be called from any other class. Thus, any code that attempts to exit the virtual machine must go through the exit method and thus through the checkExit security check without triggering a security exception.

Clearly, the integrity of the security policy depends on careful coding. The providers of system services in the standard library must be careful to always consult the security manager before attempting any sensitive operation.

When you run a Java application, the default is that no security manager is running. Your program can install a specific security manager by a call to the static setSecurityManager method in the System class. Once your program installs a security manager, any attempt to install a second security manager succeeds only if the first security manager agrees to be

replaced. This is clearly essential; otherwise, a bad applet could install its own security manager. Thus, although it is possible to have multiple class loaders, a program in the Java programming language can be governed by only one security manager. It is up to the implementor of that security manager to decide whether to grant all classes the same access or whether to take the origins of the classes into account before deciding what to do.

The default security manager of the Java 2 platform allows both programmers and system administrators fine-grained control over individual security permissions. We describe these features in the following section. First, we summarize the Java 2 platform security model. We then show how you can control permissions with *policy files*. Finally, we explain how you can define your own permission types and how you can extend the default security manager class.

Java 2 Platform Security

JDK 1.0 had a very simple security model: Local classes had full permissions, and remote classes were confined to the *sandbox*. Just like a child that can only play in a sandbox, remote code was only allowed to paint on the screen and interact with the user. The applet security manager denied all access to local resources. JDK 1.1 implemented a slight modification: Remote code that was signed by a trusted entity was granted the same permissions as local classes. However, both versions of the JDK provided an all-or-nothing approach. Programs either had full access or they had to play in the sandbox.

The Java 2 platform has a much more flexible mechanism. A *security policy* maps *code sources to permission sets* (see Figure 9–4).

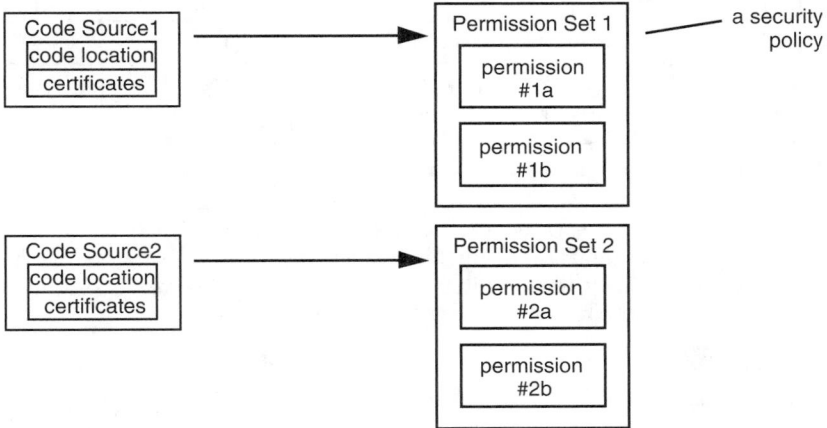

Figure 9–4: A security policy

A *code source* has two properties: the *code location* (for example, an HTTP URL for remote code, or a file URL for local code in a JAR file) and *certificates*. You see later in this chapter how code can be certified by trusted parties.

A *permission* is any property that is checked by a security manager. JDK 1.2 implementation supports a number of permission classes, each of which encapsulates the details of a particular permission. For example, the following instance of the FilePermission class states that it is okay to read and write any file in the /tmp directory.

```
FilePermission p = new FilePermission("/tmp/*", "read,write");
```

More important, the default implementation of the Policy class in JDK 1.2 reads permissions from a *permission file*. Inside a permission file, the same read permission is expressed as

```
permission java.io.FilePermission "/tmp/*", "read,write";
```

We discuss permission files in the next section.

Figure 9–5 shows the hierarchy of the permission classes that were supplied with JDK 1.2. Many more permission classes have been added in subsequent JDK versions.

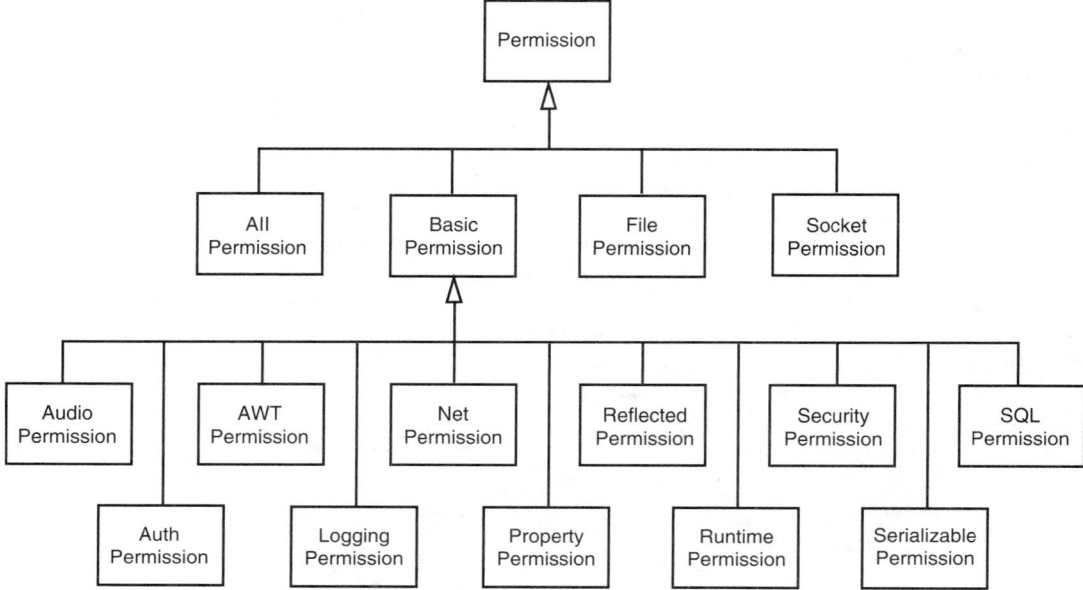

Figure 9–5: The hierarchy of permission classes

In the preceding section, you saw that the SecurityManager class has security check methods such as checkExit. These methods exist only for the convenience of the programmer and for backward compatibility. They all map into standard permission checks. For example, here is the source code for the checkExit method:

```
public void checkExit()
{
   checkPermission(new RuntimePermission("exitVM"));
}
```

Each security manager is free to provide its own implementation of the checkPermission method. However, the JDK provides a "standard model" of how to carry out permission checks. For the remainder of this section, we describe this standard model.

Each class has a *protection domain,* an object that encapsulates both the code source and the collection of permissions of the class. When the SecurityManager needs to check a permission, it looks at the classes of all methods currently on the call stack. It then gets the protection domains of all classes and asks each protection domain if its permission collection allows the operation that is currently being checked. If all domains agree, then the check passes. Otherwise, a SecurityException is thrown.

Why do all methods on the call stack need to allow a particular operation? Let us work through an example. Suppose the `init` method of an applet wants to open a file. It might call

```
Reader in = new FileReader(name);
```

The `FileReader` constructor calls the `FileInputStream` constructor, which calls the `checkRead` method of the security manager, which finally calls `checkPermission` with a `FilePermission(name,` "read" object. Table 9–1 shows the call stack.

Table 9–1: Call Stack During Permission Checking

Class	Method	Code Source	Permissions
SecurityManager	checkPermission	null	AllPermission
SecurityManager	checkRead	null	AllPermission
FileInputStream	constructor	null	AllPermission
FileReader	constructor	null	AllPermission
applet	init	applet code source	applet permissions
. . .			

The `FileInputStream` and `SecurityManager` classes are *system classes* whose CodeSource is `null` and whose permissions consist of an instance of the `AllPermission` class, which allows all operations. Clearly, their permissions alone can't determine the outcome of the check. As you can see, the `checkPermission` method must take into account the restricted permissions of the applet class. By checking the entire call stack, the security mechanism ensures that one class can never ask another class to carry out a sensitive operation on its behalf.

NOTE: This brief discussion of permission checking explains the basic concepts. However, we omit a number of technical details here. With security, the devil lies in the details, and we encourage you to read the book by Li Gong for more information. For a more critical view of the Java platform security model, see the book *Securing Java* by Gary McGraw and Ed Felten [John Wiley & Sons 1999]. You can find an online version of that book at http://www.securingjava.com.

java.lang.SecurityManager 1.0

- void checkPermission(Permission p) **1.2**
  check whether this security manager grants the given permission. The method throws a SecurityException if the permission is not granted.

java.lang.Class 1.0

- ProtectionDomain getProtectionDomain() **1.2**
  gets the protection domain for this class, or null if this class was loaded without a protection domain.

java.security.ProtectionDomain 1.2

- ProtectionDomain(CodeSource source, PermissionCollection permissions)
  constructs a protection domain with the given code source and permissions.
- CodeSource getCodeSource()
  gets the code source of this protection domain.
- boolean implies(Permission p)
  returns true if the given permission is allowed by this protection domain.

710

 java.security.CodeSource 1.2

- Certificate[] getCertificates()
  gets the certificates for class file signature associated with this code source.
- URL getLocation()
  gets the location of class files associated with this code source.

Security Policy Files

In the preceding section, you saw how the SecureClassLoader assigns permissions when loading classes, that is, by asking a Policy object to look up the permissions for the code source of each class. In principle, you can install your own Policy class to carry out the mapping from code sources to permissions. However, in this section, you learn about the standard policy class that the Java 2 virtual machine uses.

 NOTE: The policy class is set in the file java.security in the *jre*/lib/security subdirectory of the JDK home directory. By default, this file contains the line

```
policy.provider=sun.security.provider.PolicyFile
```

You can supply your own policy class and install it by changing this file.

The standard policy reads *policy files* that contain instructions for mapping code sources to permissions. You have seen these policy files in Chapter 5, where you saw that they were required to grant network access to programs that use the RMISecurityManager. Here is a typical policy file:

```
grant codeBase "http://www.horstmann.com/classes"
{
  permission java.io.FilePermission "/tmp/*", "read,write";
};
```

This file grants permission to read and write files in the /tmp directory to all code that was downloaded from http://www.horstmann.com/classes.

You can install policy files in standard locations. By default, there are two locations:

- The file java.policy in the Java platform home directory
- The file .java.policy (notice the period at the beginning of the file name) in the user home directory

 NOTE: You can change the locations of these files in the java.security configuration file. The defaults are specified as

```
policy.url.1=file:${java.home}/lib/security/java.policy
policy.url.2=file:${user.home}/.java.policy
```

A system administrator can modify the java.security file and specify policy URLs that reside on another server and that cannot be edited by users. There can be any number of policy URLs (with consecutive numbers) in the policy file. The permissions of all files are combined.

During testing, we don't like to constantly modify these standard files. Therefore, we prefer to explicitly name the policy file that is required for each application. Simply place the permissions into a separate file, say, MyApp.policy, and start the virtual machine as

```
java -Djava.security.policy=MyApp.policy MyApp
```

For applets, you instead use

```
appletviewer -J-Djava.security.policy=MyApplet.policy MyApplet.html
```

(You can use the -J option of the appletviewer to pass any command-line argument to the virtual machine.)

In these examples, the MyApp.policy file is added to the other policies in effect. If you add a second equal sign, such as

```
java -Djava.security.policy==MyApp.policy MyApp
```

then your application uses *only* the specified policy file, and the standard policy files are ignored.

CAUTION: An easy mistake during testing is to accidentally leave a .java.policy file that grants a lot of permissions, perhaps even AllPermission, in the current directory. If you find that your application doesn't seem to pay attention to the restrictions in your policy file, check for a left-behind .java.policy file in your current directory. If you use a UNIX system, this is a particularly easy mistake to make because files with names that start with a period are not displayed by default.

As you saw previously, Java applications by default do not install a security manager. Therefore, you won't see the effect of policy files until you install one. You can, of course, add a line

```
System.setSecurityManager(new SecurityManager());
```

into your main method. Or you can add the command-line option -Djava.security.manager when starting the virtual machine.

```
java -Djava.security.manager -Djava.security.policy=MyApp.policy MyApp
```

In the remainder of this section, we show you in detail how to describe permissions in the policy file. We describe the entire policy file format, except for code certificates, which we cover later in this chapter.

A policy file contains a sequence of grant entries. Each entry has the following form:

```
grant codesource
{
    permission₁;
    permission₂;
    . . .
};
```

The code source contains a code base (which can be omitted if the entry applies to code from all sources) and the names of trusted principals and certificate signers (which can be omitted if signatures are not required for this entry).

The code base is specified as

```
codeBase "url"
```

If the URL ends in a /, then it refers to a directory. Otherwise, it is taken to be the name of a JAR file. For example,

```
grant codeBase "www.horstmann.com/classes/" { . . . };
grant codeBase "www.horstmann.com/classes/MyApp.jar" { . . . };
```

The code base is a URL and should always contain forward slashes as file separators, even for file URLs in Windows. For example,

```
grant codeBase "file:C:/myapps/classes/" { . . . };
```

NOTE: Everyone knows that http URLs start with two slashes (http://). But there seems sufficient confusion about file URLs that the policy file reader accepts two forms of file URLs, namely, file://*localFile* and file:*localFile*. Furthermore, a slash before a Windows drive letter is optional. That is, all of the following are acceptable:

```
file:C:/dir/filename.ext
file:/C:/dir/filename.ext
file://C:/dir/filename.ext
file:///C:/dir/filename.ext
```

Actually, in our tests, the `file:////C:/dir/filename.ext` is acceptable as well, and we have no explanation for that. In UNIX/Linux, you should use the form

```
file:/dir/filename.ext
```

The permissions have the following structure:

permission *className targetName*, *actionList*;

The class name is the fully qualified class name of the permission class (such as `java.io.FilePermission`). The *target name* is a permission-specific value, for example, a file or directory name for the file permission, or a host and port for a socket permission. The *actionList* is also permission specific. It is a list of actions, such as read or connect, separated by commas. Some permission classes don't need target names and action lists. Table 9–2 lists the commonly used permission classes and their actions.

Table 9–2: Permissions and Their Associated Targets and Actions

Permission	Target	Action
`java.io.FilePermission`	file target (see text)	`read`, `write`, `execute`, `delete`
`java.net.SocketPermission`	socket target (see text)	`accept`, `connect`, `listen`, `resolve`
`java.util.PropertyPermission`	property target (see text)	`read`, `write`
`java.lang.RuntimePermission`	`createClassLoader` `getClassLoader` `setContextClassLoader` `enableContextClassLoaderOverride` `createSecurityManager` `setSecurityManager` `exitVM` `getenv.`*variableName* `shutdownHooks` `setFactory` `setIO` `modifyThread` `stopThread` `modifyThreadGroup` `getProtectionDomain` `readFileDescriptor` `writeFileDescriptor` `loadLibrary.`*libraryName* `accessClassInPackage.`*packageName* `defineClassInPackage.`*packageName* `accessDeclaredMembers.`*className* `queuePrintJob` `getStackTrace` `setDefaultUncaughtExceptionHandler` `preferences`	

Table 9–2: Permissions and Their Associated Targets and Actions (continued)

Permission	Target	Action
java.awt.AWTPermission	showWindowWithoutWarningBanner accessClipboard accessEventQueue createRobot fullScreenExclusive listenToAllAWTEvents readDisplayPixels replaceKeyboardFocusManager watchMousePointer setWindowAlwaysOnTop setAppletStub	
java.net.NetPermission	setDefaultAuthenticator specifyStreamHandler requestPasswordAuthentication setProxySelector getProxySelector setCookieHandler getCookieHandler setResponseCache getResponseCache	
java.lang.reflect.ReflectPermission	suppressAccessChecks	
java.io.SerializablePermission	enableSubclassImplementation enableSubstitution	
java.security.SecurityPermission	createAccessControlContext getDomainCombiner getPolicy setPolicy getProperty.*keyName* setProperty.*keyName* insertProvider.*providerName* removeProvider.*providerName* setSystemScope setIdentityPublicKey setIdentityInfo addIdentityCertificate removeIdentityCertificate printIdentity clearProviderProperties.*providerName* putProviderProperty.*providerName* removeProviderProperty.*providerName* getSignerPrivateKey setSignerKeyPair	
java.security.AllPermission		
javax.audio.AudioPermission	play record	

Table 9–2: Permissions and Their Associated Targets and Actions (continued)

Permission	Target	Action

`javax.security.auth.AuthPermission`	`doAs`
	`doAsPrivileged`
	`getSubject`
	`getSubjectFromDomainCombiner`
	`setReadOnly`
	`modifyPrincipals`
	`modifyPublicCredentials`
	`modifyPrivateCredentials`
	`refreshCredential`
	`destroyCredential`
	`createLoginContext.`*contextName*
	`getLoginConfiguration`
	`setLoginConfiguration`
	`refreshLoginConfiguration`	

`java.util.logging.LoggingPermission`	`control`	
`java.sql.SQLPermission`	`setLog`	

As you can see from Table 9–2, most permissions simply permit a particular operation. You can think of the operation as the target with an implied action "permit". These permission classes all extend the `BasicPermission` class (see Figure 9–5 on page 708). However, the targets for the file, socket, and property permissions are more complex, and we need to investigate them in detail.

File permission targets can have the following form:

file	a file
directory/	a directory
directory/*	all files in the directory
*	all files in the current directory
directory/-	all files in the directory or one of its subdirectories
-	all files in the current directory or one of its subdirectories
`<<ALL FILES>>`	all files in the file system

For example, the following permission entry gives access to all files in the directory /myapp and any of its subdirectories.

```
permission java.io.FilePermission "/myapp/-", "read,write,delete";
```

You must use the \\ escape sequence to denote a backslash in a Windows file name.

```
permission java.io.FilePermission "c:\\myapp\\-", "read,write,delete";
```

Socket permission targets consist of a host and a port range. Host specifications have the following form:

hostname or *IPaddress*	a single host
`localhost` or the empty string	the local host
*.domainSuffix	any host whose domain ends with the given suffix
*	all hosts

Port ranges are optional and have the form:

:*n*	a single port
:*n-*	all ports numbered *n* and above
:*-n*	all ports numbered *n* and below
:*n1-n2*	all ports in the given range

Here is an example:

```
permission java.net.SocketPermission "*.horstmann.com:8000-8999", "connect";
```

Finally, property permission targets can have one of two forms:

property	a specific property
*propertyPrefix.**	all properties with the given prefix

Examples are "java.home" and "java.vm.*".

For example, the following permission entry allows a program to read all properties that start with java.vm.

```
permission java.util.PropertyPermission "java.vm.*", "read";
```

You can use system properties in policy files. The token ${*property*} is replaced by the property value. For example, ${user.home} is replaced by the home directory of the user. Here is a typical use of this system property in a permission entry.

```
permission java.io.FilePermission "${user.home}", "read,write";
```

To create platform-independent policy files, it is a good idea to use the file.separator property instead of explicit / or \\ separators. To make this simpler, the special notation ${/} is a shortcut for ${file.separator}. For example,

```
permission java.io.FilePermission "${user.home}${/}-", "read,write";
```

is a portable entry for granting permission to read and write in the user's home directory and any of its subdirectories.

 NOTE: The JDK comes with a rudimentary tool, called policytool, that you can use to edit policy files (see Figure 9–6). Of course, this tool is not suitable for end users who would be completely mystified by most of the settings. We view it as a proof of concept for an administration tool that might be used by system administrators who prefer point-and-click over syntax. Still, what's missing is a sensible set of categories (such as low, medium, or high security) that is meaningful to nonexperts. As a general observation, we believe that the Java 2 platform certainly contains all the pieces for a fine-grained security model but that it could benefit from some polish in delivering these pieces to end users and system administrators.

Custom Permissions

In this section, you see how you can supply your own permission class that users can refer to in their policy files.

To implement your permission class, you extend the Permission class and supply the following methods:

- A constructor with two String parameters, for the target and the action list
- String getActions()
- boolean equals()
- int hashCode()
- boolean implies(Permission other)

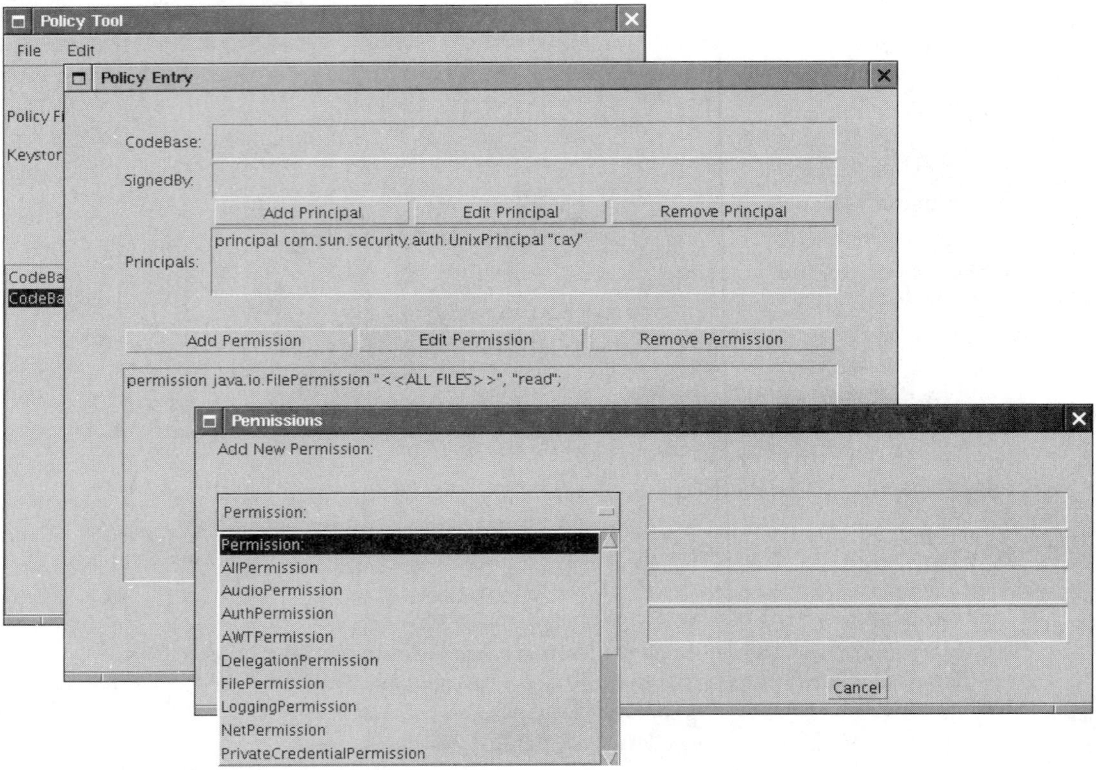

Figure 9–6: The policy tool

The last method is the most important. Permissions have an *ordering*, in which more general permissions *imply* more specific ones. Consider the file permission

```
p1 = new FilePermission("/tmp/-", "read, write");
```

This permission allows reading and writing of any file in the /tmp directory and any of its subdirectories.

This permission implies other, more specific permissions:

```
p2 = new FilePermission("/tmp/-", "read");
p3 = new FilePermission("/tmp/aFile", "read, write");
p4 = new FilePermission("/tmp/aDirectory/-", "write");
```

In other words, a file permission p1 implies another file permission p2 if

1. The target file set of p1 contains the target file set of p2;
2. The action set of p1 contains the action set of p2.

Consider the following example of the use of the implies method. When the FileInputStream constructor wants to open a file for reading, it checks whether it has permission to do so. For that check, a *specific* file permission object is passed to the checkPermission method:

```
checkPermission(new FilePermission(fileName, "read"));
```

The security manager now asks all applicable permissions whether they imply this permission. If any one of them implies it, then the check passes.

In particular, the AllPermission implies all other permissions.

If you define your own permission classes, then you need to define a suitable notion of implication for your permission objects. Suppose, for example, that you define a TVPermission for a set-top box powered by Java technology. A permission

```
new TVPermission("Tommy:2-12:1900-2200", "watch,record")
```

might allow Tommy to watch and record television channels 2–12 between 19:00 and 22:00. You need to implement the implies method so that this permission implies a more specific one, such as

```
new TVPermission("Tommy:4:2000-2100", "watch")
```

Implementation of a Permission Class

In the next sample program, we implement a new permission for monitoring the insertion of text into a text area. The program ensures that you cannot add "bad words" such as *sex, drugs,* and *C++* into a text area. We use a custom permission class so that the list of bad words can be supplied in a policy file.

The following subclass of JTextArea asks the security manager whether it is okay to add new text.

```
class WordCheckTextArea extends JTextArea
{
   public void append(String text)
   {
      WordCheckPermission p = new WordCheckPermission(text, "insert");
      SecurityManager manager = System.getSecurityManager();
      if (manager != null) manager.checkPermission(p);
      super.append(text);
   }
}
```

If the security manager grants the WordCheckPermission, then the text is appended. Otherwise, the checkPermission method throws an exception.

Word check permissions have two possible actions: insert (the permission to insert a specific text) and avoid (the permission to add any text that avoids certain bad words). You should run this program with the following policy file:

```
grant
{
   permission WordCheckPermission "sex,drugs,C++", "avoid";
};
```

This policy file grants the permission to insert any text that avoids the bad words *sex, drugs,* and *C++.*

When designing the WordCheckPermission class, we must pay particular attention to the implies method. Here are the rules that control whether permission p1 implies permission p2.

1. If p1 has action avoid and p2 has action insert, then the target of p2 must avoid all words in p1. For example, the permission

    ```
    WordCheckPermission "sex,drugs,C++", "avoid"
    ```

    implies the permission

    ```
    WordCheckPermission "Mary had a little lamb", "insert"
    ```

2. If p1 and p2 both have action avoid, then the word set of p2 must contain all words in the word set of p1. For example, the permission

    ```
    WordCheckPermission "sex,drugs", "avoid"
    ```

implies the permission

```
WordCheckPermission "sex,drugs,C++", "avoid"
```

3. If p1 and p2 both have action `insert`, then the text of p1 must contain the text of p2. For example, the permission

```
WordCheckPermission "Mary had a little lamb", "insert"
```

implies the permission

```
WordCheckPermission "a little lamb", "insert"
```

You can find the implementation of this class in Example 9–5.

Note that you retrieve the permission target with the confusingly named `getName` method of the `Permission` class.

Since permissions are described by a pair of strings in policy files, permission classes need to be prepared to parse these strings. In particular, we use the following method to transform the comma-separated list of bad words of an `avoid` permission into a genuine `Set`.

```java
public Set<String> badWordSet()
{
   Set<String> set = new HashSet<String>();
   set.addAll(Arrays.asList(getName().split(",")));
   return set;
}
```

This code allows us to use the `equals` and `containsAll` methods to compare sets. As you saw in Chapter 2, the `equals` method of a set class finds two sets to be equal if they contain the same elements in any order. For example, the sets resulting from `"sex,drugs,C++"` and `"C++,drugs,sex"` are equal.

 CAUTION: Make sure that your permission class is a public class. The policy file loader cannot load classes with package visibility outside the boot class path, and it silently ignores any classes that it cannot find.

The program in Example 9-4 shows how the `WordCheckPermission` class works. Type any text into the text field and click the Insert button. If the security check passes, the text is appended to the text area. If not, an error message is displayed (see Figure 9–7).

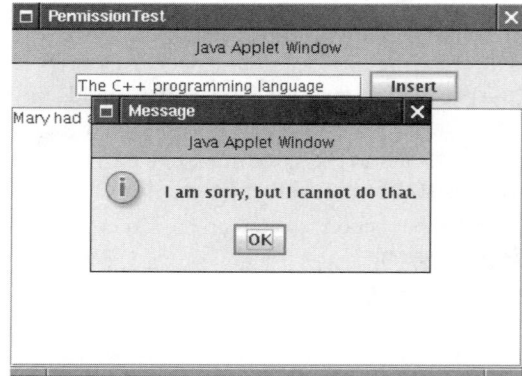

Figure 9–7: The `PermissionTest` program

Make sure to start the program with the appropriate policy file.

```
java -Djava.security.policy=PermissionTest.policy PermissionTest
```

Otherwise, all attempts to insert text will fail.

 CAUTION: If you carefully look at Figure 9–7, you will see that the frame window has a warning border with the misleading caption "Java Applet Window." The window caption is determined by the showWindowWithoutWarningBanner target of the java.awt.AWTPermission. If you like, you can edit the policy file to grant that permission.

Example 9–4: PermissionTest.java

```
 1. import java.awt.*;
 2. import java.awt.event.*;
 3. import java.io.*;
 4. import java.net.*;
 5. import java.security.*;
 6. import java.util.*;
 7. import javax.swing.*;
 8.
 9. /**
10.    This class demonstrates the custom WordCheckPermission.
11. */
12. public class PermissionTest
13. {
14.    public static void main(String[] args)
15.    {
16.       System.setSecurityManager(new SecurityManager());
17.       JFrame frame = new PermissionTestFrame();
18.       frame.setDefaultCloseOperation(JFrame.EXIT_ON_CLOSE);
19.       frame.setVisible(true);
20.    }
21. }
22.
23. /**
24.    This frame contains a text field for inserting words into
25.    a text area that is protected from "bad words".
26. */
27. class PermissionTestFrame extends JFrame
28. {
29.    public PermissionTestFrame()
30.    {
31.       setTitle("PermissionTest");
32.       setSize(DEFAULT_WIDTH, DEFAULT_HEIGHT);
33.
34.       textField = new JTextField(20);
35.       JPanel panel = new JPanel();
36.       panel.add(textField);
37.       JButton openButton = new JButton("Insert");
38.       panel.add(openButton);
39.       openButton.addActionListener(new
40.          ActionListener()
41.          {
42.             public void actionPerformed(ActionEvent event)
43.             {
```

```
44.            insertWords(textField.getText());
45.         }
46.      });
47.
48.    add(panel, BorderLayout.NORTH);
49.
50.    textArea = new WordCheckTextArea();
51.    add(new JScrollPane(textArea), BorderLayout.CENTER);
52.   }
53.
54.   /**
55.      Tries to insert words into the text area.
56.      Displays a dialog if the attempt fails.
57.      @param words the words to insert
58.   */
59.   public void insertWords(String words)
60.   {
61.      try
62.      {
63.         textArea.append(words + "\n");
64.      }
65.      catch (SecurityException e)
66.      {
67.         JOptionPane.showMessageDialog(this, "I am sorry, but I cannot do that.");
68.      }
69.   }
70.
71.   private JTextField textField;
72.   private WordCheckTextArea textArea;
73.   private static final int DEFAULT_WIDTH = 400;
74.   private static final int DEFAULT_HEIGHT = 300;
75. }
76.
77. /**
78.    A text area whose append method makes a security check
79.    to see that no bad words are added.
80. */
81. class WordCheckTextArea extends JTextArea
82. {
83.   public void append(String text)
84.   {
85.      WordCheckPermission p = new WordCheckPermission(text, "insert");
86.      SecurityManager manager = System.getSecurityManager();
87.      if (manager != null) manager.checkPermission(p);
88.      super.append(text);
89.   }
90. }
```

Example 9–5: WordCheckPermission.java

```
1. import java.security.*;
2. import java.util.*;
3.
4. /**
5.    A permission that checks for bad words.
6. */
7. public class WordCheckPermission extends Permission
```

```
8.   {
9.      /**
10.        Constructs a word check permission
11.        @param target a comma separated word list
12.        @param anAction "insert" or "avoid"
13.      */
14.      public WordCheckPermission(String target, String anAction)
15.      {
16.         super(target);
17.         action = anAction;
18.      }
19.
20.      public String getActions() { return action; }
21.
22.      public boolean equals(Object other)
23.      {
24.         if (other == null) return false;
25.         if (!getClass().equals(other.getClass())) return false;
26.         WordCheckPermission b = (WordCheckPermission) other;
27.         if (!action.equals(b.action)) return false;
28.         if (action.equals("insert"))
29.            return getName().equals(b.getName());
30.         else if (action.equals("avoid"))
31.            return badWordSet().equals(b.badWordSet());
32.         else return false;
33.      }
34.
35.      public int hashCode()
36.      {
37.         return getName().hashCode() + action.hashCode();
38.      }
39.
40.      public boolean implies(Permission other)
41.      {
42.         if (!(other instanceof WordCheckPermission)) return false;
43.         WordCheckPermission b = (WordCheckPermission) other;
44.         if (action.equals("insert"))
45.         {
46.            return b.action.equals("insert") &&
47.               getName().indexOf(b.getName()) >= 0;
48.         }
49.         else if (action.equals("avoid"))
50.         {
51.            if (b.action.equals("avoid"))
52.               return b.badWordSet().containsAll(badWordSet());
53.            else if (b.action.equals("insert"))
54.            {
55.               for (String badWord : badWordSet())
56.                  if (b.getName().indexOf(badWord) >= 0)
57.                     return false;
58.               return true;
59.            }
60.            else return false;
61.         }
62.         else return false;
63.      }
```

```
64.
65.    /**
66.       Gets the bad words that this permission rule describes.
67.       @return a set of the bad words
68.    */
69.    public Set<String> badWordSet()
70.    {
71.       Set<String> set = new HashSet<String>();
72.       set.addAll(Arrays.asList(getName().split(",")));
73.       return set;
74.    }
75.
76.    private String action;
77. }
```

API **java.security.Permission 1.2**

- Permission(String name)
  constructs a permission with the given target name.

- String getName()
  returns the target name of this permission.

- boolean implies(Permission other)
  checks whether this permission implies the other permission. That is the case if the other permission describes a more specific condition that is a consequence of the condition described by this permission.

A Custom Security Manager

In this section, we show you how to build a simple security manager. In your own programs, you are better off using custom permissions rather than implementing a full security manager, but we thought you might find it interesting to see how a security manager works internally. Our security manager monitors all file access and ensures that you can't open a text file if it contains forbidden words such as *sex, drugs,* and *C++*.

We monitor file access by overriding the checkPermission method of the standard security manager class. If the permission isn't a file read permission, then we simply call super.checkPermission. To check that it is permissible to read from a file, we open the file and scan its contents. We grant access to the file only when it doesn't contain any of the forbidden words. (We only monitor files with extension .txt since we don't want to block access to system and property files.)

```
public class WordCheckSecurityManager extends SecurityManager
{
   public void checkPermission(Permission p)
   {
      if (p instanceof FilePermission && p.getActions().equals("read"))
      {
         String fileName = p.getName();
         if (containsBadWords(fileName))
            throw new SecurityException("Bad words in " + fileName);
      }
      else super.checkPermission(p);
   }
   . . .
}
```

 NOTE: Another way of being notified of file read requests is to override the checkRead method. The SecurityManager class implements this method to call the checkPermission method with a FilePermission object. Close to 30 similar methods in the SecurityManager exist for historical reasons. The permission system has been introduced in the Java 2 platform. We recommend that you do not override these methods but instead carry out all permission checks in the checkPermission method.

There is just one catch in our file check scenario. Consider one possible flow of events.

- A method of some class opens a file.
- Then, the security manager springs into action and uses its checkPermission method.
- The checkPermission method calls the containsBadWords method.

But the containsBadWords method must itself read the file to check its contents, which calls the security manager again! This would result in an infinite regression unless the security manager has a way of finding out in which context it was called. The getClassContext method is the way to find out how the method was called. This method returns an array of class objects that gives all the classes whose calls are currently pending. For example, when the security manager is called for the first time, that array is

```
class WordCheckSecurityManager
class SecurityManager
class java.io.FileInputStream
class java.io.FileReader
class SecurityManagerFrame
. . .
class java.awt.EventDispatchThread
```

The class at index 0 gives the currently executing call. Unfortunately, you only get to see the classes, not the names of the pending methods. When the security manager itself attempts to open the file, it is called again and the getClassContext method returns the following array:

```
class WordCheckSecurityManager
class SecurityManager
class java.io.FileInputStream
class java.io.FileReader
class WordCheckSecurityManager
class WordCheckSecurityManager
class SecurityManager
class java.io.FileInputStream
class java.io.FileReader
class SecurityManagerFrame
. . .
class java.awt.EventDispatchThread
```

In this case, the security manager should permit the file access. How can we do this? We could test whether

```
getClassContext()[0] == getClassContext()[4]
```

but this approach is fragile. Here's an obvious case of where it can go wrong: Imagine that if the implementation changed, for example, so the FileReader constructor calls the security manager directly, then the test would be meaningless because the positions would not be the same in the array. It is far more robust to test whether *any* of the pending calls came from the same security manager.

Here is a method that carries out this test. Since this method is called from checkPermission, there are at least two copies of the security manager class on the call stack. We skip these first and then look for another instance of the same security manager.

```
boolean inSameManager()
{
    Class[] cc = getClassContext();

    // skip past current set of calls to this manager
    int i = 0;
    while (i < cc.length && cc[0] == cc[i])
        i++;

    // check if there is another call to this manager
    while (i < cc.length)
    {
        if (cc[0] == cc[i]) return true;
        i++;
    }
    return false;
}
```

We call this method in the checkPermission method. If we find that the security manager is invoked recursively, then we do not call the containsBadWords method again.

```
if (p instanceof FilePermission && p.getActions().equals("read"))
{
    if (inSameManager())
        return;
    String fileName = p.getName();
    if (containsBadWords(fileName))
        throw new SecurityException("Bad words in " + fileName);
}
```

Example 9–6 shows a program that puts this security manager to work. The security manager is installed in the main method. When running the program, you can specify a file. The program will load its contents into the text area. However, if the file fails the security check, the program catches the security exception and displays a message instead (see Figure 9–8). For example, you can display "Alice in Wonderland," but the program refuses to load "The Count of Monte Cristo."

 NOTE: You may wonder why we use a text field instead of a JFileChooser to select the file name. The JFileChooser calls the isHidden method of the File class for each file in the current directory, and that method tries to get read permission from the security manager.

Be careful how you invoke this program. The WordCheckSecurityManager class itself needs to be given AllPermission. The reason for this is subtle. The WordCheckSecurityManager class calls the SecurityManager superclass for all permissions other than file read permissions. When the SecurityManager class evaluates a permission, it checks whether *all methods on the call stack should be granted that particular permission*. The WordCheckSecurityManager is one of those classes. But it is not a system class, so you must explicitly grant it all permissions without also granting all permissions to the other classes of the program.

To separate the WordCheckSecurityManager class files from the other class files, make a JAR file containing just that class file.

```
jar cvf WordCheck.jar WordCheckSecurityManager.class
```

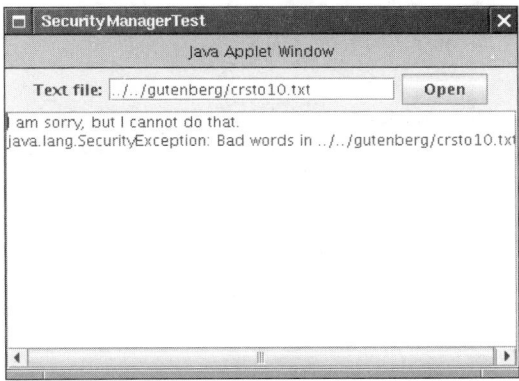

Figure 9–8: The SecurityManagerTest program

Then delete the WordCheckSecurityManager.class file.

Next, create a policy file, WordCheck.policy, with the following contents:

```
grant codeBase "file:WordCheck.jar"
{
    permission java.security.AllPermission;
};
```

This policy grants all permissions to the classes in the WordCheck.jar file. Finally, start the application as follows:

```
java -classpath .:WordCheck.jar -Djava.security.policy=WordCheck.policy SecurityManagerTest
```

On Windows, use a semicolon to separate the class path elements:

```
java -classpath .;WordCheck.jar . . .
```

 TIP: If you are thinking of changing the security manager in your own programs, you should first investigate whether you can instead use the standard security manager and a custom permission, as described in the preceding section. Writing a security manager is error prone and can cause subtle security flaws. It is much better to use the standard security manager and augment the permission system instead.

Example 9–6: SecurityManagerTest.java

```
1. import java.awt.*;
2. import java.awt.event.*;
3. import java.io.*;
4. import java.net.*;
5. import java.util.*;
6. import javax.swing.*;
7.
8. /**
9.    This class demonstrates the use of a custom security manager
10.   that prohibits the reading of text files containing bad words.
11. */
12. public class SecurityManagerTest
13. {
14.    public static void main(String[] args)
15.    {
16.       System.setSecurityManager(new WordCheckSecurityManager());
```

```
17.        JFrame frame = new SecurityManagerFrame();
18.        frame.setDefaultCloseOperation(JFrame.EXIT_ON_CLOSE);
19.        frame.setVisible(true);
20.    }
21. }
22.
23. /**
24.    This frame contains a text field to enter a file name and
25.    a text area to show the contents of the loaded file.
26. */
27. class SecurityManagerFrame extends JFrame
28. {
29.    public SecurityManagerFrame()
30.    {
31.       setTitle("SecurityManagerTest");
32.       setSize(DEFAULT_WIDTH, DEFAULT_HEIGHT);
33.
34.       fileNameField = new JTextField(20);
35.       JPanel panel = new JPanel();
36.       panel.add(new JLabel("Text file:"));
37.       panel.add(fileNameField);
38.       JButton openButton = new JButton("Open");
39.       panel.add(openButton);
40.       openButton.addActionListener(new
41.          ActionListener()
42.          {
43.             public void actionPerformed(ActionEvent event)
44.             {
45.                loadFile(fileNameField.getText());
46.             }
47.          });
48.
49.       add(panel, "North");
50.
51.       fileText = new JTextArea();
52.       add(new JScrollPane(fileText), "Center");
53.    }
54.
55.    /**
56.       Attempt to load a file into the text area. If a security exception is caught,
57.       a message is inserted into the text area instead.
58.       @param filename the file name
59.    */
60.    public void loadFile(String filename)
61.    {
62.       try
63.       {
64.          fileText.setText("");
65.          Scanner in = new Scanner(new FileReader(filename));
66.          while (in.hasNextLine()) fileText.append(in.nextLine() + "\n");
67.          in.close();
68.       }
69.       catch (IOException e)
70.       {
71.          fileText.append(e + "\n");
72.       }
```

```
73.    catch (SecurityException e)
74.    {
75.        fileText.append("I am sorry, but I cannot do that.\n");
76.        fileText.append(e + "\n");
77.    }
78.  }
79.
80.  private JTextField fileNameField;
81.  private JTextArea fileText;
82.  private static final int DEFAULT_WIDTH = 400;
83.  private static final int DEFAULT_HEIGHT = 300;
84. }
```

Example 9–7: WordCheckSecurityManager.java

```
1.  import java.io.*;
2.  import java.security.*;
3.  import java.util.*;
4.
5.  /**
6.     This security manager checks whether bad words are
7.     encountered when reading a file.
8.  */
9.  public class WordCheckSecurityManager extends SecurityManager
10. {
11.    public void checkPermission(Permission p)
12.    {
13.       if (p instanceof FilePermission && p.getActions().equals("read"))
14.       {
15.          if (inSameManager())
16.             return;
17.          String fileName = p.getName();
18.          if (containsBadWords(fileName))
19.             throw new SecurityException("Bad words in " + fileName);
20.       }
21.       else super.checkPermission(p);
22.    }
23.
24.    /**
25.       Returns true if this manager is called while there
26.       is another call to itself pending.
27.       @return true if there are multiple calls to this manager
28.    */
29.    public boolean inSameManager()
30.    {
31.       Class[] cc = getClassContext();
32.
33.       // skip past current set of calls to this manager
34.       int i = 0;
35.       while (i < cc.length && cc[0] == cc[i])
36.          i++;
37.
38.       // check if there is another call to this manager
39.       while (i < cc.length)
40.       {
41.          if (cc[0] == cc[i]) return true;
42.          i++;
43.       }
```

```
44.        return false;
45.     }
46.
47.    /**
48.       Checks if a file contains bad words.
49.       @param fileName the name of the file
50.       @return true if the file name ends with .txt and it
51.       contains at least one bad word.
52.    */
53.    boolean containsBadWords(String fileName)
54.    {
55.       if (!fileName.toLowerCase().endsWith(".txt")) return false;
56.          // only check text files
57.       Scanner in;
58.       try
59.       {
60.          in = new Scanner(new FileReader(fileName));
61.       }
62.       catch (IOException e)
63.       {
64.          return false;
65.       }
66.       while (in.hasNext())
67.          if (badWords.contains(in.next().toLowerCase()))
68.          {
69.             in.close();
70.             System.out.println(fileName);
71.             return true;
72.          }
73.       return false;
74.    }
75.
76.    private List badWords = Arrays.asList(new String[] { "sex", "drugs", "c++" });
77. }
```

java.lang.System 1.0

- void setSecurityManager(SecurityManager s)
  sets the security manager for the remainder of this application. If s is null, no action is taken. This method throws a security exception if the current security manager does not permit the installation of a new security manager.

- SecurityManager getSecurityManager()
  gets the system security manager; returns null if none is installed.

java.lang.SecurityManager 1.0

- Class[] getClassContext() **1.1**
  returns an array of the classes for the currently executing methods. The element at position 0 is the class of the currently running method, the element at position 1 is the class of the caller of the current method, and so on. Only the class names, not the method names, are available.

User Authentication

Starting with JDK 1.4, the Java Authentication and Authorization Service (JAAS) is included in the Java 2 Standard Edition. The "authentication" part is concerned with ascertaining the identity of a program user. The "authorization" part maps users to permissions.

JAAS is a "pluggable" API that isolates Java applications from the particular technology used to implement authentication. It supports, among others, UNIX logins, NT logins, Kerberos authentication, and certificate-based authentication.

Once a user has been authenticated, you can attach a set of permissions. For example, here we grant Harry a particular set of permissions that other users do not have. The syntax is like this:

```
grant principal com.sun.security.auth.UnixPrincipal "harry"
{
    permission java.util.PropertyPermission "user.*", "read";
    . . .
};
```

The com.sun.security.auth.UnixPrincipal class checks the name of the UNIX user who is running this program. Its getName method returns the UNIX login name, and we check whether that name equals "harry".

You use a LoginContext to allow the security manager to check such a grant statement. Here is the basic outline of the login code:

```
try
{
    System.setSecurityManager(new SecurityManager());
    LoginContext context = new LoginContext("Login1"); // defined in JAAS configuration file
    context.login();
    // get the authenticated Subject
    Subject subject = context.getSubject();
    . . .
    context.logout();
}
catch (LoginException exception) // thrown if login was not successful
{
    exception.printStackTrace();
}
```

Now the subject denotes the individual who has been authenticated.

The string parameter "Login1" in the LoginContext constructor refers to an entry with the same name in the JAAS configuration file. Here is a sample configuration file:

```
Login1
{
    com.sun.security.auth.module.UnixLoginModule required;
    com.whizzbang.auth.module.RetinaScanModule sufficient;
};

Login2
{
    . . .
};
```

Of course, the JDK contains no biometric login modules. The JDK contains the following modules in the com.sun.security.auth.module package:

```
UnixLoginModule
NTLoginModule
Krb5LoginModule
JndiLoginModule
KeyStoreLoginModule
```

A login policy consists of a sequence of login modules, each of which is labeled required, sufficient, requisite, or optional. The modules are executed in turn, until a sufficient module succeeds, a requisite module fails, or the end of the module list is reached. Authentication is successful if all required and requisite modules succeed, or if none of them were executed, if at least one sufficient or optional module succeeds.

A login authenticates a *subject*, which can have multiple *principals*. A principal describes some property of the subject, such as the user name, group ID, or role. As you saw in the grant statement, principals govern permissions. The com.sun.security.auth.UnixPrincipal describes the UNIX login name, and the UnixNumericGroupPrincipal can test for membership in a UNIX group.

A grant clause can test for a principal, with the syntax

```
grant principalClass "principalName"
```

For example:

```
grant com.sun.security.auth.UnixPrincipal "harry"
```

When a user has logged in, you then run, in a separate access control context, the code that requires checking of principals. Use the static doAs or doAsPrivileged method to start a new PrivilegedAction whose run method executes the code.

Both of those methods execute an action by calling the run method of an object that implements the PrivilegedAction interface, using the permissions of the subject's principals:

```
PrivilegedAction action = new
   PrivilegedAction()
   {
      public Object run()
      {
         // run with permissions of subject principals
         . . .
      }
   };
Subject.doAsPrivileged(subject, action, null); // or doAs(subject, action)
```

If the actions can throw checked exceptions, then you implement the PrivilegedExceptionAction interface instead.

The difference between the doAs and doAsPrivileged methods is subtle. The doAs method starts out with the current access control context, whereas the doAsPrivileged method starts out with a new context. The latter method allows you to separate the permissions for the login code and the "business logic." In our example application, the login code has permissions

```
permission javax.security.auth.AuthPermission "createLoginContext.Login1";
permission javax.security.auth.AuthPermission "doAsPrivileged";
```

The authenticated user has a permission

```
permission java.util.PropertyPermission "user.*", "read";
```

If we had used doAs instead of doAsPrivileged, then the login code would have also needed that permission!

The program in Example 9–8 and Example 9–9 demonstrates how to restrict permissions to certain users. The AuthTest program authenticates a user and then runs a simple action that retrieves a system property.

To make this example work, package the code for the login and the action into two separate JAR files:

```
javac AuthTest.java
jar cvf login.jar AuthTest*.class
```

```
javac SysPropAction.java
jar cvf action.jar SysPropAction.class
```

If you look at the policy file in Example 9–10, you will see that the UNIX user with the name harry has the permission to read all files. Change harry to your login name. Then run the command

```
java -classpath login.jar:action.jar
   -Djava.security.policy=AuthTest.policy
   -Djava.security.auth.login.config=jaas.config
   AuthTest
```

Example 9–11 shows the login configuration.

On Windows, change Unix to NT in both AuthTest.policy and jaas.config, and use a semicolon to separate the JAR files:

```
java -classpath login.jar;action.jar . . .
```

The AuthTest program should now display the value of the user.home property. However, if you change the login name in the AuthTest.policy file, then a security exception should be thrown because you no longer have the required permission.

 CAUTION: Be careful to follow these instructions *exactly*. It is very easy to get the setup wrong by making seemingly innocuous changes.

Example 9–8: AuthTest.java

```
1.  import java.security.*;
2.  import javax.security.auth.*;
3.  import javax.security.auth.login.*;
4.
5.  /**
6.     This program authenticates a user via a custom login and then executes the SysPropAction
7.     with the user's privileges.
8.  */
9.  public class AuthTest
10. {
11.    public static void main(final String[] args)
12.    {
13.       try
14.       {
15.          System.setSecurityManager(new SecurityManager());
16.          LoginContext context = new LoginContext("Login1");
17.          context.login();
18.          System.out.println("Authentication successful.");
19.          Subject subject = context.getSubject();
20.          System.out.println("subject=" + subject);
21.          PrivilegedAction action = new SysPropAction("user.home");
22.          Object result = Subject.doAsPrivileged(subject, action, null);
23.          System.out.println(result);
24.          context.logout();
25.       }
26.       catch (LoginException e)
27.       {
28.          e.printStackTrace();
29.       }
30.    }
31. }
```

Example 9–9: SysPropAction.java

```
1. import java.security.*;
2.
3. /**
4.    This action looks up a system property.
5. */
6. public class SysPropAction implements PrivilegedAction
7. {
8.    /**
9.       Constructs an action for looking up a given property.
10.       @param propertyName the property name (such as "user.home")
11.    */
12.    public SysPropAction(String propertyName) { this.propertyName = propertyName; }
13.
14.    public Object run()
15.    {
16.       return System.getProperty(propertyName);
17.    }
18.
19.    private String propertyName;
20. }
```

Example 9–10: AuthTest.policy

```
1. grant codebase "file:login.jar"
2. {
3.    permission javax.security.auth.AuthPermission "createLoginContext.Login1";
4.    permission javax.security.auth.AuthPermission "doAsPrivileged";
5. };
6.
7. grant principal com.sun.security.auth.UnixPrincipal "harry"
8. {
9.    permission java.util.PropertyPermission "user.*", "read";
10. };
```

---

javax.security.auth.login.LoginContext 1.4

- LoginContext(String name)
  constructs a login context. The name corresponds to the login descriptor in the JAAS configuration file.

- void login()
  establishes a login or throws LoginException if the login failed. Invokes the login method on the managers in the JAAS configuration file.

- void logout()
  logs out the subject. Invokes the logout method on the managers in the JAAS configuration file.

- Subject getSubject()
  returns the authenticated subject.

---

javax.security.auth.Subject 1.4

- Set<Principal> getPrincipals()
  gets the principals of this subject.

- `static Object doAs(Subject subject, PrivilegedAction action)`
- `static Object doAs(Subject subject, PrivilegedExceptionAction action)`
- `static Object doAsPrivileged(Subject subject, PrivilegedAction action,`
  `AccessControlContext context)`
- `static Object doAsPrivileged(Subject subject, PrivilegedExceptionAction action,`
  `AccessControlContext context)`

  execute the privileged action on behalf of the subject. Return the return value of the run method. The `doAsPrivileged` methods execute the action in the given access control context. You can supply a "context snapshot" that you obtained earlier by calling the static method `AccessController.getContext()`, or you can supply `null` to execute the code in a new context.

`java.security.PrivilegedAction` 1.4

- `Object run()`
  You must define this method to execute the code that you want to have executed on behalf of a subject.

`java.security.PrivilegedExceptionAction` 1.4

- `Object run()`
  You must define this method to execute the code that you want to have executed on behalf of a subject. This method may throw any checked exceptions.

`java.security.Principal` 1.1

- `String getName()`
  returns the identifying name of this principal.

JAAS Login Modules

In this section, we look at a JAAS example that shows you

- How to implement your own login module, and
- How to implement *role-based* authentication.

Supplying your own login module is useful if you store login information in a database. Even if you are happy with the default module, studying a custom module will help you understand the JAAS configuration file options.

Role-based authentication is essential if you manage a large number of users. It would be impractical to put the names of all legitimate users into a policy file. Instead, the login module should map users to roles such as "admin" or "HR," and the permissions should be based on these roles.

One job of the login module is to populate the principal set of the subject that is being authenticated. If a login module supports roles, it adds `Principal` objects that describe roles. The JDK does not provide a class for this purpose, so we wrote our own (see Example 9–12). The class simply stores a description/value pair, such as role=admin. Its `getName` method returns that pair, so we can add role-based permissions into a policy file:

```
grant principal SimplePrincipal "role=admin" { . . . }
```

Our login module (see Example 9–13) looks up users, passwords, and roles in a text file that contains lines like this:

```
harry|wombat|admin
carl|mockturtle|HR
```

Of course, in a realistic login module, you would store this information in a database or directory.

You can find the code for the SimpleLoginModule in Example 9–13. The checkLogin method checks whether the user name and password match a user record in the password file. If so, we add two SimplePrincipal objects to the subject's principal set:

```
Set<Principal> principals = subject.getPrincipals();
principals.add(new SimplePrincipal("username", username));
principals.add(new SimplePrincipal("role", role));
```

The remainder of SimpleLoginModule is straightforward plumbing. The initialize method receives

- The Subject that is being authenticated;
- A handler to retrieve login information;
- A sharedState map that can be used for communication between login modules; and
- An options map that contains name/value pairs that are set in the login configuration.

For example, we configure our module as follows:

```
SimpleLoginModule required pwfile="password.txt";
```

The login module retrieves the pwfile settings from the options map.

The login module does not gather the user name and password; that is the job of a separate handler. This separation allows you to use the same login module without worrying whether the login information comes from a GUI dialog, a console prompt, or a configuration file.

The handler is specified when you construct the LoginContext, for example,

```
LoginContext context = new LoginContext("Login1",
    new com.sun.security.auth.callback.DialogCallbackHandler());
```

The DialogCallbackHandler pops up a simple GUI dialog box to retrieve the user name and password. com.sun.security.auth.callback.TextCallbackHandler gets the information from the console.

However, in our application, we have our own GUI for collecting the user name and password (see Figure 9–9). We produce a simple handler that merely stores and returns that information (see Example 9–14).

The handler has a single method, handle, that processes an array of Callback objects. A number of predefined classes, such as NameCallback and PasswordCallback, implement the Callback interface. You could also add your own class, such as RetinaScanCallback. The handler code is a bit unsightly because it needs to analyze the types of the callback objects:

```
public void handle(Callback[] callbacks)
{
   for (Callback callback : callbacks)
   {
      if (callback instanceof NameCallback) . . .
      else if (callback instanceof PasswordCallback) . . .
      else . . .
   }
}
```

The login module prepares an array of the callbacks that it needs for authentication:

```
NameCallback nameCall = new NameCallback("username: ");
PasswordCallback passCall = new PasswordCallback("password: ", false);
callbackHandler.handle(new Callback[] { nameCall, passCall });
```

Then it retrieves the information from the callbacks.

Figure 9–9: A custom login module

The program in Example 9–11 displays a form for entering the login information and the name of a system property. If the user is authenticated, the property value is retrieved in a PrivilegedAction. As you can see from the policy file in Example 9–15, only users with the admin role have permission to read properties.

As in the preceding section, you must separate the login and action code. Create two JAR files:

```
javac *.java
jar cvf login.jar JAAS*.class Simple*.class
jar cvf action.jar SysPropAction.class
```

Then run the program as

```
java -classpath login.jar:action.jar
    -Djava.security.policy=JAASTest.policy
    -Djava.security.auth.login.config=jaas.config
    JAASTest
```

Example 9–16 shows the login configuration.

It is possible to support a more complex two-phase protocol, whereby a login is *committed* if all modules in the login configuration were successful. For more information, see the login module developer's guide at http://java.sun.com/j2se/5.0/docs/guide/security/jaas/JAASLMDevGuide.html.

Example 9–11: JAASTest.java

```
1. import java.awt.*;
2. import java.awt.event.*;
3. import javax.security.auth.*;
4. import javax.security.auth.login.*;
5. import javax.swing.*;
6.
7. /**
8.    This program authenticates a user via a custom login and then executes the SysPropAction
9.    with the user's privileges.
10. */
11. public class JAASTest
12. {
13.    public static void main(final String[] args)
14.    {
15.       System.setSecurityManager(new SecurityManager());
16.       JFrame frame = new JAASFrame();
17.       frame.setDefaultCloseOperation(JFrame.EXIT_ON_CLOSE);
18.       frame.setVisible(true);
19.    }
20. }
21.
22. /**
23.    This frame has text fields for user name and password, a field for the name of the requested
24.    system property, and a field to show the property value.
25. */
```

```
26. class JAASFrame extends JFrame
27. {
28.    public JAASFrame()
29.    {
30.       setTitle("JAASTest");
31.
32.       username = new JTextField(20);
33.       password = new JPasswordField(20);
34.       propertyName = new JTextField(20);
35.       propertyValue = new JTextField(20);
36.       propertyValue.setEditable(false);
37.
38.       JPanel panel = new JPanel();
39.       panel.setLayout(new GridLayout(0, 2));
40.       panel.add(new JLabel("username:"));
41.       panel.add(username);
42.       panel.add(new JLabel("password:"));
43.       panel.add(password);
44.       panel.add(propertyName);
45.       panel.add(propertyValue);
46.       add(panel, BorderLayout.CENTER);
47.
48.       JButton getValueButton = new JButton("Get Value");
49.       getValueButton.addActionListener(new
50.          ActionListener()
51.          {
52.             public void actionPerformed(ActionEvent event) { getValue(); }
53.          });
54.       JPanel buttonPanel = new JPanel();
55.       buttonPanel.add(getValueButton);
56.       add(buttonPanel, BorderLayout.SOUTH);
57.       pack();
58.    }
59.
60.    public void getValue()
61.    {
62.       try
63.       {
64.          LoginContext context = new LoginContext("Login1",
65.             new SimpleCallbackHandler(username.getText(), password.getPassword()));
66.          context.login();
67.          Subject subject = context.getSubject();
68.          propertyValue.setText(
69.             "" + Subject.doAsPrivileged(subject, new SysPropAction(propertyName.getText()), null));
70.          context.logout();
71.       }
72.       catch (LoginException e )
73.       {
74.          JOptionPane.showMessageDialog(this, e);
75.       }
76.    }
77.
78.    private JTextField username;
79.    private JPasswordField password;
80.    private JTextField propertyName;
81.    private JTextField propertyValue;
82. }
```

Example 9–12: SimplePrincipal.java

```
1.  import java.security.*;
2.
3.  /**
4.     A principal with a named value (such as "role=HR" or "username=harry").
5.  */
6.  public class SimplePrincipal implements Principal
7.  {
8.     /**
9.        Constructs a SimplePrincipal to hold a description and a value.
10.       @param roleName the role name
11.    */
12.    public SimplePrincipal(String descr, String value) { this.descr = descr; this.value = value; }
13.
14.    /**
15.       Returns the role name of this principal
16.       @return the role name
17.    */
18.    public String getName() { return descr + "=" + value; }
19.
20.    public boolean equals(Object otherObject)
21.    {
22.       if (this == otherObject) return true;
23.       if (otherObject == null) return false;
24.       if (getClass() != otherObject.getClass()) return false;
25.       SimplePrincipal other = (SimplePrincipal) otherObject;
26.       return getName().equals(other.getName());
27.    }
28.    public int hashCode() { return getName().hashCode(); }
29.
30.    private String descr;
31.    private String value;
32. }
```

Example 9–13: SimpleLoginModule.java

```
1.  import java.io.*;
2.  import java.lang.reflect.*;
3.  import java.security.*;
4.  import java.util.*;
5.  import javax.security.auth.*;
6.  import javax.security.auth.login.*;
7.  import javax.security.auth.callback.*;
8.  import javax.security.auth.spi.*;
9.
10. import javax.swing.*;
11.
12. /**
13.    This login module authenticates users by reading usernames, passwords, and roles
14.    from a text file.
15. */
16. public class SimpleLoginModule implements LoginModule
17. {
18.    public void initialize(Subject subject, CallbackHandler callbackHandler,
19.       Map<String, ?> sharedState, Map<String, ?> options)
20.    {
```

```
21.         this.subject = subject;
22.         this.callbackHandler = callbackHandler;
23.         this.sharedState = sharedState;
24.         this.options = options;
25.     }
26.
27.     public boolean login() throws LoginException
28.     {
29.         if (callbackHandler == null)
30.             throw new LoginException("no handler");
31.
32.         NameCallback nameCall = new NameCallback("username: ");
33.         PasswordCallback passCall = new PasswordCallback("password: ", false);
34.         try
35.         {
36.             callbackHandler.handle(new Callback[] { nameCall, passCall });
37.         }
38.         catch (UnsupportedCallbackException e)
39.         {
40.             LoginException e2 = new LoginException("Unsupported callback");
41.             e2.initCause(e);
42.             throw e2;
43.         }
44.         catch (IOException e)
45.         {
46.             LoginException e2 = new LoginException("I/O exception in callback");
47.             e2.initCause(e);
48.             throw e2;
49.         }
50.
51.         return checkLogin(nameCall.getName(), passCall.getPassword());
52.     }
53.
54.     /**
55.        Checks whether the authentication information is valid. If it is, the subject acquires
56.        principals for the user name and role.
57.        @param username the user name
58.        @param password a character array containing the password
59.        @return true if the authentication information is valid
60.     */
61.     private boolean checkLogin(String username, char[] password) throws LoginException
62.     {
63.         try
64.         {
65.             Scanner in = new Scanner(new FileReader("" + options.get("pwfile")));
66.             while (in.hasNextLine())
67.             {
68.                 String[] inputs = in.nextLine().split("\\|");
69.                 if (inputs[0].equals(username) && Arrays.equals(inputs[1].toCharArray(), password))
70.                 {
71.                     String role = inputs[2];
72.                     Set<Principal> principals = subject.getPrincipals();
73.                     principals.add(new SimplePrincipal("username", username));
74.                     principals.add(new SimplePrincipal("role", role));
75.                     return true;
76.                 }
```

```
77.          }
78.          in.close();
79.          return false;
80.       }
81.       catch (IOException e)
82.       {
83.          LoginException e2 = new LoginException("Can't open password file");
84.          e2.initCause(e);
85.          throw e2;
86.       }
87.    }
88.
89.    public boolean logout() { return true; }
90.    public boolean abort() { return true; }
91.    public boolean commit() { return true; }
92.
93.    private Subject subject;
94.    private CallbackHandler callbackHandler;
95.    private Map<String, ?> sharedState;
96.    private Map<String, ?> options;
97. }
```

Example 9–14: SimpleCallbackHandler.java

```
1. import javax.security.auth.callback.*;
2.
3. /**
4.    This simple callback handler presents the given user name and password.
5. */
6. public class SimpleCallbackHandler implements CallbackHandler
7. {
8.    /**
9.       Constructs the callback handler.
10.      @param username the user name
11.      @param password a character array containing the password
12.   */
13.   public SimpleCallbackHandler(String username, char[] password)
14.   {
15.      this.username = username;
16.      this.password = password;
17.   }
18.
19.   public void handle(Callback[] callbacks)
20.   {
21.      for (Callback callback : callbacks)
22.      {
23.         if (callback instanceof NameCallback)
24.         {
25.            ((NameCallback) callback).setName(username);
26.         }
27.         else if (callback instanceof PasswordCallback)
28.         {
29.            ((PasswordCallback) callback).setPassword(password);
30.         }
31.      }
32.   }
33.
```

```
34.     private String username;
35.     private char[] password;
36.  }
```

Example 9–15: JAASTest.policy

```
1.  grant codebase "file:login.jar"
2.  {
3.      permission java.awt.AWTPermission "showWindowWithoutWarningBanner";
4.      permission javax.security.auth.AuthPermission "createLoginContext.Login1";
5.      permission javax.security.auth.AuthPermission "doAsPrivileged";
6.      permission javax.security.auth.AuthPermission "modifyPrincipals";
7.      permission java.io.FilePermission "password.txt", "read";
8.  };
9.
10. grant principal SimplePrincipal "role=admin"
11. {
12.     permission java.util.PropertyPermission "*", "read";
13. };
```

Example 9–16: jaas.config

```
1.  Login1
2.  {
3.      SimpleLoginModule required pwfile="password.txt";
4.  };
```

API   **javax.security.auth.callback.CallbackHandler** 1.4

- void handle(Callback[] callbacks)
  handles the given callbacks, interacting with the user if desired, and stores the security information in the callback objects.

API   **javax.security.auth.callback.NameCallback** 1.4

- NameCallback(String prompt)
- NameCallback(String prompt, String defaultName)
  construct a NameCallback with the given prompt and default name.

- void setName(String name)
- String getName()
  set or get the name gathered by this callback.

- String getPrompt()
  gets the prompt to use when querying this name.

- String getDefaultName()
  gets the default name to use when querying this name.

API   **javax.security.auth.callback.PasswordCallback** 1.4

- PasswordCallback(String prompt, boolean echoOn)
  constructs a PasswordCallback with the given prompt and echo flag.

- void setPassword(char[] password)
- char[] getPassword()
  set or get the password gathered by this callback.

- String getPrompt()
  gets the prompt to use when querying this password.

- boolean isEchoOn()
  gets the echo flag to use when querying this password.

API   *javax.security.auth.spi.LoginModule* 1.4

- `void initialize(Subject subject, CallbackHandler handler, Map<String,?> sharedState, Map<String,?> options)`
  initializes this `LoginModule` for authenticating the given subject. During login processing, use the given handler to gather login information. Use the sharedState map for communication with other login modules. The options map contains the name/value pairs specified in the login configuration for this module instance.

- `boolean login()`
  carries out the authentication process and populate the subject's principals. Returns true if the login was successful.

- `boolean commit()`
  is called after all login modules were successful, for login scenarios that require a two-phase commit. Returns true if the operation was successful.

- `boolean abort()`
  is called if the failure of another login module caused the login process to abort. Returns true if the operation was successful.

- `boolean logout()`
  logs out this subject. Returns true if the operation was successful.

Digital Signatures

As we said earlier, applets were what started the craze over the Java platform. In practice, people discovered that although they could write animated applets like the famous "nervous text" applet, applets could not do a whole lot of useful stuff in the JDK 1.0 security model. For example, because applets under JDK 1.0 were so closely supervised, they couldn't do much good on a corporate intranet, even though relatively little risk attaches to executing an applet from your company's secure intranet. It quickly became clear to Sun that for applets to become truly useful, it was important for users to be able to assign *different* levels of security, depending on where the applet originated. If an applet comes from a trusted supplier and it has not been tampered with, the user of that applet can then decide whether to give the applet more privileges.

This added control is now possible because of the applet-signing mechanism in Java 1.1. To give more trust to an applet, we need to know two things:

1. Where did the applet come from?
2. Was the code corrupted in transit?

In the past 50 years, mathematicians and computer scientists have developed sophisticated algorithms for ensuring the integrity of data and for electronic signatures. The java.security package contains implementations of many of these algorithms. Fortunately, you don't need to understand the underlying mathematics to use the algorithms in the java.security package. In the next sections, we show you how message digests can detect changes in data files and how digital signatures can prove the identity of the signer.

Message Digests

A message digest is a digital fingerprint of a block of data. For example, the so-called SHA1 (secure hash algorithm #1) condenses any data block, no matter how long, into a sequence of 160 bits (20 bytes). As with real fingerprints, one hopes that no two messages have the same SHA1 fingerprint. Of course, that cannot be true—there are only 2^{160} SHA1 fingerprints, so there must be some messages with the same fingerprint. But 2^{160} is so large that the probability of duplication occurring is negligible. How negligible? According to James

Walsh in *True Odds: How Risks Affect Your Everyday Life* [Merritt Publishing 1996], the chance that you will die from being struck by lightning is about one in 30,000. Now, think of nine other people, for example, your nine least favorite managers or professors. The chance that you and *all of them* will die from lightning strikes is higher than that of a forged message having the same SHA1 fingerprint as the original. (Of course, more than 10 people, none of whom you are likely to know, will die from lightning. However, we are talking about the far slimmer chance that *your particular choice* of people will be wiped out.)

A message digest has two essential properties:

1. If one bit or several bits of the data are changed, then the message digest also changes.
2. A forger who is in possession of a given message cannot construct a fake message that has the same message digest as the original.

The second property is again a matter of probabilities, of course. Consider the following message by the billionaire father:

> *"Upon my death, my property shall be divided equally among my children; however, my son George shall receive nothing."*

That message has an SHA1 fingerprint of

```
2D 8B 35 F3 BF 49 CD B1 94 04 E0 66 21 2B 5E 57 70 49 E1 7E
```

The distrustful father has deposited the message with one attorney and the fingerprint with another. Now, suppose George can bribe the lawyer holding the message. He wants to change the message so that Bill gets nothing. Of course, that changes the fingerprint to a completely different bit pattern:

```
2A 33 0B 4B B3 FE CC 1C 9D 5C 01 A7 09 51 0B 49 AC 8F 98 92
```

Can George find some other wording that matches the fingerprint? If he had been the proud owner of a billion computers from the time the Earth was formed, each computing a million messages a second, he would not yet have found a message he could substitute.

A number of algorithms have been designed to compute these message digests. The two best-known are SHA1, the secure hash algorithm developed by the National Institute of Standards and Technology, and MD5, an algorithm invented by Ronald Rivest of MIT. Both algorithms scramble the bits of a message in ingenious ways. For details about these algorithms, see, for example, *Cryptography and Network Security* by William Stallings [Prentice Hall 1998]. Note that recently, subtle regularities have been discovered in MD5. Most cryptographers recommend avoiding it and using SHA1 for that reason. (Both algorithms are easy to compute.)

The Java programming language implements both SHA1 and MD5. The MessageDigest class is a *factory* for creating objects that encapsulate the fingerprinting algorithms. It has a static method, called getInstance, that returns an object of a class that extends the MessageDigest class. This means the MessageDigest class serves double duty:

*   As a factory class
*   As the superclass for all message digest algorithms

For example, here is how you obtain an object that can compute SHA fingerprints.

```
MessageDigest alg = MessageDigest.getInstance("SHA-1");
```

(To get an object that can compute MD5, use the string "MD5" as the argument to getInstance.)

After you have obtained a MessageDigest object, you feed it all the bytes in the message by repeatedly calling the update method. For example, the following code passes all bytes in a file to the alg object created above to do the fingerprinting:

```
InputStream in = . . .
int ch;
while ((ch = in.read()) != -1)
   alg.update((byte) ch);
```

Alternatively, if you have the bytes in an array, you can update the entire array at once:

```
byte[] bytes = . . .;
alg.update(bytes);
```

When you are done, call the `digest` method. This method pads the input—as required by the fingerprinting algorithm—does the computation, and returns the digest as an array of bytes.

```
byte[] hash = alg.digest();
```

The program in Example 9–17 computes a message digest, using either SHA or MD5. You can load the data to be digested from a file, or you can type a message in the text area. Figure 9–10 shows the application.

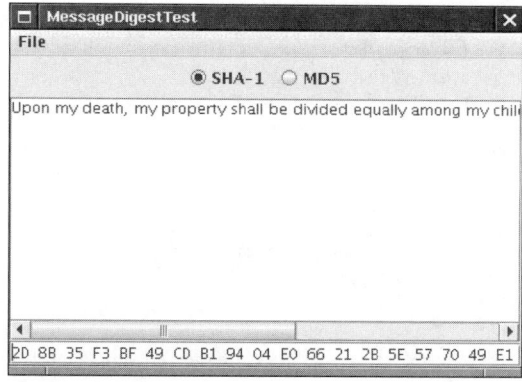

Figure 9–10: Computing a message digest

Example 9–17: MessageDigestTest.java

```
1.  import java.io.*;
2.  import java.security.*;
3.  import java.awt.*;
4.  import java.awt.event.*;
5.  import javax.swing.*;
6.
7.  /**
8.     This program computes the message digest of a file
9.     or the contents of a text area.
10. */
11. public class MessageDigestTest
12. {
13.    public static void main(String[] args)
14.    {
15.       JFrame frame = new MessageDigestFrame();
16.       frame.setDefaultCloseOperation(JFrame.EXIT_ON_CLOSE);
17.       frame.setVisible(true);
18.    }
19. }
20.
```

```
21. /**
22.     This frame contains a menu for computing the message
23.     digest of a file or text area, radio buttons to toggle between
24.     SHA-1 and MD5, a text area, and a text field to show the
25.     message digest.
26. */
27. class MessageDigestFrame extends JFrame
28. {
29.     public MessageDigestFrame()
30.     {
31.        setTitle("MessageDigestTest");
32.        setSize(DEFAULT_WIDTH, DEFAULT_HEIGHT);
33.
34.        JPanel panel = new JPanel();
35.        ButtonGroup group = new ButtonGroup();
36.        addRadioButton(panel, "SHA-1", group);
37.        addRadioButton(panel, "MD5", group);
38.
39.        add(panel, BorderLayout.NORTH);
40.        add(new JScrollPane(message), BorderLayout.CENTER);
41.        add(digest, BorderLayout.SOUTH);
42.        digest.setFont(new Font("Monospaced", Font.PLAIN, 12));
43.
44.        setAlgorithm("SHA-1");
45.
46.        JMenuBar menuBar = new JMenuBar();
47.        JMenu menu = new JMenu("File");
48.        JMenuItem fileDigestItem = new JMenuItem("File digest");
49.        fileDigestItem.addActionListener(new
50.           ActionListener()
51.           {
52.              public void actionPerformed(ActionEvent event) { loadFile(); }
53.           });
54.        menu.add(fileDigestItem);
55.        JMenuItem textDigestItem = new JMenuItem("Text area digest");
56.        textDigestItem.addActionListener(new
57.           ActionListener()
58.           {
59.              public void actionPerformed(ActionEvent event)
60.              {
61.                 String m = message.getText();
62.                 computeDigest(m.getBytes());
63.              }
64.           });
65.        menu.add(textDigestItem);
66.        menuBar.add(menu);
67.        setJMenuBar(menuBar);
68.     }
69.
70.     /**
71.        Adds a radio button to select an algorithm.
72.        @param c the container into which to place the button
73.        @param name the algorithm name
74.        @param g the button group
75.     */
76.     public void addRadioButton(Container c, final String name, ButtonGroup g)
```

```
77.     {
78.        ActionListener listener = new
79.           ActionListener()
80.           { public void actionPerformed(ActionEvent event) { setAlgorithm(name); }
81.           };
82.        JRadioButton b = new JRadioButton(name, g.getButtonCount() == 0);
83.        c.add(b);
84.        g.add(b);
85.        b.addActionListener(listener);
86.     }
87.
88.     /**
89.        Sets the algorithm used for computing the digest.
90.        @param alg the algorithm name
91.     */
92.     public void setAlgorithm(String alg)
93.     {
94.        try
95.        {
96.           currentAlgorithm = MessageDigest.getInstance(alg);
97.           digest.setText("");
98.        }
99.        catch (NoSuchAlgorithmException e)
100.        {
101.           digest.setText("" + e);
102.        }
103.     }
104.
105.     /**
106.        Loads a file and computes its message digest.
107.     */
108.     public void loadFile()
109.     {
110.        JFileChooser chooser = new JFileChooser();
111.        chooser.setCurrentDirectory(new File("."));
112.
113.        int r = chooser.showOpenDialog(this);
114.        if (r == JFileChooser.APPROVE_OPTION)
115.        {
116.           try
117.           {
118.              String name = chooser.getSelectedFile().getAbsolutePath();
119.              computeDigest(loadBytes(name));
120.           }
121.           catch (IOException e)
122.           {
123.              JOptionPane.showMessageDialog(null, e);
124.           }
125.        }
126.     }
127.
128.     /**
129.        Loads the bytes in a file.
130.        @param name the file name
131.        @return an array with the bytes in the file
132.     */
```

```
133.    public byte[] loadBytes(String name) throws IOException
134.    {
135.       FileInputStream in = null;
136.
137.       in = new FileInputStream(name);
138.       try
139.       {
140.          ByteArrayOutputStream buffer = new ByteArrayOutputStream();
141.          int ch;
142.          while ((ch = in.read()) != -1)
143.             buffer.write(ch);
144.          return buffer.toByteArray();
145.       }
146.       finally
147.       {
148.          in.close();
149.       }
150.    }
151.
152.    /**
153.       Computes the message digest of an array of bytes
154.       and displays it in the text field.
155.       @param b the bytes for which the message digest should
156.       be computed.
157.    */
158.    public void computeDigest(byte[] b)
159.    {
160.       currentAlgorithm.reset();
161.       currentAlgorithm.update(b);
162.       byte[] hash = currentAlgorithm.digest();
163.       String d = "";
164.       for (int i = 0; i < hash.length; i++)
165.       {
166.          int v = hash[i] & 0xFF;
167.          if (v < 16) d += "0";
168.          d += Integer.toString(v, 16).toUpperCase() + " ";
169.       }
170.       digest.setText(d);
171.    }
172.
173.    private JTextArea message = new JTextArea();
174.    private JTextField digest = new JTextField();
175.    private MessageDigest currentAlgorithm;
176.    private static final int DEFAULT_WIDTH = 400;
177.    private static final int DEFAULT_HEIGHT = 300;
178. }
```

`[API]` **java.security.MessageDigest 1.1**

- static MessageDigest getInstance(String algorithm)
  returns a MessageDigest object that implements the specified algorithm. Throws NoSuchAlgorithmException if the algorithm is not provided.

  Parameters: algorithm   The name of the algorithm, such as "SHA-1" or "MD5"

- `void update(byte input)`
- `void update(byte[] input)`
- `void update(byte[] input, int offset, int len)`
  update the digest, using the specified bytes.
- `byte[] digest()`
  completes the hash computation, returns the computed digest, and resets the algorithm object.
- `void reset()`
  resets the digest.

Message Signing

In the last section, you saw how to compute a message digest, a fingerprint for the original message. If the message is altered, then the fingerprint of the altered message will not match the fingerprint of the original. If the message and its fingerprint are delivered separately, then the recipient can check whether the message has been tampered with. However, if both the message and the fingerprint were intercepted, it is an easy matter to modify the message and then recompute the fingerprint. After all, the message digest algorithms are publicly known, and they don't require secret keys. In that case, the recipient of the forged message and the recomputed fingerprint would never know that the message has been altered. In this section, you will see how *digital signatures can authenticate* a message. When a message is authenticated, you *know*

- The message was not altered;
- The message came from the claimed sender.

To help you understand how digital signatures work, we explain a few concepts from the field called *public key cryptography*. Public key cryptography is based on the notion of a *public* key and *private* key. The idea is that you tell everyone in the world your public key. However, only you hold the private key, and it is important that you safeguard it and don't release it to anyone else. The keys are matched by mathematical relationships, but it is believed to be practically impossible to compute one from the other. That is, even though everyone knows your public key, they can't compute your private key in your lifetime, no matter how many computing resources they have available.

It may seem difficult to believe that nobody can compute the private key from the public keys, but nobody has ever found an algorithm to do this for the encryption algorithms that are in common use today. If the keys are sufficiently long, brute force—simply trying all possible keys—would require more computers than can be built from all the atoms in the solar system, crunching away for thousands of years. Of course, it is possible that someone could come up with algorithms for computing keys that are much more clever than brute force. For example, the RSA algorithm (the encryption algorithm invented by Rivest, Shamir, and Adleman) depends on the difficulty of factoring large numbers. For the last 20 years, many of the best mathematicians have tried to come up with good factoring algorithms, but so far with no success. For that reason, most cryptographers believe that keys with a "modulus" of 2,000 bits or more are currently completely safe from any attack.

There are two kinds of public/private key pairs: for *encryption* and for *authentication*. If anyone sends you a message that was encrypted with your public encryption key, then you can decrypt it with your private decryption key, but nobody else can. Conversely, if you sign a message with your private authentication key, then anyone else can verify the signature by checking with your public key. The verification passes only for messages that you signed, and it fails if anyone else used his or her key to sign the message. (Kahn remarks in

the new edition of his book *The Codebreakers* that this was the first *new* idea in cryptography in hundreds of years.)

Many cryptographic algorithms, such as RSA and DSA (the Digital Signature Algorithm), use this idea. The exact structure of the keys and what it means for them to match depend on the algorithm. For example, here is a matching pair of public and private DSA keys.

Public key:

```
p: fca682ce8e12caba26efccf7110e526db078b05edecbcd1eb4a208f3ae16
17ae01f35b91a47e6df63413c5e12ed0899bcd132acd50d99151bdc43ee7375
92e17

q: 962eddcc369cba8ebb260ee6b6a126d9346e38c5

g: 678471b27a9cf44ee91a49c5147db1a9aaf244f05a434d6486931d2d1427
1b9e35030b71fd73da179069b32e2935630e1c2062354d0da20a6c416e50be794ca4

y: c0b6e67b4ac098eb1a32c5f8c4c1f0e7e6fb9d832532e27d0bdab9ca2d2a
8123ce5a8018b8161a760480fadd040b927281ddb22cb9bc4df596d7de4d1b977d50
```

Private key:

```
p: fca682ce8e12caba26efccf7110e526db078b05edecbcd1eb4a208f3ae16
17ae01f35b91a47e6df63413c5e12ed0899bcd132acd50d99151bdc43ee737592e17

q: 962eddcc369cba8ebb260ee6b6a126d9346e38c5

g: 678471b27a9cf44ee91a49c5147db1a9aaf244f05a434d6486931d2d1427
1b9e35030b71fd73da179069b32e2935630e1c2062354d0da20a6c416e50be794ca4

x: 146c09f881656cc6c51f27ea6c3a91b85ed1d70a
```

These keys have a mathematical relationship, but the exact nature of the relationship is not interesting for practical programming. (If you are interested, you can look it up in *The Handbook of Applied Cryptography* at http://www.cacr.math.uwaterloo.ca/hac/.)

The obvious question is how to generate the pair of keys. Usually, you do this by feeding the result of some random process to a deterministic procedure that returns the key pair to you. Luckily, how to get a random key pair for public key cryptography is not a question anyone but cryptographers and mathematicians need to worry about.

Here is how it works in practice. Suppose Alice wants to send Bob a message, and Bob wants to know this message came from Alice and not an impostor. Alice writes the message and then *signs* the message digest with her private key. Bob gets a copy of her public key. Bob then applies the public key to *verify* the signature. If the verification passes, then Bob can be assured of two facts:

1. The original message has not been altered.
2. The message was signed by Alice, the holder of the private key that matches the public key that Bob used for verification.

See Figure 9–11.

You can see why security for private keys is all-important. If someone steals Alice's private key or if a government can require her to turn it over, then she is in trouble. The thief or a government agent can impersonate her by sending messages, money transfer instructions, and so on, that others will believe came from Alice.

Let us put the DSA algorithm to work. Actually, there are three algorithms:

1. To generate a key pair
2. To sign a message
3. To verify a signature

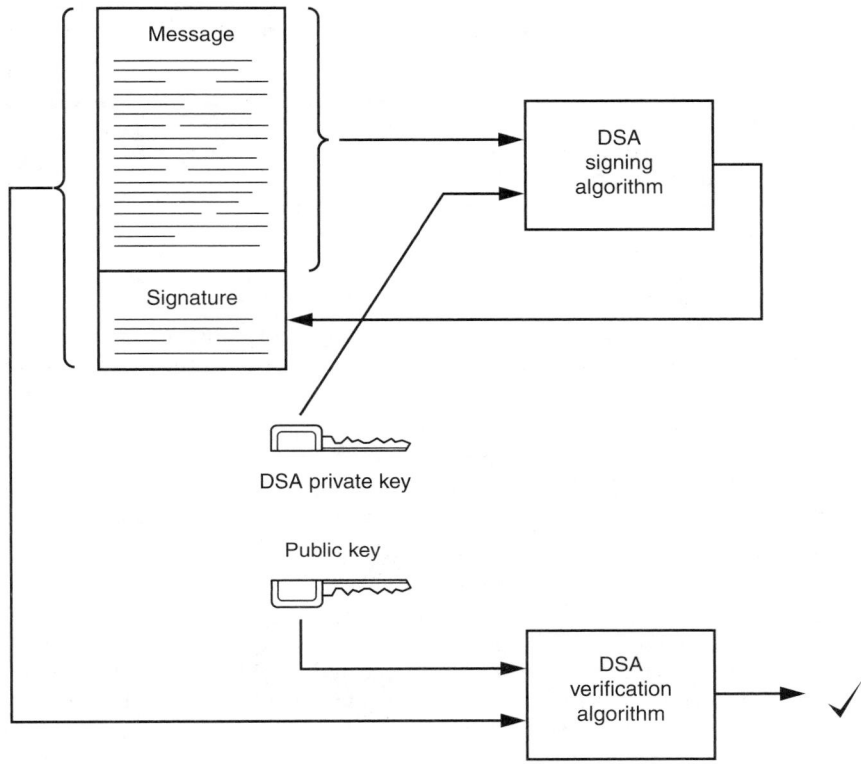

Figure 9–11: Public key signature exchange with DSA

Of course, you generate a key pair only once and then use it for signing and verifying many messages. To generate a new random key pair, make sure you use *truly random* numbers. For example, the regular random number generator in the Random class, seeded by the current date and time, is not random enough. (The jargon says the basic random number generator in java.util is not "cryptographically secure.") For example, supposing the computer clock is accurate to 1/10 of a second; then, there are at most 864,000 seeds per day. If an attacker knows the day a key was issued (as can often be deduced from the expiration date), then it is an easy matter to generate all possible seeds for that day.

The SecureRandom class generates random numbers that are far more secure than those produced by the Random class. You still need to provide a seed to start the number sequence at a random spot. The best method for doing this is to obtain random input from a hardware device such as a white-noise generator. Another reasonable source for random input is to ask the user to type away aimlessly on the keyboard, but each keystroke should contribute only one or two bits to the random seed. Once you gather such random bits in an array of bytes, you pass it to the setSeed method.

```
SecureRandom secrand = new SecureRandom();
byte[] b = new byte[20];
// fill with truly random bits
secrand.setSeed(b);
```

If you don't seed the random number generator, then it will compute its own 20-byte seed by launching threads, putting them to sleep, and measuring the exact time when they are awakened.

 NOTE: This is an innovative algorithm that, at this point, is *not* known to be safe. And, in the past, algorithms that relied on timing other components of the computer, such as hard disk access time, were later shown not to be completely random.

Once you seed the generator, you can then draw random bytes with the nextBytes method.

```
byte[] randomBytes = new byte[64];
secrand.nextBytes(randomBytes);
```

Actually, to compute a new DSA key, you don't compute the random numbers yourself. You just pass the random number generator object to the DSA key generation algorithm.

To make a new key pair, you need a KeyPairGenerator object. Just as with the MessageDigest class of the preceding section, the KeyPairGenerator class is both a factory class and the superclass for actual key-pair-generation algorithms. To get a DSA key pair generator, you call the getInstance method with the string "DSA".

```
KeyPairGenerator keygen = KeyPairGenerator.getInstance("DSA");
```

The returned object is actually an object of the class sun.security.provider.DSAKeyPairGenerator, which is a subclass of KeyPairGenerator.

To generate keys, you must initialize the key generation algorithm object with the key strength and a secure random number generator. Note that the key strength is not the length of the generated keys but the size of one of the building blocks of the key. In the case of DSA, it is the number of bits in the modulus, one of the mathematical quantities that makes up the public and private keys. Suppose you want to generate a key with a modulus of 512 bits:

```
SecureRandom secrand = new SecureRandom();
secrand.setSeed(...);
keygen.initialize(512, secrand);
```

Now you are ready to generate key pairs.

```
KeyPair keys = keygen.generateKeyPair();
KeyPair morekeys = keygen.generateKeyPair();
```

Each key pair has a public and a private key.

```
PublicKey pubkey = keys.getPublic();
PrivateKey privkey = keys.getPrivate();
```

To sign a message, you need a signature algorithm object. You use the Signature factory class:

```
Signature signalg = Signature.getInstance("DSA");
```

Signature algorithm objects can be used both to sign and to verify a message. To prepare the object for message signing, use the initSign method and pass the private key to the signature algorithm.

```
signalg.initSign(privkey);
```

Now, use the update method to add bytes to the algorithm objects, in the same way as with the message digest algorithm.

```
byte[] bytes = . . .;
while (. . .) signalg.update(bytes);
```

Finally, compute the signature with the sign method. The signature is returned as an array of bytes.

```
byte[] signature = signalg.sign();
```

The recipient of the message must obtain a DSA signature algorithm object and prepare it for signature verification by calling the initVerify method with the public key as parameter.

```
Signature verifyalg = Signature.getInstance("DSA");
verifyalg.initVerify(pubkey);
```

Then, send the message to the algorithm object.

```
byte[] bytes = . . .;
while (. . .) verifyalg.update(bytes);
```

Finally, verify the signature.

```
boolean check = verifyalg.verify(signature);
```

If the verify method returns true, then the signature was a valid signature of the message that was signed with the matching private key. That is, both the sender and the contents of the message have been authenticated.

Example 9–18 demonstrates the key generation, signing, and verification processes. Run the program like this:

```
java SignatureTest -genkey public.key private.key
java SignatureTest -sign sample.txt sample.txt.signed private.key
java SignatureTest -verify sample.txt.signed public.key
```

The program should print the message "verified". Then use a hex editor to make a small change to sample.txt.signed, and run the last command again. You should now get a message "not verified".

Example 9–18: SignatureTest.java

```
1. import java.io.*;
2. import java.security.*;
3.
4. /**
5.    This program demonstrates how to sign a message with a private DSA key
6.    and verify it with the matching public key. Usage:
7.    java SignatureTest -genkey public private
8.    java SignatureTest -sign message signed private
9.    java SignatureTest -verify signed public
10. */
11. public class SignatureTest
12. {
13.    public static void main(String[] args)
14.    {
15.       try
16.       {
17.          if (args[0].equals("-genkey"))
18.          {
19.             KeyPairGenerator pairgen = KeyPairGenerator.getInstance("DSA");
20.             SecureRandom random = new SecureRandom();
21.             pairgen.initialize(KEYSIZE, random);
22.             KeyPair keyPair = pairgen.generateKeyPair();
23.             ObjectOutputStream out = new ObjectOutputStream(new FileOutputStream(args[1]));
24.             out.writeObject(keyPair.getPublic());
25.             out.close();
26.             out = new ObjectOutputStream(new FileOutputStream(args[2]));
27.             out.writeObject(keyPair.getPrivate());
28.             out.close();
29.          }
```

```
30.        else if (args[0].equals("-sign"))
31.        {
32.            ObjectInputStream keyIn = new ObjectInputStream(new FileInputStream(args[3]));
33.            PrivateKey privkey = (PrivateKey) keyIn.readObject();
34.            keyIn.close();
35.
36.            Signature signalg = Signature.getInstance("DSA");
37.            signalg.initSign(privkey);
38.
39.            File infile = new File(args[1]);
40.            InputStream in = new FileInputStream(infile);
41.            int length = (int) infile.length();
42.            byte[] message = new byte[length];
43.            in.read(message, 0, length);
44.            in.close();
45.
46.            signalg.update(message);
47.            byte[] signature = signalg.sign();
48.
49.            DataOutputStream out = new DataOutputStream(new FileOutputStream(args[2]));
50.            int signlength = signature.length;
51.            out.writeInt(signlength);
52.            out.write(signature, 0, signlength);
53.            out.write(message, 0, length);
54.            out.close();
55.        }
56.        else if (args[0].equals("-verify"))
57.        {
58.            ObjectInputStream keyIn = new ObjectInputStream(new FileInputStream(args[2]));
59.            PublicKey pubkey = (PublicKey) keyIn.readObject();
60.            keyIn.close();
61.
62.            Signature verifyalg = Signature.getInstance("DSA");
63.            verifyalg.initVerify(pubkey);
64.
65.            File infile = new File(args[1]);
66.            DataInputStream in = new DataInputStream(new FileInputStream(infile));
67.            int signlength = in.readInt();
68.            byte[] signature = new byte[signlength];
69.            in.read(signature, 0, signlength);
70.
71.            int length = (int) infile.length() - signlength - 4;
72.            byte[] message = new byte[length];
73.            in.read(message, 0, length);
74.            in.close();
75.
76.            verifyalg.update(message);
77.            if (!verifyalg.verify(signature))
78.                System.out.print("not ");
79.            System.out.println("verified");
80.        }
81.    }
82.    catch (Exception e)
83.    {
84.        e.printStackTrace();
85.    }
86. }
```

753

```
87.
88.    private static final int KEYSIZE = 512;
89. }
```

 java.security.KeyPairGenerator 1.1

- static KeyPairGenerator getInstance(String algorithm)
  returns a KeyPairGenerator object that implements the specified algorithm. Throws a NoSuchAlgorithmException if the algorithm is not provided.

  Parameters: algorithm   The name of the algorithm, such as "DSA"

- void initialize(int strength, SecureRandom random)
  initializes this KeyPairGenerator.

  Parameters: strength   An algorithm-specific measurement, typically, the number of bits of one of the algorithm parameters

                  random   The source of random bits for generating keys

- KeyPair generateKeyPair()
  generates a new key pair.

 java.security.KeyPair 1.1

- PrivateKey getPrivate()
  returns the private key from the key pair.
- PublicKey getPublic()
  returns the public key from the key pair.

 java.security.Signature 1.1

- static Signature getInstance(String algorithm)
  returns a Signature object that implements the specified algorithm. Throws NoSuchAlgorithmException if the algorithm is not provided.

  Parameters: algorithm   The name of the algorithm, such as "DSA"

- void initSign(PrivateKey privateKey)
  initializes this object for signing. Throws InvalidKeyException if the key type does not match the algorithm type.

  Parameters: privateKey   The private key of the identity whose signature is being computed

- void update(byte input)
- void update(byte[] input)
- void update(byte[] input, int offset, int len)
  update the message buffer, using the specified bytes.
- byte[] sign()
  completes the signature computation and returns the computed signature.
- void initVerify(PublicKey publicKey)
  initializes this object for verification. Throws InvalidKeyException if the key type does not match the algorithm type.

  Parameters: publicKey   The public key of the identity to be verified

- boolean verify(byte[] signature)
  checks whether the signature is valid.

Message Authentication

Suppose you get a message from your friend, signed by your friend with his private key, using the method we just showed you. You may already have his public key, or you can easily get it by asking him for a copy or by getting it from your friend's web page. Then, you can verify that the message was in fact authored by your friend and has not been tampered with. Now, suppose you get a message from a stranger who claims to represent a famous software company, urging you to run the program that is attached to the message. The stranger even sends you a copy of his public key so you can verify that he authored the message. You check that the signature is valid. This proves that the message was signed with the matching private key and that it has not been corrupted.

Be careful: *You still have no idea who wrote the message.* Anyone could have generated a pair of public and private keys, signed the message with the private key, and sent the signed message and the public key to you. The problem of determining the identity of the sender is called the *authentication problem.*

The usual way to solve the authentication problem is simple. Suppose the stranger and you have a common acquaintance you both trust. Suppose the stranger meets your acquaintance in person and hands over a disk with the public key. Your acquaintance later meets you, assures you that he met the stranger and that the stranger indeed works for the famous software company, and then gives you the disk (see Figure 9–12). That way, your acquaintance vouches for the authenticity of the stranger.

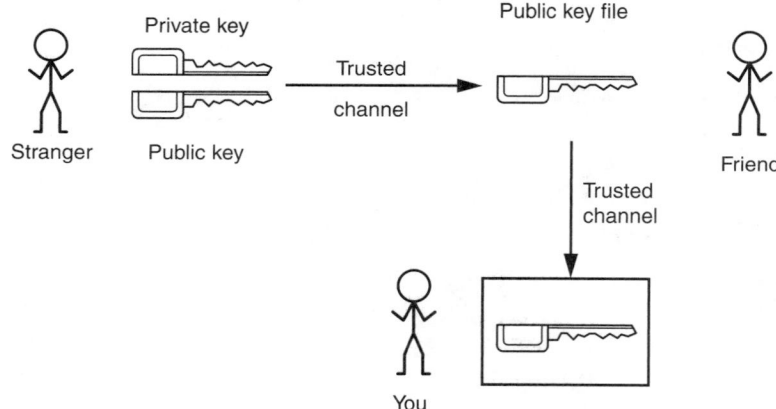

Figure 9–12: Authentication through a trusted intermediary

In fact, your acquaintance does not actually need to meet you. Instead, he can apply his private signature to the stranger's public key file (see Figure 9–13).

When you get the public key file, you verify the signature of your acquaintance, and because you trust him, you are confident that he did check the stranger's credentials before applying his signature.

However, you may not have a common acquaintance. Some trust models assume that there is always a "chain of trust"—a chain of mutual acquaintances—so that you trust every member of that chain. In practice, of course, that isn't always true. You may trust your acquaintance, Alice, and you know that Alice trusts Bob, but you don't know Bob and aren't sure that you trust him. Other trust models assume that there is a benevolent

big brother in whom we all trust. The best known of these companies is VeriSign, Inc. (http://www.verisign.com).

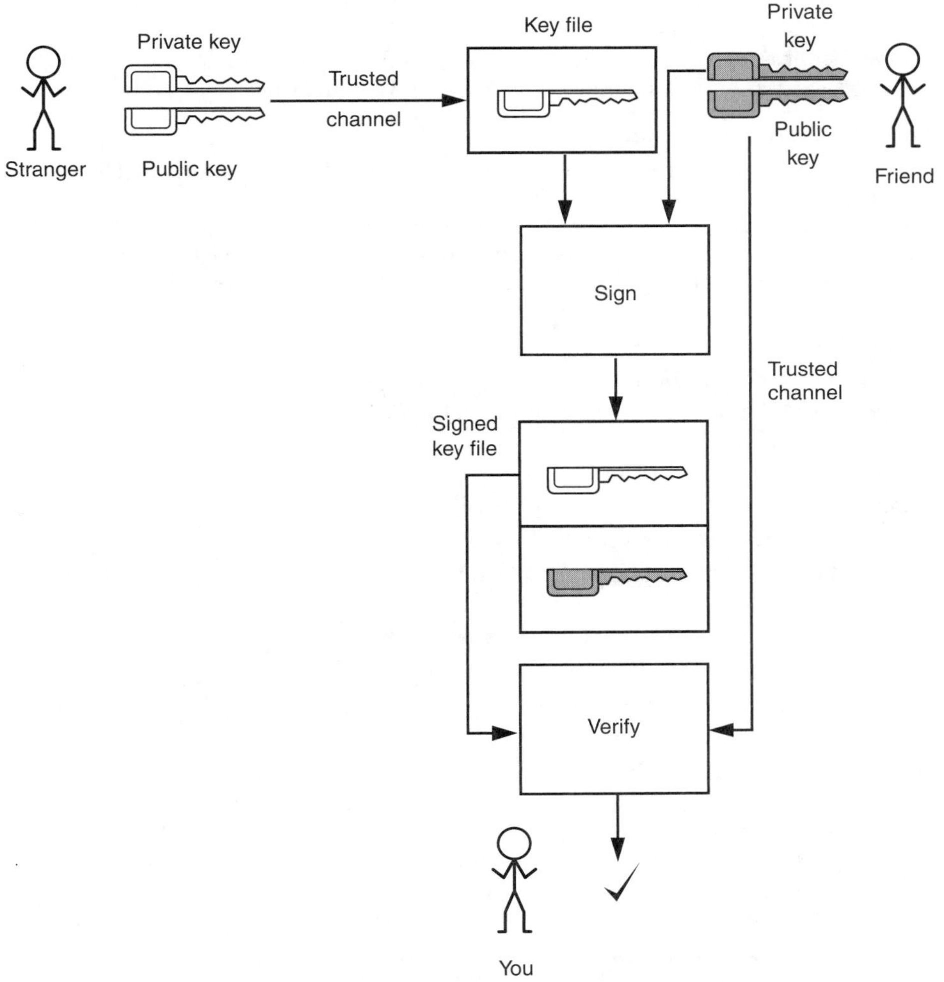

Figure 9–13: Authentication through a trusted intermediary's signature

You will often encounter digital signatures that are signed by one or more entities who will vouch for the authenticity, and you will need to evaluate to what degree you trust the authenticators. You might place a great deal of trust in VeriSign, perhaps because you saw their logo on many web pages or because you heard that they require multiple people with black attaché cases to come together into a secure chamber whenever new master keys are to be minted.

However, you should have realistic expectations about what is actually being authenticated. The CEO of VeriSign does not personally meet every individual or company representative when authenticating a public key. You can get a "class 1" ID simply by filling out

a web form and paying a small fee. The key is mailed to the e-mail address included in the certificate. Thus, you can be reasonably assured that the e-mail address is genuine, but the requestor could have filled in *any* name and organization. There are more stringent classes of IDs. For example, with a "class 3" ID, VeriSign will require an individual requestor to appear before a notary public, and it will check the financial rating of a corporate requestor. Other authenticators will have different procedures. Thus, when you receive an authenticated message, it is important that you understand what, in fact, is being authenticated.

The X.509 Certificate Format

One of the most common formats for signed certificates is the X.509 format. X.509 certificates are widely used by VeriSign, Microsoft, Netscape, and many other companies, for signing e-mail messages, authenticating program code, and certifying many other kinds of data. The X.509 standard is part of the X.500 series of recommendations for a directory service by the international telephone standards body, the CCITT. In its simplest form, an X.509 certificate contains the following data:

- Version of certificate format
- Serial number of certificate
- Signature algorithm identifier (algorithm ID + parameters of the algorithm used to sign the certificate)
- Name of the signer of the certificate
- Period of validity (begin/end date)
- Name of the identity being certified
- Public key of identity being certified (algorithm ID + parameters of the algorithm + public key value)
- Signature (hash code of all preceding fields, encoded with private key of signer)

Thus, the signer guarantees that a certain identity has a particular public key.

Extensions to the basic X.509 format make it possible for the certificates to contain additional information.

The precise structure of X.509 certificates is described in a formal notation, called "abstract syntax notation #1" or ASN.1. Figure 9–14 shows the ASN.1 definition of version 3 of the X.509 format. The exact syntax is not important for us, but, as you can see, ASN.1 gives a precise definition of the structure of a certificate file. The *basic encoding rules,* or BER, describe precisely how to save this structure in a binary file. That is, BER describes how to encode integers, character strings, bit strings, and constructs such as SEQUENCE, CHOICE, and OPTIONAL.

 NOTE: You can find more information on ASN.1 in *ASN.1—Communication Between Heterogeneous Systems* by Olivier Dubuisson [Academic Press 2000] (http://www.oss.com/asn1/dubuisson.html) and *ASN.1 Complete* by John Larmouth [Morgan Kaufmann Publishers 1999] (http://www.nokalva.com/asn1/larmouth.html).

Actually, the BER rules are not unique; there are several ways of specifying some elements. The *distinguished encoding rules* (DER) remove these ambiguities. For a readable description of the BER encoding format, we recommend *A Layman's Guide to a Subset of ASN.1, BER, and DER* by Burton S. Kaliski, Jr., available from ftp://ftp.rsa.com/pub/pkcs/ps/layman.ps. For the source code of a useful program for dumping BER encoded files, go to http://www.cs.auckland.ac.nz/~pgut001/dumpasn1.c.

```
[Certificate  ::=  SEQUENCE  {
        tbsCertificate        TBSCertificate,
        signatureAlgorithm    AlgorithmIdentifier,
        signature             BIT STRING  }

   TBSCertificate  ::=  SEQUENCE  {
        version       [0]  EXPLICIT Version DEFAULT v1,
        serialNumber       CertificateSerialNumber,
        signature          AlgorithmIdentifier,
        issuer             Name,
        validity           Validity,
        subject            Name,
        subjectPublicKeyInfo  SubjectPublicKeyInfo,
        issuerUniqueID [1]  IMPLICIT UniqueIdentifier OPTIONAL,
                           -- If present, version must be v2
                              or v3
        subjectUniqueID [2]  IMPLICIT UniqueIdentifier OPTIONAL,
                           -- If present, version must be v2
                              or v3
        extensions    [3]  EXPLICIT Extensions OPTIONAL
                           -- If present, version must be v3
        }

   Version  ::=  INTEGER  {  v1(0), v2(1), v3(2)  }

   CertificateSerialNumber  ::=  INTEGER

   Validity ::= SEQUENCE {
        notBefore     CertificateValidityDate,
        notAfter      CertificateValidityDate }

   CertificateValidityDate ::= CHOICE {
        utcTime       UTCTime,
        generalTime   GeneralizedTime }

   UniqueIdentifier  ::=  BIT STRING

   SubjectPublicKeyInfo  ::=  SEQUENCE  {
        algorithm          AlgorithmIdentifier,
        subjectPublicKey   BIT STRING  }

   Extensions  ::=  SEQUENCE OF Extension

   Extension  ::=  SEQUENCE  {
        extnID     OBJECT IDENTIFIER,
        critical   BOOLEAN DEFAULT FALSE,
        extnValue  OCTET STRING  }
```

Figure 9–14: ASN.1 definition of X.509v3

 NOTE: Peter Gutmann's web site (http://www.cs.auckland.ac.nz/~pgut001/pubs/x509guide.txt) contains an entertaining and informative description of the many discrepancies in the X.509 format as implemented by different vendors.

Certificate Generation

The JDK comes with the keytool program, which is a command-line tool to generate and manage a set of certificates. We expect that ultimately the functionality of this tool will be embedded in other, more user-friendly programs. But right now, we use keytool to show how Alice can sign a document and send it to Bob, and how Bob can verify that the document really was signed by Alice and not an impostor. We do not discuss all of the keytool features—see the JDK documentation for complete information.

The keytool program manages *keystores,* databases of certificates and private keys. Each entry in the keystore has an *alias.* Here is how Alice creates a keystore, alice.store, and generates a key pair with alias alice.

```
keytool -genkey -keystore alice.store -alias alice
```

When creating or opening a keystore, you are prompted for a keystore password. For this example, just use password. If you were to use the keytool-generated keystore for any serious purpose, you would need to choose a good password and safeguard this file—it contains private signature keys.

When generating a key, you are prompted for the following information:

```
Enter keystore password:  password
What is your first and last name?
  [Unknown]:  Alice Lee
What is the name of your organizational unit?
  [Unknown]:  Engineering Department
What is the name of your organization?
  [Unknown]:  ACME Software
What is the name of your City or Locality?
  [Unknown]:  Cupertino
What is the name of your State or Province?
  [Unknown]:  California
What is the two-letter country code for this unit?
  [Unknown]:  US
Is <CN=Alice Lee, OU=Engineering Department, O=ACME Software, L=Cupertino, ST=California,
C=US> correct?
  [no]:  Y
```

The keytool uses X.500 distinguished names, with components Common Name (CN), Organizational Unit (OU), Organization (O), Location (L), State (ST), and Country (C) to identify key owners and certificate issuers.

Finally, specify a key password, or press ENTER to use the keystore password as the key password.

Suppose Alice wants to give her public key to Bob. She needs to export a certificate file:

```
keytool -export -keystore alice.store -alias alice -file alice.cert
```

Now Alice can send the certificate to Bob. When Bob receives the certificate, he can print it:

```
keytool -printcert -file alice.cert
```

The printout looks like this:

```
Owner: CN=Alice Lee, OU=Engineering Department, O=ACME Software, L=Cupertino, ST=California, C=US
Issuer: CN=Alice Lee, OU=Engineering Department, O=ACME Software, L=Cupertino, ST=California, C=US
Serial number: 4145f46b
Valid from: Mon Sep 13 12:26:35 PDT 2004 until: Sun Dec 12 11:26:35 PST 2004
Certificate fingerprints:
        MD5:  B6:12:34:88:7C:5E:63:28:21:0D:DC:C9:F1:C1:9C:94
        SHA1: 05:AF:B6:0B:8A:D6:86:0A:0D:06:97:FA:9A:63:F4:09:0B:64:68:10
```

This certificate is *self-signed*. Therefore, Bob cannot use another trusted certificate to check that this certificate is valid. Instead, he can call Alice and have her read the certificate fingerprint over the phone.

 NOTE: Some certificate issuers publish certificate fingerprints on their web sites. For example, the JRE includes the keystore cacerts in the *jre*/lib/security directory. It contains certificates from Thawte and VeriSign. To list the contents of a keystore, use the -list option:

```
keytool -list -v -keystore jre/lib/security/cacerts
```

The password for this keystore is changeit. One of the certificates in this keystore is

```
Owner: OU=VeriSign Trust Network, OU="(c) 1998 VeriSign, Inc. - For authorized use only",
OU=Class 1 Public Primary Certification Authority - G2, O="VeriSign, Inc.", C=US
Issuer: OU=VeriSign Trust Network, OU="(c) 1998 VeriSign, Inc. - For authorized
use only", OU=Class 1 Public Primary Certification Authority - G2, O="VeriSign, Inc.", C=US
Serial number: 4cc7eaaa983e71d39310f83d3a899192
Valid from: Sun May 17 17:00:00 PDT 1998 until: Tue Aug 01 16:59:59 PDT 2028
Certificate fingerprints:
        MD5:  DB:23:3D:F9:69:FA:4B:B9:95:80:44:73:5E:7D:41:83
        SHA1: 27:3E:E1:24:57:FD:C4:F9:0C:55:E8:2B:56:16:7F:62:F5:32:E5:47
```

You can check that your certificate is valid by visiting the web site http://www.verisign.com/repository/root.html.

Once Bob trusts the certificate, he can import it into his keystore.

```
keytool -import -keystore bob.store -alias alice -file alice.cert
```

 CAUTION: Never import into a keystore a certificate that you don't fully trust. Once a certificate is added to the keystore, any program that uses the keystore assumes that the certificate can be used to verify signatures.

Now Alice can start sending signed documents to Bob. The jarsigner tool signs and verifies JAR files. Alice simply adds the document to be signed into a JAR file.

```
jar cvf document.jar document.txt
```

Then she uses the jarsigner tool to add the signature to the file. She needs to specify the keystore, the JAR file, and the alias of the key to use.

```
jarsigner -keystore alice.store document.jar alice
```

When Bob receives the file, he uses the -verify option of the jarsigner program.

```
jarsigner -verify -keystore bob.store document.jar
```

Bob does not need to specify the key alias. The jarsigner program finds the X.500 name of the key owner in the digital signature and looks for matching certificates in the keystore.

If the JAR file is not corrupted and the signature matches, then the jarsigner program prints

```
jar verified.
```

Otherwise, the program displays an error message.

Certificate Signing

In the preceding section, you saw how to use a self-signed certificate to distribute a public key to another party. However, the recipient of the certificate needed to ensure that the certificate was valid by verifying the fingerprint with the issuer. More commonly, a certificate is signed by a trusted intermediary.

The JDK does not contain tools for certificate signing. In this section, you see how to write a program that signs a certificate with a private key from a keystore. This program is useful in its own right, and it shows you how to write programs that access the contents of certificates and keystores.

Before looking inside the program code, let's see how to put it to use. Suppose Alice wants to send her colleague Cindy a signed message. But Cindy doesn't want to call up everyone who sends her a signature file to verify the signature fingerprint. There needs to be an entity that Cindy trusts to verify signatures. In this example, we suppose that Cindy trusts the Information Resources Department at ACME Software to perform this service. To simulate this process, you'll need to create an added keystore `acmesoft.store`. Generate a key and export the self-signed certificate.

```
keytool -genkey -keystore acmesoft.store -alias acmeroot
keytool -export -alias acmeroot -keystore acmesoft.store -file acmeroot.cert
```

Then add it to Cindy's keystore.

```
keytool -import -alias acmeroot -keystore cindy.store -file acmeroot.cert
```

Cindy still needs to verify the fingerprint of that *root certificate*, but from now on, she can simply accept all certificates that are signed by it.

For Alice to send messages to Cindy and to everyone else at ACME Software, she needs to bring her certificate to the Information Resources Department and have it signed. However, the `keytool` program in the JDK does not have this functionality. That is where the certificate signer program in Example 9–19 comes in. The program reads a certificate file and signs it with a private key in a keystore. An authorized staff member at ACME Software would verify Alice's identity and generate a signed certificate as follows:

```
java CertificateSigner -keystore acmesoft.store -alias acmeroot
   -infile alice.cert -outfile alice_signedby_acmeroot.cert
```

The certificate signer program must have access to the ACME Software keystore, and the staff member must know the keystore password. Clearly, this is a sensitive operation.

Now Alice gives the file `alice_signedby_acmeroot.cert` file to Cindy and to anyone else in ACME Software. Alternatively, ACME Software can simply store the file in a company directory. Remember, this file contains Alice's public key and an assertion by ACME Software that this key really belongs to Alice.

 NOTE: The `keytool` program supports a different mechanism for key signing. The `-certreq` option produces a certificate request in a standard format that can be processed by certificate authorities such as VeriSign, or by local authorities running software such as the Netscape certificate server.

When Cindy imports the signed certificate into her keystore, the keystore verifies that the key was signed by a trusted root key that is already present in the keystore and she is not asked to verify the certificate fingerprint.

Once Cindy has added the root certificate and the certificates of the people who regularly send her documents, she never has to worry about the keystore again.

 CAUTION: This scenario is for illustration only. The keytool is really not suitable as a tool for end users. The keytool silently accepts certificates that are signed by a party that it already trusts, and it asks the user to confirm those that it cannot verify. It never rejects a certificate. It is all too easy for a confused user to accept an invalid certificate.

Now let us look at the source code of Example 9–19. First, we load the keystore. The get-Instance factory method of the KeyStore class creates a keystore instance of the appropriate type. The keytool-generated keystore has a type of "JKS". The provider of this keystore type is "SUN".

```
KeyStore store = KeyStore.getInstance("JKS", "SUN");
```

Now, we load the keystore data. The load method requires an input stream and a password. Note that the password is specified as a char[] array, not a string. The JVM can keep strings around for a long time before they are garbage-collected. Hackers could potentially find these strings, for example, by examining the contents of swap files. However, character arrays can be cleared immediately after they are used.

Here is the code for loading the keystore. Note that we fill the password with spaces immediately after use.

```
InputStream in = . . .;
char[] password = . . .;
store.load(in, password);
Arrays.fill(password, ' ');
in.close();
```

Next, we use the getKey method to retrieve the private key for signing. The getKey method requires the key alias and key password. Its return type is Key, and we cast it to PrivateKey since we know that the retrieved key is a private key.

```
char[] keyPassword = . . .;
PrivateKey issuerPrivateKey = (PrivateKey) store.getKey(alias, keyPassword);
Arrays.fill(keyPassword, ' ');
```

Now we are ready to read in the certificate that needs to be signed. The CertificateFactory class can read in certificates from an input stream. First, we get a factory of the appropriate type:

```
CertificateFactory factory = CertificateFactory.getInstance("X.509");
```

Then, we call the generateCertificate method with an input stream:

```
in = new FileInputStream(inname);
X509Certificate inCert = (X509Certificate) factory.generateCertificate(in);
in.close();
```

The return type of the generateCertificate method is the abstract Certificate class that is the superclass of concrete classes such as X509Certificate. Because we know that the input file actually contains an X509Certificate, we use a cast.

 CAUTION: Two types are called Certificate: a deprecated interface in the java.security package and an abstract class in the java.security.cert package, which is the class that you want to use. If you import both the java.security and the java.security.cert package into your program, be sure to resolve the ambiguity and explicitly reference the java.security.cert.Certificate class.

The purpose of this program is to sign the bytes in the certificate. We retrieve the bytes with the getTBSCertificate method:

```
byte[] inCertBytes = inCert.getTBSCertificate();
```

Next, we need the distinguished name of the issuer, which we insert into the signed certificate. The name is stored in the issuer certificate in the keystore. We fetch certificates from the keystore with the getCertificate method. Since certificates are public information, we supply only the alias, not a password.

```
X509Certificate issuerCert = (X509Certificate) store.getCertificate(alias);
```

The getCertificate method has return type Certificate, but once again we know that the returned value is actually X509Certificate. We obtain the issuer identity from the certificate by calling the getSubjectDN method. That method returns an object of some type that implements the Principal interface. Conceptually, a *principal* is a real-world entity such as a person, organization, or company.

```
Principal issuer = issuerCert.getSubjectDN();
```

We also retrieve the name of the signing algorithm.

```
String issuerSigAlg = issuerCert.getSigAlgName()
```

Now we must leave the realm of the standard security library. The standard library contains no methods for generating new certificates. Libraries for certificate generation are available from third-party vendors such as RSA Security, Inc., and the Legion of Bouncy Castle (http://www.bouncycastle.org). However, we use the classes in the sun.security.x509 package. The usual caveats apply. This package might not be supplied by third-party vendors of Java technology, and Sun Microsystems might change the behavior at any time.

The following code segment carries out these steps:

1. Generates a certificate information object from the bytes in the certificate that is to be signed;
2. Sets the issuer name;
3. Creates the certificate and signs it with the issuer's private key;
4. Saves the signed certificate to a file.

```
X509CertInfo info = new X509CertInfo(inCertBytes);
info.set(X509CertInfo.ISSUER, new CertificateIssuerName((X500Name) issuer));
X509CertImpl outCert = new X509CertImpl(info);
outCert.sign(issuerPrivateKey, issuerSigAlg);
outCert.derEncode(out);
```

We do not discuss the use of these classes in detail because we do not recommend the use of Sun libraries for production code. A future version of the JDK may contain classes for certificate generation. In the meantime, you may want to rely on third-party libraries or simply use existing certificate generation software.

Example 9–19: CertificateSigner.java

```
1. import java.io.*;
2. import java.security.*;
3. import java.security.cert.*;
4. import java.util.*;
5.
6. import sun.security.x509.X509CertInfo;
7. import sun.security.x509.X509CertImpl;
8. import sun.security.x509.X500Name;
9. import sun.security.x509.CertificateIssuerName;
10.
11. /**
12.    This program signs a certificate, using the private key of
13.    another certificate in a keystore.
14. */
```

```
15. public class CertificateSigner
16. {
17.    public static void main(String[] args)
18.    {
19.       String ksname = null; // the keystore name
20.       String alias = null; // the private key alias
21.       String inname = null; // the input file name
22.       String outname = null; // the output file name
23.       for (int i = 0; i < args.length; i += 2)
24.       {
25.          if (args[i].equals("-keystore"))
26.             ksname = args[i + 1];
27.          else if (args[i].equals("-alias"))
28.             alias = args[i + 1];
29.          else if (args[i].equals("-infile"))
30.             inname = args[i + 1];
31.          else if (args[i].equals("-outfile"))
32.             outname = args[i + 1];
33.          else usage();
34.       }
35.
36.       if (ksname == null || alias == null || inname == null || outname == null) usage();
37.
38.       try
39.       {
40.          PushbackReader console = new PushbackReader(new InputStreamReader(System.in));
41.
42.          KeyStore store = KeyStore.getInstance("JKS", "SUN");
43.          InputStream in = new FileInputStream(ksname);
44.          System.out.print("Keystore password: ");
45.          System.out.flush();
46.          char[] password = readPassword(console);
47.          store.load(in, password);
48.          Arrays.fill(password, ' ');
49.          in.close();
50.
51.          System.out.print("Key password for " + alias + ": ");
52.          System.out.flush();
53.          char[] keyPassword = readPassword(console);
54.          PrivateKey issuerPrivateKey = (PrivateKey) store.getKey(alias, keyPassword);
55.          Arrays.fill(keyPassword, ' ');
56.
57.          if (issuerPrivateKey == null) error("No such private key");
58.
59.          in = new FileInputStream(inname);
60.
61.          CertificateFactory factory = CertificateFactory.getInstance("X.509");
62.
63.          X509Certificate inCert = (X509Certificate) factory.generateCertificate(in);
64.          in.close();
65.          byte[] inCertBytes = inCert.getTBSCertificate();
66.
67.          X509Certificate issuerCert = (X509Certificate) store.getCertificate(alias);
68.          Principal issuer = issuerCert.getSubjectDN();
69.          String issuerSigAlg = issuerCert.getSigAlgName();
70.
71.          FileOutputStream out = new FileOutputStream(outname);
```

Core Java

```
72.
73.         X509CertInfo info = new X509CertInfo(inCertBytes);
74.         info.set(X509CertInfo.ISSUER, new CertificateIssuerName((X500Name) issuer));
75.
76.         X509CertImpl outCert = new X509CertImpl(info);
77.         outCert.sign(issuerPrivateKey, issuerSigAlg);
78.         outCert.derEncode(out);
79.
80.         out.close();
81.      }
82.      catch (Exception e)
83.      {
84.         e.printStackTrace();
85.      }
86.   }
87.
88.   /**
89.      Reads a password.
90.      @param in the reader from which to read the password
91.      @return an array of characters containing the password
92.   */
93.   public static char[] readPassword(PushbackReader in)
94.      throws IOException
95.   {
96.      final int MAX_PASSWORD_LENGTH = 100;
97.      int length = 0;
98.      char[] buffer = new char[MAX_PASSWORD_LENGTH];
99.
100.     while (true)
101.     {
102.        int ch = in.read();
103.        if (ch == '\r' || ch == '\n' || ch == -1
104.           || length == MAX_PASSWORD_LENGTH)
105.        {
106.           if (ch == '\r') // handle DOS "\r\n" line ends
107.           {
108.              ch = in.read();
109.              if (ch != '\n' && ch != -1) in.unread(ch);
110.           }
111.           char[] password = new char[length];
112.           System.arraycopy(buffer, 0, password, 0, length);
113.           Arrays.fill(buffer, ' ');
114.           return password;
115.        }
116.        else
117.        {
118.           buffer[length] = (char) ch;
119.           length++;
120.        }
121.     }
122.   }
123.
124.   /**
125.      Prints an error message and exits.
126.      @param message
127.   */
128.   public static void error(String message)
```

```
129.    {
130.       System.out.println(message);
131.       System.exit(1);
132.    }
133.
134.    /**
135.       Prints a usage message and exits.
136.    */
137.    public static void usage()
138.    {
139.       System.out.println("Usage: java CertificateSigner"
140.          + " -keystore keyStore -alias issuerKeyAlias"
141.          + " -infile inputFile -outfile outputFile");
142.       System.exit(1);
143.    }
144. }
```

 java.security.KeyStore 1.2

- static getInstance(String type)
- static getInstance(String type, String provider)
  construct a keystore object of the given type. If no provider is specified, the default provider is used. To work with keystores generated by the keytool, specify "JKS" as the type and "SUN" as the provider.

- void load(InputStream in, char[] password)
  loads a keystore from a stream. The password is kept in a character array so that it does not become part of the JVM string pool.

- Key getKey(String alias, char[] password)
  returns a private key with the given alias that is stored in this keystore.

- Certificate getCertificate(String alias)
  returns a certificate for a public key with the given alias that is stored in this keystore.

java.security.cert.CertificateFactory 1.2

- CertificateFactory getInstance(String type)
  creates a certificate factory for the given type. The type is a certificate type such as "X509".

- Certificate generateCertificate(InputStream in)
  loads a certificate from an input stream.

java.security.cert.Certificate 1.2

- PublicKey getPublicKey()
  returns the public key that is being guaranteed by this certificate.

- byte[] getEncoded()
  gets the encoded form of this certificate.

- String getType()
  returns the type of this certificate, such as "X509".

java.security.cert.X509Certificate 1.2

- Principal getSubjectDN()
- Principal getIssuerDN()
  get the owner (or subject) and issuer distinguished names from the certificate.

- Date getNotBefore()
- Date getNotAfter()
  get the validity period start and end dates of the certificate.
- BigInteger getSerialNumber()
  gets the serial number value from the certificate.
- String getSigAlgName()
- byte[] getSignature()
  get the signature algorithm name and the owner signature from the certificate.
- byte[] getTBSCertificate()
  gets the DER-encoded certificate information that needs to be signed by the certificate issuer.

Code Signing

One of the most important uses of authentication technology is signing executable programs. If you download a program, you are naturally concerned about damage that a program can do. For example, the program could have been infected by a virus. If you know where the code comes from *and* that it has not been tampered with since it left its origin, then your comfort level will be a lot higher than without this knowledge. In fact, if the program was also written in the Java programming language, you can then use this information to make a rational decision about what privileges you will allow that program to have. You might want it to run just in a sandbox as a regular applet, or you might want to grant it a different set of rights and restrictions. For example, if you download a word processing program, you might want to grant it access to your printer and to files in a certain subdirectory. However, you may not want to give it the right to make network connections, so that the program can't try to send your files to a third party without your knowledge.

You now know how to implement this sophisticated scheme.

1. First, use authentication to verify where the code came from.
2. Then, run the code with a security policy that enforces the permissions that you want to grant the program, depending on its origin.

JAR File Signing

In this section, we show you how to sign applets and web start applications for use with the Java Plug-in software. There are two scenarios:

1. Delivery in an intranet
2. Delivery over the public Internet

In the first scenario, a system administrator installs certificates and policy files on local machines. Whenever the Java Plug-in tool loads signed code, it consults the keystore for signatures and the policy file for the permissions. Installing the certificates and policies is straightforward and can be done once per desktop. End users can then run signed corporate code outside the sandbox. Whenever a new program is created or an existing one is updated, it must be signed and deployed on the web server. However, no desktops need to be touched as the programs evolve. We think this is a reasonable scenario that can be an attractive alternative to deploying corporate applications on every desktop.

In the second scenario, software vendors obtain certificates that are signed by certificate authorities such as VeriSign. When an end user visits a web site that contains a signed applet, a pop-up dialog box identifies the software vendor and gives the end user two choices: to run the applet with full privileges or to confine it to the sandbox. We discuss this scenario in detail on page 770.

For the remainder of this section, we describe how you can build policy files that grant specific permissions to code from known sources. Building and deploying these policy files is not for casual end users. However, system administrators can carry out these tasks in preparation for distributing intranet programs.

Suppose ACME Software wants its users to run certain programs that require local file access, and it wants to deploy the program through a browser, as applets or web start applications. Because these programs cannot run inside the sandbox, ACME Software needs to install policy files on employee machines. As you saw earlier in this chapter, ACME could identify the applets by their code base. But that means that ACME would need to update the policy files each time the applet code is moved to a different web server. Instead, ACME decides to *sign* the JAR files that contain the applet code.

To make a signed JAR file, first add your class files to a JAR file. For example,

```
javac FileReadApplet.java
jar cvf FileReadApplet.jar *.class
```

Then run the jarsigner tool and specify the JAR file and the alias of the private key:

```
keytool -genkey -keystore acmesoft.store -alias acmeroot
jarsigner -keystore acmesoft.store FileReadApplet.jar acmeroot
```

In this example, the JAR file is signed with the self-signed root key. Alternatively, ACME could issue keys to its programmers and sign them with the root key.

Of course, the keystore containing the private root key must be kept at a safe place. Let's make a second keystore certs.store for certificates and add the acmeroot certificate into it.

```
keytool -export -keystore acmesoft.store -alias acmeroot -file acmeroot.cert
keytool -import -keystore certs.store -alias acmeroot -file acmeroot.cert
```

Next, create a policy file that gives the permission for all applets that are signed with signatures in that keystore.

Include the location of your keystore in the policy file. Add a line

```
keystore "keystoreURL", "keystoreType";
```

to the top of the policy file. The type is JKS if the keystore was generated by keytool.

```
keystore "file:certs.store", "JKS";
```

Then add signedBy "*alias*" to one or more grant clauses in the policy file. For example,

```
grant signedBy "acmeroot"
{
    . . .
};
```

Any signed code that can be verified with the public key associated with the alias is now granted the permissions inside the grant clause.

 NOTE: Because the Java platform combines authentication and control over code permissions, it offers vastly superior security than Microsoft's ActiveX technology. ActiveX code is authenticated, but once it gains permission to run, it cannot be controlled at all. Microsoft has introduced a more comprehensive security model in the .NET platform.

You can try out the code signing process with the applet in Example 9–20. The applet tries to read from a local file. The default security policy only lets the applet read files from its code base and any subdirectories. Use appletviewer to run the applet and verify that you can view files from the code base directory, but not from other directories.

Now place the applet in a JAR file and sign it with the acmeroot key. Then create a policy file applet.policy with the contents:

```
keystore "file:///home/mydir/certs.store", "JKS";
grant signedBy "acmeroot"
{
    permission java.io.FilePermission "<<ALL FILES>>", "read";
};
```

Finally, tell the applet viewer to use the policy file:

```
appletviewer -J-Djava.security.policy=applet.policy FileReadApplet.html
```

Now the applet can read all files, thus demonstrating that the signing mechanism works.

As a final test, you can run your applet inside the browser (see Figure 9–15). Modify the deployment.properties file. If you run UNIX or Linux, the file is contained inside the .java/deployment subdirectory of your home directory. In Windows, the file is located inside the C:\Documents and Settings*yourLoginName*\Application Data\Sun\Java\Deployment directory.

Add a line with a file URL for the policy file, such as

```
deployment.user.security.policy=file:///home/mydir/applet.policy
```

Load the FileReadApplet.html file into the browser. *Do not* accept the signature of the JAR file. (Doing so would automatically give the applet all permissions.) Nevertheless, you should be able to load any local file, proving that the security manager has given the applet additional rights.

When you are done, remember to clean up your deployment.properties file and remove the policy file setting. If you load the applet again after cleaning up, you should no longer be able to read files from the local file system.

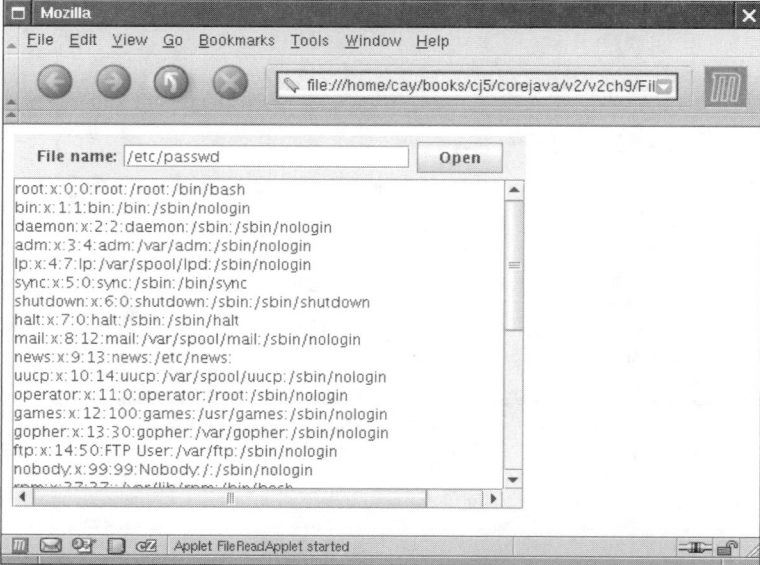

Figure 9–15: A signed applet can read local files

 CAUTION: When you test your applet in the browser instead of the applet viewer, be aware that the plug-in reads the deployment.properties file *only once*, when it is loaded for the first time. If you made a mistake, then close down the browser, fix your mistake, and restart the browser. Simply reloading the web page containing the applet does *not* work.

 TIP: If you decide to roll out signed applets or web start applications in an intranet, you should configure the deployment.properties files of your users' machines. The sections on "Deployment Configuration File and Properties" and "Java Control Panel" in the deployment guide at http://java.sun.com/j2se/1.5.0/docs/guide/deployment/deployment-guide/contents.html contain detailed instructions.

Example 9–20: FileReadApplet.java

```
1. import java.awt.*;
2. import java.awt.event.*;
3. import java.io.*;
4. import java.util.*;
5. import javax.swing.*;
6.
7. /**
8.    This applet can run "outside the sandbox" and read local files
9.    when it is given the right permissions.
10. */
11. public class FileReadApplet extends JApplet
12. {
13.    public FileReadApplet()
14.    {
15.       fileNameField = new JTextField(20);
16.       JPanel panel = new JPanel();
17.       panel.add(new JLabel("File name:"));
18.       panel.add(fileNameField);
19.       JButton openButton = new JButton("Open");
20.       panel.add(openButton);
21.       openButton.addActionListener(new
22.          ActionListener()
23.          {
24.             public void actionPerformed(ActionEvent event)
25.             {
26.                loadFile(fileNameField.getText());
27.             }
28.          });
29.
30.       add(panel, "North");
31.
32.       fileText = new JTextArea();
33.       add(new JScrollPane(fileText), "Center");
34.    }
35.
36.    /**
37.       Loads the contents of a file into the text area.
38.       @param filename the file name
39.    */
40.    public void loadFile(String filename)
```

```
41.    {
42.        try
43.        {
44.            fileText.setText("");
45.            Scanner in = new Scanner(new FileReader(filename));
46.            while (in.hasNextLine())
47.            fileText.append(in.nextLine() + "\n");
48.            in.close();
49.        }
50.        catch (IOException e)
51.        {
52.            fileText.append(e + "\n");
53.        }
54.        catch (SecurityException e)
55.        {
56.            fileText.append("I am sorry, but I cannot do that.\n");
57.            fileText.append(e + "\n");
58.        }
59.    }
60.
61.    private JTextField fileNameField;
62.    private JTextArea fileText;
63. }
```

Software Developer Certificates

Up to now, we discussed scenarios in which programs are delivered in an intranet and for which a system administrator configures a security policy that controls the privileges of the programs. However, that strategy only works with programs from known sources.

Suppose while surfing the Internet, you encounter a web site that offers to run an applet or web start application from an unfamiliar vendor, provided you grant it the permission to do so (see Figure 9–16). Such a program is signed with a *software developer* certificate that is issued by a certificate authority. The pop-up dialog box identifies the software developer and the certificate issuer. You now have two choices:

- To run the program with full privileges, or
- To confine the program to the sandbox.

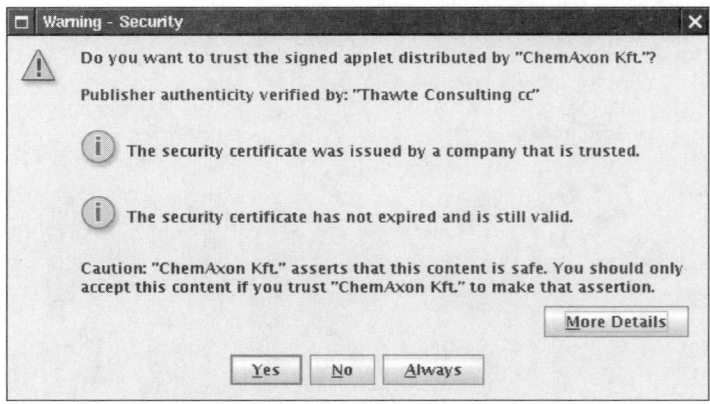

Figure 9–16: Launching a signed applet

What facts do you have at your disposal that might influence your decision? Here is what you know:

1. Thawte sold a certificate to the software developer.
2. The program really was signed with that certificate, and it hasn't been modified in transit.
3. The certificate really was signed by Thawte—it was verified by the public key in the local cacerts file.

Does that tell you whether the code is safe to run? Do you trust the vendor if all you know is the vendor name and the fact that Thawte sold them a software developer certificate? Presumably Thawte went to some degree of trouble to assure itself that ChemAxon Kft. is not an outright cracker. However, no certificate issuer carries out a comprehensive audit of the honesty and competence of software vendors.

In the situation of an unknown vendor, an end user is ill-equipped to make an intelligent decision whether to let this program run outside the sandbox, with all permissions of a local application. If the vendor is a well-known company, then the user can at least take the past track record of the company into account.

 NOTE: It is possible to use very weak certificates to sign code—see http://www.dallaway.com/acad/webstart for a sobering example. Some developers even instruct users to add untrusted certificates into their certificate store—for example, http://www.agsrhichome.bnl.gov/Controls/doc/javaws/javaws_howto.html. From a security standpoint, this seems very bad.

We don't like situations in which a program demands "give me all rights, or I won't run at all." Naïve users are too often cowed into granting access that can put them in danger.

Would it help if each program explained what rights it needs and requested specific permission for those rights? Unfortunately, as you have seen, that can get pretty technical. It doesn't seem reasonable for an end user to have to ponder whether a program should really have the right to inspect the AWT event queue.

We remain unenthusiastic about programs that are signed with software developer certificates and whose execution is approved by end users. We suggest that you limit code signing to corporate applications in which the certificates are configured by a system administrator.

Encryption

So far, we have discussed one important cryptographic technique that is implemented in the Java security API, namely, authentication through digital signatures. A second important aspect of security is *encryption*. When information is authenticated, the information itself is plainly visible. The digital signature merely verifies that the information has not been changed. In contrast, when information is encrypted, it is not visible. It can only be decrypted with a matching key.

Authentication is sufficient for code signing—there is no need for hiding the code. However, encryption is necessary when applets or applications transfer confidential information, such as credit card numbers and other personal data.

Until recently, patents and export controls have prevented many companies, including Sun, from offering strong encryption. Fortunately, export controls are now much less stringent, and the patent for an important algorithm has expired. As of JDK 1.4, good encryption support is part of the standard library. Cryptographic support is also available as a separate extension (called JCE) for older versions of the JDK.

Symmetric Ciphers

The Java cryptographic extensions contain a class Cipher that is the superclass for all encryption algorithms. You get a cipher object by calling the getInstance method:

```
Cipher cipher = Cipher.getInstance(algorithmName);
```

or

```
Cipher cipher = Cipher.getInstance(algorithmName, providerName);
```

The JDK comes with ciphers by the provider named "SunJCE". It is the default provider that is used if you don't specify another provider name. You might want another provider if you need specialized algorithms that Sun does not support.

The algorithm name is a string such as "AES" or "DES/CBC/PKCS5Padding".

DES, the Data Encryption Standard, is a venerable block cipher with a key length of 56 bits. Nowadays, the DES algorithm is considered obsolete because it can be cracked with brute force (see, for example, http://www.eff.org/Privacy/Crypto/Crypto_misc/DESCracker/). A far better alternative is its successor, the Advanced Encryption Standard (AES). See http://csrc.nist.gov/encryption/aes/ for more information on AES. We use AES for our example.

Once you have a cipher object, you initialize it by setting the mode and the key:

```
int mode = . . .;
Key key = . . .;
cipher.init(mode, key);
```

The mode is one of

```
Cipher.ENCRYPT_MODE
Cipher.DECRYPT_MODE
Cipher.WRAP_MODE
Cipher.UNWRAP_MODE
```

The wrap and unwrap modes encrypt one key with another—see the next section for an example.

Now you can repeatedly call the update method to encrypt blocks of data:

```
int blockSize = cipher.getBlockSize();
byte[] inBytes = new byte[blockSize];
. . . // read inBytes
int outputSize= cipher.getOutputSize(inLength);
byte[] outBytes = new byte[outputSize];
int outLength = cipher.update(inBytes, 0, outputSize, outBytes);
. . . // write outBytes
```

When you are done, you must call the doFinal method once. If a final block of input data is available (with fewer than blockSize bytes), then call

```
outBytes = cipher.doFinal(inBytes, 0, inLength);
```

If all input data have been encrypted, instead call

```
outBytes = cipher.doFinal();
```

The call to doFinal is necessary to carry out *padding* of the final block. Consider the DES cipher. It has a block size of 8 bytes. Suppose the last block of the input data has fewer than 8 bytes. Of course, we can fill the remaining bytes with 0, to obtain one final block of 8 bytes, and encrypt it. But when the blocks are decrypted, the result will have several trailing 0 bytes appended to it, and therefore it will be slightly different from the original input file. That may well be a problem, and, to avoid it, we need a *padding scheme*. A commonly used padding scheme is the one described in the Public Key Cryptography Standard

(PKCS) #5 by RSA Security Inc. (ftp://ftp.rsasecurity.com/pub/pkcs/pkcs-5v2/pkcs5v2-0.pdf). In this scheme, the last block is not padded with a pad value of zero, but with a pad value that equals the number of pad bytes. In other words, if L is the last (incomplete) block, then it is padded as follows:

```
L 01                              if length(L) = 7
L 02 02                           if length(L) = 6
L 03 03 03                        if length(L) = 5
 . . .
L 07 07 07 07 07 07 07            if length(L) = 1
```

Finally, if the length of the input is actually divisible by 8, then one block

```
08 08 08 08 08 08 08 08
```

is appended to the input and encrypted. For decryption, the very last byte of the plaintext is a count of the padding characters to discard.

Finally, we explain how you obtain a key. You can generate a completely random key by following these steps.

1. Get a KeyGenerator for your algorithm.
2. Initialize the generator with a source for randomness. If the block length of the cipher is variable, also specify the desired block length.
3. Call the generateKey method.

For example, here is how you generate an AES key.

```
KeyGenerator keygen = KeyGenerator.getInstance("AES");
SecureRandom random = new SecureRandom();
keygen.init(random);
Key key = keygen.generateKey();
```

Alternatively, you may want to produce a key from a fixed set of raw data (perhaps derived from a password or the timing of keystrokes). Then use a SecretKeyFactory, like this:

```
SecretKeyFactory keyFactory = SecretKeyFactory.getInstance("AES");
byte[] keyData = . . .; // 16 bytes for AES
SecretKeySpec keySpec = new SecretKeySpec(keyData, "AES");
Key key = keyFactory.generateSecret(keySpec);
```

The sample program at the end of this section puts the AES cipher to work (see Example 9–21). To use the program, you first generate a secret key. Run

```
java AESTest -genkey secret.key
```

The secret key is saved in the file secret.key.

Now you can encrypt with the command

```
java AESTest -encrypt plaintextFile encryptedFile secret.key
```

Decrypt with the command

```
java AESTest -decrypt encryptedFile decryptedFile secret.key
```

The program is straightforward. The -genkey option produces a new secret key and serializes it in the given file. That operation takes a long time because the initialization of the secure random generator is time consuming. The -encrypt and -decrypt options both call into the same crypt method that calls the update and doFinal methods of the cipher. Note how the update method is called as long as the input blocks have the full length, and the doFinal method is either called with a partial input block (which is then padded) or with no additional data (to generate one pad block).

Example 9–21: AESTest.java

```java
1. import java.io.*;
2. import java.security.*;
3. import javax.crypto.*;
4. import javax.crypto.spec.*;
5.
6. /**
7.    This program tests the AES cipher. Usage:
8.    java AESTest -genkey keyfile
9.    java AESTest -encrypt plaintext encrypted keyfile
10.   java AESTest -decrypt encrypted decrypted keyfile
11. */
12. public class AESTest
13. {
14.    public static void main(String[] args)
15.    {
16.       try
17.       {
18.          if (args[0].equals("-genkey"))
19.          {
20.             KeyGenerator keygen = KeyGenerator.getInstance("AES");
21.             SecureRandom random = new SecureRandom();
22.             keygen.init(random);
23.             SecretKey key = keygen.generateKey();
24.             ObjectOutputStream out = new ObjectOutputStream(new FileOutputStream(args[1]));
25.             out.writeObject(key);
26.             out.close();
27.          }
28.          else
29.          {
30.             int mode;
31.             if (args[0].equals("-encrypt"))
32.                mode = Cipher.ENCRYPT_MODE;
33.             else
34.                mode = Cipher.DECRYPT_MODE;
35.
36.             ObjectInputStream keyIn = new ObjectInputStream(new FileInputStream(args[3]));
37.             Key key = (Key) keyIn.readObject();
38.             keyIn.close();
39.
40.             InputStream in = new FileInputStream(args[1]);
41.             OutputStream out = new FileOutputStream(args[2]);
42.             Cipher cipher = Cipher.getInstance("AES");
43.             cipher.init(mode, key);
44.
45.             crypt(in, out, cipher);
46.             in.close();
47.             out.close();
48.          }
49.       }
50.       catch (IOException e)
51.       {
52.          e.printStackTrace();
53.       }
54.       catch (GeneralSecurityException e)
```

```
55.       {
56.          e.printStackTrace();
57.       }
58.       catch (ClassNotFoundException e)
59.       {
60.          e.printStackTrace();
61.       }
62.    }
63.
64.    /**
65.       Uses a cipher to transform the bytes in an input stream
66.       and sends the transformed bytes to an output stream.
67.       @param in the input stream
68.       @param out the output stream
69.       @param cipher the cipher that transforms the bytes
70.    */
71.    public static void crypt(InputStream in, OutputStream out, Cipher cipher)
72.          throws IOException, GeneralSecurityException
73.    {
74.       int blockSize = cipher.getBlockSize();
75.       int outputSize = cipher.getOutputSize(blockSize);
76.       byte[] inBytes = new byte[blockSize];
77.       byte[] outBytes = new byte[outputSize];
78.
79.       int inLength = 0;
80.       boolean more = true;
81.       while (more)
82.       {
83.          inLength = in.read(inBytes);
84.          if (inLength == blockSize)
85.          {
86.             int outLength = cipher.update(inBytes, 0, blockSize, outBytes);
87.             out.write(outBytes, 0, outLength);
88.          }
89.          else more = false;
90.       }
91.       if (inLength > 0)
92.          outBytes = cipher.doFinal(inBytes, 0, inLength);
93.       else
94.          outBytes = cipher.doFinal();
95.       out.write(outBytes);
96.    }
97. }
```

---

javax.crypto.Cipher 1.4

- static Cipher getInstance(String algorithm)
- static Cipher getInstance(String algorithm, String provider)

return a Cipher object that implements the specified algorithm. Throw a NoSuchAlgorithmException if the algorithm is not provided.

| *Parameters:* | algorithm | The algorithm name, such as "DES" or "DES/CBC/PKCS5Padding". Contact your provider for information on valid algorithm names. |
| | provider | The provider name, such as "SunJCE" or "BC". |

- int getBlockSize()
  returns the size (in bytes) of a cipher block, or 0 if the cipher is not a block cipher.
- int getOutputSize(int inputLength)
  returns the size of an output buffer that is needed if the next input has the given number of bytes. This method takes into account any buffered bytes in the cipher object.
- void init(int mode, Key key)
  initializes the cipher algorithm object.

Parameters	mode	ENCRYPT_MODE, DECRYPT_MODE, WRAP_MODE, or UNWRAP_MODE
	key	The key to use for the transformation

- byte[] update(byte[] in)
- byte[] update(byte[] in, int offset, int length)
- int update(byte[] in, int offset, int length, byte[] out)
  transform one block of input data. The first two methods return the output. The third method returns the number of bytes placed into out.

Parameters:	in	The new input bytes to process
	offset	The starting index of input bytes in the array in
	length	The number of input bytes
	out	The array into which to place the output bytes

- byte[] doFinal()
- byte[] doFinal(byte[] in)
- byte[] doFinal(byte[] in, int offset, int length)
- int doFinal(byte[] in, int offset, int length, byte[] out)
  transform the last block of input data and flush the buffer of this algorithm object. The first three methods return the output. The fourth method returns the number of bytes placed into out.

Parameters:	in	The new input bytes to process
	offset	The starting index of input bytes in the array in
	length	The number of input bytes
	out	The array into which to place the output bytes

 javax.crypto.KeyGenerator 1.4

- static KeyGenerator getInstance(String algorithm)
  returns a KeyGenerator object that implements the specified algorithm. Throws a NoSuchAlgorithmException if the algorithm is not provided.

Parameters:	algorithm	The name of the algorithm, such as "DES"

- void init(SecureRandom random)
- void init(int keySize, SecureRandom random)
  initialize the key generator.

Parameters:	keySize	The desired key size
	random	The source of randomness for generating keys

- SecretKey generateKey()
  generates a new key.

 javax.crypto.SecretKeyFactory 1.4

- static SecretKeyFactory getInstance(String algorithm)
- static SecretKeyFactory getInstance(String algorithm, String provider)
  return a SecretKeyFactory object for the specified algorithm.

    Parameters: algorithm   The algorithm name, such as "DES"

    provider   The provider name, such as "SunJCE" or "BC"

- SecretKey generateSecret(KeySpec spec)
  generates a new secret key from the given specification.

 javax.crypto.spec.SecretKeySpec 1.4

- SecretKeySpec(byte[] key, String algorithm)
  constructs a key specification.

    Parameters: key   The bytes to use to make the key

    algorithm   The algorithm name, such as "DES"

Cipher Streams

The JCE library provides a convenient set of stream classes that automatically encrypt or decrypt stream data. For example, here is how you can encrypt data to a file:

```
Cipher cipher = . . .;
cipher.init(Cipher.ENCRYPT_MODE, key);
CipherOutputStream out = new CipherOutputStream(new FileOutputStream(outputFileName), cipher);
byte[] bytes = new byte[BLOCKSIZE];
int inLength = getData(bytes); // get data from data source
while (inLength != -1)
{
   out.write(bytes, 0, inLength);
   inLength = getData(bytes); // get more data from data source
}
out.flush();
```

Similarly, you can use a CipherInputStream to read and decrypt data from a file:

```
Cipher cipher = . . .;
cipher.init(Cipher.DECRYPT_MODE, key);
CipherInputStream in = new CipherInputStream(new FileInputStream(inputFileName), cipher);
byte[] bytes = new byte[BLOCKSIZE];
int inLength = in.read(bytes);
while (inLength != -1)
{
   putData(bytes, inLength); // put data to destination
   inLength = in.read(bytes);
}
```

The cipher stream classes transparently handle the calls to update and doFinal, which is clearly a convenience.

 javax.crypto.CipherInputStream 1.4

- CipherInputStream(InputStream in, Cipher cipher)
  constructs an input stream that reads data from in and decrypts or encrypts them by using the given cipher.

- `int read()`
- `int read(byte[] b, int off, int len)`
  read data from the input stream, which is automatically decrypted or encrypted.

 javax.crypto.CipherOutputStream 1.4

- `CipherOutputStream(OutputStream out, Cipher cipher)`
  constructs an output stream that writes data to `out` and encrypts or decrypts them using the given cipher.
- `void write(int ch)`
- `void write(byte[] b, int off, int len)`
  write data to the output stream, which is automatically encrypted or decrypted.
- `void flush()`
  flushes the cipher buffer and carries out padding if necessary.

Public Key Ciphers

The AES cipher that you have seen in the preceding section is a *symmetric* cipher. The same key is used for encryption and for decryption. The Achilles heel of symmetric ciphers is key distribution. If Alice sends Bob an encrypted method, then Bob needs the same key that Alice used. If Alice changes the key, then she needs to send Bob both the message and, through a secure channel, the new key. But perhaps she has no secure channel to Bob, which is why she encrypts her messages to him in the first place.

Public key cryptography solves that problem. In a public key cipher, Bob has a key pair consisting of a public key and a matching private key. Bob can publish the public key anywhere, but he must closely guard the private key. Alice simply uses the public key to encrypt her messages to Bob.

Actually, it's not quite that simple. All known public key algorithms are *much* slower than symmetric key algorithms such as DES or AES. It would not be practical to use a public key algorithm to encrypt large amounts of information. However, that problem can easily be overcome by combining a public key cipher with a fast symmetric cipher, like this:

1. Alice generates a random symmetric encryption key. She uses it to encrypt her plaintext.
2. Alice encrypts the symmetric key with Bob's public key.
3. Alice sends Bob both the encrypted symmetric key and the encrypted plaintext.
4. Bob uses his private key to decrypt the symmetric key.
5. Bob uses the decrypted symmetric key to decrypt the message.

Nobody but Bob can decrypt the symmetric key because only Bob has the private key for decryption. Thus, the expensive public key encryption is only applied to a small amount of key data.

The most commonly used public key algorithm is the RSA algorithm invented by Rivest, Shamir, and Adleman. Until October 2000, the algorithm was protected by a patent assigned to RSA Security Inc. Licenses were not cheap—typically a 3% royalty, with a minimum payment of $50,000 per year. Now the algorithm is in the public domain. The RSA algorithm is supported in JDK 5.0 and above.

 NOTE: If you use an older version of the JDK, check out the Legion of Bouncy Castle (`http://www.bouncycastle.org`). It supplies a cryptography provider that includes RSA as well as a number of other features missing from the SunJCE provider. The Legion of Bouncy Castle provider has been signed by Sun Microsystems so that you can combine it with the JDK.

To use the RSA algorithm, you need a public/private key pair. You use a KeyPairGenerator like this:

```
KeyPairGenerator pairgen = KeyPairGenerator.getInstance("RSA");
SecureRandom random = new SecureRandom();
pairgen.initialize(KEYSIZE, random);
KeyPair keyPair = pairgen.generateKeyPair();
Key publicKey = keyPair.getPublic();
Key privateKey = keyPair.getPrivate();
```

The program in Example 9–22 has three options. The -genkey option produces a key pair. The -encrypt option generates an AES key and *wraps* it with the public key.

```
Key key = . . .; // an AES key
Key publicKey = . . .; // a public RSA key
Cipher cipher = Cipher.getInstance("RSA");
cipher.init(Cipher.WRAP_MODE, publicKey);
byte[] wrappedKey = cipher.wrap(key);
```

It then produces a file that contains

- the length of the wrapped key,
- the wrapped key bytes, and
- the plaintext encrypted with the AES key.

The -decrypt option decrypts such a file. To try out the program, first generate the RSA keys:

```
java RSATest -genkey public.key private.key
```

Then encrypt a file:

```
java RSATest -encrypt plaintextFile encryptedFile public.key
```

Finally, decrypt it and verify that the decrypted file matches the plaintext:

```
java RSATest -decrypt encryptedFile decryptedFile private.key
```

This example brings us to the end of our discussion on Java security. You have seen how the virtual machine and the security manager provide tight security for programs, and how to use the Java library for authentication and encryption. We did not cover a number of advanced and specialized issues, among them:

- The GSS-API for "generic security services" that provides support for the Kerberos protocol (and, in principle, other protocols for secure message exchange). The JDK has a tutorial at http://java.sun.com/j2se/5.0/docs/guide/security/jgss/tutorials/index.html.

- Support for SASL, the Simple Authentication and Security Layer, used by the LDAP and IMAP protocols. If you need to implement SASL in your own application, look at http://java.sun.com/j2se/5.0/docs/guide/security/sasl/sasl-refguide.html.

- Support for SSL, the Secure Sockets Layer. Using SSL over HTTP is transparent to application programmers; simply use URLs that start with https. If you want to add SSL to your own application, see the JSEE (Java Secure Socket Extension) reference at http://java.sun.com/j2se/5.0/docs/guide/security/jsse/JSSERefGuide.html.

Example 9–22: RSATest.java

```
 1. import java.io.*;
 2. import java.security.*;
 3. import javax.crypto.*;
 4. import javax.crypto.spec.*;
 5.
 6. /**
 7.    This program tests the RSA cipher. Usage:
 8.    java RSATest -genkey public private
```

```
 9.    java RSATest -encrypt plaintext encrypted public
10.    java RSATest -decrypt encrypted decrypted private
11. */
12. public class RSATest
13. {
14.    public static void main(String[] args)
15.    {
16.       try
17.       {
18.          if (args[0].equals("-genkey"))
19.          {
20.             KeyPairGenerator pairgen = KeyPairGenerator.getInstance("RSA");
21.             SecureRandom random = new SecureRandom();
22.             pairgen.initialize(KEYSIZE, random);
23.             KeyPair keyPair = pairgen.generateKeyPair();
24.             ObjectOutputStream out = new ObjectOutputStream(new FileOutputStream(args[1]));
25.             out.writeObject(keyPair.getPublic());
26.             out.close();
27.             out = new ObjectOutputStream(new FileOutputStream(args[2]));
28.             out.writeObject(keyPair.getPrivate());
29.             out.close();
30.          }
31.          else if (args[0].equals("-encrypt"))
32.          {
33.             KeyGenerator keygen = KeyGenerator.getInstance("AES");
34.             SecureRandom random = new SecureRandom();
35.             keygen.init(random);
36.             SecretKey key = keygen.generateKey();
37.
38.             // wrap with RSA public key
39.             ObjectInputStream keyIn = new ObjectInputStream(new FileInputStream(args[3]));
40.             Key publicKey = (Key) keyIn.readObject();
41.             keyIn.close();
42.
43.             Cipher cipher = Cipher.getInstance("RSA");
44.             cipher.init(Cipher.WRAP_MODE, publicKey);
45.             byte[] wrappedKey = cipher.wrap(key);
46.             DataOutputStream out = new DataOutputStream(new FileOutputStream(args[2]));
47.             out.writeInt(wrappedKey.length);
48.             out.write(wrappedKey);
49.
50.             InputStream in = new FileInputStream(args[1]);
51.             cipher = Cipher.getInstance("AES");
52.             cipher.init(Cipher.ENCRYPT_MODE, key);
53.             crypt(in, out, cipher);
54.             in.close();
55.             out.close();
56.          }
57.          else
58.          {
59.             DataInputStream in = new DataInputStream(new FileInputStream(args[1]));
60.             int length = in.readInt();
61.             byte[] wrappedKey = new byte[length];
62.             in.read(wrappedKey, 0, length);
63.
64.             // unwrap with RSA private key
```

```
65.          ObjectInputStream keyIn = new ObjectInputStream(new FileInputStream(args[3]));
66.          Key privateKey = (Key) keyIn.readObject();
67.          keyIn.close();
68.
69.          Cipher cipher = Cipher.getInstance("RSA");
70.          cipher.init(Cipher.UNWRAP_MODE, privateKey);
71.          Key key = cipher.unwrap(wrappedKey, "AES", Cipher.SECRET_KEY);
72.
73.          OutputStream out = new FileOutputStream(args[2]);
74.          cipher = Cipher.getInstance("AES");
75.          cipher.init(Cipher.DECRYPT_MODE, key);
76.
77.          crypt(in, out, cipher);
78.          in.close();
79.          out.close();
80.       }
81.    }
82.    catch (IOException e)
83.    {
84.       e.printStackTrace();
85.    }
86.    catch (GeneralSecurityException e)
87.    {
88.       e.printStackTrace();
89.    }
90.    catch (ClassNotFoundException e)
91.    {
92.       e.printStackTrace();
93.    }
94. }
95.
96. /**
97.    Uses a cipher to transform the bytes in an input stream
98.    and sends the transformed bytes to an output stream.
99.    @param in the input stream
100.   @param out the output stream
101.   @param cipher the cipher that transforms the bytes
102. */
103. public static void crypt(InputStream in, OutputStream out,
104.    Cipher cipher) throws IOException, GeneralSecurityException
105. {
106.    int blockSize = cipher.getBlockSize();
107.    int outputSize = cipher.getOutputSize(blockSize);
108.    byte[] inBytes = new byte[blockSize];
109.    byte[] outBytes = new byte[outputSize];
110.
111.    int inLength = 0;;
112.    boolean more = true;
113.    while (more)
114.    {
115.       inLength = in.read(inBytes);
116.       if (inLength == blockSize)
117.       {
118.          int outLength = cipher.update(inBytes, 0, blockSize, outBytes);
119.          out.write(outBytes, 0, outLength);
120.       }
```

```
121.          else more = false;
122.      }
123.      if (inLength > 0)
124.          outBytes = cipher.doFinal(inBytes, 0, inLength);
125.      else
126.          outBytes = cipher.doFinal();
127.      out.write(outBytes);
128.   }
129.
130.   private static final int KEYSIZE = 512;
131. }
```

Chapter 10

Internationalization

▼ Locales
▼ Number Formats
▼ Date and Time
▼ Collation
▼ Message Formatting
▼ Text Files and Character Sets
▼ Resource Bundles
▼ A Complete Example

There's a big world out there; we hope that lots of its inhabitants will be interested in your software. The Internet, after all, effortlessly spans the barriers between countries. On the other hand, when you pay no attention to an international audience, *you* are putting up a barrier.

The Java programming language was the first language designed from the ground up to support internationalization. From the beginning, it had the one essential feature needed for effective internationalization: It used Unicode for all strings. Unicode support makes it easy to write programs in the Java programming language that manipulate strings in any one of multiple languages.

Many programmers believe that all they need to do to internationalize their application is to support Unicode and to translate the messages in the user interface. However, as this chapter demonstrates, there is a lot more to internationalizing programs than just Unicode support. Dates, times, currencies—even numbers—are formatted differently in different parts of the world. You need an easy way to configure menu and button names, message strings, and keyboard shortcuts for different languages.

In this chapter, we show you how to write internationalized Java applications and applets and how to localize date, time, numbers, text, and graphical user interfaces. We show you tools that the JDK offers for writing internationalized programs. We close this chapter with a complete example, a retirement calculator applet that can change how it displays its results *depending on the location of the machine that is downloading it.*

>   NOTE: For additional information on internationalization, check out the informative web site `http://www.joconner.com/javai18n`, as well as the official Sun site `http://java.sun.com/j2se/corejava/intl`.

Locales

When you look at an application that is adapted to an international market, the most obvious difference you notice is the language. This observation is actually a bit too limiting for true internationalization: Countries can share a common language, but you still may need to do some work to make computer users of both countries happy.[1]

In all cases, menus, button labels, and program messages will need to be translated to the local language; they may also need to be rendered in a different script. There are many more subtle differences; for example, numbers are formatted quite differently in English and in German. The number

    123,456.78

should be displayed as

    123.456,78

for a German user. That is, the role of the decimal point and the decimal comma separator are reversed! There are similar variations in the display of dates. In the United States, dates are somewhat irrationally displayed as month/day/year. Germany uses the more sensible order of day/month/year, whereas in China, the usage is year/month/day. Thus, the date

    3/22/61

should be presented as

    22.03.1961

to a German user. Of course, if the month names are written out explicitly, then the difference in languages becomes apparent. The English

    March 22, 1961

should be presented as

    22. März 1961

in German, or

    1961年3月22日

in Chinese.

There are several formatter classes that take these differences into account. In order to control the formatting, you use the Locale class. A *locale* describes

- A language;
- Optionally, a location; and
- Optionally, a variant.

For example, in the United States, you use a locale with

    language=English, location=United States.

In Germany, you use a locale with

    language=German, location=Germany.

---

1. "We have really everything in common with America nowadays, except, of course, language." Oscar Wilde.

Switzerland has four official languages (German, French, Italian, and Rhaeto-Romance). A German speaker in Switzerland would want to use a locale with

> language=German, location=Switzerland

This locale would make formatting work similarly to how it would work for the German locale; however, currency values would be expressed in Swiss francs, not German marks.

If you only specify the language, say,

> language=German

then the locale cannot be used for country-specific issues such as currencies.

Variants are, fortunately, rare and are needed only for exceptional or system-dependent situations. For example, the Norwegians are having a hard time agreeing on the spelling of their language (a derivative of Danish). They use two spelling rule sets: a traditional one called Bokmål and a new one called Nynorsk. The traditional spelling would be expressed as a variant

> language=Norwegian, location=Norway, variant=Bokmål

To express the language and location in a concise and standardized manner, the Java programming language uses codes that were defined by the International Organization for Standardization. The local language is expressed as a lowercase two-letter code, following ISO-639, and the country code is expressed as an uppercase two-letter code, following ISO-3166. Tables 10–1 and 10–2 show some of the most common codes.

 NOTE: For a full list of ISO-639 codes, see, for example, `http://www.ics.uci.edu/pub/ietf/http/related/iso639.txt`. You can find a full list of the ISO-3166 codes at a number of sites, including `http://www.niso.org/3166.html`.

Table 10–1: Common ISO-639 Language Codes

Language	Code
Chinese	zh
Danish	da
Dutch	nl
English	en
French	fr
Finnish	fi
German	de
Greek	el
Italian	it
Japanese	ja
Korean	ko
Norwegian	no
Portuguese	pt
Spanish	sp
Swedish	sv
Turkish	tr

Table 10–2: Common ISO-3166 Country Codes

Country	Code
Austria	AT
Belgium	BE
Canada	CA
China	CN
Denmark	DK
Finland	FI
Germany	DE
Great Britain	GB
Greece	GR
Ireland	IE
Italy	IT
Japan	JP
Korea	KR
The Netherlands	NL
Norway	NO
Portugal	PT
Spain	ES
Sweden	SE
Switzerland	CH
Taiwan	TW
Turkey	TR
United States	US

These codes do seem a bit random, especially since some of them are derived from local languages (German = Deutsch = de, Chinese = zhongwen = zh), but at least they are standardized.

To describe a locale, you concatenate the language, country code, and variant (if any) and pass this string to the constructor of the Locale class.

```
Locale german = new Locale("de");
Locale germanGermany = new Locale("de", "DE");
Locale germanSwitzerland = new Locale("de", "CH");
Locale norwegianNorwayBokmål = new Locale("no", "NO", "B");
```

For your convenience, the JDK predefines a number of locale objects:

```
Locale.CANADA
Locale.CANADA_FRENCH
Locale.CHINA
Locale.FRANCE
Locale.GERMANY
Locale.ITALY
Locale.JAPAN
Locale.KOREA
```

```
Locale.PRC
Locale.TAIWAN
Locale.UK
Locale.US
```

The JDK also predefines a number of language locales that specify just a language without a location:

```
Locale.CHINESE
Locale.ENGLISH
Locale.FRENCH
Locale.GERMAN
Locale.ITALIAN
Locale.JAPANESE
Locale.KOREAN
Locale.SIMPLIFIED_CHINESE
Locale.TRADITIONAL_CHINESE
```

Besides constructing a locale or using a predefined one, you have two other methods for obtaining a locale object.

The static getDefault method of the Locale class initially gets the default locale as stored by the local operating system. You can change the default Java locale by calling setDefault; however, that change only affects your program, not the operating system. Similarly, in an applet, the getLocale method returns the locale of the user viewing the applet.

Finally, all locale-dependent utility classes can return an array of the locales they support. For example,

```
Locale[] supportedLocales = DateFormat.getAvailableLocales();
```

returns all locales that the DateFormat class can handle.

 TIP: For testing, you may want to switch the default locale of your program. Supply language and region properties when you launch your program. For example, here we set the default locale to German (Switzerland):

```
java -Duser.language=de -Duser.region=CH Program
```

Once you have a locale, what can you do with it? Not much, as it turns out. The only useful methods in the Locale class are the ones for identifying the language and country codes. The most important one is getDisplayName. It returns a string describing the locale. This string does not contain the cryptic two-letter codes, but it is in a form that can be presented to a user, such as

```
German (Switzerland)
```

Actually, there is a problem here. The display name is issued in the default locale. That may not be appropriate. If your user already selected German as the preferred language, you probably want to present the string in German. You can do just that by giving the German locale as a parameter: The code

```
Locale loc = new Locale("de", "CH");
System.out.println(loc.getDisplayName(Locale.GERMAN));
```

prints

```
Deutsch (Schweiz)
```

This example shows why you need Locale objects. You feed it to locale-aware methods that produce text that is presented to users in different locations. You can see many examples in the following sections.

 java.util.Locale 1.1

- Locale(String language)
- Locale(String language, String country)
- Locale(String language, String country, String variant)
  construct a locale with the given language, country, and variant
- static Locale getDefault()
  returns the default locale.
- static void setDefault(Locale loc)
  sets the default locale.
- String getDisplayName()
  returns a name describing the locale, expressed in the current locale.
- String getDisplayName(Locale loc)
  returns a name describing the locale, expressed in the given locale.
- String getLanguage()
  returns the language code, a lowercase two-letter ISO-639 code.
- String getDisplayLanguage()
  returns the name of the language, expressed in the current locale.
- String getDisplayLanguage(Locale loc)
  returns the name of the language, expressed in the given locale.
- String getCountry()
  returns the country code as an uppercase two-letter ISO-3166 code.
- String getDisplayCountry()
  returns the name of the country, expressed in the current locale.
- String getDisplayCountry(Locale loc)
  returns the name of the country, expressed in the given locale.
- String getVariant()
  returns the variant string.
- String getDisplayVariant()
  returns the name of the variant, expressed in the current locale.
- String getDisplayVariant(Locale loc)
  returns the name of the variant, expressed in the given locale.
- String toString()
  returns a description of the locale, with the language, country, and variant separated by underscores (e.g., "de_CH").

java.awt.Applet 1.0

- Locale getLocale() [1.1]
  gets the locale for this applet.

Number Formats

We already mentioned how number and currency formatting is highly locale dependent. The Java programming language supplies a collection of formatter objects that can format and parse numeric values in the java.text class. You go through the following steps to format a number for a particular locale.

1. Get the locale object, as described in the preceding section.
2. Use a "factory method" to obtain a formatter object.

3. Use the formatter object for formatting and parsing.

The factory methods are static methods of the NumberFormat class that take a Locale argument. There are three factory methods: getNumberInstance, getCurrencyInstance, and getPercentInstance. These methods return objects that can format and parse numbers, currency amounts, and percentages, respectively. For example, here is how you can format a currency value in German.

```
Locale loc = new Locale("de", "DE");
NumberFormat currFmt = NumberFormat.getCurrencyInstance(loc);
double amt = 123456.78;
System.out.println(currFmt.format(amt));
```

This code prints

```
123.456,78 DM
```

Note that the currency symbol is DM and that it is placed at the end of the string. Also, note the reversal of decimal points and decimal commas.

Conversely, to read in a number that was entered or stored with the conventions of a certain locale, use the parse method. For example, the following code parses the value that the user typed into a text field. The parse method can deal with decimal points and commas, as well as digits in other languages.

```
TextField inputField;

. . .

NumberFormat fmt = NumberFormat.getNumberInstance();
// get number formatter for default locale
Number input = fmt.parse(inputField.getText().trim());
double x = input.doubleValue();
```

The return type of parse is the abstract type Number. The returned object is either a Double or a Long wrapper object, depending on whether the parsed number was a floating-point number. If you don't care about the distinction, you can simply use the doubleValue method of the Number class to retrieve the wrapped number.

CAUTION: Objects of type Number are not automatically unboxed—you cannot simply assign a Number object to a primitive type. Instead, use the doubleValue or intValue method.

If the text for the number is not in the correct form, the method throws a ParseException. For example, leading whitespace in the string is *not* allowed. (Call trim to remove it.) However, any characters that follow the number in the string are simply ignored, so no exception is thrown.

Note that the classes returned by the get*Xxx*Instance factory methods are not actually of type NumberFormat. The NumberFormat type is an abstract class, and the actual formatters belong to one of its subclasses. The factory methods merely know how to locate the object that belongs to a particular locale.

You can get a list of the currently supported locales with the static getAvailableLocales method. That method returns an array of the locales for which number formatter objects can be obtained.

The sample program for this section lets you experiment with number formatters (see Figure 10–1). The combo box at the top of the figure contains all locales with number formatters. You can choose between number, currency, and percentage formatters. Each time you make another choice, the number in the text field is reformatted. If you go through a few locales, then you get a good impression of how many ways a number or currency value can

be formatted. You can also type a different number and click the Parse button to call the parse method, which tries to parse what you entered. If your input is successfully parsed, then it is passed to format and the result is displayed. If parsing fails, then a "Parse error" message is displayed in the text field.

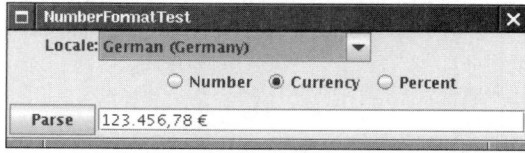

Figure 10–1: The NumberFormatTest program

The code, shown in Example 10–1, is fairly straightforward. In the constructor, we call NumberFormat.getAvailableLocales. For each locale, we call getDisplayName, and we fill a combo box with the strings that the getDisplayName method returns. (The strings are not sorted; we tackle this issue with a custom combo box later in this chapter.) Whenever the user selects another locale or clicks on one of the radio buttons, we create a new formatter object and update the text field. When the user clicks on the Parse button, we call the parse method to do the actual parsing, based on the locale selected.

Example 10–1: NumberFormatTest.java

```
 1. import java.awt.*;
 2. import java.awt.event.*;
 3. import java.text.*;
 4. import java.util.*;
 5. import javax.swing.*;
 6.
 7. /**
 8.    This program demonstrates formatting numbers under
 9.    various locales.
10. */
11. public class NumberFormatTest
12. {
13.    public static void main(String[] args)
14.    {
15.       JFrame frame = new NumberFormatFrame();
16.       frame.setDefaultCloseOperation(JFrame.EXIT_ON_CLOSE);
17.       frame.setVisible(true);
18.    }
19. }
20.
21. /**
22.    This frame contains radio buttons to select a number format,
23.    a combo box to pick a locale, a text field to display
24.    a formatted number, and a button to parse the text field
25.    contents.
26. */
27. class NumberFormatFrame extends JFrame
28. {
29.    public NumberFormatFrame()
30.    {
31.       setTitle("NumberFormatTest");
32.       setLayout(new GridBagLayout());
33.
```

```
34.      ActionListener listener = new
35.         ActionListener()
36.         {
37.            public void actionPerformed(ActionEvent event) { updateDisplay(); }
38.         };
39.
40.      JPanel p = new JPanel();
41.      addRadioButton(p, numberRadioButton, rbGroup, listener);
42.      addRadioButton(p, currencyRadioButton, rbGroup, listener);
43.      addRadioButton(p, percentRadioButton, rbGroup, listener);
44.
45.      add(new JLabel("Locale:"), new GBC(0, 0).setAnchor(GBC.EAST));
46.      add(p, new GBC(1, 1));
47.      add(parseButton, new GBC(0, 2).setInsets(2));
48.      add(localeCombo, new GBC(1, 0).setAnchor(GBC.WEST));
49.      add(numberText, new GBC(1, 2).setFill(GBC.HORIZONTAL));
50.      locales = NumberFormat.getAvailableLocales();
51.      for (Locale loc : locales) localeCombo.addItem(loc.getDisplayName());
52.      localeCombo.setSelectedItem(Locale.getDefault().getDisplayName());
53.      currentNumber = 123456.78;
54.      updateDisplay();
55.
56.      localeCombo.addActionListener(listener);
57.
58.      parseButton.addActionListener(new
59.         ActionListener()
60.         {
61.            public void actionPerformed(ActionEvent event)
62.            {
63.               String s = numberText.getText().trim();
64.               try
65.               {
66.                  Number n = currentNumberFormat.parse(s);
67.                  if (n != null)
68.                  {
69.                     currentNumber = n.doubleValue();
70.                     updateDisplay();
71.                  }
72.                  else
73.                  {
74.                     numberText.setText("Parse error: " + s);
75.                  }
76.               }
77.               catch (ParseException e)
78.               {
79.                  numberText.setText("Parse error: " + s);
80.               }
81.            }
82.         });
83.      pack();
84.   }
85.
86.   /**
87.      Adds a radio button to a container.
88.      @param p the container into which to place the button
89.      @param b the button
```

```
90.        @param g the button group
91.        @param listener the button listener
92.     */
93.     public void addRadioButton(Container p, JRadioButton b,
94.        ButtonGroup g, ActionListener listener)
95.     {
96.        b.setSelected(g.getButtonCount() == 0);
97.        b.addActionListener(listener);
98.        g.add(b);
99.        p.add(b);
100.    }
101.
102.    /**
103.       Updates the display and formats the number according
104.       to the user settings.
105.    */
106.    public void updateDisplay()
107.    {
108.       Locale currentLocale = locales[localeCombo.getSelectedIndex()];
109.       currentNumberFormat = null;
110.       if (numberRadioButton.isSelected())
111.          currentNumberFormat = NumberFormat.getNumberInstance(currentLocale);
112.       else if (currencyRadioButton.isSelected())
113.          currentNumberFormat = NumberFormat.getCurrencyInstance(currentLocale);
114.       else if (percentRadioButton.isSelected())
115.          currentNumberFormat = NumberFormat.getPercentInstance(currentLocale);
116.       String n = currentNumberFormat.format(currentNumber);
117.       numberText.setText(n);
118.    }
119.
120.    private Locale[] locales;
121.    private double currentNumber;
122.    private JComboBox localeCombo = new JComboBox();
123.    private JButton parseButton = new JButton("Parse");
124.    private JTextField numberText = new JTextField(30);
125.    private JRadioButton numberRadioButton = new JRadioButton("Number");
126.    private JRadioButton currencyRadioButton = new JRadioButton("Currency");
127.    private JRadioButton percentRadioButton = new JRadioButton("Percent");
128.    private ButtonGroup rbGroup = new ButtonGroup();
129.    private NumberFormat currentNumberFormat;
130. }
```

java.text.NumberFormat 1.1

- static Locale[] getAvailableLocales()
  returns an array of Locale objects for which NumberFormat formatters are available.

- static NumberFormat getNumberInstance()
- static NumberFormat getNumberInstance(Locale l)
- static NumberFormat getCurrencyInstance()
- static NumberFormat getCurrencyInstance(Locale l)
- static NumberFormat getPercentInstance()
- static NumberFormat getPercentInstance(Locale l)
  return a formatter for numbers, currency amounts, or percentage values for the current locale or for the given locale.

- `String format(double x)`
- `String format(long x)`

  return the string resulting from formatting the given floating-point number or integer.

- `Number parse(String s)`

  parses the given string and returns the number value, as a Double if the input string described a floating-point number, and as a Long otherwise. The beginning of the string must contain a number; no leading whitespace is allowed. The number can be followed by other characters, which are ignored. Throws `ParseException` if parsing was not successful.

- `void setParseIntegerOnly(boolean b)`
- `boolean isParseIntegerOnly()`

  set or get a flag to indicate whether this formatter should parse only integer values.

- `void setGroupingUsed(boolean b)`
- `boolean isGroupingUsed()`

  set or get a flag to indicate whether this formatter emits and recognizes decimal separators (such as `100,000`).

- `void setMinimumIntegerDigits(int n)`
- `int getMinimumIntegerDigits()`
- `void setMaximumIntegerDigits(int n)`
- `int getMaximumIntegerDigits()`
- `void setMinimumFractionDigits(int n)`
- `int getMinimumFractionDigits()`
- `void setMaximumFractionDigits(int n)`
- `int getMaximumFractionDigits()`

  set or get the maximum or minimum number of digits allowed in the integer or fractional part of a number.

Currencies

To format a currency value, you can use the `NumberFormat.getCurrencyInstance` method. However, that method is not very flexible—it returns a formatter for a single currency. Suppose you prepare an invoice for an American customer in which some amounts are in dollars, and others in Euros. You can't just use two formatters

```
NumberFormat dollarFormatter = NumberFormat.getCurrencyInstance(Locale.US);
NumberFormat euroFormatter = NumberFormat.getCurrencyInstance(Locale.GERMANY);
```

Your invoice would look very strange, with some values formatted like $100,000 and others like 100.000 €. (Note that the Euro value uses a decimal point, not a comma.)

Instead, use the `Currency` class to control the currency that is used by the formatters. You get a `Currency` object by passing a currency identifier to the static `Currency.getInstance` method. Then call the `setCurrency` method for each formatter. Here is how you would set up the Euro formatter for your American customer:

```
NumberFormat euroFormatter = NumberFormat.getCurrencyInstance(Locale.US);
euroFormatter.setCurrency(Currency.getInstance("EUR"));
```

The currency identifiers are defined by ISO 4217—see http://en.wikipedia.org/wiki/ISO_4217 for a list. Table 10–3 provides a partial list. (The official maintainer of the standard charges £70 for this information—see http://www.bsi-global.com/Technical+Information/Publications/_Publications/tig90.xalter.)

Table 10–3: Common Currency Identifiers

US Dollar	USD
Euro	EUR
British Pound	GBP
Japanese Yen	JPY
Chinese Renminbi (Yuan)	CNY
Indian Rupee	INR
Russian Ruble	RUB

API `java.util.Currency` 1.4

- `static Currency getInstance(String currencyCode)`
- `static Currency getInstance(Locale locale)`
  return the `Currency` instance for the given ISO 4217 currency code or the country of the given locale.

- `String toString()`
- `String getCurrencyCode()`
  get the ISO 4217 currency code of this currency.

- `String getSymbol()`
- `String getSymbol(Locale locale)`
  get the formatting symbol of this currency for the default locale or the given locale. For example, the symbol for USD may be "$" or "US$", depending on the locale.

- `int getDefaultFractionDigits()`
  gets the default number of fraction digits of this currency.

Date and Time

When you are formatting date and time, you should be concerned with four locale-dependent issues:

- The names of months and weekdays should be presented in the local language.
- There will be local preferences for the order of year, month, and day.
- The Gregorian calendar may not be the local preference for expressing dates.
- The time zone of the location must be taken into account.

The Java `DateFormat` class handles these issues. It is easy to use and quite similar to the `Number-Format` class. First, you get a locale. You can use the default locale or call the static `getAvailableLocales` method to obtain an array of locales that support date formatting. Then, you call one of the three factory methods:

```
fmt = DateFormat.getDateInstance(dateStyle, loc);
fmt = DateFormat.getTimeInstance(timeStyle, loc);
fmt = DateFormat.getDateTimeInstance(dateStyle, timeStyle, loc);
```

To specify the desired style, these factory methods have a parameter that is one of the following constants:

`DateFormat.DEFAULT`
`DateFormat.FULL` (e.g., Wednesday, September 15, 2004 8:51:03 PM PDT for the U.S. locale)
`DateFormat.LONG` (e.g., September 15, 2004 8:51:03 PM PDT for the U.S. locale)
`DateFormat.MEDIUM` (e.g., Sep 15, 2004 8:51:03 PM for the U.S. locale)
`DateFormat.SHORT` (e.g., 9/15/04 8:51 PM for the U.S. locale)

The factory method returns a formatting object that you can then use to format dates.

```
Date now = new Date();
String s = fmt.format(now);
```

Just as with the `NumberFormat` class, you can use the `parse` method to parse a date that the user typed. For example, the following code parses the value that the user typed into a text field, using the default locale.

```
TextField inputField;

. . .

DateFormat fmt = DateFormat.getDateInstance(DateFormat.MEDIUM);
Date input = fmt.parse(inputField.getText().trim());
```

If the number was not typed correctly, this code throws a `ParseException`. Note that leading whitespace in the string is *not* allowed here, either. You should again call `trim` to remove it. However, any characters that follow the number in the string will again be ignored. Unfortunately, the user must type the date exactly in the expected format. For example, if the format is set to `MEDIUM` in the U.S. locale, then dates are expected to look like

```
Sep 18, 1997
```

If the user types

```
Sep 18 1997
```

(without the comma) or the short format

```
9/18/97
```

then a parse error results.

A `lenient` flag interprets dates leniently. For example, `February 30, 1999` will be automatically converted to `March 2, 1999`. This seems dangerous, but, unfortunately, it is the default. You should probably turn off this feature. The calendar object that interprets the parsed date will throw `IllegalArgumentException` when the user enters an invalid day/month/year combination.

Example 10–2 shows the `DateFormat` class in action. You can select a locale and see how the date and time are formatted in different places around the world. If you see question-mark characters in the output, then you don't have the fonts installed for displaying characters in the local language. For example, if you pick a Chinese locale, the date may be expressed as

```
1997年9月18日
```

Figure 10–2 shows the program (after Chinese fonts were installed). As you can see, it correctly displays the output.

You can also experiment with parsing. Enter a date or time, click the Parse lenient checkbox if desired, and click the Parse date or Parse time button.

We use a helper class `EnumCombo` to solve a technical problem (see Example 10–3). We wanted to fill a combo with values such as `Short`, `Medium`, and `Long` and then automatically convert the user's selection to integer values `DateFormat.SHORT`, `DateFormat.MEDIUM`, and `DateFormat.LONG`. Rather than writing repetitive code, we use reflection: We convert the user's choice to upper case, replace all spaces with underscores, and then find the value of the static field with that name. (See Volume 1, Chapter 5 for more details about reflection.)

 TIP: To compute times in different time zones, use the `TimeZone` class. See http://java.sun.com/developer/JDCTechTips/2003/tt1104.html#2 for a brief tutorial.

Figure 10–2: The DateFormatTest program

Example 10–2: DateFormatTest.java

```
1.  import java.awt.*;
2.  import java.awt.event.*;
3.  import java.text.*;
4.  import java.util.*;
5.  import javax.swing.*;
6.
7.  /**
8.     This program demonstrates formatting dates under various locales.
9.  */
10. public class DateFormatTest
11. {
12.    public static void main(String[] args)
13.    {
14.       JFrame frame = new DateFormatFrame();
15.       frame.setDefaultCloseOperation(JFrame.EXIT_ON_CLOSE);
16.       frame.setVisible(true);
17.    }
18. }
19.
20. /**
21.    This frame contains combo boxes to pick a locale, date and
22.    time formats, text fields to display formatted date and time,
23.    buttons to parse the text field contents, and a "lenient"
24.    checkbox.
25. */
26. class DateFormatFrame extends JFrame
27. {
28.    public DateFormatFrame()
29.    {
30.       setTitle("DateFormatTest");
31.
32.       setLayout(new GridBagLayout());
33.       add(new JLabel("Locale"), new GBC(0, 0).setAnchor(GBC.EAST));
34.       add(new JLabel("Date style"), new GBC(0, 1).setAnchor(GBC.EAST));
35.       add(new JLabel("Time style"), new GBC(2, 1).setAnchor(GBC.EAST));
36.       add(new JLabel("Date"), new GBC(0, 2).setAnchor(GBC.EAST));
37.       add(new JLabel("Time"), new GBC(0, 3).setAnchor(GBC.EAST));
38.       add(localeCombo, new GBC(1, 0, 2, 1).setAnchor(GBC.WEST));
39.       add(dateStyleCombo, new GBC(1, 1).setAnchor(GBC.WEST));
40.       add(timeStyleCombo, new GBC(3, 1).setAnchor(GBC.WEST));
41.       add(dateParseButton, new GBC(3, 2).setAnchor(GBC.WEST));
42.       add(timeParseButton, new GBC(3, 3).setAnchor(GBC.WEST));
43.       add(lenientCheckbox, new GBC(0, 4, 2, 1).setAnchor(GBC.WEST));
44.       add(dateText, new GBC(1, 2, 2, 1).setFill(GBC.HORIZONTAL));
45.       add(timeText, new GBC(1, 3, 2, 1).setFill(GBC.HORIZONTAL));
```

```
46.
47.       locales = DateFormat.getAvailableLocales();
48.       for (Locale loc : locales) localeCombo.addItem(loc.getDisplayName());
49.       localeCombo.setSelectedItem(Locale.getDefault().getDisplayName());
50.       currentDate = new Date();
51.       currentTime = new Date();
52.       updateDisplay();
53.
54.       ActionListener listener = new
55.          ActionListener()
56.          {
57.             public void actionPerformed(ActionEvent event)
58.             {
59.                updateDisplay();
60.             }
61.          };
62.
63.       localeCombo.addActionListener(listener);
64.       dateStyleCombo.addActionListener(listener);
65.       timeStyleCombo.addActionListener(listener);
66.
67.       dateParseButton.addActionListener(new
68.          ActionListener()
69.          {
70.             public void actionPerformed(ActionEvent event)
71.             {
72.                String d = dateText.getText().trim();
73.                try
74.                {
75.                   currentDateFormat.setLenient(lenientCheckbox.isSelected());
76.                   Date date = currentDateFormat.parse(d);
77.                   currentDate = date;
78.                   updateDisplay();
79.                }
80.                catch (ParseException e)
81.                {
82.                   dateText.setText("Parse error: " + d);
83.                }
84.                catch (IllegalArgumentException e)
85.                {
86.                   dateText.setText("Argument error: " + d);
87.                }
88.             }
89.          });
90.
91.       timeParseButton.addActionListener(new
92.          ActionListener()
93.          {
94.             public void actionPerformed(ActionEvent event)
95.             {
96.                String t = timeText.getText().trim();
97.                try
98.                {
99.                   currentDateFormat.setLenient(lenientCheckbox.isSelected());
100.                  Date date = currentTimeFormat.parse(t);
101.                  currentTime = date;
102.                  updateDisplay();
```

```
103.          }
104.          catch (ParseException e)
105.          {
106.              timeText.setText("Parse error: " + t);
107.          }
108.          catch (IllegalArgumentException e)
109.          {
110.              timeText.setText("Argument error: " + t);
111.          }
112.        }
113.     });
114.     pack();
115.  }
116.
117.  /**
118.     Updates the display and formats the date according
119.     to the user settings.
120.  */
121.  public void updateDisplay()
122.  {
123.     Locale currentLocale = locales[localeCombo.getSelectedIndex()];
124.     int dateStyle = dateStyleCombo.getValue();
125.     currentDateFormat = DateFormat.getDateInstance(dateStyle, currentLocale);
126.     String d = currentDateFormat.format(currentDate);
127.     dateText.setText(d);
128.     int timeStyle = timeStyleCombo.getValue();
129.     currentTimeFormat = DateFormat.getTimeInstance(timeStyle, currentLocale);
130.     String t = currentTimeFormat.format(currentTime);
131.     timeText.setText(t);
132.  }
133.
134.  private Locale[] locales;
135.  private Date currentDate;
136.  private Date currentTime;
137.  private DateFormat currentDateFormat;
138.  private DateFormat currentTimeFormat;
139.  private JComboBox localeCombo = new JComboBox();
140.  private EnumCombo dateStyleCombo = new EnumCombo(DateFormat.class,
141.     new String[] { "Default", "Full", "Long", "Medium", "Short" });
142.  private EnumCombo timeStyleCombo = new EnumCombo(DateFormat.class,
143.     new String[] { "Default", "Full", "Long", "Medium", "Short" });
144.  private JButton dateParseButton = new JButton("Parse date");
145.  private JButton timeParseButton = new JButton("Parse time");
146.  private JTextField dateText = new JTextField(30);
147.  private JTextField timeText = new JTextField(30);
148.  private JTextField parseText = new JTextField(30);
149.  private JCheckBox lenientCheckbox = new JCheckBox("Parse lenient", true);
150. }
```

Example 10–3: EnumCombo.java

```
1. import java.util.*;
2. import javax.swing.*;
3.
4. /**
5.    A combo box that lets users choose from among static field
6.    values whose names are given in the constructor.
7. */
```

```
 8. public class EnumCombo extends JComboBox
 9. {
10.    /**
11.       Constructs an EnumCombo.
12.       @param cl a class
13.       @param labels an array of static field names of cl
14.    */
15.    public EnumCombo(Class cl, String[] labels)
16.    {
17.       for (int i = 0; i < labels.length; i++)
18.       {
19.          String label = labels[i];
20.          String name = label.toUpperCase().replace(' ', '_');
21.          int value = 0;
22.          try
23.          {
24.             java.lang.reflect.Field f = cl.getField(name);
25.             value = f.getInt(cl);
26.          }
27.          catch (Exception e)
28.          {
29.             label = "(" + label + ")";
30.          }
31.          table.put(label, value);
32.          addItem(label);
33.       }
34.       setSelectedItem(labels[0]);
35.    }
36.
37.    /**
38.       Returns the value of the field that the user selected.
39.       @return the static field value
40.    */
41.    public int getValue()
42.    {
43.       return table.get(getSelectedItem());
44.    }
45.
46.    private Map<String, Integer> table = new TreeMap<String, Integer>();
47. }
```

API   **java.text.DateFormat** 1.1

- static Locale[] getAvailableLocales()
  returns an array of Locale objects for which DateFormat formatters are available.

- static DateFormat getDateInstance(int dateStyle)
- static DateFormat getDateInstance(int dateStyle, Locale l)
- static DateFormat getTimeInstance(int timeStyle)
- static DateFormat getTimeInstance(int timeStyle, Locale l)
- static DateFormat getDateTimeInstance(int dateStyle, int timeStyle)
- static DateFormat getDateTimeInstance(int dateStyle, int timeStyle, Locale l)
  return a formatter for date, time, or date and time for the default locale or the given locale.

  Parameters: dateStyle, timeStyle   One of DEFAULT, FULL, LONG, MEDIUM, SHORT

- `String format(Date d)`
  returns the string resulting from formatting the given date/time.
- `Date parse(String s)`
  parses the given string and returns the date/time described in it. The beginning of the string must contain a date or time; no leading whitespace is allowed. The date can be followed by other characters, which are ignored. Throws a `ParseException` if parsing was not successful.
- `void setLenient(boolean b)`
- `boolean isLenient()`
  set or get a flag to indicate whether parsing should be lenient or strict. In lenient mode, dates such as `February 30, 1999` will be automatically converted to `March 2, 1999`. The default is lenient mode.
- `void setCalendar(Calendar cal)`
- `Calendar getCalendar()`
  set or get the calendar object used for extracting year, month, day, hour, minute, and second from the `Date` object. Use this method if you do not want to use the default calendar for the locale (usually the Gregorian calendar).
- `void setTimeZone(TimeZone tz)`
- `TimeZone getTimeZone()`
  set or get the time zone object used for formatting the time. Use this method if you do not want to use the default time zone for the locale. The default time zone is the time zone of the default locale, as obtained from the operating system. For the other locales, it is the preferred time zone in the geographical location.
- `void setNumberFormat(NumberFormat f)`
- `NumberFormat getNumberFormat()`
  set or get the number format used for formatting the numbers used for representing year, month, day, hour, minute, and second.

API   java.util.TimeZone 1.1

- `static String[] getAvailableIDs()`
  gets all supported time zone IDs.
- `static TimeZone getDefault()`
  gets the default `TimeZone` for this computer.
- `static TimeZone getTimeZone(String timeZoneId)`
  gets the `TimeZone` for the given ID.
- `String getID()`
  gets the ID of this time zone.
- `String getDisplayName()`
- `String getDisplayName(Locale locale)`
- `String getDisplayName(boolean daylight, int style)`
- `String getDisplayName(boolean daylight, int style, Locale locale)`
  get the display name of this time zone in the default locale or in the given locale. If the daylight parameter is true, the daylight-savings name is returned. The style parameter can be `SHORT` or `LONG`.
- `boolean useDaylightTime()`
  returns true if this `TimeZone` uses daylight-savings time.
- `boolean inDaylightTime(Date date)`
  returns true if the given date is in daylight-savings time in this `TimeZone`.

Collation

Sorting strings in alphabetical order is easy when the strings are made up of only English ASCII characters. You just compare the strings with the compareTo method of the String class. The value of

```
a.compareTo(b)
```

is a negative number if a is lexicographically less than b, 0 if they are identical, and positive otherwise.

Unfortunately, unless all your words are in uppercase English ASCII characters, this method is useless. The problem is that the compareTo method in the Java programming language uses the values of the Unicode character to determine the ordering. For example, lowercase characters have a higher Unicode value than do uppercase characters, and accented characters have even higher values. This leads to absurd results; for example, the following five strings are ordered according to the compareTo method:

```
America
Zulu
ant
zebra
Ångström
```

For dictionary ordering, you want to consider upper case and lower case to be equivalent. To an English speaker, the sample list of words would be ordered as

```
America
Ångström
ant
zebra
Zulu
```

However, that order would not be acceptable to a Swedish user. In Swedish, the letter Å is different from the letter A, and it is collated *after* the letter Z! That is, a Swedish user would want the words to be sorted as

```
America
ant
zebra
Zulu
Ångström
```

Fortunately, once you are aware of the problem, collation is quite easy. As always, you start by obtaining a Locale object. Then, you call the getInstance factory method to obtain a Collator object. Finally, you use the compare method of the collator, *not* the compareTo method of the String class, whenever you want to sort strings.

```
Locale loc = . . .;
Collator coll = Collator.getInstance(loc);
if (coll.compare(a, b) < 0) // a comes before b . . .;
```

Most important, the Collator class implements the Comparator interface. Therefore, you can pass a collator object to the Collections.sort method to sort a list of strings:

```
Collections.sort(strings, coll);
```

You can set a collator's *strength* to select how selective it should be. Character differences are classified as *primary, secondary,* and *tertiary.* For example, in English, the difference between "A" and "Z" is considered primary, the difference between "A" and "Å" is secondary, and between "A" and "a" is tertiary.

By setting the strength of the collator to Collator.PRIMARY, you tell it to pay attention only to primary differences. By setting the strength to Collator.SECONDARY, you instruct the collator to

take secondary differences into account. That is, two strings will be more likely to be considered different when the strength is set to "secondary." Table 10–4 shows how a sample set of strings is sorted with the three collation strengths. Note that the strength indicates only whether two strings are considered identical.

Table 10–4: Collations with Different Strengths (English Locale)

Primary	Secondary	Tertiary
Angstrom = Ångström	Angstrom	Angstrom
Ant = ant	Ångström	Ångström
	Ant = ant	Ant
		ant

Finally, there is one technical setting, the *decomposition mode*. The default, "canonical decomposition," is appropriate for most uses. If you choose "no decomposition," then accented characters are not decomposed into their base form + accent. This option is faster, but it gives correct results only when the input does not contain accented characters. Finally, "full decomposition" analyzes Unicode variants, that is, Unicode characters that ought to be considered identical. For example, Japanese displays have two versions of English, Katakana and Hiragana characters, called half-width and full-width. The half-width characters have normal character spacing, whereas the full-width characters are spaced in the same grid as the ideographs. (One could argue that this is a presentation issue and it should not have resulted in different Unicode characters, but we don't make the rules.) With full decomposition, half-width and full-width variants of the same letter are recognized as identical.

It is wasteful to have the collator decompose a string many times. If one string is compared many times against other strings, then you can save the decomposition in a *collation* key object. The getCollationKey method returns a CollationKey object that you can use for further, faster comparisons. Here is an example:

```
String a = . . .;
CollationKey aKey = coll.getCollationKey(a);
if(aKey.compareTo(coll.getCollationKey(b)) == 0) // fast comparison
    . . .
```

The program in Example 10–4 lets you experiment with collation order. Type a word into the text field and click the Add button to add it to the list of words. Each time you add another word, or change the locale, strength, or decomposition mode, the list of words is sorted again. An = sign indicates words that are considered identical (see Figure 10–3).

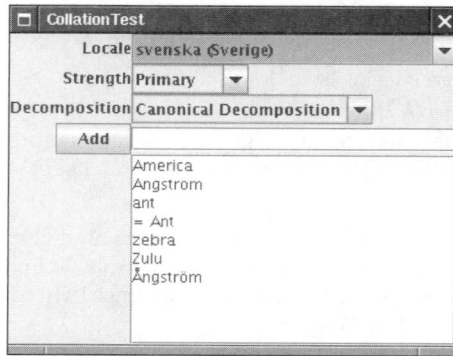

Figure 10–3: The CollationTest program

In this program, we supply an improved combo box for selecting the locale (see Example 10–5). The combo box solves two problems:

- The locale strings are sorted, according to the collation order of the current locale. We install a custom model that holds the sorted strings and replace it when the component's locale is changed. (Note how the locale names change when you change the locale.)
- The combo box holds Locale objects, not strings. We install a custom renderer so that the getDisplayName method of the component's locale is used for rendering.

Example 10–4: CollationTest.java

```
1. import java.awt.*;
2. import java.awt.event.*;
3. import java.text.*;
4. import java.util.*;
5. import java.util.List;
6. import javax.swing.*;
7.
8. /**
9.    This program demonstrates collating strings under
10.   various locales.
11. */
12. public class CollationTest
13. {
14.    public static void main(String[] args)
15.    {
16.       JFrame frame = new CollationFrame();
17.       frame.setDefaultCloseOperation(JFrame.EXIT_ON_CLOSE);
18.       frame.setVisible(true);
19.    }
20. }
21.
22. /**
23.    This frame contains combo boxes to pick a locale, collation
24.    strength and decomposition rules, a text field and button
25.    to add new strings, and a text area to list the collated
26.    strings.
27. */
28. class CollationFrame extends JFrame
29. {
30.    public CollationFrame()
31.    {
32.       setTitle("CollationTest");
33.
34.       setLayout(new GridBagLayout());
35.       add(new JLabel("Locale"), new GBC(0, 0).setAnchor(GBC.EAST));
36.       add(new JLabel("Strength"), new GBC(0, 1).setAnchor(GBC.EAST));
37.       add(new JLabel("Decomposition"), new GBC(0, 2).setAnchor(GBC.EAST));
38.       add(addButton, new GBC(0, 3).setAnchor(GBC.EAST));
39.       add(localeCombo, new GBC(1, 0).setAnchor(GBC.WEST));
40.       add(strengthCombo, new GBC(1, 1).setAnchor(GBC.WEST));
41.       add(decompositionCombo, new GBC(1, 2).setAnchor(GBC.WEST));
42.       add(newWord, new GBC(1, 3).setFill(GBC.HORIZONTAL));
43.       add(new JScrollPane(sortedWords), new GBC(1, 4).setFill(GBC.BOTH));
44.
45.       strings.add("America");
```

```
46.     strings.add("ant");
47.     strings.add("Zulu");
48.     strings.add("zebra");
49.     strings.add("\u00C5ngstr\u00F6m");
50.     strings.add("Angstrom");
51.     strings.add("Ant");
52.     updateDisplay();
53.
54.     addButton.addActionListener(new
55.        ActionListener()
56.        {
57.           public void actionPerformed(ActionEvent event)
58.           {
59.              strings.add(newWord.getText());
60.              updateDisplay();
61.           }
62.        });
63.
64.     ActionListener listener = new
65.        ActionListener()
66.        {
67.           public void actionPerformed(ActionEvent event) { updateDisplay(); }
68.        };
69.
70.     localeCombo.addActionListener(listener);
71.     strengthCombo.addActionListener(listener);
72.     decompositionCombo.addActionListener(listener);
73.     pack();
74.  }
75.  /**
76.     Updates the display and collates the strings according
77.     to the user settings.
78.  */
79.  public void updateDisplay()
80.  {
81.     Locale currentLocale = (Locale) localeCombo.getSelectedItem();
82.     localeCombo.setLocale(currentLocale);
83.
84.     currentCollator = Collator.getInstance(currentLocale);
85.     currentCollator.setStrength(strengthCombo.getValue());
86.     currentCollator.setDecomposition(decompositionCombo.getValue());
87.
88.     Collections.sort(strings, currentCollator);
89.
90.     sortedWords.setText("");
91.     for (int i = 0; i < strings.size(); i++)
92.     {
93.        String s = strings.get(i);
94.        if (i > 0 && currentCollator.compare(s, strings.get(i - 1)) == 0)
95.           sortedWords.append("= ");
96.        sortedWords.append(s + "\n");
97.     }
98.     pack();
99.  }
100.
101. private Locale[] locales;
```

```
102.  private List<String> strings = new ArrayList<String>();
103.  private Collator currentCollator;
104.  private JComboBox localeCombo = new LocaleCombo(Collator.getAvailableLocales());
105.
106.  private EnumCombo strengthCombo = new EnumCombo(Collator.class,
107.     new String[] { "Primary", "Secondary", "Tertiary" });
108.  private EnumCombo decompositionCombo = new EnumCombo(Collator.class,
109.     new String[] { "Canonical Decomposition", "Full Decomposition", "No Decomposition" });
110.  private JTextField newWord = new JTextField(20);
111.  private JTextArea sortedWords = new JTextArea(10, 20);
112.  private JButton addButton = new JButton("Add");
113. }
```

Example 10–5: LocaleCombo.java

```
 1. import java.awt.*;
 2. import java.text.*;
 3. import java.util.*;
 4. import javax.swing.*;
 5. import javax.swing.event.*;
 6.
 7. /**
 8.    This combo box lets a user pick a locale. The locales are displayed in the locale of
 9.    the combo box, and sorted according to the collator of the display locale.
10. */
11. public class LocaleCombo extends JComboBox
12. {
13.    /**
14.       Constructs a locale combo that displays an immutable collection of locales.
15.       @param locales the locales to display in this combo box
16.    */
17.    public LocaleCombo(Locale[] locales)
18.    {
19.       this.locales = (Locale[]) locales.clone();
20.       sort();
21.       setSelectedItem(getLocale());
22.    }
23.
24.    public void setLocale(Locale newValue)
25.    {
26.       super.setLocale(newValue);
27.       sort();
28.    }
29.
30.    private void sort()
31.    {
32.       Object selected = getSelectedItem();
33.       final Locale loc = getLocale();
34.       final Collator collator = Collator.getInstance(loc);
35.       final Comparator<Locale> comp = new
36.          Comparator<Locale>()
37.          {
38.             public int compare(Locale a, Locale b)
39.             {
40.                return collator.compare(a.getDisplayName(loc), b.getDisplayName(loc));
41.             }
42.          };
```

```
43.      Arrays.sort(locales, comp);
44.      setModel(new
45.         ComboBoxModel()
46.         {
47.            public Object getElementAt(int i) { return locales[i]; }
48.            public int getSize() { return locales.length; }
49.            public void addListDataListener(ListDataListener l) {}
50.            public void removeListDataListener(ListDataListener l) {}
51.            public Object getSelectedItem() { return selected >= 0 ? locales[selected] : null; }
52.            public void setSelectedItem(Object anItem)
53.            {
54.               if (anItem == null) selected = -1;
55.               else selected = Arrays.binarySearch(locales, (Locale) anItem, comp);
56.            }
57.
58.            private int selected;
59.         });
60.      setSelectedItem(selected);
61.   }
62.
63.   public ListCellRenderer getRenderer()
64.   {
65.      if (renderer == null)
66.      {
67.         final ListCellRenderer originalRenderer = super.getRenderer();
68.         if (originalRenderer == null) return null;
69.         renderer = new
70.            ListCellRenderer()
71.            {
72.               public Component getListCellRendererComponent(JList list,
73.                  Object value, int index, boolean isSelected, boolean cellHasFocus)
74.               {
75.                  String renderedValue = ((Locale) value).getDisplayName(getLocale());
76.                  return originalRenderer.getListCellRendererComponent(
77.                     list, renderedValue, index, isSelected, cellHasFocus);
78.               }
79.            };
80.      }
81.      return renderer;
82.   }
83.
84.   public void setRenderer(ListCellRenderer newValue)
85.   {
86.      renderer = null;
87.      super.setRenderer(newValue);
88.   }
89.
90.   private Locale[] locales;
91.   private ListCellRenderer renderer;
92. }
```

API **java.text.Collator 1.1**

- static Locale[] getAvailableLocales()
  returns an array of Locale objects for which Collator objects are available.

- static Collator getInstance()
- static Collator getInstance(Locale l)
  return a collator for the default locale or the given locale.

- int compare(String a, String b)
  returns a negative value if a comes before b, 0 if they are considered identical, and a positive value otherwise.

- boolean equals(String a, String b)
  returns true if they are considered identical, false otherwise.

- void setStrength(int strength)
- int getStrength()
  set or get the strength of the collator. Stronger collators tell more words apart. Strength values are Collator.PRIMARY, Collator.SECONDARY, and Collator.TERTIARY.

- void setDecomposition(int decomp)
- int getDecompositon()
  set or get the decomposition mode of the collator. The more a collator decomposes a string, the more strict it will be in deciding whether two strings ought to be considered identical. Decomposition values are Collator.NO_DECOMPOSITION, Collator.CANONICAL_DECOMPOSITION, and Collator.FULL_DECOMPOSITION.

- CollationKey getCollationKey(String a)
  returns a collation key that contains a decomposition of the characters in a form that can be quickly compared against another collation key.

 java.text.CollationKey 1.1

- int compareTo(CollationKey b)
  returns a negative value if this key comes before b, 0 if they are considered identical, and a positive value otherwise.

Message Formatting

The Java library has a MessageFormat class that formats text with variable parts, like this:

```
"On {2}, a {0} destroyed {1} houses and caused {3} of damage."
```

The numbers in braces are placeholders for actual names and values. The static method MessageFormat.format lets you substitute values for the variables. As of JDK 5.0, it is a "varargs" method, so you can simply supply the parameters as follows:

```
String msg = MessageFormat.format("On {2}, a {0} destroyed {1} houses and caused {3} of damage.",
    "hurricane", 99, new GregorianCalendar(1999, 0, 1).getTime(), 10.0E7);
```

Before JDK 5.0, you had to put the values of the placeholders inside an Object[] array.

In this example, the placeholder {0} is replaced with "hurricane", {1} is replaced with 99, and so on.

 CAUTION: The static format method uses the current locale to format the values. To use the MessageFormat class with an arbitrary locale, you have to work harder:

```
MessageFormat mf = new MessageFormat(pattern, loc);
String msg = mf.format(new Object[] { values });
```

Here, we call the format method from the Format superclass. Unfortunately, the MessageFormat class does not supply an equivalent "varargs" method.

The result of our example is the string

`On 1/1/99 12:00 AM, a hurricane destroyed 99 houses and caused 100,000,000 of damage.`

That is a start, but it is not perfect. We don't want to display the time "12:00 AM," and we want the damage amount printed as a currency value. The way we do this is by supplying an optional format for some of the placeholders:

`"On {2,date,long}, a {0} destroyed {1} houses and caused {3,number,currency} of damage."`

This example code prints:

`On January 1, 1999, a hurricane destroyed 99 houses and caused $100,000,000 of damage.`

In general, the placeholder index can be followed by a *type* and a *style*. Separate the index, type, and style by commas. The type can be any of

```
number
time
date
choice
```

If the type is `number`, then the style can be

```
integer
currency
percent
```

or it can be a number format pattern such as `$,##0`. (See the documentation of the `DecimalFormat` class for more information about the possible formats.)

If the type is either `time` or `date`, then the style can be

```
short
medium
long
full
```

or a date format pattern such as `yyyy-MM-dd`. (See the documentation of the `SimpleDateFormat` class for more information about the possible formats.)

Choice formats are more complex, and we take them up in the next section.

API `java.text.MessageFormat 1.1`

- `MessageFormat(String pattern)`
- `MessageFormat(String pattern, Locale loc)`
  construct a message format object with the specified pattern and locale.

- `void applyPattern(String pattern)`
  sets the pattern of a message format object to the specified pattern.

- `void setLocale(Locale loc)`
- `Locale getLocale()`
  set or get the locale to be used for the placeholders in the message. The locale is *only* used for subsequent patterns that you set by calling the `applyPattern` method.

- `static String format(String pattern, Object... args)`
  formats the pattern string by using args[i] as input for placeholder {i}.

- `StringBuffer format(Object args, StringBuffer result, FieldPosition pos)`
  formats the pattern of this `MessageFormat`. The args parameter must be an array of objects. The formatted string is appended to `result`, and `result` is returned. If pos equals `new FieldPosition(MessageFormat.Field.ARGUMENT)`, its beginIndex and endIndex properties are set to the location of the text that replaces the {1} placeholder. Supply `null` if you are not interested in position information.

API   `java.text.Format` `1.1`

- `String format(Object obj)`
  formats the given object, according to the rules of this formatter. This method calls `format(obj, new StringBuffer(), new FieldPosition(1)).toString()`.

Choice Formats

Let's look closer at the pattern of the preceding section:

```
"On {2}, a {0} destroyed {1} houses and caused {3} of damage."
```

If we replace the disaster placeholder {0} with "earthquake", then the sentence is not grammatically correct in English.

```
On January 1, 1999, a earthquake destroyed . . .
```

That means what we really want to do is integrate the article "a" into the placeholder:

```
"On {2}, {0} destroyed {1} houses and caused {3} of damage."
```

The {0} would then be replaced with "a hurricane" or "an earthquake". That is especially appropriate if this message needs to be translated into a language where the gender of a word affects the article. For example, in German, the pattern would be

```
"{0} zerstörte am {2} {1} Häuser und richtete einen Schaden von {3} an."
```

The placeholder would then be replaced with the grammatically correct combination of article and noun, such as "Ein Wirbelsturm", "Eine Naturkatastrophe".

Now let us turn to the {1} parameter. If the disaster isn't all that catastrophic, then {1} might be replaced with the number 1, and the message would read:

```
On January 1, 1999, a mudslide destroyed 1 houses and . . .
```

We would ideally like the message to vary according to the placeholder value, so that it can read

```
no houses
one house
2 houses
. . .
```

depending on the placeholder value. The `choice` formatting option was designed for this purpose.

A choice format is a sequence of pairs, each of which contains

- a *lower limit*
- a *format string*

The lower limit and format string are separated by a # character, and the pairs are separated by | characters.

For example,

```
{1,choice,0#no houses|1#one house|2#{1} houses}
```

Table 10–5 shows the effect of this format string for various values of {1}.

Why do we use {1} twice in the format string? When the message format applies the choice format on the {1} placeholder and the value is ≥ 2, the choice format returns "{1} houses". That string is then formatted again by the message format, and the answer is spliced into the result.

Table 10–5: String Formatted by Choice Format

{1}	Result
0	"no houses"
1	"one houses"
3	"3 houses"
-1	"no houses"

NOTE: This example shows that the designer of the choice format was a bit muddleheaded. If you have three format strings, you need two limits to separate them. In general, you need *one fewer limit* than you have format strings. As you saw in Table 10–4, the MessageFormat class ignores the first limit.

The syntax would have been a lot clearer if the designer of this class realized that the limits belong *between* the choices, such as

```
no houses|1|one house|2|{1} houses // not the actual format
```

You can use the < symbol to denote that a choice should be selected if the lower bound is strictly less than the value.

You can also use the ≤ symbol (expressed as the Unicode character code \u2264) as a synonym for #. If you like, you can even specify a lower bound of -∞ as -\u221E for the first value.

For example,

```
-∞<no houses|0<one house|2≤{1} houses
```

or, using Unicode escapes,

```
-\u221E<no houses|0<one house|2\u2264{1} houses
```

Let's finish our natural disaster scenario. If we put the choice string inside the original message string, then we get the following format instruction:

```
String pattern = "On {2,date,long}, {0} destroyed {1,choice,0#no houses|1#one house|2#{1} houses}"
   + "and caused {3,number,currency} of damage.";
```

Or, in German,

```
String pattern = "{0} zerstörte am {2,date,long} {1,choice,0#kein Haus|1#ein Haus|2#{1} Häuser}"
   + "und richtete einen Schaden von {3,number,currency} an.";
```

Note that the ordering of the words is different in German, but the array of objects you pass to the format method is the *same*. The order of the placeholders in the format string takes care of the changes in the word ordering.

Text Files and Character Sets

As you know, the Java programming language itself is fully Unicode based. However, operating systems typically have their own character encoding, such as ISO-8859-1 (an 8-bit code sometimes called the "ANSI" code) in the United States, or Big5 in Taiwan.

When you save data to a text file, you should respect the local character encoding so that the users of your program can open the text file with their other applications. Specify the character encoding in the FileWriter constructor:

```
out = new FileWriter(filename, "ISO-8859-1");
```

You can find a complete list of the supported encodings in Volume 1, Chapter 12.

Unfortunately, there is currently no connection between locales and character encodings. For example, if your user has selected the Taiwanese locale zh_TW, no method in the Java programming language tells you that the Big5 character encoding would be the most appropriate.

Character Encoding of Source Files

It is worth keeping in mind that you, the programmer, will need to communicate with the Java compiler. And *you do that with tools on your local system.* For example, you can use the Chinese version of Notepad to write your Java source code files. The resulting source code files are *not portable* because they use the local character encoding (GB or Big5, depending on which Chinese operating system you use). Only the compiled class files are portable—they will automatically use the "modified UTF-8" encoding for identifiers and strings. That means that even when a program is compiling and running, three character encodings are involved:

- Source files: local encoding
- Class files: modified UTF-8
- Virtual machine: UTF-16

(See Volume 1, Chapter 12 for a definition of the modified UTF-8 and UTF-16 formats.)

 TIP: You can specify the character encoding of your source files with the -encoding flag, for example,

```
java -encoding Big5 Myfile.java
```

To make your source files portable, restrict yourself to using the plain ASCII encoding. That is, you should change all non-ASCII characters to their equivalent Unicode encodings. For example, rather than using the string "Häuser", use "H\u0084user". The JDK contains a utility, native2ascii, that you can use to convert the native character encoding to plain ASCII. This utility simply replaces every non-ASCII character in the input with a \u followed by the four hex digits of the Unicode value. To use the native2ascii program, provide the input and output file names.

```
native2ascii Myfile.java Myfile.temp
```

You can convert the other way with the -reverse option:

```
native2ascii -reverse Myfile.temp Myfile.java
```

You can specify another encoding with the -encoding option. The encoding name must be one of those listed in the encodings table in Volume 1, Chapter 12.

```
native2ascii -encoding Big5 Myfile.java Myfile.temp
```

 TIP: It is a good idea to restrict yourself to plain ASCII class names. Because the name of the class also turns into the name of the *class file,* you are at the mercy of the local file system to handle any non-ASCII coded names. Here is a depressing example. Windows 95 uses the so-called *Code Page 437* or *original PC* encoding, for its file names. If you make a class Bär and try to run it in Windows 95, you get an error message "cannot find class BΣr".

Resource Bundles

When localizing an application, you'll probably have a dauntingly large number of message strings, button labels, and so on, that all need to be translated. To make this task feasible, you'll want to define the message strings in an external location, usually called a *resource.* The person carrying out the translation can then simply edit the resource files without having to touch the source code of the program.

In Java, you use property files to specify string resources, and you implement classes for resources of other types.

 NOTE: Java technology resources are not the same as Windows or Macintosh resources. A Macintosh or Windows executable program stores resources such as menus, dialog boxes, icons, and messages in a section separate from the program code. A resource editor can inspect and update these resources without affecting the program code.

 NOTE: Volume 1, Chapter 10 describes a concept of JAR file resources, whereby data files, sounds, and images can be placed in a JAR file. The getResource method of the class Class finds the file, opens it, and returns a URL to the resource. By placing the files into the JAR file, you leave the job of finding the files to the class loader, which already knows how to locate items in a JAR file. However, that mechanism has no locale support.

Locating Resource Bundles

When localizing an application, you produce a set of *resource bundles*. Each bundle is a property file or a class that describes locale-specific items (such as messages, labels, and so on). For each bundle, you provide versions for all locales that you want to support.

You need to use a specific naming convention for these bundles. For example, resources specific for Germany go to a file *bundleName_de_DE*, while those that are shared by all German-speaking countries go into *bundleName_de*. In general, use

> *bundleName_language_country*

for all country-specific resources, and use

> *bundleName_language*

for all language-specific resources. Finally, as a fallback, you can put defaults into a file without any suffix.

You load a bundle with the command

```
ResourceBundle currentResources = ResourceBundle.getBundle(bundleName, currentLocale);
```

The getBundle method attempts to load the bundle that matches the current locale by language, country, and variant. If it is not successful, then the variant, country, and language are dropped in turn. Then the same search is applied to the default locale, and finally, the default bundle file is consulted. If even that attempt fails, the method throws a MissingResourceException.

That is, the getBundle method tries to load one of the following bundles until it is successful.

> *bundleName_currentLocaleLanguage_currentLocaleCountry_currentLocaleVariant*
> *bundleName_currentLocaleLanguage_currentLocaleCountry*
> *bundleName_currentLocaleLanguage*
> *bundleName_defaultLocaleLanguage_defaultLocaleCountry_defaultLocaleVariant*
> *bundleName_defaultLocaleLanguage_defaultLocaleCountry*
> *bundleName_defaultLocaleLanguage*
> *bundleName*

Once the getBundle method has located a bundle, say, *bundleName_de_DE*, it will still keep looking for *bundleName_de* and *bundleName*. If these bundles exist, they become the *parents* of the *bundleName_de_DE* bundle in a *resource hierarchy*. Later, when looking up a resource, the parents are searched if a lookup was not successful in the current bundle. That is, if a particular resource was not found in *bundleName_de_DE*, then the *bundleName_de* and *bundleName* will be queried as well.

This is clearly a very useful service and one that would be tedious to program by hand. The resource bundle mechanism of the Java programming language automatically locates the items that are the best match for a given locale. It is easy to add more and more localizations to an existing program: All you have to do is add additional resource bundles.

 TIP: You need not place all resources for your application into a single bundle. You could have one bundle for button labels, one for error messages, and so on.

Property Files

Internationalizing strings is quite straightforward. You place all your strings into a property file such as `MyProgramStrings.properties`. This is simply a text file with one key/value pair per line. A typical file would look like this:

```
computeButton=Rechnen
colorName=black
defaultPaperSize=210x297
```

Then you name your property files as described in the preceding section, for example:

```
MyProgramStrings.properties
MyProgramStrings_en.properties
MyProgramStrings_de_DE.properties
```

You can load the bundle simply as

```
ResourceBundle bundle = ResourceBundle.getBundle("MyProgramStrings", locale);
```

To look up a specific string, call

```
String computeButtonLabel = bundle.getString("computeButton");
```

 CAUTION: Files for storing properties are always ASCII files. If you need to place Unicode characters into a properties file, encode them by using the \uxxxx encoding. For example, to specify "colorName=Grün", use

```
colorName=Gr\u00FCn
```

You can use the native2ascii tool to generate these files.

Bundle Classes

In order to provide resources that are not strings, you define classes that extend the `ResourceBundle` class. You use the standard naming convention to name your classes, for example

```
MyProgramResources.java
MyProgramResources_en.java
MyProgramResources_de_DE.java
```

You load the class with the same `getBundle` method that you use to load a property file:

```
ResourceBundle bundle = ResourceBundle.getBundle("MyProgramResources", locale);
```

 CAUTION: When searching for bundles, a bundle in a class is given prefererence over a property file when the two bundles have the same base names.

Each resource bundle class implements a lookup table. You provide a key string for each setting you want to localize, and you use that key string to retrieve the setting. For example,

```
Color backgroundColor = (Color) bundle.getObject("backgroundColor");
double[] paperSize = (double[]) bundle.getObject("defaultPaperSize");
```

The simplest way of implementing resource bundle classes is to extend the ListResourceBundle class. The ListResourceBundle lets you place all your resources into an object array and then does the lookup for you. Follow this code outline:

```
public class bundleName_language_country extends ListResourceBundle
{
    public Object[][] getContents() { return contents;  }
    private static final Object[][] contents =
    {
        { key₁,  value₂},
        { key₂,  value₂},
        . . .
    }
}
```

For example,

```
public class ProgramResources_de extends ListResourceBundle
{
    public Object[][] getContents() { return contents; }
    private static final Object[][] contents =
    {
        { "backgroundColor", Color.black },
        { "defaultPaperSize", new double[] { 210, 297 } }
    }
}
```

```
public class ProgramResources_en_US extends ListResourceBundle
{
    public Object[][] getContents() { return contents; }
    private static final Object[][] contents =
    {
        { "backgroundColor", Color.blue },
        { "defaultPaperSize", new double[] { 216, 279 } }
    }
}
```

 NOTE: Everyone on the planet, with the exception of the United States and Canada, uses ISO 216 paper sizes. For more information, see http://www.cl.cam.ac.uk/~mgk25/iso-paper.html. According to the U.S. Metric Association (http://lamar.colostate.edu/~hillger), only three countries in the world have not yet officially adopted the metric system, namely, Liberia, Myanmar (Burma), and the United States of America. U.S. businesses that wish to extend their export market further need to go metric. See http://ts.nist.gov/ts/htdocs/200/202/mpo_reso.htm for a useful set of links to information about the metric (SI) system.

Alternatively, your resource bundle classes can extend the ResourceBundle class. Then you need to implement two methods, to enumerate all keys and to look up the value for a given key:

```
Enumeration<String> getKeys()
Object handleGetObject(String key)
```

The getObject method of the ResourceBundle class calls the handleGetObject method that you supply.

API **java.util.ResourceBundle 1.1**

- static ResourceBundle getBundle(String baseName, Locale loc)
- static ResourceBundle getBundle(String baseName)
  load the resource bundle class with the given name, for the given locale or the default locale, and its parent classes. If the resource bundle classes are located in a package, then the base name must contain the full package name, such as "intl.ProgramResources". The resource bundle classes must be public so that the getBundle method can access them.
- Object getObject(String name)
  looks up an object from the resource bundle or its parents.
- String getString(String name)
  looks up an object from the resource bundle or its parents and casts it as a string.
- String[] getStringArray(String name)
  looks up an object from the resource bundle or its parents and casts it as a string array.
- Enumeration<String> getKeys()
  returns an enumeration object to enumerate the keys of this resource bundle. It enumerates the keys in the parent bundles as well.
- Object handleGetObject(String key)
  should be overridden to look up the resource value associated with the given key if you define your own resource lookup mechanism.

A Complete Example

In this section, we apply the material from this chapter to localize a retirement calculator applet. The applet calculates whether or not you are saving enough money for your retirement. You enter your age, how much money you save every month, and so on (see Figure 10–4).

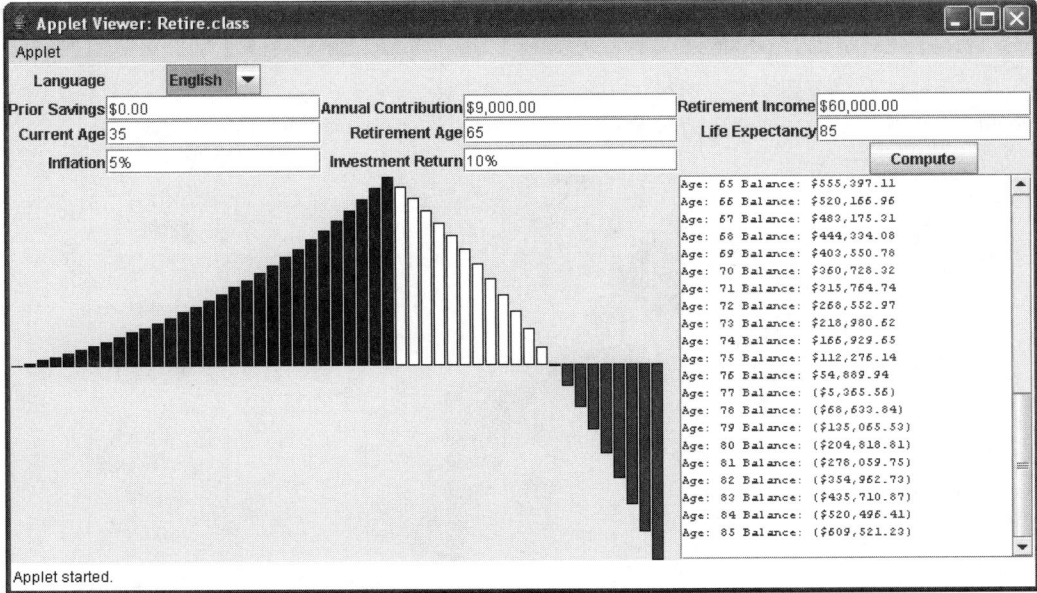

Figure 10–4: The retirement calculator in English

The text area and the graph show the balance of the retirement account for every year. If the numbers turn negative toward the later part of your life and the bars in the graph show up below the x-axis, you need to do something; for example, save more money, postpone your retirement, die earlier, or be younger.

The retirement calculator works in three locales (English, German, and Chinese). Here are some of the highlights of the internationalization.

- The labels, buttons, and messages are translated into German and Chinese. You can find them in the classes RetireResources_de, RetireResources_zh. English is used as the fall-back—see the RetireResources file. To generate the Chinese messages, we first typed the file, using Notepad running in Chinese Windows, and then we used the native2ascii utility to convert the characters to Unicode.

- Whenever the locale changes, we reset the labels and reformat the contents of the text fields.

- The text fields handle numbers, currency amounts, and percentages in the local format.

- The computation field uses a MessageFormat. The format string is stored in the resource bundle of each language.

- Just to show that it can be done, we use different colors for the bar graph, depending on the language chosen by the user.

Examples 10–6 through 10–9 show the code. Examples 10–10 through 10–12 are the property files for the localized strings. Figures 10–5 and 10–6 show the outputs in German and Chinese. To see Chinese characters, install the Chinese fonts. Otherwise, all Chinese characters show up as "missing character" icons.

In sum, while the localization mechanism of the Java programming language still has some rough edges, it does have one major virtue. Once you have organized your application for localization, it is extremely easy to add more localized versions. You simply provide more resource files, and they will be automatically loaded when a user wants them.

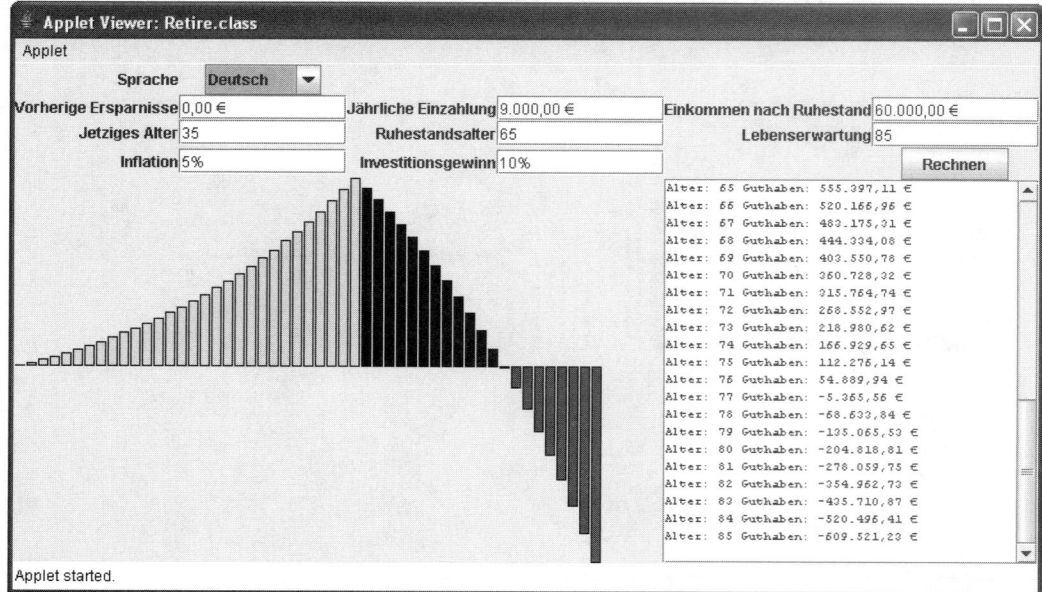

Figure 10–5: The retirement calculator in German

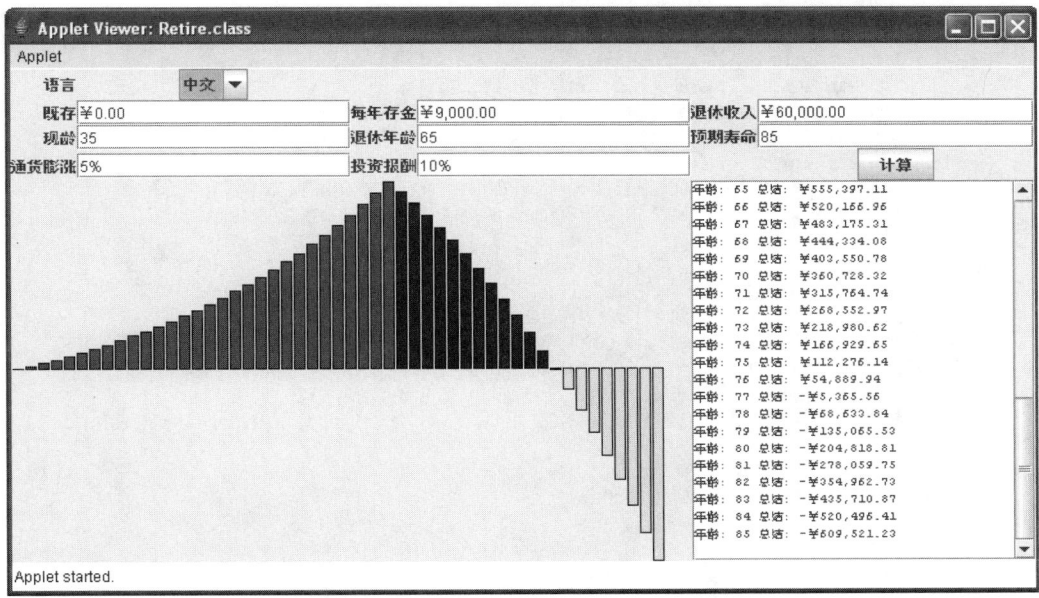

Figure 10–6: The retirement calculator in Chinese

 NOTE: This applet was harder to write than a typical localized application because the user can change the locale on the fly. The applet, therefore, had to be prepared to redraw itself whenever the user selects another locale. If you simply want to display your applet in the user's default locale, you will not need to work so hard. You can simply call getLocale() to find the locale of your user's system and then use it for the entire duration of the applet.

Example 10–6: Retire.java

```
1. import java.awt.*;
2. import java.awt.event.*;
3. import java.awt.geom.*;
4. import java.applet.*;
5. import java.util.*;
6. import java.text.*;
7. import java.io.*;
8. import javax.swing.*;
9.
10. /**
11.    This applet shows a retirement calculator. The UI is displayed
12.    in English, German, and Chinese.
13. */
14. public class Retire extends JApplet
15. {
16.    public void init()
17.    {
18.       setLayout(new GridBagLayout());
19.       add(languageLabel, new GBC(0, 0).setAnchor(GBC.EAST));
20.       add(savingsLabel, new GBC(0, 1).setAnchor(GBC.EAST));
21.       add(contribLabel, new GBC(2, 1).setAnchor(GBC.EAST));
```

```
22.      add(incomeLabel, new GBC(4, 1).setAnchor(GBC.EAST));
23.      add(currentAgeLabel, new GBC(0, 2).setAnchor(GBC.EAST));
24.      add(retireAgeLabel, new GBC(2, 2).setAnchor(GBC.EAST));
25.      add(deathAgeLabel, new GBC(4, 2).setAnchor(GBC.EAST));
26.      add(inflationPercentLabel, new GBC(0, 3).setAnchor(GBC.EAST));
27.      add(investPercentLabel, new GBC(2, 3).setAnchor(GBC.EAST));
28.      add(localeCombo, new GBC(1, 0));
29.      add(savingsField, new GBC(1, 1).setWeight(100, 0).setFill(GBC.HORIZONTAL));
30.      add(contribField, new GBC(3, 1).setWeight(100, 0).setFill(GBC.HORIZONTAL));
31.      add(incomeField, new GBC(5, 1).setWeight(100, 0).setFill(GBC.HORIZONTAL));
32.      add(currentAgeField, new GBC(1, 2).setWeight(100, 0).setFill(GBC.HORIZONTAL));
33.      add(retireAgeField, new GBC(3, 2).setWeight(100, 0).setFill(GBC.HORIZONTAL));
34.      add(deathAgeField, new GBC(5, 2).setWeight(100, 0).setFill(GBC.HORIZONTAL));
35.      add(inflationPercentField, new GBC(1, 3).setWeight(100, 0).setFill(GBC.HORIZONTAL));
36.      add(investPercentField, new GBC(3, 3).setWeight(100, 0).setFill(GBC.HORIZONTAL));
37.      add(retireCanvas, new GBC(0, 4, 4, 1).setWeight(0, 100).setFill(GBC.BOTH));
38.      add(new JScrollPane(retireText), new GBC(4, 4, 2, 1).setWeight(0, 100).setFill(GBC.BOTH));
39.
40.      computeButton.setName("computeButton");
41.      computeButton.addActionListener(new
42.        ActionListener()
43.        {
44.            public void actionPerformed(ActionEvent event)
45.            {
46.               getInfo();
47.               updateData();
48.               updateGraph();
49.            }
50.        });
51.      add(computeButton, new GBC(5, 3));
52.
53.      retireText.setEditable(false);
54.      retireText.setFont(new Font("Monospaced", Font.PLAIN, 10));
55.
56.      info.setSavings(0);
57.      info.setContrib(9000);
58.      info.setIncome(60000);
59.      info.setCurrentAge(35);
60.      info.setRetireAge(65);
61.      info.setDeathAge(85);
62.      info.setInvestPercent(0.1);
63.      info.setInflationPercent(0.05);
64.
65.      int localeIndex = 0; // US locale is default selection
66.      for (int i = 0; i < locales.length; i++) // if current locale one of the choices, select it
67.         if (getLocale().equals(locales[i])) localeIndex = i;
68.      setCurrentLocale(locales[localeIndex]);
69.
70.      localeCombo.addActionListener(new
71.        ActionListener()
72.        {
73.            public void actionPerformed(ActionEvent event)
74.            {
75.               setCurrentLocale((Locale) localeCombo.getSelectedItem());
76.            }
77.        });
```

```
78.     }
79.
80.     /**
81.        Sets the current locale.
82.        @param locale the desired locale
83.     */
84.     public void setCurrentLocale(Locale locale)
85.     {
86.        currentLocale = locale;
87.        localeCombo.setSelectedItem(currentLocale);
88.        localeCombo.setLocale(currentLocale);
89.
90.        res = ResourceBundle.getBundle("RetireResources", currentLocale);
91.        resStrings = ResourceBundle.getBundle("RetireStrings", currentLocale);
92.        currencyFmt = NumberFormat.getCurrencyInstance(currentLocale);
93.        numberFmt = NumberFormat.getNumberInstance(currentLocale);
94.        percentFmt = NumberFormat.getPercentInstance(currentLocale);
95.
96.        updateDisplay();
97.        updateInfo();
98.        updateData();
99.        updateGraph();
100.    }
101.
102.    /**
103.       Updates all labels in the display.
104.    */
105.    public void updateDisplay()
106.    {
107.       languageLabel.setText(resStrings.getString("language"));
108.       savingsLabel.setText(resStrings.getString("savings"));
109.       contribLabel.setText(resStrings.getString("contrib"));
110.       incomeLabel.setText(resStrings.getString("income"));
111.       currentAgeLabel.setText(resStrings.getString("currentAge"));
112.       retireAgeLabel.setText(resStrings.getString("retireAge"));
113.       deathAgeLabel.setText(resStrings.getString("deathAge"));
114.       inflationPercentLabel.setText(resStrings.getString("inflationPercent"));
115.       investPercentLabel.setText(resStrings.getString("investPercent"));
116.       computeButton.setText(resStrings.getString("computeButton"));
117.       validate();
118.    }
119.
120.    /**
121.       Updates the information in the text fields.
122.    */
123.    public void updateInfo()
124.    {
125.       savingsField.setText(currencyFmt.format(info.getSavings()));
126.       contribField.setText(currencyFmt.format(info.getContrib()));
127.       incomeField.setText(currencyFmt.format(info.getIncome()));
128.       currentAgeField.setText(numberFmt.format(info.getCurrentAge()));
129.       retireAgeField.setText(numberFmt.format(info.getRetireAge()));
130.       deathAgeField.setText(numberFmt.format(info.getDeathAge()));
131.       investPercentField.setText(percentFmt.format(info.getInvestPercent()));
132.       inflationPercentField.setText(percentFmt.format(info.getInflationPercent()));
133.    }
```

```
134.
135.    /**
136.       Updates the data displayed in the text area.
137.    */
138.    public void updateData()
139.    {
140.       retireText.setText("");
141.       MessageFormat retireMsg = new MessageFormat("");
142.       retireMsg.setLocale(currentLocale);
143.       retireMsg.applyPattern(resStrings.getString("retire"));
144.
145.       for (int i = info.getCurrentAge(); i <= info.getDeathAge(); i++)
146.       {
147.          Object[] args = { i, info.getBalance(i) };
148.          retireText.append(retireMsg.format(args) + "\n");
149.       }
150.    }
151.
152.    /**
153.       Updates the graph.
154.    */
155.    public void updateGraph()
156.    {
157.       retireCanvas.setColorPre((Color) res.getObject("colorPre"));
158.       retireCanvas.setColorGain((Color) res.getObject("colorGain"));
159.       retireCanvas.setColorLoss((Color) res.getObject("colorLoss"));
160.       retireCanvas.setInfo(info);
161.       repaint();
162.    }
163.
164.    /**
165.       Reads the user input from the text fields.
166.    */
167.    public void getInfo()
168.    {
169.       try
170.       {
171.          info.setSavings(currencyFmt.parse(savingsField.getText()).doubleValue());
172.          info.setContrib(currencyFmt.parse(contribField.getText()).doubleValue());
173.          info.setIncome(currencyFmt.parse(incomeField.getText()).doubleValue());
174.          info.setCurrentAge(numberFmt.parse(currentAgeField.getText()).intValue());
175.          info.setRetireAge(numberFmt.parse(retireAgeField.getText()).intValue());
176.          info.setDeathAge(numberFmt.parse(deathAgeField.getText()).intValue());
177.          info.setInvestPercent(percentFmt.parse(investPercentField.getText()).doubleValue());
178.         info.setInflationPercent(percentFmt.parse(inflationPercentField.getText()).doubleValue());
179.       }
180.       catch (ParseException e)
181.       {
182.       }
183.    }
184.
185.    private JTextField savingsField = new JTextField(10);
186.    private JTextField contribField = new JTextField(10);
187.    private JTextField incomeField = new JTextField(10);
188.    private JTextField currentAgeField = new JTextField(4);
189.    private JTextField retireAgeField = new JTextField(4);
```

```
190.    private JTextField deathAgeField = new JTextField(4);
191.    private JTextField inflationPercentField = new JTextField(6);
192.    private JTextField investPercentField = new JTextField(6);
193.    private JTextArea retireText = new JTextArea(10, 25);
194.    private RetireCanvas retireCanvas = new RetireCanvas();
195.    private JButton computeButton = new JButton();
196.    private JLabel languageLabel = new JLabel();
197.    private JLabel savingsLabel = new JLabel();
198.    private JLabel contribLabel = new JLabel();
199.    private JLabel incomeLabel = new JLabel();
200.    private JLabel currentAgeLabel = new JLabel();
201.    private JLabel retireAgeLabel = new JLabel();
202.    private JLabel deathAgeLabel = new JLabel();
203.    private JLabel inflationPercentLabel = new JLabel();
204.    private JLabel investPercentLabel = new JLabel();
205.
206.    private RetireInfo info = new RetireInfo();
207.
208.    private Locale[] locales = { Locale.US, Locale.CHINA, Locale.GERMANY };
209.    private Locale currentLocale;
210.    private JComboBox localeCombo = new LocaleCombo(locales);
211.    private ResourceBundle res;
212.    private ResourceBundle resStrings;
213.    private NumberFormat currencyFmt;
214.    private NumberFormat numberFmt;
215.    private NumberFormat percentFmt;
216. }
217.
218. /**
219.    The information required to compute retirement income data.
220. */
221. class RetireInfo
222. {
223.    /**
224.       Gets the available balance for a given year.
225.       @param year the year for which to compute the balance
226.       @return the amount of money available (or required) in
227.       that year
228.    */
229.    public double getBalance(int year)
230.    {
231.       if (year < currentAge) return 0;
232.       else if (year == currentAge)
233.       {
234.          age = year;
235.          balance = savings;
236.          return balance;
237.       }
238.       else if (year == age) return balance;
239.       if (year != age + 1) getBalance(year - 1);
240.       age = year;
241.       if (age < retireAge) balance += contrib;
242.       else balance -= income;
243.       balance = balance * (1 + (investPercent - inflationPercent));
244.       return balance;
245.    }
```

```
246.
247.    /**
248.        Gets the amount of prior savings.
249.        @return the savings amount
250.    */
251.    public double getSavings() { return savings; }
252.
253.    /**
254.        Sets the amount of prior savings.
255.        @param newValue the savings amount
256.    */
257.    public void setSavings(double newValue) { savings = newValue; }
258.
259.    /**
260.        Gets the annual contribution to the retirement account.
261.        @return the contribution amount
262.    */
263.    public double getContrib() { return contrib; }
264.
265.    /**
266.        Sets the annual contribution to the retirement account.
267.        @param newValue the contribution amount
268.    */
269.    public void setContrib(double newValue) { contrib = newValue; }
270.
271.    /**
272.        Gets the annual income.
273.        @return the income amount
274.    */
275.    public double getIncome() { return income; }
276.
277.    /**
278.        Sets the annual income.
279.        @param newValue the income amount
280.    */
281.    public void setIncome(double newValue) { income = newValue; }
282.
283.    /**
284.        Gets the current age.
285.        @return the age
286.    */
287.    public int getCurrentAge() { return currentAge; }
288.
289.    /**
290.        Sets the current age.
291.        @param newValue the age
292.    */
293.    public void setCurrentAge(int newValue) { currentAge = newValue; }
294.
295.    /**
296.        Gets the desired retirement age.
297.        @return the age
298.    */
299.    public int getRetireAge() { return retireAge; }
300.
301.    /**
```

```
302.      Sets the desired retirement age.
303.      @param newValue the age
304.   */
305.   public void setRetireAge(int newValue) { retireAge = newValue; }
306.
307.   /**
308.      Gets the expected age of death.
309.      @return the age
310.   */
311.   public int getDeathAge() { return deathAge; }
312.
313.   /**
314.      Sets the expected age of death.
315.      @param newValue the age
316.   */
317.   public void setDeathAge(int newValue) { deathAge = newValue; }
318.
319.   /**
320.      Gets the estimated percentage of inflation.
321.      @return the percentage
322.   */
323.   public double getInflationPercent() { return inflationPercent; }
324.
325.   /**
326.      Sets the estimated percentage of inflation.
327.      @param newValue the percentage
328.   */
329.   public void setInflationPercent(double newValue) { inflationPercent = newValue; }
330.
331.   /**
332.      Gets the estimated yield of the investment.
333.      @return the percentage
334.   */
335.   public double getInvestPercent() { return investPercent; }
336.
337.   /**
338.      Sets the estimated yield of the investment.
339.      @param newValue the percentage
340.   */
341.   public void setInvestPercent(double newValue) { investPercent = newValue; }
342.
343.   private double savings;
344.   private double contrib;
345.   private double income;
346.   private int currentAge;
347.   private int retireAge;
348.   private int deathAge;
349.   private double inflationPercent;
350.   private double investPercent;
351.
352.   private int age;
353.   private double balance;
354. }
355.
356. /**
357.    This panel draws a graph of the investment result.
```

```
358.  */
359.  class RetireCanvas extends JPanel
360.  {
361.     public RetireCanvas()
362.     {
363.        setSize(PANEL_WIDTH, PANEL_HEIGHT);
364.     }
365.
366.     /**
367.        Sets the retirement information to be plotted.
368.        @param newInfo the new retirement info.
369.     */
370.     public void setInfo(RetireInfo newInfo)
371.     {
372.        info = newInfo;
373.        repaint();
374.     }
375.
376.     public void paintComponent(Graphics g)
377.     {
378.        Graphics2D g2 = (Graphics2D) g;
379.        if (info == null) return;
380.
381.        double minValue = 0;
382.        double maxValue = 0;
383.        int i;
384.        for (i = info.getCurrentAge(); i <= info.getDeathAge(); i++)
385.        {
386.           double v = info.getBalance(i);
387.           if (minValue > v) minValue = v;
388.           if (maxValue < v) maxValue = v;
389.        }
390.        if (maxValue == minValue) return;
391.
392.        int barWidth = getWidth() / (info.getDeathAge() - info.getCurrentAge() + 1);
393.        double scale = getHeight() / (maxValue - minValue);
394.
395.        for (i = info.getCurrentAge(); i <= info.getDeathAge(); i++)
396.        {
397.           int x1 = (i - info.getCurrentAge()) * barWidth + 1;
398.           int y1;
399.           double v = info.getBalance(i);
400.           int height;
401.           int yOrigin = (int) (maxValue * scale);
402.
403.           if (v >= 0)
404.           {
405.              y1 = (int) ((maxValue - v) * scale);
406.              height = yOrigin - y1;
407.           }
408.           else
409.           {
410.              y1 = yOrigin;
411.              height = (int) (-v * scale);
412.           }
413.
```

```
414.        if (i < info.getRetireAge()) g2.setPaint(colorPre);
415.        else if (v >= 0) g2.setPaint(colorGain);
416.        else g2.setPaint(colorLoss);
417.        Rectangle2D bar = new Rectangle2D.Double(x1, y1, barWidth - 2, height);
418.        g2.fill(bar);
419.        g2.setPaint(Color.black);
420.        g2.draw(bar);
421.      }
422.    }
423.
424.    /**
425.       Sets the color to be used before retirement.
426.       @param color the desired color
427.    */
428.    public void setColorPre(Color color)
429.    {
430.       colorPre = color;
431.       repaint();
432.    }
433.
434.    /**
435.       Sets the color to be used after retirement while
436.       the account balance is positive.
437.       @param color the desired color
438.    */
439.    public void setColorGain(Color color)
440.    {
441.       colorGain = color;
442.       repaint();
443.    }
444.
445.    /**
446.       Sets the color to be used after retirement when
447.       the account balance is negative.
448.       @param color the desired color
449.    */
450.    public void setColorLoss(Color color)
451.    {
452.       colorLoss = color;
453.       repaint();
454.    }
455.
456.    private RetireInfo info = null;
457.    private Color colorPre;
458.    private Color colorGain;
459.    private Color colorLoss;
460.    private static final int PANEL_WIDTH = 400;
461.    private static final int PANEL_HEIGHT = 200;
462. }
```

Example 10–7: RetireResources.java

```
1. import java.util.*;
2. import java.awt.*;
3.
4. /**
5.    These are the English non-string resources for the retirement
```

```
 6.    calculator.
 7. */
 8. public class RetireResources
 9.    extends java.util.ListResourceBundle
10. {
11.    public Object[][] getContents() { return contents; }
12.    static final Object[][] contents =
13.    {
14.       // BEGIN LOCALIZE
15.       { "colorPre", Color.blue },
16.       { "colorGain", Color.white },
17.       { "colorLoss", Color.red }
18.       // END LOCALIZE
19.    };
20. }
```

Example 10–8: RetireResources_de.java

```
 1. import java.util.*;
 2. import java.awt.*;
 3.
 4. /**
 5.    These are the German non-string resources for the retirement
 6.    calculator.
 7. */
 8. public class RetireResources_de
 9.    extends java.util.ListResourceBundle
10. {
11.    public Object[][] getContents() { return contents; }
12.    static final Object[][] contents =
13.    {
14.       // BEGIN LOCALIZE
15.       { "colorPre", Color.yellow },
16.       { "colorGain", Color.black },
17.       { "colorLoss", Color.red }
18.       // END LOCALIZE
19.    };
20. }
```

Example 10–9: RetireResources_zh.java

```
 1. import java.util.*;
 2. import java.awt.*;
 3.
 4. /**
 5.    These are the Chinese non-string resources for the retirement
 6.    calculator.
 7. */
 8. public class RetireResources_zh
 9.    extends java.util.ListResourceBundle
10. {
11.    public Object[][] getContents() { return contents; }
12.    static final Object[][] contents =
13.    {
14.       // BEGIN LOCALIZE
15.       { "colorPre", Color.red },
16.       { "colorGain", Color.blue },
17.       { "colorLoss", Color.yellow }
```

827

```
18.    // END LOCALIZE
19.   };
20. }
```

Example 10–10: RetireStrings.properties

```
1. language=Language
2. computeButton=Compute
3. savings=Prior Savings
4. contrib=Annual Contribution
5. income=Retirement Income
6. currentAge=Current Age
7. retireAge=Retirement Age
8. deathAge=Life Expectancy
9. inflationPercent=Inflation
10. investPercent=Investment Return
11. retire=Age: {0,number} Balance: {1,number,currency}
```

Example 10–11: RetireStrings_de.properties

```
1. language=Sprache
2. computeButton=Rechnen
3. savings=Vorherige Ersparnisse
4. contrib=J\u00e4hrliche Einzahlung
5. income=Einkommen nach Ruhestand
6. currentAge=Jetziges Alter
7. retireAge=Ruhestandsalter
8. deathAge=Lebenserwartung
9. inflationPercent=Inflation
10. investPercent=Investitionsgewinn
11. retire=Alter: {0,number} Guthaben: {1,number,currency}
```

Example 10–12: RetireStrings_zh.properties

```
1. language=\u8bed\u8a00
2. computeButton=\u8ba1\u7b97
3. savings=\u65e2\u5b58
4. contrib=\u6bcf\u5e74\u5b58\u91d1
5. income=\u9000\u4f11\u6536\u5165
6. currentAge=\u73b0\u9f84
7. retireAge=\u9000\u4f11\u5e74\u9f84
8. deathAge=\u9884\u671f\u5bff\u547d
9. inflationPercent=\u901a\u8d27\u81a8\u6da8
10. investPercent=\u6295\u8d44\u62a5\u916c
11. retire=\u5e74\u9f84: {0,number} \u603b\u7ed3: {1,number,currency}
```

 java.applet.Applet 1.0

- Locale getLocale() **1.1**

    gets the current locale of the applet. The current locale is determined from the client computer that executes the applet.

Chapter 11

Native Methods

We hope we have convinced you that code written in the Java programming language has a number of advantages over code written in languages like C or C++—even for platform-specific applications. Here, of course, portability is not the issue but rather features like these:

- You are more likely to produce bug-free code with the Java programming language than with C or C++.

- Multithreading is probably easier to code in the Java programming language than in most other languages.

- Networking code is a breeze.

Portability is simply a bonus that you may or may not want to take advantage of down the line.

While a "100% Pure Java" solution is nice in principle, realistically, for an application, there are situations in which you will want to write (or use) code written in another language. (Such code is usually called *native* code.) There are three obvious reasons why that may be the right choice:

1. You have substantial amounts of tested and debugged code available in that language. Porting the code to the Java programming language would be time consuming, and the resulting code would need to be tested and debugged again.

2. Your application requires access to system features or devices, and using Java technology would be cumbersome at best, or impossible at worst.

3. Maximizing the speed of the code is essential. For example, the task may be time critical, or it may be code that is used so often that optimizing it has a big payoff. This is actually the least plausible reason. With just-in-time (JIT) compilation, intensive computations coded in the Java programming language are not that much slower than compiled C code.

If you are in one of these three situations, it *might* make sense to call the native code from programs written in the Java programming language. Of course, with the usual security manager in place, once you start using native code, you are restricted to applications rather than applets. In particular, the native code library you are calling must exist on the client machine, and it must work with the client machine architecture.

To make calling native methods possible, Java technology comes with hooks for working with system libraries, and the JDK has a few tools to relieve some (but not all) of the programming tedium.

 NOTE: The language you use for your native code doesn't have to be C or C++; you could use code compiled with a FORTRAN compiler if you have access to a binding between Java code and FORTRAN.

Still, keep this in mind: If you use native methods, you lose portability. Even when you distribute your program as an application, you must supply a separate native method library for every platform you want to support. This means you must also educate your users on how to install these libraries! Also, whereas users may trust that applets can neither damage data nor steal confidential information, they may not want to extend the same trust to code that uses native method libraries. For that reason, many potential users will be reluctant to use programs in the Java programming language that require native code. Aside from the security issue, native libraries are unlikely to be as safe as Java code, especially if they are written in a language like C or C++ that offers no protection against overwriting memory through invalid pointer usage. It is easy to write native methods that corrupt the Java virtual machine, compromise its security, or trash the operating system.

Thus, we suggest using native code only as a last resort. If you must gain access to a device, such as a serial port, in a program, then you may need to write native code. If you need to access an existing body of code, why not consider native methods as a stopgap measure and eventually port the code to the Java programming language? If you are concerned about efficiency, benchmark a Java platform implementation. In most cases, the speed with a just-in-time compiler will be sufficient. A talk at the 1996 JavaOne conference showed this clearly. The implementors of the cryptography library at Sun Microsystems reported that a pure Java platform implementation of their cryptographic functions was more than adequate. It was true that the code was not as fast as a C implementation would have been, but it turned out not to matter. The Java platform implementation was far faster than the network I/O. And this turns out to be the real bottleneck.

In summary, there is no point in sacrificing portability for a meaningless speed improvement; don't go native until you determine that you have no other choice.

 NOTE: In this chapter, we describe the so-called Java Native Interface (JNI) binding. An earlier language binding (sometimes called the raw native interface) was used with Java 1.0, and a variation of that earlier binding was used by the Microsoft Virtual Machine. Sun Microsystems has assured developers that the JNI binding described here is a permanent part of the Java platform and that it needs to be supported by all Java virtual machines.

Finally, we use C as our language for native methods in this chapter because C is probably the language most often used for native methods. In particular, you'll see how to make the correspondence between Java data types, feature names, and function calls and those of C. (This correspondence is usually called the C *binding*.)

 C++ NOTE: You can also use C++ instead of C to write native methods. There are a few advantages—type checking is slightly stricter, and accessing the JNI functions is a bit more convenient. However, JNI does not support any direct correspondence between Java platform classes and those in C++.

Calling a C Function from the Java Programming Language

Suppose you have a C function that does something you like and, for one reason or another, you don't want to bother reimplementing it in the Java programming language. For the sake of illustration, we assume it is the useful and venerable printf function. You want to be able to call printf from your programs. The Java programming language uses the keyword native for a native method, and you will obviously need to encapsulate the printf function in a class. So, you might write something like this:

```
public class Printf
{
    public native String printf(String s);
}
```

You actually can compile this class, but when you go to use it in a program, then the virtual machine will tell you it doesn't know how to find printf—reporting an UnsatisfiedLinkError. So the trick is to give the run time enough information so that it can link in this class. As you will soon see, under the JDK this requires a three-step process:

1. Generate a C stub for a function that translates between the Java call and the actual C function. The stub does this translation by taking parameter information off the virtual machine stack and passing it to the compiled C function.

2. Create a special shared library and export the stub from it.

3. Use a special method, called System.loadLibrary, to tell the Java runtime environment to load the library from Step 2.

We now show you how to carry out these steps for various kinds of examples, starting from a trivial special-case use of printf and ending with a realistic example involving the registry functions for Windows—platform-dependent functions that are obviously not available directly from the Java platform.

Working with the printf Function

Let's start with just about the simplest possible situation using printf: calling a native method that prints the message, "Hello, Native World." Obviously we are not even tapping into the useful formatting features of printf! Still, this is a good way for you to test that your C compiler works as expected before you try implementing more ambitious native methods.

You first declare the native method in a class. The native keyword alerts the compiler that the method will be defined externally. Of course, native methods will contain no code in the Java programming language, and the method header is followed immediately by a terminating semicolon. This means, as you saw in the example above, native method declarations look similar to abstract method declarations.

```
class HelloNative
{
    public native static void greeting();
    . . .
}
```

In this particular example, note that the native method is also declared as static. Native methods can be both static and non-static. We start with a static method because we do not yet want to deal with parameter passing.

Next, write a corresponding C function. You must name that function *exactly* the way the Java runtime environment expects. Here are the rules:

1. Use the full Java method name, such as HelloNative.greeting. If the class is in a package, then prepend the package name, such as com.horstmann.HelloNative.greeting.

2. Replace every period with an underscore, and append the prefix Java_. For example, Java_HelloNative_greeting or Java_com_horstmann_HelloNative_greeting.

3. If the class name contains characters that are not ASCII letters or digits—that is, '_', '$', or Unicode characters with code greater than '\u007F'—replace them with _0xxxx, where *xxxx* is the sequence of four hexadecimal digits of the character's Unicode value.

 NOTE: If you *overload* native methods, that is, if you provide multiple native methods with the same name, then you must append a double underscore followed by the encoded argument types. We describe the encoding of the argument types later in this chapter. For example, if you have a native method, greeting, and another native method, greeting(int repeat), then the first one is called Java_HelloNative_greeting__, and the second, Java_HelloNative_greeting__I.

Actually, nobody does this by hand; instead, you run the javah utility, which automatically generates the function names. To use javah, first, compile the source file (given in Example 11–3 on page 834).

```
javac HelloNative.java
```

Next, call the javah utility to produce a C header file. The javah executable can be found in the jdk/bin directory.

```
javah HelloNative
```

Using javah creates a header file, HelloNative.h, as in Example 11–1.

Example 11–1: HelloNative.h

```
1.  /* DO NOT EDIT THIS FILE - it is machine generated */
2.  #include <jni.h>
3.  /* Header for class HelloNative */
4.
5.  #ifndef _Included_HelloNative
6.  #define _Included_HelloNative
7.  #ifdef __cplusplus
8.  extern "C" {
9.  #endif
10. /*
11.  * Class:     HelloNative
12.  * Method:    greeting
13.  * Signature: ()V
14.  */
15. JNIEXPORT void JNICALL Java_HelloNative_greeting(JNIEnv *, jclass);
```

```
16.
17. ifdef __cplusplus
18. }
19. #endif
20. #endif
```

As you can see, this file contains the declaration of a function `Java_HelloNative_greeting`. (The strings `JNIEXPORT` and `JNICALL` are defined in the header file `jni.h`. They denote compiler-dependent specifiers for exported functions that come from a dynamically loaded library.)

Now, you simply have to copy the function prototype from the header file into the source file and give the implementation code for the function, as shown in Example 11–2.

Example 11–2: HelloNative.c

```
1. #include "HelloNative.h"
2. #include <stdio.h>
3.
4. JNIEXPORT void JNICALL Java_HelloNative_greeting(JNIEnv* env, jclass cl)
5. {
6.    printf("Hello Native World!\n");
7. }
```

In this simple function, ignore the `env` and `cl` arguments. You'll see their use later.

 C++ NOTE: You can use C++ to implement native methods. However, you must then declare the functions that implement the native methods as `extern "C"`. (This stops the C++ compiler generating C++-specific code.) For example,

```
#include "HelloNative.h"
#include <stdio.h>

extern "C"
JNIEXPORT void JNICALL Java_HelloNative_greeting(JNIEnv* env, jclass cl)
{
   printf("Hello, Native World!\n");
}
```

You compile the native C code into a dynamically loaded library. The details depend on your compiler.

For example, with the Gnu C compiler on Linux, use these commands:

```
gcc -fPIC -I jdk/include -I jdk/include/linux -shared -o libHelloNative.so HelloNative.c
```

With the Sun compiler under the Solaris Operating System, the command is

```
cc -G -I jdk/include -I jdk/include/solaris -o libHelloNative.so HelloNative.c
```

With the Microsoft C++ compiler under Windows, the command is

```
cl -I jdk\include -I jdk\include\win32 -LD HelloNative.c -FeHelloNative.dll
```

Here, *jdk* is the directory that contains the JDK.

 TIP: If you use the Microsoft C++ compiler to compile DLLs from a command shell, first run the batch file `vcvars32.net` or `vsvars32.bat`. That batch file properly configures the command-line compiler by setting up the path and the environment variables needed by the compiler. You can find it in the directory `c:\Program Files\Microsoft Visual Studio .NET 2003\Common7\tools` (or a similar monstrosity).

You can also use the freely available Cygwin programming environment, available from http://www.cygwin.com. It contains the Gnu C compiler and libraries for UNIX-style programming on Windows. With Cygwin, use the command

```
gcc --mno-cygwin -D __int64="long long" -I jdk/include/ -I jdk/include/win32
   -shared -Wl,--add-stdcall-alias -o HelloNative.dll HelloNative.c
```

Type the entire command on a single line.

 NOTE: The Windows version of the header file jni_md.h contains the type declaration

```
typedef __int64 jlong;
```

which is specific to the Microsoft compiler. If you use the Gnu compiler, you may want to edit that file, for example,

```
#ifdef __GNUC__
   typedef long long jlong;
#else
   typedef __int64 jlong;
#endif
```

Alternatively, compile with -D __int64="long long", as shown in the sample compiler invocation.

Finally, add a call to the System.loadLibrary method in the Java class that defines the native method. This ensures that the virtual machine will load the library before the first use of the class. The easiest way to do this is with a static initialization block, as in Example 11–3.

Example 11–3: HelloNative.java

```
1.  class HelloNative
2.  {
3.     public static native void greeting();
4.
5.     static
6.     {
7.        System.loadLibrary("HelloNative");
8.     }
9.  }
```

Assuming you have followed all the steps given above, you are now ready to run the HelloNativeTest application shown in Example 11–4.

Example 11–4: HelloNativeTest.java

```
1.  class HelloNativeTest
2.  {
3.     public static void main(String[] args)
4.     {
5.        HelloNative.greeting();
6.     }
7.  }
```

If you compile and run this program, the message "Hello, Native World!" is displayed in a terminal window.

 NOTE: If you run Linux, you must add the current directory to the library path. Either set the LD_LIBRARY_PATH environment variable,

```
export LD_LIBRARY_PATH=.:$LD_LIBRARY_PATH
```

or set the java.library.path system property:

```
java -Djava.library.path=. HelloNativeTest
```

Of course, this is not particularly impressive by itself. However, if you keep in mind that this message is generated by the C printf command and not by any Java programming language code, you will see that we have taken the first steps toward bridging the gap between the two languages!

 java.lang.System 1.0

- void loadLibrary(String libname)
  loads the library with the given name. The library is located in the library search path. The exact method for locating the library is operating-system dependent. Under Windows, this method searches first the current directory, then the directories listed in the PATH environment variable.

- void load(String filename)
  loads the library with the given file name. If the library is not found, then an UnsatisfiedLinkError is thrown.

 NOTE: Some shared libraries for native code must run initialization code. You can place any initialization code into a JNI_OnLoad method. Similarly, when the VM shuts down, it will call the JNI_OnUnload method if you provide it. The prototypes are

```
jint JNI_OnLoad(JavaVM* vm, void* reserved);
void JNI_OnUnload(JavaVM* vm, void* reserved);
```

The JNI_OnLoad method needs to return the minimum version of the VM that it requires, such as JNI_VERSION_1_1.

Numeric Parameters and Return Values

When passing numbers between C and the Java programming language, you should understand which types correspond to each other. For example, although C does have data types called int and long, their implementation is platform dependent. On some platforms, ints are 16-bit quantities, and on others they are 32-bit quantities. In the Java platform, of course, an int is *always* a 32-bit integer. For that reason, the Java Native Interface defines types jint, jlong, and so on.

Table 11–1 shows the correspondence between Java types and C types.

Table 11–1: Java Types and C Types

Java Programming Language	C Programming Language	Bytes
boolean	jboolean	1
byte	jbyte	1
char	jchar	2
short	jshort	2
int	jint	4
long	jlong	8
float	jfloat	4
double	jdouble	8

In the header file jni.h, these types are declared with typedef statements as the equivalent types on the target platform. That header file also defines the constants JNI_FALSE = 0 and JNI_TRUE = 1.

Using *printf* for Formatting Numbers

Until JDK 5.0, Java had no direct analog to the C printf function. Let's suppose you are stuck with an older JDK release and decide to implement the same functionality by calling the C printf function in a native method.

Example 11–5 shows a class called Printf1 that uses a native method to print a floating-point number with a given field width and precision.

Example 11–5: Printf1.java

```
1. class Printf1
2. {
3.    public static native int print(int width, int precision, double x);
4.
5.    static
6.    {
7.       System.loadLibrary("Printf1");
8.    }
9. }
```

Notice that when the method is implemented in C, all int and double parameters are changed to jint and jdouble, as shown in Example 11–6.

Example 11–6: Printf1.c

```
1. #include "Printf1.h"
2. #include <stdio.h>
3.
4. JNIEXPORT jint JNICALL Java_Printf1_print(JNIEnv* env, jclass cl,
5.    jint width, jint precision, jdouble x)
6. {
7.    char fmt[30];
8.    jint ret;
9.    sprintf(fmt, "%%%d.%df", width, precision);
10.   ret = printf(fmt, x);
11.   fflush(stdout);
12.   return ret;
13. }
```

The function simply assembles a format string "%w.pf" in the variable fmt, then calls printf. It then returns the number of characters printed.

Example 11–7 shows the test program that demonstrates the Printf1 class.

Example 11–7: Printf1Test.java

```
1. class Printf1Test
2. {
3.    public static void main(String[] args)
4.    {
5.       int count = Printf1.print(8, 4, 3.14);
6.       count += Printf1.print(8, 4, count);
7.       System.out.println();
8.       for (int i = 0; i < count; i++)
9.          System.out.print("-");
10.      System.out.println();
11.   }
12. }
```

String Parameters

Next, we want to consider how to transfer strings to and from native methods. As you know, strings in the Java programming language are sequences of UTF-16 code points whereas C strings are null-terminated sequences of bytes, so strings are quite different in the two languages. The Java Native Interface has two sets of functions for manipulating strings, one that converts Java strings to "modified UTF-8" byte sequences and one that converts them to arrays of UTF-16 values, that is, to jchar arrays. (The UTF-8, "modified UTF-8", and UTF-16 formats were discussed in Volume 1, Chapter 12. Recall that the "modified UTF-8" encoding leaves ASCII characters unchanged, but all other Unicode characters are encoded as multibyte sequences.)

 NOTE: The standard UTF-8 encoding and the "modified UTF-8" encoding differ only for "supplementary" characters with code higher than 0xFFFF. In the standard UTF-8 encoding, these characters are encoded as a 4-byte sequence. However, in the "modified" encoding, the character is first encoded as a pair of "surrogates" in the UTF-16 encoding, and then each surrogate is encoded with UTF-8, yielding a total of 6 bytes. This is clumsy, but it is a historical accident—the JVM specification was written when Unicode was still limited to 16 bits.

If your C code already uses Unicode, you'll want to use the second set of conversion functions. On the other hand, if all your strings are restricted to ASCII characters, you can use the "modified UTF-8" conversion functions.

A native method with a String parameter actually receives a value of an opaque type called jstring. A native method with a return value of type String must return a value of type jstring. JNI functions read and construct these jstring objects. For example, the NewStringUTF function makes a new jstring object out of a char array that contains ASCII characters or, more generally, "modified UTF-8"-encoded byte sequences.

JNI functions have a somewhat odd calling convention. Here is a call to the NewStringUTF function.

```
JNIEXPORT jstring JNICALL Java_HelloNative_getGreeting(JNIEnv* env, jclass cl)
{
   jstring jstr;
   char greeting[] = "Hello, Native World\n";
   jstr = (*env)->NewStringUTF(env, greeting);
   return jstr;
}
```

All calls to JNI functions use the env pointer that is the first argument of every native method. The env pointer is a pointer to a table of function pointers (see Figure 11–1). Therefore, you must prefix every JNI call with (*env)-> to actually dereference the function pointer. Furthermore, env is the first parameter of every JNI function.

 C++ NOTE: It is simpler to access JNI functions in C++. The C++ version of the JNIEnv class has inline member functions that take care of the function pointer lookup for you. For example, you can call the NewStringUTF function as

```
jstr = env->NewStringUTF(greeting);
```
Note that you omit the JNIEnv pointer from the parameter list of the call.

The NewStringUTF function lets you construct a new jstring. To read the contents of an existing jstring object, use the GetStringUTFChars function. This function returns a const jbyte* pointer to the "modified UTF-8" characters that describe the character string. Note that a specific vir-

tual machine is free to choose this character encoding for its internal string representation, so you may get a character pointer into the actual Java string. Because Java strings are meant to be immutable, it is *very* important that you treat the const seriously and do not try to write into this character array. On the other hand, if the virtual machine uses UTF-16 or UTF-32 characters for its internal string representation, then this function call allocates a new memory block that will be filled with the "modified UTF-8" equivalents.

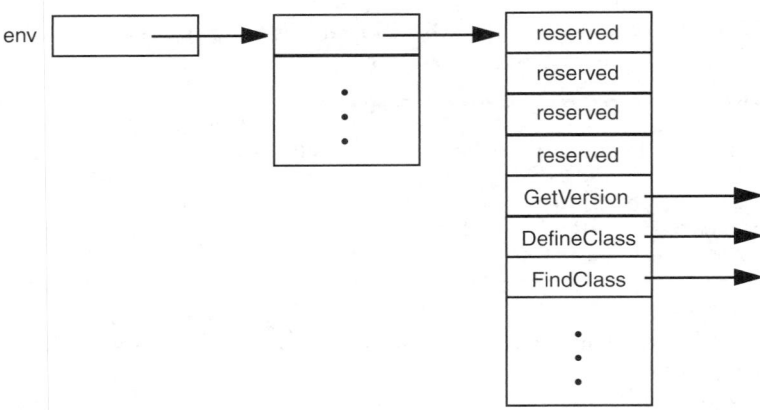

Figure 11–1: The env pointer

The virtual machine must know when you are finished using the string so that it can garbage-collect it. (The garbage collector runs in a separate thread, and it can interrupt the execution of native methods.) For that reason, you must call the ReleaseStringUTFChars function.

Alternatively, you can supply your own buffer to hold the string characters by calling the GetStringRegion or GetStringUTFRegion methods.

Finally, the GetStringUTFLength function returns the number of characters needed for the "modified UTF-8" encoding of the string.

NOTE: You can find the JNI API at http://java.sun.com/j2se/5.0/docs/guide/jni/spec/functions.html.

 Accessing Java Strings from C Code

- jstring NewStringUTF(JNIEnv* env, const char bytes[])
  returns a new Java string object from a "modified UTF-8" byte sequence, or NULL if the string cannot be constructed.

Parameters:	env	The JNI interface pointer
	bytes	The null-terminated "modified UTF-8" bytes

- jsize GetStringUTFLength(JNIEnv* env, jstring string)
  returns the number of bytes required for the "modified UTF-8" encoding.

Parameters:	env	The JNI interface pointer
	string	A Java string object

- const jbyte* GetStringUTFChars(JNIEnv* env, jstring string, jboolean* isCopy)
  returns a pointer to the "modified UTF-8" encoding of a string, or NULL if the character array cannot be constructed. The pointer is valid until ReleaseStringUTFChars is called.

Parameters:	env	The JNI interface pointer
	string	A Java string object
	isCopy	Points to a jboolean that is filled with JNI_TRUE if a copy is made; with JNI_FALSE otherwise

- void ReleaseStringUTFChars(JNIEnv* env, jstring string, const jbyte bytes[])
  informs the virtual machine that the native code no longer needs access to the Java string through bytes.

Parameters:	env	The JNI interface pointer
	string	A Java string object
	bytes	A pointer returned by GetStringUTFChars

- void GetStringRegion(JNIEnv *env, jstring string, jsize start, jsize length, jchar *buffer)
  copies a sequence of Unicode characters from a string to a user-supplied buffer.

Parameters:	env	The JNI interface pointer
	string	A Java string object
	start	The starting index
	length	The number of characters to copy
	buffer	The user-supplied buffer

- void GetStringUTFRegion(JNIEnv *env, jstring string, jsize start, jsize length, jbyte *buffer)
  copies a sequence of "modified UTF-8" bytes from a string to a user-supplied buffer. The buffer must be long enough to hold the bytes. In the worst case, 3 × length bytes are copied.

- jstring NewString(JNIEnv* env, const jchar chars[], jsize length)
  returns a new Java string object from a Unicode string, or NULL if the string cannot be constructed.

Parameters:	env	The JNI interface pointer
	chars	The null-terminated UTF16 string
	length	The number of characters in the string

- jsize GetStringLength(JNIEnv* env, jstring string)
  returns the number of characters in the string.

Parameters:	env	The JNI interface pointer
	string	A Java string object

- const jchar* GetStringChars(JNIEnv* env, jstring string, jboolean* isCopy)
  returns a pointer to the Unicode encoding of a string, or NULL if the character array cannot be constructed. The pointer is valid until ReleaseStringChars is called.

Parameters:	env	The JNI interface pointer
	string	A Java string object
	isCopy	Is either NULL or points to a jboolean that is filled with JNI_TRUE if a copy is made; with JNI_FALSE otherwise

- void ReleaseStringChars(JNIEnv* env, jstring string, const jchar chars[])
  informs the virtual machine that the native code no longer needs access to the
  Java string through chars.

Parameters:	env	The JNI interface pointer
	string	A Java string object
	chars	A pointer returned by GetStringChars

Calling *sprint* in a Native Method

Let us put these functions we just described to work and write a class that calls the C function sprintf. We would like to call the function as shown in Example 11–8.

Example 11–8: Printf2Test.java

```
1. class Printf2Test
2. {
3.    public static void main(String[] args)
4.    {
5.       double price = 44.95;
6.       double tax = 7.75;
7.       double amountDue = price * (1 + tax / 100);
8.
9.       String s = Printf2.sprint("Amount due = %8.2f", amountDue);
10.      System.out.println(s);
11.   }
12. }
```

Example 11–9 shows the class with the native sprint method.

Example 11–9: Printf2.java

```
1. class Printf2
2. {
3.    public static native String sprint(String format, double x);
4.
5.    static
6.    {
7.       System.loadLibrary("Printf2");
8.    }
9. }
```

Therefore, the C function that formats a floating-point number has the prototype

```
JNIEXPORT jstring JNICALL Java_Printf2_sprint(JNIEnv* env, jclass cl, jstring format, jdouble x)
```

Example 11–10 shows the code for the C implementation. Note the calls to GetStringUTFChars to read the format argument, NewStringUTF to generate the return value, and ReleaseStringUTF-Chars to inform the virtual machine that access to the string is no longer required.

Example 11–10: Printf2.c

```
1. #include "Printf2.h"
2. #include <string.h>
3. #include <stdlib.h>
4. #include <float.h>
5.
6. /**
7.    @param format a string containing a printf format specifier
8.    (such as "%8.2f"). Substrings "%%" are skipped.
9.    @return a pointer to the format specifier (skipping the '%')
```

```
10.     or NULL if there wasn't a unique format specifier
11.  */
12.  char* find_format(const char format[])
13.  {
14.     char* p;
15.     char* q;
16.
17.     p = strchr(format, '%');
18.     while (p != NULL && *(p + 1) == '%') /* skip %% */
19.        p = strchr(p + 2, '%');
20.     if (p == NULL) return NULL;
21.     /* now check that % is unique */
22.     p++;
23.     q = strchr(p, '%');
24.     while (q != NULL && *(q + 1) == '%') /* skip %% */
25.        q = strchr(q + 2, '%');
26.     if (q != NULL) return NULL; /* % not unique */
27.     q = p + strspn(p, " -0+#"); /* skip past flags */
28.     q += strspn(q, "0123456789"); /* skip past field width */
29.     if (*q == '.') { q++; q += strspn(q, "0123456789"); }
30.        /* skip past precision */
31.     if (strchr("eEfFgG", *q) == NULL) return NULL;
32.        /* not a floating point format */
33.     return p;
34.  }
35.
36.  JNIEXPORT jstring JNICALL Java_Printf2_sprint(JNIEnv* env, jclass cl,
37.     jstring format, jdouble x)
38.  {
39.     const char* cformat;
40.     char* fmt;
41.     jstring ret;
42.
43.     cformat = (*env)->GetStringUTFChars(env, format, NULL);
44.     fmt = find_format(cformat);
45.     if (fmt == NULL)
46.        ret = format;
47.     else
48.     {
49.        char* cret;
50.        int width = atoi(fmt);
51.        if (width == 0) width = DBL_DIG + 10;
52.        cret = (char*) malloc(strlen(cformat) + width);
53.        sprintf(cret, cformat, x);
54.        ret = (*env)->NewStringUTF(env, cret);
55.        free(cret);
56.     }
57.     (*env)->ReleaseStringUTFChars(env, format, cformat);
58.     return ret;
59.  }
```

In this function, we chose to keep the error handling simple. If the format code to print a floating-point number is not of the form %w.pc, where c is one of the characters e, E, f, g, or G, then what we simply do is *not* format the number. We show you later how to make a native method throw an exception.

Accessing Fields

All the native methods that you saw so far were static methods with number and string parameters. We next consider native methods that operate on objects. As an exercise, we implement a method of the Employee class that was introduced in Volume 1, Chapter 4, using a native method. Again, this is not something you would normally want to do, but it does illustrate how to access fields from a native method when you need to do so.

Accessing Instance Fields

In order to see how to access instance fields from a native method, we will reimplement the raiseSalary method. In the Java programming language, the code was simple.

```
public void raiseSalary(double byPercent)
{
    salary *= 1 + byPercent / 100;
}
```

Let us rewrite this as a native method. Unlike the previous examples of native methods, this is not a static method. Running javah gives the following prototype:

```
JNIEXPORT void JNICALL Java_Employee_raiseSalary(JNIEnv *, jobject, jdouble);
```

Note the second argument. It is no longer of type jclass but of type jobject. In fact, it is the equivalent of the this reference. Static methods obtain a reference to the class, whereas non-static methods obtain a reference to the implicit this argument object.

Now we access the salary field of the implicit argument. In the "raw" Java-to-C binding of Java 1.0, this was easy—a programmer could directly access object data fields. However, direct access requires all virtual machines to expose their internal data layout. For that reason, the JNI requires programmers to get and set the values of data fields by calling special JNI functions.

In our case, we need to use the GetDoubleField and SetDoubleField functions because the type of salary is a double. There are other functions—GetIntField/SetIntField, GetObjectField/SetObjectField, and so on—for other field types. The general syntax is:

```
x = (*env)->GetXxxField(env, this_obj, fieldID);
(*env)->SetXxxField(env, this_obj, fieldID, x);
```

Here, class is a value that represents a Java object of type Class, fieldID is a value of a special type, jfieldID, that identifies a field in a structure, and Xxx represents a Java data type (Object, Boolean, Byte, and so on). There are two ways to obtain the class object. The GetObjectClass function returns the class of any object. For example:

```
jclass class_Employee = (*env)->GetObjectClass(env, this_obj);
```

The FindClass function lets you specify the class name as a string (curiously, with / instead of periods as package name separators).

```
jclass class_String = (*env)->FindClass(env, "java/lang/String");
```

Use the GetFieldID function to obtain the fieldID. You must supply the name of the field and its *signature*, an encoding of its type. For example, here is the code to obtain the field ID of the salary field.

```
jfieldID id_salary = (*env)->GetFieldID(env, class_Employee, "salary", "D");
```

The string "D" denotes the type double. You learn the complete rules for encoding signatures in the next section.

You may be thinking that accessing a data field seems quite convoluted. The designers of the JNI did not want to expose the data fields directly, so they had to supply functions for getting and setting field values. To minimize the cost of these functions, computing the

field ID from the field name—which is the most expensive step—is factored out into a separate step. That is, if you repeatedly get and set the value of a particular field, you incur only once the cost of computing the field identifier.

Let us put all the pieces together. The following code reimplements the raiseSalary method as a native method.

```
JNIEXPORT void JNICALL Java_Employee_raiseSalary(JNIEnv* env, jobject this_obj, jdouble byPercent)
{
   /* get the class */
   jclass class_Employee = (*env)->GetObjectClass(env, this_obj);

   /* get the field ID */
   jfieldID id_salary = (*env)->GetFieldID(env, class_Employee, "salary", "D");

   /* get the field value */
   jdouble salary = (*env)->GetDoubleField(env, this_obj, id_salary);

   salary *= 1 + byPercent / 100;

   /* set the field value */
   (*env)->SetDoubleField(env, this_obj, id_salary, salary);
}
```

 CAUTION: Class references are only valid until the native method returns. Thus, you cannot cache the return values of GetObjectClass in your code. Do *not* store away a class reference for reuse in a later method call. You must call GetObjectClass every time the native method executes. If this is intolerable, you can lock the reference with a call to NewGlobalRef:

```
static jclass class_X = 0;
static jfieldID id_a;
. . .
if (class_X == 0)
{
   jclass cx = (*env)->GetObjectClass(env, obj);
   class_X = (*env)->NewGlobalRef(env, cx);
   id_a = (*env)->GetFieldID(env, cls, "a", ". . .");
}
```

Now you can use the class reference and field IDs in subsequent calls. When you are done using the class, make sure to call

```
(*env)->DeleteGlobalRef(env, class_X);
```

Examples 11–11 and 11–12 show the Java code for a test program and the Employee class. Example 11–13 contains the C code for the native raiseSalary method.

Example 11–11: EmployeeTest.java

```
1. public class EmployeeTest
2. {
3.    public static void main(String[] args)
4.    {
5.       Employee[] staff = new Employee[3];
6.
7.       staff[0] = new Employee("Harry Hacker", 35000);
8.       staff[1] = new Employee("Carl Cracker", 75000);
9.       staff[2] = new Employee("Tony Tester", 38000);
```

```
10.
11.      int i;
12.      for (Employee e : staff) e.raiseSalary(5);
13.      for (Employee e : staff) e.print();
14.   }
15. }
```

Example 11–12: Employee.java

```
1. public class Employee
2. {
3.    public Employee(String n, double s)
4.    {
5.       name = n;
6.       salary = s;
7.    }
8.
9.    public native void raiseSalary(double byPercent);
10.
11.   public void print()
12.   {
13.      System.out.println(name + " " + salary);
14.   }
15.
16.   private String name;
17.   private double salary;
18.
19.   static
20.   {
21.      System.loadLibrary("Employee");
22.   }
23. }
```

Example 11–13: Employee.c

```
1. #include "Employee.h"
2.
3. #include <stdio.h>
4.
5. JNIEXPORT void JNICALL Java_Employee_raiseSalary(JNIEnv* env, jobject this_obj, jdouble byPercent)
6. {
7.    /* get the class */
8.    jclass class_Employee = (*env)->GetObjectClass(env, this_obj);
9.
10.   /* get the field ID */
11.   jfieldID id_salary = (*env)->GetFieldID(env, class_Employee, "salary", "D");
12.
13.   /* get the field value */
14.   jdouble salary = (*env)->GetDoubleField(env, this_obj, id_salary);
15.
16.   salary *= 1 + byPercent / 100;
17.
18.   /* set the field value */
19.   (*env)->SetDoubleField(env, this_obj, id_salary, salary);
20. }
```

Accessing Instance Fields

- jfieldID GetFieldID(JNIEnv *env, jclass cl, const char name[], const char sig[])
  returns the identifier of a field in a class.

  Parameters:
  env   The JNI interface pointer
  cl   The class object
  name   The field name
  sig   The encoded field signature

- *Xxx* GetXxxField(JNIEnv *env, jobject obj, jfieldID id)
  returns the value of a field. The field type *Xxx* is one of Object, Boolean, Byte, Char, Short, Int, Long, Float, or Double.

  Parameters:
  env   The JNI interface pointer
  obj   The object whose field is being returned
  id   The field identifier

- void SetXxxField(JNIEnv *env, jobject obj, jfieldID id, *Xxx* value)
  sets a field to a new value. The field type *Xxx* is one of Object, Boolean, Byte, Char, Short, Int, Long, Float, or Double.

  Parameters:
  env   The JNI interface pointer
  obj   The object whose field is being set
  id   The field identifier
  value   The new field value

- jfieldID GetStaticFieldID(JNIEnv *env, jclass cl, const char name[], const char sig[])
  returns the identifier of a static field in a class.

  Parameters:
  env   The JNI interface pointer
  cl   The class object
  name   The field name
  sig   The encoded field signature

- *Xxx* GetStaticXxxField(JNIEnv *env, jclass cl, jfieldID id)
  returns the value of a static field. The field type *Xxx* is one of Object, Boolean, Byte, Char, Short, Int, Long, Float, or Double.

  Parameters:
  env   The JNI interface pointer
  cl   The class object whose static field is being returned
  id   The field identifier

- void SetStaticXxxField(JNIEnv *env, jclass cl, jfieldID id, *Xxx* value)
  sets a static field to a new value. The field type *Xxx* is one of Object, Boolean, Byte, Char, Short, Int, Long, Float, or Double.

  Parameters:
  env   The JNI interface pointer
  cl   The class object whose static field is being set
  id   The field identifier
  value   The new field value

Accessing Static Fields

Accessing static fields is similar to accessing non-static fields. You use the GetStaticFieldID and GetStaticXxxField/SetStaticXxxField functions. They work almost identically to their non-static counterpart, with two differences:

- Since you have no object, you must use FindClass instead of GetObjectClass to obtain the class reference.
- You supply the class, not the instance object, when accessing the field.

For example, here is how you can get a reference to System.out.

```
/* get the class */
jclass class_System = (*env)->FindClass(env, "java/lang/System");

/* get the field ID */
jfieldID id_out = (*env)->GetStaticFieldID(env, class_System, "out", "Ljava/io/PrintStream;");

/* get the field value */
jobject obj_out = (*env)->GetStaticObjectField(env, class_System, id_out);
```

Encoding Signatures

To access instance fields and call methods that are defined in the Java programming language, you need to learn the rules for "mangling" the names of data types and method signatures. (A method signature describes the parameters and return type of the method.) Here is the encoding scheme:

B	byte
C	char
D	double
F	float
I	int
J	long
L*classname*;	a class type
S	short
V	void
Z	boolean

Note that the semicolon at the end of the L expression is the terminator of the type expression, not a separator between parameters. For example, the constructor

```
Employee(java.lang.String, double, java.util.Date)
```

has a signature

```
"(Ljava/lang/String;DLjava/util/Date;)V"
```

Note that there is no separator between the D and Ljava/util/Date;.

Also note that in this encoding scheme, you must use / instead of . to separate the package and class names.

To describe an array type, use a [. For example, an array of strings is

```
[Ljava/lang/String;
```

A float[][] is mangled into

```
[[F
```

For the complete signature of a method, you list the parameter types inside a pair of parentheses and then list the return type. For example, a method receiving two integers and returning an integer is encoded as

(II)I

The print method that we used in the preceding example has a mangled signature of

`(Ljava/lang/String;)V`

That is, the method receives a string and returns `void`.

 TIP: You can use the `javap` command with option `-s` to generate the method signatures from class files. For example, run

```
javap -s -private Employee
```

You get the following output, displaying the signatures of all fields and methods.

```
Compiled from "Employee.java"
public class Employee extends java.lang.Object{
private java.lang.String name;
  Signature: Ljava/lang/String;
private double salary;
  Signature: D
public Employee(java.lang.String, double);
  Signature: (Ljava/lang/String;D)V
public native void raiseSalary(double);
  Signature: (D)V
public void print();
  Signature: ()V
static {};
  Signature: ()V
}
```

 NOTE: There is no rationale whatsoever for forcing programmers to use this mangling scheme for describing signatures. The designers of the native calling mechanism could have just as easily written a function that reads signatures in the Java programming language style, such as `void(int,java.lang.String)`, and encodes them into whatever internal representation they prefer. Then again, using the mangled signatures lets you partake in the mystique of programming close to the virtual machine.

Calling Java Methods

Of course, Java programming language functions can call C functions—that is what native methods are for. Can we go the other way? Why would we want to do this anyway? The answer is that it often happens that a native method needs to request a service from an object that was passed to it. We first show you how to do it for non-static methods, and then we show you how to do it for static methods.

Non-Static Methods

As an example of calling a Java method from native code, let's enhance the `Printf` class and add a method that works similarly to the C function `fprintf`. That is, it should be able to print a string on an arbitrary `PrintWriter` object.

```
class Printf3
{
    public native static void fprint(PrintWriter out, String s, double x);
    . . .
}
```

We first assemble the string to be printed into a String object str, as in the sprint method that we already implemented. Then, we call the print method of the PrintWriter class from the C function that implements the native method.

You can call any Java method from C by using the function call

```
(*env)->CallXxxMethod(env, implicit parameter, methodID, explicit parameters)
```

Replace *Xxx* with Void, Int, Object, etc., depending on the return type of the method. Just as you need a fieldID to access a field of an object, you need a method ID to call a method. You obtain a method ID by calling the JNI function GetMethodID and supplying the class, the name of the method, and the method signature.

In our example, we want to obtain the ID of the print method of the PrintWriter class. As you saw in Volume 1, Chapter 12, the PrintWriter class has several overloaded methods called print. For that reason, you must also supply a string describing the parameters and return the value of the specific function that you want to use. For example, we want to use void print(java.lang.String). As described in the preceding section, we must now "mangle" the signature into the string "(Ljava/lang/String;)V".

Here is the complete code to make the method call, by

1. Obtaining the class of the implicit parameter;
2. Obtaining the method ID;
3. Making the call.

```
/* get the class */
class_PrintWriter = (*env)->GetObjectClass(env, out);

/* get the method ID */
id_print = (*env)->GetMethodID(env, class_PrintWriter, "print", "(Ljava/lang/String;)V");

/* call the method */
(*env)->CallVoidMethod(env, out, id_print, str);
```

Examples 11–14 and 11–15 show the Java code for a test program and the Printf3 class. Example 11–16 contains the C code for the native fprint method.

 NOTE: The numerical method IDs and field IDs are conceptually similar to Method and Field objects in the reflection API. You can convert between them with the following functions:

```
jobject ToReflectedMethod(JNIEnv* env, jclass class, jmethodID methodID);
    // returns Method object
methodID FromReflectedMethod(JNIEnv* env, jobject method);
jobject ToReflectedField(JNIEnv* env, jclass class, jfieldID fieldID);
    // returns Field object
fieldID FromReflectedField(JNIEnv* env, jobject field);
```

Static Methods

Calling static methods from native methods is similar to calling non-static methods. There are two differences.

*   You use the GetStaticMethodID and CallStaticXxxMethod functions.
*   You supply a class object, not an implicit parameter object, when invoking the method.

As an example of this, let's make the call to the static method

```
System.getProperty("java.class.path")
```

from a native method. The return value of this call is a string that gives the current class path.

First, we have to find the class to use. Because we have no object of the class System readily available, we use FindClass rather than GetObjectClass.

```
jclass class_System = (*env)->FindClass(env, "java/lang/System");
```

Next, we need the ID of the static getProperty method. The encoded signature of that method is

```
"(Ljava/lang/String;)Ljava/lang/String;"
```

since both the parameter and the return value are a string. Hence, we obtain the method ID as follows:

```
jmethodID id_getProperty = (*env)->GetStaticMethodID(env, class_System, "getProperty",
    "(Ljava/lang/String;)Ljava/lang/String;");
```

Finally, we can make the call. Note that the class object is passed to the CallStaticObjectMethod function.

```
jobject obj_ret = (*env)->CallStaticObjectMethod(env, class_System, id_getProperty,
    (*env)->NewStringUTF(env, "java.class.path"));
```

The return value of this method is of type jobject. If we want to manipulate it as a string, we must cast it to jstring:

```
jstring str_ret = (jstring) obj_ret;
```

 C++ NOTE: In C, the types jstring and jclass, as well as the array types that are introduced later, are all type equivalent to jobject. The cast of the preceding example is therefore not strictly necessary in C. But in C++, these types are defined as pointers to "dummy classes" that have the correct inheritance hierarchy. For example, the assignment of a jstring to a jobject is legal without a cast in C++, but the assignment from a jobject to a jstring requires a cast.

Constructors

A native method can create a new Java object by invoking its constructor. You invoke the constructor by calling the NewObject function.

```
jobject obj_new = (*env)->NewObject(env, class, methodID, construction parameters);
```

You obtain the method ID needed for this call from the GetMethodID function by specifying the method name as "<init>" and the encoded signature of the constructor (with return type void). For example, here is how a native method can create a FileOutputStream object.

```
const char[] fileName = ". . .";
jstring str_fileName = (*env)->NewStringUTF(env, fileName);
jclass class_FileOutputStream = (*env)->FindClass(env, "java/io/FileOutputStream");
jmethodID id_FileOutputStream
    = (*env)->GetMethodID(env, class_FileOutputStream, "<init>", "(Ljava/lang/String;)V");
jobject obj_stream
    = (*env)->NewObject(env, class_FileOutputStream, id_FileOutputStream, str_fileName);
```

Note that the signature of the constructor takes a parameter of type java.lang.String and has a return type of void.

Alternative Method Invocations

Several variants of the JNI functions call a Java method from native code. These are not as important as the functions that we already discussed, but they are occasionally useful.

The CallNonvirtual*Xxx*Method functions receive an implicit argument, a method ID, a class object (which must correspond to a superclass of the implicit argument), and explicit arguments. The function calls the version of the method in the specified class, bypassing the normal dynamic dispatch mechanism.

All call functions have versions with suffixes "A" and "V" that receive the explicit parameters in an array or a va_list (as defined in the C header stdarg.h).

Example 11–14: Printf3Test.java

```
1.  import java.io.*;
2.
3.  class Printf3Test
4.  {
5.     public static void main(String[] args)
6.     {
7.        double price = 44.95;
8.        double tax = 7.75;
9.        double amountDue = price * (1 + tax / 100);
10.       PrintWriter out = new PrintWriter(System.out);
11.       Printf3.fprint(out, "Amount due = %8.2f\n", amountDue);
12.       out.flush();
13.    }
14. }
```

Example 11–15: Printf3.java

```
1.  import java.io.*;
2.
3.  class Printf3
4.  {
5.     public static native void fprint(PrintWriter out, String format, double x);
6.
7.     static
8.     {
9.        System.loadLibrary("Printf3");
10.    }
11. }
```

Example 11–16: Printf3.c

```
1.  #include "Printf3.h"
2.  #include <string.h>
3.  #include <stdlib.h>
4.  #include <float.h>
5.
6.  /**
7.     @param format a string containing a printf format specifier
8.     (such as "%8.2f"). Substrings "%%" are skipped.
9.     @return a pointer to the format specifier (skipping the '%')
10.    or NULL if there wasn't a unique format specifier
11. */
12. char* find_format(const char format[])
13. {
14.    char* p;
15.    char* q;
16.
17.    p = strchr(format, '%');
18.    while (p != NULL && *(p + 1) == '%') /* skip %% */
19.       p = strchr(p + 2, '%');
20.    if (p == NULL) return NULL;
21.    /* now check that % is unique */
22.    p++;
23.    q = strchr(p, '%');
24.    while (q != NULL && *(q + 1) == '%') /* skip %% */
25.       q = strchr(q + 2, '%');
```

```
26.    if (q != NULL) return NULL; /* % not unique */
27.    q = p + strspn(p, " -0+#"); /* skip past flags */
28.    q += strspn(q, "0123456789"); /* skip past field width */
29.    if (*q == '.') { q++; q += strspn(q, "0123456789"); }
30.        /* skip past precision */
31.    if (strchr("eEfFgG", *q) == NULL) return NULL;
32.        /* not a floating point format */
33.    return p;
34. }
35.
36. JNIEXPORT void JNICALL Java_Printf3_fprint(JNIEnv* env, jclass cl,
37.    jobject out, jstring format, jdouble x)
38. {
39.    const char* cformat;
40.    char* fmt;
41.    jstring str;
42.    jclass class_PrintWriter;
43.    jmethodID id_print;
44.
45.    cformat = (*env)->GetStringUTFChars(env, format, NULL);
46.    fmt = find_format(cformat);
47.    if (fmt == NULL)
48.        str = format;
49.    else
50.    {
51.        char* cstr;
52.        int width = atoi(fmt);
53.        if (width == 0) width = DBL_DIG + 10;
54.        cstr = (char*) malloc(strlen(cformat) + width);
55.        sprintf(cstr, cformat, x);
56.        str = (*env)->NewStringUTF(env, cstr);
57.        free(cstr);
58.    }
59.    (*env)->ReleaseStringUTFChars(env, format, cformat);
60.
61.    /* now call ps.print(str) */
62.
63.    /* get the class */
64.    class_PrintWriter = (*env)->GetObjectClass(env, out);
65.
66.    /* get the method ID */
67.    id_print = (*env)->GetMethodID(env, class_PrintWriter, "print", "(Ljava/lang/String;)V");
68.
69.    /* call the method */
70.    (*env)->CallVoidMethod(env, out, id_print, str);
71. }
```

Executing Java Methods from C Code

- jmethodID GetMethodID(JNIEnv *env, jclass cl, const char name[], const char sig[])
  returns the identifier of a method in a class.

Parameters:	env	The JNI interface pointer
	cl	The class object
	name	The method name
	sig	The encoded method signature

- *Xxx* CallXxxMethod(JNIEnv *env, jobject obj, jmethodID id, args)
- *Xxx* CallXxxMethodA(JNIEnv *env, jobject obj, jmethodID id, jvalue args[])
- *Xxx* CallXxxMethodV(JNIEnv *env, jobject obj, jmethodID id, va_list args)

  call a method. The return type *Xxx* is one of Object, Boolean, Byte, Char, Short, Int, Long, Float, or Double. The first function has a variable number of arguments—simply append the method parameters after the method ID. The second function receives the method arguments in an array of jvalue, where jvalue is a union defined as

  ```
  typedef union jvalue
  {
      jboolean z;
      jbyte b;
      jchar c;
      jshort s;
      jint i;
      jlong j;
      jfloat f;
      jdouble d;
      jobject l;
  } jvalue;
  ```

  The third function receives the method parameters in a va_list, as defined in the C header stdarg.h.

Parameters:	env	The JNI interface pointer
	obj	The implicit argument of the method
	id	The method identifier
	args	The method arguments

- *Xxx* CallNonvirtualXxxMethod(JNIEnv *env, jobject obj, jclass cl, jmethodID id, args)
- *Xxx* CallNonvirtualXxxMethodA(JNIEnv *env, jobject obj, jclass cl, jmethodID id, jvalue args[])
- *Xxx* CallNonvirtualXxxMethodV(JNIEnv *env, jobject obj, jclass cl, jmethodID id, va_list args)

  call a method, bypassing dynamic dispatch. The return type *Xxx* is one of Object, Boolean, Byte, Char, Short, Int, Long, Float, or Double. The first function has a variable number of arguments—simply append the method parameters after the method ID. The second function receives the method arguments in an array of jvalue. The third function receives the method parameters in a va_list, as defined in the C header stdarg.h.

Parameters:	env	The JNI interface pointer
	obj	The implicit argument of the method
	cl	The class whose implementation of the method is to be called
	id	The method identifier
	args	The method arguments

- jmethodID GetStaticMethodID(JNIEnv *env, jclass cl, const char name[], const char sig[])

  returns the identifier of a static method in a class.

Parameters:	env	The JNI interface pointer
	cl	The class object
	name	The method name
	sig	The encoded method signature

- *Xxx* CallStatic*Xxx*Method(JNIEnv *env, jclass cl, jmethodID id, args)
- *Xxx* CallStatic*Xxx*MethodA(JNIEnv *env, jclass cl, jmethodID id, jvalue args[])
- *Xxx* CallStatic*Xxx*MethodV(JNIEnv *env, jclass cl, jmethodID id, va_list args)

   call a static method. The return type *Xxx* is one of Object, Boolean, Byte, Char, Short, Int, Long, Float, or Double. The first function has a variable number of arguments—simply append the method parameters after the method ID. The second function receives the method arguments in an array of jvalue. The third function receives the method parameters in a va_list, as defined in the C header stdarg.h.

Parameters:	env	The JNI interface pointer
	cl	The class of the static method
	id	The method identifier
	args	The method arguments

- jobject NewObject(JNIEnv *env, jclass cl, jmethodID id, args)
- jobject NewObjectA(JNIEnv *env, jclass cl, jmethodID id, jvalue args[])
- jobject NewObjectV(JNIEnv *env, jclass cl, jmethodID id, va_list args)

   call a constructor. The method ID is obtained from GetMethodID with a method name of "<init>" and a return type of void. The first function has a variable number of arguments—simply append the method parameters after the method ID. The second function receives the method arguments in an array of jvalue. The third function receives the method parameters in a va_list, as defined in the C header stdarg.h.

Parameters:	env	The JNI interface pointer
	cl	The class to be instantiated
	id	The constructor method identifier
	args	The constructor arguments

Accessing Array Elements

All array types of the Java programming language have corresponding C types, as shown in Table 11–2.

Table 11–2: Correspondence Between Java Array Types and C Types

Java Type	C Type
boolean[]	jbooleanArray
byte[]	jbyteArray
char[]	jcharArray
int[]	jintArray
short[]	jshortArray
long[]	jlongArray
float[]	jfloatArray
double[]	jdoubleArray
Object[]	jobjectArray

The type jarray denotes a generic array.

 C++ NOTE: In C, all these array types are actually type synonyms of jobject. In C++, however, they are arranged in the inheritance hierarchy shown in Figure 11–2.

854

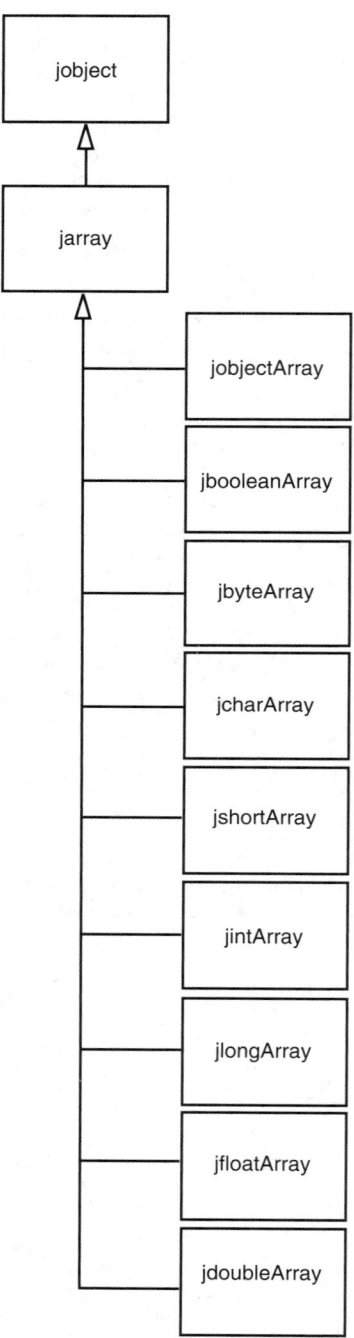

Figure 11–2: Inheritance hierarchy of array types

The GetArrayLength function returns the length of an array.

```
jarray array = . . .;
jsize length = (*env)->GetArrayLength(env, array);
```

How you access elements in the array depends on whether the array stores objects or a primitive type (bool, char, or a numeric type). You access elements in an object array with the GetObjectArrayElement and SetObjectArrayElement methods.

```
jobjectArray array = . . .;
int i, j;
jobject x = (*env)->GetObjectArrayElement(env, array, i);
(*env)->SetObjectArrayElement(env, array, j, x);
```

While simple, this approach is also clearly inefficient; you want to be able to access array elements directly, especially when doing vector and matrix computations.

The GetXxxArrayElements function returns a C pointer to the starting element of the array. As with ordinary strings, you must remember to call the corresponding ReleaseXxxArrayElements function to tell the virtual machine when you no longer need that pointer. Here, the type Xxx must be a primitive type, that is, not Object. You can then read and write the array elements directly. However, since the pointer *may point to a copy*, any changes that you make are guaranteed to be reflected in the original array only when you call the corresponding ReleaseXxxArrayElements function!

NOTE: You can find out if an array is a copy by passing a pointer to a jboolean variable as the third parameter to a GetXxxArrayElements method. The variable is filled with JNI_TRUE if the array is a copy. If you aren't interested in that information, just pass a NULL pointer.

Here is a code sample that multiplies all elements in an array of double values by a constant. We obtain a C pointer a into the Java array and then access individual elements as a[i].

```
jdoubleArray array_a = . . .;
double scaleFactor = . . .;
double* a = (*env)->GetDoubleArrayElements(env, array_a, NULL);
for (i = 0; i < (*env)->GetArrayLength(env, array_a); i++)
    a[i] = a[i] * scaleFactor;
(*env)->ReleaseDoubleArrayElements(env, array_a, a, 0);
```

Whether the virtual machine actually copies the array depends on how it allocates arrays and does its garbage collection. Some "copying" garbage collectors routinely move objects around and update object references. That strategy is not compatible with "pinning" an array to a particular location, because the collector cannot update the pointer values in native code.

NOTE: In the Sun JVM implementation, boolean arrays are represented as packed arrays of 32-bit words. The GetBooleanArrayElements method copies them into unpacked arrays of jboolean values.

To access just a few elements of a large array, use the GetXxxArrayRegion and SetXxxArrayRegion methods that copy a range of elements from the Java array into a C array and back.

You can create new Java arrays in native methods with the NewXxxArray function. To create a new array of objects, you specify the length, the type of the array elements, and an initial element for all entries (typically, NULL). Here is an example.

```
jclass class_Employee = (*env)->FindClass(env, "Employee");
jobjectArray array_e = (*env)->NewObjectArray(env, 100, class_Employee, NULL);
```

Arrays of primitive types are simpler. You just supply the length of the array.

```
jdoubleArray array_d = (*env)->NewDoubleArray(env, 100);
```

The array is then filled with zeroes.

> **NOTE:** JDK 1.4 adds three methods to the JNI API:
>
> ```
> jobject NewDirectByteBuffer(JNIEnv* env, void* address, jlong capacity)
> void* GetDirectBufferAddress(JNIEnv* env, jobject buf)
> jlong GetDirectBufferCapacity(JNIEnv* env, jobject buf)
> ```
>
> Direct buffers are used in the java.nio package to support more efficient input/output operations and to minimize the copying of data between native and Java arrays.

Manipulating Java Arrays in C Code

- jsize GetArrayLength(JNIEnv *env, jarray array)
  returns the number of elements in the array.

  Parameters: env   The JNI interface pointer

            array   The array object

- jobject GetObjectArrayElement(JNIEnv *env, jobjectArray array, jsize index)
  returns the value of an array element.

  Parameters: env   The JNI interface pointer

            array   The array object

            index   The array offset

- void SetObjectArrayElement(JNIEnv *env, jobjectArray array, jsize index, jobject value)
  sets an array element to a new value.

  Parameters: env   The JNI interface pointer

            array   The array object

            index   The array offset

            value   The new value

- *Xxx** Get*Xxx*ArrayElements(JNIEnv *env, jarray array, jboolean* isCopy)
  yields a C pointer to the elements of a Java array. The field type *Xxx* is one of Boolean, Byte, Char, Short, Int, Long, Float, or Double. The pointer must be passed to Release*Xxx*ArrayElements when it is no longer needed.

  Parameters: env   The JNI interface pointer

            array   The array object

            isCopy   Is either NULL or points to a jboolean that is filled with JNI_TRUE if a copy is made; with JNI_FALSE otherwise

- void Release*Xxx*ArrayElements(JNIEnv *env, jarray array, *Xxx* elems[], jint mode)
  notifies the virtual machine that a pointer obtained by Get*Xxx*ArrayElements is no longer needed.

  Parameters: env   The JNI interface pointer

            array   The array object

elems	The pointer to the array elements that is no longer needed
mode	0 = free the elems buffer after updating the array elements
	JNI_COMMIT = do not free the elems buffer after updating the array elements
	JNI_ABORT = free the elems buffer without updating the array elements

- void Get*Xxx*ArrayRegion(JNIEnv *env, jarray array, jint start, jint length, *Xxx* elems[]) copies elements from a Java array to a C array. The field type *Xxx* is one of Boolean, Byte, Char, Short, Int, Long, Float, or Double.

Parameters:	env	The JNI interface pointer
	array	The array object
	start	The starting index
	length	The number of elements to copy
	elems	The C array that holds the elements

- void Set*Xxx*ArrayRegion(JNIEnv *env, jarray array, jint start, jint length, *Xxx* elems[]) copies elements from a C array to a Java array. The field type *Xxx* is one of Boolean, Byte, Char, Short, Int, Long, Float, or Double.

Parameters:	env	The JNI interface pointer
	array	The array object
	start	The starting index
	length	The number of elements to copy
	elems	The C array that holds the elements

Handling Errors

Native methods are a significant security risk to programs in the Java programming language. The C runtime system has no protection against array bounds errors, indirection through bad pointers, and so on. It is particularly important that programmers of native methods handle all error conditions to preserve the integrity of the Java platform. In particular, when your native method diagnoses a problem that it cannot handle, then it should report this problem to the Java virtual machine. Then, you would naturally throw an exception in this situation. However, C has no exceptions. Instead, you must call the Throw or ThrowNew function to create a new exception object. When the native method exits, the Java virtual machine throws that exception.

To use the Throw function, call NewObject to create an object of a subtype of Throwable. For example, here we allocate an EOFException object and throw it.

```
jclass class_EOFException = (*env)->FindClass(env, "java/io/EOFException");
jmethodID id_EOFException = (*env)->GetMethodID(env, class_EOFException, "<init>", "()V");
   /* ID of default constructor */
jthrowable obj_exc = (*env)->NewObject(env, class_EOFException, id_EOFException);
(*env)->Throw(env, obj_exc);
```

It is usually more convenient to call ThrowNew, which constructs an exception object, given a class and a "modified UTF-8" byte sequence.

```
(*env)->ThrowNew(env, (*env)->FindClass(env, "java/io/EOFException"), "Unexpected end of file");
```

Both Throw and ThrowNew merely *post* the exception; they do not interrupt the control flow of the native method. Only when the method returns does the Java virtual machine throw the exception. Therefore, every call to Throw and ThrowNew should always immediately be followed by a return statement.

 C++ NOTE: If you implement native methods in C++, you cannot throw a Java exception object in your C++ code. In a C++ binding, it would be possible to implement a translation between exceptions in the C++ and Java programming languages—however, this is not currently implemented. Use Throw or ThrowNew to throw a Java exception in a native C++ method, and make sure that your native methods throw no C++ exceptions.

Normally, native code need not be concerned with catching Java exceptions. However, when a native method calls a Java method, that method might throw an exception. Moreover, a number of the JNI functions throw exceptions as well. For example, SetObjectArrayElement throws an ArrayIndexOutOfBoundsException if the index is out of bounds, and an ArrayStoreException if the class of the stored object is not a subclass of the element class of the array. In situations like these, a native method should call the ExceptionOccurred method to determine whether an exception has been thrown. The call

```
jthrowable obj_exc = (*env)->ExceptionOccurred(env);
```

returns NULL if no exception is pending, or it returns a reference to the current exception object. If you just want to check whether an exception has been thrown, without obtaining a reference to the exception object, use

```
jboolean occurred = (*env)->ExceptionCheck(env);
```

Normally, a native method should simply return when an exception has occurred so that the virtual machine can propagate it to the Java code. However, a native method *may* analyze the exception object to determine if it can handle the exception. If it can, then the function

```
(*env)->ExceptionClear(env);
```

must be called to turn off the exception.

In our next example, we implement the fprint native method with the paranoia that is appropriate for a native method. Here are the exceptions that we throw:

- A NullPointerException if the format string is NULL
- An IllegalArgumentException if the format string doesn't contain a % specifier that is appropriate for printing a double
- An OutOfMemoryError if the call to malloc fails

Finally, to demonstrate how to check for an exception when calling a Java method from a native method, we send the string to the stream, a character at a time, and call ExceptionOccurred after each call. Example 11–17 shows the code for the native method, and Example 11–18 contains the definition of the class containing the native method. Notice that the native method does not immediately terminate when an exception occurs in the call to PrintWriter.print—it first frees the cstr buffer. When the native method returns, the virtual machine again raises the exception. The test program in Example 11–19 demonstrates how the native method throws an exception when the formatting string is not valid.

Example 11–17: Printf4.c

```
1. #include "Printf4.h"
2. #include <string.h>
3. #include <stdlib.h>
4. #include <float.h>
5.
```

```
6.  /**
7.      @param format a string containing a printf format specifier
8.      (such as "%8.2f"). Substrings "%%" are skipped.
9.      @return a pointer to the format specifier (skipping the '%')
10.     or NULL if there wasn't a unique format specifier
11.  */
12.  char* find_format(const char format[])
13.  {
14.      char* p;
15.      char* q;
16.
17.      p = strchr(format, '%');
18.      while (p != NULL && *(p + 1) == '%') /* skip %% */
19.         p = strchr(p + 2, '%');
20.      if (p == NULL) return NULL;
21.      /* now check that % is unique */
22.      p++;
23.      q = strchr(p, '%');
24.      while (q != NULL && *(q + 1) == '%') /* skip %% */
25.         q = strchr(q + 2, '%');
26.      if (q != NULL) return NULL; /* % not unique */
27.      q = p + strspn(p, " -0+#"); /* skip past flags */
28.      q += strspn(q, "0123456789"); /* skip past field width */
29.      if (*q == '.') { q++; q += strspn(q, "0123456789"); }
30.         /* skip past precision */
31.      if (strchr("eEfFgG", *q) == NULL) return NULL;
32.         /* not a floating point format */
33.      return p;
34.  }
35.
36.  JNIEXPORT void JNICALL Java_Printf4_fprint(JNIEnv* env, jclass cl,
37.      jobject out, jstring format, jdouble x)
38.  {
39.      const char* cformat;
40.      char* fmt;
41.      jclass class_PrintWriter;
42.      jmethodID id_print;
43.      char* cstr;
44.      int width;
45.      int i;
46.
47.      if (format == NULL)
48.      {
49.         (*env)->ThrowNew(env,
50.            (*env)->FindClass(env,
51.            "java/lang/NullPointerException"),
52.            "Printf4.fprint: format is null");
53.         return;
54.      }
55.
56.      cformat = (*env)->GetStringUTFChars(env, format, NULL);
57.      fmt = find_format(cformat);
58.
59.      if (fmt == NULL)
60.      {
61.         (*env)->ThrowNew(env,
```

```
62.        (*env)->FindClass(env,
63.          "java/lang/IllegalArgumentException"),
64.          "Printf4.fprint: format is invalid");
65.      return;
66.    }
67.
68.    width = atoi(fmt);
69.    if (width == 0) width = DBL_DIG + 10;
70.    cstr = (char*)malloc(strlen(cformat) + width);
71.
72.    if (cstr == NULL)
73.    {
74.      (*env)->ThrowNew(env,
75.        (*env)->FindClass(env, "java/lang/OutOfMemoryError"),
76.        "Printf4.fprint: malloc failed");
77.      return;
78.    }
79.
80.    sprintf(cstr, cformat, x);
81.
82.    (*env)->ReleaseStringUTFChars(env, format, cformat);
83.
84.    /* now call ps.print(str) */
85.
86.    /* get the class */
87.    class_PrintWriter = (*env)->GetObjectClass(env, out);
88.
89.    /* get the method ID */
90.    id_print = (*env)->GetMethodID(env, class_PrintWriter, "print", "(C)V");
91.
92.    /* call the method */
93.    for (i = 0; cstr[i] != 0 && !(*env)->ExceptionOccurred(env); i++)
94.      (*env)->CallVoidMethod(env, out, id_print, cstr[i]);
95.
96.    free(cstr);
97. }
```

Example 11–18: Printf4.java

```
1. import java.io.*;
2.
3. class Printf4
4. {
5.    public static native void fprint(PrintWriter ps, String format, double x);
6.
7.    static
8.    {
9.      System.loadLibrary("Printf4");
10.   }
11. }
```

Example 11–19: Printf4Test.java

```
1. import java.io.*;
2.
3. class Printf4Test
4. {
5.    public static void main(String[] args)
```

```
6.   {
7.       double price = 44.95;
8.       double tax = 7.75;
9.       double amountDue = price * (1 + tax / 100);
10.      PrintWriter out = new PrintWriter(System.out);
11.      /* This call will throw an exception--note the %% */
12.      Printf4.fprint(out, "Amount due = %%8.2f\n", amountDue);
13.      out.flush();
14.  }
15. }
```

Error Handling in C Code

- `jint Throw(JNIEnv *env, jthrowable obj)`
  prepares an exception to be thrown upon exiting from the native code. Returns 0 on success, a negative value on failure.

Parameters:	env	The JNI interface pointer
	obj	The exception object to throw

- `jint ThrowNew(JNIEnv *env, jclass clazz, const char msg[])`
  prepares an exception to be thrown upon exiting from the native code. Returns 0 on success, a negative value on failure.

Parameters:	env	The JNI interface pointer
	cl	The class of the exception object to throw
	msg	A "modified UTF-8" byte sequence denoting the String construction argument of the exception object

- `jthrowable ExceptionOccurred(JNIEnv *env)`
  returns the exception object if an exception is pending, or NULL otherwise.

Parameters:	env	The JNI interface pointer

- `jboolean ExceptionCheck(JNIEnv *env)`
  returns true if an exception is pending.

Parameters:	env	The JNI interface pointer

- `void ExceptionClear(JNIEnv *env)`
  clears any pending exceptions.

Parameters:	env	The JNI interface pointer

Using the Invocation API

Up to now, we have considered programs in the Java programming language that made a few C calls, presumably because C was faster or allowed access to functionality that was inaccessible from the Java platform. Suppose you are in the opposite situation. You have a C or C++ program and would like to make a few calls to Java code, perhaps because the Java code is easier to program. Of course, you know how to call the Java methods. But you still need to add the Java virtual machine to your program so that the Java code can be interpreted. The so-called *invocation API* enables you to embed the Java virtual machine into a C or C++ program. Here is the minimal code that you need to initialize a virtual machine.

```
JavaVMOption options[1];
JavaVMInitArgs vm_args;
JavaVM *jvm;
```

```
JNIEnv *env;

options[0].optionString = "-Djava.class.path=.";

memset(&vm_args, 0, sizeof(vm_args));
vm_args.version = JNI_VERSION_1_2;
vm_args.nOptions = 1;
vm_args.options = options;

JNI_CreateJavaVM(&jvm, (void**) &env, &vm_args);
```

The call to `JNI_CreateJavaVM` creates the virtual machine and fills in a pointer, `jvm`, to the virtual machine and a pointer, `env`, to the execution environment.

You can supply any number of options to the virtual machine. Simply increase the size of the `options` array and the value of `vm_args.nOptions`. For example,

```
options[i].optionString = "-Djava.compiler=NONE";
```

deactivates the just-in-time compiler.

 TIP: When you run into trouble and your program crashes, refuses to initialize the JVM, or can't load your classes, then turn on the JNI debugging mode. Set an option to

```
options[i].optionString = "-verbose:jni";
```

You will see a flurry of messages that indicate the progress in initializing the JVM. If you don't see your classes loaded, check both your path and your class path settings.

Once you have set up the virtual machine, you can call Java methods in the way described in the preceding sections: Simply use the `env` pointer in the usual way. You need the `jvm` pointer only to call other functions in the invocation API. Currently, there are only four such functions. The most important one is the function to terminate the virtual machine:

```
(*jvm)->DestroyJavaVM(jvm);
```

The C program in Example 11–20 sets up a virtual machine and then calls the `main` method of the `Welcome` class, which was discussed in Volume 1, Chapter 2. (Make sure to compile the `Welcome.java` file before starting the invocation test program.)

Example 11–20: InvocationTest.c

```
 1. #include <jni.h>
 2. #include <stdlib.h>
 3.
 4. int main()
 5. {
 6.     JavaVMOption options[2];
 7.     JavaVMInitArgs vm_args;
 8.     JavaVM *jvm;
 9.     JNIEnv *env;
10.     long status;
11.
12.     jclass class_Welcome;
13.     jclass class_String;
14.     jobjectArray args;
15.     jmethodID id_main;
16.
17.     options[0].optionString = "-Djava.class.path=.";
```

```
18.
19.    memset(&vm_args, 0, sizeof(vm_args));
20.    vm_args.version = JNI_VERSION_1_2;
21.    vm_args.nOptions = 1;
22.    vm_args.options = options;
23.
24.    status = JNI_CreateJavaVM(&jvm, (void**) &env, &vm_args);
25.    if (status == JNI_ERR)
26.    {
27.       printf("Error creating VM\n");
28.       return 1;
29.    }
30.
31.    class_Welcome = (*env)->FindClass(env, "Welcome");
32.    id_main = (*env)->GetStaticMethodID(env, class_Welcome, "main", "([Ljava/lang/String;)V");
33.
34.    class_String = (*env)->FindClass(env, "java/lang/String");
35.    args = (*env)->NewObjectArray(env, 0, class_String, NULL);
36.    (*env)->CallStaticVoidMethod(env, class_Welcome, id_main, args);
37.
38.    (*jvm)->DestroyJavaVM(jvm);
39.
40.    return 0;
41. }
```

To compile this program under Linux, use

```
gcc -I jdk/include -I jdk/include/linux -o InvocationTest
   -L jdk/jre/lib/i386/client -ljvm InvocationTest.c
```

Under Solaris, use

```
cc -I jdk/include -I jdk/include/solaris -o InvocationTest
   -L jdk/jre/lib/sparc -ljvm InvocationTest.c
```

When compiling in Windows with the Microsoft C compiler, use the command line

```
cl -I jdk\include -I jdk\include\win32 InvocationTest.c jdk\lib\jvm.lib
```

With Cygwin, you have to work a little harder. First make a file, jvm.def, that contains the statement

```
EXPORTS
   JNI_CreateJavaVM@12
```

Run the command

```
dlltool -k --input-def jvm.def --dll jdk\\jre\\bin\\client\\jvm.dll --output-lib jvm.a
```

 CAUTION: If you issue this command from the bash shell, supply *four* backslashes \\\\ for each file separator.

Then compile with

```
gcc -I jdk\include -I jdk\include\win32 -D__int64="long long" -o InvocationTest
   InvocationTest.c jvm.a
```

Before you run the program under Linux/UNIX, make sure that the LD_LIBRARY_PATH contains the directories for the shared libraries. For example, if you use the bash shell on Linux, issue the following command:

```
export LD_LIBRARY_PATH=jdk/jre/lib/i386/client:$LD_LIBRARY_PATH
```

On Windows, make sure the directory

> *jdk*\jre\bin\client

is on the PATH.

 CAUTION: The exact locations of the various library files varies somewhat from one release of the JDK to the next. You may need to search for files called libjvm.so, jvm.dll, or (with older JDK versions) libjava.so, in the jdk/bin, jdk/lib, and jdk/jre/lib directories and adjust the instructions accordingly.

 TIP: If you develop an application that invokes the virtual machine by using a Windows launcher, then you may not trust your users to set the library path. You can help your users and load the shared library or DLL manually. The javac and java programs do just that. For sample code, see the file launcher/java_md.c in the src.jar file that is a part of the JDK.

 Invocation API Functions

- jint JNI_CreateJavaVM(JavaVM** p_jvm, void** p_env, JavaVMInitArgs* vm_args)
  initializes the Java virtual machine. The function returns 0 if successful, JNI_ERR on failure.

Parameters:	p_jvm	Filled with a pointer to the invocation API function table
	p_env	Filled with a pointer to the JNI function table
	vm_args	The virtual machine arguments

- jint DestroyJavaVM(JavaVM* jvm)
  destroys the virtual machine. Returns 0 on success, a negative number on failure. This function must be called through a virtual machine pointer, i.e., (*jvm)->DestroyJavaVM(jvm).

Parameters:	jvm	The virtual machine pointer

A Complete Example: Accessing the Windows Registry

In this section, we describe a full, working example that covers everything we discussed in this chapter: using native methods with strings, arrays, objects, constructor calls, and error handling. We show you how to put a Java platform wrapper around a subset of the ordinary C-based API used to work with the Windows registry. Of course, being a Windows-specific feature, a program using the Windows registry is inherently nonportable. For that reason, the standard Java library has no support for the registry, and it makes sense to use native methods to gain access to it.

Overview of the Windows Registry

The Windows registry is a data depository that holds configuration information for the Windows operating system and application programs. It provides a single point for administration and backup of system and application preferences.

On the downside, the registry is also a single point of failure—if you mess up the registry, your computer may malfunction or even fail to boot! The sample program that we present in this section is safe, but if you plan to make any modifications to it, you should learn how to back up the registry before proceeding.

We don't suggest that you use the registry to store configuration parameters for your Java programs. The Java preferences API is a better solution—see Volume 1, Chapter 10 for more information. We simply use the registry to demonstrate how to wrap a nontrivial native API into a Java class.

The principal tool for inspecting the registry is the *registry editor*. Because of the potential for error by naïve but enthusiastic users, there is no icon for launching the registry editor. Instead, start a DOS shell (or open the Start -> Run dialog box) and type regedit. Figure 11–3 shows the registry editor in action.

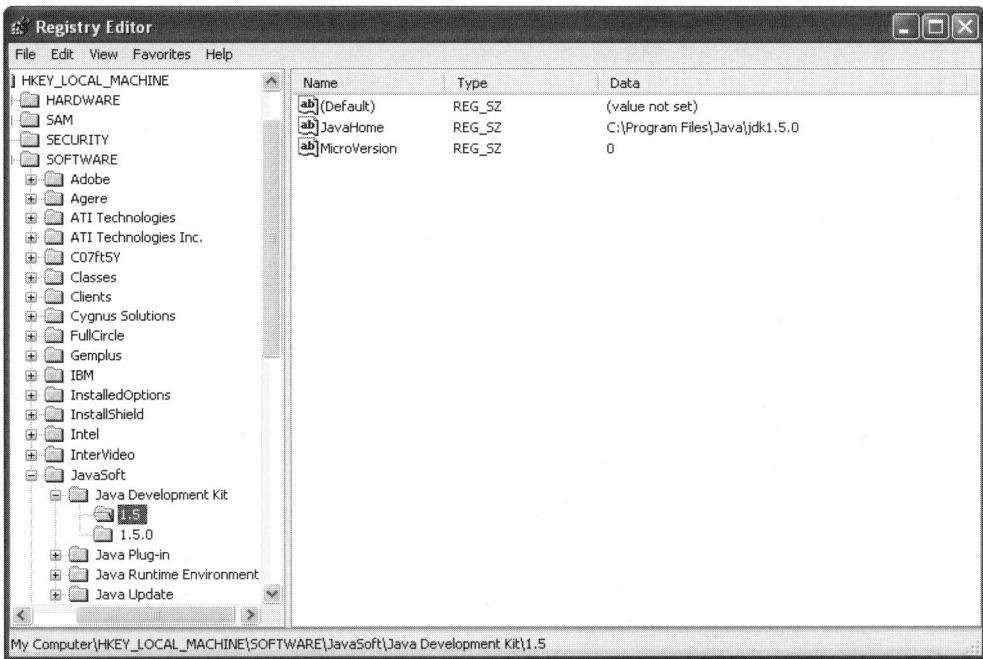

Figure 11–3: The registry editor

The left side shows the keys, which are arranged in a tree structure. Note that each key starts with one of the HKEY nodes like

```
HKEY_CLASSES_ROOT
HKEY_CURRENT_USER
HKEY_LOCAL_MACHINE
```

. . .

The right side shows the name/value pairs that are associated with a particular key. For example, the key

```
HKEY_LOCAL_MACHINE\SOFTWARE\JavaSoft\Java Development Kit\1.5
```

has two name/value pairs, such as,

```
JavaHome="c:\jdk1.5.0"
MicroVersion="0"
```

In this case, the values are strings. The values can also be integers or arrays of bytes.

A Java Platform Interface for Accessing the Registry

We implement a simple interface to access the registry from Java code, and then implement this interface with native code. Our interface allows only a few registry operations; to keep the code size down, we omitted other important operations such as adding, deleting, and enumerating keys. (It would be easy to add the remaining registry API functions.)

Even with the limited subset that we supply, you can

- Enumerate all names stored in a key;
- Read the value stored with a name;
- Set the value stored with a name.

Here is the Java platform class that encapsulates a registry key.

```java
public class Win32RegKey
{
    public Win32RegKey(int theRoot, String thePath) { . . . }
    public Enumeration names() { . . . }
    public native Object getValue(String name);
    public native void setValue(String name, Object value);

    public static final int HKEY_CLASSES_ROOT = 0x80000000;
    public static final int HKEY_CURRENT_USER = 0x80000001;
    public static final int HKEY_LOCAL_MACHINE = 0x80000002;
    . . .
}
```

The names method returns an enumeration that holds all the names stored with the key. You can get at them with the familiar hasMoreElements/nextElement methods. The getValue method returns an object that is either a string, an Integer object, or a byte array. The value parameter of the setValue method must also be of one of these three types.

Here is a simple function that lists the strings that are stored with the key

```
HKEY_LOCAL_MACHINE\SOFTWARE\JavaSoft\Java Development Kit\1.5
```

(You should change the key to the version of the JDK that is installed on your system.)

```java
public static void main(String[] args)
{
    Win32RegKey key = new Win32RegKey(Win32RegKey.HKEY_LOCAL_MACHINE,
        "SOFTWARE\JavaSoft\Java Development Kit\1.5");

    Enumeration<String> e = key.names();

    while (e.hasMoreElements())
    {
        String name = e.nextElement();
        System.out.println(name + "=" + key.getValue(name));
    }
}
```

A typical output of this program is as follows:

```
JavaHome=c:\jdk1.5.0
MicroVersion=0
```

Implementation of Registry Access Functions as Native Methods

We need to implement three actions:

- Get the value of a key;

- Set the value of a key;
- Iterate through the names of a key.

Fortunately, you have seen essentially all the tools that are required, such as the conversion between Java strings and arrays and those of C. And you saw how to raise a Java exception in case something goes wrong.

Two issues make these native methods more complex than the preceding examples. The getValue and setValue methods deal with the type Object, which can be one of String, Integer, or byte[]. The enumeration object stores the state between successive calls to hasMoreElements and nextElement.

Let us first look at the getValue method. The code (which is shown in Example 11–22) goes through the following steps.

1. Open the registry key. To read their values, the registry API requires that keys be open.
2. Query the type and size of the value that is associated with the name.
3. Read the data into a buffer.
4. If the type is REG_SZ (a string), then call NewStringUTF to create a new string with the value data.
5. If the type is REG_DWORD (a 32-bit integer), then invoke the Integer constructor.
6. If the type is REG_BINARY, then call NewByteArray to create a new byte array and call SetByteArrayRegion to copy the value data into the byte array.
7. If the type is none of these or if an error occurred when an API function was called, throw an exception and carefully release all resources that had been acquired up to that point.
8. Close the key and return the object (String, Integer, or byte[]) that had been created.

As you can see, this example illustrates quite nicely how to generate Java objects of different types.

In this native method, coping with the generic return type is not difficult. The jstring, jobject, or jarray reference is simply returned as a jobject. However, the setValue method receives a reference to an Object and must determine the Object's exact type in order to save the Object as a string, integer, or byte array. We can make this determination by querying the class of the value object, finding the class references for java.lang.String, java.lang.Integer, and byte[], and comparing them with the IsAssignableFrom function.

If class1 and class2 are two class references, then the call

```
(*env)->IsAssignableFrom(env, class1, class2)
```

returns JNI_TRUE when class1 and class2 are the same class or when class1 is a subclass of class2. In either case, references to objects of class1 can be cast to class2. For example, when

```
(*env)->IsAssignableFrom(env, (*env)->GetObjectClass(env, value), (*env)->FindClass(env, "[B"))
```

is true, then we know that value is a byte array.

Here is an overview of the code of the setValue method.

1. Open the registry key for writing.
2. Find the type of the value to write.
3. If the type is String, call GetStringUTFChars to get a pointer to the characters. Also, obtain the string length.
4. If the type is Integer, call the intValue method to get the integer stored in the wrapper object.

5. If the type is byte[], call GetByteArrayElements to get a pointer to the bytes. Also, obtain the string length.

6. Pass the data and length to the registry.

7. Close the key. If the type is String or byte[], then also release the pointer to the characters or bytes.

Finally, let us turn to the native methods that enumerate keys. These are methods of the Win32RegKeyNameEnumeration class (see Example 11–21). When the enumeration process starts, we must open the key. For the duration of the enumeration, we must retain the key handle. That is, the key handle must be stored with the enumeration object. The key handle is of type DWORD, a 32-bit quantity, and, hence, can be stored in a Java integer. It is stored in the hkey field of the enumeration class. When the enumeration starts, the field is initialized with SetIntField. Subsequent calls read the value with GetIntField.

In this example, we store three other data items with the enumeration object. When the enumeration first starts, we can query the registry for the count of name/value pairs and the length of the longest name, which we need so we can allocate C character arrays to hold the names. These values are stored in the count and maxsize fields of the enumeration object. Finally, the index field is initialized with –1 to indicate the start of the enumeration, is set to 0 once the other instance fields are initialized, and is incremented after every enumeration step.

Let's walk through the native methods that support the enumeration. The hasMoreElements method is simple.

1. Retrieve the index and count fields.

2. If the index is -1, call the startNameEnumeration function, which opens the key, queries the count and maximum length, and initializes the hkey, count, maxsize, and index fields.

3. Return JNI_TRUE if index is less than count; JNI_FALSE otherwise.

The nextElement method needs to work a little harder.

1. Retrieve the index and count fields.

2. If the index is -1, call the startNameEnumeration function, which opens the key, queries the count and maximum length, and initializes the hkey, count, maxsize, and index fields.

3. If index equals count, throw a NoSuchElementException.

4. Read the next name from the registry.

5. Increment index.

6. If index equals count, close the key.

Before compiling, remember to run javah on both Win32RegKey and Win32RegKeyNameEnumeration. The complete command line for Microsoft C++ is

```
cl -I jdk\include -I jdk\include\win32 -LD Win32RegKey.c advapi32.lib -FeWin32RegKey.dll
```

With Cygwin, use

```
gcc --mno-cygwin -D __int64="long long" -I jdk\include -I jdk\include\win32
    -I c:\cygwin\usr\include\w32api -shared -Wl,--add-stdcall-alias -o Win32RegKey.dll Win32RegKey.c
```

Example 11–23 shows a program to test our new registry functions. We add three name/value pairs, a string, an integer, and a byte array to the key.

```
HKEY_LOCAL_MACHINE\SOFTWARE\JavaSoft\Java Development Kit\1.5
```

You should edit the version number to match your JDK installation (or simply use some other existing registry key).

We then enumerate all names of that key and retrieve their values. The program will print

```
JavaHome=c:\jdk1.5.0
MicroVersion=0
Default user=Harry Hacker
Lucky number=13
Small primes=2 3 5 7 11 13
```

Although adding these name/value pairs to that key probably does no harm, you may want to use the registry editor to remove them after running this program.

Example 11–21: Win32RegKey.java

```java
 1. import java.util.*;
 2.
 3. /**
 4.    A Win32RegKey object can be used to get and set values of
 5.    a registry key in the Windows registry.
 6. */
 7. public class Win32RegKey
 8. {
 9.    /**
10.       Construct a registry key object.
11.       @param theRoot one of HKEY_CLASSES_ROOT, HKEY_CURRENT_USER,
12.       HKEY_LOCAL_MACHINE, HKEY_USERS, HKEY_CURRENT_CONFIG,
13.       HKEY_DYN_DATA
14.       @param thePath the registry key path
15.    */
16.    public Win32RegKey(int theRoot, String thePath)
17.    {
18.       root = theRoot;
19.       path = thePath;
20.    }
21.
22.    /**
23.       Enumerates all names of registry entries under the path
24.       that this object describes.
25.       @return an enumeration listing all entry names
26.    */
27.    public Enumeration<String> names()
28.    {
29.       return new Win32RegKeyNameEnumeration(root, path);
30.    }
31.
32.    /**
33.       Gets the value of a registry entry.
34.       @param name the entry name
35.       @return the associated value
36.    */
37.    public native Object getValue(String name);
38.
39.    /**
40.       Sets the value of a registry entry.
41.       @param name the entry name
42.       @param value the new value
43.    */
44.    public native void setValue(String name, Object value);
45.
46.    public static final int HKEY_CLASSES_ROOT = 0x80000000;
```

```
47.    public static final int HKEY_CURRENT_USER = 0x80000001;
48.    public static final int HKEY_LOCAL_MACHINE = 0x80000002;
49.    public static final int HKEY_USERS = 0x80000003;
50.    public static final int HKEY_CURRENT_CONFIG = 0x80000005;
51.    public static final int HKEY_DYN_DATA = 0x80000006;
52.
53.    private int root;
54.    private String path;
55.
56.    static
57.    {
58.       System.loadLibrary("Win32RegKey");
59.    }
60. }
61.
62. class Win32RegKeyNameEnumeration implements Enumeration<String>
63. {
64.    Win32RegKeyNameEnumeration(int theRoot, String thePath)
65.    {
66.       root = theRoot;
67.       path = thePath;
68.    }
69.
70.    public native String nextElement();
71.    public native boolean hasMoreElements();
72.
73.    private int root;
74.    private String path;
75.    private int index = -1;
76.    private int hkey = 0;
77.    private int maxsize;
78.    private int count;
79. }
80.
81. class Win32RegKeyException extends RuntimeException
82. {
83.    public Win32RegKeyException() {}
84.    public Win32RegKeyException(String why)
85.    {
86.       super(why);
87.    }
88. }
```

Example 11–22: Win32RegKey.c

```
1. #include "Win32RegKey.h"
2. #include "Win32RegKeyNameEnumeration.h"
3. #include <string.h>
4. #include <stdlib.h>
5. #include <windows.h>
6.
7. JNIEXPORT jobject JNICALL Java_Win32RegKey_getValue(JNIEnv* env, jobject this_obj, jobject name)
8. {
9.    const char* cname;
10.   jstring path;
11.   const char* cpath;
12.   HKEY hkey;
```

```
13.   DWORD type;
14.   DWORD size;
15.   jclass this_class;
16.   jfieldID id_root;
17.   jfieldID id_path;
18.   HKEY root;
19.   jobject ret;
20.   char* cret;
21.
22.   /* get the class */
23.   this_class = (*env)->GetObjectClass(env, this_obj);
24.
25.   /* get the field IDs */
26.   id_root = (*env)->GetFieldID(env, this_class, "root", "I");
27.   id_path = (*env)->GetFieldID(env, this_class, "path", "Ljava/lang/String;");
28.
29.   /* get the fields */
30.   root = (HKEY) (*env)->GetIntField(env, this_obj, id_root);
31.   path = (jstring)(*env)->GetObjectField(env, this_obj, id_path);
32.   cpath = (*env)->GetStringUTFChars(env, path, NULL);
33.
34.   /* open the registry key */
35.   if (RegOpenKeyEx(root, cpath, 0, KEY_READ, &hkey) != ERROR_SUCCESS)
36.   {
37.      (*env)->ThrowNew(env, (*env)->FindClass(env, "Win32RegKeyException"),
38.         "Open key failed");
39.      (*env)->ReleaseStringUTFChars(env, path, cpath);
40.      return NULL;
41.   }
42.
43.   (*env)->ReleaseStringUTFChars(env, path, cpath);
44.   cname = (*env)->GetStringUTFChars(env, name, NULL);
45.
46.   /* find the type and size of the value */
47.   if (RegQueryValueEx(hkey, cname, NULL, &type, NULL, &size) != ERROR_SUCCESS)
48.   {
49.      (*env)->ThrowNew(env, (*env)->FindClass(env, "Win32RegKeyException"),
50.         "Query value key failed");
51.      RegCloseKey(hkey);
52.      (*env)->ReleaseStringUTFChars(env, name, cname);
53.      return NULL;
54.   }
55.
56.   /* get memory to hold the value */
57.   cret = (char*)malloc(size);
58.
59.   /* read the value */
60.   if (RegQueryValueEx(hkey, cname, NULL, &type, cret, &size) != ERROR_SUCCESS)
61.   {
62.      (*env)->ThrowNew(env, (*env)->FindClass(env, "Win32RegKeyException"),
63.         "Query value key failed");
64.      free(cret);
65.      RegCloseKey(hkey);
66.      (*env)->ReleaseStringUTFChars(env, name, cname);
67.      return NULL;
68.   }
```

```
69.
70.    /* depending on the type, store the value in a string,
71.       integer or byte array */
72.    if (type == REG_SZ)
73.    {
74.       ret = (*env)->NewStringUTF(env, cret);
75.    }
76.    else if (type == REG_DWORD)
77.    {
78.       jclass class_Integer = (*env)->FindClass(env, "java/lang/Integer");
79.       /* get the method ID of the constructor */
80.       jmethodID id_Integer = (*env)->GetMethodID(env, class_Integer, "<init>", "(I)V");
81.       int value = *(int*) cret;
82.       /* invoke the constructor */
83.       ret = (*env)->NewObject(env, class_Integer, id_Integer, value);
84.    }
85.    else if (type == REG_BINARY)
86.    {
87.       ret = (*env)->NewByteArray(env, size);
88.       (*env)->SetByteArrayRegion(env, (jarray) ret, 0, size, cret);
89.    }
90.    else
91.    {
92.       (*env)->ThrowNew(env, (*env)->FindClass(env, "Win32RegKeyException"),
93.          "Unsupported value type");
94.       ret = NULL;
95.    }
96.
97.    free(cret);
98.    RegCloseKey(hkey);
99.    (*env)->ReleaseStringUTFChars(env, name, cname);
100.
101.    return ret;
102. }
103.
104. JNIEXPORT void JNICALL Java_Win32RegKey_setValue(JNIEnv* env, jobject this_obj,
105.    jstring name, jobject value)
106. {
107.    const char* cname;
108.    jstring path;
109.    const char* cpath;
110.    HKEY hkey;
111.    DWORD type;
112.    DWORD size;
113.    jclass this_class;
114.    jclass class_value;
115.    jclass class_Integer;
116.    jfieldID id_root;
117.    jfieldID id_path;
118.    HKEY root;
119.    const char* cvalue;
120.    int ivalue;
121.
122.    /* get the class */
123.    this_class = (*env)->GetObjectClass(env, this_obj);
124.
```

```
125.    /* get the field IDs */
126.    id_root = (*env)->GetFieldID(env, this_class, "root", "I");
127.    id_path = (*env)->GetFieldID(env, this_class, "path", "Ljava/lang/String;");
128.
129.    /* get the fields */
130.    root = (HKEY)(*env)->GetIntField(env, this_obj, id_root);
131.    path = (jstring)(*env)->GetObjectField(env, this_obj, id_path);
132.    cpath = (*env)->GetStringUTFChars(env, path, NULL);
133.
134.    /* open the registry key */
135.    if (RegOpenKeyEx(root, cpath, 0, KEY_WRITE, &hkey) != ERROR_SUCCESS)
136.    {
137.       (*env)->ThrowNew(env, (*env)->FindClass(env, "Win32RegKeyException"),
138.          "Open key failed");
139.       (*env)->ReleaseStringUTFChars(env, path, cpath);
140.       return;
141.    }
142.
143.    (*env)->ReleaseStringUTFChars(env, path, cpath);
144.    cname = (*env)->GetStringUTFChars(env, name, NULL);
145.
146.    class_value = (*env)->GetObjectClass(env, value);
147.    class_Integer = (*env)->FindClass(env, "java/lang/Integer");
148.    /* determine the type of the value object */
149.    if ((*env)->IsAssignableFrom(env, class_value, (*env)->FindClass(env, "java/lang/String")))
150.    {
151.       /* it is a string--get a pointer to the characters */
152.       cvalue = (*env)->GetStringUTFChars(env, (jstring) value, NULL);
153.       type = REG_SZ;
154.       size = (*env)->GetStringLength(env, (jstring) value) + 1;
155.    }
156.    else if ((*env)->IsAssignableFrom(env, class_value, class_Integer))
157.    {
158.       /* it is an integer--call intValue to get the value */
159.       jmethodID id_intValue = (*env)->GetMethodID(env, class_Integer, "intValue", "()I");
160.       ivalue = (*env)->CallIntMethod(env, value, id_intValue);
161.       type = REG_DWORD;
162.       cvalue = (char*)&ivalue;
163.       size = 4;
164.    }
165.    else if ((*env)->IsAssignableFrom(env, class_value, (*env)->FindClass(env, "[B")))
166.    {
167.       /* it is a byte array--get a pointer to the bytes */
168.       type = REG_BINARY;
169.       cvalue = (char*)(*env)->GetByteArrayElements(env, (jarray) value, NULL);
170.       size = (*env)->GetArrayLength(env, (jarray) value);
171.    }
172.    else
173.    {
174.       /* we don't know how to handle this type */
175.       (*env)->ThrowNew(env, (*env)->FindClass(env, "Win32RegKeyException"),
176.          "Unsupported value type");
177.       RegCloseKey(hkey);
178.       (*env)->ReleaseStringUTFChars(env, name, cname);
179.       return;
180.    }
```

```
181.
182.    /* set the value */
183.    if (RegSetValueEx(hkey, cname, 0, type, cvalue, size) != ERROR_SUCCESS)
184.    {
185.       (*env)->ThrowNew(env, (*env)->FindClass(env, "Win32RegKeyException"),
186.          "Set value failed");
187.    }
188.
189.    RegCloseKey(hkey);
190.    (*env)->ReleaseStringUTFChars(env, name, cname);
191.
192.    /* if the value was a string or byte array, release the pointer */
193.    if (type == REG_SZ)
194.    {
195.       (*env)->ReleaseStringUTFChars(env, (jstring) value, cvalue);
196.    }
197.    else if (type == REG_BINARY)
198.    {
199.       (*env)->ReleaseByteArrayElements(env, (jarray) value, (jbyte*) cvalue, 0);
200.    }
201. }
202.
203. /* helper function to start enumeration of names */
204. static int startNameEnumeration(JNIEnv* env, jobject this_obj, jclass this_class)
205. {
206.    jfieldID id_index;
207.    jfieldID id_count;
208.    jfieldID id_root;
209.    jfieldID id_path;
210.    jfieldID id_hkey;
211.    jfieldID id_maxsize;
212.
213.    HKEY root;
214.    jstring path;
215.    const char* cpath;
216.    HKEY hkey;
217.    DWORD maxsize = 0;
218.    DWORD count = 0;
219.
220.    /* get the field IDs */
221.    id_root = (*env)->GetFieldID(env, this_class, "root", "I");
222.    id_path = (*env)->GetFieldID(env, this_class, "path", "Ljava/lang/String;");
223.    id_hkey = (*env)->GetFieldID(env, this_class, "hkey", "I");
224.    id_maxsize = (*env)->GetFieldID(env, this_class, "maxsize", "I");
225.    id_index = (*env)->GetFieldID(env, this_class, "index", "I");
226.    id_count = (*env)->GetFieldID(env, this_class, "count", "I");
227.
228.    /* get the field values */
229.    root = (HKEY)(*env)->GetIntField(env, this_obj, id_root);
230.    path = (jstring)(*env)->GetObjectField(env, this_obj, id_path);
231.    cpath = (*env)->GetStringUTFChars(env, path, NULL);
232.
233.    /* open the registry key */
234.    if (RegOpenKeyEx(root, cpath, 0, KEY_READ, &hkey) != ERROR_SUCCESS)
235.    {
```

```
236.        (*env)->ThrowNew(env, (*env)->FindClass(env, "Win32RegKeyException"),
237.           "Open key failed");
238.        (*env)->ReleaseStringUTFChars(env, path, cpath);
239.        return -1;
240.     }
241.     (*env)->ReleaseStringUTFChars(env, path, cpath);
242.
243.     /* query count and max length of names */
244.     if (RegQueryInfoKey(hkey, NULL, NULL, NULL, NULL, NULL, NULL, &count, &maxsize,
245.           NULL, NULL, NULL) != ERROR_SUCCESS)
246.     {
247.        (*env)->ThrowNew(env, (*env)->FindClass(env, "Win32RegKeyException"),
248.           "Query info key failed");
249.        RegCloseKey(hkey);
250.        return -1;
251.     }
252.
253.     /* set the field values */
254.     (*env)->SetIntField(env, this_obj, id_hkey, (DWORD) hkey);
255.     (*env)->SetIntField(env, this_obj, id_maxsize, maxsize + 1);
256.     (*env)->SetIntField(env, this_obj, id_index, 0);
257.     (*env)->SetIntField(env, this_obj, id_count, count);
258.     return count;
259. }
260.
261. JNIEXPORT jboolean JNICALL Java_Win32RegKeyNameEnumeration_hasMoreElements(JNIEnv* env,
262.     jobject this_obj)
263. {   jclass this_class;
264.     jfieldID id_index;
265.     jfieldID id_count;
266.     int index;
267.     int count;
268.     /* get the class */
269.     this_class = (*env)->GetObjectClass(env, this_obj);
270.
271.     /* get the field IDs */
272.     id_index = (*env)->GetFieldID(env, this_class, "index", "I");
273.     id_count = (*env)->GetFieldID(env, this_class, "count", "I");
274.
275.     index = (*env)->GetIntField(env, this_obj, id_index);
276.     if (index == -1) /* first time */
277.     {
278.        count = startNameEnumeration(env, this_obj, this_class);
279.        index = 0;
280.     }
281.     else
282.        count = (*env)->GetIntField(env, this_obj, id_count);
283.     return index < count;
284. }
285.
286. JNIEXPORT jobject JNICALL Java_Win32RegKeyNameEnumeration_nextElement(JNIEnv* env,
287.     jobject this_obj)
288. {
289.     jclass this_class;
290.     jfieldID id_index;
```

```
291.   jfieldID id_hkey;
292.   jfieldID id_count;
293.   jfieldID id_maxsize;
294.
295.   HKEY hkey;
296.   int index;
297.   int count;
298.   DWORD maxsize;
299.
300.   char* cret;
301.   jstring ret;
302.
303.   /* get the class */
304.   this_class = (*env)->GetObjectClass(env, this_obj);
305.
306.   /* get the field IDs */
307.   id_index = (*env)->GetFieldID(env, this_class, "index", "I");
308.   id_count = (*env)->GetFieldID(env, this_class, "count", "I");
309.   id_hkey = (*env)->GetFieldID(env, this_class, "hkey", "I");
310.   id_maxsize = (*env)->GetFieldID(env, this_class, "maxsize", "I");
311.
312.   index = (*env)->GetIntField(env, this_obj, id_index);
313.   if (index == -1) /* first time */
314.   {
315.      count = startNameEnumeration(env, this_obj, this_class);
316.      index = 0;
317.   }
318.   else
319.      count = (*env)->GetIntField(env, this_obj, id_count);
320.
321.   if (index >= count) /* already at end */
322.   {
323.      (*env)->ThrowNew(env, (*env)->FindClass(env, "java/util/NoSuchElementException"),
324.         "past end of enumeration");
325.      return NULL;
326.   }
327.
328.   maxsize = (*env)->GetIntField(env, this_obj, id_maxsize);
329.   hkey = (HKEY)(*env)->GetIntField(env, this_obj, id_hkey);
330.   cret = (char*)malloc(maxsize);
331.
332.   /* find the next name */
333.   if (RegEnumValue(hkey, index, cret, &maxsize, NULL, NULL, NULL, NULL) != ERROR_SUCCESS)
334.   {
335.      (*env)->ThrowNew(env, (*env)->FindClass(env, "Win32RegKeyException"),
336.         "Enum value failed");
337.      free(cret);
338.      RegCloseKey(hkey);
339.      (*env)->SetIntField(env, this_obj, id_index, count);
340.      return NULL;
341.   }
342.
343.   ret = (*env)->NewStringUTF(env, cret);
344.   free(cret);
345.
346.   /* increment index */
```

```
347.    index++;
348.    (*env)->SetIntField(env, this_obj, id_index, index);
349.
350.    if (index == count) /* at end */
351.    {
352.       RegCloseKey(hkey);
353.    }
354.
355.    return ret;
356. }
```

Example 11–23: Win32RegKeyTest.java

```
1. import java.util.*;
2.
3. public class Win32RegKeyTest
4. {
5.    public static void main(String[] args)
6.    {
7.       Win32RegKey key = new Win32RegKey(
8.          Win32RegKey.HKEY_LOCAL_MACHINE, "SOFTWARE\\JavaSoft\\Java Development Kit\\1.5");
9.
10.      key.setValue("Default user", "Harry Hacker");
11.      key.setValue("Lucky number", new Integer(13));
12.      key.setValue("Small primes", new byte[] { 2, 3, 5, 7, 11 });
13.
14.      Enumeration<String> e = key.names();
15.
16.      while (e.hasMoreElements())
17.      {
18.         String name = e.nextElement();
19.         System.out.print(name + "=");
20.
21.         Object value = key.getValue(name);
22.
23.         if (value instanceof byte[])
24.            for (byte b : (byte[]) value) System.out.print((b & 0xFF) + " ");
25.         else
26.            System.out.print(value);
27.
28.         System.out.println();
29.      }
30.    }
31. }
```

Type Inquiry Functions

- jboolean IsAssignableFrom(JNIEnv *env, jclass cl1, jclass cl2)

  returns JNI_TRUE if objects of the first class can be assigned to objects of the second class; JNI_FALSE otherwise. This is the case in which the classes are the same, cl1 is a subclass of cl2, or cl2 represents an interface that is implemented by cl1 or one of its superclasses.

  Parameters: env   The JNI interface pointer

                                cl1, cl2   Class references

- jclass GetSuperClass(JNIEnv *env, jclass cl)
  returns the superclass of a class. If cl represents the class Object or an interface, returns NULL.

  Parameters: env   The JNI interface pointer

                    cl   A class reference

XML

The preface of the book *Essential XML* by Don Box, et al. [Addison-Wesley 2000] states only half-jokingly: "The Extensible Markup Language (XML) has replaced Java, Design Patterns, and Object Technology as the software industry's solution to world hunger." Indeed, as you will see in this chapter, XML is a very useful technology for describing structured information. XML tools make it easy to process and transform that information. However, XML is not a silver bullet. You need domain-specific standards and code libraries to use it effectively. Moreover, far from making Java technology obsolete, XML works very well with Java. Essentially all important XML libraries have been implemented first in the Java programming language, and many of them are unavailable in any other programming language. Since the late 1990s, IBM, Apache, and others have been instrumental in producing high-quality Java libraries for XML processing. Starting with JDK 1.4, Sun has integrated the most important libraries into the Java 2 Platform, Standard Edition.

 NOTE: You can download the Java API for XML Processing (JAXP) library from `http://java.sun.com/xml` to add the same XML processing capabilities to older Java installations.

This chapter introduces XML and covers the XML features of the Java library. As always, we point out along the way when the hype surrounding XML is justified and when you have to take it with a grain of salt and solve your problems the old-fashioned way, through good design and code.

Introducing XML

You have seen several examples (for instance, in Chapters 4 and 10) of the use of *property files* to describe the configuration of a program. A property file contains a set of name/value pairs, such as

```
fontname=Times Roman
fontsize=12
windowsize=400 200
color=0 50 100
```

You can use the Properties class to read in such a file with a single method call. That's a nice feature, but it doesn't really go far enough. In many cases, the information that you want to describe has more structure than the property file format can comfortably handle. Consider the fontname/fontsize entries in the example. It would be more object oriented to have a single entry:

```
font=Times Roman 12
```

But then parsing the font description gets ugly—you have to figure out when the font name ends and when the font size starts.

Property files have a single flat hierarchy. You can often see programmers work around that limitation with key names such as

```
title.fontname=Helvetica
title.fontsize=36
body.fontname=Times Roman
body.fontsize=12
```

Another shortcoming of the property file format is caused by the requirement that keys be unique. To store a sequence of values, you need another workaround, such as

```
menu.item.1=Times Roman
menu.item.2=Helvetica
menu.item.3=Goudy Old Style
```

The XML format solves these problems because it can express hierarchical structures and thus is more flexible than the flat table structure of a property file.

An XML file for describing a program configuration might look like this:

```
<configuration>
   <title>
      <font>
         <name>Helvetica</name>
         <size>36</size>
      </font>
   </title>
   <body>
      <font>
         <name>Times Roman</name>
         <size>12</size>
      </font>
   </body>
   <window>
      <width>400</width>
      <height>200</height>
   </window>
   <color>
      <red>0</red>
      <green>50</green>
      <blue>100</blue>
   </color>
```

```
<menu>
    <item>Times Roman</item>
    <item>Helvetica</item>
    <item>Goudy Old Style</item>
</menu>
</configuration>
```

The XML format allows you to express the structure hierarchy and repeated elements without contortions.

As you can see, the format of an XML file is straightforward. It looks similar to an HTML file. There is a good reason—both the XML and HTML formats are descendants of the venerable Standard Generalized Markup Language (SGML).

SGML has been around since the 1970s for describing the structure of complex documents. It has been used with good success in some industries that require ongoing maintenance of massive documentation, in particular, the aircraft industry. However, SGML is quite complex, so it has never caught on in a big way. Much of that complexity arises because SGML has two conflicting goals. SGML wants to make sure that documents are formed according to the rules for their document type, but it also wants to make data entry easy by allowing shortcuts that reduce typing. XML was designed as a simplified version of SGML for use on the Internet. As is often true, simpler is better, and XML has enjoyed the immediate and enthusiastic reception that has eluded SGML for so long.

 NOTE: You can find a very nice version of the XML standard, with annotations by Tim Bray, at `http://www.xml.com/axml/axml.html`.

Even though XML and HTML have common roots, there are important differences between the two.

- Unlike HTML, XML is case sensitive. For example, `<H1>` and `<h1>` are different XML tags.
- In HTML, you can omit end tags such as `</p>` or `</li>` tags if it is clear from the context where a paragraph or list item ends. In XML, you can never omit an end tag.
- In XML, elements that have a single tag without a matching end tag must end in a /, as in `<img src="coffeecup.png"/>`. That way, the parser knows not to look for a `</img>` tag.
- In XML, attribute values must be enclosed in quotation marks. In HTML, quotation marks are optional. For example, `<applet code="MyApplet.class" width=300 height=300>` is legal HTML but not legal XML. In XML, you would have to use quotation marks: `width="300"`.
- In HTML, you can have attribute names without values, such as `<input type="radio" name="language" value="Java" checked>`. In XML, all attributes must have values, such as `checked="true"` or (ugh) `checked="checked"`.

 NOTE: The current recommendation for web documents by the World Wide Web Consortium (W3C) is the XHTML standard, which tightens up the HTML standard to be XML compliant. You can find a copy of the XHTML standard at `http://www.w3.org/TR/xhtml1/`. XHTML is backward-compatible with current browsers, but unfortunately many current HTML authoring tools do not yet support it. Once XHTML becomes more widespread, you can use the XML tools that are described in this chapter to analyze web documents.

The Structure of an XML Document

An XML document should start with a header such as

```
<?xml version="1.0"?>
```

or

```
<?xml version="1.0" encoding="UTF-8"?>
```

Strictly speaking, a header is optional, but it is highly recommended.

 NOTE: Because SGML was created for processing of real documents, XML files are called *documents*, even though most XML files describe data sets that one would not normally call documents.

The header can be followed by a *document type definition*, such as

```
<!DOCTYPE web-app PUBLIC
    "-//Sun Microsystems, Inc.//DTD Web Application 2.2//EN"
    "http://java.sun.com/j2ee/dtds/web-app_2_2.dtd">
```

Document type definitions are an important mechanism to ensure the correctness of a document, but they are not required. We discuss them later in this chapter.

Finally, the body of the XML document contains the *root element*, which can contain other elements. For example,

```
<?xml version="1.0"?>
<!DOCTYPE configuration . . .>
<configuration>
    <title>
        <font>
            <name>Helvetica</name>
            <size>36</size>
        </font>
    </title>
    . . .
</configuration>
```

An element can contain *child elements*, text, or both. In the example above, the font element has two child elements, name and size. The name element contains the text "Helvetica".

 TIP: It is best if you structure your XML documents such that an element contains *either* child elements *or* text. In other words, you should avoid situations such as

```
<font>
    Helvetica
    <size>36</size>
</font>
```

This is called *mixed contents* in the XML specification. As you will see later in this chapter, you can design much cleaner document type definitions if you avoid mixed contents.

XML elements can contain attributes, such as

```
<size unit="pt">36</size>
```

There is some disagreement among XML designers about when to use elements and when to use attributes. For example, it would seem easier to describe a font as

```
<font name="Helvetica" size="36"/>
```

than

```
<font>
    <name>Helvetica</name>
    <size>36</size>
</font>
```

However, attributes are much less flexible. Suppose you want to add units to the size value. If you use attributes, then you must add the unit to the attribute value:

```
<font name="Helvetica" size="36 pt"/>
```

Ugh! Now you have to parse the string "36 pt", just the kind of hassle that XML was designed to avoid. Adding an attribute to the size element is much cleaner:

```
<font>
    <name>Helvetica</name>
    <size unit="pt">36</size>
</font>
```

A commonly used rule of thumb is that attributes should be used only to modify the interpretation of a value, not to specify values. If you find yourself engaged in metaphysical discussions about whether a particular setting is a modification of the interpretation of a value or not, then just say "no" to attributes and use elements throughout. Many useful DTDs don't use attributes at all.

 NOTE: In HTML, the rule for attribute usage is simple: If it isn't displayed on the web page, it's an attribute. For example, consider the hyperlink

```
<a href="http://java.sun.com">Java Technology</a>
```

The string Java Technology is displayed on the web page, but the URL of the link is not a part of the displayed page. However, the rule isn't all that helpful for most XML files since the data in an XML file aren't normally meant to be viewed by humans.

Elements and text are the "bread and butter" of XML documents. Here are a few other markup instructions that you may encounter:

- *Character references* have the form &#d; or &#xh;. Here d is a decimal Unicode value and h is a hexadecimal Unicode value. For example,

```
&#233;
&#x2122;
```

denote the characters é and ™.

- *Entity references* have the form &name;. The entity references

```
&lt;
&gt;
&amp;
&quot;
&apos;
```

have predefined meanings: the less than, greater than, ampersand, quotation mark, and apostrophe characters. You can define other entity references in a document type definition (DTD).

- *CDATA sections* are delimited by <![CDATA[and]]>. They are a special form of character data. You can use them to include strings that contain characters such as < > & without having them interpreted as markup, for example,

```
<![CDATA[< & > are my favorite delimiters]]>
```

CDATA sections cannot contain the string]]>. Use this feature with caution! It is too often used as a backdoor for smuggling legacy data into XML documents.

- *Processing instructions* are delimited by <? and ?>, for example,

```
<?xml-stylesheet href="mystyle.css" type="text/css"?>
```

These instructions are for the benefit of the application that processes the XML document. Every XML document starts with a processing instruction

```
<?xml version="1.0"?>
```

- *Comments* are delimited by `<!--` and `-->`, for example,

  ```
  <!-- This is a comment. -->
  ```

  Comments should not contain the string `--`. Comments should only be information for human readers. They should never contain hidden commands. Use processing instructions for commands.

Parsing an XML Document

To process an XML document, you need to *parse* it. A parser is a program that reads a file, confirms that the file has the correct format, breaks it up into the constituent elements, and lets a programmer access those elements. The Java library supplies two kinds of XML parsers:

- The Document Object Model (DOM) parser reads an XML document into a tree structure.
- The Simple API for XML (SAX) parser generates events as it reads an XML document.

The DOM parser is easier to use for most purposes, and we explain it first. You would consider the SAX parser if you process very long documents whose tree structures would use up a lot of memory, or if you are just interested in a few elements and you don't care about their context.

The DOM parser interface is standardized by the World Wide Web Consortium (W3C). The `org.w3c.dom` package contains the definitions of interface types such as `Document` and `Element`. Different suppliers, such as the Apache Organization and IBM, have written DOM parsers whose classes implement these interfaces. The Sun Java API for XML Processing (JAXP) library actually makes it possible to plug in any of these parsers. But Sun also includes its own DOM parser in the Java SDK. We use the Sun parser in this chapter.

To read an XML document, you need a `DocumentBuilder` object, which you get from a `Document-BuilderFactory`, like this:

```
DocumentBuilderFactory factory = DocumentBuilderFactory.newInstance();
DocumentBuilder builder = factory.newDocumentBuilder();
```

You can now read a document from a file:

```
File f = . . .
Document doc = builder.parse(f);
```

Alternatively, you can use a URL:

```
URL u = . . .
Document doc = builder.parse(u);
```

You can even specify an arbitrary input stream:

```
InputStream in = . . .
Document doc = builder.parse(in);
```

 NOTE: If you use an input stream as an input source, then the parser will not be able to locate other files that are referenced relative to the location of the document, such as a DTD in the same directory. You can install an "entity resolver" to overcome that problem.

The `Document` object is an in-memory representation of the tree structure of the XML document. It is composed of objects whose classes implement the `Node` interface and its various subinterfaces. Figure 12–1 shows the inheritance hierarchy of the subinterfaces.

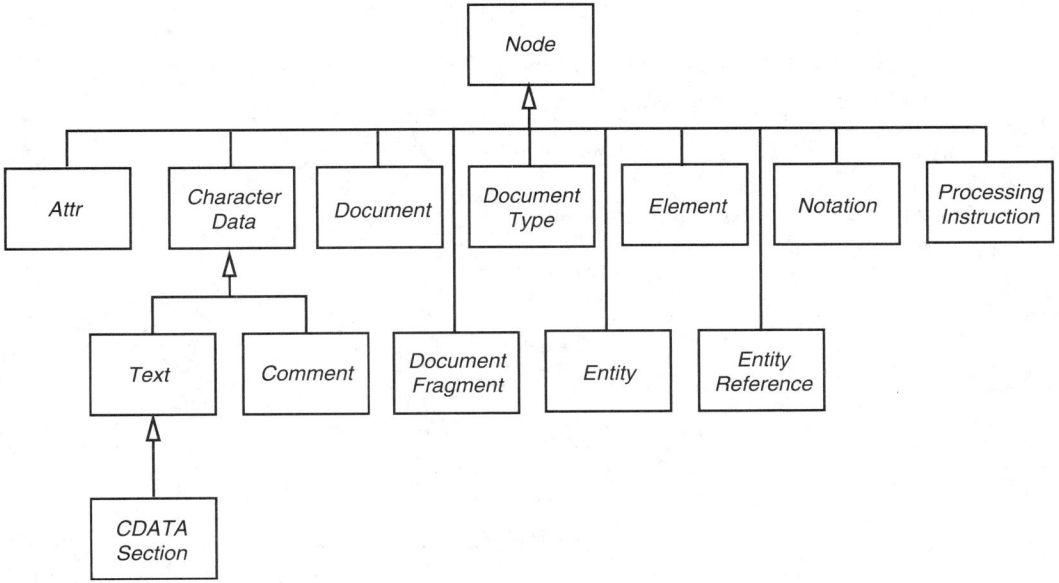

Figure 12–1: The Node interface and its subinterfaces

You start analyzing the contents of a document by calling the getDocumentElement method. It returns the root element.

```
Element root = doc.getDocumentElement();
```

For example, if you are processing a document

```
<?xml version="1.0"?>
<font>
   . . .
</font>
```

then calling getDocumentElement returns the font element.

The getTagName method returns the tag name of an element. In the preceding example, root.getTagName() returns the string "font".

To get the element's children (which may be subelements, text, comments, or other nodes), use the getChildNodes method. That method returns a collection of type NodeList. That type was invented before the standard Java collections, and it has a different access protocol. The item method gets the item with a given index, and the getLength method gives the total count of the items. Therefore, you can enumerate all children like this:

```
NodeList children = root.getChildNodes();
for (int i = 0; i < children.getLength(); i++)
{
   Node child = children.item(i);
   . . .
}
```

Be careful when analyzing the children. Suppose, for example, that you are processing the document

```
<font>
   <name>Helvetica</name>
```

```
        <size>36</size>
      </font>
```

You would expect the font element to have two children, but the parser reports five:

- The whitespace between <font> and <name>
- The name element
- The whitespace between </name> and <size>
- The size element
- The whitespace between </size> and </font>

Figure 12–2 shows the DOM tree.

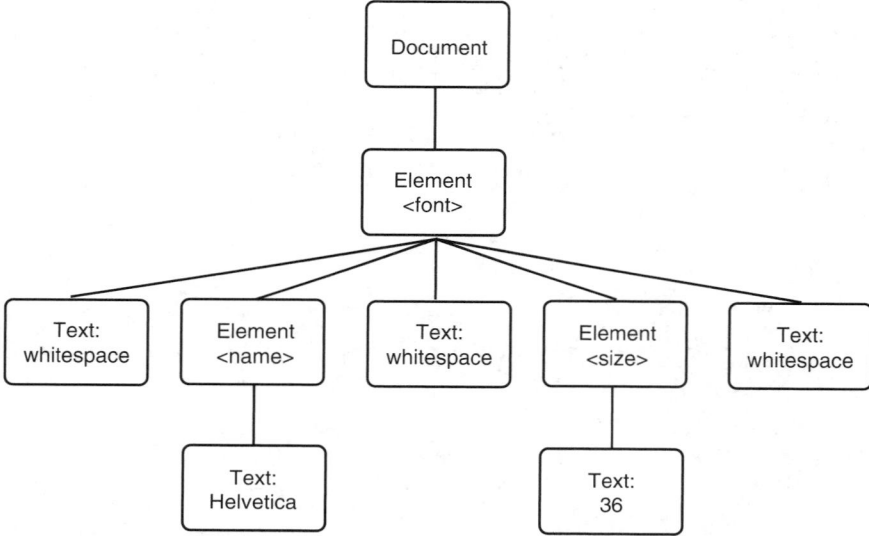

Figure 12–2: A simple DOM tree

If you expect only subelements, then you can ignore the whitespace:

```
for (int i = 0; i < children.getLength(); i++)
{
   Node child = children.item(i);
   if (child instanceof Element)
   {
      Element childElement = (Element) child;
      . . .
   }
}
```

Now you look at only two elements, with tag names name and size.

As you see in the next section, you can do even better if your document has a document type definition. Then the parser knows which elements don't have text nodes as children, and it can suppress the whitespace for you.

When analyzing the name and size elements, you want to retrieve the text strings that they contain. Those text strings are themselves contained in child nodes of type Text. Since you know that these Text nodes are the only children, you can use the getFirstChild method without having to traverse another NodeList. Then use the getData method to retrieve the string stored in the Text node.

```
for (int i = 0; i < children.getLength(); i++)
{
   Node child = children.item(i);
   if (child instanceof Element)
   {
      Element childElement = (Element) child;
      Text textNode = (Text) childElement.getFirstChild();
      String text = textNode.getData().trim();
      if (childElement.getTagName().equals("name"))
         name = text;
      else if (childElement.getTagName().equals("size"))
         size = Integer.parseInt(text);
   }
}
```

 TIP: It is a good idea to call trim on the return value of the getData method. If the author of an XML file puts the beginning and the ending tag on separate lines, such as

```
<size>
   36
</size>
```

then the parser includes all line breaks and spaces in the text node data. Calling the trim method removes the whitespace surrounding the actual data.

You can also get the last child with the getLastChild method, and the next sibling of a node with getNextSibling. Therefore, another way of traversing a set of child nodes is

```
for (Node childNode = element.getFirstChild();
   childNode != null;
   childNode = childNode.getNextSibling())
{
   . . .
}
```

To enumerate the attributes of a node, call the getAttributes method. It returns a NamedNodeMap object that contains Node objects describing the attributes. You can traverse the nodes in a NamedNodeMap in the same way as a NodeList. Then call the getNodeName and getNodeValue methods to get the attribute names and values.

```
NamedNodeMap attributes = element.getAttributes();
for (int i = 0; i < attributes.getLength(); i++)
{
   Node attribute = attributes.item(i);
   String name = attribute.getNodeName();
   String value = attribute.getNodeValue();
   . . .
}
```

Alternatively, if you know the name of an attribute, you can retrieve the corresponding value directly:

```
String unit = element.getAttribute("unit");
```

You have now seen how to analyze a DOM tree. The program in Example 12–1 puts these techniques to work. You can use the File -> Open menu option to read in an XML file. A DocumentBuilder object parses the XML file and produces a Document object. The program displays the Document object as a JTree (see Figure 12–3).

The tree display shows clearly how child elements are surrounded by text containing whitespace and comments. For greater clarity, the program displays newline and return characters as \n and \r. (Otherwise, they would show up as hollow boxes, the default symbol for a character that Swing cannot draw in a string.)

If you followed the section on trees in Chapter 6, you will recognize the techniques that this program uses to display the tree. The `DOMTreeModel` class implements the `TreeModel` interface. The `getRoot` method returns the root element of the document. The `getChild` method gets the node list of children and returns the item with the requested index. However, the tree model returns DOM `Node` objects whose `toString` methods aren't necessarily descriptive. Therefore, the program installs a tree cell renderer that extends the default cell renderer and sets the label text to a more descriptive form. The cell renderer displays the following:

- For elements, the element tag name and a table of all attributes
- For character data, the interface (Text, Comment, or CDATASection), followed by the data, with newline and return characters replaced by \n and \r
- For all other node types, the class name followed by the result of `toString`

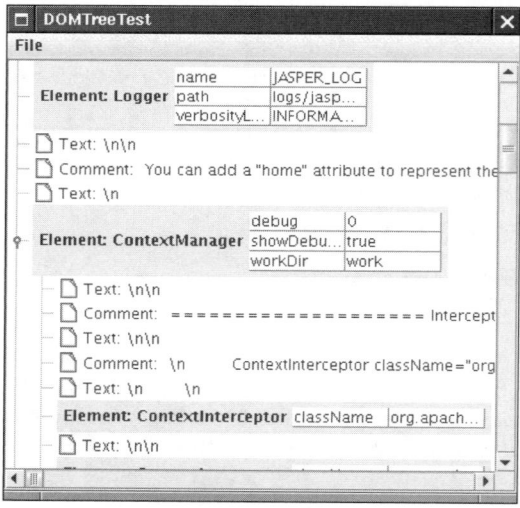

Figure 12–3: A parse tree of an XML document

Example 12–1: DOMTreeTest.java

```java
1. import java.awt.*;
2. import java.awt.event.*;
3. import java.io.*;
4. import javax.swing.*;
5. import javax.swing.event.*;
6. import javax.swing.table.*;
7. import javax.swing.tree.*;
8. import javax.xml.parsers.*;
9. import org.w3c.dom.*;
10. import org.xml.sax.*;
11.
12. /**
13.    This program displays an XML document as a tree.
```

```
14. */
15. public class DOMTreeTest
16. {
17.    public static void main(String[] args)
18.    {
19.       JFrame frame = new DOMTreeFrame();
20.       frame.setDefaultCloseOperation(JFrame.EXIT_ON_CLOSE);
21.       frame.setVisible(true);
22.    }
23. }
24.
25. /**
26.    This frame contains a tree that displays the contents of
27.    an XML document.
28. */
29. class DOMTreeFrame extends JFrame
30. {
31.    public DOMTreeFrame()
32.    {
33.       setTitle("DOMTreeTest");
34.       setSize(DEFAULT_WIDTH, DEFAULT_HEIGHT);
35.
36.       JMenu fileMenu = new JMenu("File");
37.       JMenuItem openItem = new JMenuItem("Open");
38.       openItem.addActionListener(new
39.          ActionListener()
40.          {
41.             public void actionPerformed(ActionEvent event) { openFile(); }
42.          });
43.       fileMenu.add(openItem);
44.
45.       JMenuItem exitItem = new JMenuItem("Exit");
46.       exitItem.addActionListener(new
47.          ActionListener()
48.          {
49.             public void actionPerformed(ActionEvent event) { System.exit(0); }
50.          });
51.       fileMenu.add(exitItem);
52.
53.       JMenuBar menuBar = new JMenuBar();
54.       menuBar.add(fileMenu);
55.       setJMenuBar(menuBar);
56.    }
57.
58.    /**
59.       Open a file and load the document.
60.    */
61.    public void openFile()
62.    {
63.       JFileChooser chooser = new JFileChooser();
64.       chooser.setCurrentDirectory(new File("."));
65.
66.       chooser.setFileFilter(new
67.          javax.swing.filechooser.FileFilter()
68.          {
69.             public boolean accept(File f)
```

```
70.        {
71.            return f.isDirectory() || f.getName().toLowerCase().endsWith(".xml");
72.        }
73.        public String getDescription() { return "XML files"; }
74.      });
75.   int r = chooser.showOpenDialog(this);
76.   if (r != JFileChooser.APPROVE_OPTION) return;
77.   File f = chooser.getSelectedFile();
78.   try
79.   {
80.      if (builder == null)
81.      {
82.         DocumentBuilderFactory factory = DocumentBuilderFactory.newInstance();
83.         builder = factory.newDocumentBuilder();
84.      }
85.
86.      Document doc = builder.parse(f);
87.      JTree tree = new JTree(new DOMTreeModel(doc));
88.      tree.setCellRenderer(new DOMTreeCellRenderer());
89.
90.      setContentPane(new JScrollPane(tree));
91.      validate();
92.   }
93.   catch (IOException e)
94.   {
95.      JOptionPane.showMessageDialog(this, e);
96.   }
97.   catch (ParserConfigurationException e)
98.   {
99.      JOptionPane.showMessageDialog(this, e);
100.   }
101.   catch (SAXException e)
102.   {
103.      JOptionPane.showMessageDialog(this, e);
104.   }
105. }
106.
107. private DocumentBuilder builder;
108. private static final int DEFAULT_WIDTH = 400;
109. private static final int DEFAULT_HEIGHT = 400;
110. }
111.
112. /**
113.    This tree model describes the tree structure of an XML document.
114. */
115. class DOMTreeModel implements TreeModel
116. {
117.    /**
118.       Constructs a document tree model.
119.       @param doc the document
120.    */
121.    public DOMTreeModel(Document doc) { this.doc = doc; }
122.
123.    public Object getRoot() { return doc.getDocumentElement(); }
124.
125.    public int getChildCount(Object parent)
```

```
126.     {
127.         Node node = (Node) parent;
128.         NodeList list = node.getChildNodes();
129.         return list.getLength();
130.     }
131.
132.     public Object getChild(Object parent, int index)
133.     {
134.         Node node = (Node) parent;
135.         NodeList list = node.getChildNodes();
136.         return list.item(index);
137.     }
138.
139.     public int getIndexOfChild(Object parent, Object child)
140.     {
141.         Node node = (Node) parent;
142.         NodeList list = node.getChildNodes();
143.         for (int i = 0; i < list.getLength(); i++)
144.            if (getChild(node, i) == child)
145.               return i;
146.         return -1;
147.     }
148.
149.     public boolean isLeaf(Object node) { return getChildCount(node) == 0; }
150.     public void valueForPathChanged(TreePath path, Object newValue) {}
151.     public void addTreeModelListener(TreeModelListener l) {}
152.     public void removeTreeModelListener(TreeModelListener l) {}
153.
154.     private Document doc;
155. }
156.
157. /**
158.    This class renders an XML node.
159. */
160. class DOMTreeCellRenderer extends DefaultTreeCellRenderer
161. {
162.     public Component getTreeCellRendererComponent(JTree tree, Object value,
163.         boolean selected, boolean expanded, boolean leaf, int row, boolean hasFocus)
164.     {
165.         Node node = (Node) value;
166.         if (node instanceof Element) return elementPanel((Element) node);
167.
168.         super.getTreeCellRendererComponent(tree, value,
169.            selected, expanded, leaf, row, hasFocus);
170.         if (node instanceof CharacterData)
171.            setText(characterString((CharacterData) node));
172.         else
173.            setText(node.getClass() + ": " + node.toString());
174.         return this;
175.     }
176.
177.     public static JPanel elementPanel(Element e)
178.     {
179.         JPanel panel = new JPanel();
180.         panel.add(new JLabel("Element: " + e.getTagName()));
181.         panel.add(new JTable(new AttributeTableModel(e.getAttributes())));
```

```
182.       return panel;
183.    }
184.
185.    public static String characterString(CharacterData node)
186.    {
187.       StringBuilder builder = new StringBuilder(node.getData());
188.       for (int i = 0; i < builder.length(); i++)
189.       {
190.          if (builder.charAt(i) == '\r')
191.          {
192.             builder.replace(i, i + 1, "\\r");
193.             i++;
194.          }
195.          else if (builder.charAt(i) == '\n')
196.          {
197.             builder.replace(i, i + 1, "\\n");
198.             i++;
199.          }
200.          else if (builder.charAt(i) == '\t')
201.          {
202.             builder.replace(i, i + 1, "\\t");
203.             i++;
204.          }
205.       }
206.       if (node instanceof CDATASection)
207.          builder.insert(0, "CDATASection: ");
208.       else if (node instanceof Text)
209.          builder.insert(0, "Text: ");
210.       else if (node instanceof Comment)
211.          builder.insert(0, "Comment: ");
212.
213.       return builder.toString();
214.    }
215. }
216.
217. /**
218.    This table model describes the attributes of an XML element.
219. */
220. class AttributeTableModel extends AbstractTableModel
221. {
222.    /**
223.       Constructs an attribute table model.
224.       @param map the named node map
225.    */
226.    public AttributeTableModel(NamedNodeMap map) { this.map = map; }
227.
228.    public int getRowCount() { return map.getLength(); }
229.    public int getColumnCount() { return 2; }
230.    public Object getValueAt(int r, int c)
231.    {
232.       return c == 0 ? map.item(r).getNodeName() : map.item(r).getNodeValue();
233.    }
234.
235.    private NamedNodeMap map;
236. }
```

 javax.xml.parsers.DocumentBuilderFactory 1.4

- static DocumentBuilderFactory newInstance()
  returns an instance of the DocumentBuilderFactory class.

- DocumentBuilder newDocumentBuilder()
  returns an instance of the DocumentBuilder class.

 javax.xml.parsers.DocumentBuilder 1.4

- Document parse(File f)
- Document parse(String url)
- Document parse(InputStream in)
  parse an XML document from the given file, URL, or input stream and return the
  parsed document.

 org.w3c.dom.Document 1.4

- Element getDocumentElement()
  returns the root element of the document.

org.w3c.dom.Element 1.4

- String getTagName()
  returns the name of the element.

- String getAttribute(String name)
  returns the attribute value of the attribute with the given name, or the empty string if
  there is no such attribute.

org.w3c.dom.Node 1.4

- NodeList getChildNodes()
  returns a node list that contains all children of this node.

- Node getFirstChild()
- Node getLastChild()
  get the first or last child node of this node, or null if this node has no children.

- Node getNextSibling()
- Node getPreviousSibling()
  get the next or previous sibling of this node, or null if this node has no siblings.

- Node getParentNode()
  gets the parent of this node, or null if this node is the document node.

- NamedNodeMap getAttributes()
  returns a node map that contains Attr nodes that describe all attributes of this node.

- String getNodeName()
  returns the name of this node. If the node is an Attr node, then the name is the
  attribute name.

- String getNodeValue()
  returns the value of this node. If the node is an Attr node, then the value is the
  attribute value.

 org.w3c.dom.CharacterData 1.4

- String getData()
  returns the text stored in this node.

   org.w3c.dom.NodeList `1.4`

- `int getLength()`
  returns the number of nodes in this list.
- `Node item(int index)`
  returns the node with the given index. The index is between 0 and `getLength()` − 1.

   org.w3c.dom.NamedNodeMap `1.4`

- `int getLength()`
  returns the number of nodes in this map.
- `Node item(int index)`
  returns the node with the given index. The index is between 0 and `getLength()` − 1.

Validating XML Documents

In the preceding section, you saw how to traverse the tree structure of a DOM document. However, if you simply follow that approach, you'll find that you will have quite a bit of tedious programming and error checking. Not only do you have to deal with whitespace between elements, but you also need to check whether the document contains the nodes that you expect. For example, suppose you are reading an element:

```
<font>
    <name>Helvetica</name>
    <size>36</size>
</font>
```

You get the first child. Oops...it is a text node containing whitespace "\n   ". You skip text nodes and find the first element node. Then you need to check that its tag name is `"name"`. You need to check that it has one child node of type Text. You move on to the next non-whitespace child and make the same check. What if the author of the document switched the order of the children or added another child element? It is tedious to code all the error checking, and reckless to skip the checks.

Fortunately, one of the major benefits of an XML parser is that it can automatically verify that a document has the correct structure. Then the parsing becomes much simpler. For example, if you know that the font fragment has passed validation, then you can simply get the two grandchildren, cast them as Text nodes and get the text data, without any further checking.

To specify the document structure, you can supply a document type definition (DTD) or an XML Schema definition. A DTD or schema contains rules that explain how a document should be formed, by specifying the legal child elements and attributes for each element. For example, a DTD might contain a rule:

```
<!ELEMENT font (name,size)>
```

This rule expresses that a font element must always have two children, which are name and size elements. The XML Schema language expresses the same constraint as

```
<xsd:element name="font">
    <xsd:sequence>
        <xsd:element name="name" type="xsd:string"/>
        <xsd:element name="size" type="xsd:int"/>
    </xsd:sequence>
</xsd:element>
```

XML Schema can express more sophisticated validation conditions (such as the fact that the size element must contain an integer) than can DTDs. Unlike the DTD syntax, the XML Schema syntax uses XML, which is a benefit if you need to process schema files.

The XML Schema language was designed to replace DTDs. However, as we write this chapter, DTDs are still very much alive. XML Schema is complex, and not all parsers support it. XML Schema support has been added to JDK 5.0, but, as you will see, the implementation is a bit shaky.

 NOTE: Some XML users are so annoyed by the complexity of XML Schema that they use alternative validation languages. The most common choice is Relax NG (http://www.relaxng.org).

In the next section, we discuss DTDs in detail. We then briefly cover the basics of XML Schema support. Finally, we show you a complete application that demonstrates how validation simplifies XML programming.

Document Type Definitions

There are several methods for supplying a DTD. You can include a DTD in an XML document like this:

```
<?xml version="1.0"?>
<!DOCTYPE configuration [
   <!ELEMENT configuration . . .>
   more rules
   . . .
]>
<configuration>
   . . .
</configuration>
```

As you can see, the rules are included inside a DOCTYPE declaration, in a block delimited by [. . .]. The document type must match the name of the root element, such as configuration in our example.

Supplying a DTD inside an XML document is somewhat uncommon because DTDs can grow lengthy. It makes more sense to store the DTD externally. The SYSTEM declaration can be used for that purpose. You specify a URL that contains the DTD, for example:

```
<!DOCTYPE configuration SYSTEM "config.dtd">
```

or

```
<!DOCTYPE configuration SYSTEM "http://myserver.com/config.dtd">
```

 CAUTION: If you use a relative URL for the DTD (such as "config.dtd"), then give the parser a File or URL object, not an InputStream. If you must parse from an input stream, supply an entity resolver—see the following note.

Finally, the mechanism for identifying "well known" DTDs has its origin in SGML. Here is an example:

```
<!DOCTYPE web-app
   PUBLIC "-//Sun Microsystems, Inc.//DTD Web Application 2.2//EN"
   "http://java.sun.com/j2ee/dtds/web-app_2_2.dtd">
```

If an XML processor knows how to locate the DTD with the public identifier, then it need not go to the URL.

 NOTE: If you use a DOM parser and would like to support a `PUBLIC` identifier, call the `setEntity-Resolver` method of the `DocumentBuilder` class to install an object of a class that implements the `EntityResolver` interface. That interface has a single method, `resolveEntity`. Here is the outline of a typical implementation:

```java
class MyEntityResolver implements EntityResolver
{
   public InputSource resolveEntity(String publicID,
      String systemID)
   {
      if (publicID.equals(a known ID))
         return new InputSource(DTD data);
      else
         return null; // use default behavior
   }
}
```

You can construct the input source from an `InputStream`, a `Reader`, or a string.

Now that you have seen how the parser locates the DTD, let us consider the various kinds of rules.

The `ELEMENT` rule specifies what children an element can have. You specify a regular expression, made up of the components shown in Table 12–1.

Table 12–1: Rules for Element Content

Rule	Meaning
$E*$	0 or more occurrences of E
$E+$	1 or more occurrences of E
$E?$	0 or 1 occurrences of E
$E_1|E_2| \ldots |E_n$	One of $E_1, E_2, \ldots, E_n$
$E_1, E_2, \ldots, E_n$	E_1 followed by $E_2, \ldots, E_n$
#PCDATA	Text
$(\#PCDATA|E_1|E_2| \ldots |E_n)*$	0 or more occurrences of text and $E_1, E_2, \ldots, E_n$ in any order (mixed content)
ANY	Any children allowed
EMPTY	No children allowed

Here are several simple but typical examples. The following rule states that a menu element contains 0 or more item elements.

```
<!ELEMENT menu (item)*>
```

This set of rules states that a font is described by a name followed by a size, each of which contain text.

```
<!ELEMENT font (name,size)>
<!ELEMENT name (#PCDATA)>
<!ELEMENT size (#PCDATA)>
```

The abbreviation PCDATA denotes parsed character data. The data are called "parsed" because the parser interprets the text string, looking for < characters that denote the start of a new tag, or & characters that denote the start of an entity.

An element specification can contain regular expressions that are nested and complex. For example, here is a rule that describes the makeup of a chapter in this book:

```
<!ELEMENT chapter (intro,(heading,(para|image|table|note)+)+)>
```

Each chapter starts with an introduction, which is followed by one or more sections consisting of a heading and one or more paragraphs, images, tables, or notes.

However, in one common case you can't define the rules to be as flexible as you might like. Whenever an element can contain text, then there are only two valid cases. Either the element contains nothing but text, such as

```
<!ELEMENT name (#PCDATA)>
```

Or the element contains *any combination of text and tags in any order,* such as

```
<!ELEMENT para (#PCDATA|em|strong|code)*>
```

It is not legal to specify other types of rules that contain #PCDATA. For example, the following rule is illegal:

```
<!ELEMENT captionedImage (image,#PCDATA)>
```

You have to rewrite such a rule, either by introducing another caption element or by allowing any combination of image tags and text.

This restriction simplifies the job of the XML parser when parsing *mixed content* (a mixture of tags and text). Because you lose some control when allowing mixed content, it is best to design DTDs such that all elements contain either other elements or nothing but text.

 NOTE: Actually, it isn't quite true that you can specify arbitrary regular expressions of elements in a DTD rule. An XML parser may reject certain complex rule sets that lead to "nondeterministic" parsing. For example, a regular expression $((x,y)|(x,z))$ is nondeterministic. When the parser sees x, it doesn't know which of the two alternatives to take. This expression can be rewritten in a deterministic form, as $(x,(y|z))$. However, some expressions can't be reformulated, such as $((x,y)*|x?)$. The Sun parser gives no warnings when presented with an ambiguous DTD. It simply picks the first matching alternative when parsing, which causes it to reject some correct inputs. Of course, the parser is well within its rights to do so because the XML standard allows a parser to assume that the DTD is unambiguous.

In practice, this isn't an issue over which you should lose sleep, since most DTDs are so simple that you never run into ambiguity problems.

You also specify rules to describe the legal attributes of elements. The general syntax is

```
<!ATTLIST element attribute type default>
```

Table 12–2 shows the legal attribute types, and Table 12–3 shows the syntax for the defaults.

Table 12–2: Attribute Types

Type	Meaning
CDATA	Any character string
$(A_1|A_2| \ . \ . \ . \ |A_n)$	One of the string attributes $A_1 \ A_2 \ . \ . \ . \ |A_n$
NMTOKEN, NMTOKENS	One or more name tokens
ID	A unique ID
IDREF, IDREFS	One or more references to a unique ID
ENTITY, ENTITIES	One or more unparsed entities

Table 12–3: Attribute Defaults

Default	Meaning
#REQUIRED	Attribute is required.
#IMPLIED	Attribute is optional.
A	Attribute is optional; the parser reports it to be *A* if it is not specified.
#FIXED *A*	The attribute must either be unspecified or *A*; in either case, the parser reports it to be *A*.

Here are two typical attribute specifications:

```
<!ATTLIST font style (plain|bold|italic|bold-italic) "plain">
<!ATTLIST size unit CDATA #IMPLIED>
```

The first specification describes the style attribute of a font element. There are four legal attribute values, and the default value is plain. The second specification expresses that the unit attribute of the size element can contain any character data sequence.

 NOTE: We generally recommend the use of elements, not attributes, to describe data. Following that recommendation, the font style should be a separate element, such as <font><style>plain</style>...</font>. However, attributes have an undeniable advantage for enumerated types since the parser can verify that the values are legal. For example, if the font style is an attribute, the parser checks that it is one of the four allowed values, and it supplies a default if no value was given.

The handling of a CDATA attribute value is subtly different from the processing of #PCDATA that you have seen before, and quite unrelated to the <![CDATA[...]]> sections. The attribute value is first *normalized*, that is, the parser processes character and entity references (such as é or <) and replaces whitespace with spaces.

An NMTOKEN (or name token) is similar to CDATA, but most non-alphanumeric characters and internal whitespace are disallowed, and the parser removes leading and trailing whitespace. NMTOKENS is a whitespace-separated list of name tokens.

The ID construct is quite useful. An ID is a name token that must be unique in the document—the parser checks the uniqueness. You will see an application in the next sample program. An IDREF is a reference to an ID that exists in the same document—which the parser also checks. IDREFS is a whitespace-separated list of ID references.

An ENTITY attribute value refers to an "unparsed external entity." That is a holdover from SGML that is rarely used in practice. The annotated XML specification at http://www.xml.com/axml/axml.html has an example.

A DTD can also define *entities*, or abbreviations that are replaced during parsing. You can find a good example for the use of entities in the user interface descriptions for the Mozilla/Netscape 6 browser. Those descriptions are formatted in XML and contain entity definitions such as

```
<!ENTITY back.label "Back">
```

Elsewhere, text can contain an entity reference, for example:

```
<menuitem label="&back.label;"/>
```

The parser replaces the entity reference with the replacement string. For internationalization of the application, only the string in the entity definition needs to be changed. Other uses of entities are more complex and less commonly used. Look at the XML specification for details.

This concludes the introduction to DTDs. Now that you have seen how to use DTDs, you can configure your parser to take advantage of them. First, tell the document builder factory to turn on validation.

```
factory.setValidating(true);
```

All builders produced by this factory validate their input against a DTD. The most useful benefit of validation is to ignore whitespace in element content. For example, consider the XML fragment

```
<font>
   <name>Helvetica</name>
   <size>36</size>
</font>
```

A nonvalidating parser reports the whitespace between the font, name, and size elements because it has no way of knowing if the children of font are

```
(name,size)
(#PCDATA,name,size)*
```

or perhaps

```
ANY
```

Once the DTD specifies that the children are (name,size), the parser knows that the whitespace between them is not text. Call

```
factory.setIgnoringElementContentWhitespace(true);
```

and the builder will stop reporting the whitespace in text nodes. That means you can now *rely on* the fact that a font node has two children. You no longer need to program a tedious loop:

```
for (int i = 0; i < children.getLength(); i++)
{
   Node child = children.item(i);
   if (child instanceof Element)
   {
      Element childElement = (Element) child;
      if (childElement.getTagName().equals("name")) . . .
      else if (childElement.getTagName().equals("size")) . . .
   }
}
```

Instead, you can simply access the first and second child:

```
Element nameElement = (Element) children.item(0);
Element sizeElement = (Element) children.item(1);
```

That is why DTDs are so useful. You don't overload your program with rule checking code—the parser has already done that work by the time you get the document.

 TIP: Many programmers who start using XML are uncomfortable with validation and end up analyzing the DOM tree on the fly. If you need to convince colleagues of the benefit of using validated documents, show them the two coding alternatives—it should win them over.

When the parser reports an error, your application will want to do something about it—log it, show it to the user, or throw an exception to abandon the parsing. Therefore, you should install an error handler whenever you use validation. Supply an object that implements the `ErrorHandler` interface. That interface has three methods:

```
void warning(SAXParseException exception)
void error(SAXParseException exception)
void fatalError(SAXParseException exception)
```

You install the error handler with the `setErrorHandler` method of the `DocumentBuilder` class:

```
builder.setErrorHandler(handler);
```

 javax.xml.parsers.DocumentBuilder 1.4

- void setEntityResolver(EntityResolver resolver)
  sets the resolver to locate entities that are referenced in the XML documents to be parsed.

- void setErrorHandler(ErrorHandler handler)
  sets the handler to report errors and warnings that occur during parsing.

 org.xml.sax.EntityResolver 1.4

- public InputSource resolveEntity(String publicID, String systemID)
  returns an input source that contains the data referenced by the given ID(s), or null to indicate that this resolver doesn't know how to resolve the particular name. The publicID parameter may be null if no public ID was supplied.

 org.xml.sax.InputSource 1.4

- InputSource(InputStream in)
- InputSource(Reader in)
- InputSource(String systemID)
  construct an input source from a stream, reader, or system ID (usually a relative or absolute URL).

 org.xml.sax.ErrorHandler 1.4

- void fatalError(SAXParseException exception)
- void error(SAXParseException exception)
- void warning(SAXParseException exception)
  Override these methods to provide handlers for fatal errors, nonfatal errors, and warnings.

 org.xml.sax.SAXParseException 1.4

- int getLineNumber()
- int getColumnNumber()
  return the line and column number of the end of the processed input that caused the exception.

 javax.xml.parsers.DocumentBuilderFactory 1.4

- boolean isValidating()
- void setValidating(boolean value)
  are the "validating" property of the factory. If set to true, the parsers that this factory generates validate their input.

- `boolean isIgnoringElementContentWhitespace()`
- `void setIgnoringElementContentWhitespace(boolean value)`
  are the "ignoringElementContentWhitespace" property of the factory. If set to true, the parsers that this factory generates ignore whitespace text between element nodes that don't have mixed content (i.e., a mixture of elements and #PCDATA).

XML Schema

Because XML Schema is quite a bit more complex than the DTD syntax, we cover only the basics. For more information, we recommend the tutorial at `http://www.w3.org/TR/xmlschema-0`.

To reference a Schema file in a document, you add attributes to the root element, for example:

```
<?xml version="1.0"?>
<configuration xmlns:xsi="http://www.w3.org/2001/XMLSchema-instance"
        xsi:noNamespaceSchemaLocation="config.xsd">
. . .
</configuration>
```

This declaration states that the schema file `config.xsd` should be used to validate the document. If your document uses namespaces, the syntax is a bit more complex—see the XML Schema tutorial for details. (The prefix xsi is a *namespace alias*—see page 922 for more information about namespaces.)

A schema defines a *type* for each element. The type can be a *simple type*—a string with formatting restrictions—or a *complex type*. Some simple types are built into XML Schema, including

```
xsd:string
xsd:int
xsd:boolean
```

NOTE: We use the prefix xsd: to denote the XSL Schema Definition namespace. Some authors use the prefix xs: instead.

You can define your own simple types. For example, here is an enumerated type:

```
<xsd:simpleType name="StyleType">
   <xsd:restriction base="xsd:string">
      <xsd:enumeration value="PLAIN" />
      <xsd:enumeration value="BOLD" />
      <xsd:enumeration value="ITALIC" />
      <xsd:enumeration value="BOLD_ITALIC" />
   </xsd:restriction>
</xsd:simpleType>
```

When you define an element, you specify its type:

```
<xsd:element name="name" type="xsd:string"/>
<xsd:element name="size" type="xsd:int"/>
<xsd:element name="style" type="StyleType"/>
```

The type constrains the element content. For example, the elements

```
<size>10</size>
<style>PLAIN</style>
```

will validate correctly, but the elements

```
<size>default</size>
<style>SLANTED</style>
```

will be rejected by the parser.

You can compose types into complex types, for example:

```
<xsd:complexType name="FontType">
  <xsd:sequence>
    <xsd:element ref="name"/>
    <xsd:element ref="size"/>
    <xsd:element ref="style"/>
  </xsd:sequence>
</xsd:complexType>
```

A `FontType` is a sequence of `name`, `size`, and `style` elements. In this type definition, we use the `ref` attribute and refer to definitions that are located elsewhere in the schema. You can also nest definitions, like this:

```
<xsd:complexType name="FontType">
  <xsd:sequence>
    <xsd:element name="name" type="xsd:string"/>
    <xsd:element name="size" type="xsd:int"/>
    <xsd:element name="style" type="StyleType">
      <xsd:simpleType>
        <xsd:restriction base="xsd:string">
          <xsd:enumeration value="PLAIN" />
          <xsd:enumeration value="BOLD" />
          <xsd:enumeration value="ITALIC" />
          <xsd:enumeration value="BOLD_ITALIC" />
        </xsd:restriction>
      </xsd:simpleType>
    </xsd:element>
  </xsd:sequence>
</xsd:complexType>
```

Note the *anonymous type definition* of the `style` element.

The `xsd:sequence` construct is the equivalent of the concatenation notation in DTDs. The `xsd:choice` construct is the equivalent of the | operator. For example,

```
<xsd:complexType name="contactinfo">
  <xsd:choice>
    <xsd:element ref="email"/>
    <xsd:element ref="phone"/>
  </xsd:choice>
</xsd:complexType>
```

This is the equivalent of the DTD type `email|phone`.

To allow repeated elements, you use the `minoccurs` and `maxoccurs` attributes. For example, the equivalent of the DTD type `item*` is

```
<xsd:element name="item" type=". . ." minoccurs="0" maxoccurs="unbounded">
```

To specify attributes, add `xsd:attribute` elements to `complexType` definitions:

```
<xsd:element name="size">
  <xsd:complexType>
    . . .
    <xsd:attribute name="unit" type="xsd:string" use="optional" default="cm"/>
  </xsd:complexType>
</xsd:element>
```

This is the equivalent of the DTD statement

```
<!ATTLIST size unit CDATA #IMPLIED "cm">
```

You enclose element and type definitions of your schema inside an `xsd:schema` element:

```
<xsd:schema xmlns:xsd="http://www.w3.org/2001/XMLSchema">
    . . .
</xsd:schema>
```

Parsing an XML file with a schema is similar to parsing a file with a DTD, but with three differences:

1. You need to turn on support for namespaces, even if you don't use them in your XML files.

   ```
   factory.setNamespaceAware(true);
   ```

2. You need to prepare the factory for handling schemas, with the following magic incantation:

   ```
   final String JAXP_SCHEMA_LANGUAGE = "http://java.sun.com/xml/jaxp/properties/schemaLanguage";
   final String W3C_XML_SCHEMA = "http://www.w3.org/2001/XMLSchema";
   factory.setAttribute(JAXP_SCHEMA_LANGUAGE, W3C_XML_SCHEMA);
   ```

3. At least in JDK 5.0, the parser *does not discard element content whitespace*. See the code in Example 12–4 for a workaround.

NOTE: This is definitely a bug, even though bug report #4867706 classifies it as a request for enhancement.

A Practical Example

In this section, we work through a practical example that shows the use of XML in a realistic setting. Recall from Volume 1, Chapter 9 that the GridBagLayout is the most useful layout manager for Swing components. However, it is feared not just for its complexity but also for the programming tedium. It would be much more convenient to put the layout instructions into a text file instead of producing large amounts of repetitive code. In this section, you see how to use XML to describe a grid bag layout and how to parse the layout files.

A grid bag is made up of rows and columns, very similar to an HTML table. Similar to an HTML table, we describe it as a sequence of rows, each of which contains cells:

```
<gridbag>
   <row>
      <cell>...</cell>
      <cell>...</cell>
      . . .
   </row>
   <row>
      <cell>...</cell>
      <cell>...</cell>
      . . .
   </row>
   . . .
</gridbag>
```

The gridbag.dtd specifies these rules:

```
<!ELEMENT gridbag (row)*>
<!ELEMENT row (cell)*>
```

Some cells can span multiple rows and columns. In the grid bag layout, that is achieved by setting the gridwidth and gridheight constraints to values larger than 1. We use attributes of the same name:

```
<cell gridwidth="2" gridheight="2">
```

Similarly, we use attributes for the other grid bag constraints fill, anchor, gridx, gridy, weightx, weighty, ipadx, and ipady. (We don't handle the insets constraint because its value is not a simple type, but it would be straightforward to support it.) For example,

```
<cell fill="HORIZONTAL" anchor="NORTH">
```

For most of these attributes, we provide the same defaults as the GridBagConstraints default constructor:

```
<!ATTLIST cell gridwidth CDATA "1">
<!ATTLIST cell gridheight CDATA "1">
<!ATTLIST cell fill (NONE|BOTH|HORIZONTAL|VERTICAL) "NONE">
<!ATTLIST cell anchor (CENTER|NORTH|NORTHEAST|EAST
    |SOUTHEAST|SOUTH|SOUTHWEST|WEST|NORTHWEST) "CENTER">
. . .
```

The gridx and gridy values get special treatment because it would be tedious and somewhat error prone to specify them by hand. Supplying them is optional:

```
<!ATTLIST cell gridx CDATA #IMPLIED>
<!ATTLIST cell gridy CDATA #IMPLIED>
```

If they are not supplied, the program determines them according to the following heuristic: In column 0, the default gridx is 0. Otherwise, it is the preceding gridx plus the preceding gridwidth. The default gridy is always the same as the row number. Thus, you don't have to specify gridx and gridy in the most common cases, in which a component spans multiple rows. But if a component spans multiple columns, then you must specify gridx whenever you skip over that component.

 NOTE: Grid bag experts may wonder why we don't use the RELATIVE and REMAINDER mechanism to let the grid bag layout automatically determine the gridx and gridy positions. We tried, but no amount of fussing would produce the layout of the font dialog example of Volume 1. Reading through the GridBagLayout source code, it is apparent that the algorithm just won't do the heavy lifting that would be required to recover the absolute positions.

The program parses the attributes and sets the grid bag constraints. For example, to read the grid width, the program contains a single statement:

```
constraints.gridwidth = Integer.parseInt(e.getAttribute("gridwidth"));
```

The program need not worry about a missing attribute because the parser automatically supplies the default value if no other value was specified in the document.

To test whether a gridx or gridy attribute was specified, we call the getAttribute method and check if it returns the empty string:

```
String value = e.getAttribute("gridy");
if (value.length() == 0) // use default
    constraints.gridy = r;
else
    constraints.gridx = Integer.parseInt(value);
```

A cell can contain any component, but we found it convenient to allow the user to specify more general beans. That lets us specify noncomponent types such as borders. A bean is defined by a class name and zero or more properties:

```
<!ELEMENT bean (class, property*)>
<!ELEMENT class (#PCDATA)>
```

As always when using beans, we assume that the bean class has a default constructor.

A property contains a name and a value.

```
<!ELEMENT property (name, value)>
<!ELEMENT name (#PCDATA)>
```

The value is an integer, Boolean, string, or another bean:

```
<!ELEMENT value (int|string|boolean|bean)>
<!ELEMENT int (#PCDATA)>
<!ELEMENT string (#PCDATA)>
<!ELEMENT boolean (#PCDATA)>
```

Here is a typical example, a JLabel whose text property is set to the string "Face: ".

```
<bean>
  <class>javax.swing.JLabel</class>
  <property>
    <name>text</name>
    <value><string>Face: </string></value>
  </property>
</bean>
```

It seems like a bother to surround a string with the <string> tag. Why not just use #PCDATA for strings and leave the tags for the other types? Because then we would need to use mixed content and weaken the rule for the value element to

```
<!ELEMENT value (#PCDATA|int|boolean|bean)*>
```

However, that rule would allow an arbitrary mixture of text and tags.

The program sets a property by using the BeanInfo class. BeanInfo enumerates the property descriptors of the bean. We search for the property with the matching name, and then call its setter method with the supplied value.

When our program reads in a user interface description, it has enough information to construct and arrange the user interface components. But, of course, the interface is not alive—no event listeners have been attached. To add event listeners, we have to locate the components. For that reason, we support an optional attribute of type ID for each bean:

```
<!ATTLIST bean id ID #IMPLIED>
```

For example, here is a combo box with an ID:

```
<bean id="face">
  <class>javax.swing.JComboBox</class>
</bean>
```

Recall that the parser checks that IDs are unique.

A programmer can attach event handlers like this:

```
gridbag = new GridBagPane("fontdialog.xml");
setContentPane(gridbag);
JComboBox face = (JComboBox) gridbag.get("face");
face.addListener(listener);
```

NOTE: In this example, we only use XML to describe the component layout and leave it to programmers to attach the event handlers in the Java code. You could go a step further and add the code to the XML description. The most promising approach is to use a scripting language such as JavaScript for the code. If you want to add that enhancement, check out the Rhino interpreter at http://www.mozilla.org/rhino.

The program in Example 12–2 shows how to use the GridBagPane class to do all the boring work of setting up the grid bag layout. The layout is defined in Example 12–3. Figure 12–4 shows the result. The program only initializes the combo boxes (which are too complex for

the bean property-setting mechanism that the GridBagPane supports) and attaches event listeners. The GridBagPane class in Example 12–4 parses the XML file, constructs the components, and lays them out. Example 12–5 shows the DTD.

The program can also process a schema instead of a DTD if you launch it with

```
java GridBagTest fontdialog-schema.xml
```

Example 12–6 contains the schema.

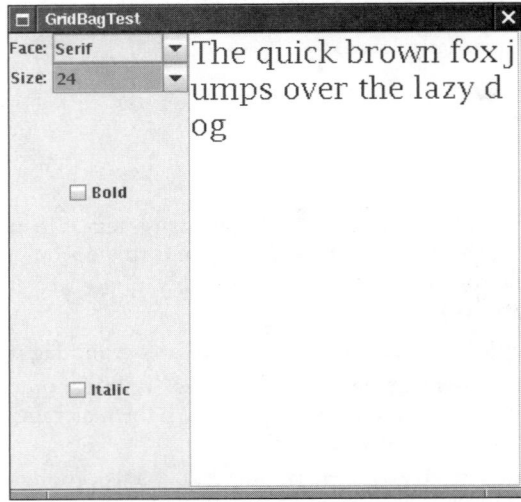

Figure 12–4: A font dialog defined by an XML layout

This example is a typical use of XML. The XML format is robust enough to express complex relationships. The XML parser adds value by taking over the routine job of validity checking and supplying defaults.

Example 12–2: GridBagTest.java

```java
 1. import java.awt.*;
 2. import java.awt.event.*;
 3. import javax.swing.*;
 4.
 5. /**
 6.    This program shows how to use an XML file to describe
 7.    a gridbag layout
 8. */
 9. public class GridBagTest
10. {
11.    public static void main(String[] args)
12.    {
13.       String filename = args.length == 0 ? "fontdialog.xml" : args[0];
14.       JFrame frame = new FontFrame(filename);
15.       frame.setDefaultCloseOperation(JFrame.EXIT_ON_CLOSE);
16.       frame.setVisible(true);
17.    }
18. }
19.
20. /**
```

```
21.     This frame contains a font selection dialog that is described by an XML file.
22.     @param filename the file containing the user interface components for the dialog.
23. */
24. class FontFrame extends JFrame
25. {
26.    public FontFrame(String filename)
27.    {
28.       setSize(DEFAULT_WIDTH, DEFAULT_HEIGHT);
29.       setTitle("GridBagTest");
30.
31.       gridbag = new GridBagPane(filename);
32.       add(gridbag);
33.
34.       face = (JComboBox) gridbag.get("face");
35.       size = (JComboBox) gridbag.get("size");
36.       bold = (JCheckBox) gridbag.get("bold");
37.       italic = (JCheckBox) gridbag.get("italic");
38.
39.       face.setModel(new DefaultComboBoxModel(new Object[]
40.          {
41.             "Serif", "SansSerif", "Monospaced", "Dialog", "DialogInput"
42.          }));
43.
44.       size.setModel(new DefaultComboBoxModel(new Object[]
45.          {
46.             "8", "10", "12", "15", "18", "24", "36", "48"
47.          }));
48.
49.       ActionListener listener = new
50.          ActionListener()
51.          {
52.             public void actionPerformed(ActionEvent event) { setSample(); }
53.          };
54.
55.       face.addActionListener(listener);
56.       size.addActionListener(listener);
57.       bold.addActionListener(listener);
58.       italic.addActionListener(listener);
59.
60.       setSample();
61.    }
62.
63.    /**
64.       This method sets the text sample to the selected font.
65.    */
66.    public void setSample()
67.    {
68.       String fontFace = (String) face.getSelectedItem();
69.       int fontSize = Integer.parseInt((String) size.getSelectedItem());
70.       JTextArea sample = (JTextArea) gridbag.get("sample");
71.       int fontStyle
72.          = (bold.isSelected() ? Font.BOLD : 0)
73.          + (italic.isSelected() ? Font.ITALIC : 0);
74.
75.       sample.setFont(new Font(fontFace, fontStyle, fontSize));
76.       sample.repaint();
```

```
77.    }
78.
79.    private GridBagPane gridbag;
80.    private JComboBox face;
81.    private JComboBox size;
82.    private JCheckBox bold;
83.    private JCheckBox italic;
84.    private static final int DEFAULT_WIDTH = 400;
85.    private static final int DEFAULT_HEIGHT = 400;
86. }
```

Example 12–3: fontdialog.xml

```
1. <?xml version="1.0"?>
2. <!DOCTYPE gridbag SYSTEM "gridbag.dtd">
3. <gridbag>
4.    <row>
5.       <cell anchor="EAST">
6.          <bean>
7.             <class>javax.swing.JLabel</class>
8.             <property>
9.                <name>text</name>
10.               <value><string>Face: </string></value>
11.            </property>
12.         </bean>
13.      </cell>
14.      <cell fill="HORIZONTAL" weightx="100">
15.         <bean id="face">
16.            <class>javax.swing.JComboBox</class>
17.         </bean>
18.      </cell>
19.      <cell gridheight="4" fill="BOTH" weightx="100" weighty="100">
20.         <bean id="sample">
21.            <class>javax.swing.JTextArea</class>
22.            <property>
23.               <name>text</name>
24.               <value><string>The quick brown fox jumps over the lazy dog</string></value>
25.            </property>
26.            <property>
27.               <name>editable</name>
28.               <value><boolean>false</boolean></value>
29.            </property>
30.            <property>
31.               <name>lineWrap</name>
32.               <value><boolean>true</boolean></value>
33.            </property>
34.            <property>
35.               <name>border</name>
36.               <value>
37.                  <bean>
38.                     <class>javax.swing.border.EtchedBorder</class>
39.                  </bean>
40.               </value>
41.            </property>
42.         </bean>
43.      </cell>
```

```
44.    </row>
45.    <row>
46.        <cell anchor="EAST">
47.            <bean>
48.                <class>javax.swing.JLabel</class>
49.                <property>
50.                    <name>text</name>
51.                    <value><string>Size: </string></value>
52.                </property>
53.            </bean>
54.        </cell>
55.        <cell fill="HORIZONTAL" weightx="100">
56.            <bean id="size">
57.                <class>javax.swing.JComboBox</class>
58.            </bean>
59.        </cell>
60.    </row>
61.    <row>
62.        <cell gridwidth="2" weighty="100">
63.            <bean id="bold">
64.                <class>javax.swing.JCheckBox</class>
65.                <property>
66.                    <name>text</name>
67.                    <value><string>Bold</string></value>
68.                </property>
69.            </bean>
70.        </cell>
71.    </row>
72.    <row>
73.        <cell gridwidth="2" weighty="100">
74.            <bean id="italic">
75.                <class>javax.swing.JCheckBox</class>
76.                <property>
77.                    <name>text</name>
78.                    <value><string>Italic</string></value>
79.                </property>
80.            </bean>
81.        </cell>
82.    </row>
83. </gridbag>
```

Example 12–4: GridBagPane.java

```java
1.  import java.awt.*;
2.  import java.beans.*;
3.  import java.io.*;
4.  import java.lang.reflect.*;
5.  import javax.swing.*;
6.  import javax.xml.parsers.*;
7.  import org.w3c.dom.*;
8.  import org.xml.sax.*;
9.
10. import org.w3c.dom.ls.*;
11. import org.w3c.dom.bootstrap.*;
12.
13. /**
```

```
14.     This panel uses an XML file to describe its
15.     components and their grid bag layout positions.
16.  */
17.  public class GridBagPane extends JPanel
18.  {
19.     /**
20.        Constructs a grid bag pane.
21.        @param filename the name of the XML file that
22.        describes the pane's components and their positions
23.     */
24.     public GridBagPane(String filename)
25.     {
26.        setLayout(new GridBagLayout());
27.        constraints = new GridBagConstraints();
28.
29.        try
30.        {
31.           DocumentBuilderFactory factory = DocumentBuilderFactory.newInstance();
32.           factory.setValidating(true);
33.
34.           if (filename.contains("-schema"))
35.           {
36.              factory.setNamespaceAware(true);
37.              final String JAXP_SCHEMA_LANGUAGE =
38.                 "http://java.sun.com/xml/jaxp/properties/schemaLanguage";
39.              final String W3C_XML_SCHEMA =
40.                 "http://www.w3.org/2001/XMLSchema";
41.              factory.setAttribute(JAXP_SCHEMA_LANGUAGE, W3C_XML_SCHEMA);
42.           }
43.
44.           factory.setIgnoringElementContentWhitespace(true);
45.
46.           DocumentBuilder builder = factory.newDocumentBuilder();
47.           Document doc = builder.parse(new File(filename));
48.
49.           if (filename.contains("-schema")) // workaround for bug #4867706
50.           {
51.              int count = removeWhitespace(doc.getDocumentElement());
52.              System.out.println(count + " whitespace nodes removed.");
53.           }
54.
55.           parseGridbag(doc.getDocumentElement());
56.        }
57.        catch (Exception e)
58.        {
59.           e.printStackTrace();
60.        }
61.     }
62.
63.     /**
64.        Removes whitespace from element content
65.        @param e the root element
66.        @return the number of whitespace nodes that were removed.
67.     */
68.     private int removeWhitespace(Element e)
69.     {
```

```
70.     NodeList children = e.getChildNodes();
71.     if (children.getLength() <= 1) return 0;
72.     int count = 0;
73.     for (int i = children.getLength() - 1; i >= 0; i--)
74.     {
75.        Node child = children.item(i);
76.        if (child instanceof Text && ((Text) child).getData().trim().length() == 0)
77.        {
78.           e.removeChild(child);
79.           count++;
80.        }
81.        else if (child instanceof Element)
82.           count += removeWhitespace((Element) child);
83.     }
84.     return count;
85.  }
86.
87.  /**
88.     Gets a component with a given name
89.     @param name a component name
90.     @return the component with the given name, or null if
91.     no component in this grid bag pane has the given name
92.  */
93.  public Component get(String name)
94.  {
95.     Component[] components = getComponents();
96.     for (int i = 0; i < components.length; i++)
97.     {
98.        if (components[i].getName().equals(name))
99.           return components[i];
100.    }
101.    return null;
102. }
103.
104. /**
105.    Parses a gridbag element.
106.    @param e a gridbag element
107. */
108. private void parseGridbag(Element e)
109. {
110.    NodeList rows = e.getChildNodes();
111.    for (int i = 0; i < rows.getLength(); i++)
112.    {
113.       Element row = (Element) rows.item(i);
114.       NodeList cells = row.getChildNodes();
115.       for (int j = 0; j < cells.getLength(); j++)
116.       {
117.          Element cell = (Element) cells.item(j);
118.          parseCell(cell, i, j);
119.       }
120.    }
121. }
122.
123. /**
124.    Parses a cell element.
125.    @param e a cell element
```

```
126.        @param r the row of the cell
127.        @param c the column of the cell
128.     */
129.     private void parseCell(Element e, int r, int c)
130.     {
131.        // get attributes
132.
133.        String value = e.getAttribute("gridx");
134.        if (value.length() == 0) // use default
135.        {
136.           if (c == 0) constraints.gridx = 0;
137.           else constraints.gridx += constraints.gridwidth;
138.        }
139.        else
140.           constraints.gridx = Integer.parseInt(value);
141.
142.        value = e.getAttribute("gridy");
143.        if (value.length() == 0) // use default
144.           constraints.gridy = r;
145.        else
146.           constraints.gridy = Integer.parseInt(value);
147.
148.        constraints.gridwidth = Integer.parseInt(e.getAttribute("gridwidth"));
149.        constraints.gridheight = Integer.parseInt(e.getAttribute("gridheight"));
150.        constraints.weightx = Integer.parseInt(e.getAttribute("weightx"));
151.        constraints.weighty = Integer.parseInt(e.getAttribute("weighty"));
152.        constraints.ipadx = Integer.parseInt(e.getAttribute("ipadx"));
153.        constraints.ipady = Integer.parseInt(e.getAttribute("ipady"));
154.
155.        // use reflection to get integer values of static fields
156.        Class cl = GridBagConstraints.class;
157.
158.        try
159.        {
160.           String name = e.getAttribute("fill");
161.           Field f = cl.getField(name);
162.           constraints.fill = f.getInt(cl);
163.
164.           name = e.getAttribute("anchor");
165.           f = cl.getField(name);
166.           constraints.anchor = f.getInt(cl);
167.        }
168.        catch (Exception ex) // the reflection methods can throw various exceptions
169.        {
170.           ex.printStackTrace();
171.        }
172.
173.        Component comp = (Component) parseBean((Element) e.getFirstChild());
174.        add(comp, constraints);
175.     }
176.
177.     /**
178.        Parses a bean element.
179.        @param e a bean element
180.     */
181.     private Object parseBean(Element e)
```

```
182.     {
183.        try
184.        {
185.            NodeList children = e.getChildNodes();
186.            Element classElement = (Element) children.item(0);
187.            String className = ((Text) classElement.getFirstChild()).getData();
188.
189.            Class cl = Class.forName(className);
190.
191.            Object obj = cl.newInstance();
192.
193.            if (obj instanceof Component)
194.               ((Component) obj).setName(e.getAttribute("id"));
195.
196.            for (int i = 1; i < children.getLength(); i++)
197.            {
198.               Node propertyElement = children.item(i);
199.               Element nameElement = (Element) propertyElement.getFirstChild();
200.               String propertyName = ((Text) nameElement.getFirstChild()).getData();
201.
202.               Element valueElement = (Element) propertyElement.getLastChild();
203.               Object value = parseValue(valueElement);
204.               BeanInfo beanInfo = Introspector.getBeanInfo(cl);
205.               PropertyDescriptor[] descriptors = beanInfo.getPropertyDescriptors();
206.               boolean done = false;
207.               for (int j = 0; !done && j < descriptors.length; j++)
208.               {
209.                  if (descriptors[j].getName().equals(propertyName))
210.                  {
211.                     descriptors[j].getWriteMethod().invoke(obj, value);
212.                     done = true;
213.                  }
214.               }
215.
216.            }
217.            return obj;
218.         }
219.         catch (Exception ex) // the reflection methods can throw various exceptions
220.         {
221.            ex.printStackTrace();
222.            return null;
223.         }
224.   }
225.
226.   /**
227.      Parses a value element.
228.      @param e a value element
229.   */
230.   private Object parseValue(Element e)
231.   {
232.      Element child = (Element) e.getFirstChild();
233.      if (child.getTagName().equals("bean")) return parseBean(child);
234.      String text = ((Text) child.getFirstChild()).getData();
235.      if (child.getTagName().equals("int")) return new Integer(text);
236.      else if (child.getTagName().equals("boolean")) return new Boolean(text);
237.      else if (child.getTagName().equals("string")) return text;
```

```
238.     else return null;
239.   }
240.
241.   private GridBagConstraints constraints;
242. }
```

Example 12–5: gridbag.dtd

```
1.  <!ELEMENT gridbag (row)*>
2.  <!ELEMENT row (cell)*>
3.  <!ELEMENT cell (bean)>
4.  <!ATTLIST cell gridx CDATA #IMPLIED>
5.  <!ATTLIST cell gridy CDATA #IMPLIED>
6.  <!ATTLIST cell gridwidth CDATA "1">
7.  <!ATTLIST cell gridheight CDATA "1">
8.  <!ATTLIST cell weightx CDATA "0">
9.  <!ATTLIST cell weighty CDATA "0">
10. <!ATTLIST cell fill (NONE|BOTH|HORIZONTAL|VERTICAL) "NONE">
11. <!ATTLIST cell anchor
12.    (CENTER|NORTH|NORTHEAST|EAST|SOUTHEAST|SOUTH|SOUTHWEST|WEST|NORTHWEST) "CENTER">
13. <!ATTLIST cell ipadx CDATA "0">
14. <!ATTLIST cell ipady CDATA "0">
15.
16. <!ELEMENT bean (class, property*)>
17. <!ATTLIST bean id ID #IMPLIED>
18.
19. <!ELEMENT class (#PCDATA)>
20. <!ELEMENT property (name, value)>
21. <!ELEMENT name (#PCDATA)>
22. <!ELEMENT value (int|string|boolean|bean)>
23. <!ELEMENT int (#PCDATA)>
24. <!ELEMENT string (#PCDATA)>
25. <!ELEMENT boolean (#PCDATA)>
```

Example 12–6: gridbag.xsd

```
1.  <xsd:schema xmlns:xsd="http://www.w3.org/2001/XMLSchema">
2.
3.    <xsd:element name="gridbag" type="GridBagType"/>
4.
5.    <xsd:element name="bean" type="BeanType"/>
6.
7.    <xsd:complexType name="GridBagType">
8.       <xsd:sequence>
9.          <xsd:element name="row" type="RowType" minOccurs="0" maxOccurs="unbounded"/>
10.      </xsd:sequence>
11.   </xsd:complexType>
12.
13.   <xsd:complexType name="RowType">
14.      <xsd:sequence>
15.         <xsd:element name="cell" type="CellType" minOccurs="0" maxOccurs="unbounded"/>
16.      </xsd:sequence>
17.   </xsd:complexType>
18.
19.   <xsd:complexType name="CellType">
20.      <xsd:sequence>
21.         <xsd:element ref="bean"/>
22.      </xsd:sequence>
```

```
23.    <xsd:attribute name="gridx" type="xsd:int" use="optional"/>
24.    <xsd:attribute name="gridy" type="xsd:int" use="optional"/>
25.    <xsd:attribute name="gridwidth" type="xsd:int" use="optional" default="1" />
26.    <xsd:attribute name="gridheight" type="xsd:int" use="optional" default="1" />
27.    <xsd:attribute name="weightx" type="xsd:int" use="optional" default="0" />
28.    <xsd:attribute name="weighty" type="xsd:int" use="optional" default="0" />
29.    <xsd:attribute name="fill" use="optional" default="NONE">
30.      <xsd:simpleType>
31.        <xsd:restriction base="xsd:string">
32.          <xsd:enumeration value="NONE" />
33.          <xsd:enumeration value="BOTH" />
34.          <xsd:enumeration value="HORIZONTAL" />
35.          <xsd:enumeration value="VERTICAL" />
36.        </xsd:restriction>
37.      </xsd:simpleType>
38.    </xsd:attribute>
39.    <xsd:attribute name="anchor" use="optional" default="CENTER">
40.      <xsd:simpleType>
41.        <xsd:restriction base="xsd:string">
42.          <xsd:enumeration value="CENTER" />
43.          <xsd:enumeration value="NORTH" />
44.          <xsd:enumeration value="NORTHEAST" />
45.          <xsd:enumeration value="EAST" />
46.          <xsd:enumeration value="SOUTHEAST" />
47.          <xsd:enumeration value="SOUTH" />
48.          <xsd:enumeration value="SOUTHWEST" />
49.          <xsd:enumeration value="WEST" />
50.          <xsd:enumeration value="NORTHWEST" />
51.        </xsd:restriction>
52.      </xsd:simpleType>
53.    </xsd:attribute>
54.    <xsd:attribute name="ipady" type="xsd:int" use="optional" default="0" />
55.    <xsd:attribute name="ipadx" type="xsd:int" use="optional" default="0" />
56.  </xsd:complexType>
57.
58.  <xsd:complexType name="BeanType">
59.    <xsd:sequence>
60.      <xsd:element name="class" type="xsd:string"/>
61.      <xsd:element name="property" type="PropertyType" minOccurs="0" maxOccurs="unbounded"/>
62.    </xsd:sequence>
63.    <xsd:attribute name="id" type="xsd:ID" use="optional" />
64.  </xsd:complexType>
65.
66.  <xsd:complexType name="PropertyType">
67.    <xsd:sequence>
68.      <xsd:element name="name" type="xsd:string"/>
69.      <xsd:element name="value" type="ValueType"/>
70.    </xsd:sequence>
71.  </xsd:complexType>
72.
73.  <xsd:complexType name="ValueType">
74.    <xsd:choice>
75.      <xsd:element ref="bean"/>
76.      <xsd:element name="int" type="xsd:int"/>
77.      <xsd:element name="string" type="xsd:string"/>
78.      <xsd:element name="boolean" type="xsd:boolean"/>
```

```
79.      </xsd:choice>
80.    </xsd:complexType>
81.  </xsd:schema>
```

Locating Information with XPath

If you want to locate a specific piece of information in an XML document, then it can be a bit of a hassle to navigate the nodes of the DOM tree. The XPath language makes it simple to access tree nodes. For example, suppose you have this XML document:

```
<configuration>
    . . .
    <database>
        <username>dbuser</username>
        <password>secret</password>
        . . .
    </database>
</configuration>
```

You can get the database user name by evaluating the XPath expression

```
/configuration/database/username
```

That's a lot simpler than the plain DOM approach:

1. Get the document node.
2. Enumerate its children.
3. Locate the database element.
4. Get its first child, the username element.
5. Get its first child, a Text node.
6. Get its data.

An XPath can describe *a set of nodes* in an XML document. For example, the XPath

```
/gridbag/row
```

describes the set of all row elements that are children of the gridbag root element. You can select a particular element with the [] operator:

```
/gridbag/row[1]
```

is the first row. (The index values start at 1.)

Use the @ operator to get attribute values. The XPath expression

```
/gridbag/row[1]/cell[1]/@anchor
```

describes the anchor attribute of the first cell in the first row. The XPath expression

```
/gridbag/row/cell/@anchor
```

describes all anchor attribute nodes of cell elements within row elements that are children of the gridbag root node.

There are a number of useful XPath functions. For example,

```
count(/gridbag/row)
```

returns the number of row children of the gridbag root. There are many more elaborate XPath expressions—see the specification at http://www.w3c.org/TR/xpath or the nifty online tutorial at http://www.zvon.org/xxl/XPathTutorial/General/examples.html.

JDK 5.0 adds an API to evaluate XPath expressions. You first create an XPath object from an XPathFactory:

```
XPathFactory xpfactory = XPathFactory.newInstance();
path = xpfactory.newXPath();
```

You then call the evaluate method to evaluate XPath expressions:

```
String username = path.evaluate("/configuration/database/username", doc);
```

You can use the same XPath object to evaluate multiple expressions.

This form of the evaluate method returns a string result. It is suitable for retrieving text, such as the text of the username node in the preceding example. If an XPath expression yields a node set, make a call such as the following:

```
NodeList nodes = (NodeList) path.evaluate("/gridbag/row", doc, XPathConstants.NODESET);
```

If the result is a single node, use XPathConstants.NODE instead:

```
Node node = (Node) path.evaluate("/gridbag/row[1]", doc, XPathConstants.NODE);
```

If the result is a number, use XPathConstants.NUMBER:

```
int count = ((Number) path.evaluate("count(/gridbag/row)", doc, XPathConstants.NUMBER)).intValue();
```

You don't have to start the search at the document root. You can start the search at any node or node list. For example, if you have a node from a previous evaluation, you can call

```
result = path.evaluate(expression, node);
```

The program in Example 12–7 demonstrates the evaluation of XPath expressions. Load an XML file and type an expression. Select the expression type and click the Evaluate button. The result of the expression is displayed at the bottom of the frame (see Figure 12–5).

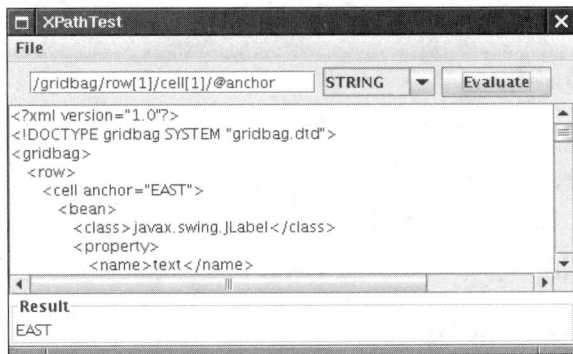

Figure 12–5: Evaluating XPath expressions

Example 12–7: XPathTest.java

```
1. import java.awt.*;
2. import java.awt.event.*;
3. import java.io.*;
4. import javax.swing.*;
5. import javax.swing.border.*;
6. import javax.xml.namespace.*;
7. import javax.xml.parsers.*;
8. import javax.xml.xpath.*;
9. import org.w3c.dom.*;
10. import org.xml.sax.*;
11.
12. /**
13.    This program evaluates XPath expressions
14. */
15. public class XPathTest
16. {
```

```
17.    public static void main(String[] args)
18.    {
19.        JFrame frame = new XPathFrame();
20.        frame.setDefaultCloseOperation(JFrame.EXIT_ON_CLOSE);
21.        frame.setVisible(true);
22.    }
23. }
24.
25. /**
26.    This frame shows an XML document, a panel to type an XPath expression,
27.    and a text field to display the result.
28. */
29. class XPathFrame extends JFrame
30. {
31.    public XPathFrame()
32.    {
33.        setTitle("XPathTest");
34.
35.        JMenu fileMenu = new JMenu("File");
36.        JMenuItem openItem = new JMenuItem("Open");
37.        openItem.addActionListener(new
38.            ActionListener()
39.            {
40.                public void actionPerformed(ActionEvent event) { openFile(); }
41.            });
42.        fileMenu.add(openItem);
43.
44.        JMenuItem exitItem = new JMenuItem("Exit");
45.        exitItem.addActionListener(new
46.            ActionListener()
47.            {
48.                public void actionPerformed(ActionEvent event) { System.exit(0); }
49.            });
50.        fileMenu.add(exitItem);
51.
52.        JMenuBar menuBar = new JMenuBar();
53.        menuBar.add(fileMenu);
54.        setJMenuBar(menuBar);
55.
56.        ActionListener listener = new
57.            ActionListener()
58.            {
59.                public void actionPerformed(ActionEvent event) { evaluate(); }
60.            };
61.        expression = new JTextField(20);
62.        expression.addActionListener(listener);
63.        JButton evaluateButton = new JButton("Evaluate");
64.        evaluateButton.addActionListener(listener);
65.
66.        typeCombo = new JComboBox(new Object[] { "STRING", "NODE", "NODESET", "NUMBER", "BOOLEAN" });
67.        typeCombo.setSelectedItem("STRING");
68.
69.        JPanel panel = new JPanel();
70.        panel.add(expression);
71.        panel.add(typeCombo);
```

```
72.     panel.add(evaluateButton);
73.     docText = new JTextArea(10, 40);
74.     result = new JTextField();
75.     result.setBorder(new TitledBorder("Result"));
76.
77.     add(panel, BorderLayout.NORTH);
78.     add(new JScrollPane(docText), BorderLayout.CENTER);
79.     add(result, BorderLayout.SOUTH);
80.
81.     try
82.     {
83.        DocumentBuilderFactory factory = DocumentBuilderFactory.newInstance();
84.        builder = factory.newDocumentBuilder();
85.     }
86.     catch (ParserConfigurationException e)
87.     {
88.        JOptionPane.showMessageDialog(this, e);
89.     }
90.
91.     XPathFactory xpfactory = XPathFactory.newInstance();
92.     path = xpfactory.newXPath();
93.     pack();
94.  }
95.
96.  /**
97.     Open a file and load the document.
98.  */
99.  public void openFile()
100. {
101.    JFileChooser chooser = new JFileChooser();
102.    chooser.setCurrentDirectory(new File("."));
103.
104.    chooser.setFileFilter(new
105.       javax.swing.filechooser.FileFilter()
106.       {
107.          public boolean accept(File f)
108.          {
109.             return f.isDirectory() || f.getName().toLowerCase().endsWith(".xml");
110.          }
111.          public String getDescription() { return "XML files"; }
112.       });
113.    int r = chooser.showOpenDialog(this);
114.    if (r != JFileChooser.APPROVE_OPTION) return;
115.    File f = chooser.getSelectedFile();
116.    try
117.    {
118.       byte[] bytes = new byte[(int) f.length()];
119.       new FileInputStream(f).read(bytes);
120.       docText.setText(new String(bytes));
121.       doc = builder.parse(f);
122.    }
123.    catch (IOException e)
124.    {
125.       JOptionPane.showMessageDialog(this, e);
126.    }
```

```
127.        catch (SAXException e)
128.        {
129.            JOptionPane.showMessageDialog(this, e);
130.        }
131.    }
132.
133.    public void evaluate()
134.    {
135.
136.        try
137.        {
138.            String typeName = (String) typeCombo.getSelectedItem();
139.            QName returnType = (QName) XPathConstants.class.getField(typeName).get(null);
140.            Object evalResult = path.evaluate(expression.getText(), doc, returnType);
141.            if (typeName.equals("NODESET"))
142.            {
143.                NodeList list = (NodeList) evalResult;
144.                StringBuilder builder = new StringBuilder();
145.                builder.append("{");
146.                for (int i = 0; i < list.getLength(); i++)
147.                {
148.                    if (i > 0) builder.append(", ");
149.                    builder.append("" + list.item(i));
150.                }
151.                builder.append("}");
152.                result.setText("" + builder);
153.            }
154.            else
155.                result.setText("" + evalResult);
156.        }
157.        catch (XPathExpressionException e)
158.        {
159.            result.setText("" + e);
160.        }
161.        catch (Exception e) // reflection exception
162.        {
163.            e.printStackTrace();
164.        }
165.    }
166.
167.    private DocumentBuilder builder;
168.    private Document doc;
169.    private XPath path;
170.    private JTextField expression;
171.    private JTextField result;
172.    private JTextArea docText;
173.    private JComboBox typeCombo;
174. }
```

API   **javax.xml.xpath.XPathFactory** 5.0

- static XPathFactory newInstance()
  returns an XPathFactory instance for creating XPath objects.
- XPath newXpath()
  constructs an XPath object for evaluating XPath expressions.

API   `javax.xml.xpath.XPath` 5.0

- `String evaluate(String expression, Object startingPoint)`
  evaluates an expression, beginning with the given starting point. The starting point can be a node or node list. If the result is a node or node set, then the returned string consists of the data of all text node children.

- `Object evaluate(String expression, Object startingPoint, QName resultType)`
  evaluates an expression, beginning with the given starting point. The starting point can be a node or node list. The `resultType` is one of the constants `STRING`, `NODE`, `NODESET`, `NUMBER`, or `BOOLEAN` in the `XPathConstants` class. The return value is a `String`, `Node`, `NodeList`, `Number`, or `Boolean`.

Using Namespaces

Java uses packages to avoid name clashes. Programmers can use the same name for different classes as long as they aren't in the same package. XML has a similar *namespace* mechanism for element and attribute names.

A namespace is identified by a Uniform Resource Identifier (URI), such as

```
http://www.w3.org/2001/XMLSchema
uuid:1c759aed-b748-475c-ab68-10679700c4f2
urn:com:books-r-us
```

The HTTP URL form is the most common. Note that the URL is just used as an identifier string, not as a locator for a document. For example, the namespace identifiers

```
http://www.horstmann.com/corejava
http://www.horstmann.com/corejava/index.html
```

denote *different* namespaces, even though a web server would serve the same document for both URLs.

There need not be any document at a namespace URL—the XML parser doesn't attempt to find anything at that location. However, as a help to programmers who encounter a possibly unfamiliar namespace, it is customary to place a document explaining the purpose of the namespace at the URL location. For example, if you point your browser to the namespace URL for the XML Schema namespace (`http://www.w3.org/2001/XMLSchema`), you will find a document describing the XML Schema standard.

Why use HTTP URLs for namespace identifiers? It is easy to ensure that they are unique. If you choose a real URL, then the host part's uniqueness is guaranteed by the domain name system. Your organization can then arrange for the uniqueness of the remainder of the URL. This is the same rationale that underlies the use of reversed domain names in Java package names.

Of course, although you want long namespace identifiers for uniqueness, you don't want to deal with long identifiers any more than you have to. In the Java programming language, you use the `import` mechanism to specify the long names of packages, and then use just the short class names. In XML, there is a similar mechanism, like this:

```
<element xmlns="namespaceURI">
    children
</element>
```

The element and its children are now part of the given namespace.

A child can provide its own namespace, for example:

```
<element xmlns="namespaceURI₁">
    <child xmlns="namespaceURI₂">
```

```
        grandchildren
      </child>
      more children
    </element>
```

Then the first child and the grandchildren are part of the second namespace.

That simple mechanism works well if you need only a single namespace or if the namespaces are naturally nested. Otherwise, you will want to use a second mechanism that has no analog in Java. You can have an *alias* for a namespace—a short identifier that you choose for a particular document. Here is a typical example:

```
<xsd:schema xmlns:xsd="http://www.w3.org/2001/XMLSchema">
  <xsd:element name="gridbag" type="GridBagType"/>
  . . .
</xsd:schema>
```

The attribute

```
xmlns:alias="namespaceURI"
```

defines a namespace and an alias. In our example, the alias is the string xsd. Thus, xsd:schema really means "schema in the namespace http://www.w3.org/2001/XMLSchema".

 NOTE: Only child elements inherit the namespace of their parent. Attributes without an explicit alias prefix are never part of a namespace. Consider this contrived example:

```
<configuration xmlns="http://www.horstmann.com/corejava"
   xmlns:si="http://www.bipm.fr/enus/3_SI/si.html">
   <size value="210" si:unit="mm"/>
   . . .
</configuration>
```

The elements configuration and size are part of the namespace with URI http://www.horst-mann.com/corejava. The attribute si:unit is part of the namespace with URI http://www.bipm.fr/enus/3_SI/si.html. However, the attribute value is not part of any namespace.

You can control how the parser deals with namespaces. By default, the Sun DOM parser is not "namespace aware."

To turn on namespace handling, call the setNamespaceAware method of the DocumentBuilderFactory:

```
factory.setNamespaceAware(true);
```

Then all builders the factory produces support namespaces. Each node has three properties:

- The *qualified name*, with an alias prefix, returned by getNodeName, getTagName, and so on
- The *local name*, without a prefix or a namespace, returned by the getLocalName method
- The namespace URI, returned by the getNamespaceURI method

Here is an example. Suppose the parser sees the following element:

```
<xsd:schema xmlns:xsl="http://www.w3.org/2001/XMLSchema">
```

It then reports the following:

- Qualified name = xsd:schema
- Local name = schema
- Namespace URI = http://www.w3.org/2001/XMLSchema

 NOTE: If namespace awareness is turned off, then getLocalName and getNamespaceURI return null.

org.w3c.dom.Node 1.4

- String getLocalName()
  returns the local name (without alias prefix), or null if the parser is not namespace aware.

- String getNamespaceURI()
  returns the namespace URI, or null if the node is not part of a namespace or if the parser is not namespace aware.

javax.xml.parsers.DocumentBuilderFactory 1.4

- boolean isNamespaceAware()
- void setNamespaceAware(boolean value)
  are the "namespaceAware" property of the factory. If set to true, the parsers that this factory generates are namespace aware.

Using the SAX Parser

The DOM parser reads an XML document in its entirety into a tree data structure. For most practical applications, DOM works fine. However, it can be inefficient if the document is large and if your processing algorithm is simple enough that you can analyze nodes on the fly, without having to see all of the tree structure. In these cases, you should use the SAX parser instead. The SAX parser reports events as it parses the components of the XML input, but it does not store the document in any way—it is up to the event handlers whether they want to build a data structure. In fact, the DOM parser is built on top of the SAX parser. It builds the DOM tree as it receives the parser events.

Whenever you use a SAX parser, you need a handler that defines the event actions for the various parse events. The ContentHandler interface defines several callback methods that the parser executes as it parses the document. Here are the most important ones:

- startElement and endElement are called when a start tag or end tag is encountered.
- characters is called whenever character data are encountered.
- startDocument and endDocument are called once each, at the start and the end of the document.

For example, when parsing the fragment

```
<font>
  <name>Helvetica</name>
  <size units="pt">36</size>
</font>
```

the parser makes sure the following calls are generated:

1. startElement, element name: font
2. startElement, element name: name
3. characters, content: Helvetica
4. endElement, element name: name
5. startElement, element name: size, attributes: units="pt"
6. characters, content: 36
7. endElement, element name: size
8. endElement, element name: font

Your handler needs to override these methods and have them carry out whatever action you want to carry out as you parse the file. The program at the end of this section prints all links <a href="..."> in an HTML file. It simply overrides the startElement method of the

handler to check for links with name a and an attribute with name href. This is potentially useful for implementing a "web crawler," a program that reaches more and more web pages by following links.

 NOTE: Unfortunately, most HTML pages deviate so much from proper XML that the example program will not be able to parse them. As already mentioned, the World Wide Web Consortium (W3C) recommends that web designers use XHTML, an HTML dialect that can be displayed by current web browsers and that is also proper XML. See http://www.w3.org/TR/xhtml1/ for more information on XHTML. Since the W3C "eats its own dog food," their web pages are written in XHTML. You can use those pages to test the example program. For example, if you run

```
java SAXTest http://www.w3.org/MarkUp
```

then you will see a list of the URLs of all links on that page.

The sample program is a good example for the use of SAX. We don't care at all in which context the a elements occur, and there is no need to store a tree structure.

Here is how you get a SAX parser:

```
SAXParserFactory factory = SAXParserFactory.newInstance();
SAXParser parser = factory.newSAXParser();
```

You can now process a document:

```
parser.parse(source, handler);
```

Here, source can be a file, URL string, or input stream. The handler belongs to a subclass of DefaultHandler. The DefaultHandler class defines do-nothing methods for the four interfaces:

```
ContentHandler
DTDHandler
EntityResolver
ErrorHandler
```

The example program defines a handler that overrides the startElement method of the ContentHandler interface to watch out for a elements with an href attribute:

```
DefaultHandler handler = new
   DefaultHandler()
   {
      public void startElement(String namespaceURI, String lname, String qname, Attributes attrs)
         throws SAXException
      {
         if (lname.equalsIgnoreCase("a") && attrs != null)
         {
            for (int i = 0; i < attrs.getLength(); i++)
            {
               String aname = attrs.getLocalName(i);
               if (aname.equalsIgnoreCase("href"))
                  System.out.println(attrs.getValue(i));
            }
         }
      }
   };
```

The startElement method has three parameters that describe the element name. The qname parameter reports the qualified name of the form alias:localname. If namespace processing is turned on, then the namespaceURI and lname parameters describe the namespace and local (unqualified) name.

As with the DOM parser, namespace processing is turned off by default. You activate namespace processing by calling the setNamespaceAware method of the factory class:

```
SAXParserFactory factory = SAXParserFactory.newInstance();
factory.setNamespaceAware(true);
SAXParser saxParser = factory.newSAXParser();
```

Example 12–8 contains the code for the web crawler program. Later in this chapter, you will see another interesting use of SAX. An easy way of turning a non-XML data source into XML is to report the SAX events that an XML parser would report. See the section on XSL transformations for details.

Example 12–8: SAXTest.java

```
1. import java.io.*;
2. import java.net.*;
3. import javax.xml.parsers.*;
4. import org.xml.sax.*;
5. import org.xml.sax.helpers.*;
6.
7. /**
8.    This program demonstrates how to use a SAX parser. The
9.    program prints all hyperlinks links of an XHTML web page.
10.   Usage: java SAXTest url
11. */
12. public class SAXTest
13. {
14.    public static void main(String[] args) throws Exception
15.    {
16.       String url;
17.       if (args.length == 0)
18.       {
19.          url = "http://www.w3c.org";
20.          System.out.println("Using " + url);
21.       }
22.       else
23.          url = args[0];
24.
25.       DefaultHandler handler = new
26.          DefaultHandler()
27.          {
28.             public void startElement(String namespaceURI,
29.                String lname, String qname, Attributes attrs)
30.             {
31.                if (lname.equalsIgnoreCase("a") && attrs != null)
32.                {
33.                   for (int i = 0; i < attrs.getLength(); i++)
34.                   {
35.                      String aname = attrs.getLocalName(i);
36.                      if (aname.equalsIgnoreCase("href"))
37.                         System.out.println(attrs.getValue(i));
38.                   }
39.                }
40.             }
41.          };
42.
43.       SAXParserFactory factory = SAXParserFactory.newInstance();
44.       factory.setNamespaceAware(true);
```

```
45.        SAXParser saxParser = factory.newSAXParser();
46.        InputStream in = new URL(url).openStream();
47.        saxParser.parse(in, handler);
48.    }
49. }
```

javax.xml.parsers.SAXParserFactory 1.4

- static SAXParserFactory newInstance()
  returns an instance of the SAXParserFactory class.

- SAXParser newSAXParser()
  returns an instance of the SAXParser class.

- boolean isNamespaceAware()
- void setNamespaceAware(boolean value)
  are the "namespaceAware" property of the factory. If set to true, the parsers that this factory generates are namespace aware.

- boolean isValidating()
- void setValidating(boolean value)
  are the "validating" property of the factory. If set to true, the parsers that this factory generates validate their input.

javax.xml.parsers.SAXParser 1.4

- void parse(File f, DefaultHandler handler)
- void parse(String url, DefaultHandler handler)
- void parse(InputStream in, DefaultHandler handler)
  parse an XML document from the given file, URL, or input stream and report parse events to the given handler.

org.xml.sax.ContentHandler 1.4

- void startDocument()
- void endDocument()
  are called at the start and the end of the document.

- void startElement(String uri, String lname, String qname, Attributes attr)
- void endElement(String uri, String lname, String qname)
  are called at the start and the end of an element.

Parameters:	uri	The URI of the namespace (if the parser is namespace aware)
	lname	The local name without alias prefix (if the parser is namespace aware)
	qname	The element name if the parser is not namespace aware, or the qualified name with alias prefix if the parser reports qualified names in addition to local names

- void characters(char[] data, int start, int length)
  is called when the parser reports character data.

Parameters:	data	An array of character data
	start	The index of the first character in the data array that is a part of the reported characters
	length	The length of the reported character string

`org.xml.sax.Attributes` 1.4

- `int getLength()`
  returns the number of attributes stored in this attribute collection.

- `String getLocalName(int index)`
  returns the local name (without alias prefix) of the attribute with the given index, or the empty string if the parser is not namespace aware.

- `String getURI(int index)`
  returns the namespace URI of the attribute with the given index, or the empty string if the node is not part of a namespace or if the parser is not namespace aware.

- `String getQName(int index)`
  returns the qualified name (with alias prefix) of the attribute with the given index, or the empty string if the qualified name is not reported by the parser.

- `String getValue(int index)`
- `String getValue(String qname)`
- `String getValue(String uri, String lname)`
  return the attribute value from a given index, qualified name, or namespace URI + local name. Return `null` if the value doesn't exist.

Generating XML Documents

You now know how to write Java programs that read XML. Let us now turn to the opposite process, producing XML output. Of course, you could write an XML file simply by making a sequence of `print` calls, printing the elements, attributes, and text content, but that would not be a good idea. The code is rather tedious, and you can easily make mistakes if you don't pay attention to special symbols (such as " or <) in the attribute values and text content.

A better approach is to build up a DOM tree with the contents of the document and then write out the tree contents. To build a DOM tree, you start out with an empty document. You can get an empty document by calling the `newDocument` method of the `DocumentBuilder` class.

```
Document doc = builder.newDocument();
```

Use the `createElement` method of the `Document` class to construct the elements of your document.

```
Element rootElement = doc.createElement(rootName);
Element childElement = doc.createElement(childName);
```

Use the `createTextNode` method to construct text nodes:

```
Text textNode = doc.createTextNode(textContents);
```

Add the root element to the document, and add the child nodes to their parents:

```
doc.appendChild(rootElement);
rootElement.appendChild(childElement);
childElement.appendChild(textNode);
```

As you build up the DOM tree, you may also need to set element attributes. Simply call the `setAttribute` method of the `Element` class:

```
rootElement.setAttribute(name, value);
```

Somewhat curiously, the DOM API currently has no support for writing a DOM tree to an output stream. To overcome this limitation, we use the XML Style Sheet Transformations (XSLT) API. We apply the "do nothing" transformation to the document and capture its output. To include a `DOCTYPE` node in the output, you also need to set the `SYSTEM` and `PUBLIC` identifiers as output properties.

```
// construct the "do nothing" transformation
Transformer t = TransformerFactory.newInstance().newTransformer();
// set output properties to get a DOCTYPE node
t.setOutputProperty(OutputKeys.DOCTYPE_SYSTEM, systemIdentifier);
t.setOutputProperty(OutputKeys.DOCTYPE_PUBLIC, publicIdentifier);
// apply the "do nothing" transformation and send the output to a file
t.transform(new DOMSource(doc), new StreamResult(new FileOutputStream(file)));
```

For more information about XSLT, turn to the next section. Right now, consider this code a "magic incantation" to produce XML output.

 NOTE: The resulting XML file contains no whitespace (that is, no line breaks or indentations). If you like whitespace, set the `"OutputKeys.INDENT"` property to the string `"yes"`.

Example 12–9 is a typical program that produces XML output. The program draws a modernist painting—a random set of colored rectangles (see Figure 12–6). To save a masterpiece, we use the Scalable Vector Graphics (SVG) format. SVG is an XML format to describe complex graphics in a device-independent fashion. You can find more information about SVG at http://www.w3c.org/Graphics/SVG. To view SVG files, download the Apache Batik viewer (http://xml.apache.org/batik) or the Adobe browser plug-in (http://www.adobe.com/svg/main.html). Figure 12–7 shows the Apache Batik viewer.

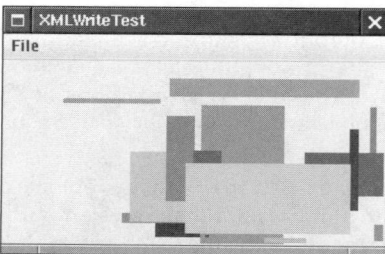

Figure 12–6: Generating modern art

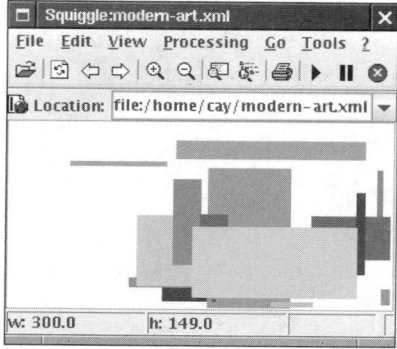

Figure 12–7: The Apache Batik SVG viewer

We don't go into details about SVG. If you are interested in SVG, we suggest you start with the tutorial on the Adobe site. For our purposes, we just need to know how to express a set of colored rectangles. Here is a sample:

```
<?xml version="1.0" encoding="UTF-8"?>
<!DOCTYPE svg PUBLIC "-//W3C//DTD SVG 20000802//EN"
    "http://www.w3.org/TR/2000/CR-SVG-20000802/DTD/svg-20000802.dtd">
<svg width="300" height="150">
<rect x="231" y="61" width="9" height="12" fill="#6e4a13"/>
<rect x="107" y="106" width="56" height="5" fill="#c406be"/>
 . . .
</svg>
```

As you can see, each rectangle is described as a rect node. The position, width, height, and fill color are attributes. The fill color is an RGB value in hexadecimal.

NOTE: As you can see, SVG uses attributes heavily. In fact, some attributes are quite complex. For example, here is a path element:

```
<path d="M 100 100 L 300 100 L 200 300 z">
```

The M denotes a "moveto" command, L is "lineto," and z is "closepath" (!). Apparently, the designers of this data format didn't have much confidence in using XML for structured data. In your own XML formats, you may want to use elements instead of complex attributes.

Here is the source code for the program. You can use the same technique whenever you need to generate XML output.

Example 12–9: XMLWriteTest.java

```
 1. import java.awt.*;
 2. import java.awt.geom.*;
 3. import java.io.*;
 4. import java.util.*;
 5. import java.awt.event.*;
 6. import javax.swing.*;
 7. import javax.xml.parsers.*;
 8. import javax.xml.transform.*;
 9. import javax.xml.transform.dom.*;
10. import javax.xml.transform.stream.*;
11. import org.w3c.dom.*;
12.
13.
14. /**
15.    This program shows how to write an XML file. It saves
16.    a file describing a modern drawing in SVG format.
17. */
18. public class XMLWriteTest
19. {
20.    public static void main(String[] args)
21.    {
22.       XMLWriteFrame frame = new XMLWriteFrame();
23.       frame.setDefaultCloseOperation(JFrame.EXIT_ON_CLOSE);
24.       frame.setVisible(true);
25.    }
26. }
27.
28. /**
29.    A frame with a panel for showing a modern drawing.
30. */
31. class XMLWriteFrame extends JFrame
```

```
32.  {
33.     public XMLWriteFrame()
34.     {
35.        setTitle("XMLWriteTest");
36.        setSize(DEFAULT_WIDTH, DEFAULT_HEIGHT);
37.
38.        chooser = new JFileChooser();
39.
40.        // add panel to frame
41.
42.        panel = new RectanglePanel();
43.        add(panel);
44.
45.        // set up menu bar
46.
47.        JMenuBar menuBar = new JMenuBar();
48.        setJMenuBar(menuBar);
49.
50.        JMenu menu = new JMenu("File");
51.        menuBar.add(menu);
52.
53.        JMenuItem newItem = new JMenuItem("New");
54.        menu.add(newItem);
55.        newItem.addActionListener(new
56.           ActionListener()
57.           {
58.              public void actionPerformed(ActionEvent event) { panel.newDrawing(); }
59.           });
60.
61.        JMenuItem saveItem = new JMenuItem("Save");
62.        menu.add(saveItem);
63.        saveItem.addActionListener(new
64.           ActionListener()
65.           {
66.              public void actionPerformed(ActionEvent event)
67.              {
68.                 try
69.                 {
70.                    saveDocument();
71.                 }
72.                 catch (TransformerException e)
73.                 {
74.                    JOptionPane.showMessageDialog(
75.                       XMLWriteFrame.this, e.toString());
76.                 }
77.                 catch (IOException e)
78.                 {
79.                    JOptionPane.showMessageDialog(
80.                       XMLWriteFrame.this, e.toString());
81.                 }
82.              }
83.           });
84.
85.        JMenuItem exitItem = new JMenuItem("Exit");
86.        menu.add(exitItem);
87.        exitItem.addActionListener(new
```

```
88.        ActionListener()
89.        {
90.           public void actionPerformed(ActionEvent event) { System.exit(0); }
91.        });
92.    }
93.
94.    /**
95.       Saves the drawing in SVG format.
96.    */
97.    public void saveDocument()
98.       throws TransformerException, IOException
99.    {
100.      if (chooser.showSaveDialog(this) != JFileChooser.APPROVE_OPTION) return;
101.      File f = chooser.getSelectedFile();
102.      Document doc = panel.buildDocument();
103.      Transformer t = TransformerFactory.newInstance().newTransformer();
104.      t.setOutputProperty(OutputKeys.DOCTYPE_SYSTEM,
105.         "http://www.w3.org/TR/2000/CR-SVG-20000802/DTD/svg-20000802.dtd");
106.      t.setOutputProperty(OutputKeys.DOCTYPE_PUBLIC, "-//W3C//DTD SVG 20000802//EN");
107.
108.      t.transform(new DOMSource(doc), new StreamResult(new FileOutputStream(f)));
109.    }
110.
111.    public static final int DEFAULT_WIDTH = 300;
112.    public static final int DEFAULT_HEIGHT = 200;
113.
114.    private RectanglePanel panel;
115.    private JFileChooser chooser;
116. }
117.
118. /**
119.    A panel that shows a set of colored rectangles
120. */
121. class RectanglePanel extends JPanel
122. {
123.    public RectanglePanel()
124.    {
125.       rects = new ArrayList<Rectangle2D>();
126.       colors = new ArrayList<Color>();
127.       generator = new Random();
128.
129.       DocumentBuilderFactory factory = DocumentBuilderFactory.newInstance();
130.       try
131.       {
132.          builder = factory.newDocumentBuilder();
133.       }
134.       catch (ParserConfigurationException e)
135.       {
136.          e.printStackTrace();
137.       }
138.    }
139.
140.    /**
141.       Create a new random drawing.
142.    */
143.    public void newDrawing()
```

```
144.    {
145.       int n = 10 + generator.nextInt(20);
146.       rects.clear();
147.       colors.clear();
148.       for (int i = 1; i <= n; i++)
149.       {
150.          int x = generator.nextInt(getWidth());
151.          int y = generator.nextInt(getHeight());
152.          int width = generator.nextInt(getWidth() - x);
153.          int height = generator.nextInt(getHeight() - y);
154.          rects.add(new Rectangle(x, y, width, height));
155.          int r = generator.nextInt(256);
156.          int g = generator.nextInt(256);
157.          int b = generator.nextInt(256);
158.          colors.add(new Color(r, g, b));
159.       }
160.       repaint();
161.    }
162.
163.    public void paintComponent(Graphics g)
164.    {
165.       if (rects.size() == 0) newDrawing();
166.       super.paintComponent(g);
167.       Graphics2D g2 = (Graphics2D) g;
168.
169.       // draw all rectangles
170.       for (int i = 0; i < rects.size(); i++)
171.       {
172.          g2.setPaint(colors.get(i));
173.          g2.fill(rects.get(i));
174.       }
175.    }
176.
177.    /**
178.       Creates an SVG document of the current drawing.
179.       @return the DOM tree of the SVG document
180.    */
181.    public Document buildDocument()
182.    {
183.
184.       Document doc = builder.newDocument();
185.       Element svgElement = doc.createElement("svg");
186.       doc.appendChild(svgElement);
187.       svgElement.setAttribute("width", "" + getWidth());
188.       svgElement.setAttribute("height", "" + getHeight());
189.       for (int i = 0; i < rects.size(); i++)
190.       {
191.          Color c = colors.get(i);
192.          Rectangle2D r = rects.get(i);
193.          Element rectElement = doc.createElement("rect");
194.          rectElement.setAttribute("x", "" + r.getX());
195.          rectElement.setAttribute("y", "" + r.getY());
196.          rectElement.setAttribute("width", "" + r.getWidth());
197.          rectElement.setAttribute("height", "" + r.getHeight());
198.          rectElement.setAttribute("fill", colorToString(c));
```

```
199.          svgElement.appendChild(rectElement);
200.        }
201.        return doc;
202.     }
203.
204.     /**
205.        Converts a color to a hex value.
206.        @param c a color
207.        @return a string of the form #rrggbb
208.     */
209.     private static String colorToString(Color c)
210.     {
211.        StringBuffer buffer = new StringBuffer();
212.        buffer.append(Integer.toHexString(c.getRGB() & 0xFFFFFF));
213.        while(buffer.length() < 6) buffer.insert(0, '0');
214.        buffer.insert(0, '#');
215.        return buffer.toString();
216.     }
217.
218.     private ArrayList<Rectangle2D> rects;
219.     private ArrayList<Color> colors;
220.     private Random generator;
221.     private DocumentBuilder builder;
222. }
```

 javax.xml.parsers.DocumentBuilder 1.4

- Document newDocument()
  returns an empty document.

 org.w3c.dom.Document 1.4

- Element createElement(String name)
  returns an element with the given name.
- Text createTextNode(String data)
  returns a text node with the given data.

 org.w3c.dom.Node 1.4

- Node appendChild(Node child)
  appends a node to the list of children of this node. Returns the appended node.

 org.w3c.dom.Element 1.4

- void setAttribute(String name, String value)
  sets the attribute with the given name to the given value.
- void setAttributeNS(String uri, String qname, String value)
  sets the attribute with the given namespace URI and qualified name to the given value.

Parameters:	uri	The URI of the namespace, or null
	qname	The qualified name. If it has an alias prefix, then uri must not be null
	value	The attribute value

 javax.xml.transform.TransformerFactory 1.4

- static TransformerFactory newInstance()
  returns an instance of the TransformerFactory class.

- Transformer newTransformer()
  returns an instance of the Transformer class that carries out an identity or "do nothing" transformation.

 javax.xml.transform.Transformer 1.4

- void setOutputProperty(String name, String value)
  sets an output property. See http://www.w3.org/TR/xslt#output for a listing of the standard output properties. The most useful ones are shown below:

Parameter:	doctype-public	The public ID to be used in the DOCTYPE declaration
	doctype-system	The system ID to be used in the DOCTYPE declaration
	indent	yes or no

- void transform(Source from, Result to)
  transforms an XML document.

 javax.xml.transform.dom.DOMSource 1.4

- DOMSource(Node n)
  constructs a source from the given node. Usually, n is a document node.

javax.xml.transform.stream.StreamResult 1.4

- StreamResult(File f)
- StreamResult(OutputStream out)
- StreamResult(Writer out)
- StreamResult(String systemID)
  construct a stream result from a file, stream, writer, or system ID (usually a relative or absolute URL).

XSL Transformations

As you have seen, the XML format is a very useful interchange format for structured data. However, most XML data are not intended for viewing by end users. In this section, we show you how to transform XML data into presentation formats such as HTML or plain text.

> NOTE: In this section, you see how to transform XML data into HTML for presentation in a browser. An alternative approach is to display XML files directly in a browser. For example, Internet Explorer shows XML documents as trees. More important, the latest versions of Netscape, Internet Explorer, and Opera let you specify a cascading style sheet (CSS) with an XML document. With a style sheet, you can control how you want the browser to display the contents of XML elements. You can find the style sheet specification at http://www.w3c.org/TR/REC-CSS2. The article "XML and CSS: Structured Markup with Display Semantics" by Pankaj Kamthan (http://tech.irt.org/articles/js198) contains a nice discussion of the pros and cons of using CSS with XML.

The purpose of a style sheet with transformation templates is to describe the conversion of XML documents into some other format (see Figure 12–8).

Here is a typical example. We want to transform XML files with employee records into HTML documents. Consider this input file.

```
<staff>
    <employee>
        <name>Carl Cracker</name>
        <salary>75000</salary>
        <hiredate year="1987" month="12" day="15"/>
    </employee>
    <employee>
        <name>Harry Hacker</name>
        <salary>50000</salary>
        <hiredate year="1989" month="10" day="1"/>
    </employee>
    <employee>
        <name>Tony Tester</name>
        <salary>40000</salary>
        <hiredate year="1990" month="3" day="15"/>
    </employee>
</staff>
```

The desired output is an HTML table:

```
<table border="1">
<tr>
<td>Carl Cracker</td><td>$75000.0</td><td>1987-12-15</td>
</tr>
<tr>
<td>Harry Hacker</td><td>$50000.0</td><td>1989-10-1</td>
</tr>
<tr>
<td>Tony Tester</td><td>$40000.0</td><td>1990-3-15</td>
</tr>
</table>
```

This table can be included in a larger HTML document, for example, a page created with JavaServer Pages technology.

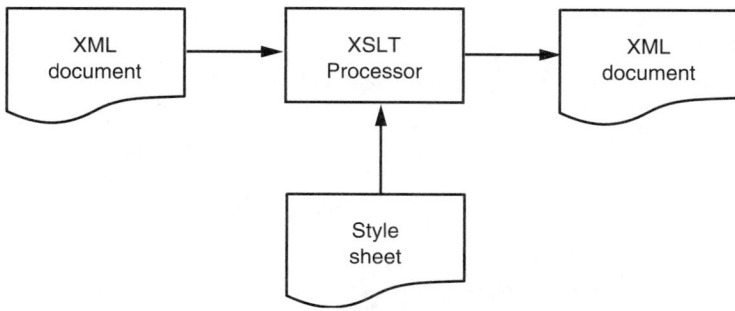

Figure 12–8: Applying XSL transformations

The XSLT specification is quite complex, and entire books have been written on the subject. We can't possibly discuss all the features of XSLT, so we just work through a representative example. You can find more information in the book *Essential XML* by Don Box et al. The XSLT specification is available at http://www.w3.org/TR/xslt.

A style sheet with transformation templates has this form:

```
<?xml version="1.0" encoding="ISO-8859-1"?>
<xsl:stylesheet
    xmlns:xsl="http://www.w3.org/1999/XSL/Transform"
    version="1.0">
    <xsl:output method="html"/>
    template₁
    template₂
    . . .
</xsl:stylesheet>
```

In our example, the `xsl:output` element specifies the method as HTML. Other valid method settings are `xml` and `text`.

Here is a typical template:

```
<xsl:template match="/staff/employee">
    <tr><xsl:apply-templates/></tr>
</xsl:template>
```

The value of the `match` attribute is an XPath expression. The template states: Whenever you see a node in the XPath set /staff/employee, do the following:

1. Emit the string `<tr>`.
2. Keep applying templates as you process its children.
3. Emit the string `</tr>` after you are done with all children.

In other words, this template generates the HTML table row markers around every employee record.

The XSLT processor starts processing by examining the root element. Whenever a node matches one of the templates, it applies the template. (If multiple templates match, the best-matching one is used—see the specification for the gory details.) If no template matches, the processor carries out a default action. For text nodes, the default is to include the contents in the output. For elements, the default action is to create no output but to keep processing the children.

Here is a template for transforming `name` nodes in an employee file:

```
<xsl:template match="/staff/employee/name">
    <td><xsl:apply-templates/></td>
</xsl:template>
```

As you can see, the template produces the `<td>...</td>` delimiters, and it asks the processor to recursively visit the children of the `name` element. There is just one child, the text node. When the processor visits that node, it emits the text contents (provided, of course, that there is no other matching template).

You have to work a little harder if you want to copy attribute values into the output. Here is an example:

```
<xsl:template match="/staff/employee/hiredate">
    <td><xsl:value-of select="@year"/>-<xsl:value-of
    select="@month"/>-<xsl:value-of select="@day"/></td>
</xsl:template>
```

When processing a `hiredate` node, this template emits

*   The string `<td>`
*   The value of the `year` attribute
*   A hyphen

- The value of the month attribute
- A hyphen
- The value of the day attribute
- A hyphen
- The string </td>

The xsl:value-of statement computes the string value of a node set. The node set is specified by the XPath value of the select attribute. In this case, the path is relative to the currently processed node. The node set is converted to a string by concatenation of the string values of all nodes. The string value of an attribute node is its value. The string value of a text node is its contents. The string value of an element node is the concatenation of the string values of its child nodes (but not its attributes).

Example 12–11 contains all transformation templates to turn an XML file with employee records into an HTML table.

Example 12–12 shows a different set of transformations. The input is the same XML file, and the output is plain text in the familiar property file format:

```
employee.1.name=Carl Cracker
employee.1.salary=75000.0
employee.1.hiredate=1987-12-15
employee.2.name=Harry Hacker
employee.2.salary=50000.0
employee.2.hiredate=1989-10-1
employee.3.name=Tony Tester
employee.3.salary=40000.0
employee.3.hiredate=1990-3-15
```

That example uses the position() function, which yields the position of the current node as seen from its parent. We get an entirely different output simply by switching the style sheet. Thus, you can safely use XML to describe your data, even if some applications need the data in another format. Just use XSLT to generate the alternative format.

It is extremely simple to generate XSL transformations in the Java platform. Set up a transformer factory for each style sheet. Then get a transformer object, and tell it to transform a source to a result.

```
File styleSheet = new File(filename);
StreamSource styleSource = new StreamSource(styleSheet);
Transformer t = TransformerFactory.newInstance().newTransformer(styleSource);
t.transform(source, result);
```

The parameters of the transform method are objects of classes that implement the Source and Result interfaces. There are three implementations of the Source interface:

```
DOMSource
SAXSource
StreamSource
```

You can construct a StreamSource from a file, stream, reader, or URL, and a DOMSource from the node of a DOM tree. For example, in the preceding section, we invoked the identity transformation as

```
t.transform(new DOMSource(doc), result);
```

In our example program, we do something slightly more interesting. Rather than starting out with an existing XML file, we produce a SAX XML reader that gives the illusion of parsing an XML file by emitting appropriate SAX events. Actually, the XML reader reads a flat file, as described in Volume 1, Chapter 12. The input file looks like this:

```
Carl Cracker|75000.0|1987|12|15
Harry Hacker|50000.0|1989|10|1
Tony Tester|40000.0|1990|3|15
```

The XML reader generates SAX events as it processes the input. Here is a part of the parse method of the EmployeeReader class that implements the XMLReader interface.

```
AttributesImpl attributes = new AttributesImpl();
handler.startDocument();
handler.startElement("", "staff", "staff", attributes);
while ((line = in.readLine()) != null)
{
   handler.startElement("", "employee", "employee", attributes);
   StringTokenizer t = new StringTokenizer(line, "|");
   handler.startElement("", "name", "name", attributes);
   String s = t.nextToken();
   handler.characters(s.toCharArray(), 0, s.length());
   handler.endElement("", "name", "name");

   . . .
   handler.endElement("", "employee", "employee");
}
handler.endElement("", rootElement, rootElement);
handler.endDocument();
```

The SAXSource for the transformer is constructed from the XML reader:

```
t.transform(new SAXSource(new EmployeeReader(),
   new InputSource(new FileInputStream(filename))), result);
```

This is an ingenious trick to convert non-XML legacy data into XML. Of course, most XSLT applications will already have XML input data, and you can simply invoke the transform method on a StreamSource, like this:

```
t.transform(new StreamSource(file), result);
```

The transformation result is an object of a class that implements the Result interface. The Java library supplies three classes:

```
DOMResult
SAXResult
StreamResult
```

To store the result in a DOM tree, use a DocumentBuilder to generate a new document node and wrap it into a DOMResult:

```
Document doc = builder.newDocument();
t.transform(source, new DOMResult(doc));
```

To save the output in a file, use a StreamResult:

```
t.transform(source, new StreamResult(file));
```

Example 12–10 contains the complete source code. Examples 12–11 and 12–12 contain two style sheets. This example concludes our discussion of the XML support in the Java library. You should now have a good perspective of the major strengths of XML, in particular, for automated parsing and validation and as a powerful transformation mechanism. Of course, all this technology is only going to work for you if you design your XML formats well. You need to make sure that the formats are rich enough to express all your business needs, that they are stable over time, and that your business partners are willing to accept your XML documents. Those issues can be far more challenging than dealing with parsers, DTDs, or transformations.

Example 12–10: TransformTest.java

```
1.  import java.io.*;
2.  import java.util.*;
3.  import javax.xml.parsers.*;
4.  import javax.xml.transform.*;
5.  import javax.xml.transform.dom.*;
6.  import javax.xml.transform.sax.*;
7.  import javax.xml.transform.stream.*;
8.  import org.xml.sax.*;
9.  import org.xml.sax.helpers.*;
10.
11. /**
12.    This program demonstrates XSL transformations. It applies
13.    a transformation to a set of employee records. The records
14.    are stored in the file employee.dat and turned into XML
15.    format. Specify the stylesheet on the command line, e.g.
16.    java TransformTest makeprop.xsl
17. */
18. public class TransformTest
19. {
20.    public static void main(String[] args) throws Exception
21.    {
22.       String filename;
23.       if (args.length > 0) filename = args[0];
24.       else filename = "makehtml.xsl";
25.       File styleSheet = new File(filename);
26.       StreamSource styleSource = new StreamSource(styleSheet);
27.
28.       Transformer t = TransformerFactory.newInstance().newTransformer(styleSource);
29.       t.transform(new SAXSource(new EmployeeReader(),
30.          new InputSource(new FileInputStream("employee.dat"))),
31.          new StreamResult(System.out));
32.    }
33. }
34.
35. /**
36.    This class reads the flat file employee.dat and reports SAX
37.    parser events to act as if it was parsing an XML file.
38. */
39. class EmployeeReader implements XMLReader
40. {
41.    public void parse(InputSource source)
42.       throws IOException, SAXException
43.    {
44.       InputStream stream = source.getByteStream();
45.       BufferedReader in = new BufferedReader(new InputStreamReader(stream));
46.       String rootElement = "staff";
47.       AttributesImpl atts = new AttributesImpl();
48.
49.       if (handler == null)
50.          throw new SAXException("No content handler");
51.
52.       handler.startDocument();
53.       handler.startElement("", rootElement, rootElement, atts);
54.       String line;
```

```
55.        while ((line = in.readLine()) != null)
56.        {
57.           handler.startElement("", "employee", "employee", atts);
58.           StringTokenizer t = new StringTokenizer(line, "|");
59.
60.           handler.startElement("", "name", "name", atts);
61.           String s = t.nextToken();
62.           handler.characters(s.toCharArray(), 0, s.length());
63.           handler.endElement("", "name", "name");
64.
65.           handler.startElement("", "salary", "salary", atts);
66.           s = t.nextToken();
67.           handler.characters(s.toCharArray(), 0, s.length());
68.           handler.endElement("", "salary", "salary");
69.
70.           atts.addAttribute("", "year", "year", "CDATA", t.nextToken());
71.           atts.addAttribute("", "month", "month", "CDATA", t.nextToken());
72.           atts.addAttribute("", "day", "day", "CDATA", t.nextToken());
73.           handler.startElement("", "hiredate", "hiredate", atts);
74.           handler.endElement("", "hiredate", "hiredate");
75.           atts.clear();
76.
77.           handler.endElement("", "employee", "employee");
78.        }
79.
80.        handler.endElement("", rootElement, rootElement);
81.        handler.endDocument();
82.     }
83.
84.     public void setContentHandler(ContentHandler newValue) {handler = newValue;}
85.     public ContentHandler getContentHandler() { return handler; }
86.
87.     // the following methods are just do-nothing implementations
88.     public void parse(String systemId) throws IOException, SAXException {}
89.     public void setErrorHandler(ErrorHandler handler) {}
90.     public ErrorHandler getErrorHandler() { return null; }
91.     public void setDTDHandler(DTDHandler handler) {}
92.     public DTDHandler getDTDHandler() { return null; }
93.     public void setEntityResolver(EntityResolver resolver) {}
94.     public EntityResolver getEntityResolver() { return null; }
95.     public void setProperty(String name, Object value) {}
96.     public Object getProperty(String name) { return null; }
97.     public void setFeature(String name, boolean value) {}
98.     public boolean getFeature(String name) { return false; }
99.
100.    private ContentHandler handler;
101. }
```

Example 12–11: makehtml.xsl

```
1. <?xml version="1.0" encoding="ISO-8859-1"?>
2.
3. <xsl:stylesheet
4.    xmlns:xsl="http://www.w3.org/1999/XSL/Transform"
5.    version="1.0">
6.
7.    <xsl:output method="html"/>
```

```
 8.
 9.    <xsl:template match="/staff">
10.       <table border="1"><xsl:apply-templates/></table>
11.    </xsl:template>
12.
13.    <xsl:template match="/staff/employee">
14.       <tr><xsl:apply-templates/></tr>
15.    </xsl:template>
16.
17.    <xsl:template match="/staff/employee/name">
18.       <td><xsl:apply-templates/></td>
19.    </xsl:template>
20.
21.    <xsl:template match="/staff/employee/salary">
22.       <td>$<xsl:apply-templates/></td>
23.    </xsl:template>
24.
25.    <xsl:template match="/staff/employee/hiredate">
26.       <td><xsl:value-of select="@year"/>-<xsl:value-of
27.       select="@month"/>-<xsl:value-of select="@day"/></td>
28.    </xsl:template>
29.
30. </xsl:stylesheet>
```

Example 12–12: makeprop.xsl

```
 1.  <?xml version="1.0"?>
 2.
 3.  <xsl:stylesheet
 4.     xmlns:xsl="http://www.w3.org/1999/XSL/Transform"
 5.     version="1.0">
 6.
 7.     <xsl:output method="text"/>
 8.
 9.     <xsl:template match="/staff/employee">
10. employee.<xsl:value-of select="position()"/>.name=<xsl:value-of select="name/text()"/>
11. employee.<xsl:value-of select="position()"/>.salary=<xsl:value-of select="salary/text()"/>
12. employee.<xsl:value-of select="position()"/>.hiredate=<xsl:value-of select="hiredate/@year"/>-
<xsl:value-of select="hiredate/@month"/>-<xsl:value-of select="hiredate/@day"/>
13.     </xsl:template>
14.
15. </xsl:stylesheet>
```

javax.xml.transform.TransformerFactory 1.4

- Transformer newTransformer(Source from)
  returns an instance of the Transformer class that reads a style sheet from the given
  source.

javax.xml.transform.stream.StreamSource 1.4

- StreamSource(File f)
- StreamSource(InputStream in)
- StreamSource(Reader in)
- StreamSource(String systemID)
  construct a stream source from a file, stream, reader, or system ID (usually a relative
  or absolute URL).

 javax.xml.transform.sax.SAXSource 1.4

- SAXSource(XMLReader reader, InputSource source)
  constructs a SAX source that obtains data from the given input source and uses the given reader to parse the input.

 org.xml.sax.XMLReader 1.4

- void setContentHandler(ContentHandler handler)
  sets the handler that is notified of parse events as the input is parsed.

- void parse(InputSource source)
  parses the input from the given input source and sends parse events to the content handler.

 javax.xml.transform.dom.DOMResult 1.4

- DOMResult(Node n)
  constructs a source from the given node. Usually, n is a new document node.

 org.xml.sax.helpers.AttributesImpl 1.4

- void addAttribute(String uri, String lname, String qname, String type, String value)
  adds an attribute to this attribute collection.

Parameters:	uri	The URI of the namespace
	lname	The local name without alias prefix
	qname	The qualified name with alias prefix
	type	The type, one of "CDATA", "ID", "IDREF", "IDREFS", "NMTOKEN", "NMTOKENS", "ENTITY", "ENTITIES", or "NOTATION"
	value	The attribute value

- void clear()
  removes all attributes from this attribute collection.

Chapter 13

Annotations

- ▼ ADDITION OF METADATA TO PROGRAMS
- ▼ AN EXAMPLE: ANNOTATING EVENT HANDLERS
- ▼ ANNOTATION SYNTAX
- ▼ STANDARD ANNOTATIONS
- ▼ THE apt TOOL FOR SOURCE-LEVEL ANNOTATION PROCESSING
- ▼ BYTECODE ENGINEERING

Annotations are tags that you insert into your source code for processing by tools. The tags can be processed at the source level, or the compiler can include them in class files.

Annotations do not change the way in which your programs are compiled. (The JDK 5.0 compiler uses a couple of annotations to generate or suppress warnings, but it generates the same class files with or without the annotations. These annotations are simple and somewhat atypical since third parties can't add new annotations to the compiler.)

In order to benefit from annotations, you need to select a *processing tool*, insert annotations into your code that your processing tool understands, and then apply the processing tool. As this chapter is written, no industrial-strength processing tools exist. Thus, we try to give you a flavor of what tools might emerge, and what capabilities you can expect of them.

There is a wide range of possible uses for annotations, and that generality can be initially confusing. Here are some possible uses for annotations:

- Automatic generation of auxiliary files, such as deployment descriptors or bean information classes.
- Automatic generation of code for testing, logging, transaction semantics, and so on.

In this chapter, we start out with the basic concepts and put them to use in a concrete example: We mark methods as event listeners for AWT components, and show you an annotation processor that analyzes the annotations and hooks up the listeners. We then discuss the syntax rules in detail. We finish the chapter with two advanced examples for

annotation processing. One of them uses apt, an annotation processing tool that is part of the JDK. The other uses the Apache Bytecode Engineering Library to inject additional byte-codes into annotated methods.

Addition of Metadata to Programs

Metadata are data about data. In the context of computer programs, metadata are data about the code. A good example for metadata is Javadoc comments. The comments describe the code, but they do not modify its meaning.

Starting with JDK 5.0, you can use *annotations* to insert arbitrary data into your source code. Why would you want to do this? Metadata are only useful in conjunction with tools. As we write this chapter, there are many promises that useful tools will soon appear. This chapter introduces you to the syntax for annotations and gives examples that demonstrate some of the possibilities. This should help you evaluate the tools that will emerge, and it might even give you ideas for building your own tools.

Here is an example of a simple annotation:

```
public class MyClass
{
    . . .
    @TestCase public void checkRandomInsertions()
}
```

The annotation @TestCase annotates the checkRandomInsertions method.

In Java, an annotation is used like a *modifier*, and it is placed before the annotated item, *without a semicolon*. (A modifier is a keyword such as public or static.) The name of each annotation is preceded by an @ symbol, similar to Javadoc comments. However, Javadoc comments occur inside /** . . . */ delimiters, whereas annotations are part of the code.

By itself, the @TestCase annotation does not do anything. It needs a tool to be useful. For example, a testing tool might call all methods that are labeled as @TestCase when testing a class. Another tool might remove all test methods from a class file so that they are not shipped with the program after it has been tested.

 NOTE: JUnit, available at http://junit.org, is a well-known testing tool. It uses a naming convention to recognize methods to be called during testing. The method names must start with the prefix test. Naming conventions are notoriously brittle—a method name such as testAndSet would confuse JUnit. The article http://www.langrsoft.com/articles/annotations.html describes how to modify JUnit for using annotations instead. It is possible that such a modification will become a part of a future version of JUnit.

Annotations can be defined to have *elements*, such as

```
@TestCase(id="3352627")
```

These elements can be processed by the tools that read the annotations. Other forms of elements are possible; we discuss them later in this chapter.

Besides methods, you can annotate classes, fields, and local variables—an annotation can be anywhere you could put a modifier such as public or static.

Each annotation must be defined by an *annotation interface*. The methods of the interface correspond to the elements of the annotation. For example, a TestCase annotation could be defined by the following interface:

```
import java.lang.annotation.*;
@Target(ElementType.METHOD)
```

```
@Retention(RetentionPolicy.RUNTIME)
public @interface TestCase
{
    String id() default "[none]";
}
```

The @interface declaration creates an actual Java interface. Tools that process annotations receive objects that implement the annotation interface. A tool would call the id method to retrieve the id element of a particular TestCase annotation.

The Target and Retention annotations are *meta-annotations*. They annotate the TestCase annotation, marking it as an annotation that can be applied to methods only and that is retained when the class file is loaded into the virtual machine. We discuss these meta-annotations in detail on page 953.

You have now seen the basic concepts of program metadata and annotations. In the next section, we walk through a concrete example of annotation processing.

An Example: Annotating Event Handlers

One of the more boring tasks in user interface programming is the wiring of listeners to event sources. Many listeners are of the form

```
myButton.addActionListener(new
    ActionListener()
    {
        public void actionPerformed(ActionEvent event)
        {
            doSomething();
        }
    });
```

In this section, we design an annotation to avoid this drudgery. The annotation has the form

```
@ActionListenerFor(source="myButton") void doSomething() { . . . }
```

The programmer no longer has to make calls to addActionListener. Instead, each method is simply tagged with an annotation. Example 13–1 shows the ButtonTest program from Volume 1, Chapter 8, reimplemented with these annotations.

We also need to define an annotation interface. The code is in Example 13–2.

Example 13–1: ButtonTest.java

```
1.  import java.awt.*;
2.  import java.awt.event.*;
3.  import javax.swing.*;
4.
5.  public class ButtonTest
6.  {
7.     public static void main(String[] args)
8.     {
9.        ButtonFrame frame = new ButtonFrame();
10.       frame.setDefaultCloseOperation(JFrame.EXIT_ON_CLOSE);
11.       frame.setVisible(true);
12.    }
13. }
14.
15. /**
16.    A frame with a button panel
17. */
```

```
18. class ButtonFrame extends JFrame
19. {
20.    public ButtonFrame()
21.    {
22.       setTitle("ButtonTest");
23.       setSize(DEFAULT_WIDTH, DEFAULT_HEIGHT);
24.
25.       panel = new JPanel();
26.       add(panel);
27.
28.       // create buttons
29.
30.       yellowButton = new JButton("Yellow");
31.       blueButton = new JButton("Blue");
32.       redButton = new JButton("Red");
33.
34.       // add buttons to panel
35.
36.       panel.add(yellowButton);
37.       panel.add(blueButton);
38.       panel.add(redButton);
39.
40.       ActionListenerInstaller.processAnnotations(this);
41.    }
42.
43.
44.    @ActionListenerFor(source="yellowButton")
45.    public void yellowBackground()
46.    {
47.       panel.setBackground(Color.YELLOW);
48.    }
49.
50.    @ActionListenerFor(source="blueButton")
51.    public void blueBackground()
52.    {
53.       panel.setBackground(Color.BLUE);
54.    }
55.
56.    @ActionListenerFor(source="redButton")
57.    public void redBackground()
58.    {
59.       panel.setBackground(Color.RED);
60.    }
61.
62.    public static final int DEFAULT_WIDTH = 300;
63.    public static final int DEFAULT_HEIGHT = 200;
64.
65.    private JPanel panel;
66.    private JButton yellowButton;
67.    private JButton blueButton;
68.    private JButton redButton;
69. }
```

Example 13–2: ActionListenerFor.java

```
1. import java.lang.annotation.*;
2.
3. @Target(ElementType.METHOD)
4. @Retention(RetentionPolicy.RUNTIME)
5. public @interface ActionListenerFor
6. {
7.    String source();
8. }
```

Of course, the annotations don't do anything by themselves. They sit in the source file. The compiler places them in the class file, and the virtual machine loads them. We now need a mechanism to analyze them and install action listeners. That is the job of the `ActionListener-Installer` class. The `ButtonFrame` constructor calls

```
ActionListenerInstaller.processAnnotations(this);
```

The static `processAnnotations` method enumerates all methods of the object that it received. For each method, it gets the `ActionListenerFor` annotation object and processes it.

```
Class cl = obj.getClass();
for (Method m : cl.getDeclaredMethods())
{
   ActionListenerFor a = m.getAnnotation(ActionListenerFor.class);
   if (a != null) . . .
}
```

Here, we use the `getAnnotation` method that is defined in the `AnnotatedElement` interface. The classes `Method`, `Constructor`, `Field`, `Class`, and `Package` implement this interface.

The name of the source field is stored in the annotation object. We retrieve it by calling the `source` method, and then look up the matching field.

```
String fieldName = a.source();
Field f = cl.getDeclaredField(fieldName);
```

This shows a limitation of our annotation. The source element must be the name of a field. It cannot be a local variable.

The remainder of the code is rather technical. For each annotated method, we construct a proxy object that implements the `ActionListener` interface and whose `actionPerformed` method calls the annotated method. (For more information about proxies, see Volume 1, Chapter 6.) The details are not important. The key observation is that the functionality of the annotations was established by the `processAnnotations` method.

In this example, the annotations were processed at run time. It would also have been possible to process them at the source level. A source code generator might have produced the code for adding the listeners. Alternatively, the annotations might have been processed at the bytecode level. A bytecode editor might have injected the calls to `addActionListener` into the frame constructor. This sounds complex, but libraries are available to make this task relatively straightforward. You can see an example on page 962.

Our example was not intended as a serious tool for user interface programmers. A utility method for adding a listener could be just as convenient for the programmer as the annotation. (In fact, the `java.beans.EventHandler` class tries to do just that. You could easily refine the class to be truly useful by supplying a method that adds the event handler instead of just constructing it.)

However, this example shows the mechanics of annotating a program and of analyzing the annotations. Having seen a concrete example, you are now more prepared (we hope) for the following sections that describe the annotation syntax in complete detail.

Example 13–3: ActionListenerInstaller.java

```
 1. import java.awt.event.*;
 2. import java.lang.annotation.*;
 3. import java.lang.reflect.*;
 4.
 5. public class ActionListenerInstaller
 6. {
 7.    /**
 8.       Processes all ActionListenerFor annotations in the given object.
 9.       @param obj an object whose methods may have ActionListenerFor annotations
10.    */
11.    public static void processAnnotations(Object obj)
12.    {
13.       try
14.       {
15.          Class cl = obj.getClass();
16.          for (Method m : cl.getDeclaredMethods())
17.          {
18.             ActionListenerFor a = m.getAnnotation(ActionListenerFor.class);
19.             if (a != null)
20.             {
21.                Field f = cl.getDeclaredField(a.source());
22.                f.setAccessible(true);
23.                addListener(f.get(obj), obj, m);
24.             }
25.          }
26.       }
27.       catch (Exception e)
28.       {
29.          e.printStackTrace();
30.       }
31.    }
32.
33.    /**
34.       Adds an action listener that calls a given method.
35.       @param source the event source to which an action listener is added
36.       @param param the implicit parameter of the method that the listener calls
37.       @param m the method that the listener calls
38.    */
39.    public static void addListener(Object source, final Object param, final Method m)
40.       throws NoSuchMethodException, IllegalAccessException, InvocationTargetException
41.    {
42.       InvocationHandler handler = new
43.          InvocationHandler()
44.          {
45.             public Object invoke(Object proxy, Method mm, Object[] args) throws Throwable
46.             {
47.                return m.invoke(param);
48.             }
49.          };
50.
```

```
51.    Object listener = Proxy.newProxyInstance(null,
52.       new Class[] { java.awt.event.ActionListener.class },
53.       handler);
54.    Method adder = source.getClass().getMethod("addActionListener", ActionListener.class);
55.    adder.invoke(source, listener);
56.    }
57. }
```

> **java.lang.AnnotatedElement 5.0**
>
> - boolean isAnnotationPresent(Class<? extends Annotation> annotationType)
>   returns true if this item has an annotation of the given type.
> - <T extends Annotation> T getAnnotation(Class<T> annotationType)
>   gets the annotation of the given type, or null if this item has no such annotation.
> - Annotation[] getAnnotations()
>   gets all annotations that are present for this item, including inherited annotations. If no annotations are present, an array of length 0 is returned.
> - Annotation[] getDeclaredAnnotations()
>   gets all annotations that are declared for this item, excluding inherited annotations. If no annotations are present, an array of length 0 is returned.

Annotation Syntax

In this section, we cover everything you need to know about the annotation syntax.

An annotation is defined by an annotation interface:

```
modifiers @interface AnnotationName
{
   element declaration₁
   element declaration₂
   . . .
}
```

Each element declaration has the form

```
type elementName();
```

or

```
type elementName() default value;
```

For example, the following annotation has two elements, assignedTo and severity.

```
public @interface BugReport
{
   String assignedTo() default "[none]";
   int severity() = 0;
}
```

Each annotation has the format

$$@AnnotationName(elementName_1=value_1, elementName_2=value_2, . . .)$$

For example,

```
@BugReport(assignedTo="Harry", severity=10)
```

The order of the elements does not matter. The annotation

```
@BugReport(severity=10, assignedTo="Harry")
```

is identical to the preceding one.

The default value of the declaration is used if an element value is not specified. For example, consider the annotation

```
@BugReport(severity=10)
```

The value of the assignedTo element is the string "[none]".

 CAUTION: Defaults are not stored with the annotation; instead, they are dynamically computed. For example, if you change the default for the assignedTo element to "[]" and recompile the BugReport interface, then the annotation @BugReport(severity=10) uses the new default, even in class files that have been compiled before the default changed.

Two special shortcuts can simplify annotations.

If no elements are specified, either because the annotation doesn't have any or because all of them use the default value, then you don't need to use parentheses. For example,

```
@BugReport
```

is the same as

```
@BugReport(assignedTo="[none]", severity=0)
```

Such an annotation is called a *marker annotation*.

The other shortcut is the *single value annotation*. If an element has the special name value, and no other element is specified, then you can omit the element name and the = symbol. For example, had we defined the ActionListenerFor annotation interface of the preceding section as

```
public @interface ActionListenerFor
{
    String value();
}
```

then we could have written the annotations as

```
@ActionListenerFor("yellowButton")
```

instead of

```
@ActionListenerFor(value="yellowButton")
```

All annotation interfaces implicitly extend the interface java.lang.annotation.Annotation. That interface is a regular interface, *not* an annotation interface. See the API notes at the end of this section for the methods provided by this interface.

You cannot extend annotation interfaces. In other words, all annotation interfaces directly extend java.lang.annotation.Annotation.

You never supply classes that implement annotation interfaces. Instead, the virtual machine generates proxy classes and objects when needed. For example, when requesting an ActionListenerFor annotation, the virtual machine carries out an operation similar to the following:

```
return Proxy.newProxyInstance(classLoader, ActionListenerFor.class,
    new
        InvocationHandler()
        {
            public Object invoke(Object proxy, Method m, Object[] args) throws Throwable
            {
                if (m.getName().equals("source")) return value of source annotation;
                . . .
            }
        });
```

The element declarations in the annotation interface are actually method declarations. The methods of an annotation interface can have no parameters and no throws clauses, and they cannot be generic.

The type of an annotation element is one of the following:

- A primitive type (int, short, long, byte, char, double, float, or boolean)
- String
- Class (with an optional type parameter such as Class<? extends MyClass>)
- An enum type
- An annotation type
- An array of the preceding types

 NOTE: An array of arrays is not a legal element type.

Here are examples for valid element declarations:

```
public @interface BugReport
{
    enum Status { UNCONFIRMED, CONFIRMED, FIXED, NOTABUG };
    boolean showStopper() default false;
    String assignedTo() default "[none]";
    Class<? extends Testable> testCase() default Testable.class;
    Status status() default Status.UNCONFIRMED;
    TestCase testCase();
    String[] reportedBy();
}
```

Because annotations are evaluated by the compiler, all element values must be compile-time constants. For example,

```
@BugReport(showStopper=true, assignedTo="Harry", testCase=MyTestCase.class,
    status=BugReport.Status.CONFIRMED, . . .)
```

 CAUTION: An annotation element can never be set to null. Not even a default of null is permissible. This can be rather inconvenient in practice. You will need to find other defaults, such as "" or Void.class.

If an element value is an array, you enclose its values in braces, like this:

```
@BugReport(. . ., reportedBy={"Harry", "Carl"})
```

You can omit the braces if the element has a single value:

```
@BugReport(. . ., reportedBy="Joe") // OK, same as {"Joe"}
```

Since an annotation element can be another annotation, you can build arbitrarily complex annotations. For example,

```
@BugReport(testCase=@TestCase(id="3352627"), . . .)
```

 NOTE: It is an error to introduce circular dependencies in annotations. For example, if BugReport has an element of the annotation type TestCase, then TestCase can't have an element of type BugReport.

You can add annotations to the following items:

- Packages
- Classes (including enum)
- Interfaces (including annotation interfaces)
- Methods
- Constructors
- Instance fields (including enum constants)
- Local variables
- Parameter variables

However, annotations for local variables can only be processed at the source level. Class files do not describe local variables. Therefore, all local variable annotations are discarded when a class is compiled. Similarly, annotations for packages are not retained beyond the source level.

 NOTE: If you want to process annotations of local variables, you have to write your own parser. The apt tool of the JDK (which we will discuss later in this chapter) does not visit local variables.

An item can have multiple annotations, provided they belong to different types. You cannot use the same annotation type more than once when annotating a particular item. For example,

```
@BugReport(showStopper=true, reportedBy="Joe")
@BugReport(reportedBy={"Harry", "Carl"})
void myMethod()
```

is a compile-time error. If this is a problem, you can design an annotation whose value is an array of simpler annotations:

```
@BugReports({
    @BugReport(showStopper=true, reportedBy="Joe"),
    @BugReport(reportedBy={"Harry", "Carl"}))
void myMethod()
```

 java.lang.annotation.Annotation 5.0

- `Class<? extends Annotation> annotationType()`
  returns the Class object that represents the annotation interface of this annotation object. Note that calling getClass on an annotation object would return the actual class, not the interface.

- `boolean equals(Object other)`
  returns true if other is an object that implements the same annotation interface as this annotation object and if all elements of this object and other are equal to another.

- `int hashCode()`
  returns a hash code that is compatible with the equals method, derived from the name of the annotation interface and the element values.

- `String toString()`
  returns a string representation that contains the annotation interface name and the element values, for example, @BugReport(assignedTo=[none], severity=0)

Standard Annotations

JDK 5.0 defines seven annotation interfaces. Three of them are regular annotations that you can use to annotate items in your source code. The other four are meta-annotations that describe the behavior of annotation interfaces. Table 13–1 shows these annotations. We discuss them in detail in the following two sections.

Table 13–1: The Standard Annotations

Annotation Interface	Applicable To	Purpose
Deprecated	All	Marks item as deprecated
SuppressWarnings	All but packages and annotations	Suppresses warnings of the given type
Override	Methods	Checks that this method overrides a superclass method
Target	Annotations	Specifies the items to which this annotation can be applied
Retention	Annotations	Specifies how long this annotation is retained
Documented	Annotations	Specifies that this annotation should be included in the documentation of annotated items
Inherited	Annotations	Specifies that this annotation, when applied to a class, is automatically inherited by its subclasses.

Regular Annotations

The @Deprecated annotation can be attached to any items whose use is no longer encouraged. The compiler will warn when you use a deprecated item. This annotation has the same role as the @deprecated Javadoc tag.

The @SuppressWarnings annotation tells the compiler to suppress warnings of a particular type, for example,

```
@SuppressWarnings("unchecked cast")
```

The initial release of the JDK 5.0 compiler does not support this annotation.

The @Override annotation applies only to methods. The compiler checks that a method with this annotation really overrides a method from the superclass. For example, if you declare

```
public MyClass
{
   @Override public boolean equals(MyClass other);
   . . .
}
```

then the compiler will report an error. After all, the equals method does *not* override the equals method of the Object class. That method has a parameter of type Object, not MyClass.

Meta-Annotations

The @Target meta-annotation is applied to an annotation, restricting the items to which the annotation applies. For example,

```
@Target({ElementType.METHOD, ElementType.CONSTRUCTOR})
public @interface TestCase
```

Table 13–2 shows all possible values. They belong to the enumerated type `ElementType`. You can specify any number of element types, enclosed in braces.

Table 13–2: Element Types for the @Target Annotation

Element Type	Annotation Applies To
ANNOTATION_TYPE	Annotation type declarations
PACKAGE	Packages
TYPE	Classes (including `enum`) and interfaces (including annotation types)
METHOD	Methods
CONSTRUCTOR	Constructors
FIELD	Fields (including `enum` constants)
PARAMETER	Method or constructor parameters
LOCAL_VARIABLE	Local variables

An annotation without an `@Target` restriction can be applied to any item. The compiler checks that you apply an annotation only to a permitted item. For example, if you apply `@TestCase` to a field, a compile-time error results.

The `@Retention` meta-annotation specifies how long an annotation is retained. You specify at most one of the values in Table 13–3. The default is `RetentionPolicy.CLASS`.

Table 13–3: Retention Policies for the @Retention Annotation

Retention Policy	Description
SOURCE	Annotations are not included in class files.
CLASS	Annotations are included in class files, but the virtual machine need not load them.
RUNTIME	Annotations are included in class files and loaded by the virtual machine. They are available through the reflection API.

In Example 13–2, the `@ActionListenerFor` annotation was declared with `RetentionPolicy.RUNTIME` because we used reflection to process annotations. In the following two sections, you will see examples of processing annotations at the source and class file levels.

The `@Documented` meta-annotation gives a hint to documentation tools such as Javadoc. Documented annotations should be treated just like other modifiers such as `protected` or `static` for documentation purposes. The use of other annotations is not included in the documentation. For example, suppose we declare `@ActionListenerFor` as a documented annotation:

```
@Documented
@Target(ElementType.METHOD)
@Retention(RetentionPolicy.RUNTIME)
public @interface ActionListenerFor
```

Now the documentation of each annotated method contains the annotation, as shown in Figure 13–1.

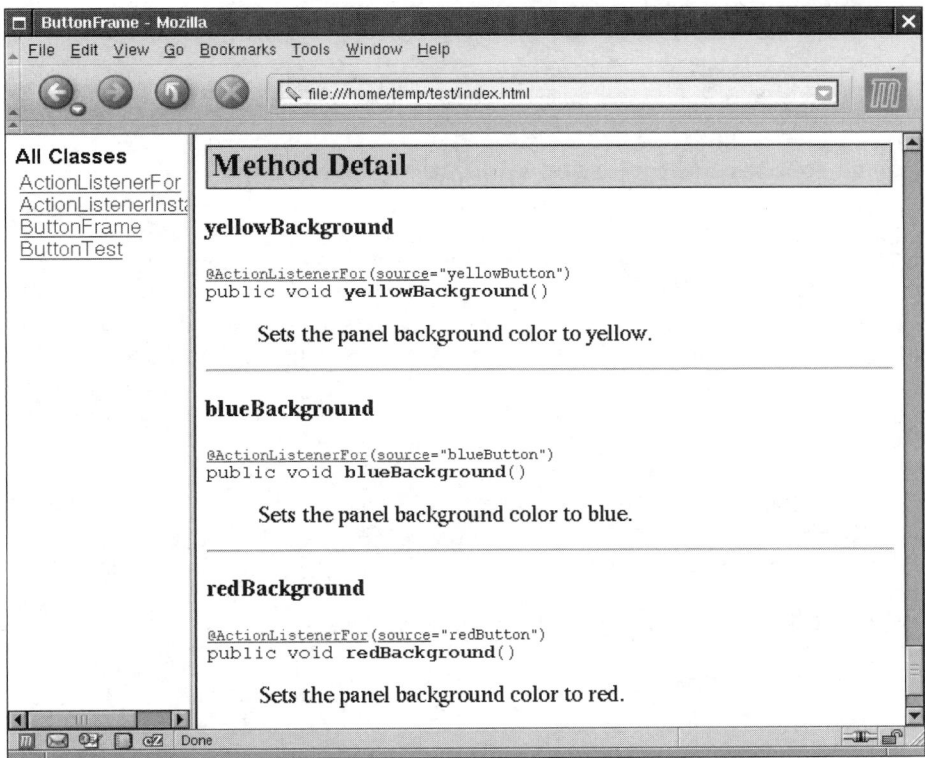

Figure 13–1: Documented annotations

If an annotation is transient (such as @BugReport) or an implementation detail (such as @Action-ListenerFor), then you should probably not document its use.

 NOTE: It is legal to apply an annotation to itself. For example, the @Documented annotation is itself annotated as @Documented. Therefore, the Javadoc documentation for annotations shows whether they are documented.

The @Inherited meta-annotation applies only to annotations for classes. When a class has an inherited annotation, then all of its subclasses automatically have the same annotation. This makes it easy to create annotations that work in the same way as marker interfaces such as Serializable.

In fact, an annotation @Serializable would be more appropriate than the Serializable marker interfaces with no methods. A class is serializable because there is runtime support for reading and writing its fields, not because of any principles of object-oriented design. An annotation describes this fact better than does interface inheritance. Of course, the Serializable interface was created in JDK 1.1, long before annotations existed.

Suppose you define an inherited annotation @Persistent to indicate that objects of a class can be saved in a database. Then the subclasses of persistent classes are automatically annotated as persistent.

```
@Inherited @Persistent { }
@Persistent class Employee { . . . }
class Manager extends Employee { . . . } // also @Persistent
```

When the persistence mechanism searches for objects to store in the database, it will detect both Employee and Manager objects.

The apt Tool for Source-Level Annotation Processing

One use for annotation is the automatic generation of "side files" that contain additional information about programs. The "Enterprise Edition" of Java is notorious for making programmers fuss with lots of boilerplate code, and an effort is underway to develop a standardized set of annotations to generate most of it automatically.

In this section, we demonstrate this technique with a simpler example. We write a program that automatically produces bean info classes. You tag bean properties with an annotation and then run a tool that parses the source file, analyzes the annotations, and writes out the source file of the bean info class. Rather than writing our own parser, we use an annotation processing tool called apt that is part of the SDK. We will first describe how to generate the bean info class, and then we will show you how to use apt.

Recall from Chapter 8 that a bean info class describes a bean more precisely than the automatic introspection process can. The bean info class lists all of the properties of the bean. Properties can have optional property editors. The ChartBeanBeanInfo class in Chapter 8 is a typical example.

To eliminate the drudgery of writing bean info classes, we supply an @Property annotation. You can tag either the property getter or setter, like this:

```
@Property String getTitle() { return title; }
```

or

```
@Property(editor="TitlePositionEditor")
public void setTitlePosition(int p) { titlePosition = p; }
```

Example 13–4 contains the definition of the @Property annotation. Note that the annotation has a retention policy of SOURCE. We analyze the annotation at the source level only. It is not included in class files and not available during reflection.

Example 13–4: Property.java

```
1. import java.lang.annotation.*;
2.
3. @Documented
4. @Target(ElementType.METHOD)
5. @Retention(RetentionPolicy.SOURCE)
6. public @interface Property
7. {
8.     String editor() default "";
9. }
```

 NOTE: It would have made sense to declare the editor element to have type Class. However, the annotation processor cannot retrieve annotations of type Class since the meaning of a class can depend on external factors (such as the class path or class loaders). Therefore, we use a string to specify the editor class name.

To automatically generate the bean info class of a class with name *BeanClass*, we carry out the following tasks:

1. Write a source file *BeanClass*BeanInfo.java. Declare the *BeanClass*BeanInfo class to extend SimpleBeanInfo, and override the getPropertyDescriptors method.

2. For each annotated method, recover the property name by stripping off the get or set prefix and "decapitalizing" the remainder.

3. For each property, write a statement for constructing a PropertyDescriptor.

4. If the property has an editor, write a method call to setPropertyEditorClass.

5. Write code for returning an array of all property descriptors.

For example, the annotation

```
@Property(editor="TitlePositionEditor")
public void setTitlePosition(int p) { titlePosition = p; }
```

in the ChartBean class is translated into

```
public class ChartBeanBeanInfo extends java.beans.SimpleBeanInfo
{
    public java.beans.PropertyDescriptor[] getProperties()
    {
        java.beans.PropertyDescriptor titlePositionDescriptor
            = new java.beans.PropertyDescriptor("titlePosition", ChartBean.class);
        titlePositionDescriptor.setPropertyEditorClass(TitlePositionEditor.class)
        . . .
        return new java.beans.PropertyDescriptor[]
        {
            titlePositionDescriptor,
            . . .
        }
    }
}
```

(The boilerplate code is printed in gray color.)

All this is easy enough to do, provided we can locate all methods that have been tagged with the @Property attribute. Rather than writing our own parser, we use apt, the *annotation processing tool*, that is a part of the JDK.

 NOTE: apt is not related to the Advanced Packaging Tool of the Debian Linux distribution.

You can find documentation for apt at http://java.sun.com/j2se/5.0/docs/guide/apt/. The tool processes annotations in source files, using *annotation factories* to locate *annotation processors*. There is a mechanism for discovering factories automatically, but for simplicity, we explicitly specify the factory on the command line. To invoke the bean info processor, run

```
apt -factory BeanInfoAnnotationFactory BeanClass.java
```

The apt program locates the annotations of the source files that are specified on the command line. It then selects the annotation processors that should be applied. Each annotation processor is executed in turn. If an annotation processor creates a new source file, then the process is repeated. If a processing round yields no further source files, then apt invokes the javac compiler on all source files.

The parser inside apt analyzes each source file and enumerates the classes, methods, fields, and variables. The API used by apt is called the "mirror API" because it is similar to the reflection API, except that it operates on the source level. Currently, the mirror API is a part of the com.sun hierarchy, and the documentation cautions that the API may change in the

future. We do not discuss the API in detail, but we do examine the program in Example 13–5 to give you a flavor of its capabilities. You can find a complete API reference in the apt documentation.

The first two methods in the BeanInfoAnnotationFactory class support the factory discovery process (which we are not using). The factory is willing to deal with annotations named Property, and it supports no command-line options. The third method yields the actual processor.

The BeanInfoAnnotationProcessor has a single public method, process, that is called for each file. In the process method, we iterate through all classes, ignore classes that are not public, then iterate through all methods and ignore methods that are not annotated with @Property. Here is the outline of the code:

```
public void process()
{
   for (TypeDeclaration t : env.getSpecifiedTypeDeclarations())
   {
      if (t.getModifiers().contains(Modifier.PUBLIC))
      {
         for (MethodDeclaration m : t.getMethods())
         {
            Property p = m.getAnnotation(Property.class);
            if (p != null)
            {
               process property
            }
         }
      }
      write bean info source file
   }
}
```

The code for writing the source file is straightforward, just a sequence of out.print statements. Note that we create the output file with a call to

```
env.getFiler().createSourceFile(beanClassName + "BeanInfo");
```

The env object encapsulates the apt processing environment. The Filer class is responsible for creating new files. The filer keeps track of the newly created source files so that they can be processed in the next processing round.

When an annotation processor detects an error, it uses the Messager to communicate with the user. For example, we issue an error message if a method has been annotated with @Property but its name doesn't start with get, set, or is:

```
if (!found)
   env.getMessager().printError(m.getPosition(),
      "@Property must be applied to getXxx, setXxx, or isXxx method");
```

When compiling the BeanInfoAnnotationFactory class, you need to add tools.jar to the class path. That file is contained in the lib subdirectory of your JDK installation:

```
javac -classpath .:jdk/lib/tools.jar BeanInfoAnnotationFactory.java
```

 NOTE: You need to add the tools.jar file to the class path only when compiling annotation processors. The apt tool locates the library automatically.

In the companion code for this book, we supply you with an annotated file, ChartBean.java.

Run

```
apt -factory BeanInfoAnnotationFactory ChartBean.java
```

and have a look at the automatically generated file ChartBeanBeanInfo.java.

This example demonstrates how tools can harvest source file annotations to produce other files. The generated files don't have to be source files. Annotation processors may choose to generate XML descriptors, property files, shell scripts, HTML documentation, and so on.

NOTE: Some people have suggested using annotations to remove an even bigger drudgery. Wouldn't it be nice if trivial getters and setters were generated automatically? For example, the annotation

```
@Property private String title;
```

could produce the methods

```
public String getTitle() {return title;}
public void setTitle(String title) { this.title = title; }
```

However, those methods need to be added to the *same class*. This requires editing a source file, not just generating another file, and is beyond the capabilities of apt. It would be possible to build another tool for this purpose, but such a tool would probably go beyond the mission of annotations. An annotation is intended as a description *about* a code item, not a directive for code editing.

The annotation facility gives programmers a lot of power, and with that power comes the potential for abuse. If annotations are used without restraint, they can result in code that becomes incomprehensible to programmers and development tools alike. (C and C++ programmers have had the same experience with unrestrained use of the C preprocessor.)

We offer the following rule of thumb for the responsible use of annotations: Your source files should compile without errors even if all annotations are removed. This rule precludes "meta-source" that is only turned into valid source by an annotation processor.

Example 13–5: BeanInfoAnnotationFactory.java

```
1.  import com.sun.mirror.apt.*;
2.  import com.sun.mirror.declaration.*;
3.  import com.sun.mirror.type.*;
4.  import com.sun.mirror.util.*;
5.
6.  import java.beans.*;
7.  import java.io.*;
8.  import java.util.*;
9.
10. /**
11.    This class is used to run an annotation processor that creates a BeanInfo file.
12. */
13. public class BeanInfoAnnotationFactory implements AnnotationProcessorFactory
14. {
15.    public Collection<String> supportedAnnotationTypes()
16.    {
17.       return Arrays.asList("Property");
18.    }
19.
20.    public Collection<String> supportedOptions()
21.    {
22.       return Arrays.asList(new String[0]);
```

```
23.    }
24.
25.    public AnnotationProcessor getProcessorFor(Set<AnnotationTypeDeclaration> atds,
26.       AnnotationProcessorEnvironment env)
27.    {
28.       return new BeanInfoAnnotationProcessor(env);
29.    }
30.
31.    /**
32.       This class is the processor that analyzes @Property annotations.
33.    */
34.    private static class BeanInfoAnnotationProcessor implements AnnotationProcessor
35.    {
36.       BeanInfoAnnotationProcessor(AnnotationProcessorEnvironment env)
37.       {
38.          this.env = env;
39.       }
40.
41.       public void process()
42.       {
43.          for (TypeDeclaration t : env.getSpecifiedTypeDeclarations())
44.          {
45.             if (t.getModifiers().contains(Modifier.PUBLIC))
46.             {
47.                System.out.println(t);
48.                Map<String, Property> props = new TreeMap<String, Property>();
49.                for (MethodDeclaration m : t.getMethods())
50.                {
51.                   Property p = m.getAnnotation(Property.class);
52.                   if (p != null)
53.                   {
54.                      String mname = m.getSimpleName();
55.                      String[] prefixes = { "get", "set", "is" };
56.                      boolean found = false;
57.                      for (int i = 0; !found && i < prefixes.length; i++)
58.                         if (mname.startsWith(prefixes[i]))
59.                         {
60.                            found = true;
61.                            int start = prefixes[i].length();
62.                            String name = Introspector.decapitalize(mname.substring(start));
63.                            props.put(name, p);
64.                         }
65.
66.                      if (!found)
67.                         env.getMessager().printError(m.getPosition(),
68.                            "@Property must be applied to getXxx, setXxx, or isXxx method");
69.                   }
70.                }
71.
72.                try
73.                {
74.                   if (props.size() > 0)
75.                      writeBeanInfoFile(t.getQualifiedName(), props);
76.                }
77.                catch (IOException e)
78.                {
```

```
79.            e.printStackTrace();
80.          }
81.        }
82.      }
83.    }
84.
85.    /**
86.      Writes the source file for the BeanInfo class.
87.      @param beanClassName the name of the bean class
88.      @param props a map of property names and their annotations
89.    */
90.    private void writeBeanInfoFile(String beanClassName, Map<String, Property> props)
91.      throws IOException
92.    {
93.      PrintWriter out = env.getFiler().createSourceFile(beanClassName + "BeanInfo");
94.      int i = beanClassName.lastIndexOf(".");
95.      if (i > 0)
96.      {
97.        out.print("package ");
98.        out.println(beanClassName.substring(0, i));
99.      }
100.     out.print("public class ");
101.     out.print(beanClassName.substring(i + 1));
102.     out.println("BeanInfo extends java.beans.SimpleBeanInfo");
103.     out.println("{");
104.     out.println("   public java.beans.PropertyDescriptor[] getPropertyDescriptors()");
105.     out.println("   {");
106.     out.println("      try");
107.     out.println("      {");
108.     for (Map.Entry<String, Property> e : props.entrySet())
109.     {
110.       out.print("         java.beans.PropertyDescriptor ");
111.       out.print(e.getKey());
112.       out.println("Descriptor");
113.       out.print("            = new java.beans.PropertyDescriptor(\"");
114.       out.print(e.getKey());
115.       out.print("\", ");
116.       out.print(beanClassName);
117.       out.println(".class);");
118.       String ed = e.getValue().editor().toString();
119.       if (!ed.equals(""))
120.       {
121.         out.print("         ");
122.         out.print(e.getKey());
123.         out.print("Descriptor.setPropertyEditorClass(");
124.         out.print(ed);
125.         out.println(".class);");
126.       }
127.     }
128.     out.println("         return new java.beans.PropertyDescriptor[]");
129.     out.print("         {");
130.     boolean first = true;
131.     for (String p : props.keySet())
132.     {
133.       if (first) first = false; else out.print(",");
134.       out.println();
```

```
135.            out.print("              ");
136.            out.print(p);
137.            out.print("Descriptor");
138.        }
139.        out.println();
140.        out.println("          };");
141.        out.println("       }");
142.        out.println("       catch (java.beans.IntrospectionException e)");
143.        out.println("       {");
144.        out.println("           e.printStackTrace();");
145.        out.println("           return null;");
146.        out.println("       }");
147.        out.println("   }");
148.        out.println("}");
149.        out.close();
150.    }
151.
152.
153.    private AnnotationProcessorEnvironment env;
154.  }
155. }
```

Bytecode Engineering

You have seen how annotations can be processed at run time or at the source code level. There is a third possibility: processing at the bytecode level. Unless annotations are removed at the source level, they are present in the class files. The class file format is documented (see http://java.sun.com/docs/books/vmspec). The format is rather complex, and it would be challenging to process class files without special libraries. One such library is BCEL, the Bytecode Engineering Library, available at http://jakarta.apache.org/bcel.

In this section, we use BCEL to add logging messages to annotated methods. If a method is annotated with

```
@LogEntry(logger=loggerName)
```

then we add the bytecodes for the following statement at the beginning of the method:

```
Logger.getLogger(loggerName).entering(className, methodName);
```

For example, if you annotate the hashCode method of the Item class as

```
@LogEntry(logger="global") public int hashCode()
```

then a message similar to the following is printed whenever the method is called:

```
Aug 17, 2004 9:32:59 PM Item hashCode
FINER: ENTRY
```

To achieve this task, we do the following:

- Load the bytecodes in the class file.
- Locate all methods.
- For each method, check whether it has a LogEntry annotation.
- If it does, add the bytecodes for the following instructions at the beginning of the method:

```
ldc loggerName
invokestatic java/util/logging/Logger.getLogger:(Ljava/lang/String;)Ljava/util/logging/Logger;
ldc className
ldc methodName
invokevirtual java/util/logging/Logger.entering:(Ljava/lang/String;Ljava/lang/String;)V
```

Inserting these bytecodes sounds tricky, but BCEL makes it fairly straightforward. However, at the time that this chapter was written, BCEL 5.1 had no support for processing annotations. Annotations are stored as "attribute" sections in the class file. Those sections store a wide variety of information, such as the settings of public, private, protected, and static modifiers and line numbers for debugging support. The class file format is extensible, and compilers are free to add custom attribute sections. Therefore, BCEL makes it possible to plug in readers for new attribute sections.

We supplied a class AnnotationsAttributeReader that processes the attribute section containing annotations. To keep the code simple, we handle only annotations whose elements have type String, and we don't handle defaults. Future versions of BCEL should include support for handling attributes.

We don't describe the process of analyzing and inserting bytecodes in detail. The important point is that the program in Example 13–6 edits a class file and inserts a logging call at the beginning of the methods that are annotated with the LogEntry annotation. If you are interested in the details of bytecode engineering, we suggest that you read through the BCEL manual at http://jakarta.apache.org/bcel/manual.html.

You need the BCEL library to compile and run the EntryLogger program. For example, here is how you add the logging instructions to the file Item.java in Example 13–7.

```
javac Item.java
javac -classpath .:bcel-5.1.jar EntryLogger.java
java -classpath .:bcel-5.1.jar EntryLogger Item
```

Try running

```
javap -c Item
```

before and after modifying the Item class file. You can see the inserted instructions at the beginning of the hashCode, equals, and compareTo methods.

```
public int hashCode();
  Code:
   0:  ldc       #85; //String global
   2:  invokestatic   #80; //Method java/util/logging/Logger.getLogger:(Ljava/lang/String;)Ljava/util/logging/Logger;
   5:  ldc       #86; //String Item
   7:  ldc       #88; //String hashCode
   9:  invokevirtual  #84; //Method java/util/logging/Logger.entering:(Ljava/lang/String;Ljava/lang/String;)V
  12:  bipush 13
  14:  aload_0
  15:  getfield      #2; //Field description:Ljava/lang/String;
  18:  invokevirtual  #15; //Method java/lang/String.hashCode:()I
  21:  imul
  22:  bipush 17
  24:  aload_0
  25:  getfield      #3; //Field partNumber:I
  28:  imul
  29:  iadd
  30:  ireturn
```

The SetTest program in Example 13–8 inserts Item objects into a hash set. When you run it with the modified class file, you will see the logging messages.

```
Aug 18, 2004 10:57:59 AM Item hashCode
FINER: ENTRY
Aug 18, 2004 10:57:59 AM Item hashCode
FINER: ENTRY
Aug 18, 2004 10:57:59 AM Item hashCode
FINER: ENTRY
Aug 18, 2004 10:57:59 AM Item equals
FINER: ENTRY
[[descripion=Toaster, partNumber=1729], [descripion=Microwave, partNumber=4562]]
```

Note the call to `equals` when we insert the same item twice.

This example shows the power of bytecode engineering. Annotations are used to add directives to a program. A bytecode editing tool picks up the directives and modifies the virtual machine instructions.

Example 13–6: EntryLogger.java

```
1.  import java.lang.annotation.*;
2.  import java.lang.reflect.Proxy;
3.  import java.lang.reflect.InvocationHandler;
4.  import java.io.*;
5.  import java.util.*;
6.
7.  import org.apache.bcel.*;
8.  import org.apache.bcel.Repository;
9.  import org.apache.bcel.classfile.*;
10. import org.apache.bcel.classfile.FieldOrMethod;
11. import org.apache.bcel.generic.*;
12. import org.apache.bcel.util.*;
13.
14. /**
15.    Adds "entering" logs to all methods of a class that have the LogEntry annotation.
16. */
17. public class EntryLogger
18. {
19.    /**
20.       Adds entry logging code to the given class
21.       @param args the name of the class file to patch
22.    */
23.    public static void main(String[] args)
24.    {
25.       try
26.       {
27.          if (args.length == 0)
28.             System.out.println("USAGE: java EntryLogger classname");
29.          else
30.          {
31.             Attribute.addAttributeReader("RuntimeVisibleAnnotations",
32.                new AnnotationsAttributeReader());
33.             JavaClass jc = Repository.lookupClass(args[0]);
34.             ClassGen cg = new ClassGen(jc);
35.             EntryLogger el = new EntryLogger(cg);
36.             el.convert();
37.             File f = new File(Repository.lookupClassFile(cg.getClassName()).getPath());
38.             cg.getJavaClass().dump(f.getPath());
39.          }
40.       }
41.       catch (Exception e)
42.       {
43.          e.printStackTrace();
44.       }
45.    }
46.
47.    /**
48.       Constructs an EntryLogger that inserts logging into annotated methods of a given class
```

```
49.      @param cg the class
50.    */
51.    public EntryLogger(ClassGen cg)
52.    {
53.       this.cg = cg;
54.       cpg = cg.getConstantPool();
55.    }
56.
57.    /**
58.       converts the class by inserting the logging calls.
59.    */
60.    public void convert() throws IOException
61.    {
62.       for (Method m : cg.getMethods())
63.       {
64.          AnnotationsAttribute attr
65.             = (AnnotationsAttribute) getAttribute(m, "RuntimeVisibleAnnotations");
66.          if (attr != null)
67.          {
68.             LogEntry logEntry = attr.getAnnotation(LogEntry.class);
69.             if (logEntry != null)
70.             {
71.                String loggerName = logEntry.logger();
72.                if (loggerName == null) loggerName = "";
73.                cg.replaceMethod(m, insertLogEntry(m, loggerName));
74.             }
75.          }
76.       }
77.    }
78.
79.    /**
80.       Adds an "entering" call to the beginning of a method.
81.       @param m the method
82.       @param loggerName the name of the logger to call
83.    */
84.    private Method insertLogEntry(Method m, String loggerName)
85.    {
86.       MethodGen mg = new MethodGen(m, cg.getClassName(), cpg);
87.       String className = cg.getClassName();
88.       String methodName = mg.getMethod().getName();
89.       System.out.printf("Adding logging instructions to %s.%s%n", className, methodName);
90.
91.
92.       int getLoggerIndex = cpg.addMethodref(
93.          "java.util.logging.Logger",
94.          "getLogger",
95.          "(Ljava/lang/String;)Ljava/util/logging/Logger;");
96.       int enteringIndex = cpg.addMethodref(
97.          "java.util.logging.Logger",
98.          "entering",
99.          "(Ljava/lang/String;Ljava/lang/String;)V");
100.
101.      InstructionList il = mg.getInstructionList();
102.      InstructionList patch = new InstructionList();
103.      patch.append(new PUSH(cpg, loggerName));
```

```
104.      patch.append(new INVOKESTATIC(getLoggerIndex));
105.      patch.append(new PUSH(cpg, className));
106.      patch.append(new PUSH(cpg, methodName));
107.      patch.append(new INVOKEVIRTUAL(enteringIndex));
108.      InstructionHandle[] ihs = il.getInstructionHandles();
109.      il.insert(ihs[0], patch);
110.
111.      mg.setMaxStack();
112.      return mg.getMethod();
113.   }
114.
115.   /**
116.      Gets the attribute of a field or method with the given name.
117.      @param fm the field or method
118.      @param name the attribute name
119.      @return the attribute, or null, if no attribute with the given name was found
120.   */
121.   public static Attribute getAttribute(FieldOrMethod fm, String name)
122.   {
123.      for (Attribute attr : fm.getAttributes())
124.      {
125.         int nameIndex = attr.getNameIndex();
126.         ConstantPool cp = attr.getConstantPool();
127.         String attrName = cp.constantToString(cp.getConstant(nameIndex));
128.         if (attrName.equals(name))
129.            return attr;
130.      }
131.      return null;
132.   }
133.
134.   private ClassGen cg;
135.   private ConstantPoolGen cpg;
136. }
137.
138. /**
139.    This is a pluggable reader for an annotations attribute for the BCEL framework.
140. */
141. class AnnotationsAttributeReader implements org.apache.bcel.classfile.AttributeReader
142. {
143.    public Attribute createAttribute(int nameIndex, int length, DataInputStream in,
144.       ConstantPool constantPool)
145.    {
146.       AnnotationsAttribute attribute = new AnnotationsAttribute(nameIndex, length, constantPool);
147.       try
148.       {
149.          attribute.read(in, constantPool);
150.          return attribute;
151.       }
152.       catch (IOException e)
153.       {
154.          e.printStackTrace();
155.          return null;
156.       }
157.    }
158. }
159.
```

```
160.  /**
161.    This attribute describes a set of annotations.
162.    Only String-valued annotation attributes are supported.
163.  */
164.  class AnnotationsAttribute extends Attribute
165.  {
166.     /**
167.        Reads this annotation.
168.        @param nameIndex the index for the name of this attribute
169.        @param length the number of bytes in this attribute
170.        @param cp the constant pool
171.     */
172.     public AnnotationsAttribute (int nameIndex, int length, ConstantPool cp)
173.     {
174.        super(Constants.ATTR_UNKNOWN, nameIndex, length, cp);
175.        annotations = new HashMap<String, Map<String, String>>();
176.     }
177.
178.     /**
179.        Reads this annotation.
180.        @param in the input stream
181.        @param cp the constant pool
182.     */
183.     public void read(DataInputStream in, ConstantPool cp)
184.        throws IOException
185.     {
186.        short numAnnotations = in.readShort();
187.        for (int i = 0; i < numAnnotations; i++)
188.        {
189.           short typeIndex = in.readShort();
190.           String type = cp.constantToString(cp.getConstant(typeIndex));
191.           Map<String, String> nvPairs = new HashMap<String, String>();
192.           annotations.put(type, nvPairs);
193.           short numElementValuePairs = in.readShort();
194.           for (int j = 0; j < numElementValuePairs; j++)
195.           {
196.              short nameIndex = in.readShort();
197.              String name = cp.constantToString(cp.getConstant(nameIndex));
198.              byte tag = in.readByte();
199.              if (tag == 's')
200.              {
201.                 short constValueIndex = in.readShort();
202.                 String value = cp.constantToString(cp.getConstant(constValueIndex));
203.                 nvPairs.put(name, value);
204.              }
205.              else
206.                 throw new UnsupportedOperationException("Can only handle String attributes");
207.           }
208.        }
209.     }
210.
211.     public void dump(DataOutputStream out)
212.        throws IOException
213.     {
214.        ConstantPoolGen cpg = new ConstantPoolGen(getConstantPool());
215.
```

```
216.    out.writeShort(getNameIndex());
217.    out.writeInt(getLength());
218.    out.writeShort(annotations.size());
219.    for (Map.Entry<String, Map<String, String>> entry : annotations.entrySet())
220.    {
221.        String type = entry.getKey();
222.        Map<String, String> nvPairs = entry.getValue();
223.        out.writeShort(cpg.lookupUtf8(type));
224.        out.writeShort(nvPairs.size());
225.        for (Map.Entry<String, String> nv : nvPairs.entrySet())
226.        {
227.            out.writeShort(cpg.lookupUtf8(nv.getKey()));
228.            out.writeByte('s');
229.            out.writeShort(cpg.lookupUtf8(nv.getValue()));
230.        }
231.    }
232. }
233.
234. /**
235.    Gets an annotation from this set of annotations.
236.    @param annotationClass the class of the annotation to get
237.    @return the annotation object, or null if no matching annotation is present
238. */
239. public <A extends Annotation> A getAnnotation(Class<A> annotationClass)
240. {
241.    String key = "L" + annotationClass.getName() + ";";
242.    final Map<String, String> nvPairs = annotations.get(key);
243.    if (nvPairs == null) return null;
244.
245.    InvocationHandler handler = new
246.        InvocationHandler()
247.        {
248.            public Object invoke(Object proxy, java.lang.reflect.Method m, Object[] args)
249.                throws Throwable
250.            {
251.                return nvPairs.get(m.getName());
252.            }
253.        };
254.
255.    return (A) Proxy.newProxyInstance(
256.        getClass().getClassLoader(),
257.        new Class[] { annotationClass },
258.        handler);
259. }
260.
261. public void accept(org.apache.bcel.classfile.Visitor v)
262. {
263.    throw new UnsupportedOperationException();
264. }
265.
266. public Attribute copy(ConstantPool cp)
267. {
268.    throw new UnsupportedOperationException();
269. }
270.
271. public String toString ()
```

```
272.    {
273.        return annotations.toString();
274.    }
275.
276.    private Map<String, Map<String, String>> annotations;
277. }
```

Example 13–7: Item.java

```
1. public class Item
2. {
3.     /**
4.         Constructs an item.
5.         @param aDescription the item's description
6.         @param aPartNumber the item's part number
7.     */
8.     public Item(String aDescription, int aPartNumber)
9.     {
10.        description = aDescription;
11.        partNumber = aPartNumber;
12.     }
13.
14.     /**
15.         Gets the description of this item.
16.         @return the description
17.     */
18.     public String getDescription()
19.     {
20.        return description;
21.     }
22.
23.     public String toString()
24.     {
25.        return "[description=" + description
26.            + ", partNumber=" + partNumber + "]";
27.     }
28.
29.     @LogEntry(logger="global") public boolean equals(Object otherObject)
30.     {
31.        if (this == otherObject) return true;
32.        if (otherObject == null) return false;
33.        if (getClass() != otherObject.getClass()) return false;
34.        Item other = (Item) otherObject;
35.        return description.equals(other.description)
36.            && partNumber == other.partNumber;
37.     }
38.
39.     @LogEntry(logger="global") public int hashCode()
40.     {
41.        return 13 * description.hashCode() + 17 * partNumber;
42.     }
43.
44.     private String description;
45.     private int partNumber;
46. }
```

Example 13–8: SetTest.java

```
1. import java.util.*;
2. import java.util.logging.*;
3.
4. /**
5.    This program logs the equals and hashCode method calls when inserting items into a hash set.
6. */
7. public class SetTest
8. {
9.    public static void main(String[] args)
10.   {
11.      Logger.global.setLevel(Level.FINEST);
12.      Handler handler = new ConsoleHandler();
13.      handler.setLevel(Level.FINEST);
14.      Logger.global.addHandler(handler);
15.
16.      Set<Item> parts = new HashSet<Item>();
17.      parts.add(new Item("Toaster", 1279));
18.      parts.add(new Item("Microwave", 4562));
19.      parts.add(new Item("Toaster", 1279));
20.      System.out.println(parts);
21.   }
22. }
```

Modifying Bytecodes at Load Time

In the preceding section, you saw a tool that edits class files. However, it can be cumbersome to add yet another tool into the build process. An attractive alternative is to defer the bytecode engineering until *load time*, when the class loader loads the class.

Before JDK 5.0, you had to write a custom classloader to achieve this task. Now, the *instrumentation API* has a hook for installing a bytecode transformer. The transformer must be installed before the main method of the program is called. You handle this requirement by defining an *agent*, a library that is loaded to monitor a program in some way. The agent code can carry out initializations in a premain method.

Here are the steps required to build an agent:

- Implement a class with a method

      public static void premain(String arg, Instrumentation instr)

  This method is called when the agent is loaded. The agent can get a single command-line argument, which is passed in the arg parameter. The instr parameter can be used to install various hooks.

- Make a manifest file that sets the Premain-Class attribute, for example:

      Premain-Class: EntryLoggingAgent

- Package the agent code and the manifest into a JAR file, for example:

      jar cvfm EntryLoggingAgent.jar EntryLoggingAgent.mf *.class

To launch a Java program together with the agent, use the following command-line options:

    java -javaagent:*AgentJARFile=agentArgument* . . .

For example, to run the SetTest program with the entry logging agent, call

    java -javaagent:EntryLoggingAgent.jar=Item -classpath .:bcel-5.1.jar SetTest

The Item argument is the name of the class that the agent should modify.

Example 13–9 shows the agent code. The agent installs a class file transformer. The transformer first checks whether the class name matches the agent argument. If so, it uses the EntryLogger class from the preceding section to modify the bytecodes. However, the modified bytecodes are not saved to a file. Instead, the transformer returns them for loading into the virtual machine. In other words, this technique carries out "just in time" modification of the bytecodes.

Example 13–9: EntryLoggingAgent.java

```
 1. import java.lang.instrument.*;
 2. import java.io.*;
 3. import java.security.*;
 4.
 5. import org.apache.bcel.classfile.*;
 6. import org.apache.bcel.generic.*;
 7.
 8. public class EntryLoggingAgent
 9. {
10.    public static void premain(final String arg, Instrumentation instr)
11.    {
12.       System.out.println(instr);
13.       instr.addTransformer(new
14.          ClassFileTransformer()
15.          {
16.             public byte[] transform(ClassLoader loader, String className, Class cl,
17.                ProtectionDomain pd, byte[] data)
18.             {
19.                if (!className.equals(arg)) return null;
20.                try
21.                {
22.                   Attribute.addAttributeReader("RuntimeVisibleAnnotations",
23.                      new AnnotationsAttributeReader());
24.                   ClassParser parser = new ClassParser(
25.                      new ByteArrayInputStream(data), className + ".java");
26.                   JavaClass jc = parser.parse();
27.                   ClassGen cg = new ClassGen(jc);
28.                   EntryLogger el = new EntryLogger(cg);
29.                   el.convert();
30.                   return cg.getJavaClass().getBytes();
31.                }
32.                catch (Exception e)
33.                {
34.                   e.printStackTrace();
35.                   return null;
36.                }
37.             }
38.          });
39.    }
40. }
```

In this chapter, you have learned

- how to add annotations to Java programs,
- how to design your own annotation interfaces, and
- how to implement tools that make use of the annotations.

It is easy to use annotations that someone else designed. It is also easy to design an annotation interface. But annotations are useless without tools. Building annotation tools is undeniably complex. The examples that we presented in this chapter give you an idea of the possibilities, and we expect many far more sophisticated tools to emerge in the future. This chapter has given you background knowledge for evaluating annotation tools, and perhaps has piqued your interest in developing your own tools.

Index

http://www.phptr.com/

Prentice Hall PTR   InformIT   InformIT Online Books   Financial Times Prentice Hall   ft.com   PTG Interactive   Reuters

TOMORROW'S SOLUTIONS FOR TODAY'S PROFESSIONALS

Prentice Hall **Professional Technical Reference**

| Browse | Book Series | What's New | User Groups | Alliances | Special Sales | Contact Us |

Search | Help | Home

Quick Search

PTR Favorites

Find a Bookstore

Book Series

Special Interests

Newsletters

Press Room

International

Best Sellers

Solutions Beyond the Book

Shopping Bag

Keep Up to Date with

PH PTR Online

We strive to stay on the cutting edge of what's happening in professional computer science and engineering. Here's a bit of what you'll find when you stop by **www.phptr.com**:

What's new at PHPTR? We don't just publish books for the professional community, we're a part of it. Check out our convention schedule, keep up with your favorite authors, and get the latest reviews and press releases on topics of interest to you.

Special interest areas offering our latest books, book series, features of the month, related links, and other useful information to help you get the job done.

User Groups Prentice Hall Professional Technical Reference's User Group Program helps volunteer, not-for-profit user groups provide their members with training and information about cutting-edge technology.

Companion Websites Our Companion Websites provide valuable solutions beyond the book. Here you can download the source code, get updates and corrections, chat with other users and the author about the book, or discover links to other websites on this topic.

Need to find a bookstore? Chances are, there's a bookseller near you that carries a broad selection of PTR titles. Locate a Magnet bookstore near you at www.phptr.com.

Subscribe today! **Join PHPTR's monthly email newsletter!** Want to be kept up-to-date on your area of interest? Choose a targeted category on our website, and we'll keep you informed of the latest PHPTR products, author events, reviews and conferences in your interest area.

Visit our mailroom to subscribe today! **http://www.phptr.com/mail_lists**